Microsoft® Windows NT® Network Administration

Microsoft Press

PUBLISHED BY
Microsoft Press
A Division of Microsoft Corporation
One Microsoft Way
Redmond, Washington 98052-6399

Copyright © 1998 by Microsoft Corporation

All rights reserved. No part of the contents of this book may be reproduced or transmitted in any form or by any means without the written permission of the publisher.

Library of Congress Cataloging-in-Publication Data
Microsoft Windows NT Network Administration Training Kit, Deluxe Multimedia Edition / Microsoft Corporation.
    p.   cm.
  Includes index.
  ISBN 1-57231-439-7
  ISBN 1-57231-832-5 (Deluxe Multimedia Edition)
    1. Microsoft Windows NT. 2. Operating systems (Computers)
I. Microsoft Corporation.
QA76.76.063M74516   1998
005.4'4769--dc21   97-52817
                                                                                      CIP

Printed and bound in the United States of America.

1 2 3 4 5 6 7 8 9 WCWC 3 2 1 0 9 8

Distributed to the book trade in Canada by Macmillan of Canada, a division of Canada Publishing Corporation.

A CIP catalogue record for this book is available from the British Library.

Microsoft Press books are available through booksellers and distributors worldwide. For further information about international editions, contact your local Microsoft Corporation office. Or contact Microsoft Press International directly at fax (425) 936-7329. Visit our Web site at mspress.microsoft.com.

Information in this document is subject to change without notice. Companies, names, and data used in examples herein are fictitious unless otherwise noted. No part of this document may be reproduced or transmitted in any form or by any means, electronic or mechanical, for any purpose, without the express written permission of Microsoft Corporation.

BackOffice, Microsoft, Microsoft Press, the Microsoft Press logo, MS, MS-DOS, Visual Basic, Windows, and Windows NT are registered trademarks of Microsoft Corporation.

Other product and company names mentioned herein may be the trademarks of their respective owners.

Project Lead and Instructional Designer: Susan Greenberg
Instructional Design and Technical Writing Contributors: Kate Knight, Tom Parker
Technical Contributors: Ryan Calafato, Jonathan Corners, Andrew Mason
Graphic Artist: Kimberly Jackson   **Graphics Contributor:** Julie Stone
Multimedia Producers: Susan Greenberg, Beverly Hare
Assistant Multimedia Producer: Sandra Alto
Interactive Lab Developer: Wendy Wahl   **Multimedia Development:** Digital Post & Graphics
Video Compression and Processing: "E.J." John Erickson, Brian Snyder
Web Page Design and Development: Kate Knight, Nikki McCormick
Web Page Graphic Design: Becky Johnson   **Editor:** Laurie Pritchard
Production Support: Irene Barnett   **Indexers:** Jane Dow, Barbara Sherman
Manufacturing Support: Bo Galford   **Product Managers:** Dean Murray, Robert Stewart, Elaine Stovall

Acquisitions Editor: Eric Stroo
Project Editor: Stuart Stuple

Part No. 097-0002005

Contents

About This Book   **xv**
    Intended Audience xvi
    Finding the Best Starting Point for You xvi
    Conventions Used in This Book xviii
        Features of This Book... xviii
        Notational Conventions xviii
        Keyboard Conventions xix
        Icons xx
        Notes xx
    Chapter and Appendix Overview xxi
Getting Started xxiii
        Cross-References to Windows NT Documentation xxiv
    Setup Procedures.. xxv
    Cleanup Procedures xxxiv
        Removing User and Group Accounts.. xxxiv
        Removing Self-Paced Training Files xxxv
    The Microsoft Certified Professional Program.................................... xxxvi
        MCSE Track xxxvii

Chapter 1   Introduction to Administering Windows NT   **1**
    About This Chapter 1
    Before You Begin.. 2
    Lesson 1: Introduction to Windows NT 3
        What Is Windows NT Workstation? 3
        What Is Windows NT Server?.. 5
        Administrative Differences... 7
    Lesson 2: Overview of Windows NT Directory Services 10
    Lesson 3: Logging On to Windows NT... 13
        Logging On... 15
    Lesson 4: Windows NT Administrative Tasks and Tools 19
        Windows NT Administrative Tasks.. 19
        Windows NT Administrative Tools.. 20

Lesson 5: The Windows NT Security Dialog Box 24
Best Practices 30
Review 31
Answer Key 32
    Procedure Answers 32
    Review Answers 32

Chapter 2 Setting Up User Accounts 35

About This Chapter 35
Before You Begin 35
Lesson 1: Introduction to User Accounts 36
    Types of User Accounts 36
    Where Accounts Are Created 37
Lesson 2: Planning New User Accounts 40
    Elements to Consider in Planning New User Accounts 40
    Naming Convention 41
    Password Requirements 41
    Logon Hours 42
    Workstation Restrictions 42
    Home Folder Location 42
Lesson 3: Creating User Accounts 48
    User Manager vs. User Manager for Domains 48
    Setting Password Options 50
    Creating a Home Folder 51
    Setting Logon Hours 55
    Setting Workstation Restrictions 57
    Setting Account Options 58
    Granting Dial-in Permission 59
    Deleting and Renaming User Accounts 61
Lesson 4: Creating User Profiles 65
    User Profiles 65
    Roaming User Profiles 67
    Creating Roaming User Profiles 68
    Copying the Profile to a Network Server 69
    Specifying the Path to the Roaming Profile 71
Best Practices 74
Review 75
Answer Key 76
    Procedure Answers 76
    Review Answers 77

Chapter 3 Setting Up Group Accounts — 79

- About This Chapter 79
- Before You Begin 80
- Lesson 1: Introduction to Groups 81
  - Permission and User Rights 81
  - Local and Global Groups 82
  - Where Local Groups Are Created 84
  - Where Global Groups Are Created 85
  - Video: Local and Global Groups 85
  - Example: Using Groups in a Single-Domain Network 87
  - Example: Using Groups in a Multiple-Domain Network 88
- Lesson 2: Planning a Group Strategy 90
- Lesson 3: Creating Local and Global Groups 96
  - Rules for Creating Groups 97
  - Creating Global Groups 97
  - Creating Local Groups 100
  - Deleting Groups 103
- Lesson 4: Implementing Built-in Groups 106
  - Determining the Rights of Built-in Groups 107
  - Built-in Groups on All Windows NT Computers 109
  - Built-in Groups on Domain Controllers Only 110
  - Built-in System Groups 113
  - Implementing Built-in Groups for Local Administration 115
  - Implementing Built-in Groups for Centralized Administration ... 116
- Best Practices 119
- Review 120
- Answer Key 122
  - Procedure Answers 122
  - Review Answers 126

Chapter 4 Administering User and Group Accounts — 129

- About This Chapter 129
- Before You Begin 130
- Lesson 1: Introduction to Administering Accounts 131
  - Administrative Tasks 131
  - Distributing Administrative Tasks 132
  - Using Templates 133
  - Using Templates to Create User Accounts 136

Lesson 2: Implementing an Account Policy 139
    Setting an Account Policy 139
    Planning an Account Policy 140
    Setting Password Options 141
    Setting Account Lockout Options 142
    Unlocking User Accounts 147
    Resetting User Account Passwords 148
Lesson 3: Modifying Multiple User Accounts 150
Lesson 4: Maintaining Domain Controllers 153
    Server Manager 154
    When the PDC Needs to Be Taken Offline 155
    When a PDC Goes Offline Unexpectedly 156
    Restoring the Original Domain Controller Roles 158
    Synchronizing Domain Controllers 160
Lesson 5: Troubleshooting Logon Problems 164
    Troubleshooting User Logon Problems 165
Review 168
Answer Key 169
    Procedure Answers 169
    Review Answers 171

Chapter 5   Securing Network Resources with Share Permissions   173

About This Chapter 173
Before You Begin 173
Lesson 1: Introduction to Shared Folders 174
    What Are Shared Folders? 174
    Share Permissions 175
    How Share Permissions Are Applied 177
    Example of Applied Permissions 178
Lesson 2: Guidelines for Planning Shared Folders 181
    Examples of Shared Folders 182
    Guidelines for Assigning Permissions 183
    Guidelines for Sharing Home Folders 187
Lesson 3: Sharing Folders 192
    Requirements for Sharing a Folder 192
    Administrative Shares 192
    Sharing a Folder 193
    Assigning Share Permissions 195
    Modifying Shared Folders 198

Lesson 4: Connecting to Shared Folders 200
Best Practices 205
Review..206
Answer Key 207
    Procedure Answers...207
    Review Answers...208

Chapter 6   Securing Network Resources with NTFS Permissions   209

About This Chapter 209
Before You Begin..210
Lesson 1: Introduction to NTFS Permissions 211
    What Are NTFS Permissions?..211
    Why Use NTFS Permissions? 212
    How NTFS Permissions Are Applied..214
Lesson 2: Combining Share Permissions and NTFS Permissions 217
    Video: Permissions 218
Lesson 3: Guidelines for Assigning NTFS Permissions 223
    Guidelines for Planning Program Folders..................................223
    Guidelines for Planning Data Folders..223
    Guidelines for Planning Home Folders......................................224
    Creating Home Folders on an NTFS Volume 224
Lesson 4: Assigning NTFS Permissions 230
    Requirements for Assigning NTFS Permissions 230
    Default NTFS Permissions 230
    Assigning NTFS Folder and File Permissions 230
    Assigning Special Access Permissions 236
Lesson 5: Taking Ownership of Folders and Files 240
    How to Take Ownership...241
    Giving Users the Ability to Take Ownership............................241
Lesson 6: Copying or Moving Folders and Files.............................245
    Copying a Folder or File..245
    Moving a Folder or File...246
    Permission Requirements 246
    Example of Copying and Moving Folders and Files 247
Lesson 7: Troubleshooting Permission Problems............................251
    Deleting a File That Has the No Access Permission.........................253

Best Practices	258
Review	259
Answer Key	261
Procedure Answers	261
Review Answers	267

Chapter 7 Setting Up a Network Print Server — 269

About This Chapter	269
Before You Begin	269
Lesson 1: Introduction to Windows NT Printing	270
Windows NT Printing Terms	270
Requirements	272
Lesson 2: Setting Up a Network Print Server and Client	274
Adding and Sharing a New Printer	275
Sharing an Existing Printer	279
Setting Up a Network Client	280
Accessing a Network Printer	281
Assigning Printer Permissions	284
Lesson 3: Configuring a Printer	290
Creating a Printing Pool	290
Setting Priorities Between Printers	292
Scheduling Printers	293
Assigning Forms to Paper Trays	296
Setting a Separator Page	297
Best Practices	300
Review	301
Answer Key	302
Procedure Answers	302
Review Answers	303

Chapter 8 Administering a Network Print Server — 305

About This Chapter	305
Before You Begin	306
Lesson 1: Introduction to Administering Print Servers	307
Print Server Administration Requirements	308
Lesson 2: Managing Documents	310
Setting a Notification, Priority, and Printing Time	310
Deleting a Document from a Printer	313

Lesson 3: Managing Printers 315
    Pausing, Resuming, and Purging a Printer 315
    Redirecting Documents..317
    Taking Ownership of a Printer 319
Lesson 4: Identifying Printing Problems 322
    How Documents Are Printed...322
    Identifying and Troubleshooting Printing Problems.......................323
Review...326
Answer Key 328
    Procedure Answers 328
    Review Answers...328

Chapter 9 Auditing Resources and Events 329

About This Chapter 329
Before You Begin...330
Lesson 1: Introduction to Auditing...331
Lesson 2: Planning and Implementing the Audit Policy 334
    Planning the Audit Policy 334
    Implementing the Audit Policy 335
    Defining the Domain Audit Policy..336
    Auditing Folders and Files...340
    Auditing a Printer 343
Lesson 3: Using Event Viewer to View the Security Log 346
    Administrative Requirements for Viewing the Security Log.............347
    Viewing the Security Log 347
    Filtering Events 350
    Locating Events 352
    Archiving the Security Log..353
Best Practices 357
Review...358
Answer Key 360
    Procedure Answers 360
    Review Answers...361

Chapter 10 Monitoring Resources — 363

- About This Chapter — 363
- Before You Begin — 364
- Lesson 1: Introduction to Monitoring Resources — 365
  - Server Manager — 365
  - Windows NT Diagnostics — 365
  - Requirements — 366
- Lesson 2: Viewing Computer Properties — 369
  - Viewing User Sessions — 371
  - Monitoring Shared Resources — 373
  - Monitoring Resources in Use — 375
- Lesson 3: Setting Alerts and Sending Messages — 379
  - Setting Administrative Alerts — 379
  - Sending Messages to Users — 380
- Lesson 4: Using Windows NT Diagnostics — 383
  - Gathering Information — 385
  - Creating and Printing a Report — 386
- Best Practices — 389
- Review — 390
- Answer Key — 391
  - Procedure Answers — 391
  - Review Answers — 391

Chapter 11 Backing Up and Restoring Files — 393

- About This Chapter — 393
- Before You Begin — 394
- Lesson 1: Introduction to the Windows NT Backup Program — 395
  - Requirements — 396
  - Creating a Backup Operator — 396
- Lesson 2: Planning a Backup Strategy — 399
  - Determining Which Files to Back Up — 400
  - Determining the Backup Type to Use — 401
  - Examples of Using Different Backup Types — 402
  - Rotating and Archiving Tapes — 403
  - Backup Sets, Catalogs, and Backup Logs — 405

Lesson 3: Backing Up Files 410
    Preparing to Back Up Files.. 410
    Selecting Drives, Folders, and Files 411
    Setting Tape, Backup Set, and Log Options 412
    Implementing a Backup 414
Lesson 4: Scheduling a Backup Using a Batch File 418
    Example of a Scheduled Backup 420
    Using the AT Command 422
    Using the Command Scheduler... 424
Lesson 5: Restoring Files.. 427
    Implementing a Restoration Strategy 427
    Creating a Restore Operator.. 428
    Examples of Restoration Strategies 429
    Preparing to Restore Files 430
    Loading the Tape and Backup Set Catalogs..................................... 430
    Selecting Backup Sets, Files, and Folders 432
    Setting Restore and Log Options 433
    Implementing the Restoration of Files 434
Best Practices 438
Review... 439
Answer Key 441
    Procedure Answers 441
    Review Answers... 442

Appendix A Planning Worksheets   445
User Accounts Planning Worksheet... 446
Group Accounts Planning Worksheet 447
Shared Folders Planning Worksheet 448
NTFS Permissions Planning Worksheet 449
Backup Planning Worksheet 450

Glossary   451

Index   485

FOREWORD

Microsoft Windows NT Network Administration

If you're buying garden gloves or an apron, one size can fit all. But your best business suit has to fit you like it fits no one else. That's because, while simple solutions are adequate for simple needs, your sophisticated needs generally require equally sophisticated solutions.

When Microsoft first introduced the Microsoft® Windows NT® operating system four years ago, it was managed in relatively simple network installations and a single, simple training course sufficed to educate IT professionals—who almost always had other, primary responsibilities—in its use. What a difference a few years can make. Today, Windows NT is the market-leading network operating system and the fastest-growing, as well. It has scaled up to support the enterprise needs of the largest corporations and, now, the new needs of intranets and the Internet.

With all this growth in the market for Windows NT, a single training course is no longer enough. At Microsoft, we build courses around specific job titles, to ensure that they're relevant for the professionals who will take them. Over the past few years, Windows NT has become important enough to most corporate users to warrant a specific, new job title: the Windows NT administrator. But those Windows NT administrators didn't have a Windows NT course just for them.

The self-study course you're holding in your hands responds to this need of Windows NT administrators. And Windows NT administrators have responded to it, in return. When the instructor-led version of this course was introduced in July, 1996, Windows NT administrators made it one of Microsoft's ten most popular courses in just two months.

And no wonder. The only thing that's growing as fast as the market for Windows NT products is the market for trained professionals to manage them. Microsoft has boosted the population of IT professionals trained on Windows NT to more than 400,000 last year and the demand continues unabated. At the end of 1996, ComputerWorld rated Windows NT administration as the fifth-hottest skill for IT professionals.

Windows NT administrators have also flocked to this course because it teaches them exactly what they need to know to make the best decisions with Windows NT. Microsoft believes in customizing each of its courses with hands-on, relevant training geared to the specific, daily needs of a single job title. This course in Windows NT administration is no exception. Forget time-consuming histories of the computer industry or the development of Windows NT. The course starts with the information you need to be more effective—and to be seen as more effective by current or prospective managers, employers, customers, or clients. After just the first chapter, you'll understand the key differences between the two Windows NT products, the tools available to administer them, and the key components of the Windows NT network.

Our emphasis on providing practical, hands-on information to help you make the best decisions about implementing Windows NT has also led to another innovation: This course is our first to be integrated with *best practices*. Windows NT administrators want to know the options available to them, but they also want to know the best option for their specific circumstances. Best practices information meets this need, based on advice from the world's leading Windows NT administrators, developers, and solutions providers, as well as from Microsoft's own Windows NT team. What's the best way to ensure the security of user accounts and disk resources? To implement a plan for backing up files? To make file and print resources available to network users? Whatever your needs, you'll find best practices tips and checklists to meet them.

As a professional in technology education management, I'm delighted to have played a key role in spurring the creation of this path-breaking course. But my enthusiasm runs even deeper, because I began my career as an IT administrator. So, I know that this is the type of information that today's IT professionals need, presented in the way that they need it. Hundreds of thousands of IT professionals already agree. I hope that very soon, you will too.

Nancy Lewis
General Manager, Training and Certification Worldwide
February 7, 1997

About This Book

Welcome to *Microsoft Windows NT Network Administration*. This book provides the knowledge and skills necessary to perform post-installation and day-to-day Windows NT administration tasks in single-domain and multiple-domain networks. It also helps prepare you to meet the certification requirements to become a Microsoft Certified Professional.

The "About This Book" provides important Setup procedures that will prepare your computer for the lessons. Read through "About This Book" thoroughly before you start the lessons. All lessons depend on the completion of the Setup procedures in "About This Book."

The chapters in this book are divided into lessons. Most lessons include hands-on procedures to practice or demonstrate key concepts and skills. At the end of each lesson is a summary of key points, and when appropriate, references to additional information on the lesson material or related topics. At the end of each chapter is a review of the critical points made throughout the chapter.

Intended Audience

This book is intended for those who administer Microsoft Windows NT Server and Windows NT Workstation, and for those who are on the Microsoft Certified Systems Engineer Windows NT 4.0 Track.

Prerequisites

- Working knowledge of an operating system, such as Microsoft MS-DOS®, UNIX, Microsoft Windows® version 3.*x*, Windows for Workgroups, Windows 95, or Windows NT.
- Proficiency using the Windows 95 or Windows NT version 4.0 interface, including the ability to use Windows Explorer to locate, create, and manipulate folders and files, to create shortcuts, and to configure the desktop environment.
- Working knowledge of major networking components, including clients, servers, local area networks (LAN), network adapter cards, drivers, protocols, and network operating systems.
- Knowledge of basic computer hardware components, including computer memory, hard disks, central processing unit (CPU), communication and printer ports, display adapters, and pointing devices.

Finding the Best Starting Point for You

The modular design of this book offers you considerable flexibility in customizing your learning. You can go through lessons in almost any order, skip lessons, and repeat lessons later to review certain skills. Lessons in each chapter build on concepts presented in previous lessons, so you may want to back up if you find that you do not understand the concepts and terminology used in a particular lesson. If the steps in one lesson require that you have completed the steps in an earlier lesson, you are told of this fact at the start of the lesson.

The following table recommends starting points depending on your Windows NT experience.

If you	Follow this learning path
Are preparing to take the Microsoft Certified Professional Exams (70–67, *Implementing and Supporting Microsoft Windows NT Server 4.0*, and 70–73, *Implementing and Supporting Microsoft Windows NT Workstation 4.0*)	Read "Getting Started" and complete the procedures in "Setup Procedures" (both located later in "About This Book"). Next, work through Chapters 1–3 and Chapters 5–6. Work through the other chapters in any order.
Want to learn key Windows NT concepts and skills	Read "Getting Started" and complete the procedures in "Setup Procedures" (both located later in "About This Book"). Next, work through Chapters 1–3 and Chapters 5–6.
Want to set up and maintain user accounts	Read "Getting Started" and complete the procedures in "Setup Procedures" (both located later in "About This Book"). Next, work through Chapters 1–4.
Want to make files available to network users	Read "Getting Started" and complete the procedures in "Setup Procedures" (both located later in "About This Book"). Next, work through Chapter 5.
Want to secure disk resources	Read "Getting Started" and complete the procedures in "Setup Procedures" (both located later in "About This Book"). Next, work through Chapters 5–6.
Want to set up a network print server	Read "Getting Started" and complete the procedures in "Setup Procedures" (both located later in "About This Book"). Next, work through Chapters 7–8.
Want to back up network files	Read "Getting Started" and complete the procedures in "Setup Procedures" (both located later in "About This Book"). Next, work through Chapter 11.
Need information on a specific topic related to Windows NT	Refer to the table of contents or index in this book, or refer to Windows NT Help.
Need to know the definition of a Windows NT term	Refer to the glossary in Windows NT Help or at the end of this book.

Conventions Used in This Book

Before you start any of the lessons, it is important that you understand the terms and notational conventions used in this book.

Features of This Book

- Each chapter opens with an "About This Chapter" section, which provides an overview of the chapter content.
- Following "About This Chapter," each chapter contains a "Before You Begin" section, which describes the prerequisites and setup required for the chapter.
- Whenever possible, lessons contain procedures that give you an opportunity to build your skills. All procedures are identified through the following procedural convention: ▶
- The "Lesson Summary" provides a summary of the key points of the lesson. Use this summary to gage whether you understood the important concepts of the lesson.
- The "For more information" table at the end of many lessons lists additional resource locations for information on the concepts and skills covered in the lesson. The information that is referred to covers product documentation, online locations, or both.
- The "Review" section at the end of each chapter is available to test what you have learned in the lesson.
- The "Answer Key" section contains all of the questions and corresponding answers for each chapter. Each question is referenced by page number.
- The "Glossary" presents a set of definitions for the technical terms that appear in this book and some related terms.

Notational Conventions

- Dialog box names, options, menu names, and menu commands appear in **bold** type.
- Characters or commands that you type appear in **bold lowercase** type (unless what you type is case-sensitive).
- *Italic* in syntax statements indicates placeholders for variable information. *Italic* is also used for important new terms, for book titles, and for emphasis in the text.
- Names of files or folders appear in Title Caps, except when you are to type them directly. Unless otherwise indicated, you can use lowercase letters when you type a folder name or file name in a dialog box or at the command prompt.

- File name extensions appear in all lowercase.
- Square brackets [ ] are used in syntax statements to enclose optional items. For example, [*file_name*] in command syntax indicates that you can choose to type a file name with the command. Type only the information within the brackets, not the brackets themselves.
- Braces { } are used in syntax statements to enclose required items. Type only the information within the braces, not the braces themselves.

Keyboard Conventions

- Names of keys that you press appear in SMALL CAPITALS—for example, TAB and SHIFT.
- A plus sign (+) between two key names means that you must press those keys at the same time. For example, "Press ALT+TAB" means that you hold down ALT while you press TAB.
- A comma (,) between two or more key names means that you must press each of the keys consecutively, not together. For example, "Press ALT, F, X" means that you press and release each key in sequence. "Press ALT+W, L" means that you first press ALT and W together, and then release them and press L.
- You can choose menu commands with the keyboard. Press the ALT key to make the menu bar active, and then sequentially press the keys that correspond to the highlighted or underlined letter of the menu name and the command name. For some commands, you can also press a key combination that is listed next to the particular menu command, such as CTRL+C for the **Copy** command.
- You can select or clear check boxes or option buttons in dialog boxes with the keyboard. Press the ALT key, and then press the key that corresponds to the underlined letter of the option name. Or you can press TAB until the option is highlighted, and then press SPACEBAR to select or clear the check box or option button.
- You can cancel the display of a dialog box by pressing the ESC key.

Icons

The following table describes the icons that are used throughout this book.

Icon	Description
	Identifies content that applies only to computers running Windows NT Server.
	Indicates a hands-on procedure for you to complete. If this symbol does not appear next to a section with steps, it is not intended as a hands-on procedure.
	Indicates instructions for starting a video. Videos are located on the Supplemental Material compact disc in an .avi format.
	Identifies content useful in planning.
	Indicates a best practice. A best practice is the way of performing a task that Microsoft recommends you follow.
	Calls out cautions or warnings. Cautions indicate a possible loss of data. Warnings indicate possible damage to hardware.
	Identifies content that is useful in identifying and troubleshooting problems.
	Indicates questions for you to answer. Sometimes the questions reference an illustration that you need to examine. Other times, the questions are for the purpose of reviewing and reinforcing key concepts.
	Indicates that two computers are required to complete the procedure. Procedures that have this icon are not required to meet the lesson objectives. Instead, they provide additional practice.

Notes

The following list describes the notes that appear throughout this book:

- Notes marked **Tip** contain explanations of possible results or alternative methods of performing a task. These tips may be suggested as best practices.
- Notes marked **Important** are items that you should check before completing an action.
- Notes marked **Note** contain supplementary information.
- Notes marked **Caution** contain warnings about possible loss of data.
- Notes marked **Warning** alert you to possible hardware damage.

Chapter and Appendix Overview

This self-paced training combines text, hands-on procedures, videos, and review questions to teach you how to administer Windows NT Workstation and Windows NT Server.

The self-paced training book is divided into the following chapters and appendix:

- Chapter 1, "Introduction to Administering Windows NT," provides you with a foundation of knowledge useful for all chapters in this book. It includes an overview of Microsoft Windows NT Server and Windows NT Workstation, describes the administrative differences between them in a workgroup and a domain, and discusses directory services, the Windows NT Server services that provide a single user logon, centralized administration, and access to domain resources. It also introduces you to the administrative tasks and tools that you will use throughout this book and the essential tasks that all users perform when using Windows NT. The hands-on procedures guide you through Windows NT basics.

- Chapter 2, "Setting Up User Accounts," introduces you to the three types of user accounts and provides you with a planning strategy for implementing them. The hands-on procedures give you an opportunity to plan and create your own user accounts.

- Chapter 3, "Setting Up Group Accounts," provides you with a groups planning strategy and procedures for creating groups. The hands-on procedures give you an opportunity to plan and implement local and global groups for a network.

- Chapter 4, "Administering User and Group Accounts," presents tasks related to maintaining existing accounts and streamlining administrative tasks, including creating template accounts, modifying multiple accounts at one time, planning and implementing an account policy, maintaining domain controllers, and troubleshooting user logon problems. The hands-on procedures give you an opportunity to implement and practice each task.

- Chapter 5, "Securing Network Resources with Share Permissions," explains how to share folders and how to assign permission for gaining access to the shared folders to user and group accounts. The hands-on procedures give you an opportunity to plan and share folders and to secure them with permissions.

- Chapter 6, "Securing Network Resources with NTFS Permissions," explains how NTFS permissions secure local resources, and how when combined with share permissions, NTFS permissions secure resources from users who connect to resources over the network. The hands-on procedures give you an opportunity to plan and implement NTFS permissions, and to troubleshoot common permission-related problems.

- Chapter 7, "Setting Up a Network Print Server," introduces you to Windows NT printing. It explains procedures and guidelines for setting up and configuring a network print server. The hands-on procedures give you an opportunity to implement and practice these tasks.

- Chapter 8, "Administering a Network Print Server," presents the post-installation and configuration print server administration tasks, including tasks related to managing documents and printers, and identifying printing problems. In the hands-on procedures, you will have an opportunity to perform many of these tasks on your own printer.

- Chapter 9, "Auditing Resources and Events," introduces auditing and provides guidance in planning and implementing a domain Audit policy. The hands-on procedures give you an opportunity to plan and implement an Audit policy, to set up auditing on files and printers, and to use Event Viewer to view audited events and archive security logs.

- Chapter 10, "Monitoring Resources," provides an overview of Server Manager and Windows NT Diagnostics and shows you how to use them to obtain key information about network and computer resources. The hands-on procedures guide you through viewing computer properties; viewing user sessions, shared resources, and resources in use; setting administrative alerts; sending messages to users; and gathering information about a computer configuration to use for inventory tracking and troubleshooting.

- Chapter 11, "Backing Up and Restoring Files," describes planning strategies for backing up files on your network and shows you how to use Windows NT Backup to back up and restore files. In the hands-on procedures, you use a Backup Simulation program to back up and restore files. This program simulates Windows NT Backup.

- Appendix A, "Planning Worksheets," provides completed planning worksheets for use with the planning exercises in Chapters 2, 3, 5, 6, and 11. Use them to check your answers or use them as guides for implementing tasks.

Getting Started

This self-paced training contains hands-on procedures to help you learn how to administer Windows NT Workstation and Windows NT Server. To complete these procedures, you must have the following:

- One computer running Windows NT Server version 4.0 configured as a domain controller, with an audio board and headphones or speakers; a CD-ROM drive; and a VGA or higher-resolution monitor, minimum of 256 color support.

Note There are a few procedures in this book that require two computers to complete them. Using a second computer is optional; it is not required to meet the lesson objectives.

It is recommended that you set up a domain controller on its own network specifically for this self-paced training because, to complete the lessons in this book, you will need to make changes to the domain controller that can affect other network users. However, you can use a domain controller on an existing network.

You can use the evaluation copy of Windows NT Server that is included with this book to set up a domain controller. The evaluation copy can be installed in a separate directory on an existing Windows NT–based computer. The evaluation copy is good for 120 days from the date that you install it. To install it, you need the following:

- On Intel and compatible systems: 486/33 MHz or higher, Pentium, or Pentium PRO processor, and 125 megabytes (MB) of free hard disk space.

    –or–

    On RISC-based systems: RISC processor compatible with Windows NT Server version 4.0, and 160 MB of free hard disk space.
- 16 MB of memory (RAM)
- VGA, Super VGA, or video graphics adapter compatible with Windows NT Server 4.0
- CD-ROM drive

Note All hardware must be on the Microsoft Windows NT 4.0 hardware compatibility list (HCL).

- Use of the built-in Administrator account on the domain controller or any user account on the domain controller with administrative privileges (one that is a member of the Administrators group).

  If you install the evaluation copy of Windows NT Server that is included with this book, an Administrator account will be created for you.

- A volume formatted with the Windows NT File System (NTFS). If you plan on using an existing domain controller and it does not already have an NTFS volume, see your network administrator before you convert one.

  If you do not have an NTFS volume and are prevented from creating one (for example, if Windows 95 is running on the same computer), you will still be able to complete most lessons in this book. However, you will not be able to complete the lessons in Chapter 7, "Securing Network Resources with NTFS Permissions" or Chapter 9, "Auditing Resources and Events."

Cross-References to Windows NT Documentation

You will find references to Windows NT documentation and Windows NT Help throughout this book. These references point you to more information about the task at hand.

- Microsoft Windows NT Server *Concepts and Planning* explains how to implement and optimize Windows NT Server. It is designed for new and experienced administrators of small networks and advanced users of operating systems. The online version of Microsoft Windows NT Server *Concepts and Planning* is included on the Windows NT Server compact disc.

- The *Microsoft Windows NT Server Resource Kit* (for version 4.0) provides detailed information on implementing Windows NT Server in larger networks.

- The *Microsoft Windows NT Workstation Resource Kit* (for version 4.0) provides detailed information on the Windows NT Workstation operating system, plus topics that are either new for version 4.0 or that reflect issues that Microsoft Technical Support Engineers consider timely and important.

- Windows NT Help, available online when you install Windows NT, provides references and how-to information for all Windows NT tasks.

Setup Procedures

The following information is a checklist of the tasks that you need to perform to prepare your computer for the lessons in this book. If you do not have experience installing Windows NT or another network operating system, you may need help from an experienced network administrator. As you complete a task, mark it off in the check box. Step-by-step instructions for each task follow.

❏ Create Windows NT Server Setup disks. These disk are required to install the evaluation copy of Windows NT Server. If you plan on completing the lessons in this book on an existing domain controller, skip this procedure.

❏ Install the evaluation copy of Windows NT Server (provided with this book), and configure it as a domain controller. If you plan on completing the lessons in this book on an existing domain controller, skip this procedure.

> **Note** The installation information provided will help you prepare a computer for use with this book. It is not intended to teach you installation. For comprehensive information on installing Windows NT Server, see the *Microsoft Windows NT Technical Support* self-paced training, also available from Microsoft Press.

❏ Install the self-paced training files. These files are required to complete the lessons. You need 6 MB of free disk space to install them.

❏ Assign the *Log on locally* user right to the Everyone group. This will ensure that all user accounts required to complete the lessons in this book have the ability to log on the computer.

❏ Create a user account named User1 with a password of **secret** (all lowercase) to prepare for the lessons in Chapter 1.

❏ Share the Users and Profiles folders to prepare for the lessons in Chapter 2. The Users and Profiles folders are created when you install the self-paced training files.

❏ Install Microsoft Internet Explorer 3.*x*. Internet Explorer 3.*x* is required only so that you can view the Web page on the Supplemental Material compact disc. It is not required to complete the lessons in this book. Skip this procedure if you already have Internet Explorer 3.*x* installed.

❏ Install the Intel Video drivers required to play the instructional videos included on the Supplemental Material compact disc.

❏ Set the color palette and desktop area for your monitor so that you can view the instructional videos included on the Supplemental Material compact disc. You only need to complete this procedure if you do not configure the color and resolution when you install the evaluation copy of Windows NT Server.

▶ **To create Windows NT Server Setup disks**

In this procedure, you create the three Setup disks that are required to install the evaluation copy of Windows NT Server. To complete this procedure, you need three blank, formatted disks.

Note This procedure requires that you have an operating system installed that provides the ability to access the CD-ROM drive on that computer.

1. Insert the Microsoft Windows NT Server compact disc into the CD-ROM drive.

   If a Windows NT CD-ROM windows appears, close it.

2. Go to a command prompt (If you are using a computer running Windows 95 or Windows NT, click the **Start** button, point to **Programs**, and then click **Command Prompt**.) and type one of the following commands:

   On a computer running MS-DOS, Windows 3.1, Windows for Workgroups, or Windows 95, type the following command, and then press ENTER.

   cd_drive**i386\winnt /ox**

   where *cd_drive* is the appropriate letter for your CD-ROM drive.

   –or–

   On a computer running Windows NT, type the following command, and then press ENTER.

   cd_drive**i386\winnt32 /ox**

   where *cd_drive* is the appropriate letter for your CD-ROM drive.

   The Windows NT 4.00 Upgrade/Installation dialog box appears, prompting for the location of the Windows NT Server files.

3. If the path to your compact disc does not already appear, type *cd_drive***:\i386** and then click **Continue**.

4. When prompted, label a blank disk as *Windows NT Server Setup Disk #3,* insert the disk into drive A, and then click **OK**.

   Setup prepares Disk #3.

5. When prompted, label a blank disk as *Windows NT Server Setup Disk #2,* insert the disk into drive A, and then click **OK**.

   Setup prepares Disk #2.

6. When prompted, label a blank disk as *Windows NT Server Setup Boot Disk,* insert the disk into drive A, and then click **OK**.

   Setup prepares the boot disk.

   When Setup has finished preparing the disks, the command prompt appears.

7. Close the Command Prompt window.
8. Remove the compact disc from the CD-ROM drive.

▶ **To install the evaluation copy of Windows NT Server**

Note If your computer is part of a part of a larger network, verify with your network administrator that the computer name, domain name, and IP address information does not conflict with network operations. If they will conflict, ask the network administrator to provide alternative values.

1. With the Windows NT Server Setup Boot Disk in drive A, restart the computer.
2. When prompted, insert Setup Disk #2, and at the subsequent prompts, insert Setup Disk #3, and then insert the CD-ROM.
3. Read the online instructions carefully. For many of the instructions, you can accept the default settings.
4. When prompted, supply the following configuration information.

When prompted for	Do this
A response to whether you are upgrading or installing a new version (fresh copy)	If you are installing the evaluation copy of Windows NT Server on the same computer as another version of Windows NT, type **N** for new version.
Partition information	Select a partition that has enough free disk space to install Windows NT Server.
File system information	Select **Leave current file system intact**.
A location to install Windows NT files	If you are installing the evaluation copy of Windows NT Server on the same computer as another version of Windows NT, type a different name (for example, \NTEval or \120Eval). Otherwise, accept \Winnt. (The location that you specify will be referred to in the lessons as *systemroot*.)

(*continued*)

When prompted for	Do this
Your name and organization	Type your name and your organization's name.
The CD key	Type **040** followed by **0048126**
The licensing mode	In the **Per Server for** box, type **10** for the maximum number of client access licenses provided with the evaluation copy of Windows NT Server.
A name for your computer	Type a name that is unique to your network.
The server type	Click **Primary Domain Controller**.
The Administrator account password	Type a password for the default Administrator account. Keep in mind that passwords are case-sensitive.
A response to the floating-point workaround (only appears on Pentium-based computers that have floating-point arithmetic problems)	Click **Do not enable the floating-point workaround**.
Emergency repair disk	Click **No, do not create an emergency repair disk** (you may want to create an Emergency Repair Disk for your computer, but it will not be used in this book).
The components to install	Click **Games** (required for some lessons). The default components should remain selected.
How this computer should participate on a network	If your computer is on a network, make sure **Wired to the network** is selected.
Install Microsoft Internet Information Server	Click to clear.
Setup to start searching for a Network Adapter	Click **Start Search**. If Setup cannot detect the installed network adapter or if your computer does not have a network adapter, click **Select from list**. If your computer does not have a network adapter, under **Network Adapter**, click **MS Loopback Adapter**. Otherwise, select your network adapter.
Network protocols	Accept **TCP/IP Protocol** and **NWLink IPX/SPX Compatible Transport**.

(continued)

When prompted for	Do this
TCP/IP setup. Do you wish to use DHCP?	Click **Yes** if your computer is connected to a network that has a DHCP server. (Check with your network administrator if you are unsure.) Otherwise, click **No**.
An IP address (appears if there is no DHCP server)	Type **131.107.2.200** (If your computer is on a network, check with the network administrator to verify that this IP address does not conflict with an existing IP address.)
A subnet mask (appears if there is no DHCP server)	Type **255.255.255.0** (If your computer is on a network, check with the network administrator for a valid subnet mask.)
A default gateway (appears if there is no DHCP server)	If your computer is on a network, check with the network administrator for a valid default gateway to use. Otherwise, leave it blank.
A name for your domain	Type a name that is unique to your network.
Time zone information	Specify your time zone.
The display properties	Set the **Color Palette** for 256 colors. Set the **Desktop Area** for 800 x 600 pixels.

5. When prompted, restart the computer.

Important If you do not have an NTFS volume, you need to convert a file allocation table (FAT) volume to NTFS. If your computer dual-boots with MS-DOS or Windows 95, do not convert the MS-DOS or Windows 95 system volume or you will no longer be able to boot those operating systems. For instructions on how to convert a volume from FAT to NTFS, see "Convert Command" in Windows NT Help.

▶ **To install the self-paced training files**

1. Log on as Administrator.
2. Insert the Supplemental Material compact disc into the CD-ROM drive.
3. In the root of the compact disc, double-click Setup.exe.

    A **Microsoft Windows NT Network Administration Setup** dialog box appears.

4. Click **Continue**.
5. In the **Name** box, type your name.

6. In the **Organization** box, type the name of your organization (optional), and then click **OK**.

7. Click **OK** to confirm that the Name and Organization information was entered correctly.

   A **Microsoft Windows NT Network Administration Setup** dialog box appears.

8. Under **Folder**, verify that the path points to a volume formatted with NTFS.

   If the path points to a volume formatted with FAT, click **Change Folder**, and then in the **Path** box, type *drive***:\Program Files\Admin Training** (where *drive* is the drive letter of your NTFS volume) and then click **OK**.

   If you are prompted to create the destination folder, click **Yes**.

9. Click the **Setup** button.

   Setup checks for free disk space and then copies the Admin Training folder to the specified path.

   The LabFiles folder is copied to the root of the drive that you specified. For example, if you specify D:\Program Files\Admin Training in the **Path** box, LabFiles will be located in D:\LabFiles. The LabFiles folder contains the folders and files required to complete the lessons in this book. You may want to record the drive location here.

   _____

10. When Setup has completed successfully, click **OK**.

    The Setup program installed the required files on your hard disk, created a **Network Administration Training** menu, and then added shortcuts to the files on the **Network Administration Training** menu.

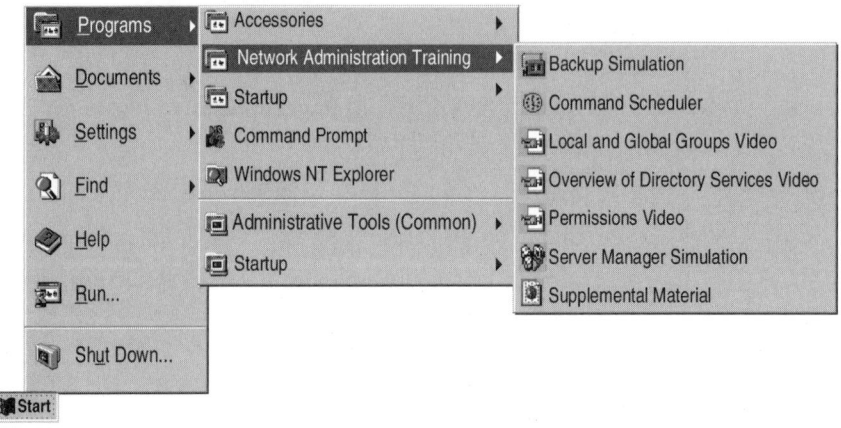

The following list describes the shortcuts that appear on the **Network Administration Training** menu:

- *Backup Simulation* is a Microsoft® Visual Basic program that simulates Windows NT Backup, but does not require a tape drive in your computer. This program is required to complete Chapter 11, "Backing Up and Restoring Files," to simulate backing up and restoring files on your hard disk.

- *Command Scheduler* is a *Microsoft Windows NT Server Resource Kit* utility (for version 4.0) that schedules batch and executable files to start a process, such as a backup, at a specified time. This utility is required to complete Chapter 11, "Backing Up and Restoring Files."

- *Local and Global Groups Video* is a six minute instructional video that defines local and global groups and explains how they are used in single-domain and multiple-domain networks. This video is required to complete Chapter 3, "Setting Up Group Accounts."

- *Overview of Directory Services Video* is a five minute instructional video that describes the components in a Windows NT network and the role of user accounts in Windows NT Directory Services. This video is required to complete Chapter 1, "Introduction to Administering Windows NT."

- *Permissions Video* is a five minute instructional video that shows the effective permissions when shared folder and NTFS permissions are combined. This video is required to complete Chapter 6, "Securing Network Resources with NTFS Permissions."

- *Server Manager Simulation* program is a Visual Basic program that simulates promoting and synchronizing multiple domain controllers in Server Manager using a single computer. This program is required to complete Chapter 4, "Administering User and Group Accounts."

- *Supplemental Material* is a Web page on the Supplemental Material compact disc. This Web page provides information on the Microsoft Certified Trainer program (including the *Administering Microsoft Windows NT 4.0* self-administered assessment), course materials, and key Web sites. To open the Web page, in the root of the Supplemental Material compact disc, double-click Open.htm.

Note The videos are the only files that are not installed on your hard disk. The menu shortcuts for the videos require that the Supplemental Material compact disc be in the CD-ROM drive. The videos can also be started directly from the Web page on the Supplemental Material compact disc.

▶ **To assign the Log on locally user right to the Everyone group**

1. Click the **Start** button, point to **Programs**, point to **Administrative Tools**, and then click **User Manager for Domains**.

   The User Manager for Domains window appears.

2. On the **Policies** menu, click **User Rights**.

   The **User Rights Policy** dialog box appears.

3. In the **Right** box, click **Log on locally**, and then click **Add**.

   The **Add Users and Groups** dialog box for your domain appears.

4. Under **Names**, click **Everyone**, and then click **Add**.

   The Everyone group appears under **Add Names**.

5. Click **OK** to return to the **User Rights Policy** dialog box.

   The Everyone group appears under **Grant To**.

6. Click **OK** to apply your changes and to return to the User Manager for Domains window.

7. On the **User** menu, click **Exit**.

▶ **To create a user account named User1 with a password of secret**

- Click the **Start** button, click **Run**, and then in the **Open** box, type *drive***:\labfiles\chapter1.cmd** (where *drive* is the drive letter that you specified when you ran the Setup.exe file to install the self-paced training files).

▶ **To share the Users and Profiles folders**

1. Click the **Start** button, point to **Programs**, and then click **Command Prompt**.

2. Type **net share users=***drive***:\labfiles\users** and then press ENTER (where *drive* is the drive letter that you specified when you ran the Setup.exe file to install the self-paced training files).

   A message appears stating that "Users" was shared successfully.

3. Type **net share profiles=***drive***:\labfiles\profiles** and then press ENTER (where *drive* is the drive letter that you specified when you ran the Setup.exe file to install the self-paced training files).

   A message appears stating that "Profiles" was shared successfully.

4. Close the Command Prompt window.

▶ **To install Internet Explorer 3.**x

1. In Windows NT Explorer, expand the IE_Setup folder on the Supplemental Material compact disc, and then double-click Msie30.exe.
2. When prompted to continue, click **Yes**.

    The **Internet Explorer License Agreement** dialog box appears.
3. Read through the license agreement, and then click **I Agree** to accept its terms.

    The Setup program copies files to your hard disk.
4. When prompted to restart your computer, click **Yes**.
5. Once your computer has restarted, log on as Administrator.

▶ **To install the Intel Video drivers required to play the videos**

1. In Windows NT Explorer, expand the Videos\Codec\32bit folder on the Supplemental Material compact disc.
2. Double-click Setup.exe.

    A **Welcome** dialog box appears.
3. Click **Next**.

    The **Software License Agreement** dialog box appears.
4. Read through the agreement, and then click **Yes** to accept its terms.

    The **Select Components** dialog box appears. **Windows NT system** is selected.
5. Click **Next**.

    The files are copied to the *systemroot*\System32 folder.
6. When prompted, if you would like to read the README file, click **Yes**; otherwise, click **No**.
7. Close all windows.

▶ **To set the color palette and desktop area for your monitor**

Complete this procedure only if you did not configure this information during installation.

1. Right-click a blank area of your desktop, and then on the menu that appears, click **Properties**.
2. In the **Display Properties** dialog box, click the **Settings** tab.
3. Under **Color Palette**, click **256**.

4. Under **Desktop Area**, move the slider to **800 x 600** pixels (if it is supported), and then click **Test**.

5. When prompted to test the new settings, click **OK**.

   A bitmap appears for five seconds, and then you are asked if you saw the test bitmap properly.

6. If you did see the bitmap properly, click **Yes**, and then click **OK**. Otherwise, click **No** and reset your the desktop area to 640 x 480 pixels.

Cleanup Procedures

Use the following procedures to remove user accounts, group accounts, and files that are created specifically for use in the lessons in this book.

Removing User and Group Accounts

Most chapters use batch files (Chapter$x$.cmd, where x is the chapter number) to create user or group accounts necessary to complete the chapter lessons. Account names include the number of the corresponding chapter. For example, User1 is created for use in Chapter 1. User5 is created for use in Chapter 5. This was done so that chapters do not depend on the completion of other chapters and can be done out of sequence.

After you complete all of the lessons in a chapter, you may want to remove the accounts that you create in the "Before You Begin" section of each chapter. You can do this at any time—when you finish all of the lessons in a chapter or when you finish all of the chapters.

▶ **To remove accounts created at the beginning of a chapter**

1. Log on as Administrator.

2. Insert the Supplemental Material compact disc into the CD-ROM drive.

3. Start Windows NT Explorer, and expand the Cleanup folder.

   The following files appear:

DeleteChapter1.cmd	DeleteChapter7.cmd
DeleteChapter3.cmd	DeleteChapter8.cmd
DeleteChapter4.cmd	DeleteChapter9.cmd
DeleteChapter5.cmd	DeleteChapter10.cmd
DeleteChapter6.cmd	DeleteChapter11.cmd

4. Double-click the DeleteChapter*x*.cmd file (where *x* is the chapter number) that corresponds to the chapter.

Note The DeleteChapter*x*.cmd files only remove the account or accounts that are created by running the corresponding Chapter*x*.cmd files. They do not remove any user or group accounts that you created as part of a lesson.

Removing Self-Paced Training Files

If you want to remove all files and shortcuts that were created when you installed the self-paced training files, you use Add/Remove Programs in Control Panel.

▶ **To remove the self-paced training files**

1. Click the **Start** button, point to **Settings**, and then click **Control Panel**.

    The Control Panel window appears.

2. Double-click the Add/Remove Programs icon.

    The **Add/Remove Programs Properties** dialog box appears.

3. On the **Install/Uninstall** tab, click **Microsoft Windows NT Network Administration**, and then click **Add/Remove**.

    The **Microsoft Windows NT Network Administration Setup** dialog box appears.

4. Click **Remove All**.

    A message appears asking if you want to remove Windows NT Network Administration.

5. Click **Yes**.

    The **Network Administration Training** menu is removed from the **Programs** menu, and all related files are removed from your hard disk, including the LabFiles folder (which does not appear on the **Network Administration Training** menu).

6. When a message appears stating that the process has successfully completed, click **OK**.

7. Click **OK** to close the **Add/Remove Programs Properties** dialog box.

8. Close Control Panel.

The Microsoft Certified Professional Program

The Microsoft Certified Professional (MCP) program provides the best method to prove your command of current Microsoft products and technologies. Anyone who must prove his or her technical expertise with Microsoft products should consider the program, including systems engineers, product developers, support technicians, system and network administrators, consultants, and trainers.

The Four Certifications

The following table describes the four certifications, based on specific areas of technical expertise.

Certification	Description
Microsoft Certified Product Specialist (MCPS)	MCPSs demonstrate in-depth knowledge of at least one Microsoft operating system. Candidates may pass additional Microsoft certification exams to further qualify their skills with Microsoft BackOffice™ integrated family of server products, development tools, or desktop programs.
Microsoft Certified Systems Engineer (MCSE)	MCSEs are qualified to effectively plan, implement, maintain, and support information systems in a wide range of computing environments with Windows NT Server and Microsoft BackOffice products.
Microsoft Certified Solution Developer (MCSD)	MCSDs are qualified to design and develop custom business solutions with Microsoft development tools, technologies, and platforms, including Microsoft Office and Microsoft BackOffice.
Microsoft Certified Trainer (MCT)	MCTs are instructionally and technically qualified to deliver Microsoft Official Curriculum through Microsoft Authorized Technical Education Centers.

Certification Requirements

The certification requirements differ for each certification and are specific to the products and job functions addressed by the certification. To become a Microsoft Certified Professional, you must pass rigorous certification exams that provide a valid and reliable measure of technical proficiency and expertise.

The following table describes exam requirements.

Certification	Exam requirements
Microsoft Certified Product Specialist (MCPS)	Pass one operating system exam. In addition, individuals seeking to validate their expertise in a desktop program must pass the appropriate elective exam.
Microsoft Certified Systems Engineer (MCSE)	Pass four operating system exams and two elective exams.
Microsoft Certified Solution Developer (MCSD)	Pass two core technology exams and two elective exams.
Microsoft Certified Trainer (MCT)	Required to meet instructional and technical requirements specific to each Microsoft Official Curriculum course that they are certified to deliver.[1]

MCSE Track

This book supports the MCSE Windows NT 4.0 track. To complete this track, we recommend that you do the steps outlined in the following table.

Step	Pass this exam	Preparation
1	70–58, *Networking Essentials*	Course 683, *Networking Essentials—Self-Paced Training Kit*
2	*Administering Microsoft Windows NT 4.0* self-administered assessment	Course 803, *Administering Microsoft Windows NT 4.0*
3	70–67, *Implementing and Supporting Microsoft Windows NT Server 4.0* and any client exam[2], such as exam 70–73, *Implementing and Supporting Microsoft Windows NT Workstation 4.0* or exam 70–63, *Implementing and Supporting Microsoft Windows 95*	Course 803, *Administering Microsoft Windows NT 4.0* Course 687, *Supporting Windows NT Core Technologies* Course 564, *Microsoft Windows 95 Training—Self-Paced Training Kit*

---

[1] *Inside the United States and Canada, call (800) 636-7544 for more information on becoming a Microsoft Certified Trainer. Outside the United States and Canada, contact your local Microsoft subsidiary.*

[2] *For a complete list of client and elective exams, see the Microsoft Training and Certification Web site at http://www.microsoft.com/train_cert/ or the Certification section of the Web page provided on the Supplemental Material compact disc.*

(*continued*)

Step	Pass this exam	Preparation
4	70–68, *Implementing and Supporting Microsoft Windows NT Server 4.0 in the Enterprise*	Course 689, *Supporting Windows NT Server 4.0 Enterprise Technologies*
5	Two elective exams	Elective exams are available for the following: Microsoft SQL Server™, BackOffice Internet-related products, Microsoft SNA Server, Microsoft Exchange Server, Microsoft Systems Management Server, and TCP/IP.

Important Microsoft Official Curriculum (MOC) courses help you to prepare for Microsoft Certified Professional (MCP) exams. However, no one-to-one correlation exists between MOC courses and MCP exams.

Administering Microsoft Windows NT 4.0 Self-Administered Assessment

The *Administering Microsoft Windows NT 4.0* self-administered assessment is a computer-based test.

▶ **To learn more about the assessment**

- If you have completed the Setup procedures in "About This Book," see the Readme file located in the *drive*:\Program Files\Admin Training\Assess folder (where *drive* is the location that you specified for the installation of the self-paced training files).

    –or–

    If you have not completed the Setup procedures in "About This Book," see "Assessment" in the "Certification" section of the Supplemental Material compact disc.

▶ To start the assessment

- If you have completed the Setup procedures in "About This Book," in Windows NT Explorer, expand *drive*:\Program Files\Admin Training\Assess folder (where *drive* is the location that you specified for the installation of the self-paced training files), and then double-click Lnchtst.exe.

    –or–

    If you have not completed the Setup procedures in "About This Book," copy the Assess folder from the Supplemental Material compact disc to your hard disk, and then in the Assess folder, double-click Lnchtst.exe.

Note Passing this self-administered assessment does not satisfy any requirements for the Microsoft Certified Professional program, nor does performance on this test guarantee or directly correlate to the success that you may have on any Microsoft certification exam. Unlike the Microsoft certification exams, this assessment is not professionally validated. If you plan to pursue Microsoft certification, see the "Certification" section of the Web page included with this book.

CHAPTER 1

Introduction to Administering Windows NT

Lesson 1 Introduction to Windows NT . . . 3

Lesson 2 Overview of Windows NT Directory Services . . . 10

Lesson 3 Logging On to Windows NT . . . 13

Lesson 4 Windows NT Administrative Tasks and Tools . . . 19

Lesson 5 The Windows NT Security Dialog Box . . . 24

Best Practices . . . 30

Review . . . 31

About This Chapter

This chapter provides you with a foundation of knowledge that is useful for all chapters in this book. It includes an overview of Microsoft® Windows NT® Server and Windows NT Workstation, describes the administrative differences between them in a workgroup and a domain, and discusses directory services, the Windows NT Server services that provide a single user logon, centralized administration, and access to domain resources. It also introduces you to the administrative tasks and tools that you will use throughout this book and the essential tasks that all users perform when using Windows NT.

The hands-on procedures guide you through Windows NT basics.

Before You Begin

To complete the lessons in this chapter, you must have completed the Setup procedures located in "About This Book."

Lesson 1: Introduction to Windows NT

Windows NT is a multipurpose network operating system that can act as both a client and a server in a network environment. Windows NT refers to two different products—Windows NT Workstation and Windows NT Server.

This lesson provides an overview of Windows NT Server and Windows NT Workstation and the key administrative differences between them.

After this lesson, you will be able to:
- Explain the key differences between Microsoft Windows NT Workstation and Windows NT Server.
- Describe the difference between a workgroup model and a domain model, and understand what the administrative differences are between these two models.

Estimated lesson time: 10 minutes

What Is Windows NT Workstation?

Windows NT Workstation is optimized for use as a high performance, secure network client and corporate desktop operating system. Windows NT Workstation can be used alone as a desktop operating system, networked in a peer-to-peer workgroup environment, or used as a workstation in a Windows NT Server domain environment. Windows NT Workstation can be used with the Microsoft BackOffice™ family of products to access resources from all of the BackOffice products.

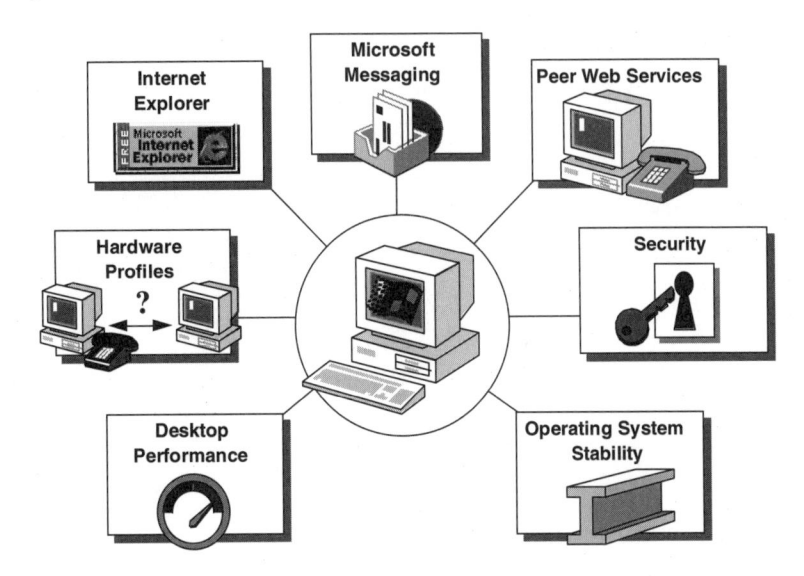

Windows NT Workstation offers the following advantages:

- *Desktop performance.* Supports preemptive multitasking for all programs. Windows NT Workstation supports multiple processors for true multitasking performance. For example, if you run a multithreaded program such as Microsoft Word, you can work on one document while another document prints.
- *Hardware profiles.* Creates and maintains a list of hardware configurations specific to a computer. For example, if you use a laptop computer and docking station at work, you can use a hardware profile to configure the laptop for use with the docking station. When you take the laptop computer home, you can use a different hardware profile with a configuration for dial-in networking.
- *Microsoft Internet Explorer.* Provides a fast and simple-to-use browser that is compatible with existing standards.
- *Microsoft messaging.* Receives and stores electronic mail, including files and objects created in other programs.
- *Peer Web services.* Provides a personal Web server, optimized to run on Windows NT Workstation version 4.0.
- *Security.* Provides local security for files, folders, printers, and other resources. Users must be authenticated by either the local computer or a domain controller in order to gain access to any resources on the computer or network.
- *Operating system stability.* Supports each program in its own memory address space. This means that malfunctioning programs will not affect other programs or the operating system.

What Is Windows NT Server?

Windows NT Server is optimized for use as a file, print, and application server that can handle tasks for organizations ranging from small workgroups to enterprise networks.

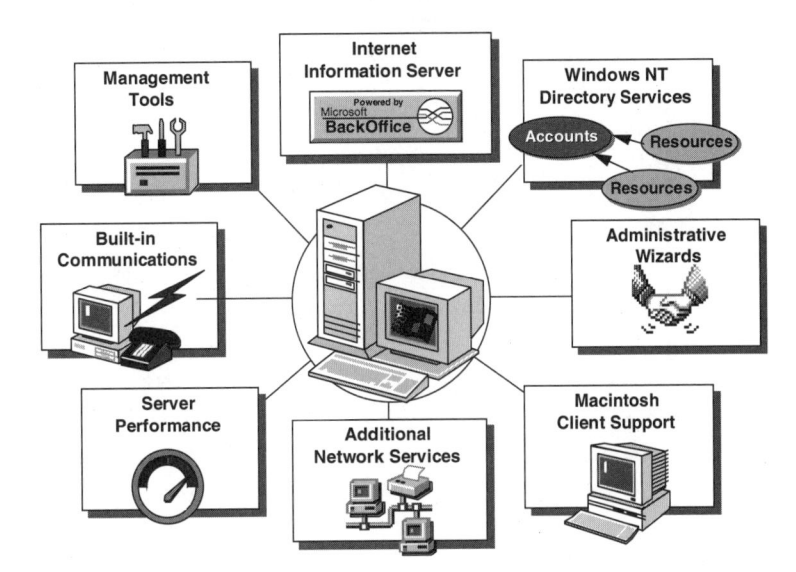

Windows NT Server offers the following advantages:

- *Server performance.* Windows NT Server version 4.0 is tuned for file, print, and application server performance. The retail version of Windows NT Server supports up to four processors in a symmetric multiprocessing environment. Original Equipment Manufacturers' (OEM) implementations of Windows NT Server support up to 32 processors in a symmetric multiprocessing environment.

- *Built-in communications.* Salespeople, home-based employees, traveling workers, and other mobile users connect to Windows NT Server 4.0 using Remote Access Service (RAS), a feature that lets remote users dial-in to the network. Windows NT provides support for 256 inbound RAS sessions.

- *Management tools.* Task Manager and Network Monitor simplify the day-to-day administration of your network server. Task Manager monitors programs, tasks, and key performance metrics of Windows NT Server 4.0, providing detailed information on each program and process running on the system. With this information, you can quickly terminate elements that are not responding, resulting in improved system reliability.

    Network Monitor examines network traffic to and from the server at the packet level and captures it for later analysis, making it easier to troubleshoot potential network problems.

- *Internet Information Server (IIS).* The integration of IIS with Windows NT Server 4.0 means that Web server installation and management are simply another part of the operating system. In addition, with IIS version 2.0 you can remotely administer your Web site from any Microsoft Windows®-based computer with a Web browser. IIS provides a fast, powerful, and secure platform for offering Hypertext Transfer Protocol (HTTP), File Transfer Protocol (FTP), and Gopher service.

- *Administrative Wizards.* Task-oriented Administrative Wizards make server management easier than ever. Wizards group the common server management tools such as User Manager for Domains and Server Manager, and walk you through the steps required to add users, create and manage groups of users, manage file and folder access for network clients, and so on.

- *Macintosh client support.* This feature provides file and print sharing services for Macintosh clients.

- *Additional network services.* These additional network services include multiprotocol routing (MPR), Domain Name System (DNS), Dynamic Host Configuration Protocol (DHCP), and Windows Internet Name Service (WINS).

- *Windows NT Directory Services.* A directory database provides a single network logon, a single point of administration, and the ability for users to access resources throughout the network.

Administrative Differences

A Microsoft Windows NT–based network can be set up using either a domain model or a workgroup model. Both Windows NT Server and Windows NT Workstation can participate in either of these two models. The administrative differences between the two products depend on the model.

Domain Model

A domain model has at least one computer running Windows NT Server configured as a domain controller. A domain is a logical grouping of computers that share common security and user account information. This information is stored in the domain controller's master directory database.

Note Windows NT Server can also be configured as a member server (a non-domain controller). A member server does not validate domain logon attempts. It maintains a local directory database just as computers running Windows NT Workstation do.

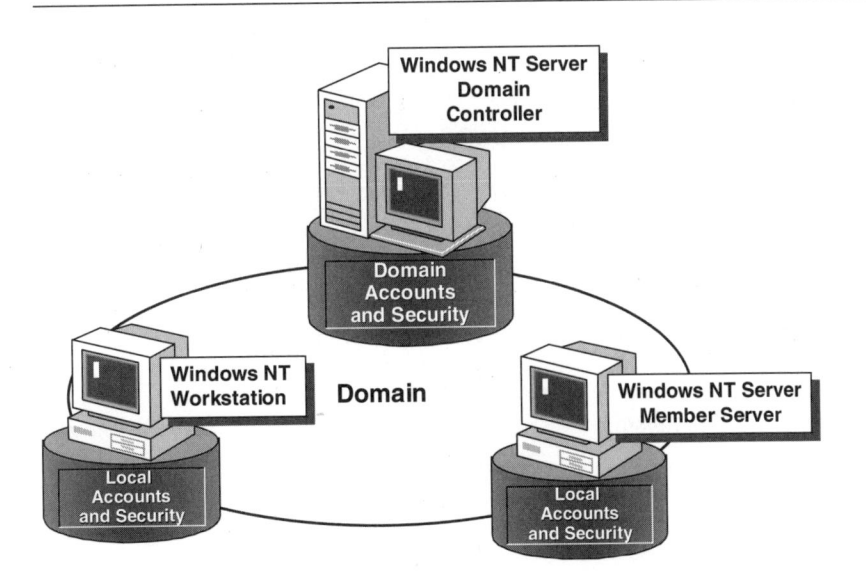

All computers running Windows NT maintain a directory database; however, it is the domain controller's master directory database that provides a central location for administering user accounts and resource security for the domain. In a domain, each user requires only one account and password to gain access to network resources. If a user changes his or her password, the change is automatically reflected throughout the domain.

Workgroup Model

A workgroup model is a Windows NT–based network that does not have a Windows NT Server domain controller. A workgroup is often referred to as a peer-to-peer network because all computers share files and printers as equals, or *peers*.

In a workgroup model, administration of user accounts and resource security is not central to any one computer. Instead, each computer running Windows NT Workstation or Windows NT Server (configured as a member server) maintains its own user accounts and resource security information in a local directory database. This means that user accounts are created on every computer that the user will access either locally or over the network.

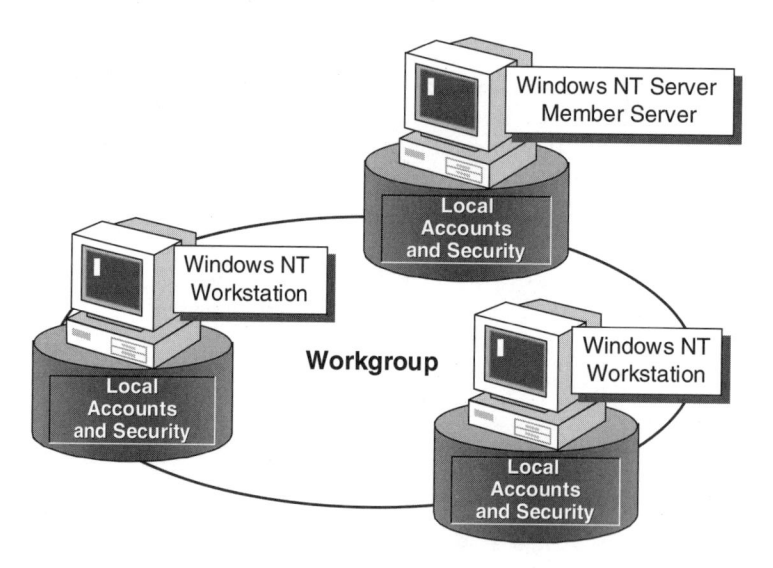

In this model, resource administration tasks are distributed to each computer in the network. For example, each time a user changes his or her password, the user must change the password at every computer where that user has an account. To administer a computer in a workgroup, changes are made on each computer. This can be a time-intensive endeavor.

Lesson Summary

The following information summarizes the key points in this lesson:

- Windows NT Server is optimized for use as a file, print, and application server.
- Windows NT Workstation is optimized for use alone as a desktop operating system, as a networked computer in a peer-to-peer workgroup environment, or as a workstation in a Windows NT Server domain environment.
- A domain is a logical grouping of computers that share common security and user account information. The domain model provides centralized administration of user accounts and resource security.
- A workgroup is a network that does not have a Windows NT Server domain controller. Windows NT Workstation and Windows NT Server member servers are administered on an individual basis.

For more information on	See
New programs and features in Windows NT	Windows NT Help.
Windows NT procedures	Windows NT Help.
Windows NT Workstation	The Microsoft World Wide Web site at http://www.microsoft.com/ntworkstation/
Windows NT Server	The Microsoft World Wide Web site at http://www.microsoft.com/ntserver/
BackOffice family of products	The Microsoft World Wide Web site at http://www.microsoft.com/backoffice/

Lesson 2: Overview of Windows NT Directory Services

Directory services is one of the services provided by Windows NT Server. Directory services provides users with a single user name and password, and allows access to resources throughout the network. It provides administrators with the ability to view and manage users and network resources from any computer on the network. This lesson provides an instructional video on directory services, which focuses on a Windows NT environment and the role that user accounts play in it.

After this lesson, you will be able to:
- Describe the components in a Windows NT network and the role of user accounts in Windows NT Directory Services.
- Describe the function of primary and backup domain controllers, and the role of member servers.
- Explain the function of a trust relationship between domains.

Estimated lesson time: 10 minutes

The five minute video describes the components in a Windows NT network and the role of user accounts in Windows NT Directory Services. In addition, the video defines key terminology that is used throughout this book. The complete video script is available under "Course Materials" on the accompanying Supplemental Material compact disc.

▶ **To start the video from the Start menu**
1. Insert the Supplemental Material compact disc into the CD-ROM drive.
2. Click the **Start** button, point to **Programs**, point to **Network Administration Training**, and then click **Overview of Directory Services Video**.

▶ **To start the video from the compact disc**
1. Start Windows NT Explorer.
2. In the root of the Supplemental Material compact disc, double-click Open.htm.
3. Click the center of the screen to continue to the home page.
4. Click **Course Materials**.

5. Under **Contents**, click **Overview of Windows NT Directory Services**.
6. Follow the instructions in the text box to install the required DLL files and to start the video.

Note If you completed the Setup procedures described in "About This Book," or if you have run a video on this computer before, you do *not* need to install the DLL files.

▶ **To review the video**

The following study guide highlights the main points of the video. Complete the guide as you view the video, or use the guide as a follow-up test (recommended).

1. Name three benefits of Windows NT Server Directory Services.

   _____

   _____

2. Name the three Windows NT Server configurations.

   _____

   _____

3. How many primary domain controllers can there be in each domain? How many backup domain controllers?

   _____

   _____

4. How does a domain differ from a peer-to-peer network?

   _____

   _____

5. Name the logical link that combines domains into one administrative unit.

   _____

   _____

Lesson Summary

The following information summarizes the key points in this lesson:

- Directory services is one of the services provided by Windows NT Server.
- A domain is the administrative unit of directory services.
- A domain consists of one or more domain controllers that maintain a common directory database.
- Directory services provides users with a single user account and password. This means that users can log on to the domain from any computer on the network and have access to resources throughout it.
- Directory services also provides administrators with the ability to view and manage users and network resources from any computer on the network.

For more information on	See
Directory services	Chapter 1, "Managing Windows NT Server Domains," in Microsoft Windows NT Server *Concepts and Planning*.
Security	Chapter 5, "Securing Network Resources with Share Permissions" and Chapter 6, "Securing Network Resources with NTFS Permissions," in this book.

Lesson 3: Logging On to Windows NT

Although resources are protected at several levels by different processes, overall access to a domain or a computer is protected by logon security. This lesson introduces the process of logging on to the domain or a local computer.

After this lesson, you will be able to:
- Log on to the domain or local computer.
- Describe the authentication process in a domain and workgroup.

Estimated lesson time: 10 minutes

To gain access to any part of the operating system, users must first identify themselves to the domain or the computer through the logon process.

Each time you start a computer running Windows NT, you are prompted to press CTRL+ALT+DELETE to log on.

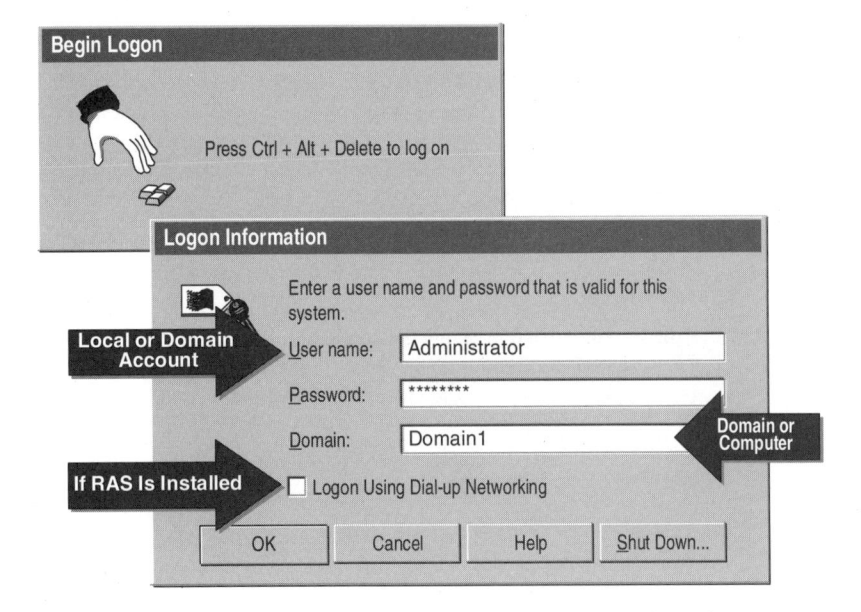

The following table describes the **Logon Information** dialog box options.

Option	Description
User name	Enter the unique user account that was assigned by an administrator. To log on to a domain, this account must reside in the directory database on domain controllers. To log on to the local computer, this account must reside in the directory database of the local computer.
Password	Enter the password assigned to the user name. Passwords are case-sensitive. The password appears on the screen as asterisks (*) to protect it from onlookers.
Domain	To log on to the domain, select the name of the domain. When a user logs on to the domain, the domain controller's directory database is checked for a valid match. The account is validated if the user name, password, and domain name match the domain controller's directory database.
	To log on to the local computer, select the name of the computer. When a user logs on to a local computer, the local computer's directory database is checked for a valid match. The account is validated if the user name, password, and computer name match the local directory database.
	A user can only log on to a local computer with a user name that resides in the local computer's directory database. Member servers and computers running Windows NT Workstation have a local Administrator and a Guest account by default. Other local accounts must be created.
Logon Using Dial-up Networking	When Remote Access Service (RAS) is installed, selecting this check box allows a user to log on to a remote network using RAS.
Shut Down	Closes all files, saves all operating system data, and prepares the computer to be safely turned off. On Windows NT Server, this button is disabled to prevent an unauthorized user from shutting down the server.

Logging On

To log on, the information that the user supplies in the **User name** and **Password** boxes must be either a valid domain user account or a local user account, depending on whether the user is logging on to the domain or the local computer.

In the **Domain** box, the user selects either the name of a domain or the name of the local computer to which he or she is logging on.

- If the computer is participating in a domain, the **Domain** box contains both the computer name and the domain name, as well as any domains trusted by the computer account's domain. The **Domain** box lists every domain where user accounts can be authenticated. To log on to a domain, the user selects the name of the domain where the user account resides.

- If the computer is participating in a workgroup, the **Domain** box contains only the local computer name. The user name and password must reside in the local computer's directory database. This is the only place where user accounts can be authenticated.

> **Important** A user cannot log on to either the domain or the local computer from any computer running Windows NT Server, unless that user has been assigned the *Log on locally* user right by an administrator or has administrative privileges for the server. This feature helps to secure the server.

The Validation Process for a Domain Account

When the user clicks **OK**, the computer sends the domain name, user name, and password to a domain controller. The domain controller first checks the domain name, and then checks the user name and password against that domain's directory database.

One of the following three processes occurs:

- If the domain name is correct and the user name and password match a domain account, the server notifies the computer that the logon is approved.

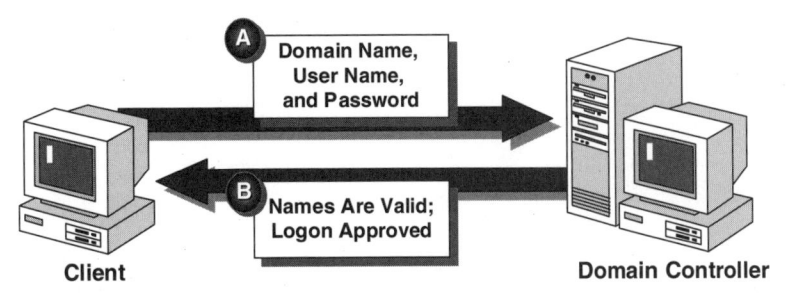

A Domain Name, User Name, and Password

B Names Are Valid; Logon Approved

Client   Domain Controller

- If the domain name is different and the domain controller recognizes the domain as a trusted domain, the domain controller passes the information to the appropriate domain, which authenticates the logon and sends the information back to the original domain controller.

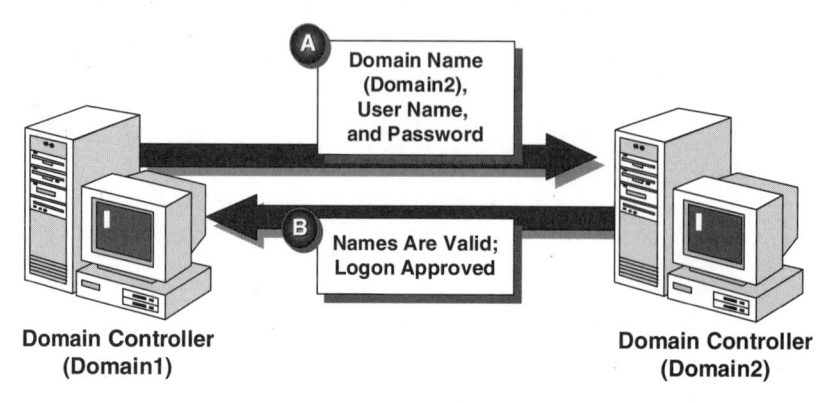

Domain Controller (Domain1) — A: Domain Name (Domain2), User Name, and Password → **Domain Controller (Domain2)**; B: Names Are Valid; Logon Approved

- If the domain name is different and the domain controller does not recognize the domain, the controller denies domain access.

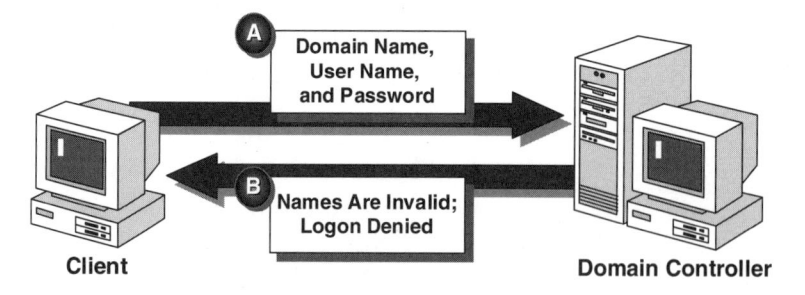

Client — A: Domain Name, User Name, and Password → **Domain Controller**; B: Names Are Invalid; Logon Denied

A Windows NT–based client keeps track of the last 10 successful logon attempts. This means that if the user account cannot be validated by a domain controller, but has been validated from that client within the last 10 previous successful logon attempts, the user will still have access to the local computer.

The Validation Process for a Local Account

When the user clicks **OK**, the computer checks the computer name, and then checks the user name and password against the local directory database. If the names match, the user account is validated and the user gains access to local resources. If the user account in not validated, the user does not gain access to the computer.

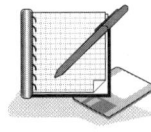

▶ **To log on to your domain**

1. Press CTRL+ALT+DELETE.

    The **Welcome** dialog box appears.

2. In the **User name** box, type **user1** (your domain user account name). By default, the account name that was last used to log on appears in this box. If this is the first time logging on, the default Administrator account appears in this box.

3. In the **Password** box, type **secret** (the password that is assigned to the account). Keep in mind that passwords are case-sensitive, and note that for security reasons, the password appears as asterisks to shield the password from onlookers.

4. In the **Domain** box, select your domain (where your account was created). By default the domain or computer name that was last used to log on appears in this box.

5. Click **OK**.

Using CTRL+ALT+DELETE to Prevent Trojan Horse Attacks

By requiring the user to press CTRL+ALT+DELETE to display the **Begin Logon** dialog box, Windows NT provides an important safeguard against Trojan horse programs. A Trojan horse program is an MS-DOS®-based program that tries to trick users into typing their user ID and password. The Trojan horse program then captures and saves the user's user name and password, giving the Trojan horse programmer access to the network.

Because most operating systems use CTRL+ALT+DELTE to restart a computer, it is difficult for programs to stay resident during a CTRL+ALT+DELETE keystroke operation. To ensure effective security, educate your users to always press CTRL+ALT+DELETE before logging on at a computer, even if the logon window already appears on the screen. The reason to always press CTRL+ALT+DELETE is to guarantee that you are providing your user name and password only to the operating system itself.

Lesson Summary

The following information summarizes the key points in this lesson:

- To log on, each user must supply a valid domain user account or a local user account.
- If a user supplies a valid domain user account, the user name and password are validated by the domain controller.
- If a user supplies a valid local user account, the user name and password are validated by the local computer.
- A user cannot log on from any computer running Windows NT Server unless that user has been assigned the Log on locally user right or the user has administrative privileges.

For more information on	See
User accounts	Chapter 2, "Working with User and Group Accounts," in Microsoft Windows NT Server *Concepts and Planning*.
	Chapter 2, "Setting Up User Accounts," in this book.
User rights	Chapter 1, "Managing Windows NT Server Domains," in Microsoft Windows NT Server *Concepts and Planning*.
	Chapter 2, "Working with User and Group Accounts," in Microsoft Windows NT Server *Concepts and Planning*.
The Administrators group	Chapter 2, "Working with User and Group Accounts," in Microsoft Windows NT Server *Concepts and Planning*.
	Chapter 3, "Setting Up Group Accounts," in this book.

Lesson 4: Windows NT Administrative Tasks and Tools

This lesson presents an overview of Windows NT administrative tasks and introduces the administrative tools. You will use many of these tools in the hands-on exercises that accompany the lessons throughout this book.

After this lesson, you will be able to:
- Describe the tasks required for administering Windows NT Workstation and Windows NT Server.
- Describe the functions of the Windows NT administrative tools for Windows NT Server and Windows NT Workstation.

Estimated lesson time: 10 minutes

Windows NT Administrative Tasks

Administering Windows NT involves both post-installation and day-to-day maintenance tasks. Administrative tasks for Windows NT Workstation and Windows NT Server are similar; however, the tools included with each product vary.

Administrative tasks can be grouped into the five categories described in the following table.

Administrative category	Specific tasks
User and group account administration	Planning, creating, and maintaining user and group accounts to ensure that each user can log on to the network and gain access to necessary resources.
Security administration	Planning, implementing, and enforcing a security policy to ensure protection of data and shared network resources, including folders, files, and printers.
Printer administration	Setting up local and network printers to ensure that users can connect to and use printer resources easily. Troubleshooting common printing problems.
Monitoring network events and resources	Planning and implementing a policy to audit network events so that you can find security breaches. Monitoring and controlling resource usage.
Backing up and restoring data	Planning, scheduling, and performing regular backups to ensure quick restoration of critical data.

The structure of this book maps to these five categories. The tasks in each category are described in detail in the corresponding chapters of this book.

Windows NT Administrative Tools

Both Windows NT Server and Windows NT Workstation include administrative tools. The Windows NT Workstation administrative tools are only used to administer the local computer. The Windows NT Server Administrative Tools are used to administer any computer in the domain.

The following illustration shows the administrative tools that are installed on a computer running Windows NT Workstation.

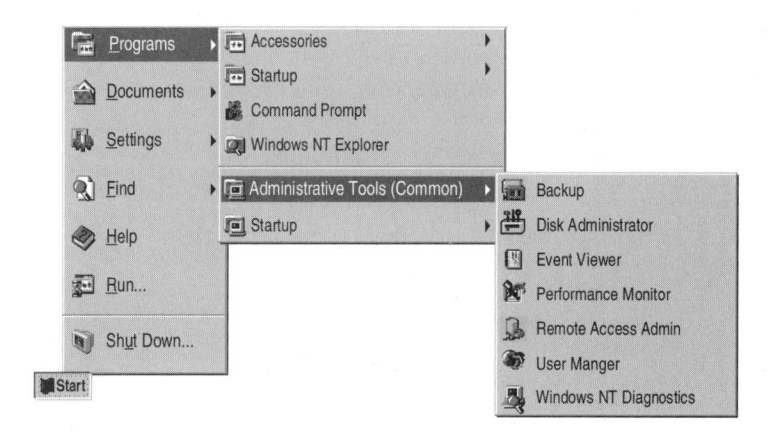

The following illustration shows the administrative tools that are installed on a computer running Windows NT Server.

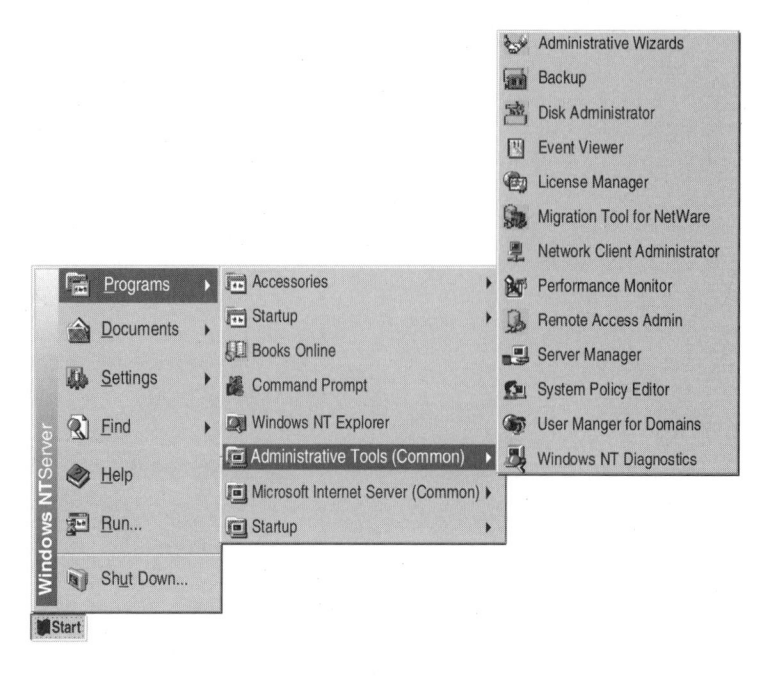

The following table describes the administrative tools that will be used throughout this book. Administrative Wizards, User Manager for Domains, and Server Manager are available on Windows NT Server only. User Manager is installed on Windows NT Workstation only. All other administrative tools are installed on computers running Windows NT Server and those running Windows NT Workstation.

Tool		Function
	Administrative Wizards	The administrative wizards are Windows NT Server tools that guide you through tasks, such as creating user accounts, creating and modifying group accounts, setting permissions on files and folders, and setting up network printers.
	User Manager for Domains	User Manager for Domains is a Windows NT Server tool that enables you to establish, delete, or disable domain user accounts. You can also set security policies and add user accounts to groups.
	User Manager	User Manager is a Windows NT Workstation tool that enables you to establish, delete, or disable local user and group accounts.
	Server Manager	Server Manager is a Windows NT Server tool that enables you to view and manage computers and domains.
	Event Viewer	In Windows NT, an event is any significant occurrence in the system or in a program that requires you to be notified. Event Viewer notifies you and/or puts the event in a log. It provides information about errors, warnings, and the success or failure of a task, such as a user logon attempt.
	Windows NT Diagnostics	Windows NT Diagnostics displays and prints system configuration information, such as data about memory, drives, and installed services.
	Backup	Backup is a tool used to back up information to your local tape drive. Backing up your computer protects your data from accidental loss and media failures.

Using Windows NT Server Client-based Tools

You can install the Windows NT Server client-based tools on any computer running Microsoft Windows 95 or Windows NT Workstation. This gives an administrator the ability to perform domain administration from a client. This is useful in networks where the server is locked in a room and is not easily accessible.

The client-based tools are located on the Windows NT Server compact disc in the Clients\Srvtools folder.

- To install the tools on a computer running Windows NT Workstation, run Setup.bat from the Clients\Srvtools\Winnt folder, and then create a shortcut to each tool. The following tools that are useful for performing tasks covered in this book are installed in the *systemroot*\System32 folder.
    - Usrgmgr.exe (User Manager for Domains)
    - Srvmgr.exe (Server Manager)
- To install the tools on a computer running Windows 95, see the Readme.txt file in the Clients\Srvtools\Win95 folder.

▶ **To open Administrative Tools**

In this procedure, you view the Administrative Tools on a computer running Windows NT Server.

1. Click the **Start** button, point to **Programs**, and then point to **Administrative Tools**.

    Notice all of the tools in the Administrative Tools group. To learn more about each tool, click a tool, and then on the **Help** menu, click **Contents**.

2. Click **Administrative Wizards** to view the wizards.

    The following table describes the wizards.

This wizard	Is used to
Add User Accounts	Create new user accounts.
Group Management	Create and modify group accounts.
Managing File and Folder Access	Set permissions on files and folders.
Add Printer	Set up printers that are connected to your computer or are on a network.
Add/Remove Programs	Install or remove programs from your computer.
Install New Modem	Set up modems that are connected to your computer.
Network Client Administrator	Install or update network client.
License Compliance	Check licensing for installed programs.

3. Click **Close**.

Lesson Summary

The following information summarizes the key points in this lesson:

- The Windows NT Workstation administrative tools are only used to administer the local computer.
- The Windows NT Server administrative tools are used to administer any computer in the domain.
- Windows NT Server Administrative Tools (with the exception of the Administrative Wizards) can be installed from the Windows NT Server compact disc on any computer running Windows NT Workstation or Windows 95.

For more information on	See
Each tool in the Administrative Tools group	Help provided in each tool.
User Manager and User Manager for Domains	Chapter 2, "Working with User and Group Accounts," in Microsoft Windows NT Server *Concepts and Planning*.
	Chapter 2, "Setting Up User Accounts," in this book.
	Chapter 3, "Setting Up Group Accounts," in this book.
Event Viewer	Chapter 9, "Auditing Resources and Events," in this book.
	Chapter 9, "Monitoring Events," in Microsoft Windows NT Server *Concepts and Planning*.
Server Manager	Chapter 4, "Administering User and Group Accounts," in this book.
	Chapter 10, "Monitoring Resources," in this book.
Windows NT Diagnostics	Chapter 10, "Monitoring Resources," in this book.
	Chapter 7, "Protecting Data," in Microsoft Windows NT Server *Concepts and Planning*.
Backup	Chapter 11, "Backing Up and Restoring Files," in this book.
	Chapter 6, "Backing Up and Restoring Network Files," in Microsoft Windows NT Server *Concepts and Planning*.
Installing client-based network administration tools	Chapter 11, "Managing Client Administration," in Microsoft Windows NT Server *Concepts and Planning*.

Lesson 5: The Windows NT Security Dialog Box

Once you are logged on, you can use the CTRL+ALT+DELETE key sequence, also referred to as the *secure attention sequence*, to access the **Windows NT Security** dialog box. You can use the **Windows NT Security** dialog box to perform key tasks.

After this lesson, you will be able to:
- Lock a workstation.
- Change your password.
- Use Task Manager.
- Log off Windows NT.
- Log on as a different user.
- Shut down the computer.

Estimated lesson time: 20 minutes

The **Windows NT Security** dialog box provides easy access to important security options. You will need to educate your users to use the features provided in this dialog box.

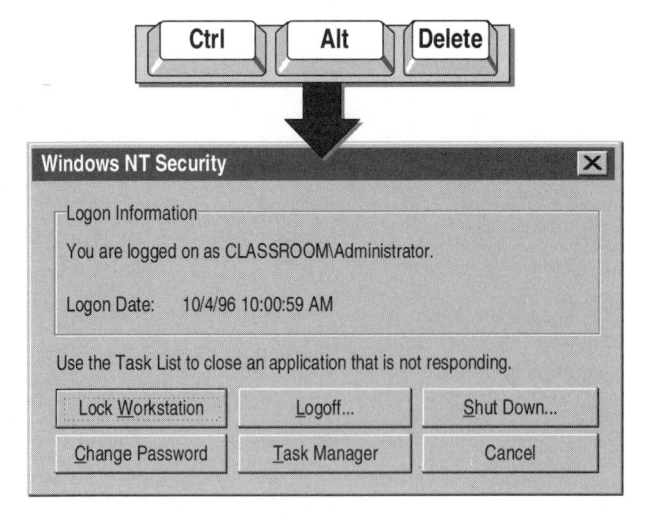

Chapter 1 Introduction to Administering Windows NT

The following table describes the **Windows NT Security** dialog box options.

Option	Function
Lock Workstation	Secures the computer without logging off. All programs remain running. Lock your workstation when leaving your workstation momentarily. The user who locks the workstation must unlock it by entering the valid password.
	If a user forgets the password, an administrator can unlock the workstation, log the user off the system, and then reassign a new password.
Change Password	Allows a user to change the user account password. The user must know the old password before a new one can be created. This prevents users from changing other users' passwords. This is the only way for users to change their passwords.
	Administrators should require users to change their passwords regularly and should set password restrictions as part of account policy.
Logoff	Logs off the current user, but leaves Windows NT running. This means that network users can still connect to and use shared resources on the computer. Always log off when you no longer need to use the computer.
Task Manager	Lists the current programs that are running. Task Manager gives you a summary of overall CPU and memory usage and a quick view of how each program, program component, or system process is using CPU and memory resources. Task Manager is also used to switch between programs and to stop a program that is not responding.
Shut Down	Closes all files, saves all operating system data, and prepares the computer to be safely turned off.
Cancel	Closes the **Windows NT Security** dialog box.

▶ **To lock your workstation**

1. Press CTRL+ALT+DELETE.

    The **Windows NT Security** dialog box appears.

2. Click **Lock Workstation**.

    The Workstation Locked window appears, indicating that the workstation is in use, but locked, and can only be opened by an administrator or by the authenticated user.

3. Press CTRL+ALT+DELETE.

    The **Unlock Workstation** dialog box appears.

4. In the **Password** box, enter your password, and then click **OK** to unlock your workstation.

▶ **To change your password**

1. Press CTRL+ALT+DELETE.

    The **Windows NT Security** dialog box appears.

2. Click **Change Password**.

    The **Change Password** dialog box appears.

    Notice that the **User name** and **Domain** boxes show the current user account and domain.

3. In the **Old Password** box, enter the current password.

4. In the **New Password** and **Confirm New Password** boxes, enter the new password, and then click **OK**.

    Your password change is confirmed.

5. Click **OK** to return to the **Windows NT Security** dialog box.

6. Click **Cancel**.

▶ **To close a program from Task Manager**

In this procedure, you open WordPad and then close it using Task Manager. Use this procedure anytime a program has stopped responding.

1. Click the **Start** button, point to **Programs**, point to **Accessories**, and then click **WordPad**.

    WordPad opens.

2. Press CTRL+ALT+DELETE.

    The **Windows NT Security** dialog box appears.

3. Click **Task Manager**.

    The Windows NT Task Manager window appears.

4. Click the **Applications** tab, if it is not already the default.

    A list of open program appears.

5. Under **Task**, click **WordPad**, and then click **End Task**.

   If the program has stopped responding, the following message appears.

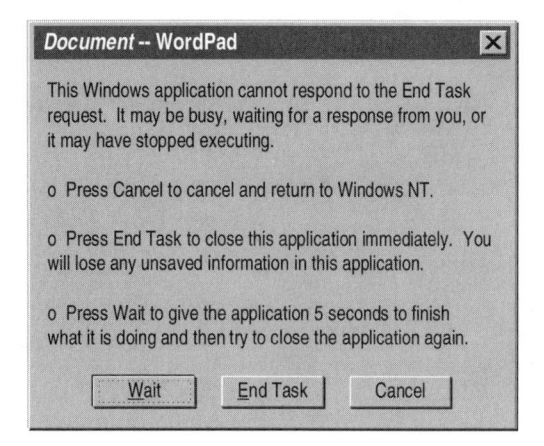

   > **Document -- WordPad**
   >
   > This Windows application cannot respond to the End Task request. It may be busy, waiting for a response from you, or it may have stopped executing.
   >
   > o Press Cancel to cancel and return to Windows NT.
   >
   > o Press End Task to close this application immediately. You will lose any unsaved information in this application.
   >
   > o Press Wait to give the application 5 seconds to finish what it is doing and then try to close the application again.
   >
   > [Wait]   [End Task]   [Cancel]

   If you did not get a chance to save changes to a document before your program stopped responding, click **Wait**. Clicking **Wait** gives the program five seconds to respond. If the program does respond, this message disappears and you are returned to your program. If your program still does not respond, click **End Task** to close the program.

   Important When Task Manager closes a program, all unsaved data is lost.

6. Exit Task Manager.

▶ **To log off**

1. Press CTRL+ALT+DELETE.

   The **Windows NT Security** dialog box appears.

2. Click **Logoff**.

   A message appears, stating that this will end your Windows NT session.

3. Click **OK**.

Note Another method to log off is to click the **Start** button, click **Shut Down**, and then click **Close all programs and log on as a different user**.

▶ **To shut down your workstation**

1. Press CTRL+ALT+DELETE.

    The **Windows NT Security** dialog box appears.

2. Click **Shut Down**.

    The **Shutdown Computer** dialog box appears. The default is **Shutdown and Restart**.

3. Click **OK** to shut down, or click **Cancel** to return to the **Windows NT Security** dialog box.

Lesson Summary

The following information summarizes the key points in this lesson:

- Use the CTRL+ALT+DELETE key sequence to gain access to the **Windows NT Security** dialog box.
- Using the **Windows NT Security** dialog box is the only way that users can change their passwords.
- Educate all users to lock their workstations anytime they leave them, to log off their workstations when they no longer need to use the computer, and to shut down their computers before turning them off.
- Use Task Manager as a troubleshooting tool anytime a program stops responding.

For more information on	See
Task Manager	Task Manager Help.

Best Practices

The following checklist provides best practices for ensuring security and safety. Educate your users to do the following:

- Always press CTRL+ALT+DELETE before logging on at a computer, even if the logon window already appears on the screen. This will ensure effective security and prevent Trojan horse attacks.
- Use the **Shut Down** command to safely prepare the computer to be turned off. This ensures that Windows NT will close all open files, save system settings, update the user environment settings, and avoid file corruption.
- Keep passwords absolutely secret. This ensures each user that no one else can access her computer and network resources by using her password.
- Enable the password protection on the computer's screen savers. This ensures that workstations will lock automatically when left unattended.
- Lock computers when stepping away from a workstation. The user's programs remain open, but the operating system remains locked until the user who locked the workstation unlocks it by entering a valid password.
- Log off computers when leaving a workstation. When a user logs off the system, all of the user's open files are closed. Windows NT remains running, however, so that another user can log on.

Additionally, for convenience:

- Install the Windows NT Server Administrative Tools (from the Clients\Srvtools folder on the Windows NT Server compact disc) on a client computer running the Windows NT Workstation or Windows 95 client, so that domain administration can be done from the client, allowing the server to be locked in a room for additional security.

Note If you want to remove the User1 user account that was created for use in this chapter only, log on as Administrator, and then double-click DeleteChapter1.cmd in the Cleanup folder on the Supplemental Material compact disc.

Review

The following questions are intended to reinforce key information presented in this chapter. If you are unable to answer a question, review the lesson and then try the question again.

1. What is the primary difference between Windows NT Server and Windows NT Workstation?

   _____

   _____

2. Which of the following describe a workgroup? (Circle all that apply.)

   a. A workgroup has only computers running Windows NT Workstation.

   b. A workgroup is a peer-to-peer network.

   c. A workgroup has at least one Windows NT Server domain controller.

   d. A workgroup does not have a Windows NT Server domain controller.

   e. Resource administration tasks are distributed to each computer in the network.

3. Which of the following describe a domain? (Circle all that apply.)

   a. A domain is a logical grouping of computers that share common security and user account information.

   b. A domain has at least one Windows NT Server member server.

   c. A domain has at least one Windows NT Server domain controller.

   d. A domain does not have a Windows NT Server domain controller.

   e. Resource administration is centralized at the domain controller.

4. Which of the following accurately describe differences between a domain controller and a member server? (Circle all that apply.)

   a. A domain controller is a computer running Windows NT Server that validates user logons for the domain.

   b. A domain controller maintains the master directory database for the domain.

   c. A member server is a computer running Windows NT Server that does not validate user logons for the domain.

   d. A member server is often used as an application server.

5. What key sequence is used to log on to the computer or a domain and to access the **Window NT Security** dialog box?

   _____

   _____

Answer Key

Procedure Answers

Page 11

▶ **To review the video**

1. Name three benefits of Windows NT Server Directory Services.

   Single user logon, universal access to resources, and centralized administration.

2. Name the three Windows NT Server configurations.

   Primary domain controller, backup domain controller, and member server.

3. How many primary domain controllers can there be in each domain? How many backup domain controllers?

   Each domain must have one and *only* one primary domain controller. A domain can have more than one backup domain controller.

4. How does a domain differ from a peer-to-peer network?

   In a domain, all domain controllers maintain a common directory database; therefore, a user can log on from any computer using a single user name and password. In a peer-to-peer network, each computer maintains its own directory database; therefore, a separate user account for each user must exist in each computer's directory database.

5. Name the logical link that combines domains into one administrative unit.

   A trust relationship, or trust.

Page 31

Review Answers

1. What is the primary difference between Windows NT Server and Windows NT Workstation?

   Windows NT Server is optimized for use as a file, print, and application server. Windows NT Workstation is optimized for use as a high-performance desktop operating system.

2. Which of the following describe a workgroup? (Circle all that apply.)

   Answers b, d, and e are correct.

3. Which of the following describe a domain? (Circle all that apply.)

   Answers a, c, and e are correct.

4. Which of the following accurately describe differences between a domain controller and a member server? (Circle all that apply.)

   All answers are correct.

5. What key sequence is used to log on to the computer or a domain and to access the **Window NT Security** dialog box?

   The correct key sequence is CTRL+ALT+DELETE.

CHAPTER 2

Setting Up User Accounts

Lesson 1 Introduction to User Accounts . . . 36

Lesson 2 Planning New User Accounts . . . 40

Lesson 3 Creating User Accounts . . . 48

Lesson 4 Creating User Profiles . . . 65

Best Practices . . . 74

Review . . . 75

About This Chapter

User accounts enable users to participate in a network and to access network resources. This chapter introduces you to the three types of user accounts and provides you with a planning strategy for implementing them. The hands-on procedures give you an opportunity to plan and create your own user accounts.

Before You Begin

To complete the lessons in this chapter, you must have:

- Viewed the *Overview of Directory Services* video referred to in Chapter 1, "Introduction to Administering Windows NT."
- Knowledge about the difference between a workgroup and a domain.
- Knowledge about the difference between a domain controller and a member server.
- Experience logging on and off Windows NT.

Lesson 1: Introduction to User Accounts

Windows NT security is based on the concept of user accounts. A user account is the user's unique credential that allows the user to access resources. This lesson provides an overview of user accounts.

After this lesson, you will be able to:
- Describe the types of user accounts.
- Describe the difference between a domain user account and a local user account.

Estimated lesson time: 10 minutes

Each person who will regularly use the network and participate in a domain, or who will log on to a local computer to access local resources, must have a user account. With user accounts, you can control how a user gains access to the domain or a local computer. For example, you can limit the number of hours a user can log on to the domain.

Types of User Accounts

There are three types of user accounts; one is the type of accounts that you create, and two are built-in user accounts that are created automatically when Windows NT Server or Windows NT Workstation is installed. The two built-in accounts are the Guest account and the Administrator account.

The following table describes the three types of user accounts.

Account	Description
Accounts that you create	A user account enables the user to log on to the local computer or domain and, with the appropriate permissions, allows access to network resources. User accounts contain information about the user, including the user's name and password.
Guest	The built-in Guest account is used to give occasional users the ability to log on and gain access to resources on the local computer. For example, an employee who needs to access the computer for a short time can use the Guest account. The Guest account is disabled by default.
Administrator	The built-in Administrator account is used to manage the overall computer and domain configuration and resources. The Administrator account is used when performing administrative tasks, such as creating or modifying user and group accounts, managing security policies, creating printers, and assigning permissions and rights to user accounts to access resources.

Where Accounts Are Created

A computer's operating system determines the type of accounts that you can create and manage, as well as the tool that you use to create and manage them:

- On computers running Windows NT Workstation, the account management tool is User Manager. It is used to manage the accounts of that computer only. Accounts created with User Manager are local accounts.
- On computers running Windows NT Server, the account management tool is User Manager for Domains. It is used to manage accounts on the local domain or on any computer, member server, or other domains to which you have access. Accounts created with User Manager for Domains can be local accounts or domain accounts.

Domain User Account

A domain user account contains information that defines a user to the domain. With a domain user account, a user can log on to the domain and gain access to domain resources from any computer on the network using a single user account and password.

A domain user account is always created in User Manager for Domains. Although a domain user account can be created from any computer running User Manager for Domains, the account is always created in the master directory database on the primary domain controller (PDC).

A copy of the master directory database is stored on all backup domain controllers (BDCs). The copy is automatically synchronized every five minutes with the master directory database on the primary domain controller.

Create domain user accounts for all users.

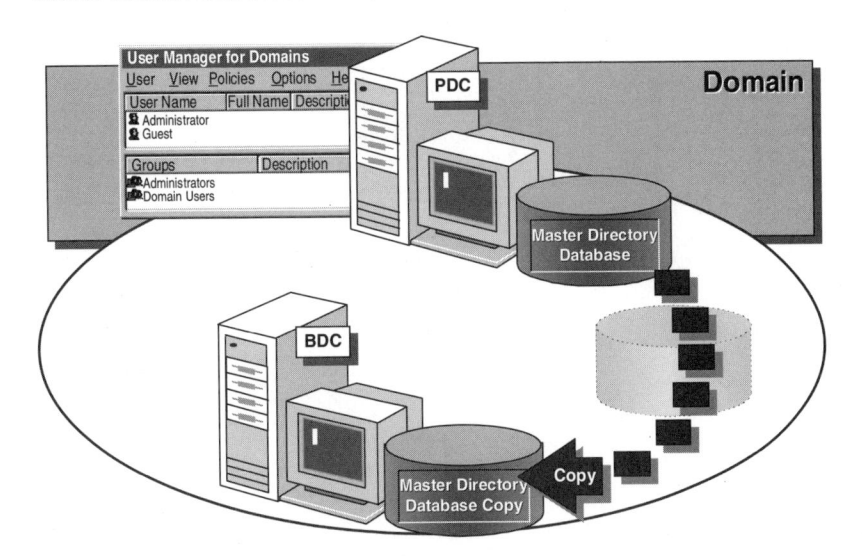

Note You can install User Manager for Domains on a computer running Windows NT Workstation or Windows® 95 by installing the Windows NT Server client-based administration tools.

Local User Account

A local user account contains information that defines a user to the local computer. With a local user account, a user can log on to and access local resources. To access resources on another computer, the user must have a separate user account on the other computer.

Although User Manager for Domains allows you to create accounts for the domain and for local computers, User Manager only allows you to create an account for the local computer.

Local user accounts should only be created within a workgroup, as shown in the following illustration.

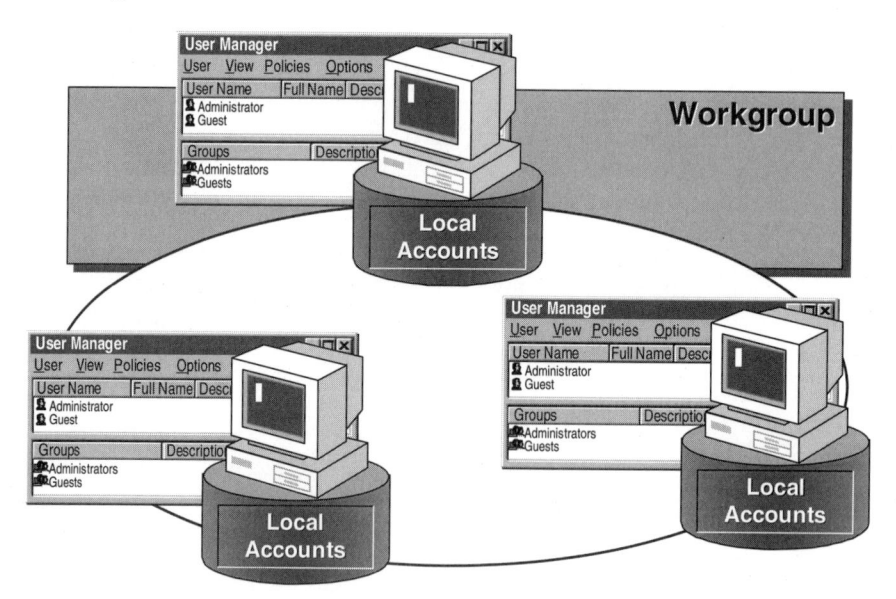

Lesson Summary

The following information summarizes the key points in this lesson:

- Windows NT security is based on the concept of user accounts.
- The Administrator account is a built-in account on all computers running Windows NT. It is used for overall management of computer resources and configuration.
- The Guest account is a built-in account on all computers running Windows NT. It provides occasional users the ability to use local computer resources. It is disabled by default.
- A domain user account gives a user the ability to log on to and access domain resources from any computer on the network using a single user account and password.
- Create a domain user account for all users.
- A local user account gives a user the ability to log on to the local computer and access local resources. To access resources on another computer, the user must have a separate account on the other computer.
- Create local user accounts only in a workgroup environment.

For more information on	See
Creating user accounts	Chapter 2, "Working With User and Group Accounts," in Microsoft Windows NT Server *Concepts and Planning*.
Installing client-based network administration tools	Chapter 11, "Managing Client Administration," in Microsoft Windows NT Server *Concepts and Planning*.

Lesson 2: Planning New User Accounts

Before you create user accounts, determine the requirements for each user based on the security level of your network. This lesson explores the strategies for creating new user accounts in networks with minimum, medium, and high levels of security.

After this lesson, you will be able to:
- Describe five elements of good user account planning.
- Plan a strategy for creating new user accounts.
- Explain how password requirements affect security levels.
- Describe the function and possible locations of a home folder.

Estimated lesson time: 30 minutes

Elements to Consider in Planning New User Accounts

To streamline the administration process, and to implement the most appropriate security measures for your organization, consider these elements in determining your planning strategy:

- *Naming convention.* Use a convention that ensures unique but consistent user account names.
- *Password requirements.* Select your password enforcement options, including whether a user can, or must, change his or her own password.
- *Logon hours.* Determine the hours that each user is allowed to log on.
- *Workstation restrictions.* Determine the computer names of the Windows NT computers that the user is permitted to work from. You can limit the choices. By default, the user can use any workstation.
- *Home folder location.* Determine location of home folders on the local computer or on a server for centralized backup and administration.

Naming Convention

A naming convention establishes how users will be identified on the network. A consistent naming convention makes it easy for you and your users to remember user names and locate them in lists.

To decide your naming convention, consider the following points:

- User names must be unique. Domain user accounts must be unique to the domain. Local user accounts must be unique to the local computer.

- User names can contain up to 20 uppercase or lowercase characters except for the following: " / \ [ ] : ; | = , + * ? < >. You can use a combination of special and alphanumeric characters.

- If you have a large number of users, establish a naming convention that accommodates employees with duplicate names. Two suggestions for handling duplicate names are:

    - Use the first name and the last initial, and then add additional letters from the last name to accommodate duplicate names. For example, if you have two users named Eric Lang, use EricL as one user name, and use EricLa for the other.

    - Add numbers to the user name. For example, EricL1 and EricL2.

- In large organizations, it is useful to identify temporary employees by their user account. For example, to identify temporary employees, use a "T" and a dash in front of the user name, as in, for example, T-EricL.

Password Requirements

The next element in planning new user accounts is identifying the password requirements. To protect access to the domain or a computer, every user account requires a password. This is especially important in networks with a medium to high level of security or in networks that are part of the Internet.

Consider the following guidelines for passwords:

- Always assign the Administrator account a password to prevent unauthorized users from using the account.

- Determine who will control the password. You may want to:

    - Assign users unique passwords and then prevent users from changing them. This gives control to administrators.

    - Assign users an initial password and then require users to change them the first time they log on. This way, the account is always protected and only individual users will know their passwords. This gives control to users.

- Determine whether an account needs to expire. For temporary employees, set their user accounts to expire when their contract or work assignment ends.
- Educate users on ways to protect their passwords by selecting passwords that deter computer hackers. Follow these guidelines:
  - Avoid using an obvious association, such as the name of a family member or pet.
  - Avoid using the user account name in any part of the password.
  - Use long passwords. Passwords can be up to 14 characters in length.
  - Use a combination of uppercase and lowercase characters. Passwords are case-sensitive. For example, the password *SeCret* is different from *secret*.
  - Include numbers in the password.

Logon Hours

By default, users can connect to a server 24 hours a day, 7 days a week. In a high-security network, restrict the hours when a user can log on to the network. For example, you may want to restrict hours in the following types of environments:

- Where logon hours are a condition for security certification, such as in a government network.
- Where there are multiple shifts; in this case, allow night shift workers to log on only during their working hours.

Workstation Restrictions

By default, any user with a valid account can log on to the network from any computer running Windows NT. In a high-security network where sensitive data is stored on the local computer, restrict which users can log on from that computer. For example, User1 can only log on from a computer named Computer1.

Home Folder Location

A home folder is a user's folder for storing files and programs. A home folder is useful because it provides a central location for a user's files, making it easy to locate files to back up or delete to clean up the hard disk. Each user should be assigned his or her own home folder.

If you create a home folder for a user, the home folder becomes the default folder whenever the user performs any of the following tasks within Windows NT or a program:

- Opens a file by clicking **Open** on the **File** menu.
- Saves a file by clicking **Save As** on the **File** menu.
- Starts a command prompt.

If you do not assign a home folder to a user, the default folder is Users\Default on the local computer.

A home folder can be stored on a network server or on a user's local computer.

Storing Home Folders on a Server

The following are considerations for storing home folders on a server.

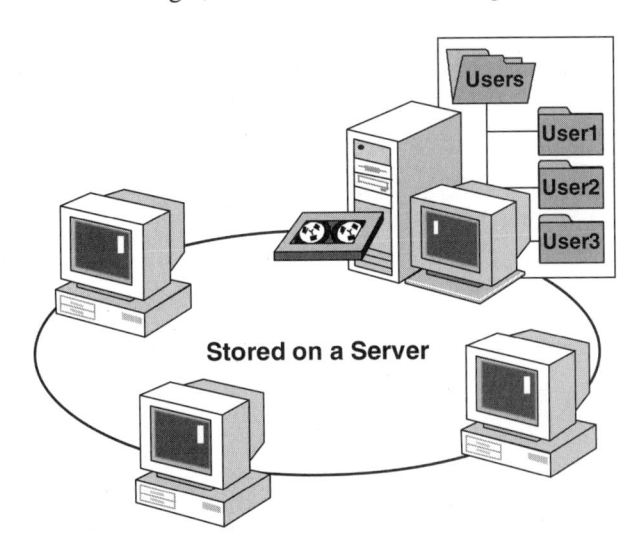

Stored on a Server

- *Backup and restore.* Preventing the loss of data is your primary responsibility. It is much easier to ensure files are backed up when they are located in a central location on a server. If users' home folders are located on their local computers, you would need to perform regular backups on each computer.
- *Space on the server.* Is there enough hard disk space on the server to store users' data? Windows NT does not provide the ability to limit the amount of hard disk space used by each user.
- *Security.* In any network with sensitive data, it is easier to maintain security on data if it is in a central location.
- *Use RAS or share computers.* If users connect to the network using Remote Access Service (RAS), or if they share their computers, having a home folder on a server makes the users' data available from any location or computer.

Storing Home Folders on Users' Computers

If it is not important to you to have a central location for maintaining data, you can create a home folder for each user on his or her local computer. Having a home folder gives the user a familiar and central place for storing data. The following are considerations for storing home folders on a user's computer.

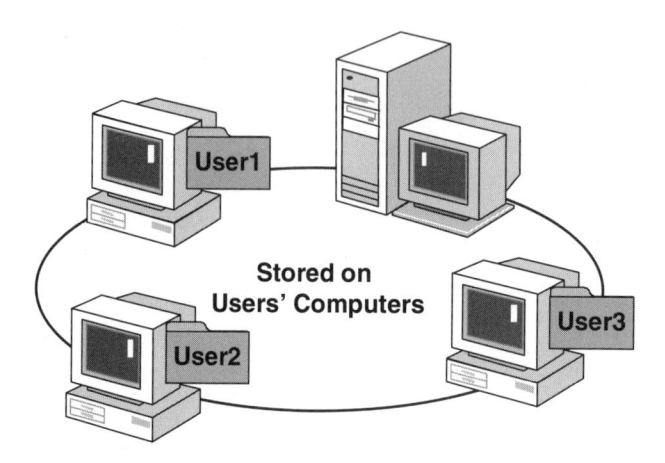

- *Space on the users' computers.* If users have space on their computers and it is not important to have centralized backup, locate home folders on users' computers.

- *Performance.* There is less network traffic if each user's home folder is located on the user's local computer.

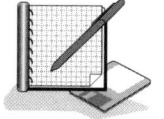

▶ **To plan new user accounts**

Scenario: World Wide Importers hires approximately 300 new employees a year. Approximately 20 of those employees are temporary contract employees hired on a one-year contract; the others are permanent staff. Each employee requires his or her own user account.

As the administrator for World Wide Importers, you would set up the user accounts for their Quebec office. In this exercise, however, you will work with only 9 user accounts that are representative of the accounts that you would create for World Wide Importers.

You will record your planning strategies on the "User Accounts Planning Worksheet" located at the end of this lesson. Notice that the Description column in the "User Accounts Planning Worksheet" identifies the job title for each of the nine employees. After completing the exercise, turn to Appendix A, "Planning Worksheets," and compare your worksheet to the sample provided. (The sample presents only one set of possible answers. You may have planned your accounts differently.)

To complete the "User Accounts Planning Worksheet," you need to:

1. Specify a full name of your choice for each user, except where already noted. Record it under Full Name.
2. Define your naming convention. Then determine each user name based on your naming convention. Record it under User Account.
3. Under Description, the job title for each employee is already noted.
4. Determine each user's password requirements (for example, Change at next logon). Record it under Password Requirements.
5. Under Home Folder Location, record either "local computer" or "server."
6. Under Logon Hours, record the access hours for each user (for example, 24/7 for 24 hour access, 7 days per week).
7. Under Workstation Restrictions, record "Yes" if the user will be restricted, and "No," if not (Y/N).

Use the following criteria to make your decisions:

- Two employees have the same name. The vice president's name is Linda Mitchell; the customer service representative who works the night shift is also named Linda Mitchell.
- For permanent employees, allow each password to be controlled by the employee.
- For temporary employees, allow each password to be controlled by the administrator for tighter security.
- Each employee requires a home folder. All home folders need to be backed up each night.
- Permanent employees who work the night shift need access to the network from 6 P.M. to 6 A.M.
- Permanent employees who work the day shift require access to the network 24 hours a day, 7 days a week.
- Temporary employees should be able to log on to *only* their assigned computers and only from 8 A.M. to 5 P.M.

Lesson Summary

The following information summarizes the key points in this lesson:

- There are five key planning elements you need to consider before implementing user accounts: naming convention, password requirements, home folder location, logon hours, and workstation restrictions.
- Require passwords for all users.
- In medium-security and high-security networks, or if your network is on the Internet, require long passwords that use a combination of uppercase and lowercase characters, and numbers. Educate users to avoid obvious associations when they select a password.
- In high-security networks, restrict the hours that a user can log on to the network.
- If sensitive data is stored on a local computer, restrict who can log on to the network from that computer.
- Assign users their own home folders so that they have a familiar and central place to store data.
- Store home folders on a network server to simplify backing up user data and to maintain sensitive data centrally.

User Accounts Planning Worksheet
Naming Convention: _____

Full Name	User Account	Description	Password Requirements	Home Folder Location	Logon Hours	Workstation Restrictions
Linda Mitchell		Vice president				
		Director of human resources				
		Sales manager				
		Sales representative				
Linda Mitchell		Customer service representative (night)				
		Customer service representative (day)				
		Accounting manager				
		Accountant				
		Temporary employee				

Lesson 3: Creating User Accounts

User accounts are created using User Manager or User Manager for Domains. To use either tool, you must have administrator privileges. This lesson explains the differences between User Manager and User Manager for Domains and takes you step-by-step through creating, deleting, and renaming user accounts.

After this lesson, you will be able to:
- Explain the difference between User Manager and User Manager for Domains.
- Create user accounts.
- Set password options.
- Create home folders.
- Set logon hours.
- Set workstation restrictions.
- Set account options.
- Grant dial-in permissions.
- Delete and rename user accounts.

Estimated lesson time: 40 minutes

User Manager vs. User Manager for Domains

User Manager and User Manager for Domains are very similar. In User Manager, you create, delete, or disable local user accounts on the local computer in a workgroup. In User Manager for Domains, you create, delete, or disable domain user accounts on the primary domain controller (PDC) or local user accounts on any computer in the domain.

The following illustration shows User Manager for Domains. All user account options appear in User Manager, except for **Select Domain**. The **Select Domain** option allows an administrator to select a different domain or computer in which to create or manage user accounts.

Chapter 2 Setting Up User Accounts   49

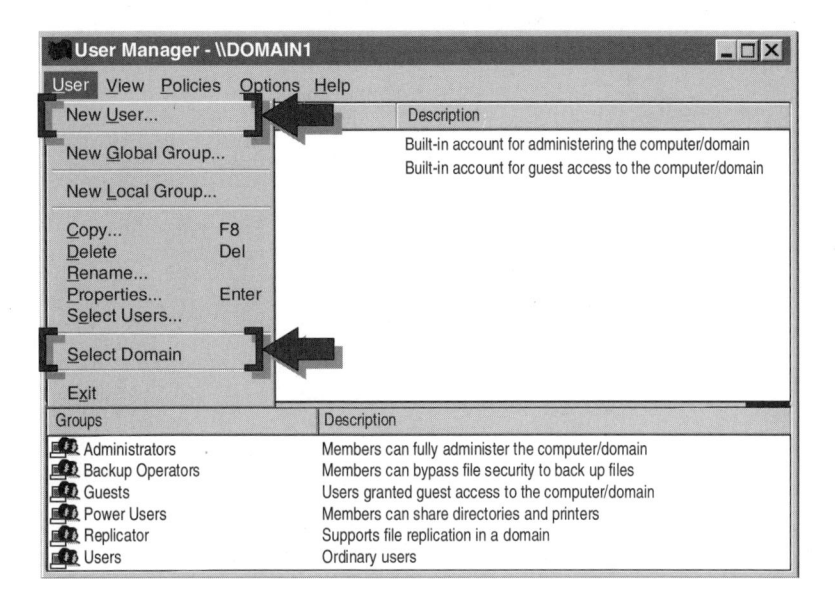

[User Manager menu screenshot showing User menu open with New User... and Select Domain highlighted by arrows, displaying built-in accounts and Groups list including Administrators, Backup Operators, Guests, Power Users, Replicator, and Users.]

The following **New User** dialog box is from User Manager for Domains. You can gain access to this dialog box by clicking **New User** on the **User** menu.

[New User dialog box screenshot with fields: Username: ericla, Full Name: Eric Lang, Description: Sales, Password and Confirm Password fields filled. Checkboxes: User Must Change Password at Next Logon (checked), User Cannot Change Password, Password Never Expires, Account Disabled, Account Locked Out. Buttons at bottom: Groups, Profile, Hours, Logon To, Account, Dialin. Hours, Logon To, and Account are bracketed as "User Manager for Domains only".]

All options in the **New User** dialog box appear in User Manager except for the **Hours**, **Logon To**, and **Account** buttons. On domain user accounts, these buttons are used to set logon hours, restrict workstation access, and set an expiration on an account.

The following table describes the user name and password options in User Manager and User Manager for Domains.

In this box	Type
Username	A unique name based on your naming convention. This is the only required option.
Full Name	The complete name of the user, to determine which person belongs to an account. This is optional.
Description	A description that is useful for identifying users. It can be a job classification, a department, or an office location. This is optional.
Password	An initial password for the account. In medium-security to high-security networks, you should always assign an initial password to keep the account secure. By default, when the user logs on for the first time, he or she must change the password. Notice that the password is not displayed. Instead, once you enter the password, it is represented on the screen by a series of 14 asterisks, regardless of the length of the password.
Confirm Password	The password a second time to make sure that you typed the password correctly. This is required if you assign the password.

Setting Password Options

Whether or not you assign a password to a new user account, by default, the user will be required to assign a new password to the account the first time the user logs on. Password options are set in the **New User** dialog box.

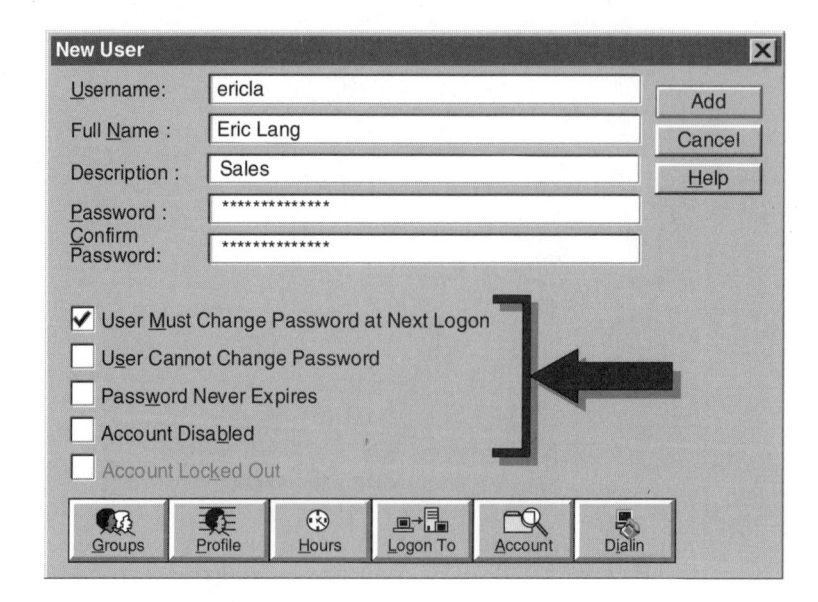

The following table describes the situations when you would select each password option.

Select this check box	If you
User Must Change Password at Next Logon (selected by default)	Want users to change their password the first time that they log on. This ensures that the user is the only person who knows his or her password. Even if you do not assign an initial password, you should require that users do this.
User Cannot Change Password	Have more than one person using the same user account (such as Guest) or want to maintain control over user passwords.
Password Never Expires	Have a user account for which you never want the password to change. For example, user accounts that will be used by Windows NT services (such as the Replicator service).
	This option overrides the selection of **User Must Change Password at Next Logon**.
Account Disabled	Want to temporarily prevent use of this account. For example, use when an employee takes a leave of absence.

Creating a Home Folder

To create home folders for users, you specify the name of the computer where the home folders will be located and names for the home folders.

The following checklist provides an overview of the tasks that you will need to do if you centralize home folders on a server. To create centralized home folders, do the following:

❑ On a server, create a folder named Users. This folder will be used to organize individual home folders. This task only needs to be done once.

❑ Share the folder and assign the Full Control permission to all users so that they can connect to it. This task only needs to be done once.

> **Note** The Users folder was created and shared for you in the Setup procedures described in "About This Book." Sharing folders and assigning permissions is covered in more detail in Chapter 5, "Securing Network Resources with Share Permissions" and Chapter 6, "Securing Network Resources with NTFS Permissions."

❑ Specify a home folder name and location for a user account in the **User Environment Profile** dialog box.

If you use %Username% in place of the home folder name, Windows NT will substitute %Username% with the user account name.

❑ Specify a network drive letter that will be used to connect to the user's home folder automatically when the user logs on.

The following **User Environment Profile** dialog box shows an example of how you specify a home folder location for a domain user account.

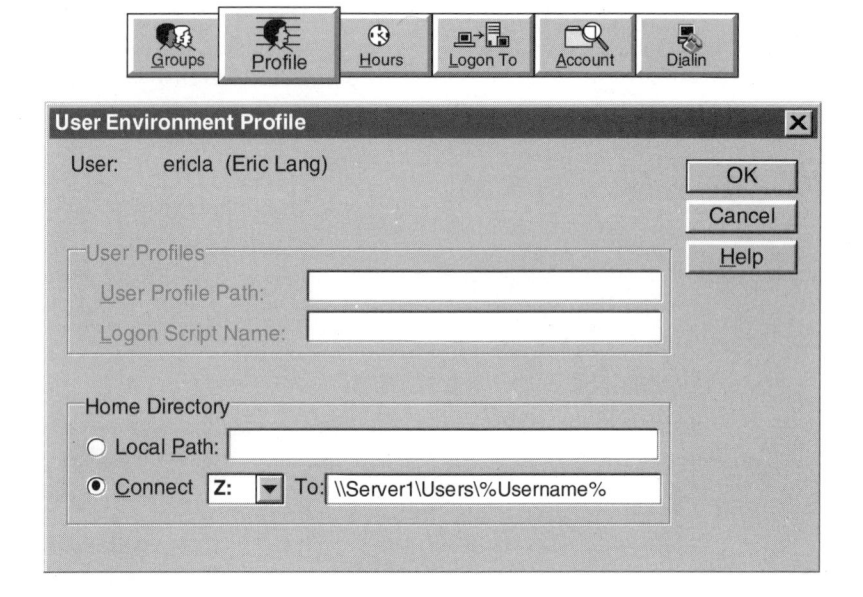

Note In a workgroup, you must specify the home folder for a local user account while sitting at the local computer. In the **Local Path** box, enter the local path; for example, type **c:***folder_name* and Windows NT creates the folder that you specify.

To create user accounts

In User Manager for Domains, you create the accounts that you planned in the hands-on procedure in the previous lesson, "Planning New User Accounts." If you did not complete the "User Accounts Planning Worksheet" from the lesson, use the sample plan provided in Appendix A, "Planning Worksheets."

1. Log on as Administrator.
2. Click the **Start** button, point to **Programs**, point to **Administrative Tools**, and then click **User Manager for Domains**.
3. On the **User** menu, click **New User**.

    The **New User** dialog box appears.

4. Configure the following options based on the information from the "User Accounts Planning Worksheet" that you completed in the previous lesson or from the sample plan provided. For each user account on the worksheet, fill in the following options:
    - **Username**
    - **Full Name**
    - **Description**
    - **Password** (leave blank)
    - **Confirm Password**

5. Select the appropriate password options, and then click **Add**.

    The **New User** dialog box reappears and is cleared so that you can add another user.

6. Create the remaining user accounts.
7. When you have created all of the accounts on the "User Accounts Planning Worksheet," click **Close** to return to the User Manager window.

To create a home folder

In this procedure, you create a home folder for a user account on the "User Accounts Planning Worksheet."

1. In the User Manager window, double-click a user account that you just created.

    The **User Properties** dialog box appears. Notice that this dialog box looks the same as the **New User** dialog box. The **User Properties** dialog box appears whenever you modify an existing user account (one that appears in the User Manager window).

2. Click **Profile**.

    The **User Environment Profile** dialog box appears.

3. Under **Home Directory**, click **Connect**.

   Notice that **Z:** appears in the **Connect** box. This is the drive letter that you will use to connect the user to the home folder upon logon.

4. In the **To** box, type *computer_name***users****%username%** (where *computer_name* is the name of your computer).

   Remember, Users is the folder that was created and shared for you during the setup process.

5. Click **OK** to return to the **User Properties** dialog box.

6. Click **OK** to return to the User Manager window.

▶ **To assign home folders to multiple accounts at one time**

In this procedure, you create a home folder for the remaining user accounts on the "User Accounts Planning Worksheet."

1. In the User Manager window, select all of the remaining accounts that you created by holding down the CTRL key while you click each account.

2. On the **User** menu, click **Properties**.

3. In the **User Properties** dialog box, click **Profile**.

4. In the **Connect box**, click **Z:** so that drive Z will be used to connect to the user's home folder.

5. In the **To** box, type *computer_name***users****%username%** (where *computer_name* is the name of your computer).

6. Click **OK** to return to the **User Properties** dialog box.

7. Click **OK** to return to the User Manager window.

Setting Logon Hours

When you set logon hours for a user account, you select the days of the week and the range of time for each day that you want to allow or disallow the user to have access the network.

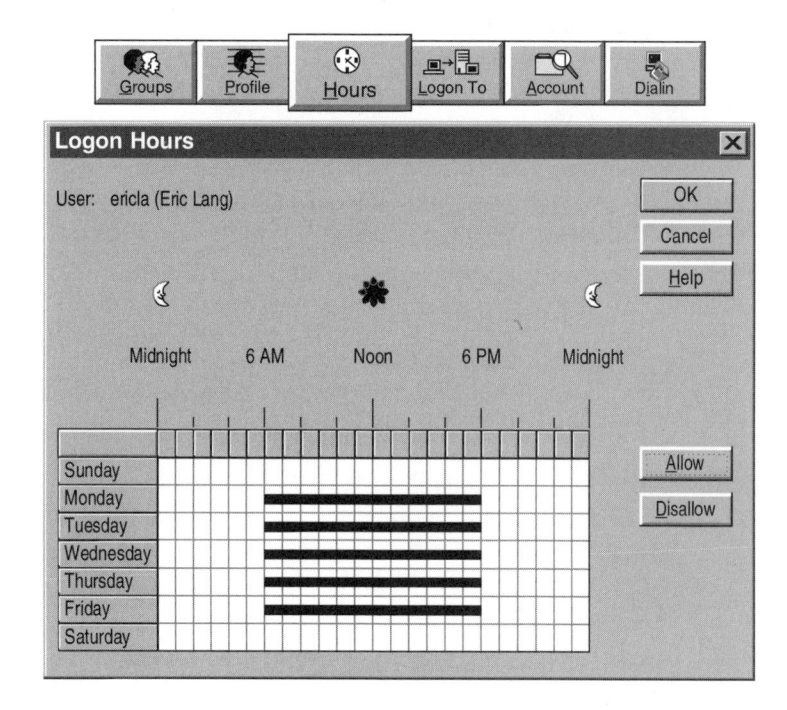

Setting logon hours lets you control when a user can log on to the domain. Restricting logon hours limits the hours that users can explore the network, or the times that someone can try to break into the network.

Note A user who is connected to a network resource on the domain is not disconnected when the user's logon hours run out. However, the user will be unable to make any new connections.

To specify logon hours

1. In the User Manager window, double-click a user account that requires logon hour restrictions (refer to the "User Accounts Planning Worksheet").
2. In the **User Properties** dialog box, click **Hours**.

   By default, all hours on all days are allowed. This is represented by a filled box for every hour of every day. A *filled* box indicates that the user is allowed to log on during that hour. An *empty* box indicates that the user cannot log on.
3. Position the mouse pointer on the rectangle on the day and hour that you want to disallow access. Press the mouse button, and drag the pointer through the last hour that you want to disallow. The area that you want to disallow should now be shaded.
4. Click **Disallow**. The area will still be shaded, but the line indicating hours of access should be gone.

   For more information about using the **Logon Hours** dialog box, click **Help**.
5. Repeat steps 3 and 4 for all of the times that you want the user to be disallowed.
6. Click **OK** to return to the **User Properties** dialog box.
7. Click **OK** to return to the User Manager window.
8. Restrict logon hours for any other users who only need to log on during specified times.

To test logon hours

1. Log off and then attempt to log on as the user account that you created for the sales representative.
2. If prompted, change the password to **student**.

   Remember, passwords are case-sensitive.

   Were you able to successfully log on? Why or why not?

   _____

3. Log off and then attempt to log on as the user who is restricted to logging on during night time hours.
4. If prompted, change the password to **student**.

   Were you able to successfully log on? Why or why not?

   _____

Setting Workstation Restrictions

To set workstation restrictions, you can specify up to eight computer names from which a user can log on. Setting workstation access allows you to control which computers a user can use to log on to the domain. This prevents users from accessing another user's local data and can be used to require users to log on to workstations that are in an observed location. Set workstation restrictions in high-security networks.

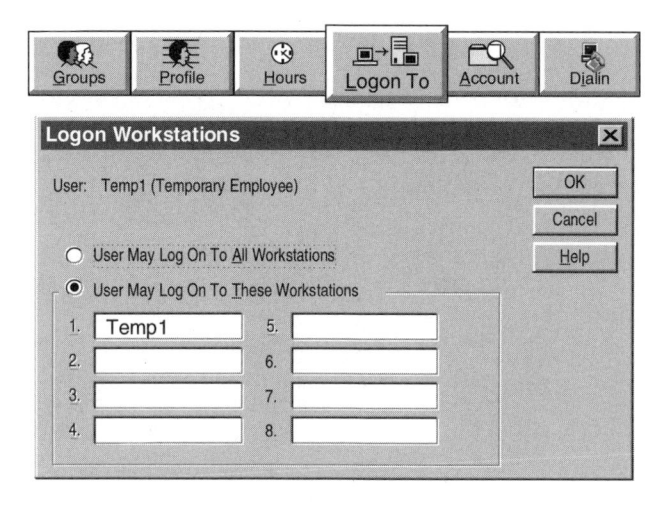

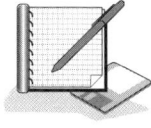

▶ **To specify the workstation from which a user can log on**

1. In the User Manager window, double-click the user account that you created for the temporary employee.

2. In the **User Properties** dialog box, click **Logon To**.

    The **Logon Workstations** dialog box appears. By default, each user account can log on from all computers.

3. Click **User May Log On To These Workstations**.

4. In the first box, type **Temp1** (the name of the computer from which the user is allowed to log on).

5. Click **OK** to return to the **User Properties** dialog box.

6. Click **OK** to return to the User Manager window.

▸ **To test workstation restrictions**

1. Log on to your computer as the user account that you created for the temporary employee.

2. If prompted, change the password to **student**.

   You were restricted from logging on to the computer, because the temporary employee can only log on to a computer named Temp1.

Setting Account Options

The following two options can be set in the **Account Information** dialog box:

- *Account Expires*. Use this to set a date when the account will be automatically disabled. To specify when a user account expires, type the date of expiration. This is useful for temporary accounts for contractors or part-time employees.

- *Account Type*. Use this to create a local account for a user from an untrusted domain who needs access to a network resource in your domain. A local account can be used to connect to a resource over the network. It cannot be used to log on from a computer in the domain where it was created.

  You only use the **Local Account for users from untrusted domains** option under **Account Type** if you want to assign permission to a user who has an account in a domain that does not have the appropriate trust relationship to your domain.

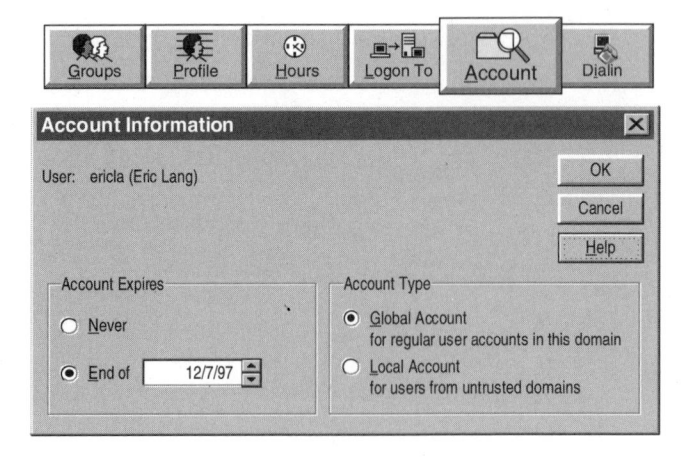

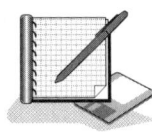

▶ **To set the account restriction**

In this procedure, you configure the Temporary Employee user account to expire in 30 days.

1. In the User Manager window, double-click the user account that you created for the temporary employee (refer to the "User Accounts Planning Worksheet").
2. In the **User Properties** dialog box, click **Account**.

   The **Account Information** dialog box appears.

   Notice that the default option for **Account Expires** is **Never**.
3. Click **End of**, and then type the date that is 30 days from today.
4. Click **OK** to return to the **User Properties** dialog box.
5. Click **OK** to return to the User Manager window.

Granting Dial-in Permission

Windows NT dial-up networking client software gives a user access to server-based dial-in packages, such as Windows NT Server Remote Access Service (RAS). Once the connection is made from the RAS client to the RAS server, users at remote sites can use the network as if their computers were directly connected to the network.

Before a user can log on to the network using RAS, the user must have dial-in permission assigned to his or her user account.

Note Additionally, the Remote Access Service must already be installed and configured on the server, and the client must already be configured for dial-up networking.

You can specify an option for the RAS server to call the dial-in user back. The RAS server can dial the number specified by the user so that the company is billed for the call. Or, the RAS server can dial a number that you specify, which restricts the user to a specific dial-in location.

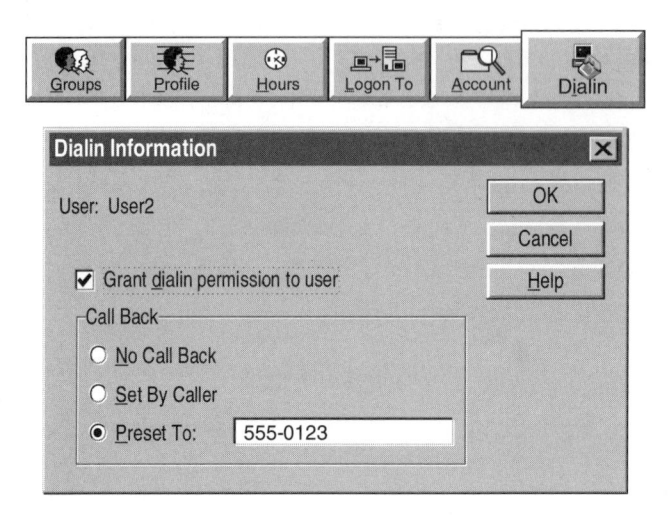

The following table describes the **Dialin Information** dialog box options.

Option	Description
No Call Back	When selected, the RAS server will not call back the user, and the user will incur the telephone charges for the session. This is the default.
Set By Caller	When selected, lets the user specify a telephone number so that the RAS server can call the user back. This means that the organization that owns the RAS server will incur the telephone charges for the session.
Preset To	When selected, lets you specify a telephone number that the RAS server will use to call back the user. This reduces the risk of an unauthorized person using the user's account, because the user must be at the specified phone number in order to connect to the RAS server. In high-security networks, use this option and restrict users to dialing in from only one telephone number.

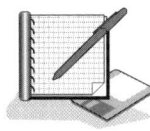

▸ **To grant dial-in permission**

In this procedure, you grant dial-in permission for the Accounting Manager who requires dial-in privileges from home.

1. In the User Manager window, double-click the user account that you created for the accounting manager (refer to the "User Accounts Planning Worksheet").
2. In the **User Properties** dialog box, click **Dialin**.

   The **Dialin Permission** dialog box appears.
3. Select the **Grant dialin permission to user** check box.
4. Click **OK** to return to the **User Properties** dialog box.
5. Click **OK** to return to the User Manager window.

Deleting and Renaming User Accounts

In Windows NT, every account is assigned a unique security identifier (SID) when the account is first created. A SID is a unique number that identifies the account. Internal processes in Windows NT refer to an account's SID rather than the account's user or group name.

Deleting an account permanently removes the account and the permissions and rights associated with it. For example, if you create an account, delete it, and then create an account with the same user name, the new account will not have the rights or permissions previously granted to the old account because the accounts have different SID numbers.

Renaming an account retains the permissions and rights associated with it because the SID was not deleted.

The following table describes the situations in which you should delete or rename an account.

Do this	When
Rename an account	You want to retain all rights, permissions, and group memberships for the account for a different user. For example, when a new employee replaces another employee, rename the user account and have the new employee change his or her password when he or she first logs on.
Delete an account	The account is no longer needed. When an account is deleted, all of the account information is lost. This information includes account properties, rights, permissions, and group memberships. The Administrator and Guest accounts cannot be deleted.

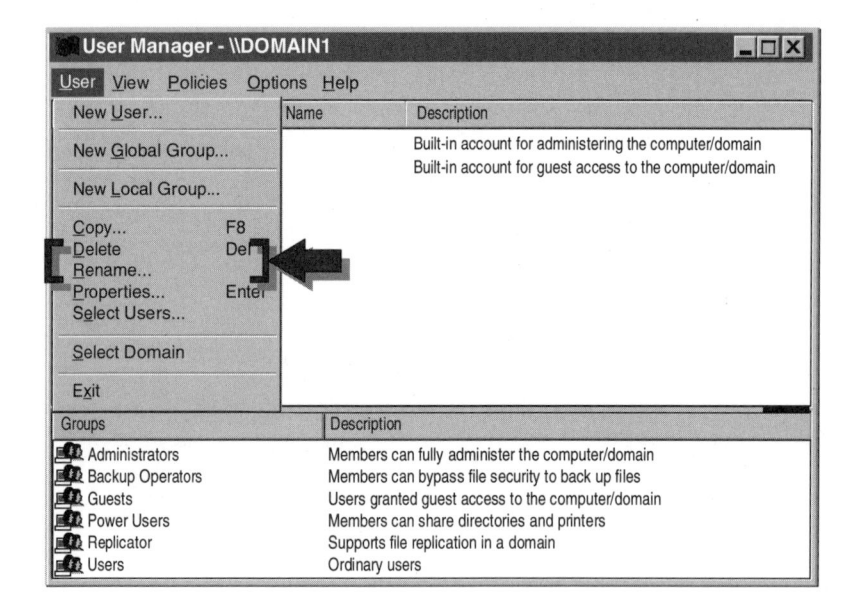

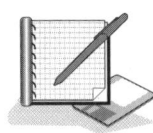

▶ **To rename a user account**

In this procedure, you create a user account and then rename it.

1. Create a new user account named Temp2.
2. In the User Manager window, select Temp2.
3. On the **User** menu, click **Rename**.
4. In the **Change To** box, type **temp3** and then click **OK**.

   The User Manager window is updated immediately.

▶ **To delete a user account**

1. In the User Manager window, select Temp3.
2. Press the DELETE key or, on the **User** menu, click **Delete**.

   A message appears warning you that once the account is deleted, even recreating it will not make the resources available to the newly created account that were available to the account that you deleted.

3. Click **OK** to acknowledge the warning.

   A message appears asking if you want to delete the user.

4. Click **Yes** and the user account is deleted.

Lesson Summary

The following information summarizes the key points in this lesson:

- In User Manager, you create, delete, or disable local accounts on a local computer in a workgroup.
- In User Manager for Domains, you create, delete, or disable domain and local accounts on the primary domain controller.
- Assign an initial password to an account and then require the user to change the password the first time that they log on. This ensures that the account is protected and only the user knows the password.
- When you create home folders for users, you specify the drive to which the user will connect, the server name, and the share name. In place of the user name, use %Username% to automatically name the home folder after the user name.
- When you set logon hours for a user account, you specify the days of the week and the time range for each day that you want to allow or disallow a user to log on.
- When you set workstation restrictions for a user account, you can specify up to eight names of the computers from which a user can log on.
- When you set account options, you specify the expiration date of a user account or you specify that the account is a local account for users from untrusted domains.

For more information on	See
Creating user accounts	Chapter 2, "Working With User and Group Accounts," in Microsoft Windows NT Server *Concepts and Planning*.
Trusted relationships between domains	Chapter 1, "Managing Windows NT Server Domains," in Microsoft Windows NT Server *Concepts and Planning*.
	Chapter 2, "Network Security and Domain Planning," in the *Networking Guide* of the *Microsoft Windows NT Server Resource Kit*.
Dial-up networking and Remote Access Service (RAS)	Chapter 7, "RAS Security," in the Microsoft Windows NT Server *Networking Supplement*.

Lesson 4: Creating User Profiles

User profiles are useful for configuring or managing a user's desktop environment. This lesson introduces user profiles and explains the differences between personal user profiles, which are profiles users can change, and mandatory user profiles, which are profiles that users cannot change.

After this lesson, you will be able to:
- Explain the difference between a roaming personal user profile and a mandatory user profile.
- Configure a local user profile.
- Create a roaming personal user profile.
- Create a roaming mandatory user profile.

Estimated lesson time: 30 minutes

User Profiles

In Windows NT, a user's computing environment is determined primarily by the user profile. Windows NT security requires a user profile for each account that has access to the system.

The user profile contains all user-definable settings for the work environment of a computer running Windows NT, including display, regional, mouse, and sounds settings, and network and printer connections.

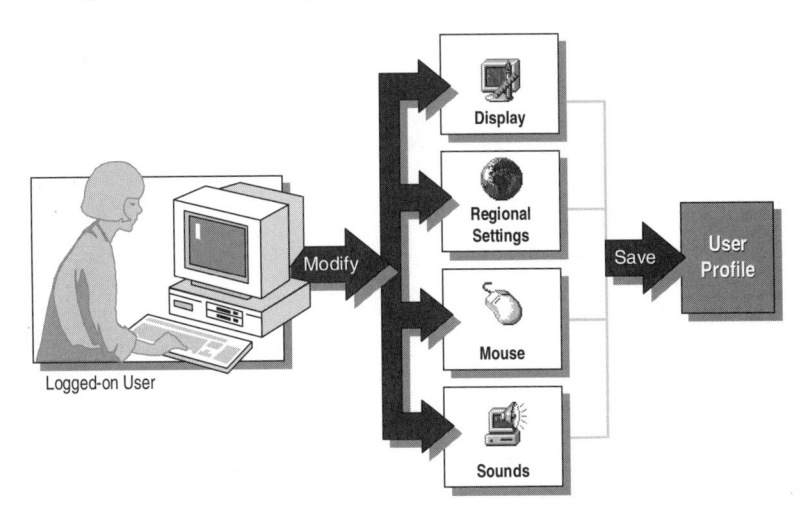

When a user logs on for the first time from a Windows NT–based client, a default user profile is created for that user. All user-specific settings are automatically saved into the Profiles folder within the system root folder (typically C:\Winnt\Profiles*user_name*).

A user profile can also be customized to restrict what users see in their interface and what tools they have available to use when they log on. For example, an administrator can remove the Administrative Tools folder to prevent a user from changing a configuration.

The following table describes the settings that are automatically saved in a user profile.

Source	Parameters saved
Windows NT Explorer	All user-definable settings for Windows NT Explorer.
Taskbar	All personal program groups and their properties, all program items and their properties, and all Taskbar settings.
Printers Settings	Network printer connections.
Control Panel	All user-defined settings made in Control Panel.
Accessories	All user-specific program settings affecting the user's Windows NT environment, including Calculator, Clock, Notepad, Paint, and HyperTerminal, among others.
Windows NT–based programs	Any program written specifically for Windows can be designed so that it tracks program settings on a per-user basis. If this information exists, it is saved in the user profile.
Online Help bookmarks	Any bookmarks placed in the Windows NT Help system.

Note User profiles cannot be set for users who log on from LAN Manager, MS-DOS, Windows for Workgroups, or Windows 3.*x* clients. For these clients, you can write a logon script to configure the user's network and printer connections. For information on creating logon scripts, see Microsoft Windows NT Server *Concepts and Planning*.

Roaming User Profiles

Unlike a default user profile, roaming user profiles provide users with the same working environment, no matter which Windows NT–based computer a user logs on to. Roaming user profiles are stored centrally on a network server rather than on the user's local computer.

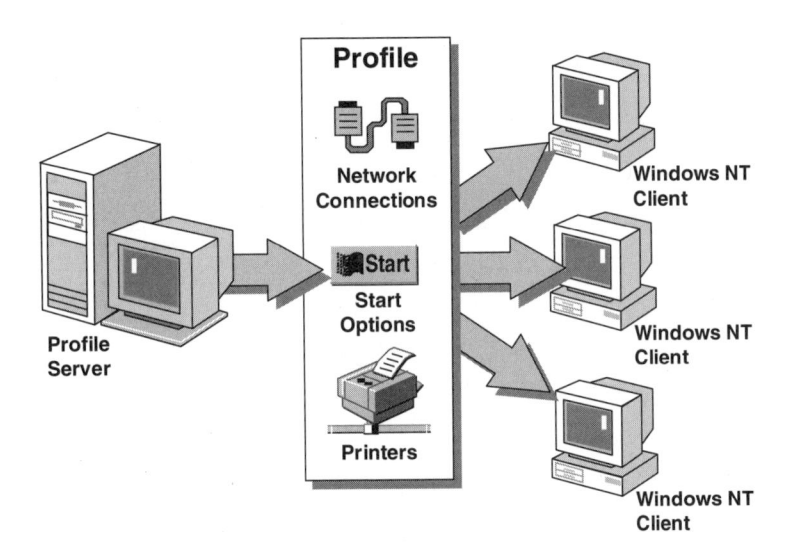

You can specify one of the following two roaming profiles for a user account:

- *Roaming personal user profile.* This is a user profile that a user can change. It is updated to include any changes made by the user when the user logs off. When the same user logs on again, the profile is loaded as it was last saved. If you use roaming personal user profiles, each user should be assigned his or her own profile.

  Roaming personal user profiles are named Ntuser.dat.

- *Roaming mandatory user profile.* This is a preconfigured user profile that users cannot change. One mandatory profile can be assigned to many users. This means that by changing one profile, you can change several desktop environments. You use this type of profile to assign common settings for all users who require identical desktop configurations—for example, bank tellers.

  Mandatory user profiles require an .man extension. You can make a personal profile mandatory by renaming it—for example, Ntuser.man.

Note Windows NT user profiles are not compatible with Windows 95 user profiles. Windows 95–based client profiles must be created on a computer running Windows 95.

Creating Roaming User Profiles

The following checklist provides an overview of the tasks required to implement roaming user profiles:

- ❏ Create a template user profile with the appropriate configuration. You do this by creating a user account, and then configuring the appropriate desktop settings.
- ❏ Create and share a folder named Profiles. (For this lesson, this step was done for you during the Setup process.) This will allow users to access the profiles from a remote computer.
- ❏ Copy the template user profile to a network server and specify the users who are permitted to use the profile.
- ❏ Specify the path to the profile for the user account in the **User Environment Profile** dialog box.

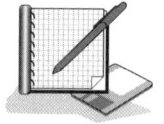

▶ **To create a template user profile**

In this procedure, you create a user account named Template Profile. This user account will be the model for a profile. Then, you configure the settings for the template profile.

1. In the **New User** dialog box, create a user account named **Template Profile** with no password. Clear the **User Must Change Password at Next Logon** check box.

2. Log on as **Template Profile**.

    A local user profile is automatically created for the Template Profile user on the local computer in the *drive:\systemroot*\Profiles folder.

3. Right-click anywhere on the desktop, and then on the shortcut menu, click **Properties**.

    The **Display Properties** dialog box appears.

4. Click **Appearance**.

    Notice the current color scheme.

5. In the **Color Schemes** box, select a different color scheme, and then click **OK**. The change will take effect immediately.

6. Log off and log on as the same user.

    Notice that the screen colors were those saved in the user's profile.

Copying the Profile to a Network Server

You copy a user profile using the System program in Control Panel. When you click the **User Profiles** tab of the **System Properties** dialog box, the default profiles appear for all users who have previously logged on to the computer.

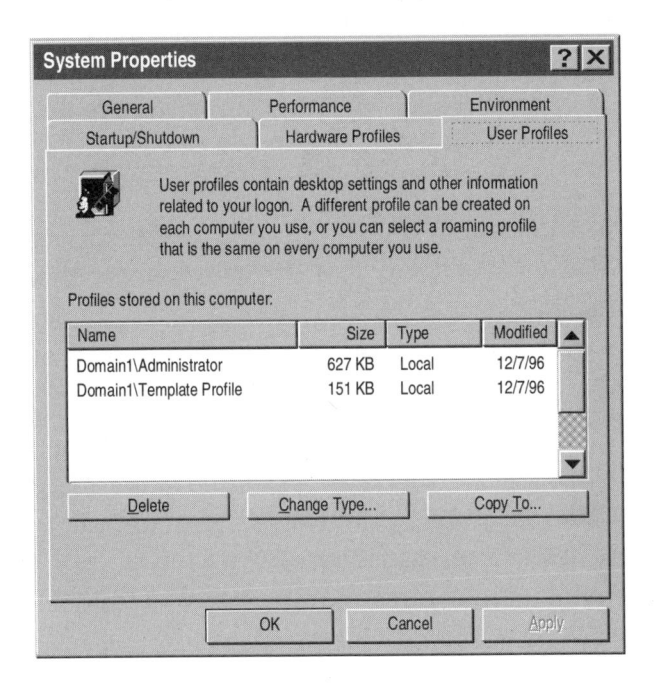

▶ **To copy the template user profile to a network server**

In this procedure, you copy the Template Profile user profile to the server for User2. (This folder was created and shared if you completed the Setup procedures described in "About This Book.")

1. Log off and log on as Administrator.
2. In User Manager for Domains, create a user account named User2 with no password requirements.
3. Click the **Start** button, point to **Settings**, and then click **Control Panel**.
4. In Control Panel, double-click System.

   The **System Properties** dialog box appears.
5. Click the **User Profiles** tab.

   Notice that a user profile has been created for all users who have previously logged on to the computer, including a user profile named Template Profile.

6. Under **Profiles stored on this computer**, click **Template Profile**, and then click **Copy To**.

   The **Copy To** dialog box appears.

7. In the **Copy profile to** box, type *computer_name***profiles****user2** (where *computer_name* is the name of your computer).

   Important If you were to make the Template Profile mandatory, in the **Copy profile to** box, you would type *computer_name***profiles** (do not specify a user name).

▸ **To specify the users who are permitted to use the profile**

1. In the **Copy To** dialog box, under **Permitted to use**, click **Change**.

   The **Choose User** dialog box appears.

2. In the **List Names From** box, make sure the domain where your accounts reside appears, and then click **Show Users**.

3. In the **Names** box, click **User2**, and then click **Add**.

   Domain\User2 appears in the **Add Name** box.

4. Click **OK**.

   Domain\User2 appears as the user permitted to use this profile.

5. Click **OK**.

   A folder named after the user name you specified is created in the Profiles folder with all the desktop settings configured for the Template Profile user account.

6. In Windows NT Explorer, view Profiles\User2. Notice the folders for the desktop settings that are stored in the Template Profile folder and the file Ntuser.dat.

   Important If you were to make the Template Profile mandatory, you would rename the Ntuser.dat file to Ntuser.man. If you did not specify a user name, this file would be located in the Profiles folder.

▶ **To delete the Template Profile user profile**

In this procedure, you delete the Template Profile user profile because it is no longer required. Only the profile on the server will be used.

1. On the **User Profiles** tab, under **Profiles stored on this computer**, click the profile that was created for the template, and then click **Delete**.

   A **Confirm Delete** message appears.

2. Click **Yes** to delete the local profile.

   The Template Profile user profile is deleted from the local computer.

Specifying the Path to the Roaming Profile

After you copy the roaming profile to a network server, specify the path to the profile for a user account in the **User Environment Profile** dialog box in User Manager for Domains.

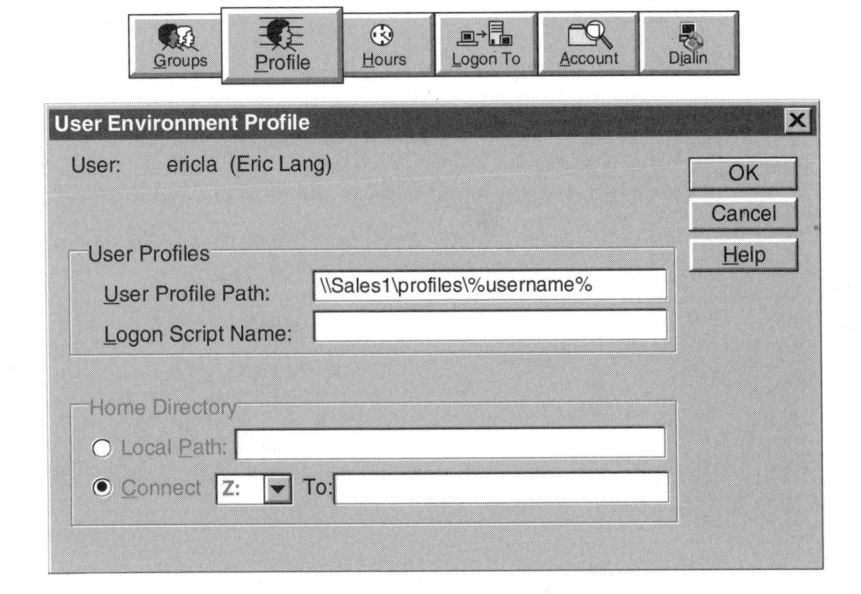

In the **User Profile Path** box, specify the server location of the user profile.

- If the profile is a roaming personal profile, enter the name of the server, the share name to the Profiles folder (in this lesson, the Profiles folder is shared as "Profiles"), and %Username%. If you use %Username%, Windows NT will substitute %Username% with the user account name.

- If the profile is a roaming mandatory profile, enter the name of the server, the share name to the Profiles folder, and the actual profile name. For example: \\Server1\Profiles\Ntuser.man.

> **Note** If you have many users that require roaming profiles, you can specify the path to the profile for multiple user accounts at one time by doing the following: 1) In the User Manager window, select multiple accounts. 2) On the **User** menu, click **Properties**. 3) In the **User Properties** dialog box, click **Profile**.

▸ **To specify a path to the roaming profile**

1. In the User Manager window, double-click User2.

   The **User Properties** dialog box appears.

2. In the **User Properties** dialog box, click **Profile**.

3. In the **User Profile Path** box, type *****computer_name***\profiles\%username%** (where *computer_name* is the name of your computer).

4. Click **OK** twice to apply your changes.

5. Exit User Manager for Domains and log off Windows NT.

▸ **To test the roaming profile**

- Log off and log on as User2.

   Notice that the screen colors are the same as the screen colors set for Template Profile.

▸ **To test the roaming profile from another computer**

If you have access to two computers on the same network, complete this procedure from the second computer.

1. Log on to the second computer as User2.

2. If a dialog box appears which provides profile options, click **Download**.

   Notice that the screen colors are the same as those set on the first computer because the roaming profile for the template user account is downloaded from the server and applied to the computer that the template user logs on to.

3. Log off.

▸ **To determine the type of profile assigned to a user**

1. Log on as an Administrator, and start Control Panel.

2. Double-click System, and then click **User Profiles**.

   Notice that the profile type for User2 is a roaming profile.

3. Exit all programs and log off Windows NT.

Lesson Summary

The following information summarizes the key points in this lesson:

- User profiles define a user's desktop environment and are created by default when a user logs on for the first time.
- A local user profile contains all user-definable settings controlling a user's desktop environment on the local computer.
- Roaming user profiles provide users with the same desktop environment from any Windows NT–based computer on a network.
- A roaming personal user profile is updated whenever a user makes a change to his or her desktop configuration. Each user has his or her own personal profile.
- A roaming mandatory user profile cannot be changed by users. One profile is assigned to many users.

For more information on	See
Logon scripts	Chapter 3, "Managing User Work Environments," in Microsoft Windows NT Server *Concepts and Planning*.
User profiles	Chapter 3, "Managing User Work Environments," in Microsoft Windows NT Server *Concepts and Planning*.
Creating Windows 95 user profiles	Chapter 15, "User Profiles and System Policies," in the *Microsoft Windows 95 Resource Kit*.

Best Practices

Review this checklist before you begin to create user accounts.

The following checklist provides best practices for setting up user accounts:

- ❏ To provide a greater degree of security, create a user account that you can use to perform non-administrative tasks; only log on as Administrator to perform administrative tasks.
- ❏ Only enable the Guest account in low-security networks and always assign it a password. This account is disabled by default.
- ❏ Always assign a password to an account.
- ❏ Always require new users to change their passwords the first time that they log on (this is the default setting). This will force users to protect their user account.
- ❏ In medium-security and high-security networks, create random initial passwords for all user accounts.
- ❏ Use roaming profiles if users frequently log on from different computers. This ensures that the user's familiar desktop configuration will always appears.
- ❏ Use the %Username% variable whenever you create a home folder or personal user profile. This variable will automatically be replaced with the user account name.
- ❏ If your server is on an Internet, rename the Administrator account. This will help to deter hackers.

Review

The following questions are intended to reinforce key information presented in this chapter. If you are unable to answer a question, review the lesson and then try the question again.

1. What is the difference between a domain user account and a local user account?

   _____

   _____

2. User Manager for Domains is (circle all that apply):

   a. Used to create and manage accounts on the local domain or on any computer, member server, or other domains to which you have access.

   b. Used to create and manage accounts on the local domain only.

   c. The account management tool on computers running Windows NT Server.

   d. Can be installed on a computer running Windows NT Workstation or Windows 95 using the client-based administration tools.

3. User Manager is (circle all that apply):

   a. Used to create and manage user accounts on the local computer only.

   b. The account management tool on computers running Windows NT Workstation and Windows NT Server.

   c. The account management tool on computers running Windows NT Workstation only.

4. In a high-security network, what can you do to make the Administrator and Guest accounts more secure?

   _____

   _____

5. What is the difference between a local and a roaming profile?

   _____

   _____

Answer Key

Procedure Answers

Page 44

▶ **To plan new user accounts**

Sample Answer:

User Account: One common naming convention uses first name, plus the first initial of the last name. When a duplicate first name exists, use additional characters from the last name. For example, use Lindam for the vice president, and Lindami for the night shift customer service representative.

Password Requirements: For all permanent employees, the administrator will select the User Must Change Password at Next Logon check box in User Manager for Domains. For all temporary contract employees, the administrator will select the User Cannot Change Password check box and will provide the password.

Home Folder Location: Home folders will be stored on the server.

Logon Hours: The night shift customer service representative's logon hours will be restricted to 6 P.M. through 6 A.M., 7 days a week. The temporary contract employee will be restricted to 8 A.M. to 5 P.M. All other employees will have 24-hour access, 7 days per week.

Workstation Restrictions: The temporary contract employee will only be able to log on at his or her own computer.

Page 56

▶ **To test logon hours**

2. Were you able to successfully log on? Why or why not?

   Yes, because the sales representative has access to the network 24 hours a day, 7 days a week.

4. Were you able to successfully log on?

   No, because night shift personnel are only allowed to log on between 6 P.M. and 6 A.M.

   -or-

   Yes, if the current time is between 6 P.M. and 6 A.M.

Review Answers

1. What is the difference between a domain user account and a local user account?

   A domain user account defines a user to the domain. A user can log on to the domain and access domain resources from any computer on the network using a single user account and password.

   A local user account defines a user to the local computer only. To access resources on another computer, the user must have a separate user account on the other computer.

2. User Manager for Domains is (circle all that apply):

   Answers a, c, and d are correct.

3. User Manager is (circle all that apply):

   Answers a and c correct.

4. In a high-security network, what can you do to make the Administrator and Guest accounts more secure?

   Assign the Administrator account a password. Rename the Administrator account. The Guest account should remain disabled.

5. What is the difference between a local and a roaming profile?

   A local profile is created and stored on the computer where the user logs on and is only applied at that computer for the user. A roaming profile is stored in a shared folder on a network server and is applied at whichever computer the user logs on from.

CHAPTER 3

Setting Up Group Accounts

Lesson 1　Introduction to Groups . . . 81

Lesson 2　Planning a Group Strategy . . . 90

Lesson 3　Creating Local and Global Groups . . . 96

Lesson 4　Implementing Built-in Groups . . . 106

Best Practices . . . 119

Review . . . 120

About This Chapter

Groups simplify administration by organizing user accounts into units. This chapter provides you with a groups planning strategy and procedures for creating groups. The hands-on procedures give you an opportunity to plan and implement local and global groups for a network.

Before You Begin

To complete the lessons in this chapter, you must have:

- Completed the Setup procedures located in "About This Book."
- The knowledge and skills covered in Chapter 2, "Setting Up User Accounts."
- Knowledge about the difference between a workgroup and a domain, and between a domain controller and a member server.
- Nine user accounts created, named VicePresident3, Director3, SalesMgr3, SalesRep3, CustomerService3-A, CustomerService3-B, AccountingMgr3, Accountant3, and Temp3.

  Log on as Administrator. In Windows NT Explorer, expand the LabFiles folder, and then double-click Chapter3.cmd to create these accounts.

Lesson 1: Introduction to Groups

Group accounts are collections of user accounts that share similar needs. By organizing accounts into groups, you can greatly simplify administration tasks. This lesson introduces you to the basics about groups.

After this lesson, you will be able to:
- Explain the purpose of local and global groups.
- Compare and contrast local and global groups.
- Explain where local and global groups are created.

Estimated lesson time: 30 minutes

Group memberships govern much of what one can do on the network and on a particular computer. Adding a user account to a group makes the user a member and gives the user all the rights and permissions granted to the group. Group membership provides an easy way to assign permissions and user rights to sets of users at one time. For example, if several users need to read a file, the user accounts are added to a group. Permission to read the file is assigned just once, to the group, rather than to each user.

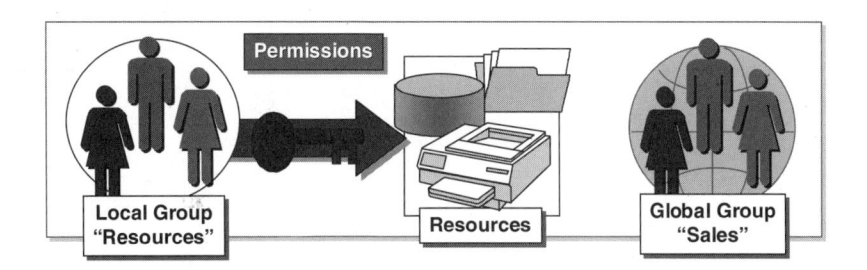

Permission and User Rights

Permissions are rules that regulate which users can use a resource, such as a folder, file, or printer. Because maintaining permissions for a group is easier than maintaining permissions for many user accounts, you generally want to use groups to manage access to resources.

User rights are rules that regulate which users can perform certain tasks on the system, such as creating a user account, logging on to the local computer, or shutting down a server.

A user can be a member of one or more groups. A user who is a member of more than one group possesses all user rights and permissions of all groups of which he or she is a member.

Local and Global Groups

There are two types of groups, local and global.

Local Groups

Local groups are used to provide users with permission to access a network resource on the local computer. You assign resource permissions to a local group, and then add user accounts or global groups to the local group from one or more domains.

Local groups are also used to provide users with rights to perform system tasks, such as changing the system time on a computer, or backing up and restoring files. Windows NT includes several built-in local groups with pre-assigned user rights. For example, the built-in Administrators group gives members the rights to perform tasks such as creating user and group accounts, backing up data, and making changes to a Windows NT configuration.

The following illustration shows two local groups with permissions for network resources and the built-in local Administrators group with user rights to perform administrative tasks.

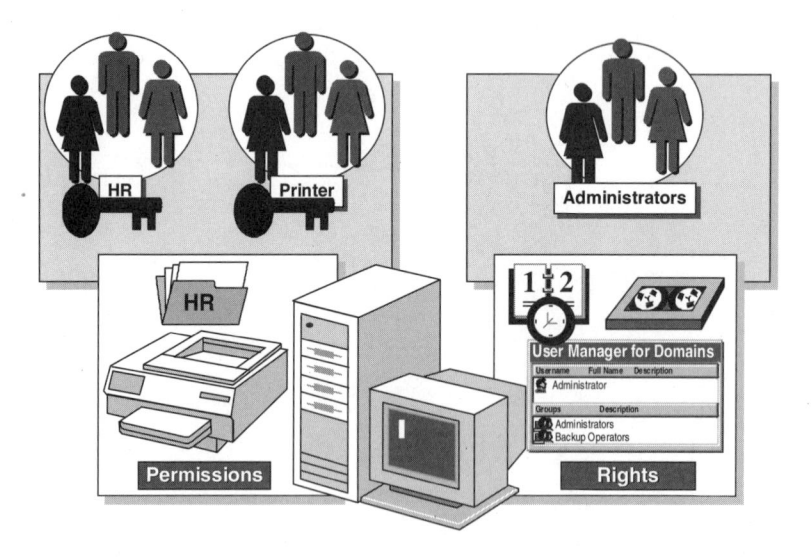

Local groups can contain user accounts and global groups from any domain (with the appropriate trust relationship). However, local groups cannot contain other local groups.

Global Groups

Global groups are used to organize domain user accounts, typically by function or geographical location. Global groups can contain only user accounts from the domain where the global group is created. They cannot contain local groups or other global groups.

The following illustration shows three global groups in Domain1.

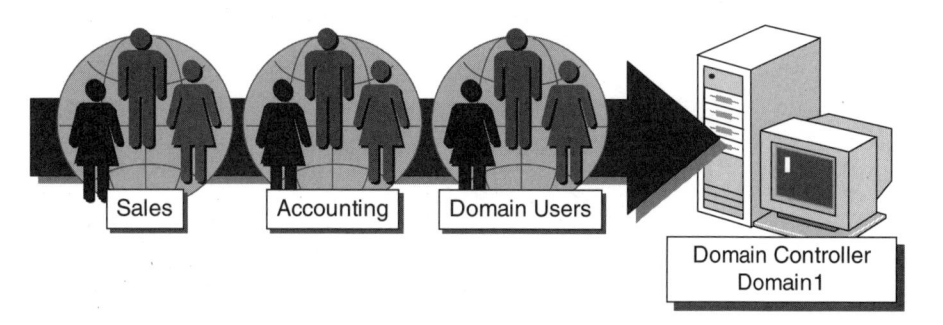

Although global groups can be assigned permissions to resources, use global groups only for grouping domain user accounts. Members of global groups obtain resource permissions when the global group is added to a local group.

Windows NT includes several built-in global groups—for example, the Domain Users group. By default, all domain user accounts are added to the Domain Users group. Unlike built-in local groups, built-in global groups do not have any inherent user rights.

Where Local Groups Are Created

If a resource resides on a member server or computer running Windows NT Workstation, the local group for the resource must be created on that computer. If the resource resides on any domain controller, the local group is created on the primary domain controller (PDC). The PDC will then provide its user account and security information to all other domain controllers in the domain.

The following illustration shows the local group Database on the computer where the database resides, and the local group Printer on either the primary domain controller (PDC) or the backup domain controller (BDC), which allows access to the network printer located on the PDC.

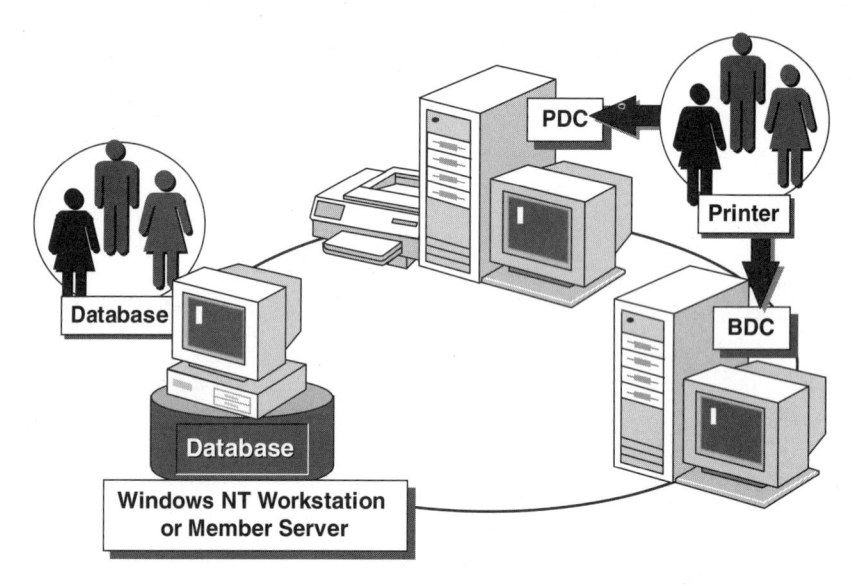

For resources on computers running Windows NT Workstation and on member servers, you use User Manager or User Manager for Domains to create local groups. For resources on any domain controller, you create local groups on the PDC from any computer running User Manager for Domains.

Where Global Groups Are Created

Global groups are always created on the primary domain controller (PDC) in the domain where the user accounts reside. For example, global groups in Domain1 are created on the PDC in Domain1. Global groups in Domain2 are created on the PDC in Domain2.

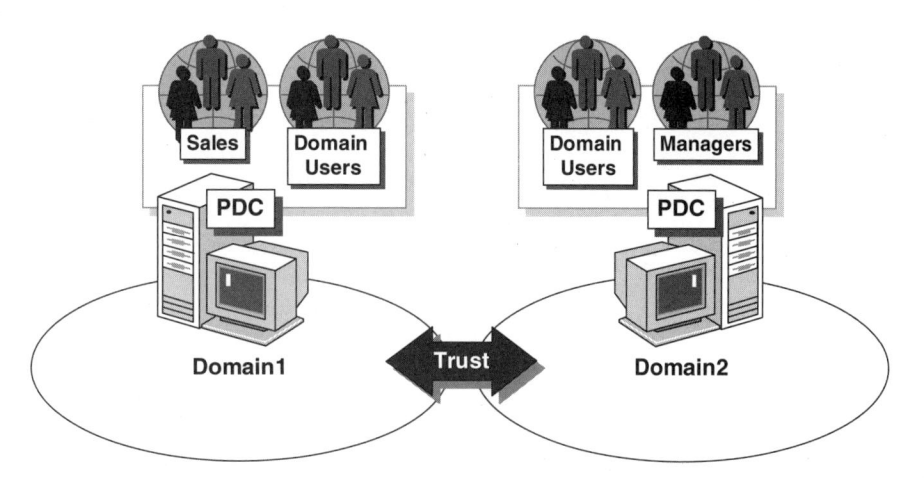

Global groups can be created on the PDC from any computer running User Manager for Domains.

Video: Local and Global Groups

This six minute video defines local and global groups and explains how they are used in single-domain and multiple-domain networks. The complete video script is available under "Course Materials" on the accompanying Supplemental Material compact disc.

▶ **To start the video from the Start menu**

1. Insert the Supplemental Material compact disc into the CD-ROM drive.
2. Click the **Start** button, point to **Programs**, point to **Network Administration Training**, and then click **Local and Global Groups Video**.

▶ **To start the video from the compact disc**

1. Start Windows NT Explorer.
2. In the root of the Supplemental Material compact disc, double-click Open.htm.
3. Click the center of the screen to continue to the home page.
4. Click **Course Materials**.

5. Under **Contents**, click **Local and Global Groups Video**.
6. Follow the instructions in the text box to install the required DLL files and to start the video.

   Note If you completed the Setup procedures located in "About This Book," or if you have run a video on this computer before, you do *not* need to install the DLL files.

▶ **To review the video**

The following study guide highlights the main points of the video. Complete the guide as you view the video, or use the guide as a follow-up test (recommended).

1. What is the purpose of a local group?

2. What is the purpose of a global group?

3. Where are local groups created?

4. Where are global groups created?

Example: Using Groups in a Single-Domain Network

Scenario: The Paris office of World Wide Importers has a single-domain network with a PDC, a BDC, and a member server (non-domain controller). The BDC has an accounts payable database, and the member server has an inventory database. All users need access to both databases.

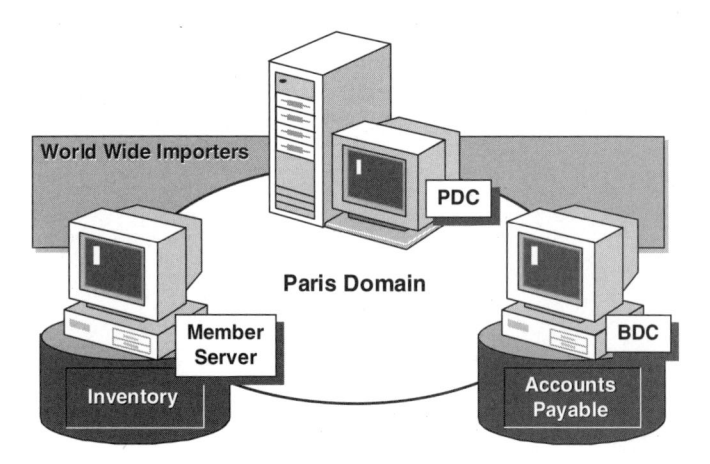

1. On which computer would you create a global group for organizing the user accounts? Why?

2. On which computer would you create a local group to provide users with access to the Accounts Payable database? Why?

3. On which computer would you create a local group to provide users with access to the Inventory database? Why?

4. How would you give members of the global group access to both databases?

Example: Using Groups in a Multiple-Domain Network

Scenario: The Paris office of World Wide Importers has expanded its network to include a second domain for its London office. Both London and Paris maintain an Inventory database. All users in the London office need access to the Inventory database in the Paris domain, and all users in the Paris office need access to Inventory database in the London domain. The appropriate trust relationship exists between the two domains.

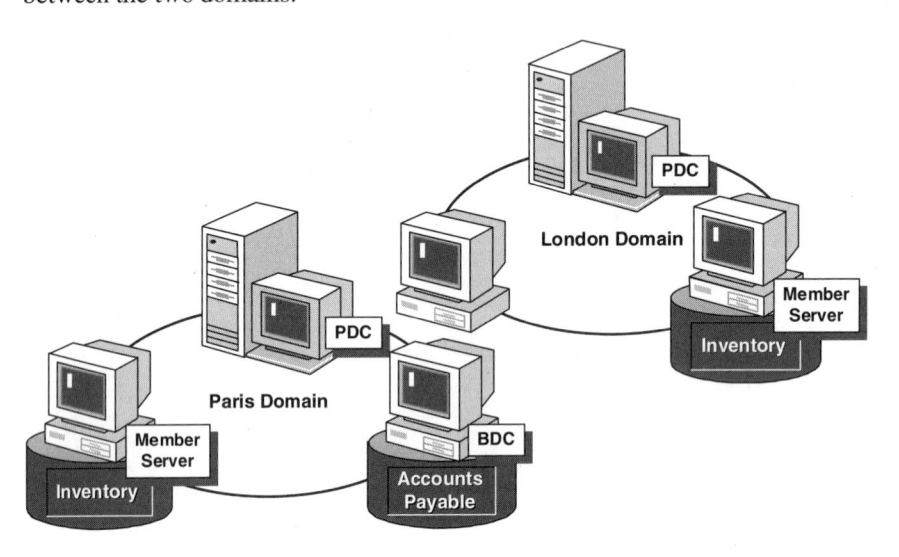

1. On which computers would you create a global group for organizing the user accounts? Why?

   _____

   _____

2. On which computers would you create a local group to provide users with access to the Inventory databases? Why?

   _____

   _____

3. How would you give members of the global groups that you just created in London and in Paris access to the Inventory databases in each other's domain?

   _____

   _____

Lesson Summary

The following information summarizes the key points in this lesson:

- Groups simplify administration by providing an easy way to assign permissions and grant user rights to sets of users.
- Local groups are used to provide users with permission to access a network resource on the local computer. You assign resource permissions to a local group, and then add user accounts or global groups to the local group from one or more domains.
- On computers running Windows NT Workstation or on member servers, local groups are created where the resource resides. On domain controllers, local groups are created on the PDC.
- Global groups are used to organize domain user accounts, typically by function or geographical location. Global groups can contain only user accounts from the domain where the global group is created.
- Global groups are created on the PDC.

For more information on	See
Group accounts	Chapter 2, "Working With User and Group Accounts," in Microsoft Windows NT Server *Concepts and Planning*.
Assigning permissions	Chapter 4, "Managing Shared Resources and Resource Security," in Microsoft Windows NT Server *Concepts and Planning*.
	Chapter 5, "Securing Network Resources with Share Permissions," in this book.
	Chapter 6, "Securing Network Resources with NTFS Permissions," in this book.
User rights	Chapter 2, "Working With User and Group Accounts," in Microsoft Windows NT Server *Concepts and Planning*.

Lesson 2: Planning a Group Strategy

Having a strategy for implementing groups will simplify administration. This lesson presents the guidelines for implementing local and global groups.

After this lesson, you will be able to:
- Describe the steps of a sound implementation strategy.
- Plan a strategy for creating local and global groups in a multiple-domain network.

Estimated lesson time: 30 minutes

For better control over user and resource management, first organize users into global groups, and then add global groups to local groups.

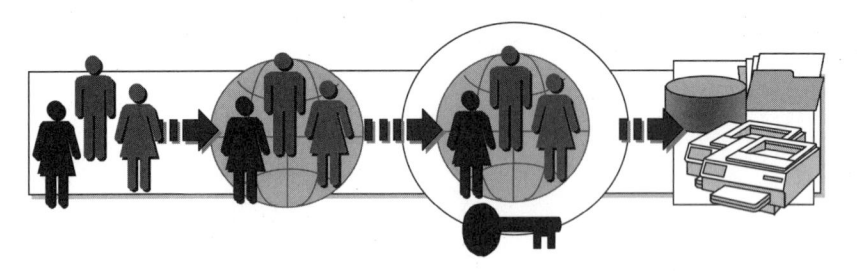

To create groups, follow these general guidelines:

1. Logically organize domain users based on the common needs of your users. For example, if all sales personnel need access to a color printer and all managers need access to an employee records file, organize users by sales personnel and managers.
2. In each domain where user accounts reside, create a global group for each logical group of users. Then add the appropriate user accounts to the appropriate global groups.
3. Create local groups based on resource access needs. For example, if managers need full control of files in the EmployeeHandbook folder and sales personnel only need to read the files, create one local group for the managers and another local group for the sales personnel.
    - If the resource is on a member server or a computer running Windows NT Workstation, create the local group where the resource is located.
    - If the resource is on a primary domain controller (PDC) or backup domain controller (BDC), create the local group on the PDC.

4. Assign the appropriate permissions to the local groups.
5. Add the global groups to the local groups.

> **Note** To add global groups from one domain to local groups in another domain, the appropriate trust relationship must have been established.

▶ **To plan group accounts**

Scenario: Users from the Istanbul domain and the Quebec domain of World Wide Importers need to access resources in each other's domain.

As the administrator, you need to determine:

- The global groups and global group memberships for each domain.
- The local groups for each resource, and the computer and domain where they need to be created.
- Which global groups to add to each local group to give members access to a resource.

You will record your planning strategies on the "Group Accounts Planning Worksheet" located at the end of this lesson. After completing the exercise, turn to Appendix A, "Planning Worksheets" and compare your worksheet to the sample provided. (The sample presents only one set of possible answers. You may have planned your accounts differently.)

To complete the "Group Accounts Planning Worksheet," do the following:

1. On the worksheet, provide a name for each group. Record each name in the Group Account column.
2. Specify whether the account is to be a local or global group. Record it in the Local or Global column.
3. List the user accounts that will be added as members to the global groups. Record these in the Members column for each global group that you specify. The following table lists the user accounts for the Istanbul and Quebec domains (both domains have the same set of user accounts).

User account	Description
VicePresident3	Vice President
Director3	Director of Human Resources
SalesMgr3	Sales Manager
SalesRep3	Sales Representative

(continued)

User account	Description
CustomerService3-A	Customer Service Representative (night shift)
CustomerService3-B	Customer Service Representative (day shift)
AccountingMgr3	Accounting Manager
Accountant3	Accountant
Temp3	Temporary employee

Note To distinguish between the same user name in each domain, include the domain name when you record it. For example: Istanbul\VicePresident3 and Quebec\VicePresident3.

4. List the global groups that will be added as members to the local groups. Record them in the Members column for each local group that you specify.
5. Provide the server location—either the PDC, BDC, or member server. Record it in the Location column.

Base your implementation plan on the following illustration and criteria.

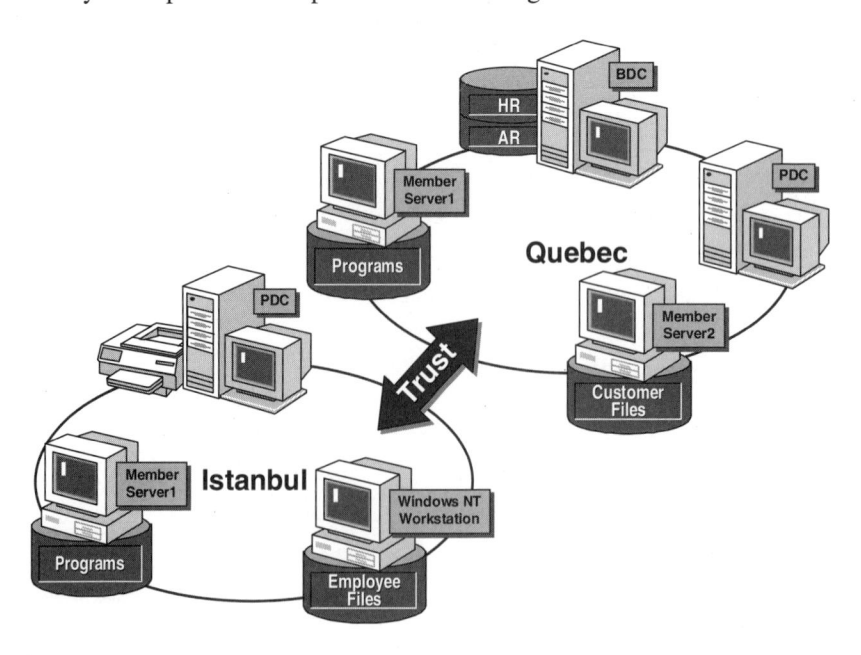

Use the following criteria to make your decisions:

- All employees need access to the programs in their own domain.
- All employees need access to the printer in the Istanbul domain.
- The executives and managers from both domains need access to the Human Resources (HR) information in the Quebec domain.
- The executives, managers, and customer service and sales representatives from both domains need access to the Customer Files in the Quebec domain.
- The accountants from both domains need access to Accounts Receivable (AR) information in the Quebec domain.
- The managers from both domains need access to Employee Files in the Istanbul domain.

Lesson Summary

The following information summarizes the key points in this lesson:

- As an effective planning strategy, use groups for organizing user accounts and for assigning permissions.
- Logically organize domain users into global groups, typically by geographic location or organizational structure.
- Create local groups based on resource access needs and assign the appropriate permissions to the local groups.
- Add global groups as members of the local groups.

For more information on	See
Group strategies	Chapter 2, "Working With Users and Group Accounts," in Microsoft Windows NT Server *Concepts and Planning*.
Assigning permissions	Chapter 5, "Securing Network Resources with Share Permissions," in this book.
	Chapter 6, "Securing Network Resources with NTFS Permissions," in this book.
	Chapter 4, "Managing Shared Resources and Resource Security," in Microsoft Windows NT Server *Concepts and Planning*.

Group Accounts Planning Worksheet

Group Account	Local or Global	Members	Location

Lesson 3: Creating Local and Global Groups

You create local groups to give sets of users permissions to access a resource. You create global groups to logically organize domain user accounts. This lesson shows you how to create and use local and global groups.

After this lesson, you will be able to:
- Create local groups and add members from local or trusted domains.
- Create global groups and add members.
- Delete local and global groups.

Estimated lesson time: 30 minutes

In a domain, local and global groups are created using User Manager for Domains. In a workgroup, local groups are created using User Manager. Global groups cannot be created in a workgroup.

The following illustration shows User Manager for Domains. All group account menu commands appear on the **User** menu in User Manager, except for **New Global Group** and **Select Domain**. The **Select Domain** menu command allows an administrator to select a different domain or computer in which to create or manage local or global groups.

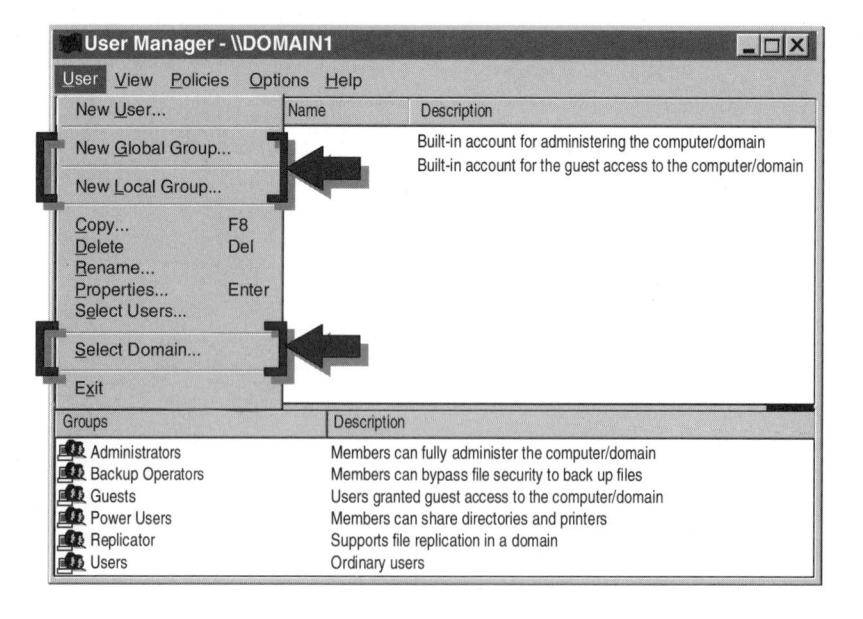

Rules for Creating Groups

When you create local and global groups, the following rules apply:

- You must be a member of the built-in Administrators or built-in Account Operators group on the computer where the group is being created.
- A local group can be created on any computer running Windows NT.
- A global group must be created on a primary domain controller (PDC), but can be created from any computer running User Manager for Domains. This includes:
  - A backup domain controller (BDC).
  - A member server that is part of the domain.
  - A computer running Windows NT Workstation or Microsoft Windows 95 with the client-based administration tools installed.
- Group names must be unique to the domain. They cannot be identical to other user names or group names.

Creating Global Groups

Your implementation strategy begins with organization. Your users must be logically organized in order to create global group accounts for them.

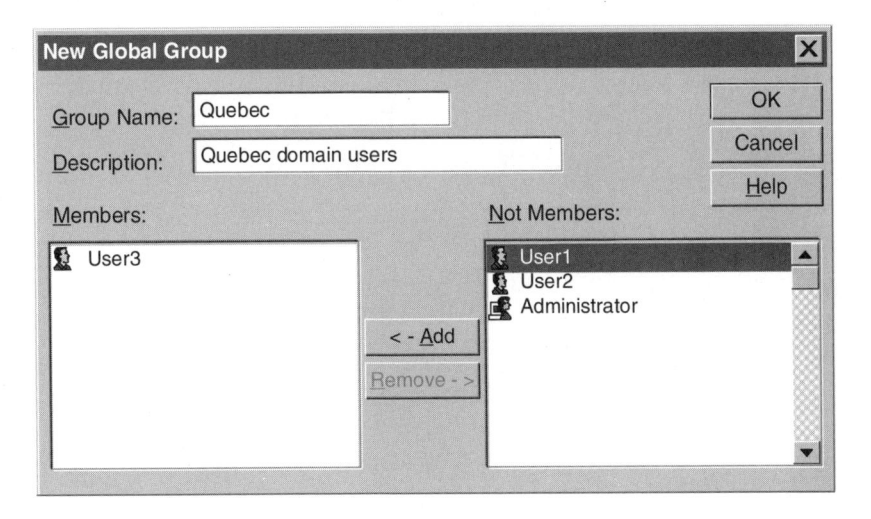

To create a new global group, you give the group a name and then add members (user accounts in the local domain) to it.

To create a global group

In User Manager for Domains, you create the groups that you planned in the hands-on procedures from the previous lesson, "Planning a Group Strategy." If you did not complete the "Groups Planning Worksheet" from the lesson, use the sample plan provided in Appendix A, "Planning Worksheets."

To simplify the exercise, assume that all groups that you create are for the Quebec domain only.

1. Log on as Administrator.
2. Click the **Start** button, point to **Programs**, point to **Administrative Tools**, and then click **User Manager for Domains**.
3. On the **User** menu, click **New Global Group**.

   The **New Global Group** dialog box appears.
4. In the **Group Name** box, type a name for your global group (from the "Group Accounts Planning Worksheet" planned for the Quebec domain only). The global group name:
   - Can contain any uppercase or lowercase characters except for the following: " / \ [ ] : ; | = , + ? < >
   - Is especially useful if it describes the function of the group.
   - Is limited to 20 characters.
5. In the **Description** box, type a description for the global group, such as the type of users that the group contains. Although the description is optional, it can be helpful in identifying the function of a group.

   Do not close the **New Global Group** dialog box.

▶ **To add members to a global group**

The user accounts that you will add as members to global groups were created in "Before You Begin" by running the Chapter3.cmd batch file located in the LabFiles folder. To distinguish these user accounts from user accounts that you may have created in other chapters, the number 3 has been appended to each user name.

1. In the **New Global Group** dialog box, in the **Not Members** box, select one user account (from those accounts in the "Group Accounts Planning Worksheet" planned for the Quebec domain only) or select multiple user accounts by holding down the CTRL key while clicking each user.

2. Click **Add**.

   Notice that each new member appears in the **Members** box.

3. Add the remaining user accounts (if any) to the same group, and then click **OK** to create the global group containing all of the users you added as members.

   Notice that the global group appears under **Groups** with a globe as part of the icon.

▶ **To complete the exercise**

- Create the remaining global groups and add members from the "Group Accounts Planning Worksheet" (of those planned for the Quebec domain only).

Tip As a shortcut to adding users to a global group, in User Manager for Domains hold down the CTRL key, select each user that you want to add to the group, and then on the **User** menu, click **New Global Group**. The **New Global Group** dialog box will appear with the selected members in the **Members** box.

Creating Local Groups

Once you have organized your domain user accounts into global groups, the next step is to create your local groups.

To create a new local group, give the group a name and add members (user accounts and global groups from the local domain or a trusted domain) to it. Even though user accounts and global groups can be added to local groups, it is easier to administer group accounts than individual user accounts.

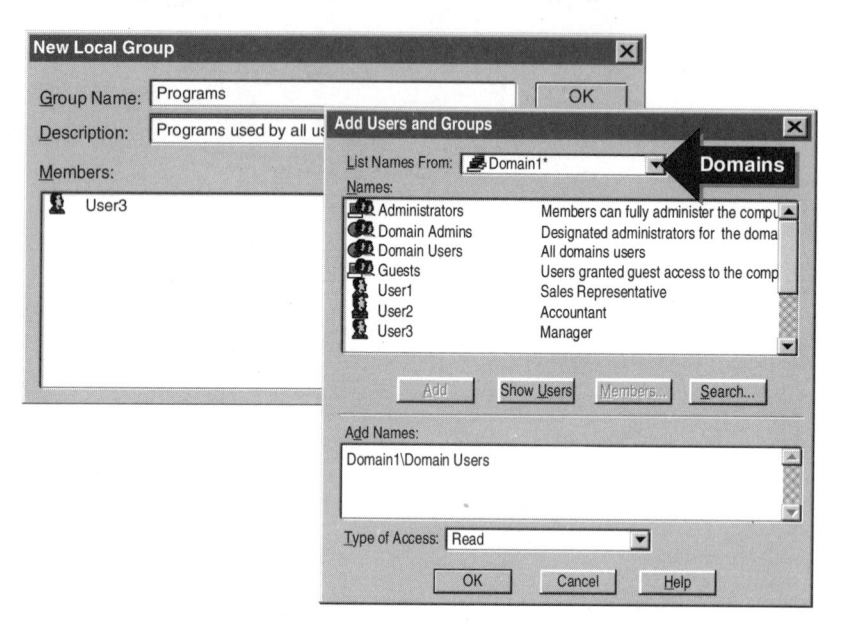

▸ **To create a local group**

1. In the User Manager window, on the **User** menu, click **New Local Group**.

   The **New Local Group** dialog box appears.

   Note In real-world situations, if you want to create the local group on a computer that is not a domain controller, select the computer on which to create the local group first. To do this, click **Select Domain** on the **User** menu, and then in the **Domain** box, type the name of the computer. For example, you may type **\\computer1**

2. In the **Group Name** box, type a unique, descriptive name for a local group (from the "Group Accounts Planning Worksheet"). Type a name that meets the following criteria:

   - Describes the function of the group.
   - Contains any uppercase or lowercase characters except for the backslash (\).
   - Is up to 256 characters in length; however, remember that only the first 22 characters display in most of the windows.

3. In the **Description** box, type a description of the local group, such as the name of the resource that the local group will be used for.

▶ **To add members to a local group**

1. In the **New Local Group** dialog box, click **Add**.

   The **Add Users and Groups** dialog box appears.

2. Make sure that your domain name appears in the **List Names From** box. If it does not appear, in the **List Names From** box, click your domain name.

3. Under **Names**, click one or more global groups (of those planned for the Quebec domain only), and then click **Add**.

   Notice that the selected names appear in the **Add Names** box.

   Note In a real-world situation where you need to add global groups from other domains, select the domain where the global group resides in the **List Names From** box. If other domains do not appear in the **List Names From** box, either you do not have other domains in your network or the appropriate trust relationship is not set up.

4. Click **Add**, and then click **OK**.

   The selected global groups appear in the **Members** box of the **New Local Group** dialog box.

5. Click **OK** to create the local group.

6. Click **OK**.

   Notice that the new local group appears under **Groups** with a computer as part of the icon.

▶ To complete the exercise

- Create the remaining local groups and add members, as planned for the Quebec domain only, from the "Group Accounts Planning Worksheet."

> **Tip** As a shortcut to adding users and global groups from the local domain to a new local group, in User Manager for Domains hold down the CTRL key, select each user that you want to add to the group, and then on the **User** menu, click **New Local Group**.

▶ To determine the possible group combinations

In this procedure, you test four different group combinations to determine whether one group can be added as a member to another group.

- Using User Manager for Domains, try the following:
    a. Add a global group to a global group.
    b. Add a global group to a local group.
    c. Add a local group to a local group.
    d. Add a local group to a global group.

    Which group combination or combinations are possible?

    _____

    _____

> **Note** In real-world situations, you would assign permissions to local groups before you add accounts to them. Assigning permissions is covered in detail in Chapter 5, "Securing Network Resources with Share Permissions," and Chapter 6, "Securing Network Resources with NTFS Permissions."

Deleting Groups

Deleting a group deletes the name of the group, its description, and the rights or permissions associated with it. It does not delete the user accounts that it contains.

A deleted group cannot be recovered, so be sure that you want to delete a group before you do so. When you delete a group, the SID for the group account is deleted, and SIDs are used only once. For this reason, resource permissions associated with the group cannot be reestablished by creating a new group using the same account name.

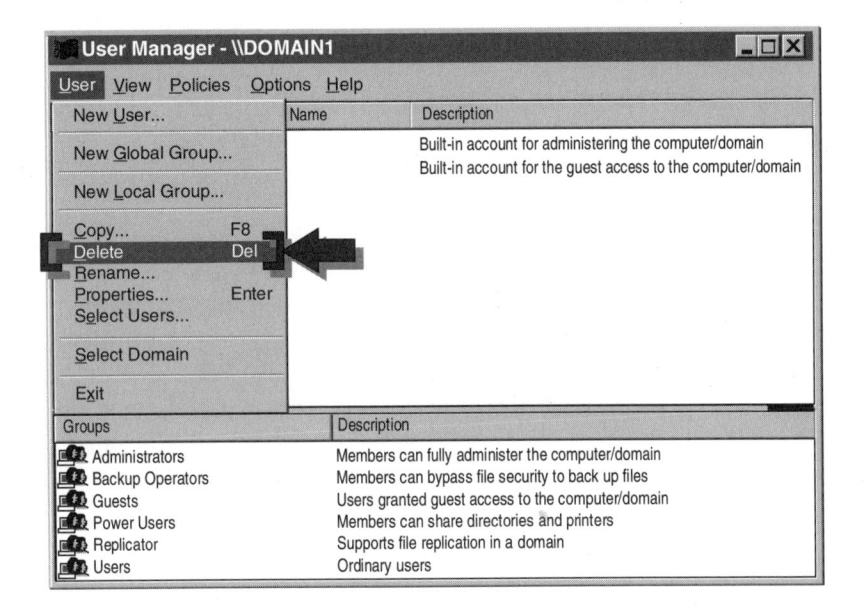

▶ **To delete a group account**

1. In User Manager for Domains, double-click the global group that you created for the Accountants.

   Notice the members of the group that appears in the **Global Group Properties** dialog box.

2. Click **Cancel** to return to the User Manager window.

3. Make sure that the same group is selected, and then on the **User** menu, click **Delete**.

   The following message appears:

   Each group is represented by a unique identifier that is independent of the group name. Once this group is deleted, even creating an identically named group in the future will not restore access to resources that currently name this group in the access control list.

4. Click **OK**, and the group is deleted.

   Notice that the members of that group have not been deleted. They still appear in the User Manager window because deleting a group account does not delete its members.

5. Quit User Manager for Domains.

Lesson Summary

The following information summarizes the key points in this lesson:

- In a domain, local and global groups are created using User Manager for Domains.
- In a workgroup, local groups are created using User Manager.
- Creating groups requires that you be a member of the Administrators or Account Operators group.
- A local group can be created on any computer running Windows NT. A global group can only be created on the PDC.
- A global group can only be a member of a local group. A local group cannot be a member of any other groups.

For more information on	See
Creating groups	Chapter 2, "Working With User and Group Accounts," in Microsoft Windows NT Server *Concepts and Planning*.
Trusted domains	Chapter 1, "Managing Windows NT Server Domains," in Microsoft Windows NT Server *Concepts and Planning*.
Assigning permissions to groups	Chapter 5, "Securing Network Resources with Share Permissions," in this book.
	Chapter 6, "Securing Network Resources with NTFS Permissions," in this book.

Lesson 4: Implementing Built-in Groups

Built-in groups are predefined groups that have a predetermined set of user rights. User rights determine the system tasks that a user or member of a built-in group can perform. This lesson explains how built-in groups are used.

After this lesson, you will be able to:
- Determine the user rights associated with a built-in group.
- Determine the default membership of a built-in group.

Estimated lesson time: 30 minutes

Even though individual user rights can be assigned directly to a user, in most cases, it is not recommended.

Computers running Windows NT have three types of built-in groups:

- *Built-in local groups*. These groups give users rights to perform system tasks, such as backing up and restoring files, changing the system time, and administering system resources.

  Built-in local groups are on all computers running Windows NT.

- *Built-in global groups*. These groups give administrators an easy way of controlling all users in a domain.

  Built-in global groups are on domain controllers only.

- *System groups*. These groups automatically organize users for system use. Administrators do not assign users to them. Rather, users are either members by default or become members during network activity.

  System groups are on all computers running Windows NT.

Note Built-in groups cannot be deleted or renamed.

Determining the Rights of Built-in Groups

You can determine the inherent rights of the built-in local groups in the **User Rights Policy** dialog box.

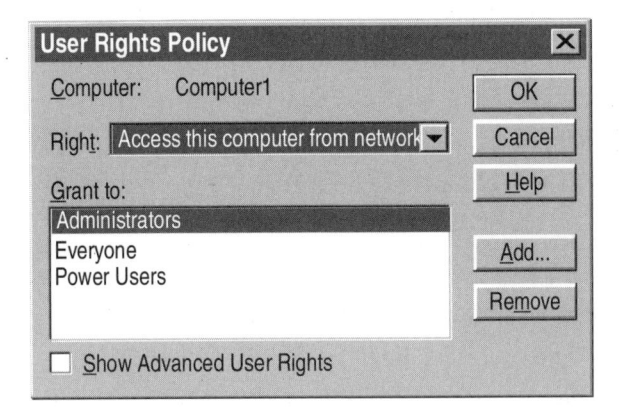

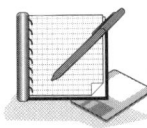

```
User Rights Policy
Computer:   Computer1
Right: Access this computer from network
Grant to:
  Administrators
  Everyone
  Power Users

  [ ] Show Advanced User Rights

  [OK]  [Cancel]  [Help]  [Add...]  [Remove]
```

▶ **To determine which groups have access to the computer**

- Start User Manager for Domains, and then on the **Policies** menu, click **User Rights**.

  The **User Rights Policy** dialog box appears. The listed right is **Access this computer from network**.

  Which built-in groups have been granted this right?

  _____

▶ **To determine which groups can log on locally**

- In the **Right** box, click **Log on locally**.

  Which built-in groups have been granted this right?

  _____

Note The group Everyone does not have the Log on locally right by default on Windows NT Server domain controllers. This user right was assigned to the Everyone group when you completed the Setup procedures located in "About This Book."

▶ **To determine which groups can change the system time**
- In the **Right** box, click **Change the system time**.
  Which built-in groups have been granted this right?

  _____

▶ **To determine which groups can shut down the system**
- In the **Right** box, click **Shut down the system**.
  Which built-in groups have been granted this right?

  _____

▶ **To determine which groups can back up files and directories**
- In the **Right** box, click **Back up files and directories**.
  Which built-in groups have been granted this right?

  _____

▶ **To determine which groups can restore files and directories**
- In the **Right** box, click **Restore files and directories**.
  Which built-in groups have been granted this right?

  _____

▶ **To determine the inherent rights that are *only* assigned to the Administrators group**
- Select each right to determine which ones are automatically assigned to *only* the Administrators group, and then mark all the check boxes in the following list that apply:
  - ❑ **Access this computer from network**
  - ❑ **Back up files and directories**
  - ❑ **Change the system time**
  - ❑ **Force shutdown from a remote system**
  - ❑ **Load and unload device drivers**
  - ❑ **Log on locally**
  - ❑ **Manage auditing and security log**
  - ❑ **Restore files and directories**
  - ❑ **Shut down the system**
  - ❑ **Take ownership of files or other objects**

Built-in Groups on All Windows NT Computers

All computers running Windows NT have built-in Users, Guests, Administrators, and Backup Operators groups. Member servers and computers running Windows NT Workstation also have a Power Users group.

A built-in group on a domain controller determines what its members can do in the domain. A built-in group on non-domain controllers determines what its members can do on the local computer.

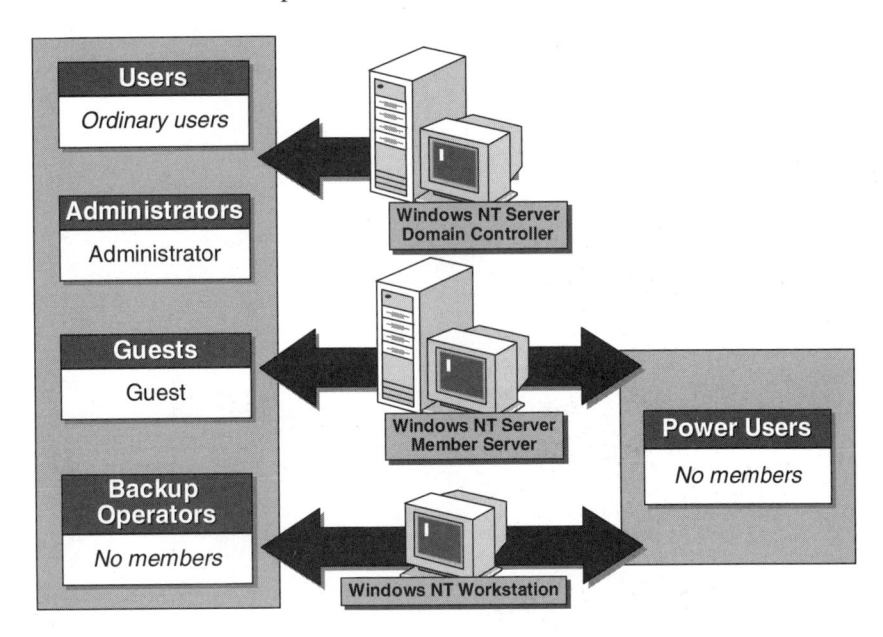

The following table describes the built-in local groups that reside on all computers running Windows NT.

Local group	Members can
Users	Perform tasks for which they have been granted rights, and access resources to which they have been assigned permissions. By default, all user accounts in the local directory database are members of the Users group.
Administrators	Can perform all administrative tasks on the local computer. If the computer is a domain controller, members can fully administer the domain. By default, the local Administrator user account is a member of the Administrators group.
Guests	Perform tasks for which they have been given rights, and access resources to which they have been assigned permissions.
	Members of Guests cannot make permanent changes to their local environment. By default, the local Guest user account is a member of the Guests group.

(continued)

Local group	Members can
Backup Operators	Back up and restore files on the local computer using the Windows NT Backup program. There are no default members.
Power Users	Create and modify accounts, and share resources on the local computer. This group is only on member servers and computers running Windows NT Workstation. There are no default members.

Note The built-in Replicator group is used by the Directory Replicator Service. This group is not used for administration and therefore, it is not covered in the book.

Built-in Groups on Domain Controllers Only

Domain controllers have three additional built-in local groups—Account Operators, Server Operators, and Print Operators; Domain controllers also have three additional built-in global groups—Domain Users, Domain Admins, and Domain Guests.

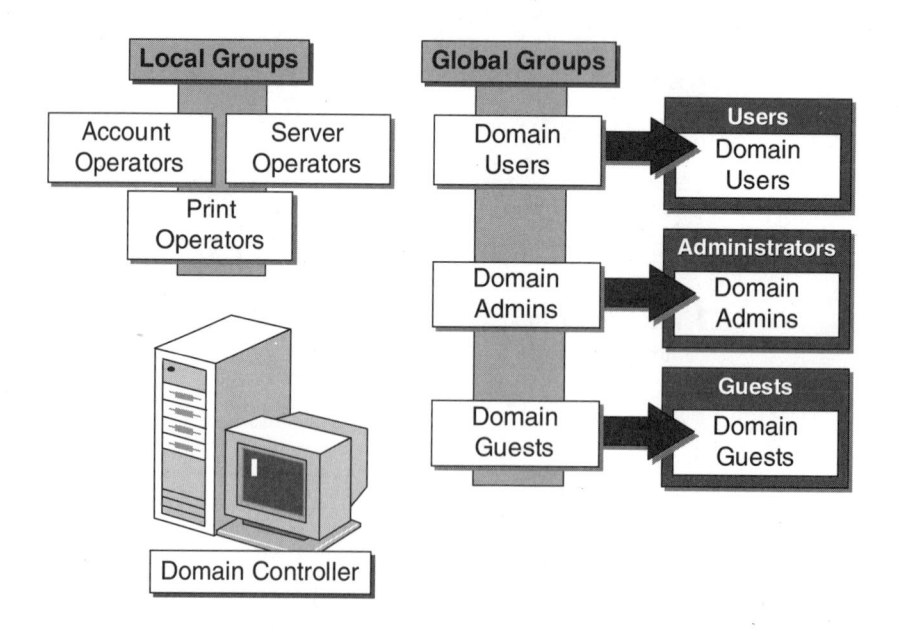

Local Groups

The following table describes the built-in local groups on domain controllers only. There are no initial members of these groups.

Local group	Capabilities
Account Operators	Create, delete, and modify users, global groups, and local groups. Cannot modify the Administrators or Server Operators groups.
Server Operators	Share disk resources, and back up and restore server.
Printer Operators	Set up and manage network printers.

Global Groups

When Windows NT Server is installed as a domain controller, three global groups are created in the domain's directory database—Domain Admins, Domain Users, and Domain Guests. By default, built-in global groups do not have any inherent rights. They get rights when they are added to local groups or when they are assigned user rights or permissions.

The following table describes what happens to built-in global groups when a Windows NT computer is added to the domain.

This group	Is automatically added to this group
Domain Admins	Local Administrators group. Members of the Domain Admins group can then perform administrative tasks on the local computer. The Administrator account is a member by default.
Domain Users	Local Users group. When a domain user account is created, it is automatically made a member of this group. The Administrator account is a member by default.
Domain Guests	Local Guests group. The Guest account is a member by default.

112   Microsoft Windows NT Network Administration

▶ **To determine the default membership of the global group Domain Admins**

1. Log on as Administrator.
2. Start User Manager for Domains.
3. Under **Groups**, double-click the global group **Domain Admins**.

   By *default*, what built-in user accounts or groups are members of Domain Admins?

   _____

4. Click **Cancel** to return to the User Manager window.

▶ **To determine membership of the local group Administrators**

- Under **Groups**, double-click the local group **Administrators**.

  By default, what built-in user accounts or global groups are members of the Administrators group?

  _____

▶ **To determine the default membership of other built-in global groups**

- Under **Groups**, double-click each of the following global groups.
  - Domain Users contains the following user accounts:

    _____

  - Domain Guests contains the following user accounts:

    _____

▶ **To determine the default membership of the built-in local group Guests**

- Under **Groups**, double-click **Guests**.

    What user accounts or groups are members of the Guests group?

▶ **To determine the default membership of the built-in local group Users**

- Under **Groups**, double-click **Users**.

    What user accounts or groups are members of the Users group?

Built-in System Groups

System groups are installed on all computers running Windows NT. Unlike other built-in groups, users become members of system groups during network activity. Membership cannot be altered.

Built-in system groups reside on all computers running Windows NT. Users become members by default during network activity. Membership cannot be modified.

The following table describes the key system groups used for network administration.

System group	Description
Everyone	Includes all local and remote users who have connected to the computer, including those who connect as Guest. You cannot control who becomes a member of the Everyone group. However, you can assign permissions and rights to the Everyone group. The Everyone group is useful when you do not need to restrict resource access to specific users and groups.
Creator Owner	Includes the user that created or took ownership of a resource. If a member of the Administrators group takes ownership of a resource, the new owner is the Administrators group. This group can be used to manage access to files and folders on NTFS volumes.

The following table describes the system groups that are not used for network administration.

System group	Description
Network	Includes any user who is currently connected from another computer on the network to a shared resource on your computer.
Interactive	Automatically includes a user who logs on to the computer locally. Interactive members access resources on the computer at which they are physically sitting. They log on and access resources by "interacting" with the computer.

Note The Everyone and Creator Owner groups are covered in more detail later in this book.

System groups can only be viewed on an NTFS volume. They do not appear in User Manager.

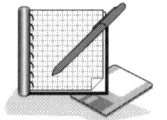

▶ **To view system groups**

1. Start Windows NT Explorer.
2. Right-click any NTFS volume.
3. On the shortcut menu, click **Properties**.

    The *drive_name*: **Properties** dialog box appears.

4. Click the **Security** tab.
5. Click **Permissions**.

    The **Directory Permissions** dialog box appears.

6. Click **Add**.

    The **Add Users and Groups** dialog box appears.

    The following system groups appear under Names. If there are many accounts, you may need to scroll through the **Names** list to see the four system groups:

    - Creator Owner
    - Interactive
    - Network
    - System

7. Close all dialog boxes and Windows NT Explorer.

Implementing Built-in Groups for Local Administration

You can give administrative privileges to a user by adding the user's account to the built-in local Administrators groups. This will give the user administrative privileges on the local computer. This is useful when you want to give a user administrative privileges for his or her own computer.

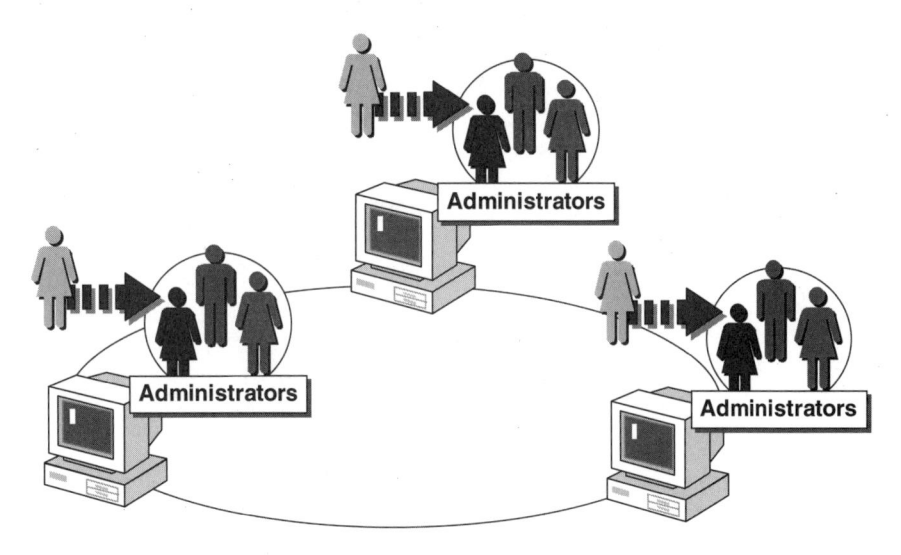

Note If you add a user account to the Administrators group on a PDC, the user will have administrative privileges on all domain controllers in the domain.

▶ **To add a user to the local Administrators group**

In this procedure, you give the administrative privileges to the Vice President of World Wide Importers.

1. Log on as Administrator.
2. In User Manager for Domains, add the user account VicePresident3 to the Administrators group.
3. Log off Windows NT.

▶ **To test the administrative privileges for a user**

1. Log on as VicePresident3.
2. Start User Manager for Domains, and try to create a user account.

    Were you successful? Why or why not?

    _____

3. Log off Windows NT.

Implementing Built-in Groups for Centralized Administration

You can give members of an Administrators group in one domain the ability to administer resources in another domain. You can do this by using the built-in global group Domain Admins.

On the PDC of a domain, add the Domain Admins group from another domain to the local Administrators group. This will give members of the Domain Admins group from the other domain the ability to administer domain user accounts and security for resources on any domain controller.

The following illustration shows the addition of the Domain Admins group from Domain2 to the Administrators group on the PDC in Domain1; as a result, Domain Admins in Domain2 have administrative privileges in Domain1.

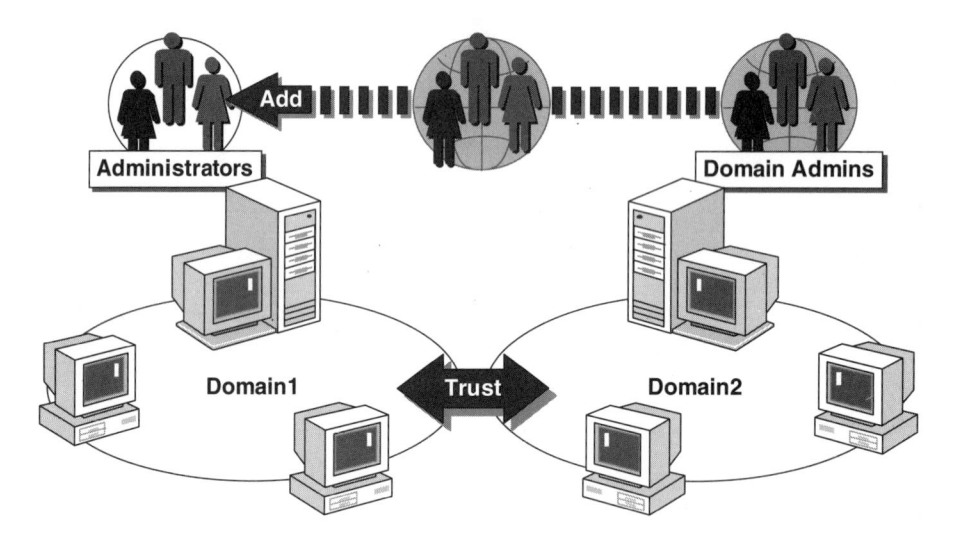

In a domain with computers running Windows NT Workstation or running Windows NT Server configured as a member server, the Domain Admins group for the local domain is automatically added to the local Administrators group. If you want Domain Admins from a different domain to administer computers running Windows NT Workstation or running Windows NT Server configured as a member server, you need to add Domain Admins to each computer's Administrators group.

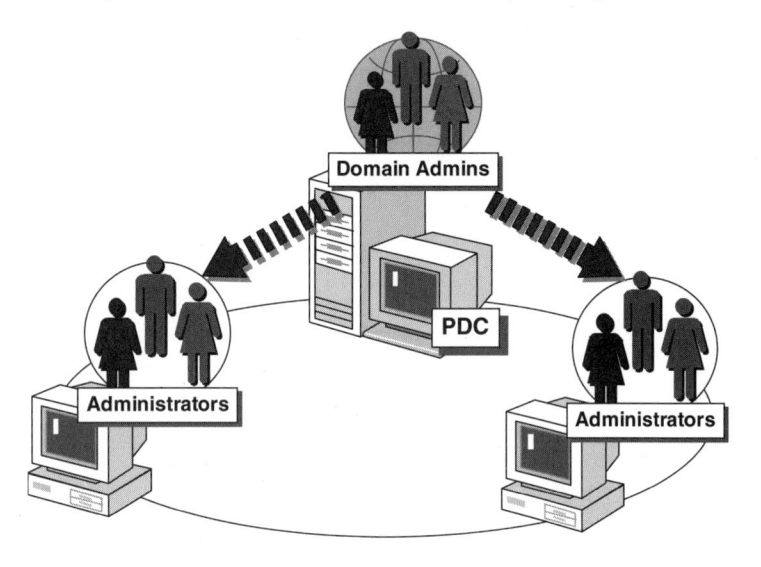

▶ **To add a user to the global group Domain Admins**

1. Log on as Administrator.
2. Start User Manager for Domains, and remove VicePresident3 from the local Administrators group.
3. Add VicePresident3 to the global Domain Admins group.

▶ **To test the user account as a member of the Domain Admins group**

1. Log off and log on as VicePresident3.
2. Start User Manager for Domains, and try to create another user account.

    Were you successful? Why or why not?

    _____

3. Exit User Manager for Domains and log off Windows NT.

Lesson Summary

The following information summarizes the key points in this lesson:

- A built-in group on a domain controller determines what its members can do in the domain.
- A built-in group on all Windows NT non-domain controllers determines what its members can do on the local computer.
- Built-in local groups are on all computers running Windows NT and give user rights to perform system tasks. Built-in local groups have inherent user rights.
- Built-in global groups are on domain controllers only and provide administrators with control of all users in a given domain. Built-in global groups do not have any inherent user rights.
- System groups are on all computers running Windows NT and automatically organize users for system use. Membership of system groups cannot be changed.

For more information on	See
Built-in groups	Chapter 2, "Working With User and Group Accounts," in Microsoft Windows NT Server *Concepts and Planning*.
NTFS volumes	Chapter 4, "Managing Shared Resources and Resource Security," in Microsoft Windows NT Server *Concepts and Planning*.

Best Practices

The following checklist provides the best practices for implementing local and global groups. Review this checklist before you begin assigning users to groups or creating group accounts:

❑ Apply the following strategy when using local and global groups:
- Organize user accounts into global groups
- Assign permissions to local groups
- Add global groups to local groups

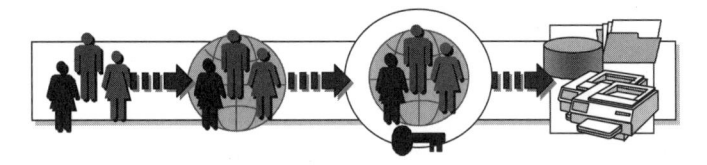

❑ For increased security, use the global group Domain Users instead of the Everyone group. The Domain Users group contains only accounts in the domain, and not the Guest account or other accounts that have connected to the network.

❑ To enable administrators to perform administration tasks in other domains, add the global group Domain Admins to the local Administrators group on the computer in the domain that you want to administer.

❑ If the rights of a built-in group meet your needs, add a user account to the group. Otherwise, create a local group and assign the appropriate user rights.

For example, if for security reasons you want a user to have the right to back up files but *not* the right to restore files, create a local group named *Backup Only* and assign it the *Back up files and directories* right.

❑ Always add users to built-in groups that are the most restrictive, yet still allow them to accomplish all necessary tasks.

Note If you want to remove the accounts that were created by running the Chapter3.cmd file at the beginning of this chapter, log on as Administrator, and then double-click DeleteChapter3.cmd in the Cleanup folder on the Supplemental Material compact disc.

Review

The following questions are intended to reinforce key information presented in this chapter. If you are unable to answer a question, review the lesson and then try the question again.

1. Which of the following describe a local group? (Circle all that apply.)
   a. Are used to provide users with permission to access a network resource and with rights to perform system tasks.
   b. Are used to organize domain user accounts.
   c. Are assigned resource permissions.
   d. Can contain user accounts and global groups.
   e. Are created on the computer where the resource resides, unless the resource resides on a domain controller. If the resource resides on a domain controller, the local group is created on the PDC.
   f. Are always created on the PDC.
   g. Can be created using User Manager or User Manager for Domains.
   h. Can only be created using User Manager for Domains.

2. Which of the following describe a global group? (Circle all that apply.)
   a. Are used to provide users with permission to gain access to a network resource and with rights to perform system tasks.
   b. Are used to organize domain user accounts.
   c. Are assigned resource permissions.
   d. Can contain user accounts and global groups.
   e. Are created on the computer where the resource resides, unless the resource resides on a domain controller. If the resources resides on a domain controller, the local group is created on the PDC.
   f. Are always created on the PDC.
   g. Can be created using User Manager or User Manager for Domains.
   h. Can only be created using User Manager for Domains.

3. What is the difference between a built-in local group and a built-in global group?

   _____

   _____

4. Which of the following tasks will work? (Circle all that apply.)

    a. To give a user administrative privileges on his or her computer running Windows NT Workstation, add the user account to the built-in Administrators group.

    b. To give administrators from Domain1 the ability to administer all domain controllers in Domain2, add the Domain Admins group from Domain1 to the Administrators group on the PDC of Domain2.

    c. To give administrators from Domain2 the ability to administer all computers in Domain2, add the Domain Admins group from Domain1 to the Administrators group on the PDC of Domain2.

    d. To give administrators from Domain1 the ability to administer computers in Domain2 running Windows NT Workstation and member servers, add the Domain Admins group from Domain1 to the Administrators group on those computers in Domain2.

5. What is the recommended strategy for implementing local and global groups?

   _____

   _____

6. What is the difference between the Domain Users group and the Everyone group?

   _____

   _____

Answer Key

Procedure Answers

Page 86

▶ **To review the video**

1. What is the purpose of a local group?

   The purpose is to provide users with permission to access a resource, such as a printer or file. Local groups are also used to provide users with rights to perform system tasks, such as changing the system time on a computer or logging on to the local computer.

2. What is the purpose of a global group?

   The purpose is to organize domain user accounts, typically by function or geographical location.

3. Where are local groups created?

   Local groups are created on the computer where the resource is located.

4. Where are global groups created?

   Global groups are always created on the PDC in the domain where the accounts reside.

Page 87

Example: Using Groups in a Single-Domain Network

1. On which computer would you create a global group for organizing the user accounts? Why?

   You would create a global group from any computer running User Manager for Domains. User Manager for Domains creates the global group on the PDC because global groups always reside in the domain's directory database.

2. On which computer would you create a local group to provide users with access to the Accounts Payable database? Why?

   You would create a local group from any computer running User Manager for Domains. User Manager for Domains creates the local group on the PDC even though the Accounts Payable database is on the BDC. This is because all domain controllers share account information with each other and maintain a common directory database.

3. On which computer would you create a local group to provide users with access to the Inventory database? Why?

   You would create a local group on the member server because that is where the Inventory database resides. The local group is then stored in the local directory database.

4. How would you give members of the global group access to both databases?

   Add the global group to both local groups, the one created for the Inventory database and the other created for the Accounts Payable database. Members of the local groups now have access to both databases, assuming that the appropriate permissions are assigned to the local groups.

Example: Using Groups in a Multiple-Domain Network

Page 88

1. On which computers would you create a global group for organizing the user accounts? Why?

   You would create two global groups, one from any computer running User Manager for Domains in the London domain and the other on the from any computer running User Manager for Domains in the Paris domain. User Manager for Domains creates the global group on the PDC in each domain because global groups always reside in the domain's directory database where the user accounts reside.

2. On which computers would you create a local group to provide users with access to the Inventory databases? Why?

   In each domain, you would create a local group on the member server because each member server has its own directory database.

3. How would you give members of the global groups that you just created in London and in Paris access to the Inventory databases in each other's domain?

   Add the global group created for London users to the local group created for the Paris Inventory database. Add the global group created for Paris users to the local group created for the London Inventory database. Members of the local groups now have access to the Inventory databases, assuming that the appropriate permissions are assigned to the local groups.

Page 102

▶ **To determine the possible group combinations**

- Which group combination or combinations are possible?

  Only b is correct. A global group can be added to a local group.

Microsoft Windows NT Network Administration

Page 107

▶ **To determine which groups have access to the computer**

- Which built-in groups have been granted this right?

    On Windows NT Workstation and member servers: Administrators, Everyone, and Power Users.

    On domain controllers: Administrators and Everyone.

Page 107

▶ **To determine which groups can log on locally**

- Which built-in groups have been granted this right?

    On Windows NT Workstation and member servers: Administrators, Backup Operators, Everyone, Guests, IUSR_*computer_name* (if Internet Information Server or Peer Web Server is installed), Power Users, and Users.

    On domain controllers: Account Operators, Administrators, Backup Operators, Everyone, IUSR_*computer_name* (if Internet Information Server is installed), Print Operators, and Server Operators.

Page 108

▶ **To determine which groups can change the system time**

- Which built-in groups have been granted this right?

    On Windows NT Workstation and member servers: Administrators and Power Users.

    On domain controllers: Administrators and Server Operators.

Page 108

▶ **To determine which groups can shut down the system**

- Which built-in groups have been granted this right?

    On Windows NT Workstation and member servers: Administrators, Backup Operators, Everyone, Power Users, and Users.

    On domain controllers: Account Operators, Administrators, Backup Operators, Print Operators, and Server Operators.

Page 108

▶ **To determine which groups can back up files and directories**

- Which built-in groups have been granted this right?

    On Windows NT Workstation and member servers: Administrators and Backup Operators.

    On domain controllers: Administrators, Backup Operators, and Server Operators.

Chapter 3 Setting Up Group Accounts   125

Page 108

▶ **To determine which groups can restore files and directories**

- Which built-in groups have been granted this right?

    On Windows NT Workstation and member servers: Administrators and Backup Operators.

    On domain controllers: Administrators, Backup Operators, and Server Operators.

Page 108

▶ **To determine the inherent rights that are *only* assigned to the Administrators group**

- Select each user right to determine which ones are automatically assigned to *only* the Administrators group, and then mark all the check boxes in the following list that apply:

    Load and unload device drivers, Manage auditing and security log, and Take ownership of files or other objects.

Page 112

▶ **To determine the default membership of the global group Domain Admins**

- By *default*, what built-in user accounts or groups are members of Domain Admins?

    Administrator is the only user account. There are no groups. Domain Admins only exists on domain controllers.

Page 112

▶ **To determine membership of the local group Administrators**

- By default, what built-in user accounts or global groups are members of the Administrators group?

    On computers running Windows NT Workstation and on member servers that are in a domain, Administrator is the only user account.

    On domain controllers, Administrator is the only user account and Domain Admins is the only global group.

Page 112

▶ **To determine the default membership of other built-in global groups**

- Domain Users contains the following user accounts:

    The Administrator and all domain user accounts except for the Guest account.

- Domain Guests contains the following user account:

    Guest.

Page 113

▶ **To determine the default membership of the built-in local group Guests**

- What user accounts or groups are members of the Guests group?

    On Windows NT Workstation and member servers, the Guest user account is a member. If Internet Information Server or Peer Web Server is installed, a user account IUSR_*computer_name* (where *computer_name* is the name of your computer) is also a member.

    On domain controllers, the global group Domain Guests. If Internet Information Server is installed, a user account IUSR_*computer_name* (where *computer_name* is the name of your computer) is also a member.

Page 113

▶ **To determine the default membership of the built-in local group Users**

- What user accounts or groups are members of the Users group?

    On all Windows NT–based computers that have been added to the domain, the global group Domain Users.

Page 115

▶ **To test the administrative privileges for a user**

2. Start User Manager for Domains, and try to create a user account.

    Were you successful? Why or why not?

    Yes, because VicePresident3 is a member of the Administrators group and has all of the user rights inherent in the Administrators group.

Page 117

▶ **To test the user account as a member of the Domain Admins group**

2. Start User Manager for Domains, and try to create another user account.

    Were you successful? Why or why not?

    Yes, because the Domain Admins group is a member of the Administrators group.

Page 120

Review Answers

1. Which of the following describe a local group? (Circle all that apply.)

    Answers a, c, d, e, and g are correct.

2. Which of the following describe a global group? (Circle all that apply.)

    Answers b, f, and h are correct.

3. What is the difference between a built-in local group and a built-in global group?

    Built-in local groups have a predetermined set of user rights. Built-in global groups get their rights from other local groups.

4. Which of the following tasks will work? (Circle all that apply.)

   Answers a, b, and d are correct.

5. What is the recommended strategy for implementing local and global groups?

   Organize users into global groups, assign permissions to local groups, and add global groups to local groups.

6. What is the difference between the Domain Users group and the Everyone group?

   The Domain Users group is a built-in global group on domain controllers that only contains domain accounts. The Everyone group is a system group on all computers that contains all local and remote users that have connected to the computer, including guest users.

CHAPTER 4

Administering User and Group Accounts

Lesson 1 Introduction to Administering Accounts . . . 131

Lesson 2 Implementing an Account Policy . . . 139

Lesson 3 Modifying Multiple User Accounts . . . 150

Lesson 4 Maintaining Domain Controllers . . . 153

Lesson 5 Troubleshooting Logon Problems . . . 164

Review . . . 168

About This Chapter

This chapter presents tasks related to maintaining existing accounts and streamlining administrative tasks, including creating template accounts, modifying multiple accounts at one time, planning and implementing an account policy, maintaining domain controllers, and troubleshooting user logon problems. The hands-on procedures give you an opportunity to implement and practice each task.

Before You Begin

To complete the lessons in this chapter, you must have:

- Completed the Setup procedures located in "About This Book."
- The knowledge and skills covered in Chapter 2, "Setting Up User Accounts."
- Knowledge and skills covered in Chapter 3, "Setting Up Group Accounts."
- A user account named User4 and two global groups—Managers4 and CustomerService4. Log on as Administrator. In Windows NT Explorer, expand the LabFiles folder, and then double-click Chapter4.cmd to create these accounts.

Lesson 1: Introduction to Administering Accounts

In this lesson, you are introduced to procedures and tools used by network administrators. Starting with an overview of the key elements that will be examined throughout this chapter, the lesson then steps you through several tasks.

After this lesson, you will be able to:
- Assign Account Operator privileges.
- Create and use account templates.

Estimated lesson time: 20 minutes

Administrative Tasks

There are several procedures that an administrator can use to efficiently administer accounts and keep the network running smoothly. Some of the most useful are:

- *Creating Templates*. Creating templates for adding new user accounts streamlines the work.
- *Modifying Accounts*. Making changes to multiple user accounts at one time, (for example, moving home folders) lightens the work load.
- *Planning Policies*. Planning and implementing an account policy helps to keep the network secure.
- *Maintaining Domain Controllers*. Maintaining domain controllers means that user accounts can always be successfully validated.
- *Troubleshooting*. Solving problems associated with user accounts ensures that users can log on.

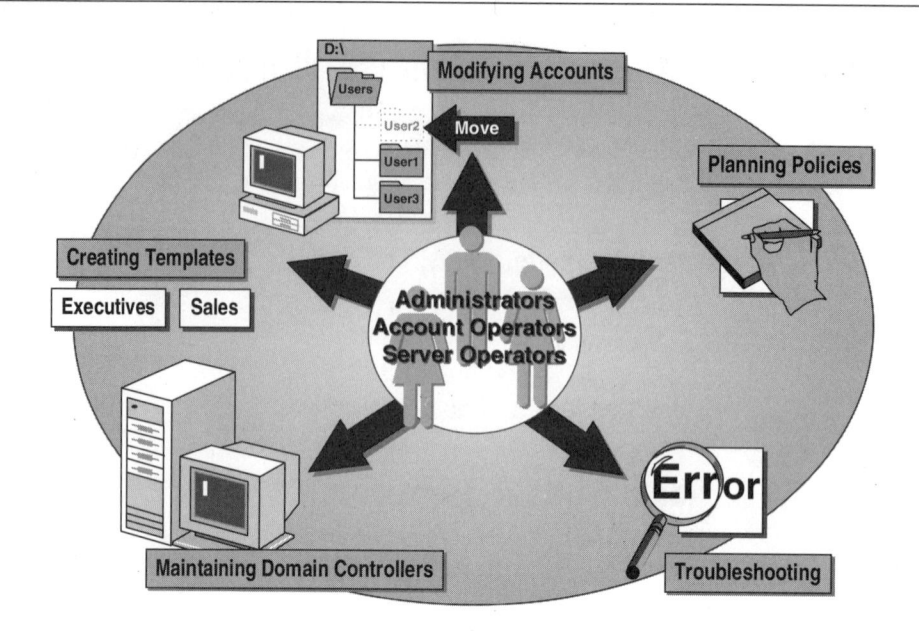

Distributing Administrative Tasks

To distribute some of your administrative tasks, you can grant administrative privileges to a user account by adding the user to one of the following groups:

- *Administrators*. Members of the Administrators group have full administrative capabilities. They are responsible for planning and maintaining network security.
- *Account Operators*. Members of the Account Operators group can create, delete, and modify user accounts, global groups, and local groups, and they can set account policies.

▶ **To give Account Operator privileges to a user account**

In this procedure, you add a user account to the Account Operators group.

1. Log on as Administrator and start User Manager for Domains.
2. In the **Username** list, double-click User4.
3. In the **User Properties** dialog box, click **Groups**.

    The **Group Memberships** dialog box appears.
4. In the **Not member of** list, click **Account Operators**, and then click **Add**.

    Notice that **Account Operators** appears in the **Member of** list.
5. Click **OK** to close the **Group Memberships** dialog box.
6. Click **OK** to close the **User Properties** dialog box, but do not exit User Manager for Domains.

▶ **To determine the inherent rights that are assigned to Account Operators**
1. In the User Manager window, on the **Policies** menu, click **User Rights**.
2. In the **Right** box, select each user right one at a time to determine which of the following rights are automatically assigned to the Account Operators group, and then mark the check boxes that apply in the following list:
   - ❑ **Access this computer from network**
   - ❑ **Add workstations to domain**
   - ❑ **Back up files and directories**
   - ❑ **Change the system time**
   - ❑ **Force shutdown from a remote system**
   - ❑ **Load and unload device drivers**
   - ❑ **Log on locally**
   - ❑ **Manage auditing and security log**
   - ❑ **Restore files and directories**
   - ❑ **Shut down the system**
   - ❑ **Take ownership of files or other objects**
3. Click **Cancel**.

Using Templates

A user account template is a standard user account that you create with the properties that apply to users who have common needs. User account templates are useful administrative tools for creating new user accounts. For example, if all sales personnel require membership in the Sales group, you can create a template that includes membership to that group.

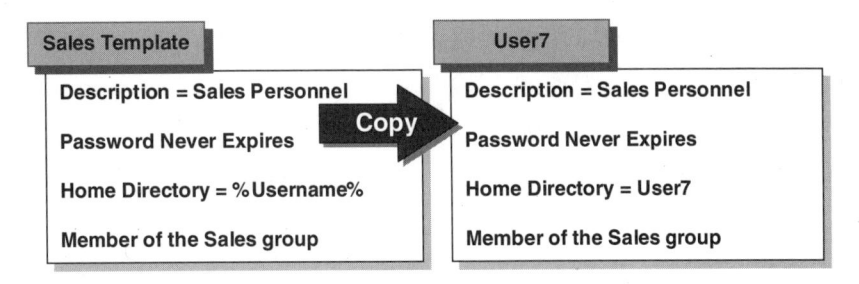

Sales Template	User7
Description = Sales Personnel	Description = Sales Personnel
Password Never Expires	Password Never Expires
Home Directory = %Username%	Home Directory = User7
Member of the Sales group	Member of the Sales group

Copy

To use a template to create a new user account, copy the template account and assign a user name and password for the new user. The following options become properties of the new user account:

Description	Profile
User Must Change Password at Next Logon	Hours (domain controllers only)
User Cannot Change Password	Logon to (domain controllers only)
Password Never Expires	Account (domain controllers only)
Groups	Dialin

Note Rights and permissions granted to an individual user account are not copied.

Suggestions for creating templates include the following:

- Make a template for each classification of employee, such as sales, accountants, managers, and so on.
- If you commonly have short-term or temporary network users, create a template with limited logon hours, workstation specifications, and other necessary restrictions.

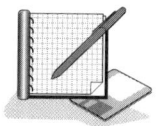

▶ **To define the user account template for new managers**

In this procedure, you create a user account template that will be used to create accounts for new managers.

1. Log on as User4 (the user that you added to the Account Operators group) and start User Manager for Domains.
2. In the **User** menu, click **New User**.
3. Provide the following information:
   - **Username**: *name* **Manager_Template**
   - **Description**: the description that you want to appear for each user account that is created using the template

Tip Add any valid non-alphabetic character, such as the underscore (_), as the first character of all template account names to make them appear at the top of the **Username** list. For example, "_Manager_Template."

▶ **To define the password requirements for new managers**

1. In the **New User** dialog box, make sure that the **User Must Change Password At Next Logon** check box is selected.
2. Select the **Account Disabled** check box.

▶ **To define the template home folder path**
  1. In the **New User** dialog box, click **Profile**.
  2. Under **Home Folder**, click **Connect**, and then click **Z**.
  3. In the **To** box, type *computer_name***users****%username%** (where *computer_name* is the name of your computer), and then click **OK**.

▶ **To define the group accounts for new managers**
  1. In the **New User** dialog box, click **Groups**.
  2. Add the managers template to the following groups:
     - Managers4
     - Domain Users

▶ **To define the template for new night shift employees**

  In this procedure, you define a template account for employees who work the night shift.

  1. Create a template for the new night shift employees, using the same properties as the managers template (except for groups).
  2. Add the night shift employees template to the following groups:
     - CustomerService4
     - Domain Users
  3. Restrict the logon hours for night shift employees to 6:00 P.M. through 6:00 A.M., Monday through Friday.

Using Templates to Create User Accounts

To create a new user account using a template, copy the template.

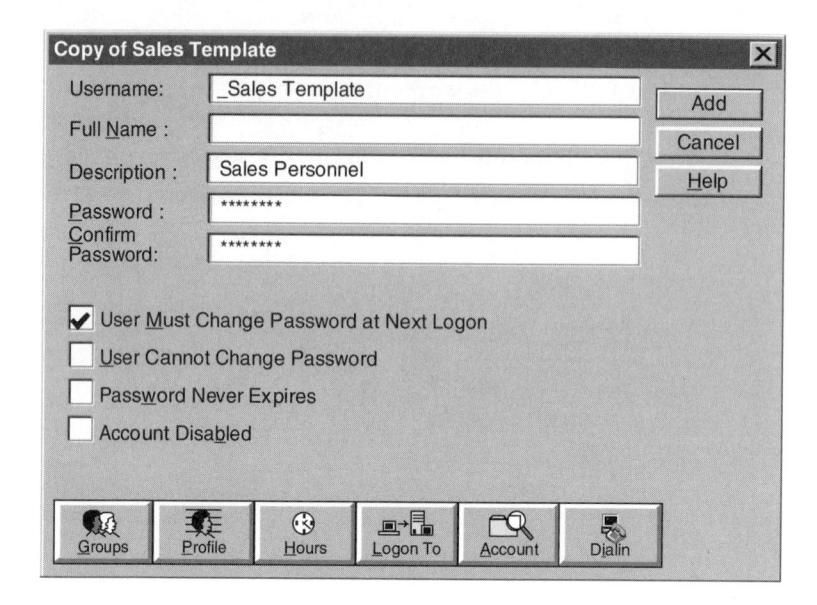

```
Copy of Sales Template
Username:        _Sales Template              [ Add ]
Full Name :                                   [ Cancel ]
Description :    Sales Personnel              [ Help ]
Password :       ********
Confirm
Password:        ********

[✓] User Must Change Password at Next Logon
[ ] User Cannot Change Password
[ ] Password Never Expires
[ ] Account Disabled

  Groups   Profile   Hours   Logon To   Account   Dialin
```

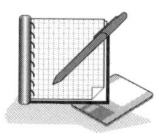

▶ **To create a user account using a template**

1. In the User Manager window, under **Username**, select one of your templates.
2. On the **User** menu, click **Copy**.
3. Type a **Username**, **Full Name**, and **Password** for the user, and then click **Add**.
4. Repeat this procedure using the other template that you created.

Chapter 4 Administering User and Group Accounts

▶ **To determine which account options were copied**

- In the User Manager window, double-click the user account that you created using the night shift employees template. Compare the following account options with those in the template account. In the following list, mark the check boxes next to those options that were copied:

  ❑ **Username**
  ❑ **Full Name**
  ❑ **Description**
  ❑ **Password** and **Confirm Password**
  ❑ **User Must Change Password at Next Logon**
  ❑ **User Cannot Change Password**
  ❑ **Password Never Expires**
  ❑ **Account Disabled**
  ❑ **Profile button options**
  ❑ **Groups button options**
  ❑ **Hours button options**

Lesson Summary

The following information summarizes the key points in this lesson:

- Administrative tasks can be distributed by granting administrative privileges to a user account by adding the user to the Administrators or Account Operators groups.

- Create template accounts with the properties that apply to users who have common needs.

Lesson 2: Implementing an Account Policy

The account policy determines how passwords must be used by all user accounts for a computer or domain and also determines the account lockout policy. This lesson provides conceptual and procedural information on setting up and using an account policy.

This lesson requires that you have completed Lesson 1.

After this lesson, you will be able to:
- Implement an account policy for all accounts in a domain.
- Reset user account passwords.
- Unlock a user account.

Estimated lesson time: 20 minutes

Setting an Account Policy

The account policy sets the requirements for:

- Password minimum and maximum ages
- Password minimum length
- Password uniqueness
- Account lockout options

Changes that you make to the account policy go into effect for users at one of the following two times:

- The next time the user logs on.
- The next time the user makes a change covered by the policy. For example, the minimum password length does not apply to existing passwords, but it will apply the next time a user changes his or her password.

Planning an Account Policy

By default, the only password requirement for user accounts is that users change their passwords the first time that they log on. To use an account policy to provide additional security for user accounts, consider the following:

- Never allow blank passwords. Blank passwords mean *no* security. Do not allow the use of blank passwords on any system connected to the Internet or any system that has dial-in capabilities.
- Require a minimum length for all passwords. The longer the password, the more difficult it is to guess.
  - In a medium-security network, require 6–8 characters.
  - In a high-security network, require 8–14 characters.
- Require users to change their passwords frequently. This helps to prevent unauthorized users from guessing them.
  - In a medium-security network, change passwords every 45–90 days.
  - In a high-security network, change passwords every 14–45 days.
- Require users to use a different password each time they change it. Make sure that once it is changed, it cannot be changed back to a previous password.
  - In a medium-security network, require 8–12 different passwords.
  - In a high-security network, require 12–24 different passwords.
- Lock out accounts after multiple failed logon attempts. This reduces the chance of an unauthorized person gaining access to the network.
  - In a medium-security network, lock out a user after five failed logon attempts.
  - In a high-security network, lock out a user account after three failed logon attempts.
- Require that all locked accounts be unlocked by an administrator. This guarantees that you will be aware of unauthorized users attempting to guess passwords for an account until it becomes locked out.
- Require that users with restricted logon hours are disconnected from the network during off hours. This will prevent users from dialing in to the network.

Setting Password Options

The password options set the requirements for user account passwords. Account policies allow control over password implementation.

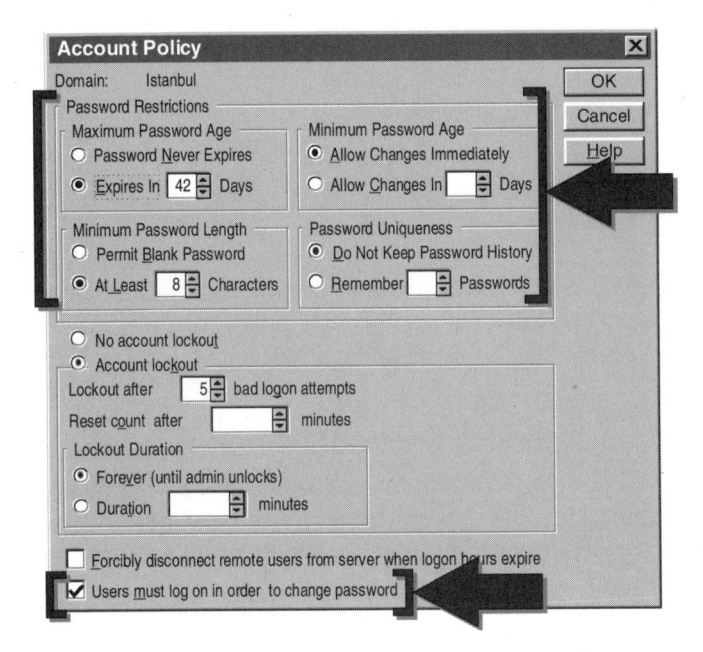

The following table describes the password options.

Option	Description
Maximum Password Age	The period of time that a password can be used before the user is required to change it.
	Range of values: 1–999 days.
Minimum Password Age	The period of time that a password must be kept before the user can change it. Do not allow immediate changes if a password uniqueness value will be entered. The value of the **Minimum Password Age** must be less than the value of the **Maximum Password Age**.
	Range of values: 1–999 days.
Minimum Password Length	The minimum number of characters required in a password.
	Range of values: 1–14 characters.

(continued)

Option	Description
Password Uniqueness	The number of new passwords that must be used by a user before an old password can be reused. For uniqueness to be effective, immediate changes should not be allowed by the **Minimum Password Age** parameter.
	Range of values: 1–24 passwords.
Users must log on in order to change password	If selected, users cannot change their own expired passwords.
	If cleared, users can change their own expired passwords.

Important If the **Password Never Expires** check box is selected in the **New User** or **User Properties** dialog boxes for an individual user account, that setting overrides the **Maximum Password Age** setting.

Setting Account Lockout Options

The account lockout feature enables you to make Windows NT more secure from intruders who try to log on by guessing the passwords of existing user accounts. The account lockout options set the requirements for locking out a user account after failed logon attempts.

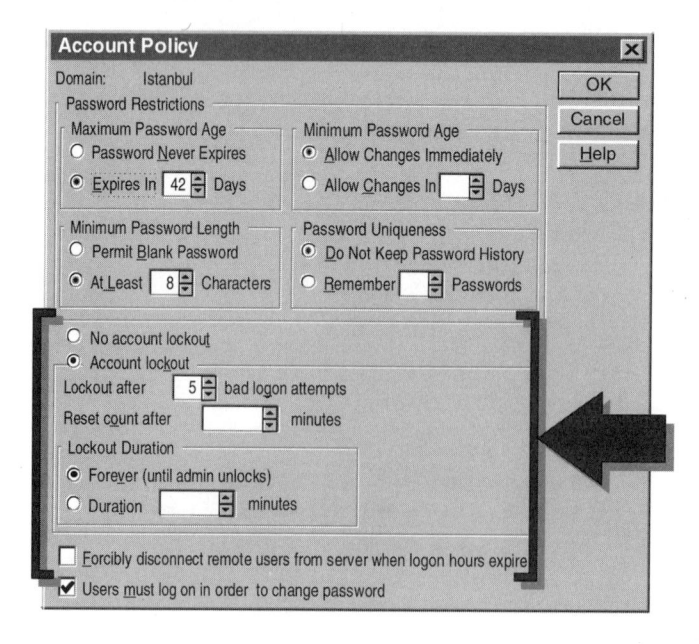

Chapter 4 Administering User and Group Accounts

The following table describes the account lockout options.

Option	Description
Account Lockout	If you click **Account Lockout**, the next three options are available.
Lockout After	The number of incorrect logon attempts that will cause the account to be locked.
	Range of values: 1–999.
Reset Count After	The maximum number of minutes that can elapse between any two bad logon attempts before lockout occurs.
	Range of values: 1–99999 minutes.
Lockout Duration	**Forever** option: Causes locked accounts to remain locked until an administrator unlocks them. (The Administrator account set up during installation cannot be locked out.)
	Duration option: Causes accounts to remain locked for the specified number of minutes. If a lockout duration expires, a locked out account will become unlocked automatically.
	Range of values: 1–99,999 minutes.
Forcibly disconnect remote users from server when logon hours expire	If selected, the user account is disconnected from any server in the domain when the account exceeds logon hours.
	If cleared, the user account is not automatically disconnected, but no new connections are allowed.
	Available only on Microsoft Windows NT Server.

▶ **To plan an account policy**

In this exercise, you plan an account policy for the Quebec domain. You need to determine the following:

- Password restrictions
- Account lockout requirements

To make your decisions, use the following criteria:

- Require users to change their passwords once a month.
- Do not allow users to reuse a password for at least six months.
- Make every effort to prevent unauthorized users from breaking into the system.
- Disconnect employees with restricted logon hours from the network during off hours.

Record your decisions by marking the appropriate options on the following reproduction of the **Account Policy** dialog box.

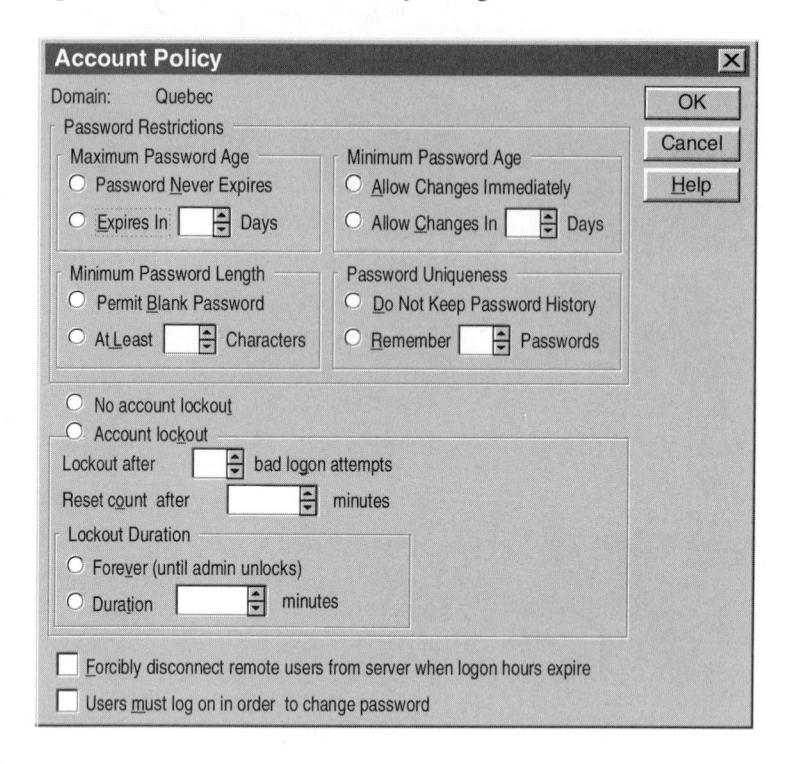

```
┌─ Account Policy ──────────────────────────────────────────── × ─┐
  Domain:    Quebec                                    ┌──────────┐
  ┌─ Password Restrictions ─────────────────────────┐  │    OK    │
  │ ┌─ Maximum Password Age ──┐ ┌─ Minimum Password Age ──┐ ├──────────┤
  │ │ ○ Password Never Expires│ │ ○ Allow Changes Immediately │ │  Cancel  │
  │ │ ○ Expires In [  ] Days  │ │ ○ Allow Changes In [  ] Days │ ├──────────┤
  │ └─────────────────────────┘ └──────────────────────────┘ │   Help   │
  │ ┌─ Minimum Password Length ┐ ┌─ Password Uniqueness ──┐ └──────────┘
  │ │ ○ Permit Blank Password  │ │ ○ Do Not Keep Password History │
  │ │ ○ At Least [  ] Characters │ │ ○ Remember [  ] Passwords │
  │ └──────────────────────────┘ └────────────────────────┘
  └─────────────────────────────────────────────────┘

      ○ No account lockout
      ○ Account lockout
      Lockout after    [  ] bad logon attempts
      Reset count after [     ] minutes
      ┌─ Lockout Duration ──────────────────┐
      │ ○ Forever (until admin unlocks)     │
      │ ○ Duration [     ] minutes          │
      └─────────────────────────────────────┘

      ☐ Forcibly disconnect remote users from server when logon hours expire
      ☐ Users must log on in order to change password
```

▶ **To set the account policy**

In this procedure, you set an account policy for all domain user accounts in a medium-security network.

1. Log on as Administrator.
2. In the User Manager window, on the **Policies** menu, click **Account**.

   The **Account Policy** dialog box appears.

3. Set the following account policy for password restrictions and account lockout based on a medium level of security.

Password or account lockout restrictions	Set this way for medium security
Maximum Password Age	Expires in 90 days
Minimum Password Age	Allow changes in 30 days
Minimum Password Length	8 characters
Password Uniqueness	Remember 8 passwords
Account Lockout	Yes
Lockout After	3 bad logon attempts
Reset Count After	30 minutes
Lockout Duration	Forever (until administrator unlocks)

4. Click **OK** to set the account policy.

▶ **To test the password restriction portion of the account policy**

In this procedure, you test how passwords are affected by the new account policy.

1. Try to create a user account with no password.

    An error message appears stating that the password you typed is invalid. This error occurred because your account policy requires passwords to be a minimum of eight characters. Blank passwords are not permitted.

2. Click **OK** to acknowledge the message.

3. In the **Password** and **Confirm Password** boxes, type a password that is at least eight characters, and then click **Add**.

    Make sure that the **User Must Change Password at Next Logon** check box is selected.

4. Log off and then log on using the new user account.

    A message box appears, indicating that you are required to change your password at first logon attempt. Even though this was not set in your account policy, it was set by default when you created the user account.

5. Click **OK** to acknowledge the message.

6. In the **New Password** and **Confirm New Password** boxes, type **watermelon** and then click **OK**.

    A message appears indicating that the password was changed.

7. Press CTRL+ALT+DELETE to access the **Windows NT Security** dialog box, and then click **Change Password**.

8. In the **Old Password** box, type **watermelon**

9. In the **New Password** and **Confirm New Password** boxes, type **cantaloupe** and then click **OK**.

    A message appears stating that the account cannot be changed at this time. This occurs because the account policy does not permit password changes more than once in 30 days. You were able to change your password the first time because it was required when the account was created.

10. Click **OK**.

▶ **To test the account lockout portion of the account policy**

In this procedure, you incorrectly type a password several times to see the effect of the account lockout policy.

1. Log off and try to log on again as the same user, without specifying a password.

    You receive an error message indicating that the system could not log you on.

2. Click **OK**.
3. Log off and log on two more times with no password.
4. Now log on with the correct password.

    Why were you unable to log on using the correct password?

    _____

    How should the user solve the problem?

    _____

5. Click **OK**.

Unlocking User Accounts

If you have an account policy set up that locks out the user after several failed logon attempts, you may need to unlock the account.

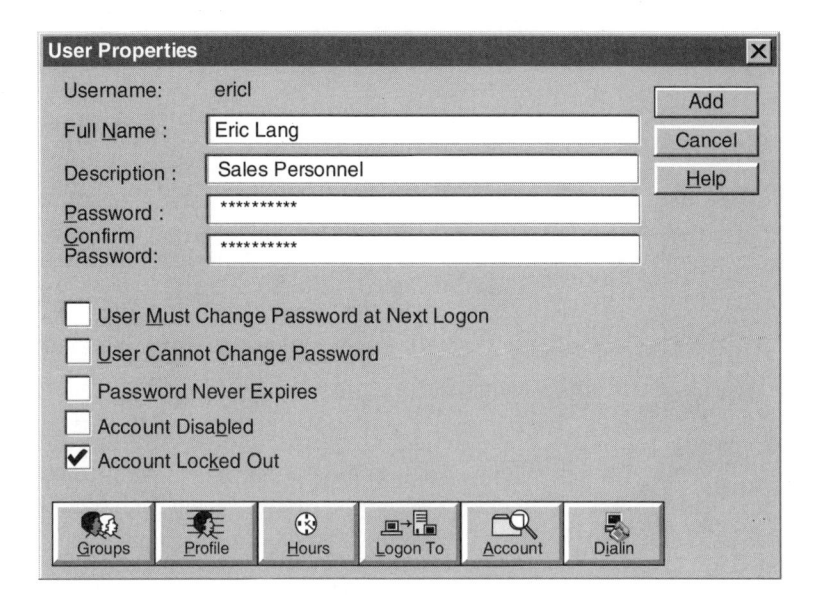

> **To unlock a locked account**
>
> 1. Log on as Administrator, and start User Manager for Domains.
> 2. In the **Username** list, double-click the locked account (from the previous exercise).
> 3. Clear the **Account Locked Out** check box.
> 4. Click **OK**.
> 5. Exit User Manager for Domains.
>
> **To verify that the account is unlocked**
>
> - Log on as the user whose account you unlocked.

Tip If the user has failed several times in trying to log on to the domain, the user may have forgotten his or her password. If that is the case, reset it while you are unlocking it.

Resetting User Account Passwords

If a user's password expires before the user has a chance to change it, or if a user forgets a password, you can reset the password by deleting it and typing a new one.

▶ **To reset a user account password**

1. Log on as Administrator.
2. Start User Manager for Domains.
3. Double-click the user that you used in the previous exercise.

    The **User Properties** dialog box appears.
4. In the **Password** box, double-click the entry, and then press DELETE.
5. In the **Password** box, type a new password.
6. In the **Confirm Password** box, retype the password, and then click **OK**.
7. Exit User Manager for Domains.

Note Before you continue, you may want to clear the account policy settings. Clearing the settings will allow you to experiment with other user accounts used throughout this book without the restrictions set in the account policy.

Lesson Summary

The following information summarizes the key points in this lesson:

- The account policy sets the requirements for passwords and lockout options for all domain user accounts.
- To protect accounts from unauthorized use, never allow blank passwords.
- To make passwords difficult to guess, require a minimum password length.
- Require that users change their passwords frequently and that they are unique each time. This will help deter unauthorized access.
- To catch computer hackers, lock out accounts after multiple failed attempts.

For more information on	See
Domain security policies	Chapter 1, "Managing Windows NT Server Domains," in Microsoft Windows NT Server *Concepts and Planning*.

Lesson 3: Modifying Multiple User Accounts

Windows NT provides a shortcut for making modifications to multiple user accounts at one time. This is especially useful for moving user home folders to a different server or volume.

This lesson guides you through the steps to modify multiple user accounts at one time.

After this lesson, you will be able to:
- Modify multiple accounts at one time.

Estimated lesson time: 10 minutes

You can easily modify multiple user accounts at one time by selecting multiple user accounts and then modifying the properties. Use this procedure when you need to modify multiple user accounts in the same manner—for example, when you need to move home folders to another server or volume, or set the logon hours for 100 users.

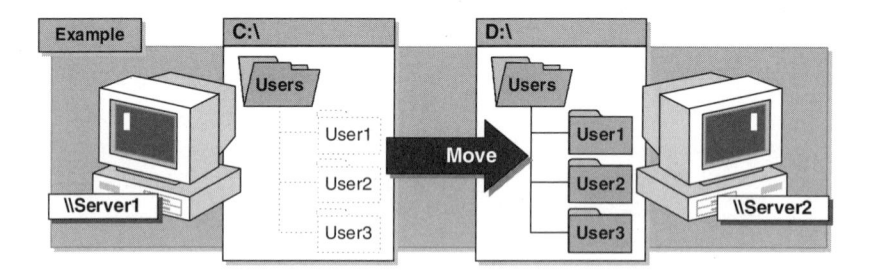

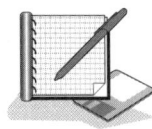

▶ **To modify multiple user accounts at one time**

1. Start User Manager for Domains.
2. Select the user accounts that you created using the Manager and Night Shift employee templates (in Lesson 1). Use one of the following methods:

   To select accounts in random order, click the first account, hold down the CTRL key, and then click the remaining accounts.

   –or–

   To select accounts in consecutive order, click the first account, hold down the SHIFT key, and then click the last account.
3. On the **User** menu, click **Properties**.

   The **User Properties** dialog box appears with both of the user account names listed in the **Users** box.
4. Click **Dialin**.

   The **Dialin Information** dialog box appears.
5. Select the **Grant dialin permissions to user** check box and then click **OK** twice to apply your changes.
6. View the properties of each account to verify that the Dialin permission has been granted.

Lesson Summary

The following information summarizes the key points in this lesson:

- Modify multiple user accounts at one time by selecting multiple user accounts and then modifying the properties. This method is especially useful for moving user home folders to a different server or volume.

For more information on	See
User accounts	Chapter 2, "Working With User and Group Accounts," in Microsoft Windows NT Server *Concepts and Planning*.
	Chapter 2, "Setting Up User Accounts," in this book.

Lesson 4: Maintaining Domain Controllers

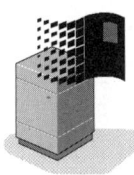

Maintaining domain controllers means making sure that a primary domain controller (PDC) is always online and that all copies of the directory database are current.

This lesson provides an overview of the procedures required to maintain domain controllers when a PDC needs to be taken offline, and when a PDC goes offline unexpectedly.

After this lesson, you will be able to:
- Describe the function of Server Manager.
- Promote a backup domain controller to a primary domain controller.
- Restore a primary domain controller.
- Synchronize domain controllers.

Estimated lesson time: 20 minutes

If your PDC goes offline for any reason, you need to perform a series of tasks to be sure that your security account database is maintained. The PDC maintains the master copy of the domain's directory database.

If the PDC goes offline, users can still log on, but you can no longer administer accounts. Maintaining domain controllers means making sure that a primary domain controller (PDC) is always online and that all copies of the directory database are current.

Every domain has only one PDC. The PDC maintains the master copy of the domain's directory database. The directory database is automatically replicated to all the backup domain controllers (BDCs) in the domain every five minutes.

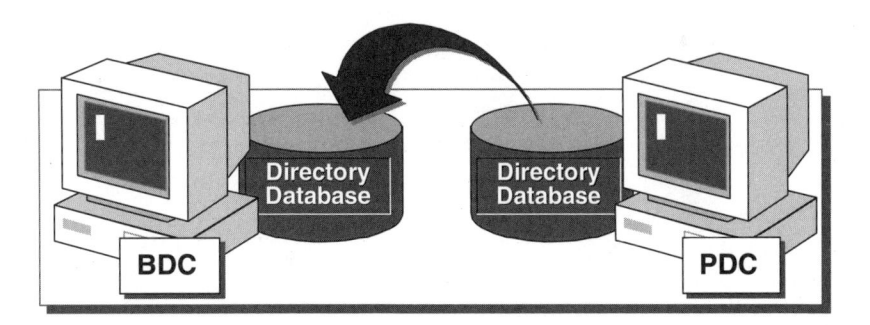

If the PDC goes offline for any reason, users will still be able to log on and be validated by the BDC. But you will no longer be able to do any account administration.

Server Manager

Server Manager is a Windows NT Server tool that you can use to maintain domain controllers. Using Server Manager, you can promote a backup domain controller to become the primary domain controller, synchronize servers with the primary domain controller, and add computers to and remove computers from the domain. To start Server Manager, click the **Start** button, point to **Programs**, point to **Administrative Tools**, and then click **Server Manager**.

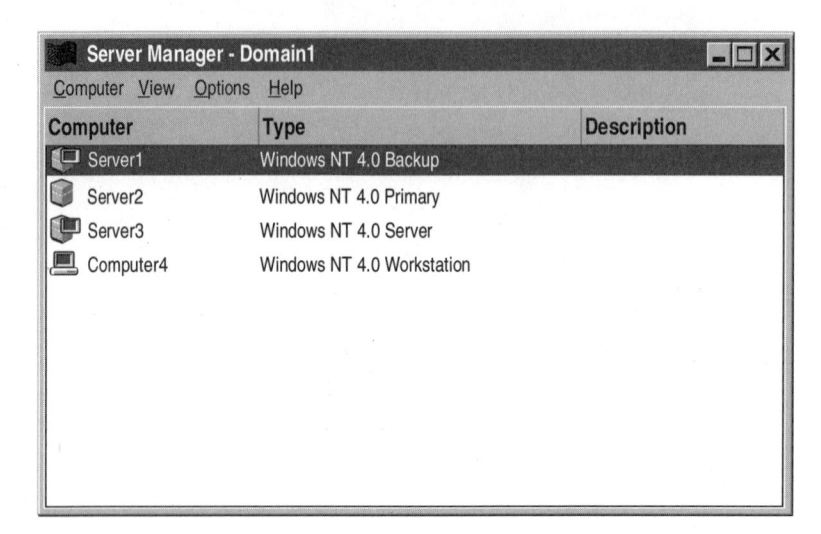

Computer	Type	Description
Server1	Windows NT 4.0 Backup	
Server2	Windows NT 4.0 Primary	
Server3	Windows NT 4.0 Server	
Computer4	Windows NT 4.0 Workstation	

The following information appears in the Server Manager window for the current domain:

- The computer name and the operating system and version it is running.
- An icon indicating whether the computer is a primary domain controller, a backup domain controller or member server, or a computer running Windows NT Workstation or another client.

  In the previous illustration, the icon for Server1 and Server3 indicates a backup domain controller or a member server. The icon for Server2 indicates a primary domain controller. The icon for Computer4 indicates a computer running Windows NT Workstation or another client.

- If a computer is not running, the icon for the computer appears dimmed.
- A description (configured during installation).

When the PDC Needs to Be Taken Offline

When you need to take a PDC offline, perform the following tasks:

❑ Promote a BDC to take the place of the PDC while its offline. This will force the PDC to become a BDC. When you promote a BDC, an up-to-date copy of the domain directory database is replicated from the old PDC to the new one. The original PDC is automatically demoted to a BDC.

❑ When the original PDC is brought back online, promote it back to a PDC, which forces the temporary PDC to demote itself to a BDC.

Scenario

Your PDC needs to be taken offline for some routine maintenance. You will use Server Manager to promote a BDC to a PDC while demoting the original PDC to a BDC. When this is accomplished, you can then take the original PDC offline for maintenance.

Note For this lesson, you use the Server Manager Simulation. This is a program that simulates a BDC in a domain.

▶ **To promote a BDC to a PDC**

1. Click the **Start** button, point to **Programs**, point to **Network Administration Training**, and then click **Server Manager Simulation**.

2. In the **Server Manager Simulation** dialog box, click **Promoting a BDC When the PDC Needs to Be Taken Offline**.

   The Server Manager window appears.

   Notice that the current BDC is Server1 and the current PDC is Server2.

3. Select the BDC, and then on the **Computer** menu, click **Promote to Primary Domain Controller**.

   The following message appears:

   ```
   Promoting Server1 to Primary may take a few minutes.
   Promoting Server1 will also close client connections to Server1 and
   to the current domain controller (if any). Press 'Help' for details
   if either machine is a Remote Access server.
   Do you want to make the change?
   ```

4. When prompted for confirmation of the change, click **Yes**.

   The Server Manager status box appears. Notice the following actions as they occur during the promotion.

   ```
   Synchronizing Server1 with its primary domain controller
   Synchronizing Server1 with its primary
   Stopping Net Logon Service on Server1
   Stopping Net Logon Service on Server2
   Changing Server2's role to Backup
   Changing Server1's role to Primary
   Starting Net Logon service on Server2
   Starting Net Logon service on Server1
   ```

   When this procedure is finished, the original PDC (Server2) automatically becomes a BDC.

▶ **To return the BDC to PDC status**

1. In the Server Manager window, select Server2 (the original PDC).
2. Promote the BDC to a primary domain controller.

   The following message appears:

   ```
   Promoting Server2 to Primary may take a few minutes.
   Promoting Server2 will also close client connections to Server2 and
   to the current domain controller (if any). Press 'Help' for details
   if either machine is a Remote Access server.
   Do you want to make the change?
   ```

   The Server Manager status box appears. Notice the following actions as they occur during the promotion.

   ```
   Synchronizing Server2 with its primary
   Stopping Net Logon Service on Server2
   Stopping Net Logon Service on Server1
   Changing Server1's role to Backup
   Changing Server2's role to Primary
   Starting Net Logon service on Server1
   Starting Net Logon service on Server2
   ```

   Notice that the current PDC (Server1) was automatically demoted to a BDC.

When a PDC Goes Offline Unexpectedly

When a PDC goes offline unexpectedly, you need to perform the following steps:

❑ Promote a BDC to take the place of the PDC.

❑ Once the original PDC is fixed and brought back online, demote it to a BDC. This will force the temporary PDC to become a BDC.

❑ Promote the original PDC again.

Scenario

Your primary domain controller goes offline unexpectedly. The computer failed, and when you ran diagnostics on it, you discovered that some of the memory was corrupted. It will take a week before you can get the replacement memory chips, and users need access to their files on the network.

▶ **To promote a BDC to PDC when the PDC is already offline**

1. In the **Server Manager Simulation** dialog box, click **Promote a BDC When the PDC Goes Offline Unexpectedly**.

   The Server Manager window appears.

   Notice that the current BDC is Server2 and the current PDC is Server1. The PDC icon appears dimmed because it is currently offline.

2. In **Server Manager**, select the BDC.

3. On the **Computer** menu, click **Promote to Primary Domain Controller**.

   The following message appears:

   ```
   Promoting Server2 to Primary may take a few minutes.
   Promoting Server2 will also close any client connections to Server2
   and to the current domain controller (if any). Press 'Help' for
   details if either machine is a Remote Access server.
   Do you want to make the change?
   ```

4. Click **Yes**.

   The following message appears:

   ```
   Cannot find the Primary for domain_name. Continuing with the
   promotion may result in errors when domain_name's old Primary comes
   back online. Do you want to continue with the promotion?
   ```

5. Click **OK**.

   The Server Manager status box appears. Notice the following actions as they occur during the promotion.

   ```
   Stopping Net Logon Service on Server2
   Changing Server2's role to Primary
   Starting Net Logon service on Server2
   ```

Restoring the Original Domain Controller Roles

If your PDC goes offline and you promote a BDC to be the PDC, you may want to restore the original PDC. To do this, you will need to demote the current PDC.

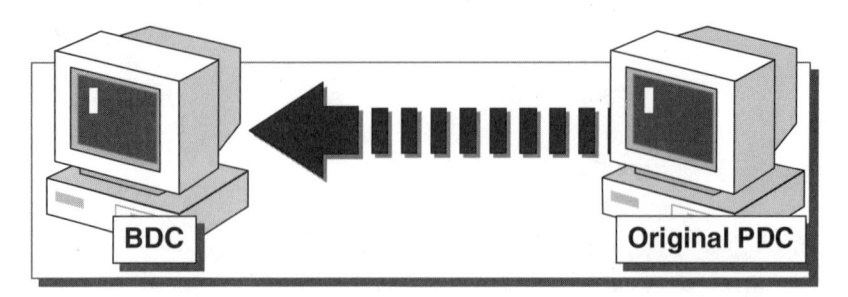

You can also promote a BDC to a PDC after the PDC has gone offline, but the PDC will not automatically be demoted. Also, because the PDC is offline, no automatic replication of the accounts database can occur between the two PDCs.

When the original PDC is brought back online, there is already a PDC in the domain, so its Net Logon service will fail to start. You will need to restore the original PDC.

▶ **To restore the original PDC to the role of PDC**

1. In the **Server Manager Simulation** dialog box, click **Restoring the Original Domain Controller Roles**.

    The Server Manager window appears.

    Note If this were not a simulation, you would start Server Manager on the computer that was originally functioning as the PDC.

    Notice that both the original and the current PDC are listed as primary domain controllers, but the icon for the original PDC (Server2) is unavailable. The Net Logon service on the original PDC was not started at system boot when the original PDC detected that a PDC was already running on the network; with the Net Logon service stopped, the original PDC cannot validate logon requests.

2. Select the original PDC.

3. On the **Computer** menu, click **Demote to Backup Domain Controller**.

    The following message appears:

    ```
    Demoting Server2 to Backup Domain Controller may take a few minutes.
    Demoting Server2 will also close client connections to Server2. Press
    'Help' for details if Server2 is a Remote Access server.
    Do you want to make the change?
    ```

4. When prompted, click **Yes** to make the change.

   The Server Manager status box appears. Notice the following actions as they occur during the promotion.

5. Try to start the Net Logon service on Server2.

   The PDC is demoted to a BDC and the Net Logon service is started. Now Server2 is a functioning BDC in the domain as indicated by its icon.

6. Select the BDC that was the original PDC, and on the **Computer** menu, click **Promote to Primary Domain Controller**.

   The following message appears:

   ```
   Promoting Server2 to Primary may take a few minutes.
   Promoting Server2 will also close client connections to Server2 and
   to the current domain controller (if any). Press 'Help' for details
   if either machine is a Remote Access server.
   Do you want to make the change?
   ```

7. Click **Yes** to make the change. Notice the following actions.

   ```
   Synchronizing Server2 with its primary
   Stopping Net Logon service on Server2
   Stopping Net Logon service on Server1
   Changing Server1's role to Backup
   Changing Server2's role to Primary
   Starting the Net Logon service on Server2
   Starting the Net Logon service on Server1
   ```

   Observe that the original BDC is demoted back to BDC. Also, notice that you receive messages indicating that the directory database on the current PDC was synchronized with the directory database on the current BDC before it is promoted to a PDC.

   If any administration, such as adding user accounts or changing passwords, was done while the original PDC was down, this automatic synchronization of the directory databases ensures that these changes are not lost.

Synchronizing Domain Controllers

Synchronizing domain controllers ensures that all directory databases in the domain are up-to-date. By default, Windows NT synchronizes domain controllers every few minutes. You may want to synchronize domain controllers manually after you make changes to an account database, to apply the changes immediately.

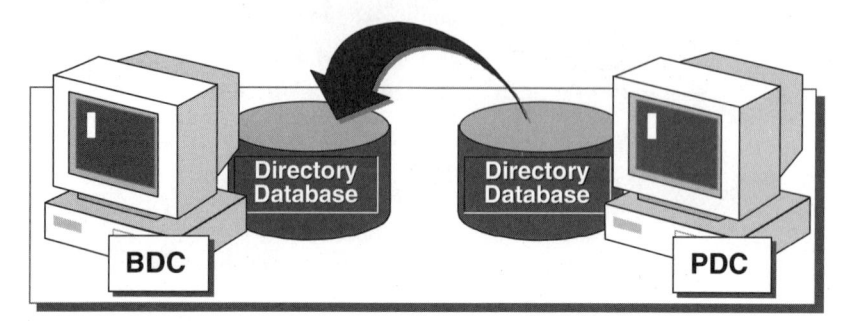

The greater the number of BDCs, the longer it takes to synchronize them.

You can manually synchronize domain controllers for the following reasons:

- To apply changes made to the domain's directory database immediately.
- To solve problems related to password mismatches. If users change their passwords, it takes time for new passwords to be distributed automatically to all the BDCs in a large domain.

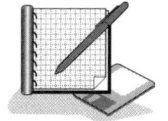

▶ **To synchronize a BDC with the PDC**

1. In the **Server Manager Simulation** dialog box, click **Synchronizing Domain Controllers**.

    The Server Manager window appears.

    Notice that the current BDC is Server1 and the current PDC is Server2.

2. Select the BDC, and then on the **Computer** menu, click **Synchronize with Primary Domain Controller**.

    The following message appears:

    ```
    Resynching Server1 with its Primary may take a few minutes. Do you
    want to make the change?
    ```

    Note If there are multiple BDCs in the domain, you can synchronize all of them by clicking **Synchronize Entire Domain**.

3. Click **Yes** to make the change.

   The following message appears:

   ```
   Backup Domain Controller Server1 will synchronize its account
   database with the Primary Domain Controller. Check the Event Log on
   Backup Domain Controller Server1 and on the Primary Domain Controller
   to determine whether synchronization was successful.
   ```

4. Click **OK**.
5. On the **Computer** menu, click **Exit**.
6. In the Server Manager Simulation window, click **Exit**.

Verifying the Synchronization

You can determine if a synchronization is successful by using Event Viewer to view the system log for Net Logon events.

Note The Server Manager Simulation does not generate any system log events, so you will not be able to view the Net Logon service events resulting from the previous procedures.

To view the system log, follow these steps:

1. Click the **Start** button, point to **Programs**, point to **Administrative Tools**, and then click **Event Viewer**.
2. On the **Log** menu, click **System**.

   The System event log appears.
3. Under **Source**, select the most recent NETLOGON event.
4. On the **View** menu, click **Detail**.
5. Read the event details by clicking **Next**, until you find confirmation of synchronization.
6. Exit Event Viewer.

About Windows NT Services

Most of the functionality of Windows NT is implemented as a service. For example, the Workstation service must be running before you can connect to resources on other computers; the Server service must be running before you can share resources. On domain controllers, the Net Logon service must be running before user logon attempts can be validated.

Some services are dependent on other services. For example, the Server service must be started before the Net Logon service can start.

You can determine which services are running by typing **net start** from a command prompt, by starting the Services program in Control Panel, or in Server Manager by clicking **Services** on the **Computer** menu.

Lesson Summary

The following information summarizes the key points in this lesson:

- Maintaining domain controllers means making sure that a primary domain controller (PDC) is always online and that all copies of the directory database are current.
- Administrators must be able to perform a series of tasks to ensure that the network security account database is maintained if the PDC goes offline for any reason.
- When a PDC needs to be taken offline, promote a backup domain controller (BDC) to take its place.
- When a PDC goes offline unexpectedly, temporarily promote a BDC to take its place. Once the original PDC is repaired and brought back online, demote it to a BDC and promote the original PDC again.

For more information on	See
Promoting and demoting domain controllers	Chapter 1, "Managing Windows NT Server Domains," in Microsoft Windows NT Server *Concepts and Planning*.
The Net Logon service	Chapter 2, "Network Security and Domain Planning," in the *Networking Guide* of the *Microsoft Windows NT Server Resource Kit*.

Lesson 5: Troubleshooting Logon Problems

One of the most common problems that users encounter is the inability to log on to the network successfully. This lesson describes the error messages and solutions to common user logon problems.

After this lesson, you will be able to:
- Identify and troubleshoot logon problems.

Estimated lesson time: 20 minutes

The following table describes common error messages and solutions to logon problems.

User error message	Solution
The system could not log you on. Make sure your user name and domain name are correct, and then type your password again. Letters in passwords must be typed using the correct case. Make sure that CAPS LOCK is not accidentally on.	Verify that the user name, domain name, and password are correct; check the CAPS LOCK key—passwords are case sensitive. (The domain name can be verified using the Network program in Control Panel.) If a user has forgotten the password, delete or reset the user's password. If the user account is new, it may not have been synchronized with BDCs. Synchronize domain controllers.
A domain controller for your domain could not be contacted. You have been logged on using cached account information. Changes made to your profile since you last logged on may not be available.	Check to see if this is the only computer having difficulty. Verify that domain controllers are online. If the PDC is still online, select a BDC and promote it to a PDC. If the PDC is offline, promote a BDC to a PDC. If it is the only computer having the problem, verify that a cable connects the computer to the network. Check the network adapter card. If the network adapter has a light on or is blinking. If the problem is not obvious, restart the computer.
Your account has time restrictions that prevent you from logging on at this time. Please try again later.	The logon hours for the user are not allowed for the current time. To allow a user to log on, modify the user's logon hours.
Your account is configured to prevent you from using this workstation. Please try another workstation.	The user has been restricted from using that workstation. To allow the user to use the workstation, modify the Logon To restrictions.

Troubleshooting User Logon Problems

In the following procedures, you troubleshoot two problems related to users logging on to the network. You produce each problem by running a batch file.

Scenario 1

You have just added a new user account, and you want to test it before allowing the user to use the account. The user account is *PDC1* and the password is *password*.

▶ **To produce the problem**

1. Log on as Administrator.
2. Start Windows NT Explorer, expand the LabFiles folder and double-click Scenario1.cmd.

   A Command Prompt window opens briefly and then closes automatically. The screen is blank to prevent you from guessing the answer to the scenario as it is being created.

▶ **To test the problem for Scenario 1**

- Log off and then log on as PDC1.

  What is the symptom of the problem?

  _____

  _____

▶ **To solve the problem for Scenario 1**

- Use User Manager for Domains to determine the problem and solve it.

  What is the problem?

  _____

  _____

  What is the solution to the problem?

  _____

  _____

Scenario 2

A user needs to change her password, but is having problems logging on. The user account is *PDC2* and the password is *password*.

▶ **To produce the problem**

1. Log on as Administrator.
2. In Windows NT Explorer, expand the LabFiles folder, and double-click Scenario2.cmd.

   A Command Prompt window opens briefly and then closes automatically. The screen is blank to prevent you from guessing the answer to the scenario as it is being created.

▶ **To test the problem for Scenario 2**

- Log off and then log on as PDC2 (the name specified in the scenario).

   What is the symptom of the problem?

   _____

   _____

▶ **To solve the problem for Scenario 2**

- Use User Manager for Domains to determine the problem and solve it.

   What is the problem?

   _____

   _____

   What are possible solutions to the problem?

   _____

   _____

Lesson Summary

The following information summarizes the key points in this lesson:

- Always verify that the user typed the user name, domain name, and password correctly, and that he or she used the correct case for the password. This is the most common problem.
- If the user name, domain name, and password are correct, check the restrictions set on the account.
- If other users have problems logging on, make sure that the domain controller is functioning properly.

For more information on	See
How the user logon process works	Chapter 1, "Managing Windows NT Server Domains," in Microsoft Windows NT Server *Concepts and Planning*.

Note If you want to remove the accounts that were created by running the Chapter4.cmd file at the beginning of this chapter, log on as Administrator, and then double-click DeleteChapter4.cmd in the Cleanup folder on the Supplemental Material compact disc.

Review

The following questions are intended to reinforce key information presented in this chapter. If you are unable to answer a question, review the lesson and then try the question again.

1. When and why would you create a template for creating new user accounts?

2. What is included in the account policy and why is it important?

3. If your PDC goes offline unexpectedly, what do you need to do to maintain the directory database?

4. What are some possible reasons why a user cannot log on?

Answer Key

Procedure Answers

Page 133

▶ **To determine the inherent rights that are assigned to Account Operators**

2. In the **Right** box, select each user right one at a time to determine which of the following rights are automatically assigned to the Account Operators group, and then mark the check boxes that apply in the following list:

Log on locally and Shut down the system are inherent rights of the Account Operators group.

Page 137

▶ **To determine which account options were copied**

- In the User Manager window, double-click the user account that you created using the night shift employees template. Compare the following options with the template account. In the following list, mark the check boxes next to those options that were copied:

All options were copied except for Username, Full Name, Password, Confirm Password, and Account Disabled.

Page 168

▶ **To plan an account policy**

Suggested answers:

Maximum Password Age: 28–31 days.

Minimum Password Age: 7–14 days.

Minimum Password Length: 8–10 characters.

Password Uniqueness: Remember 6–24 passwords.

Lockout after 3–5 bad logon attempts. Reset count after 15–30 minutes.

Lockout Duration: Forever. The administrator should unlock accounts.

Select the Forcibly Disconnect Remote Users From Server When Logon Hours Expire check box.

Page 145

▶ **To test the account lockout portion of the account policy**

4. Now log on with the correct password.

Why were you unable to log on using the correct password?

Your account has been locked out based on the account policy.

How should the user solve the problem?

The user should contact the administrator.

Page 164

▶ **To test the problem for Scenario 1**

- Log off and then log on as PDC1.

What is the symptom of the problem?

For the first *x* logon attempts, an error message appeared indicating that the name or password was incorrect. At *x*+1 logon attempts, an error message appeared indicating that the account was locked out.

Page 164

▶ **To solve the problem for Scenario 1**

- Use User Manager for Domains to determine the problem and solve it.

What is the problem?

The password was incorrect. It was set up using all uppercase characters, and the user typed all lowercase characters. This is a typical logon problem, even though there is no way for the administrator to know if the user typed the password incorrectly.

What is the solution to the problem?

Log on as Administrator and clear or reset the password.

Page 165

▶ **To test the problem for Scenario 2**

- Log off and then log on as PDC2 (the name specified in the scenario).

What is the symptom of the problem?

A message appears indicating that the account has been disabled. Once the account is enabled, a new message indicates that the account has expired. Once the account has been made active again, a message appears indicating that the user does not have permission to change his or her password.

Page 165

▶ **To solve the problem for Scenario 2**

- Use User Manager for Domains to determine the problem and solve it.

What is the problem?

The account has been disabled. The account expired at the end of 1995. The user has been restricted from changing the password.

What are possible solutions to the problem?

Log on as Administrator, and then change the user properties to enable the account.

Log on as Administrator, and then set the account to never expire.

Log on as Administrator, and then change the password for the user, or enable the user to change the password.

Review Answers

1. When and why would you create a template for creating new user accounts?

   Create templates when you need to create new user accounts that have similar requirements.

2. What is included in the account policy and why is it important?

   Account Policy settings include password and account lockout options. The account policy is important because the selections you make will determine how secure your network is.

3. If your PDC goes offline unexpectedly, what do you need to do to maintain the directory database?

   Initially, promote a BDC to a PDC. When the original PDC goes back online, you restore the original PDC, which automatically demotes the temporary PDC.

4. What are some possible reasons why a user cannot log on?

   Possible reasons include the following: password not entered correctly, workstation restrictions set for the user account, or the computer is not connected to a domain controller.

CHAPTER 5

Securing Network Resources with Share Permissions

Lesson 1 Introduction to Shared Folders . . . 174

Lesson 2 Guidelines for Planning Shared Folders . . . 181

Lesson 3 Sharing Folders . . . 192

Lesson 4 Connecting to Shared Folders . . . 200

Best Practices . . . 205

Review . . . 206

About This Chapter

Shared folders give users centralized access to network files. This chapter explains how to share folders and how to assign permission for gaining access to the shared folders to user and group accounts.

The hands-on procedures give you an opportunity to plan and share folders and to secure them with permissions.

Before You Begin

To complete the lessons in this chapter, you must have:

- Completed the Setup procedures located in "About This Book."
- The knowledge and skills covered in Chapter 3, "Setting Up Group Accounts."
- A user account named SalesRep5. Log on as Administrator. In Windows NT Explorer, expand the LabFiles folder, and then double-click Chapter5.cmd to create this account.

Lesson 1: Introduction to Shared Folders

Windows NT enables you to designate disk resources that you want to share with others. For example, when a folder is shared, authorized users can make connections to the folder (and access its files) from their own computers. This lesson introduces you to shared folders and how they are used.

After this lesson, you will be able to:
- Explain the situations in which shared folders are used.
- Describe the four levels of share permissions.
- Describe the result when share permissions are applied.

Estimated lesson time: 20 minutes

What Are Shared Folders?

Shared folders give network users centralized access to network files. When a folder is shared, all users by default can connect to the shared folder and gain access to the folder's content.

You can assign *share permissions* to user and group accounts to control what users can do with the content of a shared folder. For example, if you want a user to only view files, you can assign the user's account (or a group of which the user is a member) the Read permission; if you want a user to modify and add new files and folders, you can assign the Change permission.

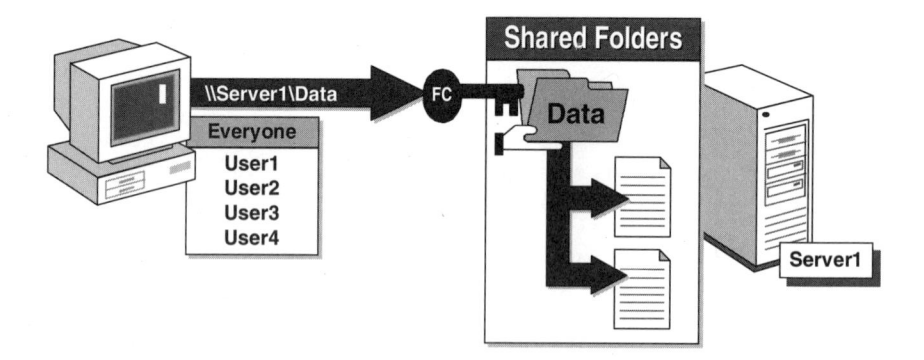

A shared folder appears in Windows NT Explorer and My Computer as an icon of a hand holding the shared folder and is often referred to simply as a *share*.

Note By default, the built-in Everyone group is automatically assigned Full Control permission to all shared folders.

Why Share Folders?

Shared folders are used to give users access to network programs, data, and user home folders:

- Network program folders centralize administration by designating one location for configuring and upgrading software. In this way, you avoid maintaining programs on clients.
- Data folders provide a central location for users to store and access common files.
- User home folders provide a central location for users to store their own files. If home folders are stored on a network server, they provide a central location for maintaining and backing up users' data.

Note If the volume where the folder is located is formatted as FAT (file allocation table), share permissions are the only way to secure disk resources. If the volume is formatted with the Windows NT File System (NTFS), NTFS permissions can be assigned for additional security. NTFS permissions are covered in Chapter 6, "Securing Network Resources with NTFS Permissions."

Share Permissions

To control how users access a shared folder, you can assign share permissions to users, groups, or both.

The following illustration shows the hierarchy of share permissions, from most restrictive at the bottom to least restrictive at the top.

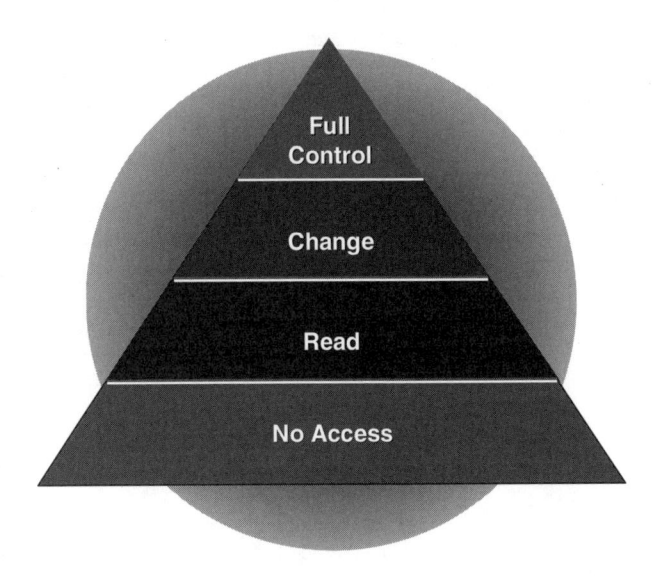

The following table describes the four share permissions.

This permission	Gives users the ability to
Full Control (default permission to Everyone group)	Modify file permissions. Take ownership of files on NTFS volumes. Perform all tasks permitted by the Change and Read permissions.
Change	Create folders and add files. Change data in files. Append data to files. Change file attributes. Delete folders and files. Perform all tasks permitted by the Read permission.
Read	Display folder names and file names. Display the data and attributes of files. Run program files. Access other folders within that folder.
No Access	Establish only a connection to the shared folder. Access to the folder is denied and the contents do not appear. This is the most restrictive permission, and is useful for high security. The No Access permission overrides other permissions.

Limitations of Share Permissions

Share permissions are effective only when a user connects to the folder over the network. They do not prevent users from gaining access to the folder while sitting at the computer where the folder resides.

On computers running Windows NT Server, where users do not have the Log on locally user right, this is not a problem. However, on computers running Windows NT Workstation, users are automatically assigned this user right and can bypass share permissions on their local computer.

If the volume where the folder resides is formatted with NTFS, you can secure local resources with NTFS permissions.

How Share Permissions Are Applied

You can assign a user permission to access a shared folder directly or as a member of a group. If you assign different permissions to multiple groups of which the user is a member, the user gets all the permissions, unless one of the permissions is the No Access permission.

There are two rules for how share permissions are applied:

1. When you assign permissions to a user and also to a group of which the user is a member, the user's effective permissions are the least restrictive permissions that result from the combination of the user and group permissions.
2. When you assign the No Access permission, the No Access permission overrides all other permissions that are assigned to the user or to the groups of which the user is a member. No Access always becomes the effective permission.

Multiple Permissions

In the following illustration, User1 is assigned the Full Control permission to the shared folder named *Public*. Full Control is the least restrictive permission. User1 is also a member of the Everyone group to which a different permission, Read, is assigned. User1's effective permissions are the combination of the user and group permissions, in this case, Full Control. (Full Control includes the permissions Read and Change.)

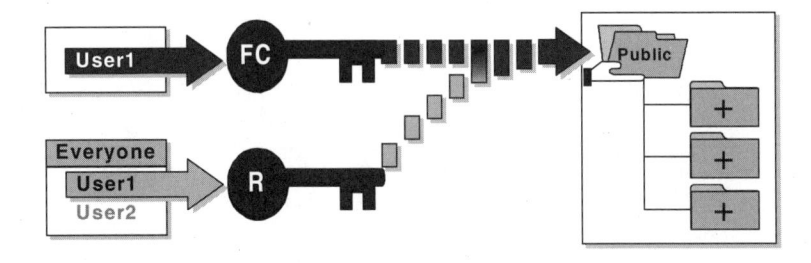

The No Access Permission

In the following illustration, User1 is assigned Read permission to the shared folder named *Public*. User1 is also a member of the Sales group to which a different permission, No Access, is assigned. Therefore, User1's effective permissions are none because the No Access permission overrides any other permissions assigned to a user or to groups to which the user belongs.

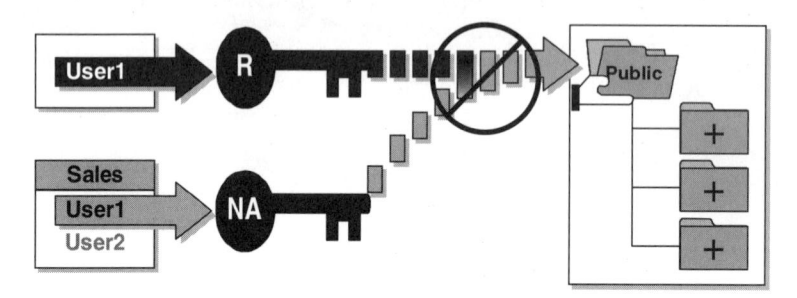

Example of Applied Permissions

The following two illustrations show two examples of applied share permissions. Examine each illustration and determine the effective permissions for User1.

Example A shows that User1 is a member of Group1, Group2, Group3, and Group4. Group1 does not have any permissions for Folder-A. Group2 has Read permission, Group3 has Change permission, and Group4 has Full Control permission for shared Folder-A.

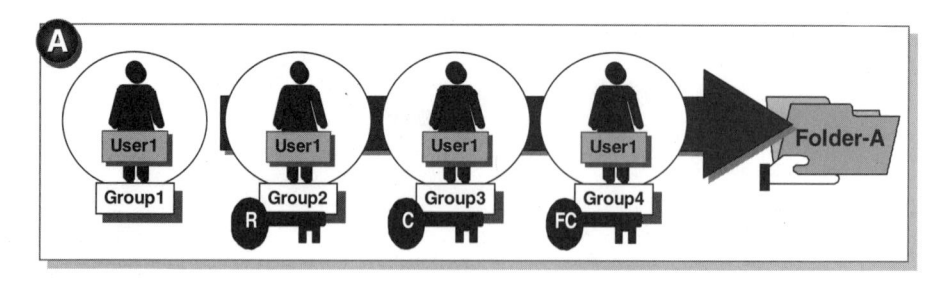

- In Example A, what are User1's effective permissions for Folder-A?

  _____

  _____

Chapter 5 Securing Network Resources with Share Permissions 179

Example B shows that User1 is a member of Group1, Group2, and Group3. Group1 does not have any permissions for Folder-B. Group2 has Change permission and Group3 has Read permission. Additionally, User1 is assigned the No Access permission.

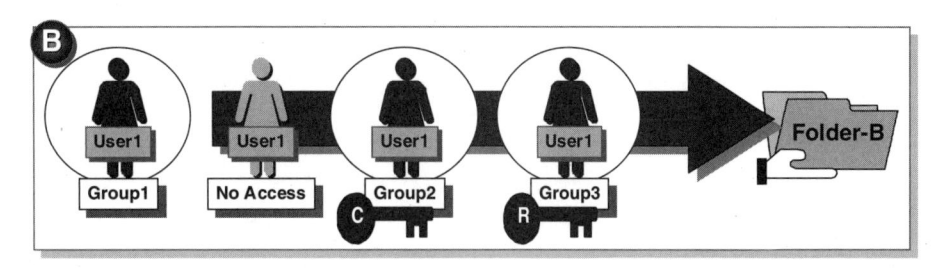

- In Example B, what are User1's effective permissions for Folder-B?

_____

_____

Lesson Summary

The following information summarizes the key points in this lesson:

- Shared folders give network users centralized access to network programs, data, and user home folders.
- Folder permissions are assigned to users, groups, or both, to control how users access a shared folder.
- There are four levels of share permissions: Full Control, Change, Read, and No Access.
- A user's effective permissions are the least restrictive permissions that result from the combination of the user and group permissions.
- The No Access permission overrides all other permissions assigned to a user or to a group to which the user is a member. It always becomes the effective permission.

For more information on	See
Procedures for setting share permissions	Windows NT Help.
Share permissions	Chapter 4, "Managing Shared Resources and Resource Security," in Microsoft Windows NT Server *Concepts and Planning*.
NTFS permissions	Chapter 4, "Managing Shared Resources and Resource Security," in Microsoft Windows NT Server *Concepts and Planning*.
	Chapter 6, "Securing Network Resources with NTFS Permissions," in this book.
FAT and NTFS volumes	Chapter 17, "Disk and File System Basics," in the *Microsoft Windows NT Workstation Resource Kit*.
Group accounts	Chapter 2, "Working with User and Group Accounts," in Microsoft Windows NT Server *Concepts and Planning*.
	Chapter 3, "Setting Up Group Accounts," in this book.

Lesson 2: Guidelines for Planning Shared Folders

Before you begin sharing folders, you need to determine what resources to share and to whom. For a network to be successful, network programs, public and working data, and user home folders must be easily accessible to authorized users. This lesson presents planning guidelines for shared folders.

After this lesson, you will be able to:
- Outline the tasks required to plan shared folders.
- Plan what permissions to assign to groups or users for network programs, data, and home folders.

Estimated lesson time: 20 minutes

When sharing folders, consider the following points:

- Determine which folders on your servers users are to use, and then organize them so that folders with the same security requirements are located within one folder hierarchy. For example, if users require Read permission to several program folders, store those folders within the same folder.
- Use intuitive share names so that users can easily recognize and locate resources. For example, for the folder *Application,* use the share name *Apps.*
- Use share names and folder names that are readable by all client operating systems. The following table describes share and folder naming conventions.

Client	Share name	Folder name
Windows NT and Windows 95	12 characters	255 characters
MS-DOS, Windows 3.*x*, and Windows for Workgroups	8.3 characters	8.3 characters

Note For client operating systems that can only read 8.3 characters, Windows NT provides 8.3 character equivalent names, but the resulting names are not always intuitive to users. For example, a folder named *Accountants Database,* would appear as *Accoun~1* to clients running MS-DOS, Windows 3.*x*, and Windows for Workgroups.

Examples of Shared Folders

How you organize folders may help you to secure data. For example, if you group folders with the same security requirements in one hierarchy, you only have to share the top-level folder. Users with the appropriate permissions have the same level of access to the contents of the shared folder, but cannot access folders that are at a higher level or at the same level as the shared folder.

The following illustrations show two examples of how to share folders to secure multiple folder hierarchies.

Example A shows program folders organized in the same hierarchy. In this example, the top-level folder, Apps, is shared. The built-in Users group is assigned the Read permission. When members of the Users group connect to the Apps shared folder, they automatically gain access to App1 and App2 because they are in the same hierarchy. Users will not gain access to the Data, Data1, and Data2 folders because the Data folder is in a different hierarchy.

When users connect to Apps, the Apps shared folder appears to users as a root folder. Users will not be able to see folders that are at a higher level or at the same level as the shared folder to which they are connected.

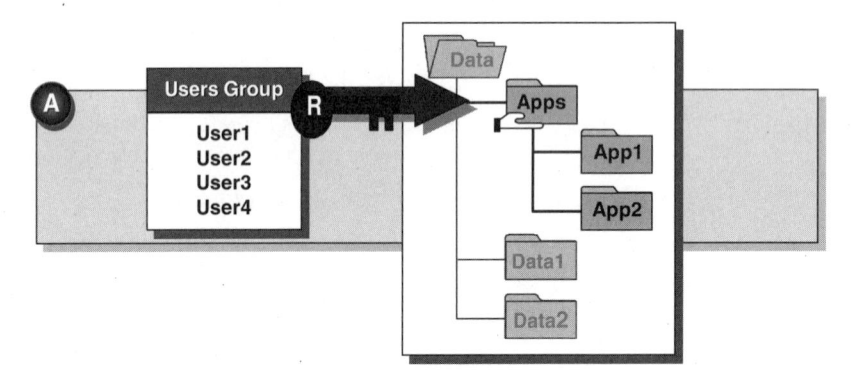

Example B shows how grouping folder hierarchies can simplify administrative access. For example, if you share the Data folder and assign only the built-in Administrators group the Full Control permission, members of the Administrators group can connect to directly to Data and gain access to the entire hierarchy, including the Apps hierarchy.

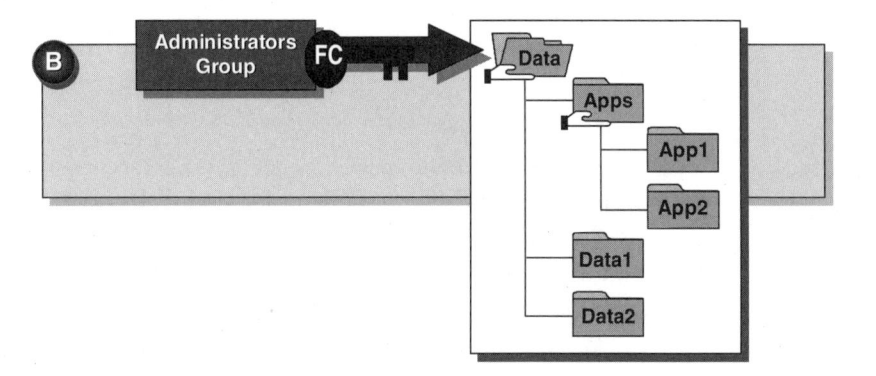

Guidelines for Assigning Permissions

When you assign share permissions to users and groups, use the following general guidelines:

- Determine which groups need access to each resource and what level of access they require. For example, for a Sales Data folder, the Sales group may require Change permission, the Administrators group may require Full Control permission, and the Executives group may require Read permission.
- Create a local group on the computer for each shared resource. If the resource resides on a member server or computer running Windows NT Workstation, the local group for the resource is created on that computer. If the resource resides on a domain controller, the local group is created from any computer running User Manager for Domains.
- Assign permissions to only the groups that need access to the resource.
- Assign the most restrictive permission (but one that allows users to perform required tasks) for the resource to the local group.

    For example, if users need only to read information in a folder, and they will never delete or create files, then assign the Read permission for those users.

- For greater security, remove the Full Control permission from the Everyone group because the Everyone group contains all user accounts who have access to your network, and Everyone includes the Guest account. If you want all users to have access to the resource, use the Users group instead. In a domain, the Users group only contains domain user accounts that you created. In a workgroup, the Users group contains local user accounts.

Guidelines for Sharing Network Program Folders

In a large network, one or more servers may be dedicated to storing programs. In a small network, one server may be used for both programs and data. The program folders that you share will vary with each network.

Consider these guidelines when planning network program folders:

- Create a shared folder for organizing your programs—for example, Apps.
- Assign the Administrators group Full Control permission to the Apps folder for administrative access.
- Remove the Full Control permission from the Everyone group and assign Read permission to the Users group to provide tighter security.
- Assign the Change permission to groups responsible for upgrading and troubleshooting software.
- Share individual program folders to the appropriate groups only when you need to restrict access to those folders. For example, to give members of Group1 access to only the spreadsheet program, share the folder for the spreadsheet program and assign Group1 the appropriate permission.

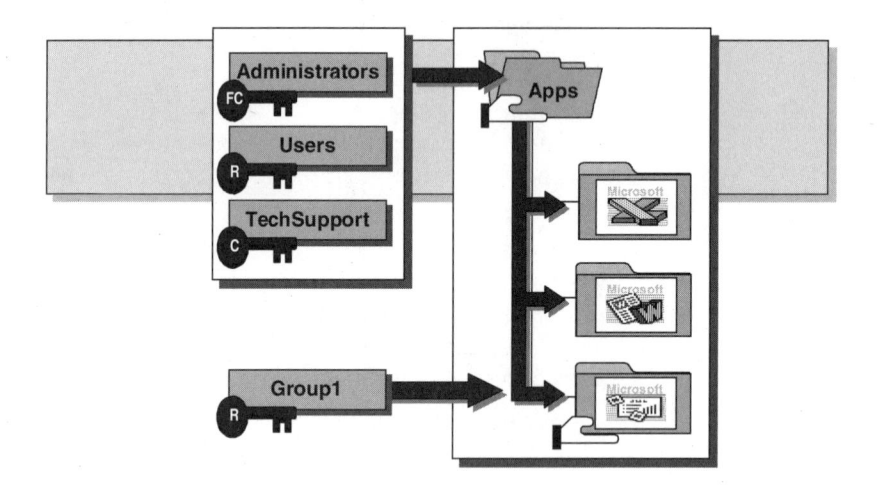

Guidelines for Sharing Data Folders

Data folders are used by network users to exchange or share common files. In planning shared data folders, consider creating shared folders for keeping information that is public to employees of the company. Also, consider creating shared folders that employees can use to exchange files with others.

If your hard disk has more than one volume, create and share a data folders on a volume separate from the operating system and programs. Having data folders in one location streamlines backup procedures. Additionally, in the unlikely event that the operating system volume needs to be reformatted, public data will remain intact.

Public Data Folders

Public data folders contain files that employees need to gain access to for reading purposes only—for example, employee benefits information or blank expense report forms.

Consider these guidelines when sharing a public folder:

- Assign the Full Control permission to the users who provide the information in the public folders and to the Administrators group (for administrative access).
- Assign the Read permission to all users who need to gain access to the data.

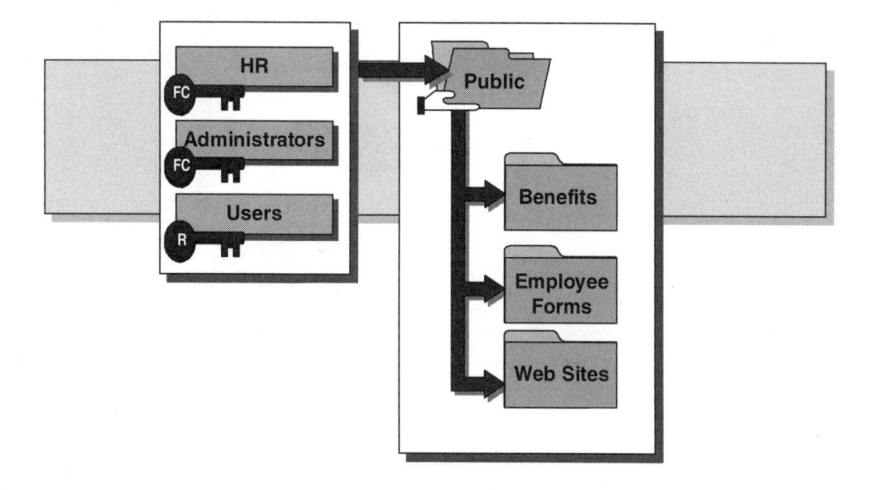

Working Data Folders

Working data folders give employees a central location for storing and exchanging working files. Typically, employees need the ability to add and remove files from common working data folders.

Consider these guidelines when sharing a data folder for working files:

- Assign the Change permission to all users who need to exchange files with others.
- Assign the Full Control permission to the Administrators group.
- Share lower-level data folders to the appropriate groups when you need to restrict access to those folders.

For example, to protect data in the Accountants folder, share that folder to only the Accountants group and assign that group Change permission. Then, members of the Accountants group can access the Accountants shared folder. Administrators have access by connecting to the Data shared folder.

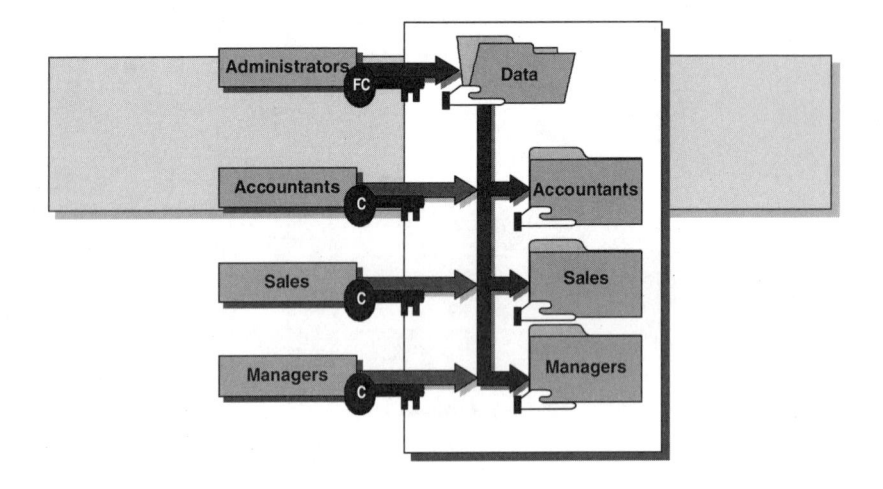

Guidelines for Sharing Home Folders

On FAT volumes, when you create a user account and you want that user to have a home folder, you must first create a home folder structure on the server. You share individual home folders on a FAT volume because share permissions are the only way to restrict access.

To create home folders for users on a FAT volume using only share permissions to restrict access, follow these general guidelines:

1. Create a central folder named Users on a volume separate from the operating system and programs.

    This streamlines backup and restore procedures. If the operating system volume requires reformatting, the volume containing the home folders will remain intact.

2. Create a folder in the Users folder for each user account, with the same name as his or her user name. For example, for the user name Ericb, create a folder named Ericb.

    Note On a FAT volume, you need to create and share home folders before you specify the home folder path in User Manager for Domains. On an NTFS volume, this step is not necessary.

3. Share each user's home folder and assign *only* the respective user Full Control permission to his or her home folder. This guarantees privacy to the user because he or she is the only person who can connect to his or her home folder. This is the only way to protect users' folders on a FAT volume.

4. In User Manager for Domains, assign a home folder to each user account.

5. Only shared the top-level folder to the Administrators group.

    You will also be able to perform administrative tasks on home folders by logging on to the server locally, or by connecting to an administrative share (C$, D$, and so on), which provides access to the root of the respective volume.

Note Creating home folders on an NTFS volume is covered in Chapter 6, "Securing Network Resources with NTFS Permissions."

▶ To plan shared folders

Scenario: World Wide Importers has opened its first office in Istanbul. As the administrator, you plan how to share resources on servers in the new Istanbul office and make them available to Istanbul office network users as appropriate.

As the administrator, you need to determine:

- Which folders to share and the share name for each folder.
- Whether to create a local group for the resource or to use a built-in local group.
- The appropriate permissions for the members of the local groups.

Record your planning decisions on the "Shared Folders Planning Worksheet" located at the end of this lesson. After completing the exercise, turn to Appendix A, "Planning Worksheets," and compare your worksheet to the sample provided. (The sample presents only one set of possible answers. You may have planned your folders differently.)

To complete the "Shared Folders Planning Worksheet," you need to:

1. Specify the name of the folder that you want shared and record it under Folder Name.
2. Specify the server name and share name for each shared folder, and record it under UNC Name using the universal naming convention format (*server_name**share_name*).
3. Specify a local group for each shared folder. Record it in the Local Group column. For some shared resources, you may want to use the following built-in local groups.

Group	Description
Users	Built-in local group that contains all domain user accounts on each computer.
Administrators	Built-in local group that gives members administrative privileges.

4. List the group accounts that require access to the shared folders and that will become members of the local groups. Record them under Members. The following table describes the group accounts for the Istanbul office.

Group	Description
Managers	Global group that contains all user accounts for the managers.
Executives	Global group that contains all user accounts for the executives.
HR	Global group that contains all user accounts in the Human Resources department.
Accountants	Global group that contains all user accounts for the accountants.

5. Specify the appropriate permissions for members of each local group. Record them under Share Permissions (for example, specify permissions as Read, Change, Full Control, or No Access).

Base your implementation plan on the following illustration and criteria. This illustration shows the PDC, the BDC, and the member server in the Istanbul office along with the folder structure on each server.

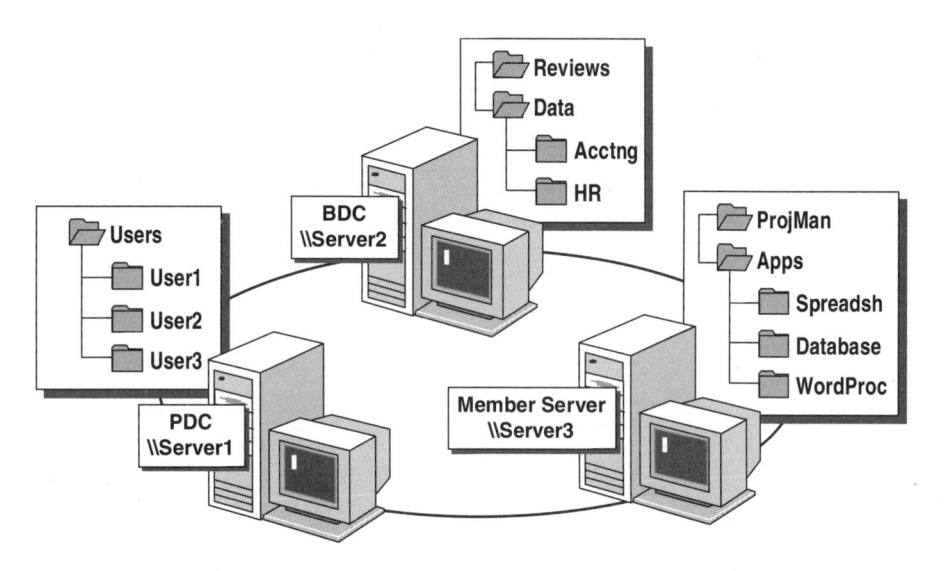

Use the following criteria to make your decisions:

- All employees need to run the spreadsheet, database, and word processing programs. Administrators need to administer all folders.
- The managers need to exchange project management files. Administrators need to administer the data.
- The Accounting and Human Resources departments require their own network location to store their working files. Each department will handle its own administration tasks. Executives will need to review the working files.
- Managers and Executives require a network location to store employee performance review forms. All employees need access to these forms. Administrators need to administer the forms.
- User1, User2, and User3 each need a home folder. Each folder must be accessible only by that user. Administrators need to administer all folders.

Note Share names must be accessible from Microsoft Windows NT, Microsoft Windows 95, and non-Windows NT platforms.

Lesson Summary

The following information summarizes the key points in this lesson:

- Determine what resources need to be shared and with whom prior to sharing folders.
- Use intuitive share names so that users can easily recognize and locate resources.
- Use share names and folder names that are readable by all client operating systems.
- Organize disk resources so that folders with the same security requirements are located within one folder hierarchy.
- Create a local group for each shared resource. If the resource resides on a member server or a computer running Windows NT Workstation, create the local group on that computer. If the resource resides on a domain controller, create the local group from any computer running User Manager for Domains.
- Follow the general guidelines provided in this lesson provided in this lesson for assigning permissions to users and groups for shared folders.

For more information on	See
Procedures for sharing a folder	Windows NT Help.
Differences between NTFS and FAT volume security	Chapter 4, "Managing Shared Resources and Resource Security," in Microsoft Windows NT Server *Concepts and Planning*.
Controlling access to files and folders	Chapter 3, "Disk Management Basics," in the *Resource Guide* of the *Microsoft Windows NT Server Resource Kit*.
Protecting files and directories in Windows NT Workstation	Chapter 6, "Windows NT Security," in the *Microsoft Windows NT Workstation Resource Kit*.
Choosing a file system	Chapter 18, "Choosing a File System," in the *Microsoft Windows NT Workstation Resource Kit*.

Shared Folders Planning Worksheet

Folder Name	UNC Name	Local Group	Members	Share Permissions

Lesson 3: Sharing Folders

This lesson guides you through the steps to share folders and assign permissions.

After this lesson, you will be able to:
- Describe the requirements for sharing folders.
- Create and modify shared folders.
- Assign share permissions to users and groups.

Estimated lesson time: 20 minutes

Requirements for Sharing a Folder

To share a folder, you must be a member of the built-in Administrators, Server Operators, or Power Users groups on the computer where the shared folder is being shared.

Note On NTFS volumes, you can give a user the ability to share folders by assigning the user the List permission to the folder.

Administrative Shares

Windows NT provides administrative shares to make it easy to gain access to the root of a volume. The root of each volume on a hard disk is automatically shared, using the drive letter appended with a dollar sign ($)—for example C$, D$, E$, and so on. The dollar sign hides the shared folder from users who browse the computer. When you connect to this folder, you have access to the entire volume. You use the administrative shares to remotely connect to the computer to perform administrative tasks.

Note Windows NT also shares the *systemroot* folder as Admin$. This is a special shared folder that is required by the system only during remote administration.

Sharing a Folder

The first step in sharing a folder is to assign it a share name. Share names are assigned on the **Sharing** tab in the *folder_name* **Properties** dialog box.

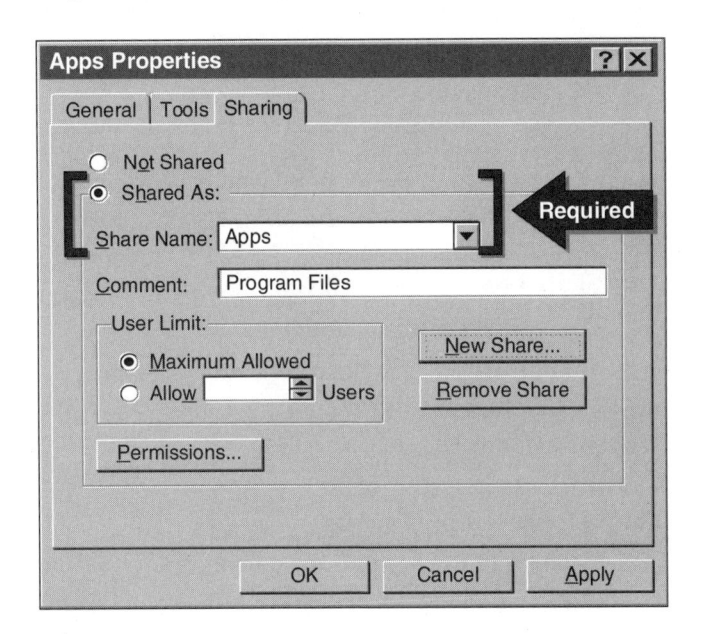

[Screenshot of Apps Properties dialog box, Sharing tab, with "Shared As:" and "Share Name: Apps" marked as Required. Comment: Program Files. User Limit section with Maximum Allowed selected. Buttons: New Share, Remove Share, Permissions, OK, Cancel, Apply.]

The following table describes the **Sharing** tab options.

Option	Description
Share Name	Provides the name that network users will use to connect to the folder. You must enter a share name. If you append a $ to the share name, the share will be hidden from users when they browse network resources.
Comment	Provides a description for the share name. The comment appears in the **Map Network Drive** dialog box when users browse shared folders on a server. It is helpful if this comment clearly identifies the contents of the shared folder.
User Limit	Sets the number of users that can simultaneously connect to the shared folder. Limiting the number of connections can reduce network traffic. The Windows NT Workstation maximum is 10. Windows NT Server is unlimited.
Permissions	Sets the permissions on the folder *only* when it is accessed over the network. The Everyone group is automatically assigned Full Control permission for all new shared folders.
New Share	Appears when the selected folder is already shared. A folder can be shared multiple times with different names and permissions. However, keeping track of multiple share names requires more administration, and in most situations, it is unnecessary.

▶ To share a folder for programs

1. Log on as Administrator, and start Windows NT Explorer.
2. Expand *drive*:\LabFiles, right-click the Apps folder, and then click **Properties**.
   The **Apps Properties** dialog box appears.
3. Click the **Sharing** tab.

> **Tip** When you right-click the Apps folder, notice that the **Sharing** command appears on the shortcut menu. If you click **Sharing** on this menu, you will switch directly to the **Sharing** tab of the **Apps Properties** dialog box.

4. Click **Shared As**.
   Notice that the default share name is the name of the folder.
5. In the **Comment** box, type **Shared Productivity Programs** and then click **OK**.
   Notice that in Windows NT Explorer, a hand appears under the Apps folder. The hand indicates that the folder is shared.

▶ To share a folder for public data

1. In the LabFiles folder, right-click the Public folder, and then click **Sharing**.
   The **Public Properties** dialog box appears with the **Sharing** tab active.
2. Click **Shared As**.
   Notice that the default share name is the name of the folder.
3. In the **Comment** box, type **Public Files** and then click **OK**.
   Notice that in Windows NT Explorer, a hand appears under the Public folder. The hand indicates that the folder is shared.

▶ To create a hidden shared folder

1. In the LabFiles folder, create a folder named Secret.
2. Right-click the Secret folder and then click **Sharing**.
3. Click **Shared As**.
4. In the **Shared Name** box, type **secret$** and then click **OK**.
   Notice in Windows NT Explorer that a hand appears under the Secret folder, indicating that the folder is shared.

Assigning Share Permissions

After you assign a share name, the next step is to specify which users can access the shared folder by assigning permissions to selected users or groups. By default, when a folder is shared, the Everyone group is assigned the Full Control permission. For most folders, you will want to remove the Full Control permission from Everyone and assign permissions to specific user and group accounts.

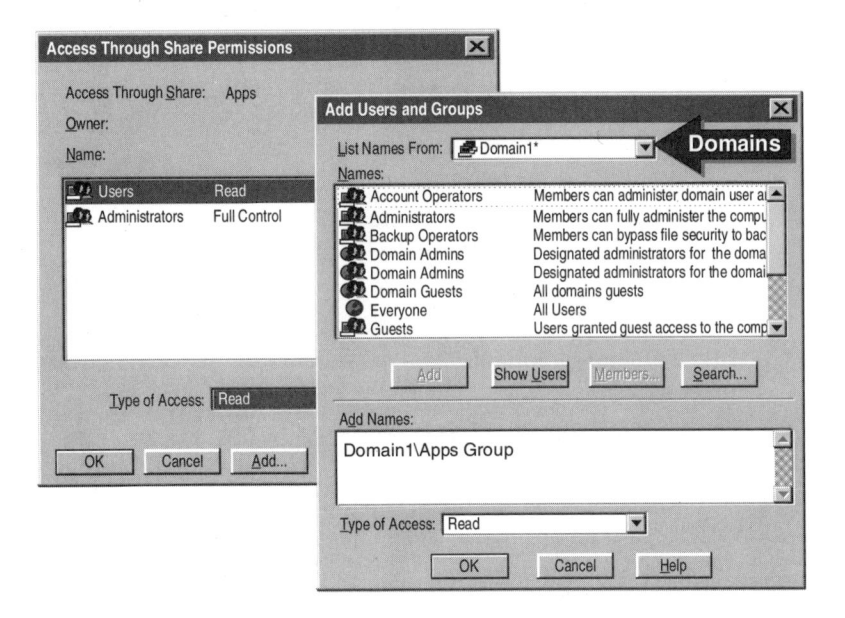

If you want to assign permission to a user or group in a different domain:

- A trust must exist between your computer's domain and another domain on your network. To verify that your computer fits this criteria, log off, press CTRL+ALT+DELETE, and then view the names that appear in the **Domain** box. If more than one domain name appears, a trust relationship exists with the other domains that appear.

- You must have Administrator privileges for that domain. To enable the Administrators group to perform administration tasks in other domains, add the global group Domain Admins to the local Administrators group on the computer in the domain that you want Administrators to administer.

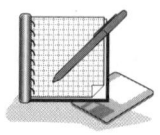

▶ **To determine the current permissions for the Apps shared folder**

1. In Windows NT Explorer, right-click the LabFiles\Apps folder, and then click **Sharing**.

   The **Apps Properties** dialog box appears.

2. Click **Permissions**.

   The **Access Through Share Permissions** dialog box appears.

   What are the default permissions for the Apps shared folder?

   _____

▶ **To remove permissions from a group**

- In the **Access Through Share Permissions** dialog box, under **Names**, make sure that **Everyone** is selected, and then click **Remove**.

   The entry disappears.

▶ **To assign the Full Control permission to the Administrators group**

1. In the **Access Through Share Permissions** dialog box, click **Add**.

   The **Add Users and Groups** dialog box appears.

   Note In a multiple-domain network, click the **List Names From** arrow to reveal other domains from which you can list user and group names for assigning permissions.

2. Under **Names**, click **Administrators**, and then click **Add**.

   Notice that *domain***Administrators** appears in the **Add Names** box. It indicates the location of the directory database where the selected name resides.

3. In the **Type of Access** box, click **Full Control**, and then click **OK**.

   The **Access Through Share Permissions** dialog box reappears. Notice that the Administrators group has Full Control permission.

▶ **To assign the Read permission to the Users group**
 1. In the **Access Through Share Permissions** dialog box, click **Add**.
 2. Under **Names**, click **Users**, and then click **Add**.
    The *domain*\Users group appears in the **Add Names** box.
 3. In the **Type of Access** box, click **Read**, and then click **OK**.
 4. Click **OK** to return to the **Apps Properties** dialog box, and then click **OK** to return to Windows NT Explorer.

▶ **To test share permissions by starting a program**
 1. Log off and log on as SalesRep5.
 2. Click the **Start** button, and then click **Run**.
 3. In the **Open** box, type *computer_name***apps** (where *computer_name* is the name of your computer).
    The Apps on *computer_name* window appears.
 4. Expand the LabFiles\Apps\Games folder, and then double-click Kolumz.exe to start it.
    Were you successful? Why or why not?

    _____

    _____

 5. Quit Kolumz.exe.

▶ **To test share permissions**
 1. In the Games window, delete Kolumz.exe.
    Were you successful? Why or why not?

    _____

    _____

 2. Quit Windows NT Explorer and log off.

Modifying Shared Folders

You can modify all shared folder options on the *folder_name* **Properties** dialog box.

The following table lists the steps to stop sharing a folder, to modify the share name, and to modify permissions.

To	Do this
Stop sharing a folder	Click **Not Shared** to stop sharing the folder, and then click **OK**. If you stop sharing a folder when a user has a file open, the user may lose data. When you click **Not Shared**, a message appears to notify you that a user is connected to the shared folder.
Modify the share name	Click **Not Shared** to stop sharing the folder. Click **Apply** to apply the change. Then, click **Shared As**, and type in a new share name.
Modify share permissions	Click **Permissions**. In the **Access Through Share Permissions** dialog box, select the user or group whose permissions are to be modified. In the **Type of Access** box, click the permission that you want to apply, and then click **OK**.

Lesson Summary

The following information summarizes the key points in this lesson:

- To share a folder, you must be a member of the built-in Administrators, Server Operators, or Power Users groups on the computer where the shared folder is being shared.
- The first step in sharing a folder is to assign a share name.
- The next step is to assign permissions to users or groups to provide access to the shared folder.
- All shared folder options are set and modified in the *folder_name* **Properties** dialog box.

For more information on	See
Organizing disk resources	Chapter 3, "Disk Management Basics," in the *Resource Guide* of the *Microsoft Windows NT Server Resource Kit*.
Windows NT security features overview	Chapter 6, "Windows NT Security," in the *Microsoft Windows NT Workstation Resource Kit*.
Trust relationships	Chapter 1, "Managing Windows NT Server Domains," in Microsoft Windows NT Server *Concepts and Planning*.
	Chapter 2, "Network Security and Domain Planning," in the *Networking Guide* of the *Microsoft Windows NT Server Resource Kit*.
Centralizing administration	Chapter 3, "Setting Up Group Accounts," in this book.
Browsing network resources	Chapter 3, "Windows NT Browser Service," in the *Networking Guide* of the *Microsoft Windows NT Server Resource Kit*.

Lesson 4: Connecting to Shared Folders

There are two ways to locate and connect to shared folders. This lesson guides you through the steps to connect to shared folders, and it also explains the differences between the two methods.

This lesson requires that you have completed Lesson 3.

After this lesson, you will be able to:
- Connect to a shared folder using the **Map Network Drive** command.
- Connect to a shared folder using the **Run** command.

Estimated lesson time: 10 minutes

Once you share a folder, network users can connect to it using the **Map Network Drive** command in Windows NT Explorer or the **Run** command on the **Start** menu.

Using the Map Network Drive Command

Using the **Map Network Drive** command to connect to a network resource provides a connection that is retained until the drive letter is manually disconnected, giving you the ability to select the drive from within a program.

You can use the **Map Network Drive** command in Windows NT Explorer, My Computer, and Network Neighborhood. In Windows NT Explorer, on the **Tools** menu, click **Map Network Drive**. In My Computer or Network Neighborhood, right-click the My Computer or Network Neighborhood desktop icons, and then click **Map Network Drive**.

When you connect to a shared folder using the **Map Network Drive** command, the shared folder appears as a drive on your computer, and the contents of the shared folder can be viewed as if they were on your computer. Because the drive letter is saved in a user profile, you can have the connection re-established each time you log on.

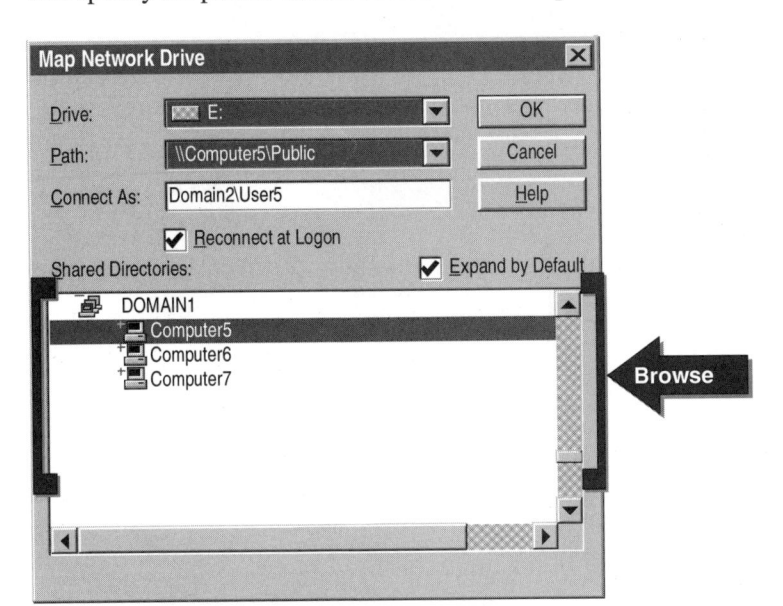

You specify the path to a shared folder in the **Map Network Drive** dialog box.

[Map Network Drive dialog box showing Drive: E:, Path: \\Computer5\Public, Connect As: Domain2\User5, Reconnect at Logon checked, Expand by Default checked, Shared Directories list showing DOMAIN1 with Computer5, Computer6, Computer7. A "Browse" arrow points to the Shared Directories area.]

The following table describes the **Map Network Drive** dialog box options.

Option	Purpose
Drive	Assigns a drive letter to the shared folder so that it appears and functions like a local drive. The user can assign up to 26 drive letters. Drive letters that are used by local devices do not appear in the **Drive** list. If a drive letter is not selected, Windows NT assigns the next available drive.
Path	Specifies the computer where the shared folder resides and the share name assigned to the folder. Use the following format: *server_name**share_name*
Connect As	Connects to a shared folder using a different user account. For example, the administrator is at another user's computer and needs to connect to a resource that the user does not have access to. The **Connect As** option requires the domain name and the user account name in the following format: *domain**user_name*
	If there is a password on the user account, the user is prompted for it.
Reconnect at Logon	If selected, will reconnect the user to the shared folder each time the user logs on.
Shared Directories	Provides the ability to browse computers in the local and trusted domains for shared folders.

To connect to a shared folder using Map Network Drive

1. Log on as SalesRep5.
2. On the desktop, right-click either the My Computer icon or the Network Neighborhood icon, and then click **Map Network Drive**.
3. In the **Drive** box, click **P**.
4. In the Path box, type *computer_name***public** (where *computer_name* is the name of your computer).
5. Clear the **Reconnect at Logon** check box, and then click **OK**.
6. Close the Public on '*computer_name*' (P:) window if it appears.
7. Start Windows NT Explorer and view the drives under My Computer.

   Notice that drive P has been added as Public on '*computer_name*' (P:).
8. If your computer is connected to a network, use the **Map Network Drive** command to search for and connect to a shared folder on another computer in your network.

Using the Run Command

Using the **Run** command you user can browse all shared folders on a computer without knowing the share name assigned to a specific shared folder. You only need to know the name of the computer.

The Run command does not assign a drive letter to the shared folder, so the connection does not appear within a program.

To use the **Run** command, click the **Start** button, and then click **Run**. In the **Open** box, type the name of the computer where the shared folder resides and the share name assigned to the folder (for example, *computer_name**share_name*), or type only the computer name (for example, *computer_name*), and then click **OK**.

If you only type the computer name, Windows NT opens the *computer_name* window, containing all shared folders on the computer. Clicking a shared folder completes the connection.

▶ **To connect to a network drive using the Run command**

1. Click the **Start** button, and then click **Run**.
2. In the **Open** box, type *computer_name* (where *computer_name* is the name of your computer), and then click **OK**.

   The *computer_name* window appears.
3. Double-click any folder to connect to it.
4. Close the *computer_name* window.
5. If your computer is connected to a network, use the **Run** command to view the shared folders on another computer in your network.
6. Quit Windows NT Explorer.

▶ **To connect to a hidden shared folder using the Run command**

1. Click the **Start** button, and then click **Run**.
2. In the **Open** box, type *computer_name***secret$** (where *computer_name* is the name of your computer), and then click **OK**.

   The Secret$ on *computer_name* window appears.
3. Quit Windows NT Explorer.

▶ **To disconnect a network drive using Windows NT Explorer**

1. Start Windows NT Explorer, and then right-click drive P.
2. Click **Disconnect**.

   Drive P is removed from the left pane of Windows NT Explorer and from the User Profile.
3. Quit Windows NT Explorer and log off.

Lesson Summary

The following information summarizes the key points in this lesson:

- You can connect to shared folders using the **Map Network Drive** command or the **Run** command.

- Using the **Run** command, you can browse all shared folders on a computer using only the name of the computer. You do not need to know the share name assigned to a specific shared folder.

For more information on	See
Procedures for opening a shared folder	Windows NT Help.
Mapping a network drive	Windows NT Help.

Best Practices

The following checklist provides the best practices for sharing folders. Review this checklist before you begin to share folders:

- ❏ Organize disk resources so that folders with the same security requirements are located within one folder hierarchy. This simplifies administration by streamlining how you assign permissions.
- ❏ Store all data and home folders on volumes separate from the operating system and programs. This separates data files from system and program files and therefore streamlines backup and restore procedures. In the unlikely event that the operating system volume requires reformatting, the volume containing the data will remain intact.
- ❏ Remove the Everyone group from the permissions list to prevent resource access. Instead, use the local Users group, which provides more security because the group only contains accounts that you created.
- ❏ Create shortcuts for network resources that users will connect to often.
- ❏ Document decisions made about shared folders and assigned permissions. Update this document when changes are made to the server, such as upgrades of software, changes to shared folder names, and changes to assigned permissions.

Note If you want to remove the account that was created by running the Chapter5.cmd file at the beginning of this chapter, log on as Administrator, and then double-click DeleteChapter5.cmd in the Cleanup folder on the Supplemental Material compact disc.

Review

The following questions are intended to reinforce key information presented in this chapter. If you are unable to answer a question, review the lesson and then try the question again.

1. What are the requirements to share a folder?

2. When a folder is shared, a user with the appropriate permissions has access to: (Circle all that apply.)
    a. All folders in the shared folder.
    b. All files in the shared folder.
    c. Any resource within the network.
    e. Any folder on a volume separate from the operating system.

3. Which, if any, permissions can be assigned to a shared folder? (Circle all that apply.)
    a. Full Control
    b. Change
    c. Read
    d. No Access
    e. All of the above

4. What is the default permission on a shared folder? What group is assigned this permission?

Answer Key

Procedure Answers

Page 178

- In Example A, what are User1's effective permissions for Folder-A?

    User1's effective permissions for Folder-A is Full Control. This is because User1 is a member of Group2, which has Read, and Group3, which has Change, and Group4, which has Full Control. Full Control includes the permissions Read and Change, so that when they are combined, User1's permissions equal Full Control. Although Group1 has no specified permissions, User1 still has permission to Folder-A through membership of the other groups.

Page 179

- In Example B, what are User1's effective permissions for Folder-B?

    User1's effective permission for Folder-B is No Access. This is because User1's account has been assigned No Access, which overrides all other permissions.

Page 188

▶ **To plan shared folders**

Strategy used in sample planning worksheet (see Appendix A, "Planning Worksheets"):

Create a local group for each resource that will be restricted to certain users.

Use the built-in local Users group whenever all users require access to a resource. In a domain, the Users group contains all domain user accounts. In a workgroup, the Users group contains all user accounts local to the computer where the folder is located.

Assign the built-in Administrators group the Full Control permission for any folders that its members will manage.

Assign the Change permission to all local group members that need the ability to add, delete, and make changes to working files.

Assign the Read permission to all local group members that only need to review and get copies of files, such as blank expense report forms.

Page 196

▶ **To determine the current permissions for the Apps shared folder**

2. What are the default permissions for the Apps shared folder?

    The group Everyone has Full Control permission.

Page 197

▶ **To test share permissions by starting a program**

4. Were you successful? Why or why not?

Yes, because SalesRep5 user account is a member of the Users group that has Read access to the Apps share. The Read permissions allows users to run program files.

Page 197

▶ **To test share permissions**

1. Were you successful? Why or why not?

No, because SalesRep5 has Read permission (as a member of Users) for the Apps folder and therefore cannot delete files.

Page 206

Review Answers

1. What are the requirements to share a folder?

   You must be a member of the built-in Administrators, Server Operators, or Power Users group on the computer where the shared folder is being shared.

2. When a folder is shared, a user with the appropriate permissions has access to: (Circle all that apply.)

   Answers a and b are correct.

3. Which, if any, permissions can be assigned to a shared folder? (Circle all that apply.)

   Answer e is correct.

4. What is the default permission on a shared folder? What group is assigned this permission?

   Full Control is the default permission on a shared folder. The Everyone group is assigned this permission.

CHAPTER 6

Securing Network Resources with NTFS Permissions

Lesson 1 Introduction to NTFS Permissions . . . 211

Lesson 2 Combining Share Permissions and NTFS Permissions . . . 217

Lesson 3 Guidelines for Assigning NTFS Permissions . . . 223

Lesson 4 Assigning NTFS Permissions . . . 230

Lesson 5 Taking Ownership of Folders and Files . . . 240

Lesson 6 Copying or Moving Folders and Files . . . 245

Lesson 7 Troubleshooting Permission Problems . . . 251

Best Practices . . . 258

Review . . . 259

About This Chapter

NTFS permissions secure folders and files on the local computer. This chapter explains how NTFS permissions secure local resources. It also explains how NTFS permissions, when they are combined with share permissions, secure resources from users who connect to resources over the network. The hands-on procedures give you an opportunity to plan and implement NTFS permissions, and to troubleshoot common permission-related problems.

Before You Begin

To complete the lessons in this chapter, you must have:

- Completed the Setup procedures located in "About This Book."
- Knowledge and skills covered in Chapter 3, "Setting Up Group Accounts."
- The knowledge and skills covered in Chapter 5, "Securing Network Resources with Share Permissions."
- Shared the LabFiles\Public folder as Public. If the Public folder is not shared, click the **Start** button, click **Run**, type **net share public=***drive***:\labfiles\public** (where *drive* is the location of the LabFiles folder), and then click **OK**.
- Shared the LabFiles\Apps folder as Apps. If the Apps folder is not shared, click the **Start** button, click **Run**, type **net share apps=***drive***:\labfiles\apps** (where *drive* is the location of the LabFiles folder), and then click **OK**.
- Three user accounts created that are named User6, SalesMgr6, and CustomerService6, three global groups created that are named Accountants6, Executives6, and Managers6, and three local groups created that are named Spreadsheet6, Database6, and Library6.

  Log on as Administrator. In Windows NT Explorer, expand the LabFiles folder, and then double-click Chapter6.cmd to create these accounts.

Lesson 1: Introduction to NTFS Permissions

On NTFS volumes, you can set NTFS permissions on folders and files. NTFS permissions secure resources on the local computer and when users connect to resources over the network. This lesson provides an introduction to securing resources through NTFS permissions.

After this lesson, you will be able to:
- Describe the situations that require Microsoft Windows NT file system (NTFS) folder and file permissions.
- Define NTFS folder and file permissions.
- Describe the result when multiple NTFS permissions are applied to a resource.

Estimated lesson time: 20 minutes

What Are NTFS Permissions?

NTFS permissions are permissions that are only available on a volume that has been formatted with the Windows NT file system (NTFS). NTFS permissions provide a greater degree of security because they can be assigned to folders and to individual files. NTFS folder and file permissions apply both to users working at the computer where the folder or file is stored and to users accessing the folder or file over the network by connecting to a shared folder.

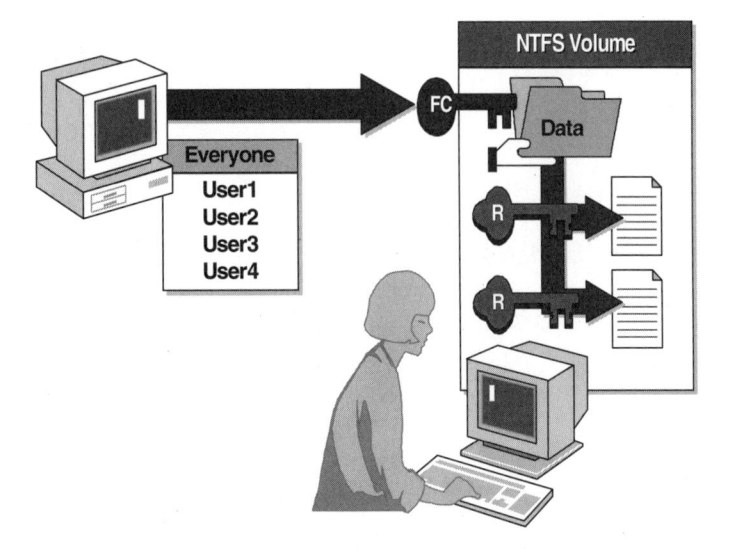

Why Use NTFS Permissions?

You use NTFS permissions to protect resources from users who can access the computer in the following ways:

- Locally, by sitting at the computer where the resource is stored.
- Remotely, by connecting to a shared folder.

You can set file permissions to a fine degree of granularity. For example, you can set different permissions for each file in a folder. You can let one user read the contents of a file and change it, let another user only read the file, and prevent all other users from any access to the file.

Note When a volume is formatted with NTFS, the Everyone group is automatically assigned Full Control permission to the volume. Folders and files created on the volume inherit this default permission.

Individual NTFS Permissions

Windows NT provides six individual NTFS permissions. Each permission specifies the access that a user or group can have to the folder or file.

The following table describes the actions that a user can take when individual permissions are assigned for a folder or file.

NTFS individual permissions	For a folder, a user can	For a file, a user can
Read (R)	Display folder names, attributes, owner, and permissions.	Display file data, attributes, owner, and permissions.
Write (W)	Add files and folders, change a folder's attributes, and display owner and permissions.	Display owner and permissions, change file attributes, create data in, and append data to, a file.
Execute (X)	Display folder attributes, make changes to folders within a folder, and display owner and permissions.	Display file attributes, owner, and permissions. Run a file if it is an executable.
Delete (D)	Delete a folder.	Delete a file.
Change Permissions (P)	Change a folder's permissions.	Change a file's permissions.
Take Ownership (O)	Take ownership of a folder.	Take ownership of a file.

Note On an NTFS volume, the user who creates a folder or file becomes the owner. If the user is a member of the Administrators group, the Administrators group becomes the owner. The owner can always assign and change permissions on a folder or file.

Standard Permissions

In most situations, you will use the NTFS standard permissions. Standard permissions are combinations of individual NTFS permissions and allow you to assign multiple NTFS permissions at one time.

By assigning combinations of individual permissions at one time, you can simplify your administrative tasks. When you set a standard permission, the abbreviations for the individual permissions appear in the interface beside the standard permission. For example, when you set the standard permission Read on a file, the abbreviation RX appears beside it.

Standard Folder Permissions

The following table lists the standard folder permissions and the individual NTFS permissions that each standard permission represents.

Standard permission	Individual permissions on folders	Individual permissions on files in the folder
No Access	None	None
List	RX	Not specified
Read	RX	RX
Add	WX	Not specified
Add & Read	RWX	RX
Change	RWXD	RWXD
Full Control	All	All

Note No Access means that the user cannot access the folder or file in any way, even if the user is a member of a group that has been granted access to the folder. "Not specified" means that the standard permission does not apply to files.

Standard File Permissions

The following table lists the standard file permissions and the individual NTFS permissions that each standard file permission represents.

Standard permission	Individual permissions
No Access	None
Read	RX
Change	RWXD
Full Control	All

Note The difference between the Full Control permission and the Change permission is that Change does not include the ability to modify permissions or to take ownership of folders and files.

How NTFS Permissions Are Applied

NTFS permissions are assigned to user and group accounts in the same way that share permissions are assigned—a user can be assigned NTFS permissions directly or as a member of one or more groups.

NTFS folder permissions are applied as follows:

- Like share permissions, NTFS permissions provide effective permissions for users that are the combination of the user and group permissions, with the exception of No Access. The No Access permission overrides all other permissions.
- Unlike share permissions, NTFS permissions protect local resources and can be assigned to other folders and files in the same folder hierarchy.

NTFS file permissions take precedence over the permissions assigned for the folder that the file is contained in. For example, if a user has Read permission to a folder and Write permission to a file in that folder, then the user will be able to write to the file, but will be unable to create a new file in the folder.

Example of NTFS Folder Permissions

In the following illustration, User1 is assigned the Write permission to the folder named *Data*. User1 is also a member of the Everyone group to which the Read permission is assigned. Therefore, User1's effective permissions are both Read and Write to the Data folder only.

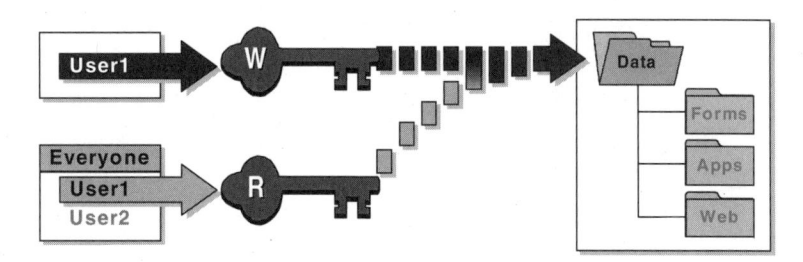

Unlike share permissions, NTFS permissions do not automatically allow User1 to gain access to the other folders within the hierarchy.

Example of NTFS File Permissions

In the following illustration, User1 is assigned the Read and Write permissions to File1 in the folder named *Data*. User1 is also a member of the Sales group to which a different permission, Read, is assigned for the Data folder. User1's effective permission to the Data folder is Read, but is Read and Write to File1 because NTFS file permissions override NTFS folder permissions.

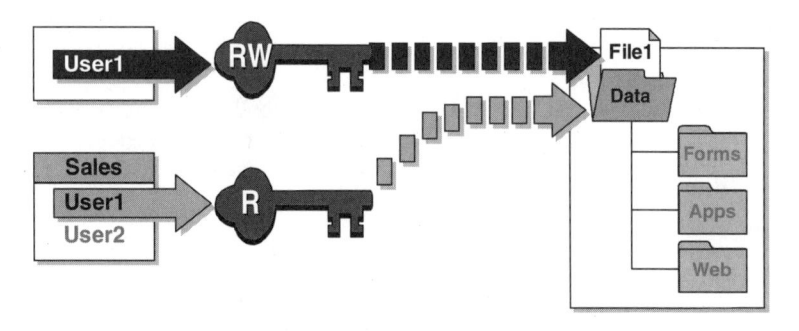

Lesson Summary

The following information summarizes the key points in this lesson:

- NTFS permissions provide a high degree of security to folders and individual files on volumes that have been formatted with the Windows NT file system (NTFS).
- NTFS folder and file permissions apply both to users working at the computer where the folder or file is located and to users accessing the folder or file over the network.
- Like share permissions, NTFS permissions can be assigned to a user directly or as a member of one or more groups.
- Like share permissions, a user's effective permissions are the combination of the user and group permissions, with the exception of No Access. The No Access permission overrides all other permissions.
- Unlike share permissions, NTFS permissions can be assigned to other folders and files in the same folder hierarchy.
- NTFS file permissions take precedence over the permissions assigned for the folder that the file is contained in.

For more information on	See
NTFS permissions	Chapter 4, "Managing Shared Resources and Resource Security," in Microsoft Windows NT Server *Concepts and Planning*.
FAT and NTFS volumes	Chapter 17, "Disk and File System Basics," in the *Microsoft Windows NT Workstation Resource Kit*.
Group accounts	Chapter 2, "Working With User and Group Accounts," in Microsoft Windows NT Server *Concepts and Planning*.

Lesson 2: Combining Share Permissions and NTFS Permissions

Share permissions for NTFS volumes work in combination with file and folder permissions. This lesson explains how share permissions are combined with NTFS permissions to secure disk resources.

After this lesson, you will be able to:
- Describe the result when folder permissions are different from those of the files in the folder.
- Describe the result when share permissions and NTFS permissions are combined.

Estimated lesson time: 20 minutes

To provide users with network access to disk resources, the folders containing those resources must be shared. Once the folder is shared, you can protect it by assigning share permissions to users and groups. However, share permissions offer limited security because they:

- Give the user the same level of access to all folders and files within the shared folder.
- Have no effect when a user gains access to the resource locally by sitting at the computer where the resource is located.
- Cannot be used to secure individual files.

If the shared folder is on an NTFS volume, you can use NTFS permissions to effectively block or change a user's access to other folders or files in the shared folder hierarchy. You gain the greatest degree of security by combining NTFS permissions with share permissions.

Note The easiest way to combine share permissions and NTFS permissions is to leave the default share permission Full Control assigned to the Everyone group, and then to assign NTFS permissions to specific user and group accounts for the folders and files within the shared folder hierarchy.

When combining share permissions with NTFS permissions, the most restrictive permission *always* becomes the effective permission. For example, if the share permission for a folder is Full Control and the NTFS permission for the same folder is Read, the effective permission is Read because it is the most restrictive.

The following illustration shows that User2 has the share permission Read for the shared folder named Public on Computer1 (when connecting over the network), and the NTFS Full Control permission to File-A. User2's effective permission for File-A is Read because Read is the most restrictive permission. User2's effective permission for File-B is Read because the NTFS Read permission has the same restrictions as the share permission Read.

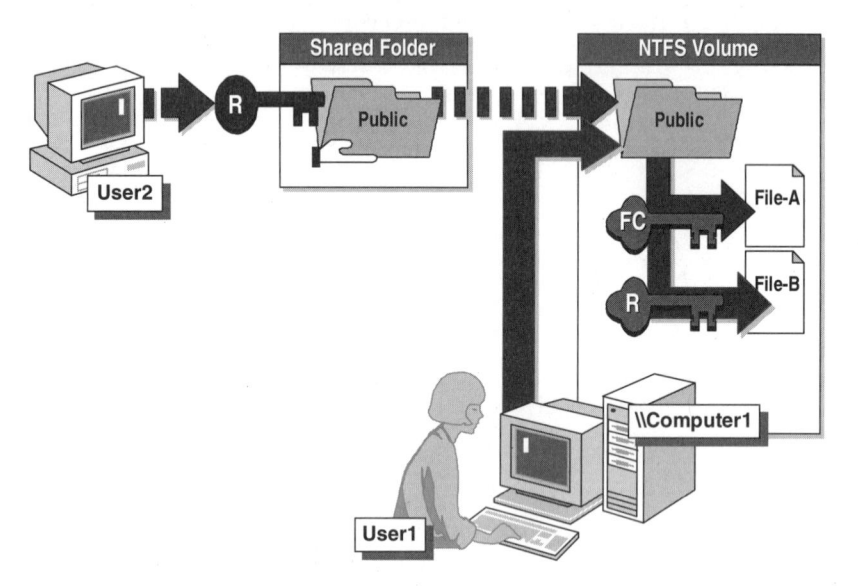

When User1 sits at Computer1, User1 is not restricted by the share folder permission for the Public folder. However, User1 has the Full Control permission for File-A and the Read permission for File-B because those are NTFS permissions. If User1 connects to the shared folder Public, User1 has the share permission Read to the Public folder just like User2.

Video: Permissions

This five minute video shows the effective permissions when shared folder and NTFS permissions are combined.

▶ **To start the video from the Start menu**
  1. Insert the Supplemental Material compact disc into the CD-ROM drive.
  2. Click the **Start** button, point to **Programs**, point to **Network Administration Training**, and then click **Permissions Video**.

Chapter 6 Securing Network Resources with NTFS Permissions

▶ **To start the video from the compact disc**

1. Start Windows NT Explorer.
2. In the root of the Supplemental Material compact disc, double-click Open.htm.
3. Click the center of the screen to continue to the home page.
4. Click **Course Materials**.
5. Under **Contents**, click **Permissions**.
6. Follow the instructions in the text box to install the required DLL files and to start the video.

> **Note** If you completed the Setup procedures described in "About This Book," or if you have run a video on this computer before, you do *not* need to install the DLL files.

▶ **To review the video**

The following study guide highlights the main points of the video. Complete the guide as you view the video, or use the guide as a follow-up test (recommended).

1. What do shared folders provide access to?

   _____

2. What can share permissions be assigned to?

   _____

3. What can NTFS permissions be assigned to?

   _____

4. When you combine a share permission with an NTFS permission what permission becomes the *effective* permission?

   _____

Example of Combined NTFS Permissions and Share Permissions

The following illustrations show two examples of shared folders that contain folders or files that have been assigned NTFS permissions. Examine each illustration and determine the effective permissions for User1 and User2.

Example A shows that the Users folder has been shared. The Users group has been assigned the share permission Full Control for the Users folder. User1, User2, and User3, however, have been assigned the NTFS permission Full Control for only their own home folder. These users are all members of the Users group.

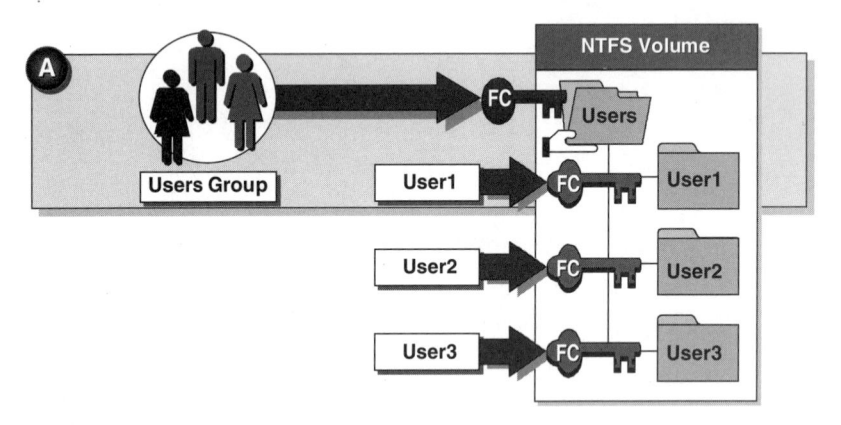

- In Example A, what is User1's effective permission when he or she accesses the User1 folder by connecting to the Users shared folder? What is User2's effective permission for the User1 folder?

_____

_____

Chapter 6 Securing Network Resources with NTFS Permissions 221

Example B shows that the Data folder has been shared. The Sales group has been assigned the share permission Read for the Data shared folder and the NTFS permission Full Control for the Sales folder.

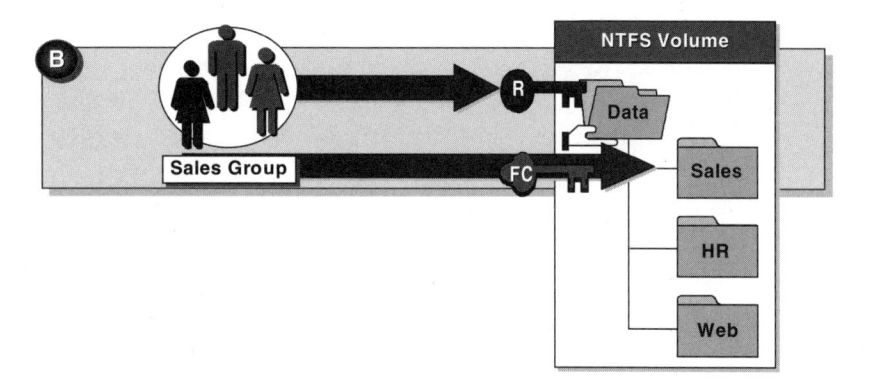

- In Example B, what are the Sales group's effective permissions when they access the Sales folder by connecting to the Data shared folder?

_____

_____

Lesson Summary

The following information summarizes the key points in this lesson:

- You gain the greatest degree of security by using a combination of share permissions and NTFS permissions.
- The easiest way to combine share and NTFS permissions is to leave the default share permission Full Control assigned to the Everyone group, and then assign NTFS permissions to specific user and group accounts for the folders and files within the shared folder hierarchy.
- The most restrictive permission is always the effective permission when share permissions are combined with NTFS permissions.

For more information on	See
Share permissions	Windows NT Help.
NTFS file system	Chapter 3, "Disk Management Basics," in the *Resource Guide* of the *Microsoft Windows NT Server Resource Kit*.
	Chapter 17, "Disk and File System Basics," in the *Microsoft Windows NT Workstation Resource Kit*.

Lesson 3: Guidelines for Assigning NTFS Permissions

Before you begin assigning NTFS permissions to folders and files, it is best to determine what permissions are required and to whom they should be assigned. This lesson presents guidelines for planning NTFS permissions.

After this lesson, you will be able to:
- Plan what permissions to assign to users or groups for network programs, data, and home folders.
- Outline the tasks required to create home folders on NTFS volumes.

Estimated lesson time: 20 minutes

Guidelines for Planning Program Folders

The following are general guidelines for assigning NTFS permissions to program folders:

- Remove the default NTFS permission Full Control from the Everyone group and assign it to the Administrators group.
- Assign groups that are responsible for upgrading and troubleshooting software the Full Control or Change permission for the appropriate folders.
- If network programs are contained in shared folders, assign the Users group the Read permission.

Guidelines for Planning Data Folders

The following are general guidelines for assigning NTFS permissions to data folders:

- Remove the default permission Full Control from the Everyone group and assign it to the Administrators group.
- Assign the Users group the Add & Read permission and the Creator Owner group the Full Control permission. This gives users who log on locally the ability to delete and modify only the folders and files that they copy or create on the computer.

Guidelines for Planning Home Folders

The following are general guidelines for assigning NTFS permissions to home folders:

- Centralize home folders on an NTFS volume (on a network server) that is separate from programs and the operating system to streamline administration and the backing up of data.
- Use %Username% to automatically assign a user's account name to the folder and to automatically assign the NTFS permission Full Control to the respective user.

Creating Home Folders on an NTFS Volume

A big advantage to storing home folders on an NTFS volume is that you can organize them in one hierarchy and restrict access to the respective users without sharing each folder.

Follow these steps to create home folders on NTFS volumes:

1. Create a folder named *Users* on a volume that is separate from the operating system and programs. By doing so, the home folders will remain intact if the operating system volume requires reformatting.
2. Share the Users folder to provide a single access point for network users and a single administration point for administrators.
3. Remove the default permission Full Control from the Everyone group and assign the share permission Full Control to the Users group.
4. Use the %Username% variable to automatically name home folders using users' user account names. The %Username% variable also automatically assigns the NTFS permission Full Control to the respective user. (On FAT volumes, home folders can only be restricted by share permissions.)

    a. In User Manager for Domains, create a new user account or double-click an existing account.

    b. In the **New User** or **User Properties** dialog box, click **Profile**, and then, in the **Home Directory To** box, type *server_name***Users****%Username%**

Tip Educate users to store their personal and work data in their home folders. If users' home folders are stored on a network server and are moved to a different server, only the home folder path will require modification.

To plan NTFS folder and file permissions

Scenario: As the administrator for World Wide Importers, you need to secure disk resources for their Quebec office. In this exercise, you plan your NTFS permissions for a server that all employees need to access. Your goal is to create a plan that will make the needed resources available to network users, and secure these resources according to the needs of the company. You will secure the folders in the hierarchy by using NTFS permissions. (In this scenario, the volume has been formatted with NTFS.)

As the administrator, you need to determine:

- Whether to create a local group for the resource or use a built-in local group.
- What NTFS permissions users will require to gain access to the appropriate folders and files.

Record your planning decisions on the "NTFS Permissions Planning Worksheet" located at the end of this lesson. After completing the exercise, turn to Appendix A, "Planning Worksheets," and compare your worksheet to the sample provided. (The sample represents only one set of possible answers. You may have planned your permissions differently.)

To complete the "NTFS Permissions Planning Worksheet," you need to:

1. Specify the folder or file that requires NTFS permissions. Record it in the Folder or File column.
2. Specify a local group for each resource. Record it under Local Group. For some folders, you may want to use the following built-in groups.

Built-in group	Description
Users	Built-in local group that contains all domain user accounts on each computer.
Administrators	Built-in local group that gives members administrative privileges.
Creator Owner	Built-in system group that is used to assign access to the creator and owner of a resource.

3. List the group accounts that require access to the folders and that will become members of the local groups. Record them under Members. The following table describes the group accounts for the Quebec office.

Group	Description
Accountants6	Global group that contains all user accounts for the accountants.
Executives6	Global group that contains all user accounts for the executives.
Managers6	Global group that contains all user accounts for the managers.
Spreadsheet6	Local group for the Spreadsheet program.
Database6	Local group for the Database program.
Library6	Local group for the Library information.

4. Specify the appropriate standard NTFS permissions for members of each local group. Record them under NTFS Permissions (for example, List, Read, Add, Add & Read, Change, Full Control, or No Access).

Base your implementation plan on the following illustration and criteria. The illustration shows the folder hierarchies. Notice that the Public folder and the Apps folder have been shared. The Everyone group has the share permission Full Control.

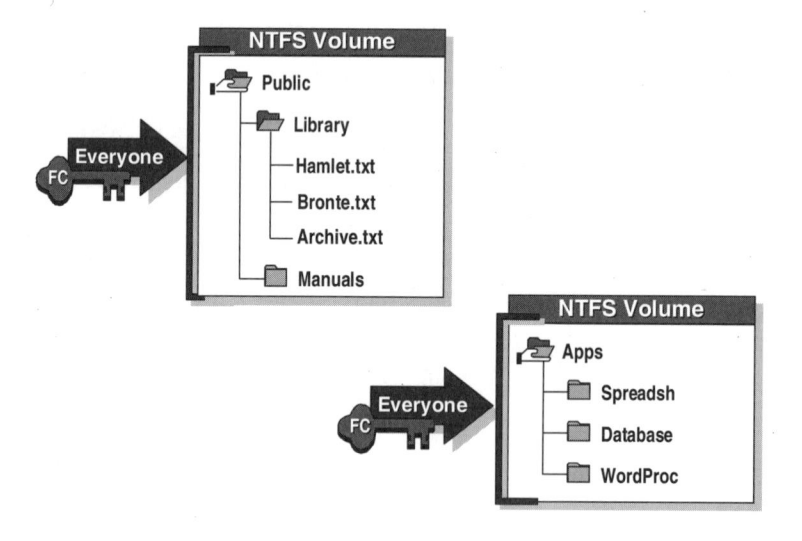

```
NTFS Volume
  Public
    Library
      Hamlet.txt
      Bronte.txt
      Archive.txt
    Manuals
```
Everyone FC

```
NTFS Volume
  Apps
    Spreadsh
    Database
    WordProc
```
Everyone FC

Use the following criteria to make your decisions:

- Administrators need to administer all folders and files.
- All users need to run programs in the WordProc folder, but they should not be able to modify the files in the WordProc folder.
- Only members of the Accountants6, Managers6, and Executives6 global groups need to run the programs in the Spreadsh and Database folders, but they should not be able to modify the files in those folders.
- All users need to copy their files to the Public folder and then modify only their own files as needed. They all need to read each others files.
- Members of the Managers6 global group need to contribute new files to the Library folder.
- All users need to open and view files in the Library and Manuals folders.
- User6 needs to update the Archive.txt file whenever a new file is added to the Library folder.
- User6 needs to modify files in the Manuals folder, including assigning permissions for files to other users and groups.

Lesson Summary

The following information summarizes the key points in this lesson:

- Determine what permissions are required and to whom they should be assigned before you begin to assign NTFS permissions to folders and files.
- For program folders, assign the Full Control permission to the Administrators group and to groups responsible for upgrading and troubleshooting software. Assign the Read permission to the Users group.
- For data folders, assign the Full Control permission to the Administrators group only. Assign the Users group the Add & Read permission, and assign the Creator Owner group the Full Control permission. This will give users the ability to delete and modify only the folders and files that they copy or create.
- Use %Username% to automatically assign a user's account name to a home folder and to automatically assign the NTFS permission Full Control to the respective user.

For more information on	See
Creating home folders on FAT volumes	Chapter 5, "Securing Network Resources with Share Permissions," in this book.
%Username%	Chapter 2, "Setting Up User Accounts," in this book.
Creator Owner	Chapter 2, "Working With User and Group Accounts," in Microsoft Windows NT Server *Concepts and Planning*.

NTFS Permissions Planning Worksheet

Folder or File	Local Group	Members	NTFS Permissions

Lesson 4: Assigning NTFS Permissions

This lesson guides you through the steps to assign NTFS permissions.

After this lesson, you will be able to:
- Describe the requirements for assigning NTFS permissions.
- Assign NTFS folder and file permissions to user and group accounts.

Estimated lesson time: 30 minutes

Requirements for Assigning NTFS Permissions

To assign NTFS permissions, you need to be the owner of the folder or file, or have one of the following permissions:

- Standard permission: Full Control
- Special access (or individual) permission: Change Permissions
- Special access (or individual) permission: Take Ownership (With this permission a user can take ownership of a folder or file, and then change permissions on the resource.)

Default NTFS Permissions

The following are the default NTFS permissions:

- When a volume is formatted with NTFS, the permission Full Control is automatically assigned to the Everyone group. This gives all users with the Log on locally user right complete access to the volume.
- When a new folder or file is created on an NTFS volume, the folder or file inherits the permissions of the folder that contains it.

Caution When Windows NT is installed on an NTFS volume, NTFS permissions are automatically assigned to some system folders. Do not modify the permissions on system files. For a complete list of these permissions, see Microsoft Windows NT Server *Concepts and Planning*.

Assigning NTFS Folder and File Permissions

You modify permissions by right-clicking the folder or file in Windows NT Explorer, clicking **Properties**, clicking the **Security** tab, and then clicking **Permissions**.

If you are modifying files, the **File Permissions** dialog box appears. If you are modifying folders, the **Directory Permissions** dialog box appears.

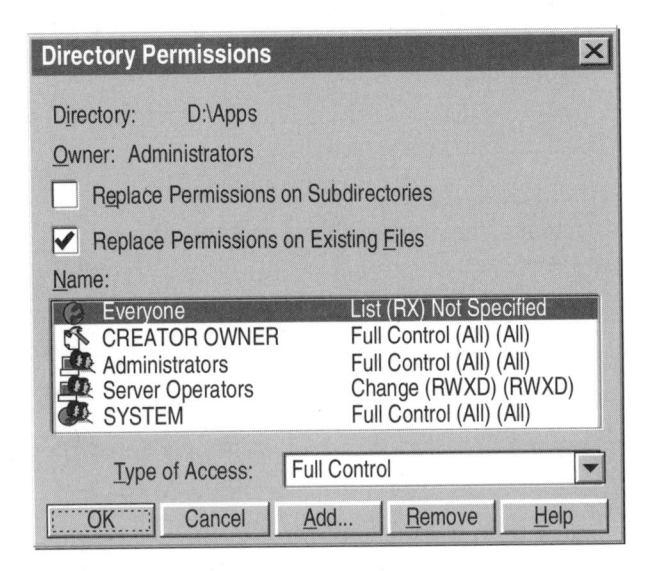

```
Directory Permissions                              [X]
  Directory:   D:\Apps
  Owner:  Administrators
  [ ] Replace Permissions on Subdirectories
  [✓] Replace Permissions on Existing Files
  Name:
    Everyone             List (RX) Not Specified
    CREATOR OWNER        Full Control (All) (All)
    Administrators       Full Control (All) (All)
    Server Operators     Change (RWXD) (RWXD)
    SYSTEM               Full Control (All) (All)

  Type of Access:  [ Full Control            ▼ ]
  [  OK  ]  [ Cancel ]  [ Add... ]  [ Remove ]  [ Help ]
```

The following table describes the **Directory Permissions** or *file_name* **Permissions** dialog box.

Option	Purpose
Replace Permissions on Subdirectories	If selected, changes existing permissions for all folders within the selected folder's hierarchy. This option does not change permissions on existing files in the folder hierarchy. This check box is cleared by default and is an option *only* when assigning folder permissions.
Replace Permissions on Existing Files	If selected, changes existing permissions for all files within the selected folder only. It does not change file permissions for folders within the same folder hierarchy. This check box is cleared by default and is an option only when assigning folder permissions.
Name	Displays the folder or file permissions assigned to a group or user for the resource. The first set of parentheses indicates the folder permissions, and the second set of parentheses indicates the permissions for any new files created in the folder.
Type of Access	Displays the folder or file permissions for the selected group or user in the **Name** box and allows you to change the permission assigned to the selection.

▶ **To assign permissions to Users for the Public folder**

In this procedure, you assign the Add & Read permission to the Users group and remove the default permissions from the Everyone group.

1. Log on as Administrator and start Windows NT Explorer.
2. Expand the LabFiles folder, right-click the Public folder, and then on the shortcut menu click **Properties**.
3. Click the **Security** tab, and then click **Permissions**.

   The **Directory Permissions** dialog box appears.

   Notice that the Everyone group is assigned the NTFS permission Full Control by default.

4. In the **Directory Permissions** dialog box, click **Add**.

   The **Add Users and Groups** dialog box appears.

5. Make sure that your domain name appears in the **List Names From** box.
6. Under **Names**, click **Users**, and then click **Add**.

   Users appears under **Add Names**.

7. In the **Type of Access** box, click **Add & Read**, and then click **OK**.

   Users appears in the **Directory Permissions** dialog box. Notice that (RWX) (RX) appears next to Add & Read. The first set of parentheses indicates the permissions that apply to the folder; the second set of parentheses indicates the permissions that apply to the files in the folder.

8. Under **Name**, click **Everyone** (if it is not already selected), and then click **Remove**.

   The Everyone group is removed from the list.

▶ **To assign permissions to Creator Owner for the Public folder**

In this procedure, you assign the Full Control permission to the Creator Owner group so that users will have the ability to modify their own files.

1. In the **Directory Permissions** dialog box, click **Add**.

   The **Add Users and Groups** dialog box appears.

2. Make sure that your domain name appears in the **List Names From** box.
3. Under **Names**, click **CREATOR OWNER**, and then click **Add**.
4. In the **Type of Access** box, click **Full Control**, and then click **OK**.

   The Creator Owner group appears with the Full Control permission in the **Directory Permissions** dialog box.

▶ **To assign permissions to Administrators for the Public folder**

1. In the **Directory Permissions** dialog box, click **Add**.

    The **Add Users and Groups** dialog box appears.

2. Make sure that your domain name appears in the **List Names From** box.

3. Under **Names**, click **Administrators**, and then click **Add**.

4. In the **Type of Access** box, click **Full Control**, and then click **OK**.

    In the **Directory Permissions** dialog box, notice that the Administrators group and the Creator Owner group have Full Control permission, and that the Users group has the Add & Read permission.

5. Select the **Replace Permissions on Subdirectories** check box so that the permissions will be applied to all folders in the hierarchy.

6. Verify that the **Replace Permissions on Existing Files** check box is selected, and then click **OK**.

    The following message appears:

    ```
    Do you want to replace the security information on all existing
    subdirectories within drive:\LabFiles\Public?
    ```

7. Click **Yes** to return to the **Public Properties** dialog box, and then click **OK** to apply your changes.

8. Use Notepad to create a file named Chapter6.txt in LabFiles\Public.

▶ **To test the NTFS permissions assigned for the Public folder**

In this procedure, you test NTFS permissions by attempting to open, modify, and delete a file created by two different users.

1. Log on as CustomerService6, and then start Windows NT Explorer.

2. Expand the LabFiles\Public folder.

3. Attempt to create a file in the Public folder.

    Were you successful? Why or why not?

    _____

    _____

4. Attempt to perform the following tasks for the file that you just created. In the following list, mark those which you are able to complete:

    ❑ Open the file

    ❑ Modify the file

    ❑ Delete the file

5. Attempt to perform the following tasks for the Chapter6.txt file created by Administrator. In the following list, mark the task or tasks that you are able to complete:
   - ❑ Open the file
   - ❑ Modify the file
   - ❑ Delete the file
6. Quit all programs and log off.

▶ **To assign NTFS permissions**

In this procedure, you assign NTFS permissions based on the sample "NTFS Permission Planning Worksheet" plan provided in Appendix A, "Planning Worksheets."

1. In Appendix A, "Planning Worksheets," locate the "NTFS Permission Planning Worksheet."
2. Log on as Administrator.
3. Start Windows NT Explorer, and then expand the LabFiles folder.
4. In the LabFiles folder, right-click a folder or file (from those listed on the "NTFS Permission Planning Worksheet"), and then click **Properties**.

   The *folder_name* **Properties** or *file_name* **Properties** dialog box appears.

5. In the *folder-name* **Properties** or *file_name* **Properties** dialog box, click the **Security** tab, and then click **Permissions**.

   The **File Permissions** or **Directory Permissions** dialog box appears.

6. If you are assigning permissions for a folder, configure the following options. Otherwise, skip this step.

For this option	Do this
Replace permissions on subdirectories	Click to select this check box.
Replace permissions on existing files	Verify that this check box is selected.

7. To add permissions for users or local groups to the folder or file, click **Add**.

   The **Add Users and Groups** dialog box appears.

8. Click **Show Users**.
9. Under **Names**, click a user or local group (from those listed on the "NTFS Permissions Planning Worksheet") and then click **Add**.

   The user or local group appears in the **Add Names** box.

10. In the **Type of Access** box, click the appropriate permissions.

Chapter 6 Securing Network Resources with NTFS Permissions 235

11. Assign the appropriate permissions to the remaining users and groups for all of the folders and files on the "NTFS Permissions Planning Worksheet." (This applies to all but the Public folder; permissions for Public were assigned in a previous procedure.)
12. Quit Windows NT Explorer and log off.

▶ **To test permissions for the Manuals folder when User6 connects over the network**

In this procedure, you connect to your own computer to test permissions for the Manuals folder. Connecting to your own computer mimics connecting over the network.

1. Log on as User6.
2. Click the **Start** button, click **Run**, and then in the **Open** box, type *\\computer_name***Public** (where *computer_name* is the name of your computer), and then click **OK**.

    The Public on *computer_name* window appears.

3. Open the Manuals folder and then attempt to create a file in it.

    Were you successful? Why or why not?

    _____

    _____

4. Quit Windows NT Explorer and log off.

▶ **To test permissions for the Manuals folders when CustomerService6 connects over the network**

In this procedure, you connect to your own computer to test permissions for the Manuals folder. Connecting to your own computer mimics connecting over the network.

1. Log on as CustomerService6.
2. Click the **Start** button, click **Run**, and then in the **Open** box, type *\\computer_name***Public** (where *computer_name* is the name of your computer), and then click **OK**.
3. Start Windows NT Explorer and expand the LabFiles\Public\Manuals folder.
4. Attempt to create a file in the Manuals folder.

    Were you successful? Why or why not?

    _____

    _____

5. Quit Windows NT Explorer and log off.

Assigning Special Access Permissions

In most situations, standard permissions are all you need to secure folders and files. However, in a few situations, you will need to assign special access permissions, which give you the ability to assign individual permissions to user and group accounts. For example, you need to assign special access permissions to do the following:

- To allow another user to manage permissions for files that you own, assign that user the permission Change Permissions (P).
- To protect program files from being deleted accidentally or infected by viruses, assign all user accounts, including administrative accounts, the permission Read (R) for executable files.
- To allow administrators to modify executable files, assign the Administrators group the permission Change Permissions (P). This permission gives administrators the ability to change the permissions on Read only files if necessary.

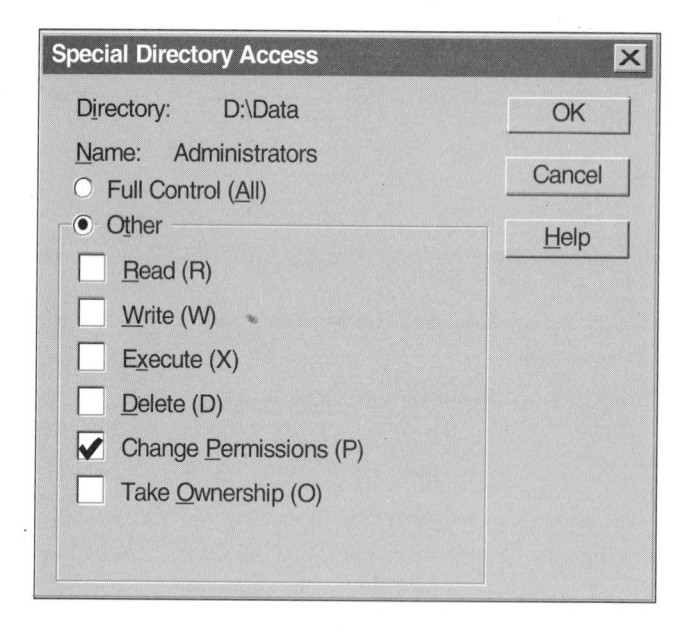

```
┌─ Special Directory Access ─────────────────── X ─┐
│                                                  │
│   Directory:     D:\Data              ┌────────┐ │
│                                       │   OK   │ │
│   Name:     Administrators            └────────┘ │
│   ○ Full Control (All)                ┌────────┐ │
│  ┌─ ⦿ Other ─────────────────┐        │ Cancel │ │
│  │                           │        └────────┘ │
│  │   ☐ Read (R)              │        ┌────────┐ │
│  │   ☐ Write (W)             │        │  Help  │ │
│  │                           │        └────────┘ │
│  │   ☐ Execute (X)           │                   │
│  │   ☐ Delete (D)            │                   │
│  │   ☑ Change Permissions (P)│                   │
│  │   ☐ Take Ownership (O)    │                   │
│  └───────────────────────────┘                   │
└──────────────────────────────────────────────────┘
```

Note The special access permissions are identical for both files and folders.

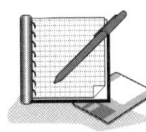

▶ **To assign standard permissions for the Games folder**

In this procedure, you assign the standard permission Read to the local Administrators and Users groups to prepare for the next procedure.

1. Log on as Administrator.
2. Start Windows NT Explorer, and expand the LabFiles\Apps folder.
3. Right-click the Games folder, and then click **Properties**.
4. In the **Games Properties** dialog box, click the **Security** tab, and then click **Permissions**.

   The **Directory Permissions** dialog box appears.
5. Select **Everyone** (if it is not already selected), click **Remove**, and then click **Add**.
6. Make sure your domain name appears in the **List Names From** box.
7. In the **Names** box, click **Administrators**, and then click **Add**.
8. In the **Names** box, click **Users**, and then click **Add**.
9. In the **Type of Access** box, click **Read** and then click **OK**.

   Administrators and Users appear in the Directory Permissions dialog box with Read (RX) (RX) as the permission. This is because the standard permission Read includes the special access permissions Read and Execute.

▶ **To assign special access permissions for files**

In this procedure, you assign the special access permission Change Permissions to the Administrators group to give its members the ability to change the permissions on the files in the Games folder.

1. In the **Directory Permissions** dialog box, select **Administrators**, and then in the **Type of Access** box, click **Special File Access**.

   The **Special File Access** dialog box appears.

   Notice that the Read and Execute permissions are selected. These are the special file access permissions included with the standard permission Read.
2. Select **Change Permissions (P)**, and then click **OK**.

   Notice that the permissions for Administrators is now indicated by Special Access (RX)(RXP). The first set of parentheses specifies the permissions for the folder and the second set of parentheses specifies the permissions for the files within the folder.
3. Verify that the **Replace Permissions on Existing Files** check box is selected. This applies the selected permission to all the files in the folder.
4. Click **OK** twice to return to Windows NT Explorer.

▶ **To test special access permissions for files**

1. In Windows NT Explorer, expand the LabFiles\Apps\Games folder.
2. Attempt to run Kolumz.exe.

    Were you successful? Why or why not?

    _____

    _____

3. Attempt to delete Kolumz.exe.

    Were you successful? Why or why not?

    _____

    _____

4. Attempt to assign the Administrators group the Full Control permission for Kolumz.exe.

    Were you successful? Why or why not?

    _____

    _____

Lesson Summary

The following information summarizes the key points in this lesson:

- To assign NTFS permissions, you must be the owner of the folder or file, have the standard permission Full Control, or have the special access permission Change Permissions or Take Ownership.
- When a volume is formatted with NTFS, the permission Full Control is automatically assigned to the Everyone group.
- Special access permissions are used when you need to assign a combination of individual permissions.

For more information on	See
Strategies for using NTFS file permissions	Chapter 4, "Managing Shared Resources and Resource Security," in Microsoft Windows NT Server *Concepts and Planning*.
Setting customized special access permissions	Chapter 4, "Managing Shared Resources and Resource Security," in Microsoft Windows NT Server *Concepts and Planning*.
Controlling access to files and folders	Chapter 3, "Disk Management Basics," in the *Resource Guide* of the *Microsoft Windows NT Server Resource Kit*.

Lesson 5: Taking Ownership of Folders and Files

By default, the user who creates a folder or file is the owner. As owner, a user can assign permissions to control what others can do with the folder or file. In some situations, it may be necessary for an administrator to remove control from a user by taking ownership of the folder or file. This lesson outlines the requirements and procedures to take ownership of a folder or file.

After this lesson, you will be able to:
- Explain the concept of taking ownership of a folder or file.
- Explain how to give users the ability to take ownership of a folder or file.
- Determine the current owner of a folder or file.
- Take ownership of a folder or file.

Estimated lesson time: 20 minutes

The user who creates a folder or file is the owner of that folder or file. As the owner of a folder or file, a user can share the folder and assign the Take Ownership permission (O) to other users and groups.

The owner can always control access to the folder or file by changing the permissions set on it. A user cannot share folders or assign permissions for folders that he or she does not own.

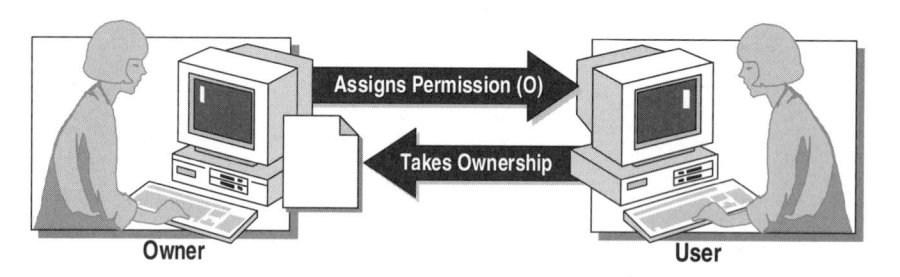

If a user has denied others from gaining access to a file and then leaves the company, the administrator can take ownership of the file and change the permissions so that others can gain access to the file.

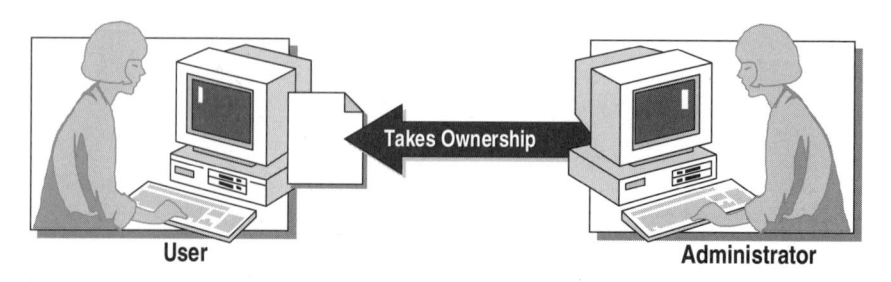

How to Take Ownership

By default, users who are members of the Administrators group always have the ability to take ownership of a folder or file. If a member of this group takes ownership of a resource, the Administrators group becomes the resource's owner and any member of the Administrators group can gain access to the resource.

The following checklist provides an overview of the tasks that you will need to do if you take ownership of a file:

- ❏ Log on as Administrator.
- ❏ On the **Security** tab of the *folder_name* **Properties** or the *file_name* **Properties** dialog box, click **Ownership** (to determine the current owner).
- ❏ In the **Owner** dialog box, click **Take Ownership**.

Giving Users the Ability to Take Ownership

An owner cannot change the ownership of a resource that they own. The owner can only give another user or group permission to take ownership of a resource. Security of the resource is maintained by preventing users from creating or editing files and then making them look as if they belonged to someone else.

The owner can assign another group or user the *ability* to take ownership of a folder or file by assigning one of the following permissions:

- Standard permission: Full Control
- The special access permission: Take Ownership
- The special access permission: Change Permissions (With this permission, users can assign the Take Ownership permission to themselves or to another user or group.)

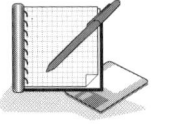

▶ **To determine the owner and permissions of a file**

1. Log on as Administrator.
2. Start Windows NT Explorer, and then in the LabFiles folder, create a text file named Owner.txt.
3. Right-click Owner.txt, and then click **Properties**.

   The **Owner.txt Properties** dialog box appears.
4. Click the **Security** tab, and then click **Ownership**.

   Notice that the current owner is the Administrators group.
5. Click **Close**, and then click **Permissions**.

   The **File Permissions** dialog box appears. The Everyone group has the Full Control permission.

▶ To assign the Take Ownership permission to a user

1. In the **File Permissions** dialog box, click **Add**.

    The **Add Users and Groups** dialog box appears.

2. Make sure that your domain name appears in the **List Names From** box.
3. Click **Show Users**.
4. Select SalesMgr6, and then click **Add**.
5. In the **Type of Access** box, click **Read** (if is does not already appear), and then click **OK**.

    SalesMgr6 appears in the **File Permissions** dialog box and has Read permission.

6. Click SalesMgr6, and then in the **Type of Access** box, click **Special Access**.

    The **Special Access** dialog box appears.

    Notice that the special access permissions Read and Execute are selected, because the standard Read permission assigned to the SalesMgr6 for the Owner.txt file includes both Read and Execute.

7. Select the **Take Ownership (O)** check box, click **OK** three times to apply your changes, and then exit to Windows NT Explorer.
8. Quit Windows NT Explorer, and then log off.

▶ To take ownership of a file

1. Log on as SalesMgr6, and start Windows NT Explorer.
2. In the LabFiles folder, right-click Owner.txt, and then click **Properties**.

    The **Owner Properties** dialog box appears.

3. On the **Security** tab, click **Ownership**.

    Notice that the Administrators group is the owner of the file. When any member of the Administrators group creates a file, the entire group becomes the owner of the file.

4. In the **Owner** dialog box, click **Take Ownership**.
5. On the **Security** tab, click **Ownership**.

    Notice that SalesMgr6 is the new owner of the Owner.txt file. By assigning SalesMgr6 the special access permission Take Ownership, SalesMgr6 was able to take ownership away from the Administrators group.

6. Click **Close** to return to the **Security** tab.

▶ **To test file permissions as the owner**

1. Assign SalesMgr6 the permission Full Control for the Owner.txt file.
2. Remove permissions for all other users and groups from the Owner.txt file. Were you successful? Why or why not?

   _____

   _____

3. Close the **Owner Properties** dialog box.
4. Quit Windows NT Explorer, and then Log off.

Lesson Summary

The following information summarizes the key points in this lesson:

- By default, the person who creates a folder or file is the owner.
- By default, members of the Administrators group always have the ability to take ownership of a folder or file.
- The owner can assign another group or user the *ability* to take ownership of a folder or file by assigning the Full Control permission, or by assigning the special access permissions Change Permissions or Take Ownership.

For more information on	See
The procedure to take ownership	Windows NT Help.
Take Ownership permission	Windows NT Help.
Taking ownership of folders and files	Chapter 4, "Managing Shared Resources and Resource Security," in Microsoft Windows NT Server *Concepts and Planning*.

Lesson 6: Copying or Moving Folders and Files

Copying and moving folders or files within and between NTFS volumes can affect the original permissions on a folder or file. This lesson explains what happens to permissions when a folder or file is copied or moved.

After this lesson, you will be able to:
- Describe what happens to permissions on folders and files that are copied or moved within the same or to different volumes.
- Describe what happens to the ownership of folders and files that are copied or moved within the same or to different volumes.
- List the required permissions for copying or moving folders or files.

Estimated lesson time: 20 minutes

Copying a Folder or File

When you copy a folder or file within the same NTFS volume or to a different NTFS volume, the folder or file inherits the permissions of the destination folder, and the user who copies a folder or file becomes the owner.

In the following illustration, File-A will inherit the Change permission at the destination folder even though the permission at the source folder is Read. User6 copied the file and will become the new owner of it at the destination folder.

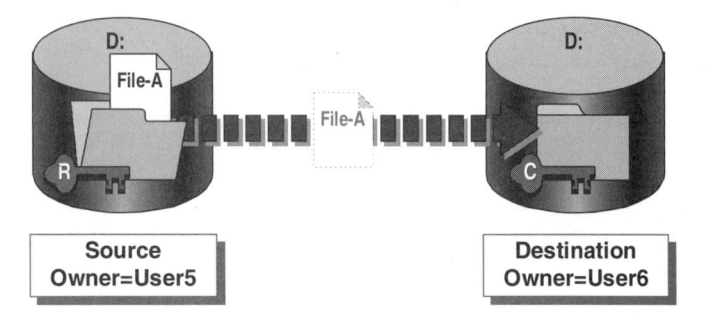

Moving a Folder or File

When you move a folder or file within the same NTFS volume, the folder or file retains its original permissions and owner. However, if you move a folder or file to a different NTFS volume, the folder or file inherits the permissions of the destination folder and the new owner is the user who moved it, just like when a user copies a folder or file.

In the following illustration, File-A will retain the Read permission because it is being moved within the same volume. User6 moved the file, but User5 remains the owner of it at the destination folder.

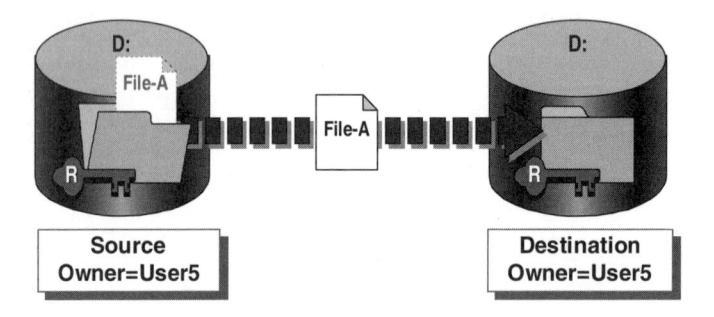

Permission Requirements

A user cannot copy or move folders or files within or between NTFS volumes, unless the user has the correct permissions.

The following table describes the required permissions to copy or move a folder or file to another folder on an NTFS volume or to another NTFS volume.

Action	Permission required
Copy	The Add permission for the destination folder.
Move	The Add permission for the destination folder and the Delete permission for the source folder. Delete is required because when a folder or file is moved, it is deleted from the source folder after it is placed in the destination folder.

Important Folders and files that are copied or moved to FAT volumes lose their permissions because FAT volumes do not support NTFS permissions.

Example of Copying and Moving Folders and Files

In the following illustration, File-A is stored in the C:\Users\Mary folder. The Users group has the following NTFS permissions to folders on drives C and D:

- Read permission for C:\Users\Mary and the files contained within it.
- Change permission for C:\Public.
- Full Control permission for D:\Data.

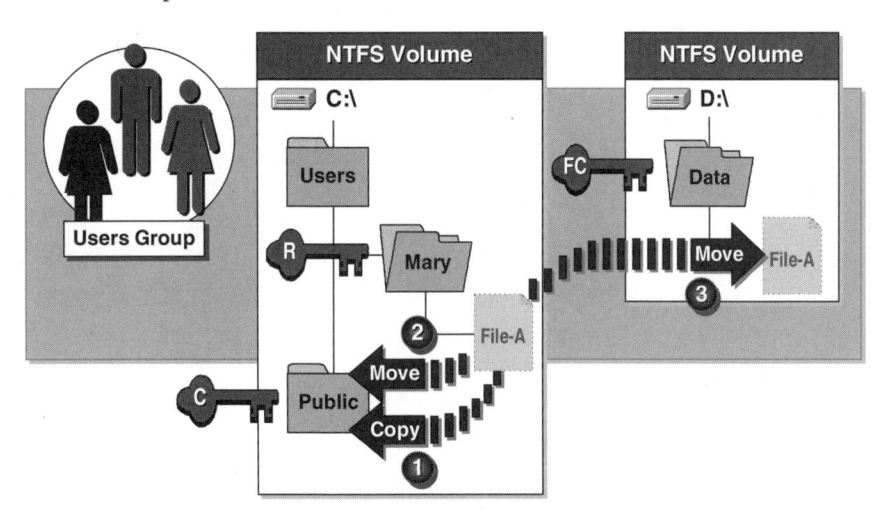

1. What permission does the Users group have to File-A after it is copied to the C:\Public folder?

2. What permission does the Users group have to File-A after it is moved to the C:\Public folder?

3. What permission does the Users group have to File-A if it is moved to the D:\Data folder?

▶ To create a folder while logged on as a user

In this procedure, you create a folder and view its default properties. This folder will be used in subsequent procedures to see how the permissions and ownership are affected when it is moved or copied.

1. Log on as SalesMgr6.
2. In Windows NT Explorer, expand the LabFiles folder.
3. In LabFiles, create a folder named Temp1.
4. Right-click the folder, click **Properties**, and then click **Permissions**.

    What are the permissions assigned to the folder?

    _____

    _____

5. Click **Cancel**.
6. Click **Ownership**.

    Who is the owner? Why?

    _____

    _____

7. Click **Close**, and then click **OK**.
8. Log off.

▶ To create a folder while logged on as Administrator

1. Log on as Administrator.
2. Start Windows NT Explorer, and expand the LabFiles folder.
3. In LabFiles, create the following folders:
    - Temp2
    - Temp3
4. View each folder's properties.

    What are the permissions assigned to the folders that you just created?

    _____

    Who is the owner of the Temp2 and Temp3 folders?

    _____

5. Remove the Everyone group from the permissions list for both folders and then assign the following permissions to the Temp2 and Temp3 folders.

Folder	Assign these permissions
Temp2	Administrators: Full Control
	Users: Read
Temp3	Backup Operators: Read
	Users: Full Control

▶ **To copy a folder within the same NTFS volume**

1. Copy the Temp2 folder into the Temp1 folder. (Hint: Hold down the CTRL key and use the mouse to drag the Temp2 folder to the Temp1 folder.)

2. Select LabFiles\Temp1\Temp2 and compare the permissions and ownership with LabFiles\Temp2, created by Administrator. Then, compare the permissions of LabFiles\Temp1\Temp2 with LabFiles\Temp1, created by SalesMgr6.

   Who is the owner of LabFiles\Temp1\Temp2 and what are the permissions? Why?

   _____

   _____

3. Log off Windows NT.

▶ **To move a folder within the same NTFS volume**

1. Log on as the SalesMgr6 and start Windows NT Explorer.

2. Expand the LabFiles folder.

3. Move the LabFiles\Temp3 folder to the LabFiles\Temp1 folder. (Hint: Use the mouse to drag the Temp3 folder to the Temp1 folder.)

   Who is the owner of the LabFiles\Temp1\Temp3 folder and what are the permissions? Why?

   _____

   _____

Lesson Summary

The following information summarizes the key points in this lesson:

- When a folder or file is copied from one folder to another, it inherits the permissions of the destination folder and the user who performed the copy becomes the owner of the folder or file in its new destination.
- When a folder or file is moved within the same volume, the permissions and owner are retained. If a folder or file is moved to a different volume, the same rules apply as when a folder or file is copied.
- To copy a folder or file, a user needs the Add permission for the destination folder. To move a folder or file, a user needs the Add permission for the destination folder and the Delete permission for the source folder.

Lesson 7: Troubleshooting Permission Problems

One of the most common problems that users encounter is the inability to gain access to resources. This lesson describes common permission-related problems and their solutions.

After this lesson, you will be able to:
- Recognize common reasons why users cannot gain access to resources.
- Solve common permission-related problems.

Estimated lesson time: 20 minutes

The following information provides solutions to common permission-related problems.

Problem 1
A user cannot gain access to a resource.

Solution
Check the permissions assigned to the user's account and to groups to which the user is a member. If the No Access permission is assigned to the user or to a group that the user is a member of, then the user does not have permission for the resource.

If a file was copied within an NTFS volume, or copied or moved to another NTFS volume, the file permissions may have changed by inheriting new permissions from the destination folder.

Problem 2
A user deletes a file, even though that user was assigned the No Access permission for the file.

In UNIX file systems, users who have the Write permission to a folder can delete files in the folder. Because Windows NT supports POSIX programs that are designed to run on UNIX file systems, the NTFS Full Control permission allows users to delete files in a folder even if the user has the No Access permission for the file. Therefore, a user with the Full Control permission to a folder can delete a file in the folder, even though the user was assigned the No Access permission to the file.

Solution

Remove the standard NTFS permission Full Control from the user for the folder. Instead, assign the user all of the individual special access permissions for the folder. This gives the user all of the abilities of the Full Control permission for the folder, but prevents the user from deleting files in the folder (for which he or she has been assigned the No Access permission).

Note The scenario described in Problem 2 is the only exception to the rule that file permissions override folder permissions.

Problem 3

You add a user to a group to give that user permission for a resource, but the user still cannot gain access to the resource.

Solution

Have the user log off and then log back on or ask the user to disconnect completely from the remote computer and attempt to connect again. This will update the list of groups that the user is identified as being a member of.

An object called an *access token* is created for a user every time that user logs on and is authenticated by a computer running Windows NT. The access token contains information about the groups to which the user belongs. For the access token to be updated to include the new group to which you have added the user, the user must log off and then log on again, or disconnect completely from the remote computer and then reconnect.

▶ **To identify incorrect permissions**

Scenario: You are the administrator for a server that contains the following folder hierarchy.

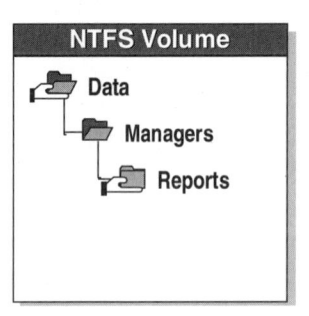

```
NTFS Volume
  📁 Data
     📁 Managers
        📁 Reports
```

Chapter 6 Securing Network Resources with NTFS Permissions

The following share permissions have been assigned to the Data and Reports folders.

Folder	Share name	User or group	Share permissions
Data	Data	Administrators	Full Control
		Managers	Read
Data\Managers\Reports	Mgr_Reports	Administrators	Full Control
		Managers	Full Control

The following NTFS permissions have been assigned.

Folder	User or group	NTFS permissions
Data	Administrators	Full Control
	Managers	Read
Managers	Managers	Add & Read
	Creator Owner	Full Control
Reports	Managers	Add & Read
	Creator Owner	Full Control

User1 calls you, saying that she does not have proper access to the Reports folder. She is a member of the Managers group. When she connects to the shared Data folder, she can browse the Managers and Reports folders. She cannot create new files or modify files that she owns. What is the problem and how would you solve it?

Deleting a File That Has the No Access Permission

In this exercise, you simulate the scenario described in Problem 2 of this lesson to observe the result when a user has Full Control permission for a folder and No Access permission to a file in that folder. To do this, you first assign these permissions.

▶ **To create a folder with the Full Control permission**

1. Log on as Administrator, and then start Windows NT Explorer.
2. In LabFiles, create a folder named FullAccess.
3. Verify that the Everyone group has the NTFS permission Full Control for the LabFiles\FullAccess folder.

▶ **To create and assign the No Access permission for the NoAccess.txt file**

1. In the FullAccess folder, create a text file named NoAccess.txt.
2. Assign the Everyone group No Access permission for the NoAccess.txt file.

   The following error message appears:

   ```
   You have denied access to drive:\LabFiles\FullAccess\NoAccess.txt.
   Nobody will be able to access drive:\LabFiles\FullAccess\NoAccess.txt
   and only the owner will be able to change the permissions. Do you
   wish to continue?
   ```

3. Click **Yes**, and then click **OK** to return to Windows NT Explorer.

▶ **To view the result of the Full Control permission for the FullAccess folder**

1. In the LabFiles\FullAccess folder, double-click the NoAccess.txt file to open it.
   Were you successful? Why or why not?

   _____

   _____

2. Click the **Start** button, point to **Programs**, and then click **Command Prompt**.
3. Change to the *drive*:\LabFiles\FullAccess folder.
4. Delete NoAccess.txt by typing the following command:

   delete noaccess.txt

   Were you successful? Why or why not?

   _____

   _____

   How would you prevent users with Full Control permission for a folder from deleting a file in that folder to which they have been assigned the No Access permission?

   _____

   _____

▶ **To create and assign special directory access permissions to a folder**

In this procedure, you assign special access permissions for the FullAccess folder to the Everyone group.

1. Switch to Windows NT Explorer, right-click the FullAccess folder, and then click **Properties**.
2. Click the **Security** tab, and then click **Permissions**.

    Notice that Everyone is selected by default.

3. In the **Type of Access** box, select **Special Directory Access**.

    The **Special Directory Access** dialog box appears.

4. Click **Other**, click to select the check boxes for all individual permissions, and then click **OK**.
5. Click **OK** to return to the **FullAccess Properties** dialog box, and then click **OK** to apply your changes.

    The Everyone group now has permission for the FullAccess folder.

▶ **To create a file and assign it the No Access permission**

1. In the FullAccess folder, create a text file named NoDelete.txt.
2. Assign the Everyone group the No Access permission for the file NoDelete.txt.

    The following error message appears:

    ```
    You have denied access to drive:\LabFiles\FullAccess\NoDelete.txt.
    Nobody will be able to access drive:\LabFiles\FullAccess\NoDelete.txt
    and only the owner will be able to change the permissions. Do you
    wish to continue?
    ```

3. Click **Yes**, and then click **OK**.

▶ **To view the result of the Full Control permission for the FullAccess folder**
1. Double-click to open LabFiles\FullAccess\NoDelete.txt.
   Were you successful? Why or why not?

   _____

   _____

2. Click the **Start** button, point to **Programs**, and then click **Command Prompt**.
3. Change to the *drive*:\LabFiles\FullAccess folder.
4. Delete NoDelete.txt by typing the following command:
   delete nodelete.txt
   Were you successful? Why or why not?

   _____

   _____

Lesson Summary

The following information summarizes the key points in this lesson:

- If a user has a problem gaining access to a resource, check the permissions on the user account and on any groups to which the user is a member.
- The NTFS folder permission Full Control allows users to delete files in the folder, even if they have the No Access permission for the file. To avoid this, remove the Full Control permission and, instead, assign the user all of the special directory access permissions for the folder.
- If a user cannot gain access to a resource after being added to a group that has permission to the resource, have the user log off and then log back on, or have the user disconnect from the resource and then reconnect.

For more information on	See
NTFS permissions	Chapter 4, "Managing Shared Resources and Resource Security," in Microsoft Windows NT Server *Concepts and Planning*.
FAT and NTFS volumes	Chapter 17, "Disk and File System Basics," in the *Microsoft Windows NT Workstation Resource Kit*.
NTFS file system	Chapter 3, "Disk Management Basics," in the *Resource Guide* of the *Microsoft Windows NT Server Resource Kit*.
NTFS file system overview	Chapter 17, "Disk and File System Basics," in the *Microsoft Windows NT Workstation Resource Kit*.
Access tokens	Chapter 2, "Network Security and Domain Planning," in the *Networking Guide* of the *Microsoft Windows NT Server Resource Kit*.

Best Practices

The following checklist provides best practices for implementing NTFS permissions. Review this checklist before you begin to assign NTFS permissions:

- ❑ Assign NTFS permissions before sharing a folder. In this way, you avoid the issue of users connecting to and gaining access to folders and files before you fully secure them.

- ❑ Assign permissions to groups rather than to individual users. If the user is a member of a group that has access to certain files, you can end the user's access by removing the user from the group rather than by changing the permissions on each of the files.

- ❑ Assign the Read permission to the Users and Administrators groups for all program executable files.

- ❑ Educate users that share a computer to assign NTFS permissions to the folders and files that they own.

- ❑ Damage to program files is usually a result of accidents and viruses. To prevent this type of file damage, assign the Read permission to all user accounts, including Administrator, for program files. By doing so, you prevent users and viruses from modifying or deleting these files. In addition, assign the Administrators group the special access permission Change Permissions (P) so that members can assign themselves less restrictive permissions when changes to the program files are required.

- ❑ Use the %Username% variable to create home folders—this simplifies administration by automatically assigning each user the NTFS permission Full Control for his or her home folder.

- ❑ Assign the Creator Owner group the Full Control permission for Data folders. This gives users the Full Control permission for only the folders or files that they create in the Data folder.

- ❑ Use long, descriptive names if the resource will only be accessed locally. If a folder will eventually be shared, then use folder and file names that are accessible by all client computers.

Note If you want to remove the accounts that were created by running the Chapter6.cmd file at the beginning of this chapter, log on as Administrator, and then double-click DeleteChapter6.cmd in the Cleanup folder on the Supplemental Material compact disc.

Review

The following questions are intended to reinforce key information presented in this chapter. If you are unable to answer a question, review the lesson and then try the question again.

1. Which of the following statements are true about NTFS permissions? (Circle all that apply.)

    a. They are available only on NTFS volumes.
    b. They protect resources from users who sit at the computer where the resource is located.
    c. They protect resources from users who connect to them over the network.
    d. They can be assigned to folders and files.
    e. A user's effective permissions are the combination of the user and group permissions.
    f. All of the above.

2. Complete this sentence. When share permissions are combined with NTFS permissions the _____ permission becomes the effective permission.

3. How would you create a home folder to which the respective user is automatically assigned the NTFS permission Full Control?

    _____

    _____

4. Which of the following are requirements for assigning NTFS permissions? (Circle all that apply.)

    a. Must be owner of the folder or file.
    b. Must have the standard permission Full Control, or either the Change Permissions or the Take Ownership special access permission.
    c. Must have the standard permission Change.

5. What is the default permission once a volume is formatted with NTFS?

    _____

    _____

6. Which of the following statements are true? (Circle all that apply.)

   a. Whenever a folder or file is copied, the folder or file inherits the permissions of the destination folder and the user who performed the copy becomes the owner of the copied folder or file.

   b. Whenever a folder or file is copied, the folder or file inherits the permissions of the destination folder and the ownership is retained.

   c. Whenever a folder or file is moved within the same volume, the folder or file retains its permissions and owner.

   d. Whenever a folder or file is moved to a different volume, the folder or file inherits the permissions of the destination folder and the user who performed the move becomes the owner of the moved folder or file.

   e. All of the above.

7. What should you always check when a user cannot access a resource?

   _____

   _____

Answer Key

Procedure Answers

Page 219

▶ **To review the video**

1. What do shared folders provide access to?

   Network resources.

2. What can share permissions be assigned to?

   Folders only.

3. What can NTFS permissions be assigned to?

   To folders and to individual files.

4. When you combine a share permission with an NTFS permission what permission becomes the *effective* permission?

   The most restrictive permission becomes the effective permission.

Example of Combined NTFS Permissions and Share Permissions

Page 220

- In Example A, what is User1's effective permission when he or she accesses the User1 folder by connecting to the Users shared folder? What is User2's effective permission for the User1 folder?

  User1 has Full Control permission to the Users folder and to the User1 folder.

  User2 does not have permission to gain access to the User1 folder, because the NTFS permission Full Control has been assigned to only the individual user for his or her home folder; therefore, only the individual user has Full Control permission to his or her home folder.

Page 221

- In Example B, what are the Sales group's effective permissions when they access the Sales folder by connecting to the Data shared folder?

  Read, because when share permissions are combined with NTFS permissions, the most restrictive permission applies.

Page 225

▶ **To plan NTFS folder and file permissions**

Strategy used in sample planning worksheet (see Appendix A, "Planning Worksheets):

Create a local group for each resource that will be restricted to certain users—for example, Spreadsheet, Database, and Library.

Use the built-in local Users group whenever all users require access to a resource. In a domain, the Users group contains all domain user accounts. In a workgroup, the Users group contains all user accounts local to the computer where the folder is located.

Assign the built-in Administrators group the Full Control permission for any folders that its members will manage.

Assign the Change permission to all local group members that need the ability to add, delete, and make changes to folders or files, but do not need to assign permissions to other users and groups.

Assign the Read permission to all local group members that only need to run programs or read files.

Assign the built-in Creator Owner system group the Full Control permission. This will give users with the Add & Read permission who copy or create a file the ability to modify the files they add to the Public folder. As a result, when a user copies or creates a file in the Public folder, the new file will have the following permission.

User or group	Permission
Users	Read
User account that copied or created the file	Full Control

Page 233

▶ **To test the NTFS permissions assigned for the Public folder**

3. Were you successful? Why or why not?

   Yes, because the Users group has been assigned the NTFS permission Add & Read for the LabFiles\Public folder.

4. Attempt to perform the following tasks for the file that you just created. In the following list, mark those which you are able to complete:

   CustomerService6 was successful at all three tasks because when CustomerService6 created the file, the account was added to the Creator Owner group, which has the NTFS permission Full Control for the LabFiles\Public folder.

Chapter 6   Securing Network Resources with NTFS Permissions   263

5. Attempt to perform the following tasks for the Chapter6.txt file created by Administrator. In the following list, mark the task or tasks that you are able to complete:

    CustomerService6 can only open the file because the account is a member of the Users group, which has the NTFS permission Add & Read for the LabFiles\Public folder, and because the file was created by another user.

Page 235

▶ **To test permissions for the Manuals folder when User6 connects over the network**

3. Were you successful? Why or why not?

    Yes, because the Everyone group has the share permission Full Control for the Public folder and User6 has the NTFS permission Full Control for the Manuals folder. If the Everyone group had the share permission Read, User6 would not have been able to create a file in the Manuals folder, because the share permission Read would be the effective permission.

Page 235

▶ **To test permissions for the Manuals folders when CustomerService6 connects over the network**

4. Were you successful? Why or why not?

    No, because CustomerService6, as a member of the Users group, only has the NTFS permission Read for the Manuals folder. CustomerService6 does have the ability to create a file in the Public folder because the share permission on Public is Full Control.

Page 238

▶ **To test special access permissions for files**

2. Attempt to run Kolumz.exe.

    Were you successful? Why or why not?

    Yes, because Users and Administrators have Read access to the Games folder and the files it contains.

3. Attempt to delete Kolumz.exe.

    Were you successful? Why or why not?

    No, because Users and Administrators only have Read access to the Games folder and the files that it contains.

4. Attempt to assign the Administrators group the Full Control permission for Kolumz.exe.

    Were you successful? Why or why not?

    Yes, because Administrators have the special access permission Change Permissions (P) for Kolumz.exe.

Page 243

▶ **To test file permissions as the owner**

2. Remove permissions for all other users and groups from the Owner.txt file.

   Were you successful? Why or why not?

   Yes, because SalesMgr6 is the owner of Owner.txt, and the owner of a folder or file always has the ability to change the permissions on folders and files that he or she owns.

Page 247

Example of Copying and Moving Folders and Files

1. What permission does the Users group have to File-A after it is copied to the C:\Public folder?

   The Users group has Change permission to File-A, because File-A inherits the Change permission after it is copied.

2. What permission does the Users group have to File-A after it is moved to the C:\Public folder?

   The Users group has Read permission, because permissions are retained for files that are moved between folders on the same NTFS volume.

3. What permission does the Users group have to File-A if it is moved to the D:\Data folder?

   The Users group has Full Control permission to File-A once it is moved to D:\Data, because moving a file to a different NTFS volume is treated as a copy; the file permissions are inherited from the destination folder.

Page 248

▶ **To create a folder while logged on as a user**

4. What are the permissions assigned to the folder?

   The Everyone group has Full Control (by default).

6. Who is the owner? Why?

   SalesMgr6, because the user who creates a folder or file is the owner.

Page 248

▶ **To create a folder while logged on as Administrator**

4. What are the permissions assigned to the folders that you just created?

   The Everyone group is assigned the Full Control permission by default.

   Who is the owner of the Temp2 and Temp3 folders?

   The Administrators group is the owner because a member of the group created the folders.

Chapter 6 Securing Network Resources with NTFS Permissions

Page 249

▶ **To copy a folder within an NTFS volume**

2. Who is the owner of LabFiles\Temp1\Temp2 and what are the permissions? Why?

The Administrators group became the owner of the folder when it was copied to its new location even though SalesMgr6 was the owner of Temp1, because whoever copies a folder or file becomes the owner. However, the folder inherited the permissions set by SalesMgr6 (Everyone: Full Control) because when a folder or file is copied within a volume, it always inherits the permissions of the destination folder.

Page 249

▶ **To move a folder within the same NTFS volume**

3. Who is the owner of the LabFiles\Temp1\Temp3 folder and what are the permissions? Why?

The Administrators group retained ownership of the folder because when a folder or file is moved within the same volume, the ownership stays the same.

The permissions were also retained (Backup Operators: Read; Users: Full Control) because when a folder or file is moved within the same volume the permissions also stay the same.

Page 252–253

▶ **To identify incorrect permissions**

User1 calls you, saying that she does not have proper access to the Reports folder. She is a member of the Managers group. When she connects to the shared Data folder, she can browse the Managers and Reports folders. She cannot create or modify any files that she owns. What is the problem and how would you solve it?

The problem is that User1 is connecting to the shared Data folder. She only has Read permission to this folder. To solve this problem, User1 needs to connect to the shared folder Mgr_Reports. Because she is a member of the Managers group, she has Full Control permission to access the Mgr_Reports shared folder.

266   Microsoft Windows NT Network Administration

Page 254

▶ **To view the result of the Full Control permission for the FullAccess folder**

1. Were you successful? Why or why not?

   No, because the Everyone group has the No Access permission for FullAccess\NoAccess.txt. The Administrator is a member of the Everyone group.

4. Were you successful? Why or why not?

   Yes, because the NTFS folder permission Full Control includes a hidden permission for POSIX compliance that allows users to delete files in the root of a folder to which the user has been assigned the Full Control permission. This hidden permission overrides No Access.

   How would you prevent users with Full Control permission to a folder from deleting a file in that folder to which they have been assigned the No Access permission?

   Assign users all of the individual special directory access permissions. These permissions provide the same level of access as the Full Control permission, but they do not allow the user to delete a file with the No Access permission.

Page 256

▶ **To view the result of the Full Control permission for the FullAccess folder**

1. Were you successful? Why or why not?

   No. Everyone has had all permissions removed for LabFiles\FullAccess\NoDelete.txt. The Administrator is a member of the Everyone group.

4. Were you successful? Why or why not?

   No, because the hidden permission for POSIX compliance that allows users to delete files in the root of a folder is only included with the standard permission Full Control.

Review Answers

Page 259

1. Which of the following statements are true about NTFS permissions? (Circle all that apply.)

   Answer f is correct.

2. Complete this sentence. When share permissions are combined with NTFS permissions the _____ permission becomes the effective permission.

   "Most restrictive" is the correct answer.

3. How would you create a home folder to which the respective user is automatically assigned the NTFS permission Full Control?

   Use %Username% to assign the user's account name to the home folder and to automatically assign the NTFS permission Full Control for the respective user's home folder.

4. Which of the following are requirements for assigning NTFS permissions? (Circle all that apply.)

   Answers a and b are correct.

5. What is the default permission once a volume is formatted with NTFS?

   The Everyone group is assigned Full Control permission.

6. Which of the following statements are true? (Circle all that apply.)

   Answers a, c, and d are correct.

7. What should you always check when a user cannot access a resource?

   You should always check the permissions for the resource to ensure that the user has the proper permissions or that the user is a member of a group with the proper permissions.

CHAPTER 7

Setting Up a Network Print Server

Lesson 1 Introduction to Windows NT Printing . . . 270

Lesson 2 Setting Up a Network Print Server and Client . . . 274

Lesson 3 Configuring a Printer . . . 290

Best Practices . . . 300

Review . . . 301

About This Chapter

This chapter introduces you to Microsoft Windows NT printing. It explains procedures and guidelines for setting up and configuring a network print server. The hands-on procedures give you an opportunity to implement and practice these tasks.

Before You Begin

To complete the lessons in this chapter, you must have:

- Completed the Setup procedures located in "About This Book."
- Knowledge about user accounts.
- Knowledge about the Administrators, Print Operators, Server Operators, and Power Users groups.
- The Microsoft Windows NT Server compact disc.
- Two user accounts created named User7-A and User7-B. Log on as Administrator. In Windows NT Explorer, expand the LabFiles folder, and then double-click Chapter7.cmd to create these accounts.

Lesson 1: Introduction to Windows NT Printing

Windows NT offers several advanced printing features. For example, as an administrator, you can remotely administer Windows NT print servers. Another advanced feature is the fact that you do not have to install a printer driver on a Windows NT client computer to enable it to use a Windows NT print server.

This lesson introduces Windows NT printing by defining key concepts and terms, and describes the requirements to set up printing.

After this lesson, you will be able to:
- Define Windows NT printing terms.
- Describe the requirements for setting up Windows NT printing.

Estimated lesson time: 10 minutes

Windows NT Printing Terms

In Windows NT, a *print device* refers to the actual hardware device that produces printed documents.

A *printer* is a software interface between the operating system and the print device. The printer defines where the document will go before it reaches the print device (to a local port, to a file, or to a remote print share), when it will go, and various other aspects of the printing process.

Network-interface print devices are print devices with their own network cards; they need not be physically connected to a print server because they are directly connected to the network.

A *print server* is the computer that runs the printer software, and that receives and processes documents from clients.

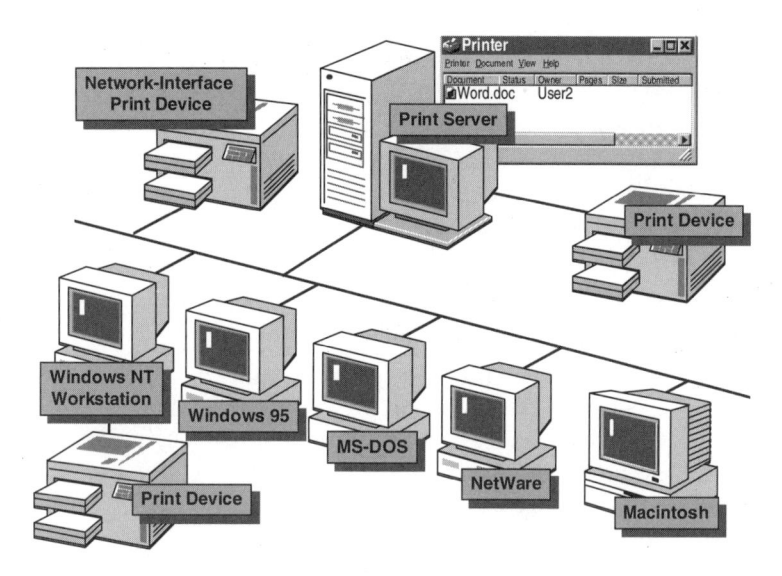

In Windows NT terminology, a *queue* is a group of documents waiting to be printed. In the NetWare and OS/2 environments, queues are the primary software interface between the program and print device: users submit documents to a queue. However, with Windows NT, the printer is that interface; therefore, the document is sent to a printer, not to a queue.

The *print spooler* is a collection of dynamic-link libraries (DLLs) that receive, process, schedule, and distribute documents. *Spooling* is the process of writing the contents of a print job to a file on disk. This file is called a spool file.

Requirements

Setting up printing on a Windows NT network requires:

- At least one computer configured as a *print server*, and running Windows NT Server or Windows NT Workstation.

    Both Windows NT Workstation and Windows NT Server can operate in either client or print server roles. However, Windows NT Workstation is limited to 10 concurrent connections from other computers and does not support Macintosh and NetWare clients.

- 16 megabytes (MB) of RAM for *x86*-based print servers controlling a small number of print devices. Managing a large number of printers or managing many large documents requires more memory.

- Sufficient disk space, especially in cases where documents are large or many of them are likely to accumulate. For example, if 10 users print large documents at the same time, the print server must have enough disk space to spool all of the documents.

- A dedicated print server, if the server is to manage many heavily used printers. When you use Windows NT for both file and print sharing, file operations have first priority. Printing transactions never slow access to files. Moreover, file operations have negligible impact on print devices attached directly to the server; parallel and serial ports are always the primary bottleneck.

- Client computers running any of the following network operating systems:
    - Windows NT
    - Windows 95
    - Windows for Workgroups
    - LAN Manager 2.*x*
    - OS/2
    - UNIX
    - NetWare*
    - Macintosh*

Note *NetWare and Macintosh clients can only access network printers on print servers running Windows NT Server. Windows NT Workstation does not support these clients.

Lesson Summary

The following information summarizes the key points in this lesson:

- In Windows NT, a *print device* refers to the actual hardware device that produces printed documents; a *printer* is a software interface between the operating system and the print device.
- Setting up printing on a Windows NT network requires one computer configured as a *print server*, running Windows NT Server or Windows NT Workstation.

Lesson 2: Setting Up a Network Print Server and Client

This lesson guides you through the steps needed to set up a network print server and client. Setting up a network print server allows multiple clients to centralize printing by using a single, high-quality print device.

After this lesson, you will be able to:
- Add and share a printer.
- Set up clients for printing.
- Access a network printer.
- Assign printer permissions to users and groups.

Estimated lesson time: 30 minutes

When setting up a network print server, you need to complete the following four key tasks:

❏ Check to see if the print device is on the Windows NT 4.0 hardware compatibility list (HCL). The HCL is included with Windows NT Workstation and Windows NT Server.
- If your print device is on the list, then the required printer driver is included with Windows NT.
- If the print device is not on the list, you will need to get a printer driver from the manufacturer of the print device, or you may be able to use a driver for a supported print device that your print device can emulate.

❏ Log on as a user who has the Full Control print permission.

The following table lists the built-in groups with the Full Control print permissions and their printer administration capabilities.

A member of this group	Can administer a printer
Administrators	On any computer in the domain running Windows NT Workstation or Windows NT Server.
Print Operators	On any domain controller.
Server Operators	On any domain controller.
Power Users	On any local computer in the domain in which the group exists.

- Add a printer—this installs the *printer driver* for the print device on the print server. The printer driver is a program that converts graphics commands into a specific printer language, such as PostScript or PCL. Windows NT supplies drivers for most of the available print devices.
- Share a printer—this allows users to connect to the printer over the network, and print to the print device. You can share a printer when you add it for the first time, or you can share a printer that was previously added but not shared.

Adding and Sharing a New Printer

If the print device is on the HCL, and you are logged on as a member of the appropriate group, you can add and share a printer. Users can then connect to it over the network.

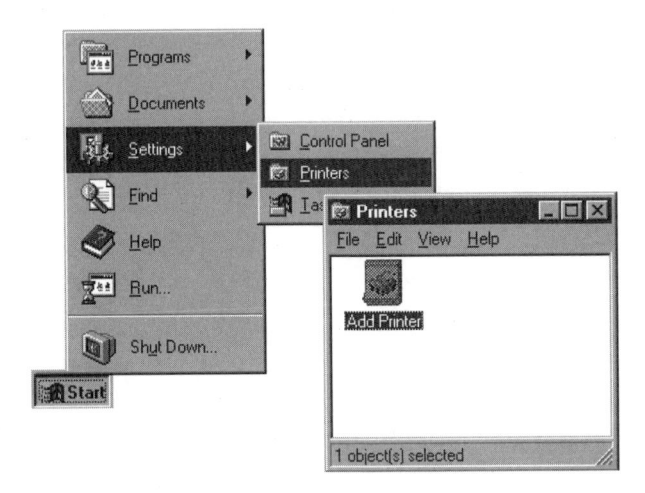

You add and share a new printer using the Add Printer Wizard. The wizard guides you through the steps needed to add a printer. The following table describes the options to add and share a new printer.

Option	Use this option to
My Computer	Designate the computer as the print server for the print device.
Available ports	Specify which port on the print server is attached to the print device.
Manufacturers and **Printers**	Install the correct printer driver on the print server. If the driver that you want is not listed, click **Other**, and then provide a driver.
Printer name	Identify the printer to the users. Type a name that is intuitive and descriptive of the print device.

(*continued*)

Option	Use this option to
Default printer	Set the default printer for all Windows-based programs on the local computer. When you add the first printer on the print server, it is automatically set as the default, and therefore, this option does not appear in the wizard until you add another printer.
Shared	Make it possible for users with the appropriate permission to connect to the printer over the network.
Share Name	Assign a share name. Select a name that tells users the type of print device or its location. Try to make this name compatible with all client computers on the network. The default share name is the printer name truncated to 8.3 characters. If you use a share name longer than an 8.3 name, not all clients will be able to connect to it.
Operating systems	Identify the types of clients, such as Windows NT and Windows 95, that will use the printer. This ensures that the appropriate printer drivers are installed on the print server.
Would you like to print a test page?	Print a test page to verify that the printer is installed correctly.

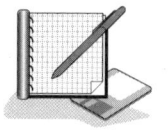

▶ **To add and share a printer**

In this procedure, you add a new printer for an HP LaserJet 4Si print device and then share it so that network clients can access it. You do not need the actual print device to do this procedure; however, if you have a printing device connected to your computer, you can substitute your print device information for the HP LaserJet 4Si.

1. Log on as Administrator.
2. Click the **Start** button, point to **Settings**, and then click **Printers**.

   The Printers window appears.
3. Double-click the Add Printer icon.

   The Add Printer Wizard starts. Notice that My Computer is selected by default. This option must be selected to set up a print server.
4. Click **Next** to add a printer on this computer.
5. Under **Available ports**, select the **LPT1** check box, and then click **Next**.
6. Under **Manufacturers**, click **HP**.

7. Under **Printers**, click **HP LaserJet 4Si**, and then click **Next**.

   Note If a printer driver for the selected print device is already installed on your computer, the Add Printer Wizard will prompt you to either keep or replace the existing driver. Replacing the existing driver is useful if you want to update it with a later version.

   In the **Printer name** box, notice that the name defaults to the selected print device. This name will appear at the top of the printer window that you will use for administering the printer. If you had multiple print devices of the same type, you would assign a printer name that easily distinguishes one printer from another. Also, if you have previously added a printer, notice that the wizard asks you if you want this new printer to be the default printer.

8. To accept the default settings, click **Next**.
9. Click **Shared**.
10. In the **Share Name** box, type **hplaser4**

    Notice the box with a list of operating systems. If you want clients to be able to automatically copy the correct printer driver when they access this printer, you must select all of the operating systems that will be printing to this computer.

    For example, select Windows 95 so that the 16-bit driver is installed on the print server. When a Windows 95 client connects to the printer, the driver is copied to the client automatically. This means that you will not need to install the driver manually on the client.

11. Click **Windows 95**, and then click **Next**.
12. When asked if you want to print a test page, click **No**, and then click **Finish**.

    If the printer driver is not already on the print server, you are prompted for the path to the files. You will find these files on both the Windows NT Server and the Windows NT Workstation compact discs.

13. If prompted for the path to the files, insert the Windows NT Server compact disc into the CD-ROM drive, and then in the **Copy files from** box, type *cd_drive***i386** (or Alpha, MIPS, or PPC if you are running Windows NT on a different platform than i386), and click **OK**.

    The printer files are copied.

    The shared printer is created, and an icon for the HP LaserJet 4Si printer appears. Notice that an open hand appears under the printer icon. This indicates that the printer is shared.

▶ To add a second printer

In this procedure, you add a second printer, but you do not share it.

1. In the Printers window, double-click the Add Printer icon.

   The Add Printer Wizard starts.

2. Click **My Computer**, and then click **Next**.

3. Under **Available ports**, select the **LPT3** check box, and then click **Next**.

4. Under **Manufacturers**, click **Canon**.

5. Under **Printers**, click **Canon Bubble-Jet BJC-600e**, and then click **Next**.

   In the **Printer name** box, notice that Windows NT automatically defaults to the printer name Canon Bubble-Jet BJC-600e.

6. Click **Next** to accept the default printer name and to avoid making this the default printer.

7. Verify that **Not Shared** is selected, and then click **Next** again.

8. When asked if you want to print a test page, click **No**, and then click **Finish**.

   If the printer driver is not already on the print server, you are prompted for the path to the files. You will find these files on the Windows NT Server and the Windows NT Workstation compact discs.

9. If prompted, in the **Copy files from** box, type the path to the files, and then click **OK**.

   An icon for the Canon Bubble-Jet BJC-600e printer appears. Notice that there is no hand under the icon, which indicates that it is not shared.

▶ To set an existing printer as the default printer

In this procedure, you set the HP LaserJet 4Si as the default printer. When a user prints a document from a program, the document will automatically be sent to this printer.

1. In the Printers window, select the HP LaserJet 4Si icon.

2. On the **File** menu, click **Set As Default**.

▶ To pause the HP LaserJet 4Si printer

In this procedure, you pause the printer to prevent it from trying to communicate with a non-existent print device. Doing this will eliminate error messages in later procedures when documents are sent to the printer.

1. In the Printers window, double-click the HP LaserJet 4Si icon.

   The HP LaserJet 4Si window appears.

2. On the **Printer** menu, click **Pause Printing**.

▶ **To print a test document to the HP LaserJet 4Si printer**

1. Click the **Start** button, point to **Programs**, point to **Accessories**, and then click **Notepad**.

2. In Notepad, type some text.

3. Arrange the Notepad window and the HP LaserJet 4Si window so that you can see the contents of each.

4. On the **File** menu, click **Print**.

    You receive a message stating that the document is printing.

    The document appears in the HP LaserJet 4Si window while it is waiting to be printed.

5. Close Notepad without saving the file.

Sharing an Existing Printer

If your computer has an existing, non-shared printer, all you have to do to share it is assign it a share name and specify the client platforms that will use the printer.

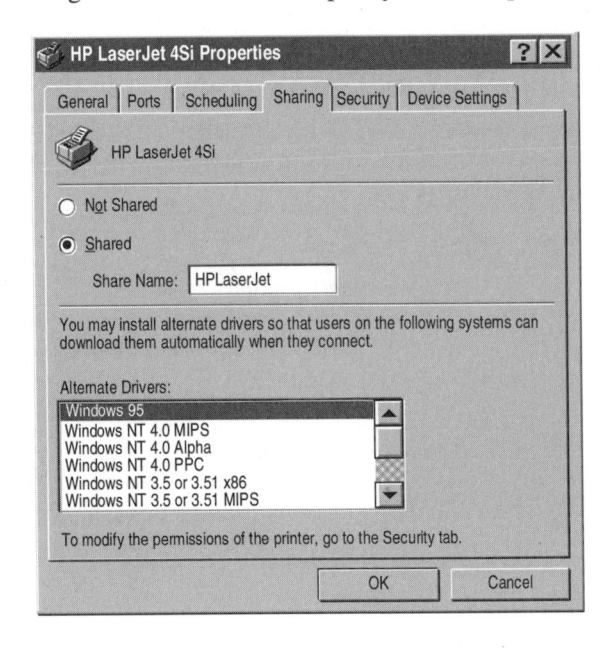

![HP LaserJet 4Si Properties dialog box showing the Sharing tab. The Shared radio button is selected with Share Name "HPLaserJet". A list of Alternate Drivers is shown including Windows 95, Windows NT 4.0 MIPS, Windows NT 4.0 Alpha, Windows NT 4.0 PPC, Windows NT 3.5 or 3.51 x86, and Windows NT 3.5 or 3.51 MIPS.]

▶ **To share an existing printer**
1. In the Printers window, select the Canon Bubble-Jet BJC-600e icon.
2. On the **File** menu, click **Sharing**.

   The **Canon Bubble-Jet BJC-600e Properties** dialog box appears.
3. Click **Shared**, and then in the **Share Name** box, type **BubbleJet**
4. Click **OK**.

   An open hand appears under the printer icon in the Printers window. This indicates that the printer is shared.

▶ **To delete a printer**
1. In the Printers window, select the Canon Bubble-Jet BJC-600e icon.
2. On the **File** menu, click **Delete**.

   You receive a message asking you to confirm that you want to delete the printer.
3. Click **Yes**.

   The printer disappears from the Printers folder.

Setting Up a Network Client

You need to make sure that users can print after you add and share a printer. The tasks that you need to perform to ensure that users can print depend on which client computers are in your network.

Windows NT and Windows 95 clients

Once you have a shared printer, and you have specified that Windows NT and Windows 95 clients will be using the printer, you do not need to do anything further. The user only needs to connect to the shared printer; the correct printer driver is automatically copied to the client.

Other Microsoft Clients

For the following clients to print to a Windows NT shared printer, you must install the appropriate printer driver locally on the client computer.

- LAN Manager 2.*x*
- Windows for Workgroups
- Windows 3.1, MS-DOS, and OS/2 (each with LAN Manager Client version 2.2c installed)

Non-Microsoft-based Clients

For non-Microsoft-based clients, you must install the appropriate printer driver locally on the client computer. Also, the print server must have the appropriate service installed.

The following table lists the non-Microsoft-based clients and their required services.

Client computer	Service
Macintosh	Services for Macintosh
NetWare	File and Print Services for NetWare (FPNW)
UNIX	TCP/IP Printer Service

Note For more information about setting up non-Microsoft-based clients, see Microsoft Windows NT Server *Concepts and Planning*.

Accessing a Network Printer

When users connect to printers, they are connecting to logical printer names that represent one or more print devices. Clients use different interfaces depending on which operating systems are used. The following illustration shows the interface for Windows NT and Windows 95 clients.

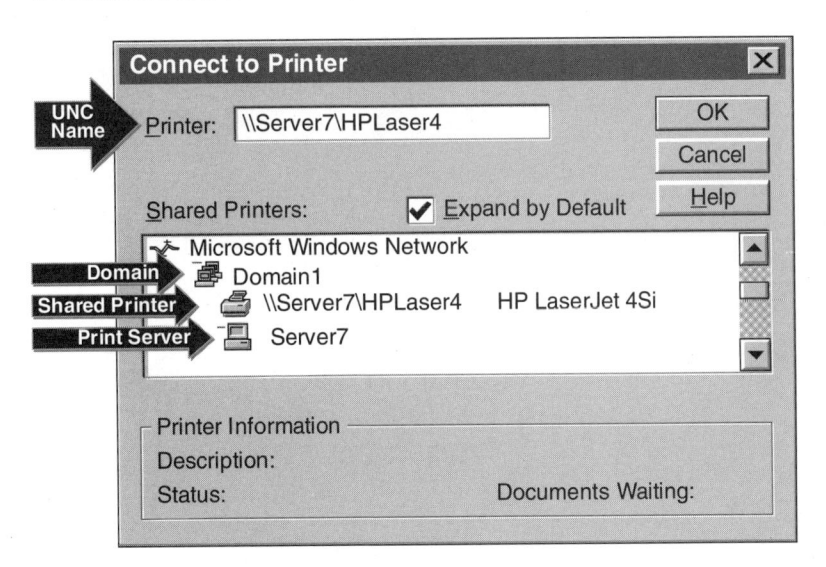

```
Connect to Printer                                          [X]

UNC
Name      Printer:  \\Server7\HPLaser4                    [ OK ]
                                                          [Cancel]
          Shared Printers:       [✓] Expand by Default    [ Help ]
                   Microsoft Windows Network
     Domain         Domain1
Shared Printer      \\Server7\HPLaser4      HP LaserJet 4Si
  Print Server      Server7

          Printer Information
          Description:
          Status:                          Documents Waiting:
```

The default print permission for all users is Print, which makes it possible for them to access any network printer.

Connecting from Clients Running Windows NT 4.0 and Windows 95

Clients running Windows NT 4.0 and Windows 95 use the Add Printer Wizard to connect to a shared printer. When they first connect, the appropriate printer driver is automatically installed into client memory.

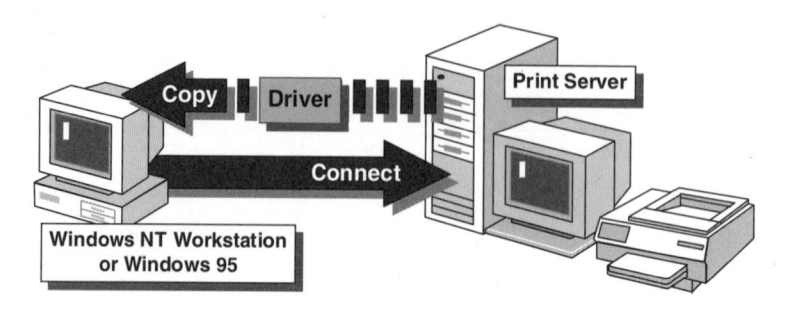

Thereafter, Windows NT–based clients and Windows 95–based clients do the following:

- A Windows NT–based client checks the printer driver each time it reconnects. If the driver is not current, a copy of the new driver is downloaded automatically.
- The printer driver for a Windows 95–based client is not automatically kept current. If you update the driver on the print server, you must manually install the driver on the Windows 95–based client.

Note Windows version 3.1 and Windows for Workgroups clients use Print Manager to connect to a printer.

▶ **To connect to a printer**

If you have two computers, do this procedure from the secondary computer.

1. In the Printers window, double-click the Add Printer icon.

   The Add Printer Wizard starts.

2. Click **Network printer server**, and then click **Next**.

   The **Connect to Printer** dialog box appears.

3. In the **Printer** box, type *print_server***hplaser4** and then click **OK**.

   –or–

   In the **Shared Printers** box, double-click *print_server*\\hplaser4.

   Note If the **Expand by Default** check box is not selected, you will need to double-click your domain name to display your print server.

   The Add Printer Wizard prompts you to use the printer as the default printer. **No** is selected by default.

4. Click **Next**.

   A message indicates that the network printer has been successfully installed. This means that the printer driver was copied to the client computer. An icon for the connected printer appears in the Printers window.

5. Click **Finish**.

Connecting from Other Clients

To connect to a printer from clients running operating systems other than Windows NT and Windows 95, use the commands specific to the clients.

- For LAN Manager clients, (either MS-DOS-based or OS/2-based), use the **net use** command. For example, type:

  net use lpt*x* *server_name**share_name*

- For NetWare clients configured with a Monolithic IPX and NetWare VLM, use the NetWare **capture** command. For example, type:

  capture *queue_name*

- For UNIX clients running TCP/IP, use the LPR utility. For example, type:

  lpr -S*server_name* **-P***share_name file_name*

- For the Apple Macintosh, use Chooser.

Assigning Printer Permissions

Once you have added and shared a printer, you need to verify that users have the appropriate permissions to print.

Printer permissions control not only who can print, but also which printing tasks a user can do. For security reasons, you may need to limit user access to certain printers. In large organizations, you may need to delegate printer administration.

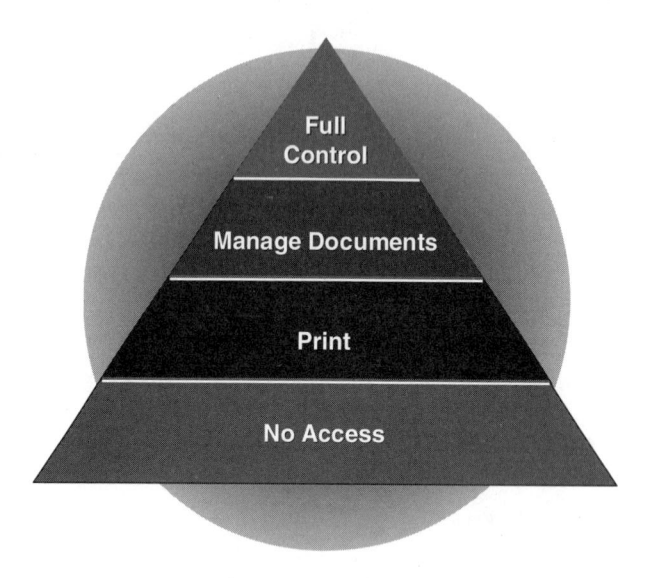

There are four levels of printer permissions: No Access, Print, Manage Documents, and Full Control. By default, all users have the Print permission as members of the Everyone group.

The following table lists the capabilities of the four levels of permissions.

Capabilities	No Access	Print (default)	Manage Documents	Full Control
Print documents		X	X	X
Pause, resume, restart, and cancel the user's own document		X	X	X
Connect to a printer		X	X	X
Control job settings for all documents			X	X

(*continued*)

Capabilities	No Access	Print (default)	Manage Documents	Full Control
Pause, restart, and delete all documents			X	X
Share a printer				X
Change printer properties				X
Delete printers				X
Change printer permissions				X

Guidelines for Assigning Permissions

Most users will only require the default Print permission. Use the following guidelines to assign other permissions:

- Remove the default Print permission from the Everyone group.
- Create a global group (or groups for larger organizations) to organize users with similar printing needs. Create a local group on the print server, add the global group to the local group, and then assign the local group the appropriate print permissions.
- Use the existing built-in Print Operators group for printer administration. Members of this group have the ability to create, delete, and manage printer shares (that is, they have the Manage Documents permission).

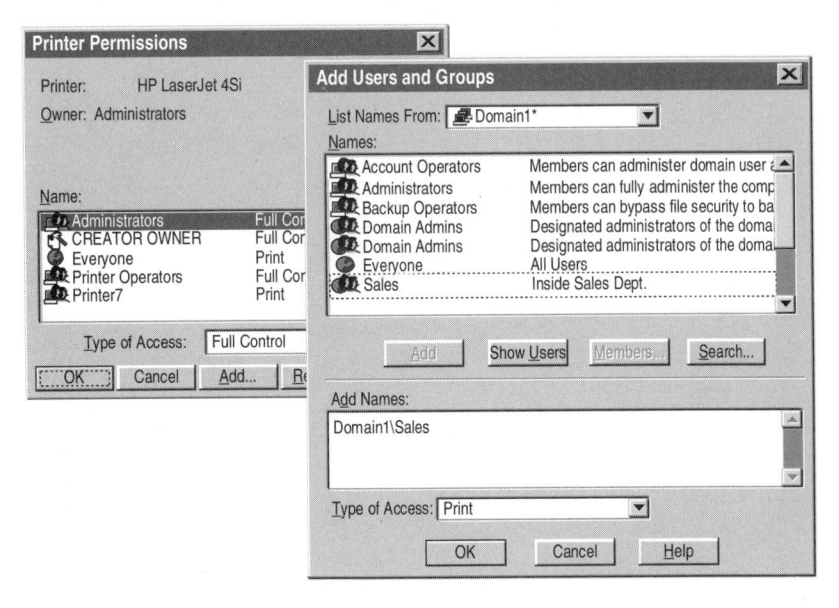

To assign permissions to a group

In this procedure, you assign the Print permission to the local groups Users, and then you remove the Print permission from the built-in group Everyone.

1. In the Printers window, select the HP LaserJet 4Si icon, and then, on the **File** menu, click **Properties**.

   The **HP LaserJet 4Si Properties** dialog box appears.

2. Click the **Security** tab, and then click **Permissions**.

   The **Printer Permissions** dialog box appears.

   Under **Name**, which built-in local groups are assigned the Full Control permission by default?

   _____

   Under **Name**, which system groups are assigned the Manage Documents permission by default?

   _____

3. Select the Everyone group, and then click **Remove**.

   The Everyone group no longer appears under **Name**.

4. Click **Add**.

   The **Add Users and Groups** dialog box appears.

5. Click **Users**, and then click **Add**.

   The Users group appears in the **Add Names** box.

6. In the **Type of Access** box, verify that **Print** is selected, and then click **OK** to return to the **Printer Permissions** dialog box.

   Notice that the User group appears with the Print permission.

7. Click **OK** to return to the **HP LaserJet 4Si Properties** dialog box.

▶ **To assign permissions to a user**

In this procedure, you assign the User7-A and User7-B user accounts different print permissions. These user accounts were created in "Before You Begin" by running the Chapter7.cmd batch file located in the LabFiles folder. To distinguish these user accounts from user accounts you may have created in other chapters, the number 7 has been appended to each user name.

- Use the same steps that you used in the previous procedure to assign the following permissions for the HP LaserJet 4Si printer to each user:
    - User7-A: Manage Documents
    - User7-B: Full Control

Note In the **Add Users and Groups** dialog box, you may need to click **Show Users** to display the user names.

▶ **To test the Manage Documents permission for User7-A**

In this procedure, you test the permission assigned to User7-A to see the options that are available.

1. Log on as User7-A.
2. Make sure that the HP LaserJet 4Si printer is paused and that there is a document waiting to be printed.
3. In the Printers window, double-click the Add Printer icon.

    What options are available to User7-A in the first **Add Printer Wizard** dialog box?

    _____

4. Close the Add Printer Wizard by clicking **Cancel**.
5. In the Printers window, select the HP LaserJet 4Si icon, and then on the **File** menu, click **Properties**.
6. Click the **Security** tab, and then click **Permissions**.

    Can you change permissions?

    _____

7. Click the **Sharing** tab.

    Are the options to share a printer available?

    _____

8. Click the **Scheduling** tab.

   Are the options to change printing hours available?

   _____

9. Click the **Ports** tab.

   Can you add a port?

   _____

10. Close the **HP LaserJet 4Si Properties** dialog box.

11. In the Printers window, with the HP LaserJet 4Si icon selected, click **File** to view the available menu options, and then click **Purge Print Documents**.

    Can you purge documents from the printer?

    _____

▶ **To test the Full Control permission for User7-B**

In this procedure, you test the permission assigned to User7-B to see the options that are available.

1. Log on as User7-B.
2. Try to perform the following tasks. In the following list, mark the tasks that are available with the Full Control permission:
   - ❑ Add a printer
   - ❑ Change a permission
   - ❑ Share a printer
   - ❑ Schedule a printer
   - ❑ Add additional ports
   - ❑ Purge a printer
3. Log off.

Lesson Summary

The following information summarizes the key points in this lesson:

- Windows NT includes printer drivers for all print devices on the Windows NT 4.0 hardware compatibility list (HCL).
- Setting up a network print server requires that you are a member of the built-in Administrators, Print Operators, Server Operators, or Power Users group.
- When you add a printer, specify all of the Windows NT and Windows 95 client operating systems (under **Alternate Drivers** on the **Sharing** tab) that will be connecting to the print server. Windows NT will then install the appropriate printer drivers on the print server for clients to download.
- If the appropriate printer drivers have been installed on the print server, Windows NT and Windows 95 clients download these automatically when they connect to the shared printer.
- There are four different print permissions—Full Control, Manage Documents, Print, and No Access. By default, the built-in Everyone group is assigned the Print permission.

For more information on	See
Setting up a print server and client	Chapter 5, "Setting Up Print Servers," in Microsoft Windows NT Server *Concepts and Planning*.
	Chapter 7, "Printing," in the *Microsoft Windows NT Workstation Resource Kit*.
Connecting to printers from non-Microsoft clients	The third-party product documentation specific to the client operating system.

Lesson 3: Configuring a Printer

This lesson shows you how to create a printing pool and set priorities between printers.

This lesson requires that you have completed Lesson 2.

After this lesson, you will be able to:
- Create a printing pool.
- Set priorities between printers.
- Schedule printers to print during specified hours.
- Assign forms to paper trays.
- Set separator pages between print jobs.

Estimated lesson time: 20 minutes

Creating a Printing Pool

If a print device is heavily used, you can create a printing pool to automatically distribute the print jobs to an available print device. A printing pool is one printer connected to multiple print devices through multiple ports of the print server. A printing pool is useful in a network with a high volume of printing because it decreases the time that documents wait in the print queue. It also simplifies administration because multiple print devices can be managed from a single printer.

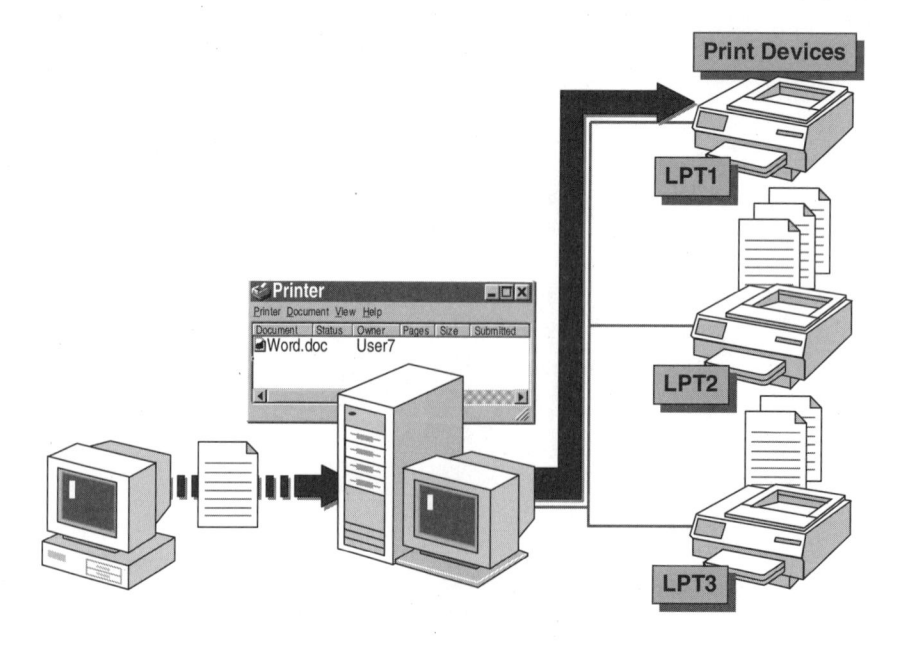

With a printing pool created, the user prints a document without having to find out which print device is available. The printer checks for an available port and sends documents to ports in the order that they were added. Adding the port connected to the fastest print device first ensures that documents are sent to the device that can print the fastest before they are routed to slower print devices in the printing pool.

To create a printing pool, you must first enable printer pooling, and then specify the ports for the print devices that will be pooled on the **Ports** tab of the *printer_name* Properties dialog box. You can also enable printer pooling in the Add Printer Wizard when you add the printer. All print devices to be pooled must use the same printer driver.

Tip Locate the print devices in a printing pool in close proximity, so that users do not have to search several locations for their documents.

▶ **To create a printing pool**

In this procedure, you create a printing pool for three HP LaserJet 4Si print devices attached to LPT1, LPT2, and COM2.

1. Log on as Administrator.
2. In the Printers window, select the HP LaserJet 4Si icon.
3. On the **File** menu, click **Properties**.

   The **HP LaserJet 4Si Properties** dialog box appears.
4. Click the **Ports** tab.

   The **Ports** tab appears, and **LPT1** is selected.
5. Select **Enable printer pooling**.
6. Click **COM2**, and then click **LPT2**.
7. Click **OK**.

Setting Priorities Between Printers

You may need to set priorities between groups of documents if a user prints time-sensitive documents (for example, a proposal for a sales meeting) after large documents have already been sent to the printer (for example, a weekly accounting report).

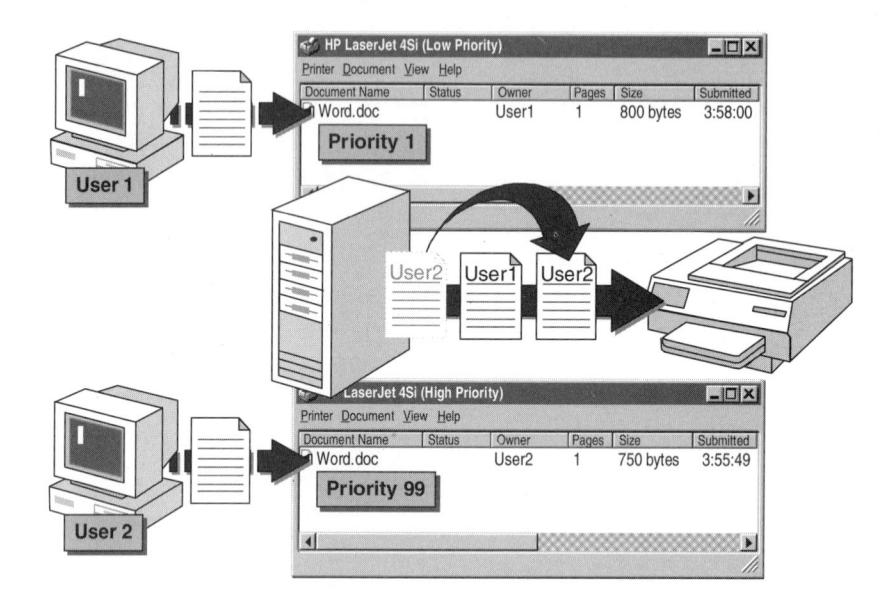

Setting priorities between printers makes it possible for you to set priorities between groups of documents. For example, you can set priorities so that all documents from executives print before other users, or so that critical documents always print before lower priority documents.

Setting priorities between printers requires that you do the following:

- Add two or more printers for the same print device. These printers must:
    - Be on the same print server.
    - Use the same port to connect to the print device. The port can be either a physical port on the print server or the UNC name of a network printer. For example: \\Server7\HPLaserJet
- Set a different priority for each printer connected to the print device. Then have users print to printers with the appropriate priority.

    For example, if User1 sends documents to a printer with the lowest priority, which is 1, while User2 sends documents to a printer with the highest priority, which is 99, User2's documents will always print before User1's.

Scheduling Printers

You can control when documents are printed by setting the priority on a printer, by setting the available printing times, and by changing how the printer processes documents. You perform these tasks in the *printer_name* **Properties** dialog box.

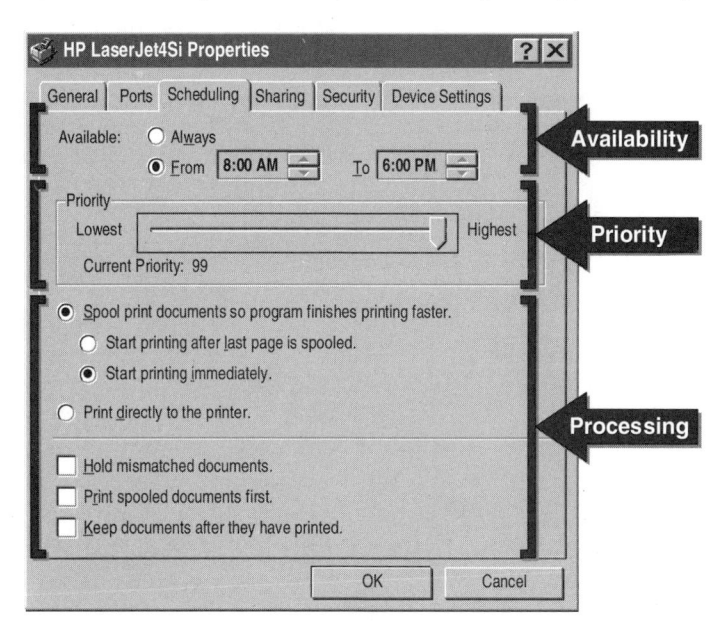

The following table describes tasks to schedule printers and under what circumstances you would set them.

Perform this task	If you want
Set available printing times	To print large documents during off-peak hours.
Set priorities between printers	To always print critical documents first. 1 is the lowest priority (and the default setting); 99 is the highest priority.
Change how the printer processes documents	To start printing large documents immediately, before they are completely processed.

The following table describes the options for scheduling a task.

Options	Description
Spool print documents so program finishes printing faster	Either this option or the **Print directly to the printer** option is selected. If you choose this option, the documents will spool. This option has two related options that you must choose between.
• **Start printing after last page is spooled**	The printer will not print a document until it is completely spooled. This is useful for documents that are assigned a low priority. Documents that are assigned a higher priority will start printing immediately.
• **Start printing immediately**	The printer starts printing a document before it is completely spooled, which means that it is printed sooner. This is useful for documents that are assigned a high priority.
Print directly to the printer	The document does not spool, which decreases printing time. Select this option only for a non-shared printer. This may be useful for third-party programs that use their own spooling process.
Hold mismatched documents	Documents that do not match the configuration of the printer will not be printed. This prevents errors resulting from documents that use paper sizes different than letter.
Print spooled documents first	A spooled document is printed before a partially spooled document.
Keep documents after they have printed	Documents remain in the print spooler after they are printed, and can be quickly resubmitted for printing.

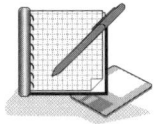

▶ **To set a printer priority**

In this procedure, you set the priority on a printer to the highest priority, so that all documents sent to that printer will be printed before documents that are sent to a printer with a lower priority.

1. In the Printers window, select the HP LaserJet 4Si icon.
2. On the **File** menu, click **Properties**.

    The **HP LaserJet 4Si Properties** dialog box appears.

3. Click the **Scheduling** tab.

    Under **Priority**, notice that the default priority is set to 1, the lowest priority.

4. Move the slider to the highest priority.

    Notice that the highest priority is 99. Documents in a printer with this priority will be printed before documents in a printer with lower priorities.

    Leave the **HP LaserJet 4Si Properties** dialog box open for the next procedure.

▶ **To set the available printing hours**

In this procedure, you set the available printing hours so that print jobs are printed during off-peak hours.

1. In the **HP LaserJet 4Si Properties** dialog box, notice that by default, the printer is available during all hours.
2. Click **From**.
3. Set the available printer hours from 12:00 A.M. until 4:00 A.M.
4. Click **OK**.

▶ **To test the available printing hours**

1. In the Printers window, double-click the HP LaserJet 4Si icon.

    The **HP LaserJet 4Si** window appears.
2. On the **Printer** menu, verify that the **Set As Default Printer** command is selected.
3. On the **Printer** menu, click **Pause Printing** to cancel the selection (remove the check mark).

    Note that if you already turned off the **Pause Printing** menu command for the printer in a previous procedure, this menu command will already appear without a check mark next to it.
4. In the LabFiles\Public\Library folder, double-click the file named Bronte.txt.
5. Arrange the Bronte–Notepad window and the HP LaserJet 4Si window so that you can see the contents of each.
6. Print Bronte.txt.

    Look at the status of the file to be printed in the HP LaserJet 4Si window and notice that the status of the document is blank (after it has finished spooling). This indicates that the printer is not attempting to print the document.
7. Close Notepad.

Assigning Forms to Paper Trays

In Windows NT, a *form* refers to the paper size and type used by a print device. If a print device has multiple trays that hold different types of forms, you can assign a form to a specific paper tray. Users can then select the form from within the program that they are using. When they print a document, the print job will be routed to the correct paper tray.

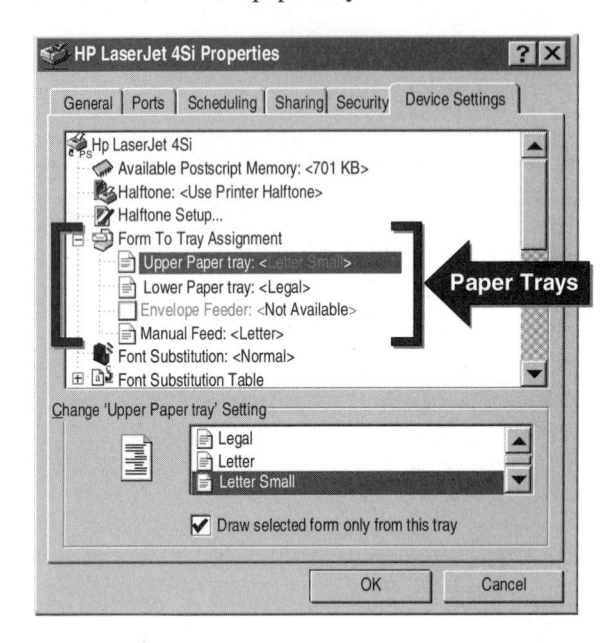

The default form setting for a paper tray is Letter. Examples of forms are:

- Legal size
- Envelopes #10
- Note size
- Letter small

▶ **To assign a form type to a paper tray**

In this procedure, you assign a paper type (form) to a paper tray so that when users print a document using a specified form, the print job will automatically be routed to and adjusted for the correct tray.

1. Make sure that the HP LaserJet 4Si window is open.
2. On the **Printer** menu, click **Properties**.

    The **HP LaserJet 4Si Properties** dialog box appears.

3. Click the **Device Settings** tab.

   Notice that there are multiple selections under **Form To Tray Assignment**. This is because no specific tray assignments have been configured.

4. Click **Upper Paper tray**.

5. Under **Change 'Upper Paper tray' Setting**, click **Letter Small**.

   Notice that **Upper Paper tray** indicates that Letter Small is the default paper size.

6. Click **OK**.

Setting a Separator Page

Separator pages have two functions:

- To identify and separate printed documents.
- To switch print devices between the different print modes. Print modes process documents into a format that the print device understands.

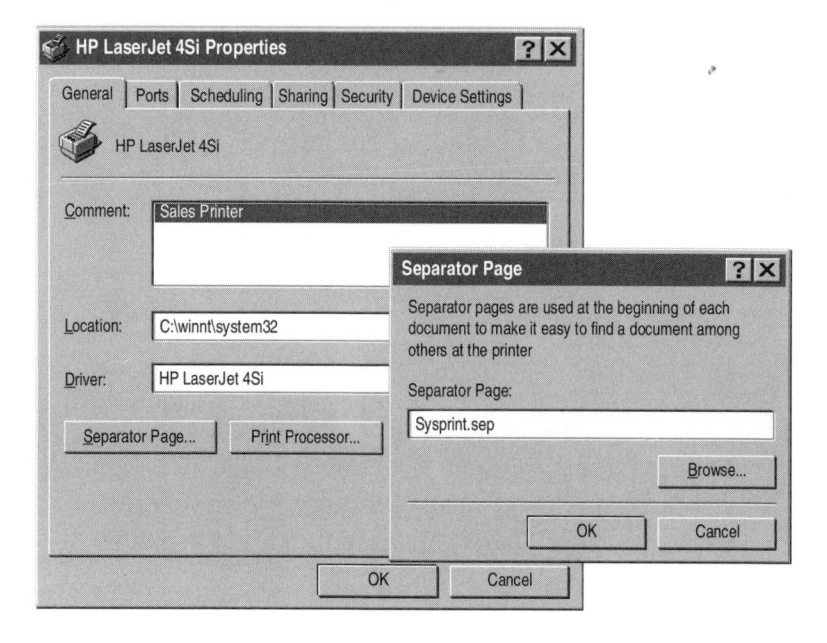

Windows NT includes three separator page files. They are located in the *systemroot*\System32 folder.

The following table describes the function of the default separator pages.

File name	Function
Sysprint.sep	Prints a page before each document. Compatible with PostScript printing devices.
Pcl.sep	Switches the printing mode to PCL for HP-series printing devices and prints a page before each document.
Pscript.sep	Switches the printing mode to PostScript for HP-series printing devices, but does not print a page before each document.

▶ **To set up a separator page**

In this procedure, you set up a separator page to print between documents. This separator page includes the user's name and the date and time that the document was printed.

1. Make sure that the **HP LaserJet 4Si** window is open.
2. On the **Printer** menu, click **Properties**.

   The **HP LaserJet 4Si Properties** dialog box appears.
3. On the **General** tab, click **Separator Page**.

   The **Separator Page** dialog box appears.
4. Click **Browse**.

   Another **Separator Page** dialog box appears.

   Notice the three default separator page files in the System32 folder.
5. Click Sysprint.sep, and then click **Open**.

   The first **Separator Page** dialog box appears, and it has the path and file name of the selected separator page.
6. Click **OK** to return to the **HP LaserJet 4Si Properties** dialog box.
7. Click **OK**, and then log off.

Lesson Summary

The following information summarizes the key points in this lesson:

- A printing pool is one printer connected to multiple print devices through multiple ports of the print server.

- You can create a printing pool to automatically distribute print jobs to an available print device. The distribution is transparent to users.

- Setting priorities between printers makes it possible for you to set priorities between groups' documents.

- Setting priorities between printers requires two or more printers for the same print device. The printers must be on the same print server.

- Documents can be scheduled to print between certain hours, reducing print device load during peak traffic hours.

For more information on	See
Configuring printers	Chapter 5, "Setting Up Print Servers," in Microsoft Windows NT Server *Concepts and Planning*.
	Chapter 7, "Printing," in the *Microsoft Windows NT Workstation Resource Kit*.

Best Practices

The following checklist provides best practices for setting up a network printer:

- ❏ Use the same guidelines that apply to any shared resource. Create a local "*printer_name* Users" group with Print permissions and then put global groups into the local group.
- ❏ Remove the Print permission from the default group Everyone. Instead, assign the Print permission to the built-in group Users. This will limit printer use to those users in the domain for which you have created accounts.
- ❏ Distribute the administrative load. If security is not an issue, assign the "*printer_name* Users" group the Manage Documents or Full Control print permission, or add a user to the Print Operators group to manage the printer.
- ❏ Secure the print device in a locked room if it is used for confidential information. Let only members of the Administrators group manage the printer.
- ❏ For printing pools, place the print devices physically close to each other. Then users do not have to check separate locations for their printed documents.
- ❏ Create multiple printers with different schedules to reduce printer traffic during peak hours. Have users send large documents, such as accounting reports, to a printer that is available only at night so that those documents will wait until off-peak hours to be printed.
- ❏ Document information about printers and the users who have the ability to administer them.
- ❏ Use the Windows NT auditing feature to keep track of changes made by users who manage network printers. Auditing is covered in Chapter 9, "Auditing Resources and Events."

Note If you want to remove the accounts that were created by running the Chapter7.cmd file at the beginning of this chapter, log on as Administrator, and then double-click DeleteChapter7.cmd in the Cleanup folder on the Supplemental Material compact disc.

Review

The following questions are intended to reinforce key information presented in this chapter. If you are unable to answer a question, review the lesson and then try the question again.

1. What is the difference between a printer and a print device?

2. What is the default print permission for users?

3. Scenario: You have added and shared a printer. What do you do to set up clients running Windows NT 4.0 so that they can print, and why?

4. What can you do to make sure one user's documents are printed before another user's documents?

5. Why would you create a printing pool?

Answer Key

Procedure Answers

Page 286

▶ **To assign permissions to a group**

2. Under **Name**, which built-in local groups are assigned the Full Control permission by default?

   The Administrators, Print Operators, and Server Operators groups.

   Under **Name**, which system groups are assigned the Manage Documents permission by default?

   The CREATOR OWNER system group.

Page 287–288

▶ **To test the Manage Documents permission for User7-A**

3. What options are available to User7-A in the first **Add Printer Wizard** dialog box?

   User7-A can connect to a printer on another computer.

6. Can you change permissions?

   No, because User7-A only has permission to view security information.

7. Are the options to share a printer available?

   No, because the Manage Documents permission does not give you the capability to share a printer.

8. Are the options to change printing hours available?

   No, because the Manage Documents permission only allows you to control settings on all print jobs, not settings on the printer.

9. Can you add a port?

   No, because the Manage Documents permission does not give you the capability to change printer properties.

11. Can you purge documents from the printer?

    No, because the Manage Documents permission does not give you the capability to delete other user's print jobs.

Page 288

▶ **To test the Full Control permission for User7-B**

2. Try to perform the following tasks. In the following list, mark the tasks that are available with the Full Control permission:

   User7-B can perform all of these tasks except add a printer.

Review Answers

1. What is the difference between a printer and a print device?

   A printer is the software interface between the operating system and the print device. The print device is the hardware that produces printed documents.

2. What is the default print permission for users?

   The Everyone group is assigned the Print permission. All users are automatically members of that group by default.

3. Scenario: You have added and shared a printer. What do you do to set up clients running Windows NT 4.0 so that they can print, and why?

   Do nothing to set them up to print. When the client connects to the shared printer, Windows NT automatically copies the printer driver to the client.

4. What can you do to make sure one user's documents are printed before another user's documents?

   Add an additional printer with a higher priority for the same print device. For the user whose documents you want printed first, set that user's default printer to be the one with the higher priority.

5. Why would you create a printing pool?

   To automatically distribute print jobs to multiple print devices so that they are printed faster. It is easier to manage one printer than to manage a printer for each print device.

CHAPTER 8

Administering a Network Print Server

Lesson 1 Introduction to Administering Print Servers . . . 307

Lesson 2 Managing Documents . . . 310

Lesson 3 Managing Printers . . . 315

Lesson 4 Identifying Printing Problems . . . 322

Review . . . 326

About This Chapter

This chapter presents the post-installation and configuration print server administration tasks, including tasks related to managing documents and printers, and identifying printing problems. In the hands-on procedures, you will have an opportunity to perform many of these tasks on your own printer.

Before You Begin

To complete the lessons in this chapter, you must have:

- Completed the Setup procedures located in "About This Book."
- The knowledge and skills covered in Chapter 7, "Setting Up a Network Print Server."
- Installed a printer on your computer. If your server does not have a printer installed, see Chapter 7, "Setting Up a Network Print Server," for instructions on how to install it.
- Knowledge about the Administrators, Print Operators, Server Operators, and Power Users groups.
- A user account created named User8 that is a member of the local Print Operators group. Log on as Administrator. In Windows NT Explorer, expand the LabFiles folder, and then double-click Chapter8.cmd to create the user account and add it to the Print Operators group.

Lesson 1: Introduction to Administering Print Servers

This lesson introduces you to print server administration tasks and the requirements for performing the tasks.

After this lesson, you will be able to:
- List the print server administration tasks.
- Describe the requirements for administering printers.

Estimated lesson time: 10 minutes

The term *administering a print server* refers to tasks that are done *after* the print server is installed and configured.

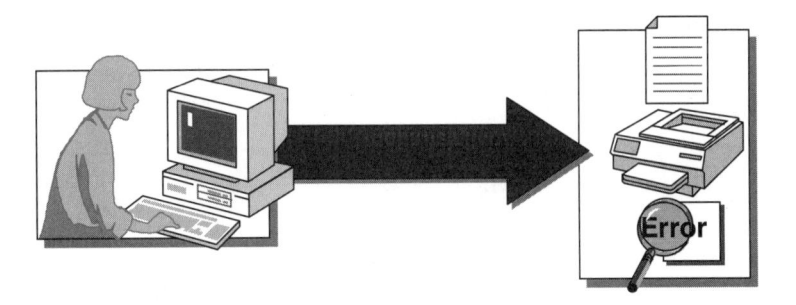

You can administer a print server locally or remotely over the network. Administration tasks include:

- Managing documents, which includes the following tasks:
    - Deleting a document
    - Setting a notification
    - Changing a document priority
    - Setting a printing time for a document

- Managing printers, which includes the following tasks:
    - Pausing and resuming a printer
    - Redirecting documents
    - Changing print device settings
    - Purging a printer
    - Taking ownership of a printer

- Identifying and solving common printing problems.

Print Server Administration Requirements

Print server administration can be done from any computer running Windows NT.

To perform administration tasks, you must meet one of the following requirements:

- You must be a member of the Administrators, Print Operators, Server Operators, or Power Users groups on the print server.

    The following table describes the built-in capabilities required for administration.

Group	Built-in capabilities
Print Operators and Server Operators	Add and remove printers
	Share printers
	Take ownership of a printer
Power Users (on Windows NT Workstation and member servers only)	Add and remove printers
	Share printers
	Take ownership of a printer

- You must have the Full Control print permission for the printer. The Full Control print permission is assigned to the Administrators, Print Operators, Server Operators, and Power Users group by default.

Note If you have the Manage Documents print permission for the printer, you can perform administration tasks on documents only.

Lesson Summary

The following information summarizes key points in this lesson:

- Print server administration tasks include administering documents and printers and troubleshooting printing problems.
- The term *administering a print server* refers to tasks that are done *after* the print server is installed and configured.
- Print server administration can be done from any computer running Windows NT as long as you have the appropriate permissions.
- To perform printer administration tasks, you must be a member of the Administrators, Print Operators, Server Operators, or Power Users group on the print server or have the Full Control print permission for the printer.
- Administering documents only requires the Manage Documents print permission for the printer.

For more information on	See
Administrators, Print Operators, Server Operators, or Power Users groups	Chapter 3, "Setting Up Group Accounts," in this book.
	Chapter 2, "Working With User and Group Accounts," in Microsoft Windows NT Server *Concepts and Planning*.
Print permissions	Chapter 7, "Setting Up a Network Print Server," in this book.

Lesson 2: Managing Documents

The term *managing documents* refers to tasks that control when users' documents are printed, and who gets notified when the documents are printed. This lesson explains how to control print jobs by setting the notification, priority, and available printing time for a document.

After this lesson, you will be able to:
- Set a notification for a document.
- Set the printing time for a document to print.
- Delete a document from a printer.

Estimated lesson time: 20 minutes

Setting a Notification, Priority, and Printing Time

You can control print jobs by setting the notification, priority, and printing hours. To set the notification, priority, and printing hours for a document, a user must have the Full Control or Manage Documents print permission for the appropriate printer.

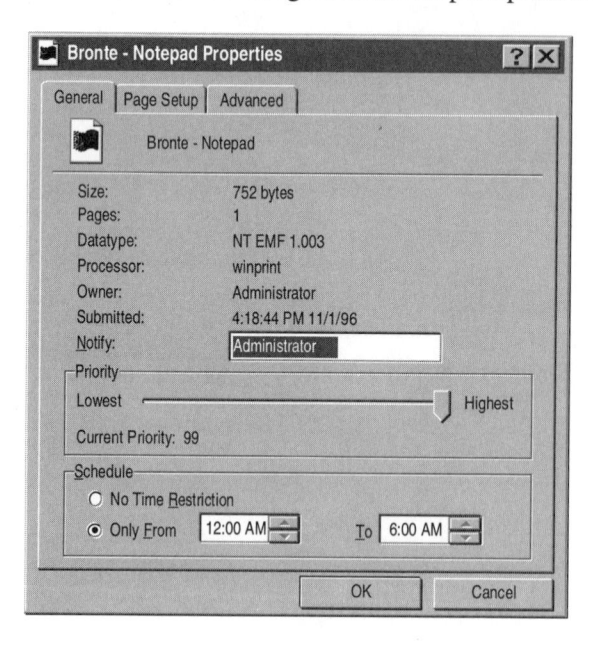

The following table describes the situations in which you would set a notification, change a document priority, or set available printing hours.

Do this	In this situation
Set a notification	Change the print notification when someone other than the user who printed the document needs to retrieve it—for example, to notify an editor when the document is ready for him or her to pick up.
Change a document priority	Change a priority so that a critical document is printed before other documents.
Set available printing hours	Set night hours for large documents that take a long time to be printed. This allows you to make sure that the document spools correctly during work hours, but that it is printed at night.

▶ **To prepare the printer**

In this procedure, you pause the printer and then print two documents to provide documents to manage.

1. Log on as Administrator.
2. Click the **Start** button, point to **Settings**, and then click **Printers**.

    The Printers window appears.
3. Double-click the icon for your printer.

    The *printer_name* window appears.
4. On the **Printer** menu, click **Set As Default Printer**.
5. On the **Printer** menu, click **Pause Printing** to pause the printer.

    Notice that the title bar now shows that your printer is paused.
6. Leave the *printer_name* window open, and switch to Windows NT Explorer.
7. Expand the LabFiles\Public\Library folder, hold down the SHIFT key, and then click both Hamlet.txt and Bronte.txt.
8. Right-click the selected documents, and then, on the shortcut menu that appears, click **Print**.
9. Switch back to the *printer_name* window.

    Both documents appear in the *printer_name* window.

▶ To set a notification

In this procedure, you set a notification so that User8 receives a message when a document has finished printing.

1. In the *printer_name* window, click Bronte.txt.
2. On the **Document** menu, click **Properties**.

   The **Bronte-Notepad Properties** dialog box appears.

3. In the **Notify** box, type **user8**

   Leave the dialog box open and continue to the next procedure.

▶ To change a document priority

In this procedure, you increase the priority of Bronte.txt for User8.

1. On the **General** tab of the **Bronte-Notepad Properties** dialog box, notice the default priority of 1, which is the lowest priority.
2. Use the slider to increase the priority of the document to 50, and then click **OK**.

   Nothing visibly changes in the *printer_name* window, but the document will be printed before other documents with a priority lower than 50, and after documents with a priority higher than 50.

   Leave the dialog box open and continue to the next procedure.

▶ To set available printing hours for a document

1. In the *printer_name* window, click Hamlet.txt.
2. On the **Document** menu, click **Properties**.

   The **Hamlet-Notepad Properties** dialog box appears.

3. Under **Schedule**, make sure that **Only From** is selected.
4. In the **Only From** box, type **12:30 AM**
5. In the **To** box, type **3:30 AM** and then click **OK**.

   Nothing changes visibly in the *printer_name* window, but the printer will not begin to print the Hamlet.txt file before 12:30 A.M. or after 3:30 A.M. If the printer has not completed printing the documents ahead of Hamlet.txt before 3:30 A.M., the Hamlet.txt will be held until 12:20 A.M. on the following day.

   Leave the *printer_name* window open and continue to the next topic.

Deleting a Document from a Printer

You may need to delete a document before it is printed. For example, if the document has the wrong printer settings, delete it before it is printed incorrectly.

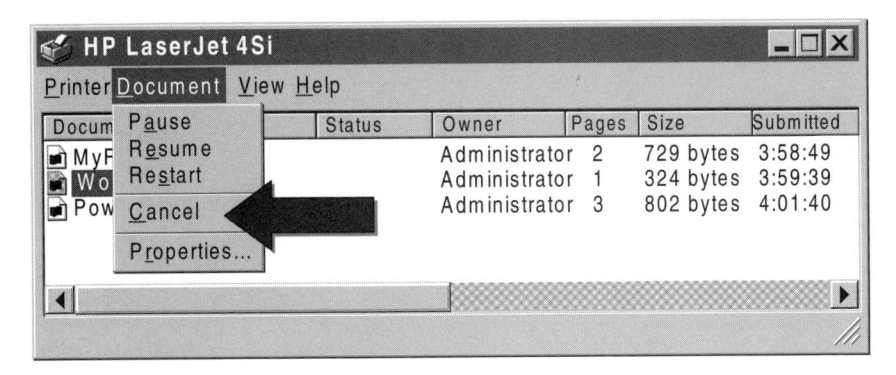

To delete other users' documents, a user must have the Full Control or Manage Documents print permission. Users with the Print permission can delete their own documents.

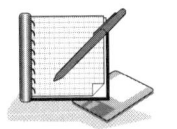

▶ **To delete a document using the DELETE key**

1. In the *printer_name* window, click Bronte.txt.
2. Press the DELETE key.

   Notice that the document disappears from the window.

▶ **To delete a document using the Cancel command**

1. In the *printer_name* window, click Hamlet.txt.
2. On the **Document** menu, click **Cancel**.

   Notice that the document disappears from the window.
3. Close the *printer_name* window.
4. Log off.

Lesson Summary

The following information summarizes the key points in this lesson:

- To set the notification, priority, and printing hours for a document, a user must have the Full Control or Manage Documents print permission for the appropriate printer.
- Users with the Print permission can delete their own documents. A user must have the Full Control or Manage Documents permission to delete other users' documents.
- Set a notification when someone other than the user who prints a documents needs to retrieve it.
- Increase a document's priority so that critical documents are printed before other documents.
- Set available printing hours to schedule large documents so that they are printed during off-peak hours.

For more information on	See
Print permissions	Chapter 7, "Setting Up a Network Print Server," in this book.

Lesson 3: Managing Printers

The term *managing printers* refers to tasks that affect the entire printer, not individual documents. This lesson guides you through the steps to perform printer management tasks and explains the situations in which these tasks are useful.

After this lesson, you will be able to:
- Redirect documents to a different printer.
- Pause and resume a printer.
- Purge all the documents in a printer.
- Take ownership of a printer.

Estimated lesson time: 20 minutes

Pausing, Resuming, and Purging a Printer

When you manage a printer, your actions affect all of the documents that are sent to the printer. Pausing, resuming, and purging a printer may be necessary if there is a printing problem.

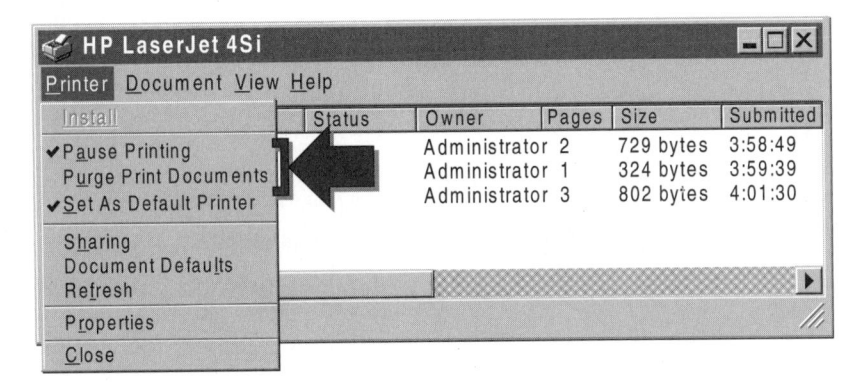

The following table describes the situations in which you would pause, resume, or purge a printer.

Do this	In this situation
Pause a printer	If there is a problem with the print device.
Resume a printer	When a non-operational print device is repaired.
Purge a printer	If you need to delete all documents, such as old documents in the spooler.

▶ **To prepare the printer**

In this procedure, you pause the printer and then print two documents to prepare the printer for the following procedures.

1. Log on as Administrator.
2. Click the **Start** button, point to **Settings**, and then select the icon for your printer.
3. On the **Printer** menu, make sure that **Pause Printing** is selected and that this printer is set as the default printer.
4. Switch to Windows NT Explorer, and then expand the LabFiles\Public folder.
5. Right-click Expenses.doc, and then on the shortcut menu that appears, click **Print**.
6. Repeat step 5 to print the document a second time.

▶ **To purge a printer**

1. Switch to the *printer_name* window.
2. On the **Printer** menu, click **Purge Print Documents**.

   Notice that all documents disappear from the *printer_name* window.

▶ **To resume the *printer_name* printer**

- On the **Printer** menu, click **Pause Printing** to resume the printer.

  The check mark next to the **Pause Printing** menu command is removed. Also, the title bar on the printer no longer says "Paused."

Redirecting Documents

If a print device becomes faulty, you may need to redirect documents in a printer to a different print device. This will prevent users from having to resubmit print jobs that are already in the printer. You can redirect documents to a print device on the local print server or on a different print server. However, both print devices must use the same printer driver.

Redirecting Documents on the Local Print Server

To redirect documents to a different print device on the same print server, you need to select the port of the other print device.

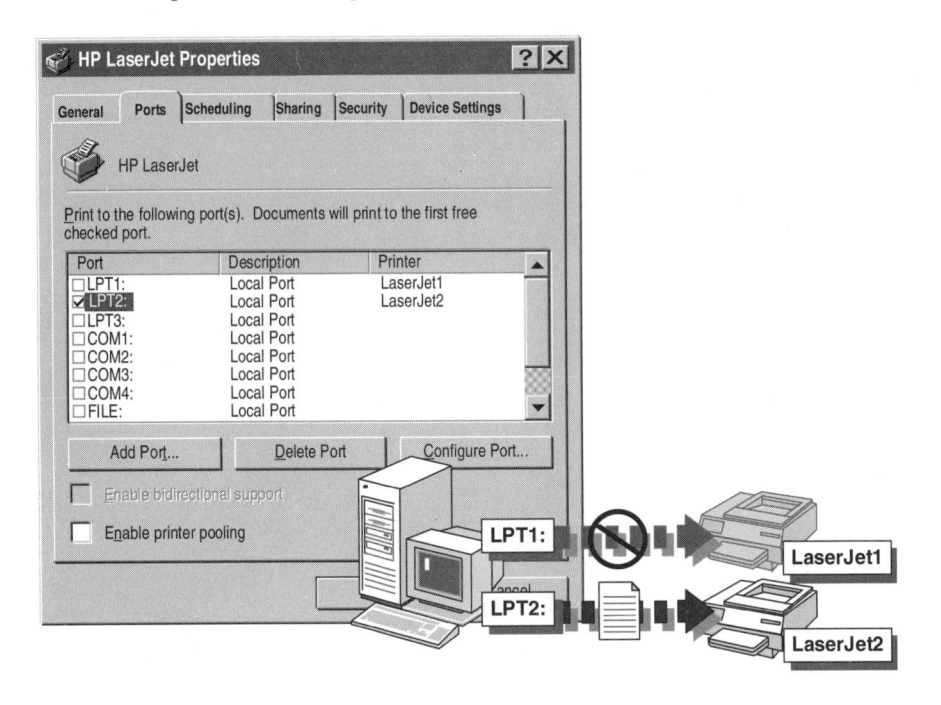

▶ **To redirect documents to a local print device**

In this procedure, you go through the steps to redirect documents to a different print device on the local print server even though you do not have a second print device.

1. In the *printer_name* window, on the **Printer** menu, click **Properties**.

   The *printer_name* **Properties** dialog box appears.

2. Click the **Ports** tab.

   The **Ports** tab displays the current configuration of the ports.

3. Select the **LPT2** check box, and then click **OK**.

   Note You may need to remove the original port to ensure that the documents print to the redirected port.

4. Click **OK**.

   If you had two print devices, the document would begin printing on the other print device.

5. Log off.

Redirecting Documents to a Different Print Server

To redirect documents to a print device on a different print server, you have to add a local port for the other print server and provide the print server name and the appropriate share name for the print device, as shown in the following illustration.

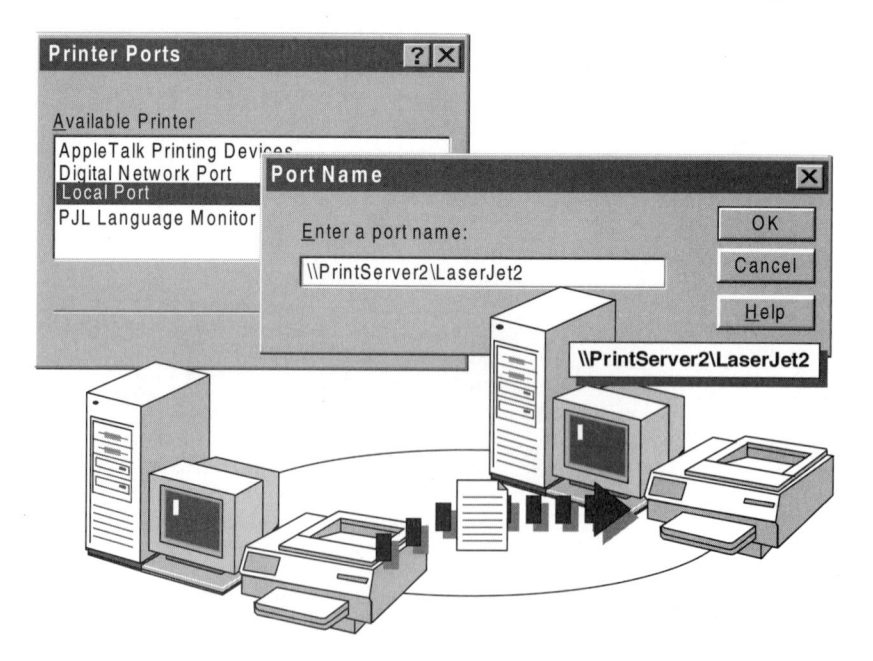

To redirect documents to a different print server, the other print device must already exist and be shared on the print server.

The following checklist provides an overview of the tasks required to redirect documents to a different print server. These tasks must be performed on the original print server from any computer running Windows NT:

- On the **Ports** tab of the *printer_name* **Properties** dialog box, click to clear the check box of the port that you want to discontinue using, and then click **Add Port**.

- In the **Printer Ports** dialog box, click **Local Port**, and then click **New Port**.

    When adding a network port, you can only add an existing port. Also, you cannot create, delete, or configure ports over the network. You must do this at the local print server.

- Type the name of the other print server and share name of the shared print device, click **OK,** and then click **Close**. (For example: *other_print_server**share_name*)

    The new port appears as the selected port for the printer.

Taking Ownership of a Printer

Taking ownership of a printer lets you change printer administrators. This is useful if the printer administrator leaves the company or if you need to change printer permissions.

Taking ownership of a printer is similar to taking ownership of a folder or file. The user who installed the printer owns it. If the user who installed the printer is a member of the Administrators group, the Administrators group owns it. Members of the Administrators group can take ownership of any printer.

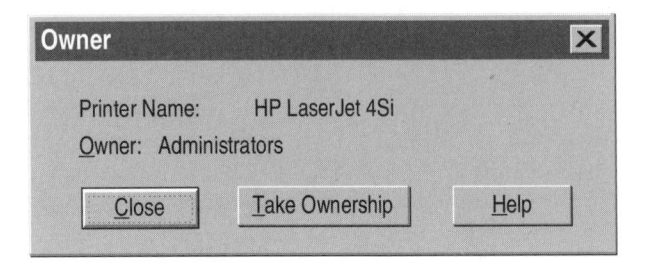

```
Owner                                          [X]

   Printer Name:    HP LaserJet 4Si
   Owner:  Administrators

        [ Close ]   [ Take Ownership ]   [ Help ]
```

▶ **To take ownership of a printer**

In this procedure, you take ownership of a printer that is owned by another user.

1. Log on as User8.
2. In the Printers window, double-click the icon for your printer.

    The *printer_name* window appears.

3. On the **Printer** menu, click **Properties**.

    The *printer_name* **Properties** dialog box appears.

4. Click the **Security** tab, and then click **Ownership**.

   Notice the current owner of the printer. If the owner is Administrators, it is because the user who created the printer was either logged on as Administrator or as a user who was a member of the Administrators group.

5. Click **Take Ownership**.

   Were you able to take ownership? Why or why not?

   _____

6. Click **Owner** to verify that User8 is the new owner.
7. Click **OK** to close the *printer_name* dialog box.

Lesson Summary

The following information summarizes key points in this lesson:

- To redirect documents in a printer to a different print device, both print devices must use the same printer driver.
- To redirect documents to a different print device on the same print server, you need to select the port of the other print device.
- To redirect documents to a print device on a different print server, you have to add a local port for the other print server and provide the print server name and the appropriate share name for the print device.
- Taking ownership of a printer lets you change printer administrators. The user who installed the printer owns it.
- Members of the Administrators group can take ownership of any printer. If any member takes ownership of a printer, the Administrators group becomes the owner.

Lesson 4: Identifying Printing Problems

Printing problems are among the most common problems that users encounter. This lesson describes the printing process, and it also discusses common printing problems and possible solutions.

After this lesson, you will be able to:
- Describe how documents are printed.
- Recognize common reasons why users cannot print.

Estimated lesson time: 20 minutes

How Documents Are Printed

An overview of the printing process will help you understand how to manage a printer and identify problems. Windows NT has a *spooler* on the print server, which processes and schedules documents for printing. If a document becomes stuck in this spooler, you might need to stop and restart the spooler using the Services program in Control Panel.

Windows NT–based and Windows® 95–based Clients

Windows NT–based and Windows 95–based clients have an additional spooler, which helps to improve printing performance. After a user sends a document to the printer, the following occurs:

1. The printer driver partially processes the document to an acceptable format for the print device.
2. The document goes to the spooler on the client computer where it stays until there is room in the spooler on the print server.
3. When the print server is available, the spooler on the client sends the job to the print server, where the print server spooler finishes processing the document. The document waits in the spooler until a print device is available. Then, it is printed.

Other Clients

The printing process is the same for client computers that are not running Windows 95 or Windows NT operating systems. For non-Microsoft clients, there is a spooler only on the print server. After the user sends a document to be printed, the following occurs:

1. The printer driver completely processes the document to an acceptable format for the print device.
2. The document waits in the spooler until a print device is available. Then, it is printed.

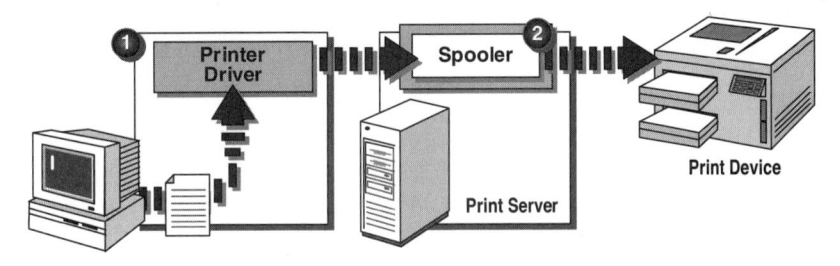

Identifying and Troubleshooting Printing Problems

One of the most frequent administrative tasks is solving printing problems. Most printing problems can be identified quickly by using the following checklist:

- ❑ Verify that the print device is operational. If some users can print normally, then the problem is not with the print server or print device.
- ❑ Verify that the printer on the print server is using the correct printer driver.
- ❑ Verify that the print server is operational and that there is enough disk space to spool files. For example, if 10 users are all printing large documents at the same time, the print server must have enough disk space to spool all of the documents.
- ❑ If the client is running an operating system other than Windows 95 or Windows NT, verify that the client has the correct printer driver. Computers running Windows NT and Windows 95 automatically copy the correct printer driver when they connect to a network printer.

If a user still has printing problems after you complete the items in the previous checklist, refer to the following table for a description of common problems and solutions.

Problem	Solutions
User receives an Access Denied message when trying to configure a printer from within a program (for example, from within Microsoft Excel).	The user does not have the appropriate permission to change printer configurations. Change the user's permission, or configure the printer for the user.
The document does not print completely or comes out garbled.	Make sure that the correct printer driver is installed on the client.
The hard disk starts thrashing and the document does not reach the print server.	There may be insufficient hard disk space for spooling the document. Create more free space, or, in the registry, move the spooler location to another volume.
There are documents on the print server that will not print and that you cannot delete.	The print spooler may be stalled. On the print server, start the Services program in Control Panel, and then stop and restart the Spooler service.
A user cannot print a document.	Verify that the user's printer is not paused and that the correct default printer is set. Make sure that the print device is online and that it is not out of paper or toner.
	Verify that the available printing time is configured properly for the user.
A user cannot connect to a printer.	Make sure that the user has the Print permission (for computers running Windows NT or Windows 95).
	Make sure that the proper printer driver is installed on the computer (for non-Windows NT–based clients).
A 16-bit Windows-based program gives an out-of-memory error on startup.	A default printer is not selected. Create a printer and set it as the default printer.
A user sends a document from an MS-DOS–based program on a Windows NT–based client to the printer, but it is never printed.	Some programs will not print a document until the program terminates. Make sure that the printer driver is correctly installed and then quit the program.

Lesson Summary

The following information summarizes key points in this lesson:

- Knowing the basics of the printing process will help you understand how to manage a printer and identify problems.
- Printing problems may require you to install the correct printer driver, verify a user's print permissions, and perform the tasks of pausing, resuming, and purging a printer.

For more information on	See
Troubleshooting printing problems	http://www.microsoft.com/support/
	Chapter 7, "Printing," in the *Microsoft Windows NT Workstation Resource Kit*.
	Chapter 2, "Printing," in the *Resource Guide* of the *Microsoft Windows NT Server Resource Kit*.
The registry	Appendix A, "Windows NT Registry," in Microsoft Windows NT Server *Concepts and Planning*.
The Services program in Control Panel	Windows NT Help.
Print spooler	Chapter 7, "Printing," in the *Microsoft Windows NT Workstation Resource Kit*.
	Chapter 2, "Printing," in the *Resource Guide* of the *Microsoft Windows NT Server Resource Kit*.

Review

The following questions are intended to reinforce key information presented in this chapter. If you are unable to answer a question, review the lesson and then try the question again.

1. Which of the following are true statements about the requirements for administering print servers? (Circle all that apply.)

    a. You must be a member of the Administrators or Print Operators groups on the print server.

    b. You must be a member of the Administrators, Print Operators, or Server Operators groups on the print server.

    c. You must have the Full Control or Manage Documents print permission for the printer.

    d. You must have the Full Control print permission for the printer.

2. What print permission does a user need to manage documents in a printer?

   _____

   _____

3. Scenario: The editor has a 1,000-page book that needs to be printed and sent to the printer by 8:00 A.M. tomorrow morning. The editor shares a printer with 10 sales people who are busy preparing and printing customer presentations that need to be ready by 5:00 P.M. today. What can you do to distribute the printing load so that everyone gets his or her documents printed on time?

   _____

   _____

4. Scenario: The Printer-A print device becomes faulty and needs to be repaired. There are 10 documents in the printer for Printer-A waiting to be printed. There are two other print devices: Printer-B is on the same print server, but it is a different type of print device than Printer-A. Printer-C is on a different print server, but it is the same type as Printer-A. What can you do to print the 10 documents without having users resubmit their print jobs? Please explain your decision.

_____

_____

5. Scenario: A user sends a document to a printer, but the printer does not print the document. Which of the following tasks would you perform to identify the problem? (Circle all that apply.)

    a. Verify that the user has the correct print permission.

    b. Verify that the print server and the client have the correct printer drivers.

    c. Check the available disk space on the print server to make sure that there is enough space to spool print jobs.

    d. Verify that the print device is online and that it is not out of paper or toner.

Answer Key

Procedure Answers

Page 319

▶ **To take ownership of a printer**

5. Were you able to take ownership? Why or why not?

Yes, because User8 is a member of the Print Operators group.

Page 326

Review Answers

1. Which of the following are true statements about the requirements for administering print servers? (Circle all that apply.)

    Answers b and d are correct.

2. What print permission does a user need to manage documents in a printer?

    The Manage Documents or Full Control print permission for the printer.

3. Scenario: The editor has a 1,000-page book that needs to be printed and sent to the printer by 8:00 A.M. tomorrow morning. The editor shares a printer with 10 sales people who are busy preparing and printing customer presentations that need to be ready by 5:00 P.M. today. What can you do to distribute the printing load so that everyone gets his or her documents printed on time?

    You can schedule the 1,000-page book to be printed after 5:00 P.M., when the sales people have finished with their presentations.

4. Scenario: The Printer-A print device becomes faulty and needs to be repaired. There are 10 documents in the printer for Printer-A waiting to be printed. There are two other print devices: Printer-B is on the same print server, but it is a different type of print device than Printer-A. Printer-C is on a different print server, but it is the same type as Printer-A. What can you do to print the 10 documents without having users resubmit their print jobs? Please explain your decision.

    Redirect the printer on Printer-A to Printer-C. You can only redirect printers to print devices that use the same printer driver.

5. Scenario: A user sends a document to a printer, but the printer does not print the document. Which of the following tasks would you perform to identify the problem? (Circle all that apply.)

    Answers b, c, and d are correct.

CHAPTER 9

Auditing Resources and Events

Lesson 1   Introduction to Auditing . . . 331

Lesson 2   Planning and Implementing the Audit Policy . . . 334

Lesson 3   Using Event Viewer to View the Security Log . . . 346

Best Practices . . . 357

Review . . . 358

About This Chapter

Through auditing, you can track selected activities of users. This chapter introduces auditing and provides guidance in planning and implementing a domain Audit policy. The hands-on procedures give you an opportunity to plan and implement an Audit policy, set up auditing on files and printers, and use Event Viewer to view audited events and to archive security logs.

Before You Begin

To complete the lessons in this chapter, you must have:

- Completed the Setup procedures located in "About This Book."
- Knowledge about domains, domain controllers, and member servers.
- Knowledge and skills to create user accounts.
- Knowledge about group accounts, including Administrators, Server Operators, and Everyone.
- A printer installed. If you have not installed a printer, see Chapter 7, "Setting Up a Network Print Server."
- A user account named User9. Log on as Administrator. In Windows NT Explorer, expand the LabFiles folder, and then double-click Chapter9.cmd to create this account.

Lesson 1: Introduction to Auditing

Auditing is a function of Windows NT for maintaining network security. With auditing, you can track user activities and system-wide events on a network, such as:

- The action performed.
- The user who performed the action.
- The date and time of the action.

This lesson provides an introduction to Windows NT auditing.

After this lesson, you will be able to:
- Describe the purpose of the Audit policy.
- Describe the requirements to set up and administer the Audit policy.

Estimated lesson time: 10 minutes

You use the Audit policy to select the types of security events that will be audited. When such an event occurs, an entry is added to the computer's security log. The security log becomes your tool for tracking the events that you specify.

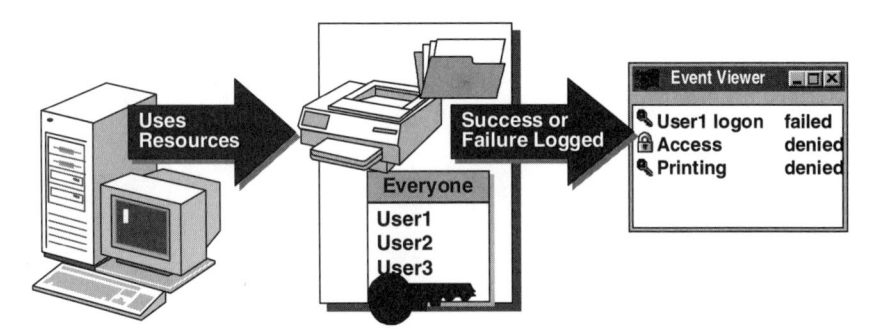

On a domain controller, the Audit polity determines the amount and type of security logging that Windows NT Server performs on all domain controllers in the domain. On computers running Windows NT Workstation or on member servers, the Audit policy determines the amount and type of security logging performed on the individual computer.

You can set up one Audit policy for a domain to:

- Track the success and failure of events, such as when users attempt to log on, read a file, make changes to user and group permissions, change the security policy, and make a network connection.
- Eliminate or minimize the risk of unauthorized use of resources.
- Track trends over time by maintaining an archive of security logs. Tracking these trends is useful in determining the use of printers or files.

Auditing Requirements

Auditing can be set up on any computer running Windows NT. However, to audit folders and files, the folders and files must be located on an NTFS volume.

To set up an Audit policy, you must meet the following requirements:

- You must be a member of the Administrators group on the computer where the Audit policy is being set.
- If you are not a member of the Administrators group, you must have the user right *Manage auditing and security log*. This user right is granted to the Administrators group by default.

Note Members of the Server Operators group are unable to set up an Audit policy; however, they can administer security logs—performing tasks such as viewing and archiving them.

Lesson Summary

The following information summarizes the key points in this lesson:

- Auditing is a function of Windows NT for maintaining network security that allows you to track user activities and system-wide events on a network.
- The Audit policy allows you to select the types of security events that will be recorded and will appear in the security log.
- On a domain controller, the Audit policy applies to all domain controllers in the domain.
- On a computer running Windows NT Workstation, or on a member server, the Audit policy applies only to that specific computer.
- To audit folders and files, the folders and files must be located on an NTFS volume.
- To set up an Audit policy, you must have administrative privileges for the computer.

For more information on	See
Overview of auditing	Windows NT Help.
Overview of Windows NT security	Chapter 6, "Windows NT Security," in the *Microsoft Windows NT Workstation Resource Kit*.
User rights and group accounts	Chapter 2, "Working With User and Group Accounts," in Microsoft Windows NT Server *Concepts and Planning*.
Domains, domain controllers, and member servers	Chapter 1, "Introduction to Windows NT," in this book.

Lesson 2: Planning and Implementing the Audit Policy

This lesson provides guidelines for planning a domain Audit policy in networks that have minimum, medium, and high levels of security. The lesson also covers how to define the Audit policy and how to audit folders, files, and printers.

After this lesson, you will be able to:
- Plan an Audit policy and determine which events to audit.
- Set up an Audit policy for the domain in User Manager for Domains.
- Set up auditing on folders and files in Windows NT Explorer.
- Set up auditing on printers using menu commands in the Printers window.

Estimated lesson time: 30 minutes

Planning the Audit Policy

The Audit policy determines the types of events to audit and how to track each event—by its success or its failure. Before you implement the Audit policy, it is important to determine the following:

- Determine the events to audit for your network.

To track	Consider auditing
Unauthorized logon attempts	Users logging on and off
Unauthorized attempts to use resources	Use of folder and file resources
System tasks performed by a user	Use of user rights
Changes made to user and group accounts	User and group management
Changes made to the user rights or audit policy	Security policy changes
Tampering with a server	Restarting or shutting down the system
Which programs users are using	Process tracking

- Determine whether to audit the success or failure of an event, or both.
    - Tracking the success of events can tell you how often users gain access to specific files or printers. You can use this information in resource planning.
    - Tracking the failure of events will alert you to possible security breaches.

    In minimum-security networks, consider auditing:
    - Successful use of resources, only if you need this information for planning purposes.
    - Successful use of sensitive and confidential data, such as payroll files.

In medium-security networks, consider auditing:

- Successful use of key resources.
- Successful and unsuccessful administrative and security policy changes.
- Successful use of sensitive and confidential data, such as payroll files.

In high-security networks, consider auditing:

- Successful and unsuccessful user logons.
- Successful and unsuccessful use of all resources.
- Successful and unsuccessful administrative and security policy changes.

Important Because auditing creates overhead on the CPU and on the hard disk, always audit only those events that provide information that is useful in your network.

Implementing the Audit Policy

The Audit policy is set on a computer-by-computer basis. For example, to audit events that occur on the primary domain controller, such as user logon attempts and changes made to user accounts, you must set the Audit policy on the primary domain controller.

To audit events on any other computer in the domain, such as access to a file on a member server, you must set the Audit policy on that computer.

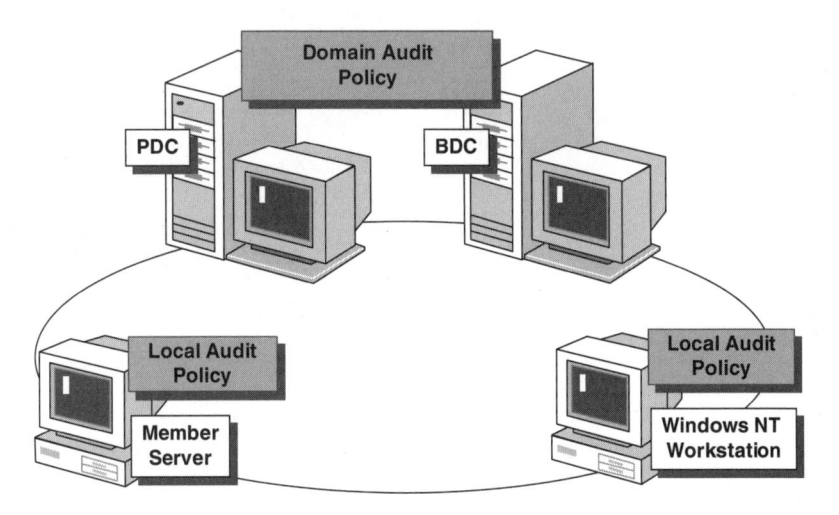

Events are recorded in the local computer's security log, but they can be viewed from any computer by a user who has administrative privileges on the computer where the events occurred.

Setting up auditing is a two-part process:

- Defining the Audit policy by selecting the events to audit in User Manager for Domains (or in User Manager on computers running Windows NT Workstation or on member servers).

- Specifying the files, folders, and printers to audit and the users and groups that you want to track. You use Windows NT Explorer to specify the folder and file events to audit. You use the Printers window to specify printer events to audit.

Defining the Domain Audit Policy

The first step of setting up the Audit policy is to select the events to audit in User Manager for Domains. To gain access to the **Audit Policy** dialog box, on the **Policies** menu, click **Audit**.

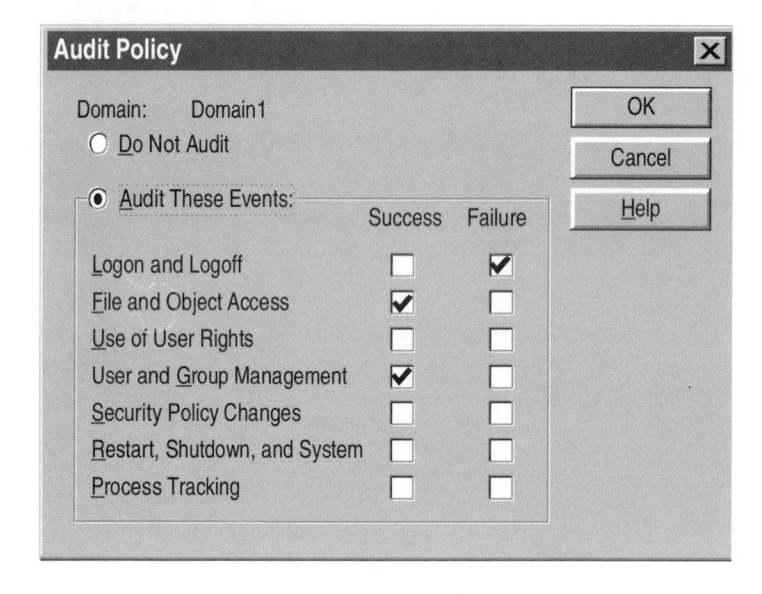

The following table describes the types of events that you can audit.

This event	Is used to track when
Logon and Logoff	A user logs on or off, or makes or breaks a network connection.
File and Object Access	A user accesses a folder, file, or printer that is set for auditing. This event must be selected to audit file or print resources.
Use of User Rights	A user exercises a right (except those rights related to logging on and logging off).
User and Group Management	A user account or group is created, modified (renamed, disabled, password changed, and so on), deleted, or when account restrictions, such as logon hours and workstation restrictions, are modified.
Security Policy Changes	A change is made to the user rights, audit, or trust relationship policies.
Restart, Shutdown, and System	A user restarts or shuts down the computer, causing an event to occur that affects system security. (For example, the audit log fills up and entries are discarded.)
Process Tracking	Events occur that cause programs to start—for example, selecting a program on the **Start** menu, or clicking a link on a Web page that starts a Setup program.

Note If you set up an Audit policy on a computer running Windows NT Workstation or on a member server, you use User Manager. All **Audit Policy** dialog box options in User Manager are identical to those in User Manager for Domains.

▶ **To plan an Audit policy**

Scenario: As the administrator for the Quebec office of World Wide Importers, you need to plan the Audit policy for the Quebec domain. World Wide Importers is a medium-security to high-security network. You need to determine:

- Which types of events to audit.
- Whether to audit the success or the failure of an event, or both.

Use the following criteria to make your decisions:

- Record unsuccessful attempts to gain access to the network.
- Record unauthorized access to the database that contains the payroll and employee files.
- For billing purposes, track color printer usage.
- Track any time that someone tries to tamper with the server hardware.
- Keep a record of actions performed by an administrator to track unauthorized changes.
- Track backup procedures to prevent data theft.
- Track which users are playing computer games.

Record your decisions by marking them directly onto the following illustration of the **Audit Policy** dialog box.

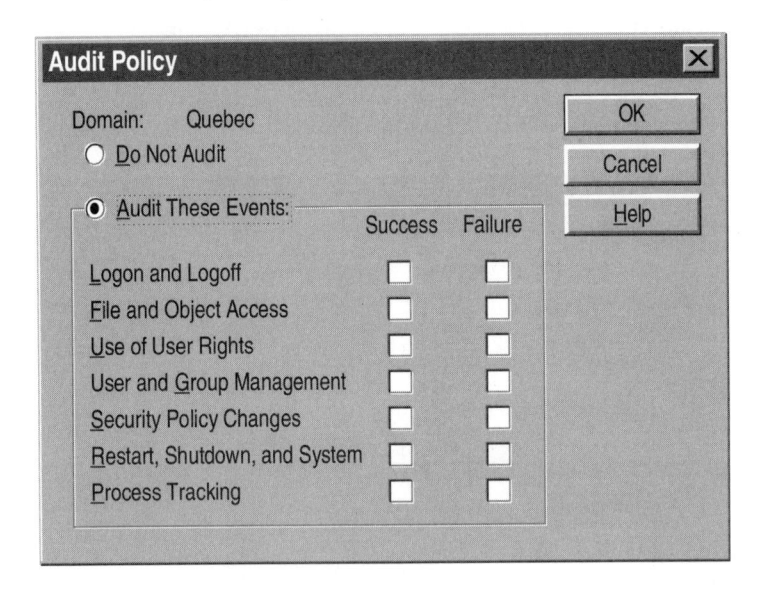

```
Audit Policy                                              [X]
    Domain:   Quebec                              ┌─────────┐
      ○ Do Not Audit                              │   OK    │
                                                  ├─────────┤
                                                  │ Cancel  │
      ⦿ Audit These Events:                       ├─────────┤
                              Success   Failure   │  Help   │
                                                  └─────────┘
        Logon and Logoff        ☐        ☐
        File and Object Access  ☐        ☐
        Use of User Rights      ☐        ☐
        User and Group Management ☐      ☐
        Security Policy Changes ☐        ☐
        Restart, Shutdown, and System ☐  ☐
        Process Tracking        ☐        ☐
```

▸ **To define the Audit policy**

In this procedure, you define the Audit policy based on your plan in the previous procedure.

1. Log on as Administrator.
2. Click the **Start** button, point to **Programs**, point to **Administrative Tools**, and then click **User Manager for Domains**.
3. On the **Policies** menu, click **Audit**.

   The **Audit Policy** dialog box appears.
4. Click **Audit These Events**.
5. Select the **Success** or **Failure** check box (or both) for the events that you planned.
6. Click **OK**.
7. Quit User Manager for Domains.

Auditing Folders and Files

Once you define the Audit policy, the next step is to specify the folders or files to audit, the events to audit for the folders or files, and which users and groups you want to track using them. To gain access to the **Directory Auditing** dialog box, in Windows NT Explorer, right-click the folder or file, click **Properties,** click the **Security** tab, and then click **Auditing**.

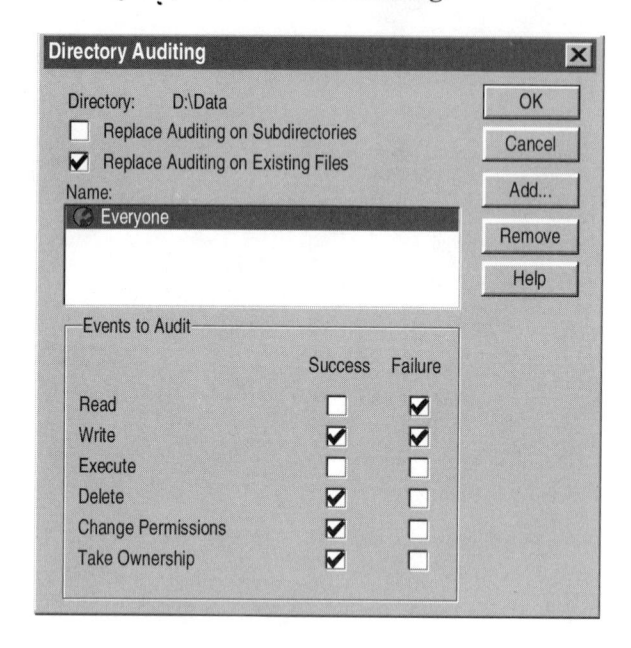

The following table explains the options for auditing folders. These options do not appear if you are auditing files.

Do this	If you want to
Select the **Replace Auditing on Subdirectories** check box.	Have auditing changes apply to all folders within the folder. By default, auditing changes apply only to the selected folder and its files.
Click to clear the **Replace Auditing on Existing Files** check box.	Apply auditing changes to the folder only. This check box is selected by default. Clearing this check box means that existing files will not be modified.

The following table describes the events that you can audit for both folders and files.

Audit this event	To track
Read	When a user opens a file; views its attributes, permissions, or owner; or copies the file.
	When a user views a folder's content, attributes, permissions, or owner. Audit Read for all sensitive data.
Write	When a user changes a file's content or attributes; views its permissions or owner; or copies the file.
	When a user creates a folder or file, changes attributes, or views the permissions or owner. Audit Write for all sensitive data.
Execute	When a user views a file's attributes, permissions, or owner; or starts a program.
	When a user changes a folder; or views its attributes, permissions, or owner. Audit Execute in high-security networks.
Delete	Deleted folders or files. Tracks copying of files.
	Audit Delete for all sensitive data and in medium- and high-security networks.
Change Permissions	Changes to folder or file permissions. Audit Change Permissions in medium- and high-security networks.
Take Ownership	Changes to folder or file ownership. Audit Take Ownership in medium- and high-security networks.

Auditing the Everyone Group

Auditing is a good example of when you would use the Everyone group. The Everyone group includes all local and remote users who have connected to the computer, including those who connect as Guest. By auditing the Everyone group, you can track use of a resource by anyone who can connect to the resource, and not just the users that you have created accounts for in the domain.

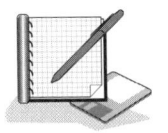

▶ **To audit a file**

In this procedure, you audit the Bronte.txt file and any member of the Everyone group who successfully deletes it, changes permission on it, or takes ownership of it.

1. Start Windows NT Explorer and expand the LabFiles\Public\Library folder.
2. Right-click Bronte.txt, and then on the menu that appears, click **Properties**.

   The **Bronte Properties** dialog box appears.

3. Click the **Security** tab.

   Note Auditing can only be done on NTFS partitions. If there is no **Security** tab, the selected file is not on an NTFS partition.

4. Click **Auditing**.

   The **File Auditing** dialog box appears.

5. Click **Add**.

   The **Add Users and Groups** dialog box appears.

6. Under **Names**, click **Everyone**, and then click **Add**.
7. Click **OK**.

   The **Everyone** group appears under **Name** in the **File Auditing** dialog box.

   Note You can easily remove a user or group from auditing by selecting its name and then clicking **Remove**.

8. Under **Events to Audit**, select the **Success** check box for the following events:
   - **Delete**
   - **Change Permission**
   - **Take Ownership**

9. Click **OK** to apply your changes and return to the **Bronte Properties** dialog box.
10. Click **OK** to return to Windows NT Explorer.
11. Quit Windows NT Explorer.

Auditing a Printer

Setting up auditing on a printer is similar to setting up auditing on folders and files. First you define the Audit policy, and then you specify the printer events to audit, and the users and groups that you want to track using the printer. To gain access to the **Printer Auditing** dialog box, in the Printers window, double-click the printer, on the **Printer** menu, click **Properties**, click the **Security** tab, and then click **Auditing**.

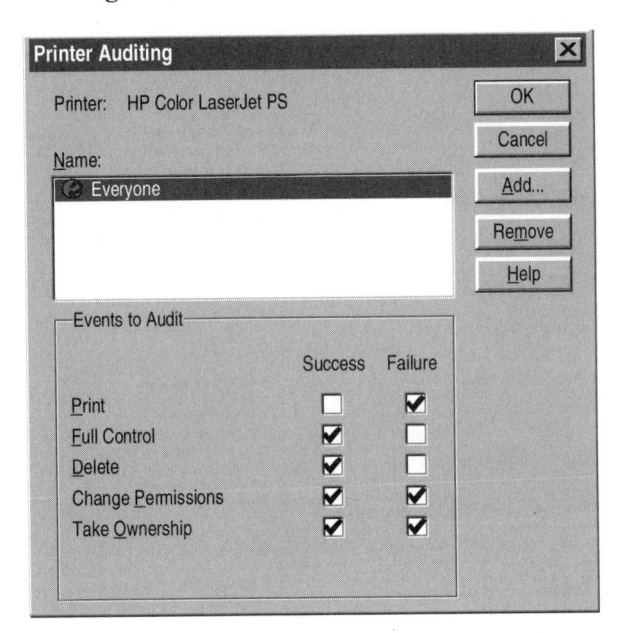

The following table explains the options for auditing printers.

Audit this event	To track
Print	Printer usage. This is useful for billing individual departments.
Full Control	Changes to job settings; pausing, restarting, moving, or deleting documents; sharing a printer; or changing printer properties. This is useful in high-security networks.
Delete	Deleted print jobs. This is useful in high-security networks.
Change Permissions	Changes to printer permissions. This is useful in medium- and high-security networks.
Take Ownership	Changes to printer ownership. This is useful in medium- and high-security networks.

▶ **To audit a printer**

In this procedure, you audit a printer and any member of the Everyone group who successfully prints to it, changes permission on it, or takes ownership of it.

1. Click the **Start** button, point to **Settings**, and then click **Printers**.
2. In the Printers window, double-click any printer.
3. On the **Printer** menu, click **Properties**.

   The *printer_name* **Properties** dialog box appears.
4. Click the **Security** tab, and then click **Auditing**.

   The **Printer Auditing** dialog box appears.
5. Click **Add**.

   The **Add Users and Groups** dialog box appears.
6. Under **Names**, click **Everyone**, and then click **Add**.
7. Click **OK**.

   The **Everyone** group appears under **Name** in the **Printer Auditing** dialog box.
8. Under **Events to Audit**, select the **Success** check box for the following events:
   - **Print**
   - **Change Permissions**
   - **Take Ownership**
9. Click **OK** to apply your changes.
10. Click **OK** to close the *printer_name* **Properties** dialog box.
11. Close the *printer_name* window.
12. Close the Printers window.
13. Log off.

Lesson Summary

The following information summarizes the key points in this lesson:

- When planning the Audit policy, determine what resources and actions are necessary to monitor.
- The Audit policy is set on a computer-by-computer basis. If it is set on the PDC, you can audit events that occur on all domain controllers. If it is set on a computer running Windows NT Workstation or on a member server, you can only audit events on that particular computer.
- To set up auditing, first define the Audit policy for the domain or the computer, specify the folder, file, and printer events to audit, and then specify the users and groups whose use of the resources you want to track.
- Audit the Everyone group to track use of a resource by all users that can connect to it, and not just its use by domain users.

For more information on	See
The procedure for auditing a file or directory	Windows NT Help.
The procedure for changing the printer settings	Windows NT Help.
Setting up auditing	Chapter 9, "Monitoring Events," in Microsoft Windows NT Server *Concepts and Planning*.
Auditing file and folder access	Chapter 37, "Windows NT Workstation Troubleshooting," in the *Microsoft Windows NT Workstation Resource Kit*.
The Everyone group	Chapter 3, "Setting Up Group Accounts," in this book.
	Chapter 2, "Working With User and Group Accounts," in Microsoft Windows NT Server *Concepts and Planning*.

Lesson 3: Using Event Viewer to View the Security Log

Event Viewer provides information about errors, warnings, and the successes or failures of tasks. This lesson describes the three types of logs created in Event Viewer, but focuses on the security log. The lesson also shows you how to use Event Viewer to view information recorded as a result of an audited event.

This lesson requires that you have completed Lesson 2.

After this lesson, you will be able to:
- Use Event Viewer to view the security log of a local and remote computer.
- Use the **Filter Events** menu command to filter and view specific events.
- Use the **Find** menu command to locate events in the security log.

Estimated lesson time: 30 minutes

Event Viewer provides information about errors, warnings, and the successes or failures of tasks. This information is stored in one of three types of logs:

- *System log*. Contains errors, warnings, and information generated by Windows NT and third-party components, such as a network adapter card driver. The selection of events that are recorded is preset by Windows NT and the third-party components.
- *Security log*. Contains information about the success or failure of audited events. The events that are recorded are a result of your Audit policy.

- *Application log.* Contains errors, warnings, or information generated by programs, such as a database or e-mail program. The selection of events that are recorded is preset by the program developer.

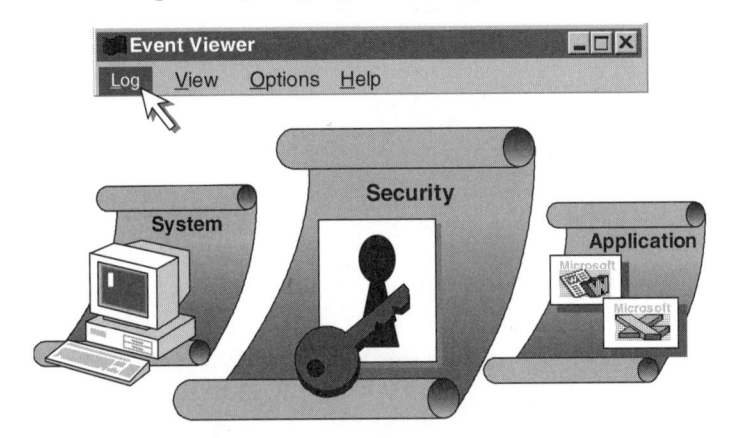

Event Viewer provides the ability to view logs on any computer running Windows NT. Event Viewer on computers running Windows NT Workstation is identical to Event Viewer on computers running Windows NT Server.

Administrative Requirements for Viewing the Security Log

The security log resides on the computer where the Audit policy was set. To view a security log, you must be a member of the Administrators or Server Operators groups on the computer where the security log resides.

For example, if the Audit policy was set on a computer running Windows NT Workstation or on a member server, you must have administrative privileges on that computer. If the Audit policy was set on the primary domain controller (PDC), you must have administrative privileges on the PDC.

Note To view a security log on a computer in a different domain, the appropriate trust relationship must exist.

Viewing the Security Log

The security log is where audited events are recorded. Successful events appear with a key icon; unsuccessful events appear with a lock icon. Other key information includes the date and time that the event occurred, and the category of the event. The **Category** indicates the type of event that was audited (set in the Audit policy).

The following table lists the Event Viewer categories and specifies which type of event in the Audit policy each category corresponds to.

This Event Viewer category	Corresponds to this type of event
Object Access	File and Object Access
System Event	Restart, Shutdown, and System
Privilege Use	Use of User Rights
Account Management	User and Group Management
Logon/Logoff	Logon and Logoff
Detailed Tracking	Process Tracking
Policy Change	Security Policy Changes

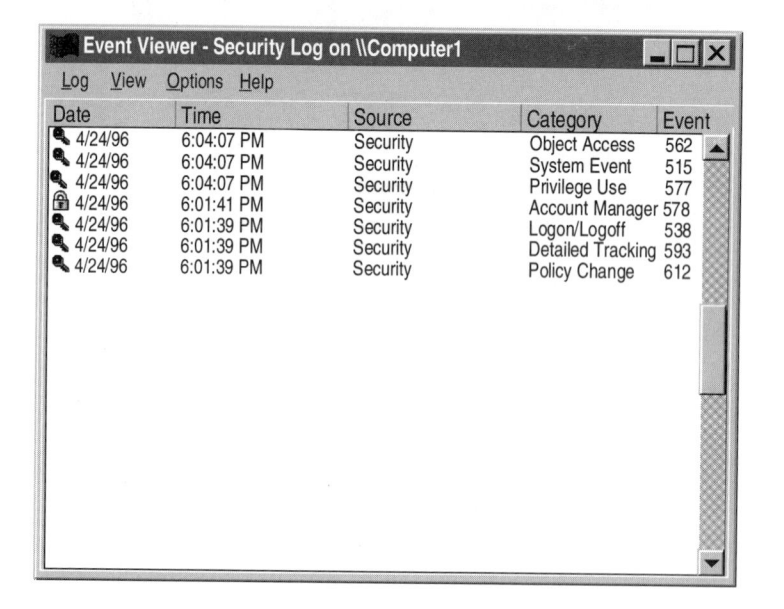

```
Event Viewer - Security Log on \\Computer1            _ □ X
Log   View   Options   Help
Date       Time           Source      Category           Event
4/24/96    6:04:07 PM     Security    Object Access      562
4/24/96    6:04:07 PM     Security    System Event       515
4/24/96    6:04:07 PM     Security    Privilege Use      577
4/24/96    6:01:41 PM     Security    Account Manager    578
4/24/96    6:01:39 PM     Security    Logon/Logoff       538
4/24/96    6:01:39 PM     Security    Detailed Tracking  593
4/24/96    6:01:39 PM     Security    Policy Change      612
```

▶ **To create log file entries in the security log**

In this procedure, you perform tasks that create entries in the security log to see the effects of your Audit policy.

1. Log on as User9.
2. In Windows NT Explorer, expand the LabFiles\Public\Library folder, and then double-click Bronte.txt to open it.
3. Close the file.
4. Log off and then log on as Administrator.
5. Create a user account.
6. Shut down and restart your computer.

▶ **To view the security log on the local computer**

1. Log on as Administrator.
2. Click the **Start** button, point to **Programs**, point to **Administrative Tools**, and then click **Event Viewer**.

   If this is the first time that you started Event Viewer, the system log for your computer appears. Otherwise, the last log that you viewed appears.
3. On the **Log** menu, click **Security** (if it does not already appear).
4. Scroll through the log and look for the following categories of events.
   - **Logon/Logoff**
   - **Object Access**
   - **Privilege Use**
   - **Account Management**
5. Double-click the different events for a description of them, or select the event and then on the **View** menu, click **Detail**.

▶ **To view the security log on a remote computer**

If you have two computers, log on as Administrator on the secondary computer and complete this procedure.

Note If your computers are connected to each other by a modem (using connections slower than 28.8), on the **Options** menu click **Low Speed Connection**, or on the **Log** menu, click **Select Computer**, and then click to select the **Low Speed Connection** check box. If this option is selected, Windows NT does not list all the computers in the default domain, thereby minimizing network traffic across the link.

---

1. On the **Log** menu, click **Select Computer**.

   The **Select Computer** dialog box appears.
2. In the **Computer** box, type the name of the remote computer, or double-click the domain and select the computer from the list.

Filtering Events

By default, Event Viewer lists all events recorded in the selected log. To view a subset of events that have specific characteristics, click **Filter Events** on the **View** menu. When filtering is on, a check mark appears by the **Filter Events** command on the **View** menu and "(Filtered)" appears on the Event Viewer title bar. If **Save Settings On Exit** on the **Options** menu is turned on (you see a check mark next to it), when you quit Event Viewer, the filter remains in effect the next time you start Event Viewer.

Filtering has no effect on the actual content of the log; it changes only the view. All events are logged continuously, whether the filter is active or not.

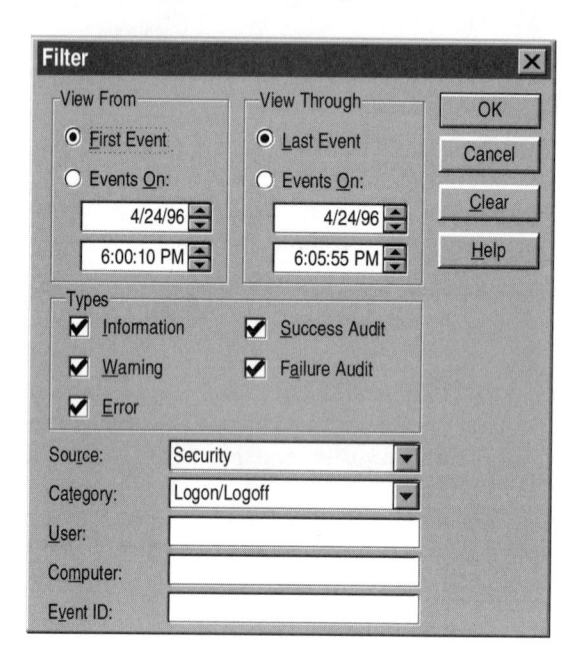

The following table describes how to use the options in the **Filter** dialog box.

Use this option	To
View From/ View Through	Specify the range of dates for which you want to view events.
Types	Select the types of events that you want to view.
Source	Specify the software or component driver that generated the event.
Category	Select the classification of the event as defined by the source; for example, a security log category is Logon/Logoff.
User	Specify a user account to locate events resulting from a specific user.
Computer	Specify a computer name to locate events resulting from a specific computer.
Event ID	Look at an event number to identify the event. This number helps product support representatives to track events.

▶ **To filter for Logon/Logoff events**

1. In Event Viewer, on the **Log** menu, click **Open**.

    The **Open** dialog box appears.

2. In the LabFiles folder, double-click Security.evt.

    The **Open File Type** dialog box appears. The **System** file type is selected by default.

3. Under **Open File of Type**, click **Security**, and then click **OK**.

    The security event log for Security.evt appears.

4. On the **View** menu, click **Filter Events**.

    The **Filter** dialog box appears.

5. In the **Source** box, click **Security**.

6. In the **Category** box, click **Logon/Logoff**, and then click **OK**.

    Notice that the lock icon appears next to each event indicating that the event failed.

7. Double-click each event for a description.

    Under **Description**, notice the reason that the event failed and the user who caused it to fail, possibly attempting to breach security.

▶ **To filter for unauthorized access to folders and files**

1. On the **View** menu, click **Filter Events**.

    The **Filter** dialog box appears.

2. In the **Source** box, click **Security**.

3. In the **Category** box, click **Object Access**.

4. Under **Types**, make sure that only the **Failure Audit** check box is selected (click to clear all of the other check boxes).

5. Click **OK**.

6. Double-click each event to see a description.

    On what file did the failed event occur?

    _____

    What action was attempted on the file? (Scroll through the **Description** and look at **Accesses**.)

    _____

Locating Events

To search for events that match a specific type, source, or category, click **Find** on the **View** menu. Searches can be useful when you are viewing large logs. For example, you can search for all Warning events related to a specific program, or you can search for all Error events from all sources.

Unlike the **Filter Events** command, the **Find** command does not enable you to search for events based on dates. You can, however, search on text that would appear in the description of the event.

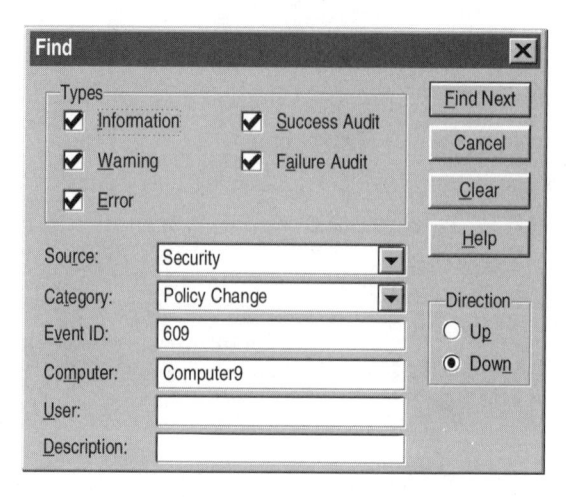

▶ **To search for printer usage events**

1. On the **View** menu, click **All Events**.
2. On the **View** menu, click **Find**.

   The **Find** dialog box appears.
3. In the **Description** box, type **printer** and then click **Find Next**.

   The first printer event is highlighted.
4. On the **View** menu, click **Detail**.

   Under **Description**, notice that the action the user performed was to print the file.
5. Click **Close**.

▶ **To search for server hardware events**

1. On the **View** menu, click **Find**.

   The **Find** dialog box appears.
2. Click **Clear** to reset the **Find** dialog box options.
3. In the **Description** box, type **shutdown** and then click **Find Next**.

   The first shutdown event is highlighted.
4. On the **View** menu, click **Detail**.

   Notice the last time that the computer was shut down.
5. Click **Close**.

Archiving the Security Log

You can track trends in your system by archiving event logs. Viewing trends helps you to determine resource use and to plan for growth. You can also determine a pattern if unauthorized use of resources is a problem.

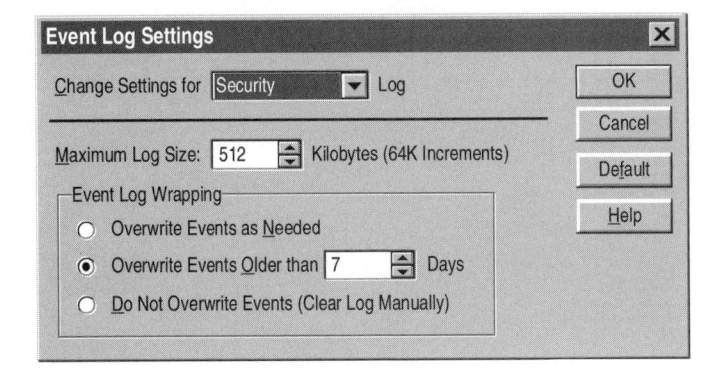

When you select events to audit, you need to keep in mind that the log can become full, which makes it unable to record any more events; however, you can avoid this problem. In the **Event Log Settings** dialog box, you can control:

- The size of the logs that you choose to archive:
    - Logs can be from 64 kilobytes (KB) to 4,194,240 KB.
    - The default is 512 KB.
- How events are recorded, by selecting any of the following options:
    - **Overwrite Events as Needed**.
    - **Overwrite Events Older than *x* Days**, and then entering the number of days.
    - **Do Not Overwrite Events (Clear Log Manually)**.
    - If you select **Do Not Overwrite Events**, you may need to archive the information in the current log before you clear it.

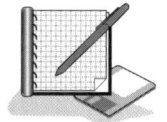

▶ **To control the size and content of a log file**

1. On the **Log** menu, click **Log Settings**.

    The **Event Log Settings** dialog box appears.

2. Click **Overwrite Events as Needed**.

    Older events will now be overwritten by new events. Note that because some events repeat at frequent intervals, use of this option may result in important events being overwritten.

3. Click **OK** when finished.

▶ **To archive the security log**

1. On the **Log** menu, make sure that the **Security** command is turned on (that it has a check mark by it), and then click **Save As**.

2. Save the log in the LabFiles folder using a name that easily identifies the file.

    Tip If you archive security logs, include the date as part of the file name to help you locate the file quickly.

▶ To clear the security log

1. On the **Log** menu, click **Clear All Events**.

    A message appears, asking you if you want to save the event log before closing it.

2. Click **No**.

    Another message appears, warning that this is an irreversible action and requesting verification.

3. Click **Yes**.

    Notice that a system event appears in the security log.

4. Double-click the event to see the description.

    Notice that the description states that the audit log was cleared.

5. Click **Close**.

▶ To view an archived security log

1. On the **Log** menu, click **Open**.
2. In the **Open** dialog box, locate and double-click the log that you archived.

    The **Open File Type** dialog box appears.

3. Under **Open File of Type**, click **Security**, and then click **OK**.
4. Quit Event Viewer and log off.

Lesson Summary

The following information summarizes the key points in this lesson:

- Event Viewer is the administrative tool that is used to view a security log on any computer running Windows NT.
- The security log is where Event Viewer records the success or failure (whichever of these you are auditing) of each audited event.
- To view a security log, you must be a member of the Administrators or Server Operators group on the computer where the security log resides. If the computer is in a different domain, the appropriate trust relationship must exist between the domains.
- Use the **Filter Events** menu command to set which events and characteristics appear in the security log when you start Event Viewer.
- Use the **Find** menu command to locate events in the security log.
- Archive security logs to track trends. This is useful in determining resource use and in planning for growth.

For more information on	See
How to use Event Viewer	Event Viewer Help.
	Chapter 9, "Monitoring Events," in Microsoft Windows NT Server *Concepts and Planning*.
	Chapter 37, "Monitoring Events," in the *Microsoft Windows NT Workstation Resource Kit*.
Trust relationships	Chapter 1, "Managing Windows NT Server Domains," in Microsoft Windows NT Server *Concepts and Planning*.
Administrative privileges	Chapter 3, "Setting Up Group Accounts," in this book.
	Chapter 2, "Working With User and Group Accounts," in Microsoft Windows NT Server *Concepts and Planning*.
Interpreting events	Chapter 9, "Monitoring Events," in Microsoft Windows NT Server *Concepts and Planning*.
	Chapter 37, "Monitoring Events," in the *Microsoft Windows NT Workstation Resource Kit*.

Best Practices

The following checklist provides best practices for auditing resources and events. Use this checklist when planning and maintaining an Audit policy:

❏ Define an Audit policy that is useful, but manageable. Audit only those events that will provide you with meaningful information about your network environment. This will minimize use of server resources and make key information easier to locate.

- In minimum-security networks, track successful events if you need to determine resource use. In medium-security networks, track successful events of key resources and of administrative and security policy changes. In high-security networks, track all successful events.
- In medium-security networks, track unsuccessful events to alert you to possible security breaches. In high-security networks, track all unsuccessful events.
- In all networks, audit sensitive and confidential data.

❏ Audit the Everyone group instead of the Users group. This ensures that anyone who can connect to the network is audited, not just the users that you create accounts for in the domain.

❏ Set up a schedule for viewing audit logs. Make it a regular part of your network administration tasks.

❏ Archive audit logs regularly to track trends. Doing so is useful for determining resource use and for planning purposes.

Note If you want to remove the account that was created by running the Chapter9.cmd file at the beginning of this chapter, log on as Administrator, and then double-click DeleteChapter9.cmd in the Cleanup folder on the Supplemental Material compact disc.

Review

The following questions are intended to reinforce key information presented in this chapter. If you are unable to answer a question, review the lesson and then try the question again.

1. On which computer would you have to set the Audit policy to audit domain logon attempts?

   _____

   _____

2. On which computer would you have to set the Audit policy to audit a folder located on a computer running Windows NT Workstation that is part of the domain?

   _____

   _____

3. Which of the following are true statements about setting up and administering auditing? (Circle all that apply.)

   a. Only members of the Administrators group can set up auditing.

   b. Only members of the Administrators and Server Operators groups can set up auditing.

   c. Users with the user right *Manage auditing and security log* can set up and administer auditing.

   d. Only members of the Administrators and Server Operator groups can administer auditing once it is set up.

   e. Only members of the Server Operators group can administer auditing once it is set up.

4. What event must be set in the **Audit Policy** dialog box before you can audit files, folders, and printers?

   _____

   _____

5. Complete this sentence. Folders and files can be audited on _____ volumes only.

6. In which event log are audited events recorded?

   a. System log

   b. Security log

   c. Application log

   d. Error log

Answer Key

Procedure Answers

Page 338

▶ **To plan an Audit policy**

Suggested answers:

Logon and Logoff: Failure (for attempts to gain access to the network).

File and Object Access: Success (for printer use) and Failure (for unauthorized access to the database).

Use of User Rights: Success (for Administrator actions and backup procedures).

User and Group Management: Success (for Administrator actions).

Security Policy Changes: Success (for Administrator actions).

Restart, Shutdown, and System: Success and Failure (for attempts to breach the server).

Process Tracking: Success.

Page 352

▶ **To filter for unauthorized access to folders and files**

6. On what file did the failed event occur?

   Wuthering Heights.txt.

   What action was attempted on the file? (Scroll through the **Description** and look at **Accesses**.)

   The Administrator attempted to delete the file.

Page 358

Review Answers

1. On which computer would you have to set the Audit policy to audit domain logon attempts?

   The Audit policy must be set on the primary domain controller.

2. On which computer would you have to set the Audit policy to audit a folder located on a computer running Windows NT Workstation that is part of the domain?

   The Audit policy must be set on the computer where the file is located—in this situation, on the computer running Windows NT Workstation.

3. Which of the following are true statements about setting up and administering auditing? (Circle all that apply.)

   Answers a, c, and d are true.

4. What event must be set in the **Audit Policy** dialog box before you can audit files, folders, and printers?

   File and Object Access.

5. Complete this sentence. Folders and files can be audited on _____ volumes only.

   "NTFS" is the correct answer.

6. In which event log are audited events recorded?

   Answer b is correct.

CHAPTER 10

Monitoring Resources

Lesson 1   Introduction to Monitoring Resources . . . 365

Lesson 2   Viewing Computer Properties . . . 369

Lesson 3   Setting Alerts and Sending Messages . . . 379

Lesson 4   Using Windows NT Diagnostics . . . 383

Best Practices . . . 389

Review . . . 390

About This Chapter

This chapter provides an overview of Server Manager and Windows NT Diagnostics and shows you how to use them to obtain key information about network and computer resources.

The hands-on procedures guide you through viewing computer properties; viewing user sessions, shared resources, and resources in use; setting administrative alerts; sending messages to users; and gathering information about a computer configuration to use for inventory tracking and troubleshooting.

Before You Begin

To complete the lessons in this chapter, you must have:

- Completed the Setup procedures located in "About This Book."
- Knowledge about the Administrators, Server Operators, and Power Users groups and the skills to add user accounts to them.
- Knowledge about shared resources, and about share and NTFS permissions.
- Shared the LabFiles\Public folder as Public. If the Public folder is not shared, see Chapter 5, "Securing Network Resources with Share Permissions" for instructions. Or, click the **Start** button, and then click **Run**. Then, in the **Open** box, type **net share public=***drive***:\LabFiles\Public** and click **OK**.
- A user account named User10. Log on as Administrator. In Windows NT Explorer, expand the LabFiles folder, and then double-click Chapter10.cmd to create it.

Lesson 1: Introduction to Monitoring Resources

You use Server Manager to assess server usage. You use Windows NT Diagnostics to obtain configuration information about a computer. This lesson describes the information provided by each and the requirements for using them.

After this lesson, you will be able to:
- Describe the function of Server Manager.
- Describe the function of Windows NT Diagnostics.
- Name the built-in group accounts that have the administrative user rights required for gaining access to Server Manager.

Estimated lesson time: 20 minutes

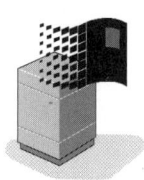

Server Manager

Server Manager is a Windows NT Server tool that you use to assess resource usage on computers running Windows NT. With Server Manager, you can view a list of connected users, view shared and open resources, manage a list of administrative alert recipients, manage services and shared folders, and send messages to connected users.

Note You can install Server Manager on any computer running Windows NT Workstation or Windows 95 by installing the client-based administration tools located in the Clients\Srvtools folder on the Windows NT Server compact disc.

Windows NT Diagnostics

Windows NT Diagnostics (Winmsd.exe) is a Windows NT Workstation and Windows NT Server diagnostic tool that you use to view and print configuration information for a local or remote computer. With Windows NT Diagnostics, you can view the following:

- Operating system information, such as the version number, system boot options, services, system settings, and user environment variables
- Hardware details, such as BIOS information, video resolution, CPU type, and CPU settings
- Physical memory, paging file information, and DMA (Direct Memory Access) usage
- The current state of each driver and service on the computer

- Drives and devices installed on the computer, plus related interrupt request line (IRQ) and port information
- Network information, including transports, configuration settings, and statistics
- Printer settings, fonts settings, and system processes that are running

Requirements

The following list describes the requirements for using Windows NT Diagnostics and Server Manager:

- To use Windows NT Diagnostics, you can be logged on as any user. Because Windows NT Diagnostics does not allow you to make configuration changes, all users can use it. However, a few of the settings are only available to members of the Administrators, Server Operators, and Power Users groups.
- To use Server Manager, you must be a member of the Administrators, Server Operators, or Power Users group on the computer that you are monitoring.

    If you are a member of the Server Operators group on a domain controller, you will have Server Operator privileges on all domain controllers in the domain.

    A few Server Manager functions are accessible only by members of the Administrators group. When Server Operators, Account Operators, or Power Users attempt to perform these functions, a message appears indicating that access is denied.

▶ **To add a user to the Server Operators group**

In this procedure, you give a user the necessary rights to administer the server by adding his or her account to the Server Operators group.

1. Log on as Administrator.
2. In User Manager for Domains, add User10 to the Server Operators group.

▶ **To determine the built-in rights that are assigned to Server Operators**

1. In the User Manager for Domains window, on the **Policies** menu, click **User Rights**.

2. In the **Right** box, click each item in the list to determine which rights are automatically assigned to the Server Operators group (that is, which rights cause **Server Operators** to appear in the **Grant To** box). In the following list, mark the check box next to each right that is granted automatically to the Server Operators group:

   ❑ **Access this computer from network**

   ❑ **Add workstations to domain**

   ❑ **Back up files and directories**

   ❑ **Change the system time**

   ❑ **Force shutdown from a remote system**

   ❑ **Load and unload device drivers**

   ❑ **Log on locally**

   ❑ **Manage auditing and security log**

   ❑ **Restore files and directories**

   ❑ **Shut down the system**

   ❑ **Take ownership of files or other objects**

3. Quit User Manager for Domains and log off.

Lesson Summary

The following information summarizes the key points in this lesson:

- Server Manager is a Windows NT Server tool that enables you to assess server usage.
- Windows NT Diagnostics (Winmsd.exe) is a Windows NT Workstation and Windows NT Server diagnostic tool that enables all users to view and print configuration information for a local or remote computer.
- To use Server Manager, you must be a member of the Administrators, Server Operators, or Power Users group on the computer that you are monitoring.

For more information on	See
Installing client-based administration tools	Chapter 11, "Managing Client Administration," in Microsoft Windows NT Server *Concepts and Planning*.

Lesson 2: Viewing Computer Properties

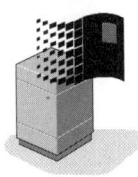

The computer properties that you can view in Server Manager show you information about system resources. This information is useful in determining how many users are connected to the computer and how many shared resources are in use. This lesson guides you through the steps to view the properties on a local or remote computer.

After this lesson, you will be able to:
- Use Server Manager to view server usage.
- Use Server Manager to view server properties.

Estimated lesson time: 20 minutes

Computer properties are viewed using Server Manager.

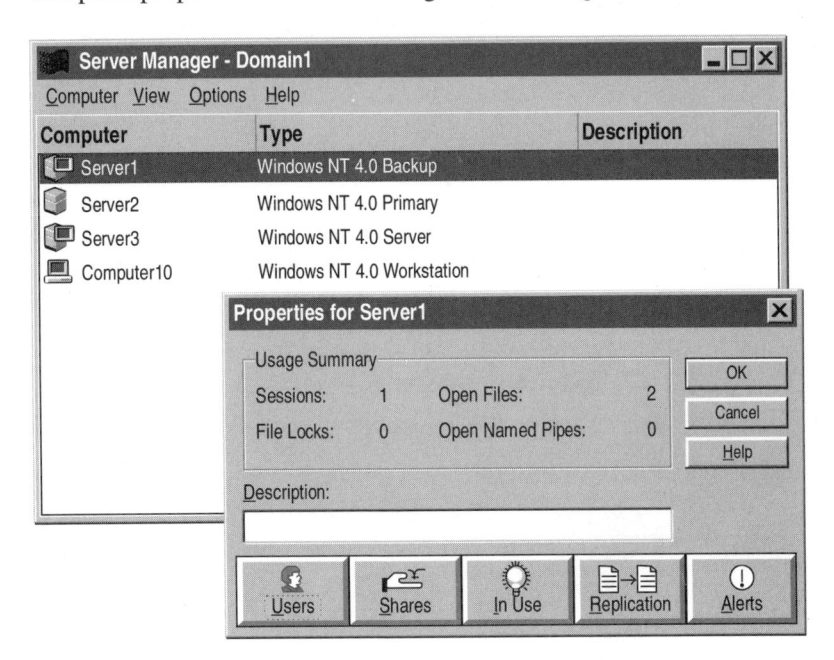

▶ **To start Server Manager**

1. Log on as Administrator.
2. Click the **Start** button, point to **Programs**, point to **Administrative Tools**, and then click **Server Manager**.

    The following information appears in the Server Manager window for the current domain:

    - The computer name, and the operating system and version it is running. (If the computer is inactive, the operating system is displayed without the version.)
    - An icon indicating whether the computer is a primary domain controller, a backup domain controller or member server, or a computer running Windows NT Workstation or another client.

       In the previous illustration, the icon for Server1 and Server3 indicates a backup domain controller or a member server. The icon for Server2 indicates a primary domain controller. The icon for Computer10 indicates a computer running Windows NT Workstation or another client.
    - If a computer is not running, the icon for the computer appears dimmed.
    - A description (configured during installation).

    Note To view computers in another domain, on the **Computer** menu, click **Select Domain,** type the domain name, and then click **OK**. To view all computers in the domain that are running Windows NT, view just the servers, or view just the workstations, click the appropriate option on the **View** menu.

▶ **To view computer properties**

- In the Server Manager window, double-click the name of your computer to view its properties.

    –or–

    Click the computer name, and then on the **Computer** menu, click **Properties**.

    The **Properties for** *computer_name* dialog box appears.

    The following table describes the information for the selected computer.

Item	Description
Sessions	The number of users remotely connected to the computer.
Open Files	The number of shared resources opened on the computer.
File Locks	The number of file locks by users on the computer.
Open Named Pipes	The number of named pipes opened on the computer.

Viewing User Sessions

The **Users** button provides information on user sessions. User session information is useful in determining which users you need to contact when you have to shut down the server, and which users you need to contact when another user is trying to access a file that is already in use. Using the **Users** button, you can:

- View users connected to the computer, and view the shared folders that they are connected to.
- View the files opened by each user.
- Disconnect users from the computer to:
  - Force the user to reconnect to a shared folder, so that changes made to a user's group membership for the resource take effect. Windows NT checks a user's group membership when the user connects to a resource. If the user's permissions for the resource change as a result of becoming a member of a new group, those permissions will not take effect until the next time the user connects to the resource.
  - Free idle connections on a computer running Windows NT Workstation. Windows NT Workstation allows only 10 incoming network connections.
  - Shut down a server.

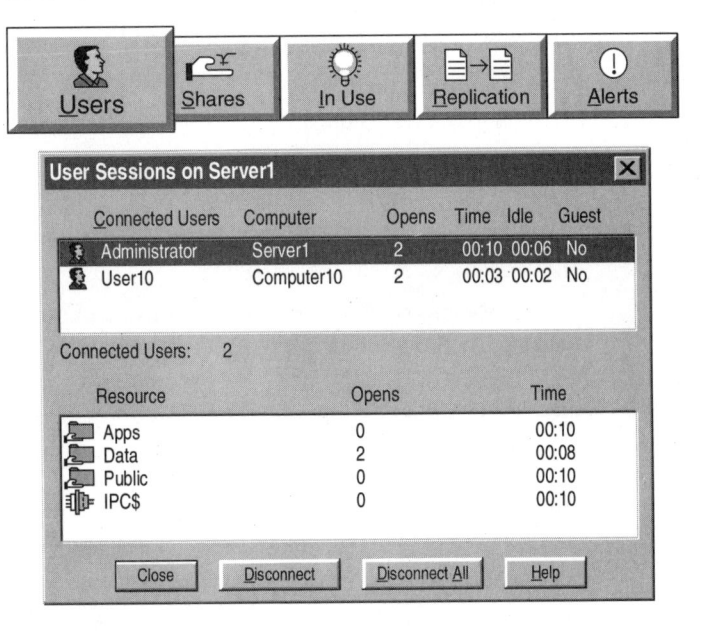

Connected Users	Computer	Opens	Time	Idle	Guest
Administrator	Server1	2	00:10	00:06	No
User10	Computer10	2	00:03	00:02	No

Connected Users: 2

Resource	Opens	Time
Apps	0	00:10
Data	2	00:08
Public	0	00:10
IPC$	0	00:10

When you select a user under **Connected Users**, the shared resources to which the user is connected appear under **Resource**, including the name of the resource, the number of files that the user has open, and the time that has elapsed since the resource was first opened.

The following table describes the information under **Connected Users** at the top of the dialog box.

Item	Description
Connected Users	The user name of a connected user.
Computer	The name of the computer where the user is logged on.
Opens	The number of resources that the user has open on this computer.
Time	The time elapsed since this session was established.
Idle	The time elapsed since the user last accessed the resource.
Guest	Whether this user has guest status on the computer.

▶ **To view user sessions**

In this procedure, you view user sessions for your user account. You create a session by connecting to your own computer.

1. In the **Properties for** *computer_name* dialog box, click **Users**.

    The **User Sessions on** *computer_name* dialog box appears.

2. Click the **Start** button, and then click **Run**.

3. In the **Open** box, type *****computer_name***\users** (where *computer_name* is the name of your computer), and then click **OK**.

    A window that shows the contents of the Users shared folder appears.

4. Switch to Server Manager.

5. Update the contents of the **User Sessions on** *computer_name* dialog box by closing the dialog box and then opening it.

6. Under **Connected Users**, click the user account that you logged on with (if it is not already selected).

    Under **Resource**, notice the connections that have been established to your server. The Users folder appears as a connection.

▶ **To disconnect users from shared resources**

In this procedure, you disconnect a user who has connected to a shared resource.

1. In the **User Sessions on** *computer_name* dialog box, make sure your user account is selected, and then click **Disconnect**.

    A message appears, prompting you to confirm the operation.

2. Click **Yes** to disconnect the user from the Users folder.

    Notice that all entries for your user account were removed.

    Note If you wanted to disconnect all users, you would click **Disconnect All**.

3. Click **Close** to return to the **Properties for** *computer_name* dialog box.
4. Click **OK** to return to the Server Manager window.
5. Quit Server Manager and log off.

Caution Always notify users before you disconnect them or shut down the server so that you give them an opportunity to save their files; otherwise, they may lose data.

Monitoring Shared Resources

The **Shares** button provides a list of shared resources on the computer and the users that are connected to each resource. Use this button to:

- Determine if the maximum number of users that are permitted to gain access to a particular resource has been reached. This may be one reason why a user cannot connect to a shared resource.

- Disconnect users. If users turned off their computers without either logging off or disconnecting from the network resource, their connection may still be active.

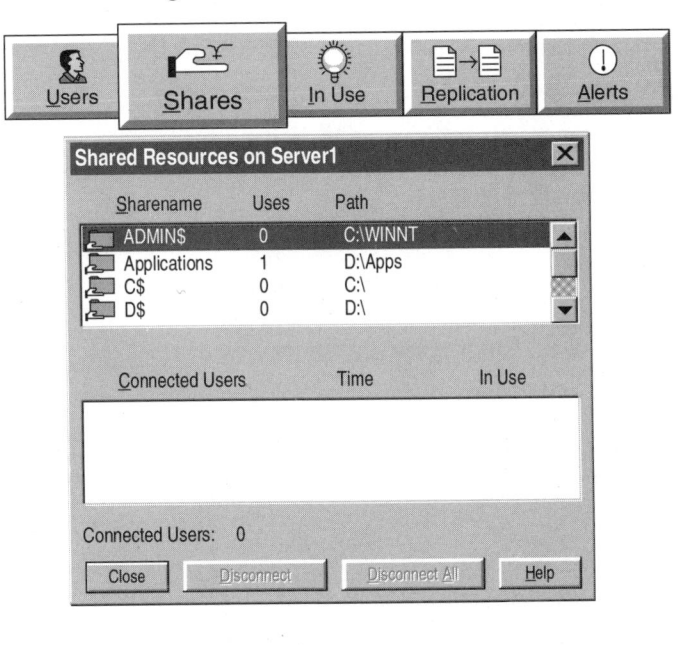

The following table describes the information in the dialog box options.

Item	Description
Sharename	The name of the shared resource. This can be a shared folder, a printer, or a named pipe.
Uses	The number of connections to the shared resource.
Path	The path of the shared resource.
Connected Users	The names of the users connected to the selected shared resource.
Time	The time that has elapsed since the user first connected to this resource.
In Use	Whether the user currently has any files open from this shared resource.

▶ **To connect to a shared resource**

In this procedure, you connect to your own computer. This procedure mimics what occurs when another user connects to your computer.

1. Log on as User10 (or as Administrator, if you did not complete Lesson 1).
2. Right-click Network Neighborhood or My Computer, and then click **Map Network Drive**.

   The **Map Network Drive** dialog box appears.
3. In the **Drive** box, click **P**, and in the **Path** box type *computer_name***public** and then click **OK**.

   A *drive* window appears for the Public shared folder.
4. Minimize, but do not close, the window.

▶ **To view a list of resources shared by computers**

In this procedure, you use Server Manager to view resources shared by other computers so that you can see which resources are currently in use on the computer.

1. Start Server Manager and double-click your computer name.
2. In the **Properties for** *computer_name* dialog box, click **Shares**.

   The **Shared Resources on** *computer_name* dialog box appears.
3. Under **Sharename**, click **Public**.

   Notice that your user account appears as a user connected to the Public shared folder. If other network users have connected to your Public shared folder, their user accounts will also appear here.

4. Under **Sharename**, click IPC$.

   Notice that your user account appears as a user connected to IPC$.

   IPC$ indicates that a resource is sharing the named pipes that are essential for communication between programs. IPC$ is used during remote administration of a computer, and when viewing a computer's shared resources.

5. Click **Close** to return to the **Properties for** *computer_name* dialog box.

Monitoring Resources in Use

The **In Use** button provides a list of the users that are connected to a shared resource and the files that they have open. Use this button to:

- Determine if a file is in use. For example, if a user cannot access a specific file because another user has the file open, you can notify this user of the file that another user needs to access the file.

- Close a file. For example, if you make changes to NTFS permissions for a file, for those changes to be immediately effective, the file has to be closed and then reopened.

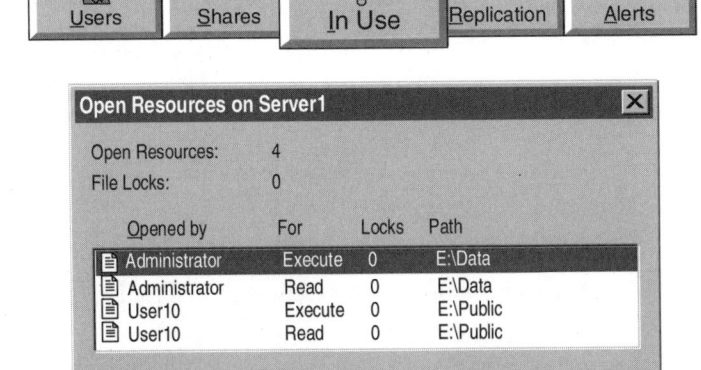

| Users | Shares | In Use | Replication | Alerts |

Open Resources on Server1

Open Resources: 4
File Locks: 0

Opened by	For	Locks	Path
Administrator	Execute	0	E:\Data
Administrator	Read	0	E:\Data
User10	Execute	0	E:\Public
User10	Read	0	E:\Public

Close | Refresh | Close Resource | Close All Resources | Help

The following table describes the information in the **Open Resources on** *computer_name* dialog box.

Item	Description
Open Resources	The total number of open resources (files, printers, or named pipes) on the computer.
File Locks	The total number of file locks on open resources.
Opened by	The user name of the user who opened the resource.
For	The permissions granted when the resource was opened.
Locks	The number of locks on the resource by that user.
Path	The path of the open resource.

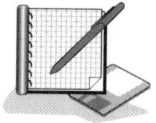

▶ **To view a list of open resources on the server**

In this procedure, you open a resource and then use the **In Use** button to view it as being open.

1. Click the **Start** button, point to **Programs**, point to **Accessories**, and then click **WordPad**.
2. Open P:\Expenses.doc.
3. Minimize WordPad.
4. In the **Properties for** *computer_name* dialog box, click **In Use**.

   Notice the resources in use on your computer.
5. Click the **Start** button, and then click **Run**.
6. In the **Open** box, type *****computer_name***users** (where *computer_name* is your computer), and then click **OK**.

   A window that shows the contents of the Users shared folder appears.
7. Minimize the window for the Users shared folder.
8. In the **Open Resources on** *computer_name* dialog box, click **Refresh** to update the list of open resources. It does not update automatically.

   Notice that an additional open resource appears.

▶ **To close a single resource**

1. In the **Open Resources on** *computer_name* dialog box, click the Public folder, and then click **Close Resource**.

   A message appears, warning you that disconnecting users may cause loss of data.

2. Click **Yes**.

   Notice that the entry was removed.

   Note To close all resources, you would click **Close All Resources**.

3. Close all windows, quit Server Manager, and then log off.

Lesson Summary

The following information summarizes the key points in this lesson:

- The computer properties that you can view in Server Manager show you information about system resources.
- The **Users** button provides information on user sessions.
- The **Shares** button provides a list of shared resources on the computer and the users that are connected to each resource.
- The **In Use** button provides a list of the users that are connected to a shared resource and the files that they have open.

For more information on	See
Viewing resources in use	Server Manager Help.
Viewing shared resources	Server Manager Help.
Server Manager	Chapter 4, "Managing Shared Resources and Resource Security," in Microsoft Windows NT Server *Concepts and Planning*.

Lesson 3: Setting Alerts and Sending Messages

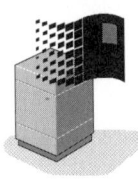

You can set administrative alerts so that Windows NT notifies administrators that operating system problems exist. You can notify users that a server event will occur by sending a Windows NT message. This lesson guides you through the steps to set administrative alerts and to send messages to users.

After this lesson, you will be able to:
- Set administrative alerts.
- Send messages to users to notify them of disruptions in service.

Estimated lesson time: 20 minutes

Setting Administrative Alerts

The **Alerts** button allows you to create a list of users or computers that need to receive an alert when there are Windows NT operating system problems, such as security and access problems, user session problems, and printer problems. For example, you can notify the Administrators group when a computer is running low on disk space so that appropriate action can be taken.

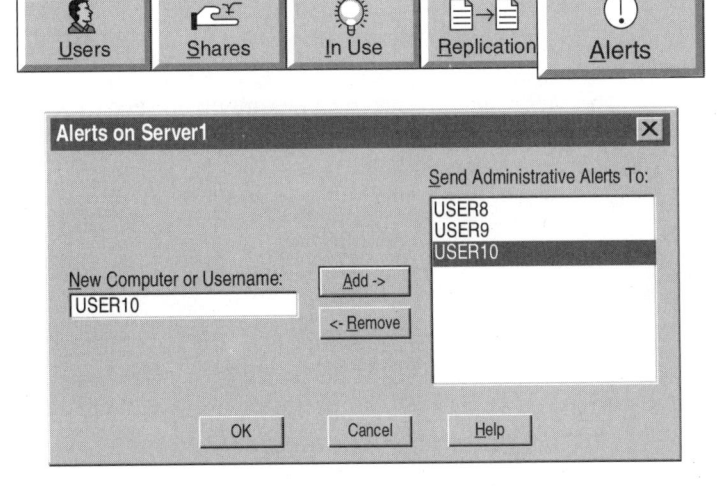

Note Administrative alerts are generated *only* by the Windows NT Alerter service. They are not generated by programs, such as Microsoft Word.

▶ **To set an administrative alert**

1. Log on as Administrator.
2. Start Server Manager, and then double-click your computer name.
3. In the **Properties for** *computer_name* dialog box, click **Alerts**.

   The **Alerts on** *computer_name* dialog box appears.
4. In the **New Computer or Username** box, type **user10** and then click **Add**.

   User10 appears under **Send Administrative Alerts To**.
5. Click **OK** twice to apply your changes and to return to the Server Manager window.

   When an operating system problem occurs, an alert will be sent to User10.

Sending Messages to Users

Always send messages to all users connected to a particular computer when there will be a disruption to the server or the resource availability. This gives users an opportunity to save their files.

Send messages to users before:

- Performing a backup or restore operation on a user's files.
- Disconnecting users from a resource.
- Shutting down the server.

Note The Messenger service must be running to send messages. It is started by default. Computers running Windows 95 must be running WinPopUp.exe to receive messages.

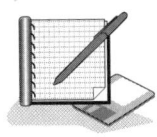

▶ **To send a message to all users connected to your computer**

1. In the Server Manager window, make sure that your computer is selected.
2. On the **Computer** menu, click **Send Message**.

   The **Send Message** dialog box appears.
3. Under **Message**, type a message notifying users to save and close their files because they will be disconnected within the next few minutes.
4. Click **OK** to send the message.

   The message is sent to all users who are currently connected to your computer and have started the Messenger service. Because you have opened a shared resource on your server, your own computer will also receive the message. Notice that the message includes the name of the computer from which the message was sent, as well as the date and time.
5. Click **OK** to close the message.
6. Quit Server Manager, and then log off.

Lesson Summary

The following information summarizes the key points in this lesson:

- By setting administrative alerts, you can notify administrators when operating system problems occur.
- When there will be a disruption to the server or the resource availability, always send a message to all users connected to a particular computer.

For more information on	See
Managing administrative alerts	Server Manager Help.
Starting and stopping services	Server Manager Help.
Configuring service startup	Server Manager Help.
Administrative alerts	Chapter 4, "Managing Shared Resources and Resource Security," in Microsoft Windows NT Server *Concepts and Planning*.
Windows NT services	Windows NT Help.

Lesson 4: Using Windows NT Diagnostics

It is recommended that you have a log book for every computer that contains information about the computer's configuration. Having current information makes it easier to rebuild a computer in the event of a serious system failure. This information also helps product support personnel to troubleshoot problems.

This lesson describes the Windows NT Diagnostics options and guides you through the steps to gather information about a computer's configuration. The lesson also covers how to save and print a report for your log book.

After this lesson, you will be able to:
- Describe the Windows NT Diagnostics options.
- View system configuration information.
- Save or print a report.

Estimated lesson time: 20 minutes

Windows NT Diagnostics is a useful tool for gathering information about a computer's hardware and software configuration and for printing a report containing this information.

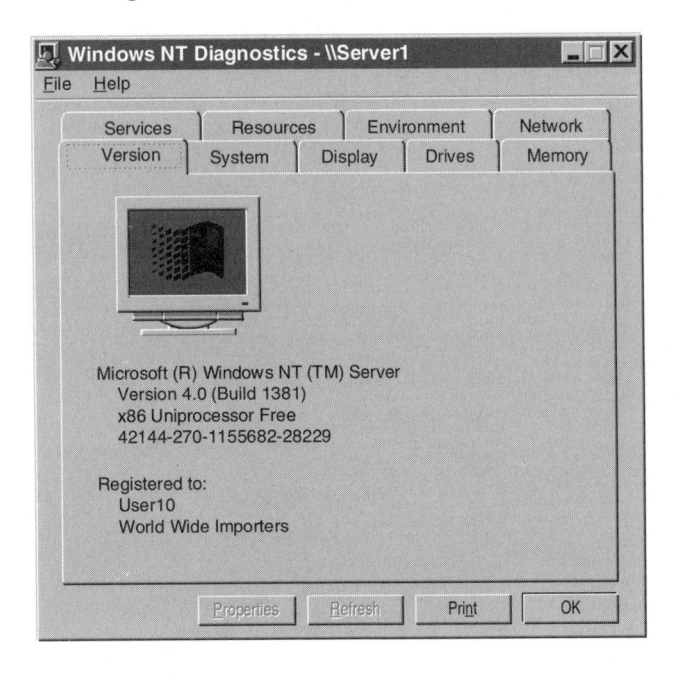

The following table describes the types of information that you can view in Windows NT Diagnostics.

Tab	Description
Version	Operating system information, including version numbers, build and service pack information, and the identity of the registered owner.
System	ROM BIOS and CPU information, including the CPU type and the number of CPUs in the computer.
Display	Information about the video driver and adapter.
Drives	Available drives and their types, including removable (floppy or optical), non-removable (hard disk), and remote (network connections).
Memory	Information about physical and virtual memory. Specifics about the paging file (Pagefile.sys), total memory, available memory, and a memory load index are displayed.
Services	Services listed in the **CurrentControlSet**, along with the state of the service, either running or stopped.
Resources	Active devices and details about each resource, including direct memory access (DMA), interrupt request line (IRQ) status, memory, and port information.
	Information about IRQ interrupts within the computer and which device has locked a particular interrupt for use.
	Information about DMA channels that are used by devices or drivers.
Environment	Environment variables, such as the path command (which is the same information you see when you type **set** at a command prompt).
Network	Network-related configuration information, including current network statistics.

Note If you view information on a remote computer, the **Drives** and **Memory** tabs do not appear.

Gathering Information

When you call Microsoft Technical Support, the support engineer will ask you a number of questions about the computer for which you are requesting support. You will be asked to provide information about the computer's hardware and software configuration and settings.

Having the answers to these questions ready will speed up the process of creating a customer record and if needed, escalating your call to the secondary response group.

▶ **To gather information about your computer**

In this procedure, you locate the configuration information for your computer that is typically requested when you call Microsoft Technical Support.

1. Log on as Administrator.
2. Click the **Start** button, point to **Programs**, point to **Administrative Tools**, and then click **Windows NT Diagnostics**.
3. Locate the information in the following table by performing the steps under **Do this**.

For this information	Do this
Version of Windows NT installed	Click the **Version** tab.
Computer BIOS (*x86*-based computers) or firmware revision level (RISC-based computers)	Click the **System** tab, and then look under **BIOS Information**.
Processor and HAL type	Click the **System** tab, and then look at **HAL** and **Processor(s)**.
File systems in use	Click the **Drives** tab, expand Local Hard Drives, double-click a drive, and then click the **File System** tab.
Total memory (RAM)	Click the **Memory** tab, and then look under **Physical Memory**.
Services installed	Click the **Services** tab, and then look under **Service**.
Hardware IRQs, I/O ports, DMA addresses, and similar information	Click the **Resources** tab. For IRQs, click the **IRQ** button. For the I\O ports, click the **I\O Port** button. For DMA addresses, click the **DMA** button.
Folder where Windows NT is installed	Click the **Environment** tab, and then look at **windir**.

(*continued*)

For this information	Do this
Name of the domain that you are currently logged into	Click the **Network** tab, and then look at **Logon Domain**.
Name of the domain controller that validated your user account	Click the **Network** tab, and then look at **Logon Server**.
Name of the workgroup or domain that your computer is a member of	Click the **Network** tab, and then look at **Workgroup or Domain**.
Protocols installed	Click the **Network** tab, click the **Transports** button, and then look under **Transport**.

Creating and Printing a Report

In addition to providing a support organization with key information about a computer, a Windows NT Diagnostics report is valuable for inventory and record keeping purposes. It can help you keep track of the RAM, hard disks, and devices installed on each computer.

The following table describes the available print options.

Click an option under	To
Scope	Either print the information on the current tab or on all tabs.
Detail Level	Either print a summary or a complete report.
Destination	Either print the information to a file, to the Clipboard, or to the default printer.

▶ **To print or save a report**

1. On the Windows NT Diagnostics **File** menu, click **Print Report**.

    Note To view and print the diagnostics for another computer, on the **File** menu, click **Select Computer**, and then type of the name of the computer. Note, however, that the printout does not necessarily contain the same data as the onscreen report.

    The **Create Report** dialog box appears.

2. Under **Scope**, click **All tabs** to include the information provided on all tabs in the saved report.
3. Under **Detail Level**, click **Complete**.

4. If your computer is connected to a printer, under **Destination**, click **Default Printer**, and then click **OK**.

   –or–

   If your computer is not connected to a printer, under **Destination**, click **File**, and then click **OK**. In the **Save in** box, click **C**, and accept the default file name **msdrpt** by clicking **Save**.

   A Generating WinMSD Report message appears.

5. Retrieve the printed report, or start Notepad and open C:\MsdRpt.txt.

   Compare the information in the report to the information displayed in Windows NT Diagnostics.

6. Close C:\MsdRpt.txt when you are done.
7. Quit Windows NT Diagnostics, and then log off.

Lesson Summary

The following information summarizes the key points in this lesson:

- For every computer, create a log book that contains information about the computer's configuration.
- Having current information makes it easier to rebuild a computer in the event of a serious system failure. This information also helps product support personnel to troubleshoot problems.
- Windows NT Diagnostics helps you to gather information about a computer's hardware and software configuration, and to create and print a report for your log book.

For more information on	See
Using Windows NT Diagnostics for system diagnosis	Chapter 7, "Protecting Data," in Microsoft Windows NT Server *Concepts and Planning*.
Using Windows NT Diagnostics to view system configuration data	Chapter 7, "Protecting Data," in Microsoft Windows NT Server *Concepts and Planning*.
Using Windows NT Diagnostics for troubleshooting	Chapter 8, "General Troubleshooting," in the *Resource Guide* of the *Microsoft Windows NT Server Resource Kit*.
Keeping a log book	Chapter 20, "Preparing for and Performing Recovery," in the *Microsoft Windows NT Workstation Resource Kit*.

Best Practices

The following checklist provides best practices for monitoring network resources. Review this checklist before you monitor network resources:

- ❏ Install the client-based administration tools (available on the Clients\Srvtools folder on the Windows NT Server compact disc) on a computer running Windows NT Workstation or Windows 95. This allows you to administer any computer running Windows NT Server from the client.
- ❏ To give users an opportunity to save their files, always notify them before disconnecting them from the server or shutting it down.
- ❏ Set administrative alerts so that they are sent to the computers of users who are responsible for maintaining the server.
- ❏ For every computer, maintain a log book that contains information about the computer's configuration. Having this information makes it easier to rebuild a computer in the event of a serious system failure. This information also helps product support personnel to troubleshoot problems.

Note If you want to remove the account that was created by running the Chapter10.cmd file at the beginning of this chapter, log on as Administrator, and then double-click DeleteChapter10.cmd in the Cleanup folder on the Supplemental Material compact disc.

Review

The following questions are intended to reinforce key information presented in this chapter. If you are unable to answer a question, review the lesson and then try the question again.

1. Scenario: You want to give a user the ability to monitor resource usage on Server1 and Server2 (in the same domain), but you do not want the user to have full administrative capabilities on either server. Server1 is the primary domain controller (PDC) and Server2 is the backup domain controller (BDC). To which group would you add the user, and on which computer or computers?

   _____

   _____

2. Which of the following tasks can you perform using Server Manager? (Circle all that apply.)

   a. View a list of connected users.
   b. View operating system information, such as the version number, services, system settings, and environment variables.
   c. View shared and open resources.
   d. View network-related information, such as the name of the domain, or the logon server.
   e. Set an administrative alert to notify an administrator of an operating system problem.
   f. Send a message to all users.

3. Scenario: So that User10 can update files in the Public shared folder, you have changed User10's permission for the Public folder from Read to Change by adding his user account to a group. User10 said that he tried adding a file to the Public folder, but was denied access. You checked the NTFS permission and determined that the Everyone group has the Full Control permission. What is the problem, and what Server Manager task can you perform to solve it?

   _____

   _____

4. What is the difference between the **Alerts** option and the **Send Message** command?

   _____

   _____

Answer Key

Procedure Answers

Page 367

▶ **To determine the built-in rights that are assigned to Server Operators**

2. In the **Right** box, click each item in the list to determine which rights are automatically assigned to the Server Operators group (that is, which rights cause **Server Operators** to appear in the **Grant To** box). In the following list, mark the check box next to each right that is granted automatically to the Server Operators group:

   The following check boxes should be marked: Back up files and directories, Change the system time, Force shutdown from a remote system, Log on locally, Restore files and directories, and Shut down the system.

Page 390

Review Answers

1. Scenario: You want to give a user the ability to monitor resource usage on Server1 and Server2 (in the same domain), but you do not want the user to have full administrative capabilities on either server. Server1 is the primary domain controller (PDC) and Server2 is the backup domain controller (BDC). To which group would you add the user, and on which computer or computers?

   Add the user to the Server Operators group on Server1. Because Server1 is a PDC, the user will have Server Operator privileges on all domain controllers in the domain.

2. Which of the following tasks can you perform using Server Manager? (Circle all that apply.)

   Answers a, c, e, and f are correct.

3. Scenario: So that User10 can update files in the Public shared folder, you have changed User10's permission for the Public folder from Read to Change by adding his user account to a group. User10 said that he tried adding a file to the Public folder, but was denied access. You checked the NTFS permission and determined that the Everyone group has the Full Control permission. What is the problem, and what Server Manager task can you perform to solve it?

   The problem is that User10 was connected to the Public folder when his permission for the folder was changed. Because Windows NT only checks a user's membership to a group when the user connects to a shared folder, the effective permission for User10 is still Read. In Server Manager, disconnect User10 from the Public folder. When User10 tries to gain access to the folder, he will automatically be reconnected.

4. What is the difference between the **Alerts** option and the **Send Message** command?

   The Alerts option only sends alerts from the Windows NT operating system to the users that have been added to the Send Administrative Alerts To box. The Send Message command gives you the ability to send a message to all users who are connected to the server.

CHAPTER 11

Backing Up and Restoring Files

Lesson 1 Introduction to the Windows NT Backup Program . . . 395

Lesson 2 Planning a Backup Strategy . . . 399

Lesson 3 Backing Up Files . . . 410

Lesson 4 Scheduling a Backup Using a Batch File . . . 418

Lesson 5 Restoring Files . . . 427

Best Practices . . . 438

Review . . . 439

About This Chapter

This chapter describes planning strategies for backing up and restoring files on your network and provides instruction on how to back up and restore files using the Windows NT Backup program. In the hands-on procedures, you use a Backup Simulation program to back up and restore files. This program simulates Windows NT Backup.

Before You Begin

To complete the lessons in this chapter, you must have:

- Completed the Setup procedures located in "About This Book."
- Knowledge and skills to create local and global groups and add user accounts to them.
- Knowledge and skills to assign user rights to accounts.
- Knowledge about the built-in Administrators, Server Operators, and Backup Operators groups.
- Knowledge about NTFS permissions.
- Two user accounts named User11-A and User11-B. Log on as Administrator. In Windows NT Explorer, expand the LabFiles folder, and then double-click Chapter11.cmd to create these accounts.

Lesson 1: Introduction to the Windows NT Backup Program

Regular backup of servers and local hard disks prevents data loss and damage caused by disk-drive failures, power outages, virus infections, and other potential disasters. Backup operations based on careful planning and reliable equipment make file recovery a relatively painless process. This lesson explains the underlying concepts of the Windows NT Backup program and the requirements that must be in place to use it.

After this lesson, you will be able to:
- Describe the requirements for backing up and restoring data.

Estimated lesson time: 10 minutes

The Windows NT Backup program is a graphical tool that you can use to back up and restore files to NTFS or FAT volumes, either manually or automatically.

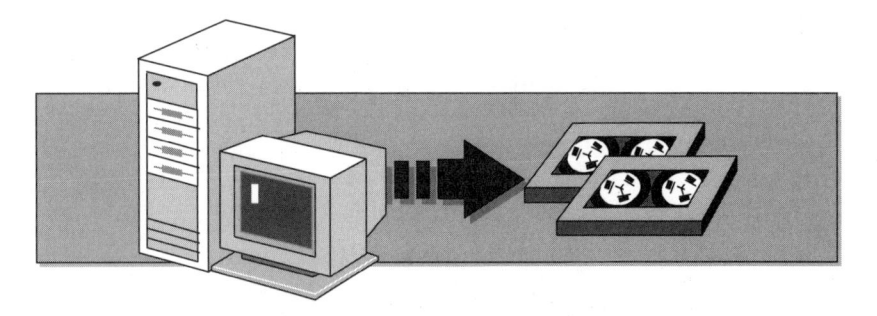

Note Windows NT Backup only supports backing up to tape. To back up information to floppy disks or other non-tape media, use the **xcopy** or **backup** commands.

Requirements

The following requirements must be met to back up and restore files using the Windows NT Backup program:

- A computer running Windows NT Workstation or Windows NT Server with a tape drive that is supported on the hardware compatibility list (HCL).

  To back up the directory database (security and user account information) for the domain, the tape drive must be located on a domain controller.

- The user who performs the backup must have the appropriate user right on the computer where Windows NT Backup is running.
  - All users can back up any files and folders on the network for which they have the Read permission.
  - To back up all files and folders on a network, a user must have the *Back up files and directories* user right.
  - To restore all files and folders on a network, a user must have the *Restore files and directories* user right.
  - By default, the Backup Operators and Server Operators groups have both the Back up files and directories user right and the Restore files and directories user right. If you want to assign the ability to back up files to a user, the easiest way is to add him or her to either the Backup Operators or Server Operators group.

Creating a Backup Operator

You can give a user the right to back up and restore all files on a computer running Windows NT, regardless of the NTFS permissions assigned to those files, by adding the user to the Backup Operators group. In networks where security is an issue, it is recommended that the user who performs the backup not have the right to restore files.

This prevents the user from restoring the files to a FAT volume, which removes NTFS security, or restoring files to a computer where the user has administrator privileges and can assign the NTFS permission Full Control to all files.

To give a user only the backup right, following these guidelines:

❑ Create a local group named Backup Only Operators on the computer where the tape drive is located and assign it the following user rights:
  - Log on locally. This user right is required to back up the registry. The registry is a database where Windows NT stores its configuration information, including the security and user account information in the directory database.
  - Back up files and directories. This user right provides the capability to perform a backup.

❑ Create a global group named Backup Only on the primary domain controller. This group will be used to organize all user accounts that you want to give backup rights to.

❑ Add the global group Backup Only to the local group Backup Only Operators. Add the user account to the global group Backup Only.

▶ **To create a local group with the appropriate user rights**

1. Log on as Administrator.

2. Start User Manager for Domains, and create a local group named *Backup Only Operators*.

3. Grant the following user rights to the Backup Only Operators group:
   - Back up files and directories
   - Log on locally

▶ **To create a global group to organize users who can back up data**

1. Create a global group named *Backup Only*.

2. Add the global group Backup Only to the local group Backup Only Operators.

▶ **To give a user the rights to back up the computer**

1. Add the user account User11-A to the global group Backup Only.

2. Quit User Manager for Domains.

3. Log off.

Lesson Summary

The following information summarizes the key points in this lesson:

- To use Windows NT Backup, you must have a computer running Windows NT Workstation or Windows NT Server with a tape drive supported on the hardware compatibility list (HCL).
- To back up the directory database (security and user account information) for the domain, the tape drive must be located on a domain controller.
- All users can back up any folders and files on the network for which they have the Read permission.
- You can give a user the right to back up and restore all files on a computer running Windows NT by adding the user to the Backup Operators group or by assigning the user right Back up files and directories (to back up files) and the user right Restore files and directories (to restore files) to a user account or group of which the user is a member.

For more information on	See
Hardware considerations	Chapter 6, "Backing Up and Restoring Network Files," in Microsoft Windows NT Server *Concepts and Planning*.
User rights	Chapter 2, "Working With User and Group Accounts," in Microsoft Windows NT Server *Concepts and Planning*.
NTFS permissions	Chapter 6, "Securing Network Resources with NTFS Permissions," in this book.
Groups	Chapter 3, "Setting Up Group Accounts," in this book.

Lesson 2: Planning a Backup Strategy

Before you begin backing up files, you need a backup strategy that meets the needs of your organization, and that guarantees the recovery of lost data. Effective information backup and retrieval are an administrator's most critical functions. It is important to create backup policies. This lesson describes important issues to consider for planning an effective backup strategy.

After this lesson, you will be able to:
- Describe the considerations for backing up files.
- Determine which folders and files to back up.
- Determine the backup type to use.
- Determine whether to rotate or archive tapes.
- Describe the difference between a backup set, catalog, and backup log.

Estimated lesson time: 30 minutes

A good backup strategy ensures that you can quickly recover your data if it is lost. Consider the following points to create an effective backup strategy that is best suited to your network:

- To determine which files to back up, use the following general backup rule: if you cannot get along without it, back it up.

- Deciding whether to perform a network backup or multiple local backups depends on which computers your organization uses for storing critical data.

    - Do a network backup when the critical data is on multiple servers or you want to perform a backup over the network. The following table describes the advantages and disadvantages of performing a network backup.

Advantages	Disadvantages
Backs up the entire network.	Users must copy their important files to the servers.
Requires fewer tape drives.	Cannot back up the registry on remote computers.
Less media to manage.	Increases network traffic.
One user can do the backup.	Requires greater planning and preparation.

- Do multiple local backups when the critical data is on client computers. The following table describes the advantages and disadvantages of performing a local backup.

Advantages	Disadvantages
Fewer network resources committed.	Requires more tape drives and tapes.
	Users are responsible for backing up the data on their computers. The users may not be reliable.

- Do both network and local backups when the critical data is on servers and workstations.
- How frequently to back up the data depends on the following:
  - How critical the data is to your company. You would want to back up critical data more often.
  - How frequently the data changes. For example, if users create or modify reports only on Fridays, a weekly backup for the report files would be sufficient.

Tip Plan to perform backups when network usage is low. If files are in use, Windows NT only backs up the last saved version of the file.

Determining Which Files to Back Up

There are folders and files that you need to always back up, some that you need to back up intermittently, and some that you never need to back up.

Use the following guidelines to help you determine which files to back up.

- Always back up:
  - Critical files that your organization needs to operate.
  - The registry on any domain controller—a BDC or PDC. Each domain controller maintains a copy of the directory database. Backing up the registry on a domain controller prevents loss of all user accounts and security information.

Important Windows NT Backup can only back up the registry on the computer where the tape drive is installed. If possible, you should have your tape drive installed on a domain controller.

- Periodically back up files that seldom change or are not critical to your organization.
- Do not back up temporary files, as they change constantly and are rarely used to recover data. Backing up temporary files not only uses extra tapes, it results in the creation of unnecessary files that take additional time to sort through when you need to look for key files to restore.

Note Windows NT Backup is not intended for volume recovery; it does not back up data at the sector level and cannot restore the boot partition. This means that to restore the operating system volume, you must format a volume, reinstall Windows NT, and then use Windows NT Backup to restore the registry and any additional files from the latest backup tape.

Determining the Backup Type to Use

Windows NT Backup provides five backup types—normal, copy, incremental, differential, and daily copy. Some backup types use *backup markers*, also known as archive attributes, to track when a file has been backed up. An effective backup strategy may combine different backup types, depending on the amount of time available to perform the backup and how quickly you would need to locate and restore files.

The following table describes the backup types.

This backup type	Backs up
Normal (also called full)	Selected files and marks each as having been backed up. With normal backups, you can restore files quickly because files on the last tape are the most current.
	Always perform a normal backup of all files as the initial backup.
Incremental	Only those files created or changed since the last normal or incremental backup. It marks files as having been backed up. If you use a combination of normal and incremental backups, restoring requires starting with your last normal backup and then working through all the incremental tapes.
Differential	Those files created or changed since the last normal (or incremental) backup. It does not mark files as having been backed up. If you are doing normal and differential backups, restoring requires only the last normal and last differential backup tape.

(*continued*)

This backup type	Backs up
Copy	Selected files, but does not mark each file as having been backed up. Copying is useful if you want to back up files between normal and incremental backups, because copying does not invalidate these other backup operations.
Daily copy	Selected files that have been modified the day the daily backup is performed. The backed up files are not marked as having been backed up. (This can be useful if you want to take work home and need a quick way to select the files that you worked on that day.)

Examples of Using Different Backup Types

You can combine backup types to create a backup strategy to fit your particular needs. Some backup types require more time to back up data, but less time to restore. Others require less time to back up, but more time to restore. You need to consider which task you want to spend your time on, and how quickly you need access to lost data.

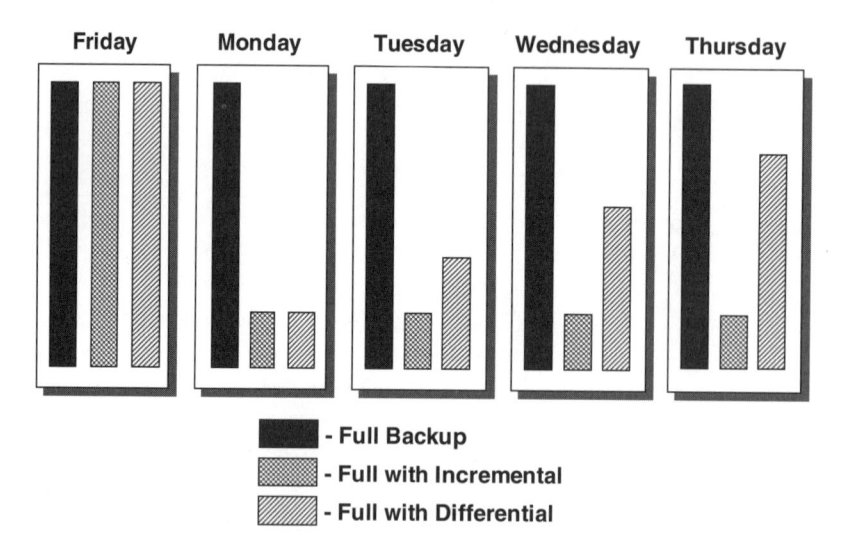

■ - Full Backup
▦ - Full with Incremental
▨ - Full with Differential

The time necessary for backup and restore operations varies depending on the backup strategy used. Each strategy has advantages and disadvantages.

Normal Backup

Using this strategy (as shown in the previous illustration), a full backup is performed every day. The disadvantage of this strategy is that this type of backup takes the longest amount of time each day and requires the most tapes. The advantage of this strategy is that if there is a catastrophic system failure on Thursday, only one tape will be required to perform a full restore.

Normal with Incremental

Using this strategy (as shown in the previous illustration), a full backup is performed each Friday. On Monday, everything that has changed since Friday is backed up. On Tuesday, everything that has changed since Monday is backed up, on Wednesday, everything that has changed since Tuesday is backed up, and so on. The advantage with this strategy is that the amount of time to do daily backup is minimal. The disadvantage is that if there is a catastrophic system failure on Thursday, it is possible that five tapes will be required to perform a full restore.

Normal with Differential

Using this strategy (as shown in the previous illustration), a full backup is performed on Friday. On Monday, everything that has changed since Friday is backed up. On Tuesday, everything that has changed since Friday is backed up, on Wednesday, everything that has changed since Friday is backed up, and so on. The disadvantage with this strategy is that backing up files takes progressively longer each day. The advantage is that if there is a catastrophic system failure on Thursday, only two tapes will be required to perform a full restore, the Friday tape and the Wednesday tape.

Tip Because the copy backup type does not set a backup marker, use it to make tape copies that will not interfere with ongoing backups—for example, an archive tape.

Rotating and Archiving Tapes

Rotating tapes ensures that you can always go to a previous tape for a lost file, even though it may not be the most current version of the file. If you perform a backup using the same tape, you run the risk of not being able to recover lost files in the event that the tape becomes damaged.

You may want to archive some tapes. Archived tapes are useful for maintaining a record of data for a specific date and time—for example, a quarterly record of financial data in case of an IRS audit. When you archive a tape, you remove it from the tape rotation.

The following are two examples of tape rotation.

Example 1

Each day of the week is on a different tape. The tape for one day of the week is archived and removed from rotation. In this example, six tapes are used. The tape for each Friday is archived.

For the following weeks, use the Monday through Thursday tapes for the same day of the week; for example, put the Monday backup on the Monday tape. These backups can either replace or append the previous backup on the tape.

Monday	Tuesday	Wednesday	Thursday	Friday
1	2	3	4	Archive 5
1	2	3	4	Archive 6

Example 2

The Monday through Thursday backups use the same tape with each new backup appended to the previous one. The Friday backup is on a different tape that is archived. The next week you would start all over again with tape 1.

Monday	Tuesday	Wednesday	Thursday	Friday
1	1	1	1	Archive 2

Note The number of tapes you need is determined not only by tape rotation, but also by the size of the files that you back up and by the life cycle of the tape.

The life cycle of a tape depends on the manufacturer and on storage conditions. If your company does not have a suitable storage facility, consider using a third-party company that specializes in off-site storage for backup media.

Backup Sets, Catalogs, and Backup Logs

Before you do a backup, it is helpful for you to know the differences between backup sets, catalogs, and backup logs.

- A *backup set* is the term used to describe a group of files or folders on a single volume from a single backup operation. One tape can contain many backup sets.

  If a single backup operation requires multiple tapes, the group of tapes is called a family set.

- The *catalog* is a graphical representation of the backup. Windows NT automatically creates catalogs during a backup and stores them on the tape. There are two different catalogs:
  - The *tape catalog* shows all the backup sets on a tape.
  - The *backup set catalog* shows all of the files and folders in the backup set.

  Before you restore files, you must load the catalogs. Then, you can select the backup sets, files, and folders that you want to restore.

- A *backup log* is a text file that records backup operations. The backup log is helpful when restoring data, in that you can print it or read it using any text editor. The backup log is stored on disk, so if the tape containing the backup set catalog is corrupted, the backup log will help you locate a file.

  A backup log may contain some or all of the following information, depending on which log options you select:

  - Date of backup
  - Who performed the backup
  - Location of the tape drive
  - Tape-set number
  - Files backed up
  - Type of backup
  - Computers backed up

▶ **To plan a backup schedule**

In this exercise, you plan a backup schedule for the Quebec domain. The Quebec domain has four servers—two servers are configured as domain controllers, and two are configured as member servers. The tape drive is installed on the primary domain controller (PDC).

You need to determine:

- Whether files need to be backed up daily or weekly.
- A weekly backup schedule that includes a backup type for each day, which tape to use, and whether that tape will be archived or reused.

Record your decisions on the "Backup Planning Worksheet," located at the end of this lesson.

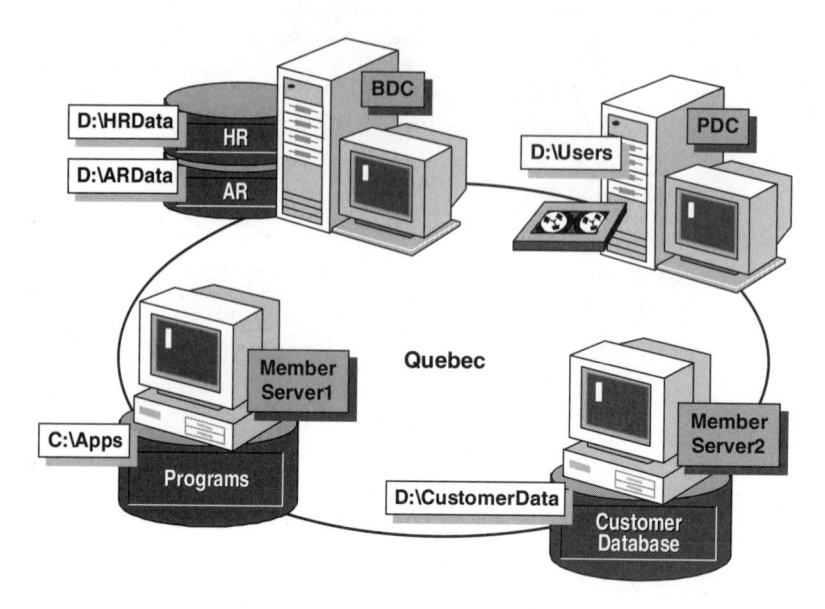

Diagram: Quebec network showing BDC with D:\HRData (HR) and D:\ARData (AR); PDC with D:\Users; Member Server1 with C:\Apps (Programs); Member Server2 with D:\CustomerData (Customer Database).

Use the following criteria to make your decisions:

- Programs are upgraded approximately every three months. Minor updates are applied as necessary.
- The Accounts Receivable (AR) database is updated each day with full and partial payments received from customers.
- The Human Resources (HR) database is updated every time a new employee is hired or an existing employee goes on vacation.
- Users store letters, memos, and archived e-mail in their home folders. Most data does not change frequently.
- Critical customer files are stored in the Customer database.
- Lost data must be restorable in a quick and easy manner.
- All backups should be well documented.

To complete the "Backup Planning Worksheet," you need to:

1. Provide the path to the folders and files that will be backed up. Record it under Folders and Files to Backup.
2. Specify whether the backup is daily (record it under Daily) or, if weekly, the day of the backup (record it under Weekly).
3. Fill in the weekly backup schedule with the backup type, tape number (record this information under Weekly Backup Schedule), and type of backup log (record it under Type of Backup Log).
4. When you are done, compare your answers to the answers on the "Backup Planning Worksheet" in Appendix A of this book.

Lesson Summary

The following information summarizes the key points in this lesson:

- Plan an effective backup strategy to ensure that you can quickly recover lost or corrupted files.
- Always back up critical files and the registry.
- Use backup types to create a backup strategy to fit your needs. Always do a normal backup of all files as your initial backup.
- Rotate your tapes so that you can always go back to a previous tape for a file. If you always back up to the same tape and that tape becomes damaged, you will not be able to recover files.
- Always create and print your backup logs. This will help you to locate lost files quickly.

For more information on	See
Planning a backup	Chapter 6, "Backing Up and Restoring Network Files," in Microsoft Windows NT Server *Concepts and Planning*.
Backup strategies	Chapter 4, "Planning a Reliable Configuration," in the *Resource Guide* of the *Microsoft Windows NT Server Resource Kit*.

Backup Planning Worksheet

Tape Drive Location _____ **Tape Storage Location** _____

Folders and Files to Back Up (Provide Path)	Daily	Weekly (Provide Day)

Weekly Backup Schedule

Monday	Tuesday	Wednesday	Thursday	Friday
Backup Type_____	Backup Type_____	Backup Type_____	Backup Type_____	Backup Type_____
Tape_____	Tape_____	Tape_____	Tape_____	Tape_____
Archive Y__N__	Archive Y__N__	Archive Y__N__	Archive Y__N__	Archive Y__N__

Backup Types

N = Normal   D = Differential   I = Incremental   C = Copy   DC = Daily Copy

Type of Backup Log

☐ Full Detail   ☐ Summary Only   ☐ Don't Log

Lesson 3: Backing Up Files

This lesson guides you through the steps required to back up data. When you create a backup, you need to conduct several preliminary tasks, and then you perform a number of tasks using the Windows NT Backup program.

After this lesson, you will be able to:
- Prepare for a backup.
- Perform a backup to tape.

Estimated lesson time: 20 minutes

Preparing to Back Up Files

Before you begin backing up files, you need to do the following tasks:

❑ Prepare your tapes. If you are beginning your backups with tapes that contain obsolete files, it is recommended that you erase the tapes first by clicking **Erase Tape** on the Windows NT Backup **Operations** menu. You can do either a **Quick Erase**, during which the tape header is simply rewritten, or a **Secure Erase**, during which the entire tape is overwritten. The secure erase method may take several hours to complete, depending on the drive technology and tape length.

If you are using a new tape that is not pre-formatted, you must format the tape by clicking **Format Tape** on the Windows NT Backup **Operations** menu. Formatting a tape may take a while, so plan ahead.

❑ Connect to all shared folders on other computers that need to be backed up.

Note Windows NT Backup can only back up the registry or event logs on the computer where the tape drive is located.

❑ Notify users to close their files before you begin the backup. If backups are performed at night, have users log off their computers before they go home. This will ensure that all files are closed.

Windows NT Backup does not back up files that are locked open by programs; for example, it would not back up a Microsoft Word document that is currently being edited. Windows NT operating system files are the exception; they can be backed up while they are in use.

You can send a message to users to notify them of the backup. To send a message to users, follow these steps:

1. Click the **Start** button, point to **Programs**, point to **Administrative Tools**, and then click **Server Manager**.
2. On the **Computer** menu, click **Send Message**.
3. Type the message to your users, and then click **OK**.

Selecting Drives, Folders, and Files

After you have connected to remote drives and notified users, the next step is to start Windows NT Backup (in Administrative Tools) and select the drives, folders, and files that you want to back up, as shown in the following illustration.

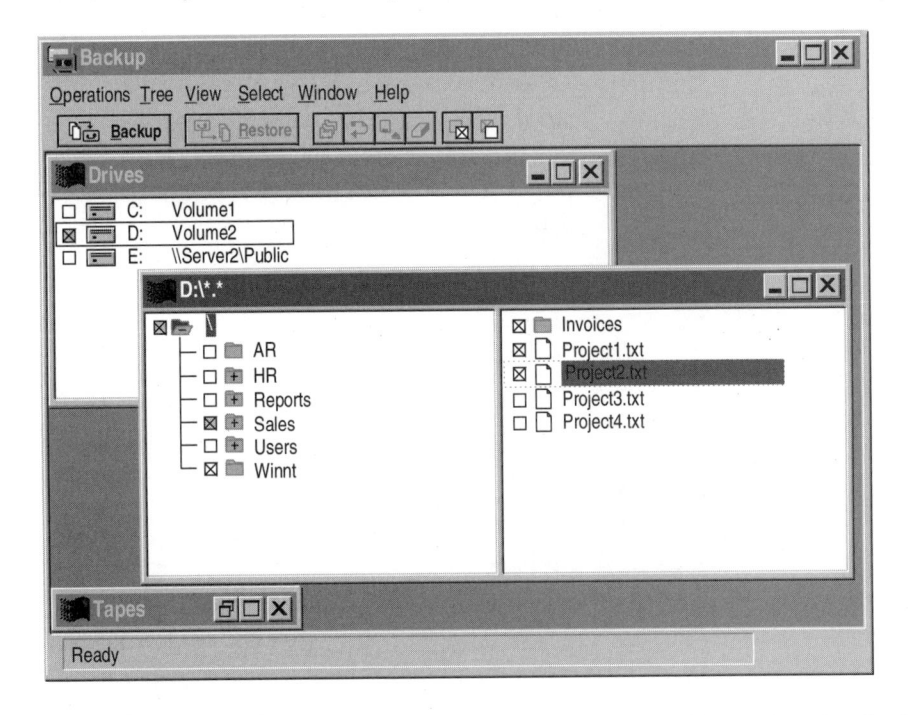

To back up all folders and files on a drive, in the Drives window, select the check box next to the drive icon.

To select specific folders and files on a drive, in the Drives window, double-click the drive icon. The window for the drive appears. This window shows a graphical view of the drive, which is similar to Windows NT Explorer. You can use one of the following methods to select folders and files:

- Select the check box next to each folder or file.

  –or–

- Select the folder or file that you want to back up, and then, on the **Select** menu, click **Check**.

Note If you do not select all the folders and files on a drive or parent folder, the selected check box appears shaded. This indicates a partial selection.

Setting Tape, Backup Set, and Log Options

After you select the drives, folders, or files to back up, the next step is to set the tape, backup set, and log options. Click **Backup** to gain access to the **Backup Information** dialog box. At the top of the dialog box is tape information, which includes the current tape name, creation date, and the owner of the tape.

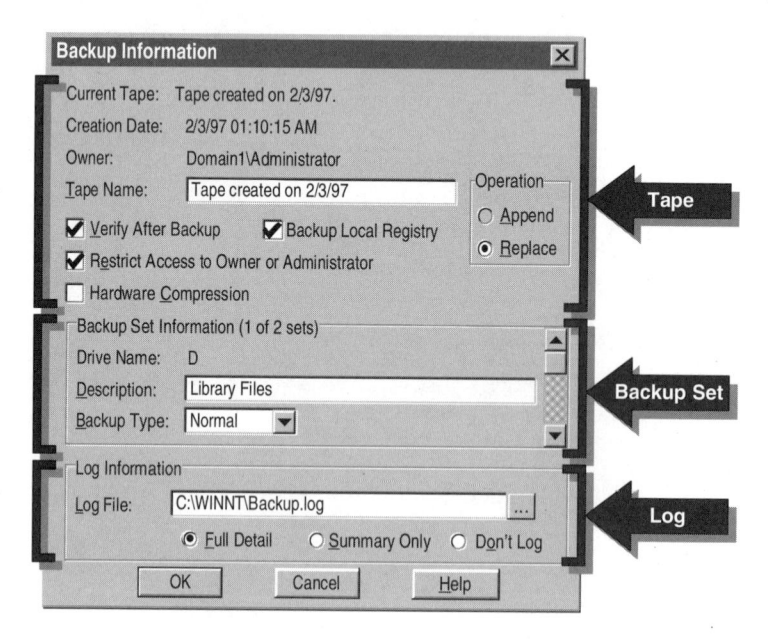

The following table describes the **Backup Information** dialog box options.

Option	Description
Tape Name	A name that you assign to identify where the tape fits into your backup strategy—for example, the name of the server you are backing up. This name can have up to 32 characters. If you select the **Append** option, the **Tape Name** box is not available.
Append	Adds a new backup set after the last backup set on the tape.
Replace	Overwrites all of the data on the tape with the new backup set.
Verify After Backup	Confirms that files are backed up accurately.
Backup Local Registry	Adds a copy of the registry to the backup set. Because you are unable to back up the registry alone, this option is available only if you select at least one other file on the local volume containing the registry file.
Restrict Access to Owner or Administrator	Limits access to the tape to Administrators, Backup Operators, or the user who performed the backup. If you back up the registry, you should select this option.
Hardware Compression	Select this option if you are using a tape drive that supports data compression. This option is available only if the tape drive supports it.
Backup Set Information	**Description**: Describes the backup set. This description should be intuitive, for example—**Server1Drive C**
	If there are multiple backup sets, you can type a description for each one. Use the scroll bar on the right side of the **Backup Set Information** box to move between backup sets.
	Backup Type: Specifies the type of backup, either Normal, Copy, Incremental, Differential, or Daily Copy.
Log Information	**Log File**: Specifies the name of the text file used to store the log. The default name is Backup.log. It is stored in the *systemroot* folder. (In most installations, *systemroot* is Winnt.)
	Full Detail: Logs all backup information, including the names of all the files and folders that are backed up, skipped, and corrupted.
	Summary Only: Logs only the major backup operations, such as loading a tape, starting backup, and failing to open a file.
	Don't Log: No information is logged.

Tip Print each backup log. Keep the printed copy in a log book.

Implementing a Backup

In this exercise, you use a Backup Simulation program to simulate backing up files to tape. The Backup Simulation is a Visual Basic® program that was developed so that you can practice backing up files without a tape drive in your computer.

With this simulation, you can:

- Erase the tape.
- Select drives, folders, and files to back up.
- Select the backup type.
- Select backup and log options.

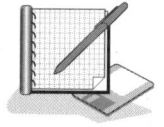

▶ **To start the Backup Simulation program**

1. Log on as Administrator.
2. Click the **Start** button, point to **Programs**, point to **Network Administration Training**, and then click **Backup Simulation**.

   The Backup Simulation window appears.

   Note If you were using the actual Windows NT Backup program, you would start it by clicking the **Start** button, pointing to **Programs**, pointing to **Administrative Tools**, and then clicking **Backup**.

▶ **To erase a tape**

In this procedure, you perform a secure erase to ensure that all old files are removed from the tape.

1. In the Backup Simulation window, on the **Operations** menu, click **Erase Tape**.

   The **Erase Tape** dialog box appears with a warning message that all information on the tape will be destroyed.

2. Click **Secure Erase**, and then click **Continue**.

   The Erase Status window appears and shows you a summary of the process.

3. When the operation is finished, click **OK**.

▶ **To select folders and files to be backed up**

In this procedure, you specify folders and files on drive D to be backed up.

1. Click to clear the check box next to drive D.
2. Double-click the disk icon for drive D.

   The D:*.* window appears.
3. Expand the folder hierarchy for drive D.

   Notice that on drive D there are two folders—the Data folder and the Public folder.
4. Expand the Data folder, and then select the check box next to the Managers folder.

   Notice that when you selected Managers, the file in Managers was automatically selected.
5. Expand the Public\Library folder, and then select the check box next to the Bronte folder.

   Notice that when you selected Bronte, the file in Bronte was automatically selected.
6. Click the Public\Templates folder (do not select the check box next to it), and then select the check boxes next to the following files:
   - Timesheet.dot
   - Timerecord.doc
   - Timesheet.doc

▶ **To begin the backup process**

1. In the Backup Simulation window, click **Backup**.

   –or–

   On the **Operations** menu, click **Backup**.

   The **Backup Information** dialog box appears. Notice that the current tape is blank and the creation date is the date that the tape was erased.
2. If you want a tape name other than the default, in the **Tape Name** box, type a descriptive name for your tape. For example, **Archive data** *today's date*
3. Select the following options:
   - **Verify After Backup** to confirm that the files were backed up correctly.
   - **Restrict Access to Owner or Administrator** so that only members of the Administrators and Backup Operators groups can restore files from this tape.

   Notice under **Operation**, that **Replace** is selected and **Append** appears dimmed. This is because no data is on the tape to append to.

▶ **To specify a backup set description and the type of log information**

1. In the **Description** box, type a descriptive name for your backup. For example, type **classics**
2. In the **Backup Type** box, click **Normal** (if it is not already selected).
3. Accept the default path of *drive*:*systemroot*\Backup.log for the log file.
4. Under **Log Information**, make sure that **Full Detail** is selected, and then click **OK**.

   Note The Backup Simulation program will only create a Full Detail log.

   The Backup Status window appears and shows you a summary of the operation.

5. When the backup process is finished, click **OK**.

   A Tapes window appears in the Backup Simulation window. Notice that it shows the date the tape was created, the drive that contained the files that were backed up, and the type of backup (normal).

▶ **To prepare the Backup Simulation for Lesson 5, "Restoring Files"**

- Minimize the Backup Simulation window.

   Important The Backup Simulation program is designed to back up and restore files in a single operation. This means that if you close the program, you will need to perform another backup before you are able to restore files in Lesson 5 of this chapter, "Restoring Files."

▶ **To view the backup log**

In this procedure, you view the backup log to see the files that were backed up.

1. Start Windows NT Explorer.
2. In the *drive*:*systemroot* folder, double-click Backup.log. (Backup.log may appear in Windows NT Explorer as Backup.)

   The Backup.log file appears in Notepad. Notice that the files in Backup.log are those that you backed up. Each file includes the date and time that the file was created, and the size of the file in bytes.

3. Quit Notepad.
4. Quit Windows NT Explorer.

Lesson Summary

The following information summarizes the key points in this lesson:

- Before you begin to back up files, you need to prepare your tapes, connect to shared folders on remote computers that need to be backed up, and then notify users to close their files.
- Select the drives, folders, and files to be backed up based on your backup strategy.
- Assign descriptive names to your tapes and backup sets. This makes it easier to identify their contents.
- When you back up the registry, always restrict tape access to members of the Administrators or the Backup Operators group.

For more information on	See
Backing up files	Chapter 6, "Backing Up and Restoring Network Files," in Microsoft Windows NT Server *Concepts and Planning*.

Lesson 4: Scheduling a Backup Using a Batch File

This lesson shows you how to automate the backup process by using a batch file and a Windows NT command scheduling program.

After this lesson, you will be able to:
- Write a batch file to back up your data.
- Use the Microsoft Windows NT **at** command (At.exe) to schedule backups.
- Use the Microsoft Windows NT Command Scheduler (WinAt.exe) to schedule backups.

Estimated lesson time: 20 minutes

There are two steps to scheduling an automatic backup. In the first step, you create a batch file with the **ntbackup** command and the details of the backup. In the second step, you schedule the batch file to run using either the Windows NT **at** command (which is included with Windows NT), or the Windows NT Command Scheduler (which is included in the *Microsoft Windows NT Server Resource Kit* version 4.0). The following illustration provides an overview of the required steps.

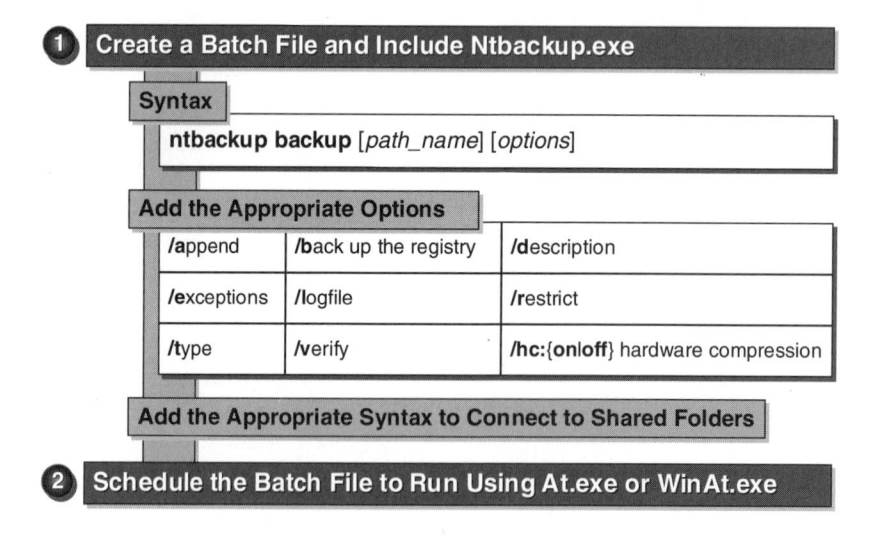

1. Create a Batch File and Include Ntbackup.exe

Syntax

ntbackup backup [*path_name*] [*options*]

Add the Appropriate Options

/append	/back up the registry	/description
/exceptions	/logfile	/restrict
/type	/verify	/hc:{on|off} hardware compression

Add the Appropriate Syntax to Connect to Shared Folders

2. Schedule the Batch File to Run Using At.exe or WinAt.exe

Chapter 11 Backing Up and Restoring Files

The following table describes options that you can use when you create the batch file.

Option	Description
/a	Appends the backup set after any existing backup sets, rather than replacing it. This is not available for a blank tape.
/b	Backs up the local registry, but only if you back up another file from the same volume.
/d "*text*"	Describes the backup set. This description appears when you view the tape catalog.
/e	Logs exceptions, such as summary log. If this option is not used, a full detail log is created.
/l *file_name*	Assigns a file name to the log file. The default is Backup.log in the *systemroot* folder.
/r	Limits access to the tape to Administrators, Backup Operators, or the user who performed the backup. If not used, anyone with the restore right can restore the backup set.
/t {**Normal**	**Copy**	**Incremental**	**Differential**	**Daily**}	Specifies the backup type. The default backup type is normal.
/v	Confirms that the files were backed up accurately.
/hc: {**on**	**off**}	Enables or disables hardware compression for tape drives that support it. The default is hardware compression off.
net use *x*:	Connects to a shared folder. Use this command at the beginning of the batch file if you are backing up files on a remote computer, and if you need to connect to a shared folder as a different user—for example: **net use x: \\Server1\Data /u:Domain1\User11**
net use *x*: **/delete**	Disconnects from a shared folder. Use this command at the end of the batch file to disconnect from any remote shares.
*server_name**share_name*	Connects to a shared folder. If you do not need to connect to a shared folder as a different user, you can use the UNC path of the shared folder with the **ntbackup backup** command. By using the UNC name, you do not need to disconnect from the shared folder.

Example of a Scheduled Backup

This example shows a batch file with the **ntbackup** command.

Batch File

```
net use x: \\computer1\public /u:domain1\user11
ntbackup backup c: d: x: \\server1\public
/t incremental /b /hc:on /v /l "c:\weekly.log"
net use x: /delete
```

Examine the example to determine the answers to the following questions.

1. What tasks will this batch file perform?

   _____

   _____

2. What would you add to this batch file to make it easier to identify the contents of the tape that this batch file creates?

   _____

   _____

3. What command would you add to the batch file to back up files (owned by the Administrators group) in the Data folder on a computer named Server2?

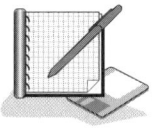

   _____

   _____

▶ **To write a batch file to back up data**

In this exercise, you write a batch file to schedule a backup for servers in the Quebec domain of World Wide Importers.

You need to create a batch file that does the following:

- Performs a differential backup of the shared CustomerData and ARData folders.
- Provides the description "Customer Data" on the backup tape.
- Create a log named "Tuesday.log."
- Verifies the backup.
- Adds the backup to the Tuesday backup tape.
- Does not implement hardware compression.

Chapter 11 Backing Up and Restoring Files 421

The following illustration shows the network servers and the data that they contain.

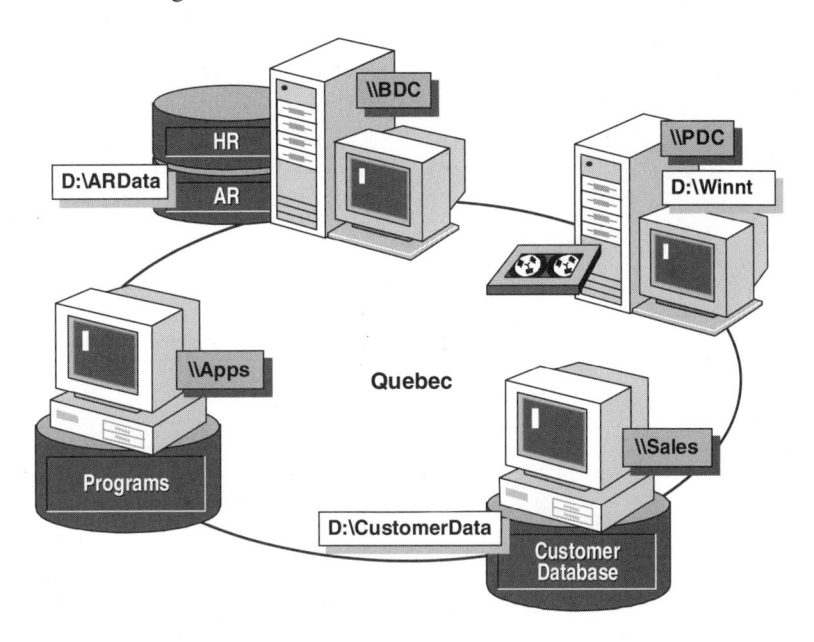

```
                    \\BDC
        HR                         \\PDC
D:\ARData                       D:\Winnt
        AR

                  Quebec
    \\Apps
                            \\Sales
  Programs
              D:\CustomerData
                         Customer
                         Database
```

Write down the commands that need to appear in the batch file.

_____

_____

_____

_____

_____

_____

▶ **To get help on Ntbackup command syntax**

  1. At a command prompt, type **ntbackup /?** and then press ENTER.
  2. Read through the information in Backup Help, and then close it.

Using the AT Command

Once you have a batch file that includes Ntbackup.exe, you can use At.exe to schedule the batch file to run at a specific time. The **at** command schedules commands from a command line.

> **Example: AT Command**
>
> ```
> at \\computer1 00:00 /every: 5,10,15,20,25,30
> "backup.bat"
> ```

Starting the Schedule Service

To use the **at** command, the Schedule service must be started on the computer that will run the scheduled backup. The Schedule service is a Windows NT service used to schedule tasks, such as backing up files. If you use the **at** command to perform a backup on a regular basis, you should configure the Schedule service to start automatically when Windows NT is started. You can start the Schedule service using Server Manager or the Services program in Control Panel.

▶ **To configure the Schedule service to start automatically using Server Manager**

1. Click the **Start** button, point to **Programs**, point to **Administrative Tools**, and then click Server Manager.

2. Under **Computer**, click your computer name, and then on the **Computer** menu, click **Services**.

    The Services on *computer_name* window appears.

3. Under **Service**, click **Schedule**, and then click **Startup**.

    The Service on *computer_name* window appears.

4. Under **Startup Type**, click **Automatic**, and then click **OK**. The Services on *computer_name* window appears.

    The Schedule service will now automatically start the next time the computer is shut down and restarted.

5. Under **Service**, click **Schedule**, and then click **Start**.

    The Service Control message window appears with the following message: `Attempting to Start the Schedule service on computer_name`.

6. Click **Close**, and then quit Server Manager.

Scheduling the Batch File

The **at** command uses the following syntax. Become familiar with the syntax and the command options before you schedule the batch file.

at [*computer_name*] [*id*] [**/delete**] *time* [**/interactive**][**/every**: *date*[,...] | **/next**: *date*[,...] "*command*"

The following table describes the **at** command options.

Option	Description
computer_name	Specifies a remote computer. If omitted, the commands are scheduled on the local computer.
id	Assigns an identification number to a scheduled command.
/delete	Cancels a scheduled command. If it is omitted, all of the scheduled commands on the computer are canceled.
time	Specifies the time that the command is to run. Time is expressed as hour:minutes in 24-hour notation. It runs 00:00 (midnight) through 23:59.
/interactive	Allows the job to interact with the desktop of the user who is logged on at the time that the job runs. You only use this option if Windows NT Backup is running on your computer and you want to observe it. If any errors occur, you will be able to correct them.
/every: *date*[,...]	Specifies the weekdays or days of the month that a command is to run. If omitted, the default is the current day of the month.
/next: *date*[,...]	Specifies the next weekdays or days of the month that a command is to run. If omitted, the default is the current day of the month.
"*command*"	Specifies the program or batch file to run, such as Ntbackup.exe.

▶ **To schedule a task using the AT command**

In this procedure, you schedule the game FreeCell to run at a specified time. Using FreeCell will show you how the **at** command works. If you were scheduling an actual backup, you would substitute NtBackup.exe for Freecell.exe.

1. Start a command prompt.
2. View the **at** command syntax by typing **at /?** and then pressing ENTER.

   Read the information about the **at** command.

3. Check the current system time and write it down here. You will need it to complete the next step.

4. Add two minutes to the system time, type the following command, and then press ENTER. Substitute the future time for *hh:mm* using the 24-hour format.

   at *hh:mm* **/interactive** "*drive*:*systemroot***system32\freecell.exe**"

   FreeCell should run on your computer within the next couple of minutes.

   Note If FreeCell fails to run, use the taskbar clock to verify that the time that you entered is correct for A.M. or P.M.

Using the Command Scheduler

The Command Scheduler is a utility included in the *Microsoft Windows NT Server Resource Kit* version 4.0 that provides a graphical way to schedule tasks.

This utility is included on the Supplemental Material compact disc that accompanies this book. If you completed the Setup procedures located in "About This Book," a shortcut to this tool was added to your **Network Administration Training** menu.

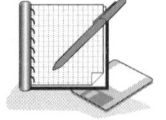

▶ **To schedule a task using the Command Scheduler**

In this procedure, you configure the Schedule service to start the game FreeCell to run at a specified time. If you do not have FreeCell on your computer, substitute Notepad.exe.

1. Click the **Start** button, point to **Programs**, point to **Network Administration Training**, and then click **Command Scheduler**.

   The Command Scheduler window appears.

   Note If the Schedule service is not running on your server, Command Scheduler will prompt you to start it.

2. Click **Add**.

   The **Add Command** dialog box appears.

3. In the **Command** box, type *drive*:*systemroot***system32\freecell.exe**

4. Under **This Occurs**, click **Today**.

   Under **Days**, notice that the current day is selected.

5. Under **Time**, add two minutes to the system time to specify a future time.

6. Click **Interactive**, and then click **OK**.

   Notice that the configured command appears in the Command Scheduler window.

7. Quit Command Scheduler and wait until the entered time arrives. FreeCell should run on your computer within the next couple of minutes.

8. Quit FreeCell.

Lesson Summary

The following information summarizes the key points in this lesson:

- You can automate the backup process using a batch file and the Windows NT **at** command (At.exe) or the Windows NT Command Scheduler (WinAt.exe).
- To schedule an automatic backup, first create a batch file with the details of the backup, and second, schedule the batch file to run using either the At.exe (included with Windows NT) or WinAt.exe (included in the *Microsoft Windows NT Server Resource Kit* version 4.0).
- The Schedule service must be started on the computer where the tape drive is installed before you can run the scheduled backup. You can start the Schedule service using Server Manager or the Services program in Control Panel.

For more information on	See
Windows NT Backup command prompt parameters	Chapter 6, "Backing Up and Restoring Network Files," in Microsoft Windows NT Server *Concepts and Planning*.
Using the **at** command scheduler	The Microsoft Knowledge Base at http://www.microsoft.com/kb/
	Chapter 22, "Disk, File System, and Backup Utilities," in the *Microsoft Windows NT Workstation Resource Kit*.
	Chapter 7, "Disk, File System, and Backup Utilities," in the *Resource Guide* of the *Microsoft Windows NT Server Resource Kit*.

Lesson 5: Restoring Files

This lesson describes the key principles that contribute to an effective data restoration strategy.

This lesson requires that you have completed Lesson 3.

After this lesson, you will be able to:
- Implement a restoration strategy.
- Create a restore operator.
- Restore files.

Estimated lesson time: 30 minutes

Implementing a Restoration Strategy

A good restoration strategy means that you can quickly locate and restore lost files. Having a good restoration strategy depends on the following:

- A good backup strategy. For example, if you always do a full backup of a volume, then in the unlikely event of a disk failure, you can restore the volume in a single operation. Rotating tapes over a period of a week ensures that you can restore an earlier version of a file.

- Keep documentation for each backup. By creating and printing a backup log of each backup, you will be able to quickly locate files that need to be restored without having to load the catalogs from all current backup sets.

  Depending upon the log that you create, the log can include information about the backup type, which folders and files are backed up, and on which tape they are located.

- Keep a record of multiple backups in a calendar format showing the days that you do backups. By each backup, note the type of backup and a tape identifier, such as a number. Then, if there is a problem, you have a quick glimpse of backups over several weeks and which tape was used for each.

- Store a set of backup tapes off-site in case of fire or other disaster. Consider using a third-party company that provides storage of magnetic media. You can even restore tapes to the offline servers at the alternate facility every time you do a backup.

- Perform a trial restoration periodically to verify that your files were properly backed up. A trial restoration can uncover hardware problems that do not show up with software verifications.

  Restore the tape to a drive other than the original drive, and then compare the restored files to the files on the original drive.

Creating a Restore Operator

In networks where security is an issue, it is recommended that the user who restores files is different from the user who backs up files. You can create a restore operator by assigning a user account the Restore files and directories user right.

The following checklist outlines the recommended method for creating a restore operator:

- ❏ Create a local group named Restore Operators on the computer where the tape drive is located and assign it the following three user rights:
    - Log on locally. This user right is required to back up the registry.
    - Restore files and directories. This user right provides the capability to do a restoration.
    - Shut down the system. This user right is required so that the server can be restarted to implemented changes made to Windows NT files, such as the registry.
- ❏ Create a global group named Restore Only on the primary domain controller. This group will be used to organize all user accounts that you want to give restore rights to.
- ❏ Add the global group Restore Only to the local group Restore Operators. Add the user account to the global group Restore Only.

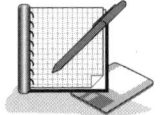

▶ **To create a local group with the appropriate user rights**

1. Start User Manager for Domains.
2. Create a local group named *Restore Operators*.
3. Grant the following user rights to the Restore Operators group:
    - Log on locally
    - Restore files and directories
    - Shut down the system

▶ **To give a user the rights to restore to the computer**

1. Create a global group named *Restore Only*.
2. Add the Restore Only group to the Restore Operators group.
3. Add the user account User11-B to the Restore Only group.
4. Quit User Manager for Domains.

Examples of Restoration Strategies

Each of the following restoration strategies uses a different combination of backup types to back up files. As a general rule, review your backup logs to identify the appropriate tapes to use to restore files for any restoration strategy.

Note If only one file is corrupted, you need to find only the last backup of that file and restore it.

Example 1: Restoring Normal and Differential Backups

On Friday an entire volume became corrupted. Based on the backup schedule, restore the normal backup from Monday. Then, because the remaining backups are differential, the only additional restoration that is necessary is the backup from Thursday.

Monday	Tuesday	Wednesday	Thursday	Friday
Normal	Differential	Differential	Differential	Differential

Example 2: Restoring Normal and Incremental Backups

On Friday an entire volume became corrupted. Based on the backup schedule, restore the normal backup from Monday. Because the remaining backups are incremental backups, you also need to restore the backups from Tuesday through Thursday, in that order.

Monday	Tuesday	Wednesday	Thursday	Friday
Normal	Incremental	Incremental	Incremental	Incremental

Example 3: Restoring a Single File

On Friday, one file became corrupted. Because after Monday the backups are incremental backups, you cannot be sure which tape has the most recent copy of the file. Use the backup log to determine when the file was last backed up and which tape contains the backup. Then, restore the file from that tape.

Monday	Tuesday	Wednesday	Thursday	Friday
Normal	Incremental	Incremental	Incremental	Incremental

Caution Make sure that the date on your computer is correct. Windows NT Backup uses the date attribute of the file to determine which file version is most current. If you change the date, you may overwrite a file with an older version.

Preparing to Restore Files

Before you begin restoring files, you need to connect to all shared folders on other computers where files will be restored.

Note Windows NT Backup can only restore the registry or event logs on computers where the tape drive is installed.

Loading the Tape and Backup Set Catalogs

The first step in restoring data is to start Windows NT Backup (in Administrative Tools) and load the tape and backup set catalogs. The tape catalog shows all the backup sets on a tape. The backup set catalog shows all of the folders and files in the backup set. You use both catalogs to verify the data you have, and to select data to restore. If a tape has only one backup set, loading the tape catalog will automatically load the backup set catalog.

The following table describes the steps that you use in Windows NT Backup to load a tape and backup catalog.

To	Do this
Load a tape catalog	On the **Operations** menu, click **Catalog**.
Load a backup catalog	Double-click the appropriate backup set folder.

After each task, the **Catalog Status** dialog box shows a summary of the backup set information. When the catalog finishes loading, click **OK**.

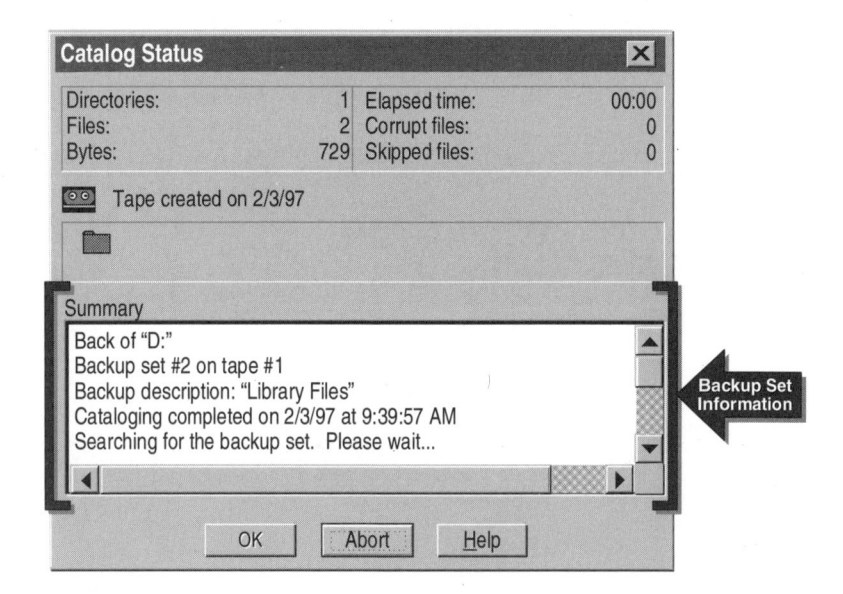

Catalog Status			
Directories:	1	Elapsed time:	00:00
Files:	2	Corrupt files:	0
Bytes:	729	Skipped files:	0

Tape created on 2/3/97

Summary
Back of "D:"
Backup set #2 on tape #1
Backup description: "Library Files"
Cataloging completed on 2/3/97 at 9:39:57 AM
Searching for the backup set. Please wait...

← Backup Set Information

Important If the last tape in a family set is missing or damaged, you can force Windows NT Backup to treat the data on each remaining tape as a single unit, by starting Windows NT Backup at the command prompt with the **/missingtape** option.

Selecting Backup Sets, Files, and Folders

After a backup set catalog is loaded, the *tape_name* window appears with the folder tree for the backup set. The question mark (?) on the folder changes to a plus sign (+). To see this, you have to maximize the *tape_name* window. If there are corrupted files on the tape, the files' corresponding folders are marked with a red X.

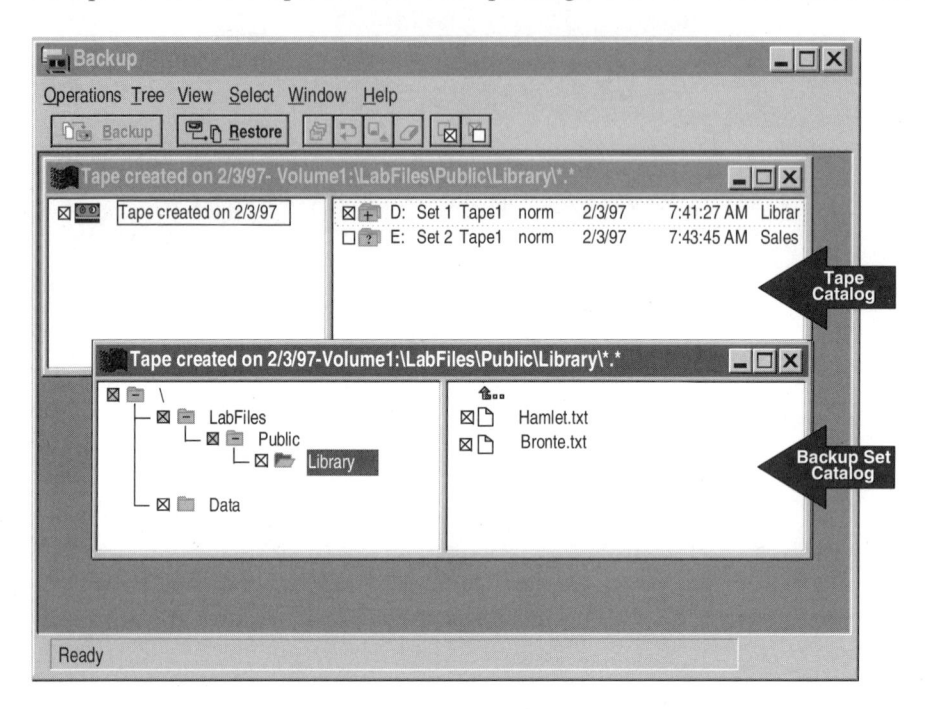

Once you have loaded the tape catalog, you can select a backup set by clicking the check boxes for the set.

To select individual folders and files in a backup set, double-click the appropriate folder to expand it and then select the check boxes for the appropriate folders and files.

An X appears in the check box of the folder or file that you select, and in the boxes of the parent folder and disk drive. If you select only some of the folders and files on a disk drive or within a parent folder, then the check box appears dimmed.

Note You can select multiple folders or files by holding down the CTRL key and clicking the folders or files.

Setting Restore and Log Options

Once you have selected the folders and files to restore, the next step is to set the restore and log options. You can access the **Restore Information** dialog box by clicking **Restore** in the Backup window.

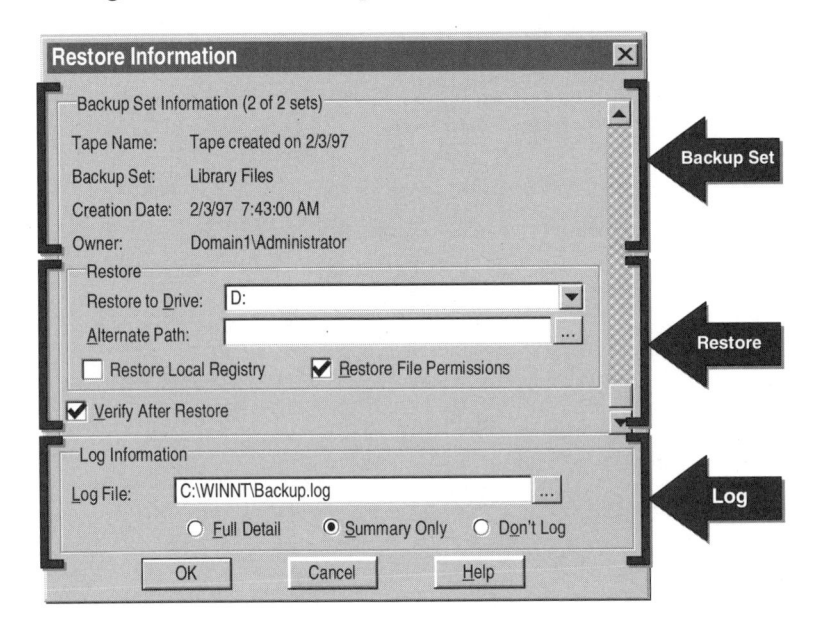

The following table describes the options under **Restore** and **Log Information** in the **Restore Information** dialog box.

Option	Description
Restore Local Registry	Restores the registry file. For the changes to the registry files to take effect, shut down and restart the computer.
Restore File Permissions	Restores the NTFS permissions. If not selected, files inherit the permissions of the folder to which they are restored.
	Do not restore file permissions if you restore to a computer that does not have the same user and group accounts.
Verify After Restore	Verifies the content of the files restored to disk against the files on the tape. Windows NT Backup logs exceptions.
Log File	The location of the text file for logging all tape operations. You can browse to find the correct name.
Full Detail	Logs all information on all restore operations including the names of all folders and files that were restored.
Summary Only	Logs only information about the major operations, such as loading a tape, starting to restore a file, and failing to restore a file.
Don't Log	Logs nothing.

Implementing the Restoration of Files

In this exercise, you use the Backup Simulation program to restore files from tape based on specific criteria. The Backup Simulation allows you to perform the following Windows NT Backup functions:

- Select a backup set and create a catalog
- Select a file to restore
- Set restore and log options

▶ **To use the Backup.log file to locate the file to restore**

In this procedure, you use the Backup.log file to determine the path to the Sven.doc file.

1. In Windows NT Explorer, expand the *systemroot* folder, and then double-click Backup.log to open it. (Backup.log may appear in Windows NT Explorer as Backup.)

2. Search Backup.log for Sven.doc, and write down its path. You will need it to restore the file.

   _____

3. Quit Notepad.

▶ **To load the backup set catalog**

This procedure requires that you have performed a backup using the Backup Simulation program and that the Backup Simulation program is still running. If you do not meet these requirements, complete all the procedures in Lesson 3 of this chapter, "Backing Up Files."

1. Click **Backup Simulation** on the taskbar to maximize the Backup Simulation window.

   The Tapes window is the active window.

   Note If you were using the actual Windows NT Backup program, you would start it by clicking the **Start** button, pointing to **Programs**, pointing to **Administrative Tools**, and then clicking **Backup**.

2. In the right pane of the Tapes window, double-click the backup set (the folder icon with the question mark [?] on it) to load the backup set catalog.

   A **Tape Created on** *date* dialog box appears. Notice that the catalog status information appears under **Summary**.

   Note The Backup Simulation creates only one backup set. Because of this fact, you need to load only a backup set catalog, and not a tape catalog.

3. When the cataloging operation is finished, click **OK**.

   The window for your backup set appears. Notice that the window name is the same as the name that you assigned to the tape.

▶ **To select a file to restore**

In this procedure, you restore the Sven.doc file to its original folder.

1. In the *tape_name* window, expand the folders to see the files on the tape. Notice that they are the same files that you selected to back up.
2. Locate Sven.doc and select its check box.
3. Click **Restore**.

   The **Restore Information** dialog box appears. Notice that Administrator is the owner of the tape. Only the owner of the tape, or a member of the Administrators or Backup Operators groups can restore files contained on the tape. This is because the Restrict Access to Owner or Administrator check box was selected when this tape was created.

▶ **To set restore and log options**

1. In the **Restore to Drive** box, type **d:** (if it does not already appear) to specify the location where Sven.doc will be restored.

   If you wanted to restore a file to a different drive and folder, you would specify the location in the **Alternative Path** box.

2. Select the **Verify After Restore** and **Restore File Permissions** check boxes to ensure that all files are restored without errors, and to guarantee that NTFS permissions assigned to the original backup files are correctly applied.

3. Under **Log Information**, make sure that **Full Detail** is selected so that the restored file and restore operation are added to the log.

▶ **To start the restoration process**

1. In the **Restore Information** dialog box, click **OK**.

   The Restore Status window appears with a summary of the restoration process, and then changes to a Verify Status window.

   If any files did not restore properly, information describing any problems would be described here.

2. When the restoration process is finished, click **OK**.

   The Backup Simulation window appears.

3. Quit the Backup Simulation program.

4. Log off.

Lesson Summary

The following information summarizes the key points in this lesson:

- A good data restoration strategy depends on creating a good backup strategy, keeping documentation of your backup, maintaining a regular backup schedule, storing tapes in a safe location, and performing trial restorations periodically.
- In networks where security is an issue, it is recommended that the user who restores files be different from the user who backs up files. You can give a user the ability to only restore files by assigning a user account to the Restore files and directories user right.
- Before you begin to restore files, connect to shared folders on remote computers where files will be restored.
- Load the tape and backup set catalogs for a list of all the files in a backup set. Use both of these catalogs to locate files to restore.
- If you restore files to a computer that does not have the same user and group accounts as the computer where the files originated, do not restore file permissions. The files will inherit the permissions of the folder to which they are restored.

For more information on	See
Restoring files	Chapter 6, "Backing Up and Restoring Network Files," in Microsoft Windows NT Server *Concepts and Planning*.
Comparing the restored files with the original files	The Windiff utility on the *Microsoft Windows NT Server Resource Kit CD-ROM*.

Best Practices

The following checklist provides best practices for backing up and restoring files. Review this checklist before you back up and restore files:

❏ In minimum-security and medium-security networks, grant one user backup rights and a different user restore rights.

- Grant backup only rights by creating a local group named Backup Operators and then assigning the *Back up files and directories* user right to the group. Then, create a global group named Backup Only and add it to the local group.

- Grant restore only rights by creating a local group named Restore Operators and then assigning the *Restore files and directories* user right to the group. Then, create a global group named Restore Only and add it to the local group.

- Train personnel with restore rights to perform all of the restore tasks in the event that the administrator is unavailable.

Note In a high-security network, only administrators should restore files.

❏ Back up an entire volume to prepare for the unlikely event of a disk failure. It is more efficient to restore the entire volume in one operation.

❏ Always back up the registry on a domain controller to prevent the loss of user account and security information.

❏ Always create and print a backup log for each backup. Keep a book of logs to make it easier to locate specific files.

❏ Keep three copies of tapes. Keep at least one copy off-site in a properly controlled environment.

❏ Perform a trial restoration periodically to verify that your files were properly backed up. A trial restoration can uncover hardware problems that do not show up with software verifications.

❏ Secure both the tape drive and the backup tapes. Someone can access the data from a stolen tape by restoring the data to another server for which they are an administrator.

Note If you want to remove the accounts that were created by running the Chapter11.cmd file at the beginning of this chapter, log on as Administrator, and then double-click DeleteChapter11.cmd in the Cleanup folder on the Supplemental Material compact disc.

Review

The following questions are intended to reinforce key information presented in this chapter. If you are unable to answer a question, review the lesson and then try the question again.

1. Which of the following should you always back up?

    a. Temporary files

    b. Files critical to your organization

    c. Registry files

    d. Program files

2. Scenario: As administrator of the World Wide Importers network, you have been assigned the task of implementing a backup strategy for the Accounts Receivable server. Because there are only a few hours in the evening when the server is not in use, you need to be able to back up all files in the least amount of time possible. If files are lost, you need to be able to restore them from only two tapes. Which of the following is the best backup strategy for World Wide Importers?

    a. Do a normal backup Monday through Friday.

    b. Do a normal backup on Monday, and incremental backups Tuesday through Friday.

    c. Do a normal backup on Monday, and differential backups Tuesday through Friday.

    d. Do a daily copy Monday through Friday.

    e. Do a normal backup on Monday, and copy backups Tuesday through Friday.

3. Which of the following would ensure that your backup and restoration procedures are successful? (Circle all that apply.)

    a. Select the **Verify After Backup** check box when backing up files.

    b. Select the **Verify After Restore** check box when restoring files.

    c. Perform a trial restoration periodically, by restoring a recent backup to a drive other than the original drive, and then comparing the restored files to the files on the original drive.

    d. Select the **Restrict Access to Owner or Administrator** check box when backing up files.

4. Scenario: You want to create a local Backup Only Operators group. Which of the following user rights do you need to assigned to that group? (Circle all that apply.)

   a. Load and unload device drivers.
   b. Log on locally.
   c. Back up files and directories.
   d. Restore files and directories.
   e. Shutdown the system.

5. Scenario: You want to create a local restore operators groups. Which of the following user rights do you need to assign to that group? (Circle all that apply.)

   a. Load and unload device drivers.
   b. Log on locally.
   c. Back up files and directories.
   d. Restore files and directories.
   e. Shut down the system.

6. Scenario: You need to restore a particular file. You did a normal backup yesterday, but you forgot to create a backup log. How do you find the file?

   _____

   _____

7. Scenario: You need to restore the server data. The backup for the data consists of multiple tapes of which the last tape is damaged. What can you do?

   _____

   _____

Answer Key

Procedure Answers

Page 405

▶ **To plan a backup schedule**

Strategy used in planning worksheet (see Appendix A, "Backup Planning Worksheet"):

The tape drive is at the PDC to back up the registry. Tape storage can be two tapes on-site and one tape off-site.

All folders, except for Apps, are backed up daily because they contain files that change frequently or are critical.

The Apps folder is backed up weekly because it contains program files that change infrequently.

A normal backup is done on Monday and then a differential backup is done Tuesday through Friday so that if there is a catastrophic system failure, a minimal number of tapes will be required to perform a full restore. Monday's backup is archived because it contains a copy of all files. The backups done on Tuesday through Friday are on the same tape.

A Full Detail backup log is created so that all backup events are recorded.

Page 420

Example of a Scheduled Backup

1. What tasks will this batch file perform?

    The batch file connects to \\Computer1\Public as User11 (from Domain1), and then performs an incremental backup of drives C, D, and X; of the shared folder Public on Server1; and of the local registry.

    It also verifies that the files were backed up correctly, uses hardware compression, and then records the results in the log file named C:\Weekly.log. It also disconnects from the two remote shared folders.

2. What would you add to this batch file to make it easier to identify the contents of the tape that this batch file creates?

    Add the /d option with a complete description of the backup set. For example: /d "Incremental backup of drives C, D, X, \\Server1\Public, and the registry"

3. What command would you add to the batch file to back up files (owned by the Administrators group) in the Data folder on a computer named Server2?

    Add the UNC path \\Server2\Data after the command ntbackup backup—for example, type: ntbackup backup \\server2\data

Page 420

▶ **To write a batch file to back up data**

Possible answer 1:

net use e: \\sales\customerdata

net use f: \\bdc\ardata

ntbackup backup e: f: /t differential /a /HC:off /v /d "Customer Data" /l "Tuesday.log"

net use e: /delete

net use f: /delete

Possible answer 2:

ntbackup backup \\sales\customerdata \\bdc\ardata /t differential /a /HC:off /v /d "Customer Data" /l "Tuesday.log"

Page 434

▶ **To use the Backup.log file to locate the file to restore**

2. Search Backup.log for Sven.doc, and write down its path. You will need it to restore the file.

D:\Data\Managers\Sven.doc

Page 439

Review Answers

1. Which of the following should you always back up?

   Answers b and c are correct.

2. Scenario: As administrator of the World Wide Importers network, you have been assigned the task of implementing a backup strategy for the Accounts Receivable server. Because there are only a few hours in the evening when the server is not in use, you need to be able to back up all files in the least amount of time possible. If files are lost, you need to be able to restore them from only two tapes. Which of the following is the best backup strategy for World Wide Importers?

   Answer c would be the best strategy.

3. Which of the following would ensure that your backup and restoration procedures are successful? (Circle all that apply.)

   Answers a, b, and c are correct.

4. Scenario: You want to create a local Backup Only Operators group. Which of the following user rights do you need to assigned to that group? (Circle all that apply.)

   Answers b and c are correct.

5. Scenario: You want to create a local restore operators groups. Which of the following user rights do you need to assign to that group? (Circle all that apply.)

   Answers b, d, and e are correct.

6. Scenario: You need to restore a particular file. You did a normal backup yesterday, but you forgot to create a backup log. How do you find the file?

   First load the tape catalog to determine the appropriate backup set. Then, load the backup set catalog, which shows all the folders and files in the backup set.

7. Scenario: You need to restore the server data. The backup for the data consists of multiple tapes of which the last tape is damaged. What can you do?

   You can force Windows NT Backup to treat the data on the remaining tapes as a single unit by starting Windows NT Backup at the command prompt and including the /missingtape option.

APPENDIX A

Planning Worksheets

User Accounts Planning Worksheet . . . 446

Group Accounts Planning Worksheet . . . 447

Shared Folders Planning Worksheet . . . 448

NTFS Permissions Planning Worksheet . . . 449

Backup Planning Worksheet . . . 450

User Accounts Planning Worksheet

Naming Convention: First name + Last Initial + Additional Characters

Full Name	User Account	Description	Password Requirements	Home Folder Location	Logon Hours	Workstation Restrictions
Linda Mitchell	VicePresident	Vice president	User Must Change Password at Next Logon	Server	All	N
	Director	Director of human resources	User Must Change Password at Next Logon	Server	All	N
	SalesMgr	Sales manager	User Must Change Password at Next Logon	Server	All	N
	SalesRep	Sales representative	User Must Change Password at Next Logon	Server	All	N
Linda Mitchell	CustomerService1	Customer service representative (night shift)	User Must Change Password at Next Logon	Server	6 P.M.–6 A.M. (7 days)	N
	CustomerService2	Customer service representative (day shift)	User Must Change Password at Next Logon	Server	All	N
	AccountingMgr	Accounting manager	User Must Change Password at Next Logon	Server	All	N
	Accountant	Accountant	User Must Change Password at Next Logon	Server	All	N
	Temp	Temporary employee	User Cannot Change Password	Server	8 A.M.–5 P.M. (7 days)	Y

Group Accounts Planning Worksheet

Group Account	Local or Global	Members	Location
Executives	Global	VicePresident3, Director3	PDC (in both domains)
Managers	Global	SalesMgr3, AccountingMgr3	PDC (in both domains)
Customer Service	Global	CustomerService3-A, CustomerService3-B	PDC (in both domains)
Sales	Global	SalesMgr3, SalesRep3	PDC (in both domains)
Accountants	Global	AccountingMgr3, Accountant3	PDC (in both domains)
Istanbul\Domain Users*	Global	VicePresident3, Director3, SalesMgr3, SalesRep3, CustomerService3-A, CustomerService3-B, AccountingMgr3, Accountant3, and Temp3 (all user accounts)	PDC (in the Istanbul domain)
Quebec\Domain Users*	Global	VicePresident3, Director3, SalesMgr3, SalesRep3, CustomerService3-A, CustomerService3-B, AccountingMgr3, Accountant3, and Temp3 (all user accounts)	PDC (in the Quebec domain)
Programs	Local	Istanbul\Domain Users*	Member Server1 (in the Istanbul domain)
Programs	Local	Quebec\Domain Users*	Member Server1 (in the Quebec domain)
Printer	Local	Istanbul\Domain Users* and Quebec\Domain Users*	PDC (in the Istanbul domain)
HR	Local	Global groups: Executives3 and Managers3 (from both domains)	BDC (in the Quebec domain)
Customer Files	Local	Global groups: Executives3, Managers3, Customer Service3, and Sales3 (from both domains)	Member Server2 (in the Quebec domain)
AR	Local	Global group: Accountants3 (from both domains)	PDC (in the Quebec domain)
Employee Files	Local	Global group: Managers3 (from both domains)	Windows NT Workstation (in the Istanbul domain)

*Domain Users is a built-in global group that contains all domain user accounts by default. You can either create a global group and add all domain user accounts or you can use the built-in group Domain Users.

Shared Folders Planning Worksheet

Folder Name	UNC Name	Local Group	Members	Share Permissions
Apps	\\Server3\Apps	Users Administrators	Default members Default members	Read Full Control
ProjMan	\\Server3\ProjMan	Project Managers Administrators	Managers global group Default members	Change Full Control
Data	\\Server2\Data	Data Access	Executives global group	Read
Acctng	\\Server2\Account	Accounting Access	Accountants global group	Full Control
HR	\\Server2\HR	HR Access	HR global group	Full Control
Reviews	\\Server2\Reviews	Reviews Users Administrators	Managers and Executives global groups Default members Default members	Change Read Full Control
Users	\\Server1\Users	Administrators	Default members	Full Control
User1 User2 User3	\\Server1\User1 \\Server1\User2 \\Server1\User3	None None None		User1: Full Control User2: Full Control User3: Full Control

NTFS Permissions Planning Worksheet

Folder or File	Local Group	Members	NTFS Permissions
Apps	Administrators Users	Default members Default members	Full Control Read
Apps\Wordproc	Administrators Users	Default members Default members	Full Control Read
Apps\Spreadsh	Administrators Spreadsheet6	Default members Global groups: Accountants6, Managers6, and Executives6	Full Control Read
Apps\Database	Administrators Database6	Default members Global groups: Accountants6, Managers6, and Executives6	Full Control Read
Public	Administrators Users Creator Owner (system group)	Default members Default members Users who copy or create a file in the Public folder	Full Control Add & Read Full Control
Public\Library	Administrators Users Library6	Default members Default members Global group: Managers6	Full Control Read Change
Public\Library\Archive.txt			User6: Add & Read
Public\Manuals	Administrators Users	Default members Default members	Full Control Read User 6: Full Control

Backup Planning Worksheet

Tape Drive Location: Primary domain controller   **Tape Storage Location:** Two tapes on-site, one tape off-site

Folders and Files to Back Up (Provide Path)	Daily	Weekly (Provide Day)
(PDC) D:\Users*.*	X	
(PDC) Registry	X	
(BDC) D:\ARData*.*	X	
(BDC) D:\HRData*.*	X	
(Member Server1) C:\Apps*.*		Every Monday
(Member Server2) D:\CustomerData*.*	X	

Weekly Backup Schedule

Monday	Tuesday	Wednesday	Thursday	Friday
Backup Type: **N**	Backup Type: **D**	Backup Type: **D**	Backup Type: **D**	Backup Type: **D**
Tape: **1**	Tape: **2**	Tape: **2**	Tape: **2**	Tape: **2**
Archive Y ✓ N ___	Archive Y ___ N ✓	Archive Y ___ N ✓	Archive Y ___ N ✓	Archive Y ___ N ✓

Backup Types

N = Normal   D = Differential   I = Incremental   C = Copy   DC = Daily Copy

Type of Backup Log

☑ Full Detail   ☐ Summary Only   ☐ Don't Log

Glossary

A

access permission A rule associated with an object (usually a directory, file, or printer) to regulate which users can have access to the object and in what manner. *See also* user rights.

access privileges Permissions set by Macintosh users that allow them to view and make changes to folders on a server. By setting access privileges (called *permissions* when set on the computer running Windows NT Server), you control which Macintosh can use folders in a volume. Services for Macintosh (SFM) translates access privileges set by Macintosh users to the equivalent Windows NT permissions.

access token (or security token) An object that uniquely identifies a user who has logged on. An access token is attached to all the user's processes and contains the user's security ID (SID), the SIDs of any groups to which the user belongs, any permissions that the user owns, the default owner of any objects that the user's processes create, and the default access control list (ACL) to be applied to any objects that the user's processes create. *See also* permissions.

account *See* group account; user account.

account lockout A Windows NT Server security feature that locks a user account if a number of failed logon attempts occur within a specified amount of time, based on account policy lockout settings. (Locked accounts cannot log on.)

account policy Controls the way passwords must be used by all user accounts of a domain or of an individual computer. Specifics include minimum password length, how often a user must change his or her password, and how often users can reuse old passwords. Account policy can be set for all user accounts in a domain when administering a domain, and for all user accounts of a single workstation or member server when administering a computer.

active Refers to the window or icon that you are currently using or that is currently selected. Windows NT always applies the next keystroke or command you choose to the active window. If a window is active, its title bar changes color to differentiate it from other windows. If an icon is active, its label changes color. Windows or icons on the desktop that are not selected are inactive.

adapter card *See* network adapter.

administrative account An account that is a member of the Administrators local group of a computer or domain.

administrative alerts Administrative alerts relate to server and resource use and warn about problems in areas such as security and access, user sessions, server shutdown due to power loss (when UPS is available), directory replication, and printing. When a computer generates an administrative alert, a message is sent to a predefined list of users and computers. *See also* Alerter service; uninterruptible power supply (UPS).

administrator A person responsible for setting up and managing domain controllers or local computers and their user and group accounts, assigning passwords and permissions, and helping users with networking issues. To use administrative tools such as User Manager or User Manager for Domains, an administrator must be logged on as a member of the Administrators local group for the computer or domain, respectively.

Administrator privilege One of three privilege levels you can assign to a Windows NT user account. Every user account has one of the three privilege levels (Administrator, Guest, and User). *See also* administrator; Guest privilege; User privilege.

Alerter service Notifies selected users and computers of administrative alerts that occur on a computer. Used by the Server service and other services. Requires the Messenger service. *See also* administrative alerts; Messenger service.

API *See* application programming interface.

application A computer program used for a particular kind of work, such as word processing. This term is often used interchangeably with "program."

application log The application log contains specific events logged by programs. Programs developers decide which events to monitor (for example, a database program might record a file error in the application log). Use Event Viewer to view the application log.

application programming interface (API) A set of routines that a program uses to request and carry out lower-level services performed by another component, such as the computer's operating system or a service running on a network computer. These maintenance chores are performed by the computer's operating system, and an API provides the program with a means of communicating with the system, telling it which system-level task to perform and when.

application window The main window for a program, which contains the program's menu bar and work area. A program window may contain multiple document windows.

archive bit Backup programs use the archive bit to mark the files after backing them up, if a normal or incremental backup is performed. *See also* backup types.

ASCII file Also called a text file, a text-only file, or an ASCII text file, refers to a file in the universally recognized text format called ASCII (American Standard Code for Information Interchange). An ASCII file contains characters, spaces, punctuation, carriage returns, and sometimes tabs and an end-of-file marker, but it contains no formatting information. This generic format is useful for transferring files between programs that could not otherwise understand each other's documents. *See also* text file.

associate To identify a file name extension as "belonging" to a certain program so that when you open any file with that extension, the program starts automatically.

attributes Information that indicates whether a file is a read-only, hidden, system, or compressed file, and whether the file has been changed since a backup copy of it was made.

auditing Tracking activities of users by recording selected types of events in the security log of a server or a workstation.

Audit policy For the servers of a domain or for an individual computer, defines the type of security events that will be logged.

authentication Validation of a user's logon information. When a user logs on to an account on a computer running Windows NT Workstation, the authentication is performed by that workstation. When a user logs on to an account on a Windows NT Server domain, authentication may be performed by any server of that domain. *See also* server; trust relationship.

B

backup domain controller (BDC) In a Windows NT Server domain, a computer running Windows NT Server that receives a copy of the domain's directory database, which contains all account and security policy information for the domain. The copy is synchronized periodically and automatically with the master copy on the primary domain controller (PDC). BDCs also authenticate user logons and can be promoted to function as PDCs as needed. Multiple BDCs can exist on a domain. *See also* member server; primary domain controller (PDC).

backup set A collection of files from one drive that is backed up during a single backup operation.

backup set catalog At the end of each backup set, Windows NT Backup stores a summary of file and/or directory information in a backup set catalog. Catalog information includes the number of tapes in a set of tapes as well as the date they were created and the dates of each file in the catalog. Catalogs are created for each backup set and are stored on the last tape in the set. *See also* backup set.

backup set map At the end of each tape used for backup, a backup set map maintains the exact tape location of the backup set's data and catalog.

backup types:

copy backup Copies all selected files, but does not mark each file as having been backed up. Copying is useful if you want to back up files between normal and incremental backups, because copying will not invalidate these other backup operations.

daily backup Copies all selected files that have been modified the day that the daily backup is performed.

differential backup Copies those files created or changed since the last normal (or incremental) backup. It does not mark files as having been backed up.

incremental backup Backs up only those files created or changed since the last normal (or incremental) backup. It marks files as having been backed up.

normal backup Copies all selected files and marks each as having been backed up. Normal backups give you the ability to restore files quickly because files on the last tape are the most current.

batch program An ASCII file (unformatted text file) that contains one or more Windows NT commands. A batch program's file name has a .cmd or .bat extension. When you type the file name at the command prompt, the commands are processed sequentially.

BDC *See* backup domain controller.

bits per second (bps) A measure of the speed at which a device, such as a modem, can transfer data.

blue screen The screen displayed when Windows NT encounters a serious error.

boot partition The volume, formatted for either an NTFS or FAT file system, that contains the Windows NT operating system and its support files. The boot partition can be (but does not have to be) the same as the system partition. *See also* file allocation table (FAT); partition; Windows NT file system (NTFS).

bps *See* bits per second.

browse To view available network resources by looking through lists of folders, files, user accounts, groups, domains, or computers. Browsing allows users on a Windows NT network to see what domains and computers are accessible from their local computer.

browse list A list kept by the master browser of all of the servers and domains on the network. This list is available to any workstation on the network requesting it. *See also* browse.

built-in groups Default groups, provided with Windows NT Workstation and Windows NT Server, that have been granted useful collections of rights and built-in abilities. In most cases, a built-in group provides all of the capabilities needed by a particular user. For example, if a domain user account belongs to the built-in Administrators group, logging on with that account gives a user administrative capabilities over the domain and the servers of the domain. To provide a needed set of capabilities to a user account, assign it to the appropriate built-in group. *See also* group; User Manager; User Manager for Domains.

C

cache A special memory subsystem that stores the contents of frequently accessed RAM locations and the addresses where these data items are stored. In Windows NT, for example, user profiles have a locally cached copy of part of the registry.

catalog *See* backup set catalog.

centralized network administration A centralized view of the entire network from any workstation on the network that provides the ability to track and manage information on users, groups, and resources in a distributed network.

check box A small box in a dialog box or property page that can be selected or cleared. Check boxes represent an option that you can turn on or off. When a check box is selected, an X or a check mark appears in the box.

Chooser The Macintosh desk accessory with which users select the network server and printers that they want to use.

clear To turn off an option by removing the X or check mark from a check box. To clear a check box, you can click it, or you can select it and then press the SPACEBAR.

click To press and release a mouse button quickly.

client A computer that accesses shared network resources provided by another computer, called a server. *See also* server; workstation.

client application A Windows NT application that can display and store linked or embedded objects. For distributed applications, the program that imitates a request to a server application. *See* Distributed Component Object Module (DCOM); server application.

Client Service for NetWare Included with Windows NT Workstation, enabling workstations to make direct connections to file and printer resources at NetWare servers running NetWare 2.*x* or later.

Clipboard A temporary storage area in memory, used to transfer information. You can cut or copy information onto the Clipboard and then paste it into another document or program.

close Remove a window or dialog box, or quit a program. To close a window, you can click **Close** on the **Control** menu, or you can click the close button icon in the upper right corner of the dialog box. When you close an application window, you quit the program.

collapse To hide additional directory levels below a selected directory in the directory tree.

command A word or phrase, usually found on a menu, that you click to carry out an action. You click a command on a menu or type a command at the Windows NT command prompt. You can also type a command in the **Run** dialog box, which you open by clicking **Run** on the **Start** menu.

command button A button in a dialog box that carries out or cancels the selected action. Two common command buttons are **OK** and **Cancel**. If you click a command button that contains an ellipsis (for example, **Browse...**), another dialog box appears.

common group Common groups appear in the program list on the **Start** menu for all users who log on to the computer. Only Administrators can create or change common groups.

communications settings Settings that specify how information is transferred from your computer to a device (usually a printer or modem).

computer account Each computer running Windows NT Workstation and Windows NT Server that participates in a domain has its own account in the directory database. A computer account is created when the computer is first identified to the domain during network setup at installation time.

Computer Browser service Maintains an up-to-date list of computers, and provides the list to programs when requested. Provides the computer lists displayed in the **Network Neighborhood**, **Select Computer**, and **Select Domain** dialog boxes; and (for Windows NT Server only) in the Server Manager window.

computer name A unique name of up to 15 uppercase characters that identifies a computer to the network. The name cannot be the same as any other computer or domain name in the network.

configure To change the initial setup of a client, a Macintosh-accessible volume, a server, or a network.

connect To assign a drive letter, port, or computer name to a shared resource so that you can use it with Windows NT.

connected user A user accessing a computer or a resource across the network.

connection A software link between a client and a shared resource such as a printer or a shared directory on a server. Connections require a network adapter or modem.

controller *See* backup domain controller (BDC); primary domain controller (PDC).

conventional memory Up to the first 640 KB of memory in your computer. MS-DOS uses this memory to run programs.

current directory The directory that you are currently working in. Also called "current folder."

D

default button In some dialog boxes, the command button that is selected or highlighted when the dialog box is initially displayed. The default button has a bold border, indicating that it will be chosen automatically if you press ENTER. To override a default button, you can click **Cancel** or another command button.

default gateway In TCP/IP, the intermediate network device on the local network that has knowledge of the network IDs of the other networks in the Internet, so it can forward the packets to other gateways until the packet is eventually delivered to a gateway connected to the specified destination. *See also* gateway.

default owner The person assigned ownership of a folder on the server when the account of the folder or volume's previous owner expires or is deleted. Each server has one default owner; you can specify the owner.

default printer The printer that is used if you choose the **Print** command without first specifying which printer you want to use with a program. You can have only one default printer; it should be the printer you use most often.

default profile *See* system default profile; user default profile.

default user Every user profile begins as a copy of *default user*, which is a default user profile stored on each computer running Windows NT Workstation or Windows NT Server.

dependent service A service that requires support of another service. For example, the Alerter service is dependent on the Messenger service. *See also* Alerter service; Messenger service.

desktop The background of your screen, on which windows, icons, and dialog boxes appear.

desktop pattern A design that appears across your desktop. You can create your own pattern or select a pattern provided by Windows NT.

destination directory The directory to which you intend to copy or move one or more files.

device Any piece of equipment that can be attached to a network—for example, a computer, a printer, or any other peripheral equipment.

device driver A program that enables a specific piece of hardware (device) to communicate with Windows NT. Although a device may be installed on your system, Windows NT cannot recognize the device until you have installed and configured the appropriate driver. If a device is listed in the Hardware Compatibility List, a driver is usually included with Windows NT. Drivers are installed when you run the Setup program (for a manufacturer's supplied driver) or by using Devices in Control Panel. *See also* Hardware Compatibility List (HCL).

DHCP *See* Dynamic Host Configuration Protocol.

dialog box A window that is displayed to request or supply information. Many dialog boxes have options that you must select before Windows NT can carry out a command.

dial-up line A standard dial-up connection such as telephone and ISDN lines.

dial-up networking The client version of Windows NT Remote Access Service (RAS), enabling users to connect to remote networks.

directory Part of a structure for organizing your files on a disk, a directory (also called a folder) is represented by the folder icon in Windows NT, Windows 95, and on Macintosh computers. A directory can contain files and other directories, called subdirectories or folders within folders.

With Services for Macintosh, directories on the computer running Windows NT Server appear to Macintosh users as volumes and folders if they are designated as Macintosh accessible.

See also directory tree; folder.

directory database A database of security information such as user account names and passwords, and the security policy settings. For Windows NT Workstation, the directory database is managed by using User Manager. For a Windows NT Server domain, it is managed by using User Manager for Domains. (Other Windows NT documents may refer to the directory database as the "Security Accounts Manager (SAM) database.") *See also* Windows NT Server Directory Services.

directory replication The copying of a master set of directories from a server (called an export server) to specified servers or workstations (called import computers) in the same or other domains. Replication simplifies the task of maintaining identical sets of directories and files on multiple computers, because only a single master copy of the data must be maintained. Files are replicated when they are added to an exported directory and every time a change is saved to the file. *See also* Directory Replicator service.

Directory Replicator service Replicates directories, and the files in those directories, between computers. *See also* directory replication.

directory services *See* Windows NT Server Directory Services.

directory tree A graphical display of a disk's directory hierarchy. The directories and folders on the disk are shown as a branching structure. The top-level directory is the root directory.

disabled user account A user account that does not permit logons. The account appears in the user account list of the User Manager or User Manager for Domains window and can be re-enabled at any time. *See also* user account.

Distributed Component Object Model (DCOM) Use the DCOM Configuration tool to integrate client/server applications across multiple computers. DCOM can also be used to integrate robust Web browser applications. *See also* DCOM Configuration tool.

DLL *See* dynamic-link library.

document A self-contained file created with a program and, if saved on disk, given a unique file name by which it can be retrieved. A document can be a text file, a spreadsheet, or an image file, for example.

document file A file that is associated with a program. When you open a document file, the program starts and loads the file. *See also* associate.

Document file icon Represents a file that is associated with a program. When you double-click a document file icon, the program starts and loads the file. *See also* associate.

document icon Located at the left of a document window title bar, the document icon represents the open document. Clicking the document icon opens the window menu. Also known as the control menu box.

domain In Windows NT, a collection of computers, defined by the administrator of a Windows NT Server network, that share a common directory database. A domain provides access to the centralized user accounts and group accounts maintained by the domain administrator. Each domain has a unique name. *See also* directory database; user account; workgroup.

domain controller In a Windows NT Server domain, refers to the computer running Windows NT Server that manages all aspects of user-domain interactions, and uses information in the directory database to authenticate users logging on to domain accounts. One shared directory database is used to store security and user account information for the entire domain. A domain has one primary domain controller (PDC) and one or more backup domain controllers (BDCs). *See also* backup domain controller (BDC); directory database; member server; primary domain controller (PDC).

domain database *See* directory database.

domain model A grouping of one or more domains with administration and communication links between them that are arranged for the purpose of user and resource management.

domain synchronization *See* synchronize.

double-click To rapidly press and release a mouse button twice without moving the mouse. Double-clicking carries out an action, such as starting a program.

down level A term that refers to earlier operating systems, such as Windows for Workgroups or LAN Manager, that can still interoperate with Windows NT Workstation or Windows NT Server.

drag To move an item on the screen by selecting the item and then pressing and holding down the mouse button while moving the mouse. For example, you can move a window to another location on the screen by dragging its title bar.

drive icon An icon in the All Folders column in Windows NT Explorer or the Names Column in My Computer that represents a disk drive on your system. Different icons depict floppy disk drives, hard disk drives, network drives, RAM drives, and CD-ROM drives.

driver *See* device driver.

dual boot A computer that can boot two different operating systems. *See also* multiple boot.

Dynamic Host Configuration Protocol (DHCP) A protocol that offers dynamic configuration of IP addresses and related information. DHCP provides safe, reliable, and simple TCP/IP network configuration, prevents address conflicts, and helps conserve the use of IP addresses through centralized management of address allocation. *See also* IP address.

dynamic-link library (DLL) An operating system feature that allows executable routines (generally serving a specific function or set of functions) to be stored separately as files with .dll extensions and to be loaded only when needed by the program that calls them.

E

EISA *See* Extended Industry Standard Architecture.

embedded object Presents information, created in another program, which has been pasted inside your document. Information in the embedded object does not exist in another file outside of your document.

EMS *See* Expanded Memory Specification.

encapsulated PostScript (EPS) file A file that prints at the highest possible resolution for your printer. An EPS file may print faster than other graphical representations. Some Windows NT and non-Windows NT graphical programs can import EPS files. *See also* PostScript printer; print processor.

encryption The process of making information indecipherable to protect it from unauthorized viewing or use, especially during transmission or when it is stored on a transportable magnetic medium.

enterprise server Refers to the server to which multiple primary domain controllers (PDCs) in a large organization will replicate. *See also* primary domain controller (PDC).

environment variable A string consisting of environment information, such as a drive, path, or file name, associated with a symbolic name that can be used by Windows NT. To define environment variables, use System in Control Panel or use the **set** command from the Windows NT command prompt.

EPS *See* encapsulated PostScript file.

error logging The process by which errors that cannot readily be corrected by the majority of end users are written to a file instead of being displayed on the screen. System administrators, support technicians, and users can use this log file to monitor the condition of the hardware in a computer running Windows NT to tune the configuration of the computer for better performance, and to debug problems as they occur.

event Any significant occurrence in the system or a program that requires users to be notified, or an entry to be added to a log.

Event Log service Records events in the system, security, and application logs. The Event Log service is located in Event Viewer.

expand To show hidden directory levels in the directory tree. With My Computer or Windows NT Explorer, directories that can expand have plus-sign icons which you click to expand.

expanded memory A type of memory, up to 8 megabytes, that can be added to an 8086 or 8088 computer, or to an 80286, 80386, 80486, or Pentium computer. The use of expanded memory is defined by the Expanded Memory Specification (EMS). Note: Windows NT requires an 80486 or higher computer.

Expanded Memory Specification (EMS) Describes a technique for adding memory to IBM PC systems. EMS bypasses the limits on the maximum amount of usable memory in a computer system by supporting memory boards containing a number of 16 KB banks of RAM that can be enabled or disabled by software. *See also* memory.

Explorer *See* Windows NT Explorer.

Extended Industry Standard Architecture (EISA)
A 32-bit bus standard introduced in 1988 by a consortium of nine computer industry companies. EISA maintains compatibility with the earlier Industry Standard Architecture (ISA) but provides for additional features.

extended memory Memory beyond one megabyte in 80286, 80386, 80486, and Pentium computers. Note: Windows NT requires an 80486 or higher computer.

extended partition Created from free space on a hard disk, an extended partition can be subpartitioned into zero or more logical drives. Only one of the four partitions allowed per physical disk can be an extended partition, and no primary partition needs to be present to create an extended partition. *See also* free space; logical drive; primary partition.

extension A file name extension usually indicates the type of file or directory, or the type of program associated with a file. In MS-DOS, this includes a period and up to three characters at the end of a file name. Windows NT supports long file names, up to the file name limit of 255 characters.

extension-type association The association of an MS-DOS file name extension with a Macintosh file type and file creator. Extension-type associations allow users of the PC and Macintosh versions of the same program to share the same data files on the server. Services for Macintosh has many predefined extension-type associations. *See also* name mapping.

external command A command that is stored in its own file and loaded from disk when you use the command.

F

family set A collection of related tapes containing several backup sets. *See also* backup set.

FAT *See* file allocation table.

fault tolerance Ensures data integrity when hardware failures occur. In Windows NT, fault tolerance is provided by the Ftdisk.sys driver. In Disk Administrator, fault tolerance is provided using mirror sets, stripe sets with parity, and volume sets.

file A collection of information that has been given a name and is stored on a disk. This information can be a document or a program.

file allocation table (FAT) A table or list maintained by some operating systems to keep track of the status of various segments of disk space used for file storage. Also referred to as the FAT file system.

File and Print Services for NetWare (FPNW)
A Windows NT Server component that enables a computer running Windows NT Server to provide file and print services directly to NetWare-compatible client computers.

file name The name of a file. MS-DOS supports the 8.3 naming convention of up to eight characters followed by a period and a three-character extension. Windows NT supports the FAT and NTFS file systems with file names up to 255 characters. Since MS-DOS cannot recognize long file names, Windows NT Server automatically translates long names of files and folders to 8.3 names for MS-DOS users. *See also* long name; name mapping; short name.

file name extension The characters that follow the period in a file name, following the FAT naming conventions. File name extensions can have as many as three characters and are often used to identify the type of file and the program used to create the file (for example, spreadsheet files created by Microsoft Excel have the extension .xls). With Services for Macintosh, you can create extension-type associations that map PC file name extensions with Macintosh file creators and types.

File Replication service A Windows NT service that allows specified file(s) to be replicated to remote systems, ensuring that copies on each system are kept in synchronization. The system that maintains the master copy is called the exporter, and the systems that receive updates are known as importers.

file sharing The ability for a computer running Windows NT to share parts (or all) of its local file system(s) with remote computers. An administrator creates share points by using the file sharing command in My Computer or Windows NT Explorer or by using the **net share** command from the command prompt.

file system In an operating system, the overall structure in which files are named, stored, and organized. NTFS and FAT are types of file systems.

find tab Displays the words you can use to search for related topics. Use this tab to look for topics related to a particular word. It is located in the Help button bar near the top of the Help window.

floppy disk A disk that can be inserted in and removed from a disk drive. Floppies are most commonly available in a 3.5 or 5.25 inch format.

folder A grouping of files or other folders, graphically represented by a folder icon, in both the Windows NT and Macintosh environments. A folder is analogous to a PC's file system directory, and many folders are, in fact, directories. A folder may contain other folders as well as file objects. *See also* directory.

font A graphic design applied to a collection of numbers, symbols, and characters. A font describes a certain typeface along with other qualities such as size, spacing, and pitch.

FPNW *See* File and Print Services for NetWare.

free space Free space is an unused and unformatted portion of a hard disk that can be partitioned or subpartitioned. Free space within an extended partition is available for the creation of logical drives. Free space that is not within an extended partition is available for the creation of a partition, with a maximum of four partitions allowed per disk. *See also* extended partition; logical drive; primary partition.

full name A user's complete name, usually consisting of the last name, first name, and middle initial. The full name is information that can be maintained by User Manager and User Manager for Domains as part of the information identifying and defining a user account. *See also* user account.

full-screen application A non–Windows NT application that is displayed in the entire screen, rather than a window, when running in the Windows NT environment.

full synchronization Occurs when a copy of the entire database directory is sent to a backup domain controller (BDC). Full synchronization is performed automatically when changes have been deleted from the change log before replication takes place, and when a new BDC is added to a domain. *See also* backup domain controller (BDC); directory database.

G

gateway Describes a system connected to multiple physical TCP/IP networks, capable of routing or delivering IP packets between them. A gateway translates between different transport protocols or data formats (for example IPX and IP) and is generally added to a network primarily for its translation ability. Also referred to as an IP router. *See also* IP address; IP router.

global account For Windows NT Server, a normal user account in a user's domain. Most user accounts are global accounts. If there are multiple domains in the network, it is best if each user in the network has only one user account in only one domain, and each user's access to other domains is accomplished through the establishment of domain trust relationships. *See also* local account; trust relationship.

global group For Windows NT Server, a group that can be used in its own domain, member servers and workstations of the domain, and trusting domains. In all those places it can be granted rights and permissions and can become a member of local groups. However, it can only contain user accounts from its own domain. Global groups provide a way to create handy sets of users from inside the domain, available for use both in and out of the domain.

Global groups cannot be created or maintained on computers running Windows NT Workstation. However, for Windows NT Workstation computers that participate in a domain, domain global groups can be granted rights and permissions at those workstations, and can become members of local groups at those workstations. *See also* domain; group; local group; trust relationship.

group In User Manager or User Manager for Domains, an account containing other accounts that are called members. The permissions and rights granted to a group are also provided to its members, making groups a convenient way to grant common capabilities to collections of user accounts. For Windows NT Workstation, groups are managed with User Manager. For Windows NT Server, groups are managed with User Manager for Domains. *See also* built-in groups; global group; local group; user account.

group account A collection of user accounts. Giving a user account membership in a group gives that user all the rights and permissions granted to the group. *See also* local account; user account.

group category One of three categories of users to which you can assign Macintosh permissions for a folder. The permissions assigned to the group category are available to the group associated with the folder.

group memberships The groups to which a user account belongs. Permissions and rights granted to a group are also provided to its members. In most cases, the actions a user can perform in Windows NT are determined by the group memberships of the user account the user is logged on to. *See also* group.

group name A unique name identifying a local group or a global group to Windows NT. A group's name cannot be identical to any other group name or user name of its own domain or computer. *See also* global group; local group.

guest Users of Services for Macintosh who do not have a user account or who do not provide a password are logged on as a guest, using a user account with guest privileges. When a Macintosh user assigns permissions to everyone, those permissions are given to the group's guests and users.

guest account On computers running Windows NT Workstation or Windows NT Server, a built-in account used for logons by people who do not have a user account on the computer or domain or in any of the domains trusted by the computer's domain.

Guest privilege One of three privilege levels that you can assign to a Windows NT user account. The guest account used for Macintosh guest logons must have the Guest privilege. *See also* Administrator privilege; user account; User privilege.

H

Hardware Compatibility List (HCL) The Windows NT Hardware Compatibility List lists the devices supported by Windows NT. The latest version of the HCL can be downloaded from the Microsoft Web Page (microsoft.com) on the Internet.

HCL *See* Hardware Compatibility List.

heterogeneous environment An internetwork with servers and workstations running different operating systems, such as Windows NT, Macintosh, or Novell NetWare, using a mix of different transport protocols.

high memory area (HMA) The first 64 KB of extended memory (often referred to as HMA). *See also* memory.

High-Performance File System (HPFS) The file system designed for the OS/2 version 1.2 operating system.

HMA *See* high memory area.

home directory A directory that is accessible to the user and contains files and programs for that user. A home directory can be assigned to an individual user or can be shared by many users. Also referred to as a home folder.

home folder *See* home directory.

home page The initial page of information for a collection of pages. The starting point for a Web site or section of a Web site is often referred to as the home page. Individuals also post pages that are called home pages.

HPFS *See* High-Performance File System.

HTML *See* Hypertext Markup Language.

HTTP *See* Hypertext Transport Protocol.

hyperlink A way of jumping to another place on the Internet. Hyperlinks usually appear in a different format from regular text. You initiate the jump by clicking the link.

Hypertext Markup Language (HTML) A simple markup language used to create hypertext documents that are portable from one platform to another. HTML files are simple ASCII text files with codes embedded (indicated by markup tags) to indicate formatting and hypertext links. HTML is used for formatting documents on the World Wide Web.

Hypertext Transport Protocol (HTTP) The underlying protocol by which WWW clients and servers communicate. HTTP is an application-level protocol for distributed, collaborative, hypermedia information systems. It is a generic, stateless, object-oriented protocol. A feature of HTTP is the typing and negotiation of data representation, allowing systems to be built independently of the data being transferred.

I

icon A graphical representation of an element in Windows NT, such as a disk drive, directory, group, program, or document. Click the icon to enlarge a program icon to a window when you want to use the program. Within programs, there are also toolbar icons for commands such as cut, copy, and paste.

IIS *See* Internet Information Server.

insertion point The place where text will be inserted when you type. The insertion point usually appears as a flashing vertical bar in a program's window or in a dialog box.

Integrated Services Digital Network (ISDN) A type of phone line used to enhance WAN speeds, ISDN lines can transmit at speeds of 64 or 128 kilobits per second, as opposed to standard phone lines, which typically transmit at only 9600 bits per second (bps). An ISDN line must be installed by the phone company at both the server site and the remote site. *See also* bits per second (bps).

internal command Commands that are stored in the file Cmd.exe and that reside in memory at all times.

internet In Windows NT, a collection of two or more private networks, or private inter-enterprise TCP/IP networks.

In Macintosh terminology, refers to two or more physical networks connected by routers, which maintain a map of the physical networks on the internet and forward data received from one physical network to other physical networks. Network users in an internet can share information and network devices. You can use an internet with Services for Macintosh by connecting two or more AppleTalk networks to a computer running Windows NT Server.

Internet The global network of networks. *See also* World Wide Web (WWW).

Internet Information Server (IIS) A network file and application server that supports multiple protocols. Primarily, Internet Information Server transmits information in Hypertext Markup Language (HTML) pages by using the Hypertext Transport Protocol (HTTP).

Internet service provider (ISP) A company or educational institution that enables remote users to access the Internet by providing dial-up connections or installing leased lines.

internetworks Networks that connect local area networks (LANs) together.

interprocess communication (IPC) The ability, provided by a multitasking operating system, of one task or process to exchange data with another. Common IPC methods include pipes, semaphores, shared memory, queues, signals, and mailboxes. *See also* named pipe; queue.

intranet A TCP/IP network that uses Internet technology. May be connected to the Internet. *See also* Internet; Transmission Control Protocol/Internet Protocol (TCP/IP).

IP address Used to identify a node on a network and to specify routing information. Each node on the network must be assigned a unique IP address, which is made up of the *network ID*, plus a unique *host ID* assigned by the network administrator. This address is typically represented in dotted-decimal notation, with the decimal value of each octet separated by a period (for example, 138.57.7.27).

In Windows NT, the IP address can be configured statically on the client or configured dynamically through DHCP. *See also* Dynamic Host Configuration Protocol (DHCP).

IPC *See* interprocess communication.

IP router A system connected to multiple physical TCP/IP networks that can route or deliver IP packets between the networks. *See also* Transmission Control Protocol/Internet Protocol (TCP/IP).

IPX *See* IPX/SPX.

IPX/SPX Acronym for Internetwork Packet Exchange/Sequenced Packet Exchange, which is a set of transport protocols used in Novell NetWare networks. Windows NT implements IPX through NWLink.

ISDN *See* Integrated Services Digital Network.

ISP *See* Internet service provider.

J

jump Text, graphics, or parts of graphics that provide links to other Help topics or to more information about the current topic. The pointer changes shape whenever it is over a jump. If you click a jump that is linked to another topic, that topic appears in the Help window. If you click a jump that is linked to more information, the information appears in a pop-up window on top of the main Help window.

L

LAN *See* local area network.

linked object A representation or placeholder for an object that is inserted into a destination document. The object still exists in the source file and, when it is changed, the linked object is updated to reflect these changes.

list box In a dialog box, a type of box that lists available choices—for example, a list of all files in a directory. If all the choices do not fit in the list box, there is a scroll bar.

local account For Windows NT Server, a user account provided in a domain for a user whose global account is not in a trusted domain. Not required where trust relationships exist between domains. *See also* global account; trust relationship; user account.

local area network (LAN) A group of computers and other devices dispersed over a relatively limited area and connected by a communications link that enables any device to interact with any other on the network.

local group For Windows NT Workstation, a group that can be granted permissions and rights only for its own workstation. However, it can contain user accounts from its own computer and (if the workstation participates in a domain) user accounts and global groups both from its own domain and from trusted domains.

For Windows NT Server, a group that can be granted permissions and rights only for the domain controllers of its own domain. However, it can contain user accounts and global groups both from its own domain and from trusted domains.

Local groups provide a way to create handy sets of users from both inside and outside the domain, to be used only at domain controllers of the domain. *See also* global group; group; trust relationship.

local guest logon Takes effect when a user logs on interactively at a computer running Window NT Workstation or at a member server running Windows NT Server, and specifies Guest as the user name in the **Logon Information** dialog box.

local printer A printer that is directly connected to one of the ports on your computer. *See also* port.

local user profiles User profiles that are created automatically on the computer at logon the first time a user logs on to a computer running Windows NT Workstation or Windows NT Server.

log books Kept by the system administrator to record the backup methods, dates, and contents of each tape in a backup set. *See also* backup set; backup types.

log files Created by Windows NT Backup and contain a record of the date the tapes were created and the names of files and directories successfully backed up and restored. Performance Monitor also creates log files.

logical drive A subpartition of an extended partition on a hard disk. *See also* extended partition.

log off To stop using the network and remove your user name from active use until you log on again.

log on To provide a user name and password that identifies you to the network.

logon hours For Windows NT Server, a definition of the days and hours during which a user account can connect to a server. When a user is connected to a server and the logon hours are exceeded, the user will either be disconnected from all server connections or allowed to remain connected but denied any new connections.

logon script A file that can be assigned to user accounts. Typically a batch program, a logon script runs automatically every time the user logs on. It can be used to configure a user's working environment at every logon, and it allows an administrator to affect a user's environment without managing all aspects of it. A logon script can be assigned to one or more user accounts. *See also* batch program.

logon script path When a user logs on, the computer authenticating the logon locates the specified logon script (if one has been assigned to that user account) by following that computer's local logon script path (usually C:\Winnt\System32\Repl\Imports\Scripts). *See also* authentication; logon script.

logon workstations In Windows NT Server, the computers from which a user is allowed to log on.

long name A folder name or file name longer than the 8.3 file name standard (up to eight characters followed by a period and a three-character extension) of the FAT file system. Windows NT Server automatically translates long names of files and folders to 8.3 names for MS-DOS users.

Macintosh users can assign long names to files and folders on the server, and by using Services for Macintosh, you can assign long names to Macintosh-accessible volumes when you create them. *See also* file allocation table (FAT); file name; name mapping; short name.

loopback driver A network driver that allows the packets to bypass the network adapter completely and be returned directly to the computer that is performing the test.

M

Macintosh-accessible volume Storage space on the server used for folders and files of Macintosh users. A Macintosh-accessible volume is equivalent to a shared directory for PC users. Each Macintosh-accessible volume on a computer running Windows NT Server will correspond to a directory. Both PC users and Macintosh users can be given access to files located in a directory that is designated as both a shared directory and a Macintosh-accessible volume.

Macintosh-style permissions Directory and volume permissions that are similar to the access privileges used on a Macintosh.

Make Changes The Macintosh-style permission that gives users the right to make changes to a folder's contents; for example, modifying, renaming, moving, creating, and deleting files. When Services for Macintosh translates access privileges into Windows NT Server permissions, a user who has the Make Changes privilege is given Write and Delete permissions.

mandatory user profile A profile that is downloaded to the user's desktop each time he or she logs on. A mandatory user profile is created by an administrator and assigned to one or more users to create consistent or job-specific user profiles. They cannot be changed by the user and remain the same from one logon session to the next. *See also* roaming user profile; user profile.

master domain In the master domain model, the domain that is trusted by all other domains on the network and acts as the central administrative unit for user and group accounts.

maximize To enlarge a window to its maximum size by using the **Maximize** button (at the right of the title bar) or the **Maximize** command on the window menu.

Maximize button The small button containing a window icon at the right of the title bar. Mouse users can click the **Maximize** button to enlarge a window to its maximum size. Keyboard users can use the **Maximize** command on the window menu.

maximum password age The period of time a password can be used before the system requires the user to change it. *See also* account policy.

member server A computer that runs Windows NT Server but is not a primary domain controller (PDC) or backup domain controller (BDC) of a Windows NT domain. Member servers do not receive copies of the directory database. Also called a stand-alone server. *See also* backup domain controller (BDC); directory database; primary domain controller (PDC).

memory A temporary storage area for information and programs. *See also* expanded memory; extended memory.

menu A list of available commands in a program window. Menu names appear in the menu bar near the top of the window. The window menu, represented by the program icon at the left end of the title bar, is common to all programs for Windows NT. To open a menu, click the menu name.

menu bar The horizontal bar containing the names of all the program's menus. It appears below the title bar.

Messenger service Sends and receives messages sent by administrators or by the Alerter service. *See also* Alerter service.

minimize To reduce a window to a button on the taskbar by using the **Minimize** button (at the right of the title bar) or the **Minimize** command on the **Control** menu. *See also* maximize.

Minimize button The small button containing a short line at the right of the title bar. Mouse users can click the **Minimize** button to reduce a window to a button on the taskbar. Keyboard users can use the **Minimize** command on the **Control** menu.

minimum password age The period of time a password must be used before the user can change it. *See also* account policy.

minimum password length The fewest characters a password can contain. *See also* account policy.

modem Short for modulator/demodulator, a communications device that enables a computer to transmit information over a standard telephone line.

MS-DOS-based application An application that is designed to run with MS-DOS, and therefore may not be able to take full advantage of all Windows NT features.

multiple boot A computer that runs two or more operating systems. For example, Windows 95, MS-DOS, and Windows NT operating systems can be installed on the same computer. When the computer is started, any one of the operating systems can be selected. Also known as dual boot.

N

named pipe An interprocess communication mechanism that allows one process to communicate with another local or remote process.

name mapping Is provided by Windows NT Server and Windows NT Workstation to ensure access by MS-DOS users to NTFS and FAT volumes (which can have share names of up to 255 characters, as opposed to MS-DOS, which is restricted to eight characters followed by a period and a three-character extension). With name mapping, each file or directory with a name that does not conform to the MS-DOS 8.3 standard is automatically given a second name that does. MS-DOS users connecting the file or directory over the network see the name in the 8.3 format; Windows NT Workstation and Windows NT Server users see the long name. *See also* long name.

NDS *See* NetWare Directory Services.

NetBEUI A network protocol usually used in small, department-size local area networks of 1 through 200 clients. It can use Token Ring source routing as its only method of routing. *See also* router.

NetBIOS *See* network basic input/output system.

Net Logon service For Windows NT Server, performs authentication of domain logons, and keeps the domain's directory database synchronized between the primary domain controller (PDC) and the other backup domain controllers (BDCs) of the domain. *See also* backup domain controller (BDC); directory database; primary domain controller (PDC).

NetWare Directory Services (NDS) A NetWare service that runs on NetWare servers. The service enables the location of resources on the network.

network adapter An expansion card or other device used to connect a computer to a local area network (LAN). Also called a network card; network adapter card; adapter card; network interface card (NIC).

network adapter card *See* network adapter.

network administrator A person responsible for planning, configuring, and managing the day-to-day operation of the network. This person may also be referred to as a system administrator.

network basic input/output system (NetBIOS) An application programming interface (API) that can be used by applications on a local area network. NetBIOS provides applications with a uniform set of commands for requesting the lower-level services required to conduct sessions between nodes on a network and to transmit information back and forth. *See also* application programming interface (API).

network card *See* network adapter.

network card driver A network device driver that works directly with the network card, acting as an intermediary between the card and the protocol driver. With Services for Macintosh, the AppleTalk Protocol stack on the server is implemented as a protocol driver and is bound to one or more network drivers.

network device driver Software that coordinates communication between the network adapter and the computer's hardware and other software, controlling the physical function of the network adapters.

network directory *See* shared directory.

network driver *See* network device driver.

network interface card (NIC) *See* network adapter.

network protocol Software that enables computers to communicate over a network. TCP/IP is a network protocol, used on the Internet. *See also* Transmission Control Protocol/Internet Protocol (TCP/IP).

NIC Acronym for network interface card. *See* network adapter.

nonpaged memory Memory that cannot be paged to disk. *See also* memory; paging file.

non–Windows NT application Refers to an application that is designed to run with Windows 3.*x*, MS-DOS, OS/2, or POSIX, but not specifically with Windows NT, and that may not be able to take full advantage of all Windows NT features (such as memory management). *See also* POSIX.

NT *See* Windows NT Server; Windows NT Workstation.

NT file system *See* Windows NT file system.

NTFS *See* Windows NT file system.

NWLink IPX/SPX Compatible Transport A standard network protocol that supports routing, and can support NetWare client/server applications, where NetWare-aware Sockets-based applications communicate with IPX/SPX Sockets-based applications. *See also* IPX/SPX.

O

one-way trust relationship One domain (the trusting domain) "trusts" the domain controllers in the other domain (the trusted domain) to authenticate user accounts from the trusted domain to use resources in the trusting domain. *See also* trust relationship; user account.

open To display the contents of a directory, a document, or a data file in a window.

owner In Windows NT, every file and directory on an NTFS volume has an owner, who controls how permissions are set on the file or directory and who can grant permissions to others.

In the Macintosh environment, an owner is the user responsible for setting permissions for a folder on a server. A Macintosh user who creates a folder on the server automatically becomes the owner of the folder. The owner can transfer ownership to someone else. Each Macintosh-accessible volume on the server also has an owner.

owner category In the Macintosh environment, this refers to the user category to which you assign permissions for the owner of a folder or a Macintosh volume. *See also* Macintosh-accessible volume.

P

paging file A special file on a PC hard disk. With virtual memory under Windows NT, some of the program code and other information is kept in RAM while other information is temporarily swapped into virtual memory. When that information is required again, Windows NT pulls it back into RAM and, if necessary, swaps other information to virtual memory. Also called a swap file.

partial synchronization The automatic, timed delivery to all domain BDCs (backup domain controllers) of only those directory database changes that have occurred since the last synchronization. *See also* backup domain controller (BDC); synchronize.

partition A partition is a portion of a physical disk that functions as though it were a physically separate unit. *See also* volume; extended partition; system partition.

Partition Table An area of the Master Boot Record that the computer uses to determine how to access the disk. The Partition Table can contain up to four partitions for each physical disk. *See also* Master Boot Record.

pass-through authentication When the user account must be authenticated, but the computer being used for the logon is not a domain controller in the domain where the user account is defined, nor is it the computer where the user account is defined, the computer passes the logon information through to a domain controller (directly or indirectly) where the user account is defined. *See also* domain controller; user account.

password A security measure used to restrict logons to user accounts and access to computer systems and resources. A password is a unique string of characters that must be provided before a logon or an access is authorized. For Windows NT, a password for a user account can be up to 14 characters, and is case-sensitive. There are four user-defined parameters to be entered in the **Account Policy** dialog box in User Manager or User Manager for Domains: maximum password age, minimum password age, minimum password length, and password uniqueness.

With Services for Macintosh, each Macintosh user must type a user password when accessing the Windows NT Server. You can also assign each Macintosh-accessible volume a volume password if you want, which all users must type to access the volume. *See also* account policy.

password uniqueness The number of new passwords that must be used by a user account before an old password can be reused. *See also* account policy; password.

path A sequence of directory (or folder) names that specifies the location of a directory, file, or folder within the directory tree. Each directory name and file name within the path (except the first) must be preceded by a backslash (\). For example, to specify the path of a file named Readme.wri located in the Windows directory on drive C, you type **c:\windows\readme.wri**

PC Any personal computer (such as an IBM PC or compatible) using the MS-DOS, OS/2, Windows, Windows for Workgroups, Windows 95, Windows NT Workstation, or Windows NT Server operating systems.

peer Any of the devices on a layered communications network that operate on the same protocol level.

permissions Windows NT Server settings you set on a shared resource that determine which users can use the resource and how they can use it. *See also* access permission.

Services for Macintosh automatically translates between permissions and Macintosh access privileges, so that permissions set on a directory (volume) are enforced for Macintosh users, and access privileges set by Macintosh users are enforced for PC users connected to the computer running Windows NT Server.

personal group In the **Start** menu on the **Programs** list, a program group you have created that contains program items. Personal groups are stored with your logon information and each time you log on, your personal groups appear. *See also* group.

pipe An interprocess communication mechanism. Writing to and reading from a pipe is much like writing to and reading from a file, except that the two processes are actually using a shared memory segment to communicate data. *See also* named pipe.

pointer The arrow-shaped cursor on the screen that follows the movement of a mouse (or other pointing device) and indicates which area of the screen will be affected when you press the mouse button. The pointer changes shape during certain tasks.

port A location used to pass data in and out of a computing device. This term can refer to an adapter card connecting a server to a network, a serial 232 port, a TCP/IP port, or a printer port.

POSIX Acronym for Portable Operating System Interface, an IEEE (Institute of Electrical and Electronics Engineers) standard that defines a set of operating-system services. Programs that adhere to the POSIX standard can be easily ported from one system to another.

PostScript printer A printer that uses the PostScript page description language to create text and graphics on the output medium, such as paper or overhead transparency. Examples of PostScript printers include the Apple LaserWriter, the NEC LC-890, and the QMS PS-810.

primary domain controller (PDC) In a Windows NT Server domain, the computer running Windows NT Server that authenticates domain logons and maintains the directory database for a domain. The PDC tracks changes made to accounts of all computers on a domain. It is the only computer to receive these changes directly. A domain has only one PDC. *See also* directory database.

primary group The group with which a Macintosh user usually shares documents stored on a server. You specify a user's primary group in the user's account. When a user creates a folder on the server, the user's primary group is set as the folder's associated group (by default).

primary partition A partition is a portion of a physical disk that can be marked for use by an operating system. There can be up to four primary partitions (or up to three, if there is an extended partition) per physical disk. A primary partition cannot be subpartitioned. *See also* extended partition; partition.

print device Refers to the actual hardware device that produces printed output.

printer Refers to the software interface between the operating system and the print device. The printer defines where the document will go before it reaches the print device (to a local port, to a file, or to a remote print share), when it will go, and various other aspects of the printing process.

printer driver A program that converts graphics commands into a specific printer language, such as PostScript or PCL.

printer fonts Fonts that are built into your printer. These fonts are usually located in the printer's read-only memory (ROM). *See also* font.

printer permissions Specify the type of access a user or group has to use the printer. The printer permissions are No Access, Print, Manage Documents, and Full Control.

printer window Shows information for one of the printers that you have installed or to which you are connected. For each printer, you can see what documents are waiting to be printed, who owns them, how large they are, and other information.

printing pool Consists of two or more identical print devices associated with one printer.

print job In the Macintosh environment, a document or image sent from a client to a printer.

print processor A PostScript program that understands the format of a document's image file and how to print the file to a specific printer or class of printers. *See also* encapsulated PostScript (EPS) file.

print server Refers to the computer that receives documents from clients.

Print Server for Macintosh A Services for Macintosh service that enables Macintosh clients to send documents to printers attached to a computer running Windows NT; enables PC clients to send documents to printers anywhere on the AppleTalk network; and enables Macintosh users to spool their documents to the computer running Windows NT Server, thus freeing their clients to do other tasks. Also called MacPrint.

print sharing The ability for a computer running Windows NT Workstation or Windows NT Server to share a printer on the network. This is done by using the **Printers** folder or the **net share** command.

print spooler A collection of dynamic-link libraries (DLLs) that receive, process, schedule, and distribute documents.

private volume A Macintosh-accessible volume that is accessible by only one Macintosh user. For a volume to be a private volume, the permissions on its root directory must give the volume's owner all three permissions (Make Changes, See Files, and See Folders), while giving the primary group and everyone categories no permissions at all. When a private volume's owner uses the Chooser to view the volumes available on the server, the private volume is listed; however, no other users can see the private volume when viewing the volumes available on the server. *See also* Macintosh-accessible volume.

privilege level One of three settings (User, Administrator, or Guest) assigned to each user account. The privilege level a user account has determines the actions that the user can perform on the network. *See also* Administrator privilege; Guest privilege; user account; User privilege.

process When a program runs, a Windows NT process is created. A process is an object type which consists of an executable program, a set of virtual memory addresses, and one or more threads.

program file A file that starts an application or program. A program file has an .exe, .pif, .com, or .bat file name extension.

program group On the **Start** menu, a collection of programs. Grouping your programs makes them easier to find when you want to start them. *See also* common group; personal group.

program icon Located at the left of the window title bar, the program icon represents the program being run. Clicking the program icon opens the window menu.

program item A program, accessory, or document represented as an icon in the **Start** menu or on the desktop.

protocol A set of rules and conventions for sending information over a network. These rules govern the content, format, timing, sequencing, and error control of messages exchanged among network devices.

protocol driver A network device driver that implements a protocol, communicating between Windows NT Server and one or more network adapter card drivers. With Services for Macintosh, the AppleTalk Protocol stack is implemented as an NDIS-protocol driver, and is bound to one or more network adapter card drivers.

Q

queue In Windows NT terminology, a queue refers to a group of documents waiting to be printed. (In NetWare and OS/2 environments, queues are the primary software interface between the program and print device; users submit documents to a queue. However, with Windows NT, the printer is that interface—the document is sent to a printer, not a queue.)

R

RAM An acronym for random-access memory. RAM can be read from or written to by the computer or other devices. Information stored in RAM is lost when you turn off the computer. *See also* memory.

RAS *See* Remote Access Service.

refresh To update displayed information with current data.

registry The Windows NT registry is a hierarchical database that provides a repository for information about a computer's configuration on Windows NT Workstation and about hardware and user accounts on Windows NT Server. It is organized in subtrees and their keys, hives, and value entries. *See also* user account.

Remote Access Service (RAS) A service that provides remote networking for telecommuters, mobile workers, and system administrators who monitor and manage servers at multiple branch offices. Users with RAS on a Windows NT–based computer can dial in to remotely access their networks for services such as file and printer sharing, electronic mail, scheduling, and SQL database access.

remote administration Administration of one computer by an administrator located at another computer and connected to the first computer across the network.

remote logon Occurs when a user is already logged on to a user account and makes a network connection to another computer. *See also* user account.

remote procedure call (RPC) A message-passing facility that allows a distributed program to call services available on various machines in a network. Used during remote administration of computers. *See also* remote administration.

resource Any part of a computer system or a network, such as a disk drive, printer, or memory, that can be allotted to a program or a process while it is running, or shared over a local area network.

resource domain A trusting domain that establishes a one-way trust relationship with the master (account) domain, enabling users with accounts in the master domain to use resources in all the other domains. *See also* domain; trust relationship.

right *See* permissions; user rights.

roaming user profile User profile that is enabled when an administrator enters a user profile path into the user account. The first time the user logs off, the local user profile is copied to that location. Thereafter, the server copy of the user profile is downloaded each time the user logs on (if it is more current than the local copy) and is updated each time the user logs off. *See also* user profile.

root directory The top-level directory on a computer, a partition, or Macintosh-accessible volume. *See also* directory tree.

router In the Windows NT environment, a router helps LANs and WANs achieve interoperability and connectivity and can link LANs that have different network topologies (such as Ethernet and Token Ring). Routers match packet headers to a LAN segment and choose the best path for the packet, optimizing network performance.

In the Macintosh environment, routers are necessary for computers on different physical networks to communicate with each other. Routers maintain a map of the physical networks on a Macintosh internet (network) and forward data received from one physical network to other physical networks. Computers running Windows NT Server with Services for Macintosh can act as routers, and you can also use third-party routing hardware on a network with Services for Macintosh. *See also* local area network (LAN); wide area network (WAN).

S

SAM Acronym for Security Accounts Manager. *See* directory database; Windows NT Server Directory Services.

Schedule service Supports and is required for use of the **at** command. The **at** command can schedule commands and programs to run on a computer at a specified time and date.

screen elements The parts that make up a window or dialog box, such as the title bar, the **Minimize** and **Maximize** buttons, the window borders, and the scroll bars.

screen saver A moving picture or pattern that appears on your screen when you have not used the mouse or the keyboard for a specified period of time. To select a screen saver, either use Display in Control Panel or right-click on the desktop for properties.

scroll To move through text or graphics (up, down, left, or right) in order to see parts of the file that cannot fit on the screen.

scroll arrow An arrow on either end of a scroll bar that you use to scroll through the contents of the window or list box. Click the scroll arrow to scroll one screen at a time, or continue pressing the mouse button while pointing at the scroll arrow to scroll continuously.

scroll bar A bar that appears at the right and/or bottom edge of a window or list box whose contents are not completely visible. Each scroll bar contains two scroll arrows and a scroll box, which enable you to scroll through the contents of the window or list box.

scroll box In a scroll bar, a small box that shows the position of information currently visible in the window or list box relative to the contents of the entire window.

SCSI *See* small computer system interface.

Search button *See* find tab.

secure attention sequence A series of keystrokes (CTRL+ALT+DELETE) that will always display the Windows NT operating system logon screen.

security A means of ensuring that shared files can be accessed only by authorized users.

Security Accounts Manager (SAM)
See directory database; Windows NT Server Directory Services.

security database *See* directory database.

security ID (SID) A unique name that identifies a logged-on user to the security system. Security IDs (SIDs) can identify one user or a group of users.

security identifier *See* security ID (SID).

security log Records security events. This helps track changes to the security system and identify any possible breaches of security. For example, depending on the Audit settings in User Manager or User Manager for Domains, attempts to log on to the local computer might be recorded in the security log. The security log contains both valid and invalid logon attempts as well as events related to resource use (such as creating, opening, or deleting files). *See also* event.

security policies For Windows NT Workstation, the security policies consist of the Account, User Rights, and Audit policies, and are managed by using User Manager.

For a Windows NT Server domain, the security policies consist of the Account, User Rights, Audit, and Trust Relationships policies, and are managed by using User Manager for Domains.

security token *See* access token.

See Files The Macintosh-style permission that give users the right to open a folder and see the files in the folder. For example, a folder that has See Files and See Folders Macintosh-style permissions is given the Windows NT-style R (Read) permission. *See also* permissions.

See Folders The Macintosh-style permission that gives users the right to open a folder and see the files contained in that folder. *See also* permissions.

select To mark an item so that a subsequent action can be carried out on that item. You usually select an item by clicking it with a mouse or pressing a key. After selecting an item, you choose the action that you want to affect the item.

selection cursor The marking device that shows where you are in a window, menu, or dialog box and what you have selected. The selection cursor can appear as a highlight or as a dotted rectangle around text.

server In general, refers to a computer that provides shared resources to network users. *See also* member server.

server application A Windows NT application that can create objects for linking or embedding into other documents. For distributed applications, the application that responds to a client application. *See also* client application; Distributed Component Object Model (DCOM); embedded object; linked object.

Server Manager In Windows NT Server, a program used to view and administer domains, workgroups, and computers.

Server service Provides RPC (remote procedure call) support, and file, print, and named pipe sharing. *See also* named pipe; remote procedure call (RPC).

service A process that performs a specific system function and often provides an application programming interface (API) for other processes to call. Windows NT services are RPC-enabled, meaning that their API routines can be called from remote computers. *See also* application programming interface (API); remote procedure call (RPC).

Services for Macintosh *See* Windows NT Server Services for Macintosh.

session A link between two network devices, such as a client and a server. A session between a client and server consists of one or more connections from the client to the server.

SFM Acronym for Windows NT Services for Macintosh.

share To make resources, such as directories and printers, available to others.

shared directory A directory that network users can connect to.

shared network directory *See* shared directory.

shared resource Any device, data, or program that is used by more than one other device or program. For Windows NT, shared resources refer to any resource that is made available to network users, such as directories, files, printers, and named pipes. Also refers to a resource on a server that is available to network users. *See also* named pipe.

share name A name that refers to a shared resource on a server. Each shared directory on a server has a share name, used by PC users to refer to the directory. Users of Macintosh use the name of the Macintosh-accessible volume that corresponds to a directory, which may be the same as the share name. *See also* Macintosh-accessible volume.

share permissions Are used to restrict a shared resource's availability over the network to only certain users.

shortcut key A key or key combination, available for some commands, that you can press to carry out a command without first selecting a menu. Shortcut keys are listed to the right of commands on a menu.

short name A valid 8.3 (up to eight characters followed by a period and a three-character extension) MS-DOS or OS/2 file name that the computer running Windows NT Server creates for every Macintosh folder name or file name on the server. PC users refer to files on the server by their short names; Macintosh users refer to them by their long names. *See also* long name; name mapping.

SID *See* security ID.

single user logon Windows NT network users can connect to multiple servers, domains, and programs with a single network logon.

small computer system interface (SCSI) A standard high-speed parallel interface defined by the American National Standards Institute (ANSI). A SCSI interface is used for connecting microcomputers to peripheral devices such as hard disks and printers, and to other computers and local area networks.

SMS *See* Systems Management Server.

source directory The directory that contains the file or files you intend to copy or move.

source document The document where a linked or embedded object was originally created. *See also* embedded object; linked object.

special access permission On NTFS volumes, a custom set of permissions. You can customize permissions on files and directories by selecting the individual components of the standard sets of permissions. *See also* access permission.

split bar Divides Windows NT Explorer into two parts: The directory tree is displayed on the left, and the contents of the current directory are on the right. *See also* directory tree.

spooler Software that accepts documents sent by a user to be printed, and then stores those documents and sends them, one by one, to available printer(s). *See also* spooling.

spooling A process on a server in which print documents are stored on a disk until a printing device is ready to process them. A spooler accepts each document from each client, stores it, then sends it to a printing device when it is ready.

SQL Acronym for structured query language, a database programming language used for accessing, querying, and otherwise managing information in a relational database system.

stand-alone server *See* member server.

status bar A line of information related to the program in the window. Usually located at the bottom of a window. Not all windows have a status bar.

subdirectory A directory within a directory. Also called a folder within a folder.

subnet A portion of a network, which may be a physically independent network segment, that shares a network address with other portions of the network and is distinguished by a subnet number. A subnet is to a network what a network is to an internet.

subnet mask A 32-bit value that allows the recipient of IP packets to distinguish the network ID portion of the IP address from the host ID. *See also* IP address.

swap file *See* paging file.

synchronize To replicate the domain database from the primary domain controller (PDC) to one backup domain controller (BDC) of the domain, or to all the BDCs of a domain. This is usually performed automatically by the system, but can also be invoked manually by an administrator. *See also* backup domain controller (BDC); domain; primary domain controller (PDC).

syntax The order in which you must type a command and the elements that follow the command. Windows NT commands have up to four elements: command name, parameters, switches, and values.

system default profile In Windows NT Server, the user profile that is loaded when Windows NT is running and no user is logged on. When the **Begin Logon** dialog box is visible, the system default profile is loaded. *See also* user default profile, user profile.

system disk A disk that contains the MS-DOS system files necessary to start MS-DOS.

system log The system log contains events logged by the Windows NT components. For example, the failure of a driver or other system component to load during startup is recorded in the system log. Use Event Viewer to view the system log.

system partition The volume that has the hardware-specific files needed to load Windows NT. *See also* partition.

system policy A policy, created by using the System Policy Editor, to control user work environments and actions, and to enforce system configuration for Windows 95. System policy can be implemented for specific users, groups, computers, or for all users. System policy for users overwrites settings in the current user area of the registry, and system policy for computers overwrites the current local machine area of the registry. *See also* registry.

systemroot The name of the directory that contains Windows NT files. The name of this directory is specified when Windows NT is installed.

Systems Management Server Part of the Microsoft BackOffice family of products. Systems Management Server includes desktop management and software distribution that significantly automates the task of upgrading software on client computers.

T

tape set A tape set (sometimes referred to as a tape family) in Windows NT Backup is a sequence of tapes in which each tape is a continuation of the backup on the previous tape. *See also* backup set; backup types.

Task list A window that shows all running programs and their status. View the Task list in the **Applications** tab in Task Manager.

Task Manager Task Manager enables you to start, end, or run programs, end processes (a program, program component, or system process), and view CPU and memory use data. Task Manager gives you a simple, quick view of how each process (program or service) is using CPU and memory resources. (Note: In previous versions of Windows NT, Task List handled some of these functions.)

To run Task Manager, right-click the toolbar and then click Task Manager.

TCP *See* Transmission Control Protocol.

TCP/IP *See* Transmission Control Protocol/Internet Protocol.

template accounts Accounts that are not actually used by real users but serve as a basis for the real accounts (for administrative purposes).

terminate-and-stay-resident program (TSR)
A program running under MS-DOS that remains loaded in memory even when it is not running so that it can be quickly invoked for a specific task performed while any other program is operating.

text box   In a dialog box, a box in which you type information needed to carry out a command. The text box may be blank or may contain text when the dialog box opens.

text file   A file containing text characters (letters, numbers, and symbols) but no formatting information. A text file can be a "plain" ASCII file that most computers can read. Text file can also refer to a word-processing file. *See also* ASCII file.

text-only   An ASCII file that contains no formatting. *See also* ASCII file.

time-out   If a device is not performing a task, the amount of time the computer should wait before detecting it as an error.

title bar   The horizontal bar (at the top of a window) that contains the title of the window or dialog box. On many windows, the title bar also contains the program icon and the **Maximize**, **Minimize**, and **Close** buttons.

toolbar   A series of icons or shortcut buttons providing quick access to commands. Usually located directly below the menu bar. Not all windows have a toolbar.

topic   Information in the Help window. A Help topic usually begins with a title and contains information about a particular task, command, or dialog box.

Transmission Control Protocol (TCP)
A connection-based Internet protocol responsible for breaking data into packets, which the IP protocol sends over the network. This protocol provides a reliable, sequenced communication stream for network communication. *See also* Internet Protocol (IP).

Transmission Control Protocol/Internet Protocol (TCP/IP)
A set of networking protocols that provide communications across interconnected networks made up of computers with diverse hardware architectures and various operating systems. TCP/IP includes standards for how computers communicate and conventions for connecting networks and routing traffic.

Trojan horse   A program that masquerades as another common program in an attempt to receive information. An example of a Trojan horse is a program that masquerades as a system logon to retrieve user names and password information, which the writers of the Trojan horse can use later to break into the system.

TrueType fonts   Fonts that are scalable and sometimes generated as bitmaps or soft fonts, depending on the capabilities of your printer. TrueType fonts can be sized to any height, and they print exactly as they appear on the screen.

trust   *See* trust relationship.

trust relationship A link between domains that enables pass-through authentication, in which a trusting domain honors the logon authentications of a trusted domain. With trust relationships, a user who has only one user account in one domain can potentially access the entire network. User accounts and global groups defined in a trusted domain can be given rights and resource permissions in a trusting domain, even though those accounts do not exist in the trusting domain's directory database. *See also* directory database; global group; pass-through authentication; user account.

trust relationships policy A security policy that determines which domains are trusted and which domains are trusting domains. *See also* trust relationship.

TSR *See* terminate-and-stay-resident program.

two-way trust relationship Each domain trusts user accounts in the other domain to use its resources. Users can log on from computers in either domain to the domain that contains their account. *See also* trust relationship.

U

unavailable An unavailable button or command is displayed in light gray instead of black, and it cannot be clicked.

UNC name *See* universal naming convention name.

uninterruptible power supply (UPS) A battery-operated power supply connected to a computer to keep the system running during a power failure.

universal naming convention (UNC) name A full Windows NT name of a resource on a network. It conforms to the *server_name**share_name* syntax, where *server_name* is the server's name and *share_name* is the name of the shared resource. UNC names of directories or files can also include the directory path under the share name, with the following syntax: *server_name**share_name**directory*\file_name

UPS *See* uninterruptible power supply.

UPS service Manages an uninterruptible power supply connected to a computer. *See also* uninterruptible power supply (UPS).

user account Consists of all the information that defines a user to Windows NT. This includes such things as the user name and password required for the user to log on, the groups in which the user account has membership, and the rights and permissions the user has for using the system and accessing its resources. For Windows NT Workstation, user accounts are managed with User Manager. For Windows NT Server, user accounts are managed with User Manager for Domains. *See also* group.

user account database *See* directory database.

user default profile In Windows NT Server, the user profile that is loaded by a server when a user's assigned profile cannot be accessed for any reason; when a user without an assigned profile logs on to the computer for the first time; or when a user logs on to the Guest account. *See also* system default profile; user profile.

User Manager A Windows NT Workstation tool used to manage the security for a workstation. User Manager administers user accounts, groups, and security policies.

User Manager for Domains A Windows NT Server tool used to manage security for a domain or an individual computer. User Manager for Domains administers user accounts, groups, and security policies.

user name A unique name identifying a user account to Windows NT. An account's user name cannot be identical to any other group name or user name of its own domain or workgroup. *See also* user account.

user password The password stored in each user's account. Each user generally has a unique user password and must type that password when logging on or accessing a server. *See also* password; volume password.

User privilege One of three privilege levels you can assign to a Windows NT user account. Every user account has one of the three privilege levels (Administrator, Guest, and User). Accounts with User privilege are regular users of the network; most accounts on your network probably have User privilege. *See also* Administrator privilege; Guest privilege; user account.

user profile Configuration information that can be retained on a user-by-user basis, and is saved in user profiles. This information includes all the per-user settings of the Windows NT environment, such as the desktop arrangement, personal program groups and the program items in those groups, screen colors, screen savers, network connections, printer connections, mouse settings, window size and position. When a user logs on, the user's profile is loaded and the user's Windows NT environment is configured according to that profile. *See also* personal group; program item.

user rights Define a user's access to a computer or domain and the actions that a user can perform on the computer or domain. User rights permit actions such as logging onto a computer or network, adding or deleting users in a workstation or domain, and so forth.

user rights policy Manages the assignment of rights to groups and user accounts. *See also* user account; user rights.

users In the Macintosh environment, a special group that contains all users who have user permissions on the server. When a Macintosh user assigns permissions to everyone, those permissions are given to the groups users and guests. *See also* guest.

V

variables In programming, a variable is a named storage location capable of containing a certain type of data that can be modified during program execution. System environment variables are defined by Windows NT Server and are the same no matter who is logged on at the computer. (Administrator group members can add new variables or change the values, however.) User environment variables can be different for each user of a particular computer. They include any environment variables you want to define of variables defined by your programs, such as the path where program files are located.

virtual memory The space on your hard disk that Windows NT uses as if it were actually memory. Windows NT does this through the use of paging files. The benefit of using virtual memory is that you can run more programs at one time than your system's physical memory would otherwise allow. The drawbacks are the disk space required for the virtual-memory paging file and the decreased execution speed when paging is required. *See also* paging file.

virtual printer memory In a PostScript printer, a part of memory that stores font information. The memory in PostScript printers is divided into two areas: banded memory and virtual memory. The banded memory contains graphics and page-layout information needed to print your documents. The virtual memory contains any font information that is sent to your printer either when you print a document or when you download fonts. *See also* PostScript printer.

virus A program that attempts to spread from computer to computer and either cause damage (by erasing or corrupting data) or annoy users (by printing messages or altering what is displayed on the screen).

volume A partition or collection of partitions that have been formatted for use by a file system. *See also* Macintosh-accessible volume; partition.

volume password An optional, case-sensitive password you can assign to a Macintosh-accessible volume when you configure the volume. To access the volume, a user must type the volume password. *See also* Macintosh-accessible volume; user password.

volume set A combination of partitions on a physical disk that appear as one logical drive. *See also* logical drive; partition.

W

WAN *See* wide area network.

warning beep The sound that your computer makes when you encounter an error or try to perform a task that Windows NT does not recognize.

Web browser A software program, such as Microsoft Internet Explorer, that retrieves a document from a Web server, interprets the HTML codes, and displays the document to the user with as much graphical content as the software can supply.

Web server A computer equipped with the server software to respond to HTTP requests, such as requests from a Web browser. A Web server uses the HTTP protocol to communicate with clients on a TCP/IP network.

wide area network (WAN) A communications network that connects geographically separated areas.

wildcard A character that represents one or more characters. The question mark (?) wildcard can be used to represent any single character, and the asterisk (*) wildcard can be used to represent any character or group of characters that might match that position in other file names.

window A rectangular area on your screen in which you view a program or document. You can open, close, and move windows, and change the size of most windows. You can open several windows at a time, and you can often reduce a window to an icon or enlarge it to fill the entire desktop.

Windows NT–based application Used as a shorthand term to refer to an application that is designed to run with Windows NT and does not run without Windows NT. All Windows NT–based applications follow similar conventions for arrangement of menus, style of dialog boxes, and keyboard and mouse use.

Windows NT Explorer A program that enables you to view and manage the files and folders on your computer and make network connections to other shared resources, such as a hard disk on a server. Windows NT Explorer replaces Program Manager and File Manager, which were programs available in earlier versions of Windows NT. Program Manager and File Manager are still available, and can be started in the same way you start other Windows-based programs.

Windows NT file system (NTFS) An advanced file system designed for use specifically within the Windows NT operating system. It supports file system recovery, extremely large storage media, long file names, and various features for the POSIX subsystem. It also supports object-oriented programs by treating all files as objects with user-defined and system-defined attributes. *See also* POSIX.

Windows NT Server A superset of Windows NT Workstation, Windows NT Server provides centralized management and security, fault tolerance, and additional connectivity. *See also* fault tolerance; Windows NT Workstation.

Windows NT Server Directory Services A Windows NT protected subsystem that maintains the directory database and provides an application programming interface (API) for accessing the database. *See also* application programming interface (API); directory database.

Windows NT Server Services for Macintosh A software component of Windows NT Server that allows Macintosh users access to the computer running Windows NT Server. The services provided with this component allow PC and Macintosh users to share files and resources, such as printers on the AppleTalk network or those attached to a computer running Windows NT Server. *See also* Print Server for Macintosh.

Windows NT Workstation The portable, secure, 32-bit, preemptive multitasking member of the Microsoft Windows operating system family.

workgroup For Windows NT, a workgroup is a collection of computers that are grouped for viewing purposes. Each workgroup is identified by a unique name. *See also* domain.

workstation Any networked Macintosh or PC using server resources. *See also* backup domain controller (BDC); member server; primary domain controller (PDC).

Workstation service Provides network connections and communications.

World Wide Web (WWW) The software, protocols, conventions, and information that enable hypertext and multimedia publishing of resources on different computers around the world. *See also* Hypertext Markup Language (HTML); Internet.

Index

$, administrative shares 192, 375
[] (square brackets), notational conventions used in this book xviii
{ } (brackets), notational conventions used in this book xviii
16-bit Windows programs, troubleshooting printing 324

A

Access
    permissions, definition 451
    privileges, definition 451
    restricting *See* Security; Share permissions
    to resources, auditing *See* Audit policy; Auditing
    tokens
        definition 451
        troubleshooting NTFS permissions 252
Access Denied message, troubleshooting printer problems 324
Account Expires option 58
Account Lockout 143, 451
Account Operators group
    description 110–111
    distributing administrative tasks 132–133
    requirements for monitoring resources 366
    rules for creating groups 97
Account policy
    definition 451
    description 139
    dialog box 141–146
    planning 140
    setting
        account lockout options 142–143
        password options 141–142
        password requirements 139
    unlocking user accounts 147
Account Policy dialog box 141–146
Accounts
    computer account, definition 455
    global, definition 462
    groups *See* Groups, group accounts; User accounts, group accounts
    users *See* User accounts
Active, definition 451
Adapters, network
    definition 468
    network card drivers, definition 469
    network device drivers, definition 469

Add & Read permission
    assigning 232
    NTFS standard folder permission 213
    planning NTFS permissions for data folders 223
Add permission, NTFS standard folder permission 213
Add Printer wizard
    connecting to printers from Windows NT and Windows 95 clients 282
    description 22
    enabling printer pooling 291
    overview 275–276
Add User Accounts wizard 22
Add Users and Groups dialog box 232
Add/Remove Programs wizard 22
Adding
    See also Creating
    files to folders, permissions required *See* Permissions
    members to global groups 99
    printers 275–278
    users to Administrators group 115
    users to Backup Operators group 396–397
    users to Server Operators group 366
Addresses
    DMA, checking 385
    IP, definition 464
Admin$ share 192
Administering print servers
    definition 307
    managing documents 310–313
    managing printers 315–320
    requirements 308
    tasks 307
    troubleshooting printing problems 322–324
Administering Windows NT
    administrative tasks 19
    administrative tools 20–22
    client-based tools 21–22
    creating user accounts *See* User accounts
    domain model 7
    workgroup model 8
Administration, remote, definition 474
Administrative account, definition 451
Administrative alerts
    definition 451
    setting 379–380
Administrative shares 192
Administrative tools
    account templates 133–138

Administrative tools *(continued)*
    built-in groups 132–133
    Event Viewer 161
    included with Windows NT 20–22
    monitoring resources 365–366
    Server Manager
        See also Server Manager
        maintaining domain controllers 154
        monitoring resources 365
    User Manager *See* User Manager;
      User Manager for Domains
    Windows NT Diagnostics 365, 383–387
Administrative wizards
    description 21
    opening Windows NT administrative tools 22
    Windows NT Server advantages 6
Administrator account
    description 36
    NTFS permissions
        recommendations 258
        special access 236
    password 41
    recommendations 74
Administrator privilege, definition 452
Administrators
    definition 452
    sharing network program folders 184
Administrators group
    adding Domain Admins group 116–118
    auditing requirements 332
    built-in capabilities for printer administration 308
    description 109
    distributing administrative tasks 132–133
    facilitating local administration 115
    Full Control print permission 274
    inherent user rights 108
    NTFS permissions
        planning data folders 223
        planning program folders 223
        recommendations 258
        special access 236
        taking ownership of files and folders 241
    promoting centralized administration 116–118
    requirements for monitoring resources 366
    rules for creating groups 97
    sharing folders 192
    viewing security log 347
Alerter service, definition 452
Alerts, sending to users 379–380
API (application programming interface), definition 452
Application log
    definition 452
    description 346
Application programming interface (API), definition 452

Application window, definition 452
Applications
    See also Programs
    definition 452
Archive bit, definition 452
Archiving
    backup tapes 403–404
    security logs 353–355
ASCII file, definition 452
Associate, definition 452, 460
at command
    command line options 423
    scheduling automatic backups 418, 422–424
    starting Schedule service 422
Attributes, definition 452
Audit policy
    See also Auditing
    administration requirements 332
    Audit Policy dialog box 337
    auditing
        changes to Audit policy 334–335
        printer use 343–344
    checklist 357
    defining domain Audit policy 336–337
    definition 453
    description 331–332
    implementing 335–339
    planning 334–335, 338–339
    security log
        See also Security log
        creating entries 348
        viewing 347
Audit Policy dialog box 337
Auditing
    See also Audit policy
    administration requirements 332
    definition 453
    description 331
    Everyone group 341–342
    folder and file operations
        NTFS volumes only 342
        specifying events to audit 340–341
    log file types 346
    printers 343–344
    security log
        See also Security log
        archiving 353–355
        viewing using Event Viewer 346–353
    setting up
        defining domain Audit policy 336–337
        description 335

Authentication, definition 453
Automatic backups, scheduling
   at command 422–424
   batch file options 419
   example 420–421
   ntbackup command 419–421
   overview 418
   using Windows NT Command Scheduler 424–425

B

Backing up data
   archive bit, definition 452
   backing up registry information 400
   backup logs
      description 405
      log books defined 465
      printing 414
      setting options 412–414
      viewing 416
   backup markers 401
   Backup Operators group 109–110
   backup sets
      backup set map, definition 453
      definition 453
      description 405
      family sets 405, 460
      loading when restoring data 430–431, 435
      missing or damaged tapes, restoring data 431
      setting options 412–414
   benefits 395
   catalogs
      backup set map, definition 453
      definition 453, 454
      description 405
      loading when restoring data 430–431, 435
   checklist 438
   creating backup operators 396–397
   erasing backup tapes 410, 414
   home folder considerations 43
   life cycle of tapes 404
   non-tape media 395
   planning strategy
      backup types 401–403, 453
      determining data to back up 400–401
      exercise 405–407
      guidelines 399–400
      rotating and archiving tapes 403–404
      worksheets 450
   preparatory tasks 410–411
   recommendations 438

Backing up data *(continued)*
   rotating and archiving tapes 403–404
   scheduling automatic backups
      at command 422–424
      batch file options 419
      example 420–421
      ntbackup command 419–421
      overview 418
      using Windows NT Command Scheduler 424–425
   selecting drives, folders, and files 411–412, 415
   sending messages to users 411
   setting tape, backup set, and log options 412–414
   simulation exercise 414–416
   tape devices *See* Tape drives
   tape set defined 478
   tapes
      erasing backup tapes 410, 414
      life cycle of tapes 404
      missing or damaged tapes, restoring data 431
      rotating and archiving tapes 403–404
   to floppy disks 395
   weekly backup schedule 450
   Windows NT administrative tasks 19
   Windows NT Backup
      backup types 401–403
      description 21, 395
      missing or damaged tapes, restoring data 431
      requirements for using 396
      verifying computer date when restoring data 430
   worksheets, planning 450
backup command 395
Backup domain controllers (BDCs)
   See also Domain controllers; Primary domain controllers
   definition 453
   determining data to back up 400
   maintaining
      overview 153
      using Server Manager 154
   planning group strategy 90–94
   promoting to primary domain controllers 155–157
   restoring original domain controller roles 158–159
   synchronizing domains 160–161, 478
   troubleshooting logon problems 164
   Windows NT Directory services 10–11
Backup Information dialog box 413–414
Backup Operators group
   adding users 396–397
   data backup requirements 396
   description 109–110
Backup sets
   backup set map, definition 453
   catalogs, definition 453

Backup sets *(continued)*
    definition 453
    family sets 460
    loading when restoring data 430–431
    missing or damaged tapes, restoring data 431
    setting options 412–414
Backup simulation program
    backing up data 414–416
    restoring data 434–436
    starting 414
Batch files, scheduling automatic backups
    at command 422–424
    batch file options 419
    batch programs, definition 453
    example 420–421
    ntbackup command 419–421
    overview 418
    using Windows NT Command Scheduler 424–425
Batch programs, definition 453
BDCs *See* Backup domain controllers
Beep, warning 482
BIOS information, checking 385
Bits per second (bps), definition 453
Blue screen, definition 454
Boot partition, definition 454
Brackets ({ }), notational conventions used in this book xviii
Browse list, definition 454
Browsing
    definition 454
    shared folders on other computers 202–203
    web browsers, definition 482
Built-in groups
    See also specific group names
    definition 454
    determining rights 107–108
    distributing administrative tasks 132–133
    facilitating local administration 115
    on all Windows NT computers 109–110
    on domain controllers only 110–111
    promoting centralized administration 116–118
    recommendations 119
    rules for creating groups 97
    system groups 113–114
    types 106
Built-in user accounts 36
Buttons, default 456

C

Cache, definition 454
Cancel command, deleting documents from print queues 313
Canon Bubble-Jet BJC-600e printer, installing 278

CAPS LOCK key, troubleshooting logon problems 164
Cards, network adapters
    definition 468
    network card drivers, definition 469
    network device drivers, definition 469
Catalog Status dialog box 431
Catalogs
    backup set map, definition 453
    data backup
        definition 454
        description 405
        loading when restoring data 430–431, 435
    definition 453
CD-ROM
    course
        cleanup procedures xxxiv–xxxv
        conventions xviii–xix
        deleting self-paced training files xxxv
        icons xx
        intended audience xvi
        Network Administration Training menu shortcuts xxxi
        notes xx
        overview of this book xxi–xxii
        requirements xxiii–xxiv
        setup procedures xxv–xxxiv
        starting xvi
        Windows NT 4.0 self-administered assessment xxxviii
    instructional videos
        description xxxi
        installing Intel video drivers xxxiii
        local and global groups 85
        permissions 218
        starting 10
        Windows NT Directory services 10
        Windows NT client–based tools 22
Centralized network administration, definition 454
Certified Professional (MCP) program xxxvi–xxxviii
Change Password option, Windows NT Security dialog box 25–26
Change permission
    description 176
    NTFS standard file permission 214
    NTFS standard folder permission 213
    planning NTFS permissions for program folders 223
    sharing network program folders 184
Change Permissions
    events, auditing
        files and folders 341
        printers 343
    permission
        description 212
        giving users ability to take ownership 241

Index   489

Change Permissions *(continued)*
   permission *(continued)*
      recommendations 258
      requirements for assigning NTFS permissions 230
      special access permission 236
Characters
   in user account passwords 42
   in user names 41
Check box, definition 454
Chooser, definition 454
Cleanup procedures for this course xxxiv–xxxv
Clearing
   definition 454
   log files 355
Click, definition 454
Client-based tools, Windows NT Server 21–22
Client Service for NetWare 455
Clients
   client applications, definition 455
   definition 454
   non–Windows NT clients, logon scripts 66
   print clients, network operating systems 272, 277
   Windows 95 clients, receiving administrative
      messages 380
Clipboard 455
Closing
   definition 455
   programs from Task Manager 26–27
   resources in use on servers 377
   Windows NT *See* Shutting down
Collapse, definition 455
Color palette, setting xxxiii
Command button, definition 455
Command prompt
   default home folder location 43
   determining which services are running 162
   notational conventions used in this book xviii
   scheduling automatic backups
      at command 418, 422–424
      ntbackup command 418–421, 431
   set command, environment variables 384
Command, definition 455
Commands
   external, definition 460
   internal, definition 464
   notational conventions used in this book xviii
Common group, definition 455
Communications
   Install New Modem wizard 22
   interprocess communication (IPC), definition 464
   settings, definition 455
   Windows NT Server advantages 5
Compact disc *See* CD-ROM; Course materials

Computer account, definition 455
Computer Browser service 455
Computers
   accounts, definition 455
   Audit policy 335
   clients, definition 454
   computer names, definition 455
   dual boot, definition 458
   monitoring resources
      Server Manager 365
      viewing computer properties 369–370
      viewing user sessions 371–372
      Windows NT Diagnostics 365, 384
   multiple boot, definition 468
   planning data backup strategy 399–400
   remote
      viewing computer properties 370
      viewing security log 349
   requirements for this course xxiii–xxiv
   troubleshooting
      maintaining log book 383
      Windows NT Diagnostics 365, 384
   verifying date when restoring data 430
   viewing
      properties 369–370
      security log 349
      user sessions 371–372
Configuring
   definition 455
   print servers 274–280
Connected users
   definition 455
   disconnecting 371, 372–373
   viewing open resources 371
Connecting to
   definition 455
   printers
      other print clients 283
      troubleshooting 324
      Windows NT and Windows 95 clients 281–282
      Windows NT requirements 272
   shared folders
      Map Network Drive command 200–202, 374
      Run command 202–203
   shared resources, monitoring procedures 374
Connection, definition 455
Control Panel
   copying user profiles to network server 69–70
   deleting self-paced training files xxxv
Conventional memory, definition 456
Conventions used in this book xviii–xix

Copy backup
  definition 453
  description 401
Copying
  files and folders
    auditing events 341
    permissions 245–246
  user profiles to network server 69–70
Course materials
  cleanup procedures xxxiv–xxxv
  conventions xviii–xix
  deleting self-paced training files xxxv
  icons xx
  instructional videos
    description xxxi
    installing Intel video drivers xxxiii
    local and global groups 85
    permissions 218
    starting 10
    Windows NT Directory services 10
  intended audience xvi
  Network Administration Training menu shortcuts xxxi
  notes xx
  overview of this book xxi–xxii
  requirements xxiii–xxiv
  setup procedures xxv–xxxiv
  starting xvi
  Windows NT 4.0 self-administered assessment xxxviii
Creating
  See also Adding
  entries in security log 349
  files and folders
    permissions inherited 230
    permissions required 176
  groups
    combining types 102
    global groups 85, 97–99
    guidelines 90
    local groups 84, 100–102
    planning strategy 90–94
    rules 97
    using User Manager (for Domains) 96
  home folders
    NTFS volumes 224
    overview 51–52
    procedure 53–54
  printing pools 290–291
  reports in Windows NT Diagnostics 386–387
  roaming user profiles 68
  shortcuts for shared network resources 205
  user accounts
    granting dial-in permission 59–61
    home folders 51–54, 187
    procedure 53

Creating *(continued)*
  user accounts *(continued)*
    recommendations 74
    security identifiers (SIDs) 61
    setting account options 58–59
    setting logon hours 55–56
    setting password options 50–51, 141–142
    setting workstation restrictions 57
    tools for creating 37
    User Manager vs. User Manager for Domains 48–50
    using templates 133–138
  Windows NT Server setup disks xxvi
Creator Owner group
  assigning permissions 232
  description 113
  planning NTFS permissions for data folders 223
  recommendations for NTFS permissions 258
CTRL key, selecting items 151
CTRL+ALT+DELETE
  displaying Windows NT Security dialog box 24–28
  logging on to Windows NT 13, 17
  preventing Trojan horse attacks 17
  recommendations 30
  viewing domain trust relationships 195
Current directory, definition 456

D

Daily backup
  definition 453
  description 401
Data
  backing up *See* Backing up data
  encryption, definition 459
  folders
    planning NTFS permissions 223
    recommendations for NTFS permissions 258
    sharing, planning guidelines 185–186
    sharing, procedure 194
    sharing, recommendations 205
  restoring *See* Restoring data
Database, directory *See* Directory database
Date, verifying when restoring data 430
DCOM (Distributed Component Object Model), definition 457
Default
  button, definition 456
  gateway, definition 456
  home folder location 43
  NTFS permissions 230
  owner, definition 456
  printer
    definition 456
    setting 278

Index 491

Default
    profile, definition 456
    separator pages 298
    user, definition 456
Delete events, auditing
    files and folders 341
    printers 343
DELETE key, deleting documents from print queues 313
Delete permission, description 212
Deleting
    documents from printers 313, 324
    files and folders
        auditing events 341
        No Access permission 253–256
        permissions required 176
        troubleshooting permissions 251
    groups 103–104
    print jobs, auditing 343
    printers 280
    self-paced training files xxxv
    user accounts 61–63
    user and group accounts xxxiv
    user profiles 71
Demoting primary domain controllers (PDCs) to backup domain controllers (BDCs) 158–159
Dependent service, definition 456
Desktop
    area, setting xxxiii
    definition 456
    pattern, definition 456
    performance, Windows NT Workstation advantages 4
Destination directory, definition 456
Devices
    definition 456
    print devices *See* Print devices; Printers; Printing
    viewing information using Windows NT Diagnostics 365, 384
DHCP (Dynamic Host Configuration Protocol), definition 458
Diagnostics, Windows NT *See* Windows NT Diagnostics
Dial-up line, definition 457
Dial-up networking
    definition 457
    granting dial-in permission to users 59–61
Dialin Information dialog box 60
Dialog boxes
    Account Policy 141–146
    Add Printer wizard 275–276
    Add Users and Groups 232
    Audit Policy 337
    Backup Information 413–414
    Catalog Status 431
    definition 456
    Dialin Information 60
    Directory Permissions 231

Dialog boxes *(continued)*
    Event Log Settings 354
    File Permissions 231
    Filter 351
    Logon Information options 14
    Map Network Drive 201
    New Global Group 99
    New Local Group 102
    notational conventions used in this book xviii
    Open Resources 376
    Restore Information 433
    Shared Resources 374
    Special Directory Access 236
    System Properties 69
    User Manager menu commands 96
    User Rights Policy 107
    Welcome dialog box, validating local accounts 17
    Windows NT Diagnostics 384
    Windows NT Security 24–28
Differential backup
    advantages and disadvantages 403
    definition 453
    description 401
    restoring data 429
Directories
    See also Folders
    current, definition 456
    definition 457
    directory tree, definition 457
    home directories *See* Home folders
    root, definition 474
    subdirectories, definition 477
Directory database
    definition 457
    description 7
    logon domains 14–15
    maintaining domain controllers
        See also Domain controllers
        overview 153
        using Server Manager 154
    synchronizing domain controllers 160–161
    Windows NT domain model 7
    Windows NT workgroup model 8
Directory Permissions dialog box 231
Directory permissions *See* Folder permissions; NTFS permissions; Share permissions; Shared folders
Directory replication, definition 457
Directory Replicator service 457
Directory services
    definition 483
    description 6
    instructional video 10
    overview 10–11
Directory tree, definition 457

Disabled user account, definition 457
Disconnecting network drives 203
Disconnecting remote users forcibly from server when logon hours expire 143
Disconnecting users 143, 371, 372–373
Disk space
　free space, definition 461
　home folder considerations 43–44
　troubleshooting printing problems 323
　Windows NT printing requirements 272
Disks
　See also Drives
　floppy, definition 461
　installing Windows NT Server xxvi
　system, definition 478
Display
　setting properties xxxiii
　user profiles 65–66
Displaying
　built-in system groups 114
　folder names and file names, permissions required 176
　Windows NT Security dialog box 24
Distributed Component Object Model (DCOM), definition 457
Distributing administrative tasks 132–133
DLLs (dynamic-link libraries)
　definition 458
　print spooler defined 271, 322, 477
DMA addresses, checking 385
Document
　definition 457
　file icon, definition 457
　file, definition 457
　icon, definition 458
Documents, printing
　See also Printing
　deleting from printers 313, 324
　Encapsulated PostScript (EPS) files, definition 459
　overview 322–323
　pausing, resuming, and purging printers 315–316
　print queues 271, 473
　redirecting 317–319
　setting notification, priority, and printing time 310–312
　troubleshooting 323–324
Domain Admins group 110–111, 116–118, 119
Domain controllers
　See also Backup domain controllers; Primary domain controllers
　account validation, checking 385
　Audit policy 335

Domain controllers *(continued)*
　backup
　　See also Backup domain controllers
　　promoting to primary 155–157
　　restoring original domain controller roles 158–159
　built-in groups
　　on all Windows NT computers 109–110
　　on domain controllers only 110–111
　definition 458
　determining data to back up 400
　location of
　　global groups 85
　　local groups 84
　maintaining
　　overview 153
　　using Server Manager 154
　Net Logon service 162
　planning group strategy 90–94
　primary
　　See also Primary domain controllers
　　going offline unexpectedly 156–157
　　restoring original domain controller roles 158–159
　　taking offline 155–156
　requirements for this course xxiii–xxiv
　streamlining account administration 131
　synchronizing 160–161
　troubleshooting logon problems 164–167
　validating
　　domain accounts 15–16
　　local accounts 17
　viewing security log 347
　Windows NT Directory services 10–11
　Windows NT domain model 7
　Windows NT workgroup model 8
Domain database *See* Directory database
Domain, definition 458
Domain Guests group 110–111
Domain model, definition 458
Domain synchronization, definition 478
Domain user accounts
　description 37–38
　specifying home folder location 52
Domain Users group 110–111, 119
Domains
　adding users to Administrators group 115
　assigning share permissions 195
　Audit policy 335
　controllers *See* Backup domain controllers; Domain controllers; Primary domain controllers
　current, checking 385

Index

Domains *(continued)*
  description 7
  global groups 83
  local groups 82
  logging on to Windows NT 13–15
  master domain, definition 467
  planning groups 90–94
  resource domain, definition 474
  restricting logon hours 55–56, 142–143
  Select Domain command 96
  selecting in Server Manager 370
  synchronizing *See* Synchronization
  trust relationships
    See also Trust relationships
    assigning share permissions to users in other domains 195
    definition 480
    one-way, definition 469
    policy 480
    two-way, definition 480
    viewing 195
    Windows NT Directory services video 10
  Users group 183
  validating
    domain accounts 15–16
    local accounts 17
  Windows NT domain model 7
Double-click, definition 458
Down level, definition 458
Drag, definition 458
Drive letters
  connecting to shared folders 200–202, 374
  Map Network Drive dialog box 201
  specifying home folder location 52
Drivers
  See also Printer drivers
  definition 456
  loopback, definition 466
  network card drivers, definition 469
  network device drivers, definition 469
  print devices on hardware compatibility list 274
  protocols 473
  required to view instructional videos, installing xxxiii
  viewing information using Windows NT Diagnostics 365, 384
Drives
  backing up *See* Backing up data
  backup tape devices *See* Tape drives
  icons, definition 458
  logical, definition 466
  partitions
    boot 454
    definition 470
    extended 460

Drives *(continued)*
  partitions *(continued)*
    primary 471
    system 478
    volume sets 482
  restoring *See* Restoring data
  viewing information using Windows NT Diagnostics 365, 384
Dual boot, definition 458
Dynamic Host Configuration Protocol (DHCP) 458
Dynamic-link libraries (DLLs)
  definition 458
  print spooler defined 271, 322, 477

E

EISA (Extended Industry Standard Architecture), definition 460
Electronic mail, Windows NT Workstation advantages 4
Email, Windows NT Workstation advantages 4
Embedded object, definition 459
EMS (Expanded Memory Specification), definition 459
Encapsulated PostScript (EPS) file, definition 459
Encryption, definition 459
End Task option, Windows NT Security dialog box 26–27
Enterprise networks, Windows NT Server advantages 5–6
Enterprise server, definition 459
Environment variables
  definition 459
  setting 384
EPS (Encapsulated PostScript) file, definition 459
Erasing backup tapes 410, 414
Error logging, definition 459
Error messages, troubleshooting logon problems 164
Event Log service 459
Event Log Settings dialog box 354
Event Viewer
  description 21
  event categories 348
  filtering events 350–352
  locating events 352–353
  log file types 346
  verifying domain controller synchronization 161
  viewing security log 346–353
Events
  definition 459
  Event Viewer categories 348
  filtering 350–352
  locating 352–353
  logging *See* Log files
  tracking *See* Audit policy; Auditing

Everyone group
    assigning Log on locally user right xxxii
    auditing 341–342
    description 113
    planning NTFS permissions, program folders 223
    print permissions 284
    share permissions 174, 177, 183, 205
    sharing network program folders 184
Exams, Certified Professional (MCP) program xxxvi–xxxviii
Execute events, auditing 341
Execute permission, description 212
Expand, definition 459
Expanded Memory Specification (EMS), definition 459
Expanded memory, definition 459
Expired logon hours, forcibly disconnecting remote users from server 143
Explorer *See* Internet Explorer; Windows NT Explorer
Extended Industry Standard Architecture (EISA), definition 460
Extended memory, definition 460
Extended partition, definition 460
Extension-type association, definition 460
Extensions
    definition 460, 461
    notational conventions used in this book xviii
External command, definition 460

F

Failed logon attempts, setting account lockout options 142–143
Failure of events, auditing *See* Audit policy; Auditing; Log files; Security log
Family sets, data backup
    definition 460
    description 405
    missing or damaged 431
FAT volumes
    copying files and folders, effect on permissions 246
    creating home folders 187
    definition 460
    restoring backup data, security 396
    shared folders 175
    sharing home folders 187–189
Fault tolerance, definition 460
Features of this book xviii
File allocation table (FAT)
    See also FAT volumes
    definition 460
File and Print Services for NetWare (FPNW) 460
File locks
    viewing computer properties 370
    viewing resources in use 376
File Permissions dialog box 231

File permissions, NTFS
    See also NTFS permissions; Permissions; Share permissions; Shared folders
    assigning 230–235
    backing up data 396
    giving users ability to take ownership 241–244
    overview 214–215
    restoring data 433
File Replication service 461
File systems
    definition 461
    FAT *See* FAT volumes
    HPFS, definition 463
    in use, checking 385
    NTFS *See* NTFS permissions; NTFS volumes
    UNIX, deleting files, troubleshooting permissions 251
Files
    adding, permissions required 176
    ASCII, definition 452
    attributes, definition 452
    auditing access
        See also Audit policy; Auditing
        specifying events to audit 340–341
    backing up *See* Backing up data
    copying, effect on permissions 245–246
    definition 460
    deleting
        No Access permission 253–256
        permissions required 176
        troubleshooting permissions 251
    document file, definition 457
    Encapsulated PostScript (EPS), definition 459
    filenames
        definition 460
        extensions xviii, 460, 461
        short 477
    long filenames
        definition 466
        NTFS permissions 258
        shared folders 181
    Managing File and Folder Access wizard 22
    moving, effect on permissions 245–246
    new, permissions inherited 230
    notational conventions used in this book xviii
    NTFS permissions
        See also File permissions, NTFS; NTFS permissions
        recommendations 258
        standard 214
    open files
        viewing computer properties 370
        viewing resources in use 376
        viewing user sessions 371–372
    permissions description 81

Files *(continued)*
    printing *See* Printing
    program files, definition 473
    restoring *See* Restoring data
    share naming conventions 181
    sharing
        See also Share permissions; Shared folders
        definition 461
    spooling 271, 322, 477
    taking ownership 240–244
    text, definition 479
    universal naming convention (UNC), definition 480
Filter dialog box 352
Filtering events in Event Viewer 350–352
Find command, locating events 352–353
Find tab, definition 461
Firmware revision level, RISC-based computers 385
Floppy disks, definition 461
Folder permissions, NTFS
    See also NTFS permissions; Permissions; Share permissions; Shared folders
    assigning 230–235
    backing up data 396
    giving users ability to take ownership 241–244
    overview 214–215
    restoring data 433
Folders
    administrative shares 192
    auditing access
        See also Audit policy; Auditing
        specifying events to audit 340–341
    backing up *See* Backing up data
    copying, effect on permissions 245–246
    creating, permissions required 176
    current, definition 456
    definition 461
    deleting, permissions required 176
    destination, definition 456
    directory tree, definition 457
    home folders
        assigning to multiple accounts 54
        benefits of shared folders 175
        centralizing 51–52, 224
        creating 51–54, 187
        default location 43
        definition 463
        description 42–43
        moving, modifying multiple user accounts 150–152
        NTFS volumes 224
        planning shared folders 187–189
        recommendations 74
        recommendations for NTFS permissions 258
        sharing 51
        specifying using %Username% 52, 224, 258

Folders *(continued)*
    home folders *(continued)*
        storing on a server 43
        storing on a user's computer 44
    long filenames
        See also Long filenames
        definition 466
    Managing File and Folder Access wizard 22
    moving, effect on permissions 245–246
    new, permissions inherited 230
    notational conventions used in this book xviii
    permissions
        See also Folder permissions, NTFS; NTFS permissions
        description 81
        recommendations for NTFS permissions 258
        standard NTFS permissions 213
    restoring *See* Restoring data
    root directory, definition 474
    share naming conventions 181
    sharing *See* Shared folders
    source, definition 477
    subdirectories, definition 477
    systemroot 192
    taking ownership 240–244
    universal naming convention (UNC), definition 480
    Windows NT installation, checking 385
Fonts
    definition 461
    printer fonts 472
    TrueType, definition 479
Forcibly disconnect remote users from server when logon hours expire 143
Formatting backup tapes 410
Forms
    assigning to printer paper trays 296–297
    definition 296
FPNW (File and Print Services for NetWare) 460
Free space, definition 461
Freeing idle connections 371, 372–373
FTP (file transfer protocol) service, Internet Information Server (IIS) description 6
Full backup, description 401
Full Control events, auditing 343
Full Control permission
    NTFS
        assigning to Creator Owner group 232
        giving users ability to take ownership 241
        planning data folders 223
        planning program folders 223
        recommendations 258
        requirements for assigning NTFS permissions 230
        standard file permission 214
        standard folder permission 213

Full Control permission *(continued)*
  print permission 274, 284, 308
  share permissions
    description 176
    Everyone group, shared folders 174
    illustration 177
    sharing network program folders 184
Full name, definition 461
Full-screen application, definition 461
Full synchronization, definition 461

G

Garbled printing, troubleshooting 324
Gateway
  default 456
  definition 462
Global accounts, definition 462
Global groups
  See also specific group names
  adding members 99
  assigning print permissions 285
  built-in 106, 111
  creating
    procedure 97–99
    rules 97
    using User Manager (for Domains) 96
  definition 462
  deleting 103–104
  description 83
  location 85
  recommendations 119
Glossary definitions 451–483
Gopher service, Internet Information Server (IIS) description 6
Granting dial-in permission to users 59–61
Group accounts *See* Groups, group accounts;
  User Accounts, group accounts
Group category, definition 462
Group Management wizard 22
Group memberships
  See also Groups, user accounts
  built-in groups
    on all Windows NT computers 109–110
    on domain controllers only 110–111
  definition 462
  deleting and renaming user accounts 62
  examples
    multiple-domain networks 88
    single-domain networks 87
  Full Control print permission 274
  global groups
    adding members 99
    description 83
    location 85

Group memberships *(continued)*
  local groups
    description 82
    location 84
  overview 81
  recommendations 119
Group name, definition 462
Groups
  See also specific group names
  auditing
    defining Audit policy 337
    planning Audit policy 334–335
    viewing security log events 348
  built-in
    See also specific group names
    definition 454
    determining rights 107–108
    distributing administrative tasks 132–133
    facilitating local administration 115
    on all Windows NT computers 109–110
    on domain controllers only 110–111
    promoting centralized administration 116–118
    recommendations 119
    rules for creating groups 97
    system groups 113–114
    types 106
  common group, definition 455
  creating
    combining types 102
    global groups 97–99
    guidelines 90
    local groups 100–102
    planning strategy 90–94
    rules 97
    using User Manager (for Domains) 96
  deleting 103–104
  description 79
  distributing administrative tasks 132–133
  examples
    multiple-domain networks 88
    single-domain networks 87
  Full Control print permission 274
  global
    See also specific group names
    adding members 99
    assigning print permissions 285
    built-in 106, 111
    creating 97–99
    definition 462
    description 83
    location 85
    recommendations 119

Index 497

Groups *(continued)*
  group accounts
    See also User accounts, group accounts
    definition 462
    deleting xxxiv
    description 81
    planning strategy 90–94
    planning worksheets 447
    share permissions 174
  Group Management wizard 22
  local
    See also specific group names
    built-in 106, 111
    creating 100–102
    definition 465
    description 82
    location 84
    planning share permissions 183
    recommendations 119
  Network 114
  primary, definition 471
  program groups 473
  recommendations for NTFS permissions 258
  recommendations 119
  system groups 106, 113–114
  troubleshooting permissions 252
Guests
  definition 462
  Domain Guests group 110–111
  Guest account 463
    description 36
    recommendations 74
  Guest privilege, definition 463
  Guests group 109
  security recommendations 119

H

HAL type, checking 385
Hardware
  IRQs, checking 385
  print devices 270
  profiles, Windows NT Workstation advantages 4
  viewing information using Windows NT Diagnostics 365, 384
Hardware Compatibility List (HCL)
  checking backup tape drives 396
  checking print devices 274
  definition 463
  system requirements for installing Windows NT Server xxiii
HCL *See* Hardware Compatibility List
Heterogeneous environment, definition 463
Hewlett Packard LaserJet 4Si printer, installing 276–277

Hiding share names from users 192, 194
High memory area (HMA), definition 463
High-Performance File System (HPFS), definition 463
HMA (High memory area), definition 463
Home directories *See* Home folders
Home folders
  assigning to multiple accounts 54
  benefits of shared folders 175
  centralizing 51–52, 224
  creating
    NTFS volumes 224
    overview 51–52
    planning folder sharing 187
    procedure 53–54
  default location 43
  definition 463
  description 42–43
  moving, modifying multiple user accounts 150–152
  planning
    NTFS permissions 224
    shared folders 187–189
  recommendations
    creating user accounts 74
    NTFS permissions 258
  sharing 51
  specifying using %Username% 52, 224, 258
  storing on a server 43
  storing on a user's computer 44
Home page, definition 463
Hours
  See also Scheduling; Time
  available for printing, testing 295
  forcibly disconnect remote users from server when logon hours expire 143
  logon hours defined 466
HP LaserJet 4Si printer, installing 276–277
HPFS (High-Performance File System), definition 463
HTML (Hypertext Markup Language), definition 463
HTTP *See* Hypertext Transport Protocol
Hyperlink, definition 463
Hypertext Markup Language (HTML), definition 463
Hypertext Transport Protocol (HTTP)
  definition 463
  service, Internet Information Server (IIS) description 6

I

I/O ports, checking 385
Icons
  definition 463
  documents, definition 458
  drives, definition 458
  programs 473
  shared folders 174

498   Microsoft Windows NT Network Administration

Icons *(continued)*
   success and failure events in security log 347
   used in this book xx
Idle connections, freeing 371, 372–373
IIS (Internet Information Server) 6, 464
Incremental backup
   advantages and disadvantages 403
   definition 453
   description 401
   restoring 429
Inherited permissions 230, 245–246
Insertion point, definition 464
Install New Modem wizard 22
Installing
   Canon Bubble-Jet BJC-600e printer 278
   HP LaserJet 4Si printer 276–277
   Intel video drivers xxxiii
   Internet Explorer 3.*x* xxxiii
   self-paced training files xxix
   Server Manager 365
   this course, setup procedures xxv–xxxiv
   Windows NT client–based tools 22
   Windows NT Server
      setup procedures xxv–xxix
      system requirements xxiii
Instructional videos
   description xxxi
   installing Intel video drivers xxxiii
   local and global groups 85
   permissions 218
   starting 10
   Windows NT Directory services 10
Integrated Services Digital Network (ISDN), definition 464
Intel video drivers, installing xxxiii
Interactive group 114
Internal command, definition 464
Internet Explorer
   3.*x*, installing xxxiii
   Windows NT Workstation advantages 4
Internet Information Server (IIS) 6, 464
Internet service provider (ISP), definition 464
Internet, definition 464
Internetworks, definition 464
Interprocess communication (IPC), definition 464
Interrupts, checking 385
Intranet, definition 464
IP address, definition 464
IP router, definition 464
IPC (interprocess communication), definition 464
IPC$ share 375
IPX/SPX (Internet Packet Exchange/Sequenced Packet Exchange), definition 465

IRQs, checking 385
ISDN (Integrated Services Digital Network), definition 464
ISP (Internet service provider), definition 464

J

Jump, definition 465

K

Keyboard
   conventions used in this book xix
   keys
      CAPS LOCK key, troubleshooting logon problems 164
      CTRL key, selecting items 151
      CTRL+ALT+DELETE *See* CTRL+ALT+DELETE
      DELETE key, deleting documents from print queues 313
      SHIFT key, selecting items 151
      shortcut keys, definition 476
      secure attention sequence *See* CTRL+ALT+DELETE

L

LAN (local area network), definition 465
LAN Manager 2.*x*
   logon scripts 66
   print clients
      connecting to printers 283
      enabling 277
      possible 272
      printing overview 323
      setting up 280
Lessons *See* Self-paced training
License Compliance wizard 22
Life cycle of backup tapes 404
Linked object, definition 465
List box, definition 465
List permission
   NTFS standard folder permission 213
   requirements for sharing folders 192
Local area network (LAN), definition 465
Local computers
   planning data backup strategy 399–400
   viewing security log 349
Local groups
   See also specific group names
   built-in 106, 111
   creating
      procedure 100–102
      rules 97
      using User Manager (for Domains) 96

Local groups *(continued)*
  definition 465
  deleting 103–104
  description 82
  location 84
  planning share permissions 183
  recommendations 119
Local guest logon, definition 465
Local Path, specifying home folder location 52
Local printer, definition 465
Local user accounts 38, 465
Local user profiles 465
Lock Workstation option, Windows NT Security dialog
  box 25
Locking
  files
    viewing computer properties 370
    viewing resources in use 376
  user accounts
    account lockout, definition 451
    planning account policy 140
    setting account lockout options 142–143
  workstations, security recommendations 30
Lockout After 143
Lockout Duration 143
Log books
  definition 465
  maintaining for computers 383
Log files
  application log 346, 452
  backup logs
    data restoration strategies 427
    description 405
    log books defined 465
    printing 414
    setting options 412–414, 433
    viewing 416
  clearing 355
  controlling size and content 354
  definition 466
  Event Log Settings dialog box 354
  security log
    archiving 353–355
    creating entries 348
    definition 475
    filtering events 350–352
    locating events 352–353
    viewing using Event Viewer 346–353
  system log 346, 478
Log on locally user right, assigning to Everyone group xxxii
Logging off
  See also Shutting down
  definition 466
  recommendations 30

Logging off *(continued)*
  Windows NT Security dialog box option 25, 27
Logging on
  access tokens, troubleshooting permissions 252
  auditing
    defining Audit policy 337
    planning Audit policy 334–335
    viewing security log events 348
  definition 466
  directory database
    description 7
    logon domains 14–15
    maintaining domain controllers 153–162
    synchronizing domain controllers 160–161
  failed attempts, setting account lockout options 142–143
  Logon Information dialog box options 14
  logon scripts 66
  logon workstations, definition 466
  overview 13–15
  recommendations 30
  reestablishing network connections 200–202
  remote logon, definition 474
  restricting logon hours 42, 55–56, 142–143, 164
  setting password options 142
  setting workstation restrictions 57
  single user logon, definition 477
  specifying home folder location 52
  troubleshooting problems 164–167
  validating
    domain accounts 15–16
    local accounts 17
Logical drive, definition 466
Logon hours
  See also Restricting logon hours; Time
  definition 466
  disconnecting remote users forcibly from server when
    logon hours expire 143
Logon Information dialog box options 14
Logon scripts
  definition 466
  description 66
  path 466
Logon workstations, definition 466
Long filenames
  definition 466
  NTFS permissions 258
  shared folders 181
  short filenames 477
Loopback driver, definition 466

M

Macintosh
  extension-type association, definition 460

Macintosh *(continued)*
    group category, definition 462
    internets, definition 464
    Macintosh-accessible volume, definition 466
    Owner category, definition 469
    permissions, definition 466
    print clients
        connecting to printers 283
        enabling 277
        possible 272
        printing overview 323
        setting up 281
Maintaining domain controllers
    overview 153
    using Server Manager 154
Make Changes permission 466
Manage auditing and security log user right 332
Manage Documents permission
    built-in capabilities for printer administration 308
    print permission 284
Managing File and Folder Access wizard 22
Mandatory user profiles 67, 71, 467
Map Network Drive command 200–202, 374
Mapping names, definition 468
Master domain, definition 467
Maximize button, definition 467
Maximize, definition 467
Maximum Password Age 141, 467
MCP (Microsoft Certified Professional)
    program xxxvi–xxxviii
MCSE Windows NT 4.0 Track xxxvii
Member servers
    Audit policy 335
    definition 467
    description 7
    global groups 83
    local groups 82
    planning groups 90–94
    planning share permissions 183
    Windows NT Directory services 10–11
Memory
    cache, definition 454
    conventional, definition 456
    definition 467
    DMA addresses, checking 385
    EMS, definition 459
    expanded, definition 459
    extended, definition 460
    HMA, definition 463
    nonpaged, definition 469
    paging files, definition 470
    RAM
        checking 385
        definition 473

Memory *(continued)*
    RAM *(continued)*
        system requirements for installing Windows NT
            Server xxiii
        Windows NT printing requirements 272
    troubleshooting printing 324
    viewing information using Windows NT Diagnostics 365,
        384
    virtual
        definition 481
        paging files, definition 470
Menu bar, definition 467
Menu, definition 467
Messages
    email, Windows NT Workstation advantages 4
    sending to users 380–381, 411
    troubleshooting logon problems 164
Messenger service
    definition 467
    sending messages to users 380
Microsoft Certified Professional (MCP)
    program xxxvi–xxxviii
Microsoft Internet Explorer
    3.*x*, installing xxxiii
    Windows NT Workstation advantages 4
Minimize button, definition 467
Minimize, definition 467
Minimum Password Age 141, 467
Minimum Password Length 141, 467
Missing or damaged tapes, restoring data 431
Modems
    definition 467
    Install New Modem wizard 22
Modifying
    multiple user accounts at one time 150–152
    NTFS permissions 230
    share permissions 198
    shared folder options 198
Monitor, setting desktop area xxxiii
Monitoring networks, Windows NT administrative tasks 19
Monitoring resources
    disconnecting users 371, 372–373
    resources in use 375–377
    sending messages to users 380–381
    Server Manager
        disconnecting users 371, 372–373
        domain information 370
        overview 365
        requirements 366
        resources in use 375–377
        sending messages to users 380–381
        setting administrative alerts 379–380
        shared resources 373–375
        viewing computer properties 369–370

Index

Monitoring resources *(continued)*
    Server Manager *(continued*
        viewing user sessions 371–372
        setting administrative alerts 379–380
        shared resources 373–375
        viewing computer properties 369–370
        viewing user sessions 371–372
    Windows NT Diagnostics
        description 365
        gathering information 385–386
        options 384
        overview 383–384
        reports 386–387
        requirements 366
Mouse
    click, definition 454
    double-click, definition 458
    right-click *See* Right-click
    user profiles 65–66
Moving
    files and folders, permissions 245–246
    home folders, modifying multiple user accounts 150–152
MS-DOS
    logon scripts 66
    MS-DOS-based applications 467
    print clients 280
    shared folder names 181
    short filenames 477
    troubleshooting printing 324
Multiple boot, definition 468
My Computer
    connecting to shared resources 374
    icon representing shared folders 174
    Map Network Drive command 200

N

Named pipes
    definition 468
    IPC$ share 375
    viewing computer properties 370
Names
    computer names, definition 455
    full name, definition 461
    group names, definition 462
    mapping, definition 468
    notational conventions used in this book xviii
    share names
        definition 476
        naming conventions 181
    short filenames 477
    troubleshooting logon problems 164
    UNC, printers 292

Names *(continued)*
    universal naming convention (UNC), definition 480
    user *See* User names
Naming new user accounts 41
NDS (NetWare Directory services) 468
Net Logon events, verifying domain controller synchronization 161
Net Logon service 162, 468
net start command 162
NetBEUI, definition 468
NetBIOS, definition 468
NetWare
    print clients
        connecting to printers 283
        enabling 277
        possible 272
        printing overview 323
        setting up 281
NetWare Directory services (NDS) 468
Network adapters
    definition 468
    network card drivers, definition 469
    network device drivers, definition 469
Network Administration Training menu shortcuts xxxi
Network administrator
    See also Administrators
    definition 468
Network basic input/output system (NetBIOS), definition 468
Network Client Administrator wizard 22
Network directories *See* Shared folders
Network group 114
Network interface card (NIC) *See* Network adapters
Network-interface print devices
    definition 270
    setting up 274–280
Network Monitor, description 5
Network Neighborhood
    connecting to shared resources 374
    Map Network Drive command 200
Network print clients
    See also Print clients; Printing
    setting up 280–281
Network printers *See* Printers; Printing
Network protocols
    See also Protocols; Transport protocols
    definition 469, 473
    drivers, definition 473
    installed, checking 386
    TCP 479
    TCP/IP 479
Network servers, copying user profiles 69–70
Networks
    centralized network administration, definition 454
    connecting to shared folders 200–203, 374

Networks *(continued)*
    default home folder location 43
    examples of groups 87–88
    internets, definition 464
    internetworks, definition 464
    intranets, definition 464
    LANs, definition 465
    loopback drivers, definition 466
    Map Network Drive command 200–202, 374
    monitoring *See* Monitoring resources; Server Manager; Windows NT Diagnostics
    Network Monitor 5
    planning data backup strategy 399–400
    securing resources
        NTFS permissions *See* NTFS permissions
        shared folders *See* Share permissions; Shared folders
    shared folders
        See also Shared folders
        benefits 175
        description 174
    sharing network program folders 184, 205
    subnets, definition 477
    tracking events *See* Audit policy; Auditing
    troubleshooting logon problems 164–167
    viewing information using Windows NT Diagnostics 365, 384
    WANs, definition 482
    Windows NT administrative tasks 19
    Windows NT Server advantages 5–6
New files and folders, permissions inherited 230, 245–246
New Global Group command 96, 99
New Local Group command 102
New user accounts
    creating
        granting dial-in permission 59–61
        home folders 51–54, 187
        procedure 53
        security identifiers (SIDs) 61
        setting account options 58–59
        setting logon hours 55–56
        setting password options 50–51, 141–142
        setting workstation restrictions 57
        User Manager vs. User Manager for Domains 48–50
        using templates 133–138
    planning
        home folders 42–44
        logon hours 42
        naming 41
        overview 40
        password requirements 41–42
        workstation restrictions 42
New user profiles 68

NIC (network interface cards) *See* Network adapters
    description 176
    illustration 178
    NTFS standard file permission 214
    NTFS standard folder permission 213
No Access permission
    print permission 284
    priority 177
    troubleshooting
        access denied 251
        user with No Access deleting files 251
No Call Back, Dialin Information option 60
Non–Windows NT application, definition 469
Nonpaged memory, definition 469
Normal backup
    advantages and disadvantages 402
    definition 453
    description 401
    restoring 429
Notational conventions used in this book xviii
Notifications, setting for printers 310–312
ntbackup command
    See also Backing up data; Restoring data; Windows NT Backup
    command line options 419
    example 420–421
    missing or damaged tapes, restoring data 431
    scheduling automatic backups 418
NTFS, definition 483
NTFS permissions
    See also specific permission names; File permissions, NTFS; Folder permissions, NTFS
    assigning 230–237
    backing up data 396
    benefits 212
    combining with share permissions 217–218, 220–221
    copying files and folders 245–246
    data folders 223, 258
    default 230
    description 211
    file permissions 214–215, 230–235
    folder permissions 214–215, 230–235
    home folders 224
    individual 212–213
    instructional video 218
    modifying 230
    moving files and folders 245–246
    overview 214–215
    planning
        guidelines 223–224
        worksheets 449
    program folders 223

Index

NTFS permissions *(continued)*
    recommendations 258
    restoring data 433
    special access 230, 236–237, 255, 477
    specifying home folders using %Username% 224, 258
    standard 213–214
    taking ownership of files and folders 240–244
    troubleshooting
        access denied 251
        access tokens 252
        deleting files with No Access permission 253–256
        group memberships 252
        user with No Access deleting files 251
    vs. shared folders on FAT volumes 175
    worksheets, planning 449
NTFS volumes
    auditing resources
        See also Audit policy; Auditing
        limitations 342
    backing up data 396
    copying files and folders, effect on permissions 245–246
    creating home folders 224
    new files and folders, permissions inherited 230
    permissions *See* NTFS permissions
    restoring data 433
Ntuser.dat, personal user profile 67, 71
Ntuser.man, mandatory user profile 67, 71
NWLink IPX\SPX Compatible Transport 469

O

Objects
    embedded, definition 459
    linked, definition 465
Offline, taking primary domain controllers (PDCs) offline 155–156
One-way trust relationship, definition 469
Open files
    viewing computer properties 370
    viewing resources in use 376
    viewing user sessions 371–372
Open Named Pipes
    IPC$ share 375
    viewing computer properties 370
Open Resources dialog box 376
Open, definition 469
Opening
    files, default home folder 43
    Windows NT administrative tools 22
    Windows NT Security dialog box 24
Operating systems
    down level, definition 458
    dual boot computers, definition 458

Operating systems *(continued)*
    interprocess communication (IPC), definition 464
    multiple boot, definition 468
    POSIX programs, definition 471
    preventing Trojan horse attacks 17
    print clients possible 272, 277
    shared folder names 181
    short filenames 477
    viewing information using Windows NT Diagnostics 365, 384
    Windows NT *See* Windows NT Server; Windows NT Workstation
Optimizing performance, Windows NT Server tools 5
OS/2
    print clients
        connecting to printers 283
        enabling 277
        possible 272
        printing overview 323
        setting up 280
    short filenames 477
Out-of-memory errors, troubleshooting printing 324
Overwriting events, Event Log Settings dialog box 354
Owner category, definition 469
Ownership
    default owner, definition 456
    owner, definition 469
    recommendations for NTFS permissions 258
    requirements for assigning NTFS permissions 230
    special access permissions 236
    taking
        auditing events 341, 343
        of files and folders 240–244
        of printers 308, 319–320
        permissions required 176, 213

P

Paging files, definition 470
Paper trays, assigning forms 296–297
Partial synchronization, definition 470
Partition Table, definition 470
Partitions
    boot 454
    definition 470
    extended 460
    primary 471
    system 478
    volume sets 482
Pass-through authentication, definition 470
Password Uniqueness 142, 470

Passwords
    administering user accounts
        resetting 148
        setting account policy 139–149
    Change Password option, Windows NT Security
        dialog box 25, 26
    creating user accounts 50
    definition 470
    directory database description 7
    guidelines 41–42, 140
    Logon Information dialog box 14
    maximum age 141, 467
    minimum age 141, 467
    minimum length 141, 467
    preventing Trojan horse attacks 17
    recommendations 30, 74
    setting options 50–51, 141–142
    synchronizing domain controllers 160–161
    troubleshooting logon problems 164
    user account requirements 41–42
    user passwords, definition 481
    validating
        domain accounts 15–16
        local accounts 17
    volumes 482
Path, specifying
    definition 470
    home folders 52
    logon scripts
        See also Logon scripts
        definition 466
    shared folders, Map Network Drive dialog box 201
    user profiles 71–72
Pausing printers 278, 315–316
PCL printers
    Pcl.sep, separator page 298
    printer drivers 275
Peer Web services, Windows NT Workstation advantages 4
Peer, definition 471
Performance
    home folder considerations 44
    Windows NT Server advantages 5
    Windows NT Workstation advantages 4
Permissions
    See also specific permission names
    access permissions, definition 451
    auditing changes 341
    definition 471
    deleting and renaming user accounts 62
    description 81
    dial-in, granting to users 59–61
    global groups 83
    group accounts 81
    inherited by new files and folders 230, 245–246

Permissions *(continued)*
    local groups 82
    Macintosh-style, definition 466
    modifying 230
    NTFS permissions
        See also specific permission names; File permissions,
            NTFS; Folder permissions, NTFS
        assigning 230–237
        backing up data 396
        benefits 212
        combining with share
            permissions 217–218, 220–221
        copying files and folders 245–246
        data folders 223, 258
        default 230
        description 211
        file permissions 214–215, 230–235
        folder permissions 214–215, 230–235
        home folders 224
        individual 212–213
        modifying 230
        moving files and folders 245–246
        overview 214–215
        planning exercise 225–227
        planning guidelines 223–224
        program folders 223
        recommendations 258
        restoring data 433
        special access 230, 236–237, 255, 477
        specifying home folders using
            %Username% 224, 258
        standard 213–214
        taking ownership of files and folders 240–244
        troubleshooting 251–253
        vs. shared folders on FAT volumes 175
    print permissions
        assigning 285–287
        auditing changes 343
        definition 472
        description 284
        levels 284
        testing 287
    recommendations for using groups 119
    share permissions
        See also specific permission names
        assigning 195
        combining with NTFS
            permissions 217–218, 220–221
        definition 476
        description 174
        Everyone group 174, 177, 183, 184, 205
        limitations 176, 217
        modifying 198
        multiple, illustration 177

Permissions *(continued)*
   share permissions *(continued)*
      overview 175–179
      planning guidelines 183–186
      priority of user permissions and group
         permissions 177
      recommendations 205
      users in other domains 195
   special access
      assigning 236–237, 255
      definition 477
      requirements for assigning NTFS permissions 230
   troubleshooting
      access denied 251
      access tokens 252
      deleting files with No Access permission 253–256
      group memberships 252
      user with No Access deleting files 251
Personal group, definition 471
Personal user profiles 67, 71
Pipes
   definition 471
   named *See* Named pipes
Planning
   Audit policy 334–335, 338–339
   backup strategy
      backup types 401–403, 453
      determining data to back up 400–401
      exercise 405–407
      guidelines 399–400
      rotating and archiving tapes 403–404
   data restoration strategy 427
   groups
      guidelines 90
      strategy 90–94
   NTFS permissions
      guidelines 223–224
      home folders 224
   shared folders
      considerations 181
      data folders 185–186
      examples 182–183
      home folders 187–189
      network programs 184
      permissions guidelines 183–186
   user accounts
      account policy 140
      home folders 42–44
      logon hours 42
      naming 41
      overview 40
      password requirements 41–42
      streamlining account administration 131
      workstation restrictions 42

Planning *(continued)*
   worksheets
      backup planning 450
      group accounts 447
      NTFS permissions 449
      shared folders 448
      user accounts 446
      weekly backup schedule 450
Pointer, definition 471
Policies
   account *See* Account policy
   audit *See* Audit policy
   security
      auditing changes 337
      definition 475
   system, definition 478
   trust relationships
      auditing 337, 348
      definition 480
   user rights
      auditing changes 334–335
      definition 481
Pools of printers
   creating 290–291
   definition 472
Ports
   creating printing pools 290–291
   definition 471
   I/O, checking 385
   redirecting print documents 317–319
   setting printer priority 292–294, 310–312
POSIX programs
   definition 471
   deleting files, troubleshooting permissions 251
PostScript printers
   definition 471
   print processor 472
   printer drivers 275
   Pscript.sep, separator page 298
Power Users group
   built-in capabilities for printer administration 308
   Full Control print permission 274
   requirements for monitoring resources 366
   sharing folders 192
   Windows NT Workstation built-in groups 109–110
Preset to, Dialin Information option 60
Primary domain controllers (PDCs)
   See also Backup domain controllers; Domain controllers
   adding
      Domain Admins group to local Administrators
         group 116–118
      users to Administrators group 115
   Audit policy 335
   definition 471

Primary domain controllers (PDCs) *(continued)*
    determining data to back up 400
    going offline unexpectedly 156–157
    location of global groups 85
    location of local groups 84
    maintaining, overview 153
    maintaining using Server Manager 154
    planning group strategy 90–94
    restoring original domain controller roles 158–159
    synchronizing domains 160–161, 470
    taking offline 155–156
    troubleshooting logon problems 164
    viewing security log 347
    Windows NT Directory services 10–11
Primary group, definition 471
Primary partition, definition 471
Print clients
    adding printers 277
    connecting to printers
        other print clients 283
        Windows NT and Windows 95 clients 281–282
    possible operating systems 272
    printing overview 322–323
    setting up 280–281
Print devices
    checking on hardware compatibility list 274
    creating printing pools 290–291
    definition 270, 471
    printer drivers
        definition 275, 472
        hardware compatibility list 274
        Windows NT and Windows 95 clients 282
    printer pools 290–291, 472
    redirecting documents 317–319
    separator pages 297–298
    troubleshooting printing problems 323–324
    viewing information using Windows NT Diagnostics 365, 384
Print events, auditing 343
Print jobs, definition 472
Print Manager, Windows 3.*x* 282
Print Operators group
    assigning print permissions 285
    built-in capabilities for printer administration 308
    built-in groups on domain controllers 110–111
    Full Control print permission 274
Print permission
    default print permission 281
    print permission 284
Print processor, definition 472
Print queues
    creating printing pools 290–291
    definition 271, 473

Print queues *(continued)*
    deleting documents 313, 324
    purging 315–316
Print Server for Macintosh 472
Print servers
    administering
        definition 307
        managing documents 310–313
        managing printers 315–320
        requirements 308
        tasks 307
        troubleshooting printing problems 322–324
    definition 271, 472
    printing requirements 272
    redirecting documents 317–319
    setting printer priority 292–294, 310–312
    setting up 274–280
    troubleshooting printing problems 323–324
Print sharing, definition 472
Print spooler
    definition 271, 472, 477
    printing overview 322–323
Printer drivers
    definition 275, 472
    hardware compatibility list 274
    replacing with updated version 277
    troubleshooting printing problems 323–324
    viewing information using Windows NT Diagnostics 365, 384
    Windows NT and Windows 95 clients 282
Printer fonts, definition 472
Printer window, definition 472
Printers
    See also Printing
    Add Printer wizard 22
    adding 275–278
    administering *See* Print servers, administering
    assigning forms to paper trays 296–297
    auditing use 343–344
    creating printing pools 290–291
    default
        definition 456
        setting 278
    definition 270, 472
    deleting 280
    local, definition 465
    managing 315–320
    pausing 278, 315–316
    permissions description 81
    pools
        creating 290–291
        definition 472

Printers (continued)
   PostScript
      definition 471
      print processor 472
      printer drivers 275
   printer drivers
      definition 275, 472
      hardware compatibility list 274
      Windows NT and Windows 95 clients 282
   printing overview 322–323
   purging 315–316
   redirecting documents 317–319
   resuming printing 315–316
   scheduling 293–294, 310–312
   setting as default 278
   setting priority 292–294, 310–312
   sharing
      Add Printer wizard 275–276
      adding printers 276–278
      administration requirements 308
      definition 472
      description 275
      existing printers 279–280
   taking ownership 319–320
   troubleshooting problems 323–324
   UNC names 292
   user profiles 65–66
   viewing information using Windows NT Diagnostics 365, 384
   virtual memory, definition 482
   Windows NT administrative tasks 19
   Windows NT printing terminology 270–271
Printing
   See also Printers
   backup logs 414
   forms
      assigning to printer paper trays 296–297
      definition 296
   garbled, troubleshooting 324
   overview 322–323
   pausing printers 278
   permissions
      assigning 285–287
      definition 472
      description 284
      levels 284
      testing 287
   print jobs, definition 472
   redirecting documents 317–319
   requirements 272
   resuming 315–316

Printing (continued)
   separator pages 297–298
   setting
      default printer 278
      printer priority 292–294, 310–312
   setting up network print servers and clients 274–289
   test documents 279
   testing available printing hours 295
   troubleshooting problems 323–324
   Windows NT Diagnostics reports 386–387
   Windows NT terminology 270–271
Priority
   between printers, setting 292–294, 310–312
   of user permissions and group permissions 177
Private volume, definition 472
Privilege level, definition 472
Process, definition 473
Processor
   print, definition 472
   system requirements for installing Windows NT Server xxiii
   type, checking 385
Profiles
   default, definition 456
   hardware profiles 4
   user *See* User profiles
Programs
   Add/Remove Programs wizard 22
   associating, definition 452, 460
   auditing use
      See also Audit policy; Auditing
      defining Audit policy 337
      planning Audit policy 334–335
      viewing security log events 348
   batch programs, definition 453
   client applications, definition 455
   closing from Task Manager 26–27
   full-screen, definition 461
   icons 473
   MS-DOS-based, troubleshooting printing 324
   network folders
      planning NTFS permissions 223
      sharing 184, 205
   non–Windows NT, definition 469
   POSIX, deleting files, troubleshooting permissions 251
   program files, definition 473
   program groups 473
   program items 473
   server applications, definition 476
   terminate-and-stay-resident (TSR), definition 479
   Windows NT–based, definition 482

Promoting backup domain controllers (BDCs) to primary
    domain controllers (PDCs)
    PDCs going offline unexpectedly 156–157
    restoring original domain controller roles 158–159
    taking PDCs offline 155–156
Properties
    computers, monitoring resources 369–370
    display, setting xxxiii
    modifying NTFS permissions 230
    printers
        assigning forms to paper trays 296–297
        enabling printer pooling 291
        printing times 310–312
        priority 310–312
        scheduling 293–294, 310–312
        separator pages 297–298
        setting notifications 310–312
    setting, for shared folders 193–194
Protecting against
    Trojan horse attacks
        definition 479
        prevention 17
    viruses
        backing up data 395
        definition 482
        recommendations for NTFS permissions 258
        special access permissions 236
Protocols
    definition 473
    DHCP (Dynamic Host Configuration Protocol) 458
    drivers, definition 473
    FTP (File Transfer Protocol) 6
    HTTP (Hypertext Transfer Protocol) 6, 463
    installed, checking 386
    IPX/SPX, definition 465
    NWLink IPX\SPX Compatible Transport, definition 469
    TCP 479
    TCP/IP 479
Pscript.sep, separator page 298
Public data folders
    planning NTFS permissions 223
    recommendations for NTFS permissions 258
    sharing
        planning guidelines 185–186
        procedure 194
        recommendations 205
Purging printers 315–316

Q

Queues, print
    creating printing pools 290–291
    definition 271, 473

Queues, print *(continued)*
    deleting documents 313, 324
    purging 315–316
Quick Erase, backup tapes 410
Quitting Windows NT *See* Shutting down

R

RAM
    checking 385
    definition 473
    system requirements for installing Windows NT
        Server xxiii
    Windows NT printing requirements 272
RAS *See* Remote Access Service
Read events, auditing 341
Read permission
    NTFS
        description 212
        planning program folders 223
        recommendations 258
        special access 236
        standard file permission 214
        standard folder permission 213
    share permission
        description 176
        sharing network program folders 184
Redirecting print documents 317–319
Reestablishing network connections when
    logging on 200–201
Refresh, definition 473
Regional settings, user profiles 65–66
Registry
    definition 473
    planning backup strategy 400
Remote Access Service (RAS)
    definition 473
    granting dial-in permission to users 59–61
    home folder considerations 43
    Windows NT Server advantages 5
Remote administration, definition 474
Remote computers
    viewing computer properties 370
    viewing security log 349
Remote connections, $, administrative shares 192, 375
Remote logon, definition 474
Remote procedure call (RPC), definition 474
Removing *See* Deleting
Renaming user accounts 61–63
Replace Auditing on Existing Files check box 340
Replace Auditing on Subdirectories check box 340
Replace Permissions on Existing Files check box 231
Replace Permissions on Subdirectories check box 231

Reports, Windows NT Diagnostics 386–387
Reset Count After 143
Resetting user account passwords 148
Resource domain, definition 474
Resources
    auditing *See* Audit policy; Auditing
    definition 474
    monitoring *See* Monitoring resources
    permissions *See* Permissions
    shared *See* Shared resources
Restore Information dialog box 433
Restoring data
    backup logs
        data restoration strategies 427
        description 405
        setting options 433
    Backup Operators group 109–110
    Backup program *See* Windows NT Backup
    catalogs
        definition 454
        description 405
        loading 430–431, 435
    checklist 438
    corrupted files 432
    examples of strategies 429–430
    guidelines 427
    home folder considerations 43
    limitations 401
    loading tape and backup set catalogs 430–431, 435
    missing or damaged tapes 431
    planning strategy 427
    recommendations 438
    requirements 396, 428
    selecting backup sets, folders, and files 432, 435
    simulation exercise 434–436
    verifying computer date 430
    Windows NT administrative tasks 19
Restoring original domain controller roles after promoting BDCs 158–159
Restricting
    access
        See also Security
        share permissions *See* Share permissions
    logon hours 42, 55–56, 142–143, 164
    users using user profiles 65–66
Resuming printing 315–316
Right-click
    Map Network Drive command 374
    modifying NTFS permissions 230
    sharing folders 194
Rights, user
    adding users to Server Operators group 366
    auditing requirements 332
    built-in groups 106–118

Rights, user *(continued)*
    data backup requirements 396
    data restoration requirements 428
    definition 481
    deleting and renaming user accounts 62
    description 81
    global groups 83
    group accounts 81
    local groups 82
    Log on locally user right, assigning to Everyone group xxxii
    user rights policy
        auditing 334–335
        definition 481
RISC-based computers, firmware revision level 385
Roaming user profiles
    copying to network server 69–70
    creating 68
    definition 474
    deleting 71
    description 67
    mandatory 67, 71
    personal 67, 71
    recommendations 74
    specifying path 71–72
Root directory, definition 474
Rotating backup tapes 403–404
Routers, definition 474
RPC (Remote procedure call), definition 474
Run command, connecting to shared folders 202–203

S

SAM (Security Accounts Manager)
    See also Directory database
    definition 475
Saving files, default home folder 43
Schedule service
    definition 474
    starting 422
Scheduling
    automatic backups
        at command 422–424
        batch file options 419
        example 420–421
        ntbackup command 419–421
        overview 418
        starting Schedule service 422
        using Windows NT Command Scheduler 424–425
    printers 293–294, 310–312
Screen elements, definition 474
Screen saver, definition 474
Scrolling, definition 475
SCSI (small computer system interface), definition 477

510   Microsoft Windows NT Network Administration

Search button, definition 475
Secure attention sequence (CTRL+ALT+DELETE) 24, 475
Secure Erase, backup tapes 410, 414
Security
    See also Permissions; Share permissions
    auditing *See* Audit policy; Auditing; Security log
    backing up data 396
    definition 475
    home folders 43
    logging on 13–15
    passwords
        See also Passwords
        user account requirements 41–42
    planning
        account policy 140
        shares *See* Share permissions; Shared folders
    policy
        auditing changes 337
        definition 475
    preventing Trojan horse attacks 17
    recommendations for using groups 119
    restricting logon hours 42, 164
    securing network resources *See* NTFS permissions;
        Share permissions; Shared folders
    security tokens, definition 451
    setting account lockout options 142–143
    special access permissions 236
    user accounts description 36
    user profiles 65–66
    Windows NT administrative tasks 19
    Windows NT Security dialog box 24–28
    Windows NT Workstation advantages 4
Security account database *See* Directory database;
    Domain controllers
Security Accounts Manager (SAM)
    See also Directory database
    definition 475
Security identifiers (SIDs)
    definition 475
    deleting user accounts 61
Security log
    archiving 353–355
    Audit policy *See* Audit policy
    clearing 355
    controlling size and content 354
    creating entries 348
    definition 475
    filtering events 350–352
    locating events 352–353
    viewing using Event Viewer 346–353
Select Domain command 96
Selecting
    definition 475
    domains in Server Manager 370

Selecting *(continued)*
    drives, folders, and files
        to back up 411–412, 415
        to restore 432, 435
    items 151
Selection cursor, definition 476
Self-paced training
    cleanup procedures xxxiv–xxxv
    conventions xviii–xix
    deleting files xxxv
    icons xx
    instructional videos
        description xxxi
        installing Intel video drivers xxxiii
        local and global groups 85
        permissions 218
        starting 10
        Windows NT Directory services 10
    intended audience xvi
    Network Administration Training menu shortcuts xxxi
    notes xx
    overview of this book xxi–xxii
    requirements xxiii–xxiv
    setup procedures xxv–xxxiv
    starting xvi
    Windows NT 4.0 self-administered assessment xxxviii
Sending
    administrative alerts 379–380
    messages to users 380–381, 411
Separator pages, printing 297–298
Server applications, definition 476
Server Manager
    definition 476
    description 21
    determining which services are running 162
    installing 365
    maintaining domain controllers 154
    monitoring resources
        disconnecting users 371, 372–373
        domain information 370
        overview 365
        requirements 366
        resources in use 375–377
        sending messages to users 380–381
        setting administrative alerts 379–380
        shared resources 373–375
        viewing computer properties 369–370
        viewing user sessions 371–372
    promoting backup domain controllers (BDCs) to primary
        domain controllers (PDCs)
        PDCs going offline unexpectedly 156–157
        taking PDCs offline 155–156
    restoring original domain controller roles 158–159
    starting Schedule service 422

Index

Server Manager *(continued)*
    starting 370
    synchronizing domain controllers 160–161
    Windows NT Server administrative wizards 6
Server Operators group
    adding users 366
    administering security logs 332
    built-in capabilities for printer administration 308
    data backup requirements 396
    description 110–111
    Full Control print permission 274
    requirements for monitoring resources 366
    sharing folders 192
    viewing security log 347
Server performance, Windows NT Server advantages 5
Server service 162, 476
Servers
    closing resources in use 377
    definition 476
    disk space, storing home folders 43
    enterprise, definition 459
    member servers
        Audit policy 335
        definition 467
        description 7
        global groups 83
        local groups 82
        planning groups 90–94
        planning share permissions 183
        Windows NT Directory services 10–11
    monitoring
        See also Monitoring resources
        shared resources 373–375
    network program folders, sharing 184, 205, 223
    planning data backup strategy 399–400
    print servers *See* Print servers
    server applications, definition 476
    shutting down, disconnecting users 371, 372–373
    stand-alone, definition 477
    universal naming convention (UNC), definition 480
    viewing resources in use 375–376
    Web servers, definition 482
    Windows NT Server administrative wizards 6
Services
    Alerter service, definition 452
    Computer Browser 455
    definition 476
    dependent, definition 456
    Directory Replicator 457
    directory *See* Directory services
    Event Log 459
    File Replication 461
    Messenger 380, 467
    Net Logon 162, 468

Services *(continued)*
    net start command 162
    Schedule
        definition 474
        starting 422
    Server 476
    Services for Macintosh 476
    UPS 480
    viewing information using Windows NT Diagnostics 365, 384
    Windows NT Directory services 6, 10–11, 483
    Windows NT, overview 162
    Workstation 483
Services for Macintosh 476
Services program, Control Panel, stopping and restarting spooler 322
Sessions
    definition 476
    viewing computer properties 370
    viewing user sessions 371–372
Set By Caller, Dialin Information option 60
Setting
    administrative alerts 379–380
    environment variables 384
Setting up
    auditing
        defining domain Audit policy 336–337
        description 335
    print clients 280–281
    print servers 274–280
Setup procedures for this course xxv–xxxiv
Share permissions
    See also specific permission names; Shared folders
    assigning 195
    combining with NTFS permissions 217–218, 220–221
    definition 476
    description 174
    Everyone group 174, 177, 183, 184, 205
    instructional video 218
    limitations 176, 217
    modifying 198
    multiple, illustration 177
    overview 175–179
    planning guidelines 183–186
    priority of user permissions and group permissions 177
    recommendations 205
Shared folders
    See also Share permissions; Shared resources
    administrative shares 192
    benefits 175
    browsing, on other computers 202–203
    connecting to
        Map Network Drive command 200–202, 374
        Run command 202–203

Shared folders *(continued)*
    definition 476
    description 174
    disconnecting network drives 203
    file sharing defined 461
    hiding 194
    modifying 198
    permissions *See* NTFS permissions; Share permissions
    planning
        considerations 181
        data folders 185–186
        examples 182–183
        home folders 187–189
        network programs 184
        permissions guidelines 183–186
        worksheets 448
    recommendations 205
    requirements for sharing 192
    setting folder properties 193–194
    share names
        definition 476
        naming conventions 181
    stopping sharing 198
    viewing user sessions 371–372
    worksheets, planning 448
Shared resources
    See also Shared folders
    connecting to 374
    definition 476
    monitoring 373–375
    viewing computer properties 370
    viewing user sessions 371–372
Shared Resources dialog box 374
Shares *See* Share permissions; Shared folders; Shared resources
Sharing
    computers, home folder considerations 43
    definition 476
    files
        See also Share permissions; Shared folders
        definition 461
        home folders 51
    printers
        Add Printer wizard 275–276
        adding printers 276–278
        administration requirements 308
        definition 472
        description 275
        existing printers 279–280
    resources *See* Share permissions; Shared folders; Shared resources
SHIFT key, selecting items 151
Short name, definition 477
Shortcut keys, definition 476

Shortcuts
    creating for shared network resources 205
    installing Windows NT client–based tools 22
    Network Administration Training menu xxxi
Shutting down
    auditing user actions 337
    Logoff option, Windows NT Security dialog box 25, 27
    Logon Information dialog box 14
    recommendations 30
    servers, disconnecting users 371, 372–373
    Shut Down option, Windows NT Security dialog box 25
    using Windows NT Security dialog box 28
SIDs *See* Security identifiers
Single user logon, definition 477
Small computer system interface (SCSI), definition 477
Sounds, user profiles 65–66
Source directory, definition 477
Source document, definition 477
Special access permissions
    assigning 236–237, 255
    definition 477
    requirements for assigning NTFS permissions 230
Special Directory Access dialog box 236
Split bar, definition 477
Spooler, print
    definition 271, 472, 477
    printing overview 322–323
SQL (Structured Query Language), definition 477
Square brackets([]), notational conventions used in this book xviii
Stand-alone server, definition 477
Starting
    Backup simulation program 414
    instructional videos 10
    programs, process tracking 337
    Schedule service 422
    self-paced training course xvi
    Server Manager 370
    Spooler service 322
    Windows NT administrative tools 22
    Windows NT Command Scheduler 424
Status bar, definition 477
Stopping
    sharing folders 198
    Spooler service 322
Streamlining account administration 131
Subdirectory, definition 477
Subnet mask, definition 477
Subnet, definition 477
Success of events, auditing *See* Audit policy; Auditing
Swap files *See* Paging files
Switches
    at command 423
    ntbackup command 419, 431

Synchronization
    full synchronization, definition 461
    partial synchronization, definition 470
    synchronizing domain controllers 160–161, 478
Syntax
    definition 478
    notational conventions used in this book xviii
Sysprint.sep, separator page 298
System default profile, definition 478
System disk, definition 478
System groups 106, 113–114
System log
    definition 478
    description 346
    verifying domain controller synchronization 161
System partition, definition 478
System policy, definition 478
System program, Control Panel, copying user profiles to
  network server 69–70
System Properties dialog box 69
System requirements for installing Windows NT Server xxiii
Systemroot folder 192, 478
Systems Management Server 478

T

Take Ownership events, auditing
    files and folders 341
    printers 343
Take Ownership permission
    description 212
    giving users ability to take ownership 241
    requirements for assigning NTFS permissions 230
Taking ownership
    auditing events 341, 343
    default owner, definition 456
    of files and folders 240–244
    of printers
        procedure 319–320
        requirements 308
    owner, definition 469
    permissions required 176, 213
    requirements for assigning NTFS permissions 230
    special access permissions 236
Taking primary domain controllers (PDCs) offline 155–156
Tape catalogs, data backup
    definition 454
    description 405
    loading when restoring data 430–431, 435
Tape drives
    backing up registry information 400
    checking on hardware compatibility list 396
    data restoration strategies 427
    erasing backup tapes 410, 414

Tape drives (continued)
    life cycle of tapes 404
    missing or damaged tapes, restoring data 431
    preparing to back up files 410–411
    rotating and archiving tapes 403–404
    tape set defined 478
    Windows NT Backup requirements 396
Task list, definition 478
Task Manager
    closing programs 26–27
    definition 478
    description 5
    Windows NT Security dialog box 25
TCP (Transmission Control Protocol), definition 479
TCP/IP (Transmission Control Protocol/Internet Protocol),
  definition 479
Templates
    definition 478
    streamlining account administration 131
    using to create accounts 133–138
Terminate-and-stay-resident (TSR) programs, definition 479
Terms
    glossary definitions 451–483
    Windows NT printing terminology 270–271
Testing
    available printing hours 295
    NTFS permissions 233
    print permissions 287
    printers 279
    share permissions 197
    special access permissions 238
    Windows NT 4.0 self-administered assessment xxxviii
Text box, definition 479
Text file, definition 479
Text-only, definition 479
Time
    restricting logon hours 42, 55–56, 142–143, 164
    scheduling printers 293–295, 310–312
Time-out, definition 479
Title bar, definition 479
Toolbar, definition 479
Tools
    administering accounts
        built-in groups 132–133
        templates 133–138
        useful tools and procedures 131
    maintaining domain controllers 154
    monitoring resources 365–366
    Server Manager
        See also Server Manager
        maintaining domain controllers 154
        monitoring resources 365
    user profiles 65–66
    Windows NT administrative tools 20–22

Tools *(continued)*
    Windows NT client–based tools 21–22
    Windows NT Diagnostics 365, 383–387
    Windows NT Server advantages 5
Topic, definition 479
Track, MCSE Windows NT 4.0 xxxvii
Tracking events *See* Auditing
Training *See* Self-paced training
Transmission Control Protocol (TCP) 479
Transmission Control Protocol/Internet Protocol (TCP/IP) 479
Transport protocols
    See also Network protocols; Protocols
    definition 473
    drivers, definition 473
    installed, checking 386
    NWLink IPX\SPX Compatible Transport 469
    TCP 479
    TCP/IP 479
Trojan horse attacks
    definition 479
    preventing 17
Troubleshooting
    computers
        maintaining log book 383
        using Windows NT Diagnostics 365, 384
    logon problems 164–167
    missing or damaged tapes, restoring data 431
    permission problems
        access denied 251
        access tokens 252
        deleting files with No Access permission 253–256
        group memberships 252
        user with No Access deleting files 251
    printer problems 323–324
    user accounts, streamlining account administration 131
TrueType fonts, definition 479
Trust relationships
    assigning share permissions to users in other domains 195
    definition 480
    one-way, definition 469
    policy
        definition 480
        auditing changes 337, 348
    promoting centralized administration 116–118
    two-way, definition 480
    viewing 195
    Windows NT Directory services video 10
TSR (terminate-and-stay-resident) programs, definition 479
Two-way trust relationship, definition 480

U

Unavailable, definition 480
UNC (universal naming convention) names
    definition 480
    of printers 292
Uninterruptible power supply (UPS), definition 480
Universal naming convention (UNC), definition 480
UNIX
    file systems, deleting files and troubleshooting permissions 251
    print clients
        connecting to printers 283
        enabling 277
        possible 272
        printing overview 323
        setting up 281
Unlocking
    user accounts 147
    workstations 25
UPS (uninterruptible power supply)
    definition 480
    service 480
User accounts
    Account Expires option 58
    account lockout 451
    account policy
        definition 451
        description 139
        planning 140
        setting 139
        setting account lockout options 142–143
        setting password options 141–142
        unlocking user accounts 147
    Add User Accounts wizard 22
    administering
        distributing administrative tasks 132–133
        maintaining domain controllers 153–162
        multiple accounts 150–152
        setting account policy 139–149
        troubleshooting logon problems 164–167
        useful tools and procedures 131
        using templates 133–138
    auditing
        See also Audit policy; Auditing
        defining Audit policy 337
        planning Audit policy 334–335
        viewing security log events 348

User accounts *(continued)*
  creating
    granting dial-in permission 59–61
    home folders 51–54, 187
    procedure 53
    security identifiers (SIDs) 61
    setting account options 58–59
    setting logon hours 55–56
    setting password options 50–51, 141–142
    setting workstation restrictions 57
    User Manager vs. User Manager for Domains 48–50
  definition 480
  deleting xxxiv, 61–63
  description 36
  directory database
    See also Directory database
    description 7
  disabled, definition 457
  domain user accounts 37–38
  global accounts, recommendations 119
  global, definition 462
  group accounts
    See also Groups
    definition 462
    deleting 103–104
    description 81
    global group memberships 83
    local group memberships 82
    planning strategy 90–94
    planning worksheets 447
    share permissions 174
  home folders
    assigning to multiple accounts 54
    centralizing 51–52
    creating 51–54, 187
    default location 43
    description 42–43
    NTFS volumes 224
    planning shared folders 187–189
    recommendations 74
    sharing 51
    specifying using %Username% 52, 224, 258
    storing on a server 43
    storing on a user's computer 44
  local user accounts 38, 465
  logon domains 14–15
  modifying multiple accounts 150–152
  passwords
    See also Passwords
    definition 481
    resetting 148

User accounts *(continued)*
  planning
    home folders 42–44
    logon hours 42
    naming 41
    overview 40
    password requirements 41–42
    worksheets 446
    workstation restrictions 42
  planning backup strategy 400
  recommendations 74
  renaming 61–63
  setting lockout options 142–143
  share permissions
    See also Share permissions
    description 174
  special access permissions 236
  template accounts, definition 478
  templates 133–138
  tools for creating 37, 48–50
  troubleshooting logon problems 164
  types 36
  unlocking 147
  User privilege, definition 481
  user profiles 65–66
  validating
    domain accounts 15–16
    local accounts 17
  Windows NT administrative tasks 19
  Windows NT Directory services 10–11
  worksheets, planning 446
User Manager
  creating groups
    global groups 97–99
    local groups 84, 100–102
    menu commands 96
    rules 97
  creating user accounts 37, 48–50, 53
  defining Audit policy 335
  definition 480
  deleting group accounts 103–104
  description 21
  setting password options 50–51
User Manager for Domains
  adding users to Server Operators group 366
  creating groups
    global groups 85, 97–99
    local groups 84, 100–102
    menu commands 96
    rules 97

User Manager for Domains *(continued)*
    creating user accounts 37, 48–50, 53
    defining Audit policy 335
    definition 481
    deleting group accounts 103–104
    description 21
    distributing administrative tasks 132–133
    modifying multiple user accounts at one time 150–152
    resetting user account passwords 148
    setting password options 50–51
    unlocking user accounts 147
    Windows NT Server administrative wizards 6
User names
    creating user accounts 50
    definition 481
    Logon Information dialog box 14
    new user accounts 41
    preventing Trojan horse attacks 17
    specifying home folder using %Username% 52
User privilege, definition 481
User profiles
    creating 68
    default, definition 456
    definition 481
    deleting 71
    determining type 72
    local, definition 465
    logging on from non–Windows NT clients 66
    mandatory 67, 71, 467
    overview 65–66
    personal 67, 71
    recommendations 74
    reestablishing network connections 200–202
    roaming
        copying to network server 69–70
        creating 68
        definition 474
        deleting 71
        description 67
        specifying path 71–72
    specifying home folder using %Username% 52
    specifying path 71–72
    system default, definition 478
    System Properties dialog box 69
    troubleshooting logon problems 164
    user default profiles, definition 480
    Windows 95 67
User rights
    adding users to Server Operators group 366
    auditing requirements 332
    built-in groups 106–118
    data backup requirements 396
    data restoration requirements 428
    definition 481

User rights *(continued)*
    deleting and renaming user accounts 62
    description 81
    global groups 83
    group accounts 81
    local groups 82
    Log on locally user right, assigning to Everyone group xxxii
    policy
        auditing 334–335
        definition 481
%Username% variable
    recommendations
        creating user accounts 74
        NTFS permissions 258
    specifying home folder location 52, 224
Users
    adding to Server Operators group 366
    assigning print permissions 287
    auditing events
        See also Audit policy; Auditing
        defining Audit policy 337
        planning Audit policy 334–335
        viewing security log events 348
    connected, definition 455
    default, definition 456
    definition 481
    disconnecting remote users forcibly from server when logon hours expire 143
    disconnecting 143, 371, 372–373
    permissions *See* NTFS permissions; Permissions; Share permissions
    sharing resources *See* Share permissions; Shared folders; Shared resources
    troubleshooting logon problems 164–167
    viewing user sessions 371–372
Users group
    assigning Add & Read permission 232
    overview 109
    planning NTFS permissions
        data folders 223
        program folders 223
    recommendations for NTFS permissions 258
    share permissions 183
    sharing network program folders 184
Users must log on in order to change password 142

V

Validating
    domain accounts 15–16
    local accounts 17

Index

Variables
  definition 481
  environment, definition 459
Verifying domain controller synchronization 161
Version of Windows NT installed, checking 385
Videos
  description xxxi
  installing Intel video drivers xxxiii
  local and global groups 85
  permissions 218
  starting 10
  Windows NT Directory services 10
Viewing
  backup logs 416
  built-in system groups 114
  computer properties 369–370
  files and folders, auditing 341
  resources in use 375–377
  security log using Event Viewer 346–353
  shared resources 373–375
  user sessions 371–372
Virtual memory
  definition 481
  paging files, definition 470
Virus protection
  backing up data 395
  recommendations for NTFS permissions 258
  special access permissions 236
  viruses, definition 482
Volumes
  definition 482
  FAT See FAT volumes
  Macintosh-accessible volume, definition 466
  passwords 482
  private, definition 472
  volume sets, definition 482

W

WANs (wide area networks), definition 482
Warning beep, definition 482
Web browsers, definition 482
Web servers
  definition 482
  Internet Information Server (IIS) description 6
Web services, Windows NT Workstation advantages 4
Welcome dialog box, validating local accounts 17
Wide area networks (WANs), definition 482
Wildcards, definition 482
WinAt.exe, scheduling automatic backups 418, 424–425
Windows
  application window, definition 452
  definition 482

Windows *(continued)*
  printer, definition 472
  screen elements, definition 474
Windows 3.*x*
  logon scripts 66
  print clients
    connecting to printers 282, 283
    printing overview 323
    setting up 280
  shared folder names 181
Windows 95
  print clients
    connecting to printers 281–282
    enabling 277
    possible operating systems 272
    printing overview 322
    setting up 280
  running WinPopUp.exe 380
  shared folder names 181
  user profiles 67
  Windows NT client–based tools 21–22
Windows for Workgroups
  logon scripts 66
  print clients
    connecting to printers 282–283
    enabling 277
    possible 272
    printing overview 323
    setting up 280
  shared folder names 181
Windows NT Backup
  See also Backing up data; Restoring data
  backup types 401–403, 453
  description 21, 395
  missing or damaged tapes, restoring data 431
  requirements for using 396
  verifying computer date when restoring data 430
Windows NT Command Scheduler, scheduling automatic backups 418, 424–425
Windows NT Diagnostics
  description 21
  monitoring resources
    description 365
    gathering information 385–386
    options 384
    overview 383–384
    reports 386–387
    requirements 366
Windows NT Directory services *See* Directory services
Windows NT Explorer
  definition 483
  disconnecting network drives 203
  icon representing shared folders 174
  Map Network Drive command 200

Windows NT file system *See* NTFS permissions; NTFS volumes
Windows NT Security dialog box 24–28
Windows NT Server
   administrative tasks 19
   administrative tools 20–22
   auditing resources *See* Audit policy; Auditing
   client-based tools 21–22
   creating user accounts 37, 48–50
   definition 483
   Directory services 6, 10–11, 483
   domain model 7
   installed on NTFS volumes, permissions 230
   installing
      setup procedures xxv–xxix
      system requirements xxiii
   logging on 13–15
   member servers
      Audit policy 335
      definition 467
      description 7
      global groups 83
      local groups 82
      planning groups 90–94
      planning share permissions 183
      Windows NT Directory services 10–11
   overview 5–6
   printing
      See also Printing
      connecting to printers 281–282
      overview 322
      print devices on hardware compatibility list 274
      requirements 272
      setting up clients 280
      terminology 270–271
   Services for Macintosh 483
   services overview 162
   shared folder names 181
   shutting down, Logon Information dialog box 14
   version installed, checking 385
   workgroup model 8
Windows NT Workstation
   administrative tools 20–22
   auditing resources *See* Audit policy; Auditing
   client-based tools 21–22
   creating user accounts 37, 48–50
   definition 483
   domain model 7
   freeing idle connections 371, 372–373
   installed on NTFS volumes, permissions 230
   overview 3–4

Windows NT Workstation *(continued)*
   printing
      See also Printing
      connecting to printers 281–282
      overview 322
      print devices on hardware compatibility list 274
      requirements 272
      setting up clients 280
      terminology 270–271
   services overview 162
   shared folder names 181
   version installed, checking 385
   workgroup model 8
Windows NT–based applications, definition 482
Winmsd.exe
   See also Windows NT Diagnostics
   description 365
WinPopUp.exe, Windows 95 clients 380
Wizards
   Add Printer wizard
      connecting to printers from Windows NT and Windows 95 clients 282
      description 22
      enabling printer pooling 291
      overview 275–276
   Add User Accounts wizard 22
   Add/Remove Programs wizard 22
   administrative wizards
      description 21
      opening Windows NT administrative tools 22
      Windows NT Server advantages 6
   Group Management wizard 22
   Install New Modem wizard 22
   License Compliance wizard 22
   Managing File and Folder Access wizard 22
   Network Client Administrator wizard 22
Workgroups
   creating groups
      See also Groups
      using User Manager 96
   current, checking 385
   definition 483
   logging on 13–15
   specifying home folder location 52
   Users group 183
   Windows NT Server advantages 5–6
   Windows NT workgroup model 8
Working data folders
   NTFS permissions
      planning guidelines 223
      recommendations 258

Working data folders *(continued)*
    sharing
        planning guidelines 185–186
        recommendations 205
Worksheets, planning
    backup planning 450
    group accounts 447
    NTFS permissions 449
    shared folders 448
    user accounts 446
    weekly backup schedule 450
Workstation service 162, 483
Workstations
    Audit policy 335
    clients, definition 454
    definition 483
    locking and unlocking 25
    logon workstations, definition 466
    setting restrictions 57
    troubleshooting logon problems 164–167
World Wide Web (WWW), definition 483
Write events, auditing 341
Write permission
    deleting files, troubleshooting permissions 251
    description 212
WWW (World Wide Web), definition 483

X

X86-based computers, BIOS information 385
xcopy command 395

This is how Microsoft® Windows NT® pros become incredibly resourceful.

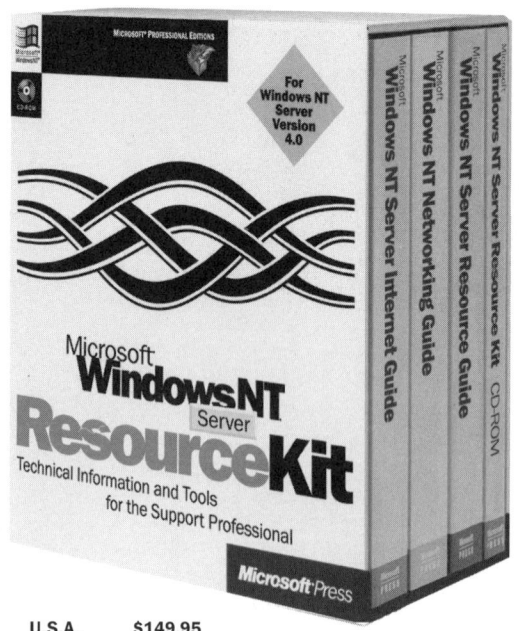

This three-volume kit provides the valuable technical and performance information and tools that you need for handling rollout and support issues surrounding Microsoft Windows NT Server 4.0. You get a full 2500 pages—plus a CD-ROM—loaded with essential information not available anywhere else. For support professionals, MICROSOFT WINDOWS NT SERVER 4.0 RESOURCE KIT is more than a guide. It's a natural resource.

U.S.A.	**$149.95**
U.K.	£140.99 [V.A.T. included]
Canada	$201.95
ISBN	1-57231-344-7

Microsoft Press® products are available worldwide wherever quality computer books are sold. For more information, contact your book retailer, computer reseller, or local Microsoft Sales Office.

To locate your nearest source for Microsoft Press products, reach us at www.microsoft.com/mspress/, or call 1-800-MSPRESS in the U.S. (in Canada: 1-800-667-1115 or 416-293-8464).

To order Microsoft Press products, call 1-800-MSPRESS in the U.S. (in Canada: 1-800-667-1115 or 416-293-8464).

Prices and availability dates are subject to change.

Microsoft Press

Microsoft® Internet Information Server 4.0 Training

Microsoft Press

PUBLISHED BY
Microsoft Press
A Division of Microsoft Corporation
One Microsoft Way
Redmond, Washington 98052-6399

Copyright © 1998 by Microsoft Corporation

All rights reserved. No part of the contents of this book may be reproduced or transmitted in any form or by any means without the written permission of the publisher.

Library of Congress Cataloging-in-Publication Data pending.
Printed and bound in the United States of America.

1 2 3 4 5 6 7 8 9 McQueen 3 2 1 0 9 8

Distributed to the book trade in Canada by Macmillan of Canada, a division of Canada Publishing Corporation.

A CIP catalogue record for this book is available from the British Library.

Microsoft Press books are available through booksellers and distributors worldwide. For further information about international editions, contact your local Microsoft Corporation office. Or contact Microsoft Press International directly at fax (425) 936-7329. Visit our Web site at mspress.microsoft.com.

ActiveX, BackOffice, FrontPage, Microsoft, Microsoft Press, MS-DOS, PowerPoint, Visual Basic, Visual C++, Windows, and Windows NT are registered trademarks and Authenticode, JScript, MSN, Outlook, and Visual J++ are trademarks of Microsoft Corporation.

Other product and company names mentioned herein may be the trademarks of their respective owners.

For Instructional Design Solutions
Instructional Designer: Jim Semick—Instructional Design Solutions
Editor: Shari G. Smith—R & S Consulting
Desktop Publishing: Irene Barnett—Barnett Communications

For Microsoft (Original Instructor-Led Course Content)
Project Lead/Instructional Designers:
   David Bramble, Steve Thues
Instructional Designer: Jennifer Kerns
Graphic Artist: Lisa Clark
Production Support: Kathy Ford (S&T Onsite)
Product Manager: David Bramble

Program Managers: W. Burl Evans, Rob Laws
Editor: Melissa Bramble
Manufacturing Support: Bo Galford
Publication/Mfg. Manager: Elaine Stovall
Group Product Manager: Robert Steward

Program Manager: Jeff Madden
Project Editors: Stuart J. Stuple, Michael D. Bolinger

Part No. 097-0002013

Contents

About This Book   xi
  Course Compact Disc xii
  Reference Materials xii
  Intended Audience. xii
  Finding the Best Starting Point for You xiv
    Where to Find Specific Skills in This Book. xv
  Conventions Used in This Book xxi
    Features of This Book. xxi
    Procedural Conventions xxi
    Notational Conventions. xxii
    Keyboard Conventions xxii
    Notes xxiii
  Getting Started xxiii
    Hardware and Software Requirements xxiii
  Chapter Overview. xxvi
  The MCP Program xxviii
    Microsoft Certification Benefits. xxix
    Requirements for Becoming a Microsoft Certified Professional xxxi
  Technical Training for Computer Professionals xxxii
    Self-paced Training xxxii
    Online Training xxxii
    Authorized Technical Education Centers xxxii
  Technical Support xxxiii
    Evaluation Edition Software Support xxxiii

Chapter 1   Introducing Microsoft Internet Information Server 4.0   1
  About This Chapter 1
  Before You Begin 1
  Lesson 1: Defining Microsoft Internet Information Server 4.0 2
    Windows NT 4.0 Option Pack. 3
  Lesson 2: Key Features of Internet Information Server 5
    Support of Internet Standards 5
    Setup and Administration 7
    Web-Based Applications. 7
    Security and Authentication. 8

            Web Publishing Tools 9
            Internet Information Server and Windows Operating Systems 9
        Review 12

Chapter 2   Installing Microsoft Internet Information Server   13
        About This Chapter 13
        Before You Begin 13
        Lesson 1: Preparing for Installation 14
            System Requirements..................................... 14
            Configuring Windows NT Server 15
        Lesson 2: Installing Microsoft Internet Information Server 18
            Installation Options 18
            Installation Changes to Windows NT Server 23
        Review 26

Chapter 3   Managing Internet Information Server   27
        About This Chapter 27
        Before You Begin 27
        Lesson 1: Microsoft Management Console 28
            Features of Microsoft Management Console..................... 29
            The Microsoft Management Console Interface 29
        Lesson 2: Internet Information Server Administrative Tools 32
            Internet Service Manager Snap-in 32
            Internet Service Manager (HTML) 35
            Windows Scripting Host 36
        Lesson 3: Internet Information Server Metabase 38
            Configuring Metabase Entries............................... 38
            Key Metabase Entries 39
        Review 41

Chapter 4   Understanding Internet Information Server Architecture   43
        About This Chapter 43
        Before You Begin 43
        Lesson 1: TCP/IP Architecture................................... 44
        Lesson 2: Server Architecture 47
            Inetinfo Process.. 48
            Connectors 50
            Windows NT System Services 51
            Web Services 52
            Application Services 54

Lesson 3: Administration Architecture	56
Review	58

Chapter 5 Configuring the WWW Service — 59

About This Chapter	59
Before You Begin	59
Lesson 1: HTTP Defined	60
Lesson 2: WWW Properties	62
Types of WWW Property Sheets	62
WWW Property Sheets	64
Web Site	65
Operators	66
Performance	67
ISAPI Filters	68
Home Directory	69
Documents	72
Directory Security	73
HTTP Headers	74
Custom Errors	75
Lesson 3: Virtual Directories	81
Virtual Directory Administration	83
Virtual Directories and FrontPage	84
Lesson 4: Virtual Servers	86
Host Headers	87
Virtual Server Administration	87
Review	90

Chapter 6 Configuring the FTP Service — 93

About This Chapter	93
Before You Begin	93
Lesson 1: The FTP Service	94
Lesson 2: FTP Properties	96
FTP Site	97
Security Accounts	98
Messages	99
Home Directory	100
Directory Security	101
Review	107

Chapter 7 Establishing Microsoft SMTP Service — 109
About This Chapter 109
Before You Begin 109
Lesson 1: Introduction to Microsoft SMTP Service 110
   Microsoft SMTP Service Features. 110
   SMTP Administration Interface 111
   SMTP Service Process Overview 113
Lesson 2: Managing and Configuring SMTP Service 115
   Configuring SMTP Service. 116
   Security Features. 123
   Monitoring the SMTP Service 124
Review 125

Chapter 8 Establishing Microsoft NNTP Service — 127
About This Chapter 127
Before You Begin 127
Lesson 1: Introduction to NNTP Service. 128
   How NNTP Service Works 130
Lesson 2: Configuring and Managing NNTP Service. 132
   Creating Virtual Directories Across Hard Disks. 134
   Configuring NNTP Service. 134
Review 141

Chapter 9 Adding Windows NT and Internet Information Server Security Features — 143
About This Chapter 143
Before You Begin 143
Lesson 1: Windows NT Server Security 144
   User Accounts. 144
   NTFS 146
   Web Server Permissions for Files and Folders 147
   Other Windows NT Security Measures 148
Lesson 2: Internet Information Server Security Features. 150
   Control Access by Logon 150
   Control Access to Folders. 152
   Control Access by IP Address. 153
Lesson 3: Secure Sockets Layer 3.0 154
   SSL Architecture. 155
   Client Certificate Authentication. 156

Contents   vii

Lesson 4: Configuring SSL 159
    External Certificate Authorities........................... 160
    Applying Your Certificate................................ 164
    Microsoft Certificate Server 165
Review... 167

Chapter 10   Issuing Digital Certificates   171

About This Chapter 171
Before You Begin 171
Lesson 1: Certificate and Authentication Background................. 172
    Cryptography... 172
    Encryption... 173
    Public-Key Algorithms................................... 174
    Digital Signatures and Digital Envelopes 174
    Digital Certificates...................................... 175
Lesson 2: Overview of Microsoft Certificate Server 176
    Certificate Server Configurations........................... 176
    Certificate Server Features 178
    Certificate Server Architecture 179
Lesson 3: Using Microsoft Certificate Server....................... 182
    Enrolling Certificates 183
    Processing Certificate Requests............................ 185
    Adding Certificate Authorities............................. 186
    Administration Tools 187
Review... 195

Chapter 11   Active Server Pages   197

About This Chapter 197
Before You Begin 197
Lesson 1: Web Server Extensions............................... 198
    ASP 199
    CGI Support 199
    ISAPI 199
    ODBC... 200
Lesson 2: Web Formats 201
    Basic Linked Content 201
    Dynamic HTML 202
    Data-Bound Applications 202
    Interactive Applications 203
    Personalization and Transaction Processing 203

Lesson 3: ASP 205
    Benefits of ASP. 205
    ASP Elements 206
    ASP Objects 208
    ASP Components. 210
    Use of the Script Tag 211
Review 218

Chapter 12 Indexing Web Sites 221

About This Chapter 221
Before You Begin 221
Lesson 1: Index Server Overview. 222
    Features of Index Server. 222
    Running Index Server 223
Lesson 2: The Indexing Process 226
    Corpus 226
    Content Filters. 227
    Word Breakers 227
    Normalizer 228
    Indexes. 228
    Catalogs 230
    The CiDaemon Process 230
    Types of Merges 231
    Index Server Manager 233
Lesson 3: Queries. 236
    Query Form Elements 237
    The Query Process. 238
    Formulating Queries and Results. 240
Lesson 4: Index Server Administration 248
    Administering an Index 248
    Error Detection and Recovery. 250
    Security Features. 251
Review 257

Chapter 13 Understanding Microsoft Transaction Server	**259**
About This Chapter	259
Before You Begin	259
Lesson 1: Overview of Transaction Processing	260
Microsoft Transaction Server Components	261
Three-Tier Architecture	262
MSMQ	263
ASP Integration	263
Components of a Transaction	264
Component-Based Programming	265
Lesson 2: Configuring and Managing Microsoft Transaction Server	267
Review	275
Chapter 14 Analyzing Web Sites	**277**
About This Chapter	277
Before You Begin	278
Lesson 1: Introduction to Site Server Express	279
Lesson 2: Using WebMaps	281
WebMaps	281
Lesson 3: Quick Search	287
Lesson 4: Site Summary Reports	289
Lesson 5: Using Log Files	293
Saving Log Files	295
Importing Log Files	295
Lesson 6: Report Writer	298
Lesson 7: Posting Acceptor	306
Review	308
Chapter 15 Tuning and Monitoring Internet Information Server	**311**
About This Chapter	311
Before You Begin	311
Lesson 1: Monitoring the Services	312
Performance Monitor	313
Event Viewer Logs and Internet Information Server Logs	314
Other Tools for Monitoring Performance	314
Important Counters to Monitor	314

Lesson 2: Factors Affecting Internet Information Server Performance 317
    Bandwidth 317
    Hardware 319
    Network Application Speeds. 321
Lesson 3: Internet Information Server Performance Tuning. 323

Questions and Answers   327

Appendix: Internet Concepts   345

Index   353

About This Book

Welcome to *Microsoft Internet Information Server 4.0 Training*. This book provides systems administrators the knowledge and skills to install, configure, and implement Microsoft® Internet Information Server (IIS) version 4.0 on the Microsoft Windows NT® version 4.0 operating system. It also prepares you for the related Microsoft Certified Professional (MCP) exam, Implementing and Supporting Microsoft Internet Information Server 4.0. Because this book focuses on implementing Internet Information Server, it does not cover publishing Web page content.

Note For more information on becoming a Microsoft Certified Professional, see the section titled The MCP Program later in this chapter.

Each chapter in this book is divided into lessons. Most lessons include hands-on practices to practice or demonstrate the concept or skill presented in the lesson. At the end of each lesson is a short summary, and at the end of most chapters is a set of review questions to test your knowledge of the chapter material. If appropriate, at the end of each chapter there are references to additional information on the lesson material or related topics.

The Getting Started section provides important setup instructions that describe the hardware and software requirements to complete the practices in this book. Read through this section thoroughly before you start the lessons.

Course Compact Disc

The compact disc provided in this kit contains optional multimedia presentations that supplement concepts covered in the book. You should view these presentations when suggested, and use them as a review tool while you work through the material.

The course compact disc also includes an online version of the book that you can view on-screen and use to launch demonstrations, link to all of the referenced articles, and work through the exercises. The screen shots in the online book do vary from those in the book, however, this does not affect the purpose of their content. Instructions for using the online book are available in the Readme.txt file in the root folder of the course compact disc.

An additional compact disc included in this kit contains an Evaluation Edition of Microsoft Windows NT Server 4.0. Either this Evaluation Edition or the retail edition of Windows NT Server is necessary to install Internet Information Server and complete the practices contained in this book.

Reference Materials

You may find the following reference material useful:

- Windows NT Server 4.0 documentation
- *Microsoft Windows NT Server Resource Kit*
- Windows NT 4.0 Option Pack online documentation
- Microsoft TechNet compact disc (the latest volume)

Intended Audience

This book is intended for System Engineers and Webmasters who are planning to use Microsoft Internet solutions to host Web sites, or who want to prepare for the related MCP exam 70-087, Implementing and Supporting Microsoft Internet Information Server 4.0.

Prerequisites

To successfully complete the material and to understand the concepts and tasks presented in this book, you are required to have, as a minimum, the following background:

- Successful completion of the following Microsoft Certified Professional exams:
    - 70-067, Implementing and Supporting Microsoft Windows NT Server 4.0 or 70-043, Implementing and Supporting Microsoft Windows NT Server 3.51
    - 70-059, Internetworking with Microsoft TCP/IP on Microsoft Windows NT 4.0 or 70-053, Internetworking with Microsoft TCP/IP on Microsoft Windows NT (3.5–3.51)

    –Or–

- Completion of the following courses:
    - #659, Supporting Microsoft Windows NT Server 3.51; #694, Microsoft Windows NT 4.0 Technical Support Training (self-study course); or #922, Supporting Microsoft Windows NT 4.0 Core Technologies
    - #688, Internetworking with Microsoft TCP/IP on Microsoft Windows NT 4.0 or #472, Internetworking with Microsoft TCP/IP on Microsoft Windows NT 3.51

    –Or–

- The ability to accomplish the following tasks:
    - Install Windows NT Server.
    - Install Transmission Control Protocol/Internet Protocol (TCP/IP) on Windows NT Server, including the ability to:

        Explain how Dynamic Host Configuration Protocol (DHCP), Microsoft Windows® Internet Name Service (WINS), and domain name system (DNS) can be used to resolve TCP/IP addresses.

        Obtain and use a TCP/IP address from a service provider.

    - Explain Windows NT Server and DNS domain structures.
    - Assign permissions to users and groups.

Finding the Best Starting Point for You

This book is designed for you to complete at your own pace, so you can skip some lessons and revisit them later. Keep in mind that you need to complete the practices in Chapter 2, "Installing Microsoft Internet Information Server," in order to perform the practices in the other chapters. Use the following table to find the best starting point for you.

If you	Follow this learning path
Are preparing to take the Microsoft Certified Professional exam.	Read the Getting Started section. Next, work through Chapters 1–4. Work through Chapters 5–15 in any order. Before starting a chapter, read through the Before You Begin section to determine any prerequisites.
Need to install and configure Windows NT 4.0 Option Pack with Internet Information Server and all available features.	Read the Getting Started section. Work through Chapter 2, and then complete Chapter 3. Work through the remaining chapters depending on your configuration. Before starting a chapter, read through the Before You Begin section to determine any prerequisites.
Need to install and configure Internet Information Server with the WWW Service and the FTP Service.	Read the Getting Started section. Work through Chapters 2 and 3. Complete Chapters 5 and 6, and then work through the remaining chapters depending on your configuration. Before starting a chapter, read through the Before You Begin section to determine any prerequisites.
Need a greater understanding of TCP/IP and the Internet, including Internet security issues.	Work through Chapters 2 and 4. Complete Chapters 9 and 10, and then work through the remaining chapters depending on your configuration. Before starting a chapter, read through the Before You Begin section to determine any prerequisites.
Need information on a specific topic related to Internet Information Server.	Refer to the table of contents or index.

Where to Find Specific Skills in This Book

The following tables provide a list of the skills measured on the certification exam, Implementing and Supporting Microsoft Internet Information Server 4.0. The tables list the skill, and where in this book you can find the lesson relating to that skill.

Note Exam skills are subject to change without prior notice and at the sole discretion of Microsoft. You can find the latest exam preparation guides at the Microsoft Training and Certification site:

http://www.microsoft.com/train_cert

Planning

Skill being measured	Location in book
Choose a security strategy for various situations. Security considerations include:	
• Controlling anonymous access.	Chapter 9, Lessons 1 and 2; Chapter 15, Lesson 1
• Controlling access to known users and groups.	Chapter 9, Lessons 1 and 2
• Controlling access by host or network.	Chapter 9, Lesson 2
• Configuring SSL to provide encryption and authentication schemes.	Chapter 9, Lessons 2–4
• Identifying the appropriate balance between security requirements and performance requirements.	Chapter 15, Lesson 3
Choose an implementation strategy for an Internet site or an intranet site for stand-alone servers, single-domain environments, and multiple-domain environments. Tasks include:	
• Resolving host header name issues by using a HOSTS file or DNS.	Chapter 5, Lesson 4
• Choosing the appropriate operating system on which to install Internet Information Server.	Chapter 1, Lesson 2

(*continued*)

Skill being measured	Location in book
Choose the appropriate technology to resolve specified problems. Technology options include:	
■ WWW Service.	Chapter 5, Lessons 2–4; Chapter 14, Lesson 5; Chapter 15, Lessons 1 and 2
■ FTP Service.	Chapter 6, Lessons 1 and 2; Chapter 14, Lesson 5; Chapter 15, Lessons 1 and 2
■ Microsoft Transaction Server.	Chapter 13, Lessons 1 and 2
■ Microsoft SMTP Service.	Chapter 7, Lessons 1 and 2
■ Microsoft NNTP Service.	Chapter 8, Lessons 1 and 2
■ Microsoft Index Server.	Chapter 12, Lessons 1–4
■ Microsoft Certificate Server.	Chapter 10, Lessons 2 and 3

Installation and Configuration

Skill being measured	Location in book
Install Internet Information Server. Tasks include:	
■ Configuring a Microsoft Windows NT Server 4.0 computer for the installation of Internet Information Server.	Chapter 2, Lesson 1
■ Identifying differences to a Windows NT Server 4.0 computer made by the installation of Internet Information Server.	Chapter 2, Lesson 2
Configure Internet Information Server to support the FTP Service. Tasks include:	
■ Setting bandwidth and user connections.	Chapter 6, Lesson 2
■ Setting user logon requirements and authentication requirements.	Chapter 6, Lesson 2; Chapter 9, Lessons 1 and 2
■ Modifying port settings.	Chapter 6, Lesson 2
■ Setting directory listing style.	Chapter 6, Lesson 2
■ Configuring virtual directories and servers.	Chapter 5, Lesson 3

(continued)

Skill being measured	Location in book
Configure Internet Information Server to support the WWW Service. Tasks include:	
■ Setting bandwidth and user connections.	Chapter 5, Lesson 2
■ Setting user logon requirements and authentication requirements.	Chapter 5, Lesson 2; Chapter 9, Lessons 1 and 2
■ Modifying port settings.	Chapter 5, Lesson 2
■ Setting default pages.	Chapter 5, Lesson 2
■ Setting HTTP 1.1 Host Header names to host multiple Web sites.	Chapter 5, Lesson 4
■ Enabling HTTP Keep-Alives.	Chapter 5, Lesson 2
Configure and save consoles by using Microsoft Management Console (MMC).	Chapter 3, Lesson 1
Verify server settings by accessing the metabase.	Chapter 3, Lesson 3
Choose the appropriate administration method.	Chapter 3, Lesson 2
Install and configure Certificate Server.	Chapter 2, Lesson 2; Chapter 10, Lesson 3
Install and configure Microsoft SMTP Service.	Chapter 2, Lesson 2; Chapter 7, Lesson 2
Install and configure Microsoft NNTP Service.	Chapter 2, Lesson 2; Chapter 8, Lesson 2
Customize the installation of Microsoft Site Server Express Content Analyzer.	Chapter 14, Lessons 1–4
Customize the installation of Site Server Express Report Writer and Usage Import.	Chapter 14, Lessons 1 and 6

Configuring and Managing Resource Access

Skill being measured	Location in book
Create and share folders with appropriate permissions. Tasks include:	
▪ Setting folder-level permissions.	Chapter 9, Lessons 1 and 2
▪ Setting file-level permissions.	Chapter 9, Lessons 1 and 2
Create and share local and remote virtual directories with appropriate permissions. Tasks include:	
▪ Creating a virtual directory and assigning an alias.	Chapter 5, Lesson 3
▪ Setting folder-level permissions.	Chapter 5, Lessons 2 and 3
▪ Setting file-level permissions.	Chapter 5, Lessons 2 and 3
Create and share virtual servers with appropriate permissions by assigning IP addresses.	Chapter 5, Lesson 4
Write scripts to manage the FTP Service or the WWW Service.	Chapter 3, Lesson 2
Manage a Web site by using Content Analyzer. Tasks include:	
▪ Creating, customizing, and navigating WebMaps.	Chapter 14, Lesson 2
▪ Examining a Web site by using the various reports provided by Content Analyzer.	Chapter 14, Lesson 6
▪ Tracking links by using a WebMap.	Chapter 14, Lesson 2
Configure Microsoft SMTP Service to host personal mailboxes.	Chapter 7, Lessons 1 and 2
Configure Microsoft NNTP Service to host a newsgroup.	Chapter 8, Lessons 1 and 2
Configure Certificate Server to issue certificates.	Chapter 10, Lesson 3
Configure Index Server to index a Web site.	Chapter 12, Lessons 2–4
Manage MIME types.	Chapter 5, Lesson 2
Manage the FTP Service.	Chapter 6, Lesson 2; Chapter 15, Lesson 1
Manage the WWW Service.	Chapter 5, Lesson 2; Chapter 15, Lesson 1

Integration and Interoperability

Skill being measured	Location in book
Configure Internet Information Server to connect to a database by configuring ODBC.	Chapter 11, Lessons 1 and 2
Configure Internet Information Server to integrate with Index Server. Tasks include:	
• Specifying query parameters by creating the .idq file.	Chapter 12, Lesson 3
• Specifying how the query results are formatted and displayed to the user by creating the .htx file.	Chapter 12, Lesson 3

Running Applications

Skill being measured	Location in book
Configure Internet Information Server to support server-side scripting.	Chapter 3, Lesson 2
Configure Internet Information Server to run ISAPI applications.	Chapter 11, Lesson 1
Configure Internet Information Server to support ADO associated with the WWW Service.	Chapter 11, Lesson 2

Monitoring and Optimization

Skill being measured	Location in book
Maintain a log for fine-tuning and auditing purposes. Tasks include:	
• Importing log files into a Report Writer and Usage Import database.	Chapter 14, Lessons 5 and 6
• Configuring the logging features of the WWW Service.	Chapter 5, Lesson 2
• Configuring the logging features of the FTP Service.	Chapter 6, Lesson 2
• Configuring Report Writer and Usage Import to analyze logs created by the WWW Service or the FTP Service.	Chapter 14, Lessons 5 and 6
• Automating the use of Report Writer and Usage Import.	Chapter 14, Lessons 5 and 6
Monitor performance of various functions by using Performance Monitor. Functions include HTTP and FTP sessions.	Chapter 15, Lesson 1

(continued)

Skill being measured	Location in book
Analyze performance. Performance issues include:	
• Identifying bottlenecks.	Chapter 5, Lesson 2; Chapter 6, Lesson 2; Chapter 15, Lesson 2
• Identifying network-related performance issues.	Chapter 5, Lesson 2; Chapter 6, Lesson 2; Chapter 15, Lesson 2
• Identifying disk-related performance issues.	Chapter 5, Lesson 2; Chapter 6, Lesson 2; Chapter 15, Lesson 2
• Identifying CPU-related performance issues.	Chapter 15, Lesson 2
Optimize performance of Internet Information Server.	Chapter 5, Lesson 2; Chapter 6, Lesson 2; Chapter 15, Lesson 3
Optimize performance of Index Server.	Chapter 12, Lesson 4
Optimize performance of Microsoft SMTP Service.	Chapter 7, Lesson 2
Optimize performance of Microsoft NNTP Service.	Chapter 8, Lesson 2
Interpret performance data.	Chapter 15, Lesson 3
Optimize a Web site by using Content Analyzer.	Chapter 14, Lessons 2, 3, 4, 5, and 6

Troubleshooting

Skill being measured	Location in book
Resolve Internet Information Server configuration problems.	Chapter 3, Lesson 2; Chapter 15, Lessons 1, 2, and 3
Resolve security problems.	Chapter 9, Lessons 1 and 2; Chapter 15, Lessons 1 and 2
Resolve resource access problems.	Chapter 5, Lesson 2; Chapter 6, Lesson 2; Chapter 9, Lessons 1 and 2; Chapter 15, Lessons 1 and 2
Resolve Index Server query problems.	Chapter 12, Lesson 4

(continued)

Skill being measured	Location in book
Resolve setup issues when installing Internet Information Server on a computer running Windows NT Server 4.0.	Chapter 2, Lessons 1 and 2
Use a WebMap to find and repair broken links, hyperlink texts, headings, and titles.	Chapter 14, Lesson 2
Resolve WWW Service problems.	Chapter 5, Lesson 2; Chapter 15, Lesson 1
Resolve FTP Service problems.	Chapter 6, Lesson 2; Chapter 15, Lesson 1

Conventions Used in This Book

Before you start any of the lessons, it is important that you understand the terms and notational conventions used in this book.

Features of This Book

- Each chapter opens with a Before You Begin section, which describes other chapters that must be completed before continuing.

- Whenever possible, lessons contain practices that give you an opportunity to use the skills being presented or explore the part of Internet Information Server being described. The hands-on practices describe the requirements for performing the practice. All practices and procedures are identified with the following procedural convention: ▶

- The Review section at the end of most chapters allows you to test what you have learned in the lessons. They are designed to familiarize you with the types of questions you will find on the Microsoft Certified Professional exam.

- The For More Information list at the end of many chapters provides additional resource locations for information on the concepts and skills covered in the chapter. The information referred to covers product documentation, online locations, or both.

- The Questions and Answers section contains all of the book's questions and corresponding answers. Each question is cross-referenced by page number.

Procedural Conventions

- Hands-on practices that you are to follow are presented in numbered lists of steps (1, 2, and so on). A triangular bullet (▶) indicates the beginning of a practice.

- The word *select* is used for highlighting folders, file names, text boxes, menu bars, and option buttons, and for selecting options in a dialog box.

- The word *click* is used for carrying out a command from a menu or dialog box.

Notational Conventions

- Characters or commands that you type appear in **bold lowercase** type.
- *Italic* in syntax statements indicates placeholders for variable information. *Italic* is also used for book titles.
- Names of files and folders appear in Title Caps, except when you are to type them directly. Unless otherwise indicated, you can use all lowercase letters when you type a file name in a dialog box or at a command prompt.
- File name extensions appear in all lowercase.
- Names of folders appear in initial caps, except when you are to type them directly. Unless otherwise indicated, you can use all lowercase letters when you type a folder name in a dialog box or at a command prompt.
- Acronyms appear in all uppercase.
- `Monospace` type represents code samples, examples of screen text, or entries that you might type at a command prompt or in initialization files.
- Braces { } are used in syntax statements to enclose required items. Type only the information within the braces, not the braces themselves.
- Icons represent specific sections in the book as follows:

Icon	Represents
	A multimedia presentation. You will find the applicable multimedia presentation on the course compact disc.
	A hands-on practice. You should perform the practice to give you an opportunity to use the skills being presented in the lesson.
	Chapter review questions. These questions at the end of most chapters allow you to test what you have learned in the lessons. You will find the answers to the review questions in the Questions and Answers section at the end of the book.

Keyboard Conventions

- A plus sign (+) between two key names means that you must press those keys at the same time. For example, "Press ALT+TAB" means that you hold down ALT while you press TAB.
- A comma (,) between two or more key names means that you must press each of the keys consecutively, not together. For example, "Press ALT, F, X" means that you press and release each key in sequence. "Press ALT+W, L" means that you first press ALT and W together, release them, and then press L.

- You can choose menu commands with the keyboard. Press the ALT key to activate the menu bar, and then sequentially press the keys that correspond to the highlighted or underlined letter of the menu name and the command name. For some commands, you can also press a key combination listed in the menu.
- You can select or clear check boxes or option buttons in dialog boxes with the keyboard. Press the ALT key, and then press the key that corresponds to the underlined letter of the option name. Or you can press TAB until the option is highlighted, and then press the spacebar to select or clear the check box or option button.
- You can cancel the display of a dialog box by pressing the ESC key.

Notes

Notes appear throughout the lessons.

- Notes marked **Note** contain supplemental information.
- Notes marked **Tip** contain explanations of possible results or alternative methods.
- Notes marked **Important** contain information that is essential to completing a task.
- Notes marked **Caution** contain warnings about possible loss of data.

Getting Started

Hardware and Software Requirements

This self-paced training book contains hands-on practices to help you learn about Internet Information Server. There are minimum hardware and software requirements to successfully perform the practices in the book.

Hardware

You must have one computer to perform the practices in this book. The computer must have the following minimum configuration:

- 66 MHz 486 or higher Intel-based processor (90 MHz Pentium recommended)
- 32 MB RAM
- 200 MB free hard disk space after installing Windows NT Server 4.0
- CD-ROM drive (3x minimum)

- VGA Monitor (SVGA recommended) capable of displaying 256 colors
- Microsoft Mouse or compatible pointing device
- Sound card with headphones or speakers (optional)

All hardware should be on the Microsoft Windows NT 4.0 Hardware Compatibility List (HCL).

Software

Before installing the Windows NT 4.0 Option Pack (which includes Internet Information Server) as described in Chapter 2, "Installing Microsoft Internet Information Server," you must have previously configured Windows NT Server version 4.0, Windows NT 4.0 Service Pack 3, and Microsoft Internet Explorer 4.01.

The following software is required to complete the hands-on practices in this book:

- Windows NT Server 4.0 retail product (or the Evaluation Edition included on the supplemental compact disc).
- Windows NT 4.0 Option Pack (included on the course compact disc). The Windows NT 4.0 Option Pack contains Internet Information Server 4.0.
- Windows NT Server 4.0 Service Pack 3 or later (Service Pack 3 is included on the course compact disc). You must install Service Pack 3 before installing the Windows NT 4.0 Option Pack.
- Internet Explorer 4.01 (included on the course compact disc). You must install Internet Explorer 4.01 before installing the Windows NT 4.0 Option Pack.

Preparing Your Computer to Complete the Practices

To complete the practices in the lessons, you must have Windows NT Server 4.0 installed and configured on your computer. The computer should be configured as a stand-alone server with Windows NT File System (NTFS) as the file system. Note that you cannot install NTFS on a computer running two or more operating systems. The lesson practices assume the installation folder is C:\Winnt.

In addition, you must install Windows NT 4.0 Service Pack 3 and Internet Explorer 4.01 before installing Internet Information Server. The following procedures outline installing the Service Pack and Internet Explorer from the course compact disc.

▶ **To install Windows NT 4.0 Service Pack 3**

1. From the Windows NT 4.0 Option Pack compact disc, double-click **nt4sp3_i.exe** in the WinntSP3\i386 folder.

   The **Welcome** dialog box appears.

About This Book xxv

2. Click **Next**.
3. Click **Yes** to accept the license agreement.
4. In the **Service Pack Setup** dialog box, select the **Install the Service Pack** option, and then click **Next**.
5. Select the option to not create an uninstall folder.
6. Click **Next**, and then click **Finish**.
7. In the **Windows NT Service Pack Setup** dialog box, click **OK** to complete Setup.
8. After the files are loaded to the computer, restart your computer.

▶ **To install Internet Explorer 4.01**

1. From the Windows NT 4.0 Option Pack compact disc, double-click **ie4setup.exe** in the ie401\x86 folder.

   The **Internet Explorer 4.0 Active Setup** dialog box appears.

2. In the **Internet Explorer 4.0 Setup** dialog box, click **Next**.
3. Select the **I accept the agreement** option.
4. In **License Agreement**, click **Next**.
5. In **Installation Option**, select **Standard Installation**, and then click **Next**.
6. In **Windows Desktop Update**, select **No**, and then click **Next**.
7. In **Active Channel Selection**, select the appropriate country, and then click **Next**.
8. In **Destination Folder**, click **Next**.

   Internet Explorer 4.0 Active Setup installs the requested components.

9. Click **OK** to finish the installation.
10. Click **OK** to restart the computer.
11. When the computer restarts, log on as Administrator.

    When you log on, the **Microsoft Internet Explorer 4.0 Setup** dialog box appears and Internet Explorer Setup continues necessary configuration changes.

12. In the **Security Warning** dialog box, click **Yes**.
13. Close the Welcome-Microsoft Internet Explorer window.
14. Double-click the Internet Explorer desktop icon.

    The **Internet Connection Wizard** dialog box appears.

15. Click **Next**.
16. Select the appropriate Internet connection option for your configuration, and then click **Next**.
17. Complete any connection information required for your configuration; and then click **Finish** and **OK**.

Chapter Overview

This self-paced training book combines hands-on practices and review questions in addition to the book material to teach you how to implement and support Internet Information Server on Windows NT 4.0. It is designed to be completed from beginning to end, but you can choose a customized track and complete only the sections that interest you. If you choose the customized track option, see the Before You Begin section in each chapter. Any hands-on practices that require preliminary work from preceding chapters refer to the appropriate chapters.

The self-paced training book is divided into the following chapters:

- This About This Book section contains a self-paced training overview and introduces the components of this training. Read this section thoroughly to get the greatest educational value from this self-paced training and to plan which lessons you will complete.

- Chapter 1, "Introducing Microsoft Internet Information Server 4.0," provides an overview of Internet Information Server and its relationship to the other Microsoft Internet services. It introduces the components of the Windows NT 4.0 Option Pack, and calls out those elements of the Windows NT 4.0 Option Pack that, for the purpose of the book, are considered core components of the Internet Information Server platform.

- Chapter 2, "Installing Microsoft Internet Information Server," explains the steps necessary to install components of the Windows NT 4.0 Option Pack—including Internet Information Server—on your computer. It describes the platform and system requirements necessary to run Internet Information Server, suggests how to configure your operating system prior to installing Internet Information Server, and details the differences between the Minimum, Typical, and Custom installation options.

- Chapter 3, "Managing Internet Information Server," introduces the various tools and interfaces used to configure Internet Information Server. It describes the functionality of Microsoft Management Console and of Internet Service Manager. It also provides an overview of the metabase, the fast-access, hierarchical database that replaces the Windows NT registry for most Internet Information Server settings.

- Chapter 4, "Understanding Internet Information Server Architecture," provides an overview of the technologies that underlie and support Internet Information Server. It reviews the TCP/IP protocols supported by Internet Information Server and introduces the components that comprise the server architecture.

- Chapter 5, "Configuring the WWW Service," describes the various features of the World Wide Web (WWW) Service running on Internet Information Server. It explains the functions of the property sheets associated with the WWW Service and demonstrates how to configure the service.

- Chapter 6, "Configuring the FTP Service," describes the features of the File Transfer Protocol (FTP) Service running on Internet Information Server. It reviews the functions of the various property sheets associated with FTP Service.

- Chapter 7, "Establishing Microsoft SMTP Service," details the features of the Microsoft Simple Mail Transfer Protocol (SMTP) Service running on Internet Information Server. It reviews the functions of the various property sheets for configuring SMTP to transmit electronic mail (e-mail) over the Internet.

- Chapter 8, "Establishing Microsoft NNTP Service," describes the features of the Microsoft Network News Transfer Protocol (NNTP) Service, which allows users in your organization to engage in newsgroup-type discussions with other users, both inside and outside the organization. The chapter reviews the functions of the various property sheets associated with NNTP Service running on Internet Information Server.

- Chapter 9, "Adding Windows NT and Internet Information Server Security Features," provides an overview of the security features of Internet Information Server. It explains and demonstrates the various Internet-related security features that are part of Windows NT Server and Internet Information Server. The chapter also reviews the steps involved with implementing the Secure Sockets Layer (SSL) protocol, and explains how to obtain digital certificates.

- Chapter 10, "Issuing Digital Certificates," provides an overview of the role of Microsoft Certificate Server and explains certificates. At the end of this chapter, you will be able to distinguish between the processes involved with creating digital signatures and digital envelopes, and describe the purpose served by Microsoft Certificate Server in the process of certifying individuals, browsers, and servers.

- Chapter 11, "Active Server Pages," introduces Active Server Pages (ASP) as a tool that enables you to combine HTML, scripts, and reusable Microsoft ActiveX™ Server components to create dynamic Web sites. The chapter discusses the elements that comprise ASP—ASP scripts, objects, and components—and distinguishes between built-in and installable objects and components.

- Chapter 12, "Indexing Web Sites," discusses Microsoft Index Server 2.0, the indexing and searching tool included with the Windows NT 4.0 Option Pack. It explains how Index Server provides an indexing service for Internet and intranet sites.

- Chapter 13, "Understanding Microsoft Transaction Server," introduces the concept of transactions in distributing computing and describes the features of Microsoft Transaction Server. The chapter provides an example of using Microsoft Transaction Server in a business environment.

- Chapter 14, "Analyzing Web Sites," provides an overview of Microsoft Site Server Express (SSE), the content management and usage analysis tool included with the Windows NT 4.0 Option Pack. The chapter describes the features and functions of the SSE components: Content Analyzer, Usage Import and Report Writer, and Posting Acceptor. The chapter also explains how to select, analyze, and report information from an SSE database.

- Chapter 15, "Tuning and Monitoring Internet Information Server," summarizes many of the monitoring tools and methods used throughout the book. It explains how you can monitor and tune Internet Information Server performance, as well as what can cause performance problems. The lessons review the available tools and methods to measure and correct performance problems.

- The appendix, "Internet Concepts," gives you an overview of the Internet, how information is transferred across the Internet, and describes the components of a Uniform Resource Locator (URL). While reading the appendix, you will view a multimedia presentation covering additional Internet concepts.

The MCP Program

The Microsoft Certified Professional (MCP) program provides the best method to prove your command of current Microsoft products and technologies. Microsoft, an industry leader in certification, is on the forefront of testing methodology. Our exams and corresponding certifications are developed to validate your mastery of critical competencies as you design and develop, or implement and support, solutions with Microsoft products and technologies. Computer professionals who become Microsoft certified are recognized as experts and are sought after industry-wide.

The Microsoft Certified Professional program offers six certifications, based on specific areas of technical expertise:

- *Microsoft Certified Professional (MCP).* MCPs have demonstrated in-depth knowledge of at least one Microsoft operating system. Candidates may pass additional Microsoft certification exams to further qualify their skills with Microsoft BackOffice® products, development tools, or desktop programs.

- *Microsoft Certified Professional + Internet.* MCPs with a specialty in the Internet are qualified to plan security, install and configure server products, manage server resources, extend servers to run Common Gateway Interface (CGI) scripts or Internet Server Application Programming Interface (ISAPI) scripts, monitor and analyze performance, and troubleshoot problems.

- *Microsoft Certified Systems Engineer (MCSE).* MCSEs are qualified to effectively plan, implement, maintain, and support information systems in a wide range of computing environments with Microsoft Windows® 95, Microsoft Windows NT, and the Microsoft BackOffice integrated family of server software.

- *Microsoft Certified Systems Engineer + Internet (MCSE + Internet).* MCSEs have an advanced qualification to enhance, deploy and manage sophisticated intranet and Internet solutions that include a browser, proxy server, host servers, database, and messaging and commerce components. In addition, an MCSE + Internet-certified professional is able to manage and analyze Web sites.
- *Microsoft Certified Solution Developer (MCSD).* MCSDs are qualified to design and develop custom business solutions with Microsoft development tools, technologies, and platforms, including Microsoft Office and Microsoft BackOffice.
- *Microsoft Certified Trainer (MCT).* An MCT is instructionally and technically qualified to deliver Microsoft Official Curriculum through a Microsoft Authorized Technical Education Center (ATEC).

Microsoft Certification Benefits

Microsoft certification, one of the most comprehensive certification programs available for assessing and maintaining software-related skills, is a valuable measure of an individual's knowledge and expertise. Microsoft certification is awarded to individuals who have successfully demonstrated their ability to perform specific tasks and implement solutions with Microsoft products and technologies. Not only does Microsoft certification provide an objective measure for employers and potential employers to consider during hiring and evaluation; it also provides guidance for what you should know to be proficient with Microsoft products and technologies. And as with any skills-assessment and benchmarking measure, certification brings a variety of benefits to the individual, and to employers and organizations.

Microsoft Certification Benefits for Individuals

As a Microsoft Certified Professional, you receive many benefits:

- Industry recognition of your knowledge and proficiency with Microsoft products and technologies.
- Access to technical and product information directly from Microsoft through a secured area of the MCP Web site.
- Material and logos to enable you to identify your Microsoft Certified Professional status to colleagues and clients.
- Invitations to Microsoft conferences, technical training sessions, and special events.
- A Microsoft Certified Professional certificate.
- Subscription to Microsoft Certified Professional Magazine (North America only), a career and professional development magazine.

Additional benefits, depending on your certification and geography, include:

- A complimentary one-year subscription to the Microsoft TechNet Technical Information Network, providing valuable information on monthly compact discs.
- A one-year subscription to the Microsoft Beta Evaluation program. This benefit provides you with up to 12 free monthly compact discs containing beta software (English only) for many of Microsoft's newest software products.

Microsoft Certification Benefits for Employers and Organizations

Through certification, computer professionals can maximize the return on investment in Microsoft technology. Research shows that Microsoft certification provides organizations with:

- Excellent return on training and certification investments by providing a standard method of determining training needs and measuring results.
- Increased customer satisfaction and decreased support costs through improved service, increased productivity, and greater technical self-sufficiency.
- Reliable benchmarks for hiring, promoting, and career planning.
- Recognition and rewards for productive employees by validating their expertise.
- Retraining options for existing employees so they can work effectively with new technologies.
- Assurance of quality when outsourcing computer services.

To learn more about how certification can help your company, see the following information available on http://www.microsoft.com/train_cert/cert/bus_bene.htm:

- The Microsoft Certified Professional Program Corporate Backgrounder.
- A white paper that evaluates the Microsoft Certified Solution Developer certification.
- A white paper that evaluates the Microsoft Certified Systems Engineer certification.
- The Jackson Hole High School Case Study.
- The Lyondel Case Study.
- The Stellcom Case Study.

Requirements for Becoming a Microsoft Certified Professional

The certification requirements differ for each certification and are specific to the products and job functions addressed by the certification.

To become a Microsoft Certified Professional, you must pass rigorous certification exams that provide a valid and reliable measure of technical proficiency and expertise. These exams are designed to test your expertise and ability to perform a role or task with a product, and are developed with the input of professionals in the software industry. Questions in the exams reflect how Microsoft products are used in actual organizations, giving them real-world relevance.

Microsoft Certified Product Specialists are required to pass one operating system exam. Candidates may pass additional Microsoft certification exams to further qualify their skills with Microsoft BackOffice products, development tools, or desktop applications.

Microsoft Certified Professional + Internet are required to pass the prescribed Microsoft Windows NT Server 4.0, TCP/IP, and Microsoft Internet Information Server exam series.

Microsoft Certified Systems Engineers are required to pass a series of core Microsoft Windows operating system and networking exams, and BackOffice technology elective exams.

Microsoft Certified Solution Developers are required to pass two core Microsoft Windows operating system technology exams and two BackOffice technology elective exams.

Microsoft Certified Trainers are required to meet instructional and technical requirements specific to each Microsoft Official Curriculum course they are certified to deliver. In the United States and Canada, call Microsoft at (800) 688-0496 for more information on becoming a Microsoft Certified Trainer. Outside the United States and Canada, contact your local Microsoft subsidiary.

Technical Training for Computer Professionals

Technical training is available in a variety of ways, with self-paced training, online instruction, or instructor-led classes available at thousands of locations worldwide.

Self-paced Training

For motivated learners who are ready for the challenge, self-paced instruction is the most flexible, cost-effective way to increase your knowledge and skills.

A full line of self-paced print and computer-based training materials are available direct from the source—Microsoft Press. Microsoft Official Curriculum courseware kits from Microsoft Press are designed for advanced computer system professionals. Self-paced training kits from Microsoft Press feature print-based instructional materials, along with compact disc-based product software, multimedia presentations, practice procedures, and practice files. The Mastering Series provides in-depth, interactive training on compact disc for experienced developers. Both are great ways to prepare for MCP exams.

Online Training

For a more flexible alternative to instructor-led classes, turn to online instruction delivered over the Internet. Learn at your own pace and on your own schedule in a virtual classroom, often with access to an online instructor. Without leaving your desk, you can gain the expertise you need. Online instruction covers a variety of Microsoft products and technologies and includes Microsoft Official Curriculum. It is training on demand, with access to learning resources 24 hours a day.

Online training is available through ATECs.

Authorized Technical Education Centers

ATECs are the best source for instructor-led training that can help you prepare to become a Microsoft Certified Professional. The Microsoft ATEC program is a worldwide network of qualified technical training organizations that provide authorized delivery of Microsoft Official Curriculum courses by Microsoft Certified Trainers to computer professionals.

For a listing of ATEC locations in the United States and Canada, call the Microsoft fax service at (800) 727-3351. Outside the United States and Canada, contact your local Microsoft subsidiary.

Technical Support

Every effort has been made to ensure the accuracy of this book and the contents of the companion compact disc. Microsoft Press provides information about known issues for books through the Web at the following address:

http://mspress.microsoft.com/support/

If you have comments, questions, or ideas regarding this book or the companion compact disc, please send them to Microsoft Press using either of the following methods:

- E-mail

    tkinput@microsoft.com

- Postal mail

    Microsoft Press
    Attn: Microsoft Internet Information Server 4.0 Training Editor
    One Microsoft Way
    Redmond, WA 98052-6399

Please note that product support is not offered through the preceding mail addresses. For further information regarding Microsoft software support options, please connect to http://www.microsoft.com/support or call Microsoft Support Network Sales at (800) 936-3500. Outside the United States, contact your local Microsoft subsidiary.

Evaluation Edition Software Support

The Evaluation Edition of Microsoft Windows NT Server 4.0 included with this book is unsupported by both Microsoft and Microsoft Press, and should not be used on a primary work computer. For online support information relating to the full version of Windows NT Server 4.0 that may also apply to the Evaluation Edition, connect to:

http://support.microsoft.com/

Information about any issues relating to the use of this Evaluation Edition with this kit are posted to the Support section of the Microsoft Press Web site:

http://mspress.microsoft.com/support/support.htm

CHAPTER 1

Introducing Microsoft Internet Information Server 4.0

Lesson 1   Defining Microsoft Internet Information Server 4.0 . . . 2

Lesson 2   Key Features of Internet Information Server . . . 5

Review . . . 12

About This Chapter

This chapter gives you an overview of Microsoft Internet Information Server (IIS) version 4.0 and describes its key features. It also details differences in functionality among installations of Microsoft Internet Information Server 4.0 running on Microsoft Windows NT Server 4.0, Microsoft Windows NT Workstation 4.0, and Microsoft Windows 95.

Before You Begin

There are no prerequisites to complete this chapter. In order to view the optional Internet Overview multimedia presentation, you must have the course compact disc.

Lesson 1: Defining Microsoft Internet Information Server 4.0

Microsoft Internet Information Server 4.0 is a network file and application server for the Microsoft Windows NT Server 4.0 operating system. Internet Information Server supports standard information protocols, and is highly extensible through the use of both Internet Server Application Programming Interface (ISAPI) and Common Gateway Interface (CGI). Internet Information Server provides a server solution for Internet, intranet, and extranet sites.

After this lesson, you will be able to:
- Define Internet Information Server 4.0.
- List and describe the key components of the Windows NT 4.0 Option Pack.

Estimated lesson time: 15 minutes

Internet Information Server is the base component for building an Internet or intranet server solution on Windows NT Server 4.0, Windows NT Workstation 4.0, and Windows 95.

Internet Information Server is fully integrated with Windows NT Server 4.0. With the tight integration of Internet Information Server and Windows NT Server, you can take advantage of the built-in security of Windows NT Server and Windows NT File System (NTFS).

You can use the additional Internet technologies provided by Internet Information Server to enhance Microsoft BackOffice. The Microsoft BackOffice family includes:

- Microsoft SQL Server client/server database management system.
- Microsoft Exchange Server client/server messaging system.
- Microsoft Proxy Server.
- Microsoft SNA Server connectivity for IBM enterprise networks.
- Microsoft Systems Management Server centralized management for distributed systems.
- Microsoft Commercial Internet Server (MCIS).

With Internet Information Server, you can deploy scalable server applications to host the latest generation of Web content. Internet Information Server fully supports Microsoft Visual Basic® programming system, VBScript, Microsoft JScript™ development software, and Java components. It also supports CGI applications for Web-based programs, and ISAPI extensions and filters.

Windows NT 4.0 Option Pack

Internet Information Server 4.0 is a component of the Windows NT 4.0 Option Pack. In addition to Internet Information Server, the Windows NT 4.0 Option Pack consists of the following core components:

- Microsoft Transaction Server 2.0 (MTS)
- Microsoft Management Console 1.0 (MMC)
- Microsoft Index Server 2.0
- Microsoft Certificate Server 1.0
- Microsoft Site Server Express 2.0 (SSE)

Microsoft Transaction Server 2.0 is a component-based transaction processing system for developing, deploying, and managing high-performance, scalable, and robust server applications. Microsoft Transaction Server defines a programming model and provides a run-time environment and graphical administration tool for managing enterprise applications.

Microsoft Management Console 1.0 is a tool to create consoles for performing administrative tasks on your network. It integrates all of the tools, information, Web pages, and views of the network an administrator needs to perform specific tasks.

Microsoft Index Server 2.0 enables users accessing a Web site to perform full-text searches and to retrieve information from the server.

Microsoft Certificate Server 1.0 provides customizable services for issuing and managing digital certificates. You can use these certificates to secure e-mail and to authenticate clients and servers on the Internet and corporate intranets.

Comprised of three tools—Content Analyzer, Usage Import and Report Writer, and Posting Acceptor—Microsoft Site Server Express 2.0 offers a subset of the functionality found in Microsoft Site Server.

- *Content Analyzer.* Provides comprehensive site visualization, content analysis, link management, and reporting capabilities for managing Web sites.
- *Usage Import and Report Writer.* Enables you to collect and analyze Internet Information Server log files from a single server using nine predefined reports that give you insight into the actual requests, users, and organizations that interact with your site.
- *Posting Acceptor.* A server add-on tool that allows Web content providers to publish their content using Hypertext Transport Protocol (HTTP) Post (RFC 1867). After installing Posting Acceptor on your Web server, you are able to provide a hosting service for users who want to post Web content to your server. You can install Posting Acceptor on Windows NT Server, Windows NT Workstation, or Windows 95.

In addition to the core components, the Windows NT 4.0 Option Pack includes the following components:

- Microsoft Data Access Components 1.5
- Microsoft Message Queue Server 1.0 (MSMQ)
- Microsoft Update to Remote Access Services 1.0 (RAS)
- Microsoft Script Debugger 1.0

Summary

Internet Information Server is a network file and application server designed for Microsoft Windows NT Server, and is a component of the Windows NT 4.0 Option Pack. Several elements of the Windows NT 4.0 Option Pack are the core components of the Internet Information Server platform.

Lesson 2: Key Features of Internet Information Server

Internet Information Server creates a Web server that is standards-based by supporting the HTTP 1.1 functionality. Additional features such as the integrated setup wizard, integrated security and authentication utilities, Web publishing tools, and support for other Web-based applications help you increase the overall performance over the Internet.

After this lesson, you will be able to:
- List and describe the key features of Internet Information Server 4.0.
- Describe the differences in functionality among installations of Internet Information Server running on Windows NT Server 4.0, Windows NT Workstation 4.0, and Windows 95.

Estimated lesson time: 25 minutes

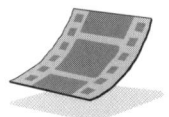

Multimedia Presentation: Internet Overview

For an overview of Internet concepts, run the Internet.exe presentation file on the course compact disc. This optional nine-minute multimedia presentation covers the most important Internet concepts, including Internet topology and Internet Protocol (IP) packets.

For more information about the history and architecture of the Internet, read the appendix, "Internet Concepts," located in this book.

Support of Internet Standards

Internet Information Server supports Internet industry standards and functionality. The features include HTTP 1.1 support, and standard Internet services such as World Wide Web (WWW), File Transfer Protocol (FTP), Simple Mail Transfer Protocol (SMTP), and Network News Transfer Protocol (NNTP).

HTTP 1.1 is the latest version of this protocol. HTTP 1.1 features improved transfer speed, tighter logon security, and additional virtual hosting abilities. Internet Information Server provides users with a Web server that is standards-based by supporting the new HTTP functionality and helping to increase overall performance over the Internet.

Internet Information Server provides support for such standard Internet services as WWW, FTP, SMTP, and NNTP.

WWW Service

Microsoft WWW Service supports HTTP, allowing users to publish content to the Internet. The Web is the most graphical service on the Internet and has the most sophisticated linking capabilities. Whether your site is on an intranet or the Internet, the principles of providing content are the same. You place your files in folders on your Web site so that users can view your files with a Web browser, such as Microsoft Internet Explorer. You can publish documents in Hypertext Markup Language (HTML) format that includes text, graphics, animation, or video. WWW Service also allows you to install business applications on your Web site so that customers can order products or fill out forms.

FTP Service

Microsoft FTP Service supports FTP. FTP is the industry-standard protocol used for transferring files between computers on a Transmission Control Protocol/Internet Protocol (TCP/IP) network. FTP was one of the earliest protocols used on TCP/IP networks and the Internet.

WWW and FTP sites enable you to use one computer to host multiple domain names. With only one computer and one installation of Internet Information Server, you are able to give the appearance of having multiple computers with a different WWW or FTP site on each virtual computer. For example, an Internet Service Provider (ISP) can use one computer running two Web sites to provide Web sites for two different companies, each with its own unique domain name and IP address. The ISP uses Internet Service Manager to create as many Web or FTP sites as needed for customers, and assigns unique identification information and property settings to each one.

You can create an unlimited number of sites. When creating a very large number of sites, be sure to consider hardware limitations and to upgrade hardware as necessary.

SMTP Service

The SMTP Service is a standards-based, secure, and scalable e-mail server. The SMTP Service supports a distributed e-mail service using SMTP and the Post Office Protocol version 3 (POP3). The SMTP Service allows the partitioning of inboxes across multiple servers and enables the server to scale to millions of user inboxes independent of the number of concurrent service connections. It also enables user inboxes to be backed up, restored, and moved easily between sites and servers.

NNTP Service

The NNTP Service is a commercial-grade, standards-based server for hosting electronic discussion groups. NNTP provides Internet sites and services with the means to:

- Create public, read-only, moderated, or private (authenticated) discussion groups.
- Provide customers with permission to access remote discussion groups, including Usenet newsgroups, which are the most popular electronic discussion groups on the Internet.
- Provide secure authentication through standard Windows NT Server mechanisms or encrypted clear-text authentication using Secure Sockets Layer (SSL).
- Provide encrypted access to newsgroups by using SSL.

Setup and Administration

The integrated setup wizard provides one-step setup for Internet Information Server and its components. During setup, you select the components you want to install and answer configuration questions. The wizard then completes the setup process.

Microsoft Management Console is a common extensible user interface for systems-management applications. Microsoft Management Console combines Internet Information Server administrative tasks with those of associated components into a single integrated management utility.

HTML-based Administration, or HTMLA, allows you to manage your Web server or individual Web sites remotely using any industry-standard Web browser that supports frames and JScript.

Command Line Administration Scripting allows you to manage Web sites from the command prompt. This means that you can write scripts to automate repetitive tasks.

Web-Based Applications

Internet Information Server includes several features that can help you develop and deploy Web-based applications.

As described in the preceding lesson, Microsoft Transaction Server is a programming model that provides support for a range of tools required for multiuser Web server applications. You can use Microsoft Transaction Server to leverage your existing knowledge of popular tools such as Visual Basic, Microsoft Visual C++®, or Microsoft Visual J++™ in creating desktop applications to create reliable and scalable data-driven Web applications.

Process isolation enables your applications to run in a memory space separate from that used by the Web and other applications. This results in a greater degree of reliability for organizations running Web applications by preventing a single unstable application from disabling the entire server.

Active Server Pages (ASP) is an open, compile-free application environment. With ASP you can combine the ease of HTML with familiar tools such as Visual Basic scripting and reusable Microsoft ActiveX server components to create dynamic and powerful Web sites. ASP enables server-side scripting for Internet Information Server with native support for both VBScript and JScript.

By integrating Internet Information Server with Microsoft Transaction Server, ASP runs as a component within the Microsoft Transaction Server environment. As a result, ASP can take advantage of Microsoft Transaction Server capabilities such as process isolation, transactions, and scalability.

Server-Side Java Virtual Machine is a system you can use to create and run Java components on the server. It is an industry standard, high-performance platform for building and deploying Java-based applications.

Security and Authentication

Internet Information Server security and authentication features include Certificate Authentication, Certificate Wildcard Mapping, and Domain Blocking.

With Certificate Authentication, you can map clients to Windows NT Server user accounts using industry standard client certificates such as X.509 digital certificates. You can use Certificate Authentication to provide users with single logon servers to network resources using client certificates.

Certificate Wildcard Mapping allows you to authenticate users without having access to the actual certificate. With this feature, you can map users to Windows NT Server user accounts using third-party certificates such as those issued by VeriSign.

You can use Domain Blocking to regulate access to content on your server selectively by domain. Domain Blocking is a reliable way for you to control access to content on your server by either granting or denying access to all users from a specified domain.

Web Publishing Tools

Internet Information Server helps to facilitate Web publishing by including the Web Publishing wizard, Posting Acceptor, and Microsoft FrontPage® 98 Server Extensions.

The Web Publishing wizard is a client-side application that helps users post Web pages to an Internet Information Server Web site by automating the process of copying files from the user's computer to the Web server. The Web Publishing wizard connects to the ISP, determines the protocol needed to copy the files successfully, and then uploads the files to the appropriate folder on the ISP computer.

The Posting Acceptor enables Internet Information Server to accept Web content from the Web Posting wizard, Netscape Navigator, Content Replication Server, and other client applications using HTTP.

Internet Information Server incorporates FrontPage 98 Server Extensions, which allow users to take advantage of the administration features of FrontPage 98 in managing their Web site.

Note For additional information on use of FrontPage 98 Server Extensions, please refer to http://www.microsoft.com/frontpage and search for FrontPage Server Extensions.

Internet Information Server and Windows Operating Systems

Internet Information Server 4.0 behaves differently according to the platform where you install it. Although this book teaches you how to install Internet Information Server on Windows NT Server 4.0, you can also install Internet Information Server on Windows NT Workstation and Windows 95.

All of the features and components of Internet Information Server are fully supported on Windows NT Server 4.0. However, when you install Internet Information Server on Windows NT Workstation or Windows 95, Internet Information Server becomes Microsoft Personal Web Server (PWS) because it lacks some of the key features associated with Windows NT Server.

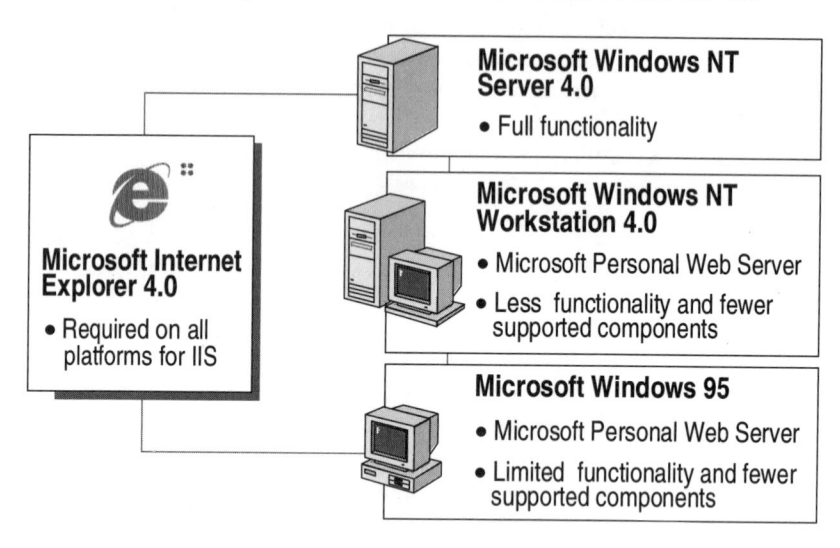

Microsoft Internet Explorer 4.0
- Required on all platforms for IIS

Microsoft Windows NT Server 4.0
- Full functionality

Microsoft Windows NT Workstation 4.0
- Microsoft Personal Web Server
- Less functionality and fewer supported components

Microsoft Windows 95
- Microsoft Personal Web Server
- Limited functionality and fewer supported components

Windows NT Workstation

Personal Web Server running on Windows NT Workstation provides all of the Internet Information Server functionality except:

- Multiple Web site hosting
- Open Database Connectivity (ODBC) logging
- IP restrictions
- Process isolation

Personal Web Server running on Windows NT Workstation works well for personal publishing, workgroup site hosting, and remote administration of Internet Information Server running on Windows NT Server.

Windows 95

Personal Web Server running on Windows 95 works well for personal publishing, and provides the same functionality of Personal Web Server running on Windows NT Workstation, except for:

- Security (Windows 95 does not have Windows NT security)
- Index Server

Summary

Internet Information Server is a standards-based Web server that supports all HTTP 1.1 functionality and includes a range of features such as the integrated setup wizard, security and authentication utilities, and Web publishing tools.

Internet Information Server loaded on a Windows 95 computer provides nearly the same functionality as Personal Web Server running on a Windows NT Workstation computer, but lacks Windows NT security features and Index Server.

Review

The following questions are intended to reinforce key information presented in this chapter. If you are unable to answer a question, review the appropriate lesson, and then try the question again.

1. Will Internet Information Server load properly on a computer running Windows NT Workstation or Windows 95 operating systems? Will the resulting Internet Information Server system be fully functional?

2. You are a consultant to a firm that wants to allow customers to search through documents at their Web site. Which component of Internet Information Server enable the user to do this? Will Internet Information Server running on a Windows 95–based computer fully support this component? What about Internet Information Server running on a computer that runs Windows NT Workstation?

3. You are working on a release of a software product for a large company. You have decided to create an intranet site to allow every member of your large team access to the current build of the product, as well as to current versions of product documentation. You would like to limit access to the site to the people on your team. What feature of Internet Information Server would allow this?

For More Information

For information about the history and organization of the Internet, refer to the appendix, "Internet Concepts."

CHAPTER 2

Installing Microsoft Internet Information Server

Lesson 1 Preparing for Installation . . . 14

Lesson 2 Installing Microsoft Internet Information Server . . . 18

Review . . . 26

About This Chapter

This chapter details how you can prepare for installing Microsoft Internet Information Server (IIS) version 4.0, and then takes you through the installation process. It also describes the changes that a full installation of Internet Information Server makes to Microsoft Windows NT Server version 4.0 operating system.

Before You Begin

To complete the lessons in this chapter, you must have:

- Configured your computer as described in the Getting Started section of About This Book.
- Installed Microsoft Windows NT Service Pack 3 and Microsoft Internet Explorer 4.01 as described in the Getting Started section of About This Book.
- The Windows NT 4.0 Option Pack file from the course compact disc.

Lesson 1: Preparing for Installation

Before installing Internet Information Server, there are some hardware and software requirements that you need to be aware of. This lesson details how to prepare for Internet Information Server installation.

After this lesson, you will be able to:
- Describe the minimum and recommended system requirements for installation of Internet Information Server on supported platforms.
- Configure Windows NT Server 4.0 to support Internet Information Server.

Estimated lesson time: 15 minutes

To install Internet Information Server successfully, you must first make sure that your computer meets at least the minimum system requirements. Once you have confirmed that your system is sufficient for installation, make sure that Windows NT Server is configured correctly.

System Requirements

Internet Information Server supports both Intel-based and Alpha-based computers. Internet Information Server installed on an Intel-based computer is fully functional. However, Internet Information Server installed on an Alpha-based computer lacks the following:

- Microsoft Visual Basic components and samples
- Microsoft Visual J++ components and samples
- Java Virtual Machine

In addition to the functional differences with different platforms, the different platforms have slightly different hardware requirements. The following two tables list the minimum and recommended hardware requirements for typical installations of Internet Information Server on the two supported platforms.

Intel *x86* Platform

Component	Requirement	Recommendation
Processor	50 MHz 486	90 MHz Pentium or greater
RAM	16 MB	32 to 64 MB
Available disk space	50 MB	200 MB
Monitor	VGA	Super VGA

Alpha Platform

Component	Requirement	Recommendation
Processor	150 MHz	200 MHz
RAM	48 MB	64 MB
Available disk space	50 MB (minimum)	200 MB
Monitor	VGA	Super VGA

Note Installing the Simple Mail Transfer Protocol (SMTP) and Network News Transfer Protocol (NNTP) services requires additional resources. See the Internet Information Server online documentation for details about these resources.

The software requirements for Internet Information Server are consistent for both Intel-based and Alpha-based computers. Internet Information Server requires the Windows NT Server 4.0, Microsoft Windows NT Workstation 4.0, or Microsoft Windows 95 operating system. The tangible differences between Internet Information Server running on each of these operating systems are outlined in Chapter 1, "Introducing Microsoft Internet Information Server 4.0."

Installing Internet Information Server on any computer requires Microsoft Internet Explorer 4.01 as a Web browser. In addition, you need to install Microsoft Windows NT Service Pack 3 prior to installing Internet Information Server.

Configuring Windows NT Server

A fully functional Internet Information Server installation on Windows NT Server 4.0 requires that you first configure the operating system with Transmission Control Protocol/Internet Protocol (TCP/IP) and Windows NT File System (NTFS). Assigning a static IP address for the server is optional for an installation of Internet Information Server.

TCP/IP provides the Internet connectivity necessary for retrieving data from, and hosting a site on, the Internet.

With NTFS you can limit permission to files and folders on a Windows NT server. This is a key factor in maintaining a secure Internet server and is a necessary component of the SMTP Service.

Windows NT Security Features

Because Internet Information Server is completely integrated with Windows NT Server 4.0, you can use all of the security options built into the operating system to help secure your Internet Information Server installation. To take advantage of these Windows NT security options, consider the following suggestions:

- Use NTFS as your file system.
- Use a complex password scheme.
- Maintain strict account policies such as limiting the Guest account to specific folders on the server.
- Limit the membership of the administrators group.
- Run only the services and protocols required by your system.
- Check permissions on network shares.
- Enable auditing.

Note Because these additional security features can slow server performance, you must be selective in choosing which services to use.

Practice

In this practice, you examine your Windows NT environment. This helps you understand the changes Internet Information Server installation makes to Windows NT.

▶ **To examine the Windows NT Server environment**

1. Log on to Windows NT Server as Administrator.
2. Click the **Start** button, point to **Settings**, and then click **Control Panel**.

   Control Panel appears.
3. In Control Panel, double-click **Services**.

   The **Services** dialog box appears.
4. Scroll through the services available.

   There should not be any Publishing services listed.
5. Close the **Services** dialog box.
6. Close Control Panel.
7. Click the **Start** button, point to **Programs**, point to **Administrative Tools**, and then click **User Manager for Domains**.

   The User Manager window appears.

8. Examine the list of names.

   There should not be an Internet Guest Account listed.

9. Close User Manager.

10. Click the **Start** button, point to **Programs**, point to **Administrative Tools**, and then click **Performance Monitor**.

    Performance Monitor appears.

11. On the **Edit** menu, click **Add To Chart**.

    The **Add to Chart** dialog box appears.

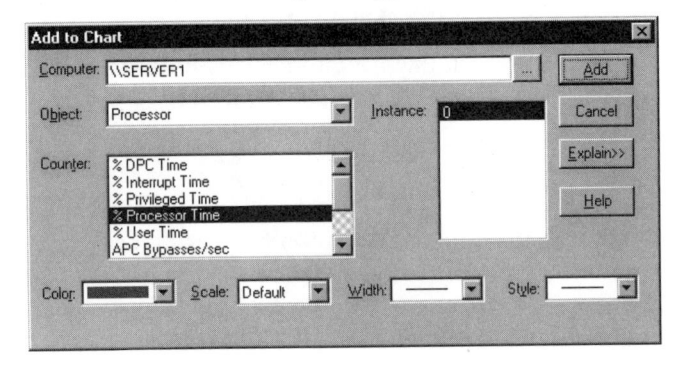

    ![Add to Chart dialog box showing Computer: \\SERVER1, Object: Processor, Counter list with %DPC Time, %Interrupt Time, %Privileged Time, %Processor Time (selected), %User Time, APC Bypasses/sec; Instance: 0; buttons Add, Cancel, Explain>>, Help; Color, Scale: Default, Width, Style options]

12. Click the **Object** box to see more options.

    The list of objects appears.

13. Examine the items in the list for Internet-related items such as File Transfer Protocol (FTP) or Hypertext Transport Protocol (HTTP) objects.

    Unless you have previously installed a version of Internet Information Server, there should not be any Internet-related items in the list.

14. Close the **Add to Chart** dialog box.

15. Close the Performance Monitor window.

Summary

Your computer must meet certain minimum system requirements and you must be sure that Windows NT Server 4.0 is configured with TCP/IP before you can successfully install Internet Information Server.

Lesson 2: Installing Microsoft Internet Information Server

Installing Internet Information Server 4.0 is managed by the integrated setup wizard. During setup, you select the components you want to install and answer a series of configuration questions. The wizard then completes the setup process. This lesson describes the different Internet Information Server installation options, outlines the procedure for installing Internet Information Server on Windows NT Server 4.0, and describes the changes that are made to your Windows NT server network as a result.

After this lesson, you will be able to:
- Install Microsoft Internet Information Server 4.0 on an Intel-based computer platform running Windows NT Server 4.0.
- Identify changes to Windows NT Server 4.0 made by the Internet Information Server installation.

Estimated lesson time: 30 minutes

You can choose from several different installation options to fit your needs and your system. The option you select only affects the installation procedure slightly.

Note Although this lesson discusses a full Internet Information Server installation on Windows NT Server 4.0, you can also install the different Internet Information Server installation options on both Windows NT Workstation and Windows 95.

Installation Options

The Internet Information Server installation procedure prompts you to select from three installation options when installing the software. Deciding which of these options you want to install before undertaking the actual installation simplifies the installation process.

Minimum

The Minimum installation option conserves disk space and offers the following limited components:

- *Internet Information Server.* A Web server that uses TCP/IP to host Web sites on the corporate intranet or the Internet.
- *Microsoft Transaction Server (MTS).* A transaction processing system for developing, deploying, and managing distributed server applications. A transaction is a server operation that succeeds or fails as a whole, even if the operation involves many steps. Microsoft Transaction Server also supports process isolation of applications.

- *Active Server Pages*. Enables you to use server-side scripting and components to create browser-independent dynamic content.
- *Microsoft Data Access Components*. Eases use of databases with support for a variety of connections including Microsoft ActiveX Data Objects with Remote Data Service, and OLE DB. OLE DB is a data-access interface that provides consistent access to Structured Query Language (SQL) and non-SQL data sources.
- *Posting Acceptor*. Makes it possible for others to upload files to your Web site.
- *FrontPage Extensions*. Allows the use of Microsoft FrontPage to manage your Web site, as well as create the site content.
- *Microsoft Management Console (MMC)*. Provides the ability to custom-design administration tools that "snap-in." Microsoft Management Console creates a uniform look and feel, regardless of the administration tool being used.
- *Internet Service Manager snap-in*. Offers complete control of your Web and FTP sites with a wizard-driven graphical interface.
- *Microsoft Transaction Server snap-in*. Manages applications and transaction components graphically. A transaction is a server operation that succeeds or fails as a whole, even if the operation involves many steps. Microsoft Transaction Server also supports process isolation of applications.
- *Index Server*. Creates a site index and search for text in a variety of formats.
- *Context-sensitive Help*. Supplies documentation for Microsoft Management Console and context-sensitive Help for the interfaces.

Typical

The Typical installation option includes all of the components offered in the Minimum installation option in addition to the following components:

- *File Transfer Protocol (FTP) Service*. Installs the necessary components to operate an FTP server.
- *Internet Service Manager (HTML)*. Administers your Web and FTP sites from across the intranet or the Internet by using a Web browser.
- *Documentation*. Provides online documentation covering server administration, content management, and content development, including indexing, scripting, and programming.
- *Programmability*. The Microsoft Script Debugger provides you with a comprehensive debugging environment for testing and correcting errors in your Web document scripts. You can use Microsoft Script Debugger to debug both client scripts and server scripts.
- *Additional Services*. The Java Virtual Machine makes it possible to run Java applications on the server.

Custom

The Custom installation option offers a choice of all components included with Internet Information Server. In addition to the previously listed components, the following options are available:

- *Site Server Express*. Enables you to analyze activity logs to determine site usage statistics and check links on your Web site to be sure they are functioning properly.
- *Windows Scripting Host*. Enables you to use Cscript or Wscript to administer servers from the command prompt.
- *Web Publishing wizard*. Makes sending files to another server for publishing quick and simple.
- *Additional Documentation*. Complete documentation for all of the installable components.
- *SMTP Service*. Supports SMTP.
- *NNTP Service*. Supports NNTP used for discussion groups.
- *Certificate Server*. Enables you to issue your own client and server certificates.

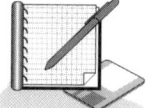

Practice

After you have made sure that your system meets the minimum requirements for Internet Information Server and you have installed Windows NT Server with TCP/IP and NTFS, you can proceed with the installation.

Perform this practice to ensure your computer is configured adequately for the subsequent practices in this book. In this practice, you install all of the optional Internet Information Server components including Site Server and Index Server. This prepares your system for practices in later chapters.

Note Certain options available to you during setup may vary if you have previous versions of Internet Information Server installed on your computer. During installation, you should select all the options available to you. In addition, for the purposes of this book, avoid changing the default folders. Subsequent references assume that files are contained in the default folders.

Caution Do not cancel the installation process once you have started it. If you decide not to install Internet Information Server, finish the installation, and then use the **Remove All** button in Setup to remove the product from your disk or select specific components to remove only those from your disk.

Chapter 2 Installing Microsoft Internet Information Server

▶ **To install Internet Information Server 4.0**
1. From the course compact disc, double-click **setup.exe** in the \Software folder.
   The **Microsoft Windows NT 4.0 Option Pack Setup** dialog box appears.
2. Click **Next**.
   The End User License Agreement appears.
3. Click **Accept**.
   You are prompted to choose Minimum, Typical, or Custom installation.

▶ **To select components and folders**
1. Click **Custom**.
   The options available for installation appear.
2. Scroll down the list and select all components, including **Certificate Server**.
3. Select **Internet Information Server (IIS)**.
4. Click **Show Subcomponents**.
5. Select **Internet NNTP Service**.
6. Click **OK**.
7. Click **Next**.
   You are prompted for the default World Wide Web (WWW) and FTP publishing folders and the application installation folder.
8. Click **Next** to accept the default folders.
   You are prompted for the Microsoft Transaction Server destination folder.
9. Click **Next**.
   You are prompted for the Administration Account (local).
10. Click **Next** to accept the default account.
    You are prompted for the Microsoft Index Server destination folder.
11. Click **Next**.
    You are prompted for the Microsoft Mail Server destination folder.
12. Click **Next**.
    You are prompted to create the mailroot path.

13. Click **Yes**.

    You are prompted for the Microsoft News Server destination folder.

14. Click **Next**.

    You are prompted to create the nntpfile path.

15. Click **Yes**.

    The **Microsoft Certificate Server** dialog box appears.

▶ To add Microsoft Certificate Server

1. Type **C:\Inetpub** in **Shared Folder** to configure the storage location for Certificate Server. Use the default database location and log location.
2. Click **Next**.
3. Click **OK** to create the C:\Winnt\System32\Certlog folder.

    You are prompted to enter identifying information for Certificate Server.

4. Complete the **Identifying Information** dialog box with your information according to the following table.

For this entry	Type
Name	Your name
Organization	The name of your organization
Organizational Unit	The name of your department or division
Locality	The name of your city or town
State	The name of your state
Country	The name of your country

Note If the **Important Notice** dialog box appears with a warning concerning the length of the CA name, click **OK** to return to the **Microsoft Certificate Server Setup** dialog box. Either add a character to the CA name or remove a character, and then click **Next**.

▶ **To finish Setup**

1. When Setup is complete, click **Finish**.

   You are prompted to restart the computer.

2. Click **Yes**.
3. Log on as **Administrator**.

Installation Changes to Windows NT Server

A complete installation of Internet Information Server modifies your Windows NT Server in several ways. It adds a metabase, a new user account, Microsoft Management Console, and counters to Performance Monitor.

The metabase is a database that the Internet Information Server installation adds to the Windows NT system to handle Internet Information Server configuration settings. The metabase performs some of the same functions as the Windows NT system registry but uses less disk space.

Note The metabase can be found at C:\Winnt\System32\Inetsvr\Metabase.bin

Windows NT services are found in Control Panel. Installing Internet Information Server adds the following services to Windows NT Server 4.0:

- Content Index (Index Server)
- FTP Publishing Service
- IIS Admin Service (Internet Service Manager snap-in)
- Microsoft Network News Transfer Protocol (NNTP) Service
- Microsoft Simple Mail Transfer Protocol (SMTP) Service
- MSDTC (Microsoft Distributed Transaction Coordinator)
- World Wide Web Publishing Service

User Manager for Domains is found on the **Administrative Tools** menu. Installing Internet Information Server adds the user account IUSR_*computername* to the system. For example, if your computer is named Server1, you will find the user account IUSR_Server1 on the list of users after installing Internet Information Server. You can use this tool to manage security for domains, member servers, and workstations.

The Internet Information Server installation adds Microsoft Management Console to the **Internet Service Manager** menu. The root folder listings provided by Microsoft Management Console allow you to configure all of the components of Internet Information Server with a single tool.

You can find Performance Monitor on the **Administrative Tools** menu of Microsoft Management Console. Performance Monitor is a Windows NT feature with which you can monitor specific kinds of performance. Installing Internet Information Server adds the following counters to Performance Monitor:

- Active Server Pages (ASP)
- Content Index
- Content Index Filter
- FTP Service
- HTTP Content Index
- Internet Information Services Global
- NNTP Server Client Requests
- NNTP Server Service
- SMTP Server
- Web Service

Practice

In this practice, you inspect the Windows NT Server environment to identify changes made by installing Internet Information Server.

▶ **To view the changes made in the Windows NT Server environment**

1. Click the **Start** button, point to **Settings**, and then click **Control Panel**.

   Control Panel appears.

2. Double-click the Services icon.

   The **Services** dialog box appears.

3. Scroll through the services available.

   Are there any publishing services listed?

   _____

4. Close the **Services** dialog box.
5. Close **Control Panel**.
6. Click the **Start** button, point to **Programs**, point to **Administrative Tools**, and then click **User Manager for Domains**.

   The User Manager window appears.

7. Examine the list of names.

   Is there an Internet Guest Account listed?

   _____

Chapter 2   Installing Microsoft Internet Information Server   25

8. Close the User Manager window.
9. Click the **Start** button, point to **Programs**, point to **Administrative Tools**, and then click **Performance Monitor**.

    Performance Monitor appears.
10. On the **Edit** menu, click **Add To Chart**.

    The **Add to Chart** dialog box appears.
11. Click the **Object** box.

    The list of objects appears.
12. Examine the items in the list for Internet-related items.

    Are there any Internet-related items in the list?

    _____

    If so, what are the names of the items that can be monitored?

    _____

    _____

    _____

    _____

13. Close the **Add to Chart** dialog box.
14. Close Performance Monitor.

Summary

Once you have met the system requirements and configured your Windows NT Server 4.0 operating system, you can install Microsoft Internet Information Server. You must choose from the Minimum, Typical, and Custom installation options to determine what is installed on your computer. A full installation of Internet Information Server adds several new components to the operating system.

Review

The following questions are intended to reinforce key information presented in this chapter. If you are unable to answer a question, review the appropriate lesson, and then try the question again.

1. Will Internet Information Server installed on an Intel platform computer differ from Internet Information Server installed on an Alpha platform computer?

2. Does Internet Information Server have any particular Web browser requirements?

3. If you want to run Microsoft SMTP Service, do you need to configure your operating system in any special way before installing Internet Information Server?

4. If you want to set up Internet Information Server to run Microsoft Transaction Server, but also want to take advantage of the remote administration features of Internet Service Manager (HTML), which installation option should you choose?

CHAPTER 3

Managing Internet Information Server

Lesson 1 Microsoft Management Console . . . 28

Lesson 2 Internet Information Server Administrative Tools . . . 32

Lesson 3 Internet Information Server Metabase . . . 38

Review . . . 41

About This Chapter

This chapter gives you an overview of Microsoft Management Console, including a description of the interface, how to use it, and how to save a console once you have created it. It also describes the different tools you have with which to administer Microsoft Internet Information Server (IIS). Finally, this chapter introduces you to the Internet Information Server metabase.

Before You Begin

To complete the lessons in this chapter, you must have installed Internet Information Server as described in Chapter 2, "Installing Microsoft Internet Information Server."

Lesson 1: Microsoft Management Console

Microsoft Management Console is the primary management interface for Microsoft Internet Information Server 4.0. This lesson introduces you to Microsoft Management Console, describes the interface, and teaches you how to save and restore a console after you have created it.

After this lesson, you will be able to:
- Describe Microsoft Management Console and how it can help you manage your server.
- Select nodes and access property sheets through Microsoft Management Console.
- Configure and save consoles using Microsoft Management Console.

Estimated lesson time: 20 minutes

Microsoft Management Console is a cross-application, shared management tool that provides a way to administer multiple network-management programs. In addition to shipping as a component of the Microsoft Windows NT 4.0 Option Pack, Microsoft Management Console will be incorporated into releases of other Microsoft products such as Windows NT and all Microsoft BackOffice products.

While Microsoft Management Console itself does not give you any additional functionality, it does provide a common environment for snap-ins. Snap-ins provide the actual management environment for each associated product. For Internet Information Server, the implemented snap-in is Internet Service Manager (ISM). When you start Internet Service Manager, Microsoft Management Console starts and loads the Internet Service Manager snap-in.

Note In future releases of all Microsoft BackOffice products, including the Windows NT operating system itself, administrative tools will be converted to Microsoft Management Console snap-ins. Microsoft Management Console specifications are also available to third-party companies, and many third-party software vendors will ship products managed by snap-ins.

▶ **To open Microsoft Management Console**
- Click the **Start** button, point to **Programs**, point to **Windows NT 4.0 Option Pack**, point to **Microsoft Internet Information Server**, and then click **Internet Service Manager**.

  Microsoft Management Console starts and displays the Internet Service Manager snap-in. If necessary, close the Tip of the Day.

Features of Microsoft Management Console

Because it is a single, fully customizable framework, Microsoft Management Console simplifies the management of your Internet implementation.

With Microsoft Management Console, you have total console customization. You can create management consoles that include only the exact administrative tools you need. Customizing consoles in this way enables you to conduct task-based administration. By creating a tool set that relates more closely to the tasks that need to be performed, you can avoid displaying a lot of unused objects and features.

Because snap-ins run within a common framework in Microsoft Management Console, you can manage multiple network products through this single integrated interface. Due to the demands of this framework, all snap-ins must conform to the same specifications. This means that all snap-ins have a similar look and feel, which makes it easy for you to learn how to use each tool.

Microsoft Management Console does not restrict you to any specific protocols. This allows you to use products of your choice with the confidence that you can manage them seamlessly and without compatibility problems.

The Microsoft Management Console Interface

With Microsoft Management Console, the interface you use to manage your server is the Microsoft Management Console window.

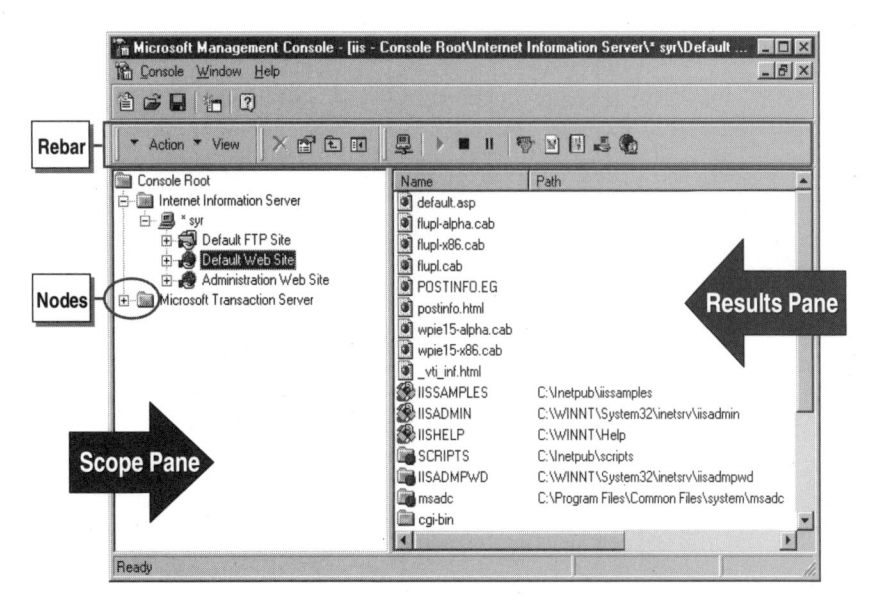

The components of the Microsoft Management Console interface are as follows:

- *Scope pane*. The scope pane is the left window in Microsoft Management Console and corresponds to the left pane in Windows NT Explorer. The scope pane lists all of the services that can be administered through Microsoft Management Console. This hierarchy of services is also called the namespace. This may include multiple (hardware) servers and multiple services, such as Microsoft Transaction Server (MTS) and FTP Server.
- *Results pane*. The right window in Microsoft Management Console is the results pane and corresponds to the right pane in Windows NT Explorer. When you select a node in the scope pane, the results pane displays a list of all elements and services that fall within the selected node's domain.
- *Rebar*. In addition to the two window panes, Microsoft Management Console has three menu bars, the lowest of which is the Rebar. The Rebar consists of **Action** and **View** menus, plus two additional toolbars, or bands. The commands associated with Rebar menus and bands all change with respect to the selected node. Functions tied to individual services, such as Performance Monitor for Internet Information Server, are all found on the Rebar.
- *Nodes*. Nodes, which appear in the tree view of the scope pane, are instances of individual services. For example, a computer on a network or a Web service on a particular (hardware) server may appear as a node in the scope pane of Microsoft Management Console. You can open the property sheets of any node by right-clicking it and then selecting **Properties** on the shortcut menu.

You can manage the services represented in Microsoft Management Console by taking action on the contents of the results pane or by using the commands in the toolbars and command menus. Command menus and bands on the Rebar change automatically to correspond to the selected node.

Tip You can create multiple windows within Microsoft Management Console. Each window can have a different view of the current namespace. The console always has one current master namespace; each child window may just provide a different view of that master namespace. Multiple windows enable you to view and switch to multiple parts of the console interface at once.

Once you have created a console you like by loading snap-ins and arranging windows, you can save the console to a file (with the .msc file extension). When you load the file later, you recreate the saved console state.

Because saved console files—called tools—are not tied to large amounts of managed data, you can create multiple console files and share them by e-mail or other means. Designating shared tools as read-only prevents the people using the tools from changing them.

Summary

Microsoft Management Console is a cross-application, shared management tool that serves as the primary management interface for Internet Information Server. The console window is the interface you use to manage your server. This interface is a fully customizable framework that you can save to a file in order to recreate the saved console state at a later time.

Lesson 2: Internet Information Server Administrative Tools

Internet Information Server relies on three tools for its administrative functionality. The Internet Service Manager snap-in allows you to configure Internet Information Server settings through Microsoft Management Console. The Hypertext Markup Language (HTML) version of Internet Service Manager allows you to configure Internet Information Server settings remotely by means of Web access. Finally, you can use the Windows Scripting Host (WSH) to automate server administration through scripts. This lesson introduces you to these three administrative tools.

After this lesson, you will be able to:
- Describe the core functionality of the Internet Service Manager snap-in for Microsoft Management Console.
- Using the Internet Service Manager snap-in for Microsoft Management Console, configure the Master Properties for the WWW Service and FTP Service.
- Describe the methods of administering Internet Information Server 4.0.

Estimated lesson time: 25 minutes

You can manage Internet Information Server both locally and remotely through the different versions of Internet Service Manager.

Internet Service Manager Snap-in

Internet Service Manager helps you configure and monitor all Internet Information Server services running on Windows NT Server. Starting Internet Service Manager adds a node to Microsoft Management Console from which you can administer Internet Information Server services.

The Internet Service Manager snap-in provides the following band of administrative tools for the server on the Rebar of the child window:

- *User Manager*. Use to manage user and group accounts.
- *Server Manager*. Use to manage server properties, services, and file sharing.
- *Event Viewer*. Use to monitor server hits and record network-related events.
- *Performance Monitor*. Use to monitor server performance.
- *Key Manager*. Use to manage user authentication codes.

Chapter 3 Managing Internet Information Server

You also get additional administrative functions, such as creating folders and configuring property sheets, through the **Action** menu on the Rebar.

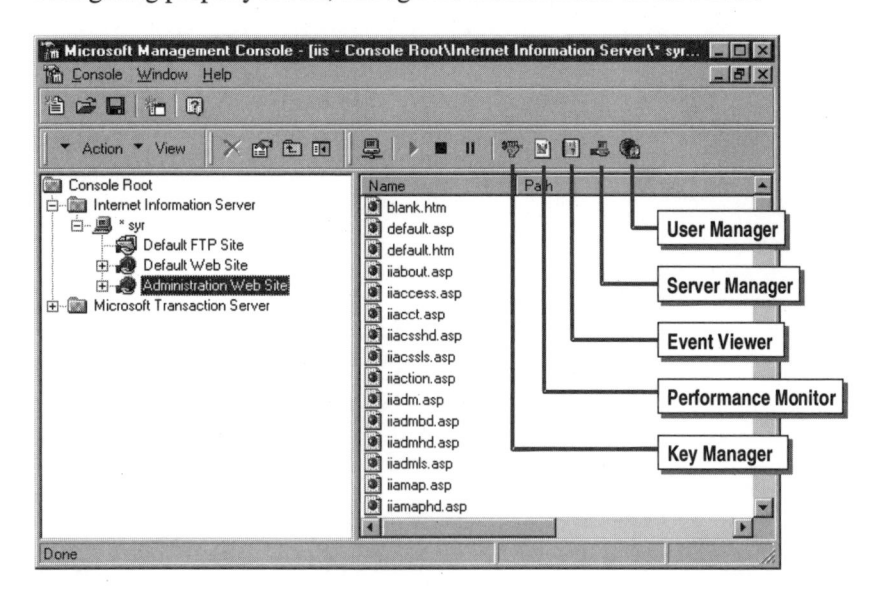

Practice

In this practice, you use Internet Service Manager to establish default settings for future World Wide Web (WWW) virtual servers by configuring the WWW Service Master Properties.

▶ **To configure the WWW Service Master Properties**

1. Click the **Start** button, point to **Programs**, point to **Windows NT 4.0 Option Pack**, point to **Microsoft Internet Information Server**, and then click **Internet Service Manager**.

    Microsoft Management Console starts and displays the Internet Service Manager snap-in. If necessary, close the Tip of the Day.

2. Click the **+** sign next to the Internet Information Server folder.

    The Internet Information Server folder opens and displays the icon for your computer.

3. Right-click the computer icon, and then click **Properties**.

   The *computername* **Properties** dialog box appears.

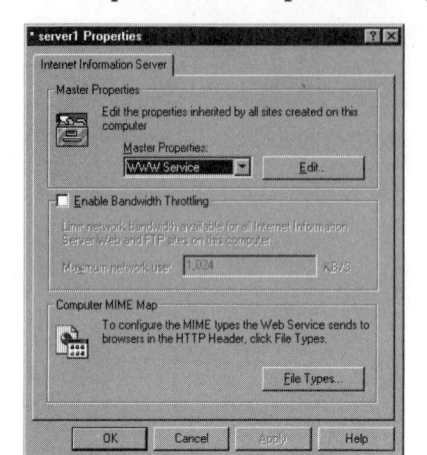

4. Under **Master Properties**, click **Edit**.

   The **WWW Service Master Properties for** *computername* dialog box appears.

5. On the **Performance** tab, move the **Performance Tuning** slider control to **Fewer than 10,000**.

6. On the **Web Site** tab, change the **Connection Timeout** to 120 seconds.

7. Click **OK**.

8. Click **OK**.

   This finishes the configuration of the WWW Service Master Properties. You learn more about configuring Master Properties in Chapter 5, "Configuring the WWW Service."

In this practice, you establish default settings for future File Transfer Protocol (FTP) virtual servers by configuring the FTP Service Master Properties.

▶ **To configure the FTP Service Master Properties**

1. Right-click the computer icon, and then click **Properties**.

   The *computername* **Properties** dialog box appears.

2. Under **Master Properties**, change the service to **FTP Service**.

3. Click **Edit**.

   The **FTP Service Master Properties for** *computername* dialog box appears.

4. On the **Home Directory** tab, click **Read**.

   A check mark appears next to **Read**.

5. On the **Messages** tab, type the welcome, exit, and maximum connections messages.

6. On the **FTP Site** tab, change the **Connection Timeout** to 60 seconds.

7. Click **OK**.

8. Click **OK**.

   This finishes the configuration of the FTP Service Master Properties.

9. Close Microsoft Management Console.

   You are prompted to save the changes to Iis.msc.

10. Click **Yes**.

    Microsoft Management Console saves your configuration changes and closes.

Internet Service Manager (HTML)

With Internet Information Server, you can also manage your server remotely from anywhere on the Internet or your company-wide intranet using HTML-based Administration, or HTMLA.

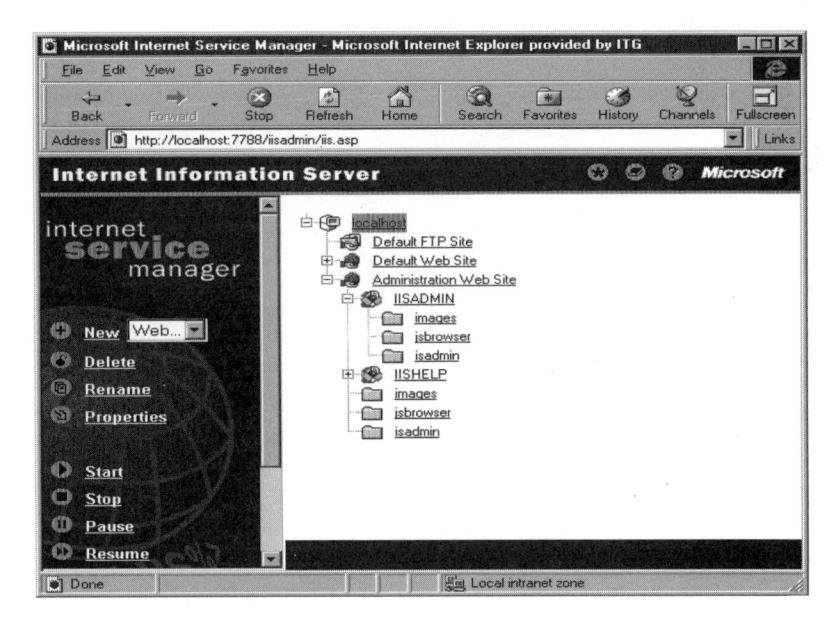

The HTML version of Internet Service Manager provides most of the same features and functions of the Internet Service Manager snap-in for Microsoft Management Console. A user can manage accounts, track event logs, monitor performance, adjust server properties, administer authentication keys, and perform other server-management functions through either HTMLA or Microsoft Management Console. Although HTMLA offers many of the same features as the snap-in, property changes such as certificate mapping—which require coordination with Windows NT utilities—cannot be made with the HTML version of Internet Service Manager.

Note For security purposes, the port number in an HTMLA connection is randomly assigned.

The HTMLA tool relies on integrated component architecture. This architecture is based on Component Object Model (COM) and Distributed Component Object Model (DCOM) standards.

COM, the basis of OLE and Microsoft ActiveX technologies, is Microsoft's software component model. COM components are encapsulated objects that have a set of structured interfaces. This standardization enables different applications or components to communicate freely with one another.

DCOM provides distributed services to COM. Such services allow various components to communicate across a network easily. As a single-vendor standard, DCOM represents a uniform interoperability mechanism. In this way, DCOM contrasts with CORBA/IIOP, a multivendor distributed-object standard for networks comprised of heterogeneous systems.

Note For additional information on COM and DCOM, please refer to *Understanding ActiveX and OLE*, by David Chappell (Microsoft Press, 1996).

Windows Scripting Host

Windows Scripting Host (WSH) is a language-independent scripting host for 32-bit Microsoft Windows platforms. WSH enables you to execute scripts directly on the Windows desktop (Wscript.exe) or command console (Cscript.exe), without embedding those scripts in an HTML document. WSH is ideal for non-interactive scripting needs such as logon scripting and administrative scripting.

Internet Information Server is scriptable in languages such as VBScript and JavaScript.

Because it employs the ActiveX scripting architecture, you can automate Internet Information Server management routines with scripts in languages such as Microsoft Visual Basic Scripting Editing (VBScript) and Microsoft JScript. Microsoft MS-DOS® command scripts are also supported.

Summary

There are three administrative tools with which you can manage Internet Information Server. The Internet Service Manager snap-in allows you to manage the server through Microsoft Management Console while the HTMLA tool allows you to do the same administrative tasks remotely by means of a Web browser. Finally, you can automate non-interactive administrative tasks with the WSH.

Lesson 3: Internet Information Server Metabase

The Internet Information Server metabase is a memory-resident data store that contains Internet Information Server configuration parameters. You can also use the metabase to store and manage configuration parameters for your custom Internet Information Server applications. In this lesson, you learn how to identify the key entries in the Internet Information Server metabase and how to configure the metabase on your own.

After this lesson, you will be able to:
- Describe the purpose and identify the key entries in the Internet Information Server metabase.
- Describe and configure the Internet Information Server metabase.

Estimated lesson time: 10 minutes

The Internet Information Server metabase is specifically designed for Internet Information Server needs. It is faster, more flexible, and more expandable than the Windows NT registry. Many registry keys that existed for previous versions of Internet Information Server have been migrated to the metabase, but the registry has not disappeared. The keys that remain in the registry are used to initiate Internet services and to enable backwards compatibility with older versions of Internet Information Server. Any new configuration information that you write, however, should be written to the metabase.

Configuring Metabase Entries

There are two programming techniques with which you can manipulate settings in the metabase.

- *IIS Admin Objects*. You can use the IIS Admin Objects with automation languages, such as Microsoft Visual Basic Scripting Edition (VBScript). With this tool you can administer IIS configuration settings through simple Active Server Page (ASP) scripts and other automation language programs. The IIS Admin Objects have been developed to COM standards.
- *IIS Admin Base Object*. The IIS Admin Base Object is designed for C++ programs and eliminates most of the overhead associated with the conversion of variant data. This object provides better performance than the IIS Admin Objects and has been developed to DCOM standards.

> **Caution** Incorrectly configuring properties in the metabase can cause problems, including the failure of a Web or FTP site. If you make mistakes, your Web or FTP site's configuration could be damaged. You should edit metabase properties only for settings that you cannot adjust in the user interface, and you should be very careful whenever you edit the metabase directly.

Metabase properties configured at higher levels, such as the Web site Master Properties level, can be passed on—or inherited—by the lower levels, such as the folder properties level. You can individually edit these inherited properties at the lower level, as well. Once you change a property on an individual server, folder, or file, changes to the settings at the higher level do not automatically override the lower individual setting. The metabase properties tables indicate whether a property is inheritable or not.

The Metabase Properties Tables

The metabase stores server properties in tables. The following table is a key to metabase entries and configuration information.

Task or functional area: A description of the task to be completed using Internet Service Manager, and the metabase property that is modified as a result.
Range: The scope of values that a property can have. **Default:** The value that a property maintains without user intervention. **Location in ISM:** Name of the property sheet or dialog box in Internet Service Manager that allows the modification of the property. **Can be configured at:** Indication of what levels in the metabase hierarchy (computer, Web site, FTP site, virtual directory, directory, or file) the property can be affected.
Description of the property and the implications of modifying it.

Key Metabase Entries

The metabase does not include all of the entries of the Windows NT registry, only those pertinent to Internet Information Server administration. For these settings, the metabase offers more advanced features including speed, scriptability, and remote administration. The following list describes the types of property settings stored in the metabase.

- *Computer and Web site properties*. Properties configurable at the computer and Web site level.
- *Logging properties*. Properties configurable for Web site activity logging.
- *FTP-specific properties*. Properties configurable for FTP services only.
- *HTTP-specific properties*. Properties configurable for Hypertext Transport Protocol (HTTP) services only.

- *Virtual directory and directory properties.* Properties configurable at the virtual directory and directory level.
- *File properties.* Properties configurable at the file level.
- *Filter properties.* Properties configurable for filters.
- *SSL key properties.* Properties configurable for Secure Sockets Layer (SSL) keys.

Summary

The Internet Information Server metabase is a fast-access, hierarchical, memory-resident data store specifically designed for Internet Information Server needs. It contains the Internet Information Server configuration parameters and is faster, more flexible, and more expandable than the Windows NT registry. There are two programming techniques with which you can manipulate settings in the metabase, but you should be very careful whenever you directly edit the metabase.

Review

The following questions are intended to reinforce key information presented in this chapter. If you are unable to answer a question, review the appropriate lesson, and then try the question again.

1. What is the primary function of Microsoft Management Console?

2. What Internet Information Server tools allow a user to administer a Web site?

3. Can you share customized consoles among the members of your group?

4. How can a user access the property sheets associated with a particular Web service?

5. What is the purpose of the Internet Information Server metabase?

CHAPTER 4

Understanding Internet Information Server Architecture

Lesson 1 TCP/IP Architecture . . . 44

Lesson 2 Server Architecture . . . 47

Lesson 3 Administration Architecture . . . 56

Review . . . 58

About This Chapter

This chapter introduces you to the Microsoft Internet Information Server (IIS) 4.0 architecture. It describes the Transmission Control Protocol/Internet Protocol (TCP/IP), Server, and Administration frameworks and their components. This chapter also discusses how each of these different pieces of Internet Information Server serve overall Internet Information Server functionality.

Before You Begin

There are no prerequisites to complete this chapter. To view the optional Overview of the TCP/IP Protocol Suite multimedia presentation, you must have the course compact disc.

Lesson 1: TCP/IP Architecture

Microsoft Internet Information Server provides Internet communication by incorporating a number of different TCP/IP protocols. This lesson introduces you to these supported protocols and describes their relationship to Internet Information Server.

After this lesson, you will be able to:
- List and describe the Internet Protocols (IPs) used between a client and Internet Information Server.

Estimated lesson time: 10 minutes

Multimedia Presentation: Overview of the TCP/IP Protocol Suite

This optional 15-minute multimedia presentation provides an overview of the TCP/IP protocol suite and explains how the protocols in the suite work internally with other protocols. The information in this presentation applies to Microsoft TCP/IP and most other implementations of TCP/IP. To view this presentation, run the Tcpip.exe presentation file on the course compact disc.

Internet Information Server supports the following TCP/IP protocols:

- Hypertext Transfer Protocol (HTTP)
- File Transfer Protocol (FTP)
- Simple Mail Transfer Protocol (SMTP)
- Network News Transfer Protocol (NNTP)
- Post Office Protocol version 3 (POP3)
- Internet Messaging Access Protocol (IMAP)

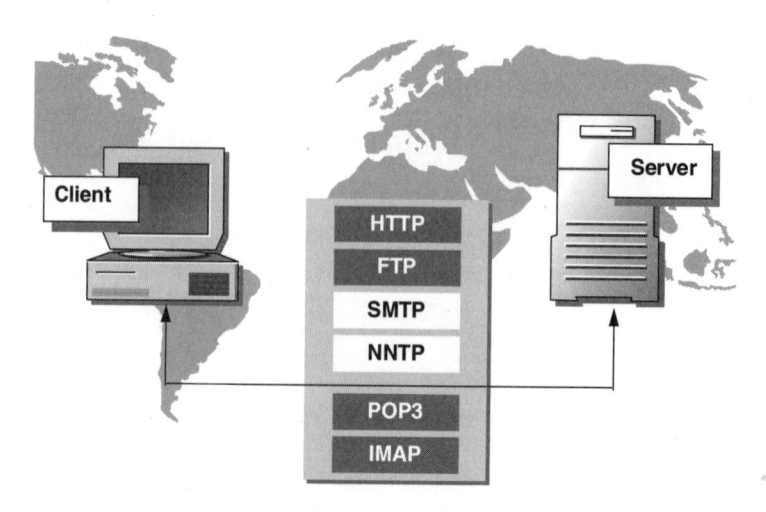

Note Internet Information Server 4.0 does not support the Gopher protocol.

HTTP

HTTP is the client/server protocol used by the WWW Service that allows clients to interact with servers in order to perform specified, Web-related tasks. For example, when a user clicks a hyperlink on a Web page, HTTP is what allows the server to replace the existing page with the new page on the user's screen. Currently, Internet Information Server interfaces to HTTP version 1.1 using Windows Sockets (WinSock).

FTP

FTP was designed to move files between two computers on a TCP/IP network. Internet Information Server supports FTP through Windows Sockets. This means that although FTP uses Transmission Control Protocol (TCP) as its transport protocol for all communication and data exchanges between the client and server, Internet Information Server first communicates with Windows Sockets and then Windows Sockets interfaces with TCP.

SMTP

SMTP is used to exchange e-mail on a TCP/IP network. Microsoft uses TCP as its transport protocol for all exchanges between the e-mail client and server.

NNTP

NNTP is used to read messages posted in news groups on the Internet. Microsoft NNTP uses TCP as its transport protocol for all exchanges between the news client and server.

POP3

POP3 is a standard e-mail server commonly used on the Internet. It provides a message store that holds incoming e-mail until a user logs on and downloads the data. POP3 is a simple system with little selectivity, meaning that all pending messages and attachments are downloaded at the same time. POP3 uses the SMTP protocol message format.

Internet Information Server supports POP3 for compatibility with Independent Software Vendor (ISV) applications.

IMAP

The IMAP service uses the IMAP protocol and is expected to be widely used on the Internet. Like POP3, IMAP provides a message store that holds incoming e-mail until a user logs on and downloads the data. However, IMAP is more sophisticated than the POP3 e-mail server. With IMAP, users can archive messages in folders, share mailboxes, and access multiple e-mail servers.

Additionally, users can opt to read only message headers; they do not have to accept and download all of their e-mail messages automatically. IMAP is also better integrated than POP3 with Multipurpose Internet Mail Extension (MIME), which is used to attach files to e-mail messages. Like POP3, IMAP accepts SMTP-formatted messages that have been routed across the Internet.

Summary

TCP/IP provides a set of networking protocols that support Internet communication. Internet Information Server supports the HTTP, FTP, SMTP, NNTP, POP3, and IMAP protocols.

Lesson 2: Server Architecture

The Internet Information Server server is constructed around several key components that provide the framework for Internet Information Server server functionality. This lesson introduces you to the key components that make up the Internet Information Server server architecture.

After this lesson, you will be able to:
- List and describe the four key components that make up the Internet Information Server server architecture.
- Describe the path that data takes through Internet Information Server.

Estimated lesson time: 40 minutes

The Internet Information Server server is made up of three distinct service layers and one additional component, which contains elements shared by the different service layers and that together provide the server's communication capabilities.

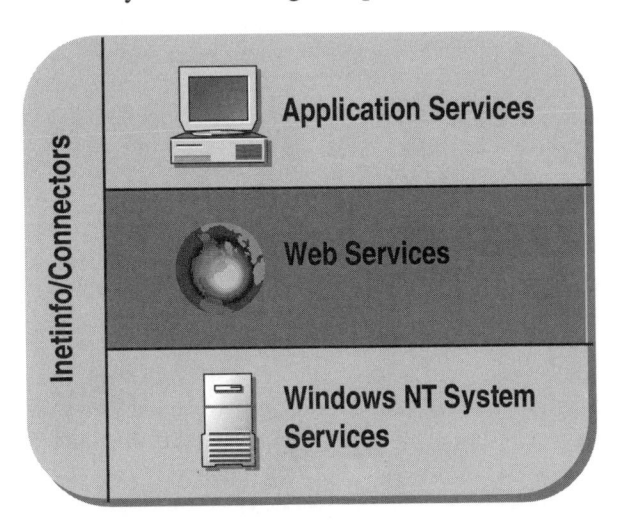

The following are the four primary components of the Internet Information Server server architecture:

- Inetinfo process/connectors
- Microsoft Windows NT system services
- Web services
- Application services

Inetinfo Process

All of the standard Internet services described in the preceding lesson are contained within a process called Internet Information Services Application (Inetinfo). In addition to Internet services, Inetinfo contains the shared thread pool, cache, logging, and simple network management protocol (SNMP) services.

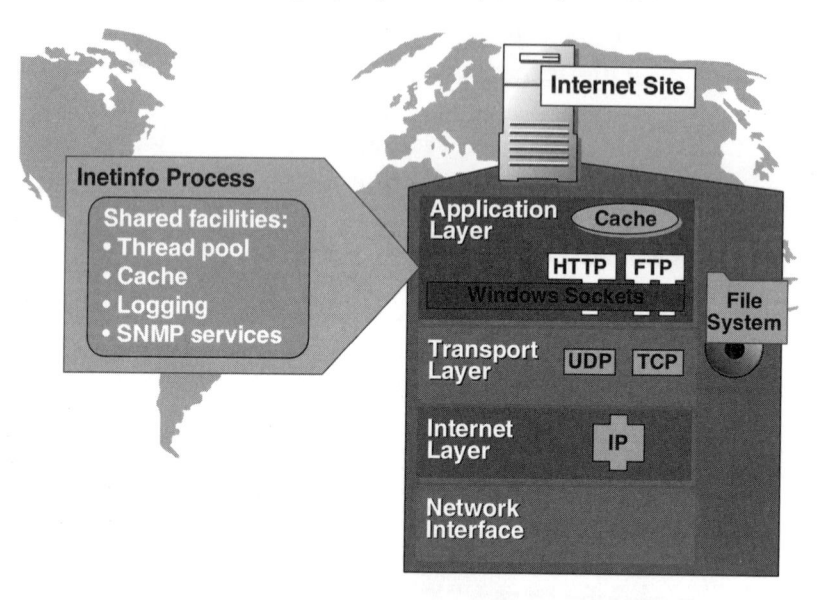

A thread is a unit of execution. It is the component of a process that is actually running at any given time. A thread runs within the process address space, using resources allocated to the process. A thread pool is a group of threads used within the process for a particular operation.

Using threads in a thread pool is an ideal way to create additional execution states. While a full-fledged process has both a separate address space, register set, and execution point, a thread has a separate register set and execution point but shares the address space. For this reason, using threads is faster and more efficient than spawning additional processes to handle tasks for the Web server.

A thread contains:

- A stack for use when running in user mode.
- A stack for use when running in kernel mode.
- A processor state including the current instruction pointer, or register.

The following table describes the eight possible thread states:

Thread state	Description
0	Initialization
1	Ready
2	Running
3	Standby
4	Termination
5	Wait
6	Transition
7	Unknown

Because HTTP and FTP run from within the same process, they are able to share cached data such as file handles, account information, and log file data for logging to text files.

Logging tracks which users access your Web site. Tracking users can help you identify security and performance issues. You can direct logging information to either a log file (that can be processed offline and offers faster performance), or to an Open Database Connectivity (ODBC) Data Source Name (DSN) for dynamic evaluation.

If you monitor your network with SNMP, you can use the SNMP Management Information Bases (MIBs) provided by Internet Information Server to monitor your Web server.

You can use the MIB files included in the software development kit (SDK) folder on the Internet Information Server compact disc with third-party SNMP monitors to enable SNMP monitoring of WWW and FTP services.

Note Internet Information Server supports SNMP monitoring only—configuring the SNMP service is not supported.

You can isolate server applications, which means they will run in a process separate from the Web server process. If an isolated application fails, it will not affect the running of the server. It also will not affect other applications, except for those that work as a unit with the failed application. Isolating an application can also be described as running it in a separate memory space.

Generally, it is a good idea to isolate applications; slightly more memory is used, but the server is less likely to fail if an application fails.

Remote Administration

With Windows NT Server and Internet Information Server, you can set up remote administration for customers. To set up remote administration, you provide each customer with a Windows NT user account and a browser that supports JavaScript and frames, and then set up a Windows NT account for each customer.

Note The customer account does not have to be a Windows NT Administrator account; any Windows NT account can be granted appropriate permissions for Web site maintenance.

You then set permissions on the appropriate virtual servers and directories so that customers can make changes only to their own Web sites. Because you grant each customer permissions for that customer's respective virtual server only, other customers sites on your computer are unaffected by any changes—or any mistakes—that any one customer makes.

If a customer wants to run dynamic Web pages that make use of Microsoft ActiveX scripting or Internet Server Application Programming Interface (ISAPI)-based programs, you can enable the Internet Information Server process isolation feature on those applications. This isolates the scripts or programs so that they cannot affect the other Web sites hosted on the server computer, thus providing protection for your server in the event an application fails.

Connectors

In Internet Information Server, connectors most often appear as extensions. A connector is an ISAPI dynamic-link library (DLL) that acts as a communications pipe between Internet Information Server and a particular service.

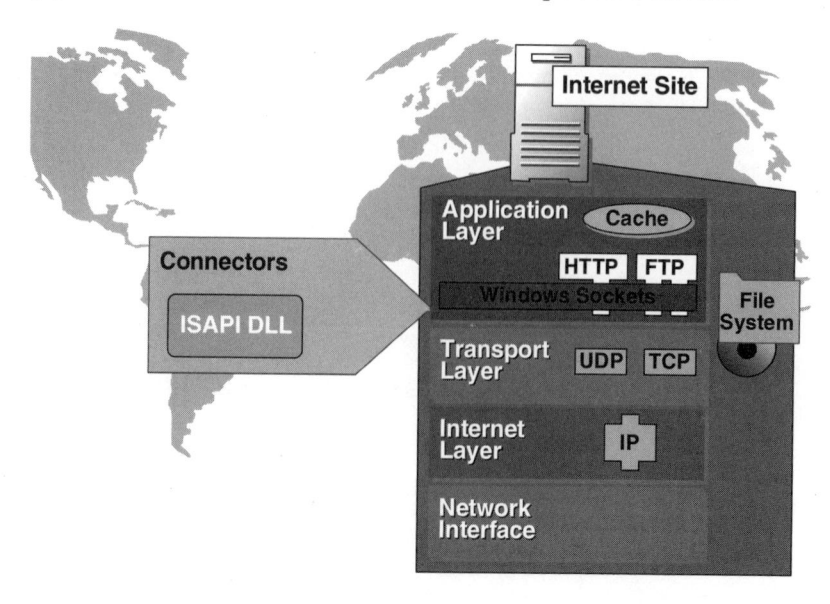

The following connectors are supported by Internet Information Server:

- *Microsoft BackOffice connectors*. These connectors include the following:
  - *The Microsoft Exchange Server/Web connector*. This connector supports public folder integration with Internet Information Server.
  - *The ODBC connector*. This connector allows communication with any ODBC-compliant database engine.
- *Common Gateway Interface (CGI)*. CGI was developed for UNIX-based systems to extend Web server software. Internet Information Server supports CGI applications for backward compatibility.
- *ISAPI filters*. ISAPI filters are used to preprocess packets before they enter or leave the Internet Information Server process. These filters give the Internet Information Server architecture added flexibility. Secure Sockets Layer (SSL) is one example of a Microsoft ISAPI filter.
- *Active Server Pages (ASPs)*. ASPs provide an open scripting system for dynamic creation of Web content.

Windows NT System Services

The Windows NT system services layer is the lowest layer of the Internet Information Server server architecture. Data enters this layer through TCP/IP and exits through Windows Sockets.

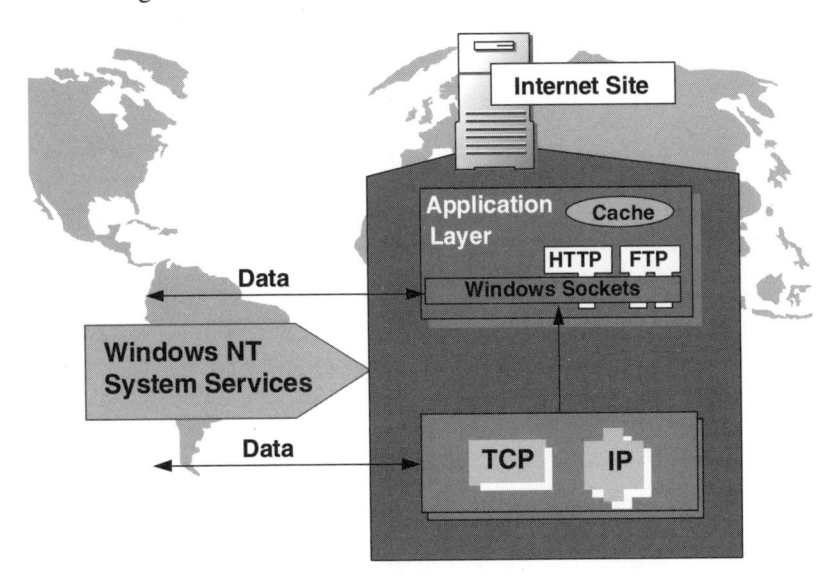

TCP/IP provides a set of networking protocols that support communication across interconnected networks made up of computers with diverse hardware architecture and operating systems.

Windows Sockets (WinSock) is a Microsoft Windows implementation of the widely used UC Berkeley sockets application programming interface (API). Windows Sockets interfaces between programs and the transport protocol and works as a bidirectional pipe for incoming and outgoing data.

The current implementation of WinSock is version 2.0.

Web Services

The middle layer of the Internet Information Server architecture is the Web services layer. This layer houses the core functionality of Internet Information Server.

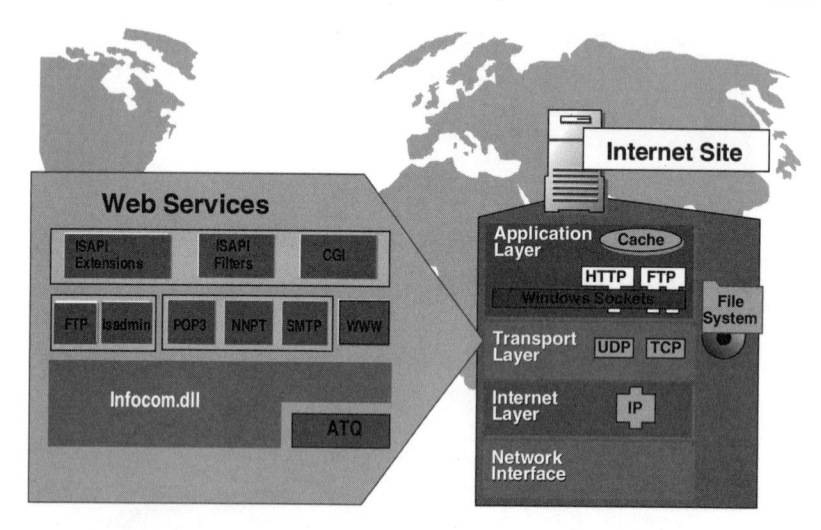

The Asynchronous Thread Queue (ATQ) component maintains the input/output (I/O) threads for handling I/O operations. ATQ handles the Internet Information Server bandwidth throttling feature, which allows you to limit the bandwidth used by the Web site. ATQ, which is included in the Isatq.dll file, also constantly monitors specific TCP sockets.

The Infocom.dll component manages the following functions for Internet Information Server:

- File handling cache
- Security
- Authentication (SSL)
- Administration support

- Utilities
- Service controller interface
- Meta cache (run-time cache)
- Instance support (implements Host Headers for the Web server and multiple domains for the NNTP Service)

The FTP component handles all FTP requests, while the WWW component handles all WWW requests.

Another component of Web services is Isadmin. This component houses the Distribute Component Object Model (DCOM) for the metabase. Isadmin is the gateway for administration of Internet Information Server services.

The SMTP, NNTP, and POP3 components support e-mail and news services for Internet Information Server. Each is a .dll and can support multiple instances of each component.

The Microsoft ISAPI is an alternative to CGI. ISAPI provides the benefits of low overhead, fast loading, better scalability, and efficient use of resources. You can use ISAPI extensions to process requests and generate custom dynamic data.

An ISAPI filter is another type of ISAPI application. You can use an ISAPI filter to receive notifications of various events during the handling of HTTP requests. When it is first loaded, the ISAPI filter (which is a DLL) lets the server know what type of HTTP notifications it can handle. Subsequently, that filter receives those notifications corresponding to those requests whether it is a file, a CGI script, or an ISAPI application.

Because they are extremely powerful, you can use ISAPI filters to facilitate a variety of procedures, including the following:

- Custom authentication schemes
- Compression
- Encryption
- Customized logging
- Traffic or other request analyses

The CGI component supports the use of CGI on an Internet Information Server server. CGI is a server-side interface that you can use to initiate software services. Included with CGI are a set of interfaces that describe how a Web server communicates with software on the same computer. CGI applications allow you to extend a Web server by running applications not native to the server.

Application Services

The Application services layer is the top layer of Internet Information Server architecture. This layer contains some primary extensibility options for Internet Information Server, including ASP and Index Server.

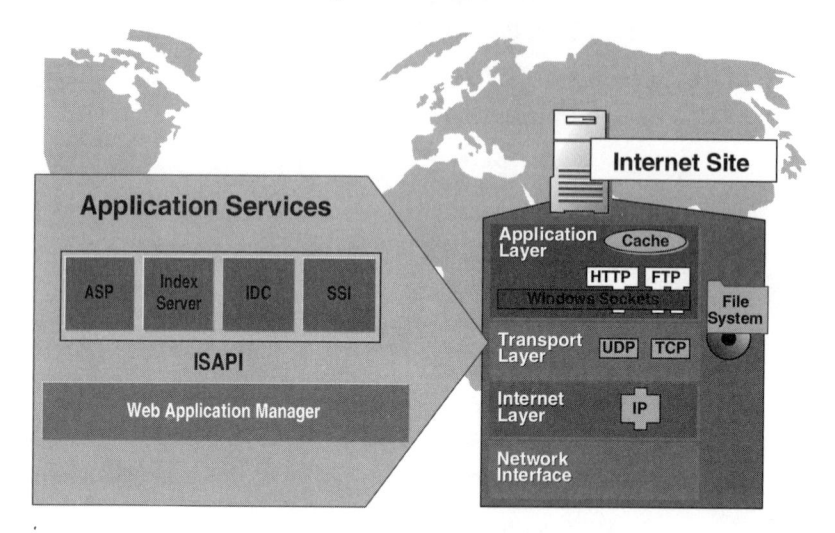

All information enters and exits the Application service layer through the Web Application Manager (WAM). You can find the WAM in the Wam.dll file. WAM sits above the Web services layer and provides Internet Information Server with the following:

- Housing components for ISAPI DLLs
- Translation from ISV to core Internet Information Server features
- Support for multiple ISAPI DLLs
- Recovery for application failure
- A unit for process isolation

ISAPI is an API that resides on a server computer. ISAPI initiates software services that have been tuned for the Windows NT operating system.

The ASP component of the Application services layer provides server-side ASP functionality.

The Index Server component provides functionality for indexing and querying files on Internet Information Server. It is implemented as a separate ISAPI DLL. Index Server objects can also be accessed from ASP.

The HTTP ODBC component supports Internet Database Connector (IDC) scripts. You can use IDC scripts to generate dynamic Web pages from data stored in ODBC-compliant databases.

Note You can access databases and generate dynamic Web pages more efficiently using ASP than through IDC scripts.

The server-side include (SSI) directives component allows Internet Information Server to include text, graphics, or application information in a Hypertext Markup Language (HTML) page just before sending the HTML page to a user. SSI can be used to include, for example, a time or date stamp, a copyright notice, or a form for a customer to fill out and return to your organization. Using SSI to include a file is an easy way to incorporate text or graphics that will be repeated in many files. Rather than typing repeated information into every file, SSI allows you to use a statement to instruct the Web server to read from a single file instead.

The Web server processes SSI directives while it is processes the HTML page. When it reaches an SSI directive, the Web server inserts the contents of the included file directly into the HTML page. If the included file in turn contains an SSI directive, that file is also inserted.

Summary

Four major components make up the Internet Information Server server architecture:

- *Inetinfo process/connectors*. This component contains all of the standard Internet services and connectors supported by Internet Information Server.
- *Windows NT system services*. This is the lowest layer in the Internet Information Server server architecture. Data enters this layer through TCP/IP and exits through Windows Sockets.
- *Web services*. This layer of the Internet Information Server architecture houses the core functionality of Internet Information Server.
- *Application services*. The top layer of Internet Information Server architecture, this layer contains the primary extensibility options for Internet Information Server.

Lesson 3: Administration Architecture

Internet Information Server stores all of its configuration information in a database called the metabase. As a result, Internet Information Server administration revolves around communication with this database. This lesson introduces you to the architecture of Internet Information Server administration.

After this lesson, you will be able to:
- Describe the Internet Information Server architecture that supports administration tools.

Estimated lesson time: 10 minutes

The architecture of Internet Information Server is administered by the metabase and Active Directory Service Interface (ADSI). The following illustration depicts the administration architecture of Internet Information Server.

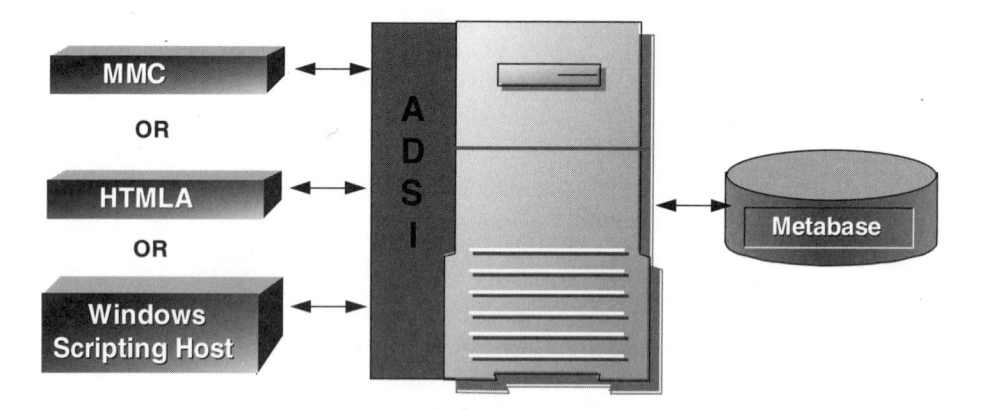

Internet Information Server stores all of its configuration information in a database called the metabase. The metabase replaces the function of the registry for Internet Information Server, as explained in Chapter 3, "Managing Internet Information Server." You can access the metabase by using ADSI. ADSI can also be used as an interface for scripting purposes.

ADSI is a general interface that you can use to administer services in Windows NT. Internet Information Server allows an ADSI provider to connect applications to the metabase using the ADSI interface. You can also use ADSI as a scripting interface.

The Microsoft Management Console (MMC) allows snap-ins hosted by the Microsoft Management Console to communicate with the Internet Information Server metabase.

HTML-based Administration (HTMLA) communicates with the Internet Information Server metabase over the Internet or intranet. This structure enables administration of the Web server even if the Web site is unavailable.

The Windows Scripting Host (WSH) controls the Microsoft ActiveX scripting engines in the same way that Microsoft Internet Explorer does. Because the scripting host is not a full Internet browser, it has a smaller memory footprint than Internet Explorer; therefore, WSH is appropriate for performing simple, quick tasks.

The scripting engine does not use the SCRIPT tag (used in HTML); instead it relies on the file name extension. This way, the script writer does not need to be familiar with the exact ProgID of various script engines. The scripting host maintains a mapping of the script extensions to ProgIDs and uses the Windows association model to launch the appropriate engine.

Summary

The metabase is a database that contains all Internet Information Server configuration information. You can access the metabase using ADSI, which also serves as a connection between your applications and the metabase. Microsoft Management Console, HTMLA, and WSH are all tools with which you can administer Internet Information Server.

Review

The following questions are intended to reinforce key information presented in this chapter. If you are unable to answer a question, review the appropriate lesson, and then try the question again.

1. Describe the features provided by the Inetinfo process.

2. Which Internet Information Server service layer provides support for process isolation? What component provides process isolation?

3. Describe how a data request is routed through the Internet Information Server architecture.

CHAPTER 5

Configuring the WWW Service

Lesson 1 HTTP Defined . . . 60

Lesson 2 WWW Properties . . . 62

Lesson 3 Virtual Directories . . . 81

Lesson 4 Virtual Servers . . . 86

Review . . . 90

About This Chapter

This chapter describes the basic functionality of Hypertext Transport Protocol (HTTP) 1.1 as it relates to the Microsoft Internet Information Server (IIS) 4.0 World Wide Web (WWW) service. It introduces you to the three different types of property sheets within Internet Information Server and how to access them in order to configure your Web sites. This chapter also describes virtual directories and servers, explaining the various methods by which you can add virtual directories and servers to Internet Information Server.

Before You Begin

To complete the lessons in this chapter, you must have installed Internet Information Server as described in Chapter 2, "Installing Microsoft Internet Information Server."

Lesson 1: HTTP Defined

Hypertext Transfer Protocol (HTTP) is the most frequently used protocol on the Internet today. This lesson describes the fundamentals of HTTP.

After this lesson, you will be able to:
- Define HTTP and describe its basic functionality as it relates to the WWW Service.

Estimated lesson time: 5 minutes

HTTP is the protocol that led to the development of the Web. It is a generic, stateless, object-oriented protocol that grew out of a need for a universal protocol to simplify the way users access information on the Internet. HTTP is a client/server protocol located in the Application layer of the Internet protocol stack.

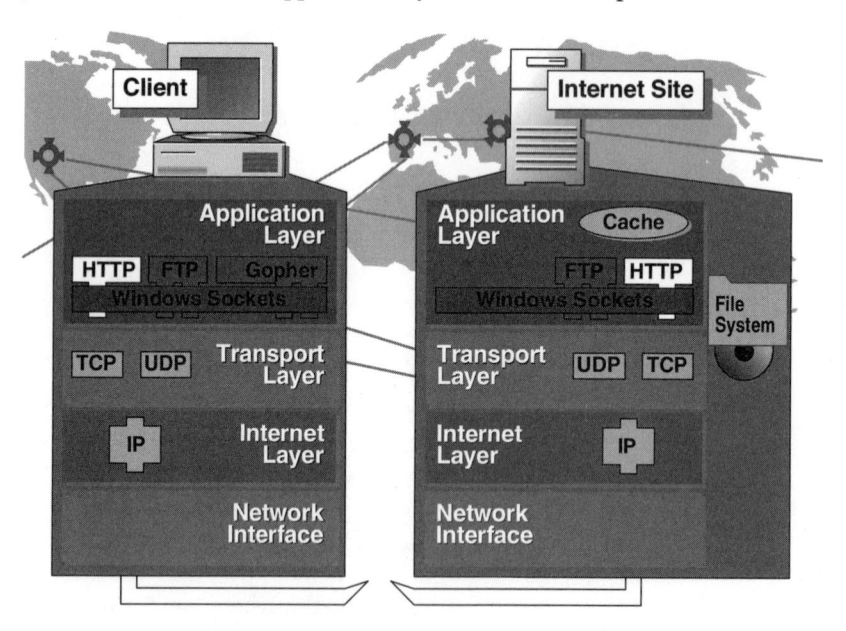

By extending its request methods, or commands, you can use HTTP for many different functions, including name servers and distributed object management systems. Because HTTP categorizes or types data, systems can be built independently of the data being transferred.

HTTP is constantly being improved. The World Wide Web Consortium (W3C) was founded in 1994 to develop common standards for the Web. You can find more information about the W3C at:

http://www.w3.org/

General discussions about HTTP and the applications that use HTTP take place on the following mailing list:

www-talk@w3.org

Summary

HTTP is a client/server protocol that was developed to simplify the way users access information on the Internet. It is a generic, stateless, object-oriented protocol that led to the Web. Because HTTP is constantly changing, the W3C was created to develop standards for the Web.

Lesson 2: WWW Properties

Each Web site that you create on your computer has its own set of property sheets. The general settings, or properties, for a site are displayed in these property sheets and stored in the metabase. In this lesson, you learn about the different types of property sheets.

This lesson describes these different property sheets and demonstrates how to access them in order to set the general properties for a site or file within a site on your computer.

After this lesson, you will be able to:
- List and describe the three types of WWW property sheets and their relationship to one another.
- Locate the WWW property sheets and use them to configure the WWW Service.
- List and describe the functions of the property sheets associated with the WWW Service.

Estimated lesson time: 70 minutes

During installation, Internet Information Server assigns default values to the various properties on the different property sheets. You can publish documents on your site without changing these default settings, and you can easily customize the settings as well.

Each Web site that you create and each file within each Web site has an individual set of property sheets that you can edit in order to customize configuration on a file-by-file or site-by-site basis. You can also edit the default property settings so that all subsequent sites or files are created with your custom configuration.

Types of WWW Property Sheets

There are three different types, or classes, of property sheets within Internet Information Server: the **Master**, **Default**, and **File** property sheets. You can customize configuration of all three types of property sheets, but where you make your changes affects the range of influence the changes have on subsequent sites or files created.

It may be helpful to think of the different types of property sheets in terms of a hierarchy with **Master** property sheets at the top of the hierarchy and **File** property sheets at the bottom. **Master** property sheets determine the properties of the virtual Web sites you create, which in turn determine the properties of the files created within each Web site.

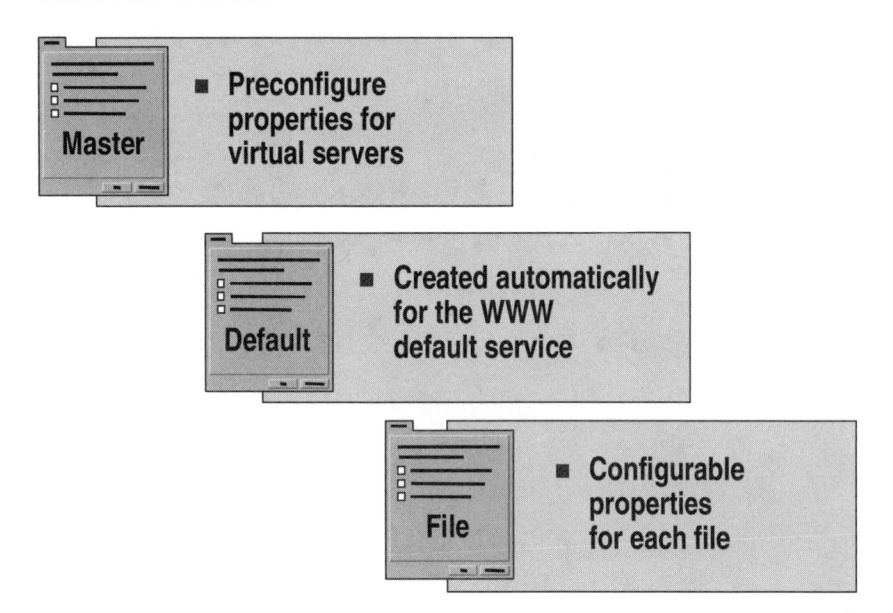

- **Master**: Preconfigure properties for virtual servers
- **Default**: Created automatically for the WWW default service
- **File**: Configurable properties for each file

Master

Master property sheets determine the default properties of every virtual Web site created with this installation of Internet Information Server. During installation, Internet Information Server applies certain default properties to the **Master** property sheets. Every virtual site you create inherits these settings. If you change the settings on the **Master** property sheets, subsequent virtual sites inherit the new settings, but previously created virtual sites do not.

Default

The installation process creates a default Web site with its own default properties. Every file you create within the default Web site inherits these settings.

File

Files created in a virtual directory inherit the virtual directory's property sheet settings, whereas files created in the default Web site inherit the settings of the **Default Web Site Properties** dialog box. After a file is created, the property sheets can be configured on the file level.

WWW Property Sheets

The WWW Service can be configured using a set of nine different property sheets:

- Web Site
- Operators
- Performance
- ISAPI Filters
- Home Directory
- Documents
- Directory Security
- HTTP Headers
- Custom Errors

You can change the settings on these property sheets as needed at any time.

All WWW property sheets can be accessed using the Internet Service Manager (ISM) snap-in for Microsoft Management Console (MMC).

▶ **To access the WWW property sheets**

1. Click the **Start** button, point to **Programs**, point to **Windows NT 4.0 Option Pack**, point to **Microsoft Internet Information Server**, and then click **Internet Service Manager**.
2. In the left pane, double-click the Internet Information Server node.
3. In the left pane, double-click the *computername* node.
4. Right-click **Default Web Site**, and then click **Properties**.

    The **Default Web Site Properties** dialog box appears with tabs for each property sheet.

Web Site

You can use the **Web Site** property sheet to set the Web site identification, specify the number of connections allowed, and enable or disable logging for a Web site.

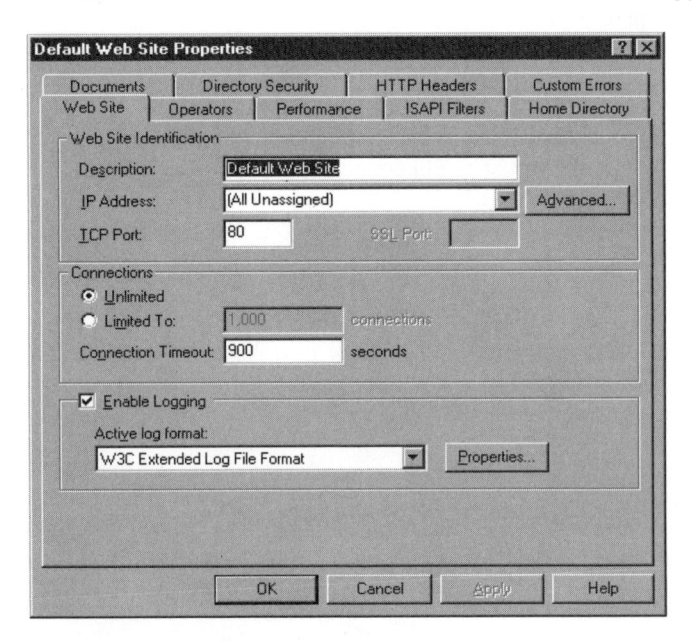

The **Web Site Identification** field allows you to choose a description for your Web site using the following settings:

- **Description**. This dialog box lists the name you choose for your Web site and appears in the tree view of the Internet Service Manager.
- **IP Address**. This dialog box lists the Internet Protocol (IP) address associated with your Web site.
- **TCP Port**. This dialog box determines the port where each service runs. The default is port 80.
- **SSL Port**. This dialog box determines the port used by Secure Sockets Layer (SSL) transmissions.
- **Advanced**. This button opens the **Advanced Multiple Web Site Configuration** dialog box where you can specify additional identities for your Web site.

The **Connections** field allows you to set the number of simultaneous connections to the server using the following settings:

- **Unlimited**. Select this option to allow an unlimited number of simultaneous connections to the server.
- **Limited To**. Select this option to limit the number of simultaneous connections to the server to the number entered in the associated text box.
- **Connection Timeout**. Use this property to set the length of time in seconds before the server disconnects an inactive user.

Select the **Enable Logging** option to activate your Web site's logging features. These can record details about user activity and create logs in your choice of format.

Click the **Properties** button to open the **Microsoft Logging Properties** dialog box. This dialog box allows you to choose how often to create new logs, to specify the file folder for the log, and to select additional extended properties for logging.

Operators

You can use the **Operators** property sheet to control which Microsoft Windows NT User Accounts have administrative privileges for your Web site.

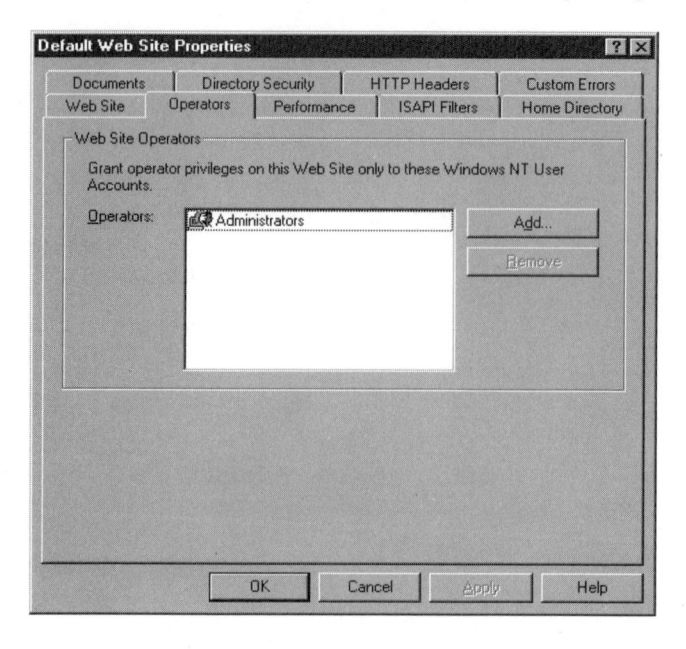

To add a Windows NT User Account to the current list of accounts that have administrative privileges, click the **Add** button. To remove a Windows NT User Account from this list, select the account in the **Operators** box, and then click **Remove**.

Performance

You can use the settings on the **Performance** property sheet to fine-tune your Web site's performance.

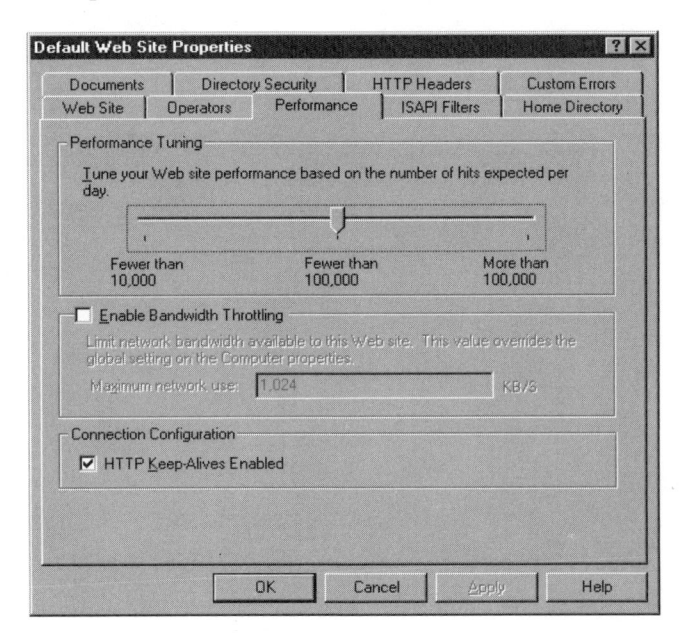

Adjust the **Performance Tuning** setting to the number of daily connections you anticipate for your site. If you set the number slightly higher than the actual number of connections, connections are made faster and server performance is improved. However, if you set it too much higher than the actual number of connection attempts, server memory is wasted and overall server performance is reduced.

The **Enable Bandwidth Throttling** option allows you to limit the bandwidth used by this Web site. For this Web site only—even if it is greater than the value set at the computer level—the bandwidth value entered here overrides the value set at the computer level.

Select the **HTTP Keep-Alives Enabled** box to allow a client to maintain an open connection with your server. This means that the client connection does not have to be reopened with each new request. Keep-Alives are enabled by default.

ISAPI Filters

The **ISAPI Filters** property sheet contains options for Internet Server Application Programming Interface (ISAPI) filters. You can use ISAPI to run remote applications. Requesting a Uniform Resource Locator (URL) that is mapped to a filter activates these applications. You can use these settings to map file name extensions to the correct filter on the Web server.

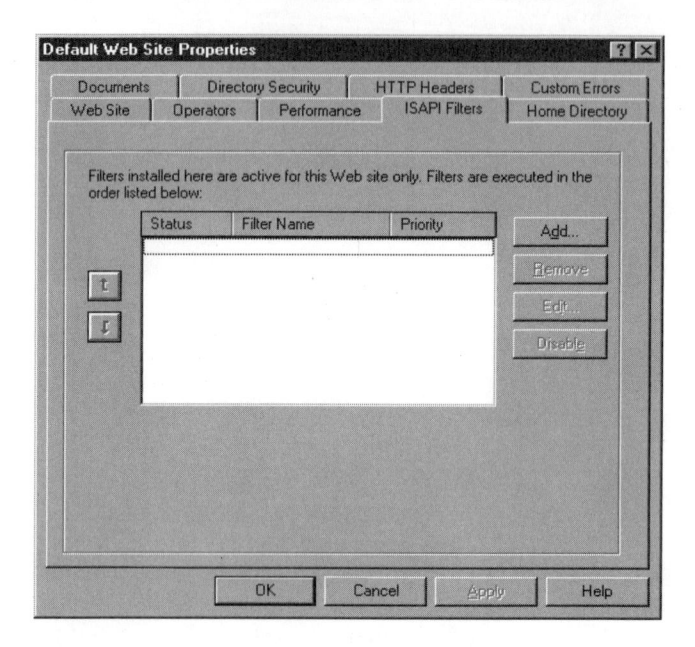

The table on this property sheet lists the status (Loaded, Unloaded, or Disabled), name, and the priority rating set inside the dynamic-link library (DLL), which is High, Medium, or Low, of each filter. You can modify filter mappings with the **Add**, **Remove**, and **Edit** buttons. You can use the **Enable** and **Disable** buttons to modify a filter's status. Select a filter and then click the up or down arrow button to change the order in which the server runs the ISAPI filters.

Home Directory

You can use the **Home Directory** property sheet to change your Web site's home folder and modify its properties.

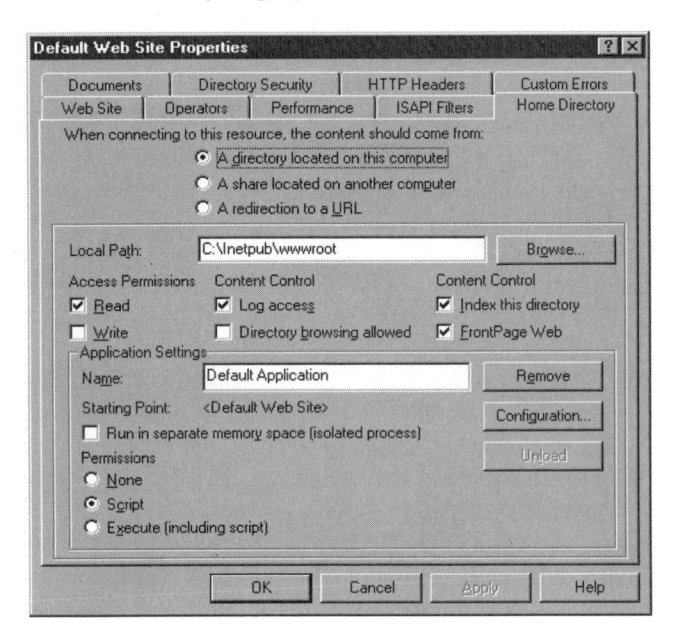

![Default Web Site Properties dialog showing the Home Directory tab with options for directory location, local path C:\Inetpub\wwwroot, access permissions, content control, and application settings]

The home folder is the central location for the files published in your Web site. Installation of the WWW Service creates a default home folder named Wwwroot. You can use the buttons at the top of this property sheet to change the location of the current Web site's home folder to one of the following:

- A folder located on the same computer
- A share located on another computer
- A redirection to a URL

If you change the home folder, type the precise path to the new folder, share, or destination URL in the **Local Path** box, or use the **Browse** button to locate the folder path.

Access Permissions properties are applicable when your home folder is a local folder or a network share. The following check boxes determine the type of access the folder allows:

- **Read**. Read access permission enables Web clients to read or download files stored in either the home folder or a virtual directory. You learn more about virtual directories later in this chapter.
- **Write**. Write access permission enables Web clients to upload files to the enabled folder on your server, or to change the content of a write-enabled file. However, Web clients can only perform Write-access procedures with a browser that supports the PUT feature of the HTTP 1.1 protocol standard.

The following **Content Control** properties are applicable when your home folder is a local folder or a network share:

- **Log access**. Log access allows you to record visits to this folder in a log file.
- **Directory browsing allowed**. By selecting this check box you allow the server to compile a hypertext listing of the files and subfolders within this folder. This listing is generated automatically and sent to the user whenever a browser request does not include a specific file name or when the server cannot find one of the specified default documents in the folder. For more information, see the discussion of the **Documents** property sheet later in this lesson. This listing allows the user to navigate through the folder structure.
- **Index this directory**. Selecting this check box instructs Microsoft Index Server to include this folder in the full-text index of your Web site.
- **FrontPage Web**. Select this check box to create a Microsoft FrontPage Web site for this folder. FrontPage allows you to manage your Web site, as well as create the site content.

Within the WWW Service, an application is defined as all of the folders and files contained within a folder. The application begins at a point marked as an application starting point and runs until another application starting point is reached. If you make your site's home folder an application starting point, then every virtual directory and physical folder within your site can participate in the application.

To dissociate this home folder from an application, click the **Remove** button. You can make this folder an application starting point (and thus create an application) by clicking the **Create** button. Type the name of the application in the **Name** box, and the name appears in the property sheets for any folder contained within the application boundary.

- **Run in separate memory space (isolated process)**. Select this check box to run this application in a process separate from the Web server process. Running an isolated application protects other applications, including the Web server itself, from being affected if this application becomes unavailable or stops responding.
- **Permissions**. Use this setting to control whether other applications can be run in this folder. Select **None** if you do not want to allow any programs or scripts to run in this folder. Selecting **Script** enables a script engine to run in this folder without having set Execute permissions. The **Execute (including script)** setting allows any application to run in this folder, including script engines and Windows NT binaries (.dll and .exe files).

Click the **Configuration** button to set application-specific properties. There are four application configuration property sheets:

- **Application Mappings**. Use this page to map file name extensions to the applications that process those files.
- **Active Server Pages (ASP)**. Use this page to set the options that control how ASP scripts run.
- **ASP Debugging**. Use this page to set debugging options for ASP scripts.
- **Other**. Use this page to set or change the CGI Script Timeout value.

Documents

You can use the **Documents** property sheet to specify default documents and attach default footers to your Web pages.

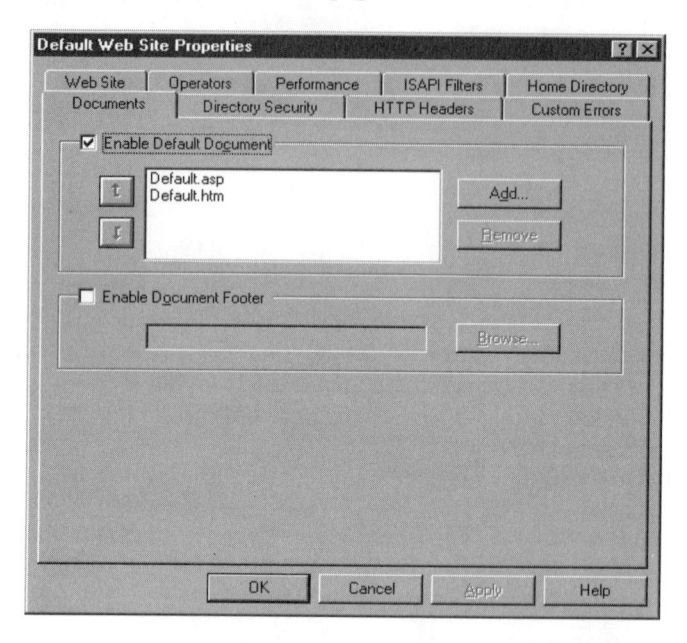

By selecting the **Enable Default Documents** check box, you can show the user a default document when a browser request does not include a specific Hypertext Markup Language (HTML) file name. Default documents can be a folder's home page or an index page that provides links to the documents in the folder. For more information, see the discussion of the **Home Directory** property sheet earlier in this lesson. You can specify more than one default document. To add a new default document, click **Add**.

When prompted by a browser, the Web server searches the folder for default documents, following the order in which the names appear in this list. The server returns the first document it finds. To change the search order, select a document, and then click the up or down arrow button.

Select the **Enable Document Footer** option to configure your Web server to insert a footer automatically. Your footer must be a separate file, but it should not be a complete HTML document. Your footer file should include only the HTML tags necessary for formatting the appearance and function of your footer content. For example, your footer file can contain HTML formatting instructions for adding a logo image and identifying text to your Web pages. You must provide the full path and file name for you footer file.

Directory Security

You can use the **Directory Security** property sheet to configure your Web server's user identification security features.

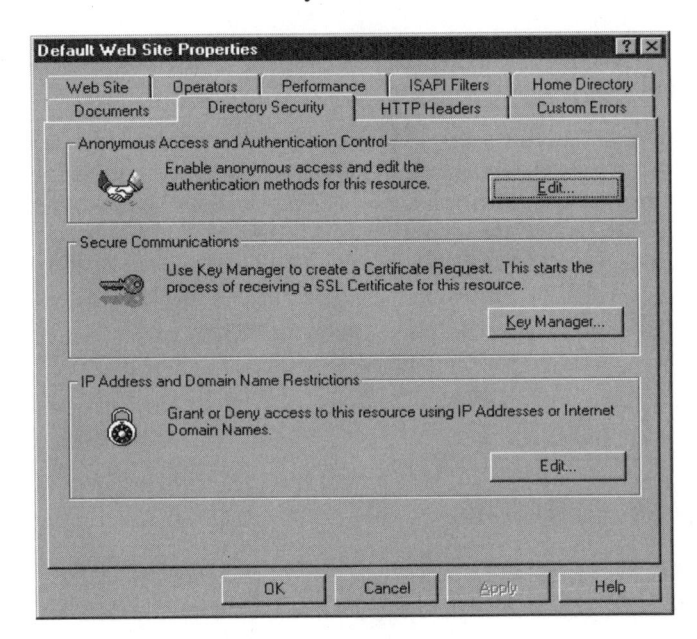

The **Anonymous Access and Authentication Control** option sets the anonymous access and authentication control methods for access to the server. Click **Edit** to select one or more authentication methods from the following options:

- **Allow Anonymous Access**. Select this box to allow anonymous users to log on to your Web server. When a user establishes an anonymous connection, your server logs the user on with an anonymous or guest account. In either case, the account used is a valid Windows NT user account. Click **Edit** to specify which Windows NT User Account to use for anonymous connections.

- **Basic Authentication**. Select this box to enable your Web server's Basic Authentication method, where the password is sent in clear text. By selecting this option, a user name and password are required when the **Allow Anonymous Access** option is disabled, or access to the server is controlled using Windows NT File System (NTFS) access control lists.

- **Windows NT Challenge/Response**. Select this box to enable your Web server's Windows NT Challenge/Response authentication methods. As with Basic Authentication, a user name and password are required when the **Allow Anonymous Access** option is disabled, or access to the server is controlled using NTFS access control lists. Windows NT Challenge/Response is supported by Microsoft Internet Explorer, version 2.0 or later.

For a discussion of authentication and password security issues, see Chapter 9, "Adding Windows NT and Internet Information Server Security Features."

The **Secure Communications** feature is available only for Windows NT Server installations. This feature uses Key Manager to create a certificate request. Click **Key Manager** to start the process of receiving a SSL digital certificate for this resource.

Use the **IP Address and Domain Name Restrictions** properties to grant or deny access to this resource using IP addresses or Internet domain names. Click **Edit** to grant or deny access to specific individuals or groups as follows:

- **Granted Access**. Click this button to grant access to all computers by default. Click **Add** to list those computers that are denied access.
- **Denied Access**. Click this button to deny access to all computers by default. Click **Add** to list those computers that are granted access.

HTTP Headers

You can use the **HTTP Headers** property sheet to set values returned to the browser in the header of specific HTML pages.

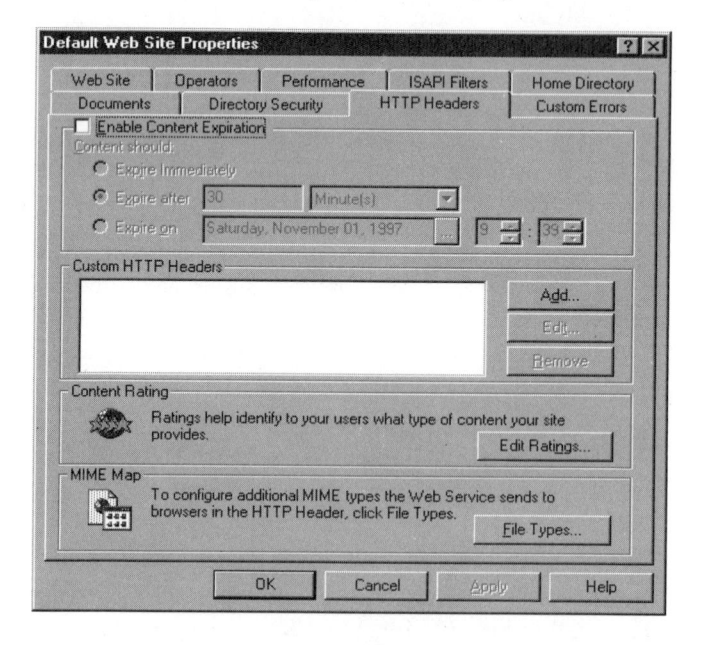

Select the **Enable Content Expiration** check box to include expiration information in the HTML page header. When you include a date in time-sensitive material, such as special offers or event announcements, the browser compares the current date to the expiration date and determines whether to display a cached page or request an updated page from the server.

You can send custom HTTP headers from your Web server to the client browser. To send a header, click **Add**, and then type the name and value of the header in the **Add Custom HTTP Header** dialog box. Click **Remove** to stop sending the header.

You can embed descriptive labels in your Web page's HTTP headers using the **Content Rating** feature. Some Web browsers, such as Microsoft Internet Explorer version 3.0 or later, can detect these content labels in order to help users identify potentially objectionable Web content. Click **Edit Ratings** to set content ratings for this Web site, folder, or file.

You can set which file types your Web service returns to browsers. Clicking the **File Types** button allows you to configure Multipurpose Internet Mail Extensions (MIME) mappings.

Custom Errors

The **Custom Errors** property sheet lists the messages returned to the browser in the event of an HTTP error.

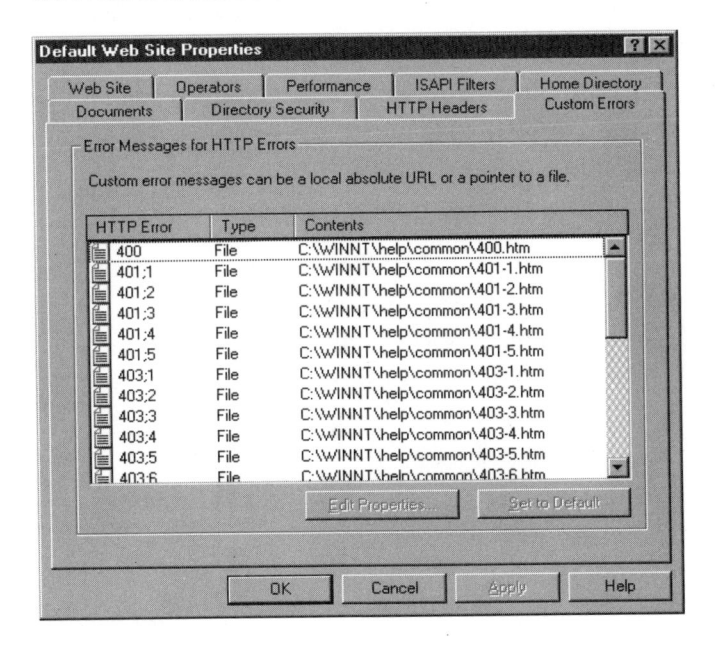

You can use either the default HTTP 1.1 errors or you can customize these error messages with your own content. When error messages are customized, the HTTP error code is still listed, as well as the output type, which can be the default HTTP 1.1 error, a local absolute URL, or a pointer to a file.

Practice

In this practice scenario, you use Internet Service Manager to take your Web site offline without stopping the WWW Service. You then create a custom error message, and replace the default error message with your custom error message. Finally, you use Internet Service Manager to bring your Web site online without restarting the WWW Service. You can use the procedures in this practice if you need to inform visitors that your site is offline due to maintenance.

In the first part of the practice, you take your default Web site offline.

▶ **To take your default Web site offline**

1. Start Microsoft Management Console with the Internet Service Manager snap-in.
2. In the left pane, double-click the Internet Information Server folder.

   The Internet Information Server folder opens displaying a computer icon.
3. In the left pane, double-click the computer icon.

   The computer tree expands displaying the default sites.
4. Right-click **Default Web Site**, and then click **Properties**.

   The **Default Web Site Properties** dialog box appears displaying the **Web Site** tab.
5. Click the **Home Directory** tab.
6. Under **Access Permissions**, click **Read**.

   The **Read** check box is cleared.
7. Click **OK**.

   The **Inheritance Overrides** dialog box appears.
8. Click **Select All**.
9. Click **OK**.

You now test your Web site for the standard error message.

▶ **To test your Web site with Internet Explorer**

1. Open Internet Explorer.
2. In the **Address** box, type your server name.
3. Click **OK**.

   The message

   HTTP Error 403 Access Forbidden
   403.2 Forbidden: Read Access Forbidden

   appears with a paragraph describing the error beneath it.

4. Minimize Internet Explorer.

Next, you create a custom error message to replace the standard error you viewed in the previous practice.

▶ **To create the custom error message by editing the existing message**

1. Open Notepad.
2. On the **File** menu, click **Open**.

   The **File name** box appears.

3. Type **c:\winnt\help\common\403-2.htm**
4. Click **Open**.

   Notepad displays the HTML code for error 403. The main error message text is in the middle of the screen. It begins "This error can…" and is bounded by a paragraph beginning marker, <p>, and a paragraph ending marker, </p>.

5. Replace the error message text with: "Our site is closed for repairs. Please try again later."
6. On the **File** menu, click **Save As**.
7. The **Save As** dialog box appears.
8. Save the file in the C:\Winnt\Help\Common folder.
9. In the **File Name** box, type **err403.htm**
10. Click **Save**.
11. Close Notepad.

In this practice, you install the custom error message on your Web site.

Note This step is necessary because you are redirecting the Help engine to a different file (Err403.htm) when encountering Error 403.2 rather than permanently replacing the standard file. This way, you can easily direct the Help engine back to the standard message when you no longer need the custom message.

If you had saved the custom message over the standard file, this step would not be necessary.

▶ **To install the custom error message**

1. Start Internet Service Manager.
2. Right-click **Default Web Site**, and then click **Properties**.

    The **Default Web Site Properties** dialog box appears.
3. Click the **Custom Errors** tab.
4. Select the 403;2 HTTP error.
5. Click **Edit Properties**.

    The **Error Mapping Properties** dialog box appears.

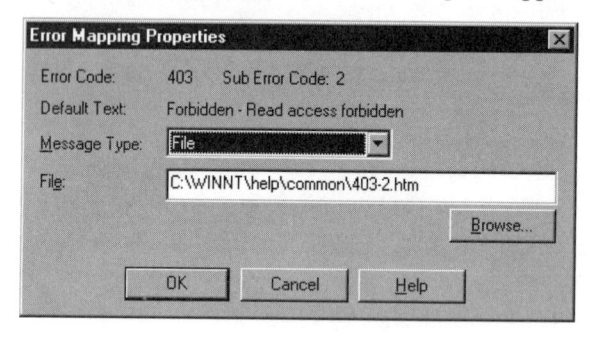

6. In the **Message Type** box, select **File**.
7. In the **File** box, type **c:\winnt\help\common\err403.htm**
8. Click **OK** to return to the **Default Web Site Properties** dialog box.
9. Click **OK**.

    The **Inheritance Overrides** dialog box appears.
10. Click **Select All**.

    In the **Child Nodes** text box, **IISADMIN** and **IISHELP** are selected.
11. Click **OK**.

You now test your Web site for the custom error message.

▶ **To test your Web site with Internet Explorer**
1. Switch to Internet Explorer.
2. Click **Refresh**.

   The message

   HTTP Error 403 Access Forbidden
   403.2 Forbidden: Read Access Forbidden

   appears with your new error text beneath it.
3. Close Internet Explorer.

To complete the practice, you bring your default Web site online.

▶ **To bring your default Web site online**
1. Switch to Internet Service Manager.
2. Right-click **Default Web Site**, and then click **Properties**.

   The **Default Web Site Properties** dialog box appears displaying the **Web Site** tab.
3. Click the **Home Directory** tab.
4. Under **Access Permissions**, click **Read**.

   The **Read** check box is selected.
5. Click **OK**.
6. Close Microsoft Management Console.

   You are prompted to save the changes to Iis.mcs.
7. Click **No**.

   Microsoft Management Console closes without saving your changes.

Summary

There are three different types, or classes, of property sheets within Internet Information Server. They are the **Master**, **Default**, and **File** property sheets. The property sheets in Internet Information Server are organized within a hierarchy such that the settings of the **Master** property sheets are passed on to the **Default** property sheets, which are passed on to the **File** property sheets.

You can use WWW property sheets to configure the different areas of your Web site, folder, or file. Each set of the WWW property sheets is made up of the following nine component property sheets:

- **Web Site**
- **Operators**
- **Performance**
- **ISAPI Filters**
- **Home Directory**
- **Documents**
- **Directory Security**
- **HTTP Headers**
- **Custom Errors**

You can change the settings on these property sheets at any time as needed.

Lesson 3: Virtual Directories

A virtual directory is a folder that is not physically contained within the Internet Information Server service (WWW or File Transfer Protocol [FTP]) home folder, but which appears as though it were to users who visit your Web site. In this lesson, you learn about the different types of virtual directories, how to create them, and how to administer them.

After this lesson, you will be able to:
- Describe the different aspects of a virtual directory.
- Create and administer a WWW Service virtual directory using the ISM snap-in.

Estimated lesson time: 20 minutes

Virtual directories increase your flexibility when determining where to store files on your server. By using virtual directories you can store files where they are most easily updated or accessed. Virtual directories also allow you to add storage capacity for your Web site without having to shut down your server.

However, you may experience a drop in performance when accessing folders contained on another computer's disk. This performance drop is due to the transfer speed of data over a LAN.

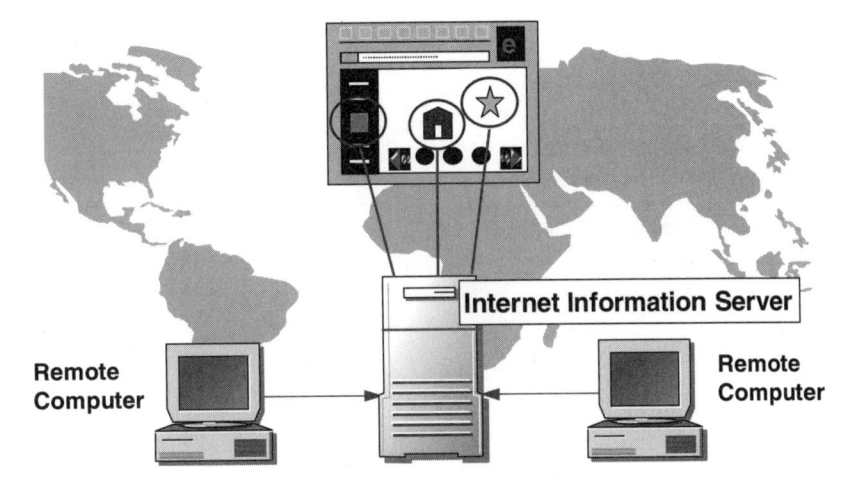

Virtual directories can be established for both WWW and FTP Services running on Internet Information Server. Virtual directories can be created for folders located on:

- The same disk as the Wwwroot or Ftproot (home) directories.
- Another disk inside the local computer.
- Another computer's disk on the network. This computer must be located within the same Windows NT Server domain as the Internet Information Server computer.

Local Virtual Directory

You can create local virtual directories for folders stored on any disk installed in the same computer as the disk running Internet Information Server.

When configuring a local virtual directory, you must assign an alias to the folder. This alias can be the folder's name or any other name that identifies the site to the user. You must also be prepared to provide the virtual directory's full path.

Remote Virtual Directory

You can use remote virtual directories for folders stored on disks installed in other computers within the Internet Information Server computer's domain.

As with local virtual directories, when configuring a remote virtual directory, you are asked to assign an alias to the folder. You must also supply the folder's universal naming convention (UNC) address. In order to access the folder with a UNC, you have to enter a valid user name and password. The user name and password you enter is automatically used by visitors who access data contained within this virtual directory.

Caution Make sure that the user account you establish to allow Internet access to a remote virtual directory provides only the minimum permissions required to use the site. Do not use the administrator's account to access virtual directories.

Virtual Directory Administration

You can create a virtual directory with any Internet Information Server administration tool. Each tool uses a different user interface for creating virtual directories.

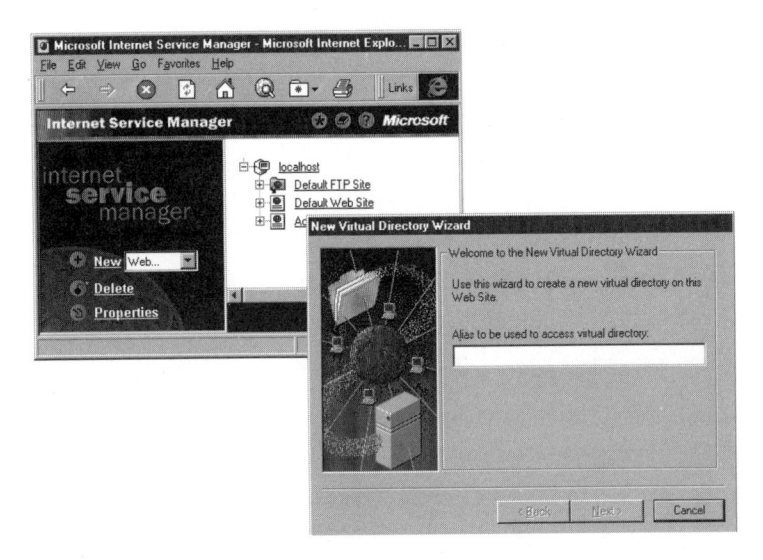

The ISM snap-in for Microsoft Management Console uses the New Virtual Directory wizard to lead you through the virtual directory creation process. After you have established the virtual directory, you can use the **Virtual Directory** property sheet to modify its configuration.

HTML-based Administration (HTMLA), the HTML-based ISM, uses a Web page to lead you through the creation of the virtual directory. You can use this administration tool to establish and modify virtual directories remotely.

With Windows Scripting Host (WSH) you can create virtual directories automatically using scripts.

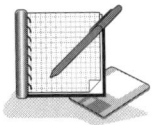

Practice

In this practice, you set up a virtual directory. To set up a virtual directory, you must use Microsoft Windows NT Explorer to create and share the folder with the appropriate permissions. You then use ISM to create the virtual directory.

▶ **To create a local virtual directory**

1. Create the C:\Inetpub\Vdir folder.
2. Copy the Default.asp file from the C:\Inetpub\Wwwroot folder to the C:\Inetpub\Vdir folder.
3. Start Internet Service Manager.

4. Right-click **Default Web Site**.

   A context menu appears.

5. Click **New**, and then click **Virtual Directory**.

   The New Virtual Directory wizard appears.

6. Type **MyVirSite** as the alias to be used.

7. Click **Next**.

8. Type the path **c:\inetpub\vdir** and then click **Next**.

9. Click **Finish**.

10. Start Internet Explorer and then in the **Address** box, type **http://*computername*/myvirsite**

    The Internet Information Server home page appears.

11. Switch to Internet Service Manager.

12. In the left pane, select **MyVirSite**, and then press **F2**.

    The ISM interface allows you to rename **MyVirSite**.

13. Rename **MyVirSite** to **OldVirSite**.

14. Switch to Internet Explorer, and then click **Refresh**.

    The HTTP/1.0 404 Object not found message appears.

15. In the **Address** box, type *computername*/**oldvirsite** and then press ENTER.

    The Internet Information Server home page appears.

Virtual Directories and FrontPage

The Microsoft FrontPage Web authoring and management tool automatically manages virtual directory use. When installed, FrontPage sets up virtual directories for the folders containing executable FrontPage server extensions. In addition, by marking folders as executable you permit them to include such executable objects as:

- Active Server Pages (.asp)
- Internet database connector files (.idc)
- Common Gateway Interface (CGI) scripts (.exe)
- ISAPI extensions (.dll)
- Practical Extraction and Report Language (PERL) scripts (.pl)

Note Because it does not support noncontiguous content areas, you cannot use virtual directories to merge noncontiguous content areas in FrontPage.

Summary

A virtual directory is a folder that is not physically contained within the Internet Information Server service (WWW or FTP) home folder. You can create two types of virtual directories with Internet Information Server, local and remote. A local virtual directory is located on a disk contained within the same computer as the disk running Internet Information Server. A remote virtual directory is located on a different computer located within the same domain as the computer running Internet Information Server. You can create virtual directories with any Internet Information Server administration tool, and use Microsoft FrontPage to automatically manage them.

Lesson 4: Virtual Servers

Multiple domain names can be hosted on a single computer running Internet Information Server by using virtual servers. This lesson describes virtual servers, their setup, and their administration.

After this lesson, you will be able to:
- Describe two methods of assigning an IP address to virtual servers running on Internet Information Server.
- Create and administer a WWW Service virtual server.

Estimated lesson time: 15 minutes

With virtual servers you can host multiple Web and FTP sites on a single computer running Internet Information Server, which means you do not need to allocate one computer and software package for each site. You simply need to obtain a unique IP address for each domain name assigned to the server, and by using Host Headers you can use a single IP address for multiple domain names. However, only WWW sites can use Host Headers. Virtual servers also centralize administration and simplify server software upgrades.

Hosting multiple virtual servers on the same computer may reduce overall server performance, and virtual Web servers using Host Headers require an HTTP version 1.1-compliant Web browser.

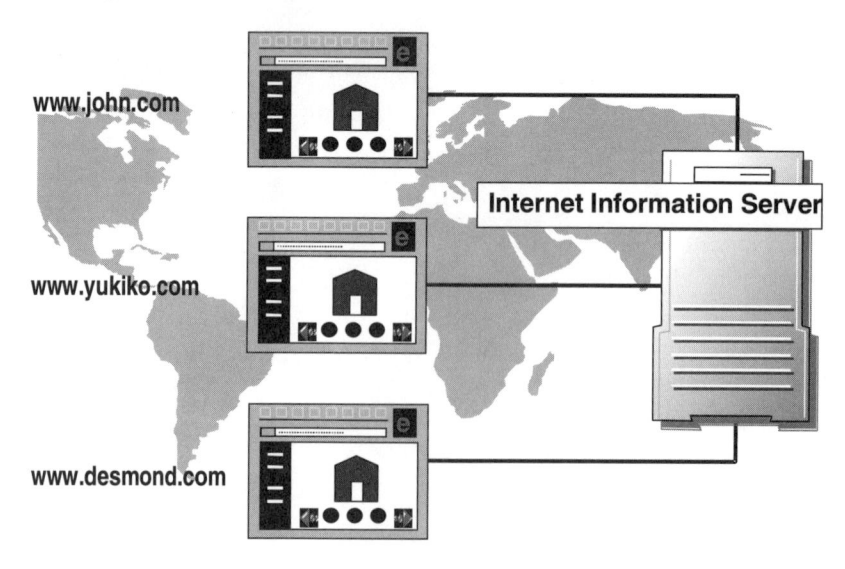

Host Headers

The Host Headers capability of HTTP 1.1 allows you to associate multiple host names with a single IP address. Internet Information Server uses Host Header information when building redirects to the different virtual host names. To use Host Headers, you must provide a host name-to-IP address resolution using either a domain name system (DNS) server or HOSTS files. A HOSTS file provides name resolution for host names to IP addresses.

Note Web browsers that are not HTTP 1.1-compliant can access URLs with Host Headers. Internet Information Server provides non-compliant browsers with a list of servers associated with a given IP address. When the user selects a server, a cookie is placed on the user's disk to direct all future access to the virtual server.

Virtual Server Administration

You can create a virtual server with any Internet Information Server administration tool. Each tool uses a different user interface for creating virtual servers.

The ISM snap-in for Microsoft Management Console uses the New Web Site wizard or New FTP Site wizard to lead you through the virtual server creation process. After you have established the virtual server, you can use the **Virtual Server** property sheets to modify its configuration.

HTLMA uses a Web page to lead you through the creation of the virtual server. You can use this administration tool to establish and modify virtual servers remotely.

With WSH, you can create virtual servers automatically using scripts.

Practice

In this practice, you configure a virtual server by using Windows NT Explorer to create and share the folder with the appropriate permissions. You then use Internet Service Manager to create the virtual server. You can use the optional loopback address to connect to your server to perform these virtual server procedures.

Note The loopback IP address is 127.0.0.1. The loopback address uses loopback drivers to reroute outgoing packets back to the source computer. The loopback drivers allow the packets to bypass the network adapter card completely and return directly to the computer that is performing the action.

▶ **To add a WWW virtual server**

1. Start Windows NT Explorer.
2. Create the C:\Inetpub\Vroot folder.
3. Copy the contents of C:\Inetpub\Wwwroot to C:\Inetpub\Vroot.
4. Start Internet Service Manager, and then right-click your computer icon.

    A context menu appears.
5. Click **New**, and then click **Web Site**.

    The New Web Site wizard appears.
6. In the **Description** box, type **copy of wwwroot**
7. Click **Next**.
8. In the **IP Address** box, select your server's IP address or your loopback address (127.0.0.1).

    Leave the entry as 80 in the **TCP Port this Web Site should use (Default: 80)** text box.
9. Click **Next**.
10. Type the path to C:\Inetpub\Vroot.
11. Click **Next**.

    Only the **Read** and **Script** boxes should be selected.
12. Click **Finish**.
13. Right-click the **Copy of WWWRoot** Web site, and then click **Properties**.

    The **Properties** dialog box appears.
14. On the **Web Site** tab, click **Advanced**.
15. Select your IP address.
16. Click **Add**.
17. In the **IP Address** box, select your IP address.

18. In the **TCP Port Of** box, type **80**
19. In the **Host Header Name** box, type *computername***A**

    For example, if your computer name is Server1, the Host Header name for your virtual server is Server1A.
20. Click **OK**.
21. In the **Advanced Multiple Web Site Configuration** box, click **OK**.
22. Click **OK** to return to Internet Service Manager.

Note This new virtual server inherits its property sheet settings from the WWW or FTP Services **Master** property sheets.

▶ **To start your new Web site**
1. Right-click **Copy of WWWRoot**.

   A context menu appears.
2. Click **Start**.

▶ **To test your virtual server**
1. Start Internet Explorer.
2. In the **Address** box, type *computername***A** and then press ENTER.

   The Microsoft Internet Information Server home page appears. This verifies that your virtual server is working using host headers.
3. Close Internet Explorer.

Summary

With virtual servers you can host multiple Web and FTP sites on a single computer running Internet Information Server. The Host Headers capability of HTTP 1.1 allows you to associate multiple host names with a single IP address. You can use any Internet Information Server administration tool to create virtual servers.

Review

The following questions are intended to reinforce key information presented in this chapter. If you are unable to answer a question, review the appropriate lesson, and then try the question again.

1. You are interested in changing your Web site configurations pertaining to connections—how many users are connecting, how many users can connect, and how long you tolerate an idle connection before dropping it. Where would you go to adjust these functions?

2. You are working on the beta release of a new product and want to allow the members of your team—and no one else—to access documentation on the intranet. Which property sheet helps you to configure your Web site in this way, and what are the steps you must take to configure your site?

3. You are concerned about users having Write privileges to your Web site. Which property sheet contains this information? Would a user require any special browser functionality in order to write to a Web site?

Chapter 5 Configuring the WWW Service 91

4. After installing Internet Information Server, you configure 10 virtual servers. To verify that the virtual servers are working, you copy the Default.asp file from Inetpub\Wwwroot into the home folder of each virtual server. When you test each of the virtual servers, none of the images on the page are displayed. After troubleshooting, you determine that all of the images are in virtual directories, and these virtual directories are only accessible from the default Web site. How do you make them accessible from all virtual servers?

5. You are the administrator for an intranet at a small accounting firm with 10 employees and 15 computers running Windows NT 4.0. After installing Internet Information Server and configuring three virtual servers, users complain they can only display the default WWW server. What must you do so that the virtual servers are working?

6. You are the administrator for an intranet at a large accounting firm with 1000 employees and 1500 computers running Windows NT 4.0. After installing Internet Information Server, creating three virtual servers, and installing DNS, users complain they can only display the default WWW server. What must you do so that the clients can display the pages on the virtual servers?

CHAPTER 6

Configuring the FTP Service

Lesson 1 The FTP Service . . . 94

Lesson 2 FTP Properties . . . 96

Review . . . 107

About This Chapter

This chapter describes the basic functionality of the Microsoft Internet Information Server (IIS) 4.0 File Transfer Protocol (FTP) service. This chapter also introduces you to the five different specific property sheets that contain FTP site configuration settings, and teaches you how to access these property sheets in order to configure your FTP sites.

Before You Begin

To complete the lessons in this chapter, you must have installed Internet Information Server as described in Chapter 2, "Installing Microsoft Internet Information Server."

Lesson 1: The FTP Service

File Transfer Protocol (FTP) is the protocol used to transfer files between two computers on a Transmission Control Protocol/Internet Protocol (TCP/IP) network. This lesson introduces you to the Internet Information Server FTP Service.

After this lesson, you will be able to:
- List the features of the FTP Service running on Internet Information Server.

Estimated lesson time: 10 minutes

FTP was one of the earliest protocols used on TCP/IP networks and the Internet. Although the World Wide Web (WWW) has replaced most functions of FTP, FTP is still used to copy files from a client computer to a server over the Internet. Unlike Hypertext Transport Protocol (HTTP), FTP uses two ports for file transfer—one to send files, and another to receive them. As a result, FTP is still more efficient than HTTP for the specialized task of transferring files.

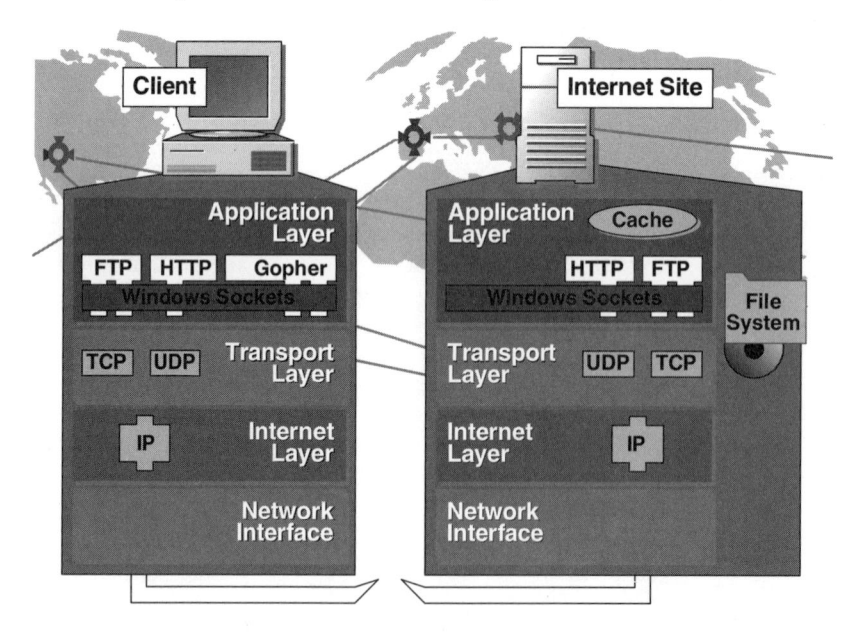

In order to use FTP to transfer files between two computers, both computers must support their respective FTP roles; one must be an FTP client and the other an FTP server. The FTP client gives the server commands for downloading and uploading files, as well as creating and changing server folders.

FTP uses Transmission Control Protocol (TCP) as its transport for all communications and data exchanges between the client and the server. TCP is a connection-oriented protocol, which means that the communications session is established between the client and the server before data is transmitted. This connection remains active during the entire FTP session. Connection-oriented sessions are known for their reliability and error-recovery due to the following features:

- *Flow control.* Because both client and server computers participate in the transmission of the packets, potential transmission problems such as packet overflows and lost packets are virtually eliminated.
- *Acknowledgment.* The computer sending data packets expects an acknowledgment (ACK) from the destination computer. This acknowledgment verifies that the destination computer received the packet successfully.
- *Retransmission.* If the transmitting computer does not receive an ACK within a specified period of time, it assumes that the packet became lost or corrupted, and then it retransmits the packet.
- *Sequencing.* All packets are numbered and sent in order so the receiving computer knows how to reorganize the data.
- *Checksum.* All packets contain a checksum to ensure integrity of the data. If the data is corrupted somewhere during the transmission, the checksum indicates that the data received is not the same as the data that was sent.

Note Do not confuse FTP with Trivial File Transfer Protocol (TFTP). TFTP is a fast, simple file transfer protocol that uses the User Datagram Protocol (UDP) transport. UDP, unlike TCP, is a connectionless protocol and cannot retransmit packets. As a result, UDP is not as reliable as TCP.

Summary

FTP is the protocol used to transfer files between two computers on a TCP/IP network. FTP uses TCP as its transport for all communications and data exchanges between the client and the server. TCP is a connection-oriented protocol, known for its reliability and error-recovery.

Lesson 2: FTP Properties

Each FTP site that you create has its own set of property sheets. The general settings, or properties, for a site are displayed in these property sheets. This lesson introduces you to each of these property sheets and demonstrates how to access them in order to set the general properties for a FTP site or file within a site on your computer.

After this lesson, you will be able to:
- List and describe the functions of the property sheets associated with the FTP Service.
- Establish an FTP Service using the Internet Service Manager (ISM) snap-in.
- Use the ISM snap-in to modify the standard FTP port (21).
- Use the command prompt FTP client and Microsoft Internet Explorer to connect to an FTP server.

Estimated lesson time: 50 minutes

The FTP Service uses five different property sheets to configure the specific FTP Service areas:

- **FTP Site**
- **Security Accounts**
- **Messages**
- **Home Directory**
- **Directory Security**

During installation, Internet Information Server assigns default values to the various settings on the different property sheets. You can publish documents on your FTP site without changing these default settings, but you can easily customize the settings as well.

Each FTP site that you create and each file within each FTP site has an individual set of property sheets that you can edit in order to customize the configuration on a site-by-site or file-by-file basis. You can also edit the default property settings so that all subsequent sites or files are created with your custom configuration.

There are three different types, or classes, of FTP property sheets within Internet Information Server and they behave similarly to the same three classes of property sheets that apply to your WWW sites. Similar to the WWW property sheets, FTP property sheet classes consist of **Master**, **Default**, and **File** property sheets. You can customize the configuration of all three types of property sheets, but where you make your changes affects the range of influence the changes have on sites or files subsequently created.

You can access all FTP property sheets using the ISM snap-in for Microsoft Management Console (MMC).

▶ **To access the FTP property sheets**

1. Click the **Start** button, point to **Programs**, point to **Windows NT 4.0 Option Pack**, point to **Microsoft Internet Information Server**, and then click **Internet Service Manager**.
2. In the left pane, double-click the Internet Information Server node.
3. In the left pane, double-click the *computername* node.
4. Right-click **Default FTP Site**, and then click **Properties**.
5. The **FTP Property Sheet** dialog box appears with tabs for each property sheet.

FTP Site

You can use the **FTP Site** property sheet to set the FTP site identification, specify the number of connections allowed, and enable or disable logging for an FTP site.

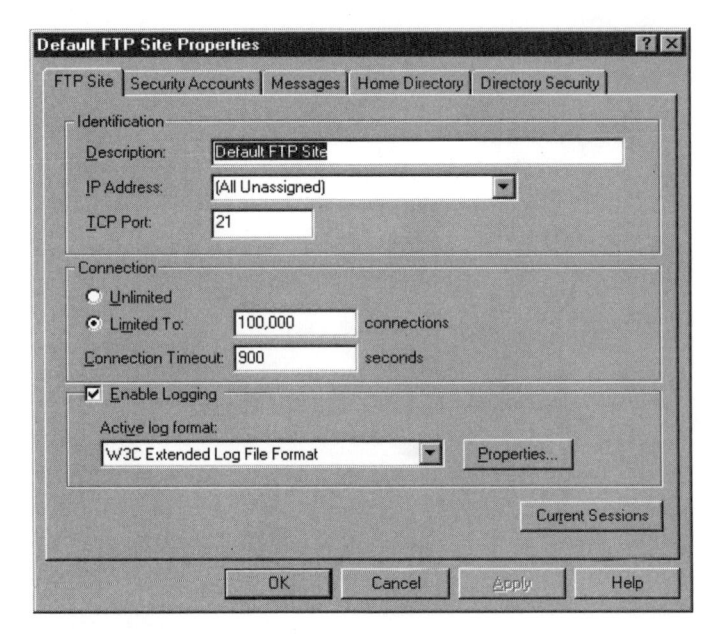

The **Identification** field allows you to choose a description for your site.

- **Description**. This box lists the name you choose for your Web site, and appears in the tree view of the Internet Service Manager.
- **IP Address**. This box lists the IP address for your FTP site.
- **TCP Port**. This box determines the port on which each service runs.

The **Connections** field allows you to set the number of simultaneous connections to the server.

- **Unlimited**. Select this option to allow an unlimited number of simultaneous connections to the server.
- **Limited To**. Select this option to limit the number of simultaneous connections to the server by typing the number of connections permitted.
- **Connection Timeout**. Select this option to set the length of time (in seconds) before the server disconnects an inactive user.

Select the **Enable Logging** option to activate your FTP site's logging features. These can record details about user activity such as which users accessed your FTP site and what information they accessed. You can create logs in Microsoft IIS Log format, W3C Extended Log File format, or ODBC Logging.

Click **Properties** to open the **Microsoft Logging Properties** dialog box. Here you can choose how often to create new logs and specify the folder for the log file.

Click **Current Sessions** to view a list of users currently connected to the FTP Service.

Security Accounts

You can use the **Security Accounts** property sheet to control server access and to specify which account is used for anonymous client logon requests.

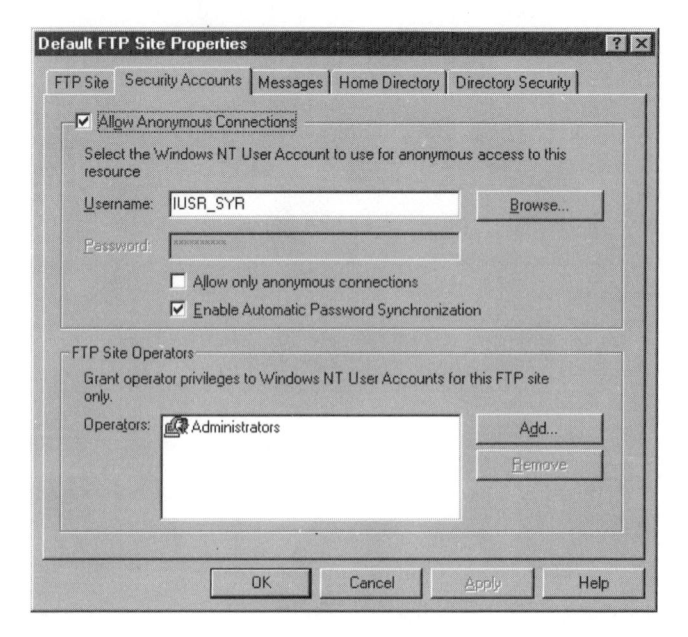

Select the **Allow Anonymous Connections** check box to allow users using the user name "anonymous" to log on to your FTP server. You can use the **User Name** and **Password** dialog boxes to establish which Windows NT User Account permissions are used for all anonymous connections. By default, Internet Information Server creates and uses the account IUSR_*computername* for all anonymous logons.

- **Browse**. Click **Browse** to browse for a Windows NT user account.
- **Allow only anonymous connections**. Select this option to prevent users from logging on with user names and passwords.
- **Enable Automatic Password Synchronization**. Select this option if you want your FTP site to automatically synchronize your anonymous password settings with those set in Windows NT.

You can designate which Windows NT User Accounts are able to administer this FTP server using the **FTP Site Operators** field. Click **Add** to add an account to the list of those that have administrative privileges. To remove an account from this list, select the account you want to remove from those shown in the **Operators** box, and then click **Remove**.

Messages

You can use the **Messages** property sheet to create the messages that are displayed to browsers that contact your site. All of the message fields are blank by default.

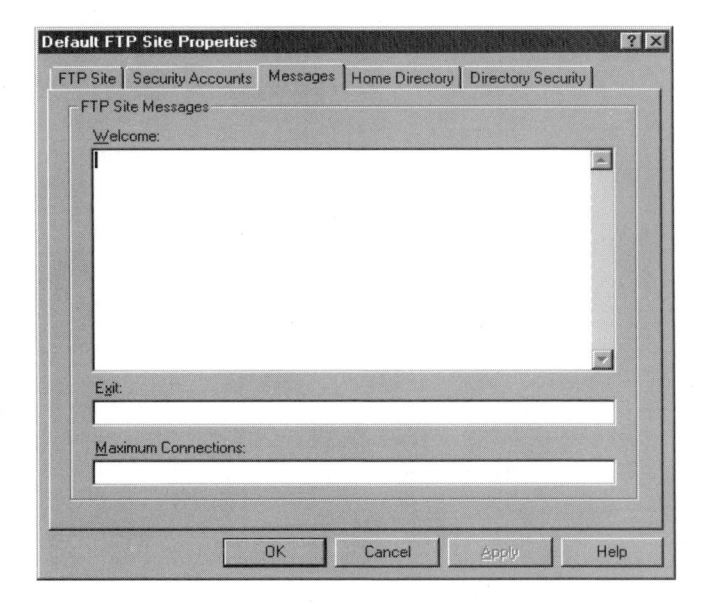

To create a message, type what you want the message to say in the text box corresponding to one of the three types of messages you want to create. The three type of messages are:

- **Welcome**. Use this dialog box to create the message displayed to clients when they first connect to the FTP server.
- **Exit**. Use this dialog box to create the message displayed to clients when they log off the FTP server.
- **Maximum Connections**. Use this dialog box to create the message displayed to clients who try to connect to the FTP server when the FTP Service is already supporting the maximum number of connections allowed.

Home Directory

You can use the **Home Directory** property sheet to change your FTP site's home directory and modify its properties.

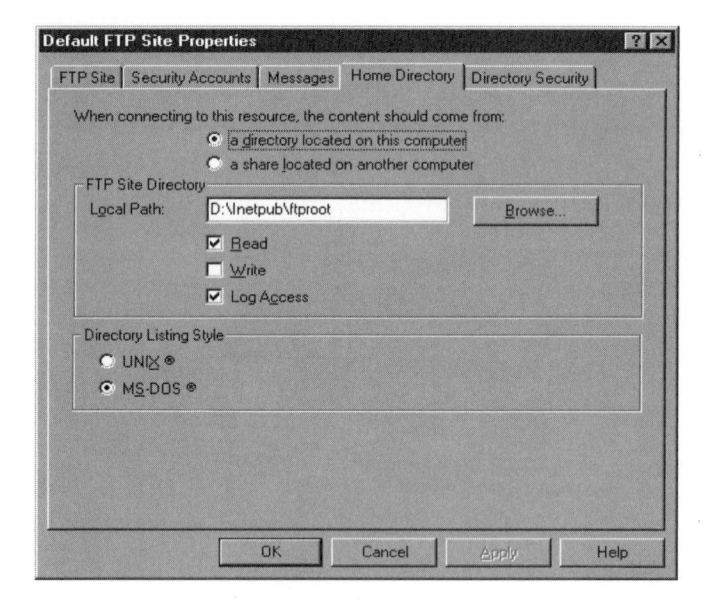

The home directory is the central location for the files published in your FTP site. Installation of the FTP Service creates a default home directory named Ftproot. You can change the location of the current FTP site's home directory to a folder located on the same computer or a share located on another computer.

If you change the home directory, type the precise path to the new folder or share in the **Local Path** box, or use the **Browse** button to locate the path.

Use the **FTP Site Directory** options to determine the type of access allowed to the folder. The **FTP Site Directory** options are:

- **Read**. **Read** access permission enables Web clients to read or download files stored in either the home directory or a virtual directory.
- **Write**. **Write** access permission enables Web clients to upload files to the enabled folder on your server, or to change the content of a write-enabled file. However, Web clients can only perform Write-access procedures with a browser that supports the PUT feature of the HTTP 1.1 protocol standard.
- **Log Access**. **Log Access** allows you to record visits to this folder in a log file.

You can choose from either the **UNIX** or **MS-DOS** folder listing style when selecting which folder listing style is sent to FTP users.

Note Because many browsers expect UNIX format, selecting **UNIX** gives you maximum compatibility.

Directory Security

You can use the **Directory Security** property sheet to set FTP server access privileges by specific IP address.

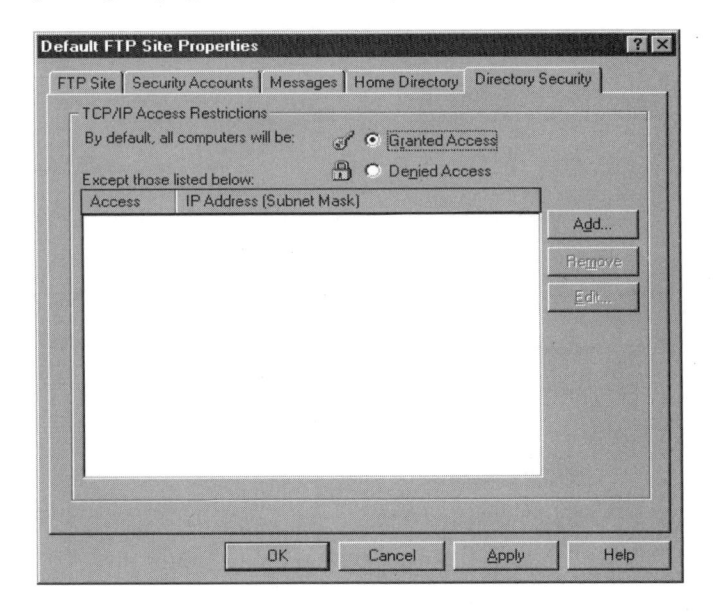

Use the following TCP/IP access restrictions to block or grant server access to specific individuals or groups:

- **Granted Access**. Select this option to grant access to all computers except those listed in the **Except those listed below:** box.
- **Denied Access**. Select this option to deny access to all computers except those listed in the **Except those listed below:** box.

Click **Add** when the **Granted Access** option is selected to add computers to the list of those computers that are denied access. Click **Add** when the **Denied Access** option is selected to add computers to the list of those that are granted access. Clicking the **Remove** button deletes selected computers from the exceptions list.

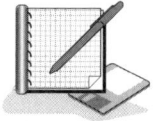

Practice

In this practice, you create FTP site messages, use the command prompt FTP client to connect to an FTP server, use Internet Explorer to connect to an FTP server, and then use the Internet Service Manager snap-in to modify the standard FTP port (21).

You can use the loopback address or your server name to connect to your server to perform these FTP procedures.

Note The loopback IP address is 127.0.0.1. The loopback address uses loopback drivers to reroute outgoing packets back to the source computer. The loopback drivers allow the packets to bypass the network adapter card completely and return directly to the computer that is performing the action.

In this practice, you populate your FTP site and create FTP site messages for visitors.

▶ **To populate your FTP site with text files**

1. Click the **Start** button, point to **Find**, and then click **Files or Folders**.

    The **Find: All Files** dialog box appears.

2. In the **Named** box, type ***.txt** and then click **Find Now**.
3. Click **Edit**, and then click **Select All**.
4. Click **Edit**, and then click **Copy**.
5. Start Windows NT Explorer, and then double-click **Inetpub**.

    The Inetpub folder opens and displays the subfolders.

6. Right-click **ftproot**, and then click **Paste**.

    The **Confirm File Replace** dialog box appears.

7. Click **Yes to All**.
8. Close the **Find:** dialog box.

Chapter 6 Configuring the FTP Service   103

▶ **To create FTP site messages**

1. Click the **Start** button, point to **Programs**, point to **Windows NT 4.0 Option Pack**, point to **Microsoft Internet Information Server**, and then click **Internet Service Manager**.

2. Expand Internet Information Server.

   The Internet Information Server folder opens displaying a computer icon with your computer name.

3. Expand the computer icon.

4. Right-click **Default FTP Site**, and then click **Properties**.

   The **Default FTP Site Properties** dialog box appears.

5. Click the **Messages** tab.

6. Under **Welcome**, type a welcome message.

7. Under **Exit**, type an exit message.

8. Under **Maximum Connections**, type a warning message.

9. Click **OK**.

10. Close Internet Service Manager.

    You are prompted to save the changes to Iis.msc.

11. Click **No**.

In this practice, you use the FTP client to transfer files and test the connection to your server.

▶ **To use the command prompt FTP client**

1. Start a command prompt.

2. Switch to the Temp folder.

3. Type the following command:

   dir

   Notice that the folder is empty.

4. At the command prompt, type **ftp** *computername* (or the loopback address 127.0.0.1) and then press ENTER.

   The FTP client responds with a user prompt.

5. At the user prompt, type **anonymous** and then press ENTER.

   The FTP client responds with a password prompt.

6. At the password prompt, press ENTER.

   The FTP client confirms that you are logged on and responds with an FTP prompt.

7. At the FTP prompt, type **prompt** and then press ENTER.

   This turns interactive mode off.

8. At the FTP prompt, type **dir** and then press ENTER.

   A list of available files from Inetpub\Ftproot appears.

9. At the FTP prompt, type **mget *.*** and then press ENTER.

   Files are transferred from the FTP server to the C:\Temp folder.

10. At the FTP prompt, type **bye** and then press ENTER.

    The FTP exit message appears.

11. At the command prompt, type **dir** and then press ENTER.

    A list of files for the C:\Temp folder appears.

12. At the command prompt, type **del *.txt** and then press ENTER.

    This deletes the files from the C:\Temp folder.

13. Close the command prompt.

▶ **To use the Internet Explorer FTP client**

1. Start Internet Explorer.

2. In the **Address** box, type **ftp://**/computername/

   Internet Explorer displays the file names.

3. Click any of the file names.

   Internet Explorer displays the file.

4. Click **Back**.

   Internet Explorer displays the file names.

5. Right-click any of the file names.

   An option menu appears.

6. Click **Save Target As**.

   The **Save As** dialog box appears.

7. Save the file in the C:\Temp folder.

8. Click **OK** to close the **Download Complete** dialog box.

9. Close Internet Explorer.

In the next part of the practice, you modify the default FTP port to discourage casual visitors from logging in to your FTP site. You then test the connection to ensure the port has been changed.

▶ **To modify the default FTP port**

1. Start Internet Service Manager.
2. Expand the computer icon.
3. Right-click **Default FTP Site**, and then click **Properties**.
4. On the **FTP Site** tab, change the **TCP Port** to **2021**.
5. Click **OK**.

▶ **To use the command prompt FTP client**

1. Start a command prompt.
2. Switch to the Temp folder.
3. At the command prompt, type **ftp** *computername* and then press ENTER.

   The server responds:
   ftp: connect:connection refused
   ftp>
4. At the ftp prompt, type **open** *computername* **2021** and then press ENTER.
5. At the user prompt, type **anonymous** and then press ENTER.

   The FTP client responds with a password prompt.
6. At the password prompt, press ENTER.

   The FTP client confirms that you are logged on and responds with an FTP prompt.
7. At the FTP prompt, type **bye** and then press ENTER.

   The FTP exit message appears.

▶ **To use the Internet Explorer FTP client**

1. Start Internet Explorer.
2. In the **Address** box, type **ftp://***computername/* and then press ENTER.

   Internet Explorer responds with an error message informing you that a connection could not be established with the server.
3. Click **OK**.
4. In the **Address** box, type **ftp://***computername***:2021** and then press ENTER.

   Internet Explorer displays the file names and their attributes.

5. Close Internet Explorer.
6. Close Internet Service Manager.

    You are prompted to save the changes to Iis.msc.
7. Click **No**.

Summary

There are three different types, or classes, of property sheets within Internet Information Server: the **Master**, **Default**, and **File** property sheets. FTP property sheets behave identically to WWW property sheets. You can use the FTP property sheets to configure the different areas of your FTP site, folder, or file. You can change the settings on these property sheets at any time as needed.

Review

The following questions are intended to reinforce key information presented in this chapter. If you are unable to answer a question, review the appropriate lesson, and then try the question again.

1. You are a consultant to a company interested in recording details about the activities of users who access their FTP site. Which feature of Internet Information Server allows the company to monitor user activity, and which property sheet is used to configure this feature?

2. You are interested in greeting the users who access your FTP site with a standard message. Does the FTP Service support custom messages? How would you go about creating one?

3. You want to restrict access to your intranet's FTP site except to one specific group in your organization. Which property sheet helps you to configure your FTP site in this way, and what are the steps you must take to configure your site?

CHAPTER 7

Establishing Microsoft SMTP Service

Lesson 1 Introduction to Microsoft SMTP Service . . . 110

Lesson 2 Managing and Configuring SMTP Service . . . 115

Review . . . 125

About This Chapter

This chapter describes the Microsoft Simple Mail Transfer Protocol (SMTP), which allows you to configure your hardware to transmitting electronic mail (e-mail) over the Internet.

Before You Begin

You must have installed Microsoft Internet Information Server (IIS) 4.0 according to the practices in Chapter 2, "Installing Microsoft Internet Information Server." This practice installs the SMTP Service with Internet Information Server.

Lesson 1: Introduction to Microsoft SMTP Service

A common component of Internet sites is e-mail delivery. Internet messages are generally transmitted and delivered through the use of the SMTP protocol. This lesson describes the features and use of the SMTP Service.

After this lesson, you will be able to:
- Describe the features of the SMTP Service.
- Describe how the SMTP Service works.

Estimated lesson time: 20 minutes

Microsoft SMTP Service allows you to configure your hardware for sending and receiving messages over the Internet. It also provides additional features that enable you to customize your hardware configuration to accommodate unique delivery and security requirements.

Microsoft SMTP Service Features

Microsoft SMTP Service features support for Internet industry standards, scalability, graphical administration tools, and advanced security. Designed for high scalability, reliability, and performance, SMTP Service supports thousands of users in a single-server configuration.

Microsoft SMTP Service provides full support for Simple Mail Transfer Protocol (SMTP) and is compatible with standard SMTP e-mail clients.

SMTP Service uses Internet Service Manager (ISM) and Internet Service Manager (HTML) for administration. In addition, SMTP Service uses other Microsoft Windows NT Server administrative features including simple network management protocol (SNMP), performance monitoring, and event logs. These tools allow administrators to track messages and transactions, collect usage statistics and examine usage patterns, monitor server performance, and identify potential problems with the e-mail service.

SMTP Service supports use of the Secure Sockets Layer (SSL) for encrypting transmissions. The available security features for the Microsoft SMTP Service are described in more detail in following lesson.

For each configured domain, SMTP Service supports the placement of all incoming messages directly into a Drop folder. This allows SMTP Service to be used as an e-mail receiver for other applications.

In addition to connecting to a Transmission Control Protocol (TCP) port to send messages, applications can also use a Pickup folder. Once a message is placed in the Pickup folder, SMTP Service delivers the message, thus simplifying the development of external e-mail services.

SMTP Administration Interface

Internet Information Server provides the server platform for Microsoft SMTP Service. Like other Internet Information Server services, such as File Transfer Protocol (FTP) and World Wide Web (WWW), SMTP Service is administered through Internet Service Manager. It has a similar look and feel to the other Internet Information Server services and is managed in the same manner. SMTP Service can also be administered through Internet Service Manager (HTML).

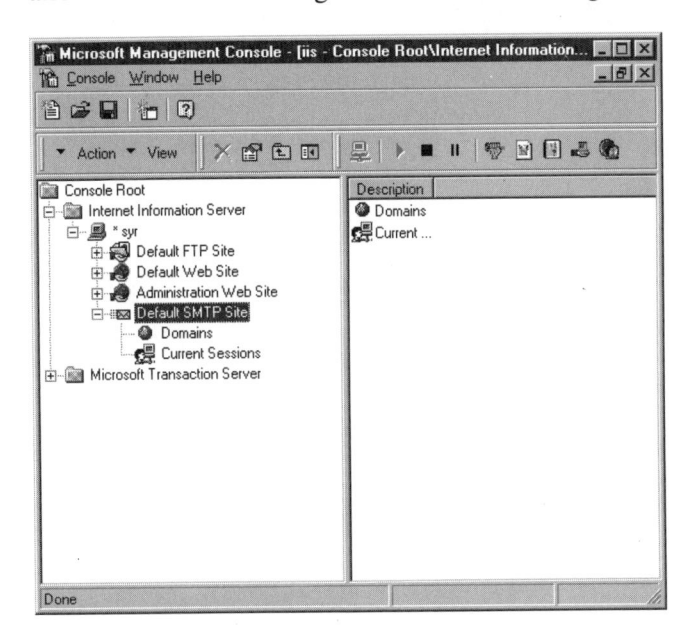

All Internet Information Server services set for the computer are displayed in the Internet Service Manager. A node in the left pane of the Internet Service Manager represents Microsoft SMTP Service. When you select one of the nodes, detailed information about it is displayed in the right pane. The following list describes the computer and SMTP Service nodes, as well as the function of the component represented:

- *Computer node.* Computers on a network or a service on a particular server appear as a node in the scope pane. Clicking the computer node displays information about Microsoft SMTP Service in the results pane, including operational status, the Internet Protocol (IP) address, and the port.

- *Default SMTP Site node.* This is the main administrative component of Microsoft SMTP Service. It provides access to the property sheets for configuring the virtual server. When you double-click the node, a list of domains and current sessions is displayed.

- *Domains node*. Domains are organizational components of Microsoft SMTP Service. The node provides access to the **Domain Properties** property sheet for creating and configuring domains, and displays information about all domains set up on the virtual server.
- *Current Sessions node*. Lists the user, source location, and connection time for each currently connected session.

The SMTP site in the Internet Service Manager is a virtual server you use to run Microsoft SMTP Service and Internet Information Server. It includes a default domain, which is used to stamp messages from addresses that do not have a domain. There is a single default domain, and it cannot be deleted. You can, however, create an alias domain. All alias domains use the default domain to stamp messages.

When you install SMTP, it installs five default folders in the Mailroot folder for Microsoft SMTP Service. The Mailroot folder must be installed on the same drive as Microsoft SMTP Service. The default location is C:\Inetpub\Mailroot, but you can designate a different location during the installation process. If you install the Mailroot folder on a Windows NT File System (NTFS) partition, you can move the Badmail and Drop folders to a different partition. The other folders must stay in the Mailroot folder on the NTFS partition.

The following list describes the Mailroot folders and their contents:

- *Badmail*. Stores undeliverable messages that cannot be returned to the sender.
- *Drop*. Receives all incoming messages. You can change the location provided you do not select a folder already designated as the Pickup folder. You can designate a different Drop folder for each domain.
- *Pickup*. Picks up outgoing messages that are manually created as a text file and copied to the folder. As soon as a message is placed in the Pickup folder, Microsoft SMTP Service picks it up and initiates delivery.
- *Queue*. Holds messages for delivery. If a message cannot be delivered because the connection is busy or unavailable, the message is stored in the queue and sent again at designated retry intervals.

SMTP Service Process Overview

Microsoft SMTP Service uses the SMTP protocol to transport and deliver messages. Messages are transferred between remote e-mail servers and the Drop folder designated for the default domain. Client and server connections to SMTP do not involve user interactions and tend to be fairly short. Microsoft SMTP Service is designed to provide quick turnaround on connections to maximize messages-per-second processing.

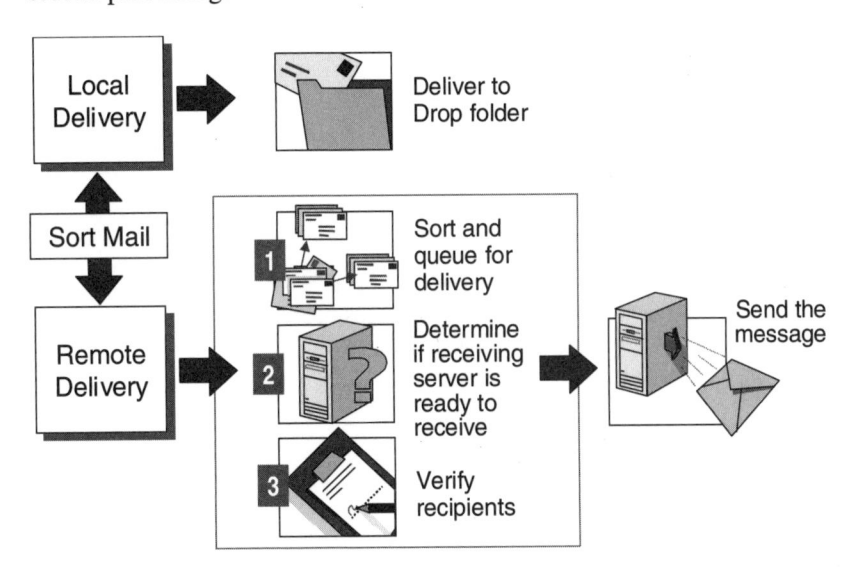

When a message is placed in the Pickup folder, or comes in through the designated TCP port, it is placed in the Queue folder. As shown in the preceding illustration, if the recipients are local, the message is delivered. If they are not local, the message is processed for remote delivery.

If a message is determined to be for a local recipient, the message is moved from the Queue folder to the Drop folder designated for the default domain. Once deposited in the Drop folder, the Microsoft SMTP Service delivery cycle is complete. The Drop folder can be designated on the **Domain Properties** property sheet.

The following list describes the processes that Microsoft SMTP Service uses to deliver remote messages:

- *Sort messages and queue for delivery*. Messages remain in the Queue folder. They are sorted by domain so that Microsoft SMTP Service can send them as a group. This enables Microsoft SMTP Service to optimize connections by delivering multiple messages in one session.
- *Determine if the receiving server is ready to receive messages*. Microsoft SMTP Service attempts to connect to the receiving e-mail server. If the server is not ready, the message is returned to the queue and delivery is attempted again at designated intervals to a maximum number of attempts. These are the retry settings, and they can be set on the **Delivery** property sheet.
- *Verify recipients*. Each message recipient is verified. If a recipient is not verified, a non-delivery report (NDR) is generated for that recipient. You can designate where to store undeliverable messages and NDRs on the **Messages** property sheet.
- *Send the message*. The message is sent. Once the receiving server acknowledges the transmission, Microsoft SMTP Service delivery is complete. Delivery options are described in the following text:
  - If you have enabled SSL for remote delivery, Microsoft SMTP Service encrypts all outgoing messages. You can also enable or disable this function for a specific remote domain. SSL can be set on the **SMTP Site** property sheet.
  - All messages can be sent to a smart host, which then sends them to recipients. The smart host can be designated on the **Delivery** property sheet.
  - Messages destined for a remote domain can also be delivered using a specific route. This option enables you to specify a route that may be quicker and less costly than a direct delivery route. This option overrides the smart host setting. Route domains can be set on the **Domain Properties** property sheet for the remote domain.

Summary

Microsoft SMTP Service uses the SMTP protocol to transmit e-mail messages. Advanced security features are provided, as well as the ability to make configuration changes for unique situations. Even with this increased security, client and server connections to SMTP are brief, so as to maximize messages-per-second processing.

Lesson 2: Managing and Configuring SMTP Service

This lesson describes how to use, configure, and manage SMTP Service.

After this lesson, you will be able to:
- Use Internet Service Manager to configure the SMTP Service.
- Use the property sheets to configure the SMTP Service.
- Select security options using the **Directory Security** and **Operators** property sheets.
- Monitor the SMTP Service using Microsoft, Extended, or National Center for Supercomputing Applications (NCSA) logging.

Estimated lesson time: 45 minutes

Microsoft SMTP Service is installed as part of Internet Information Server using the **Custom setup** option. System requirements for Microsoft SMTP Service are identical to those for Internet Information Server. If you performed the Internet Information Server installation practice outlined in Chapter 2, "Installing Microsoft Internet Information Server," you have installed the SMTP Service.

Starting, Pausing, and Stopping SMTP Service

You can start and stop SMTP Service manually. However, while it is in operation, you must be careful when stopping, pausing, and restarting the service so that users are not affected.

All Internet Information Server computers on an organization's network can be started, paused, and stopped remotely from any computer on which Internet Service Manager is installed. To administer a service remotely, the user running Internet Service Manager must be defined in the Windows NT Server Administrators group on the computer to be administered.

You can change the default startup setting using the Services program in Control Panel.

▶ **To change the default startup setting**
1. In Control Panel, double-click the Services icon.
2. Under **Service**, select **Microsoft SMTP Service**, and then click **Startup**.
3. Under **Startup**, choose **Automatic**, **Manual**, or **Disabled**.

If you set the default startup setting to Manual, you can use Internet Service Manager to start Microsoft SMTP Service.

▶ **To start the SMTP Service manually**

1. In the Internet Service Manager window, expand the SMTP tree structure.
2. Select the default SMTP server.
3. On the **Action** menu, click **Start**.

You can pause Microsoft SMTP Service for updates and maintenance. Pausing prevents new client connections but enables Microsoft SMTP Service to continue processing existing client connections and deliver queued e-mail. Messages with the .eml extension cannot be deleted from the Queue folder while the service is paused.

▶ **To pause SMTP Service manually**

1. In the Internet Service Manager window, expand the SMTP tree structure.
2. Select the default SMTP server.
3. On the **Action** menu, click **Pause**.

You can stop Microsoft SMTP Service for updates and maintenance.

▶ **To stop SMTP Service manually**

1. In the Internet Service Manager window, expand the SMTP tree structure.
2. Select the default SMTP server.
3. On the **Action** menu, click **Stop**.

Configuring SMTP Service

Microsoft SMTP Service uses five property sheets to configure different aspects of the service. All SMTP Service property sheets can be accessed using Internet Service Manager.

SMTP Site

Use this property sheet to set basic connection parameters. These include identifying what port to use, designating the number of connections that can be opened simultaneously, determining the length of time before a connection is closed due to inactivity, and enabling or disabling logging for the SMTP site.

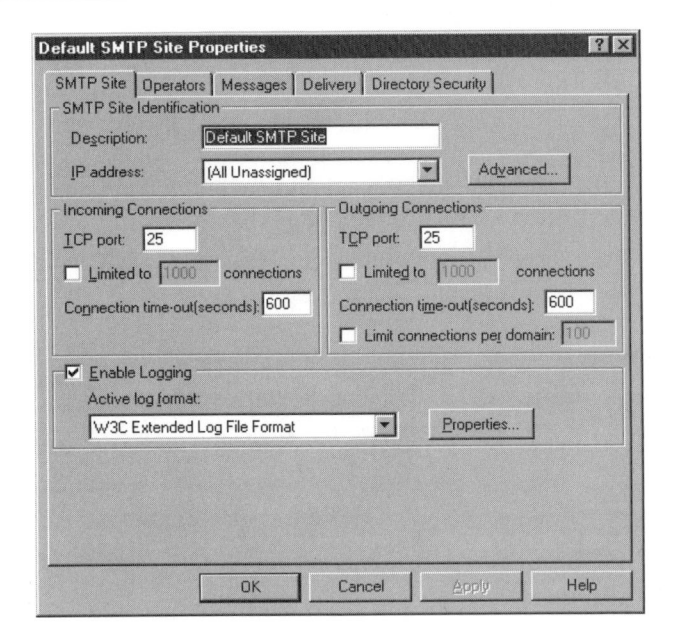

- *SMTP Site Identification*
    - *Description.* This option allows you to choose the name for the SMTP site that appears in the tree view for the SMTP Service.
    - *IP address.* This option box lists the IP address for the SMTP site.
- *Incoming and Outgoing Connections*
    - *TCP port.* Use this option to designate which port to use for Transmission Control Protocol/Internet Protocol (TCP/IP) connections. The default setting is port 25.
    - *Limited to connections.* Select this check box to specify the number of concurrent connections allowed—the default setting for incoming and outgoing message delivery is 1,000 connections.
    - *Connection time-out (seconds).* Use this option to specify the time allowed before an inactive connection is closed. The default is 600 seconds.
    - *Limit connections per domain.* Select this check box to limit outgoing connections per domain. The default setting limits the service to 100 connections.

- *Enable Logging.* Select this check box to enable or disable logging for the SMTP site.
  - *Active log format.* Use this menu to choose between Microsoft IIS Log File Format, NCSA Common Log File Format, ODBC Logging, and W3C Extended Log File Format. For more information, see the Monitoring the SMTP Service section later in this lesson.
  - *Properties.* Click this button to choose how often to create new logs, and to specify the file folder for the log.

Operators

Use this property sheet to designate permissions for specific user accounts. These options can be set in Internet Service Manager, but not Internet Service Manager (HTML).

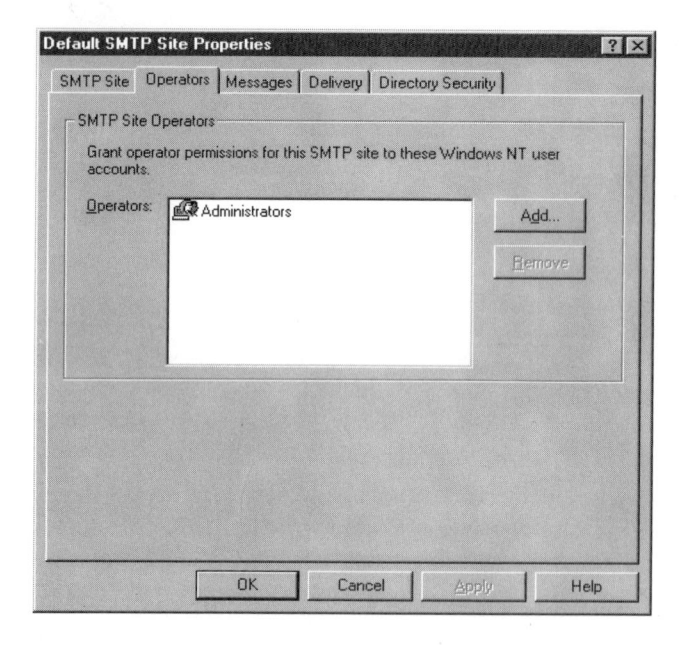

![Default SMTP Site Properties dialog showing the Operators tab with Administrators listed under Operators, and Add/Remove buttons.]

- *SMTP Site Operators.* This option designates which user accounts have operator permissions for the SMTP site. After Windows NT user accounts are set up, you can grant permissions by selecting the accounts from a list. Removing the account from the list of site operators rescinds these permissions.

Messages

Use this property sheet to set limits for messages, including size and number of recipients. If a message exceeds the limits you designate, it is undeliverable and is returned to the sender along with an NDR. If the NDR is also undeliverable, the message is sent to the Badmail folder because the message cannot be sent or returned. You can use this property sheet to designate the location for the Badmail folder and storage for NDRs and undeliverable messages that cannot be returned to the sender.

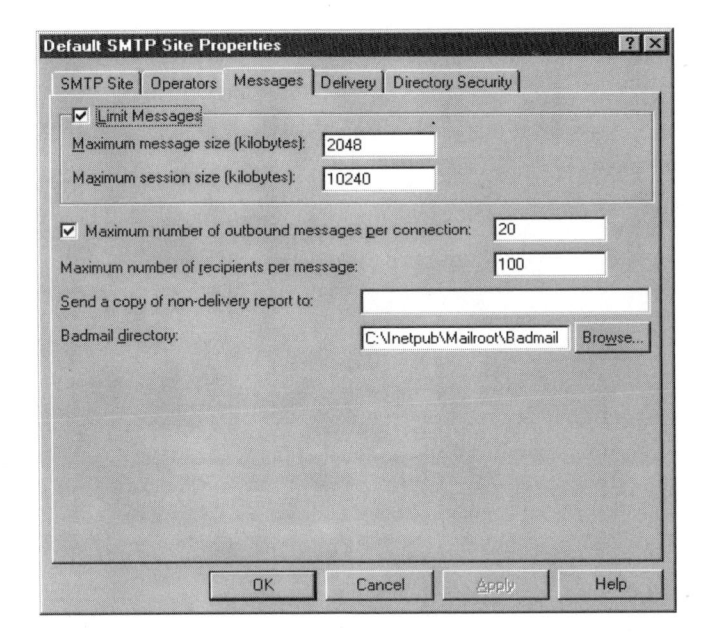

- *Limit Messages*. Select this check box to specify limitations to message or session size. These are two related message size limits.
    - *Maximum message size (kilobytes)*. Use this option to indicate a limit to message size—a preferred limit to the server. If an e-mail client sends a message that exceeds the limit, the message is still processed as long as it does not exceed the maximum session size.
    - *Maximum session size (kilobytes)*. Use this option to indicate a limit to session size, which is an absolute limit. A connection is automatically closed if a message reaches this limit.
- *Maximum number of outbound messages per connection*. Use this option to limit the number of messages sent in a single connection.

- *Maximum number of recipients per message.* Use this option to specify the maximum number of recipients allowed per message. The default setting is 100. To impose no limit, clear the dialog box and then click **OK**.
- *Send a copy of non-delivery report to.* Use this option to specify who should receive a copy of all non-delivery reports generated by Microsoft SMTP Service.
- *Badmail directory.* Use this option to set the Badmail folder. Click **Browse** to search your folder tree for a folder to use for this purpose.

Delivery

Use this property sheet to set all delivery and routing options. Settings can be grouped into three categories: transmission options, routing options, and security options.

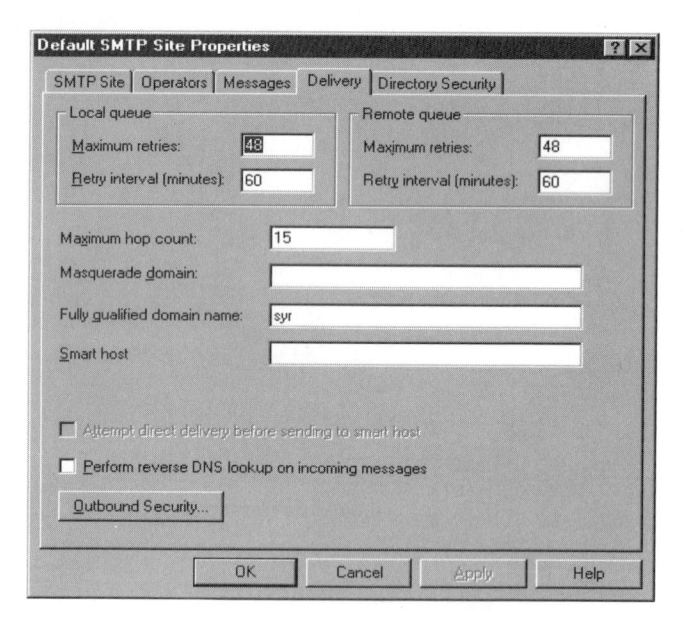

Transmissions Options, Local or Remote Queue

- *Maximum retries.* Use this option to determine how many times to resend a message before the message is considered undeliverable. After the limit is reached, the message is returned to the sender with an NDR.
- *Retry interval (minutes).* Use this option to determine at what interval to resend a message before the message is considered undeliverable.

Routing Options

- *Maximum hop count.* Use this option to determine the maximum number of servers a message is routed through before being considered undeliverable.
- *Fully qualified domain name.* Use this option to clarify the address for use in message exchanger (MX).
- *Smart host.* Use this option to designate a server through which to route all outgoing messages.

Security Options

- *Masquerade domain.* Use this option to replace any local domain used in any *From* lines in the header or *Mail From* lines in the protocol with a different domain name.
- *Perform reverse DNS lookup on incoming messages.* Select this check box to verify that the message actually originated from the computer and domain listed in the *From* field.
- *Outbound Security.* Click **Outbound Security** to choose one of four security methods for outbound messages:
  - No authentication
  - Clear-text authentication
  - Windows NT Challenge/Response authentication and encryption
  - Transport Layer Security (TLS) encryption

Directory Security

You can use this property sheet to specify the methods for anonymous access and authentication control, and to set the secure communication method. You can also use this sheet to set IP address and domain name restrictions, and to grant or deny permissions to relay e-mail through the SMTP site.

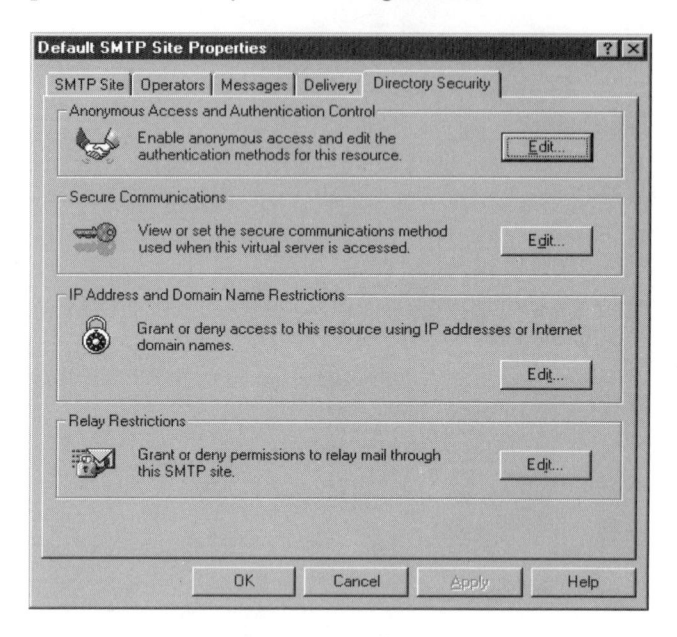

The **Anonymous Access and Authentication Control** option allows you to enable anonymous access and edit the authentication methods for this resource. Click **Edit** to select one of more authentication methods from the following options:

- *Allow Anonymous Access*. This option requires no user name or password for access to the resource.
- *Basic Authentication*. This option allows client authentication with password sent over the network in clear text using standard commands.
- *Windows NT Challenge/Response*. This option allows the client and server to negotiate the Windows NT Systems Security Provider Interface using Windows NT Challenge/Response.

The **Secure Communication** option sets the secure communication method used when the SMTP site is accessed. Once a valid key certificate from a certificate authority is installed on your virtual server, you can require that access to your virtual directory takes place on a secure channel.

You can use the **IP Address and Domain Name Restrictions** properties to block individuals or groups from gaining access to your server, or to grant access only to specific individuals or groups. Click **Edit** to set the defaults for your service.

By default, all computers are:

- *Granted access*. Select this option to grant access to all computers by default. Click **Add** to list those computers that are denied access by exception.
- *Denied access*. Select this option to deny access to all computers by default. Click **Add** to list those computers that are granted access by exception.

The **Relay Restrictions** properties determine whether to grant or deny permission to relay e-mail through the SMTP site. Click **Edit** to set the defaults for your service.

By default, all computers are:

- *Allowed to relay*. Select this option to allow all computers to relay e-mail by default. Click **Add** to list those computers that, by exception, are not allowed to relay e-mail.
- *Not allowed to relay*. Select this option not to allow all computers to relay e-mail by default. Click **Add** to list those computers that, by exception, are allowed to relay e-mail.
- *Allow any computer that successfully authenticates to relay*. Select this option to override the default for any computer that authenticates itself successfully.

Security Features

SMTP site access protection is available on several levels. To start, you can grant or deny access for specific computers or networks. For computers allowed access, you can require that SSL is used for all transmissions sent to the server. Finally, you can grant or deny access to specific user accounts. Not all of these options have to be enabled. You can choose how secure you want the SMTP site to be and use the security options to obtain the level of protection you need.

There are two property sheets available for setting security options. The **Operators** property sheet enables you to designate permissions for specific user accounts, and the **Directory Security** property sheet provides settings for SSL. It also includes IP access restrictions in Internet Service Manager, but not Internet Service Manager (HTML). Settings on these property sheets apply to all domains on the site.

You can designate which user accounts can have operator permissions for the SMTP site. Once Windows NT user accounts are set up, you can easily grant permissions by selecting the accounts from a list of site operators. These permissions can be rescinded just as easily by removing the account from the list of site operators.

You can require that all clients use SSL to connect to the server managed through the default SMTP site. This option secures the connection, but is not used for authentication.

To use SSL for the server, you must create key pairs and configure key certificates. Clients can then use SSL to submit encrypted messages to Microsoft SMTP Service, which Microsoft SMTP Service can then decode. Microsoft SMTP Service can also use SSL to encrypt messages sent to remote servers.

There are two additional SSL options available. To use SSL for all outgoing connections, you can select **Always Use SSL** on the **Delivery** property sheet. Also, if a server you commonly connect to requires the use of SSL for all incoming connections, you can create a remote domain and select **Use SSL** on the **Domain Properties** property sheet.

Monitoring the SMTP Service

You can use transaction logging to track individual message transactions, including time of receipt, delivery to a local mailbox, and recipient access. From the **SMTP Site** property sheet, you can choose which logging format to use for recording information about SMTP Service. From the format list, select a logging format. The default format is the Microsoft IIS Log File Format.

- *Microsoft logging*. A fixed ASCII format and the default option.
- *Extended logging*. An ASCII format that can be customized. You choose the items you want to track.
- *NCSA logging*. A fixed ASCII format common to the NCSA.

Summary

You can install SMTP Service when you install Internet Information Server. To configure SMTP Service, open Internet Service Manager and use the **SMTP Site**, **Operators**, **Messages**, **Delivery**, and **Directory Security** property sheets. SMTP Service provides site access protection, and you can use transaction logging to monitor message transactions.

Review

The following questions are intended to reinforce key information presented in this chapter. If you are unable to answer a question, review the appropriate lesson, and then try the question again.

1. Which tools do you use to administer SMTP Service?

2. What is the purpose of the default Mailroot folder named Badmail?

3. In terms of SMTP Service process, what happens to messages once they have reached the Queue folder?

4. What purpose is served by pausing SMTP Service?

5. Which SMTP Service property sheets are used to configure aspects related to security?

CHAPTER 8

Establishing Microsoft NNTP Service

Lesson 1   Introduction to NNTP Service . . . 128

Lesson 2   Configuring and Managing NNTP Service . . . 132

Review . . . 141

About This Chapter
This chapter describes Microsoft Network News Transfer Protocol (NNTP) service, which allows users in your organization to engage in newsgroup-type discussions with other users, both inside and outside the organization.

Before You Begin
You must have installed Microsoft Internet Information Server (IIS) 4.0 according to the practices in Chapter 2, "Installing Microsoft Internet Information Server." This practice installs the Microsoft NNTP Service with Internet Information Server.

Lesson 1: Introduction to NNTP Service

Microsoft NNTP Service allows users to read articles posted by others, post articles on their own, and join conversation threads about topics of interest. This lesson describes the features and use of the NNTP Service.

After this lesson, you will be able to:
- Describe the features of the Microsoft NNTP Service.
- Describe how the NNTP Service works.

Estimated lesson time: 15 minutes

Microsoft NNTP Service supports Internet industry standards, uses graphical administration tools, is fully integrated with Microsoft Windows NT Server, and supports three different options for securing your NNTP Service.

Microsoft NNTP Service supports the protocol that is used for both client-to-server and server-to-server communication over the Internet. Microsoft NNTP Service supports popular NNTP extensions and is fully compatible with other NNTP clients and servers.

In addition, Microsoft NNTP Service supports numerous content formats including:

- Multipurpose Internet Mail Extension (MIME)
- Hypertext Markup Language (HTML)
- Graphics interchange format (GIF)
- Joint Photographic Experts Group (JPEG)

This content format support enables users to post pictures and to include Web links in articles.

Microsoft NNTP Service offers you a choice of two graphical administration tools: Internet Service Manager and Internet Service Manager (HTML). You can perform all administration tasks with the tool that best meets your needs at the time:

- Internet Service Manager uses Microsoft Management Console (MMC) to manage Microsoft NNTP Service from a computer on the same LAN. This tool can manage all Internet Information Server components using a single interface.
- Internet Service Manager (HTML) uses a Web browser, such as Microsoft Internet Explorer, to manage Microsoft NNTP Service from a computer on the same network or on the Internet. This tool requires only a Web browser on the administrator's computer.

Microsoft NNTP Service can also write to the Internet Information Server access log to record usage statistics and transactions.

Microsoft NNTP Service takes full advantage of standard Windows NT Server administration tools for performance monitoring and event reporting. When you install Microsoft NNTP Service, Setup installs a complete set of Performance Monitor counters. All Microsoft NNTP Service status and error messages are written to event logs for viewing with Windows NT Event Viewer. Microsoft NNTP Service also includes support for simple network management protocol (SNMP) monitors.

Microsoft NNTP Service manages access to newsgroups using Windows NT Server access control lists (ACLs). By setting the permissions for the folder that contains a newsgroup, you control who can access that newsgroup. You can also specify anonymous access to allow anyone to access a newsgroup.

Microsoft NNTP Service supports full-text and property indexing of newsgroup content using Microsoft Index Server, which is included with Internet Information Server.

The optional Microsoft Content Replication System updates the ACLs for Microsoft NNTP Service automatically across multiple servers. This saves time and simplifies security administration.

Microsoft NNTP Service supports three security options for protecting your organization's private information:

- *Anonymous access*. Allows anyone to access a newsgroup without having to provide a user name or a password.
- S*tandard NNTP security extension (AUTHINFO)*. Requires users to provide a user name and a password, which are sent as clear text across the network.
- *Windows NT Challenge/Response protocol*. Requires users to provide a user name and a password, which are encrypted for secure transmission across the network. This protocol requires the Microsoft Internet Mail and News client.

To protect the information that is sent across a public network, Microsoft NNTP Service supports Secure Socket Layer (SSL) channel encryption. SSL support includes certificate support to validate the identity of clients and servers.

How NNTP Service Works

Microsoft NNTP Service implements NNTP, which is a client/server protocol. Microsoft NNTP Service is the server; Microsoft Internet Mail and News is a typical client.

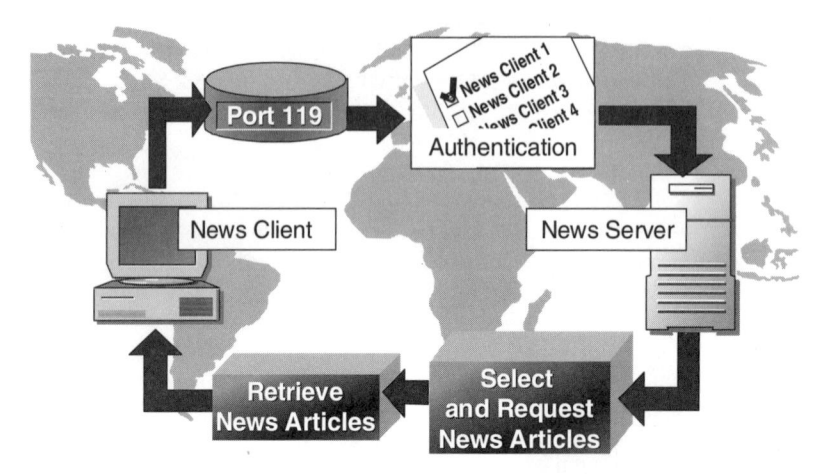

Clients connect to Microsoft NNTP Service through a Transmission Control Protocol/Internet Protocol (TCP/IP) network. The default TCP port is 119 for typical connections; for optional encrypted SSL connections, the default TCP port is 563.

Microsoft NNTP Service runs as a service on Windows NT Server and it is configured to start automatically. In the Services program in Windows NT Server Control Panel, the service name is Microsoft NNTP Service.

Posting Articles

You post newsgroup articles to Microsoft NNTP Service using a news client such as Microsoft Internet Mail and News. The client connects to Microsoft NNTP Service and requests to post the article to one or more newsgroups. Microsoft NNTP Service receives the connection request and verifies that the user is authorized to post to the specified newsgroups. Microsoft NNTP Service then adds the article to the newsgroup and updates the newsgroup index.

Viewing Articles

You view newsgroup articles on Microsoft NNTP Service using a news client such as Microsoft Internet Mail and News. The first step in viewing newsgroup articles is to get a list of available newsgroups. The client connects to Microsoft NNTP Service and requests the list of available newsgroups. Microsoft NNTP Service receives the connection request, verifies that the user is authorized to access newsgroups, and then sends the client a list of all available newsgroups.

The second step is to select the newsgroup the user wants to view. The client requests the list of articles for the selected newsgroup. Microsoft NNTP Service verifies that the user is authorized to access the specified newsgroup and sends the client a list of all articles in that newsgroup.

As the user selects articles, the client requests the selected articles from Microsoft NNTP Service. Microsoft NNTP Service then returns the contents of the specified articles.

Microsoft NNTP Service Data Structures

Microsoft NNTP Service stores newsgroup articles in one or more folder hierarchies. Each newsgroup has its own folder, and each article is stored as a file in that folder.

The main folder is C:\Inetpub\Nntproot by default, which can be changed on the **Home Directory** tab of the **Microsoft NNTP Service** property sheet. You can create additional folder hierarchies on other hard disks or other computers by defining virtual directories.

The newsgroup folder has the same name as the newsgroup. Microsoft NNTP Service automatically creates the required folders when you create new newsgroups. For example, the newsgroup named entertainment.news is stored by default in the Entertainment\News folder under the root folder C:\Inetpub\Nntproot\Entertainment\News.

Newsgroup article files have an .nws extension. Microsoft NNTP Service also creates files that list the subjects of stored articles. Microsoft NNTP Service creates one of these subject files, which has an .xix extension, for every 128 articles in a newsgroup.

Microsoft NNTP Service maintains a number of internal data structure files with .hsh, .hdr, .lst, and .txt extensions. Do not modify or delete these files. By default, they are located in C:\Inetpub\Nntpfile.

Summary

Microsoft NNTP Service runs as a service on Windows NT Server and allows users to participate in newsgroup discussions with other users. Using a news client such as Microsoft Internet Mail and News, users can post or view newsgroup articles. Microsoft NNTP Service supports common content formats and provides advanced security features.

Lesson 2: Configuring and Managing NNTP Service

You can set up and manage NNTP Service easily using standard Internet Information Server tools. This lesson describes how to use and configure NNTP Service.

After this lesson, you will be able to:
- Create newsgroups for Internet Information Server.
- Create a virtual directory for newsgroups across servers.
- Moderate, restrict, edit, and define newsgroups on Internet Information Server.

Estimated lesson time: 30 minutes

Microsoft NNTP Service is installed as part of Internet Information Server using the Custom Setup option. System requirements for Microsoft NNTP Service are identical to those for Internet Information Server.

Starting, Stopping, and Pausing NNTP Service

Microsoft NNTP Service runs as a service on Windows NT Server and is configured to start automatically. However, you can manually start, stop, and pause the service using Internet Service Manager, Internet Service Manager (HTML), or the Services program in Windows NT Server Control Panel.

When you start Microsoft NNTP Service, it accepts new connections from users. When you stop Microsoft NNTP Service, it disconnects current users and does not accept new connections. When you pause Microsoft NNTP Service, it does not accept new connections but continues to service existing connections.

▶ **To start, stop, or pause Microsoft NNTP Service using Internet Service Manager**

1. Start Internet Service Manager.
2. Select the **NNTP Site** entry.
3. On the **Action** menu, click **Start**, **Stop**, or **Pause**.

Creating a Newsgroup

You use the **Groups** property sheet in Microsoft NNTP Service to create a newsgroup. When you create a new newsgroup, Microsoft NNTP Service creates the folder for the newsgroup automatically.

In this practice, you add an NNTP newsgroup to the default newsgroup.

▶ **To add a newsgroup**

1. Click the **Start** button, point to **Programs**, point to **Windows NT 4.0 Option Pack**, point to **Microsoft Internet Information Server**, and then click **Internet Service Manager**.
2. Expand **Internet Information Server**.

   A computer icon appears with the name of your computer next to it.
3. Expand your computer icon.

   The **Default FTP Site**, the **Default Web Site**, the **Administration Web Site**, the **Default SMTP Site**, and the **Default NNTP Site** appear. Start the NNTP service if it is not started.
4. Right-click the **Default NNTP Site** folder.

   A content menu appears.
5. Click **Properties**.

   The **Default NNTP Site Properties** dialog box appears.
6. Click the **Groups** tab.
7. Click **Create new newsgroup**.

   The **Newsgroup Properties** dialog box appears.

8. In the **Newsgroup** box, type **alt.**computername (where computername is the name of your computer).
9. Click **OK**.
10. Click **OK**.
11. Close Microsoft Management Console.

    You are prompted to save console settings to Internet Information Server.
12. Click **No**.

Creating Virtual Directories Across Hard Disks

Virtual directories enable you to store newsgroup files on multiple hard disks. Using more than one hard disk can improve the performance of a heavily used disk, and it can provide more storage than a single disk. Virtual directories also enable you to change the physical location of the folder without changing the name of the newsgroup.

Virtual directories contain part of the newsgroup hierarchy. For example, a virtual directory named Research could contain all of the newsgroups named research.*.

Virtual directories can be located on a local hard disk or on a network drive. There is no advantage to creating a virtual directory on the same physical disk as the home directory.

You can create as many virtual directories as you need. You create virtual directories that match the structure of your newsgroup hierarchy.

▶ **To create a virtual directory**

1. Using either Internet Service Manager or Internet Service Manager (HTML), select **Directories**.
2. On the **Action** menu, click **New**, and then click **Virtual Directory**.
3. Follow the instructions of the New Virtual Directory wizard. Select **Help** if you need more information.

Configuring NNTP Service

Microsoft NNTP Service uses six property sheets to configure different aspects of the service. All NNTP Service property sheets can be accessed using Internet Service Manager (ISM).

- *News Site*. Use this property sheet to set NNTP site identification and Internet Protocol (IP) address, to limit the number of connections allowed, to specify a connection timeout, and to enable or disable logging for an NNTP site.
- *Security Accounts*. Use this property sheet to control which users can access your server and to specify which account to use for anonymous client logon requests.

- *NNTP Settings*. Use this property sheet to specify whether to allow clients to post messages, to limit message size or connection length, or to allow servers to pull messages from the server. You can also specify the Simple Mail Transfer Protocol (SMTP) server for moderated groups, set the default moderator domain, and set the e-mail account for the site administrator.
- *Home Directory*. Use this property sheet to specify whether content should come from a folder located on this computer or a share located elsewhere, to set access restriction for the site, to set content control specifications, and to specify the secure communications method for the server.
- *Directory Security*. Use this property sheet to set the password authentication method for non-anonymous access, and to set TCP/IP access restrictions.
- *Groups*. Use this property sheet to create new newsgroups, to limit the number of resulting newsgroup matches, and to edit or delete newsgroups from a list of matching newsgroups.

Editing and Deleting a Newsgroup

You can edit the properties of an existing Microsoft NNTP Service newsgroup or delete a newsgroup that you no longer need.

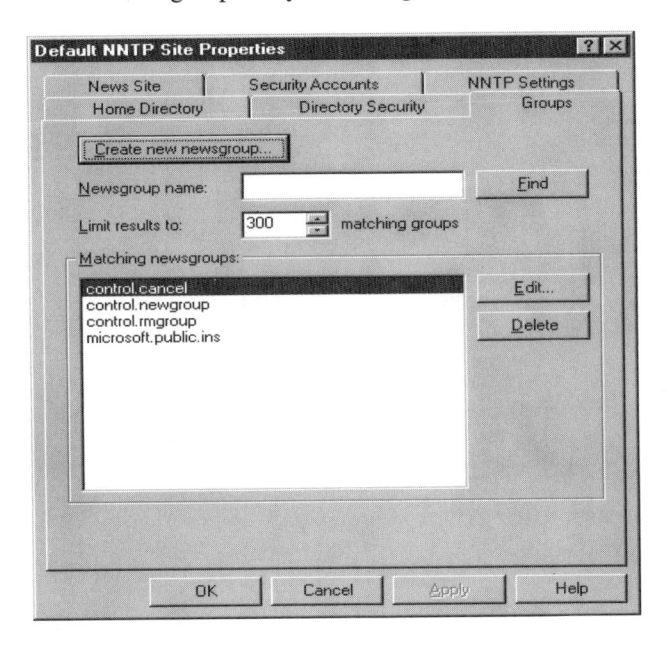

▶ **To edit or delete a newsgroup**

1. Using either Internet Service Manager or Internet Service Manager (HTML), select the **Groups** property sheet.

2. In the **Matching newsgroups** box, select a newsgroup. If you do not see the newsgroup you want, type the first few characters of the newsgroup name in the **Newsgroup name** box, and then click **Find**.

3. Click **Edit** to edit newsgroup properties, or click **Delete** to remove the newsgroup.

Defining Newsgroup Limits and Expirations

You can limit the length of time articles are kept in a Microsoft NNTP Service newsgroup and how much disk space a newsgroup can occupy by defining expiration policies for newsgroups. An expiration policy can apply to a single newsgroup or to any number of newsgroups. You can define as many policies as you need. In each case, the oldest articles are deleted first.

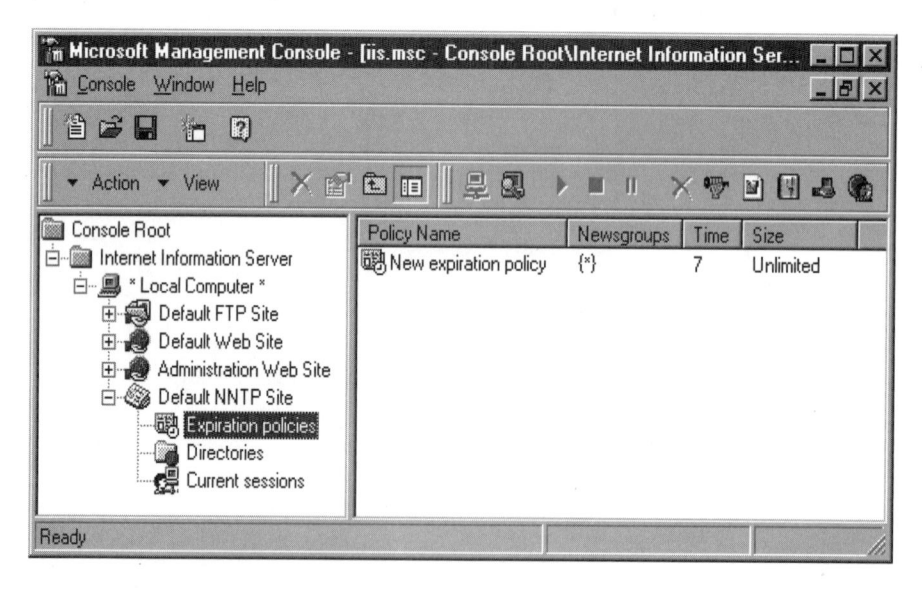

If you do not specify an expiration policy for a newsgroup, you should delete articles manually when they are no longer needed.

▶ **To create an expiration policy**

1. Using either Internet Service Manager or Internet Service Manager (HTML), select the Expiration policies node.

2. On the **Action** menu, click **New expiration policy**.

3. Follow the instructions of the New Expiration Policy wizard. Select **Help** if you need more information.

You can modify an existing expiration policy, including changing the newsgroups to which the policy applies, using the **General (Expiration Policy)** property sheet.

▶ **To modify an expiration policy**

1. Using either Internet Service Manager or Internet Service Manager (HTML), select the Expiration policies node.
2. In the right pane, select the expiration policy you want to modify.
3. On the **Action** menu, click **Properties**.
4. Change the options in the *policyname* **Properties** dialog box as needed.

Restricting Access

There are several methods you can use to restrict access and provide security. These methods include restricting access to the newsgroup, authenticating users, or limiting access by IP address.

You can control access to individual newsgroups or sets of newsgroups by setting Windows NT Server permissions for the folders that contain those newsgroups.

▶ **To restrict access to a newsgroup**

1. Create Windows NT Server accounts for users.
2. Define Windows NT Server permissions for the folder that contains the newsgroup.
3. Set the authentication method used by Microsoft NNTP Service.

Microsoft NNTP Service supports basic authentication and Windows NT Challenge/Response authentication for authentication of users.

▶ **To set the authentication method**

1. Using Internet Service Manager or Internet Service Manager (HTML), in the **Default NNTP Site** dialog box, select the **Directory Security** property sheet.
2. Under **Password Authentication Method**, click **Edit**.
3. Select the **Basic Authentication** check box, the **Windows NT Challenge/Response** check box, or both.

You can also limit access to all newsgroups by the IP address of the client computer. By default, all IP addresses can access Microsoft NNTP Service.

You can either allow access to a specified list of IP addresses or you can deny access to a specified list of IP addresses. You can also specify IP addresses using a domain name, but this adds the overhead of a domain name system (DNS) lookup for each connection.

▶ **To limit access by IP address**

1. Using Internet Service Manager or Internet Service Manager (HTML), select the **Directory Security** property sheet.
2. In the **IP Address and Domain Name Restrictions** section, click **Edit**.
3. Select **Granted Access** to deny access to a list of IP address, or select **Denied Access** to allow access to a list of IP addresses.
4. Click **Add** to add each IP address you want to allow or deny.
5. Select **Single Computer**, and then type the IP address of the computer in the **IP Address** box. If you do not know the IP address, click **DNS Lookup**.

    Select **Group of Computers**, type the IP address in the **Network ID** box, and then type the subnet mask of the group of computers in the **Subnet Mask** box.

    Select **Domain Name**, and then type the domain name of the computer in the **Domain Name** box.

Moderating a Newsgroup

If you want to control what articles are posted to a newsgroup, you can use a moderated newsgroup. Articles submitted to a moderated newsgroup are not posted until the moderator for that newsgroup approves them.

When a user submits an article to a moderated newsgroup, Microsoft NNTP Service sends the article to the newsgroup moderator as shown in the following illustration. The moderator can either approve the article and send it back to Microsoft NNTP Service to be posted, or discard the article. For discarded articles, the moderator can choose to send a message to the author of the article to explain why the article was rejected.

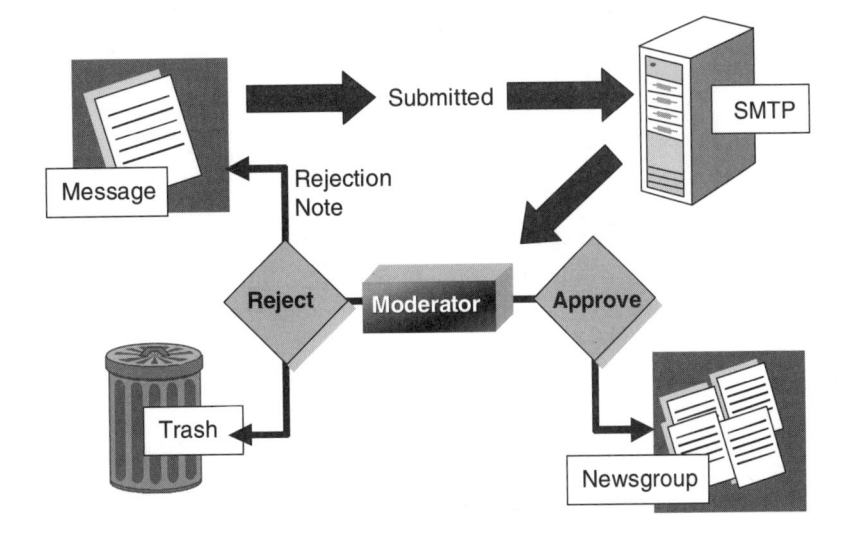

To use moderated newsgroups, you have to specify an SMTP e-mail server that is used to send articles to moderators or a folder where the articles are stored for the moderators.

You can also specify a default moderator domain. If you choose to use the default moderator for a newsgroup, articles are sent to
newsgroup_name@default_domain.

▶ **To enable moderated newsgroups**

1. Using either Internet Service Manager or Internet Service Manager (HTML), select the **NNTP Settings** property sheet.

2. In the **SMTP server for moderated groups** box, either type the DNS name or IP address of the SMTP server, or type the path to the folder where articles are stored for the moderators. The folder path must be a local folder or a network folder mapped to a drive letter.

3. In the **Default moderator domain** box, type the e-mail domain for default moderators.

4. If you specified an SMTP server, be sure that the user ID under which Microsoft NNTP Service is running (by default the System Account) is defined as an account on the SMTP server.

▶ **To create a moderated newsgroup**
1. Using either Internet Service Manager or Internet Service Manager (HTML), select the **Groups** property sheet.
2. Click **Create new newsgroup**.
3. In the **Newsgroup** box, type the name of the newsgroup you want to create.
4. In the **Description** box, type a brief description of the newsgroup function.
5. Select either **Moderated by default newsgroup moderator** or **Moderated by**, and then type the e-mail address of the moderator.

Summary

You can install NNTP Service when you install Internet Information Server. To configure NNTP Service, open the Internet Service Manager and use the **News Site**, **Security Accounts**, **NNTP Settings**, **Home Directory**, **Directory Security**, and **Groups** property sheets. You can edit and delete newsgroups, and restrict access by setting the authentication mode and limiting access by IP address. You can also establish moderated newsgroups to control content.

Review

The following questions are intended to reinforce key information presented in this chapter. If you are unable to answer a question, review the appropriate lesson, and then try the question again.

1. What is the process involved with viewing articles posted on Microsoft NNTP Service, and are there any built-in controls to prevent unauthorized users from accessing newsgroups?

2. How do you ensure that articles posted to a particular newsgroup are not offensive or inappropriate for a given audience?

CHAPTER 9

Adding Windows NT and Internet Information Server Security Features

Lesson 1 Windows NT Server Security . . . 144

Lesson 2 Internet Information Server Security Features . . . 150

Lesson 3 Secure Sockets Layer 3.0 . . . 154

Lesson 4 Configuring SSL . . . 159

Review . . . 167

About This Chapter

This chapter outlines the fundamentals of Microsoft Internet Information Server (IIS) 4.0 and its potential security risks. In doing so, it describes the various Microsoft Windows NT Server and Internet Information Server security features that you can use to secure your Internet server. The chapter also reviews the steps involved with implementing the Secure Sockets Layer (SSL) protocol, and explains how to obtain digital certificates.

Before You Begin

There are no prerequisites to complete the lessons in this chapter.

Lesson 1: Windows NT Server Security

Security is a constant concern for Internet site administrators. Internet Information Server gives you a range of tools with which you can ensure Web site security. At the core of this security is Windows NT Server. This lesson describes the various Windows NT features that can help secure your Internet site.

After this lesson, you will be able to:
- Describe the Windows NT security features used by Internet Information Server.
- Secure files and folders by using Web server permissions and Windows NT File System (NTFS) permissions.

Estimated lesson time: 25 minutes

Microsoft Windows NT is an extremely secure operating system that is C2 certifiable, depending on how the system is configured. By taking advantage of some or all of the Windows NT security features, you can significantly reduce the risk of unwanted system access. Statistics show that most system break-ins can be avoided if system administrators pay careful attention to security basics.

Windows NT secures servers primarily through user account security and NTFS security. You can take additional steps to prevent security breaches by properly configuring the services running on your computer.

User Accounts

One way that Windows NT security helps you protect your computer and its resources is by requiring assigned user accounts. You can control access to all computer resources by limiting the authority of these accounts. The user name and password used to log on to Windows NT identifies the user and defines what that user can do on that computer. Control of user and administrator accounts in conjunction with a strict account policy is a necessary part of a secure server.

Allow Anonymous Access with Internet Guest Account

The Internet Guest account is created during Internet Information Server setup. All Internet Information Server users use this account by default. In other words, users are logged on to the server computer using the Internet Guest account. This account can only log on locally, and no other rights that it has could allow an intruder using this account to damage your server or its files.

Note Because the Internet Guest account is added to the Guests group, Guest group settings apply to the Internet Guest account. You should review the settings for the Guest group to ensure that they are appropriate for the Internet Guest account.

If you grant remote access to your server through the Internet Guest account only, remote users do not provide a user name and password and have only the permissions assigned to the Guest account. This prevents anyone from gaining access to sensitive information with fraudulent or illegally obtained passwords. Often, this strategy creates the most secure system.

Require a User Name and Password

Both basic and Windows NT password authentication force users to supply a valid Windows NT user name and password in order to access the server. Windows NT authentication, supported by Microsoft Internet Explorer, encrypts the user name and password, which provides secure transmission over the Internet. Basic authentication, however, sends Windows NT user names and passwords over public networks unencrypted.

Warning Basic authentication does not encrypt user names or passwords before transmitting them. Encryption is the process of scrambling information so it is extremely difficult for anyone other than an intended recipient to retrieve the original information.

Basic authentication is only encoded with uuencode, which can be decoded easily by anyone with access to your network, or even only to a segment of the Internet that transfers your packets. Thus, Microsoft recommends only the Windows NT Challenge/Response method of password authentication.

The different password authentication schemes supported by Internet Information Server are discussed later in this chapter.

Choose Difficult Passwords

The easiest way for someone to gain unauthorized access to your system is through a stolen or easily guessed password. Make sure that all passwords used on your system, especially those with administrative rights, have difficult-to-guess passwords (long, mixed-case, alphanumeric passwords are best). You should also set appropriate account policies to further tighten system security. Use the User Manager utility to set passwords.

Manage Strict Account Policies

In addition to setting user passwords, you can use the User Manager utility to manage other aspects of user accounts. For example, you can use this utility to specify how many bad logon attempts are tolerated before the system locks a user out, as well as when account passwords expire. By setting regular password expiration dates, you force users to change passwords periodically.

By creating a strict account policy and following it closely—particularly regarding accounts with administrative access—you can thwart both exhaustive and random password attacks.

Limit Membership of the Administrators Group

By limiting the members of the Administrators group, you limit the number of users who can choose passwords. This reduces the chance that someone selects an easily detectable password that puts your system at risk. You can also rename the default Administrator account so intruders will not try to guess passwords for that account.

NTFS

In order to take full advantage of Windows NT Server security, you should apply NTFS to every drive that can be accessed from the Internet or intranet. Also, you should never configure the system drive (the drive containing the System32 folder) for Internet access.

NTFS provides security and access control for your data files and allows you to restrict the access specific users and services have in certain portions of your file system. In particular, it is a good idea to apply access control lists (ACLs) to all data files available to any Internet publishing service.

NTFS enhances your system security because it lets you control which users and groups are permitted access to what files and folders, and what type of access they may have. For example, you can grant some users Read Only access to a particular folder, while giving others Read and Write access to the same folder. You can also control whether the Internet Guest account is granted access to specific files and folders or whether authenticated accounts are required.

Permissions

NTFS has five standard levels of permissions:

- *Full Control*. Users can modify, move, delete, and change permissions.
- *No Access*. Users have absolutely no access, even if a user has access to a higher-level parent folder.
- *Read*. Users can view files.
- *Change*. Users can view and modify files, including deleting and adding files to a folder.
- *Special Access*. User access is defined by a custom set of criteria.

After you set NTFS permissions, your Web server must be configured with an authentication method to identify users prior to granting access to restricted files. You can configure your server's authentication features to require users to log on with a valid Windows NT account user name and password.

You should note that the Everyone group includes all users and groups, including the Internet Guest account and the Guest group. By default, the Everyone group has full control of all files created on an NTFS drive. In the interest of server security, you should remove permissions for the Everyone group for all resources when you set up your server for the Internet or intranet. You can then add permissions as necessary. In addition, you should remove any unneeded permissions on network shares.

If there are conflicts between your NTFS settings and Internet Information Server settings, the most restrictive settings take effect. In order to have the most secure server possible, you should review the security settings for all Internet Information Server folders and adjust them appropriately.

Web Server Permissions for Files and Folders

Web server permissions allow you to control how users access and interact with specific Web sites. You can use these permissions to control whether users visiting your Web site are allowed to view a particular page, upload information, or run scripts on the site. Unlike NTFS permissions, Web server permissions apply to all users accessing your Web site. This distinction is very important because NTFS permissions apply only to a specific user or group of users with a valid Windows NT account.

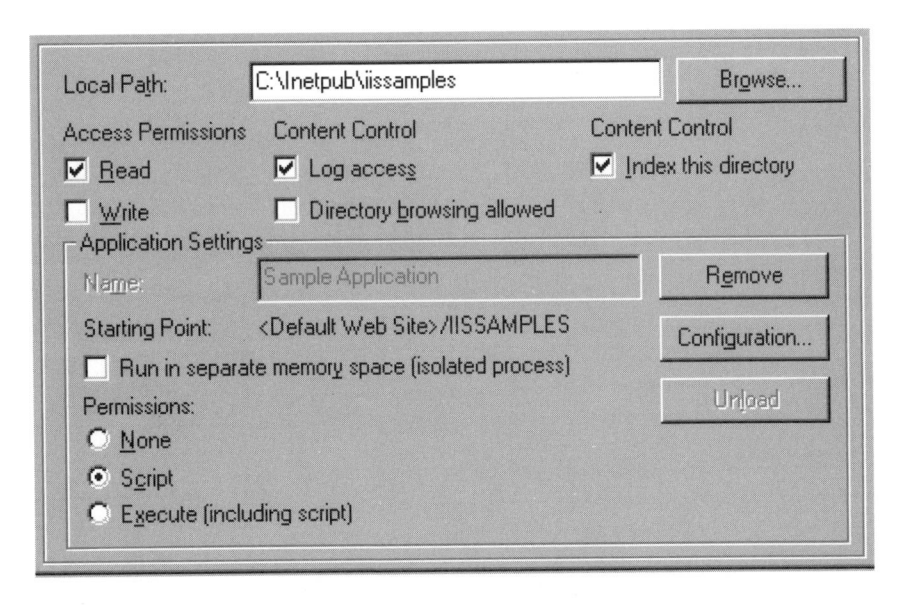

For example, disabling Web server Read permission for a particular file prevents all users from viewing that file, regardless of the NTFS permissions applied to those users' accounts. However, enabling Read permissions allows all users to view the file, unless NTFS permissions that restrict access have also been applied.

If both Web server and NTFS permissions are set, the permissions that explicitly deny access take precedence over permissions that grant access.

Warning When you select the **Write** and **Execute** check boxes, you enable users to upload and execute programs on your Web server. In that case, a user could inadvertently or intentionally upload and then run a potentially destructive program on your server. Whenever possible, select the **Script** option rather than the **Execute** option, because the **Script** option limits users to executing programs associated with an installed script engine, not any executable application.

Other Windows NT Security Measures

You can improve security by limiting the number of protocols that network adapter cards use. Reducing the number of services running on your system limits opportunities for administration mistakes. You can use the Services program in Control Panel to disable any services you do not need on your Internet server.

In addition, you can use the **Bindings** tab in the Network program in Control Panel to unbind any unnecessary services or protocols from any network adapter cards connected to the Internet. For example, if you use the Server service to upload new images and documents from computers in your internal network, but do not want remote users to have direct access to the Server service from the Internet, you should disable the Server service binding to any network adapter cards connected to the Internet.

In addition to limiting the number of protocol used by your network adapter cards, you can turn off the Windows NT Server service to prevent users from viewing shares that exist on Internet Information Server. Turning off the Server service prevents users from probing your systems for weaknesses.

The Server service uses Microsoft networking, which utilizes the server message block (SMB) protocol rather than the Hypertext Transport Protocol (HTTP) protocol. Because of this, all Windows NT Server licensing requirements apply to all connections. Windows NT Server licensing requirements do not apply to HTTP connections.

If you choose not to turn off the Server service, be sure to double-check the permissions set on the shares you have created on the system. It is also a good idea to verify the permissions set on the files contained within each share.

Summary

Microsoft Windows NT security features are the foundation of Internet Information Server security and can significantly reduce the risk of unwanted system access. Windows NT user account security and NTFS security give you a range of tools with which you can secure your Internet server. You can take additional steps to prevent security breaches by disabling unnecessary services on your computer and properly configuring the services that remain.

Lesson 2: Internet Information Server Security Features

In addition to the Windows NT security features available to you, Internet Information Server includes a number of tools that you can use to help secure your Internet site. This lesson describes the security features built into Internet Information Server.

After this lesson, you will be able to:
- Describe the Internet Information Server security features.
- Use authentication and access control to secure specific files and folders.
- Implement domain blocking and Internet Protocol (IP) blocking to secure Web sites.

Estimated lesson time: 15 minutes

Internet Information Server security allows you to control access to your Internet server in a number of ways. You can control access to the server itself both by employing password authentication schemes and by restricting or permitting access at the IP address level. You can also disable folder browsing, which prevents users from examining the folder structure of your Internet server.

Control Access by Logon

In order to control access by user name and password, you must use an SSL, Private Communication Technology (PCT) scheme, Windows NT Challenge/Response, or some equivalent authentication method.

Authentication Control

To prevent anonymous users from connecting to restricted content, you can configure your Web server to authenticate users. Authentication involves prompting users for unique user name and password information, which must correspond to a valid Windows NT user account, governed by the NTFS file and folder permissions that define the level of access for that account.

Your Web server authenticates users under the following circumstances:

- Anonymous access is disabled.
- Anonymous access fails because the anonymous user account does not have permission to access a specific NTFS file or resource.

If either of these conditions occur, your Web server refuses to establish an anonymous connection. Your Web server then uses the authentication method you have enabled to attempt to identify the user.

Basic Password Authentication Schemes

There are several authentication methods available to Internet Information Server administrators for controlling access to the server and files. These password authentication methods include Anonymous, Basic, Windows NT Challenge/Response, and digital certificates. In addition to these methods, you can add custom authentication methods by writing Internet Server Application Programming Interface (ISAPI) filters.

These password authentication schemes include:

- *Anonymous*. No password is required. Instead, Internet Information Server uses a special guest account (typically IUSR_*computername*) as the logon account.
- *HTTP basic authentication*. The user account and password are sent unencrypted from the Web browser to the server.
- *Windows NT Challenge/Response*. The server engages in a cryptographic exchange with the Web browser to determine the correctness of the supplied password. The password itself is never sent over the network. This method is significantly safer than HTTP basic authentication, but is only supported (at this time) by Internet Explorer 3.0 and later.
- *FTP authentication*. The user name and password are sent across the network in clear text.
- *Custom*. An ISAPI filter handles the authentication of the remote user. For more information on ISAPI filters, see Chapter 4, "Understanding Internet Information Server Architecture."

Note With the basic (clear text) password authentication methods, the password is contained in the frame passed on the Internet and intranet. Because it is not encrypted, the password can be decoded easily by anyone with access to your network. For this reason, Microsoft recommends only the Windows NT Challenge/Response method of password authentication.

Authentication with Certificates

Using the Web server's SSL 3.0 security feature to authenticate users, the server checks the contents of an encrypted digital identification submitted by the user's Web browser during the logon process. Users obtain these digital identifications, called client certificates, from a mutually trusted third-party organization. Client certificates usually contain identifying information about the user and the organization that issued the certificate.

Certificates are discussed in Chapter 10, "Issuing Digital Certificates."

Control Access to Folders

Unless it is part of your Internet strategy to share your entire file structure with anyone who wants to access this information, you should disable the **Directory browsing allowed** check box on the service's **Home Directory** property sheet.

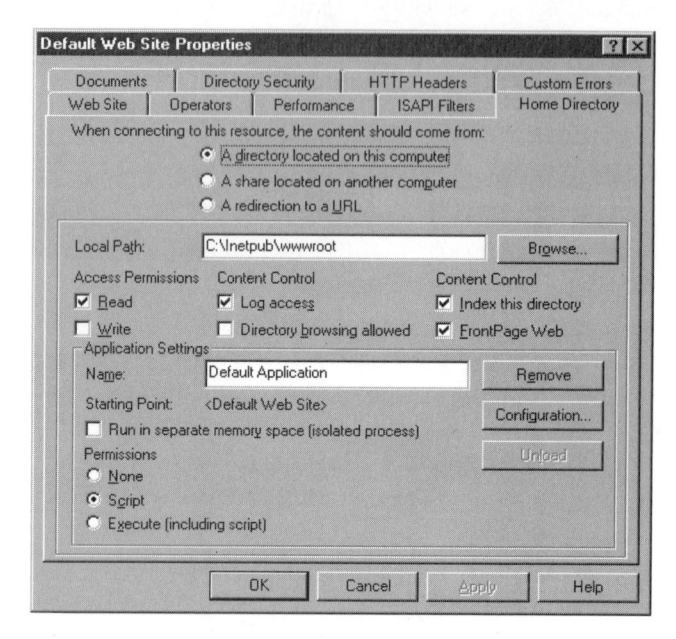

Disabled by default, folder browsing exposes the entire file structure of your Internet server. If your file structure is not configured to protect sensitive files, you risk exposing files to unauthorized access.

Control Access by IP Address

You can configure Internet Information Server to grant or deny server access at an IP address level. For example, you can prevent both individuals and entire networks from accessing your server by denying access to your server from a particular IP address.

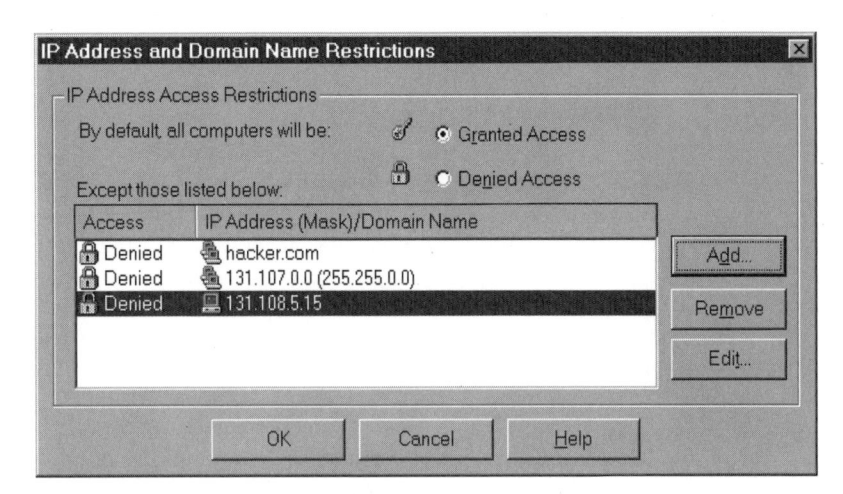

In many cases IP access security is sufficient. However, while either restricting or permitting various IP addresses, remember that packets can be intercepted and "spoofed." Spoofing is a technique where a sophisticated user can alter the contents of a packet without affecting the IP address.

IP access and domain name restrictions are configured with Internet Information Server administrative tools. When you configure a security property for a specific Web site or folder, you automatically set it for all folders and files within that site or folder, unless the security property of the individual folders and files were previously set. For those folders and files with previous security settings, you are prompted for permission to reset (replace) its security setting. This security inheritance mechanism applies to all of the Internet Information Server security methods.

Summary

Using password authentication schemes is the first step in controlling access to your Internet server. Determine which authentication scheme suits the needs of your organization. As a further security measure, you can also control access by restricting access by IP address. This means that you can prevent individuals or entire networks from accessing your server.

Lesson 3: Secure Sockets Layer 3.0

Internet Information Server provides users with a secure communication channel by supporting Secure Sockets Layer (SSL) protocol and RSA Data Security encryption on both the server and client. This lesson describes the SSL protocol layer.

After this lesson, you will be able to:
- Describe the SSL architecture and the process by which SSL authenticates clients and servers.

Estimated lesson time: 20 minutes

Users visiting commercial Web sites are sometimes reluctant to supply sensitive information (such as a credit card or bank account number) for fear that computer intruders will intercept this information. To address this type of security concern, you need to protect sensitive information transmitted over a network from all forms of interception and tampering.

The SSL 3.0 protocol, implemented as a Web server security feature, provides a secure way of establishing an encrypted communication link with users. SSL guarantees the authenticity of your Web content, while reliably verifying the identity of users accessing restricted Web sites.

Your Web server also supports the PCT 1.0 protocol. Similar to SSL, PCT 1.0 includes hardy and efficient encryption features for securing communication.

SSL Architecture

SSL is a protocol layer that, when enabled in Internet Information Server, is located between the Transmission Control Protocol/Internet Protocol (TCP/IP) layer and the Application layer, which contains HTTP.

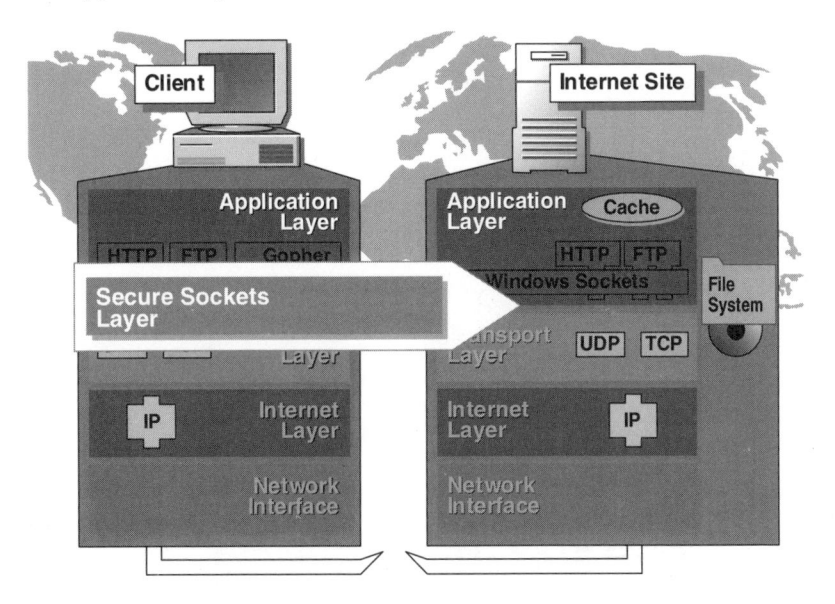

The SSL protocol secures data communication through server authentication, data encryption, and data integrity. SSL has the following benefits:

- Authentication ensures that data is sent to the correct server and that the server is secure.
- Encryption ensures that the data sent is read only by the secure target server.
- Data integrity ensures that the data received by the target server has not been altered in any way.

Using SSL, however, requires an SSL digital certificate.

Note The primary difference between SSL 2.0 and SSL 3.0 is that SSL 3.0 supports client certificates.

SSL Digital Certificates

Authentication in SSL is accomplished through the use of digital certificates. The digital certificate has the following fields:

- Version
- Serial number
- Signature algorithm ID
- Issuer name
- Validity period
- Subject user name
- Subject public key information
- Issuer unique ID
- Subject unique identifier
- Extensions
- Signature on the above fields

How SSL uses these certificates for authentication is described later in this lesson.

Client Certificate Authentication

In Internet Information Server, not only can you control whether SSL is required for access to a particular virtual server or folder, but you can also decide whether that server or folder requires a client certificate.

Client certificate authentication occurs when a client attempts to access a SSL-enabled server that requires a client certificate. When this happens, the server requests an X.509 certificate back from the client in order to authenticate the client user's identity. Only after the server verifies the user successfully does it grant the client access to the resource specified in the Uniform Resource Locator (URL). Through client certificate authentication, servers can identify and authenticate individual users.

Internet Information Server supports client authentication in a secure channel session by means of public-key certificates. However, using a secure channel and certificates requires the following:

- The protocol must be able to handle certificates at both the client and server ends. This includes handling the appropriate requests and replies.
- The client must be able to verify server certificates, request a certificate, and allow the user to present a certificate upon request. This requires that the client support certificate storage and management.
- The server must be able to request a certificate, verify client certificates, and map the client certificates it receives to access controls on the server.

Creating an SSL Session

An SSL session, which encrypts all data between the client and server, is created using the following process, as shown in the following illustration:

1. The Web browser establishes a secure communication link with the Web server.

2. The Web server sends the browser a copy of its certificate along with its public key. (The certificate enables the browser to confirm the server's identity and the integrity of the Web content.)

3. The Web browser and the server engage in a negotiating exchange to determine the degree of encryption to use for securing communications, typically 40 or 128 bits. The stronger 128-bit encryption is currently allowed only in the United States and Canada due to U.S. government export restrictions.

4. The Web browser generates a session key, and encrypts it with the server's public key. The browser then sends the encrypted session key to the Web server.

5. Using its own private key, the server decrypts the session key and establishes a secure channel.

6. The Web server and the browser then use the session key to encrypt and decrypt transmitted data.

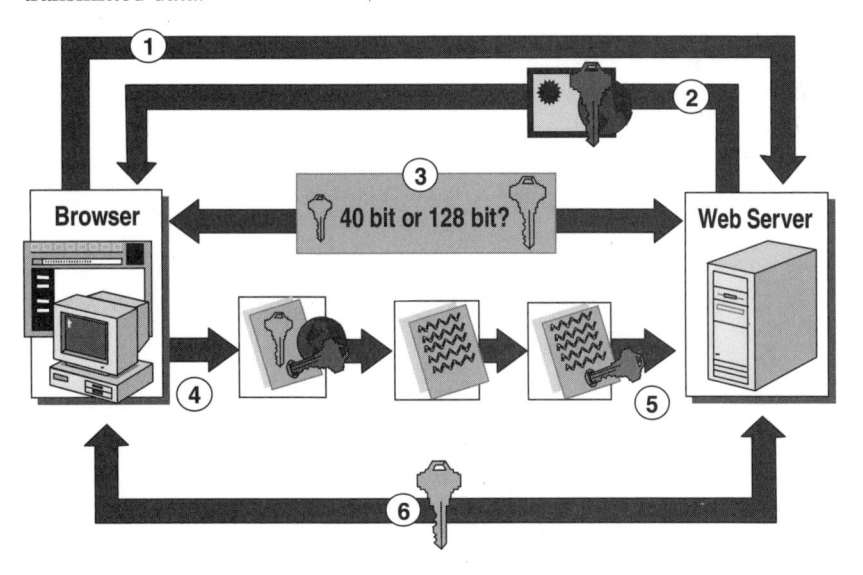

Note For more information on SSL, refer to the Web site for RSA Data Security, Inc. at:

http://www.rsa.com/

Summary

The SSL protocol enables servers to send and receive secure communication across the Internet to SSL-enabled clients. SSL secures data communication through server authentication, data encryption, and data integrity. Authentication in SSL is accomplished through the use of digital certificates. Client certificate authentication means that servers identify and authenticate individual users.

Lesson 4: Configuring SSL

Before you can implement SSL, you must have the appropriate certificates and keys. This lesson describes how to acquire the required certificates and keys, and then how to configure SSL on Internet Information Server. You will use the certificate you create in this lesson during a practice in Chapter 10, "Issuing Digital Certificates."

After this lesson, you will be able to:
- Obtain a digital certificate to use SSL to secure a Web site hosted on Internet Information Server.

Estimated lesson time: 25 minutes

Before you can apply SSL to your server, you must obtain an SSL digital certificate for it. Once you have the required certificate, you can apply SSL security features to your Web site. In order to get a digital certificate, you must first register your entity or organization with an external certificate authority who then issues the certificate to you. Once registered, your digital certificate proves your authorization to others registered with the same authentication authority.

Microsoft Certificate Server, however, eliminates the need for clients wanting to access your certificate protected server or folder from having to register with an external certificate authority; they simply have to register with you. Certificate Server allows you full control over certificate management. Certificate Server is a component of Internet Information Server.

Note Microsoft Certificate Server is covered in more detail in Chapter 10, "Issuing Digital Certificates."

External Certificate Authorities

To obtain a digital certificate from an external certificate authority, use Key Manager (Keygen.exe) to generate a key pair for your system, as described later in this lesson. Then e-mail the corresponding certificate request file to the certificate authority. The certificate authority responds by sending the verification of your digital certificate.

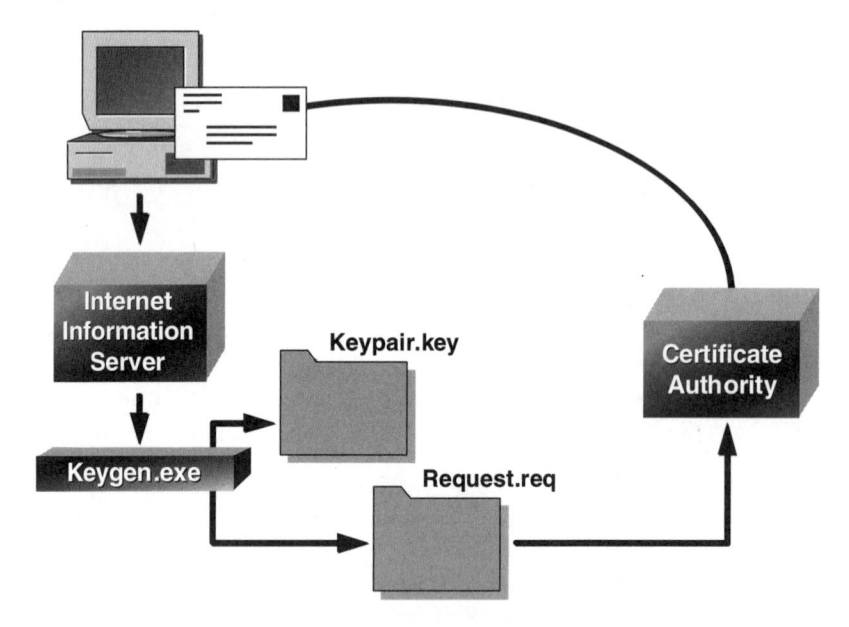

Until you send this certificate request and receive a verification, the key pair exists on its host computer (your server), but cannot be used. After you have registered with the certificate authority, you can enable SSL client certificate authentication as one aspect of your Web site security.

Chapter 9 Adding Windows NT and Internet Information Server Security Features   161

Practice

In this practice, you use Key Manager to create a certificate key.

Note You must consult your certificate authority if you intend to use the keys you create during this practice. SSL does not work unless keys are received from the certificate authority.

This practice uses Keygen.exe as part of the process to obtain an SSL digital certificate. You also use this digital certificate during a practice in Chapter 10, "Issuing Digital Certificates."

▶ **To create a folder to hold the new key**

- Use Windows NT Explorer to create the C:\Cert folder.

▶ **To generate an SSL digital key**

1. Click the **Start** button, point to **Programs**, point to **Windows NT 4.0 Option Pack**, point to **Microsoft Internet Information Server**, and then click **Internet Service Manager**.

   The Internet Service Manager snap-in appears in Microsoft Management Console (MMC).

2. Expand your computer icon.

3. Right-click the Default Web Site folder.

   A content menu appears.

4. Click **Properties**.

   The **Default Web Site Properties** dialog box appears.

5. Click the **Directory Security** property sheet.

6. Click the **Key Manager** button.

   The **Key Manager** dialog box appears.

7. Right-click **WWW**, and then click **Create New Key**.

   The Create New Key wizard appears.

8. Select **Put the request in a file that you will send to an authority**.

   The Key Request file name is C:\NewKeyRq.txt by default.

9. Click **Browse**, select the C:\Cert folder, and then click **Save**.

10. Click **Next**.

▶ To configure the new key

1. For the following screen, enter the following values:

   Key Name: **Certkey**

   Password: **password**

   Leave the bit length at 512

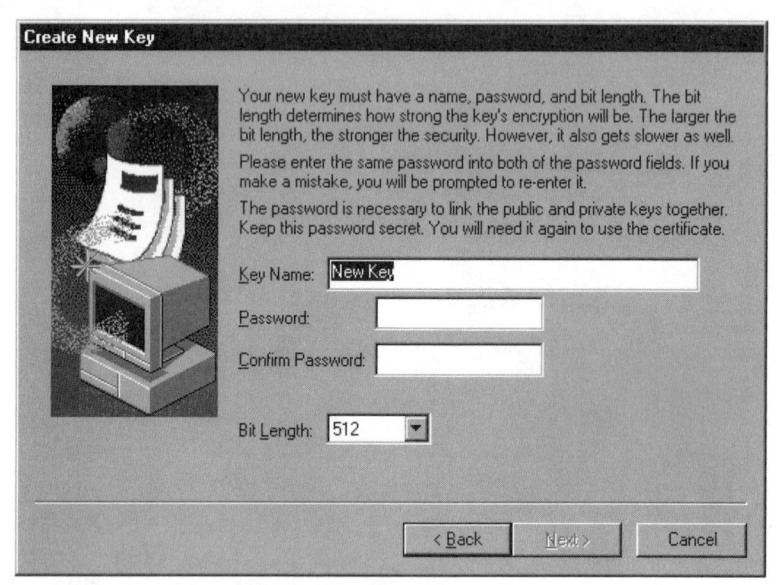

   ![Create New Key dialog box]

2. Click **Next**.
3. On the following screen, enter your information in the **Organization**, **Organizational Unit**, and **Common Name** text boxes.
4. Click **Next**.
5. On the following screen, enter your information in the **Country State/Province**, and **City/Locality** text boxes.
6. Click **Next**.
7. On the following screen, enter the values below:

   Your Name: **Administrator**

   E-mail address: **anyone@anywhere**

   Phone number: **1-234-555-0123**

8. Click **Next**.

   A dialog box appears informing you that the new key will be saved to the C:\Cert\NewKeyRq.txt file.

9. Click **Finish**.

Chapter 9 Adding Windows NT and Internet Information Server Security Features

10. Click **OK**.
11. Close Key Manager.

    A dialog box appears asking you to commit all changes.

12. Click **Yes**.
13. To close the **Default Web Site Properties** dialog box, click **OK**.

    If you were creating a certificate key for use in your organization, you would send the key to a certificate authority at this point.

    Note Do not use commas in any field. The Create New Key wizard interprets commas as the end of that field and generates an invalid request without warning.

    By default, Key Manager generates a key pair 512 bits long. You can also specify key lengths of 768 or 1024 bits in the **Create New Key and Certificate Request** dialog box.

▶ **To display the contents of the key file**

1. Start a command prompt.
2. Type **c:\cert\newkeyrq.txt**
3. Press ENTER.

   Notepad opens and displays text similar to the following message:

   ```
   -----BEGIN NEW CERTIFICATE REQUEST-----
   MIIBSzCBEQIBADAOMQwwCgYDVQQGEwNVU0EwgZ8wDQYJKoZIhvcNAQEBBQADgY0AMIGJA
   oGBaI7nOitueTDEChjJTy0pKPSlDbtRDRouhCei5SWw2t5fxc7Vs46kPTF91J9UuwpM5T
   tzqDbBDn7PkpqfV5Cea6LYaAp5U10d8s+IAAqOlRivVf8az3M8cDUBeEBbdcWS7Oa2X9/
   R44p1oXODwUnuOnGVW3rh00QgpFOi85bAVvMRAgMBAAEwDQYJKoZIhvcNAQEEBQADgYEA
   icID2qfNkttpx3zagtEEoDgDi5VQfA7bSIjXQ0RNtKKrMBa3tsqqNOUdA8KY4Abb7Yr9n
   Frjf3emSgJ2QcE2NxnEX59NS+JEbLkBTVRt/Twr3xjU8wq3sBMuy/9ReozxGWTWQB0RXy
   hDpJyOncwuSo/N8GUWAB2ddUm6+d+LraA=
   -----END NEW CERTIFICATE REQUEST-----
   ```

4. Close Notepad.
5. Close the command prompt.

To receive your SSL digital certificate, you must send this text file to the external certificate authority.

After completing your certificate request, the authentication authority sends you a digital certificate that looks similar to the following example.

```
-----BEGIN CERTIFICATE-----
JIEBSDSCEXoCHQEwLQMJSoZILvoNVQECSQAwcSETMRkOAMUTBhMuVrMmIoAnBdNVBAoTF1JT
QSBEYXRhIFN1Y3VyaXR5LCBJbmMuMRwwGgYDVQQLExNQZXJzb25hIEN1cnRpZm1jYXR1MSQw
IgYDVQQDExtPcGVuIE1hcmt1dCBUZXN0IFN1cnZ1ciAxMTAwHhcNOTUwNzE5MjAyNzMwWhcN
OTYwNTE0MjAyOTEwWjBzMQswCQYDVQQGEwJVUzEgMB4GA1UEChMXU1NBIERhdGEgU2VjdXJp
dHksIE1uYy4xHDAaBgNVBAsTE1BlcnNvbmEgQ2VydGlmaWNhdGUxJDAiBgNVBAMTG09wZW4g
TWFya2V0IFR1c3QgU2VydmVyIDExMDBcMA0GCSqGSIb3DQEBAQUAA0sAMEgCQQDU/71rgR6v
kVNX40BAq1poGdSmGkD1iN3sEPfSTGxNJXY58XH3JoZ4nrF7mIfvpghNi1taYimvhbBPNqYe
4yLPAgMBAAEwDQYJKoZIhvcNAQECBQADQQBqyCpws9EaAjKKAefuNP+z+8NY8khckgyHN2LL
pfhv+iP8m+bF66HNDU1Fz8ZrVOu3WQapgLPV90kIskNKXX3a
------END CERTIFICATE-----
```

Applying Your Certificate

Using Notepad (or a similar word processing tool), copy and save the certificate to a text file. Give it a name you can remember (for example, Certif.txt), and then use Key Manager to install your signed certificate on the server.

▶ **To install a certificate**

1. Click the **Start** button, point to **Programs**, point to **Microsoft Internet Server**, and then click **Internet Service Manager**.

   The Internet Service Manager snap-in appears in Microsoft Management Console.

2. On the **Tool** Rebar, click the Key Manager icon.

   The **Key Manager** dialog box appears.

3. On the **Key Manager** tree, click the key you want to validate.

4. On the **Key** menu, click **Install Key Certificate**.

5. Follow the on-screen instructions.

   If you do not specify an IP address, the same certificate applies to all virtual servers on the system. If one server hosts multiple sites, specify the IP address of the virtual server to which the certificate should apply.

Applying this certificate enables SSL from Internet Service Manager (ISM) for the World Wide Web (WWW) service. You can now require SSL on any virtual folder available through this Internet server. Use the **Home Directory** property sheet of the **Web Site Properties** dialog box located in ISM to configure your folders.

Note Consider using separate content folders for secure content and public content (for example, C:\Inetpub\Wwwroot\Secure-Content and C:\InetpubWwwroot\Public-Content) on your Internet server. You do not want to have an unprotected server folder that contains a folder that needs to be secure.

In addition, it is a good idea to store your key file on a disk and remove it from the local system after completing all Setup steps. Record the password you assigned to the key file in a safe place. You will need the key file and password if you have to reinstall your certificate.

Microsoft Certificate Server

Once you have your signed digital certificate, you can use Microsoft Certificate Server to manage the issuance, renewal, and revocation of SSL certificates without having to rely on external certificate authorities. Certificate Server gives you full control over your specific certificate policies as well as the format and contents of the certificates themselves.

Certificate Server's default certificate policy automatically grants certificates to a trusted set of users based on preset Windows NT user groups of administrators, accounts, and servers. While you can approve or deny certificate requests directly, Certificate Server has the ability to authenticate users based on their Windows NT logon. In addition, you can use Certificate Server's logging capabilities to track, audit, and manage certificate requests.

Certificate Server gives you the power to issue, renew, and revoke SSL certificates. Without Certificate Server, anyone who wants to access a Web site that requires a client certificate must register with the same external authority that you did. With Certificate Server, the process is as follows:

1. A potential user accesses your certificate-protected Web site and fills out a certificate request form.
2. Certificate Server's entry module (a fully customizable component of Certificate Server) processes the request. After issuing the SSL certificate to the customer, Certificate Server logs the user and policy information in a corporate database.

When the user attempts to access this Web site, the Internet server goes through the client certificate authentication process and grants access to the user based on the presentation of this certificate. If either you or the user want to invalidate this certificate—for whatever reason—you can revoke the user's certificate and deny access.

Note Contact a certifying authority such as VeriSign to acquire a VeriSign certificate. You can find instructions at VeriSign's Web site:

http://www.verisign.com/

For information on obtaining an SSL certificate for Internet Explorer, see:

http://www.microsoft.com/security

Summary

SSL security features require a digital certificate on your host computers. You can get compatible digital certificates from an external certificate authority, such as VeriSign. Microsoft Certificate Server gives you control over the issuance, renewal, and revocation of SSL certificates without having to rely on external certificate authorities.

Review

The following questions are intended to reinforce key information presented in this chapter. If you are unable to answer a question, review the appropriate lesson, and then try the question again.

1. A company has hired you as a consultant to oversee and make recommendations on the security of their Web site running Internet Information Server. The company has employees that log on to its secure Web site using the Internet. You discover that they are using basic authentication as their only security measure. What changes are you going to recommend to the company? What type of security should the company be using on their secure Web site?

2. The same company has launched a second Web site to allow customers to purchase books over the Internet using their credit card. They have hired you to review the security on this Web site. The company is using only Windows NT Challenge/Response, but they are wondering why they are not getting any customers to use the customer Web site. What changes are you going to recommend to the company? What type of security should the company be using on their customer Web site?

3. You are the LAN administrator for a small school. You are going to be setting up a Web site by installing Internet Information Server on an NTFS partition. As a security measure, what Windows NT Server group permissions should you remove?

4. You are the new administrator for a worldwide organization. While examining the C:\Inetpub\Wwwroot folder properties, you notice that NTFS has granted full Read and Write permissions to the Everyone group. Internet Information Server, on the other hand, has the Read, Write, Script, and Execute properties disabled for the same folder. Which setting applies?

5. You are the Web administrator for a banjo manufacturer. After setting up Internet Information Server, you want to ensure that all client requests are processed as anonymous requests. How would you configure password authentication to process all client requests as anonymous requests?

6. What is the difference between authentication and encryption?

7. Why is a digital certificate required for SSL encryption?

For More Information

- For additional information on configuring Windows NT Security, consult the *Windows NT Resource Kit*.
- Information on SSL for RSA Data Security, Inc. is at:

  http://www.rsa.com/
- VeriSign has produced a paper titled *Digital IDs for Servers: High-level Security at a Low Cost*. You can obtain a copy of this paper from the VeriSign Web site at:

  http://www.verisign.com/

CHAPTER 10

Issuing Digital Certificates

Lesson 1 Certificate and Authentication Background . . . 172

Lesson 2 Overview of Microsoft Certificate Server . . . 176

Lesson 3 Using Microsoft Certificate Server . . . 182

Review . . . 195

About This Chapter

This chapter provides an overview of digital certificates and data security. It explains how to protect the privacy of your network using Microsoft Certificate Server. This chapter also introduces you to the authentication and encryption protocols supported by Microsoft Internet Information (IIS) Server 4.0.

Before You Begin

To complete the lessons in this chapter, you must:

- Have installed Internet Information Server and Certificate Server as described in Chapter 2, "Installing Microsoft Internet Information Server."
- Understand the concepts presented in Chapter 9, "Adding Windows NT and Internet Information Server Security Features."
- Have used the Key Manager to create a certificate key as described in the practice in Chapter 9, "Adding Windows NT and Internet Information Server Security Features."

Lesson 1: Certificate and Authentication Background

Certificates provide a form of digital authentication to software security systems. They verify that the entity with which you are communicating is, in fact, who you think it is—even though you have no direct physical means of proof. Certificates also provide the information necessary to conduct private communications and prove the origin of communications.

After this lesson, you will be able to:
- Understand data encryption and decryption.
- Understand digital signatures and envelopes.
- Explain the role of digital certification in secure communication.
- Describe Microsoft Cryptographic application programming interface (API) (CryptoAPI) and how it can be used to secure packets over the Internet.

Estimated lesson time: 20 minutes

The need for privacy and authentication over nonsecure networks such as the Internet requires some form of data encryption and decryption—otherwise known as cryptography—as part of a software security system.

Cryptography

Cryptography provides a set of techniques for encrypting data and messages so that they can be stored and transmitted securely. Cryptography can achieve secure communications even when the transmission medium—such as the Internet—is not secure. Cryptography can also encrypt sensitive files so an intruder cannot understand them.

In order for software applications to take advantage of increasingly sophisticated and feature-rich communications technology, they require an API that provides security and encryption services.

Microsoft Cryptographic API (CryptoAPI) is a 32-bit Microsoft Windows-based API set that provides a variety of security options. CryptoAPI is supported by Microsoft Windows NT Server and is thus available to Internet Information Server. It is an ideal API if you are developing Windows-based collaborative workgroup computing applications, Internet applications, or desktop applications that require security.

A variety of applications support CryptoAPIs, including:

- Online conferencing.
- Secure WAN transport.
- Customer authentication.
- Banking applications, including smart-card technology.
- File encryption and decryption utilities.
- E-mail applications.
- Collaborative workgroup applications.

CryptoAPI is modular; replaceable components known as cryptographic service providers (CSPs) perform all of the actual cryptographic operations. Each CSP contains the core cryptographic algorithm and is independent of the application using it. As a result, an application can run with a variety of different CSPs. This allows you to choose a CSP that has an appropriate level of security without having to modify the application.

Encryption

When a message is encrypted, an encryption key is used. To decrypt the message, the corresponding decryption key must be used. It is very important to properly restrict access to the decryption key, because anyone who possesses it is able to decrypt all messages that were encrypted with the matching encryption key.

Public-Key Algorithms

Public-key algorithms use two different keys: a public key and a private key. The private key is kept private to the owner of the key pair, and the public key can be distributed to anyone who requests it, often through a digital certificate. As shown in the following illustration, if one key is used to encrypt a message, then the other key is required to decrypt the message.

Digital Signatures and Digital Envelopes

Digital signatures and digital envelopes are produced using two different but related processes. The process for creating a digital signature involves using the sender's private key, whereas the process for creating a digital envelope uses the intended recipient's public key.

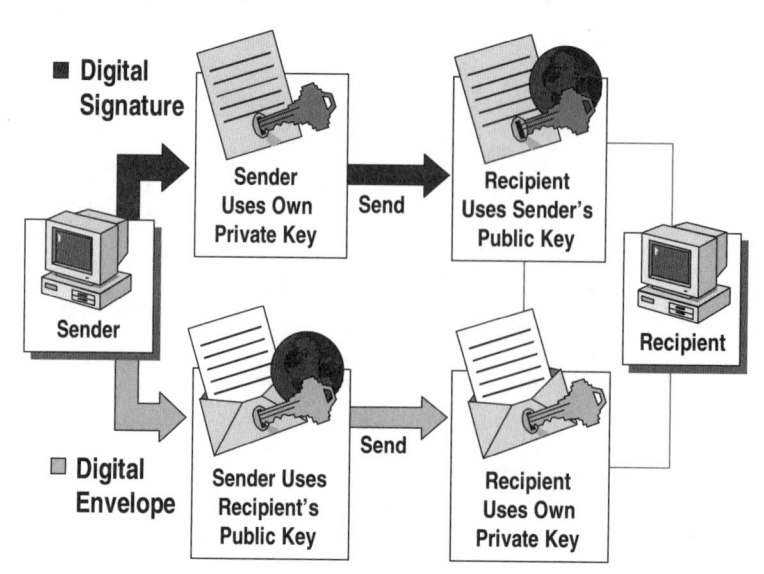

Digital signatures are used to confirm authorship, not to encrypt a message. As shown in the preceding illustration, the sender uses his or her private key to generate a digital signature string that is bundled with the message. Upon receipt of the message, the recipient uses the sender's public key to validate the signature. Because only the signer's public key can be used to validate the signature, the digital signature is proof that the message sender's identity is authentic.

Digital envelopes are used to send private messages that can only be understood by a specific recipient. To create a digital envelope, the sender encrypts the message using the recipient's public key. The message can only be decrypted using the recipient's private key, so only the recipient is able to understand the message.

Digital Certificates

The use of digital signatures and envelopes assumes that the identity of the owner of the public key used to encrypt or decrypt a message is established beyond doubt.

In order to guarantee authenticity of public keys, Microsoft Certificate Server provides digital certificates as a secure method of exchanging public keys over a nonsecure network.

A digital certificate is a set of data that completely identifies an entity, and is issued by a Certificate Authority (CA) only after that authority has verified the entity's identity. The data set includes the public cryptographic key tendered to the entity. When the sender of a message signs the message with its private key, the recipient of the message can use the sender's public key (retrieved from the certificate either sent with the message or available elsewhere in the directory service) to verify that the sender is legitimate.

Certificate Revocation Lists

Certificates, like most real-world forms of identification, can expire and no longer be valid. The CA can also revoke them for other reasons. In order to handle the existence of invalid certificates, the CA maintains a certificate revocation list (CRL). The CRL is available to network users to determine validity of any given certificate.

Summary

If members of your organization exchange information over a nonsecure network like the Internet, you need to provide data encryption and decryption methods to ensure security and authentication. This lesson described components of this process. Digital certificates verify the identity of the other party, and provide the information that is required to conduct private communications. Digital signatures confirm authorship. Digital envelopes are used to send private messages that can only be understood by a specific recipient. Public and private keys are used to encrypt and decrypt messages, and restricting access to important keys is vital to maintaining privacy.

Lesson 2: Overview of Microsoft Certificate Server

Microsoft Certificate Server provides customizable services for issuing and managing digital certificates. This lesson introduces Microsoft Certificate Server and describes its features and architecture.

After this lesson, you will be able to:
- Identify configurations where Microsoft Certificate Server might be used.
- Identify Certificate Server features.
- Explain the architecture of Certificate Server.

Estimated lesson time: 25 minutes

Microsoft Certificate Server enables an organization to manage the issuance, renewal, and revocation of digital certificates without having to rely on external certificate authorities. With Certificate Server, an organization also has full control over the policies associated with issuance, management, and revocation of certificates, as well as the format and contents of the certificates themselves. In addition, Certificate Server logs all transactions, enabling the administrator to track, audit, and manage certificate requests.

Certificate Server Configurations

Microsoft Certificate Server is designed for Web-based applications that require authentication and secure communications based on the Secure Sockets Layer (SSL) protocol. It can also support other certificate-based applications such as secure e-mail, for example, Secure/Multipurpose Internet Mail Extensions (S/MIME), secure payment such as Secure Electronic Transaction (SET), and digital signatures such as Microsoft Authenticode™. In the case of SSL, an organization can use the certificate server to issue both server and client certificates in a standard X.509 version 3.0 format. The organization may elect to issue all certificates from a single certificate server or use multiple certificate servers that are chained together in a CA hierarchy.

At the most basic level, the role of Microsoft Certificate Server is to receive a Public-Key Cryptography Standards (PKCS) #10 certificate request, verify the information in the request, and then issue a corresponding X.509 certificate (or, possibly, certificate chain) in a PKCS #7 format. In the case of a user who wants to obtain a certificate for a Web browser, a certificate request is typically generated by visiting a Web site and enrolling for a certificate. To enroll, the user enters identifying information (for example, name, address, and e-mail address) into a Hypertext Markup Language (HTML) form, a key pair is generated, and the public key is sent in a PKCS #10 to the CA. If all identifying information meets the CA criteria for granting a request, Certificate Server generates the certificate, which is downloaded to the user's browser.

Internetworking in Large Organizations

The following examples show situations where Certificate Server typically grants certificates to users within an organization so they can conduct secure communications across the Internet and gain access to the corporate intranet:

- *Branch offices.* The Internet supplements or serves as a corporate WAN.
- *Supplier/vendor relationships.* Intranet access is granted to groups of users from key partners.

The CA issuing the certificates can implement policies tailored to each specific case. An example of such a policy would include the following:

- Use authenticated remote procedure calls (RPCs) to receive certificate requests and transmit completed certificates.
- Check that the Issuer Organization and Issuer Organizational Unit information specified in certificate requests correctly identifies the CA server's organization (specified in the CA server's configuration file).
- Check that the Subject Common Name information specified in certificate requests matches the authenticated user name.

Internetworking with Partner Organizations

Certificate Server can be used to grant certificates to end-users within an organization so they can conduct secure communications across the Internet and gain access to the corporate intranet. Two examples are:

- *Branch offices.* The Internet supplements or serves as a corporate WAN.
- *Supplier/vendor relationships.* Intranet access is granted to groups of users from key partners.

The CA issuing the certificates can implement policies tailored to each specific case. An example of such a policy would include the following:

- Use authenticated RPCs to receive certificate requests and transmit completed certificates.
- Check that the Issuer Organization and Issuer Organizational Unit information specified in certificate requests correctly identifies the CA server's organization (specified in the CA server's configuration file).
- Check that the Subject Common Name information specified in certificate requests matches the authenticated user name.

Customer Registration

Certificate Server registers users for services on the Internet by following these conditions:

- Receives certificate requests and issues completed certificates over Hypertext Transport Protocol (HTTP).
- Checks information in a certificate request against an external database.
- Optionally defers completion of the request process so the customer can be personally contacted for verification.

This set of conditions comprises a typical offline approval policy that would be appropriate when there is need for a high degree of user validation.

Certificate Server Features

Certificate Server has a number of features which make it valuable to organizations that choose not to rely upon external certificate authorities and who need a flexible tool that can be adapted to the needs of their organization. The features and benefits of Certificate Server include policy independence, transport independence, adherence to cryptography standards, management of private keys, and high reliability.

Policy Independence

Certificates are granted according to policies that define the criteria that requestors must meet in order to receive a certificate. For example, one policy may be to grant commercial certificates only if applicants present their identification in person. Another policy may grant credentials based on e-mail requests. An agency that issues credit cards may choose to consult a database and make telephone inquiries before issuing a card.

Policies are implemented in policy modules written in Java, Microsoft Visual Basic, or Microsoft C/C++. Certificate Server functions are isolated from any changes in policy that an agency may implement. Such changes in policy can be fully implemented in the server policy module code.

Transport Independence

Certificates can be requested and distributed through any transport mechanism. Certificate Server accepts certificate requests from an applicant and posts certificates to the applicant through HTTP, RPC, disk file, or by custom transport.

Transports are supported by intermediary applications and exit module dynamic-link libraries (DLLs), usually written in Microsoft C/C++. The intermediary applications and exit modules isolate the Certificate Server functions from communicating with any specific transport.

Adherence to Standards

Certificate Server accepts standard PKCS #10 requests and issues X.509 version 1.0 and 3.0 certificates. Additional certificate formats can be supported by modules called extension handlers. Certificate Server works with non-Microsoft clients and browsers, and non-Microsoft Web servers. Certificate Server can write certificates to any database or directory service supported by a custom exit module.

Key Management

The security of a certification system depends on how the private keys are protected. The design of Certificate Server ensures that individuals cannot perform unauthorized access of private key information. Certificate Server relies on Microsoft CryptoAPI to perform key management, thus isolating Certificate Server from these confidential pieces of data. In addition, the CryptoAPI functions can use anything from software modules to hardware-based key engines for the generation and protection of keys, thus allowing a user to select a level of key-management system strength appropriate for their organization.

High Reliability

Certificate Server leverages the reliability features incorporated into the Windows NT Server operating system. The Windows NT architecture protects applications from damaging each other and the operating system by employing structured exception handling and the Windows NT File System (NTFS). Windows NT provides protection through its built-in security and has United States government C2 certification.

Certificate Server Architecture

Microsoft Certificate Server architectural elements include the server engine that handles certificate requests and other modules that perform tasks by communicating with the server engine.

Server Engine

The server engine is the core component of Certificate Server. The engine acts as a broker for all requests it receives from the entry modules, driving the flow of information between components during the processing of a request and generation of a certificate. At each processing stage, the engine interacts with the various modules to ensure appropriate action is taken based on the state of the request.

Intermediary

The intermediary is the architectural component that receives new certificate requests from clients and submits them to the server engine. The intermediary is composed of two parts, the intermediary application that performs actions on behalf of clients, and the Certificate Server Client Interface that handles communications between the intermediary application and the server engine.

Intermediaries can be written to handle certificate requests from different types of clients, across multiple transports, or according to policy-specific criteria. Internet Information Server 4.0 is an intermediary that provides support for clients over HTTP. Intermediaries can also check on the status of a previously submitted request and obtain the Certificate Server's configuration information.

Server Database

Certificate Server includes a server database that maintains status information and a log of all issued certificates and CRLs. The database is composed of two components, the server log and the server queue:

- *Server log*. Stores all certificates and CRLs issued by the server so administrators can track, audit, and archive server activity. In addition, the server log is used by the server engine to store pending revocations prior to publishing them in the CRL. The server log also stores recent certificate requests for a configurable period of time in case a problem is encountered when issuing a certificate. The server log is administered using the Certificate Administration Log Utility, which is explained in more detail in the next lesson.

- *Server queue*. Maintains status information (receipt, parsing, authorization, signing, and dispatch) as a certificate request is being processed by the server. The server queue is administered using the Certificate Administration Queue Utility, which is explained in more detail in the next lesson.

Administration Tools

Microsoft Certificate Server includes Web-based administration tools that provide services for accessing the data contained in the server database. These tools include the Certificate Administration Log Utility and Certificate Administration Queue Utility for administering data in the server log and server queue, respectively. Additional administration tools may be written using the administration interface. These tools are explained further in the next lesson.

Policy Module

The policy module contains the set of rules governing issuance, renewal, and revocation of certificates. All requests received by the server engine are passed to the policy module for validation. Policy modules are also used to parse any supplemental information provided within a request and set properties on the certificate accordingly.

Extension Handlers

Extension handlers work in tandem with the policy module to set custom extensions on a certificate. Each extension handler acts as a template for the custom extensions that should appear in a certificate. The policy module must load the appropriate extension handler when it is needed.

Exit Modules

Exit modules publish completed certificates and CRLs through any number of transports or protocols. By default, the server notifies each exit module installed on the server whenever a certificate or CRL is published.

Microsoft Certificate Server provides a Component Object Model (COM) interface for writing custom exit modules for different transports or protocols, or custom delivery options. For example, a Lightweight Directory Access Protocol (LDAP) exit module may be used to publish only client certificates in a Directory Service and not server certificates. LDAP makes it possible for Certificate Server to issues certificates to any other directory compliant with LDAP standard. In this case, the exit module can use the COM interface to determine the type of certificate that the server is issuing and filter out any certificates that are not client certificates.

Summary

With Microsoft Certificate Server, you can manage your organization's use of digital certificates without having to rely on external certificate authorities. Certificate Server takes advantage of the reliability features of Windows NT Server and ensures that individuals cannot perform unauthorized access of private key information. Certificate Server can write certificates to any database or directory service that is supported by a custom exit module. Microsoft Certificate Server functions are kept separate from any policy changes and can operate over any transport mechanism.

Lesson 3: Using Microsoft Certificate Server

Microsoft Certificate Server runs as a Windows NT service. This lesson explains how to run Certificate Server and use its administration tools.

After this lesson, you will be able to:
- Use Certificate Server log and queue utilities.
- Install CA certificates.

Estimated lesson time: 35 minutes

By default, Certificate Server starts automatically when the operating system loads unless the service has been configured to use the manual Startup Type setting. Additionally, the CA service stops automatically when the operating system is unloaded, or it can be stopped manually.

If the CA service has been configured to use the manual Startup Type, then the service must be started manually. The CA service always stops automatically when the operating system is unloaded. It can also be stopped manually, regardless of whether it was started automatically or manually.

▶ **To start or stop the service manually**

1. In Control Panel, double-click the Service icon.
2. Click **Certificate Authority**.
3. Click **Start** or **Stop**, and then click **Close**.

Enrolling Certificates

Certificate Server issues digital certificates that enable server and client authentication under the SSL protocol. The process of obtaining a digital certificate is called certificate enrollment. This process begins with a client submitting a certificate request and ends with the installation of the issued certificate in the client application.

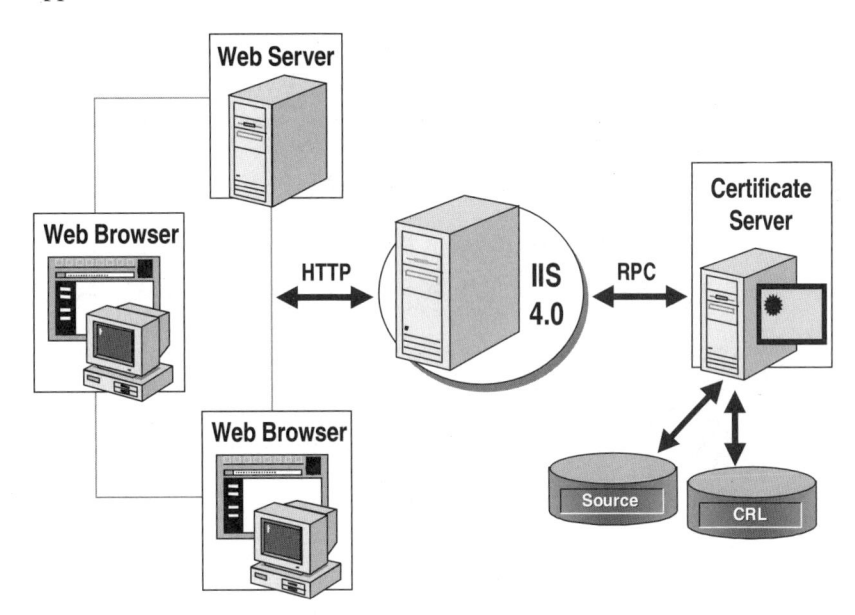

Certificate Server includes an HTTP enrollment control with forms for the following certificate enrollment tasks:

- Installing CA certificates.
- Enrolling a Web server.
- Client certificate enrollment using Microsoft Internet Explorer version 3.0 or later.
- Client certificate enrollment using Netscape Navigator 3.0.

The enrollment control and its forms are accessed through the Certificate Server Enrollment page. This page is available from the Certificate Server Administration Tools Web page at http://*computername*/certsrv/.

Web Server Enrollment Page

The Web Server Enrollment page allows you to submit a certificate request to the Certificate Server through a Web-based user interface. To do this, open a PKCS #10 certificate request file using Notepad, and use the Clipboard to copy and paste the contents of the request file into the text box on the enrollment page. (The certificate request file is generated by Key Manager.) After Certificate Server creates the certificate, it is returned to the browser to save as a file. With Internet Information Server, you then run Key Manager and install the new certificate.

Client Certificate Enrollment

Certificate Server includes support for client certificate enrollment using Internet Explorer 3.0 or later and Netscape Navigator 3.0. To obtain a client certificate with these browsers, open the client authentication page and submit your identification information. After Certificate Server creates the client certificate, it is returned to the browser, which installs the client certificate on your client.

Processing Certificate Requests

Certificate Server provides services for processing certificate requests and issuing digital certificates.

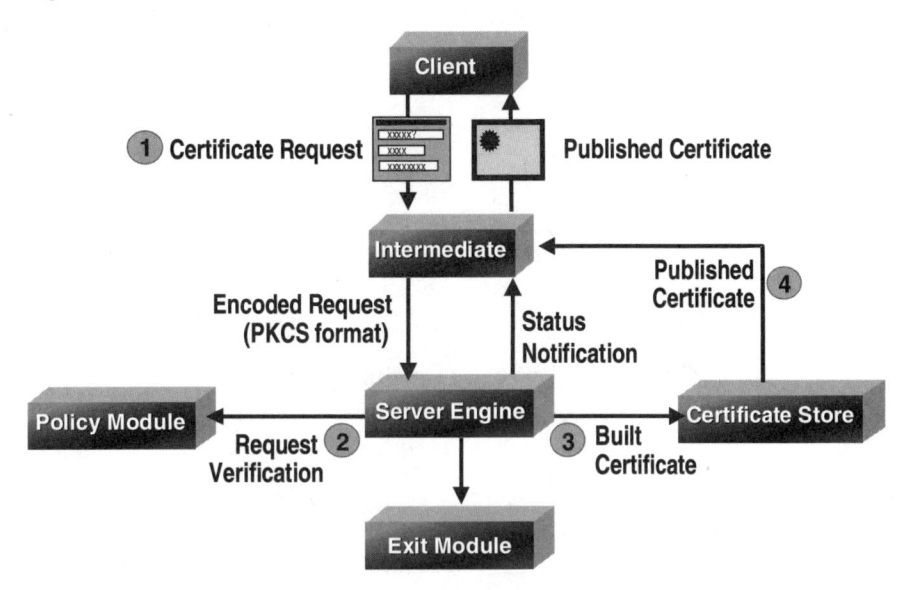

Certificate Server performs the following steps when processing a certificate request, as shown in the preceding illustration:

- *Request reception.* The certificate request is sent by the client to an intermediary application, which formats it into a PKCS #10 format request and submits it to the server engine iishelp/certsrv/concept_19.htm.
- *Request approval.* The server engine calls the policy module, which queries request properties, decides whether the request is authorized or not, and then sets optional certificate properties.
- *Certificate formation.* If the request is approved, the server engine takes the request and builds a complete certificate.
- *Certificate publication.* The server engine stores the completed certificate in the certificate store and notifies the intermediary application of the request status. If the exit module has so requested, the server engine notifies it of a certificate issuance event. This allows the exit module to perform further operations such as publishing the certificate to a directory service. Meanwhile, the intermediary gets the published certificate from the certificate store and passes it back to the client.

Adding Certificate Authorities

Certificate Server enables anyone to create digital certificates for Web servers, clients, or organizations. In the process of issuing a digital certificate, the CA validates the identity of the individual requesting the certificate and then signs the certificate with its own private key. This ensures that the certificate owner is who they claim to be.

A client application—such as Internet Explorer—checks the CA signature before accepting a certificate. If the CA signature is not valid, or if it comes from an unknown Certificate Authority, Internet Explorer warns the user by displaying a security message and may prevent the user from accepting the certificate.

If the certificates issued by your Certificate Server are to be trusted by applications such as Internet Explorer, you need to identify it as a Certificate Authority.

Certificate Authority Certificates

In addition to the server and client authentication certificates issued by Certificate Server, there are certificates that identify Certificate Authorities (CAs).

The CA certificate is a signature certificate that contains a public key used to verify digital signatures. It identifies the CA that issues server or client authentication certificates to the servers and clients that request these certificates. Clients use the CA certificate of the CA issuing the server certificate to validate the server certificate. Servers use the CA certificate of the CA issuing the client certificate to validate the client certificate.

A self-signed CA certificate is also called a root certificate because it is the certificate for the root CA. The root CA must sign its own CA certificate because by definition there is no higher certifying authority to sign its CA certificate.

Distribution and Installation of CA Certificates

CA certificates are not requested and issued in the same manner as server and client authentication certificates. Server and client authentication certificates are unique for each requesting server and client, and are not shared; they must be generated and issued by a CA upon demand. In contrast, the CA certificate does not require issuance upon demand. Instead, it is created once and then made readily available to all servers or client who request certificates from the CA.

The commonly applied technique for distributing CA certificates is to place them in a location known and accessible to anyone who requests certificates from the CA.

CA Certificate List Web Page

The CA Certificate List Web page allows Web browsers to obtain and install a CA certificate by selecting it from the list of available certificates. This page is stored with CA certificates by the Configuration wizard in the Shared folder and in the default Web location (http://*computername*/certsrv/).

Browser Installation of CA Certificates

Each browser talking to a Web server that uses a locally-generated certificate must obtain and install the CA certificate for the CA that issued the server certificate. The browser uses the CA certificate to validate the server certificate.

Browsers can install CA certificates into Internet Explorer 3.0 or later by loading the Certificate Authority Certificate List Web page at the Shared folder location.

Server Installation of CA Certificates

You must obtain and install a CA certificate provided by the CA that issues the client certificates for servers you want to perform authentication of clients. The CA certificate is needed by the server to validate the client certificates.

Internet Information Server uses CA certificates that are stored in the same location in the system registry as Internet Explorer. The procedure for installing CA certificates for use by Internet Information Server is to load Internet Explorer on the same computer and use it to install the CA certificates just as you would on a client computer.

Netscape Enterprise Server has a user interface for installing the CA certificate for the CA issuing a server certificate as part of the server certificate installation process.

Note Netscape FastTrack Server does not include a user interface to install new Microsoft Certificate Server CA certificates, so it cannot participate in client or server authentication with locally generated certificates.

Administration Tools

Certificate Server maintains a server database divided into two components, the server queue and the server log. A record of all certificate requests received in the server queue and copies of all issued certificates are kept in the server log. Certificate Server includes administration tools that can be used to view and manage the server database.

The Certificate Server administration tools are Web-based. You access the tools by browsing through Internet Information Server to the Certificate Server virtual root, which contains a link to the Certificate Server Administration Tools Web page.

From the Certificate Server Administration Tools Web page, select either the Certificate Administration Log Utility or the Certificate Administration Queue Utility.

Certificate Administration Log Utility

The Certificate Administration Log Utility generates Web pages that allow the administrator to manage certificates and CRLs in the server log. When the utility is started, the browser displays the Certificate Log Administration Web page. Initially, this page displays a list view of the beginning of the certificate data in the server log. Each row contains a database record for a certificate, and the rows appear in the order the certificates were created.

On the Certificate Log Administration Web page, click **Form View** to view the data for the currently selected certificate. You can also click the certificate's link in the far-left column of the list view, or double-click anywhere on the certificate entry.

On the Certificate Form Viewer Web page, click **Filter** to enter filter criteria for viewing certificates with the filter. Click **Apply** to apply the filter criteria, and then click **List View** to return to a list of certificates that match the filter criteria.

▶ **To revoke a certificate**

1. From http://*computername*/certsrv, start the Certificate Administration Log Utility.

    The browser display window contains a list of certificates in the server log.

2. If the certificate you want is displayed in the current page, select it. If the certificate you want is not displayed in the current page, click >> until the page containing the desired certificate is displayed.

    The certificate is displayed in form view.

3. Click **Revoke Certificate** to revoke the certificate, and then click **Requery**.

    The RevokedWhen entry now indicates the time that the certificate was revoked.

Note Certificate Server includes the Web address to its CRL in every certificate it creates. The application that uses the certificate is responsible for accessing the CRL and determining if the certificate is valid.

Certificate Administration Queue Utility

The Certificate Administration Queue Utility generates Web pages that allow the administrator to manage requests in the server queue. When the Certificate Administration Queue Utility is started, the browser displays the Certificate Server Queue Administration Web page. Initially this page displays a list view of the beginning of the requested data from the server queue. Each row contains a database record for a request, and the rows appear in the order the requests were received.

To view the data for the currently selected request, click **Form View** on the Certificate Server Queue Administration Web page. You can also click the request's link in the far-left column of the list view, or double-click anywhere on the certificate row in the list. The Web page displays the data for the selected request in form view.

On the Certificate Server Queue Administration Form Viewer Web page, click **Filter** to enter filter criteria for viewing requests with the filter. Click **Apply** to apply the filter criteria, and then click **List View** to return to the Certificate Server Queue Administration Web page. Only requests that match the filter criteria are displayed in the list view of the Web page.

Practice

To complete this practice, you must use the certificate key file you generated in Chapter 9, "Adding Windows NT and Internet Information Server Security Features." In this practice, you submit the certificate request to Microsoft Certificate Server.

▶ **To open the certification tool page**

1. Start Internet Explorer.
2. Go to the following address: http://localhost/certsrv/.
3. Click **Certificate Enrollment Tools**.
4. Click **Process Certificate Request**.
5. Copy the contents between and including the following lines:
   a. -----BEGIN NEW CERTIFICATE REQUEST-----
   b. -----END NEW CERTIFICATE REQUEST-----
6. Return to the browser and paste the certificate request file contents into the Web Server Enrollment page.
7. Click **Submit Request**.

   Note If a **Security Alert** dialog box appears, click **Yes** to clear it.

   A Web page appears which states that the certificate downloaded. If you receive an error, it is likely you did not include the Begin and End lines. If this is the case, copy the contents again and complete the procedure.

8. Click **Download**.

   A download dialog box appears.

9. Select **Save this file to disk**, and then click **OK**.

   The **Save As** dialog box appears.

10. Save the Newcert.cer file to the root of the Cert folder, C:\Cert.
11. Click **OK**.
12. Close Internet Explorer.
13. Close **Notepad**.

In this part of the practice, you test the installed Newkey.cer file using Key Manager.

▶ To open Key Manager

1. In Microsoft Management Console, right-click **Default Web Site**.
2. Select **Properties**.
3. Click the **Directory Security** tab.
4. In the **Secure Communications** section, click **Edit**.
5. Click **Key Manager**.

    The Key Manager window appears.
6. Select the **WWW** folder.
7. In the WWW folder, select **Certkey**.
8. Right-click **Certkey**, and then click **Install Key Certificate**.

    The **Open** dialog box appears.
9. Browse the certification root, C:\Cert, and then double-click the Newcert.cer file.

    You are prompted to confirm your password.
10. Type the password that you gave to the file, **password**

    Note You created this password during the practice in Chapter 9, "Adding Windows NT and Internet Information Server Security Features."

11. Click **OK**.

    The **Server Bindings** dialog box appears.
12. Click **OK**.

    Notice the status of the right pane in Key Manager. The status should read Complete and Usable.
13. Close Key Manager.

    A dialog box appears asking you to commit all changes.
14. Click **Yes**.
15. Click **OK** to close the Secure Communications window.
16. Click **OK** to close the **Default Web Site Properties** dialog box.

Microsoft Internet Information Server 4.0 Training

In this part of the practice, you enforce security for communication.

▶ **To open secure communications**
1. In Microsoft Management Console, right-click **Default Web Site**.
2. Select **Properties**.
3. Click the **Directory Security** tab.
4. In the **Secure Communications** section, click **Edit**.
5. Select **Require secure channel when accessing this resource**.
6. Click **OK**.
7. Click **OK** again.

   The **Inheritance Overrides** dialog box appears.
8. Click **OK**.

You now test the certificates for communication using a secure connection. You can do this by using the Uniform Resource Locator (URL) https:// rather than http://. In the next practice, you demonstrate that your certificate is not enabled. You then restart your computer and enable secure communications.

▶ **To open and test the certificates using the browser**
1. Start Internet Explorer.
2. Go to http://localhost/certsrv/.
3. You should receive an error message.
4. Using HTTPS, go to https://localhost/certsrv/.

   You receive an error message explaining that the page requires a secure connection.
5. Click **No**.
6. Close Internet Explorer.
7. Restart the computer.

In this part of the practice, you install the certificate from the server.

▶ **To remove the secure channel communications**
1. In Microsoft Management Console, right-click **Default Web Site**.
2. Select **Properties**.
3. Click the **Directory Security** tab.
4. In the **Secure Communications** section, click **Edit**.
5. Clear the **Require secure channel when accessing this resource** check box.
6. Click **OK**.

Chapter 10 Issuing Digital Certificates 193

7. Click **OK** again.

   The **Inheritance Overrides** dialog box appears.

8. Click **OK**.

9. Close Internet Service Manager.

10. Restart the computer.

▶ **To request a client authentication certificate**

1. Start Internet Explorer.
2. Go to http://localhost/certsrv/.
3. Select **Certificate Enrollment Tools**.
4. Select **Request a Client Authentication Certificate**.
5. Complete the Certificate Enrollment Form with your information.
6. Click **Submit Request**.

   If security alerts appear, click **Yes** to continue. The certificate download page appears.

7. Click **Download**.
8. The **Root Certificate Store** dialog box appears.
9. Click **Yes**.
10. Click **OK**.
11. Close Internet Explorer.

▶ **To reenable secure communications**

1. In Microsoft Management Console, right-click **Default Web Site**.
2. Select **Properties**.
3. Click the **Directory Security** tab.
4. In the **Secure Communications** section, click **Edit**.
5. Click **Require secure channel when accessing this resource**.
6. Click **OK**.
7. Click **OK** again.
8. If the **Inheritance Overrides** dialog box appears, click **OK**.

▶ **To open and test the certificate using the browser**

1. Start Internet Explorer.
2. Go to http://localhost/certsrv/.

    You should receive the **403.4 Forbidden: SSL required.** error message.

3. Using HTTPS, go to https://localhost/certsrv/.

    Because you have installed the certificate, this procedure will now work and you will see the **Microsoft Certificate Server** page.

Summary

Microsoft Certificate Server runs as a Windows NT service and, by default, starts automatically when the operating system loads. Microsoft Certificate Server issues digital certificates that enable server and client authentication under the SSL protocol. This process begins with a client submitting a certificate request and ends with the installation of the issued certificate in the client application. The server queue and the server log make up Certificate Server's server database. The server queue keeps a record of all certificate requests received and the server log keeps copies of all issued certificates. You can use the Certificate Administration Log Utility and the Certificate Administration Queue Utility to view and manage the server database.

Review

The following questions are intended to reinforce key information presented in this chapter. If you are unable to answer a question, review the appropriate lesson, and then try the question again.

1. How does the processes for creating a digital signature differ from that for creating a digital envelope?

2. What purpose do digital certificates serve in the process of providing for secure and private communication on the Internet? Why would an organization choose to issue its own certificates rather than relying on an independent certificate authority?

3. What is the difference between the server queue and the server log? Which allows you to revoke certificates?

For More Information

Information on SSL for RSA Data Security, Inc. is on the Web at:

http://www.rsa.com/

Information on SET is on the Microsoft Secure Technologies Web at:

http://www.microsoft.com/intdev/security/

Information on VeriSign certificates is on the Web at:

http://www.verisign.com/

CHAPTER 11

Active Server Pages

Lesson 1 Web Server Extensions . . . 198

Lesson 2 Web Formats . . . 201

Lesson 3 ASP . . . 205

Review . . . 218

About This Chapter
This chapter teaches you how to create dynamic Web pages using Active Server Pages (ASP). The lessons give you an overview of typical Web server extensions, and then details the features and functions of ASP as they relate to Microsoft Internet Information Server (IIS).

Before You Begin
To complete the lessons in this chapter, you must have:

- Installed Internet Information Server as described in Chapter 2, "Installing Microsoft Internet Information Server."
- Completed the practice adding virtual directories and servers as described in Chapter 5, "Configuring the WWW Service."
- The course compact disc containing the necessary practice files.

Lesson 1: Web Server Extensions

ASP is just one of the Web content formats available with Internet Information Server. This lesson describes the various Web publishing features that are available to you.

After this lesson, you will be able to:
- List and describe the various Web content formats.

Estimated lesson time: 10 minutes

Internet Information Server enhances the capabilities of your Microsoft Windows NT server primarily by giving you the ability to publish in a variety of formats. With Internet Information Server, you can run applications that are not native to your Web server, access databases, and embed scripts in your Hypertext Markup Language (HTML) pages. The options include, ASP, Common Gateway Interface (CGI), Internet Service Application Programming Interface (ISAPI), and Open Database Connectivity (ODBC).

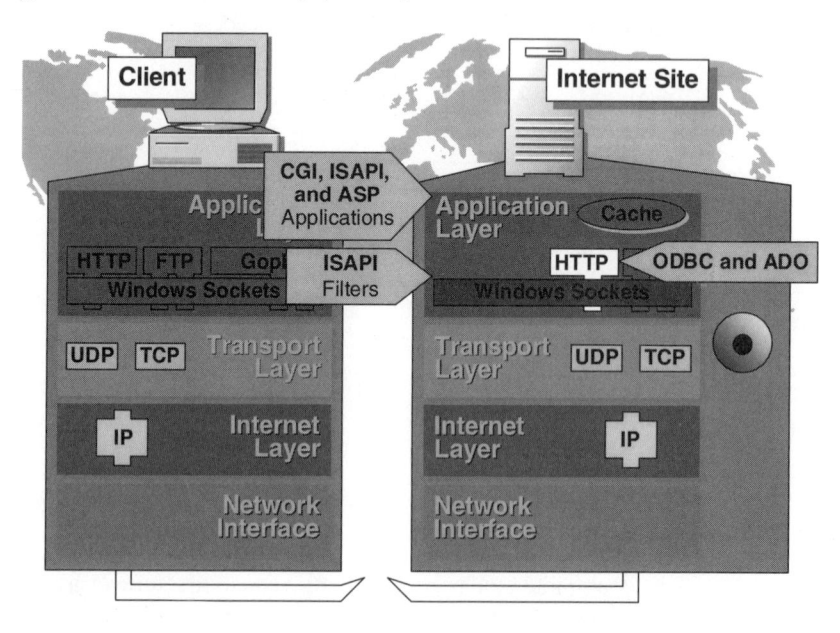

ASP

ASP gives you the ability to embed scripts in standard HTML documents. You can use these scripts to perform application logic and invoke software components that perform specialized tasks, such as database queries, file input/output (I/O), business rules, and work flow. ASP combines the simplicity of Internet Database Connector (IDC) with the flexibility of ISAPI, and because it supports the Java Virtual Machine, you can write ASP application components in a variety of programming languages, including Java and Microsoft JScript.

CGI Support

CGI is the most commonly used Web server extension. CGI gives you the ability to run applications not native to your Web server. For example, you can have users complete an HTML form on your Web site. You can use CGI to pass the user-supplied information to a remote application for processing, and then retrieve the results from the application and return them to the user by means of an HTML page.

Many CGI applications are written in scripting languages such as Practical Extraction and Report Language (PERL)—an interpretive language much like Basic. Due to their portability, these languages are a popular way to extend your Web server's capabilities. You can copy any PERL script running on a UNIX Web server and run it directly on an Internet Information Server server. Binary applications, on the other hand, must be recompiled. Internet Information Server supports PERL 5.0.

Despite their flexibility and portability, however, PERL applications are not the optimal solution for Web sites with heavy traffic because CGI must start a new process for each CGI request. After CGI services the request, it kills that process and any information associated with it. For example, you have a script that tells users how many times the current Web page has been accessed. PERL has to start the counter script every time a user accesses the page. If there is heavy traffic on a particular Web site, this process can cause performance problems, because CGI does not cache information.

ISAPI

The Internet Server Application Programming Interface (ISAPI), created by Microsoft to supplement CGI, is a set of general extensibility routines for making calls to external applications and for manipulating the flow of data between the browser and server.

ISAPI is an open specification supported by third-party Web servers on Windows NT and other operating systems. By combining ISAPI with Internet Information Server and Windows NT Server, you can create a high-performance, cost-effective, and scaleable Hypertext Transport Protocol (HTTP) platform.

ISAPI development occurs in ISAPI applications, which are used to overcome the performance issues of CGI. In addition, ISAPI filters are used to preprocess and post-process messages to and from Internet Information Server.

Though much faster and more flexible than CGI, a programmer must know the Microsoft Visual C++ development system fairly well to program in ISAPI.

ODBC

IDC is another extensibility option included in Internet Information Server. IDC is an ISAPI application that lets you tie your Web pages into any back-end database that supports ODBC.

A number of capabilities and features inherent in this ODBC connector let you take advantage of existing database solutions. These include:

- An HTML template that lets you merge database result sets.
- Interactive application development capability with the Microsoft SQL Server client/server database management system (and other ODBC data sources).
- No programming requirement; you author a query and provide an output template to attach to a data source.
- High performance; it runs in-process as an ISAPI extension.
- An ODBC driver for SQL Server.

The fact that IDC uses a simple scripting language to create database connections makes it a particularly popular server extension. Understanding Structured Query Language (SQL) can help you create IDC applications.

Summary

Internet Information Server can enhance your Web site through a variety of content formats. These include ASP, CGI support, ISAPI applications and filters, and ODBC.

Lesson 2: Web Formats

Internet Information Server allows Web authors many choices when it comes to publishing content to the Internet. This lesson describes the evolution of Web formats. In addition, this lesson describes the ODBC connector and how you can use it to access an ODBC database.

After this lesson, you will be able to:
- List and describe the various Web content formats.
- Describe the components of Active Data Objects (ADO) and ODBC technologies.

Estimated lesson time: 10 minutes

Web formats range in type from static to active. For example, basic HTML links static content. As shown in the following illustration, formats become more active as you add database interactivity and transaction processing.

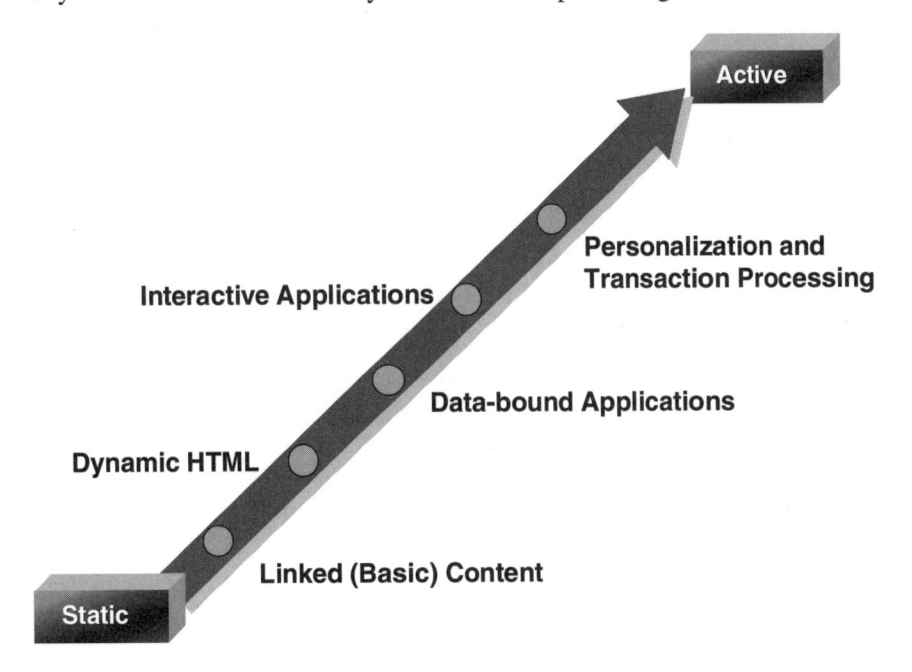

Basic Linked Content

The most basic type of Web content can be described as static and linked. Generally, this content contains basic HTML, embedded graphics, and links for navigation. The same content is shown to all visitors.

Dynamic HTML

With the introduction of Microsoft Internet Explorer 4.0, Web authors can use dynamic HTML to control any page element, and to change styles, positioning, and content at any time—even after the client loads the page.

Note Dynamic HTML is run on the client side and, therefore, is not covered as a part of this book.

Data-Bound Applications

ADO and ODBC technologies enable databases to be accessed from either an intranet or the Internet. Using ADO and ODBC, a Web browser can be an interface for a database, allowing Web authors to create interactive and customized Web content.

The ODBC connector is a high-performance connector that runs as an ISAPI extension or with database access.

ODBC Connector Components

The ODBC connector includes OLE DB because it defines a core set of interfaces for accessing all types of data. OLE DB provides data-access interfaces that give consistent access to SQL and non-SQL data sources. This allows databases to make their data available through common interfaces, without having to write the database code to support SQL functionality for the data.

ADO provides automation-based, language-independent data access. The ODBC connector implements ADO on top of OLE DB to provide a set of efficient, high-level objects that access database components.

The ODBC connector gives you simple, interactive application development with SQL Server or another ODBC data source. With the ODBC connector, you do not need to do any programming; you author a query and an output template that attaches it to a data source. In fact, the ODBC connector also includes an HTML template that allows you to merge a database results set.

Database Registration

Before you can use an ODBC database, you need to register the database with the server by defining the Data Source Name (DSN). There are three types of data source names:

- *System*. The system DSN stores connection information for the indicated database. System DSNs are available to all users of the computer for which it is defined, including Windows NT services. For this reason, it is the DSN ordinarily used with the Internet.
- *User*. The user DSN also stores connection information for the indicated database. However, user DSNs are only available to the user currently logged on and cannot be used by other users.
- *File*. The file DSN allows you to connect to a database. File DSNs can be shared by users who have the same driver installed.

You can use the ODBC program in Control Panel to register the database with your server. The exact registration steps depend upon the type of database you are registering.

ODBC works with an underlying database application to provide the executable middle step between the client's request and the server response. The specific response is based on the contents of the target database. Using the ODBC connector, the client can update as well as read the database.

Interactive Applications

To create Web-based applications, Internet Information Server provides Active Server and Active Client technologies. With these technologies, you can book a hotel reservation, complete expense reports, or check your personnel information, all from the Web browser.

You learn more about Active Server in the following lesson.

Personalization and Transaction Processing

Adding to the data-bound and interactive applications, Microsoft Personalization Server and Microsoft Transaction Server (MTS) enable users to personalize and manage Web applications. Personalization Server works with ASP to dynamically generate Web pages based on stored user preferences. It enables you to deliver targeted content to each site visitor.

Microsoft Transaction Server allows an application to be developed as if it is to run on only one computer. It speeds and simplifies the software development process so the developer does not have to worry about issues such as security, context of the users, and scalability. When an application invokes MTS, it ensures that all of the necessary issues, such as security and user context, are handled. Installing MTS enables applications that have been written to take advantage of it to run on Internet Information Server. In addition, MTS makes it easy to manage these transactional applications.

MTS is discussed in detail in Chapter 13, "Understanding Transaction Server."

Summary

With Internet Information Server, you can create Web pages that are more dynamic than typical linked content. ASP gives you the ability to embed scripts into standard HTML documents.

The ODBC connector allows your Web server to access ODBC databases. It implements ADO and OLE DB to give you simple, interactive application development with any ODBC data source.

Lesson 3: ASP

Active Server Pages (ASP) allow you to embed scripts in your HTML pages. This lesson explains how ASP works and describes the components that comprise it.

After this lesson, you will be able to:
- Explain ASP features and functions.
- Describe how using ASP enables you to create dynamic Web sites.
- Distinguish between built-in and installable objects and the features they bring to ASP.

Estimated lesson time: 50 minutes

Active Server Pages (ASP) enables you to combine HTML, scripts, and reusable Microsoft ActiveX server components to create dynamic Web sites. ASP provides server-side scripting for Internet Information Server with native support for both Microsoft Visual Basic Scripting Edition and Microsoft JScript. Processing for ASP occurs on the server. The output of an ASP file is plain HTML customized for the Web browser.

Benefits of ASP

The primary benefit of using ASP is the ability for a Web developer to provide dynamic content to users. The Web site can deliver content that is customized for that specific user based on user preferences, demographics, customer information, or a more basic criterion, such as whether the user's Web browser can view content displayed in frames.

The ADO component provides standard access to multiple data sources. Internet Information Server includes drivers for Microsoft SQL Server, Microsoft Access, and Oracle databases. Using ODBC, other databases are supported.

The OLE DB further extends the ODBC standard to permit connection to various data sources: Microsoft Excel files, text files, log files, Microsoft Exchange Servers, indexed sequential access method (ISAM), virtual storage access method (VSAM), AS/400, and many other sources.

The Internet Information Server administrator may choose to run all of the applications on the Web server in the same address space for scaling and efficiency. By default, Internet Information Server uses threads within the Web server's address space, instead of creating a new process for each user. The administrator can configure a single application to run in a separate memory space to assure that a problem with one application does not impact the remaining Web applications on the server. Keep in mind, however, that running applications in their own memory space requires additional memory.

ASP provides integrated state and user management. Because HTTP is a stateless protocol, the Web server does not maintain state information about the client. Creating dynamic applications requires state management, which ASP can provide. Through the use of the Application and Session object, the state of the application is available in both Application and Session scope. The Application object is a repository for information and objects that are available application wide. In this sense, they are global objects and data. The Session object maintains information on a per-user basis. A separate copy of the Session object is created for each user of the application.

ASP enables developers to reuse software components. Components may also be aggregated. For example, if a component provides 85 percent of the functionality required by an application, the developer may simply capitalize on the functions of that component and only code the remaining 15 percent of the functionality required.

ASP Elements

ASP consists of three major elements: scripts, objects, and components, as defined in the following list:

- *ASP scripts*. ASP scripts are compatible with any ActiveX scripting language, and contain server extensions that are compatible with HTML.
- *Objects*. Objects manage the Application state, and provide simple access to forms and HTTP parameters. They come in both built-in and installable forms.
- *Components*. Components are written in any language, reusable in other environments, and are a familiar programming model. They provide database access, and enhance browser capabilities and link navigation.

ASP Scripts

ASP scripts are an integral element necessary for process flow. For performance and scalability, COM components should be used to provide the functional processes within the page.

ASP is built on a scripting engine. This enables it to support multiple scripting languages such as Microsoft Visual Basic Scripting Edition (VBScript), JScript, and PERL. Developers may create the components to interface with the scripting engine to create new scripting languages.

Server-side scripting provides the structure for ASP. Application developers use scripting to provide input to components and may use a script for simple functions and calculations.

Note For enhanced performance and scalability, complex calculations and functions should be written with compiled languages by creating components.

ASP is built on a scripting engine that provides an object model for the Web application developer's use. VBScript—a subset of Visual Basic—is included with ASP to take advantage of the developer's knowledge of that programming model.

In addition, JScript is included in the default installation of ASP. JScript is a standard for scripting that is used in most contemporary browsers and is included to capitalize on the developer's knowledge of that language.

Note JScript is not a subset of Java.

Components Accessed Using Properties and Methods

ASP accesses components using properties and methods. Properties are data objects that control the state of the object. Methods are functions that operate on the properties.

As an example, imagine a component that converts temperature between Fahrenheit and Celsius. The two properties would be the temperature, one in Fahrenheit (Ftemp), and the other in Celsius (Ctemp).

The Web developer would first create an object representing this component and set the property that matches the temperature scale from which the developer wants to convert.

The component would have two methods:

- *Conv2Cels*. To convert a Fahrenheit temperature to Celsius.
- *Conv2Fare*. To convert a Celsius temperature to Fahrenheit.

Once an instance of the object has been created and the temperature that will be converted has been entered, the proper method is called. The component uses the method to convert the temperature, placing the result in the correct property, where it may be referenced by the ASP and used in the Web application.

The VBScript created in this example may appear as the following code:

```
<%
Dim CelsiusTemp
Set objconverter = Server.CreateObject("TempConv.Converter")
objconverter.Ftemp = 67
objconverter.Conv2Cels
CelsiusTemp = objconverter.Ctemp
Response.Write "The temperature in Celsius is " & CelsiusTemp & " degrees."
%>
```

ASP Objects

Objects are components of a programming language that provide tools for completing basic repetitive programming tasks. Objects often provide simple access to forms and manage the application state. ASP objects are defined as built-in or installable.

Built-in Objects

The ASP framework provides six built-in objects that do not need to be created before you can use them in scripts.

Server Object

The server object provides access to methods and properties on the server.

Application Object

You can use the application object to share information among all users of a given application. An ASP-based application is defined as all of the .asp files in a virtual directory and its subfolders. Because the application object can be shared by multiple users, there are lock and unlock methods to ensure that multiple users do not try to alter application properties simultaneously.

Session Object

The session object stores information needed for a particular user session. Variables stored in the session object are not discarded when the user jumps between pages in the application; rather, these variables persist for the entire user session.

The Web server creates a session object automatically when a Web page included in the application is requested by a user who does not already have a session. The server destroys the session object when the session expires or is abandoned.

Session objects are often used to store user preferences or selections. For example, an application may need to track catalog items a visitor has selected while using your site.

Note A session state is only maintained for browsers that support cookies.

Request Object

The request object retrieves the values that a client browser passes to the server during an HTTP request.

Response Object

The response object sends output to the client.

ObjectContext Object

The ObjectContext object is used either to commit or cancel a transaction initiated by an ASP script. The ObjectContext object provides for information about the transactions, and also provides information about the client and the state of the client's connection to the server. This permits the developer to avoid an expensive transaction if the user has canceled the page.

Installable Objects

You can use the built-in ActiveX components to create ASP files. These components are reusable in other environments, and you can use them with any language. They also provide a familiar programming model for use when developing your own custom components.

Database Access

The Database Access component uses ActiveX data objects (ADO) to access information stored in a database or other tabular data structure. It also uses the connection pooling feature of ODBC 3.0 to make database access more efficient.

Browser Capabilities

The Browser Capabilities component provides your scripts with a description of the capabilities of a client's Web browser.

When a browser connects to the Web server, it automatically sends a user agent HTTP header. This header is an ASCII string that identifies the browser and its version number. The Browser Capabilities component compares the header to entries in the Browscap.ini file.

If it finds a match, the Browser Capabilities component assumes the properties of the browser listing that matched the user agent header.

If the component does not find a match for the header in the Browscap.ini file, it takes on the default browser properties.

You can add properties or new browser definitions to this component by updating the Browscap.ini file.

Content Rotator

Each time a user opens or reloads the Web page, the Content Rotator component displays different content based on the information specified in the Content Schedule file.

For example, an advertising account manager can manage the placement of new advertisements using the Content Rotator. In addition, the account manager can record how many users click each advertisement by setting the Redirect parameter in the Content Schedule file. Specifying this parameter causes each click on an advertisement to be recorded in the Web server activity logs.

Content Linking

The Content Linking component manages a list of Uniform Resource Locators (URLs) in your Web site. It automatically generates and updates the table of contents and navigational links to previous and subsequent Web pages. This is ideal for applications such as online newspapers and forum message listings.

File Access

The File Access component uses the FileSystemObject and TextStream objects to retrieve and modify information stored in files on your Web server.

ASP Components

There are several installable ASP components designed to assist in building interactive and dynamic Web sites. These components include File Upload, Simple Mail Transfer Protocol (SMTP) Send Mail, Network News Transfer Protocol (NNTP) Discussions, Page Counter, and Permission Checker.

The File Upload component is a Request for Comment (RFC) 1867-compliant component that provides the ability to upload files from the client computer to the Web server. This component interoperates with the <INPUT TYPE=FILE> tag in Netscape browsers, as well as with the Web Publishing wizard and ActiveX Upload control.

With the SMPT Send Mail component your Web pages can easily and quickly send e-mail through an SMPT e-mail sever. Microsoft Exchange 5.0 and later provides an SMTP e-mail server that may be used to exchange e-mail on the Internet.

Threaded NNTP discussions are created using the NNTP Discussion object. Developers may now create either public or private NNTP newsgroups. Newsgroups are accessed using a standard NNTP newsreader such as Microsoft Outlook™ Express desktop information manager.

The Page Counter is a component designed to be launched in the Application scope of the Web application. This global location makes displaying page hits much faster and easy to implement.

The Permission Checker component tests the Web user's access rights to a file or a page. You can use the Permission Checker component to customize an ASP-based page for different types of users. For example, if a Web page contains links to pages that might be restricted, you can use the Permission Checker component to test the user's permissions for the corresponding Web pages. You can then omit or make inactive any links to which the user does not have access.

Creating Components

ActiveX server components are created to extend the functionality of ASP. They are the logical evolution of scripting. When a procedure is used repeatedly in ASP page construction, such as business rules, the application is made more scaleable and more responsive when the code is within an ActiveX server component instead of ActiveX scripting.

You can write your component in any language that generates Automation server components. Choosing a language involves many considerations: familiarity with the language, tools support, run-time performance, threading models, code complexity, and the size of the compiled code. Languages and products that can be used to write Automation server components include Microsoft Visual C++, Microsoft Visual Basic, and Java.

Components that are created for ASP follow the Component Object Model (COM). These objects are launched in memory and provide methods and properties that are in turn called from the Active Server Pages.

These components are essentially ActiveX components that do not implement a user interface. While developing components for ASP, you must use the interfaces provided by ASP to create the components in accordance with COM.

ActiveX server components are installed and run on the Web server. The browser that is used to access these components is completely independent of the browser's manufacturer or version.

The ActiveX server is extensible. Because of this, developers can create ActiveX server components that can be used in a variety of Internet and intranet scenarios.

Use of the Script Tag

The script tag is used to indicate that the text enclosed in the tag is to be interpreted, not displayed. Script may be used in both the client and the server.

Client scripting is not ASP, and is dependent on the browser for the implementation of any scripting language. Scripting language varies with browsers and may even vary within versions of the same browser. Client scripting is only mentioned here to differentiate from ASP and server-side scripting in general.

Script Tag for Non-ASP Clients

The script tag for use within browsers is as follows:

```
<SCRIPT LANGUAGE=XXX>
<!—script commands

--!>
</SCRIPT>
```

The type of language supported—and the object model for the browser—is browser-specific.

Script Tag on ASP

ASP on the server uses a similar tag, with a few changes. First, there must be a method to specify that the script is to run on the server and not to be sent to the client.

A script on an ASP may be enclosed in the following tags:

```
<SCRIPT LANGUAGE=XXX RUNAT=SERVER>
<!—Server side script
--!>
</SCRIPT>
```

Alternately, for convenience and to reduce the complexity of the scripted pages, the server-side script tag may be shortened as follows:

```
<%
<!—Server side script
--!>
%>
```

Notice that the script, in this case, runs on the server and, as a result, is not browser-specific. The output of this script can display any content to the user and may be browser-specific. In fact, ASP scripting can be used to create client-side scripting at run time.

Practice

In this practice, you create an ASP, respond to input from a form, use a Microsoft ActiveX control on a Web page, and then determine the capabilities of a browser accessing the page.

Note These practices are also available in the Internet Information Server online documentation (with minor file name and folder differences). To use the online versions of these exercises, on the Windows NT 4.0 Option Pack **Start** menu, open the Internet Information Server product documentation, and then navigate to **Microsoft Internet Information Server**, **Web Applications**, **ASP Tutorial**, **Creating ASP Pages**, and **Using ActiveX Components**.

To prepare for this practice, create a C:\LabFiles\Lab08 folder on your server. Then copy the files from the Iis\Practice\Asp folder on the course compact disc to the C:\LabFiles\Lab08 folder. The folder should be shared with the World Wide Web (WWW) service as /Lab8. Read/write permissions must be granted on this folder.

In this part of the practice, you configure a virtual directory and set up your browser.

▶ **To configure a virtual directory**

1. Click the **Start** button, point to **Programs**, point to **Windows NT 4.0 Option Pack**, point to **Microsoft Internet Information Server**, and then click **Internet Service Manager**.
2. Expand Internet Information Server.

    A computer icon appears with the name of your computer next to it.
3. Expand your computer icon.

    The following sites appear: **Default FTP**, **Default Web**, **Administration Web**, **Default SMTP**, and **Default NNTP**.
4. Right-click the **Default Web Site** folder.

    A content menu appears.
5. Click **New**, and then click **Virtual Directory**.

    The New Virtual Directory wizard appears.
6. In the **Alias to be used to access virtual directory** text box, type **Lab8** and then click **Next**.
7. In the text box, type **C:\Labfiles\Lab08** and then click **Next**.
8. Verify that **Allow Read Access** and **Allow Script Access** are selected.
9. Click **Finish**.

▶ **To change the security level of Internet Explorer**

1. Start Internet Explorer.
2. Click **View**, and then click **Internet Options**.

    The **Internet Options** dialog box appears.
3. Click the **Security** tab.

    For your local intranet zone, verify the **Safety Level** is set to **Medium**.
4. Click **OK**.
5. Close Internet Explorer.

In this part of the practice, you create an ASP by taking a simple HTML page and add scripting that repeats an action.

▶ **To create an ASP from an HTML file**

1. In the **Address** box of Internet Explorer, type **http://***computername***/Lab8/Hello.htm** (where *computername* is the name of your Web server) to open Hello.htm.

    The text "Hello World!" appears.

2. Using Microsoft Windows NT Explorer, open the **C:\Labfiles\Lab08** folder, make a copy of **Hello.htm**, and then rename it **Hello.asp**.

3. Using Windows NT Explorer, remove the Read-only attribute of all of the files in the \Lab8 folder.

    Note If you do not remove the Read-only attribute from all of the files, the remainder of the practice does not work properly.

4. Open Hello.asp with Notepad.
5. Near the top of the file, replace the title Static Hello with Active Hello.
6. In the middle of the file, delete <FONT SIZE=7> and replace it with:

    <% For I = 3 To 7 %>

    <FONT SIZE=<%= I %>>

7. Add <% Next %> after the line containing "Hello World."
8. Save Hello.asp, and then leave the file open.

    Note To make sure that Notepad saves your file with the correct file extension, in the **File Save As** box, type **Hello.asp** as the file name and file extension.

9. In the **Address** box of Internet Explorer, type **http://***computername***/Lab8/Hello.asp** to open Hello.asp.

    The text "Hello World!" is displayed in five different font sizes.

10. Right-click the browser window, and then click **View Source**.

    Notice that the source in the browser is different than the source at the server.

Many Web sites allow the user to enter information using a form. In this part of the practice, you process a form using ASP.

► **To respond to a form using ASP**

1. In the **Address** box of Internet Explorer, type **http://*computername*/Lab8/Form.htm** to open Form.htm.

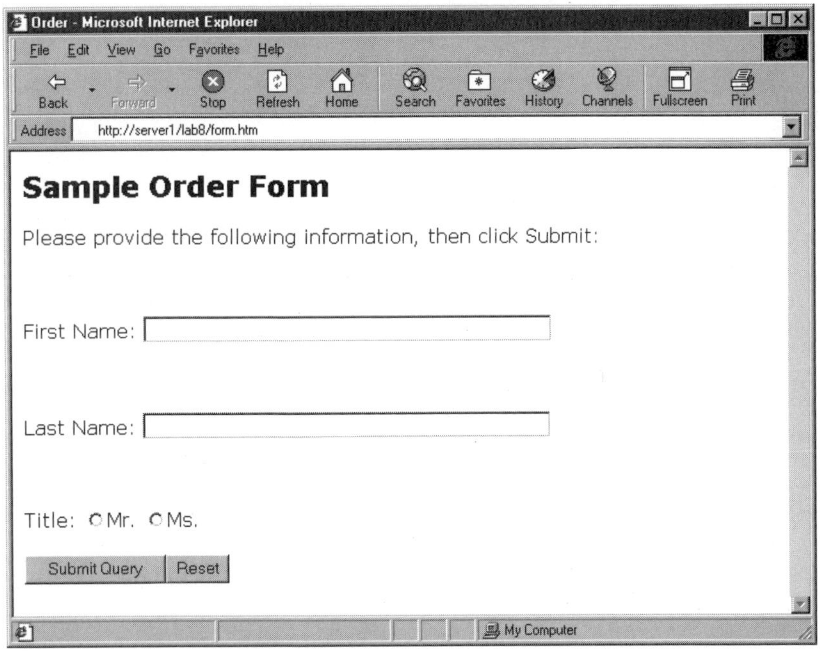

2. Fill in the form, and then click **Submit Query**.

   The message "Thank you for your order." is displayed.

3. Close Internet Explorer.
4. Use Notepad to open C:\Labfiles\Lab08\Response.asp.
5. Insert your pointer at the end of the line containing <!--Form Exercise-->, and then press ENTER.

6. Open Asp.txt, and then copy and paste the following code into Response.asp:

    ```
    <%
    Title = Request.Form("title")
    LastName = Request.Form("lname")
    If Title = "mr" Then
    %>
    Mr. <%= LastName %>
    <% ElseIf Title = "ms" Then %>
    Ms. <%= LastName %>
    <% Else %>
    <%= Request.Form("fname") & " " & LastName %>
    <% End If %>
    ```

7. Save the file as Response.asp.
8. In the **Address** box of Internet Explorer, type **http://***computername*/**Lab8/Form.htm** to open Form.htm.
9. Complete the form, and then click **Submit**.

    The message "Thank you, (Mr. / Ms.) lastname for your order." appears.

10. Click **Back**, clear the form by clicking **Reset**, select **Ms.** or **Mr.**, and then click **Submit**.

    The message "Thank You Mr. or Ms., for your order." appears.

11. Click **Back**, clear the form by clicking **Reset**, type your first and last name, and then click **Submit**.

    The message "Thank you, firstname lastname for your order." appears.

You now use an ActiveX control called the Ad Rotator to present an advertisement on a Web page. The Ad Rotator is designed to display a series of images. The Ad Rotator is different than the Content Rotator, which rotates content strings.

▶ **To add an ActiveX component to an ASP**

1. Start Internet Explorer and type **http://***computername*/**Lab8/Ad.asp** to open Ad.asp.

    Note that no advertisement is displayed.

2. Close Internet Explorer.
3. Using Windows NT Explorer, go to C:\Labfiles\Lab08 and open Ad.asp with Notepad.

4. Scroll the file, insert your pointer at the end of the line containing <!--Component Exercise-->, and then press ENTER.

5. Open Asp.txt, and then copy and paste the following code into Ad.asp:

    <% Set Ad = Server.CreateObject("MSWC.Adrotator") %>

    <%= Ad.GetAdvertisement("adrot.txt") %>

6. Save Ad.asp.

7. Open Ad.asp with Internet Explorer.

    An advertisement appears.

8. Click **Refresh**.

    A different advertisement appears.

    When you view the resulting page, it displays one of several different advertisements each time. These cycle through the list in Adrot.txt and then restart at the beginning of the list.

One of the ActiveX server objects included with Internet Information Server enables the server to find out the capabilities of the browser that requests the page.

▶ **To test browser capabilities**

1. In the Internet Explorer **Address** text box, type **http://**computername**/Lab8/Browseca.asp** to display some of the browser's capabilities.

    A list appears with information about the browser.

2. Close Internet Explorer.

Summary

ASP files are regular HTML documents that include scripting language within the HTML code. ASP supports a range of scripting languages, all of which include the ability to use components. ASP is made up of ASP scripts, objects, and components.

Review

The following questions are intended to reinforce key information presented in this chapter. If you are unable to answer a question, review the appropriate lesson, and then try the question again.

1. World Wide Importers has over 1,000 sales people worldwide. All sales people are required to use their laptops to dial-in long distance to the company's Microsoft Access database to check stock levels. This is done four or five times a day by each sales person, and results in large telephone bills for World Wide Importers. The sales force complains that the telephone lines are often tied up for hours limiting their access. Can you recommend a way using Internet Information Server to reduce the telephone costs and improve access?

2. How can using ASP enable you to create dynamic Web sites?

3. Is the object that causes a Web browser to see different content every time the user opens or reloads a file or Web page a built-in or installable object? How could this feature be useful to advertisers?

4. Will any of the installable ASP components track Web page hits or ensure that only the appropriate users are allowed to access sensitive documents or Web pages?

CHAPTER 12

Indexing Web Sites

Lesson 1 Index Server Overview . . . 222

Lesson 2 The Indexing Process . . . 226

Lesson 3 Queries . . . 236

Lesson 4 Index Server Administration . . . 248

Review . . . 257

About This Chapter

This chapter gives you an overview of Microsoft Index Server 2.0. In this chapter, you learn the details of both the indexing and the querying processes. You also learn how to manage Index Server and how to correct possible Index Server error conditions.

Before You Begin

Before completing the lessons in this chapter, you must have:

- Installed Microsoft Internet Information Server 4.0 (IIS) according to the procedures in Chapter 2, "Installing Microsoft Internet Information Server." During this procedure you should have installed Index Server. Windows NT File System (NTFS) must be the installed file system to properly run Index Server.
- The course compact disc containing the necessary practice files.

Lesson 1: Index Server Overview

Microsoft Index Server provides content indexing and searching for Internet Information Server. This lesson gives you an overview of Index Server's capabilities and its system requirements.

After this lesson, you will be able to:
- List and describe the key features of Microsoft Index Server version 2.0.

Estimated lesson time: 20 minutes

Microsoft Index Server gives you the ability to index and search the content of documents stored in your Internet Information Server site. It indexes the full text and properties of those documents, and enables clients to search the resulting indexes with queries formulated using any Web browser by filling in the fields of a simple Web query form.

You can use Index Server to index documents on intranets and for any hard disk accessible through a universal naming convention (UNC) path on the Internet. It can also index documents on more than one Web server, documents in several different languages, and documents stored in a variety of file formats. Index Server updates an index automatically whenever the files associated with the index are changed.

Features of Index Server

You can use Index Server to index the files of multiple Web servers by sharing a folder on the remote computer and creating a virtual directory on the indexing server. This includes files on Novell NetWare servers or files on a file allocation table (FAT) partition.

Index Server can also index the full text contents and property values of formatted documents, such as those created by Microsoft Word or Microsoft Excel. This allows you to publish existing documents directly on your intranet without having to convert them to a different format, such as Hypertext Markup Language (HTML).

Index Server includes the ability to index several file formats:

- Text files (.txt)
- HTML 3.0 or earlier files (.htm)
- Microsoft Word 95/97 files (.doc)
- Microsoft Excel 95/97 files (.xls)
- Microsoft PowerPoint® 95/97 files (.ppt)
- Binary files (properties only)

OLE links are also indexed. You can install additional content filters, available from independent software vendors, in order to index other file formats. A content filter reads a proprietary document format and emits words in text format that are then indexed by Index Server.

Index Server can also index Network News Transfer Protocol (NNTP) messages stored on a news server.

Index Server currently supports multilingual indexing and querying in the following languages:

- Dutch
- French
- German
- Italian
- Japanese
- Spanish
- Swedish
- International English
- U.S. English
- Traditional and simplified Chinese

With Index Server, you can index multilingual documents and switch between languages as required. For example, it can index an English paragraph, index a French paragraph, and then switch back to English. All index information is stored as Unicode characters, and all queries are converted to Unicode before processing.

As soon as you install and start Index Server, it automatically indexes all files associated with your Internet Information Server Web site. If you make changes to the files on the Web site, Index Server automatically refreshes the searchable index. Index Server also includes an automatic error detection and recovery system to handle common errors.

Running Index Server

You install Index Server on Microsoft Windows NT Server 4.0 through the Windows NT 4.0 Option Pack Setup program. If you installed Internet Information Server according to the procedure in Chapter 2, "Installing Microsoft Internet Information Server," you have installed Index Server.

Index Server System Requirements

Index Server program files require from 3 to 12 MB of hard disk space, depending upon the number of languages installed with the software. You need additional hard disk space for the Index Server data. The total amount of space you need, however, depends upon the number and type of documents to be indexed. Generally, Index Server data requires hard disk space equal to approximately 40 percent of the size of the corpus, which is the documents to be indexed. While the average usage is less than 30 percent of the corpus, the peak usage of hard disk space can be as much as 40 percent.

In other words, a site supporting multiple languages with a 100 MB corpus may require an additional 52 MB of hard disk space (40 percent of 100 MB = 40 MB +12 MB for the program files).

Note For security reasons, Microsoft recommends storing Index Server data on an NTFS hard disk. The use of NTFS is key to maintaining a secure Internet Information Server and Index Server, because NTFS allows you to limit access to files and folders.

The minimum configuration requirements for Index Server are basically the same as the requirements for Microsoft Windows NT Server 4.0; however, the configuration for optimum performance depends upon the following factors:

- The number of documents
- The size of the data corpus
- The search load on the server

A 486/DX4-100 computer with 32 MB of RAM, running Windows NT Server 4.0, services queries well if the number of simultaneous queries is not too high. This hardware configuration may be sufficient for a small organization; for a larger group serving more users, you may want to install Index Server on higher performance hardware.

You can estimate the memory you need to run Index Server for your configuration based on the following table.

Number of documents	Recommended memory (in megabytes)
Fewer than 100,000	32
100,000–250,000	64–128
250,000–500,000	128–256
500,000 or more	256 or more

A faster CPU and more memory improves the performance of indexing as well as the speed of queries. If you have a large number of documents, insufficient memory seriously affects performance. If performance is slow when Index Server is running, use Performance Monitor to determine what is causing the loss in performance.

Effects of Installation

You specify a catalog folder during installation. A catalog is the highest-level unit of organization in Index Server. Setup creates a CATALOG.WCI folder in the specified catalog folder to store the index and property cache. This folder may use up to 40 percent of the corpus size, so place it on a partition that has enough space available.

During the installation procedure, the Index Server files are copied to your computer in the following locations:

- Sample HTML and script files are copied to /Iissamples/Issamples
- Administration files are copied to /Iisadmin/Isadmin
- Documentation files are copied to /Iishelp/Ix

After installation, the Content Index service (Cisvc.exe) is started and begins indexing all documents in each of the virtual directories configured for the Internet Information Server Web server, including virtual directories for remote resources.

Index Server starts automatically when you start Internet Information Server. You can check to see if the Content Index service is running by looking under Services in Control Panel. If the Content Index service is not running, you can start it by selecting **Content Index** and then clicking **Start**. Index Server does not stop automatically when Internet Information Server is stopped.

After the initial indexing, the Content Index service continues to index whatever documents you add to Internet Information Server. You can add new documents to existing virtual directories or add new virtual directories in which to place documents. The Content Index service continues to monitor and index all virtual directories on the server even when the World Wide Web (WWW) service is not running.

Summary

With Microsoft Index Server, you can index and search the content of documents stored in your Internet Information Server site. Index Server is capable of indexing multilingual documents, documents of different file types, and documents stored on multiple Web servers. It also updates an index automatically whenever the files associated with the index are changed. The minimum Index Server configuration requirements are basically the same as for Microsoft Windows NT Server 4.0. You can start and stop the Index Server through Control Panel.

Lesson 2: The Indexing Process

The indexing process is the process by which Index Server catalogs the full text and properties of documents stored on your Internet Information Server site. This lesson describes each phase and component of the indexing process. You also learn how to use the tools provided with the Internet Server Administration Microsoft Management Console (MMC) snap-in.

After this lesson, you will be able to:
- Describe the indexing process used by Index Server.
- Describe the types of index merges performed by Index Server.
- Add documents to a corpus.
- Describe the features provided by the Index Server Manager.

Estimated lesson time: 45 minutes

The indexing process is a background activity that requires no user input. It begins with the corpus (all of the documents designated for indexing), filters out the content and properties of each, and ends with a catalog containing a corresponding index.

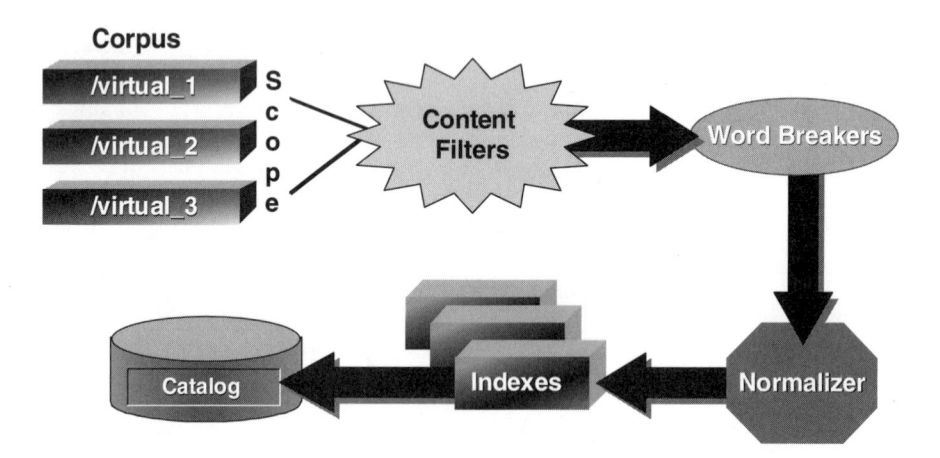

Corpus

The collection of all documents stored in an Internet Information Server site for indexing is called a corpus. You can store the corpus in one or more physical storage locations on the local machine or another connected file server; however, you must define each storage folder as either a virtual server or virtual directory. By defining which folders are indexed, you can configure the scope of the corpus.

Note You can improve performance by having Index Server data on a different hard disk than the disk or disks that contain the corpus.

Content Filters

Content filters are programs that allow you to index files of varying file types. Typically, documents are stored in proprietary file formats. For example, WordPerfect files are stored on the hard disk in a different way than Microsoft Word files. Index Server uses these content filters to index private file formats.

In order to do this, content filters must be able to:

- Extract text chunks.
- Recognize language shifts in multilingual documents.
- Handle embedded objects.

When a content filter encounters an embedded object in a document, it identifies the object's type and activates the appropriate filter. This means that Index Server indexes not only the text in a Word document, but also any text in a Microsoft Excel spreadsheet that is embedded in the Word document.

Because knowledge of the file format is contained entirely within the filter, you can index additional file formats simply by supplying an appropriate filter. In this manner, you can extend Index Server to read new formats as filters become available.

Word Breakers

Content filters emit streams of characters, but Index Server indexes words. Thus, in order to index correctly, Index Server must be able to identify the words within the character stream. This is complicated by the fact that different languages treat words and word breaks differently.

To handle this, Index Server employs language-specific word breakers that understand how to break a stream of characters into valid words. Word breakers understand a particular language's structure and syntax, and use that understanding to identify words within the character stream. The word breakers take in a stream of characters on one side and emit words on the other side.

Note To avoid problems with code pages and other double-byte character set issues, Index Server uses Unicode to store all of its index data.

Normalizer

The normalizer cleans up the words emitted by the word breaker, handling issues such as capitalization, punctuation, and noise word removal.

In most languages, written text contains a number of noise words. English noise words include "the," "of," "and," "you," and several hundred similar words. The content index does not include references to these words. The system maintains a system-wide list of noise words on a per-language basis, which you can customize to account for local slang and application-specific words. When a word breaker detects a noise word during character stream analysis, the normalizer makes sure that the noise word is ignored. Because noise words constitute a large portion of written text, noise word removal can significantly reduce the size of the overall index.

Only after words are normalized, does Index Server put them into the content index.

Indexes

Index Server includes two types of indexes: word lists and persistent indexes. Words and properties extracted from a document first appear in a word list, then move to a persistent index. This organization is optimized for query responsiveness and performance, and ensures optimal resource usage. Even though there may be multiple indexes internally, these details are completely hidden from the user. The user sees only a list of documents satisfying the posted queries.

Word Lists

Word lists are small, temporary indexes stored in the server's RAM. Each word list contains data for a small number of documents. As soon as Index Server filters a document, it stores its data in a word list. Word list creation is very quick and does not require updating data on hard disk. It is used as a temporary staging area during indexing.

There are several registry parameters that you can use to control word list behavior. All of the keys are under the following registry path:

\HKEY_LOCAL_MACHINE\SYSTEM\CurrentControlSet\Control\ Content Index

The following table shows the word list registry parameters and their explanations.

Parameter	Explanation
MaxWordLists	Maximum number of word lists that can exist at one time.
MaxWordlistSize	Maximum amount of memory consumed by an individual word list. When this limit is reached, only the document being filtered is added. Additional documents are refiled and placed in another word list at a later time. Each unit is 128 kilobytes (K) (for example, 20 = 2.5 MB).
MinSizeMergeWordlists	Minimum combined size of word lists that will force a shadow merge.
MinWordlistMemory	Minimum free memory for word list creation.

When the number of word lists exceeds the MaxWordLists parameter, Index Server merges the word lists into a shadow index by a process called the shadow merge, which is described later in this lesson. Although they compress data to some extent, because word lists are only temporary structures this compression is not very high. Additionally, because word lists are memory-resident structures, documents that have been filtered into word lists must be refiltered whenever Internet Information Server is restarted. Index Server detects when refiltering is required and performs it automatically.

Persistent Indexes

When Index Server stores data for an index on a hard disk, it is called a persistent index. Unlike word lists, persistent indexes survive shutdowns and restarts. Because it is stored on a hard disk, Index Server compresses persistent index data significantly. A persistent index is considered either a shadow or master index.

A shadow index is created by merging word lists and sometimes other shadow indexes into a single index. Catalogs can contain multiple shadow indexes. Index Server uses shadow indexes as staging areas for merging into the master index. Using shadow indexes creates up-to-date indexes without performing complex, resource-intensive procedures. However, because shadow indexes are not compressed as far as master indexes, they require more hard disk space than comparable master indexes.

A master index contains the indexed data for a large number of documents. This is usually the largest persistent data structure. The master index contains all of the data that has been indexed as of its creation date. Master indexes utilize a much more aggressive compression than shadow indexes and require more resources to complete the compression.

Index Server creates a master index by means of the master merge, which merges all shadow indexes and the current master index (if any) into a new master index. After the master merge, Index Server deletes all of the source indexes leaving only the new master index. This is the state in which queries are resolved most efficiently. Master merges are described later in this lesson.

The total number of persistent indexes (shadow indexes and master index) in a catalog cannot exceed 255.

Catalogs

A catalog is the highest organizational level in Microsoft Index Server. Each catalog is a completely self-contained unit, containing an index and cached properties for one or more scopes (virtual servers). Index Server queries cannot span multiple catalogs.

The Default Catalog

The initial catalog location configured during setup is stored in the IsapiDefaultCatalogDirectory registry entry. This is the catalog used unless you specify a different catalog in an .idq file. The default catalog contains an index of all virtual servers with read permission. You can, however, modify the scope of the catalog through administrative pages.

Multiple Catalogs

You can create multiple catalogs to distribute queries and to support virtual servers.

Because it is impossible to create a query that spans more than one catalog, you should consider the consequences of creating multiple catalogs before doing so. Multiple catalogs mean that you lose the ability to query the entire content of your Internet Information Server site, and they impair default catalog support—multiple catalogs do not support multiple IP address-specific default catalogs.

Dividing the set of physical locations between a number of catalogs improves query performance, but only if most queries are restricted to a subscope (one or more physical locations) of the Web site. This improvement occurs because the number of false hits (hits outside the query scope) is reduced.

The CiDaemon Process

The CiDaemon process is a child process created by the Index Server engine. The Index Server engine gives a list of documents to the CiDaemon process, which is responsible for filtering the documents by identifying the correct filter dynamic-link library (DLL) and word breaker DLL associated with a specific document.

Filtering is handled in the background so as not to interfere with any foreground activity. On local hard disks, if a document opened by the CiDaemon process for reading is needed by another process for writing, the CiDaemon process closes the document as quickly as possible. The document will be retried for filtering at a later time. This feature is not available on network shared folders.

If the CiDaemon process stops, the Index Server engine automatically restarts it.

Types of Merges

Merging is the process of combining data from multiple indexes into a single index. Merging reduces instances of redundant data and frees up system resources. Also, Index Server resolves queries more quickly with fewer indexes. There are three types of merges:

- Shadow merge
- Annealing merge
- Master merge

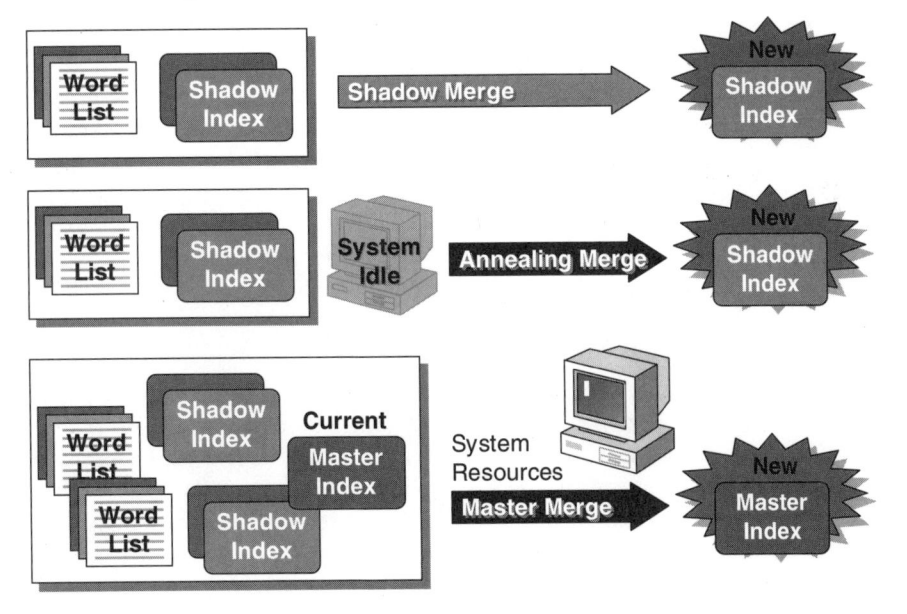

After a merge completes, a single target index replaces the multiple source indexes.

Shadow Merge

A shadow merge combines multiple word lists and shadow indexes into a single shadow index. Index Server performs shadow merges to free up memory used by word lists and to make the filtered data persistent; it is usually a quick operation.

Word lists are the most common source indexes for a shadow merge. However, if the total number of persistent indexes exceeds the maximum number configured in the registry setting MaxIndexes (default is 50), some shadow indexes are also used as source indexes.

Any one of the following conditions can trigger a shadow merge:

- The number of word lists exceeds MaxWordLists.
- The combined size of word lists exceeds MinSizeMergeWordlists.
- A master merge is performed. As a precursor to a master merge, a shadow merge is performed to merge all existing word lists into a shadow index.
- An annealing merge is performed.

Annealing Merge

An annealing merge is a type of shadow merge. Index Server performs this type of merge only when the system is idle and the total number of persistent indexes exceeds the value specified by MaxIdealIndexes in the registry. The registry parameter MinMergeIdleTime specifies the percentage of CPU time that must be idle during a time period to trigger an annealing merge. An annealing merge improves query performance and hard disk space usage by reducing the number of shadow indexes that have been formed from word lists.

Master Merge

Master merge source indexes include the existing shadow indexes and the current master index (if any). After a master merge, Index Server replaces all of the source indexes with the single resulting master index. Although the master merge itself is a very resource-intensive operation (both for CPU and hard disk space), once completed it will have freed resources and deleted redundant data, and queries will run more quickly.

Note Depending upon the size of the source indexes, a master merge can take a long time. However, you can restart a master merge after failures and shutdowns. If interrupted, a master merge continues from where it left off.

Whenever a master merge is started, restarted, or paused, an event is written to the event log.

You have several registry settings with which to configure Index Server to start a master merge, including:

- *Maintenance master merge MasterMergeTime.* You configure the nightly master merge in minutes after midnight. The default start time is midnight. Adjust this value to reflect the time when the load on the server is lowest.
- *Number of changed documents since the last master merge exceeded MaxFreshCount.* Index Server performs a master merge to reduce the number of changed documents. If the number of changed documents is too high, it puts an extra load on memory usage. A master merge reduces the FreshCount to zero.
- *Disk space remaining on the catalog drive is less than MinDiskFreeForceMerge and the cumulative space occupied by shadow indexes exceeds MaxShadowFreeForceMerge.* Index Server starts a master merge in order to combine the shadow indexes and free up hard disk space.
- *Total disk space occupied by shadow indexes exceeds MaxShadowIndexSize.* Index Server starts a master merge in order to combine the shadow indexes. This condition has higher precedence than the previous condition.

Additionally, you can force a master merge by using the administrative Web page (http://*computername*/srchadm/admin.htm). Because a master merge makes queries run faster after it completes, you may want to force a merge even before one of the preceding conditions triggers it.

Index Server Manager

The Index Server Administration Microsoft Management Console snap-in provides seven management tools for Index Server administration.

Checking Status

With the Index Server snap-in, you can check indexing status and view the properties of folders that are indexed, as well as the cached properties. To do so, highlight the Index Server folder in Microsoft Management Console. In the right pane, the number of files indexed, catalog size, documents to filter, and other information is displayed.

Setting Global Properties

At the Index Server level, you can adjust property settings for all catalogs. For example, you can choose to turn off characterization for all catalogs. In this case, no summaries or abstracts are generated for files listed on the results page of a search. You can also change a value for a specific catalog. The values you set on the catalog level override those set on the Index Server level.

Creating and Configuring Catalogs

During installation, Index Server creates the Web catalog. You can create additional catalogs. You can also separate the content in those catalogs.

Adjusting the Property Cache

To reduce the time it takes to retrieve values for frequently used queries, you can add properties to the cache on your server. If not cached, Index Server directly accesses ActiveX documents (for example, Microsoft Office documents) returned from a query and retrieves the properties at that time. Additional properties that are not indexed by default can be added to the cache properties for use in later queries. For example, adding the tag META="ServerProduct" VALUE="*product name*" to your HTML documents allows you to create queries that look for server products that match a specific name.

Note If your index becomes corrupted and is rebuilt, you need to reconfigure your property cache.

Adding and Removing Folders

You can use the Index Server snap-in to add or remove folders to be indexed by Index Server. Taking this action neither adds nor deletes physical folders. Instead, it instructs Index Server to include or exclude them from the folder it indexes.

Forcing a Scan

To re-inventory a virtual root (virtual directory), you must force Index Server to scan it. You should rescan after making certain global changes, such as the following:

- Changing the size of characterization
- Adding or removing a filter
- Changing the filtering of unrecognized extensions
- Adding a new word breaker

▶ **To force a scan**

1. Click the **Start** button, point to **Programs**, point to **Windows NT 4.0 Option Pack**, point to **Microsoft Index Server**, and then click **Index Server Manager**. Expand the catalog to display the Directories folder.
2. Click **Directories**.
3. In the right frame, right-click the folder to scan.
4. On the **Action** menu, click **Rescan**.
5. In the **Full Rescan** dialog box, click **Yes** for a full rescan, or click **No** for an incremental rescan.

Forcing a Merge

If response time for queries begins to slow down, you can free resources by combining indexes. From time to time, you must combine smaller indexes into larger ones to free space—both in memory and on the hard disk—to resolve queries quickly. To merge smaller indexes, you need to force a merge.

▶ **To force a merge**

1. In the left frame of Microsoft Management Console, select the catalog where you want to merge indexes.
2. On the **Action** menu, click **Merge**.

    The **Merge Catalog?** dialog box appears.

3. Click **Yes**.

Summary

During indexing, Index Server catalogs the full text and properties of documents stored on your Internet Information Server site. The process starts by using content filters to extract character streams from the corpus, which is all of the documents on your Internet Information Server site. Through a series of index mergers, these word lists are combined into shadow indexes which are then combined into the master index contained in the catalog. The Index Server Manager provides seven key management tools for Index Server administration.

Lesson 3: Queries

Queries are the method by which users perform content and property searches of your server from the Internet or an intranet. This lesson describes queries and explains the query process.

After this lesson, you will be able to:
- List and describe the query features of Index Server.
- Describe the steps in the query process used by Index Server.
- Describe the function of the .idq, .htx, and .asp files when hosted on Internet Information Server.

Estimated lesson time: 55 minutes

Query forms allow users to search your Web site for documents that meet specified criteria. Index Server provides several features that you can incorporate into a query form to enhance the query process, improve result reporting, and track usage:

- *Query scope*. Specifies the set of documents to be searched by the query engine. The scope is typically specified by a folder path on a storage volume, such as D:\Docs.

- *Content query restrictions*. Narrows the focus of a query by describing what type of textual content to search for.

- *Property query restrictions*. Specifies the file attributes that should be included in the search. These properties can include file size, creation and modification dates, file names, and authors.

- *Hit highlighting*. Generates an HTML page containing a list of qualifying documents, with those words corresponding to your query emphasized. The hit is displayed in red, italicized text. To view the hit highlights, click **Show Highlights (condensed)** or **Show Highlights (full text)**, located under each result abstract.

- *Query logging*. Internet Information Server logs all traffic between the client and server. Standard Internet Information Server logging picks up query information such as the querying Internet Protocol (IP) address and the queries processed by the server.

A sample query form is included with Index Server. You can use this sample query form to search the indexed files. These sample forms can be made available to Web site users or they can serve as examples of how to develop customized query forms. To open the sample query form, click **Start**, point to **Programs**, point to **Windows NT 4.0 Option Pack**, point to **Microsoft Index Server**, and then click **Index Server Sample Query Form**.

Query Form Elements

The basic query form is comprised of several elements:

- *HTML file*. This file displays a Web page where the user enters the query parameters. It also displays the results set returned by Index Server.
- *Internet Data Query (IDQ) file*. The IDQ file (a file with an .idq extension) is the intermediate form of the user's search request that Index Server runs to search the index.
- *HTML extension file (HTX)*. The HTX file (a file with an .htx extension) is an HTML file containing query results set data. This data is then added to an HTML page and sent to the Web browser to be displayed.

Note Index Server also uses another file type, .htw, as a template for formatting the hit-highlight page. The contents of the .htw with the .htx file are formatted as a Web page and sent to the Web browser.

In addition to creating basic query forms, you can use Active Server Pages (ASP) and Structured Query Language (SQL) with Microsoft Active Data Objects (ADO) to create query forms.

Building query forms with ASP allows you to use ActiveX scripting. Queries created with .asp files enable you to capitalize on scripting languages such as Microsoft Visual Basic Scripting Edition (VBScript) and Microsoft JScript to add flexibility in displaying query results.

ASP is described in detail in Chapter 11, "Active Server Pages."

Instead of using the standard forms in Index Server, you can write SQL queries in applications that use ADO. In your .asp files, use the SQL Extensions to form the query, ADO to retrieve the data, and a scripting language such as VBScript to display the data.

Note If Index Server performance becomes an issue, use the basic forms with .idq, .htx, and .htm files. ASP queries and SQL queries require more processing power to execute than the basic query forms.

The Query Process

Unlike the indexing process, which is a background process, the query process is entirely user-driven and works with Internet Information Server to accept and process queries and return result sets. Consequently, the querying process is the more complicated of the two processes.

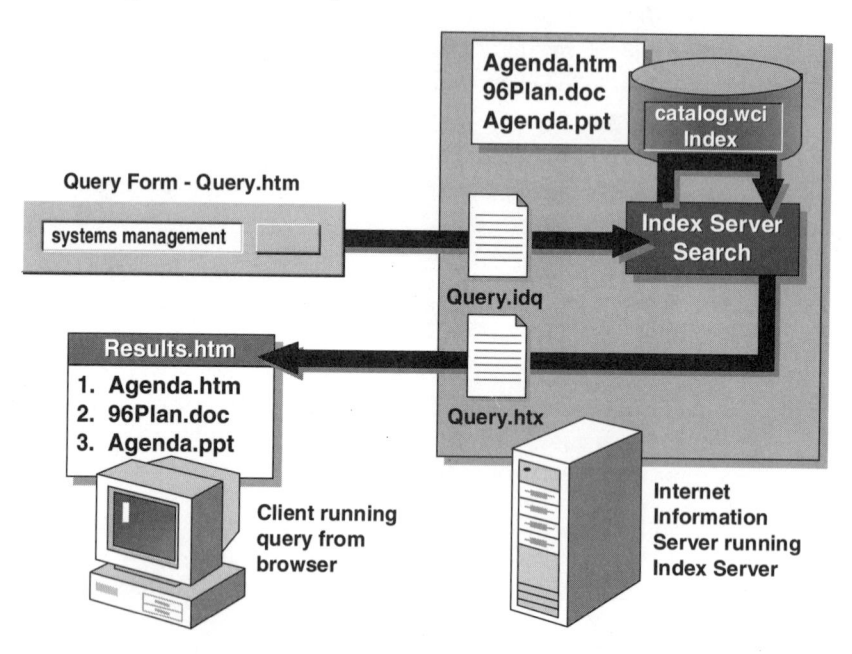

As shown in the preceding illustration, Index Server begins by converting queries from query forms into queries that are compatible with Index Server indexes. The system then carries out the query, and returns the results to the user in HTML format.

Index Server uses .idq files in the conversion of the query to a Web form, and advanced .htx files to format the query results.

Result Sets

Index Server packages query hits into result sets which are returned to the client.

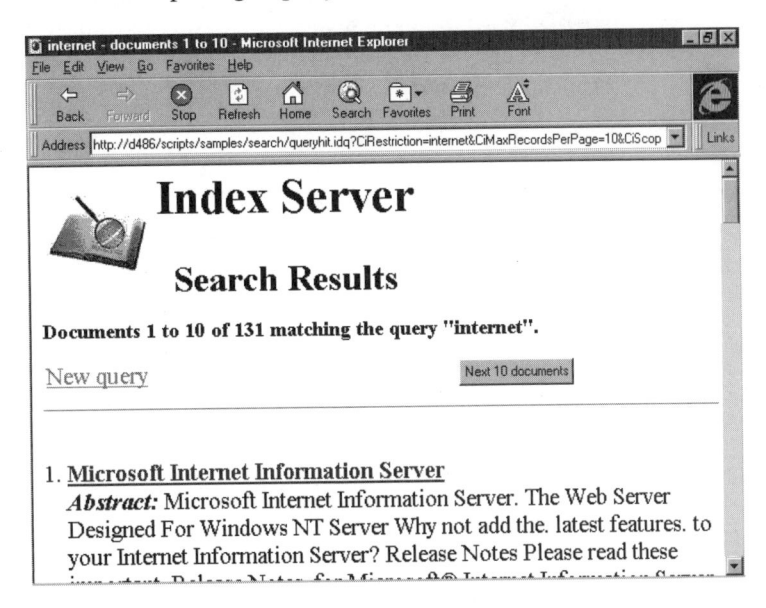

You can use the query form to limit the maximum number of hits returned on each result page. For example, you can limit a 200-item result set so that the client retrieves the information in 10 pages of 20 hits each. The user can also use the form to enable the client to determine the number of hits returned. Index Server can rank the hits in a result set according to any document property.

If you use access control lists (ACLs) as part of your Internet Information Server security and you store the corpus on an NTFS volume, Index Server respects all security restrictions by using ACL checking. Users can never see a document reference in a result set if the ACL on that object prohibits read permission to that client.

If the ACL permits access to the document, the client can specify what property data the server returns in a result set (this data corresponds to the columns in the result set).

In addition to returning properties stored with the document, the system can generate document abstracts, which can also be returned in a result set. Query restrictions can also include the document abstract.

Formulating Queries and Results

With Index Server, Internet data query files (files with an .idq extension) help convert queries. Working in tandem with .idq files, advanced .htx files format the query results. As shown in the following illustration, these advanced .htx files include extensions that handle the unique characteristics of Index Server query results.

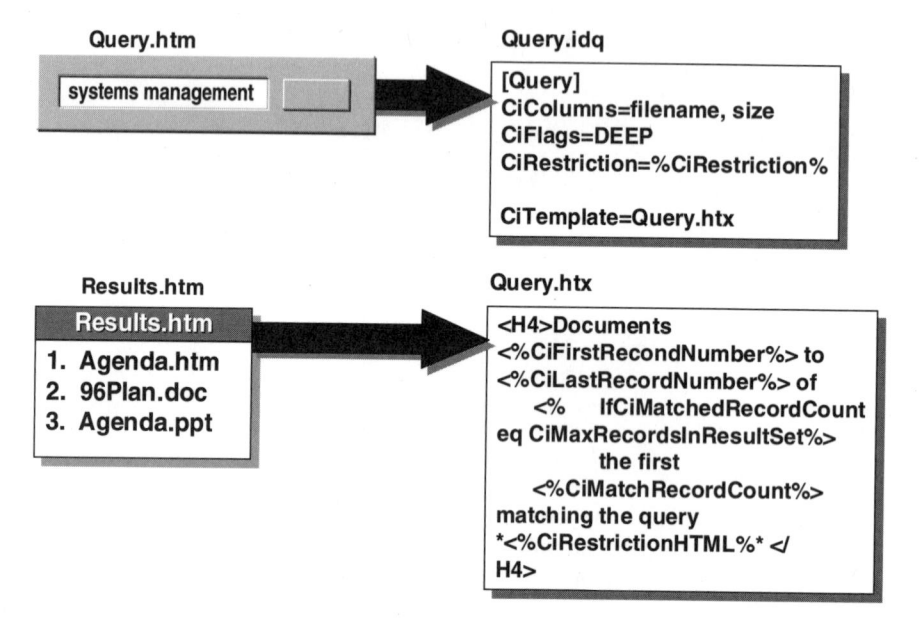

Query.htm

[systems management]

Query.idq
```
[Query]
CiColumns=filename, size
CiFlags=DEEP
CiRestriction=%CiRestriction%

CiTemplate=Query.htx
```

Results.htm

Results.htm
1. Agenda.htm
2. 96Plan.doc
3. Agenda.ppt

Query.htx
```
<H4>Documents
<%CiFirstRecordNumber%> to
<%CiLastRecordNumber%> of
    <%   IfCiMatchedRecordCount
eq CiMaxRecordsInResultSet%>
    the first
    <%CiMatchRecordCount%>
matching the query
*<%CiRestrictionHTML%>* </
H4>
```

The .idq file and its corresponding .htx file should be in a folder with Execute permission assigned.

Declaring Parameters Using .idq Files

The .idq files (together with the HTML form parameters) specifies the queries that Index Server runs.

Note All paths to .idq files must have the full path from a virtual server, and not a relative or physical path. In other words, all paths must start with a slash and cannot contain "." or ".." components, as in the following examples:

Valid Paths

```
/scripts/myquery.idq
/scripts/samples/search/query.idq
```

Invalid Paths

```
c:\inetsrv\scripts\myquery.idq
scripts/query.idq
/samples/../scripts/query.idq
```

You cannot store .idq files on a virtual server pointing to a remote UNC share.

The .idq files are divided into two sections, the names section and the query section.

The Names Section

Although the query section does the bulk of the work, the names section defines nonstandard column names that can be referred to in the query. These columns refer to ActiveX properties that have been created in document files with IPropertyStorage, or in the Microsoft Office summary and custom properties. The names section is a powerful tool with which you can customize searches for your organization's particular needs.

The names section is optional, and need not be supplied for standard queries.

The Query Section

Use the query section to specify the parameters that are actually used in the query process. These can refer to such properties as scope, restriction, and result sets, or form variables including conditional expressions that change the value of a variable depending upon some condition. The section begins with a [Query] tag, and is followed by a set of parameters.

The following example shows a basic but typical .idq file.

```
[Query]
CiColumns=filename,size,rank,characterization,vpath,DocTitle,write
CiFlags=DEEP
CiRestriction=%CiRestriction%
CiMaxRecordsInResultSet=150
CiMaxRecordsPerPage=10
CiScope=\
CiTemplate=/scripts/spdc1.htx
CiSort=rank[d]
CiCatalog=d:\
```

Each line of the file is explained in the following table.

This line in the query	Indicates or means to
[Query]	A query restriction.
CiColumns= filename, size, rank, characterization, vpath, DocTitle, write	The properties to return in the result set (file name, size, abstract, and so on).
CiFlags=DEEP	Execute the query over all child folders within the scope.
CiRestriction=%CiRestriction%	The query terms to search for.
CiMaxRecordsInResultSet=150	No more than 150 results will be returned.
CiMaxRecordsPerPage=10	Place only 10 results per Web page returned to the user.
CiScope=\	Start the query at the top (root) of the storage space.
CiTemplate=/scripts/spdc1.htx	Use the Spdc1.htx file to format the results.
CiSort=rank[d]	Sort the results based on the rank in descending ("d") order.
CiCatalog=d:\	Use the index stored on the root of drive D.

Generating Query Results Using .htx Files

The .htx file is an HTML file containing variables referring to data in the query result. For example, the following .htx code defines a page header that displays the query restriction and the range of documents included on the current page. The code is followed by the formatted HTML text produced.

```
<%if CiMatchedRecordCount eq 0%>
<H4>No documents matched the query "<%CiRestrictionHTML%>".</H4>
<%else%>
<H4>Documents <%CiFirstRecordNumber%> to <%CiLastRecordNumber%> of
<%if CiMatchedRecordCount eq CiMaxRecordsInResultSet%>
the first
<%endif%>
<%CiMatchedRecordCount%> matching the query
"<%CiRestrictionHTML%>".</H4>
<%endif%>
```

The preceding .htx text produces the following output:

> Documents 1 to 10 of the first 150 matching the query "systems management"

where the variable <%CiFirstRecordNumber%> is returned as 1 and <%CiMatchedRecordCount%> is returned as 150.

The .htx file is a standard HTML file that incorporates additional extensions provided by Internet Information Server and Index Server to include variable names and other processing information. Index Server uses the .htx file as a template when formatting the results.

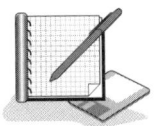

Practice

In this practice, you search a sample index. The Index Server sample query pages provide a good overview of its querying capabilities. To complete the remaining practices in this chapter, the Index Server process (Cidaemon.exe) must be running.

▶ **To make sure the Index Server process is running**

1. Press CTRL+ALT+DELETE, and then click **Task Manager**.
2. Click the **Processes** tab.

    If Index Server is running, you see the Cidaemon.exe process.

3. Close Task Manager.

▶ **To run a sample index**

1. Click the **Start** button, point to **Programs**, point to **Windows NT 4.0 Option Pack**, point to **Microsoft Index Server**, and then click **Index Server Sample Query Form**.

   Microsoft Internet Explorer starts and displays a query form.

2. In the **Enter your query below** box, type **ftp**
3. Click **Go**.

   This query starts Index Server (Cidaemon.exe), which begins building the Index.

   Note If there is a security alert, click **Yes**.

   The results page displays approximately 100 matches for ftp.

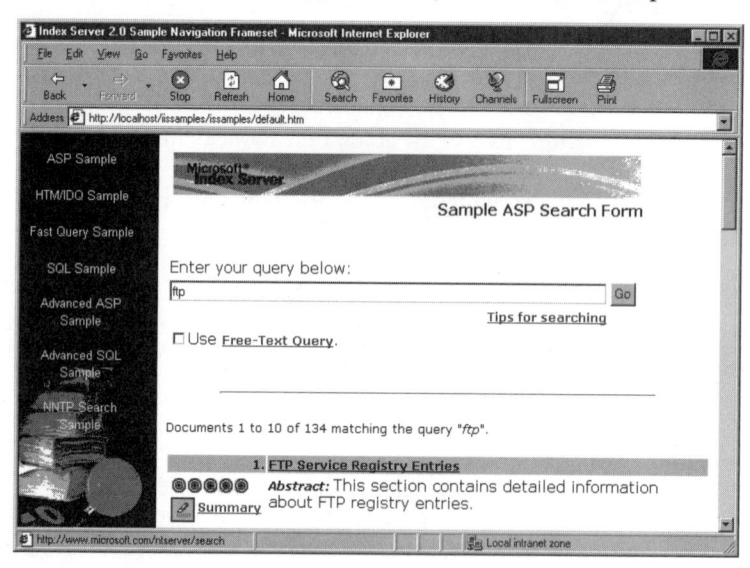

4. Close Internet Explorer.

In this part of the practice, you administer Index Server by checking the index status using Performance Monitor and Internet Explorer.

▶ **To check the index status using Performance Monitor**

1. Click the **Start** button, point to **Programs**, point to **Administrative Tools**, and then click **Performance Monitor**.
2. Press CTRL+R to display the Report view.
3. Click the **plus (+)** button to add counters to the report.

   The **Add to Report** dialog box appears.

4. In the **Object** list, click **Content Index**.
5. In the **Counters** list, select all of the counters, and then click **Add**.
6. Click **Done**.

    Performance Monitor displays the index status. You can check Performance Monitor during the remainder of the practice to determine if the indexing process has been completed.

In this part of the practice, you copy files into the virtual root of the Web site. You then perform a merge to filter and index the new documents. This increases several counters.

▶ **To update the index status using Index Server Manager merge**

1. Using Windows NT Explorer, copy the \Iis\Practice\Index folder located on the course compact disc to C:\Inetpub\Wwwroot.
2. Press ALT+TAB to return to Performance Monitor.
3. Press CTRL+U to update the report.

    The report now indicates that files to be filtered are no longer zero. Write down the number of documents filtered, files to be filtered, and the total number of documents.

    _____

    _____

    _____

    Note Because you copied the files into the virtual root of the Web site, you must perform a merge to filter and index the new documents.

4. Click the **Start** button, point to **Programs**, point to **Windows NT 4.0 Option Pack**, point to **Microsoft Index Server**, and then click **Index Server Manager**.
5. Click the **Index Server on Local Machine** node.
6. In the Catalog column of the Scope pane, right-click **Web**.
7. Click **Merge**.

    A dialog box appears asking if you want to merge the catalog.

8. Click **Yes**.

9. When the merge is complete, press ALT+TAB to return to Performance Monitor.
10. Press CTRL+U to update the Performance Monitor report.
11. Compare the three counters that you previously documented. The total number of documents should have increased, the number of documents filtered should have increased, and files to be filtered should be zero.

▶ **To check the index status using Internet Explorer**

1. Click the **Start** button, point to **Programs**, point to **Windows NT 4.0 Option Pack**, point to **Microsoft Index Server**, and then click **Index Server Manager (HTML)**.

   Internet Explorer displays the Index Server Administration page.

2. Click **Refresh** to obtain Index Statistics.

   The administration page displays two sets of statistics: cache statistics and index statistics.

3. View the index statistics.

   If the message "Index is up to date" appears, then the indexing process is complete. If the message "Index is not up to date" appears, then the indexing process is still active.

4. If the number of **Wordlists** statistic is greater than 0, click **Merge Index**.

   This optimizes the search capabilities of Index Server. Internet Explorer returns to the Index Server Administration page.

In this practice, you post a content query and a property query on Index Server and examine the differences.

Note Your results will vary in this practice as the corpus is going through its various stages of indexing.

▶ **To post extended queries**

1. Click the **Start** button, point to **Programs**, point to **Windows NT 4.0 Option Pack**, point to **Microsoft Index Server**, and then click **Index Server Sample Query Form**.

   Internet Explorer starts and displays a query form.

2. In the left pane of the page, click **Advanced ASP Sample**.

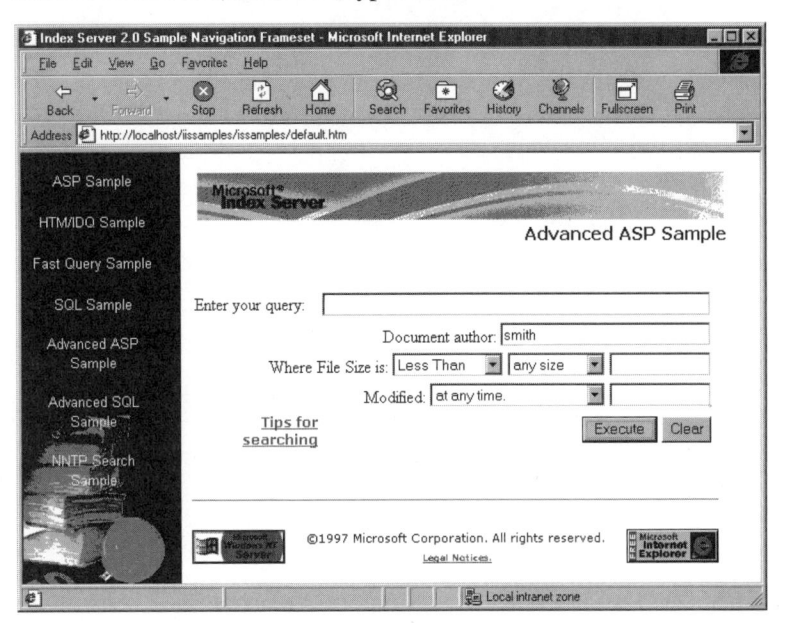

3. In the **Document author** box, type **Smith**

4. Click **Execute**.

   The query results indicates that five documents matched the content query named "smith."

   Note If you receive a security alert message, click **Yes**.

5. Click the **Start** button, point to **Programs**, point to **Windows NT 4.0 Option Pack**, point to **Microsoft Index Server**, and then click **Index Server Manager (HTML)**.

6. Internet Explorer starts and displays the Administration – Index Statistics page. Notice that the Total queries have increased since the last access.

Summary

The query process is entirely user-driven and works with Internet Information Server to accept and process queries and return results. Index Server uses .idq files in the conversion of the query to a Web form, and advanced .htx files to format the query results. You can also build query forms with ASP. By incorporating different scripting languages, you can add flexibility in displaying query results.

Lesson 4: Index Server Administration

Although Microsoft Index Server is designed to minimize administrative requirements, you can control indexing on a per-physical location basis. In this lesson, you learn how to manage indexing and understand the way in which Index Server handles error detection and recovery.

After this lesson, you will be able to:
- List and describe the tools provided with Index Server and Windows NT Server to monitor and manage Index Server.
- List the errors automatically detected by Index Server and state how they are corrected.
- Implement Index Server security features to control access to indexed files.

Estimated lesson time: 45 minutes

Microsoft Index Server is designed to minimize administrative requirements and manual intervention in the case of most errors. However, manual indexing can be managed on a location-by-location basis.

Administering an Index

By default, Index Server indexes every virtual server and virtual directory automatically, but you can perform indexing manually by first reviewing the performance statistics using either Performance Monitor or Hypertext Transport Protocol (HTTP).

Administrative Requests

Administrative requests are essentially queries, except that the administrative parameters are stored in an .ida file instead of an .idq file. The .ida files allow users with appropriate permissions to administer the Internet Information Server site.

You can find the working administration page that comes with Index Server at http://*computername*/iisadmin/isadmin/admin.htm.

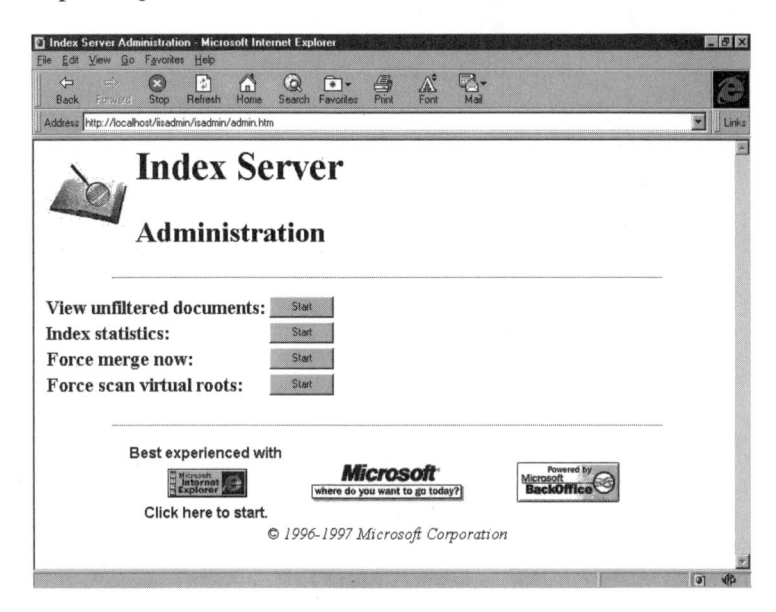

Note Do not put .ida files on a virtual server pointing to a remote UNC share.

Some administrative operations can change the state of the index. You can restrict administrative operations with an ACL.

Monitoring Performance

Index Server provides a number of different performance monitors to help you optimize query service. These monitors measure criteria such as the number of documents that need to be indexed and how fast queries are being processed.

In the practice in the preceding lesson, you learned that you can use Performance Monitor to administer Index Server. You can also monitor performance by using an .ida script. The information available is nearly identical, but the method of retrieval differs. You can use either solution both locally or from a remote client.

Performance Monitor has the advantage of automatic refresh, as well as graphing and logging capabilities. No setup is required when you use Windows NT Performance Monitor.

Using an .ida script, however, gives you more flexible .htx output formatting, which can be viewed from a client running an operating system other than Microsoft Windows. In order to use an .ida script, you must create an .ida file with CiAdminOperation=GetState. Index Server includes a sample page using an .ida script.

Error Detection and Recovery

Microsoft Index Server automatically detects several kinds of errors. Most of these errors are recoverable. Other than in the case of hardware failures or situations where the catalog drive runs out of hard disk space, you generally do not have to intervene in the error detection process in any way.

Lost File Notifications

During normal operation—and if the indexed folders are on computers running Windows NT—Index Server tracks all changes to the documents in those folders automatically. If the rate of file modification is very high, you may lose some notifications due to buffer overflows.

In the case of a buffer overflow, Index Server automatically schedules an incremental scan on the scope that lost the notifications. No manual intervention is needed.

Dropped Network Connections

When a virtual root points to a remote share and its connection to the remote share is lost, you get what is called a disconnected path. Index Server detects this situation and scans the remote shares periodically in order to detect when the connection becomes active again. No manual intervention is needed.

Corrupted Files and Faulty Filter DLLs

If the CiDaemon process detects corrupted files, Index Server marks the files as unfiltered. You can get a list of unfiltered files by issuing an administrative command to list them. It is also possible that you have a problem with the filter DLL used to filter those files.

If you see that a particular type of file is consistently not being filtered, contact the vendor of that filter DLL.

Disk-full Condition

If the catalog drive starts getting full, Index Server pauses indexing temporarily. Filtering cannot continue unless you free additional hard disk space on the catalog drive. Index Server writes a message to the event log when the hard disk starts getting full.

You should monitor the event log for these messages and take corrective action as needed.

Note You may want to stop Index Server while correcting the disk-full condition.

Corrupt Property Cache

If Index Server is shut down abruptly or it detects a corruption during normal operation, Index Server marks the property cache as corrupted. When you restart Index Server, it performs a recovery action on the property cache. Index Server writes one event log message at the beginning of the recovery action and another at the end of recovery. During the automatic recovery, Index Server allows queries but does not start filtering again until the recovery is completed. No manual intervention is needed.

Data Corruption and Internal Inconsistencies

It is possible that a power failure or other catastrophic event may corrupt the index data beyond repair. In that situation, Index Server deletes all existing data and refilters the corpus. If it detects corruption during startup, Index Server refilters automatically. However, if it detects corruption during normal operation, it writes an event log message and denies all further queries.

When this event appears in the event log, you should stop and restart the Content Index service (Cisvc.exe).

When Index Server performs automatic recovery, it writes an event to the event log. If the catalog specified in the event log message had default settings and all of the virtual roots were indexed, no action is required.

Security Features

Index Server uses the built-in security features of Windows NT Server 4.0 and Internet Information Server. To maintain a secure site without disclosing information to unauthorized users, it is necessary to be aware of authentication and access control issues. Even on sites that contain only widely-available public information, being aware of security issues helps to prevent compromising the server.

Restricted Catalog Access

When you first install Index Server, the catalog is set up with an ACL that allows only system administrators and system services to access it. In part, this assures that if the catalog folder is contained within a virtual root, ensuring that unauthorized users cannot see the files in the catalog as part of their query.

The protection on the catalog folder is also important to prevent unauthorized users (who may have access to the server by use of file-server shares) from seeing the contents of the catalog. Although the information in the catalog is in a form that would be difficult for someone without knowledge of the file formats to decipher, it is possible to read the content of files on the server by examining the catalog.

If an additional catalog folder is created manually, care should be taken to ensure that it, and the files created in it, have appropriate access controls. A catalog folder should allow access for administrators and for the System account. Index Server runs as a service, so system permission is required.

Document Access Control

When documents are filtered, any access controls on a document are kept in the catalog and checked against client permissions when a query is processed. If a client does not have access to a document, the document is not included in any of the client's query results; there is no indication that the document exists. To avoid the appearance of missing hits, a user should be properly authenticated before processing a query.

Authentication

To enforce access control properly, clients should be properly authenticated before they can send a query to the server. The easiest way to ensure that a client is authenticated is to put an access control on the form that issues a query. You can also put an access control list on the .idq, .htx, or .htw file used in a query.

Depending upon the configuration of Internet Information Server, one or more of the following authentication mechanisms can be used:

- Anonymous logon
- Basic authentication
- Windows NT Challenge/Response authentication

If anonymous logon is allowed, it will be used by default as long as all files accessed by the client are permitted to be accessed by the anonymous logon account. Whenever an attempt is made to gain access to a document for which access is denied to the anonymous user, an authentication dialog is presented, provided another authentication mechanism is available. The client can then provide authentication and thereby gain access to files that would otherwise be denied.

Note If you turn off client access to some protected files by disabling authentication on a virtual directory (that is, by setting anonymous permission only), you should also disable authentication for the .htw file. Otherwise, clients are able to see the contents of the protected files in the hit highlights returned after issuing a query.

Practice

In this practice, you implement and test the security features of Index Server by using different user accounts. To perform the practice, you must first create user accounts and change security permissions on your server as the following procedures describe.

▶ **To create the user accounts**

1. Click the **Start** button, point to **Programs**, point to **Administrative Tools**, and then click **User Manager for Domains**.
2. Create two user accounts with the information in the following table.

Property	User 1	User 2
User Name	Laurel	Megan
Password	laurel	megan
User Must Change Password	Clear the check box	Clear the check box

3. Close Windows NT User Manager.

▶ **To change security permissions on a Security.doc file**

1. Start Windows NT Explorer and then select the C:\Inetpub\Wwwroot\Index folder.
2. Open the Confidential folder.
3. Right-click Security.doc, and then click **Properties**.

    The **Security.doc Properties** dialog box appears.
4. Click the **Security** tab.
5. Click **Permissions**.

    The **File Permissions** dialog box appears.
6. Click **Add**.

    The **Add Users and Groups** dialog box appears.
7. Click **Show Users**.
8. Scroll the list of names, and then click **Laurel** and **Megan**.
9. Click **Add**.

    Laurel and Megan are added to the **Add Names** list.
10. Click **OK**.

    The **File Permissions** dialog box appears.
11. Click **Laurel**.

12. In the **Type of Access** list, click **No Access**.

    The dialog box shows that Laurel has no access.
13. Click **OK**.
14. Close **User Manager**.

You must now enable the appropriate security on Internet Information Server.

▶ **To enable security on Internet Information Server**

1. Start Internet Service Manager.
2. Right-click **Default Web Site**.
3. Click **Properties**.
4. In the Anonymous Access and Authentication Control pane on the **Directory Security** tab, click **Edit**.

    The **Authentication Methods** dialog box appears.
5. Set the authentication methods using the settings in the following table.

Authentication methods	Status
Allow Anonymous	Disabled
Basic (Clear Text)	Enabled
Windows NT Challenge/Response	Disabled

    A warning message appears.
6. Click **Yes**.
7. Click **OK** twice.
8. In the **Inheritance Overrides** box, select **IISADMIN**, and then click **OK**.

    Basic authentication is used for demonstration purposes only. Basic authentication makes the practice run more quickly by preventing you from logging off.
9. Minimize Internet Service Manager.
10. Click the **Start** button, point to **Programs**, point to **Windows NT 4.0 Option Pack**, point to **Microsoft Index Server**, and then click **Index Server Manager (HTML)**.

    Note If prompted for a user name and password, type your administrator name and password.

11. Scroll to **Index Statistics**, and then click **Refresh**.

    Notice under Index Statistics that **# Documents changed** is 163.

    Note If a security warning message appears, click **Yes**.

12. In the left frame of the **Index Statistics** page, click **Merge Index**.
13. In the **Index Statistics** page, click **Refresh**.

    Notice under **Index Statistics**, that the **# Documents changed** setting has changed. This indicates that the Security.doc file security status change has been indexed.

▶ **To test the security of Index Server**

1. Close all copies of Internet Explorer.
2. Click the **Start** button, point to **Programs**, point to **Microsoft Index Server**, and then click **Index Server Sample Query Form**.

    The **Enter Network password** dialog box appears.

3. In the **Username** box, type **laurel**
4. In the **Password** box, type **laurel**
5. Click **OK**.
6. In the **Enter your query below** box, type **confidential document**
7. Click **Go**.

    Index Server returns no documents. Laurel is not given any indication that Security.doc exists.

8. Close Internet Explorer.
9. Click the **Start** button, point to **Programs**, point to **Microsoft Index Server**, and then click **Index Server Sample Query Form**.

    The **Basic Authentication** dialog box appears.

10. In the **Username** box, type **megan**
11. In the **Password** box, type **megan**
12. Click **OK**.
13. In the **Enter your query below box**, type **confidential document**
14. Click **Go**.

    Index Server should return the Security.doc file.

15. Close Internet Explorer.

▶ **To restore password authentication settings on the WWW Service**

1. Start Internet Service Manager.
2. Right-click **Default Web Site**.
3. Click **Properties**.
4. In the Anonymous Access and Authentication Control pane on the **Directory Security** tab, click **Edit**.

   The **Authentication Methods** dialog box appears.
5. Use the information in the following table to set password authentication.

Password authentication	Check box
Allow Anonymous	Enabled
Basic (Clear Text)	Disabled
Windows NT Challenge/Response	Enabled

6. Click **OK** three times.
7. Close Internet Service Manager.

Summary

Although Index Server requires minimal administration, you can perform manual administration of your indexes using .ida files. Index Server also detects most errors automatically and, except in the event of hardware failures and data corruption, corrects the error states without manual intervention. Index Server uses the built-in security features of Windows NT Server 4.0 and Internet Information Server.

Review

The following questions are intended to reinforce key information presented in this chapter. If you are unable to answer a question, review the appropriate lesson, and then try the question again.

1. What is required in order to index files saved as proprietary formatted documents, such as Microsoft Word files?

2. What factors can impact Index Server performance?

3. What can you do to reduce the time it takes to return results for frequently queried documents?

4. What feature shows you the exact portion of a document that satisfies your query?

5. How can you exclude certain folders from being indexed?

6. If a user does not have access to a specific file on an Internet or intranet site, will they see that file returned in the results set?

CHAPTER 13

Understanding Microsoft Transaction Server

Lesson 1 Overview of Transaction Processing . . . 260

Lesson 2 Configuring and Managing Microsoft Transaction Server . . . 267

Review . . . 275

About This Chapter

This chapter introduces you to Microsoft Transaction Server (MTS). In the lessons of this chapter, you learn about the components of Microsoft Transaction Server and how to configure it. The chapter also provides an example of using Microsoft Transaction Server in a business environment.

Before You Begin

To complete the lessons in this chapter, you must have:

- Installed Microsoft Internet Information Server (IIS) according to the procedures in Chapter 2, "Installing Microsoft Internet Information Server."
- The course compact disc to install the Microsoft SQL Server 6.5 evaluation version during the chapter practice.

Lesson 1: Overview of Transaction Processing

Microsoft Transaction Server simplifies the application development process. With it, you can deploy scaleable server applications built from Microsoft ActiveX components. This lesson provides an overview of how Microsoft Transaction Server works.

After this lesson, you will be able to:
- Define a transaction.
- List and describe the Microsoft Transaction Server components.
- Describe the function Microsoft Transaction Server plays in transactions over the Internet.

Estimated lesson time: 30 minutes

Microsoft Transaction Server delivers the components—including transactions, scalability services, connection management, and point-and-click administration—that makes it possible for you to build and deploy scaleable server applications.

Microsoft Transaction Server uses a simple programming model. The basic pattern is always the same: the client requests a Component Object Model (COM) object running under Microsoft Transaction Server control. This permits Microsoft Transaction Server to create an object context and associate it with the object. When the work is done, the object either calls SetComplete to indicate success or calls SetAbort to indicate rollback.

A transaction is a unit of work that succeeds or fails as a whole. Transactions are a way to coordinate a series of changes made to a resource or sets of resources. The most common type of transactions handle this coordination through a central point, called a resource manager.

These actions have what are known as ACID properties. ACID is an acronym that stands for Atomicity, Consistency, Isolation, and Durability.

- *Atomicity—Either all changes happen or none happen*. Atomicity refers to the fact that a single transaction has an all-or-nothing behavior. An example of this is a bank account transfer. When you withdraw money from your checking account and deposit it into your savings account you expect the transaction to be atomic, that is, completed as a whole.

- *Consistency—Actions taken as a group do not violate any integrity constraints*. Consistency ensures that, in the preceding example, the deposit-withdraw pair does not violate any rules or integrity constraints, such as transferring more than $200 on any business day, or overdrawing your checking account.

- *Isolation—For actions that execute concurrently, one is either executed before or after the other, but not both.* Isolation ensures that, if two people share a joint checking account and they are both moving money at the same time, one money transaction waits for the other money transaction to be completed. If the account contains $200, each individual does not withdraw the only $200 at the same time.
- *Durability—Changes survive failures of process, network, operating system, and others.* Durability ensures that if the Automatic Teller Machine (ATM) that you are withdrawing money from experiences a power failure in the midst of the transaction, the $200 in bills that you receive is ensured to be debited from the account.

Microsoft Transaction Server Components

There are four major categories of Microsoft Transaction Server services. First, there is an Object Request Broker (ORB). When a call comes into a server and requests an object, the ORB handles this call, checks for availability, and ultimately gives the requestor an object.

Next, a Transaction Processing Monitor (TP Monitor) is, in simplest terms, an environment that inserts itself between the clients and the server resources so that it can manage transactions, manage resources, and provide load balancing and fault tolerance. The typical TP Monitor model does not acknowledge other objects. It only knows how to handle requests in the most efficient means possible.

Microsoft Transaction Server combines Object Request Brokering and TP Monitoring using the Distributed Component Object Model (DCOM) as the main element. Microsoft Transaction Server uses the Microsoft Distributed Transaction Coordinator (DTC) as the TP Monitor.

In a typical process, requests for objects come in by means of DCOM; Microsoft Transaction Server processes the requests, efficiently allocates server resources, and begins a Distributed Transaction Coordinator transaction. It then returns this object to the client. The client then uses the object to perform its intended function. Microsoft Transaction Server resides between the object and the client, and monitors all client actions. By doing this, it is acting as a TP Monitor and, as a result, can perform the duties of the TP Monitor. For example, it can schedule requests and pool resources during idle time. When the client is done with the object, the client releases the object which causes Microsoft Transaction Server to complete the transaction and free or pool the resources.

Three-Tier Architecture

Three-tiered applications, where the application server, client computer, and data source can be separated from each other, provide more deployment flexibility than two-tiered client/server programming, where application code is location-dependent. The three-tier architecture consists of:

- *Presentation*. The client application consists mostly of a graphical user interface (GUI). Services such as database connections and business services are obtained from middle-tier servers. This results in less overhead for the user, but more network traffic for the system as components are distributed among different computers.

- *Business/Data Components*. Middle-tier components can implement data rules or business rules. Business rules can consist of business algorithms, or legal or governmental regulations. Data rules consist of rules to keep the data structures consistent, within a specific database as well as among multiple databases. These can exist on a server computer to assist in resource sharing. They can be used to enforce business and data rules. Because they are not tied to a specific client, they can be used by all applications.

    Note It is time and cost effective to place business objects in a centralized location on the network. Objects can be shared among applications, and unit testing can be done before any components are deployed. Maintenance costs are decreased because rule changes only occur at a single point.

- *Data Access*. This is the actual database management system (DBMS) access layer. It can be accessed through the data/business rules layer, and on occasion by the GUI itself. It consists of data access components (rather than raw DBMS connections) to aid in resource sharing and to allow clients to be configured without installing libraries or drivers on each client.

No matter which kind of presentation interface is used, it is important to remember that all applications consist of the same basic pieces. A three-tier architecture is a logical architecture, and does not imply that you need to use three different computers. In other words, there is no required correspondence between the logical layers of a three-tier architecture and the physical topology of your network. How the pieces of an application are distributed may change, depending on the system requirements.

In a typical client/server environment it is deemed best to acquire resources early and hold them for the duration of the application. Although the amount of time that these resources were in use was small in comparison to the time the resources were acquired (and unavailable to other users), the overriding consideration was performance. Resource utilization was a secondary consideration.

MSMQ

Microsoft Message Queue Server (MSMQ) can act as a Microsoft Transaction Server resource manager. It permits asynchronous transport through an enterprise-wide queuing system. It enables scalability, because transaction-processing systems such as Microsoft Transaction Server do not have to depend on all resource managers being available all of the time, or the transaction response being dependent on the slowest resource manager. Messages can simply be queued for future delivery. MSMQ even supports independent clients, where the client delivers messages only when connected to the MSMQ server network.

MSMQ offers ActiveX support, dynamic routing and configuration, multiple delivery and acknowledgment options, and integration with Microsoft Windows NT security facilities.

ASP Integration

Internet Information Server 4.0 integrates Active Server Pages (ASP) technology and Microsoft Transaction Server. The ASP technology built into Internet Information Server makes it possible to apply the client/server model to Web-based applications. This means you obtain faster responses to queries and less network traffic.

ASP has been extended further to accommodate scaleable three-tier applications. Active Server Pages are now based on Microsoft Transaction Server. This means ASP applications can run in separate address spaces for reliability and security. A transaction cannot span multiple ASP pages. You should make sure to group objects on one ASP page if a transaction requires objects from several transactional components.

Components of a Transaction

A component is a discrete unit of code built on ActiveX technologies that delivers a well-specified set of services through well-specified interfaces. Components provide the objects that clients request at run time.

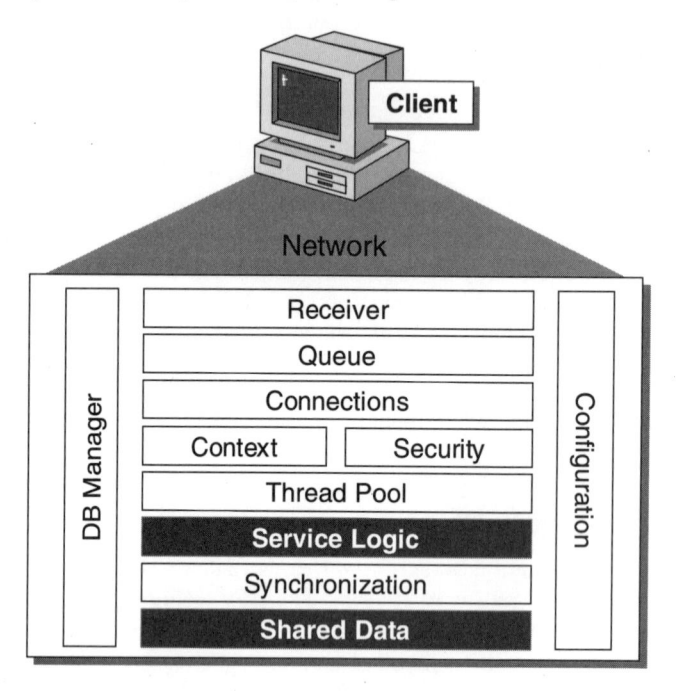

Transaction components must include:

- *Client logic*. Includes forms and the user interface.
- *Network protocol*. Links the client with the server.
- *Network receiver*. Listens to the network, accepts incoming calls from clients, and manages congestion.
- *Queue manager*. Manages client calls if they start to back up.
- *Connection manager*. Tracks work and system resources on behalf of each client.
- *Context manager*. Keeps track of each user's concurrent identity and state.
- *Security manager*. Prevents unauthorized access to the application or data.
- *Thread pool*. Keeps you from having to dedicate a thread for each user.
- *Actual service logic*. Includes all business functions the application performs.

- *Synchronization manager.* Coordinates the transaction.
- *Configuration manager.* Manages thread and server resources.
- *Database connection manager.* Allocates database connections for multiple users.
- *Data.* Includes all transaction information.

Component-Based Programming

With a component-based approach, applications can be assembled using available components. Applications no longer have to be monolithic, implying a less tight coupling between the code using the components and the components themselves.

COM allows discovering the functionality of COM objects at run time or at design time. This has a number of important repercussions:

- The user of the object can defer until run time committing to use the services provided by the object. This allows the component and client to evolve asynchronously.
- A client that only expects the base functionality has no difficulty with components that use newer functionality.
- If a client that expects enhanced functionality supplied by a later version object, but instead encounters a older version component, the client can degrade its exposed services.

This enables vendors to add functionality to components without danger of breaking code that has already been deployed.

COM also makes it unnecessary for the client of a component to know the physical location of the component in the file system or on the network. If this knowledge is unavailable to the client, it forces a consistent approach for interaction with components whether they are in-process or out-of-process.

Client code does not need to be written in the same language as the component. All that is required is that the client language permits calling of functions through pointer-to-function. For scripting languages, the script environment can act as a proxy in making such calls.

When a COM component is registered with Microsoft Transaction Server, it is run as a separate process. The InProcServer32 key from the code is replaced with LocalServer32, specifying Mtx.exe as a surrogate for the in-process server. Acting as a surrogate allows Microsoft Transaction Server to provide a wrapper for the real component.

COM provides a new specification for object description called metadata. All COM objects are required to be self-describing using this metadata. This means all objects have a standard way of advertising their services and any other requirements they may have of the COM run time.

Note There are methods you can use if you want to keep some state on the client. For example, using variant arrays, you can pass data back to the client for local user input. Another approach is to copy objects down to the client, use them locally, and then copy them back to the server to update them. This allows the server components to be stateless, but the full objects are available locally so their properties and methods can be accessed without network traffic.

Summary

A transaction is a unit of work that succeeds or fails as a whole. Transactions are composed of a number of components. Microsoft Transaction Server makes transaction management transparent to the component developer. With Microsoft Transaction Server, you can coordinate the work of many components written in different languages and running on different systems as a single, atomic unit.

Lesson 2: Configuring and Managing Microsoft Transaction Server

You can configure Microsoft Transaction Server through a series of point-and-click transaction wizards. This lesson describes how to use these wizards to configure and manage Microsoft Transaction Server.

After this lesson, you will be able to:
- Install a Microsoft Transaction Server package.
- Configure the Microsoft Transaction Server Explorer.
- Configure the Open Database Connectivity (ODBC) data source.
- Monitor Microsoft Transaction Server components and transactions.

Estimated lesson time: 45 minutes

You can use the Microsoft Transaction Server Explorer snap-in, a graphical management tool used to deploy and manage solutions across a network, to configure Microsoft Transaction Server. Microsoft Transaction Server Explorer provides you with a complete view of all of the components deployed within a solution.

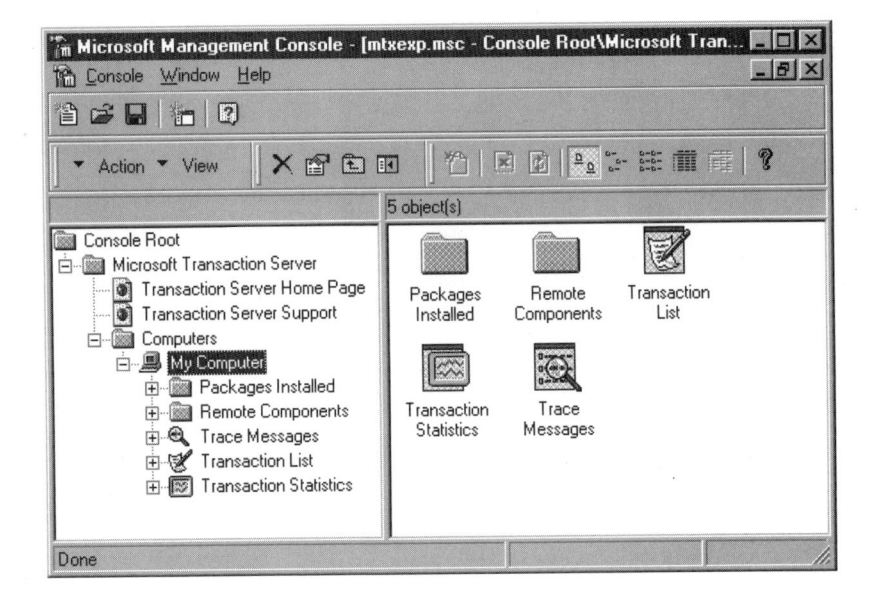

▶ **To open Microsoft Transaction Server Explorer snap-in**

- Click the **Start** button, point to **Programs**, point to **Windows NT 4.0 Option Pack**, point to **Microsoft Transaction Server**, and then click **Transaction Server Explorer**.

  The Microsoft Transaction Server Explorer snap-in opens in Microsoft Management Console (MMC).

The Microsoft Transaction Server Explorer includes point-and-click wizards for assembling and configuring a solution from prebuilt packages and components. A package is a set of components that perform related application functions. These wizards include:

- *Package wizard.* Creates packages.
- *Component wizard.* Adds components to a package. This wizard either lists all components already registered in the system, or enables you to register new components.
- *Add Server wizard.* Exports a package to a remote server, dynamically adding servers to a distributed solution.
- *Add Clients wizard.* Adds client systems to a distributed solution.
- *Configure wizard.* Sets the transactional properties of components deployed within a package.
- *Security wizard.* Configures the security attributes of components and packages.

The Microsoft Transaction Server Explorer includes the following GUI utilities:

- *Transaction lists.* Lists the properties of the running transactions.
- *Transaction statistics.* Tracks transaction performance.
- *Trace messages.* Views trace messages.

Practice

In this practice, you install the sample bank package included with Internet Information Server. You use the following information of a common transaction that occurs in the banking industry.

The bank application consists of four components:

- *Account.* Uses ODBC calls to modify an account record in a single database.
- *MoveMoney.* Performs debit, credit, and transfer operations against different bank databases.
- *Receipt.* Generates a unique ID number for each bank transaction.
- *UpdateReceipt.* Allocates ranges of unique ID numbers for receipts.

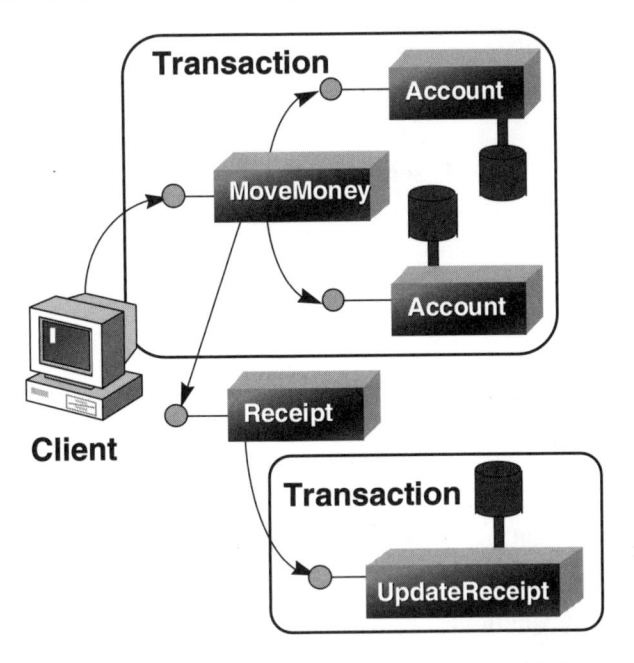

This is an example of a simple application that can receive all of the benefits of a sophisticated, high-end server infrastructure—including transactions, location transparency, thread and process management, and database connection pooling—through integration with Microsoft Transaction Server. As shown in the preceding illustration, the following process occurs:

1. The client initiates a bank transaction by invoking MoveMoney.
2. MoveMoney invokes an Account component for each database that it needs to modify. MoveMoney also invokes the Receipt component for each bank transaction.
3. Microsoft Transaction Server makes sure that the work of all of these components executes as a single unit (or transaction), even though these are different components that could be written in different languages.

    Even though each one of these components is built as a simple, single-user ActiveX component, the transaction executes as multiuser through Microsoft Transaction Server thread and process management services.
4. The Account components access the SQL Server database by means of the Microsoft Transaction Server ODBC resource dispensers, a mechanism for high-performance database access.

To complete this practice, you must install Microsoft SQL Server 6.5. You can find an evaluation copy of SQL Server 6.5 in the Mssql folder on the course compact disc.

▶ **To install the SQL Server 6.5 Evaluation Edition**

1. On the Windows NT 4.0 Option Pack compact disc, double-click **setup.bat** in the Mssql folder.

    A command prompt appears.

2. Press the ENTER key to continue to with the installation.

    The **Welcome** dialog box appears.

3. Click **Continue**.

    The **Enter Name and Organization** dialog box appears.

4. In the **Name** box, type **Student** and then in the **Company name** box, type **Microsoft**

    Leave the **Product ID** box blank.

5. Click **Continue**.

    The **Verify Name and Organization** dialog box appears.

6. Click **Continue**.

    The **Microsoft SQL Server 6.5 - Option** dialog box appears.

7. Verify that **Install SQL Server & Utilities** is selected.

8. Click **Continue**.

    The **SQL Server 6.5 - Evaluation Edition** dialog box appears.

9. Click **Continue**.

    The **SQL Server Installation Path** dialog box appears.

10. Click **Continue** to accept defaults.

    The **MASTER Device Creation** dialog box appears.

11. Click **Continue** to accept defaults.

    The **SQL Server Books Online** dialog box appears.

12. Click **Continue**.

    The **Installation Options** dialog box appears.

13. Select the **Auto Start SQL Server at boot time** option.
14. Select the **Auto Start SQL Executive at boot time** option.
15. Click **Continue**.

    The **SQL Executive Log On Account** dialog box appears.

Chapter 13 Understanding Microsoft Transaction Server

16. Select **Install** to log on as Local System Account.
17. Click **Continue**.

    Files are copied, the system is updated, and then the **Microsoft SQL Server 6.5 - Completed** dialog box appears.

18. Click **Exit to Windows NT**.
19. Restart your computer.

▶ **To install the sample bank package**

1. Click the **Start** button, point to **Programs**, point to **Windows NT 4.0 Option Pack**, and then click **Windows NT 4.0 Option Pack Setup**.
2. Click **Next**.
3. Click **Add/Remove**.
4. In the **Components** list box, select **Transaction Server**.
5. Click **Show Subcomponents**.
6. Select **Transaction Server Development**.
7. Click **OK**.
8. Click **Next**, and then follow the prompts to complete Setup.

In this part of the practice, you prepare the Microsoft Transaction Server environment to monitor the sample bank components and transactions.

▶ **To configure the Microsoft Transaction Server Explorer**

1. Click the **Start** button, point to **Programs**, point to **Windows NT 4.0 Option Pack**, point to **Microsoft Transaction Server**, and then click **Transaction Server Explorer**.

   Microsoft Management Console appears with the Microsoft Transaction Server Explorer snap-in.

2. Expand the Microsoft Transaction Server folder.
3. Expand the Computers folder.
4. Expand the My Computer node.
5. Select the Packages Installed folder.
6. Maximize Microsoft Management Console.
7. In the right pane, double-click the **Sample Bank** icon.
8. Double-click the Components folder.
9. Click **View**, and then click **Status View**.

   This displays usage information for the various components in the package.

10. Click **Window**, and then click **New Window**.

272   Microsoft Internet Information Server 4.0 Training

11. Click **Window**, and then click **Tile Horizontally**.

    Microsoft Management Console displays two windows, which are enumerated as 1 and 2.

12. Scroll the left pane of the new window (2), and then click **Transaction Statistics**.

    Transaction statistics are displayed when transactional components are used.

13. In window number 2, click **Action**.

    A menu appears.

14. Click **Scope Pane**.

    The left pane disappears in window number 2.

15. In window number 1, click **Action**.

    A menu appears.

16. Click **Scope Pane**.

    The left pane disappears in window number 1.

In this part of the practice, you configure the ODBC data source.

▶ **To configure the ODBC data source**

1. Open Control Panel.

2. Double-click **ODBC**.

    The **ODBC Data Source Administrator** dialog box appears and displays the **User DSN** tab.

3. Click **Add**.

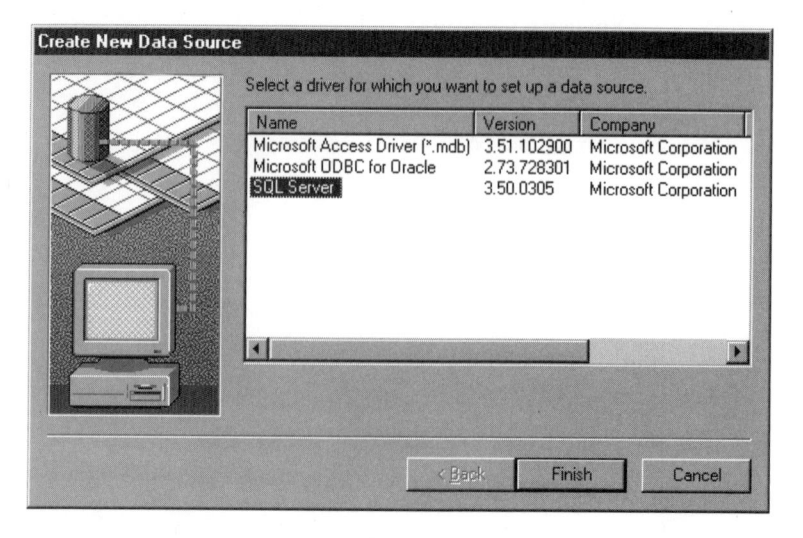

4. Select **SQL Server**, and then click **Finish**.

   The **Create a New Data Source to SQL Server** dialog box appears.

5. In the **Name** box, type **MtxSamples** and then in the **Server** box, select **(local)**.

6. Click **Next**.

   The **Create a New Data Source to SQL Server** dialog box appears.

7. Click **Next** three times, and then click **Finish**.

8. Click **OK**.

   The **ODBC Data Source Administrator** dialog box appears.

9. Click **OK**.

10. Close Control Panel.

▶ **To verify that Microsoft SQL Server is running**

1. Click the **Start** button, point to **Programs**, point to **Microsoft SQL Server 6.5**, and then click **SQL Service Manager**.

   If the stoplight is green, SQL Server is running.

2. Close the SQL Service Manager window.

In this part of the practice, you monitor Microsoft Transaction Server components and transactions.

▶ **To monitor Microsoft Transaction Server components and transactions**

1. Click the **Start** button, point to **Programs**, point to **Windows NT 4.0 Option Pack**, point to **Microsoft Transaction Server**, and then click **Bank Client**.

   Arrange the Bank Client window so that it does not overlap the Microsoft Transaction Server Explorer window.

   The form defaults to credit $1 to account number 1.

2. Click **Submit**.

   A response with the new balance should appear.

   Observe the Microsoft Transaction Server Explorer window. Notice that the component usage and transaction statistics windows have been updated.

3. Experiment with the bank client and observe the statistics using different transaction types, servers, and iterations. You might notice that the first transaction takes longer than the others. This is because the first transaction creates the sample bank database tables and inserts temporary records into them. Valid account numbers are 1 and 2. Other actions to try include:
   - Transfer amounts greater than 500.
   - Use invalid account numbers (0, 3, 4, 5).
   - Deposit a negative amount (-100).
4. Close Bank Client.
5. Close Microsoft Transaction Server Explorer.

Summary

You configure Microsoft Transaction Server using the Microsoft Transaction Server Explorer snap-in for Microsoft Management Console. The Microsoft Transaction Server Explorer includes predefined wizards to help simplify configuration. You can also use the included GUI utilities to list a current transaction's properties, track transaction performance, and view trace messages.

Review

The following questions are intended to reinforce key information presented in this chapter. If you are unable to answer a question, review the appropriate lesson, and then try the question again.

1. The Woodgrove Bank, a new bank, will have operations in 16 locations. Each location will have account information stored in separate Microsoft SQL Server databases. The bank's management is going to hire a group of software developers to write code to synchronize transactions between all 16 databases. Bank management has hired you as a consultant to oversee the consultants' work. You want to create a proposal to persuade management to use Microsoft Transaction Server. What are some items to include in your proposal?

2. What are the three tiers of the three-tier application model, and what is the function of each layer?

3. One of the board members of the Woodgrove Bank is still unclear on the need for Microsoft Transaction Server. He would like you to make a presentation at the next board meeting explaining the benefits of Microsoft Transaction Server. He would like the presentation to include an example of a bank transaction that has gone wrong. What might you present?

For More Information

For more information on Microsoft Transaction Server, refer to the following resources:

Microsoft Transaction Server on the Microsoft Web site at

http://www.microsoft.com/ntserver/guide/trans_intro.asp

Newsgroups:

microsoft.public.iis4

On-demand NetShow sessions available from events at Microsoft TechEd97 held on May 5–9, 1997:

- *Deploying and Managing Applications on Microsoft Transaction Server*
  http://www.audionet.com/video/netshow/teched/archive/mon/ent201.asx
- *Developing Distributed Applications with Microsoft Transaction Server (Part 1)*
  http://www.audionet.com/video/netshow/teched/archive/wed/ent310.asx
- *Developing Distributed Applications with Microsoft Transaction Server (Part 2)*
  http://www.audionet.com/video/netshow/teched/archive/wed/ent311.asx
- *Building Visual Basic Components for Microsoft Transaction Server*
  http://www.audionet.com/video/netshow/teched/archive/thurs/ent504.asx

CHAPTER 14

Analyzing Web Sites

Lesson 1 Introduction to Site Server Express . . . 279

Lesson 2 Using WebMaps . . . 281

Lesson 3 Quick Search . . . 287

Lesson 4 Site Summary Reports . . . 289

Lesson 5 Using Log Files . . . 293

Lesson 6 Report Writer . . . 298

Lesson 7 Posting Acceptor . . . 306

Review . . . 308

About This Chapter

This chapter describes how to use Microsoft Site Server Express 2.0 (SSE) to manage Web site performance. As Web sites become more complex and incorporate more objects and links, you need tools to better assess usage and content. With the Content Analyzer feature of Site Server Express, you can make these assessments, generate reports, and search for potential problems. Using Site Server Express, you can create logs of Web activity and generate reports with the collected information.

Before You Begin

To complete the lessons in this chapter, you must have:

- Installed Microsoft Internet Information Server (IIS) and Site Server Express according to the procedures in Chapter 2, "Installing Microsoft Internet Information Server." During this procedure you installed Site Server Express.
- The course compact disc containing the necessary practice files.

Lesson 1: Introduction to Site Server Express

Microsoft Site Server Express 2.0 is a multipurpose tool that allows you to publish content, manage content, and analyze usage on your Web sites. Site Server Express, which is included with Internet Information Server, helps you gauge the effectiveness of your Web presence by providing detailed reports about site usage. Site Server Express is a limited-functionality version of Site Server, a component of the Microsoft Site Server product.

After this lesson, you will be able to:
- Identify the principal features of Site Server Express.
- Explain the benefits of using Site Server Express.

Estimated lesson time: 5 minutes

Site Server Express can tackle many site administration tasks through the Content Analyzer, Usage Import, Report Writer, and Posting Acceptor components.

Using the Content Analyzer component of Site Server Express, site administrators can visualize how their sites are laid out, identify broken links, and create comprehensive Hypertext Markup Language (HTML) reports containing detailed information on the content of the site.

The core feature of Content Analyzer is the WebMap, its visual database. A WebMap stores information about all of the objects and links on a site, such as label text, size, and date last modified. A WebMap acts as a unifying hub for examining all of a site's resources. You can quickly scan a WebMap through two graphical representations, or views: the Tree view and the Cyberbolic view.

The Content Analyzer provides a Site Summary report, which helps you understand the mix of content on a site. Summary reports include information such as counts and sizes for objects such as pages, images, and applications. It also can include information such as the number of levels used by the site, or the average number of links per page.

The Usage Import and Report Writer components of Site Server Express enable you to analyze imported Internet Information Server log files and organize this information using any of 21 predefined reports.

The Usage Import feature reads the log files that are produced by the Web server. It then applies rules (algorithms) to the raw log data to make inferences. For example, Site Server Express can examine a series of requests from a user in order to determine how many distinct visits the user actually makes to a site. It then stores the results in the Site Server Express database.

The Report Writer module queries the data from the database and generates reports. It can then deliver these reports to you in HTML, Microsoft Word, or Microsoft Excel formats. Additionally, Site Server Express allows you to customize these standard reports to a certain extent in order to alter both their content and appearance.

Posting Acceptor is a server add-on tool that Web content providers can use to publish their content using Hypertext Transport Protocol (HTTP) Post (Request for Comment [RFC] 1867).

Summary

Site Server Express lets you generate reports that can help you assess how your Web site is being used. The major components of Site Server Express are the Content Analyzer, Usage Import, Report Writer, and Posting Acceptor. Using these components, you can increase the effectiveness of Web sites.

Lesson 2: Using WebMaps

The Content Analyzer feature of Site Server Express provides site visualization, content analysis, link management, and reporting capabilities for managing Web sites. You visualize your Web site using WebMaps, which store information about all of the objects and links on a site and provide a visual representation of your site as a whole. This lesson introduces you to WebMap features.

After this lesson, you will be able to:
- Create and customize a WebMap.
- Read and navigate the Tree and Cyberbolic views of a WebMap.

Estimated lesson time: 25 minutes

Webmasters, content authors, and Web-server administrators can use Content Analyzer to find broken links, analyze site structure and object properties, manage local and remote sites, and perform a variety of other Web site management tasks.

WebMaps

A WebMap shows every resource in a site, such as Web pages, images, audio files, video files, and Java applications. The manner in which these objects are presented indicates how they are used and how they interrelate.

The graphical representations of a WebMap are the Tree view and the Cyberbolic view.

Tree View

The Tree view is a hierarchy of objects; it will look familiar to users of Microsoft Windows NT Explorer. The Tree view is easy to read, but displays a limited amount of information on a screen at any one time.

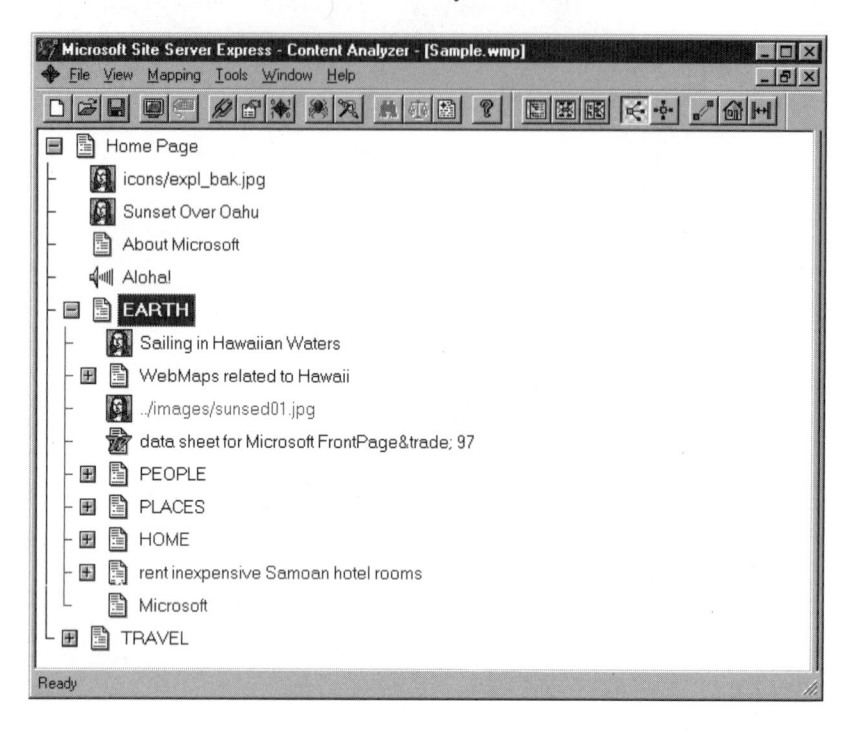

```
Microsoft Site Server Express - Content Analyzer - [Sample.wmp]
File  View  Mapping  Tools  Window  Help

□ 🗎 Home Page
   ├── 🖼 icons/expl_bak.jpg
   ├── 🖼 Sunset Over Oahu
   ├── 🗎 About Microsoft
   ├── 🔊 Aloha!
   ├── □ 🗎 EARTH
   │      ├── 🖼 Sailing in Hawaiian Waters
   │      ├── ⊞ 🗎 WebMaps related to Hawaii
   │      ├── 🖼 ../images/sunsed01.jpg
   │      └── 📄 data sheet for Microsoft FrontPage&trade; 97
   ├── ⊞ 🗎 PEOPLE
   ├── ⊞ 🗎 PLACES
   ├── ⊞ 🗎 HOME
   ├── ⊞ 🗎 rent inexpensive Samoan hotel rooms
   └── 🗎 Microsoft
└── ⊞ 🗎 TRAVEL

Ready
```

Each object in the Tree view is represented by an icon and its text label. As shown in the preceding illustration, the home page icon is at the top of a Tree. Level 2 resources (resources linked to the home page) may be pages or other objects. Their icons are indented beneath the home page icon. Level 3 resources (those resources two links from the home page) have icons indented beneath them. The result is very much like the outline of a document.

Control icons are small gray squares marked with a plus sign, minus sign, or question mark. Found to the left of the objects' icons, you can click the plus sign control icon to expand the view and show the objects that are directly linked to a given object (which is the next level down). Clicking a minus sign control icon collapses this expanded view and shortens the visible Tree to its original state. Question marks indicate that you have not yet examined a particular page to determine if there is a level of linked objects below it. Pages without control icons have been examined and have no links to any other page. They represent the end of a branch of the hierarchy.

Cyberbolic View

The WebMap Cyberbolic view represents your Web site as a matrix of links among objects and is a dynamic, nonlinear picture of a site. It shows the relationships among Web objects starting with any object you select as the point of focus. The Cyberbolic view helps you grasp the layout of an entire site immediately, as shown in the following illustration.

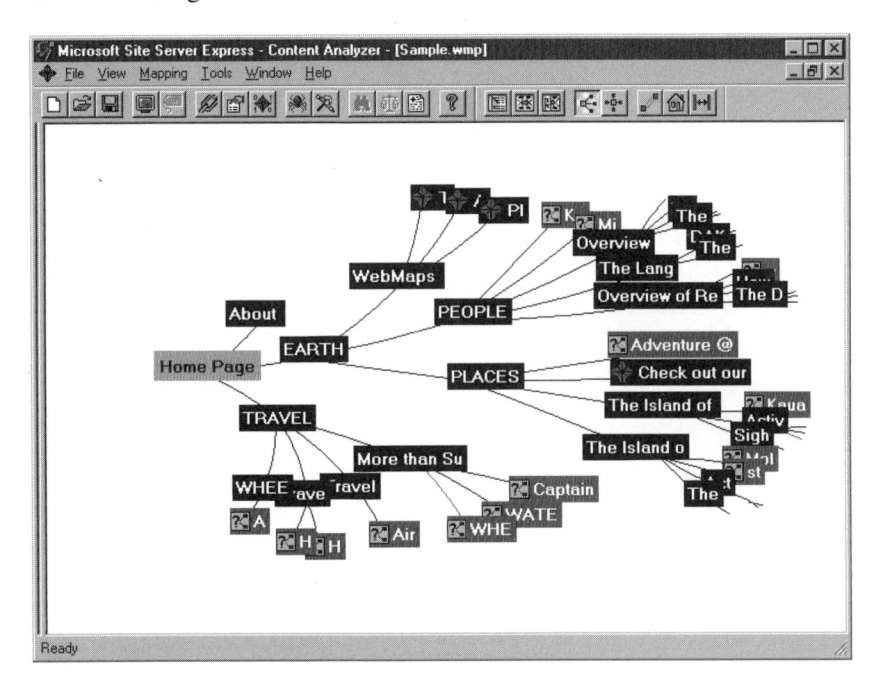

By default, clicking an object in Cyberbolic view moves that object to the left of the view. The objects linked to it fan out to the right.

By default, the Cyberbolic view shows only Web pages, as opposed to other resources, and main routes (the quickest routes to the home page). This reduces clutter within the view and allows ample room for page labels. To determine which objects to display, on the **View** menu, change settings in the **Display Options** box.

All objects have a short label. A longer descriptive label appears when you place the mouse arrow over an object.

Because all objects are always available to be viewed, there are no expanding or collapsing levels as in the Tree view.

The Cyberbolic view can seem confusing at first. The following tips can help you use the Cyberbolic view most efficiently:

- Consider showing fewer types of objects, such as pages only, for a more intelligible perspective. You can run out of room if you try to put too much on a single screen.
- To bring an object into focus, click its label.
- If you click overlapping items, the object on top becomes active.
- If you are unclear which object is active in a crowded WebMap, wait for the automatic display of the yellow pop-up label.
- You can navigate the view more quickly when Snap mode is enabled.

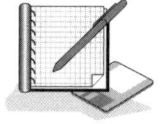

Practice

This practice uses a scenario to demonstrate some of the ways Site Server Express can be used in a corporate environment. This practices uses a sample Web site with the following problems:

- An image on the EARTH page that cannot be seen.
- The link to the HAWAIIAN HIGHWAY page on the TRAVEL page does not work.
- Text-based users are not aware of graphics on the site.
- The legal team wants to verify that all external sites that have links from this site meet the company's ethical standards.
- Management insists that there be no broken links among the pages on this site before going into production mode.

In this practice, you build a WebMap of the Bayshore Travel site and use it to find some of the problems listed in the scenario.

▶ To create a WebMap

1. Using Windows NT Explorer, create a folder named C:\Website.
2. From the course compact disc, copy the contents of the Iis\Practice\Sse\Website folder to C:\Website.
3. Click the **Start** button, point to **Programs**, point to **Windows NT 4.0 Option Pack**, point to **Microsoft Site Server Express 2.0**, and then click **Content Analyzer**.

    The Microsoft Site Server Express - Content Analyzer window appears.

4. Click **New WebMap**.
5. Select **File**, and then click **OK**.
6. In the **Home Page Path and Filename** text box, type **C:\Website\Index.htm**

7. In the **Domain and Site Root** text box, type **vacations.com**

   > **Note** You have now mapped http://vacations.com/... to C:\Website\.... This mapping is only relevant because you are creating a WebMap from a file, not from a live Web site.

8. Click **OK**.

   The **Generate Site Reports** dialog box appears.

9. Click **OK**.

   Microsoft Internet Explorer displays the Microsoft Content Analyzer Site Summary Report page.

10. Return to Microsoft Site Server Express - Site Analyst. Double-click the window title to maximize the Content Analyzer window.

11. Double-click the Vacations.com window to maximize the window inside Content Analyzer.

After the Web site files are read, the WebMap appears with the Tree view in the left pane and the Cyberbolic view in the right pane. It is identified by your chosen domain name, vacations.com.

In this part of the practice, you read information from the WebMap that helps to solve several of the problems that have been identified with the site.

▶ **To determine why one image on the EARTH page cannot be seen**

1. In the left pane, double-click **EARTH**.

   The Earth page appears in Internet Explorer.

2. Scroll through the page in Internet Explorer until you find a blank area containing an image icon (a small square with a red X).

3. Right-click the icon, and then click **Properties**.

   Notice the typographical error in the address ("sunsed" instead of "sunset").

4. Click **OK**.

5. Minimize Internet Explorer.

6. Microsoft Site Server Express - Content Analyzer should now be your current application. If it is not, switch to it.

7. Expand EARTH by clicking the plus sign (+).

   Observe the broken link to the image in red.

8. Click (-) next to EARTH to collapse this portion of the tree.

▶ **To determine why the link to the HAWAIIAN HIGHWAY page on the TRAVEL page does not work**

1. Expand TRAVEL.

   Notice that the link to the HAWAIIAN HIGHWAY image is red. This indicates that the link is broken.

2. Right-click the HAWAIIAN HIGHWAY image icon.

3. Click **Properties**.

   Notice the HTTP status of 404, which indicates the image could not be found. This is the cause of the problem.

4. Click **Cancel**.

5. Click (–) to collapse TRAVEL.

Keep the Content Analyzer open for the practice in the next lesson.

Summary

A WebMap is a visual database that contains information about all resources in a site. You can view a WebMap in Tree view or Cyberbolic view. While the Tree view is easy to read and understand, the Cyberbolic view presents a more graphical view of how objects are interrelated.

Lesson 3: Quick Search

Content Analyzer's preset searches can help you to see what maintenance is required on your site. This lesson lists each search and explains how you can use them.

After this lesson, you will be able to:
- Use Quick Search to find broken links and other Web site problems.

Estimated lesson time: 10 minutes

Content Analyzer offers eight preconfigured searches for errors or potential weaknesses throughout your site. You can access these searches on the **Tools** menu by clicking **Quick Search**.

The following list describes each search.

- *Broken Links*. Shows links that do not successfully connect to their destination object.
- *Home Site Objects*. Shows objects that share the same domain as your home page, and determines whether an object needing maintenance or repair can be accessed through the local security structure.
- *Images without ALT*. Reveals images lacking the optional ALT text string, allowing one to determine which graphics would not display a placeholder label to text-only browsers because this string is missing.
- *Load Size Over 32 K*. Shows which resources require more than 32 K of data to pass over your communications link during load, indicating which resources might need to be streamlined to reduce their download time.
- *Non-Home Site Objects*. Lists objects that do not share the same domain as your home page, thus revealing which linked pages are not under your immediate control. You may want to test the reliability of these links frequently.
- *Not Found Objects (404)*. Lists objects that could not be located when the site was mapped, revealing which objects have links that must be removed or repaired.
- *Unavailable Objects*. Reveals objects that either could not be located, or could not be accessed when located. This could be due to an unavailable host server, a broken communication link, or password protection on the object.
- *Unverified Objects*. Shows objects that have not been checked to determine whether they are accessible.

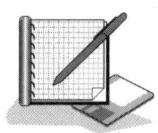

Practice

In this practice, you use Quick Search to work with some of the problems in the scenario from the previous lesson. In the first part of the practice, you want to determine why users of text-only browsers are not getting notification of each of the graphic images that they cannot view.

▶ **To locate images lacking the ALT parameter**

- Using Content Analyzer, click **Tools**, point to **Quick Search**, and then click **Images Without ALT**.

    Notice that there are nine images listed in the Images Without ALT Search Results window. The entire IMG/ALT column of the window is blank because each of these images lacks an ALT parameter in their respective image (IMG) tag. Do not confuse this with the file name of each image that appears in the left-hand (LABEL) column of the display.

    To add the missing ALT parameters to the IMG tags that lack them, you edit the HTML pages on which the images are placed by using Notepad or another HTML editor.

Summary

You may find the Site Server Express preconfigured searches helpful for locating any current or potential problems with your Web site. You should perform all nine searches when you first establish a site, and then perform selected searches later as necessary.

Lesson 4: Site Summary Reports

Content Analyzer offers a printable report, called a Site Summary report, that contains useful information about your Web site. This lesson describes how to use a Site Summary report to help you understand the mix of content on a site.

After this lesson, you will be able to:
- Examine a Web site through the Site Summary report.
- Understand the functions of specific Site Summary reports.

Estimated lesson time: 15 minutes

Content Analyzer provides Site Summary reports to help you understand the mix of content on a site. These reports include:

- Counts and sizes for objects such as pages, images, and applications.
- Counts of objects and links that are OK, missing, or in error.
- The number of levels in use by the site, where the home page is considered level one.
- The average number of links per page.

You can generate a Site Summary report in any of these three ways:

- Select the **Generate Site Reports** check box when creating a new WebMap.
- Use the **Generate Site Reports** toolbar button.
- On the **Tools** menu, click **Generate Site Reports**.

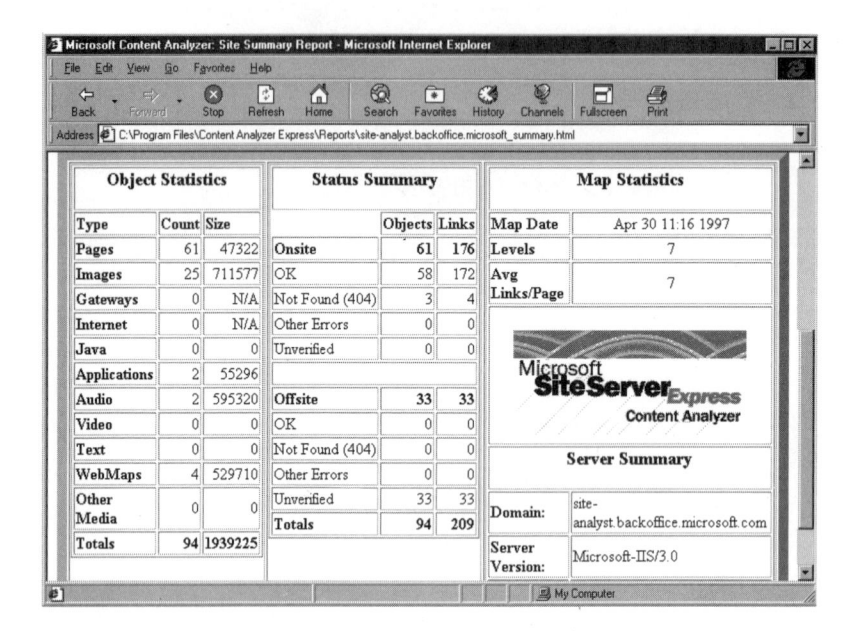

To help you understand how to use Site Summary reports, the following list shows typical questions about a Web site, and the function and purpose of specific reports.

Object Statistics—Count and Size Of

- *Pages*. Are my pages getting too large to load with minimal hardware and standard browsers?
- *Images*. Am I including enough images in my site presentation?
- *Gateways*. How many links permit browsers to run Common Gateway Interface (CGI) scripts on my server using GET or POST commands?
- *Internet*. How many links point to Internet services such as Telnet?
- *Java*. Is the number of links to Java applications appropriate considering the anticipated mix of browsers among the visitors to my site?
- *Applications*. What are the capacity planning implications of the number of links to applications?
- *Audio*. Is the number of audio links appropriate for the anticipated percentage of audio-enabled hardware among the visitors to my site?

- *Video.* Is the number of video links appropriate for the anticipated percentage of video-enabled hardware among the visitors to my site?
- *Text.* Is the number of text objects appropriate for the anticipated percentage of visitors who will be using Lynx or other text-only browsers on older hardware?
- *WebMaps.* Do I have sufficient WebMap links to assist my users in navigating the site?
- *Other Media.* Do I use links to other media?
- *Totals.* How complicated is my site? Would it be more effective if I streamlined the contents?

Status Summary—Number of Objects and Links

On-site

- *OK.* What is the condition of my on-site links? Do I need to allocate more resources to repairing and maintaining them?
- *Not Found (code 404).* What is the condition of my on-site links? Do I need to allocate more resources to repairing and maintaining them?
- *Other Errors.* What is the condition of my on-site links? Do I need to allocate more resources to repairing and maintaining them?
- *Unverified.* What is the condition of my on-site links? Do I need to allocate more resources to repairing and maintaining them?

Off-site

- *OK.* What is the condition of my off-site links? Do I need to allocate more resources to repairing and maintaining them?
- *Not Found (code 404).* What is the condition of my off-site links? Do I need to allocate more resources to repairing and maintaining them?
- *Other Errors.* What is the condition of my off-site links? Do I need to allocate more resources to repairing and maintaining them?
- *Unverified.* What is the condition of my off-site links? Do I need to allocate more resources to repairing and maintaining them?

Map Statistics

- *Map Date.* Is this report current? Do I need to remap my site at this time?
- *Levels.* How much navigating through links is necessary to get from my home page to the outer edge of my site?
- *Average Links per Page.* Has my site been logically structured? Do I have a confusing mesh of links? Should I streamline the links so that I can more closely control the ways in which visitors will use the site?

Practice

In this practice, you use Verify Links and the Site Summary report to identify a broken link.

▶ **To determine if there are broken internal links on the site**

1. On the **Tools** menu, click **Generate Site Reports**.
2. Click **OK**.

    Internet Explorer displays the Site Summary report. In the **Status Summary** box, examine the Not Found (code 404) line in the Onsite section. Notice that there are seven broken internal links to six objects. This indicates that there are two bad links pointing to the same object.

    A quick search could be used to find the broken links which could then be fixed with an HTML editor.

3. Minimize Internet Explorer.

Summary

Site Summary reports contain information that can help you assess the content of a Web site. Depending on your needs, only certain report sections and statistics may be of interest to you.

Lesson 5: Using Log Files

You can configure your Web or File Transfer Protocol (FTP) sites to log information about user activity. Internet Information Server logging is of a different caliber than the logging carried out through Windows NT Server. The logging in Internet Information Server is more extensive than Windows NT logging and, unlike Windows NT logging which you view through the Event Viewer, Internet Information Server log files are generated as ASCII text files or Open Database Connectivity (ODBC)-compliant databases. This lesson describes Internet Information Server logging capabilities.

After this lesson, you will be able to:
- Generate a log file of Web site usage.
- Choose a log file format.
- Import log files into Site Server Express.

Estimated lesson time: 20 minutes

By logging site usage, you can find out which users access your sites and the information they request. Logged data can help you regulate access to content, plan user accessibility, assess content popularity, and plan security requirements. You can also use Internet Information Server logs to detect and troubleshoot potential Web or FTP site problems.

▶ **To enable logging on a Web or FTP site**

1. From Internet Service Manager select a Web or FTP site, and then on the toolbar, click the **Properties** button.
2. On the **Web Site** or **FTP Site** property sheet, select the **Enable Logging** check box.

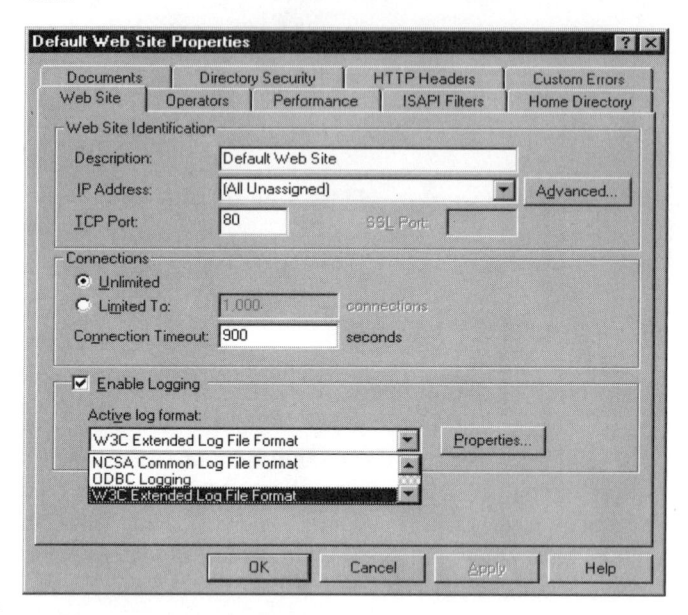

![Default Web Site Properties dialog box showing Web Site tab with Enable Logging checkbox selected and W3C Extended Log File Format selected in the Active log format dropdown]

3. In the **Active log format** list, select a format.

   By default, the **Enable Logging** check box is selected.
4. Click **OK**.

You can choose a log format for each individual Web or FTP site. Internet Information Server can log server usage in four different formats:

- *Microsoft IIS Log File Format*. A fixed ASCII format.
- *NCSA Common Log File Format*. The National Center for Supercomputing Applications (NCSA) common format; a fixed ASCII format, available for Web sites but not for FTP sites.
- *W3C Extended Log File Format*. A customizable ASCII format.
- *ODBC Logging*. A fixed format logged to a database.

Site Server Express only reads log files in Microsoft IIS Log File Format or NCSA Common Log File Format. However, you can read and edit all ASCII log files in any text editor, and the ODBC log file with an compatible database.

Saving Log Files

Internet Information Server lets you specify both where log files are saved and what to include in the log data. You can choose to save only the log entries within the most recent day, week, or month. You can also save all log entries until the log file reaches a specified size.

▶ **To save a log file**

1. Make sure logging is enabled.
2. Select a Web or FTP site, and then on the toolbar, click the **Properties** button.
3. On the **Web Site** or **FTP Site** property sheet, click **Properties**.

   The **Logging Properties** dialog box appears.
4. Under **Log file directory**, type the folder in which log files should be saved, accept the default if offered, or click **Browse** and locate the folder.
5. Click **OK**.

   A file name is displayed beneath the box showing the folder.
6. Click **OK** until you have closed all dialog boxes.

Importing Log Files

In order to create a report on a log file, you must first import the file into the Site Server Express database. You analyze a report in the next lesson.

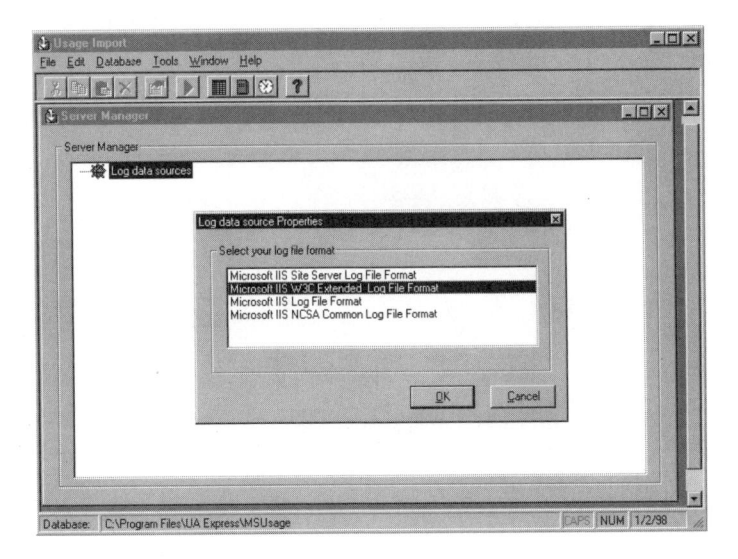

Practice

To import log files, you use the Site Server Express Usage Import feature. In this practice, you import Trey Research's log files. In the next lesson, you use the log files in a scenario to understand how Usage Analyzer is used in a corporate environment.

▶ **To import Trey Research's log files**

1. From the course compact disc, copy the Iis\Practice\Sse\Logfile folder to C:\Website.

2. Click the **Start** button, point to **Programs**, point to **Windows NT 4.0 Option Pack**, point to **Microsoft Site Server Express 2.0**, and then click **Usage Import**.

   Usage Analysis Import opens displaying a message that no Internet sites are configured for the database.

3. Click **OK**.

   The **Log data source Properties** dialog box appears.

4. Click **Microsoft IIS Log File Format**.

5. Click **OK**.

   The **Server Properties** dialog box appears.

6. In the **Local Domain** text box, type **trey.com** and then click **OK**.

   The **Site Properties** dialog box appears.

7. In the **Home page URLs** box, type **http://mstrain** and then click **OK**.

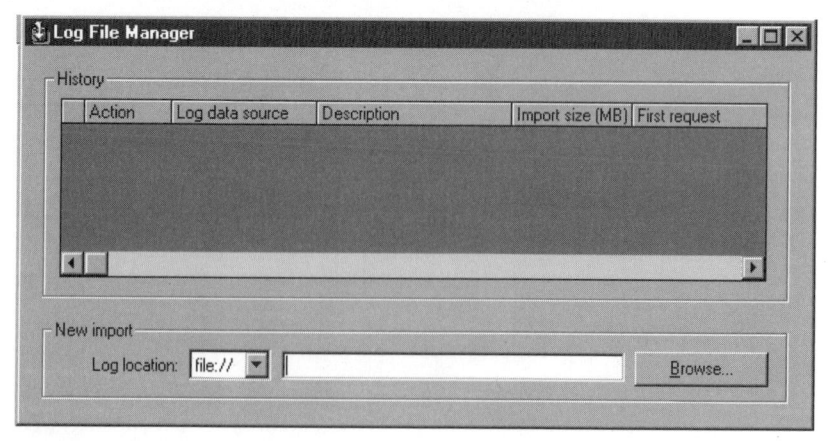

8. In the **New import** section of the **Log File Manager** dialog box, click **Browse**.

   The **Select a Log File name** dialog box appears.

9. Navigate to the C:\Website\Logfile folder, and then select the eight log files.

10. Click **Open**.
11. On the toolbar, click the **Start Import** button (the green triangle).

    After about two minutes, a message appears indicating the time it took to complete the import.
12. Click **OK**.

    Note the contents of the **Import Statistics** dialog box.
13. Click **Close**.
14. Close the Usage Import window.

Summary

You can save Web site usage information to a log file. You can configure what format to save the logs in, and how often to save log entries. Using the information collected in the logs, you can create reports to help interpret the data.

Lesson 6: Report Writer

With Report Writer, you can produce analysis reports about the activity of your Internet sites. This lesson explains how to create reports from imported log files so that you can better understand the information contained in the log files.

After this lesson, you will be able to:
- Generate a report from an imported log file.
- Select report types and settings.

Estimated lesson time: 35 minutes

Once you have imported log files into the database, you are ready to produce analysis reports about the activity of your Internet sites.

Usage Import reconstructs requests and visits from users and organizations interacting with your Internet sites. The Report Writer enables you to analyze and cross-reference several properties of those requests, visits, users, and organizations.

When you start Report Writer, you are given the option to choose an analysis from a catalog of standard reports, create your own from scratch, or select a report you have previously created. The Report Writer catalog contains more than 20 standard reports, grouped as detail reports and summary reports.

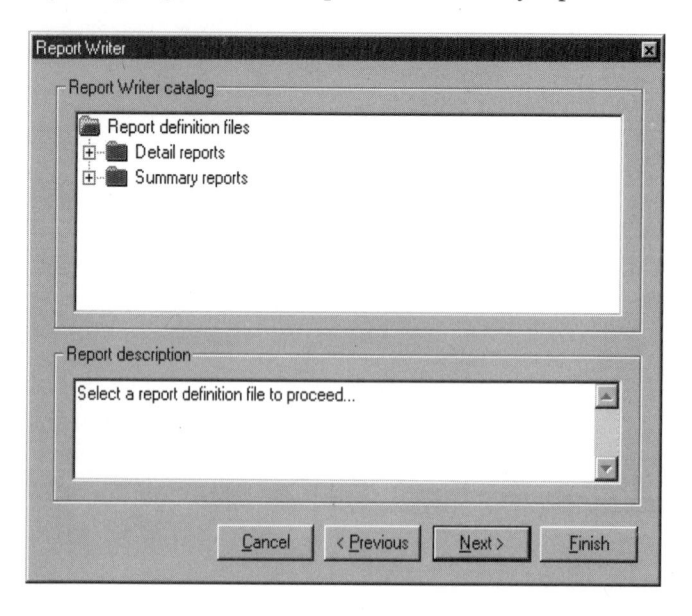

Note The preconfigured detail and summary reports contained in the Report Writer catalog can be edited.

Detail Reports

Report Writer can produce nine different preconfigured detail reports, as described in the following list:

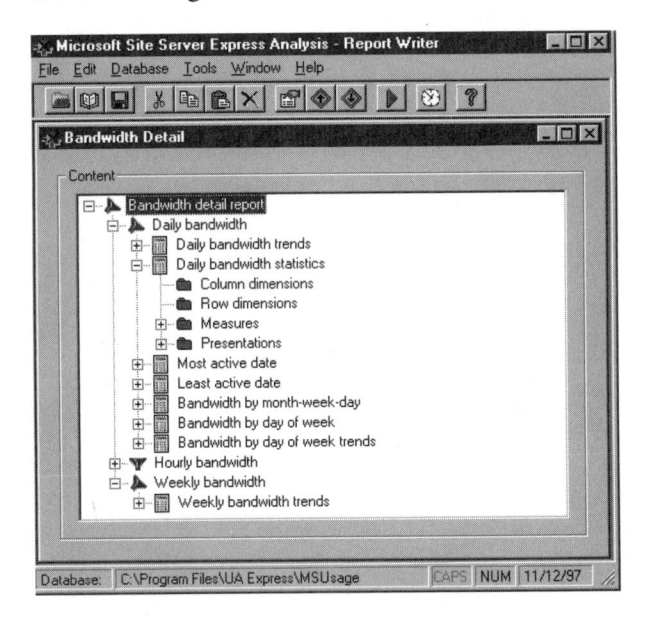

- *Bandwidth.* Shows byte transfers on an hourly, daily, and weekly basis. This report helps you to identify trends over time, as well as averages per day of week and hour of day. Use this information to plan maintenance or upgrades, or to alert you to the need for additional capacity to maintain an optimal user experience on your Web site.
- *Browser and Operating System.* Shows browser market share, trends in Netscape and Microsoft browser versions, browser security support, and user operating systems. Use this information to design your Web site for proper user experience. This report requires user agent data within your server log files.
- *Geography.* Shows the top cities, states/provinces, and regions in the United States and Canada, as well as the international countries visiting your Web site. Use this information to target your efforts towards the origin of your visitors, and to determine where to mirror your sites. This report requires that IP resolution and Who-is queries be completed before analysis.
- *Hit.* Shows the number of hits on the server each hour, day, and week in addition to the average number of hits for a day of the week and an hour of the day. This report helps to determine when to conduct maintenance and install upgrades, and how to plan for additional capacity.

- *Organization.* Shows the U.S., Canadian, and international organizations that visit your Web site. Use this information to monitor your target audience, identify new target customers, and generate leads from frequently visiting organizations. This report requires that IP resolution and Who-is queries be completed before analysis.

- *Referrer.* Shows the top external organization names and Uniform Resource Locators (URLs) that users linked from to reach your Web site. Use this information to evaluate the effectiveness of online advertising or promotions, or to identify synergistic locations for such programs. This report requires referrer data within your server log files, and IP resolution to be completed before analysis.

- *Request.* Shows the most and least requested documents over time and by folder. This report indicates if there is unnecessary material on your site, and what attracts the attention of site visitors.

- *User.* Lists the number of overall and first time visitors to the site, and the average number of visits per user, users per organization, and requests and length of visit per user. This report also charts trends in usage by registered and unregistered users over time. This report lets you know if first-time users are returning to your site, if users are relying on your site habitually, and whether your site is becoming more popular over time.

- *Visits.* Lists the number of requests made per visit by those users who do the most requesting, the average length of a visit, and the pages of your site that users are likely to access first during a visit or last just before leaving your site. It also charts visit trends. This report helps to determine the characteristics of visitors to your site, as well as whether particular content is drawing users to, or repelling them from, your site.

Summary Reports

Report Writer can produce twelve different preconfigured summary reports.

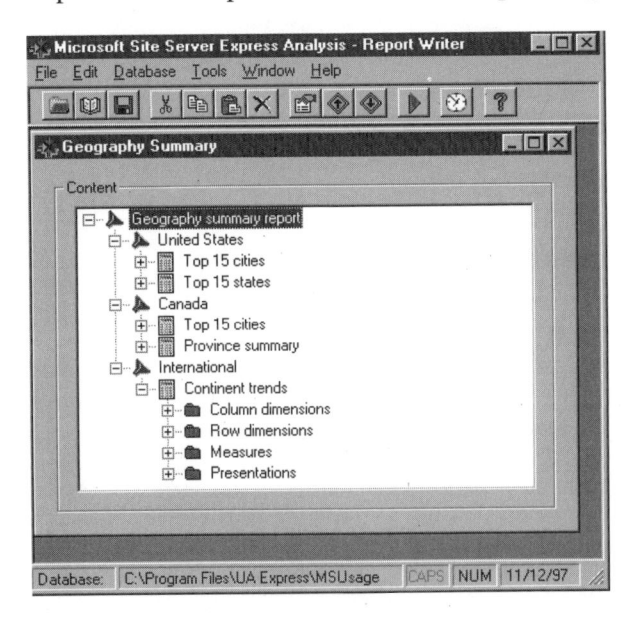

- *Bandwidth.* Lists the average amount of bandwidth used each day, and offers analyses by day of week, hour of day, and work versus non-work hours. This helps to determine if special circumstances are saturating bandwidth and causing performance problems, or if connection problems are suggested by abnormal bandwidth usage.
- *Browser and Operating System.* Indicates which browsers and operating systems the visitors to your site are using, and whether you should adjust your content to accommodate them.
- *Executive.* Highlights the information contained in the Detail reports.
- *Executive Summary for Extended Logs.* Highlights the information in the Detail reports for users of extended log files.
- *Geography.* Shows a summary of the Geography detail report.

- *Hits*. Shows a summary of the Hits detail report.
- *Organization*. Shows a summary of the Organization detail report.
- *Path*. Lists the sequence of requests that a user makes when navigating through your site, indicating whether links need to be rearranged to facilitate access to key content on your site.
- *Referrer*. Shows a summary of the Referrer detail report.
- *Request*. Shows a summary of the Request detail report.
- *User*. Shows a summary of the User detail report.
- *Visit*. Shows a summary of the Visit detail report.

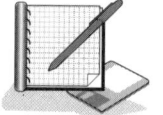

Practice

This practice uses a scenario to demonstrate how Usage Analyzer is used in a corporate environment. In order to complete the practice, you must have imported the Trey Research log files during the previous practice.

Trey Research is a software consulting company with approximately 5000 employees who need frequent training to stay current with the latest software.

In an effort to provide more cost-effective and timely training, Trey Research has implemented a pilot training server, MSTRAIN. This server hosts an intranet Web site that contains training tutorials for various Microsoft products, such as Windows NT 4.0, Microsoft FrontPage 97, Internet Information Server 3.0, and Microsoft SQL Server 6.5. Students register for a specific tutorial, read through the online materials, and then take review quizzes to ensure they understand the Web site content.

The server was pilot-tested for the week of June 23 through June 30. Most of the consultants in the company were able to try out the tutorials. You have been given the task of reporting to management how well the site performed during the pilot test. Your report must address these questions:

- How many employees used the site?
- How many times was the server visited?
- How much network bandwidth was used by employees visiting the site?
- When was the server the busiest?
- Which online tutorials had the greatest number of visits?
- How long did the employees spend studying a tutorial in an average online session?
- How many pages of each tutorial were accessed at least once by the students during an average online session?
- How many visits to the site did the average employee make to use the tutorials?

Use Usage Analysis and the following instructions to answer the questions in the scenario. During the practice, you use the Bandwidth summary, Visits detail, and User detail reports.

▶ **To generate and analyze a Bandwidth summary report**

1. Click the **Start** button, point to **Programs**, point to **Windows NT 4.0 Option Pack**, point to **Microsoft Site Server Express 2.0**, and then click **Report Writer**.

    The **Report Writer** dialog box appears.

2. Click **From The Report Writer Catalog**, and then click **OK**.
3. Expand the **Summary Reports** folder, and then click the Bandwidth summary report.
4. Click **Finish**.

    The Bandwidth summary window appears.

5. On the toolbar, click the **Create Report Document** button (the green triangle).

    The Report Document window appears.

6. In the **File Name** box, type **PilotBandSum**
7. Click **OK**.

    Report Writer generates the report and displays it in Internet Explorer. Scroll through the Bandwidth summary report.

8. What was the total network bandwidth used by employees visiting the site?

    _____

9. When was the server the busiest?

    _____

▶ **To generate and analyze a Visits detail report**

1. Return to the Microsoft Site Server Express Analysis– Report Writer.
2. Click **File**, and then click **Open Report Writer Catalog**.
3. Double-click **Detail Reports**.
4. Click **Visits Detail Report**, and then click **Finish**.

    The Visit detail window appears. This report includes all relevant imported data.

5. On the toolbar, click the **Create Report Document** button (the green triangle).

    This initiates report creation.

6. In the **File Name** box, type **VisitsDetails**

7. Click **OK**.

   Report Writer generates the report and displays it in Internet Explorer. Scroll through the Visits detail report.

8. How many times was the server visited?

   _____

9. Which online tutorials had the greatest number of visits?

   _____

▶ **To generate and analyze a User Detail report**

1. Return to the Microsoft Site Server Express Analysis – Report Writer.
2. Click **File**, and then click **Open Report Writer Catalog**.
3. Double-click **Detail Reports**.
4. Click **User Detail Report**, and then click **Finish**.

   The User Detail window appears. This report includes all relevant imported data.

5. On the toolbar, click the **Create Report Document** button (the green triangle).

   This initiates report creation.

6. In the **File Name** box, type **UserDetails**
7. Click **OK**.

   Report Writer generates the report and displays it in Internet Explorer. Scroll through the User detail report.

8. How many employees used the site?

   _____

9. What was the average number of requests per employee?

_____

10. How long did the employees spend studying a tutorial in an average online session?

_____

11. What was the average number of visits per user?

_____

Summary

You can import a log file into the Site Server Express database and select any of the Detail reports or Summary reports to generate a report of Web site usage. You can choose which type of report to generate based on what you want to measure.

Lesson 7: Posting Acceptor

Posting Acceptor enables you to provide a hosting service for users who want to post Web content to your server.

After this lesson, you will be able to:
- Explain how your Web server can receive content with Posting Acceptor.

Estimated lesson time: 5 minutes

Microsoft Posting Acceptor is a server add-on tool that Web content providers can use to publish their content using HTTP Post (RFC 1867). After installing Posting Acceptor on your Web server running Windows NT Server, Windows NT Workstation, or Windows 95, you are able to provide a hosting service for users who want to post Web content to your server.

Posting Acceptor allows Internet Information Server, Microsoft Peer Web Services, and Microsoft Personal Web Server to accept Web content from a variety of sources. Using Posting Acceptor, you can accept content from Microsoft Web Publishing wizard/API, Internet Explorer, and Netscape Navigator 2.02 or later through any standard HTTP connection. In conjunction with Microsoft Content Replication System (CRS), Posting Acceptor can also distribute content to multiple servers simultaneously.

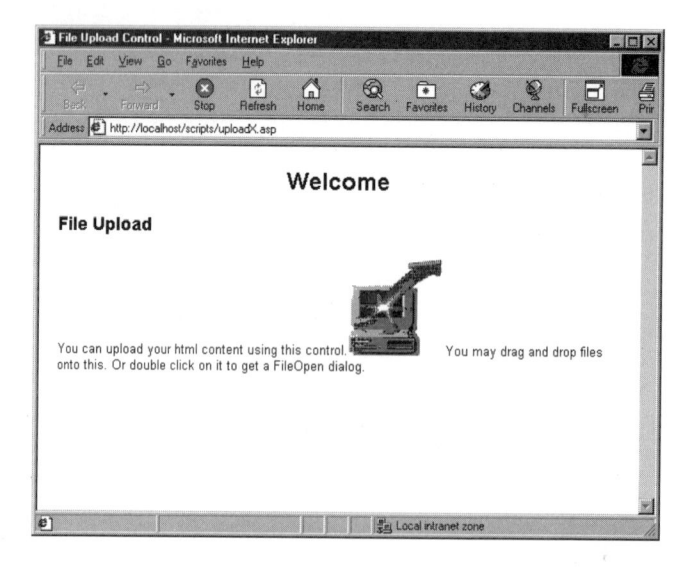

▶ **To upload content on the Web server**

1. Open Internet Explorer.
2. In the **Address** box, type **http://localhost/scripts/upload.asp** to load the Posting Acceptor upload page.
3. On the upload page, double-click the file upload image.

   A dialog box for selecting files to upload appears.
4. In the **Open File** dialog box, select the file(s) to upload, and then click **Open**.

Note For additional information on setting up and configuring Microsoft Posting Acceptor, please refer to the Windows NT 4.0 Option Pack product documentation.

Summary

You can use Posting Acceptor, a server add-on tool, to publish Web content using HTTP Post (RFC 1867).

Review

1. What is the difference between the Tree View WebMap and the Cyberbolic View WebMap?

   _____

   _____

   _____

   _____

2. Will the Site Summary report allow you to check on the number of images, video, or audio on your Web site? How could this information be useful?

   _____

   _____

   _____

   _____

3. What is the purpose of the Quick Search feature of Content Analyzer? Will any of the preconfigured searches indicate whether objects on your site are too large for users to download quickly?

   _____

   _____

   _____

   _____

4. Which detail report provides information about the individuals who visit your Web site? What kind of information does the report give you?

CHAPTER 15

Tuning and Monitoring Internet Information Server

Lesson 1 Monitoring the Services . . . 312

Lesson 2 Factors Affecting Internet Information Server Performance . . . 317

Lesson 3 Internet Information Server Performance Tuning . . . 323

About This Chapter

This chapter summarizes many of the monitoring tools and methods used throughout this book. It explains how you can monitor and tune Microsoft Internet Information Server (IIS) performance, as well as what can cause performance problems. The lessons review the available tools and methods to measure and correct performance problems.

Before You Begin

There are no prerequisites to complete this chapter.

Lesson 1: Monitoring the Services

Monitoring the server is a crucial part of server administration. By using appropriate monitoring tools, you can detect Web server problems, evaluate the result of changes to your Web site content, and plan upgrades to make your Web sites more accessible to users. This lesson details the monitoring tools that can give you both moment-to-moment and summary information.

After this lesson, you will be able to:
- Use Performance Monitor to analyze Internet Information Server performance.
- List the available Performance Monitor counters.

Estimated lesson time: 15 minutes

There are a number of tools available to you for collecting performance information about your Web server. Microsoft Windows NT includes two important tools: Performance Monitor and Event Viewer (for viewing logs). Additional logging is available in Internet Information Server, and other Windows NT tools, such as netstat and Network Monitor, provide supplementary monitoring functions.

The best choice of monitoring tool and method depends on the information you need. For example, if you want to measure the overall load on your Web server, you would use Performance Monitor to render a week-long plot, showing information such as the number of computer connections and file transfers. However, if you noticed a slowdown in your server's performance, you would check for errors in Event Viewer, which is the tool for viewing logs generated by Windows NT.

You can also monitor your server by examining logs generated by Internet Information Server. These logs provide more information than those generated by Windows NT and are viewed through Event Viewer.

Additionally, an important monitoring tool is to put feedback mechanisms on your Web site so that users can alert you when problems exist.

Performance Monitor

You can use Performance Monitor to monitor your server's activity and summarize its performance at selected intervals. With Performance Monitor, you can display performance data in real-time charts or reports, collect data in files, and generate alerts that warn you when critical events occur. Performance Monitor for Internet Information Server is found on the Rebar section of Microsoft Management Console (MMC).

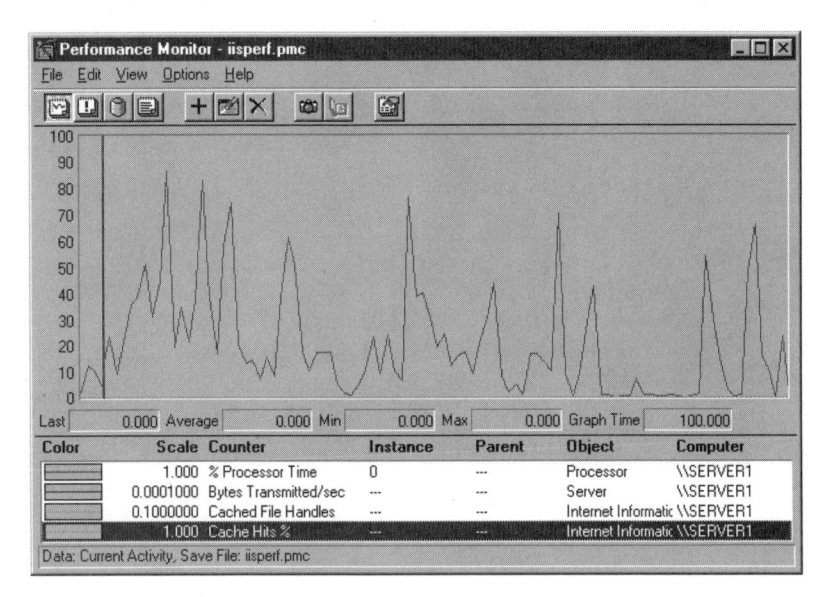

Performance Monitor contains counters that monitor the activity of specific objects that is, of specific services or mechanisms that control server resources. For example, if you view the object called Web Service, you can see counters that monitor bytes received per second or connection attempts per second.

Windows NT includes a number of counters, and you can supplement these with counters for disk usage and Transmission Control Protocol (TCP) activity by using utilities available in the Windows NT Resource Kit. For more information, see the Windows NT Resource Kit documentation.

In addition, Internet Information Server installs special counters, including Web Service counters, File Transfer Protocol (FTP) Service counters, and Global counters for Internet Information Services. The Web and FTP Service counters monitor connection activity, while the Internet Information Services Global counters monitor things such as bandwidth usage and caching activity for all Internet Information Server services.

Event Viewer Logs and Internet Information Server Logs

Windows NT includes an event-logging service, which records events such as errors and the successful starting of a service. You can view these event logs with Event Viewer. To start Event Viewer, click the **Start** button, point to **Programs**, point to **Administrative Tools**, and then click **Event Viewer**.

Event Viewer allows you to monitor System, Security, and Application event logs. With this information you can better understand the sequence and types of events that lead to particular performance problems.

Other Tools for Monitoring Performance

You can also use more advanced tools in Windows NT to collect specific performance information.

Netstat

Netstat renders a snapshot of protocol statistics and network connections over Transmission Control Protocol/Internet Protocol (TCP/IP). Use netstat to monitor TCP/IP information instantly. This includes information such as failed connection attempts, packets transmitted, or computers currently connected to your Web site.

Network Monitor

Network Monitor captures information on traffic to and from a computer, and gives detailed information about the frames being sent and received. This tool can help you analyze complex patterns of network traffic.

Important Counters to Monitor

There are numerous counters available that you can use to monitor different aspects of your network. The counters fall into four categories: bandwidth counters, Internet Server Application Programming Interface (ISAPI) and Common Gateway Interface (CGI) counters, Active Server Page (ASP) counters, and Internet Information Server cache counters.

Bandwidth Counters

The following Web Service Performance Monitor counters are useful when monitoring your site's bandwidth:

- Bytes Received/sec
- Bytes Sent/sec
- Bytes Total/sec
- Connection Attempts/sec
- Current Anonymous Users
- Current Connections

- Current NonAnonymous Users
- Maximum Connections
- Maximum NonAnonymous Users
- Total Anonymous Users
- Total Connection Attempts
- Total NonAnonymous Users

ISAPI and CGI Counters

The following Web Service Performance Monitor counters are useful when monitoring ISAPI and CGI applications:

- Bytes Received/sec
- Bytes Sent/sec
- Bytes Total/sec
- Current CGI Requests
- Current ISAPI Extension Requests
- Maximum CGI Requests
- Maximum Connections
- Maximum ISAPI Extension Requests
- Total CGI Requests
- Total Files Sent
- Total Files Transferred
- Total Get Requests
- Total ISAPI Extension Requests
- Total Other Request Methods
- Total Post Requests

ASP Counters

You may find these counters useful when monitoring Active Server Pages:

- Memory Allocated
- Request Execution Time
- Request Wait Time
- Requests Executing
- Requests Failed Total

- Requests Queued
- Requests Succeeded
- Requests Total
- Requests/Sec

Internet Information Server Cache Counters

The following Internet Information Server Global counters are useful when monitoring Internet Information Server cache usage:

- Cache Flushes
- Cache Hits %
- Cache Misses
- Cache Size
- Cache Used
- Cached File Handles
- Folder Listings
- Objects

Summary

Using the counters described in this lesson, you can monitor one Web or FTP site at a time, or monitor all sites at the same time. How you use the tools provided with Internet Information Server and Microsoft Windows NT (Performance Monitor, Event Viewer, netstat, and Network Monitor), depends on your network needs. Use the categorized list of counters in the preceding section to help determine which counters you want to use.

Lesson 2: Factors Affecting Internet Information Server Performance

There are a number of factors that can affect Internet Information Server performance, and it is important to identify any that may affect performance negatively. Identifying these factors in advance can help you tune Internet Information Server most efficiently. This lesson describes those factors that have the potential for decreasing performance, and provides tips for addressing them.

After this lesson, you will be able to:
- List various hardware and software factors that may negatively impact the performance of Internet Information Server.

Estimated lesson time: 25 minutes

Before tuning Internet Information Server, consider if there are any bandwidth, hardware, or network application speed issues that should be addressed.

Bandwidth

When addressing bandwidth issues, consider your Internet connection type and network connection capacity.

Internet Connection Type

Your Internet bandwidth determines both how fast data gets to your computer and how many requests can be serviced simultaneously. If you do not have sufficient bandwidth for the number of requests coming to your site, delays or failures can occur. The amount of bandwidth you have is a function of the type of connection you select.

You can choose the right connection by figuring the average size of your content files, the amount of time files of that size take to send, and the number of simultaneous users you want to support.

As a general rule, pages should take less than five seconds to send. This does not include external graphics, audio, or video. Typically, external files load after the text loads. A general rule for external files is that they should load in less than 30 seconds.

Once you have determined the amount of bandwidth your Web or FTP server requires, determine whether you offer other services that require bandwidth. These services can include e-mail, news, and audio or video streaming. Be sure to include enough bandwidth for these services.

Typically, your Internet connection comes to a router, and then a network adapter card connects your computer to the router. You need a high-performance network adapter card to prevent a bottleneck between your Internet connection and your computer. For example, if your connection to the Internet is a T1 line with a 1.54 Mbps bandwidth, then having your servers on an Ethernet LAN with a 10 Mbps bandwidth should be sufficient. However, if you have a T3 connection to the Internet, you should consider putting in a Fiber Distributed Data Interface (FDDI) LAN for your servers because the T3 bandwidth of 45 Mbps is much greater than the Ethernet bandwidth of 10 Mbps.

Network Connection Capacity

The type of network connection you have directly impacts server performance. Server performance is compromised whenever your network connection cannot handle the amount of data being sent across it. Additionally, other applications running on the computer (such as e-mail) that require network bandwidth affect the bandwidth available to Internet Information Server.

▶ **To determine the number of simultaneous users a connection type can support**

1. Assuming that you want to stay within a five-second transmission time for a page of text, and assuming a text file size of 63,360 bits transmitted for the user to receive the page, divide the 63,360 bits by 5 seconds = 12,672 bits per second per user.

2. Divide the connection speed by the bits per second per user. For instance, for a T1 line, divide 1,540,000 bits per second (bps) by 12,672 bps per user = 121 simultaneous users on a T1 connection.

Note This assumes text-only pages with no graphics and a complete page transmitted within five seconds. If more users attempt to connect, they are not refused, but the transmission speed of files may drop well below the five-second recommended time.

The following table provides a general guideline for the number of simultaneous users various connection types can support.

Connection type	Users supported
Dedicated PPP/SLIP	2–3
56 K (Frame Relay)	10–20
ISDN (using PPP)	10–50
T1	100–500
T3	5000+

Hardware

As Web servers have matured, performance has become increasingly important. Today, with the growth of Web applications for database publishing, content indexing, and collaboration, maximizing hardware and software performance has become a priority.

CPU Bottlenecks

The speed at which information moves between the various components of the computer, such as the CPU, hard disk, and RAM, depends on the clock speed of the CPU and the size of the data bus the CPU uses to move the information. Faster clock speeds mean more trips are made back and forth by the data bus during the same time interval. Clock speeds are usually expressed as megahertz (MHz). The data bus can carry 16, 32, or 64 bits of data on each trip, depending on the bus size. How much data is carried is also a function of the operating system used and the transfer rate on which the application is based.

CPU bottlenecks are characterized by very high CPU % utilization numbers while the network adapter card remains well below capacity. If CPU % utilization is high, you can upgrade the CPU, add additional CPUs to the same computer, or add additional computers on which you replicate your site, and then distribute traffic across them. If you are running other CPU-intensive applications on the Web server, such as a database application, you can move the other applications to another computer.

RAM Bottlenecks

Typically, when you start an application, the computer copies the necessary application files from the hard disk to RAM, and the application runs from RAM. Because RAM has much faster access time than the hard disk, the less the computer accesses the hard disk, the faster applications can run. When running, Internet Information Server uses some portion of RAM. The amount of RAM used, however, depends on a number of factors, including:

- The amount of RAM used for cache.
- The size of swap file.
- The amount of free disk space.
- The number of services running.
- The type of processor.
- The size of content files.
- The number of content files.
- Other active applications that require RAM.

> **Tip** Task Manager shows how much RAM is being used at any given time.

When Internet Information Server receives a request, the file it returns is usually cached in RAM. As it receives subsequent requests for the same file, Internet Information Server uses the copy cached in RAM, rather than going back to the hard disk to retrieve the file again. This reduces the time Internet Information Server takes to fulfill a request and makes access faster for visitors. However, the amount of time a file is kept in cache depends on a number of other things.

As requests for different files come in to Internet Information Server, older requested files are purged to make room for the newer ones. This means that if you make a large number of files available through Internet Information Server, and you only have a small amount of RAM, access may be slowed while Internet Information Server retrieves requested files from the hard disk. Additionally, other applications on the same computer that also use RAM push cached copies of files out of RAM to make room for the new files. As a result, Internet Information Server may be unable to maintain cached files in RAM. This also means slower Internet Information Server access as files are brought from the hard disk.

Because large files take up more space in RAM than small files, requests for large files, such as audio or video files, may increase turnover in cached files when the amount of RAM is small. If you publish large documents, a large number of documents, or if you run other RAM-intensive applications on the computer hosting Internet Information Server, you can improve system performance by adding RAM. However, if you publish only a very small number of files and the files are relatively small in size, adding RAM does not improve computer performance.

Network Adapter Card Bottlenecks

Different brands of network adapter cards perform differently. The drivers and driver settings you use when configuring your network adapter card can also affect its performance. Check with the maker of your network adapter card to see if updated drivers are available.

On a moderately busy site, Internet Information Server can completely saturate a 10 MB Ethernet card. To prevent the server from becoming network bound, use either multiple 10 MB Ethernet cards, or install a 100 MB Ethernet or FDDI network adapter card. If you suspect that you have achieved network saturation, check for CPU % utilization on both the client and the server. If neither the client nor the server is CPU bound, then you may have a different problem. Use the Network Monitor agent, included with Windows NT, to check network utilization. If the network is close to 100 percent utilized for either the client or the server, then the network is most likely the bottleneck.

Hard Disk Bottlenecks

The amount of RAM and the number and size of requested files directly affects how often Internet Information Server needs to access the hard disk. If you use only a small amount of RAM and there are either a large number of requests for different files, or the size of the requested files is large, Internet Information Server cannot maintain copies of the files in RAM for faster access. In this case, Internet Information Server must access files from the hard disk. The access speed and size of the hard disk determine how quickly Internet Information Server locates a requested file.

You find hard disk bottlenecks most frequently on sites with a very large file set that is accessed randomly. If your bottleneck is related to disk access, the percentage of the CPU utilized remains low, the network adapter card is not saturated, but the Physical Disk % Disk Time is high. To improve disk access in this situation, use a redundant array of inexpensive drives (RAID) and striped disk sets.

Network Application Speeds

Certain network technologies demand more processing than others. The FTP Service uses less memory than the Web Service. In addition, ASP applications, CGI scripts, database queries, and video files are more processor-intensive than static Hypertext Markup Language (HTML) pages.

ISAPI, CGI, and ASP

Internet Information Server supports two levels of server programming. The most complex level involves using ISAPI. The less complex level utilizes CGI and the new ASP interface.

ISAPI

ISAPI architecture allows multithreaded multiple-instance applications written as dynamic-link libraries (DLLs). As a result, ISAPI applications can reuse resources to achieve less processor overhead. ISAPI also lets you filter server data and extends the server itself. Extremely powerful and flexible, ISAPI requires sophisticated programming skills.

ISAPI is discussed in detail in Chapter 5, "Configuring the WWW Service."

CGI

CGI and Practical Extraction and Report Language (PERL) offer another, less complex, way to create Web-based applications. Internet Information Server supports both CGI and PERL, each of which are useful if compatibility with existing UNIX Internet servers is a key issue.

CGI and PERL are discussed in more detail in Chapter 11, "Active Server Pages."

ASP

ASP offers advantages over CGI and PERL scripting systems. ASP supports the Open Script interface, which means that you can use any scripting language that conforms to this standard. Languages that support the Open Script interface include VBScript and Microsoft JScript. These scripting languages generally require less time to learn and are common in programmer and user communities.

In ASP, you can add scripts directly to the HTML content of your Web pages. Additionally, they are run directly; there is no need to recompile the scripts. This allows you to change the nonscript content of the page without requiring you to submit the page for recompilation.

ISAPI Filters

ISAPI filters can preprocess messages and may take some action that can reduce the workload for Internet Information Server. For example, an ISAPI filter can deny users not allowed on the Web server. In this case, the ISAPI filter can communicate with the security accounts manager (SAM) to authenticate users by passing the Internet Information Server InetInfo process.

However, if you add the Secure Sockets Layer (SSL) ISAPI filter, the .dll for the SSL ISAPI would spend processor time on encrypting and decrypting data, and authenticating users.

ISAPI filters are discussed in detail in Chapter 5, "Configuring the WWW Service."

ODBC Logging

Open Database Connectivity (ODBC) logging requires more process time than writing to a simple comma-separated values (CSV) log file, that is, a text file with comma-delimited fields. Logging on to an ODBC database on a separate computer eliminates overuse of the local processor and improves server performance.

The ODBC connector is discussed in Chapter 11, "Active Server Pages."

Security Features

While basic file permissions have little or no effect on a server speed, advanced security features tend to slow performance.

Internet Information Server security features are discussed in Chapter 9, "Adding Windows NT and Internet Information Server Security Features."

Summary

Available bandwidth, hardware, and network connections can affect Internet Information Server performance. It is important to assess these items at your site to determine whether you need to make adjustments or purchase additional equipment.

Lesson 3: Internet Information Server Performance Tuning

Internet Information Server includes many property settings that make it easy for you to fine-tune your site performance. If your site is not delivering the performance you expect from it, then you may want to make changes to the default settings of one or more performance tuning properties. This lesson explains several ways by which you can fine tune site performance.

After this lesson, you will be able to:
- Optimize server performance within given network constraints.

Estimated lesson time: 15 minutes

There are several strategies you can take for tuning site performance. You can restrict bandwidth, balance memory use against response speed, limit connections and set timeout values, increase the size of the Internet Information Server cache, and maximize processor share.

Restricting Bandwidth

By restricting, or throttling, the connection bandwidth used by Internet Information Server, you can maintain available bandwidth for other applications, such as e-mail or news servers. If you run more than one site on Internet Information Server, you can throttle bandwidth on each of the sites individually using Internet Service Manager. Throttling bandwidth on individual sites assures that bandwidth is available for all of the sites sharing the network adapter card.

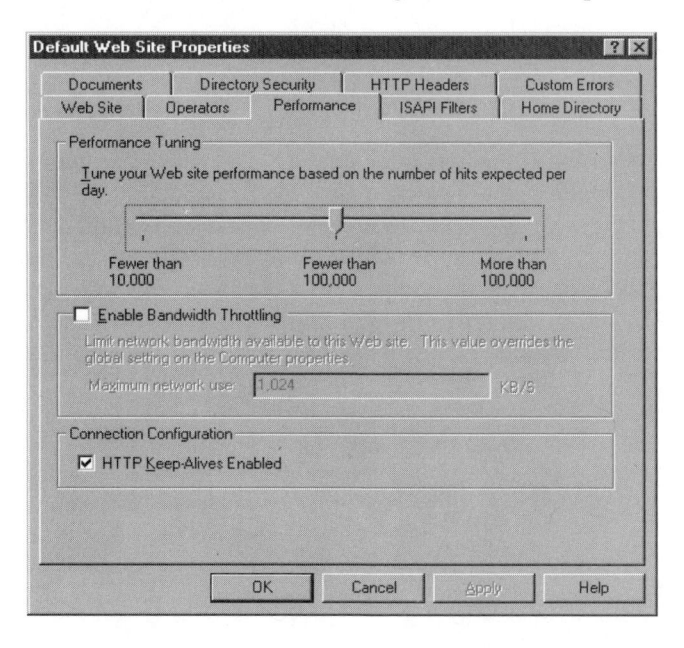

To determine whether you should throttle the bandwidth of Internet Information Server, or of an individual site, use the tools described in the Performance Monitoring section of the Internet Information Server documentation. Keep in mind that while the total number of connection attempts in a day may give you an idea of the overall activity on your site, you also need to consider changes in the connection rate (connections per second) to see if you are having congestion problems at peak times. If you use more than 50 percent of your total connection bandwidth regularly, you may need to consider upgrading your connection.

If you have a new Web site and thus no data yet to analyze, but you plan on running multiple services such as a Web server, e-mail server, and news server, you may want to start by restricting your Web server to 50 percent of the available bandwidth. Once you have been in operation for a short time, you can analyze site performance and adjust bandwidth accordingly.

Note Bandwidth throttling values set on Web sites can override the master value set at the computer level. For instance, if you set the value at the computer level to 1024 Kbps, and then set the value on a Web site as 2048 Kbps, the bandwidth of the network adapter card used by the Web site will be 2048 Kbps. Any additional sites on the computer that do not have bandwidth throttling enabled share the 1024 Kbps bandwidth set at the computer level.

Balancing Memory Use Against Response Speed

You can use a number of different performance properties to adjust memory usage or improve request response speed. Generally, increasing request response speed requires dedicating more memory or processor resources to individual connections, thereby reducing resources for other applications. Maximizing memory performance may mean slightly slower request responses for users visiting your site.

Internet Information Server includes a built-in adjustment to balance memory use against response time. By estimating the number of hits or connections you anticipate having to your site, Internet Information Server automatically adjusts the amount of memory dedicated to listening for new requests. If you set the number slightly higher than the actual number of connections, connections are made faster and server performance is improved. If the number is much greater than the actual connection attempts, server memory is wasted, reducing overall server performance.

Limiting Connections and Setting Timeout Values

By limiting connections you can conserve bandwidth for other uses. By limiting Internet Information Server connections, for example, you can increase bandwidth for other services, such as e-mail or news servers, or for another Web site running on the same installation. Internet Information Server rejects all connection attempts beyond the connection limit. When a browser stops working unexpectedly or loses a connection in midstream, the site continues to process data until the timeout value is reached. Setting a timeout value reduces loss of processing resources for broken connections.

Internet Information Server Cache

Internet Information Server maintains its own cache, separate from the one maintained by the Windows NT Server operating system. The Internet Information Server cache allocates a portion of physical memory to store objects for future requests.

Increasing cache size allows Internet Information Server to fulfill requests from the cache. This is one of the best ways by which you can optimize server performance. Keep in mind, however, that if you increase the cache size beyond the amount of available physical memory, the performance of other processes may decrease.

Maximizing Processor Share

You can use Task Manager to determine what processes are using processor time. You can access Task Manager by pressing CTRL+ALT+DEL and then selecting **Task Manager**.

In Task Manager, select the **Processes** tab and look for a process called Inetinfo.exe. This process is the sum of all of the services (HTTP, FTP, Internet Information Server cache, thread pool, and simple network management protocol [SNMP] tasks, if any).

To optimize the Internet Information Server server, run only processes necessary for the Web server. Refrain from using the Internet Information Server server as a file and print server, and avoid running other services that are not involved with the Internet and intranet server.

Summary

Every tuning strategy has tradeoffs. For example, increasing the Internet Information Server cache size may adversely affect the performance of other processes. In another strategy, you can limit the number of connections to improve performance, but the site is made less accessible. The strategies you choose to implement will depend on your situation.

Questions and Answers

Chapter 1: Introducing Microsoft Internet Information Server 4.0

Review Answers

Page 12

1. Will Internet Information Server load properly on a computer running Windows NT Workstation or Windows 95 operating systems? Will the resulting Internet Information Server system be fully functional?

   Internet Information Server loaded on a Windows NT Workstation or Windows 95 computer installs as Microsoft Personal Web Server because it lacks some of the key functionality associated with Windows NT Server.

2. You are a consultant to a firm that wants to allow customers to search through documents at their Web site. Which component of Internet Information Server enable the user to do this? Will Internet Information Server running on a Windows 95–based computer fully support this component? What about Internet Information Server running on a computer that runs Windows NT Workstation?

   The component that enables full-text searching is Index Server. Index Server works with Internet Information Server running on a computer that runs Windows NT Workstation, but is not supported by Internet Information Server running on Windows 95.

3. You are working on a release of a software product for a large company. You have decided to create an intranet site to allow every member of your large team access to the current build of the product, as well as to current versions of product documentation. You would like to limit access to the site to the people on your team. What feature of Internet Information Server would allow this?

   Domain Blocking allows you to grant access to the intranet site only to members of your team.

Chapter 2: Installing Microsoft Internet Information Server

Practice Answers

Page 24

▶ **To view the changes made in the Windows NT Server environment**

3. Scroll through the services available.

    Are there any publishing services listed?

    Yes, the FTP Publishing Service and World Wide Web Publishing Service should be listed.

7. Examine the list of names.

    Is there an Internet Guest Account listed?

    Yes, IUSR_*computername*.

12. Examine the items in the list for Internet-related items.

    Are there any Internet-related items in the list?

    Yes.

    If so, what are the names of the items that can be monitored?

    Active Server Pages, Content Index, Content Index Filter, FTP Service, HTTP Content Index, Internet Information Services Global, and Web Service.

Review Answers

Page 26

1. Will Internet Information Server installed on an Intel platform computer differ from Internet Information Server installed on an Alpha platform computer?

    Internet Information Server installed on an Alpha platform computer is nearly as functional as Internet Information Server installed on the Intel platform, but lacks Visual Basic and Visual J++ components and samples, as well as the Server-Side Java Virtual Machine.

2. Does Internet Information Server have any particular Web browser requirements?

    Yes, any installation of Internet Information Server requires Microsoft Internet Explorer 4.01.

3. If you want to run Microsoft SMTP Service, do you need to configure your operating system in any special way before installing Internet Information Server?

   Yes, Microsoft SMTP Service requires the use of NTFS.

4. If you want to set up Internet Information Server to run Microsoft Transaction Server, but also want to take advantage of the remote administration features of Internet Service Manager (HTML), which installation option should you choose?

   The Minimum installation option gives you Microsoft Transaction Server, but not Internet Service Manager (HTML). If you want both, you need to choose either the Typical or Custom installation option.

Chapter 3: Managing Internet Information Server

Review Answers

Page 41

1. What is the primary function of Microsoft Management Console?

   Instead of providing functionality by itself, Microsoft Management Console provides a common environment for snap-ins. Snap-ins provide the actual management environment for each associated product. For Internet Information Server, the implemented snap-in is Internet Service Manager. When you start Internet Service Manager, Microsoft Management Console starts and loads the Internet Service Manager snap-in.

2. What Internet Information Server tools allow a user to administer a Web site?

   The Internet Service Manager snap-in is the main administration tool for Internet Information Server. For remote administration, the HTML version of Internet Service Manager provides nearly all of the functionality of the Internet Service Manager snap-in.

3. Can you share customized consoles among the members of your group?

   Once you have created a console you like by loading snap-ins and arranging windows, you can save the console to a file with the default extension of .msc. Because saved consoles are not themselves large files, it is practical to create multiple console files and to share them with the members of your group by e-mail or other means.

4. How can a user access the property sheets associated with a particular Web service?

In the scope pane of Internet Service Manager, nodes in a tree view represent the different Web services. To access the property sheets of a particular service, right-click its node and then select Properties on the menu that appears.

5. What is the purpose of the Internet Information Server metabase?

In place of the Windows NT registry, Internet Information Server stores most of its configuration parameters in the metabase, specifically designed for Internet Information Server. The Internet Information Server metabase offers more advanced features than the Windows NT registry, including speed, scriptability, and remote administration.

Chapter 4: Understanding Internet Information Server Architecture

Review Answers

Page 58

1. Describe the features provided by the Inetinfo process.

   The Inetinfo process provides shared facilities for the thread pool, cache, logging, and SNMP services. The thread pool contains a group of threads used within the process for a specific operation. The cache stores data for file handles, account information, and log file data for logging to text files. Logging stores information about which users access a site. SNMP is used to monitor a Web server.

2. Which Internet Information Server service layer provides support for process isolation? What component provides process isolation?

   The Application services layer houses the Web Application Manager, which provides support for process isolation.

3. Describe how a data request is routed through the Internet Information Server architecture.

   A data request enters an Internet Information Server server through the Windows NT systems services, is passed to the Web services, and then forwarded to Application services. The response retraces the route of the request.

Chapter 5: Configuring the WWW Service

Review Answers

Page 90

1. You are interested in changing your Web site configurations pertaining to connections—how many users are connecting, how many users can connect, and how long you tolerate an idle connection before dropping it. Where would you go to adjust these functions?

    Use the Web Site property sheet to can adjust the number of connections allowed and the connection timeout limit. Use the Performance property sheet to adjust the anticipated number of daily connections to your site in order to optimize server performance.

2. You are working on the beta release of a new product and want to allow the members of your team—and no one else—to access documentation on the intranet. Which property sheet helps you to configure your Web site in this way, and what are the steps you must take to configure your site?

    Use the Directory Security property sheet to grant or deny access by IP address. Select the Denied Access check box to deny access to all computers by default. Then click Add to list the addresses of team members who are granted access to the Web site.

3. You are concerned about users having Write privileges to your Web site. Which property sheet contains this information? Would a user require any special browser functionality in order to write to a Web site?

    The Home Directory property sheet contains check boxes for indicating Read or Write privileges to your Web site. If the Write check box is cleared, users cannot write to your Web site. A user wanting to write to a Web site must use a browser that supports the PUT feature of the HTTP 1.1 protocol standard.

4. After installing Internet Information Server, you configure 10 virtual servers. To verify that the virtual servers are working, you copy the Default.asp file from Inetpub\Wwwroot into the home folder of each virtual server. When you test each of the virtual servers, none of the images on the page are displayed. After troubleshooting, you determine that all of the images are in virtual directories, and these virtual directories are only accessible from the default Web site. How do you make them accessible from all virtual servers?

    Create a new virtual directory for each virtual server. Make sure that each virtual directory references the physical folder where the images are stored.

5. You are the administrator for an intranet at a small accounting firm with 10 employees and 15 computers running Windows NT 4.0. After installing Internet Information Server and configuring three virtual servers, users complain they can only display the default WWW server. What must you do so that the virtual servers are working?

   You must set up a HOSTS file for each client to download, or set up and configure a DNS server.

6. You are the administrator for an intranet at a large accounting firm with 1000 employees and 1500 computers running Windows NT 4.0. After installing Internet Information Server, creating three virtual servers, and installing DNS, users complain they can only display the default WWW server. What must you do so that the clients can display the pages on the virtual servers?

   You must edit the property sheet for each virtual server and add a name in the Host Headers Name box.

Chapter 6: Configuring the FTP Service

Review Answers

Page 107

1. You are a consultant to a company interested in recording details about the activities of users who access their FTP site. Which feature of Internet Information Server allows the company to monitor user activity, and which property sheet is used to configure this feature?

   Your client is interested in the logging feature of Internet Information Server. You can enable and configure logging from the FTP Site property sheet.

2. You are interested in greeting the users who access your FTP site with a standard message. Does the FTP Service support custom messages? How would you go about creating one?

   The FTP Service supports custom Welcome, Exit, and Maximum Connections error messages. To configure this feature, use the Messages property sheet.

3. You want to restrict access to your intranet's FTP site except to one specific group in your organization. Which property sheet helps you to configure your FTP site in this way, and what are the steps you must take to configure your site?

   Use the Directory Security property sheet to grant or deny access by IP address. Select the Denied Access check box to deny access to all computers by default. Then click Add to list the addresses of group members who are granted access to the FTP site.

Chapter 7: Establishing Microsoft SMTP Service

Review Answers

Page 125

1. Which tools do you use to administer SMTP Service?

   Both Internet Service Manager and Internet Service Manager (HTML) are used to administer SMTP Service.

2. What is the purpose of the default Mailroot folder named Badmail?

   The Badmail folder is used for storing messages that cannot be delivered and also cannot be returned to their senders.

3. In terms of SMTP Service process, what happens to messages once they have reached the Queue folder?

   Messages that reach the Queue folder are sorted for local or remote delivery. Local messages are moved from the Queue to the Drop folder and delivered directly. Messages designated for remote delivery are first sorted by domain, then SMTP Service determines whether the server for the intended recipient is ready to receive messages by attempting to contact the server and deliver the message. If the server is not ready, the message is returned to the queue for a predetermined waiting period before delivery is reattempted. When SMTP Service makes contact with the recipient's server, it verifies the identity of the recipients, and sends the message, completing the process.

4. What purpose is served by pausing SMTP Service?

   An administrator may choose to pause SMTP Service in order to perform updates or maintenance on the service. When the service is paused, new client connections are prevented, while the service continues to process existing client connections and continues to deliver queued messages.

5. Which SMTP Service property sheets are used to configure aspects related to security?

   The Directory Security property sheet is used to specify the method of secure communication for the server, as well as to set TCP/IP access restrictions, and to grant or deny access to all computers by default. The Operators property sheet allows the administrators to specify which users can access the server.

Chapter 8: Establishing Microsoft NNTP Service

Review Answers

Page 141

1. What is the process involved with viewing articles posted on Microsoft NNTP Service, and are there any built-in controls to prevent unauthorized users from accessing newsgroups?

   A user wanting to view articles contacts Microsoft NNTP Service using Microsoft Internet News and Mail or another news client and requests a list of available newsgroups. Before returning such a list, NNTP Service verifies that the user is authorized to access newsgroups on the server. As the client requests specific newsgroups, and then requests particular articles posted in those newsgroups, NNTP Service continues to verify that the user is authorized to access the requested material before returning it to the user. The Microsoft NNTP Service administrator can restrict access to particular newsgroups by setting Windows NT Server permissions, or by limiting access by IP address of the client computer.

2. How do you ensure that articles posted to a particular newsgroup are not offensive or inappropriate for a given audience?

   As an administrator, you can configure properties associated with content control using the Home Directory property sheet. Another option is to use a moderated newsgroup. In establishing a moderated newsgroup, you specify a moderator using the NNTP Settings property sheet for that newsgroup. Articles submitted to the moderated newsgroup are not posted until the moderator approves them. Rejected articles are discarded, or the moderator may choose to return the article to its submitter along with a note explaining the reason it was rejected.

Chapter 9: Adding Windows NT and Internet Information Server Security Features

Review Answers

Page 167

1. A company has hired you as a consultant to oversee and make recommendations on the security of their Web site running Internet Information Server. The company has employees that log on to its secure Web site using the Internet. You discover that they are using basic authentication as their only security measure. What changes are you going to recommend to the company? What type of security should they company be using on their secure Web site?

   Remove basic authentication, because the user's password is sent unencrypted over the Internet. The appropriate authentication method for the company would be Windows NT Challenge/Response, which ensures password encryption.

2. The same company has launched a second Web site to allow customers to purchase books over the Internet using their credit card. They have hired you to review the security on this Web site. The company is using only Windows NT Challenge/Response, but they are wondering why they are not getting any customers to use the customer Web site. What changes are you going to recommend to the company? What type of security should the company be using on their customer Web site?

   Remove Windows NT Challenge/Response because it prevents anyone from gaining access to the customer Web site unless they have a valid user name and password. Instead, the company should allow anonymous logons so customers can access the Web site. To provide security for the credit card information, they should configure SSL on the folders that handle credit card numbers.

3. You are the LAN administrator for a small school. You are going to be setting up a Web site by installing Internet Information Server on an NTFS partition. As a security measure, what Windows NT Server group permissions should you remove?

   You should remove permissions for the Everyone group for all resources. You can then add permissions as necessary. In addition, you should remove any permissions on the network shares unless these permissions are necessary.

4. You are the new administrator for a worldwide organization. While examining the C:\Inetpub\Wwwroot folder properties, you notice that NTFS has granted full Read and Write permissions to the Everyone group. Internet Information Server, on the other hand, has the Read, Write, Script, and Execute properties disabled for the same folder. Which setting applies?

   The Internet Information Server setting applies in this case. The Everyone group contains all users and groups, including the Internet Guest account and the Guest group. By default, the Everyone group has full control of all files created on an NTFS drive. If there are conflicts between your NTFS and Internet Information Server settings, the most restrictive settings are used.

5. You are the Web administrator for a banjo manufacturer. After setting up Internet Information Server, you want to ensure that all client requests are processed as anonymous requests. How would you configure password authentication to process all client requests as anonymous requests?

   If the Basic and Windows NT Challenge/Response check boxes are both cleared and the Allow Anonymous check box is selected, all client requests are processed as anonymous requests.

6. What is the difference between authentication and encryption?

   Authentication is the process of confirming the identity of the entity with which you are communicating. Encryption is the process of scrambling data—often using a public and private key pair—so that only the intended recipient can unscramble the data and read the message.

7. Why is a digital certificate required for SSL encryption?

   Each entity or organization registers with an authentication authority. Once registered, you can provide a digital certificate to prove your authorization to others registered with the same authentication authority.

Chapter 10: Issuing Digital Certificates

Review Answers

Page 195

1. How does the processes for creating a digital signature differ from that for creating a digital envelope?

   The process for creating a digital signature uses the sender's private key to encrypt the signature and the recipient uses the corresponding public key to decrypt and verify the signature. The accompanying message is sent unencrypted; the role of the digital signature is only to confirm authorship. The process for creating a digital envelope involves encrypting the message using the recipient's public key so that the recipient—presumably the only person with access to the corresponding private key—can decrypt and read the message.

2. What purpose do digital certificates serve in the process of providing for secure and private communication on the Internet? Why would an organization choose to issue its own certificates rather than relying on an independent certificate authority?

   Digital certificates are used to verify the identity of the individual, browser, or server with which you are communicating. An organization may choose to issue its own digital certificates in order to have full control over the policies associated with the issuing, managing, and revoking certificates, as well as the format and content of the certificates themselves.

3. What is the difference between the server queue and the server log? Which allows you to revoke certificates?

   The server queue maintains copies of every certificate request you have ever received. The server queue includes the information contained in each request, in addition to whether you issued a certificate to the requestor. The server log maintains copies of all certificates you have issued, and is administered using the server log. This component includes information about every certificate you have issued, including whether you have chosen to revoke it. If you want to revoke a certificate you have issued, locate it using the server log and then click Revoke Certificate.

Chapter 11: Active Server Pages

Review Answers

Page 218

1. World Wide Importers has over 1,000 sales people worldwide. All sales people are required to use their laptops to dial-in long distance to the company's Microsoft Access database to check stock levels. This is done four or five times a day by each sales person, and results in large telephone bills for World Wide Importers. The sales force complains that the telephone lines are often tied up for hours limiting their access. Can you recommend a way using Internet Information Server to reduce the telephone costs and improve access?

   World Wide Importers might set up a secure Internet Information Server Web site for their sales people. After implementing the ODBC for Microsoft Access, the Web pages can be designed so that sales people can read and update the database. Each sales person can use a local Internet Service Provider (ISP) to do this, thereby reducing the telephone bills and the access problem.

2. How can using ASP enable you to create dynamic Web sites?

   Using ASP, you can combine HTML, scripts, and reusable components to publish content to the Web. ASP enables a Web developer to deliver content that is customized for specific users based on that individual's preferences, their demographics, or something more basic, such as whether the client's browser will accept content displayed in frames.

3. Is the object that causes a Web browser to see different content every time the user opens or reloads a file or Web page a built-in or installable object? How could this feature be useful to advertisers?

    The Content Rotator is an installable ASP object. It relies on information in the Content Schedule file to determine how frequently to display new content to Web browsers. The Content Schedule file can be configured to return vital information—such as how frequently users click a given advertisement—to Web administrators. The Content Rotator also allows administrators with little or no HTML experience to manage the placement of new advertisements.

4. Will any of the installable ASP components track Web page hits or ensure that only the appropriate users are allowed to access sensitive documents or Web pages?

    The Page Counter component displays hits to your Web page. Because it is launched in the Application scope, it works quickly and is easy to implement. The Permission Checker component verifies that a user has permission to access a given file or Web page before granting that individual access. You can also configure this component to automatically test permissions to all the Web pages linked to a given page so that only those links the user can access are displayed.

Chapter 12: Indexing Web Sites

Review Answers

Page 257

1. What is required in order to index files saved as proprietary formatted documents, such as Microsoft Word files?

    Indexing proprietary formatted documents requires content filters. Index Server includes several default content filters. The default filters are for text files, HTML files, Word 95 and Word 97 files, Excel 95 and Excel 97 files, PowerPoint 95 and PowerPoint 97 files, and properties on binary files.

    To index other document types you must obtain and install the appropriate content filters, which are available from independent software vendors.

2. What factors can impact Index Server performance?

    The factors that can impact Index Server performance include the number of documents indexed, the size of the data corpus, the rate of queries, and the kind of queries made.

3. What can you do to reduce the time it takes to return results for frequently queried documents?

   Using the Index Server snap-in, you can add to the property cache files that are frequently queried. Querying file properties stored in cache reduces the query response time.

4. What feature shows you the exact portion of a document that satisfies your query?

   Hit highlighting not only shows you the exact portion of the document that satisfies your query, but displays the sought-after content in red, italic text. To see the hit highlighting for a particular result abstract, click Show Highlights (condensed) or Show Highlights (full text). These links appear at the bottom of each result abstract in the results set.

5. How can you exclude certain folders from being indexed?

   Indexing and searching in Index Server is based on virtual roots, and you can exclude virtual directories from indexing through Internet Information Server Internet Service Manager by clearing the Index This Resource check box on the Directory property sheet.

   Alternatively, in your .idq files, you can specify files to be prevented from appearing in search results.

6. If a user does not have access to a specific file on an Internet or intranet site, will they see that file returned in the results set?

   When filtering the documents, Index Server also saves the associated access control setting created in the Windows NT File System (NTFS). This access control setting is used by Index Server to determine if a user has access to the file. If a user does not have access to the file, it will not appear in the results set thereby denying that individual access to the file.

Chapter 13: Understanding Microsoft Transaction Server

Review Answers

Page 275

1. The Woodgrove Bank, a new bank, will have operations in 16 locations. Each location will have account information stored in separate Microsoft SQL Server databases. The bank's management is going to hire a group of software developers to write code to synchronize transactions between all 16 databases. Bank management has hired you as a consultant to oversee the consultants' work. You want to create a proposal to persuade management to use Microsoft Transaction Server. What are some items to include in your proposal?

    Microsoft Transaction Server is a product that provides the components that synchronize the transactions between databases. This saves substantial time creating, testing, and debugging code.

    Microsoft Transaction Server guarantees that transactions are always completed or rolled back. Transactions do not stop responding in an unknown state.

    Microsoft Transaction Server supports ActiveX, which means developers can write code using Microsoft Visual Basic, Microsoft Visual C++, and Visual J++ to access ActiveX components.

    Microsoft Transaction Server manages low-level system resources such as threads, file I/O, and so on so that developers do not have to add this complexity into their applications.

2. What are the three tiers of the three-tier application model, and what is the function of each layer?

    Presentation. The client consists mostly of a GUI such as a browser used to display Web pages. Services such as database connection and business services are obtained from middle-tier servers. This results in less overhead for the user, but more network traffic for the system as components are distributed among different computers.

    Business/Data Components. Middle-tier components can implement data rules or business rules. They provide the logic between the client computer and the data source. This is the layer where necessary line-of-business rules and logic exist. Business rules can consist of business algorithms, or legal or government regulations. Data rules consist of rules to keep the data structures consistent, within a specific database as well as among multiple databases. These can exist on a server computer to assist in resource sharing. They can be used to enforce business and data rules. Because they are not tied to a specific client, they can be used by all applications.

Data Access. The data access tier represents a computer running a database where information is stored; this is the actual DBMS access layer. It can be accessed though the data/business rules layer, and on occasion directly by the Presentation layer itself. It consists of data access components (rather that raw DBMS connections) to aid in resource sharing and to allow clients to be configured without installing libraries or drivers on each client.

3. One of the board members of the Woodgrove Bank is still unclear on the need for Microsoft Transaction Server. He would like you to make a presentation at the next board meeting explaining the benefits of Microsoft Transaction Server. He would like the presentation to include an example of a bank transaction that has gone wrong. What might you present?

   A good example would include the discussion all of the components used in a transaction. For a bank transaction example, you could use the following scenario:

   A user uses his browser to connect to the bank's Web site. This uses the client, network, and receiver components.

   The receiver component would be the component of Microsoft Transaction Server to accept the call.

   In the next several minutes, 100 additional customers use their browsers to connect to the bank. Microsoft Transaction Server uses its receiver, queue manager, connection manager, context manager, and security manager components.

   The receiver manages congestion, the queue manager prioritizes the requests in the order they were received, the connection manager tracks the work of each client, the context manager keeps track of each user's identity, and the security manager prevents unauthorized users from accessing the data or applications.

   The user transfers money between two accounts, which impacts more than one database. Microsoft Transaction Server uses its thread pool, service logic, configuration manager, database connection manager, and synchronization manager components and the data for the transaction.

   The thread pool supplies the threads for the users. The service logic performs the debit, credit, and transfer functions. The synchronization manager coordinates the transaction between databases. The configuration manager manages the thread pool and other resources. The database connection manager allocates database connections.

   Before the transaction is completed, the connection between SQL servers is broken. Synchronization manager detects the incomplete transaction and rolls the databases back to their original state.

Chapter 14: Analyzing Web Sites

Practice Answers

Page 303

▶ **To generate and analyze a Bandwidth summary report**

8. What was the total network bandwidth used by employees visiting the site?
   119 MB

9. When was the server the busiest?
   June 26

Page 303

▶ **To generate and analyze a Visits detail report**

8. How many times was the server visited?
   786 times

9. Which online tutorials had the greatest number of visits?
   Windows NT 4.0, FrontPage 97, Internet Information Server 3.0

Page 304

▶ **To generate and analyze a User Detail report**

8. How many employees used the site?
   384

9. What was the average number of requests per employee?
   22.97

10. How long did the employees spend studying a tutorial in an average online session?
    30 hours and 24 minutes (30:24)

11. What was the average number of visits per user?
    2.05

Review Answers

Page 308

1. What is the difference between the Tree View WebMap and the Cyberbolic View WebMap?

   The Tree View gives a more traditional graphical representation of a Web site—it closely resembles the tree-like structure of Windows NT Explorer—whereas the Cyberbolic view display a more dynamic representation. The Tree view allows you to expand or collapse different hierarchical branches of the Web site's structure, so you can choose to see only those resources that appear a single step away from the home page, or you can view the objects on every level. The Cyberbolic view allows you to choose to view your Web site with a single object as the point-of-focus, but does not give you the option of expanding or collapsing your view.

2. Will the Site Summary report allow you to check on the number of images, video, or audio on your Web site? How could this information be useful?

   Yes, the object statistics section of the Site Summary report lists the number of images and video and audio clips you have on your site. This information could be useful in helping you to determine whether you have enough—or too much—of this sort of content on your Web site.

3. What is the purpose of the Quick Search feature of Content Analyzer? Will any of the preconfigured searches indicate whether objects on your site are too large for users to download quickly?

   The Quick Search feature of Content Analyzer enables users to search their Web sites for errors and potential weaknesses. Running the Load Size over 32 K quick search indicates which objects on your Web site are larger than 32 K, and therefore might require streamlining to reduce their download time.

4. Which detail report provides information about the individuals who visit your Web site? What kind of information does the report give you?

   The User and Visits detail reports both provide information on users who visit your Web site. The User detail report lets you know the total number of users who visit your site, how many first time visitors you have, and charts usage trends. It also provides information on averages; the average number of times individual users visit you site and the average number of visits from different users per organization, and the average number of requests and length of visit per user.

APPENDIX

Internet Concepts

The Internet has evolved dramatically from its early beginnings as a connection between universities. The first part of this appendix provides a brief history of the Internet, describes how the Internet is organized, and reviews who is responsible for its development.

Note When reading this appendix, you may want to view a multimedia presentation outlining the basic concepts of the Internet. In order to view this presentation, you must have the course compact disc. In addition, you must have a sound card and speakers or headphones for the sound portion of the presentation.

History of the Internet

In the 1960s, the RAND Corporation and educational institutions such as the Massachusetts Institute of Technology (MIT) and the University of California, Los Angeles (UCLA) designed a new network protocol. The purpose of this network protocol was to provide high-speed communication between two networked devices, even if some of the connecting links between those devices failed.

The U.S. Department of Defense (DOD) wanted to use the technology to keep its defense communications working in the event of an infrastructure failure. In 1969, the DOD Advanced Research Agency started the first network based on this technology, the Advanced Research Agency Network (ARPANET). The ARPANET initially connected four supercomputers across the United States.

By the 1970s, the original ARPANET had grown into a worldwide community of interconnected networks. Research and educational institutions began connecting their local networks together with the ARPANET to form one large collection of networks.

In the late 1970s, Transmission Control Protocol/Internet Protocol (TCP/IP) became the official protocol used to communicate across the Internet. The UNIX family of operating systems became popular in the late 1970s as servers and clients for the Internet. The popularity of UNIX has affected many of the utilities and commands available today for working with the Internet.

A high-speed network called NSFNET was built by the U.S. National Science Foundation (NSF) to replace ARPANET in the 1980s. The U.S. military created its own private network called MILNET when ARPANET was decommissioned by the U.S. Government. Private companies and organizations such as schools then began connecting their networks to the NSF network. The first European provider of Internet services for business use began in 1980.

Private companies began supporting the Internet when Internet funding by the NSF ceased in 1995. Today the Internet is funded primarily by these companies.

Defining the Internet

Because the terminology of the Internet is constantly expanding, it is important to have a common definition of the Internet.

Multimedia Presentation: Internet Concepts

Before continuing, you may want to view the Internet Concepts multimedia presentation. This presentation covers the most important concepts of the Internet. Select the **Text On** option if your computer is not equipped with a sound card. To view this presentation, double-click the Internet.exe file on the course compact disc.

Technological advancements have enabled virtually all computers to network together, resulting in the Internet. The Internet that is usually referred to is an aggregate of internetworked computers.

The Internet is a network of networks. It is a massive collection of computer networks that connect millions of computers, people, software programs, databases, and files. The parts and people from around the world interact continuously.

Any two connected computers can be considered a network. Any two connected networks become an internet. An internet enables communication between disparate computer systems, platforms, and environments. The communication between disparate computer environments is possible in part because of the communication protocols—agreed upon standards for exchanging data—that a particular network supports.

There are thousands of computer networks around the world; some are Internet-connected, while others not. Some networks are private, and others are publicly accessible. Protocols are what enable them to share data across their web of cables, computers, and users. TCP/IP is the suite of protocols used to move data over the Internet.

Many people use the term World Wide Web (WWW, or the Web) as a synonym for the Internet. Actually, the Web is just one of the many services available as part of the Internet. Other services include gopher, File Transfer Protocol (FTP), and Telnet. The graphically-based Web, however, is the fastest growing and most popular portion of the Internet today.

The reported growth rate of the Internet varies. Some estimates claim the Internet is growing by 10 percent of its total base of users every month. Other statistics say the Internet is doubling every 53 days. Because of the speed of its expansion, no paper-based document can provide accurate Internet growth rate and statistics.

Infrastructure

When you send data over the Internet, it is broken into packets that travel over many different routes between your computer and the recipient's computer.

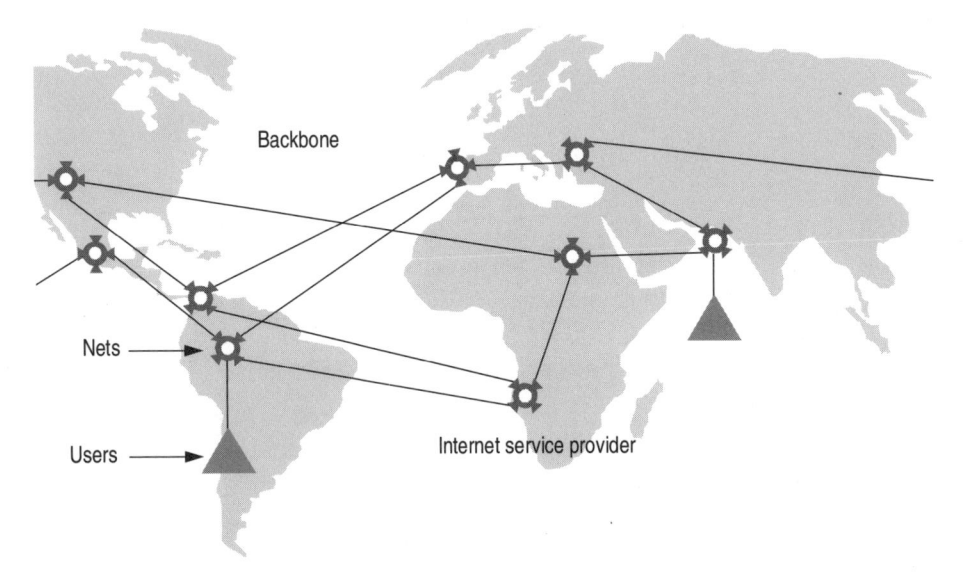

By using the standard TCP/IP protocol, computers using different operating systems are able to communicate with each other. Computers based on systems such as Microsoft MS-DOS, Microsoft Windows, Macintosh, Microsoft Windows NT, and UNIX can all use TCP/IP to connect to the Internet.

NAPs

The Internet is built on regional commercial networks which are connected to each other. Each network, called a Network Access Point (NAP), is a site that has agreed to provide services such as computers, data storage space, and communications equipment. It will also support various protocols to transfer data across the Internet.

Each regional NAP connects to at least two or more other regional NAPs by high-speed data lines. These multiple connections allow one regional NAP to temporarily drop out of service without affecting the rest of the Internet.

ISPs

With the popularity of Internet protocols, modems, and Web browsers, virtually anyone can gain access to the Internet. Before connecting to the Internet, you must have an account with, or service from, an Internet Service Provider (ISP). ISPs can be anything from a small, local operation to one of the large commercial online services.

Service providers, sometimes called access providers, are organizations that provide users with access to the Internet. Service providers generally have high-speed data connections through regular telephone lines to a regional NAP.

Users

Most users connect to the Internet using a service provider. Each user and host has a TCP/IP address. Users can connect in two different ways. One way is point-to-point, which is a dedicated line and address into the Internet. The other way is to dial in to an ISP.

Intranet

An intranet uses a network within an organization on which individuals can browse and share information using Internet software. It is a private network available only to people within the organization. Intranets are quickly becoming a popular and inexpensive way for networked organizations to share information internally.

An intranet site requires the same software and hardware as an Internet site except for the connections to an ISP. An intranet can be any network that is not connected to the Internet.

Internet Maintenance

The Internet is not "owned" by any particular group because it is a diverse network that links approximately 25 million users. However, there are organizations that administer the functioning of the Internet.

Maintenance Groups

The Internet is maintained by a group of people called the Internet Activities Board (IAB). The IAB is responsible for the broad view of the architectural structure of the Internet. This organization is divided into two groups, the Internet Research Task Force (IRTF) and the Internet Engineering Task Force (IETF).

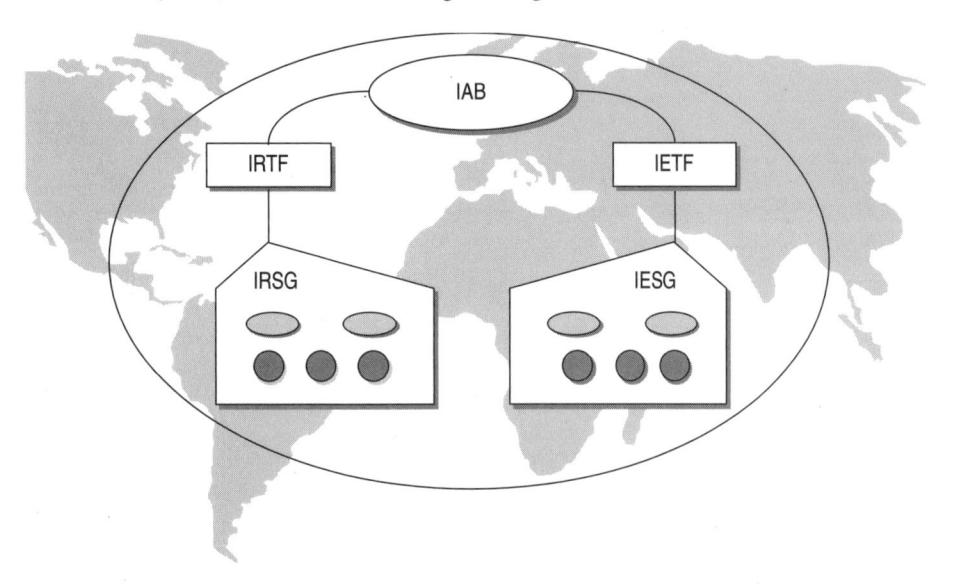

The IRTF is responsible for determining the future of the Internet. The IRTF makes long-term decisions on the direction of the Internet. Part of the IRTF is the Internet Research Steering Group (IRSG). This group is responsible for coordinating the various research groups to develop future Internet standards.

The IETF deals with implementing and maintaining the Internet on a mid- to short-term basis. The IETF and the Internet Engineering Steering Group (IESG) maintain the basic structure of the Internet.

Internet Standards

There are two sets of documents that define and describe the Internet: Internet Drafts (IDs) and Request for Comments (RFCs). Internet Drafts are dynamic, informal documents. RFCs contain the official comments of the IAB and are permanent records.

You can access IETF information from the following site:

   http://www.ietf.cnri.reston.va.us/home.html

For more information about the infrastructure of the Internet, refer to *Internetworking with TCP/IP*, by Douglas K. Comer.

URL

Every resource on the Internet has its own unique location identifier called a Uniform Resource Locator, or URL. A URL is an Internet address. When you know the URL, you can use it to immediately access that resource without browsing through folders or using keyword searches.

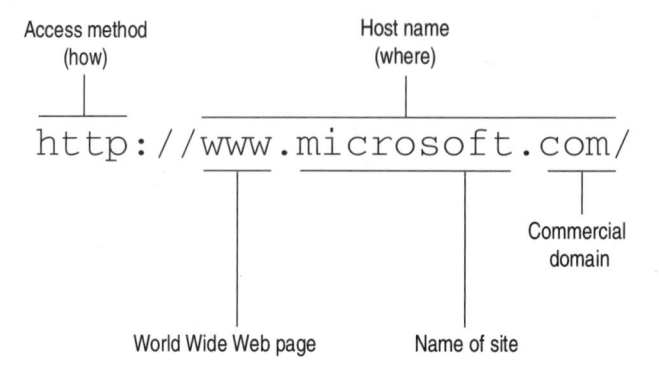

```
     Access method          Host name
         (how)               (where)
           |                    |
    ———————————        ———————————————
    http://www.microsoft.com/
           |         |          |
           |         |          |
           |         |     Commercial
           |         |       domain
           |         |
    World Wide Web page   Name of site
```

URLs follow a specific syntax. The first part of the URL indicates how the access method or protocol is used by that server. For example, the protocol for accessing the Web is specified as Hypertext Transfer Protocol (HTTP). All Web sites, therefore, would have a URL that begins with HTTP. If the site uses FTP, the access method would be FTP.

The second part of the URL is the computer's host name. The host name indicates where to find the computer on the Internet. For example, *http://www.microsoft.com/* is the locator for the Microsoft Web page. The *www* indicates it is a Web home page, *microsoft* is the domain name selected by Microsoft for this site, and *com* indicates it is in the U.S. commercial domain of the Internet.

Other locators may follow the host name. These names identify a more specific resource within the site. For example, *http://www.microsoft.com/internet.html* would identify a specific Internet page within the Microsoft site.

For the most part, domain names indicate who or what is located at the site and the type of organization that owns or supports the site. In the preceding URL example, *microsoft.com* is the domain name for the Microsoft Web page.

The following are common domain types.

Domain name	Type of domain
com	U.S. commercial organizations
edu	U.S. educational institutions
gov	U.S. government organizations (except the military)
mil	U.S. military organizations
net	Network service providers
org	U.S. organizations other than those above
au	Australian domain
uk	United Kingdom domain
de	German domain
hu	Hungarian domain

In addition, every computer—client or server—on the Internet has a unique IP address to distinguish it from other computers on the Internet. The IP address is four sets of digits separated by dots, for example: 198.105.232.1.

Because this string of numbers is not user friendly and could cause typing errors, the domain name system (DNS) was created so people would not have to remember several confusing numbers. Domain names enable short, alphabetical names to be assigned to IP addresses.

The Network Information Center (NIC) is responsible for issuing domain names. Their Web site is located at:

   http://www.internic.net/

Future URLs

URLs are being modified to keep up with the changes planned for the Internet. The following modifications will make Internet addresses more functional than they are today. For example, the modifications will allow addresses to easily change locations or give users information about the author of a Web document.

URI

One of the problems with URLs is that if the resource is moved, everyone who uses that URL must update their link to reflect the new location. The standard URL will be extended to Uniform Resource Identifiers (URIs). The URI specification is available as RFC 1630.

URC

Uniform Resource Characteristics (URCs) will provide additional information about an Internet site or document. Similar to properties, the URC could contain information about the author, keywords, expiration dates, copyright data, and even pricing or purchase information. URCs can also contain digitized signatures or even endorsements from professional organizations.

URN

Uniform Resource Names (URNs) are being developed by the IETF as a naming scheme that works with a mirrored site. If a busy site is located on the other side of a busy link (for example, a transatlantic link) the site may be mirrored on the closest side of the link. A URN looks for the nearest location that contains the requested data, whether that is the original site or a mirrored site. This type of naming convention can help increase the efficiency of the Internet.

All future Internet work is documented at the following Web site:

> http://merlin.cnri.reston.va.us/

For More Information

- Use your favorite Web search engine and search on Internet concepts.
- Search on abstracts from http://www.w3.org/.
- Microsoft has an Internet resource page at http://www.microsoft.com/.

Index

A

Abstracts, document, in index query result sets 239
Access control lists 129, 146, 239
Access protection *See* Security
Account policy
    Internet Guest account 144, 147
    limiting Administrators membership 146
    lockouts 145
    overview 144
    passwords 145
ACID properties 260
Acknowledgment, FTP 95
ACLs 129, 146, 239
Active Directory Service Interface 56–57
Active Server Pages
    benefits of 205–206
    components
        creating 211
        overview 210
    connectors 51
    counters 315
    creating query forms with 237
    creating 212–217
    effect on performance 322
    elements of, overview 206
    introduction 8
    metabase settings 38
    methods 207
    objects
        built-in 208–209
        installable 209–210
        overview 208
    overview 199, 205
    practices 212–217
    properties 207
    script tag and 211–212
    scripts 206–207
    Transaction Server and 263
Active Server Pages counter 24
ActiveX
    ASP and 8, 209–211, 216
    HTMLA and 36
ActiveX data objects
    as ASP component 205
    creating query forms with 237
    Database Access component and 209
    databases as Web content format 202–203

Adapter cards, network
    bottlenecks 320
    protocols, security considerations 148
Adding
    ActiveX components to ASP 216
    administrators 66, 99, 118
    folders, Index Server 234
    footers to documents 72
    headers 75
    ISAPI filters 68
    newsgroups 133
    virtual directories 83, 134
    virtual servers 87–89
Addresses, IP
    restricting access by
        FTP 101
        NNTP 137
        overview 153
        SMTP 123
        WWW 74
    settings
        FTP 97
        NNTP 134
        SMTP 117
        WWW 65
Addresses, MX 121
Administration
    Certificate Server
        Certificate Administration Log Utility 180, 188–189
        Certificate Administration Queue Utility 180, 189
        overview 187
    Command Line Administration Scripting 7
    features for 7
    Index Server
        administrative requests 248–249
        error detection, recovery 250–251
        MMC snap-in 233–235
        monitoring performance 249
        overview 248
    SMTP Service 111–112
    tools
        HTMLA 7, 35–36
        Internet Service Manager snap-in 7, 32–34
        overview 32
        Windows Scripting Host 36
Administration architecture 56–57
Administrative privileges 66, 99, 118
Administrative requests, Index Server 248–249
Administrators 66, 99, 118, 146

A

ADO
    as ASP component 205
    creating query forms with 237
    Database Access component and 209
    databases as Web content format 202–203
ADSI 56–57
Allowing anonymous connections
    FTP sites 99
    NNTP newsgroups 129, 134
    overview 144
    SMTP sites 122
    WWW sites 73
Alphanumeric passwords 145
Analyzer, Content *See* Content Analyzer
Analyzing Web sites *See* Site Server Express
Annealing merge 232
Anonymous authentication 151
Anonymous connections, allowing
    FTP sites 99
    NNTP newsgroups 129, 134
    overview 144
    SMTP sites 122
    WWW sites 73
Application event logs 314
Application object, ASP 208
Application services 54–55
Application speed, effect on performance
    ISAPI filters 322
    ODBC logging 322
    security features 322
    server programming 321–322
Applications
    home directory 70–71
    interactive 203
    isolating *See* Process isolation
    ISV 45
Applying digital certificates 164
Architecture
    administration 56–57
    Certificate Server 179–181
    overview 43
    server
        Application services 54–55
        connectors 50–51
        Inetinfo 48–50
        overview 47
        Web services 52–53
        Windows NT system services 51–52
    SSL 155–156
    TCP/IP 44–46
    Transaction Server 262–263
ARPANET 345

Articles, newsgroup
    indexing 223
    limits *See* Message limits
    posting 130
    viewing 130
AS/400 connections 205
ASP
    benefits of 205–206
    components
        creating 211
        overview 210
    connectors 51
    counters 315
    creating query forms with 237
    creating 212–217
    effect on performance 322
    elements of, overview 206
    introduction 8
    metabase settings 38
    methods 207
    objects
        built-in 208–209
        installable 209–210
        overview 208
    overview 199, 205
    practices 212–217
    properties 207
    script tag and 211–212
    scripts 206–207
    Transaction Server and 263
ASP component, Application services 54
Asynchronous Thread Queue 52
ATECs xxxii
Atomicity property 260
ATQ 52
Attaching footers 72
Auditing 16
Authentication
    See also Security
    Certificate Authentication 8
    Certificate Wildcard Mapping 8
    certificates
        See also Certificates
        client certificate authentication 156–158
        overview 151, 156, 172–175
    Challenge/Response
        NNTP 129
        overview 151
        SMTP 121, 122
        WWW 73
    custom schemes using ISAPI filters 53
    effect on performance 322

Index

Authentication *(continued)*
   features for 8
   Index Server and 252
   Infocom.dll and 52
   NNTP Service 7, 137
   overview 145, 150
   schemes 151
   settings 73, 122, 134
   SMTP 121
Authenticode 176
AUTHINFO 129
Authorities, certificate 160–164, 165
Authorized Technical Education Centers xxxii
Available disk space requirements
   IIS 14
   Index Server 224–225

B

BackOffice xxviii, 2, 51
Badmail folder, SMTP Service 112, 119–120
Balancing memory use, response speed 324
Bands, MMC Rebar 30
Bandwidth
   counters 314
   performance issues
      Internet connection type 317–318
      network connection capacity 318
   reports, Report Writer 299, 301, 303
   throttling 67, 323–324
Basic authentication 151
Basic linked content 201
Binary files, indexing 222
Bindings 148
Blocking, Domain 8
Book
   conventions used xxi–xxiii
   getting started xiv
   hardware requirements xxiii–xxiv
   intended audience xii
   multimedia presentations
      Internet concepts 5, 346
      overview xii
      TCP/IP protocol suite 44
   outline xxvi
   overview xi, xxvi
   prerequisites xiii, xxiv
   software requirements xxiv
   technical support xxxiii
Bottlenecks
   CPU 319
   hard disk 321
   network adapter card 320
   RAM 319–320

Breaking words for indexing 227
Broken Links search, Content Analyzer 287
Browser and Operating System reports, Report Writer 299, 301
Browser Capabilities component, ActiveX 209
Browsing, directory, disabling 152
Built-in objects, ASP 208–209

C

C++ 7, 38, 200
C2 security 144, 179
CA Certificate List Web page 186, 187
CA certificates
   browser installation 187
   CA Certificate List Web page 186, 187
   distribution, installation 186
   overview 186
   server installation 187
CA service 182
Cache
   file handling 52
   Index Server 234, 251
   Inetinfo 49
   size, adjusting 325
   usage counters 316
Capacity, network connection, effect on performance 318
Cards, network adapter
   bottlenecks 320
   protocols, security considerations 148
CAs 160–164, 175, 186–187
Catalog folder, Index Server 225
Catalog.wci 225
Catalogs
   administration 233
   default 230
   merging 232–233, 235
   multiple, creating 230
   overview 230
   persistent indexes in 230
   restricted access 251–252
   shadow indexes in 229
CD presentations
   Internet concepts 5, 346
   overview xii
   TCP/IP protocol suite 44
Certificate Administration Log Utility 180, 188–189
Certificate Administration Queue Utility 180, 189
Certificate authorities 160–164, 175, 186–187
Certificate Authority certificates
   browser installation 187
   CA Certificate List Web page 186, 187
   distribution, installation 186
   overview 186

Certificate Authority certificates *(continued)*
    server installation 187
Certificate keys, creating 161
Certificate requests 160–164, 185
Certificate revocation lists 175, 181, 188
Certificate Server
    administration
        Certificate Administration Log Utility 180, 188–189
        Certificate Administration Queue Utility 180, 189
        overview 187
    architecture 179–181
    as Certificate Authority 186–187
    as Windows NT service 182
    configurations 176
    customer registration 178
    enrollment 183–184
    features
        adherence to standards 179
        key management 179
        overview 178
        policy independence 178
        reliability 179
        transport independence 178
    internetworking in organizations 177
    overview 3, 165, 176, 182
    practices 190–194
    request processing 185
    role of 176
Certificate Wildcard Mapping 8
Certificates
    applying 164
    CA certificates *See* CA certificates
    client certificate authentication 156–158
    enrollment 183–184
    introduction 8
    issuance 175
    keys 174
    overview 151, 156, 172–175
    practices 190–194
    requests 160–164, 185
    revocation lists 175, 181, 188
    SMTP Service and 122
    vs. digital envelopes 174–175
    WWW Service and 74
Certification exams
    MCP program xxviii–xxxi
    skills for, location in book (tables) xv
    training for xxxii
Certified Professional program xxviii–xxxi
CGI
    connectors 51
    counters 315

CGI *(continued)*
    effect on performance 321
    introduction 2
    overview 199
CGI component, Web services 53
Challenge/Response authentication
    NNTP 129
    overview 151
    SMTP 121, 122
    WWW 73
Change permission 146
Change tracking, Index Server 250
Checking indexing status 233
Checksum, FTP 95
CiDaemon process 230, 250
Cisvc.exe 225, 251
Client certificate authentication 156–158
Client certificate enrollment 184
COM
    ASP and 206, 211
    certificates and 181
    HTMLA and 36
    Transaction Server and 260, 265–266
Command Line Administration Scripting 7
Command scripts, MS-DOS 36
Commercial Internet Server 2
Common Gateway Interface
    connectors 51
    counters 315
    effect on performance 321
    introduction 2
    overview 199
Compact disc presentations
    Internet concepts 5, 346
    overview xii
    TCP/IP protocol suite 44
Component Object Model
    ASP and 206, 211
    certificates and 181
    HTMLA and 36
    Transaction Server and 260, 265–266
Component-based programming 265–266
Components, IIS server architecture 47
Components, transaction 263–265
Compression, using ISAPI filters 53
Configuring applications 71
Configuring FTP Service
    See also Configuring sites
    practice 34
Configuring metabase entries 38–39
Configuring MIME mappings 75
Configuring NNTP Service 134

Index 357

Configuring sites
  FTP
    Directory Security property sheet 101
    FTP Site property sheet 97–98
    Home Directory property sheet 100–101
    Messages property sheet 99–100
    overview 96–97
    practices 102–106
    Security Accounts property sheet 98–99
  SMTP
    Delivery property sheet 120–121, 124
    Directory Security property sheet 122–123
    Messages property sheet 119–120
    Operators property sheet 118, 123
    security options overview 123–124
    SMTP Site property sheet 116–118, 124
  WWW
    Custom Errors property sheet 75
    Directory Security property sheet 73–74
    Documents property sheet 72
    Home Directory property sheet 69–71
    HTTP Headers property sheet 74–75
    ISAPI Filters property sheet 68
    Operators property sheet 66
    overview 64
    Performance property sheet 67
    practices 76–79
    Web Site property sheet 65–66
Configuring SSL 159
Configuring Transaction Server
  overview 267–268
  practices 268–274
Configuring virtual directories 82
Configuring Windows NT Server 15–16
Configuring WWW Service
  See also Configuring sites
  practice 33
Connection capacity, effect on performance 318
Connection errors, Index Server 250
Connection settings 66, 98, 117, 325
Connection type, Internet, effect on performance 317–318
Connections, NNTP Service 130, 134
Connectors
  ODBC 202
  overview 50–51
Consistency property 260
Console files
  advantages of 29
  creating 30
  sharing 30
Content
  control settings 70
  expiration 74

Content *(continued)*
  filters for indexing 227
  formats
    databases 202–203
    dynamic HTML 202
    interactive applications 203
    overview 201
    Personalization Server 203
    static, linked 201
    support for 128
    Transaction Server 203
  indexing *See* Index Server; Indexing
  queries *See* Index queries
  ratings 75
  uploading on Web server 307
Content Analyzer
  introduction 3, 279
  overview 281
  Quick Search 287–288
  Site Summary reports
    introduction 279
    Map Statistics 291
    Object Statistics 290–291
    overview 289–290
    practice 292
    Status Summary 291
  WebMaps
    creating 284
    Cyberbolic view 283–284
    overview 281
    practices 284–286
    Tree view 282
Content Index counter 24
Content Index Filter counter 24
Content Index service 23, 225, 251
Content Linking component, ActiveX 210
Content Replication Server 9
Content Replication System 129, 306
Content Rotator component, ActiveX 209
Conventions used in this book xxi–xxiii
Converting index queries, results
  .htx files 243
  .ida files 248–249
  .idq files 240–242
  overview 240
  practices 243–247
CORBA/IIOP 36
Core components of IIS platform 3
Corpus, Index Server 226
Corrupted files, Index Server 250, 251
Corrupted property cache, Index Server 251
Counters, Performance Monitor
  ASP 315
  bandwidth 314

358 Microsoft Internet Information Server 4.0 Training

Counters, Performance Monitor *(continued)*
   cache usage 316
   CGI 315
   ISAPI 315
   overview 24, 313, 314
Course
   compact disc xii
   conventions used xxi–xxiii
   getting started xiv
   hardware requirements xxiii–xxiv
   intended audience xii
   multimedia presentations
      Internet concepts 5, 346
      overview xii
      TCP/IP protocol suite 44
   outline xxvi
   overview xi, xxvi
   prerequisites xiii, xxiv
   software requirements xxiv
   technical support xxxiii
CPU bottlenecks 319
Creating
   applications in home directory 70–71
   ASP 212–217
   ASP components 211
   certificate keys 161
   console files 29, 30
   expiration policies, newsgroups 136
   indexes
      catalogs *See* Catalogs
      persistent indexes 229–230
      word lists 228–229
   moderated newsgroups 138–140
   newsgroups 133
   virtual directories 83, 134
   virtual servers 87–89
   WebMaps 284
CRLs 175, 181
CRS 306
CryptoAPI 172, 179
Cryptography
   See also Encryption
   overview 172–173
Cscript.exe 36
CSPs 173
Current FTP sessions, viewing 98
Custom authentication 151
Custom installation described 20
Custom management consoles
   advantages of 29
   creating 30
   sharing 30
Custom messages 75, 99–100

Customer registration 178
Cyberbolic view, Content Analyzer WebMaps 283–284

D

Data Access Components 4
Data corruption, Index Server 250, 251
Data Source Names 49, 203
Database Access component, ActiveX 209
Databases
   as Web content format 202–203
   metabase
      as administration architecture 56–57
      configuring entries 38–39
      introduction 23
      Isadmin and 53
      overview 37
      types of property settings in 39
   registration 203
   server database, Certificate Server 180
   Site Server Express, importing log files into
      overview 295
      practice 296–297
DCOM 36, 38, 53, 261
Declaring index query parameters with .idq files 240–242
Decreasing cache size 325
Default document, setting 72
Default property sheets
   FTP 96, 97
   WWW 63, 64
Deleting
   administrators 66, 99, 118
   application associations, home directory 70–71
   folders, Index Server 234
   headers 75
   ISAPI filters 68
   newsgroups 135
   noise words, Index Server 228
Delivery, message
   See also E-mail; SMTP Service
   settings for 120–121
   SMTP Service 113
Description, Web site 65, 97, 117, 134
Designating files for indexing 226
Detail reports, Report Writer 299–300
Detecting errors, Index Server 250–251
Digital certificates
   applying 164
   client certificate authentication 156–158
   enrollment 183–184
   introduction 8

Digital certificates *(continued)*
    issuance 175
    keys 174
    overview 151, 156, 172–175
    practices 190–194
    requests 160–164, 185
    revocation lists 175, 181, 188
    SMTP and 122
    vs. digital envelopes 174–175
    WWW and 74
Digital envelopes 174–175
Directives, SSI 55
Directories, virtual
    creating 83, 134
    FrontPage and 84
    local 82
    overview 81–82
    remote 82
    use for indexing 222, 226, 234
Directory browsing, disabling 152
Directory, home
    FTP sites 100–101
    NNTP Service 131, 134
    WWW sites 69–71
Directory properties in metabase 39
Directory security settings
    FTP sites 101
    NNTP Service 134
    SMTP sites 122–123
    WWW sites 73–74
Discussion groups *See* Newsgroups
Disk bottlenecks 321
Disk space requirements
    IIS 14
    Index Server 224–225
Disk-full errors, Index Server 250
Display requirements 14
Distributed Component Object Model 36, 38, 53, 261
DLL connectors, ISAPI 50–51
DNS lookup 121
Document abstracts in index query result sets 239
Document conventions xxi–xxiii
Documents
    footers 72
    headers 74–75
    indexing 222
Domain Blocking 8
Domain names, fully qualified (MX) 121
Drop folder, SMTP Service 110, 112, 113
Dropped network connections, Index Server 250
DSNs 203
DTC 23, 261
Durability property 260
Dynamic HTML 202

E

Editing
    content ratings 75
    expiration policies, newsgroups 137
    newsgroups 135
E-mail
    See also SMTP Service
    IMAP and 46
    POP3 and 45
    SMTP and 45
Enabling
    auditing 16
    automatic password synchronization 99
    bandwidth throttling 67
    content expiration 74
    document footers 72
    HTTP keep-alives 67
    logging 66, 98, 118, 124, 294
Encryption
    certificates
        See also Certificates
        overview 151, 156
    cryptography 172–173
    effect on performance 322
    NNTP Service 7
    overview 145, 173
    SMTP Service and 110
    Transport Layer Security 121
    using ISAPI filters 53
Enrollment, certificate 183–184
Enterprise Server, Netscape 187
Entries, metabase
    configuring 38–39
    types of 39
Envelopes, digital 174–175
Error detection, recovery, Index Server 250–251
Error messages, customizing 75
Ethernet LANs 318
Evaluation Edition, Windows NT Server, support
    limitation xxxiii
Event logging 314
Event Viewer 32, 314
Everyone group, permissions 147
Exams, certification
    MCP program xxviii–xxxi
    skills for, location in book (tables) xv
    training for xxxii
Excel spreadsheets, indexing 222
Exchange Server
    connections to 205
    connectors 51
    introduction 2

Executive summary reports, Report Writer 301
Exit modules, Certificate Server 181
Expiration
    content 74
    newsgroup articles 136
    passwords 145
Extended logging
    FTP 98
    overview 294
    SMTP 118, 124
    WWW 66
Extension handlers, Certificate Server 180
Extensions, ISAPI 53
External certificate authorities 160–164, 165

F

FastTrack Server, Netscape 187
FDDI LANs 318
Features of IIS
    See also specific feature
    for administration, management
        Command Line Administration Scripting 7
        HTMLA 7
        MMC 7
    for security, authentication
        Certificate Authentication 8
        Certificate Wildcard Mapping 8
        Domain Blocking 8
        Windows NT features 16
    for Web publishing
        FrontPage 98 Server Extensions 9
        Posting Acceptor 9
        Web Publishing wizard 9
    for Web-based application development
        ASP 8
        MTS 7
        Server-Side Java Virtual Machine 8, 14
    FTP Service 6
    HTTP 1.1 support 5
    NNTP Service 7
    overview 5
    setup wizard 7
    SMTP Service 6
    WWW Service 6
Fiber Distributed Data Interface LANs 318
File Access component, ActiveX 210
File properties
    FTP 96
    in metabase 39
    WWW 63
File system, NTFS
    certificates and 179
    Index Server and 224, 239

File system, NTFS *(continued)*
    introduction xxiv, 2
    overview 15, 16, 146
    permissions 146–147
    security and 144, 146–150, 168
    SMTP and 112
    WWW and 73
File types 75
File Upload component, ASP 210
Files for indexing, corpus 226
Filter properties in metabase 39
Filtering, Index Server
    CiDaemon process 230
    content filters 227
Filters, ISAPI
    effect on performance 322
    overview 53
    settings 68
Flow control, FTP 95
Folder browsing, disabling 152
Folder hierarchy, NNTP Service 131
Folder, home
    FTP sites 100–101
    NNTP Service 131, 134
    WWW sites 69–71
Folders, Index Server 225, 234
Folders, SMTP Service 112
Folders, virtual
    creating 83, 134
    FrontPage and 84
    local 82
    overview 81–82
    properties in metabase 39
    remote 82
    use for indexing 222, 226, 234
Footers, attaching 72
Forcing index merging 235
Forcing Index Server scans 234
Formats, log file 66, 98, 118, 124, 294
Formats, Web content
    databases 202–203
    dynamic HTML 202
    interactive applications 203
    overview 201
    Personalization Server 203
    static, linked 201
    Transaction Server 203
Forms, query
    elements of 237
    overview 236
Formulating index queries, results
    .htx files 243
    .ida files 248–249
    .idq files 240–242

Index

Formulating index queries, results *(continued)*
    overview 240
    practices 243–247
FrontPage 9, 84
FTP
    authentication 151
    overview 45, 94–95
    properties, in metabase 39
    sessions 95, 98
    support for 44
FTP component, Web services 53
FTP Publishing Service 23
FTP Service
    configuring
        See also Configuring sites
        practice 34
    introduction 6
    overview 94–95
    SNMP monitoring 49
FTP Service counter 24
FTP site property sheets
    Directory Security 101
    FTP Site 97–98
    Home Directory 100–101
    Messages 99–100
    overview 96–97
    practice using 102–106
    Security Accounts 98–99
    types of 96
FTP site usage logging *See* Logging
Full Control permission 146
Full hard disk, Index Server handling of 250
Fully qualified domain names (MX) 121

G

Generating
    certificate keys 160
    index query results with .htx files 243
    reports *See* Report Writer
Geography reports, Report Writer 299, 301
Getting started
    book practices hardware, software requirements
        xxiii–xxiv
    installing IIS *See* Installing IIS
    learning paths xiv
    overview of IIS 1–4
GIF, NNTP Service support for 128
Graphics interchange format, NNTP Service support for 128
Groups *See* Newsgroups
Guest account 144, 147

H

Handlers, extension, Certificate Server 180
Hard disk bottlenecks 321
Hard disk full, Index Server handling of 250
Hard disk space requirements
    IIS 14
    Index Server 224–225
Hardware
    bottlenecks
        CPU 319
        hard disk 321
        network adapter card 320
        RAM 319–320
    requirements
        course xxiii–xxiv
        IIS 14–15
        Index Server 224–225
Headers, HTTP 74–75
Hit highlighting 236
Hit reports, Report Writer 299, 302
Home directory
    FTP sites 100–101
    NNTP Service 131, 134
    WWW sites 69–71
Home Site Objects search, Content Analyzer 287
Hop count 121
Host Headers 87
Hosting multiple sites 86
HTML
    administration *See* HTMLA
    documents
        footers 72
        headers 74–75
        indexing 222
    dynamic HTML 202
    file indexing 222
    IIS support of 6
    NNTP Service support for 128
    SSI directives and 55
    WSH and 36
HTMLA
    administration architecture and 57
    creating virtual directories 83
    creating virtual servers 87
    introduction 7
    NNTP Service administration 128
    overview 35–36
    SMTP Service and 111–112
HTTP
    ASP and 206
    basic authentication 151

HTTP *(continued)*
    headers 74–75
    Host Headers 87
    keep-alives 67
    overview 45, 60–61
    properties in metabase 39
    security considerations 148
    support for 44
    version 1.1, features and IIS support of 5
HTTP Content Index counter 24
HTTP enrollment control 184
HTTP ODBC component, Application services 55
HTTP Post (RFC 1867) 3, 306
.htw files 237
.htx files 237, 238, 243
Hypertext Markup Language
    administration *See* HTMLA
    documents
        footers 72
        headers 74–75
        indexing 222
    dynamic HTML 202
    file indexing 222
    IIS support of 6
    NNTP Service support for 128
    SSI directives and 55
    WSH and 36
Hypertext Transport Protocol
    ASP and 206
    basic authentication 151
    headers 74–75
    Host Headers 87
    keep-alives 67
    overview 45, 60–61
    properties in metabase 39
    security considerations 148
    support for 44
    version 1.1, features and IIS support of 5

I

IAB 348
.ida files 248–249
IDC
    overview 200
    scripts 55
Identification, Web site 65, 97, 117, 134
.idq files 237, 238, 240–242
IDs 349
IETF 348
IIS
    architecture *See* Architecture
    as Windows NT 4.0 Option Pack component 3

IIS *(continued)*
    features
        See also specific feature
        for administration, management 7
        for security, authentication 8, 16
        for Web publishing 9
        for Web-based application development 7–8
        FTP Service 6
        HTTP 1.1 support 5
        NNTP Service 7
        overview 5
        setup wizard 7
        SMTP Service 6
        Web publishing tools 9
        WWW Service 6
    installing *See* Installing IIS
    Internet concepts overview, multimedia presentation 5
    metabase *See* Metabase
    overview, components 1–4
    performance monitoring *See* Monitoring performance, IIS
    platform selection, effect of 9–11, 14–15
    running on Windows NT Workstation, Windows 95 9–11
    security *See* Security
IIS Admin Base Object 38
IIS Admin Objects 38
IIS Admin Service 23
Images without ALT search, Content Analyzer 287
IMAP 44, 46
Importing log files
    overview 295
    practice 296–297
Improving performance, IIS
    balancing memory use, response speed 324
    bandwidth issues
        Internet connection type 317–318
        network connection capacity 318
    cache size, adjusting 325
    Event Viewer 314
    factors affecting performance 317
    hardware issues, bottlenecks
        CPU 319
        hard disk 321
        network adapter card 320
        RAM 319–320
    limiting connections 325
    logs 314
    maximizing processor share 325
    Netstat 314
    network application speed issues
        ISAPI filters 322
        ODBC logging 322
        security features 322
        server programming 321–322

Index

Improving performance, IIS *(continued)*
    Network Monitor 314
    overview 312, 323
    Performance Monitor
        counters 314–316
        overview 313
    restricting bandwidth 323–324
Include directives, server-side 55
Inconsistencies, internal, Index Server 251
Increasing cache size 325
Independent Software Vendor applications 45
Index queries
    administrative requests 248–249
    form elements 237
    formulating queries, results
        .htx files 243
        .ida files 248–249
        .idq files 240–242
        overview 240
    overview 236
    practices 243–247
    process overview 238
    result sets 239
Index Server
    administration
        administrative requests 248–249
        error detection, recovery 250–251
        MMC snap-in 233–235
        monitoring performance 249
        overview 248
        security 251–253
    cache 234
    catalogs
        administration 233
        default 230
        multiple, creating 230
        overview 230
        persistent indexes in 230
        shadow indexes in 229
    checking status 233
    CiDaemon process 230, 250
    content filters 227
    corpus, designating 226
    error detection, recovery 250–251
    extending to read new formats 227
    features 222–223
    folders 225, 234
    forcing scans 234
    installation 223–225
    merging
        annealing merge 232
        forcing 235
        master merge 232–233
        overview 231

Index Server *(continued)*
    merging *(continued)*
        shadow merge 232
    normalizer 228
    not supported on PWS on Windows 95 11
    overview 3, 222
    performance monitoring 249
    properties, settings 233
    queries *See* Index queries
    security 251–253
    supported languages 223
    system requirements 224–225
    types of indexes
        overview 228
        persistent indexes 229–230
        word lists 228–229
    word breakers 227
Index Server component, Application services 54
Indexes
    See also Index Server
    catalogs
        administration 233
        default 230
        merging 232–233, 235
        multiple, creating 230
        overview 230
        persistent indexes in 230
        restricted access 251–252
        shadow indexes in 229
    merging
        annealing merge 232
        forcing 235
        master merge 232–233
        overview 231
        shadow merge 232
    queries *See* Index queries
    types of
        overview 228
        persistent indexes 229–230
        word lists 228–229
Indexing
    See also Index Server
    cache 234
    catalogs
        administration 233
        default 230
        multiple, creating 230
        overview 230
        persistent indexes in 230
        shadow indexes in 229
    checking status 233
    CiDaemon process 230, 250
    content filters 227
    corpus, designating 226

Indexing *(continued)*
    forcing scans 234
    merging
        annealing merge 232
        forcing 235
        master merge 232–233
        overview 231
        shadow merge 232
    newsgroup content 129
    normalizer 228
    process overview 226
    queries *See* Index queries
    types of indexes
        overview 228
        persistent indexes 229–230
        word lists 228–229
    word breakers 227
Inetinfo
    cache 49
    logging 49
    monitoring 325
    overview 48
    process isolation 49
    remote administration 49–50
    SNMP MIBs 49
    threads 48–49
Infocom.dll 52
Information sources xii
Initialization thread state, Inetinfo 49
Installable objects, ASP 209–210
Installing
    CA certificates 186–187
    digital certificates 164
    IIS *See* Installing IIS
    Index Server 223–225
    Internet Explorer 4.01 xxiv, xxv
    SMTP Service 115
    Windows NT 4.0 Service Pack xxiv
Installing IIS
    changes made to Windows NT Server 23–25
    options
        Custom 20
        Minimum 18
        Typical 19
    overview 18
    platform selection, effect of 9–11, 14–15
    prerequisites 13
    running Setup 20–23
    setup wizard 7
    system requirements 14–15
    Windows NT Server configuration 15–16
Instance support, Infocom.dll 52
Integrated setup wizard 7, 18
Interactive applications 203

Intermediary, Certificate Server component 179
Internal inconsistencies, Index Server 251
Internet
    growth of 347
    history of 345–346
    infrastructure 347–348
    maintenance groups 348
    overview of concepts, multimedia presentation 5, 346
    standards 349
    terminology 346–347
    URLs 68, 350–352
    vs. intranet 348
Internet Activities Board 348
Internet connection type, effect on performance 317–318
Internet Database Connector scripts 55
Internet Drafts 349
Internet Engineering Task Force 348
Internet Explorer
    CA certificates, installing 187
    dynamic HTML 202
    installing xxiv, xxv
    SSL certificates for, obtaining 165
    version 4.01 required 10, 15
Internet Guest account 144, 147
Internet Information Server *See* IIS
Internet Information Services Application *See* Inetinfo
Internet Information Services Global counter 24
Internet Messaging Access Protocol 44, 46
Internet Research Task Force 348
Internet Server Application Programming Interface
    counters 315
    effect on performance 321
    extensions 53
    introduction 2
    overview 54, 199
Internet Service Manager (HTML)
    administration architecture and 57
    creating virtual directories 83
    creating virtual servers 87
    introduction 7
    NNTP Service administration 128
    overview 35–36
    SMTP Service and 111–112
Internet Service Manager snap-in
    creating virtual directories 83
    creating virtual servers 87
    FTP site property sheets 97
    NNTP Service administration 128, 134
    overview 28, 32–34
    SMTP Service and 111–112
    SMTP site property sheets 116
    WWW site property sheets 64
Internet Service Providers 348

Intranet 348
Introduction to IIS
    features
        See also Features of IIS
        overview 5
    Internet concepts overview, multimedia presentation 5
    overview, components 1–4
Introduction to this course xi, xxvi
IP addresses
    restricting access by
        FTP 101
        NNTP 137
        overview 153
        SMTP 123
        WWW 74
    settings
        FTP 97
        NNTP 134
        SMTP 117
        WWW 65
IRTF 348
Isadmin component, Web services 53
ISAM 205
ISAPI
    counters 315
    effect on performance 321
    extensions 53
    introduction 2
    overview 54, 199
ISAPI DLL connectors 50–51
ISAPI filters
    effect on performance 322
    overview 51, 53
    settings 68
Isatq.dll 52
ISM *See* Internet Service Manager snap-in
Isolation property 260
Isolation, process
    Inetinfo process and 49
    not supported on PWS 10
    provided by MTS 8
    WWW 71
ISPs 348
ISV applications 45

J

Java 2, 8
Java Virtual Machine 8, 14
JavaScript *See* JScript
Joint Photographic Experts Group 128
JPEG 128

JScript
    ASP and 206
    Index Server and 237
    support for 2, 8
    WSH and 36

K

Keep-alives 67
Key certificates 122
Key management 179
Key Manager
    generating keys 160, 161
    installing certificates 164
    on Internet Service Manager snap-in 32
    WWW Secure Communications and 74
Key pairs 160, 174
Keygen.exe *See* Key Manager

L

Languages, Index Server support for 223
Lessons
    compact disc xii
    conventions used xxi–xxiii
    getting started xiv
    hardware requirements xxiii–xxiv
    intended audience xii
    multimedia presentations
        Internet concepts 5, 346
        overview xii
        TCP/IP protocol suite 44
    outline xxvi
    overview xi, xxvi
    prerequisites xiii, xxiv
    software requirements xxiv
    technical support xxxiii
Limiting access
    See also Security
    to catalogs 251–252
    to folders 152
    to newsgroups 137
    using IP addresses
        FTP 101
        NNTP 137
        overview 153
        SMTP 123
        WWW 74
Limiting bandwidth 67, 323–324
Limiting connections 66, 98, 117, 325
Limiting permissions 15

Limits, message 119–120, 134, 136
Linked content 201
Lists, transaction 268
Load Size Over 32 K search, Content Analyzer 287
Loading console files 30
Loading snap-ins 30
Local delivery, SMTP Service 113
Local virtual directories 82
Log file formats 66, 98, 118, 124, 294
Log Utility, Certificate Administration 180, 188–189
Logging
 customized, using ISAPI filters 53
 effect on performance 322
 enabling 294
 enabling, settings 66, 98, 118, 124
 events, performance monitoring 314
 formats 294
 importing log files into Site Server Express
  overview 295
  practice 296–297
 Inetinfo 49
 ODBC *See* ODBC
 overview 293
 properties, in metabase 39
 query 236
 saving log files 294
Lookup, reverse DNS 121
Loopback address, drivers 88
Lost file notifications, Index Server 250

M

Mail, electronic
 See also SMTP Service
 IMAP and 46
 POP3 and 45
 SMTP and 45
Mailroot folder, SMTP Service 112
Management Console
 added to Internet Service Manager menu 23
 features 29
 Index Server snap-in 233–235
 interface, components 29–30
 Internet Service Manager snap-in
  creating virtual directories 83
  creating virtual servers 87
  FTP site property sheets 97
  NNTP Service administration 128
  overview 32–34
  SMTP Service and 111–112
  SMTP site property sheets 116
  WWW site property sheets 64
 introduction 7
 opening 28

Management Console *(continued)*
 overview 3, 28
 Rebar 33
 snap-ins 28–30
 Transaction Server Explorer snap-in
  overview 267–268
  practices 268–274
Management consoles, custom
 advantages of 29
 creating 30
 sharing 30
Management Information Bases 49
Managing IIS
 features for 7
 Microsoft Management Console *See* MMC
 tools
  Command Line Administration Scripting 7
  HTMLA 7, 35–36
  Internet Service Manager snap-in 7, 32–34
  overview 32
  Windows Scripting Host 36
Managing Transaction Server
 overview 267–268
 practices 268–274
Managing Web sites *See* Site Server Express
Manually starting, stopping services
 CA service 182
 Content Index service 225
 NNTP Service 132
 SMTP Service 115–116
Map Statistics, Site Summary reports 291
Maps, Web
 creating 284
 Cyberbolic view 283–284
 introduction 279
 overview 281
 practices 284–286
 Tree view 282
Masquerade domain settings 121
Master indexes 229–230
Master merge 232–233
Master namespace, MMC 30
Master property sheets 63, 96
MCIS 2
MCP program xxviii–xxxi
Memory
 balancing use against response speed 324
 bottlenecks 319–320
 requirements
  IIS 14
  Index Server 224–225
Menu bars, MMC 30
Merging indexes
 annealing merge 232

Merging indexes *(continued)*
    forcing 235
    master merge 232–233
    overview 231
    shadow merge 229, 232
Message limits 119–120, 134, 136
Message Queue Server
    as Transaction Server resource manager 263
    introduction 4
Messages
    custom 75, 99–100
    e-mail *See* E-mail; SMTP Service
    indexing of 223
    trace 268
Meta cache 52
Metabase
    as administration architecture 56–57
    configuring entries 38–39
    introduction 23
    Isadmin and 53
    overview 37
    types of property settings in 39
Methods, ASP 207
MIBs 49
Microsoft ActiveX
    ASP and 8, 209–211, 216
    HTMLA and 36
    data objects
        as ASP component 205
        creating query forms with 237
        Database Access component and 209
        databases as Web content format 202–203
Microsoft Authenticode 176
Microsoft BackOffice xxviii, 2, 51
Microsoft Certificate Server *See* Certificate Server
Microsoft Certified Professional program xxviii–xxxi
Microsoft Commercial Internet Server 2
Microsoft Content Replication System 129, 306
Microsoft Cryptographic API 172, 179
Microsoft Data Access Components 4
Microsoft Distributed Transaction Coordinator 23, 261
Microsoft Excel spreadsheets, indexing 222
Microsoft Exchange Server
    connections to 205
    connectors 51
    introduction 2
Microsoft FrontPage 9, 84
Microsoft FTP Service *See* FTP Service
Microsoft IIS Log File Format 118, 124, 294
Microsoft Index Server *See* Index Server
Microsoft Internet Explorer
    CA certificates, installing 187
    dynamic HTML 202

Microsoft Internet Explorer *(continued)*
    installing xxiv, xxv
    SSL certificates for, obtaining 165
    version 4.01 required 10, 15
Microsoft Internet Information Server *See* IIS
Microsoft JScript
    ASP and 206
    Index Server and 237
    support for 2, 8
    WSH and 36
Microsoft Management Console
    added to Internet Service Manager menu 23
    features 29
    Index Server snap-in 233–235
    interface, components 29–30
    Internet Service Manager snap-in
        creating virtual directories 83
        creating virtual servers 87
        FTP site property sheets 97
        NNTP Service administration 128
        overview 32–34
        SMTP Service and 111–112
        SMTP site property sheets 116
        WWW site property sheets 64
    introduction 7
    opening 28
    overview 3, 28
    Rebar 33
    snap-ins 28–30
    Transaction Server Explorer snap-in
        overview 267–268
        practices 268–274
Microsoft Message Queue Server
    as Transaction Server resource manager 263
    introduction 4
Microsoft MS-DOS command scripts 36
Microsoft NNTP Service *See* NNTP Service
Microsoft Personal Web Server 10–11
Microsoft Personalization Server 203
Microsoft PowerPoint files, indexing 222
Microsoft Proxy Server 2
Microsoft Script Debugger 4
Microsoft Site Server Express *See* Site Server Express
Microsoft SMTP Service *See* SMTP Service
Microsoft SNA Server 2
Microsoft SQL Server 2
Microsoft Systems Management Server 2
Microsoft Transaction Server *See* Transaction Server
Microsoft Update to Remote Access Services 4
Microsoft Visual Basic
    introduction 7, 8
    not supported on Alpha-based computers 14
    support for 2

Microsoft Visual C++ 7, 38, 200
Microsoft Visual J++ 7, 14
Microsoft Windows 95
    features not supported on 9–11
    introduction 2
Microsoft Windows NT Server *See* Windows NT Server
Microsoft Windows NT Service Pack
    installing xxiv
    required 15
Microsoft Windows NT Workstation
    features not supported on 9–11
    introduction 2
Microsoft Word documents, indexing 222
Microsoft WWW Service *See* WWW Service
MIME
    IMAP and 46
    mappings, configuring 75
    NNTP Service support for 128
Minimum installation described 18
Minimum system requirements
    IIS 14–15
    Index Server 224–225
MMC
    added to Internet Service Manager menu 23
    features 29
    Index Server snap-in 233–235
    interface, components 29–30
    Internet Service Manager snap-in
        creating virtual directories 83
        creating virtual servers 87
        FTP site property sheets 97
        NNTP Service administration 128
        overview 32–34
        SMTP Service and 111–112
        SMTP site property sheets 116
        WWW site property sheets 64
    introduction 7
    opening 28
    overview 3, 28
    Rebar 33
    snap-ins 28–30
    Transaction Server Explorer snap-in
        overview 267–268
        practices 268–274
Moderated newsgroups
    described, creating 138–140
    setting SMTP server for 134
Modifying expiration policies, newsgroups 137
Modules, Certificate Server
    exit 181
    policy 180
Monitor requirements 14

Monitoring performance
    IIS *See* Monitoring performance, IIS
    Index Server 249
    SMTP Service 124
    Web site *See* Site Server Express
Monitoring performance, IIS
    bandwidth issues
        Internet connection type 317–318
        network connection capacity 318
    Event Viewer 314
    factors affecting performance 317
    hardware issues, bottlenecks
        CPU 319
        hard disk 321
        network adapter card 320
        RAM 319–320
    logs 314
    Netstat 314
    network application speed issues
        ISAPI filters 322
        ODBC logging 322
        security features 322
        server programming 321–322
    Network Monitor 314
    overview 312
    Performance Monitor
        counters 314–316
        overview 313
    performance tuning strategies 323–325
Monitoring, SNMP 49
.msc files 30
MS-DOS command scripts 36
MSDTC 23, 261
MSMQ
    as Transaction Server resource manager 263
    introduction 4
MTS
    ASP integration 263
    component-based programming 265–266
    components 261
    configuring, managing
        overview 267–268
        practices 268–274
    effect on Web content format 203
    introduction 3, 7
    MSMQ as resource manager 263
    overview 260
    three-tier architecture 262–263
    transaction components 263–265
Multilingual indexing 223
Multimedia presentations
    Internet concepts 5, 346

Index

Multimedia presentations *(continued)*
    overview xii
    TCP/IP protocol suite 44
Multiple catalogs 230
Multipurpose Internet Mail Extension
    IMAP and 46
    mappings, configuring 75
    NNTP Service support for 128
MX addresses 121

N

Names section, .idq files 241
Namespace, MMC 30
NAPs 347
NCSA Log File Format 118, 124, 294
NDRs 114, 119–120
Netscape Enterprise Server, installing CA certificates 187
Netscape FastTrack Server 187
Netscape Navigator, accepting content from 9
Netstat 314
Network Access Points 347
Network adapter cards
    bottlenecks 320
    protocols, security considerations 148
Network application speed, effect on performance
    ISAPI filters 322
    ODBC logging 322
    security features 322
    server programming 321–322
Network connection capacity, effect on performance 318
Network connection errors, Index Server 250
Network Monitor 314
Network monitoring, SNMP 49
New expiration policies, newsgroups 136
New virtual directories 83
New virtual servers 87–89
News Site property sheet, NNTP Service 134
Newsgroups
    access control lists 129
    content formats supported 128
    content indexing 129, 223
    creating 133
    deleting 135
    editing 135
    folders 131
    introduction 7, 45
    limits, expiration policies 136
    moderated
        described, creating 138–140
        setting SMTP server for 134
    NNTP and 45
    posting articles 130
    viewing articles 130

NNTP
    message indexing 223
    overview 45
    support for 44
NNTP component, Web services 53
NNTP Discussions component, ASP 210
NNTP Server Client Requests counter 24
NNTP Server Service counter 24
NNTP Service
    access control lists 129
    administration 128
    configuring 134
    connecting to 130
    content formats supported 128
    creating newsgroups 133
    creating virtual directories 134
    deleting newsgroups 135
    editing newsgroups 135
    folder hierarchy 131
    introduction 7, 23
    moderated newsgroups 138, 140
    overview 128, 130, 132
    posting articles 130
    security 129, 137
    setting limits, expiration policies 136
    starting, stopping 132
    viewing articles 130
Nntproot folder, NNTP Service 131
No Access permission 146
Nodes, MMC scope pane 30
Noise word removal, Index Server 228
Non-delivery reports 114, 119–120
Non-Home Site Objects search, Content Analyzer 287
Normalizer, Index Server 228
Not Found Objects search, Content Analyzer 287
NSFNET 346
NT *See* Windows NT Server; Windows NT Workstation
NTFS
    certificates and 179
    Index Server and 224, 239
    introduction xxiv, 2
    overview 15, 16, 146
    permissions 146–147
    security and 144, 146–150, 168
    SMTP and 112
    WWW and 73
Number of connections, limiting 66, 98, 117, 325
Number of recipients, limiting 119–120

O

Object Request Broker, Transaction Server 261
Object Statistics, Site Summary reports 290–291
ObjectContext object, ASP 209

Objects, ASP
    built-in 208–209
    installable 209–210
    overview 208
Obtaining digital certificates 160–164, 183–184
ODBC
    ASP, OLE DB, and 205
    connectors 51, 202
    Data Source Names, logging to 49
    databases as Web content format 202–203
    IDC 200
    logging
        effect on performance 322
        FTP 98
        not supported on PWS 10
        overview 294
        SMTP 118, 124
        overview 200
ODBC component, Application services 55
OLE DB 202, 205
OLE links, indexing 223
Open Database Connectivity
    ASP, OLE DB, and 205
    connectors 51, 202
    Data Source Names, logging to 49
    databases as Web content format 202–203
    IDC 200
    logging
        effect on performance 322
        FTP 98
        not supported on PWS 10
        overview 294
        SMTP 118, 124
        overview 200
Opening MMC 28
Operators, Web site 66, 99, 118
Option Pack 3–4
ORB, Transaction Server 261
Organization reports, Report Writer 300, 302
Outline of course xxvi
Overview of IIS
    features
        See also Features of IIS
        overview 5
    Internet concepts overview, multimedia presentation 5
    introduction, components 1–4

P

Packages, Transaction Server Explorer 268
Page Counter component, ASP 210
Panes, MMC 30
Parameters, index query, declaring with .idq files 240–242
Password authentication *See* Authentication

Password synchronization 99
Passwords 16, 144, 145
Pausing NNTP Service 132
Pausing SMTP Service 115–116
PCT 150, 154
Performance Monitor
    counters 24, 314–316
    Index Server and 249
    overview 32, 313
Performance monitoring, IIS
    bandwidth issues
        Internet connection type 317–318
        network connection capacity 318
    Event Viewer 314
    factors affecting performance 317
    hardware issues, bottlenecks
        CPU 319
        hard disk 321
        network adapter card 320
        RAM 319–320
    logs 314
    Netstat 314
    network application speed issues
        ISAPI filters 322
        ODBC logging 322
        security features 322
        server programming 321–322
    Network Monitor 314
    overview 312
    Performance Monitor
        counters 314–316
        overview 313
    performance tuning strategies 323–325
Performance monitoring, Index Server 249
Performance, Web site
    managing *See* Site Server Express
    WWW sites 67
PERL 84, 199, 206, 321–322
Permission Checker component, ASP 210
Permissions
    for remote administration 49–50
    home directory 70, 101
    limiting 15
    NTFS 146–147
    Web server 147–148
Persistent indexes 229–230
Personal Web Server 10–11
Personalization Server 203
Pickup folder, SMTP Service 110, 112, 113
PKCS certificates 176, 179, 184
Platforms 2, 9–11, 14–15
Policies, Certificate Server 178, 180
Policy module, Certificate Server 180

Index 371

Policy, user account
    Internet Guest account 144, 147
    limiting Administrators membership 146
    lockouts 145
    overview 144
    passwords 145
Pools, thread, Inetinfo 48
POP3
    introduction 6
    overview 45
    support for 44
POP3 component, Web services 53
Port settings
    FTP 97
    NNTP 130
    SMTP 117
    WWW 65
Post (RFC 1867) 3, 306
Post Office Protocol
    introduction 6
    overview 45
    support for 44
Posting Acceptor 3, 9, 280, 306–307
Posting articles 130
PowerPoint files, indexing 222
Prerequisites to this course xiii, xxiv
Presentations, multimedia
    Internet concepts 5, 346
    overview xii
    TCP/IP protocol suite 44
Presentations, PowerPoint, indexing 222
Private Communication Technology 150, 154
Private keys 174
Process isolation
    Inetinfo process and 49
    not supported on PWS 10
    provided by MTS 8
    WWW 71
Processor requirements
    IIS 14
    Index Server 224–225
Processor usage, monitoring 325
Product support for this book xxxiii
Programming, component-based 265–266
Programming, server, effect on performance 321–322
Properties tables, metabase 39
Properties, ASP 207
Properties, Index Server 233
Property cache corruption, Index Server 251
Property queries *See* Index queries
Property sheets, FTP sites
    Directory Security 101
    FTP Site 97–98
    Home Directory 100–101

Property sheets, FTP sites *(continued)*
    Messages 99–100
    overview 96–97
    practice using 102–106
    Security Accounts 98–99
Property sheets, NNTP Service 134
Property sheets, SMTP sites
    Delivery 120–121, 124
    Directory Security 122–123
    Messages 119–120
    Operators 118, 123
    security options overview 123–124
    SMTP Site 116–118, 124
Property sheets, WWW sites
    Custom Errors 75
    Directory Security 73–74
    Documents 72
    Home Directory 69–71
    HTTP Headers 74–75
    ISAPI Filters 68
    Operators 66
    overview 62, 64
    Performance 67
    practice using 76–79
    types of 62–63
    Web Site 65–66
Protocols
    See also specific protocol
    not restricted by MMC 29
    security considerations 148
    TCP/IP protocol suite 44
Proxy Server 2
Public keys 174
Public-Key Cryptography Standards certificates 176, 179, 184
Publishing, Web
    content formats
        databases 202–203
        dynamic HTML 202
        interactive applications 203
        overview 201
        Personalization Server 203
        static, linked 201
        Transaction Server 203
    server extensions
        ASP 199
        CGI 199
        ISAPI 199
        ODBC, IDC 200
        overview 198
    tools
        FrontPage 98 Server Extensions 9
        Posting Acceptor 9
        Web Publishing wizard 9

PWS 10–11

Q

Queries, index
    administrative requests 248–249
    form elements 237
    formulating queries, results
        .htx files 243
        .ida files 248–249
        .idq files 240–242
        overview 240
    overview 236
    practices 243–247
    process overview 238
    result sets 239
Query logging 236
Query section, .idq files 241
Queue folder, SMTP Service 112, 113, 114
Queue Utility, Certificate Administration 180, 189
Quick Search, Content Analyzer 287–288

R

RAM
    balancing use against response speed 324
    bottlenecks 319–320
    requirements
        IIS 14
        Index Server 224–225
RAS 4
Ratings 75
Read permission 146
Reading files for indexing 227
Ready thread state, Inetinfo 49
Rebar, MMC 30, 33
Receiving e-mail
    See also SMTP Service
    IMAP and 46
    POP3 and 45
    SMTP and 45
Recipients
    limiting number of 119–120
    verifying, SMTP Service 114
Recovering from errors, Index Server 250–251
Reference materials xii
Referrer reports, Report Writer 300, 302
Registration, customer 178
Registration, database 203
Registry, Index Server entries
    default catalog 230
    for word lists 228
    master merge 233
Relay restrictions 123

Remote Access Services 4
Remote administration 49–50
Remote delivery, SMTP Service 113
Remote virtual directories 82
Removing
    administrators 66, 99, 118
    application associations, home directory 70–71
    folders, Index Server 234
    headers 75
    ISAPI filters 68
    newsgroups 135
    noise words, Index Server 228
Replication, content 9, 129, 306
Report Writer
    detail reports 299–300
    introduction 3, 280
    overview 298–299
    practices 302–305
    summary reports 301–302
Reports
    non-delivery 114, 119–120
    Report Writer
        detail 299–300
        summary 301–302
    Site Summary
        introduction 279
        Map Statistics 291
        Object Statistics 290–291
        overview 289–290
        practice 292
        Status Summary 291
Request analyses, using ISAPI filters 53
Request object, ASP 208
Request reports, Report Writer 300, 302
Requests for Comments 349
Requests, administrative, Index Server 248–249
Requests, certificate 160–164, 185
Resource management, Transaction Server 263
Resources xii
Response object, ASP 208
Response speed, balancing against memory use 324
Restarting NNTP Service 132
Restarting SMTP Service 115–116
Restricting access
    See also Security
    to catalogs 251–252
    to folders 152
    to newsgroups 137
    using IP addresses
        FTP 101
        NNTP 137
        overview 153
        SMTP 123
        WWW 74

Index

Restricting bandwidth 323–324
Restricting connections 66, 98, 117, 325
Result sets, index queries 239, 243
Results pane, MMC 30
Retransmission, FTP 95
Retry settings 120
Reverse DNS lookup 121
Revocation lists, certificate 175, 188
Revoking certificates 188
RFC 1630 351
RFC 1867 3, 306
RFCs 349
Root certificates 186
Routing options, SMTP 121
RSA Data Security 154
Running Setup 20–23
Running thread state, Inetinfo 49
Run-time cache 52

S

S/MIME 176
Sample query form 236
Saving console files 30
Saving log files 294
Scans, Index Server 234
Schemes, authentication 151
Scope pane, MMC 30
Scope, query 236
Script Debugger 4
Script tag 57, 211–212
Scripting
    ADSI and 56–57
    ASP
        See also ASP
        overview 8, 206
    Command Line Administration Scripting 7
    IDC 55
    metabase settings 38
    query forms 237
    script tag 57, 211–212
    support for 2
    Windows Scripting Host 36
Searches, Content Analyzer 287–288
Searches, index *See* Queries, index
Secure communications 74, 122
Secure Electronic Transaction 176
Secure Sockets Layer *See* SSL
Secure/Multipurpose Internet Mail Extensions 176
Security
    authentication
        See also Authentication
        Index Server and 252
        overview 150

Security *(continued)*
    authentication *(continued)*
        schemes 151
        with certificates 151, 156
    Certificate Authentication 8
    Certificate Server
        See also Certificate Server
        overview 165, 182
    Certificate Wildcard Mapping 8
    certificates
        applying 164
        enrollment 183–184
        issuance 175
        overview 151, 172–175
        requests 160–164, 185
        vs. digital envelopes 174–175
    cryptography 172–173
    digital envelopes 174–175
    directory, settings
        FTP sites 101
        NNTP Service 134
        SMTP sites 122–123
        WWW sites 73–74
    disabling directory browsing 152
    Domain Blocking 8
    effect on performance 322
    encryption
        See also Encryption
        overview 173
    event logs 314
    features for 8
    FTP sites, configuring 98–99
    Index Server 251–253
    Infocom.dll and 52
    IP address restrictions 153
    keys 174
    limitation of PWS on Windows 95 11
    NNTP Service 129, 134, 137
    NTFS
        overview 146
        permissions 146–147
    overview 144, 150, 154
    protocol settings 148
    SMTP settings 121
    SMTP sites
        access protection 123–124
        configuring 122–123
    SSL
        See also SSL
        applying certificates 164
        architecture 155–156
        certificate requests 160–164
        certificates 156
        client certificate authentication 156–158

Security *(continued)*
  SSL *(continued)*
    configuring 159
    overview 151, 154
  user account policy
    Internet Guest account 144, 147
    limiting Administrators membership 146
    lockouts 145
    overview 144
    passwords 145
  Web server permissions 147–148
  Windows NT features, taking advantage of 16
  WWW sites, configuring 73
Sending e-mail
  See also SMTP Service
  IMAP and 46
  POP3 and 45
  SMTP and 45
Sending headers 75
Sequencing, FTP 95
Server architecture
  Application services 54–55
  connectors 50–51
  Inetinfo
    cache 49
    logging 49
    overview 48
    process isolation 49
    remote administration 49–50
    SNMP MIBs 49
    threads 48–49
  overview 47
  Web services 52–53
  Windows NT system services 51–52
Server database, Certificate Server component 180
Server engine, as Certificate Server component 179
Server Manager 32
Server message block protocol 148
Server object, ASP 208
Server permissions 147–148
Server programming, effect on performance 321–322
Server Service 148
Servers, virtual
  creating 87–89
  Host Headers 87
  overview 86
Server-side include directives 55
Server-Side Java Virtual Machine 8, 14
Service layers, server architecture
  Application services 54–55
  overview 47
  Web services 52–53
  Windows NT system services 51–52

Service Pack
  installing xxiv
  required 15
Services
  See also specific service
  monitoring *See* Monitoring performance, IIS
  overview 23
Session object, ASP 208
Sessions, FTP 95, 98
Sessions, SSL 157
SET 176
Settings
  See also Property sheets
  content ratings 75
  Index Server 233
  metabase 38–39
  permissions
    for remote administration 49–50
    NTFS 146–147
    Web server 147–148
Setup
  changes made to Windows NT Server 23–25
  options
    Custom 20
    Minimum 18
    Typical 19
  overview 18
  platform selection, effect of 9–11, 14–15
  prerequisites 13
  running Setup 20–23
  system requirements 14–15
  Windows NT Server configuration 15–16
Setup wizard 7, 18
Shadow indexes
  merging word lists into 229
  overview 229–230
Shadow merge
  described 232
  introduction 229
Shared thread pools, Inetinfo 48
Sharing console files 30
Site access protection *See* Security
Site performance, managing *See* Site Server Express
Site Server Express
  Content Analyzer
    overview 281
    Quick Search 287–288
    Site Summary reports 289–292
    WebMaps 281–284
  logging
    enabling 294
    formats 294
    importing log files 295–297

Index   375

Site Server Express *(continued)*
   logging *(continued)*
      overview 293
      saving log files 294
   overview, components 3, 279–280
   Posting Acceptor 306–307
   Report Writer
      detail reports 299–300
      overview 298–299
      practices 302–305
      summary reports 301–302
Site Summary reports
   introduction 279
   Map Statistics 291
   Object Statistics 290–291
   overview 289–290
   practice 292
   Status Summary 291
Site usage logging *See* Logging
Sites *See specific type*
Size limits, messages 119–120, 134
Size, cache, adjusting 325
Smart host 121
SMB protocol 148
SMS 2
SMTP
   as server for moderated newsgroups 134
   overview 45, 110
   support for 44, 110
SMTP component, Web services 53
SMTP Send Mail component, ASP 210
SMTP Server counter 24
SMTP Service
   administration 111–112
   configuring
      See also SMTP site property sheets
      overview 116
   features 110
   installation 115
   introduction 6, 23
   monitoring, logging 124
   NTFS and 15
   overview 110
   processes 113–114
   security 123–124
   starting, stopping 115–116
SMTP site property sheets
   Delivery 120–121, 124
   Directory Security 122–123
   Messages 119–120
   Operators 118, 123
   security options overview 123–124
   SMTP Site 116–118, 124
SNA Server 2

Snap-ins, MMC
   See also specific snap-in
   overview 28–30
SNMP
   MIBs 49
   monitoring 49
Sockets 45, 52
Software requirements
   course xxiv
   IIS 14–15
   Index Server 224–225
Sorting messages, SMTP Service 114
Special Access permission 146
Speed, network application, effect on performance
   ISAPI filters 322
   ODBC logging 322
   security features 322
   server programming 321–322
Speed, response, balancing against memory use 324
Spreadsheets, indexing 222
SQL 200, 202, 237
SQL Server 2
SSE *See* Site Server Express
SSI directives 55
SSL
   architecture 155–156
   certificate requests 160–164
   Certificate Server
      See also Certificate Server
      overview 165
   certificates
      applying 164
      enrollment 183–184
      overview 151, 156, 172–175
   client certificate authentication 156–158
   configuring 159
   digital certificates 74
   IIS support of 7
   Infocom.dll and 52
   keys, properties in metabase 39
   NNTP Service support for 129
   overview 151, 154
   port 65
   sessions, creation of 157
   SMTP Service and 110
   SMTP settings 123–124
Standby thread state, Inetinfo 49
Starting, stopping services
   CA service 182
   Content Index service 225
   NNTP Service 132
   SMTP Service 115–116
States, thread, Inetinfo 49
Static content 201

Statistics, Site Summary reports
   Map 291
   Object 290–291
Statistics, transaction 268
Status Summary, Site Summary reports 291
Status, indexing, checking 233
Stopping NNTP Service 132
Stopping SMTP Service 115–116
Structured Query Language 200, 202, 237
Summary reports
   introduction 279
   Map Statistics 291
   Object Statistics 290–291
   overview 289–290
   practice 292
   Report Writer 301–302
   Status Summary 291
Super VGA recommendation 14
Support services for this book xxxiii
Synchronization, password, automatic 99
System event logs 314
System requirements
   course xxiii–xxiv
   IIS 14–15
   Index Server 224–225
Systems Management Server 2

T

T1 lines 318
T3 connections 318
Tabs *See* Property sheets
Task Manager, using to monitor performance 325
TCP ports
   FTP 97
   NNTP 130
   SMTP 110, 113, 117
   WWW 65
TCP/IP
   access restrictions, NNTP Service 134
   configuration requirements 15–16
   history of 346
   networks, IIS support of 6
   NNTP Service use of 130
   protocol suite 44
TCP/IP architecture
   overview 44
   protocols described 44–46
Technical support for this book xxxiii
Termination thread state, Inetinfo 49
Testing certificates 194
Testing virtual servers 89
Text files, indexing 222

Thread pools, Inetinfo 48
Threads, ATQ 52
Threads, Inetinfo 48–49
Three-tier architecture, Transaction Server 262–263
Throttling bandwidth 67, 323–324
Timeout, connection 66, 98, 117, 325
TLS encryption 121
Tools for administering IIS
   HTMLA 35–36
   Internet Service Manager snap-in 32–34
   overview 32
   Windows Scripting Host 36
Tools, management console *See* Console files
TP Monitor, Transaction Server 261
Trace messages 268
Traffic analyses, using ISAPI filters 53
Training programs xxxii
Transaction components 263–265
Transaction lists 268
Transaction logging *See* Logging
Transaction Processing Monitor, Transaction Server 261
Transaction Server
   ASP integration 263
   component-based programming 265–266
   components 261
   configuring, managing
      overview 267–268
      practices 268–274
   effect on Web content format 203
   introduction 3, 7
   MSMQ as resource manager 263
   overview 260
   three-tier architecture 262–263
   transaction components 263–265
Transaction Server Explorer snap-in
   overview 267–268
   practices 268–274
Transaction statistics 268
Transition thread state, Inetinfo 49
Transmission Control Protocol\Internet Protocol
   access restrictions, NNTP Service 134
   architecture 44–46
   configuration requirements 15–16
   history of 346
   networks, IIS support of 6
   NNTP Service use of 130
   protocol suite 44
Transmission options, SMTP 120
Transport Layer Security encryption 121
Transports, Certificate Server and 178
Tree view, Content Analyzer WebMaps 282
Tuning performance, IIS
   balancing memory use, response speed 324

Tuning performance, IIS *(continued)*
  bandwidth issues
    Internet connection type 317–318
    network connection capacity 318
  cache size, adjusting 325
  Event Viewer 314
  factors affecting performance 317
  hardware issues, bottlenecks
    CPU 319
    hard disk 321
    network adapter card 320
    RAM 319–320
  limiting connections 325
  logs 314
  maximizing processor share 325
  Netstat 314
  network application speed issues
    ISAPI filters 322
    ODBC logging 322
    security features 322
    server programming 321–322
  Network Monitor 314
  overview 312, 323
  Performance Monitor
    counters 314–316
    overview 313
  restricting bandwidth 323–324
Tuning performance, Web site 67
Types, file 75
Typical installation described 19
Typographical conventions xxi–xxiii

U

Unavailable Objects search, Content Analyzer 287
UNC 222
Unicode characters, index information as 223
Uniform Resource Characteristics 352
Uniform Resource Identifiers 351
Uniform Resource Locators 68, 350–352
Uniform Resource Names 352
Universal naming convention 222
Unknown thread state, Inetinfo 49
Unverified Objects search, Content Analyzer 287
Update to Remote Access Services 4
Uploading content on Web server 307
URCs 352
URIs 351
URLs 68, 350–352
URNs 352
Usage Analyzer 302
Usage Import
  introduction 3, 279
  overview 298

Usenet newsgroups
  access control lists 129
  content formats supported 128
  content indexing 129
  creating 133
  deleting 135
  editing 135
  folders 131
  indexing messages 223
  introduction 7
  limits, expiration policies 136
  moderated
    described, creating 138–140
    setting SMTP server for 134
  NNTP and 45
  overview 45
  posting articles 130
  viewing articles 130
User account policy
  Internet Guest account 144, 147
  limiting Administrators membership 146
  lockouts 145
  overview 144
  passwords 145
User Manager 23, 32
User reports, Report Writer 300, 302, 304
Users, Internet, described 348

V

VB
  introduction 7, 8
  not supported on Alpha-based computers 14
  support for 2
VBScript
  ASP and 206
  Index Server and 237
  introduction 8, 36, 38
  support for 2
Verifying recipients, SMTP Service 114
VeriSign certificates 165
VGA requirements 14
Viewing
  articles 130
  current FTP sessions 98
  trace messages 268
  Windows NT Server configuration
    after IIS installation 24–25
    before IIS installation 16–17
Views, MMC 30
Virtual directories
  creating 83, 134
  FrontPage and 84
  local 82

378   Microsoft Internet Information Server 4.0 Training

Virtual directories *(continued)*
    overview 81–82
    properties in metabase 39
    remote 82
    use for indexing 222, 226, 234
Virtual servers
    creating 87–89
    Host Headers 87
    overview 86
Visits reports, Report Writer 300, 302, 303
Visual Basic
    introduction 7, 8
    not supported on Alpha-based computers 14
    support for 2
Visual C++ 7, 38, 200
Visual J++ 7, 14
VSAM 205

W

W3C 61
W3C Extended Log File Format 66, 98, 118, 124, 294
Wait thread state, Inetinfo 49
WAM 54
Web Application Manager 54
Web content formats
    databases 202–203
    dynamic HTML 202
    interactive applications 203
    overview 201
    Personalization Server 203
    static, linked 201
    Transaction Server 203
Web publishing
    content formats
        databases 202–203
        dynamic HTML 202
        interactive applications 203
        overview 201
        Personalization Server 203
        static, linked 201
        Transaction Server 203
    server extensions
        ASP 199
        CGI 199
        ISAPI 199
        ODBC, IDC 200
        overview 198
    tools
        FrontPage 98 Server Extensions 9
        Posting Acceptor 9
        Web Publishing wizard 9
Web Publishing wizard 9

Web server
    extensions
        ASP 199
        CGI 199
        ISAPI 199
        ODBC, IDC 200
        overview 198
    permissions 147–148
    uploading content on 307
Web Server Enrollment page 184
Web Service counter 24
Web services 52–53
Web site identification 65, 97, 117, 134
Web site performance, managing *See* Site Server Express
Web Site property sheet, WWW 65–66
WebMaps
    creating 284
    Cyberbolic view 283–284
    introduction 279
    overview 281
    practices 284–286
    Tree view 282
Wildcard Mapping 8
Windows 95
    features not supported on 9–11
    introduction 2
Windows NT 4.0 Option Pack 3–4
Windows NT Challenge/Response authentication
    NNTP Service 129
    overview 151
    SMTP 121, 122
    WWW 73
Windows NT File System
    certificates and 179
    Index Server and 224, 239
    introduction xxiv, 2
    overview 15, 16, 146
    permissions 146–147
    security and 144, 146–150, 168
    SMTP and 112
    WWW and 73
Windows NT Server
    configuration
        after IIS installation, viewing 24–25
        before IIS installation, viewing 16–17
        requirements 15–16
    effect of IIS installation 23–25
    Evaluation Edition support limitation xxxiii
    integration with 2, 9, 11
    security *See* Security
Windows NT Server service 148
Windows NT Service Pack
    installing xxiv
    required 15

Windows NT system services 51–52
Windows NT Workstation
    features not supported on 9–11
    introduction 2
Windows Scripting Host
    administration architecture and 57
    creating virtual directories 83
    creating virtual servers 87
    overview 36
Windows Sockets 45, 52
WinSock 45, 52
Wizards, Transaction Server Explorer 268
Word breakers for indexing 227
Word documents, indexing 222
Word lists 228–229
World Wide Web Consortium 61
World Wide Web Publishing Service 23
Writing reports, Site Server Express *See* Report Writer
Wscript.exe 36
WSH
    administration architecture and 57
    creating virtual directories 83
    creating virtual servers 87
    overview 36
WWW Service
    configuring
        See also Configuring sites
        practice 33
    HTTP and 45
    introduction 6
    SNMP monitoring 49
WWW site property sheets
    Custom Errors 75
    Directory Security 73–74
    Documents 72
    Home Directory 69–71
    HTTP Headers 74–75
    ISAPI Filters 68
    Operators 66
    overview 62, 64
    Performance 67
    practice using 76–79
    types of 62–63
    Web Site 65–66
WWW site usage logging *See* Logging

X

X.509 certificates 8, 156, 176

The definitive resource for Microsoft Internet Information Server.

This exclusive Microsoft® resource kit was created in cooperation with the Microsoft Internet Information Server (IIS) development and support teams. That makes it comprehensive, authoritative, and indispensable for system administrators and other computer professionals who demand the best technical information and tools for rolling out and supporting Microsoft IIS within their organizations. Plus, you get more than 40 utilities, ISAPI filters, and components on the enclosed CD-ROMs. For the top performance you want with Microsoft IIS, the essential information you need is inside this kit.

U.S.A.	$49.99
U.K.	£46.99 [V.A.T. included]
Canada	$71.99
ISBN 1-57231-638-1	

Microsoft Press® products are available worldwide wherever quality computer books are sold. For more information, contact your book or computer retailer, software reseller, or local Microsoft Sales Office, or visit our Web site at mspress.microsoft.com. To locate your nearest source for Microsoft Press products, or to order directly, call 1-800-MSPRESS in the U.S. (in Canada, call 1-800-268-2222).

Prices and availability dates are subject to change.

Microsoft Press

Deluxe Multimedia Editions let you create your own best way to learn.

Microsoft® Windows NT® Server 4.0 Enterprise Technologies Training Kit, Deluxe Multimedia Edition
U.S.A. $199.99
U.K. £187.99
[V.A.T. included]
Canada $289.99
ISBN 1-57231-829-5

Networking Essentials, Second Edition, Training Kit, Deluxe Multimedia Edition
U.S.A. $199.99
U.K. £187.99
[V.A.T. included]
Canada $289.99
ISBN 1-57231-831-7

Microsoft Windows NT Technical Support Training Kit, Deluxe Multimedia Edition
U.S.A. $199.99
U.K. £187.99
[V.A.T. included]
Canada $289.99
ISBN 1-57231-833-3

Microsoft Windows NT Network Administration Training Kit, Deluxe Multimedia Edition
U.S.A. $199.99
U.K. £187.99
[V.A.T. included]
Canada $289.99
ISBN 1-57231-832-5

Microsoft Windows® 95 Training Kit, Deluxe Multimedia Edition
U.S.A. $199.99
U.K. £187.99
[V.A.T. included]
Canada $289.99
ISBN 1-57231-830-9

For success on the job and on Microsoft Certified Professional exams, no other self-paced training kits offer so much learning at such low cost. You get proven self-paced curriculum from Microsoft—training based on the same Microsoft Official Curriculum courses used by Microsoft Authorized Training and Education Centers (ATECs) worldwide. Plus, you get extra help via multimedia-based training from NETg (National Education Training Group), training that's prized industry-wide and available at retail nowhere else. Combine these materials in the ways that best suit your learning style. And get ready for success—on the exams and on the job.

Microsoft Press® products are available worldwide wherever quality computer books are sold. For more information, contact your book or computer retailer, software reseller, or local Microsoft Sales Office, or visit our Web site at mspress.microsoft.com. To locate your nearest source for Microsoft Press products, or to order directly, call 1-800-MSPRESS in the U.S. (in Canada, call 1-800-268-2222).

Prices and availability dates are subject to change.

Microsoft Press

Microsoft® TCP/IP Training

Microsoft Press

PUBLISHED BY
Microsoft Press
A Division of Microsoft Corporation
One Microsoft Way
Redmond, Washington 98052-6399

Copyright © 1998 by Microsoft Corporation

All rights reserved. No part of the contents of this book may be reproduced or transmitted in any form or by any means without the written permission of the publisher.

Library of Congress Cataloging-in-Publication Data pending.

Printed and bound in the United States of America.

1 2 3 4 5 6 7 8 9   WCWC   3 2 1 0 9 8

Distributed to the book trade in Canada by Macmillan of Canada, a division of Canada Publishing Corporation.

A CIP catalogue record for this book is available from the British Library.

Microsoft Press books are available through booksellers and distributors worldwide. For further information about international editions, contact your local Microsoft Corporation office. Or contact Microsoft Press International directly at fax (425) 936-7329. Visit our Web site at mspress.microsoft.com.

BackOffice, Microsoft, Microsoft Press, MS, MS-DOS, Win32, Windows, the Windows logo, and Windows NT are registered trademarks and MSN and NetShow are trademarks of Microsoft Corporation.

Other product and company names mentioned herein may be the trademarks of their respective owners.

For Instructional Design Solutions
Instructional Designer: Jim Semick—Instructional Design Solutions
Editor: Shari G. Smith—R & S Consulting
Desktop Publishing: Irene Barnett—Barnett Communications

For Microsoft (Original Instructor-Led Course Content)
Instructional Designers: Susan Greenberg, Nikki McCormick
Subject Matter Experts: Kelli Adam, Jeff Clark, Scott Hay, Wally Mead

For Microsoft Press
Acquisitions Editor: Eric Stroo
Project Editor: Stuart J. Stuple

Part No. 097-0002014

Contents

About This Book   xi
    Course Compact Disc xii
    Reference Materials. xii
    Intended Audience xii
    Finding the Best Starting Point for You xiii
    Conventions Used in This Book xiv
       Features of This Book xiv
       Procedural Conventions xiv
       Notational Conventions xiv
       Keyboard Conventions. xv
       Notes. xv
    Getting Started xvi
       Hardware and Software Requirements xvi
       Setup Instructions. xvii
    Chapter and Appendix Overview xix
    The Microsoft Certified Professional Program. xxi
       Microsoft Online Institute xxiii
       ATECs xxiii

Chapter 1   Introduction to TCP/IP   1
    About This Chapter 1
    Before You Begin. 1
    Lesson 1: TCP/IP Overview 2
       TCP/IP History. 2
       The Internet Standards Process 3
    Lesson 2: TCP/IP Utilities. 6
       Diagnostics Utilities. 7
    Review 8

Chapter 2   Installing and Configuring TCP/IP   9
    About This Chapter 9
    Before You Begin. 9
    Lesson 1: Installing and Configuring Microsoft TCP/IP 10
       Configuration Parameters 10
    Lesson 2: Testing TCP/IP with Ipconfig and PING 15

Lesson 3: Microsoft Network Monitor 18
    Analyzing Network Traffic 20
Review 22

Chapter 3   Architectural Overview of the TCP/IP Protocol Suite   23

About This Chapter 23
Before You Begin. 24
Lesson 1: The Microsoft TCP/IP Protocol Suite. 25
    The Four-Layer Model 26
    Network Interface Technologies 27
Lesson 2: ARP 29
    Resolving a Local IP Address 30
    Resolving a Remote IP Address. 31
    The ARP Cache 32
Lesson 3: ICMP and IGMP 40
    ICMP 40
    IGMP 41
Lesson 4: IP 42
    IP on the Router 43
Lesson 5: TCP 46
    Ports. 46
    Sockets 47
    TCP Three-Way Handshake 48
    TCP Sliding Windows 49
Lesson 6: UDP 51
Review 53

Chapter 4   IP Addressing   55

About This Chapter 55
Before You Begin. 55
Lesson 1: The IP Address 56
    Network ID and Host ID 57
    Converting IP Addresses from Binary to Decimal 57
Lesson 2: Address Classes. 60
Lesson 3: Addressing Guidelines 64
    Assigning Network IDs 64
    Assigning Host IDs. 66
Lesson 4: Subnet Mask and the IP Address 71
Lesson 5: IP Addressing with IP Version 6.0 75
Review 77

Chapter 5 Subnetting 81
- About This Chapter 81
- Before You Begin 81
- Lesson 1: Subnet Overview 82
  - Implementing Subnetting 83
  - Subnet Mask Bits 84
- Lesson 2: Defining a Subnet Mask 85
  - Subnetting More Than One Octet 87
- Lesson 3: Defining Subnet IDs 93
  - Shortcut to Defining Subnet IDs 94
- Lesson 4: Defining Host IDs for a Subnet 96
- Lesson 5: Supernetting 103
- Review 106

Chapter 6 Implementing IP Routing 111
- About This Chapter 111
- Before You Begin 111
- Lesson 1: IP Routing Overview 112
  - Static vs. Dynamic IP Routing 114
- Lesson 2: Static IP Routing 115
  - Configuring Static IP Routers 116
  - Building a Routing Table 117
- Lesson 3: Dynamic IP Routing 121
  - RIP 122
  - Integrating Static and Dynamic Routing 124
- Lesson 4: Implementing a Windows NT Router 126
  - The TRACERT Utility 126
- Review 128

Chapter 7 The Dynamic Host Configuration Protocol 129
- About This Chapter 129
- Before You Begin 129
- Lesson 1: DHCP Overview 130
  - Manual vs. Automatic Configuration 131
  - How DHCP Works 132
  - IP Lease Renewal 136
  - Using the Ipconfig Utility 138
- Lesson 2: Installing and Configuring a DHCP Server 140
  - Installing and Configuring a DHCP Server 143

Lesson 3: Enabling a DHCP Relay Agent 155
Lesson 4: Managing the DHCP Database 159
    Compacting the DHCP Database. 160
Review 162

Chapter 8 NetBIOS over TCP/IP   165
About This Chapter 165
Before You Begin... 165
Lesson 1: NetBIOS Names 166
    NetBIOS Names... 167
    NetBIOS Name Registration, Discovery, and Release. 169
    Segmenting NetBIOS Names with Scopes 169
Lesson 2: NetBIOS Name Resolution. 171
    Resolving Local NetBIOS Names Using a Broadcast 172
    Resolving Names with a NetBIOS Name Server 174
    Microsoft Methods of Resolving NetBIOS Names. 175
    NetBIOS over TCP/IP Name Resolution Nodes. 176
Lesson 3: Using the LMHOSTS File 179
    Name Resolution Problems Using LMHOSTS. 181
Review 184

Chapter 9 Windows Internet Name Service (WINS)   185
About This Chapter 185
Before You Begin... 186
Lesson 1: WINS Overview 187
Lesson 2: The WINS Resolution Process 189
    Name Registration 190
    Name Renewal 192
    Name Release.. 193
    Name Query and Name Response 194
Lesson 3: Implementing WINS 196
    WINS Requirements... 196
    Configuring a WINS Proxy Agent.................................. 201
    Configuring a DHCP Server for WINS.............................. 203
Lesson 4: Database Replication Between WINS Servers 208
    Configuring a WINS Server As a Push or Pull Partner 209
    Configuring Database Replication................................ 210

Lesson 5: Maintaining the WINS Server Database	214
Configuring the WINS Server	216
Backing Up and Restoring the WINS Database	219
Compacting the WINS Database	220
Review	222

Chapter 10   IP Internetwork Browsing and Domain Functions   225

About This Chapter	225
Before You Begin	225
Lesson 1: Browsing Overview	226
Browsing Collection and Distribution	227
Servicing Client Browsing Requests	228
Lesson 2: Browsing an IP Internetwork	230
Browsing with WINS	231
Browsing Using the LMHOSTS File	232
Lesson 3: Domain Functions in an IP Internetwork	235
Review	240

Chapter 11   Host Name Resolution   241

About This Chapter	241
Before You Begin	241
Lesson 1: TCP/IP Naming Schemes	242
Lesson 2: Host Names	243
Host Name Resolution	243
Lesson 3: The HOSTS File	249
Review	252

Chapter 12   Domain Name System (DNS)   253

About This Chapter	253
Before You Begin	253
Lesson 1: Domain Name System (DNS)	254
How DNS Works	255
Domain Name Space	257
Zones of Authority	258
Name Server Roles	259
Lesson 2: Name Resolution	261
Caching and TTL	263

Lesson 3: Configuring the DNS Files 264
    The Database File.. 264
    The Reverse Lookup File 266
    The Cache File 266
    The Boot File 267
Lesson 4: Planning a DNS Implementation 269
    Registering with the Parent Domain 270
Review 278

Chapter 13 Implementing DNS   281

About This Chapter 281
Before You Begin... 281
Lesson 1: The Microsoft DNS Server............................ 282
    Installing Microsoft DNS Server........................... 282
    Troubleshooting DNS with NSLOOKUP......................... 283
Lesson 2: Administering the DNS Server........................ 286
    Adding DNS Domains and Zones 288
    Adding Resource Records 291
    Configuring Reverse Lookup 292
Lesson 3: Integrating DNS and WINS 296
    Enabling WINS Lookup...................................... 298
Review 301

Chapter 14 Connectivity in Heterogeneous Environments   303

About This Chapter 303
Before You Begin... 303
Lesson 1: Connectivity in Heterogeneous Environments 304
    Connecting to a Remote Host with Microsoft Networking..... 304
    Microsoft TCP/IP Utilities................................ 305
Lesson 2: Remote Execution Utilities 307
Lesson 3: Data Transfer Utilities 309
    RCP... 309
    FTP 309
    Web Browsers 314
Lesson 4: Printing Utilities 316
    Using the TCP/IP Print Server (LPD)....................... 317
    Using LPR and LPQ... 317
    Using Windows NT As a Print Gateway....................... 319
Review 323

Chapter 15 Implementing the Microsoft SNMP Services   **325**
    About This Chapter 325
    Before You Begin. 325
    Lesson 1: SNMP Defined 326
        Management Systems and Agents 327
        The Microsoft SNMP Service 328
    Lesson 2: The MIB 330
        The Hierarchical Name Tree 331
    Lesson 3: Installing and Configuring the SNMP Service. 333
        Defining SNMP Communities. 333
        How SNMP Gathers Information 334
        Installing SNMP. 336
        Configuring SNMP Service Security. 338
        Configuring SNMP Agent Services. 339
        Identifying SNMP Service Errors 341
        The SNMPUTIL Utility. 344
    Review 346

Chapter 16 Troubleshooting Microsoft TCP/IP   **347**
    About This Chapter 347
    Before You Begin. 347
    Lesson 1: Windows NT Diagnostic Tools and Guidelines 348
        Windows NT Utilities 348
        Troubleshooting Guidelines. 349
    Review 353

Questions and Answers   **355**

Index   **391**

About This Book

Welcome to *Internetworking with Microsoft® TCP/IP on Microsoft Windows NT® 4.0*. This book provides systems administrators the knowledge and skills to set up, configure, use, and support Transmission Control Protocol/Internet Protocol (TCP/IP) on the Microsoft Windows NT operating system version 4.0 in a networked environment. It will also prepare you to meet the certification requirements to become a Microsoft Internet Systems Certified Professional.

Note For more information on becoming a Microsoft Certified Professional, please see the section titled "The Microsoft Certified Professional Program" later in this chapter.

Each chapter in this book is divided into lessons. Most lessons include hands-on procedures to practice or demonstrate the concept or skill presented in the lesson. At the end of each lesson is a short summary, and at the end of each chapter is a set of review questions to test your knowledge of the chapter material. If appropriate, at the end of each chapter there are references to additional information on the lesson material or related topics.

The "Getting Started" section provides important setup instructions that describe the hardware and software requirements to complete the procedures in this course. This section also provides the networking configuration for the two computers that are necessary to complete the hands-on procedures. Read through this section thoroughly before you start the lessons.

Course Compact Disc

The compact disc provided in this course contains multimedia presentations that supplement the key concepts covered in the book. You should view these presentations when suggested, and then use them as a review tool while you work through the material.

The course compact disc also contains files required to perform the hands-on procedures, and information designed to supplement the lesson material.

The multimedia presentations, additional materials, and files can all be accessed from the *Course Materials* Web page on the course compact disc. In order to view the course Web site from the compact disc, you must first install Microsoft Internet Explorer™ 3.0. See the "Getting Started" section for information on installing Internet Explorer from the course compact disc.

Reference Materials

You may find the following reference material useful:

- Documentation for Windows NT Server version 4.0
- *Microsoft Windows NT Server Resource Kit*

Intended Audience

This book is designed for network integrators, system engineers, and support professionals who implement and support TCP/IP in local and wide area network environments. This book was developed for those who plan to take the related Microsoft Certified Professional exam 70-59, Internetworking with Microsoft TCP/IP on Microsoft Windows NT 4.0.

Prerequisites

- A knowledge of the function and uses of local area network (LAN) hardware, including network cards, cabling, bridges, and routers.
- Successful completion of the following Microsoft Certified Professional exam:
  70-67, Implementing and Supporting Microsoft Windows NT Server 4.0
  –Or–
- Completion of the following course:
  #687, Supporting Microsoft Windows NT Server 4.0 Core Technologies

Finding the Best Starting Point for You

This book is designed for you to complete at your own pace, so you can skip some lessons and revisit them later. Keep in mind that you need to complete the procedures in Chapter 2, "Installing and Configuring TCP/IP," in order to perform the procedures in the other chapters. Use the following table to find the best starting point for you.

If you	Follow this learning path
Are preparing to take the Microsoft Certified Professional exam 70-59, Internetworking with Microsoft TCP/IP on Microsoft Windows NT 4.0	Read the "Getting Started" section. Next, work through Chapters 1–3. Work through the remaining chapters in any order. Before beginning a chapter, always refer to the "Before You Begin" section to determine any prerequisites.
Need to install and configure TCP/IP	Read the "Getting Started" section. Next, work through Chapter 2. Complete Chapters 1 and 3, then work through the other chapters in any order.
Need to install TCP/IP and configure multiple departments, groups, or computers	Read the "Getting Started" section. Depending on your configuration, you should read the appropriate planning chapter. For example, if your configuration requires multiple subnets, read Chapter 5, "Subnetting," for information on how to create a range of valid IP addresses. Then complete Chapter 2 and work through the other chapters in any order.
Need information on a specific topic related to TCP/IP	Refer to the table of contents or index.

Conventions Used in This Book

Before you start any of the lessons, it is important that you understand the terms and notational conventions used in this book.

Features of This Book

- Each chapter opens with a "Before You Begin" section, which describes other chapters that must be completed before continuing.

- Whenever possible, lessons contain procedures that give you an opportunity to use the skills being presented or explore the part of TCP/IP being described. All procedures are identified with the following procedural convention: ▶

- The "Review" section at the end of most lessons allows you to test what you have learned in the lesson. They are designed to familiarize you with the Microsoft Certified Professional exam.

- The "For More Information" list at the end of many chapters provides additional resource locations for information on the concepts and skills covered in the chapter. The information referred to covers product documentation, online locations, or both.

- The "Questions and Answers" section contains all of the book's questions and corresponding answers. Each question is cross-referenced by page number.

Procedural Conventions

- Hands-on procedures that you are to follow are presented in numbered lists of steps (1, 2, and so on). A triangular bullet (▶) indicates the beginning of a procedure.

- The word *select* is used for highlighting directories, file names, text boxes, menu bars, and option buttons, and for selecting options in a dialog box.

- The word *click* is used for carrying out a command from a menu or dialog box.

Notational Conventions

- Characters or commands that you type appear in **bold lowercase** type.

- *Italic* in syntax statements indicates placeholders for variable information. *Italic* is also used for important new terms, for book titles, and for emphasis in the text.

- Names of files and folders appear in Title Caps, except when you are to type them directly. Unless otherwise indicated, you can use all lowercase letters when you type a file name in a dialog box or at a command prompt.

- File name extensions appear in all lowercase.

- Names of directories appear in initial caps, except when you are to type them directly. Unless otherwise indicated, you can use all lowercase letters when you type a directory name in a dialog box or at a command prompt.

- Acronyms appear in all uppercase.
- `Monospace` type represents code samples, examples of screen text, or entries that you might type in a command line or in initialization files.
- Square brackets [ ] are used in syntax statements to enclose optional items. For example, [*filename*] in command syntax indicates that you can choose to type a file name with the command. Type only the information within the brackets, not the brackets themselves.
- Braces { } are used in syntax statements to enclose required items. Type only the information within the braces, not the braces themselves.

Keyboard Conventions

- Names of keys that you press appear in SMALL CAPITALS; for example, TAB and SHIFT.
- A plus sign (+) between two key names means that you must press those keys at the same time. For example, "Press ALT+TAB" means that you hold down ALT while you press TAB.
- A comma (,) between two or more key names means that you must press each of the keys consecutively, not together. For example, "Press ALT, F, X" means that you press and release each key in sequence. "Press ALT+W, L" means that you first press ALT and W together, and then release them and press L.
- You can choose menu commands with the keyboard. Press the ALT key to activate the menu bar, and then sequentially press the keys that correspond to the highlighted or underlined letter of the menu name and the command name. For some commands, you can also press a key combination listed in the menu.
- You can select or clear check boxes or option buttons in dialog boxes with the keyboard. Press the ALT key, and then press the key that corresponds to the underlined letter of the option name. Or you can press TAB until the option is highlighted, and then press SPACEBAR to select or clear the check box or option button.
- You can cancel the display of a dialog box by pressing the ESC key.

Notes

Notes appear throughout the lessons.

- Notes marked **Tip** contain explanations of possible results or alternative methods.
- Notes marked **Important** contain information that is essential to completing a task.
- Notes marked **Note** contain supplemental information.
- Notes marked **Caution** contain warnings about possible loss of data.

Getting Started

Hardware and Software Requirements

This self-paced training course contains hands-on procedures to help you learn about Microsoft TCP/IP on Microsoft Windows NT 4.0. To complete many of these procedures, you must have two networked computers or be connected to a larger network.

Both computers must be capable of running Microsoft Windows NT Server 4.0 and must have the following minimum configuration:

- A 486/33 or higher Intel-based processor
- 16 MB of RAM (32 MB recommended)
- A minimum of 450 MB of available hard disk space on each computer
- SVGA display adapter and monitor capable of displaying 256 colors
- Microsoft Mouse or compatible pointing device
- Network adapter card and related cables
- One 3.5-inch high-density disk drive
- CD-ROM drive
- Sound card with headphones or speakers on one computer (optional)

All hardware should be on the Microsoft Windows NT 4.0 Hardware Compatibility List (HCL).

Software

The following software is required to complete the procedures in this course:

- Windows NT Server 4.0 retail product
- Microsoft MS-DOS® 5.0 or later
- Windows NT Server 4.0 Service Pack 2 or later (Service Pack 2 is located on the course compact disc)

Setup Instructions

It is highly recommended that you have two networked computers or be part of a larger network to perform many of the procedures.

1. Set up both computers according to the manufacturer's instructions.
2. The computers need to be networked together, either cabled together using a hub so that the two computers can communicate or as part of a larger network.
3. Each computer requires 450 MB of free disk space on drive C.
4. Set up Windows NT Server on each computer. For the Evaulation Editions included with this trainingkit, the CD-ROM key is 040-0048126. Microsoft technical support does not provide assistance with Evaulation Editions.

The first computer will be configured as a primary domain controller (PDC), and will be assigned the computer account name Server1 and the domain name, Domain1. This computer will act as a domain controller, a file and print server, and an application server in Domain1.

The second computer will act as a server and workstation for most of the procedures in this course. It is a member of Domain1 and is assigned the computer account name Server2.

Caution If your computers are part of a larger network, you *must* verify with your network administrator that the computer names, domain name, and IP address information in the following table do not conflict with network operations. If they do conflict, ask your network administrator to provide alternative values and use those values throughout all of the practices in this book.

Variable	Values used in this course
Computer name for first computer (PDC)	Server1
IP address for first computer	131.107.2.200
Computer name for second computer	Server2
IP address for second computer	131.107.2.211
IP address range	131.107.2.200 — 131.107.2.211
Subnet mask	255.255.255.0
Domain name	Domain1
Default gateway	131.107.2.1

Microsoft Internet Explorer

To use the course Web site from the course compact disc, you must first install Microsoft Internet Explorer 3.0.

▶ **To install Microsoft Internet Explorer 3.0**

1. On the course compact disc, open the Ie_setup folder, and then run Msie30.exe.

    A **Microsoft Internet Explorer 3.0** dialog box appears prompting if you want to install Microsoft Internet Explorer 3.0.

2. Click **Yes** to install Microsoft Internet Explorer 3.0.

    A **Microsoft Internet Explorer 3.0** dialog box appears indicating that files are being copied to a temporary folder on your hard disk.

3. Read the End-User License Agreement for Microsoft Internet Explorer, and then click **I Agree** to accept the terms of the agreement and continue the installation.

    A **Microsoft Internet Explorer Setup** dialog box appears indicating that files are being copied and Microsoft Internet Explorer is being set up on your computer.

4. When prompted to restart your computer, click **Yes**.

Windows NT 4.0 Service Pack

If you have not already installed the Windows NT 4.0 Service Pack 2, you should do so. This procedure shows you how to install the Service Pack from the course compact disc.

▶ **To install Windows NT 4.0 Service Pack 2**

1. Log on as Administrator.
2. Insert the course compact disc into the CD-ROM drive.

    Internet Explorer starts and the Internetworking with Microsoft TCP/IP on Microsoft Windows NT 4.0 start page opens.

    –Or–

    Start Windows NT Explorer, navigate to the drive containing the course compact disc, and then double-click the Open.htm file.

3. Click the start page icon.
4. Click **Course Materials**.
5. Click **Windows NT 4.0 Service Pack 2**.
6. Click **Service Pack**.

7. Scroll and click the **Install Service Pack** hyperlink.

   An Internet Explorer dialog box appears asking if you want to open the file or save it to disk.

8. Select **Open it**, and then click **OK**.

   This launches Spsetup.bat, which begins the upgrade process.

9. At the Welcome screen, click **Next**.

10. In the **Service Pack Setup** dialog box, select **Install the Service Pack**, and then click **Next**.

11. Select whether you want to create an Uninstall directory, and then click **Next**.

12. Click **Finish** for the Service Pack setup to complete.

    Setup inspects your computer and then begins to copy the Service Pack files.

    At the end of copying files a dialog box pops up, notifying you that Windows NT 4.0 has been updated.

13. Click **OK** to restart your computer.

Chapter and Appendix Overview

This self-paced training course combines notes, hands-on procedures, multimedia presentations, and review questions to teach you Microsoft TCP/IP on Microsoft Windows NT 4.0. It is designed to be completed from beginning to end, but you can choose a customized track and complete only the sections that interest you. If you choose the customized track option, see the "Before You Begin" section in each chapter. Any hands-on procedures that require preliminary work from preceding chapters refer to the appropriate chapters.

The self-paced training book is divided into the following chapters:

- The "About This Book" section contains a self-paced training overview and introduces the components of this training. Read this section thoroughly to get the greatest educational value from this self-paced training and to plan which lessons you will complete.
- Chapter 1, "Introduction to TCP/IP," provides an overview of TCP/IP and the Internet standards process.
- Chapter 2, "Installing and Configuring TCP/IP," covers installing and manually configuring an IP address, subnet mask, and default gateway. An overview is also provided on basic configuration testing procedures using Ipconfig, PING, and Microsoft Network Monitor.
- Chapter 3, "Architectural Overview of the TCP/IP Protocol Suite," describes the four layers of the TCP/IP protocol suite and explains how protocols at each layer work internally and in association with other protocols.

- Chapter 4, "IP Addressing," introduces IP addressing, including the differences between IP address classes, IP addressing guidelines, network components that require an IP address, and common addressing problems.

- Chapter 5, "Subnetting," teaches you fundamental subnetting and supernetting concepts and procedures, including: when subnetting is necessary, how to use a default subnet mask, how to define a custom subnet mask, and how to create a range of valid IP addresses for each subnet in an intranet from one IP address.

- Chapter 6, "Implementing IP Routing," provides an overview of IP routing concepts and terminology, and detailed information on implementing IP routing in Microsoft network environments.

- Chapter 7, "The Dynamic Host Configuration Protocol," addresses how the Dynamic Host Configuration Protocol (DHCP) centralizes and manages the allocation of TCP/IP configuration information by automatically assigning IP addresses to computers configured to use DHCP.

- Chapter 8, "NetBIOS over TCP/IP," provides an overview of NetBIOS name resolution concepts and methods.

- Chapter 9, "Windows Internet Name Service (WINS)," discusses how WINS reduces broadcast traffic with NetBIOS over TCP/IP, addresses database replication between WINS servers, and provides the knowledge and skills required to support WINS in an intranet.

- Chapter 10, "IP Internetwork Browsing and Domain Functions," discusses how browsing for NetBIOS resources occurs in a TCP/IP internetwork.

- Chapter 11, "Host Name Resolution," covers host name resolution concepts and issues.

- Chapter 12, "Domain Name System (DNS)," gives you an overview of the structure and components of the Domain Name System (DNS). You will learn about DNS database files, and how to resolve TCP/IP addresses.

- Chapter 13, "Implementing DNS," addresses installing and configuring DNS, and integrating DNS and WINS.

- Chapter 14, "Connectivity in Heterogeneous Environments," covers the options for using TCP/IP to operate in a heterogeneous environment.

- Chapter 15, "Implementing the Microsoft SNMP Services," provides an overview of the Simple Network Management Protocol (SNMP), including the functions performed by an SNMP management station and the Microsoft SNMP service (SNMP agent).

- Chapter 16, "Troubleshooting Microsoft TCP/IP," combines a review of important topics with troubleshooting guidelines. Topics include common TCP/IP-related problems, symptoms, possible causes, and the Windows NT and TCP/IP utilities useful in troubleshooting problems.

The Microsoft Certified Professional Program

The Microsoft Certified Professional (MCP) program provides the best method to prove your command of current Microsoft products and technologies. Microsoft, an industry leader in certification, is on the forefront of testing methodology. Our exams and corresponding certifications are developed to validate your mastery of critical competencies as you design and develop, or implement and support, solutions with Microsoft products and technologies. Computer professionals who become Microsoft certified are recognized as experts and are sought after industry-wide.

The Microsoft Certified Professional program offers four certifications, based on specific areas of technical expertise:

- *Microsoft Certified Product Specialists.* Demonstrated in-depth knowledge of at least one Microsoft operating system. Candidates may pass additional Microsoft certification exams to further qualify their skills with Microsoft BackOffice™ products, development tools, or desktop programs.

- *Microsoft Certified Systems Engineers.* Qualified to effectively plan, implement, maintain, and support information systems with Microsoft Windows® 95, Microsoft Windows NT, and the Microsoft BackOffice integrated family of server software.

- *Microsoft Certified Solution Developers.* Qualified to design and develop custom business solutions with Microsoft development tools, technologies, and platforms, including Microsoft Office and Microsoft BackOffice.

- *Microsoft Certified Trainers.* Instructionally and technically qualified to deliver Microsoft Official Curriculum through a Microsoft Authorized Technical Education Center (ATEC).

What Are the Requirements for Becoming a Microsoft Certified Professional?

The certification requirements differ for each certification and are specific to the products and job functions addressed by the certification.

To become a Microsoft Certified Professional, you must pass rigorous certification exams that provide a valid and reliable measure of technical proficiency and expertise. These exams are designed to test your expertise and ability to perform a role or task with a product, and are developed with the input of professionals in the industry. Questions in the exams reflect how Microsoft products are used in actual organizations, giving them "real-world" relevance.

- *Microsoft Certified Product Specialists* are required to pass one operating system exam. In addition, individuals seeking to validate their expertise in a program must pass the appropriate elective exam.
- *Microsoft Certified Systems Engineers* are required to pass a series of operating system exams and elective exams.
- *Microsoft Certified Solution Developers* are required to pass two core technology exams and two elective exams.
- *Microsoft Certified Trainers* are required to meet instructional and technical requirements specific to each Microsoft Official Curriculum course they are certified to deliver. In the United States and Canada, call Microsoft at (800) 636-7544 for more information on becoming a Microsoft Certified Trainer. Outside the United States and Canada, contact your local Microsoft subsidiary.

How to Order the Microsoft Roadmap to Education and Certification

It is easy to find the road that leads to your successful future—just use the Microsoft Roadmap to Education and Certification. The Roadmap contains everything you need to take advantage of Microsoft Education and Certification, including detailed descriptions of all of the most current Microsoft Official Curriculum courses; complete information about the Microsoft Certified Professional Program; Microsoft Certified Professional Assessment exams; and the Planning wizard, an easy-to-use tool to help you quickly map out a plan designed to meet your training goals. The Roadmap can be obtained from the following sources:

- Internet: ftp://ftp.microsoft.com/services/msedcert/e&cmap.zip
- CompuServe: Go MECFORUM, Library #2, e&cmap.zip
- TechNet: Search for "Roadmap" and install from the built-in setup link.
- Microsoft: Call us at (800) 636-7544 and ask for the Roadmap. Outside the United States and Canada, contact your local Microsoft subsidiary.

Microsoft Online Institute

The Microsoft Online Institute is an online interactive learning and information resource available on the World Wide Web (WWW) and the Microsoft Network (MSN™). The Microsoft Online Institute provides access to learning materials, instructor expertise, product information, developer articles, user forums, and other resources for Microsoft product and technology information.

Anyone with access to the Web or to an MSN account can access the Microsoft Online Institute to attend a class, join user forums, research library materials, purchase learning materials, or investigate other Microsoft Online Institute offerings.

To access the Microsoft Online Institute on the Web, connect to http://moli.microsoft.com. For more information about classes and other offerings, contact the Microsoft Online Institute by e-mail at moli_quest@msn.com.

ATECs

Authorized Technical Education Centers (ATECs) are the best source for instructor-led training that can help you prepare to become a Microsoft Certified Professional. The Microsoft ATEC program is a worldwide network of qualified technical training organizations that provide authorized delivery of Microsoft Official Curriculum courses by Microsoft Certified Trainers to computer professionals.

For a listing of ATEC locations in the United States and Canada, call the Microsoft fax service at (800) 727-3351. Outside the United States and Canada, call the fax service at (206) 635-2233.

CHAPTER 1

Introduction to TCP/IP

Lesson 1   TCP/IP Overview . . . 2

Lesson 2   TCP/IP Utilities . . . 6

Review . . . 8

About This Chapter
This chapter gives you an overview of TCP/IP. The lessons provide a brief history of TCP/IP, discuss the Internet standards process, and review TCP/IP utilities.

Before You Begin
To complete the lessons in this chapter, you must have the course compact disc to view the additional technical information.

Lesson 1: TCP/IP Overview

Transmission Control Protocol/Internet Protocol (TCP/IP) is an industry-standard suite of protocols designed for wide area networks (WANs). This lesson gives you an overview of TCP/IP concepts, terminology, and how the Internet Society creates Internet standards.

After this lesson, you will be able to:
- Define TCP/IP and describe its advantages on Microsoft Windows NT 4.0.
- Describe the Internet standards process.
- Explain the purpose of a Request for Comments (RFC) document.

Estimated lesson time: 15 minutes

TCP/IP History

TCP/IP originated with the packet-switching network experiments conducted by the U.S. Department of Defense Advanced Research Projects Agency (DARPA) in the late 1960s and early 1970s. There have been several important milestones during the history of TCP/IP:

1970	Advanced Research Agency Network (ARPANET) hosts started to use Network Control Protocol (NCP).
1972	The first Telnet specification, "Ad hoc Telnet Protocol," was submitted as RFC 318.
1973	RFC 454, "File Transfer Protocol," was introduced.
1974	The Transmission Control Program (TCP) was specified in detail.
1981	The IP standard was published in RFC 791.
1982	Defense Communications Agency (DCA) and ARPA established the Transmission Control Protocol (TCP) and Internet Protocol (IP) as the TCP/IP protocol suite.
1983	ARPANET switched from NCP to TCP/IP.
1984	Domain Name System (DNS) was introduced.

Microsoft TCP/IP

Microsoft TCP/IP on Windows NT 4.0 provides enterprise networking and connectivity on computers running Windows NT. Adding TCP/IP to a Windows NT configuration offers several advantages. The primary advantage of TCP/IP is its distinction as the most complete and accepted enterprise networking protocol available today. All modern operating systems offer TCP/IP support, and most large networks rely on TCP/IP for much of their network traffic. TCP/IP is also the protocol standard for the Internet.

Another advantage of using TCP/IP technology is the ability to connect dissimilar systems. Many standard connectivity utilities are available to access and transfer data between dissimilar systems. Several of these standard utilities such as File Transfer Protocol (FTP) and Telnet are included with Windows NT Server.

TCP/IP is also a scaleable client/server framework. Microsoft TCP/IP offers the Windows Sockets interface, which is a standard networking application programming interface (API) used for Windows-based applications. You can use the Windows Sockets interface to develop client/server applications that can run on Windows Sockets-compliant stacks. Windows Sockets applications can take advantage of other networking protocols such as Microsoft NWLink used in Novell NetWare networks.

The Internet Standards Process

An international group of volunteers called the Internet Society manages the TCP/IP suite of protocols. The standards for TCP/IP are published in a series of documents called Request for Comments, or RFCs. Though no organization owns the Internet or its technologies, several are responsible for its direction.

ISOC

The Internet Society (ISOC) was created in 1992 and is a global organization responsible for the internetworking technologies and applications of the Internet. Though its principal purpose is to encourage the development and availability of the Internet, it is in turn responsible for the further development of the standards and protocols that allow the Internet to function.

IAB

The Internet Architecture Board (IAB) is the technical advisory group of the Internet Society responsible for setting Internet standards, publishing RFCs, and overseeing the Internet standards process.

The IAB governs the Internet Engineering Task Force (IETF), Internet Assigned Numbers Authority (IANA), and Internet Research Task Force (IRTF). The IETF develops Internet standards and protocols, and will develop solutions to technical problems as they arise on the Internet. The IANA oversees and coordinates the assignment of every unique protocol identifier used on the Internet. The IRTF group is responsible for coordinating all TCP/IP-related research projects.

RFCs

The standards for TCP/IP are published in a series of documents called Request for Comments (RFCs). RFCs describe the internal workings of the Internet. TCP/IP standards are always published as RFCs, although not all RFCs specify standards.

TCP/IP standards are not developed by a committee, but rather by consensus. Any member of the Internet Society can submit a document for publication as an RFC. The documents are then reviewed by a technical expert, a task force, or the RFC editor, and then assigned a *classification*. The classification specifies whether a document is being considered as a standard. There are five classifications of RFCs.

Classification	Description
Required	This must be implemented on all TCP/IP-based hosts and gateways.
Recommended	It is encouraged that all TCP/IP-based hosts and gateways implement the RFC specifications. Recommended RFCs are usually implemented.
Elective	Implementation of this is optional. Its application has been agreed to, but never became widely used.
Limited use	This is not intended for general use.
Not recommended	This is not recommended for implementation.

If a document is being considered as a standard, it goes through stages of development, testing, and acceptance. Within the Internet standards process, these stages are formally labeled *maturity levels*. There are three maturity levels of Internet standards.

Maturity level	Description
Proposed Standard	A Proposed Standard specification is generally stable, has resolved known design choices, is believed to be well understood, has received significant community review, and appears to enjoy enough community interest to be considered valuable.
Draft Standard	A Draft Standard must be well understood and known to be quite stable, both in its semantics and as a basis for developing an implementation.
Internet Standard	The Internet Standard specification (which may simply be referred to as a Standard) is characterized by a high degree of technical maturity and by a generally held belief that the specified protocol or service provides significant benefit to the Internet community.

When a document is published, it is assigned an RFC number. The original RFC is never updated. If the RFC requires changes, a new RFC is published with a new number. Therefore, it is important to verify that you have the most recent RFC on a particular topic. The IAB publishes the *IAB Official Protocol Standard*, a quarterly memo that is useful in determining the current RFC for each protocol.

Note Several RFCs are referenced throughout this course. For a copy of the RFCs, see the *Course Materials* Web page on the course compact disc.

Summary

TCP/IP is an industry-standard suite of protocols designed for WANs. Adding TCP/IP to a Windows NT configuration offers several advantages. The standards for TCP/IP are published in a series of documents called Request for Comments, or RFCs.

Lesson 2: TCP/IP Utilities

Windows NT supplies a number of application utilities that build on the lower-level protocols. This lesson introduces you to these utilities. You learn more about, and use several of, these utilities throughout this course.

After this lesson, you will be able to:
- Describe the TCP/IP utilities included with Windows NT.

Estimated lesson time: 5 minutes

Microsoft TCP/IP utilities work with TCP/IP protocols to provide access to foreign hosts and the TCP/IP-based Internet. On Windows NT, all utilities are implemented as client software except for FTP, which is implemented as both client and server software.

Data Transfer Utilities

Windows NT 4.0 provides the utilities for connecting to other TCP/IP-based hosts. The most commonly used data transfer utility is FTP. FTP provides bidirectional file transfers between two TCP/IP hosts, where one is running FTP server software.

Other utilities used for transferring data include Trivial File Transfer Protocol (TFTP) and Remote Copy Protocol (RCP). TFTP, like FTP, provides bidirectional file transfers between two TCP/IP hosts where one is running TFTP server software. RCP copies files between a computer running Windows NT and a UNIX host.

Remote Execution Utilities

Windows NT also provides the utilities for connecting to and remotely operating other TCP/IP-based hosts. The most frequently used remote execution utility is Telnet, which provides terminal emulation to a TCP/IP host running Telnet server software. Other utilities include Remote Shell (RSH), which runs commands on a UNIX host, and Remote Execution (REXEC), which runs a process on a remote computer.

Printing Utilities

Two TCP/IP utilities provide the ability to print and obtain print status on a TCP/IP printer. Line Printer Remote (LPR) prints a file to a host running the Line Printing Daemon (LPD) service. Line Printer Queue (LPQ) obtains status of a print queue on a host running the LPD service.

Note These utilities require software on both the client and server sides. Microsoft provides FTP and LPD server applications. You learn more about these utilities in Chapter 14, "Connectivity in Heterogeneous Environments."

Diagnostics Utilities

Windows NT 4.0 provides several utilities for diagnosing TCP/IP-related problems. You will use several of these utilities throughout this course.

Diagnostics utility	Function
Packet InterNet Groper (PING)	Verifies that TCP/IP is configured correctly and that another host is available.
IPCONFIG	Verifies a TCP/IP configuration, including DHCP, DNS, and WINS server addresses.
Finger	Retrieves system information from a remote computer that supports the TCP/IP Finger service.
NSLOOKUP	Examines entries in the DNS database that pertain to a particular host or domain.
HOSTNAME	Returns the local computer's host name for authentication.
NETSTAT	Displays protocol statistics and the current state of TCP/IP connections.
NBTSTAT	Checks the state of current NetBIOS over TCP/IP connections, updates the LMHOSTS cache, or determines your registered name and scope ID.
Route	Views or modifies the local routing table.
Tracert	Verifies the route used from the local host to a remote host.
Address Resolution Protocol (ARP)	Displays a cache of locally resolved IP addresses to Media Access Control (MAC) addresses.

Summary

Windows NT supplies a number of application utilities that can help you connect to other TCP/IP-based hosts or help you troubleshoot TCP/IP connection problems.

Review

The following questions are intended to reinforce key information presented in this chapter. If you are unable to answer a question, review the appropriate lesson and then try the question again.

1. What is TCP/IP?

   _____

   _____

2. Are all TCP/IP standards published as RFCs? Do all RFCs specify standards?

   _____

   _____

For More Information

- The *Course Materials* Web page on the course compact disc contains technical information on TCP/IP.
- Read the white paper titled *Microsoft Windows NT 3.5/3.51/4.0: TCP/IP Implementation Details TCP/IP Protocol Stack and Services, Version 2.0.*
- Read *Internetworking with TCP/IP Volume I*, by Douglas E. Comer.

CHAPTER 2

Installing and Configuring TCP/IP

Lesson 1 Installing and Configuring Microsoft TCP/IP . . . 10

Lesson 2 Testing TCP/IP with Ipconfig and PING . . . 15

Lesson 3 Microsoft Network Monitor . . . 18

Review . . . 22

About This Chapter

This chapter provides the procedures for installing and manually configuring an IP address, subnet mask, and default gateway. During the lessons you install and manually configure Microsoft TCP/IP. The lessons also give you an overview of basic configuration testing procedures using Ipconfig, PING, and Microsoft Network Monitor.

Before You Begin

To complete the lessons in this chapter, you must set up your computer(s) as described in the Setup Instructions section in About This Book.

Lesson 1: Installing and Configuring Microsoft TCP/IP

This lesson describes the procedure for installing Microsoft TCP/IP. Follow this procedure if you have not previously installed the TCP/IP network protocol on the computer(s) you are using to perform the practice procedures during this course.

After this lesson, you will be able to:
- Install and configure Microsoft TCP/IP.

Estimated lesson time: 20 minutes

TCP/IP installs several system and name resolution files to your Windows NT System32\Drivers and System32\Drivers\Etc directories. TCP/IP uses the name resolution files shown in the following table. You learn more about these files later in the course.

Configuration file	Description
HOSTS	Provides name resolution for host names to IP addresses.
LMHOSTS	Provides name resolution for NetBIOS names to IP addresses.
NETWORKS	Provides name resolution for network names to IP network IDs.
PROTOCOL	Provides resolution from a protocol name to an RFC-defined protocol number. The protocol number is a field in the IP header that identifies to which upper-layer protocol (such as TCP or UDP) the IP data should be passed.
SERVICES	Provides resolution from a service name to a port number and protocol name. The port number is a field in the TCP or UDP header that identifies the TCP or UDP process.

Configuration Parameters

TCP/IP uses an IP address, subnet mask, and default gateway to communicate with hosts. TCP/IP hosts running on a WAN require all three configuration parameters. Each network adapter card in the computer that uses TCP/IP requires these parameters.

IP Address

An IP address is a logical 32-bit address that identifies a TCP/IP host. Each IP address has two parts: the network ID and the host ID. The network ID identifies all hosts that are on the same physical network. The host ID identifies a host on the network. Each computer running TCP/IP requires a unique IP address. An example of an IP address is 131.107.2.200.

Chapter 4, "IP Addressing," covers the essential details of assigning IP addresses.

Subnet Mask

A subnet mask blocks out a portion of the IP address so that TCP/IP can distinguish the network ID from the host ID. When TCP/IP hosts try to communicate, they use the subnet mask to determine whether the destination host is on a local or remote network. An example of a subnet mask is 255.255.255.0. Chapter 5, "Subnetting," teaches you how to assign a valid subnet mask.

Default Gateway

To communicate with a host on another network, you must configure an IP address for the default gateway. TCP/IP sends packets that are destined for remote networks to the default gateway, but only if no other route is configured on the local host to the destination network. If you have not configured a default gateway, communication may be limited to the local network. A sample default gateway is 131.107.2.1.

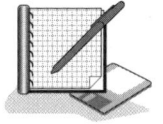

Practice

You install and configure TCP/IP through the Network program in Control Panel. In this procedure, you first view the network protocols currently installed on your machine. If TCP/IP is not present, you continue with the installation.

Note If you have two networked computers available to you, perform this procedure on both computers.

▶ **To view the network protocols on your machine**

1. Log on as Administrator.
2. Click the **Start** button, point to **Settings**, and then click **Control Panel**.

   Control Panel appears.
3. Double-click the Network icon.

   The **Network** dialog box appears.
4. Click the **Protocols** tab.

   If the TCP/IP protocol does not appear in the list of network protocols, complete the following procedure.

▶ **To install Microsoft TCP/IP on Windows NT 4.0**

1. On the **Protocols** tab, click **Add**.

    The **Select Network Protocol** dialog box appears.

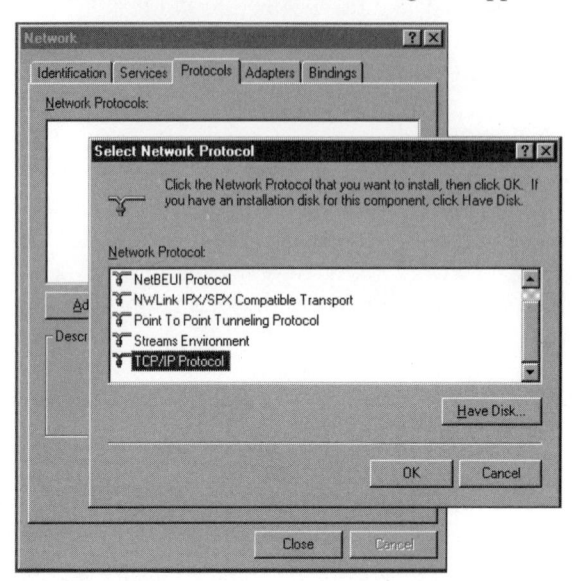

2. Select **TCP/IP Protocol**, and then click **OK**.

    The **DHCP Server** dialog box appears.

    Note You manually configure TCP/IP parameters later during this procedure. Chapter 7, "The Dynamic Host Configuration Protocol," provides details about the DHCP service.

3. Click **No**.

    The **Windows NT Setup** dialog box appears, requesting the full path to the Windows NT distribution files.

4. Type the complete path to the Windows NT Server source files.
5. Click **Continue**.

   Setup installs the files from the path you provide.
6. Click **Close**.

   The **Microsoft TCP/IP Properties** dialog box appears.
7. If a DHCP server is not available, you can specify an IP address, a subnet mask, and a default gateway to manually configure TCP/IP. If you need to connect to hosts beyond the local network, assign a default gateway. Type your TCP/IP configuration parameters as described in the following table.

Caution If your computer(s) are part of a larger network, you *must* verify with your network administrator that the following computer names, domain name, and IP address information do not conflict with network operations. If they do conflict, ask your network administrator to provide alternative values and use those values throughout all of the practices in this course.

Parameter	Description
IP address	An IP address is required. If you are configuring two networked computers for the procedures, the IP address for Server1 should be 131.107.2.200, and the IP address for Server2 should be 131.107.2.211.
Subnet mask	A subnet mask is required. If configuring your computers for the procedures, the subnet mask is 255.255.255.0.
Default gateway	The default gateway is an optional parameter (unless you connect with hosts on a remote network). If you are configuring your computers for the procedures, the default gateway is 131.107.2.1.

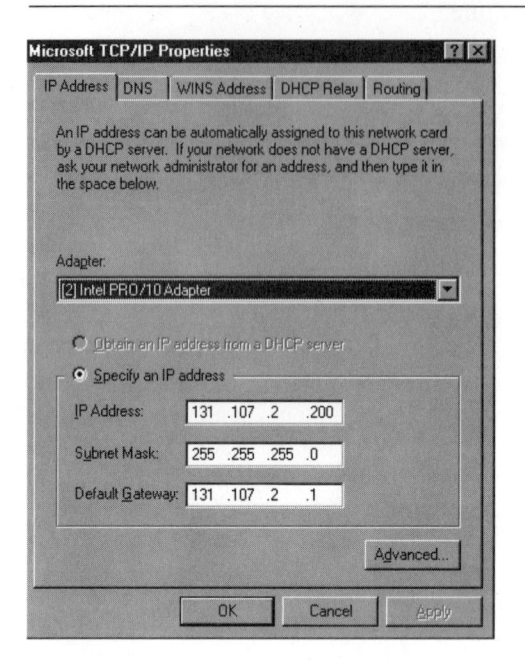

Note IP communications can fail if multiple devices use the same IP address.

[Screenshot: Microsoft TCP/IP Properties dialog, IP Address tab, showing Adapter [2] Intel PRO/10 Adapter, Specify an IP address selected, IP Address 131.107.2.200, Subnet Mask 255.255.255.0, Default Gateway 131.107.2.1]

8. Click **OK**.

   A **Network Settings Change** dialog box appears, prompting you to restart your computer.

9. Click **Yes**.

   The computer restarts with your new IP address settings.

Summary

During the TCP/IP installation, several system and name resolution files are copied to your Windows NT directories. If you configure TCP/IP manually, you must assign an IP address and a subnet mask.

Lesson 2: Testing TCP/IP with Ipconfig and PING

After you install TCP/IP, it is a good idea to verify and test the configuration and any connections to other TCP/IP hosts and networks. This lesson explains basic TCP/IP configuration testing procedures using Ipconfig and PING utilities.

After this lesson, you will be able to:
- Verify TCP/IP configuration parameters with the Ipconfig utility.
- Test a TCP/IP configuration and IP connection with the PING utility.

Estimated lesson time: 10 minutes

The Ipconfig Utility

You can use the Ipconfig utility to verify the TCP/IP configuration parameters on a host, including the IP address, subnet mask, and default gateway. This is useful in determining whether the configuration is initialized or if a duplicate IP address is configured. The command syntax is:

ipconfig

If a configuration has initialized, the configured IP address, subnet mask, and default gateway appear. If a duplicate address is configured, the IP address appears as configured, but the subnet mask appears as 0.0.0.0.

Note The WINIPCFG utility, included in Microsoft Windows 95, also verifies the TCP/IP configuration.

The PING Utility

After you verify the configuration with the Ipconfig utility, you can use the Packet InterNet Groper (PING) utility to test connectivity. The PING utility is a diagnostic tool that tests TCP/IP configurations and diagnoses connection failures. PING uses the Internet Control Message Protocol (ICMP) *echo request* and *echo reply* messages to determine whether a particular TCP/IP host is available and functional. The command syntax is:

ping *IP_address*

If PING is successful, a message similar to the following appears:

```
Pinging IP_address with 32 bytes of data:
Reply from IP_address: bytes= x time<10ms TTL= x
Reply from IP_address: bytes= x time<10ms TTL= x
Reply from IP_address: bytes= x time<10ms TTL= x
Reply from IP_address: bytes= x time<10ms TTL= x
```

Practice

In this procedure, you use the Ipconfig utility to view an IP configuration and the PING utility to test your workstation configuration and connections to another TCP/IP host.

Note You must have a second networked computer to perform part of this procedure. Review the Setup Instructions section of About This Book before you begin. Perform this procedure from the computer you designated as Server1.

▶ **To verify a computer's configuration and for test router connections**

1. Use the Ipconfig utility to verify that your TCP/IP configuration has initialized. At a command prompt, type:

   ipconfig

   If the configuration is correctly initialized, the IP address, subnet mask, and default gateway (if configured) values display.

2. Ping the loopback address to verify that TCP/IP is installed and loaded correctly. At a command prompt, type:

   ping 127.0.0.1

   and then press ENTER.

   Note The loopback address (127.0.0.1) uses loopback drivers to reroute outgoing packets back to the source computer. These loopback drivers bypass the network adapter card completely. If you are using the procedures on a stand-alone computer, you can use the loopback address to perform many of the TCP/IP procedures contained in this course.

3. Ping the IP address of your computer to verify that you added it correctly. Type:

   ping 131.107.2.200

4. Ping the IP address of your second computer to verify that you can communicate with a host on the local network. Type:

   ping 131.107.2.211

5. If a remote host is available on your configuration, ping the IP address of the remote host to verify that you can communicate through a router. Type:

   ping *IP_address_of_remote_host*

Tips If Ipconfig verifies that TCP/IP is properly installed and using the correct IP address, you may not need to perform steps 2 and 3.

If you start with step 5 and can ping successfully, then steps 2 through 4 are successful by default.

If the address is incorrect, or you have not properly configured TCP/IP, PING times out.

Summary

The Ipconfig and the PING utilities can help you verify and test your configuration after you install TCP/IP. Ipconfig verifies the IP address, subnet mask, and default gateway. The PING utility tests connectivity and can help you diagnose connection failures.

Lesson 3: Microsoft Network Monitor

Microsoft Network Monitor is a tool that simplifies the task of troubleshooting complex network problems. This lesson gives you an overview of Network Monitor. You use Network Monitor to view packets in Chapter 3, "Architectural Overview of the TCP/IP Protocol Suite."

After this lesson, you will be able to:
- Install and configure Microsoft Network Monitor.

Estimated lesson time: 15 minutes

Microsoft Network Monitor troubleshoots network problems by monitoring and capturing network traffic for analysis. Network Monitor works by configuring the network adapter card to capture all incoming and outgoing packets.

You can define capture filters so that you save only specific frames for analysis. You can define filters based on source and destination Media Access Control addresses, source and destination protocol addresses, and pattern matches. Once Network Monitor captures a packet, you can use display filtering to further analyze a problem. Once Network Monitor captures and filters a packet, it interprets trace data and presents a real-time report.

Note The version of Network Monitor included with Windows NT is limited to only capturing data for the local computer. The full version of Network Monitor is available with Microsoft Systems Management Server, a centralized management for distributed systems.

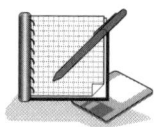

Practice

In this procedure you will install Network Monitor from the Services tab. This will prepare your computer(s) for viewing packets in Chapter 3, "Architectural Overview of the TCP/IP Protocol Suite."

▶ **To install Network Monitor**

1. Log on as Administrator.
2. Double-click the Network icon in Control Panel, and then click the **Services** tab.

Chapter 2 Installing and Configuring TCP/IP 19

3. Click **Add**.

   The **Select Network Service** dialog box appears.

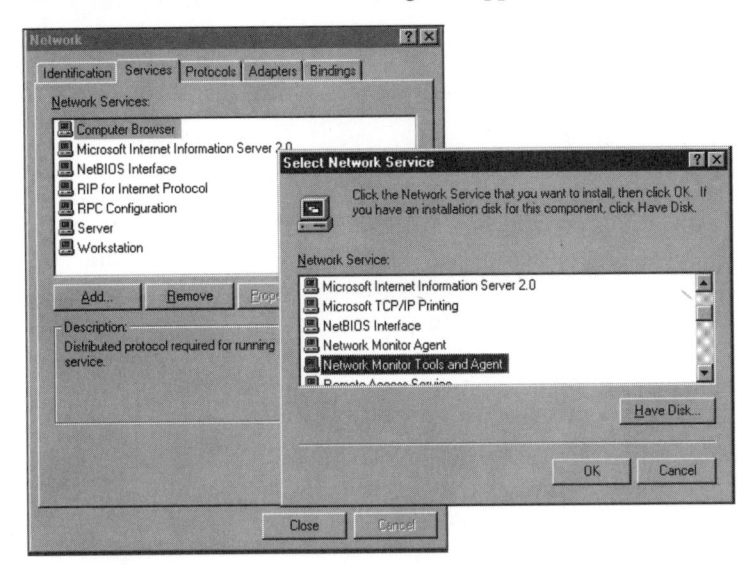

4. Click **Network Monitor Tools and Agent** in the **Network Service** list, and then click **OK**.

   Windows NT Setup displays a dialog box that asks for the full path to the Windows NT distribution files.

5. Type the path to the source files, and then click **Continue**.

6. In the **Network** dialog box, click **Close**.

7. Click **Yes** when prompted to restart your computer.

Analyzing Network Traffic

To analyze network traffic with Network Monitor, you need to start the capture process, generate the network traffic you are observing, then stop the capture and view the data. To use Network Monitor, click the **Start** button, point to **Programs**, point to **Administrative Tools**, and then click **Network Monitor**.

Starting a Capture

Network Monitor uses many windows for displaying different data. One of the primary windows is the Capture window. When this window has the focus, the toolbar shows you options to start, pause, stop, or stop and view captured data. On the **Capture** menu, click **Start** to start a capture. While the capture process is running, Network Monitor displays statistical information in the Capture window.

Stopping a Capture

After you have generated the network traffic you are analyzing, on the **Capture** menu, click **Stop** to stop the capture. You can then create another capture or display the current capture data. Then, on the **Capture** menu, click **Stop and View** to stop a capture and immediately open it for viewing.

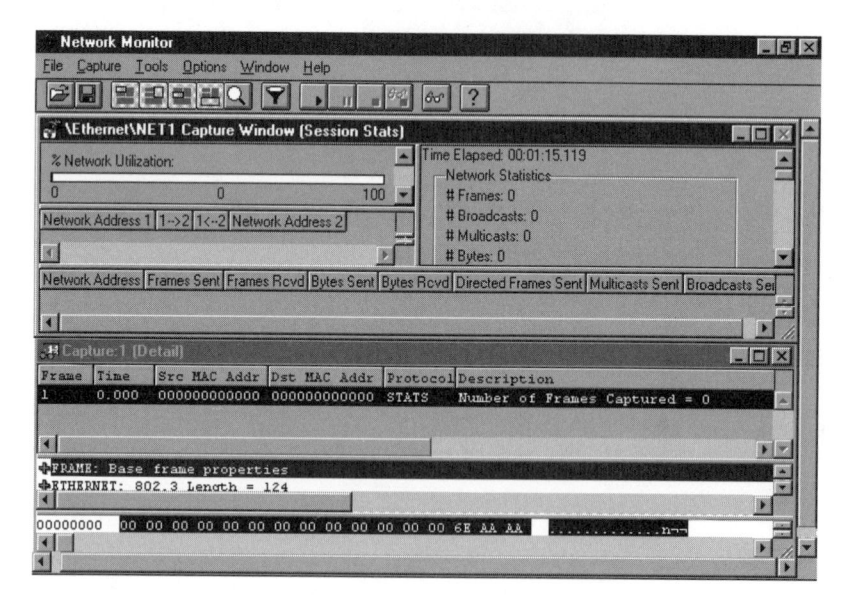

Viewing the Data

When opening a capture to view, a Summary window appears, showing each frame capture. The Summary window contains a frame number, time of frame reception, and source and destination addresses. It also contains the highest-layer protocol used in the frame and a description of the frame.

For more detailed information on a specific frame, on the **Window** menu, click **Zoom**. In the zoom view you get two additional windows, the **Detail** frame and **Hexadecimal** frame. The **Detail** frame shows the protocol information in detail. The **Hexadecimal** frame shows the raw bytes in the frame.

Note You use Network Monitor to view packets in Chapter 3, "Architectural Overview of the TCP/IP Protocol Suite."

Summary

Network Monitor can help you troubleshoot difficult network problems. The three steps to using Network Monitor are starting the capture process, generating network traffic, and then stopping the capture to review the data.

Review

The following questions are intended to reinforce key information presented in this chapter. If you are unable to answer a question, review the appropriate lesson and then try the question again.

1. What TCP/IP utilities are used to verify and test a TCP/IP configuration?

   _____

2. What parameters are required on a Windows NT-based computer running TCP/IP on a WAN?

   _____

   _____

For More Information

- Read the Microsoft Network Monitor product documentation.

CHAPTER 3

Architectural Overview of the TCP/IP Protocol Suite

Lesson 1 The Microsoft TCP/IP Protocol Suite . . . 25

Lesson 2 ARP . . . 29

Lesson 3 ICMP and IGMP . . . 40

Lesson 4 IP . . . 42

Lesson 5 TCP . . . 46

Lesson 6 UDP . . . 51

Review . . . 53

About This Chapter

This chapter describes the four layers of the TCP/IP protocol suite and explains in detail how protocols at each layer work with other protocols. This chapter contains two multimedia presentations that acquaint you with TCP/IP. During the lessons you view and modify the Address Resolution Protocol (ARP) cache, and view packets with Network Monitor.

Before You Begin

To complete the lessons in this chapter, you must have:

- Installed Microsoft Windows NT Server 4.0 with the TCP/IP network protocol.
- Installed the Network Monitor Tools and Agent Network service (covered in Chapter 2, "Installing TCP/IP").
- The course compact disc to view the multimedia presentations.
- A sound card with headphones or speakers (optional).

Lesson 1: The Microsoft TCP/IP Protocol Suite

This lesson describes the four layers of the TCP/IP protocol suite and explains how protocols at each layer work internally and in association with other protocols. At the beginning of the lesson, you view a multimedia presentation covering the essentials of TCP/IP.

After this lesson, you will be able to:
- Describe how the TCP/IP protocol suite maps to a four-layer model.
- Describe the network interface layer protocols that Internet Protocol (IP) supports.

Estimated lesson time: 30 minutes

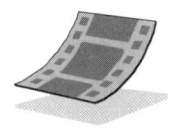

Multimedia Presentation: Overview of the TCP/IP Protocol Suite

This 15-minute multimedia presentation provides an overview of the TCP/IP protocol suite and explains how the protocols in the suite work internally and with other protocols. It describes how the TCP/IP protocol suite maps to a four-layer model. The information in this presentation applies to Microsoft TCP/IP and most other implementations of TCP/IP.

▶ **To start the Overview of the TCP/IP Protocol Suite multimedia presentation**

1. Insert the course compact disc into the CD-ROM drive.

   Microsoft Internet Explorer starts and The Internetworking with Microsoft TCP/IP on Microsoft Windows NT 4.0 start page opens.

   –Or–

   Start Windows NT Explorer, navigate to the drive containing the course compact disc, and then double-click the Open.htm file.

2. Click the start page icon.
3. Click **Course Materials**.
4. Click **Multimedia Presentations**.
5. Click **Overview of the TCP/IP Protocol Suite**.

   An Internet Explorer dialog box appears asking if you want to open the file or save it to disk.

6. Select **Open it**, and then click **OK**.
7. Click **Yes** if a security box appears.

   The multimedia presentation begins. Click the **Text On** button if you do not have a sound card and speakers.

The Four-Layer Model

TCP/IP protocols follow a four-layer conceptual model: Application, Transport, Internet, and Network Interface. The Microsoft TCP/IP core protocols provide a set of standards for how computers communicate and how networks are interconnected.

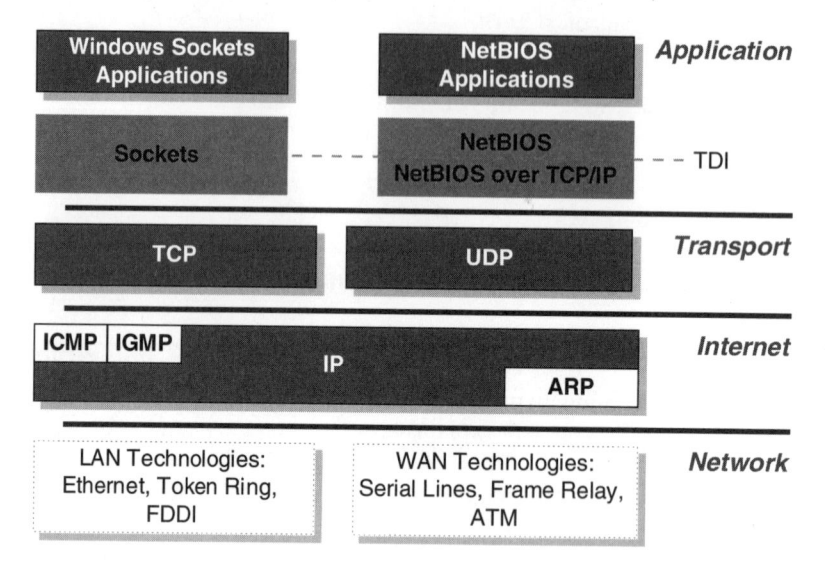

Application		
Windows Sockets Applications	NetBIOS Applications	*Application*
Sockets	NetBIOS / NetBIOS over TCP/IP --- TDI	
TCP	UDP	*Transport*
ICMP / IGMP / IP / ARP		*Internet*
LAN Technologies: Ethernet, Token Ring, FDDI	WAN Technologies: Serial Lines, Frame Relay, ATM	*Network*

Network Interface Layer

At the base of the model is the Network Interface layer. This layer is responsible for sending and receiving frames, which are packets of information transmitted on a network as a single unit. The Network Interface layer puts frames on the network, and pulls frames off the network.

Internet Layer

Internet protocols encapsulate packets into Internet datagrams and run all of the necessary routing algorithms. The four Internet protocols are Internet Protocol (IP), Address Resolution Protocol (ARP), Internet Control Message Protocol (ICMP), and Internet Group Management Protocol (IGMP).

- IP is primarily responsible for addressing and routing packets between hosts and networks.
- ARP obtains hardware addresses of hosts located on the same physical network.
- ICMP sends messages and reports errors regarding the delivery of a packet.
- IGMP is used by IP hosts to report host group memberships to local multicast routers.

Transport Layer

Transport protocols provide communication sessions between computers. The two Transport protocols are Transmission Control Protocol and User Datagram Protocol (UDP). The transport protocol used depends upon the preferred method of data delivery.

TCP provides connection-oriented, reliable communications for applications that typically transfer large amounts of data at one time. It is also used for applications that require an acknowledgment for data received.

UDP provides connectionless communications and does not guarantee to deliver packets. Applications that use UDP typically transfer small amounts of data at one time. Reliable delivery of data is the responsibility of the application.

Application Layer

At the top of the TCP/IP model is the Application layer. This layer is where applications gain access to the network. There are many standard TCP/IP utilities and services at the Application layer such as FTP, Telnet, SNMP, and DNS.

Microsoft TCP/IP provides two interfaces for network applications to use the services of the TCP/IP protocol stack. The first, called Windows Sockets, provides a standard application programming interface (API) under Microsoft Windows for transport protocols such as TCP/IP and IPX.

The second interface for network applications is NetBIOS. This interface provides a standard interface to protocols that support the NetBIOS naming and messaging services, such as TCP/IP and NetBEUI.

Network Interface Technologies

IP uses the network device interface specification (NDIS) to submit frames to the network interface layer. IP supports LAN and WAN interface technologies.

LAN technologies supported by TCP/IP include Ethernet (Ethernet II and 802.3), Token Ring, ArcNet and Metropolitan Area Network (MAN) technologies such as fiber distributed data interface (FDDI).

Using TCP/IP in a WAN environment may require the Windows NT Remote Access Service (RAS) or additional hardware. There are two major categories of WAN technologies supported by TCP/IP: serial lines and packet-switched networks. Serial lines include dial-up analog, digital lines, and leased lines. Packet-switched networks include X.25, frame relay, and asynchronous transfer mode (ATM).

Serial Line Protocols

TCP/IP is typically transported across a serial line using either the Serial Line Internet Protocol (SLIP) or the Point-to-Point Protocol (PPP).

SLIP is an industry standard developed in the early 1980s to support TCP/IP networking over low-speed serial interfaces. With the Windows NT RAS, computers running Windows NT can use TCP/IP and SLIP to communicate with remote hosts.

Note Windows NT supports only SLIP client functionality, not SLIP server functionality. Windows NT RAS servers do not accept SLIP client connections.

The Point-to-Point Protocol (PPP) was designed as an enhancement to the original SLIP specification. PPP is a data-link protocol that provides a standard method of sending network packets over a point-to-point link. Because PPP provides greater security, configuration handling, and error detection than SLIP, it is the recommended protocol for serial line communication.

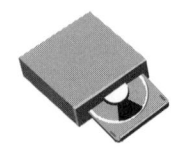

Note The transmission of IP over serial lines is described in RFC 1055. The Point-to-Point Protocol is defined in RFCs 1547 and 1661. For copies of these RFCs, see the *Course Materials* Web page on the course compact disc.

Summary

TCP/IP protocols use a four-layer conceptual model: Application, Transport, Internet, and Network Interface. IP supports both LAN and WAN interface technologies.

Lesson 2: ARP

Hosts must know the hardware address of other hosts to communicate on a network. Address resolution is the process of mapping a host's IP address to its hardware address. The Address Resolution Protocol (ARP), part of the TCP/IP Internet layer, obtains hardware addresses of hosts located on the same physical network.

After this lesson, you will be able to:
- Explain how ARP resolves an IP address to a hardware address.
- Explain how ARP adds and deletes entries to cache.
- View and modify the ARP cache.

Estimated lesson time: 45 minutes

ARP is responsible for obtaining hardware addresses of TCP/IP hosts on broadcast-based networks. ARP uses a local broadcast of the destination IP address to acquire the hardware address of the destination host or gateway.

Once ARP obtains the hardware address, both the IP address and hardware address are stored as one entry in the ARP cache. ARP always checks the ARP cache for an IP address and hardware address mapping before initiating an ARP request broadcast.

Reverse address resolution is the process of mapping a host's hardware address to its IP address. Microsoft TCP/IP does not support reverse address resolution.

Note ARP is defined in RFC 826. For a copy of this RFC, see the *Course Materials* Web page on the course compact disc.

Resolving a Local IP Address

Before communication between two hosts can occur, the IP address of each host must be resolved to the host's hardware address. The address resolution process includes an ARP request and an ARP reply, as the following example illustrates:

1. An ARP request initiates any time a host tries to communicate with another host. When IP determines that the IP address is for the local network, the source host checks its own ARP cache for the hardware address of the destination host.

2. If it finds no mapping, ARP builds a request with the question "Who is this IP address, and what is your hardware address?" The source host's IP address and hardware address are included in the request. The ARP request is sent as a broadcast so that all local hosts can receive and process it.

3. Each host on the local network receives the broadcast and checks for a match to its own IP address. If a host does not find a match, it ignores the request.

4. The destination host determines that the IP address in the request matches its own IP address and sends an ARP reply directly to the source host with its hardware address. It then updates its ARP cache with the IP address/hardware address mapping of the source host. Communication is established when the source host receives the reply.

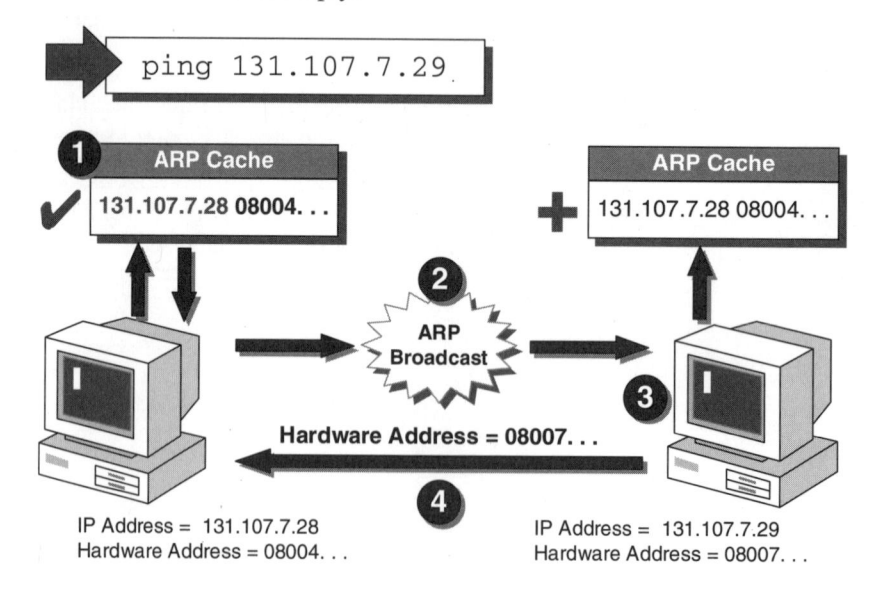

Resolving a Remote IP Address

ARP also allows two hosts on different networks to communicate. In this situation, the ARP broadcast is for the default gateway of the source host and not the IP address of the destination host.

If the destination IP address belongs to a host on a remote network, the ARP broadcast is for a router that can forward datagrams to the destination host's network, as the following example illustrates:

1. When a request for communications initiates, the destination IP address is identified as a remote address.

    The source host checks the local routing table for a route to the destination host or network. If it finds no mapping, the source host determines the IP address of the default gateway. The source host then checks the ARP cache for the IP address/hardware address mapping of the specified gateway.

2. If it finds no mapping for the specified gateway, an ARP request is broadcast for the gateway's address rather than the address of the destination host.

    The router responds to the source host's ARP request with its hardware address. The source host then sends the data packet to the router to deliver to the destination host's network, and ultimately the destination host.

3. At the router, IP determines whether the destination IP address is local or remote. If it is local, the router uses ARP (either cache or broadcast) to obtain its hardware address. If it is remote, the router checks its routing table for a specified gateway, and then uses ARP (either cache or broadcast) to obtain the gateway's hardware address. The packet is sent directly to the next destination host.

4. After the destination host receives the request, it formulates an ICMP echo reply. Because the source host is on a remote network, the local routing table is checked for a specified gateway to the source host's network. When it finds a gateway, ARP obtains its hardware address.

5. If the specified gateway's hardware address is not in the ARP cache, an ARP broadcast obtains it. Once it obtains the hardware address, the ICMP echo reply is sent to the router to be routed to the source host.

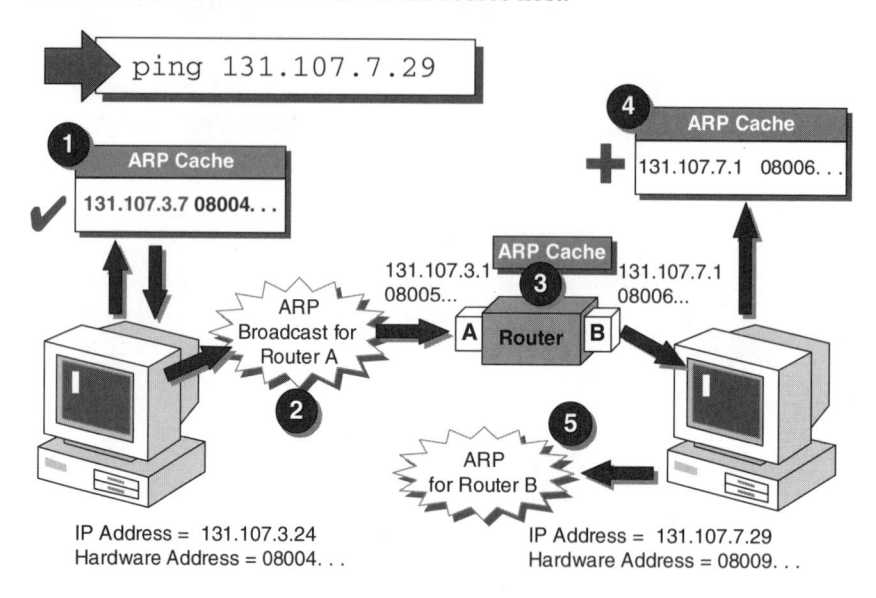

The ARP Cache

To minimize the number of broadcasts, ARP maintains address mappings in cache for future use. The ARP cache maintains both dynamic and static entries. Dynamic entries are added and deleted automatically. Static entries remain in cache until the computer is restarted.

Additionally, the ARP cache always maintains the hardware broadcast address (FFFFFFFFFFFF) for the local subnet as a permanent entry. This entry allows a host to accept ARP broadcasts. The address does not appear when you view the cache.

Each ARP cache entry has a potential lifetime of 10 minutes. As each entry is added to the ARP cache, it is timestamped. If it is not used within two minutes, the entry is deleted; otherwise, if it is used, it is deleted after 10 minutes. If the ARP cache reaches its maximum capacity before entries expire, the oldest entry is deleted so that a new entry can be added.

Note There is a separate ARP cache for each IP address on a computer running Windows NT.

ARP Cache Aging

The default for ARP cache time-outs is two minutes on unused entries and 10 minutes on used entries. Adding the **ARPCacheLife** parameter to the registry and setting a value in seconds overrides both default values.

Note In some TCP/IP implementations, when an entry is reused, it is given a new timestamp, adding another 10 minutes to its life. Windows NT 4.0 has not implemented this feature.

Adding Static (Permanent) Entries

Adding a static ARP entry decreases the number of ARP requests for frequently accessed hosts. Under Windows NT 4.0, if a static entry is added to the ARP cache, it is available until one of the following conditions is met:

- The computer restarts.
- The entry is deleted manually with **arp-d**.
- An ARP broadcast is received indicating a different hardware address. In this case, the entry changes from static to dynamic, and the newly received hardware address replaces the current hardware address.

Note If you manually insert an entry into the ARP cache, the hardware address must contain hyphens.

ARP Packet Structure

Although created for IP address resolution, the ARP packet structure is adaptable to other types of address resolution. ARP has an EtherType of 0x08-06. The fields of the ARP structure are as shown in the following table.

Field	Function
Hardware Type	The type of hardware (Network Access Layer) being used.
Protocol Type	The protocol being used for the resolution process using the EtherType value. Hence, the Protocol Type for IP is 0x08–00.
Hardware Address Length	Length in bytes of the hardware address. For Ethernet and Token Ring, the length is 6 bytes.
Protocol Address Length	Length in bytes of the protocol address. For IP, the length is 4 bytes.
Operation (Opcode)	The operation field specifies the operation being performed.
Sender's Hardware Address	The hardware address of the sender (the ARP requester).
Sender's Protocol Address	The protocol address of the sender (the ARP requester).
Target's Hardware Address	The hardware address of the target (the ARP responder).
Target's Protocol Address	The protocol address of the target (the ARP responder).

Practice

You can use Network Monitor to capture and display packets. In this procedure, you capture and display ARP packets. You then examine ARP request and ARP reply details.

Note To complete this procedure, you need two networked computers as described in About This Book. Perform the procedure from the computer acting as Server1.

▶ **To start Network Monitor**

1. Log on as Administrator.
2. Click the **Start** button, point to **Programs**, point to **Administrative Tools**, and then click **Network Monitor**.

    The Network Monitor window appears.
3. Maximize the Network Monitor window.
4. Maximize the Capture window.

To capture network data

1. On the **Capture** menu, click **Start**.

   This starts the data capture process. Network Monitor allocates buffer space for network data and begins capturing frames.

2. At a command prompt, type:

   ping 131.107.2.211

To stop the network data capture

1. Switch back to **Network Monitor**.
2. On the **Capture** menu in **Network Monitor**, click **Stop**.

   Network Monitor stops capturing frames and displays four panes: **Graph**, **Total Stats**, **Session Stats**, and **Station Stats**.

To view captured data

- On the **Capture** menu, click **Display Captured Data**.

   The Network Monitor Capture Summary window appears, displaying the summary record of all frames captured.

In the following procedure, you change the color of all frames that use ARP. This is useful when viewing frames for a particular protocol.

To highlight captured data

1. On the **Display** menu, click **Colors**.

   The **Protocol Colors** dialog box appears.

2. Under **Name**, select **ARP_RARP**.
3. Under **Colors**, set **Foreground** to **Red**, and then click **OK**.

   The Network Monitor Capture Summary window appears, displaying all ARP frames in red.

To view the ARP request frame details

1. Under **Description**, double-click the **ARP: Request**.

   Three separate windows appear. The top window displays the frame summary, the middle window displays the selected frame details, and the bottom window displays the selected frame details in hexadecimal notation.

2. In the Detail window, click **Frame** with a plus sign (**+**) preceding it.

3. Expand the **Frame** details by clicking the plus sign.

   The **Frame** details properties expand to show more detail. The contents of the packet are highlighted and displayed in hexadecimal notation in the bottom window.

   View the size of the base frame.

4. Collapse the base frame properties.

5. In the Detail window, expand **ETHERNET**.

   The **ETHERNET** frame properties are displayed.

   What is the destination address?

   _____

   Does the destination address refer to a physical address?

   _____

   What is the source address?

   _____

   What type of Ethernet frame is this?

   _____

6. Collapse the **ETHERNET** properties.

7. In the Detail window, expand **ARP_RARP**.

   What is the sender's hardware address?

   _____

   What is the target's hardware address?

   _____

   What is the target's protocol address?

   _____

Chapter 3 Architectural Overview of the TCP/IP Protocol Suite 37

▶ **To examine an ARP reply frame details**
1. Under **Description**, double-click **ARP: Reply**.
2. In the Detail window, expand **ETHERNET: ETYPE**.
   The **ETHERNET: ETYPE** frame properties are displayed.
   What is the destination address?

   _____

   Does the destination address refer to a physical address?

   _____

   What is the source address?

   _____

   What type of Ethernet frame is this?

   _____

3. Collapse the **ETHERNET** properties.
4. In the Detail window, expand **ARP_RARP**.
   What is the sender's hardware address?

   _____

If you want to save captured data for later analysis, use the following procedure.

▶ **To save the capture**
1. On the **File** menu, click **Save As**.
2. Under **File Name**, type a file name and then click **OK**.
3. On the **File** menu, click **Close**.
   The Network Monitor Capture window appears, still displaying the statistics from the last capture.
4. Exit Network Monitor.

Practice

In this procedure, you first use the ARP utility to view entries in your computer's ARP cache. You then use the ARP utility to modify entries in your computer's ARP cache.

Note In order to complete this procedure, you need two networked computers as described in About This Book. If it has been several minutes since you completed the preceding procedure, you may need to refresh the ARP cache by pinging your second computer.

▶ To view the ARP cache

1. At a command prompt, type **arp-g** and then press ENTER to view the ARP cache.
2. Document the entry for your default gateway (if configured)—for example: 131.107.2.1 08-00-02-6c-28-93.

_____

▶ To ping a local host

1. Ping the IP address of your second computer.

   This adds an entry to the cache.
2. View the new entry in the ARP cache.

   What entry was added?

   _____

   What is the entry's type?

   _____

Note The default gateway address is added to the ARP cache when pinging a remote host. This is because PING must use the default gateway to get to the remote host.

▶ **To add an ARP entry**

1. Type the following **arp** command to add the entry from step 1 to the cache:
   arp-s 131.107.2.1 *hardware_address*

   Note Make sure that you type the physical address using hyphens between as listed in step 1.

2. View the ARP cache to verify that the entry has been added.

   What is the entry's type?

   _____

   Why was this entry's type different from preceding entries?

   _____

IP Address Resolution Problems

You may encounter situations when ARP cannot resolve an IP address to a hardware address. If the ARP cache contains an invalid hardware address, communications with a remote host times out.

Summary

Address resolution is the process of mapping a host's IP address to its hardware address. Address resolution consists of an ARP request and an ARP reply. The ARP cache maintains both dynamic and static entries. Static entries remain in cache until you restart the computer, while dynamic entries will expire after a period of time.

Lesson 3: ICMP and IGMP

While the IP protocol is for IP internetwork routing, Internet Control Message Protocol (ICMP) reports errors and controls messages on behalf of IP. IP uses Internet Group Management Protocol (IGMP) to inform routers that hosts of a specific group are available on a network.

After this lesson, you will be able to:
- Explain how ICMP reports IP errors.
- Define IGMP and understand its packet structure.

Estimated lesson time: 10 minutes

ICMP

ICMP does not attempt to make IP a reliable protocol. It merely attempts to report errors and provide feedback on specific conditions. ICMP messages are carried as IP datagrams, and are therefore unreliable.

If a TCP/IP host is sending datagrams to another host at a rate that is saturating the routers or links between them, the router can send an *ICMP Source Quench* message. This source quench message asks the host to slow down the rate of the transmission. A Windows NT TCP/IP host honors a source quench message and slows the sending rate of datagrams. However, if a computer running Windows NT is being used as a router and is unable to forward datagrams at the rate they are arriving, it drops any datagrams that cannot be buffered. In this case, it does not send ICMP source quench messages to the senders.

ICMP Packet Structure

All ICMP packets have the same structure, as shown in the following table.

Field	Function
Type	An 8-bit Type field indicates the type of ICMP packet (Echo Request versus Echo Reply, and so on).
Code	An 8-bit Code field indicates one of possible multiple functions within a given type. If there is only one function within a type, the Code field is set to 0.
Checksum	A 16-bit checksum over the ICMP portion of the packet.
Type-Specific Data	Additional data that varies for each ICMP type.

Note ICMP is defined in RFC 792. For a copy of this RFC, see the *Course Materials* Web page on the course compact disc.

IGMP

IGMP information passes to other routers so that each router that supports multicasting is aware of which host groups are on which network. IGMP packets are carried by IP datagrams, and are therefore unreliable.

IGMP Packet Structure

The fields in the IGMP packet are as shown in the following table.

Field	Function
Version	The version of IGMP that is fixed at 0x1.
Type	The type of IGMP message. A type of 0x1 is called a Host Membership Query and is used by a multicast router to poll a network for any members of a specified multicast group. A type of 0x2 is called a Host Membership Report, and is used by hosts to either declare membership in a specific group or to respond to a router's Host Membership Query.
Unused	An unused field that is zeroed by the sender and ignored by the receiver.
Checksum	A 16-bit checksum on the 8-byte IGMP header.
Group Address	The group address is used by hosts in a Host Membership Report to store the IP multicast address. In the Host Membership Query, the group address is set to all 0's and the hardware-level multicast address is used to identify the host group.

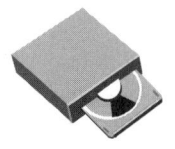

Note IGMP is defined in RFC 1112. For a copy of this RFC, see the *Course Materials* Web page on the course compact disc.

Summary

ICMP reports errors and controls messages on behalf of IP. Routers can send an ICMP Source Quench message asking a TCP/IP host to slow down the rate of transmission if it is sending datagrams too fast.

IGMP informs routers that hosts of a specific multicast group are available on a given network.

Lesson 4: IP

IP is a connectionless protocol primarily responsible for addressing and routing packets between hosts. This lesson describes the process IP uses to route packets.

After this lesson, you will be able to:
- Explain how IP fragments and routes IP packets.
- Describe the IP packet structure.

Estimated lesson time: 15 minutes

IP is connectionless because it does not establish a session before exchanging data. IP is unreliable because it does not guarantee delivery. It always makes a "best effort" attempt to deliver a packet. Along the way, a packet might be lost, delivered out of sequence, duplicated, or delayed.

IP does not require an acknowledgment when data is received. The sender or receiver is not informed when a packet is lost or sent out of sequence. The acknowledgment of packets is the responsibility of a higher-layer transport, such as TCP.

The IP datagram fields in the following table are added to the header when a packet is passed down from the Transport layer.

Field	Function
Source IP Address	Identifies the sender of the datagram by the IP address.
Destination IP Address	Identifies the destination of the datagram by the IP address.
Protocol	Informs IP at the destination host whether to pass the packet up to TCP or UDP.
Checksum	A simple mathematical computation that is used to verify that the packet arrived intact.
Time to Live (TTL)	Designates the number of seconds a datagram is allowed to stay on the wire before it's discarded. This prevents packets from endlessly looping around an internetwork. Routers are required to decrement the TTL by the number of seconds the datagram was stuck in the router. The TTL is decremented by at least one second each time the datagram passes through a router. The default TTL in Windows NT 4.0 is 128 seconds.

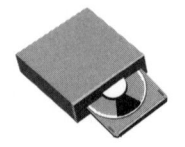

Note IP is defined in RFC 791. For a copy of this RFC, see the *Course Materials* Web page on the course compact disc.

If IP identifies a destination address as a *local* address, IP transmits the packet directly to that host. If the destination IP address is identified as a *remote* address, IP checks the local routing table for a route to the remote host. If it finds a route, IP sends the packet using that route. If IP does *not* find a route, it sends the packet to the source host's default gateway, also called a router.

IP on the Router

When a router receives a packet, the packet is passed up to IP, which does the following:

1. IP decrements the TTL by at least 1 or more if the packet is stuck at the router due to congestion.

    If the TTL reaches zero, the packet is discarded.

2. IP may fragment the packet into smaller packets if the packet is too large for the underlying network.

3. If the packet is fragmented, IP creates a new header for each new packet, which includes:

    - A *Flag* to indicate that other fragments follow.
    - A *Fragment ID* to identify all fragments that belong together.
    - A *Fragment Offset* to tell the receiving host how to reassemble the packet.

4. IP calculates a new checksum.

5. IP obtains the destination hardware address of the next router.

6. IP forwards the packet.

At the next host, the packet passes up the stack to either TCP or UDP. This entire process is repeated at each router until the packet reaches its final destination. When the packets arrive at their final destination, IP assembles the pieces into the original packet.

IP Packet Structure

The fields in the IP (version 4) header are as shown in the following table.

Field	Function
Version	4 bits are used to indicate the version of IP. The current version is version 4. The next version of IP will be version 6. This next version is discussed in Chapter 4, "IP Addressing."
Header Length	4 bits are used to indicate the number of 32-bit words in the IP header. IP headers have a minimum size of 20 bytes; therefore, the smallest header length is 0x5. IP options can extend the minimum IP header size 4 bytes at a time. If an IP option does not use all 4 bytes of the IP option field, the remaining bits are padded with 0's so that the entire IP header is an integral number of 32 bits (4 bytes).
Type of Service	8 bits are used to indicate the quality of service expected by this datagram for delivery through routers across the IP internetwork. Within the 8 bits are bits for precedence, delay, throughput, and reliability characteristics.
Total Length	16 bits are used to indicate the total length of the IP datagram (IP header + IP payload); the total length does not include the Network Access Layer framing.
Identification	16 bits are used as an identifier for this specific IP packet. If the IP packet is fragmented, all of the fragments have the same original identification to be used for reassembly by the destination node.
Fragmentation Flags	3 bits are reserved as flags for the fragmentation process; however, only 2 bits are defined for current use. There is a flag to indicate whether the IP datagram may be fragmented and a flag to indicate whether more fragments are to follow.
Fragment Offset	13 bits are used as an offset counter to indicate the position of the fragment relative to the original IP payload. If unfragmented, the fragment offset is 0x0.
Time to Live	8 bits are used as an indicator of the amount of time or *hops* an IP packet can travel before being discarded. The Time to Live field (TTL) was originally used as a time count during which an IP router timed how long it took (in seconds) to forward the IP packet and decremented the TTL accordingly. Modern routers almost always forward an IP datagram in less than a second and are required by RFC 791 to decrement the TTL by at least one. Therefore, the TTL becomes a maximum hop count. A suggested default value is twice the diameter of the IP internetwork, where the diameter is the maximum number of hops between any two IP nodes.

(*continued*)

Field	Function
Protocol	8 bits are used as an identifier of the IP client protocol, the protocol that gave a payload for IP to send. The protocol field is used to demultiplex an IP packet to the upper-layer protocol.
Header Checksum	16 bits are used as a checksum on the IP header only. The IP payload is not included and may include its own checksum to check for errors. When an IP node receives an IP packet, it performs a checksum verification and discards the IP packet if invalid. When a router forwards a IP packet, it minimally decrements the TTL. Therefore, the checksum is recomputed at each hop in its journey from source to destination.
Source Address	32 bits are used to store the IP address of the originating host.
Destination Address	32 bits are used to store the IP address of the destination host.
Options and Padding	A multiple of 32 bits is used to store IP options. If the IP option does not use all 32 bits, it must pad the additional bits with 0's so that the IP header is an integral number of 32 bits, which can be indicated by the header length field.

Summary

IP is a connectionless protocol that addresses and routes packets between hosts. IP is unreliable because delivery is not guaranteed. If a packet is destined for a local address, it is sent directly to that host. If the destination IP address is for a remote address, IP checks the local routing table for a route.

Lesson 5: TCP

TCP is a reliable, connection-oriented delivery service. In this lesson, you learn how TCP transmits data. You also learn about related TCP ports and sockets.

After this lesson, you will be able to:
- Describe how TCP transmits data.
- Define ports and sockets.

Estimated lesson time: 25 minutes

TCP data is transmitted in segments, and a session must be established before hosts can exchange data. TCP uses byte-stream communications, which means that the data is treated as a sequence of bytes.

It achieves reliability by assigning a sequence number to each segment transmitted by TCP. If a segment is broken into smaller pieces, the receiving host knows whether all pieces have been received. An acknowledgment verifies that the other host received the data. For each segment sent, the receiving host must return an acknowledgment (ACK) within a specified period.

If the sender does not receive an ACK, then the data is retransmitted. If the segment is received damaged, the receiving host discards it. Because an ACK is not sent, the sender retransmits the segment.

Note TCP is defined in RFC 793. For a copy of this RFC, see the *Course Materials* Web page on the course compact disc.

Ports

Sockets applications identify themselves uniquely within a computer by using a *protocol port number*. For example, the FTP Server application uses a specific TCP port so that other applications can communicate with it.

Ports can use any number between 0 and 65,536. Port numbers for client-side applications are dynamically assigned by the operating system when there is a request for service. Port numbers for *well-known* server-side applications are pre-assigned by the Internet Assigned Numbers Authority (IANA) and do not change.

Tip You can examine port numbers by looking at the file *systemroot*\System32\Drivers\Etc\Services.

Well-known port numbers range from 1 to 1024. The complete list of well-known port numbers is documented in RFC 1700. For a copy of this RFC, see the *Course Materials* Web page on the course compact disc.

Sockets

A socket is similar in concept to a file handle in that it functions as an endpoint for network communication. An application creates a socket by specifying three items: the IP address of the host, the type of service (TCP for connection-based service, UDP for connectionless), and the port the application is using.

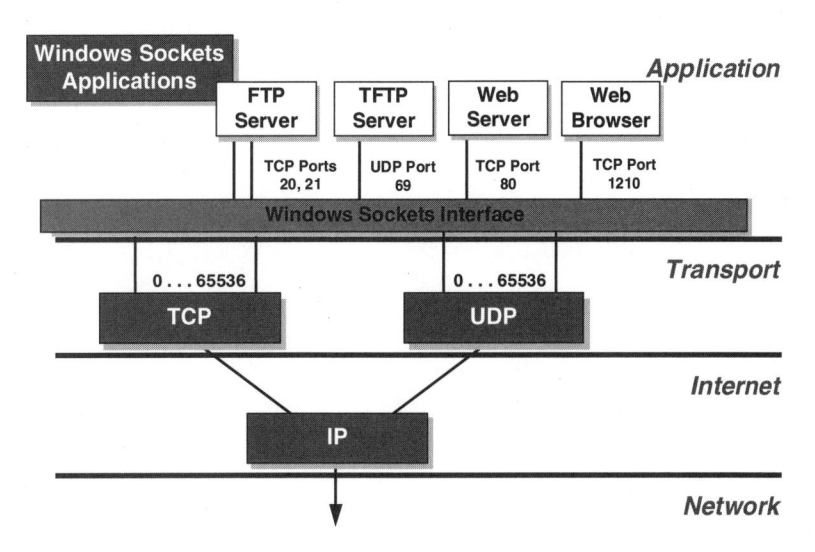

An application can create a socket and use it to send connectionless traffic to remote applications. An application can also create a socket and connect it to another application's socket. Data can then be reliably sent over this connection.

TCP Ports

A TCP port provides a specific location for delivery of messages. Port numbers below 256 are defined as commonly used ports. The following table shows a few commonly used TCP ports.

Port number	Description
21	FTP
23	Telnet
53	Domain Name System (DNS)
139	NetBIOS session service

TCP Three-Way Handshake

A TCP session is initialized through a three-way handshake. The purpose of the three-way handshake is to synchronize the sending and receiving of segments, inform the other host of the amount of data it is able to receive at once, and establish a virtual connection.

The following steps outline the three-way handshake process.

1. The initiating host requests a session by sending out a segment with the synchronization (SYN) flag set to **on**.
2. The receiving host acknowledges the request by sending back a segment with:
   - The synchronization flag set to **on**.
   - A sequence number to indicate the starting byte for a segment it may send.
   - An acknowledgment with the byte sequence number of the next segment it expects to receive.
3. The requesting host sends back a segment with the acknowledged sequence number and acknowledgment number.

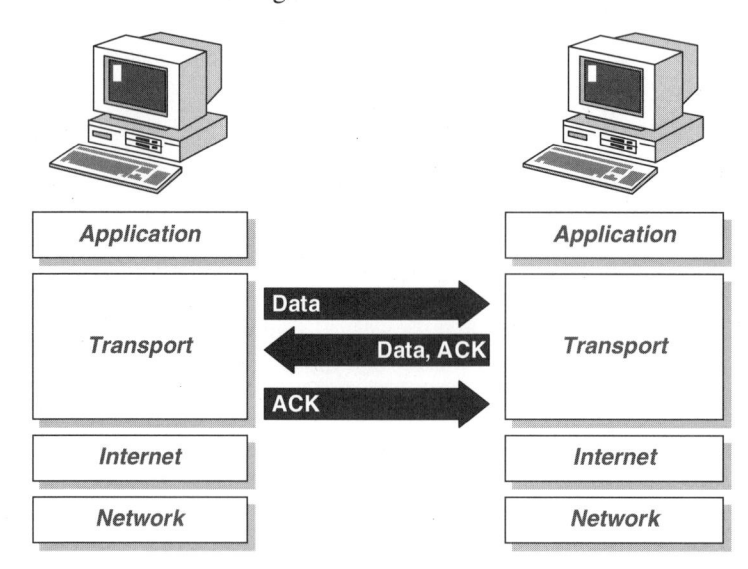

TCP uses a similar handshake process to end a connection. This guarantees that both hosts have finished transmitting and that they received all of the data.

TCP Sliding Windows

TCP buffers data for transmission between two hosts by using sliding windows. Each TCP/IP host maintains two sliding windows: one for receiving data, and the other for sending data. The size of the window indicates the amount of data that can be buffered on a computer.

Multimedia Presentation: TCP Sliding Windows

In this seven-minute presentation, you see how TCP sliding windows work and how the size of a sliding window can affect performance.

▶ **To start the TCP Sliding Windows multimedia presentation**

1. Insert the course compact disc into the CD-ROM drive.

   Internet Explorer starts and The Internetworking with Microsoft TCP/IP on Microsoft Windows NT 4.0 start page opens.

   –Or–

   Start Windows NT Explorer, navigate to the drive containing the course compact disc, and then double-click the Open.htm file.

2. Click the start page icon.
3. Click **Course Materials**.
4. Click **Multimedia Presentations**.
5. Click **TCP Sliding Windows**.

   An Internet Explorer dialog box appears asking if you want to open the file or save it to disk.

6. Select **Open it**, and then click **OK**.
7. Click **Yes** if a security box appears.

   The multimedia presentation begins. Click the **Text On** button if you do not have a sound card and speakers.

TCP Packet Structure

All TCP segments have two parts: data and header. The following table lists fields that are added to a TCP header.

Field	Function
Source Port	TCP port of sending host.
Destination Port	TCP port of destination host. This provides an endpoint for communications.
Sequence Number	The sequence of bytes transmitted in a segment. The sequence number is used to verify that all bytes have been received.
Acknowledgment Number	The sequence number of the byte the local host expects to receive next.
Data Length	Length of the TCP segment.
Reserved	Reserved for future use.
Flags	This field specifies what content is in the segment.
Window	How much space is currently available in the TCP window.
Checksum	Verifies that the header is not corrupted.
Urgent Pointer	When urgent data is being sent (as specified in the Flags field), this field points to the end of the urgent data in the segment.

Summary

TCP is a reliable, connection-oriented delivery service. Sockets applications use a unique port number. A socket functions as an endpoint for network communication. Ports and sockets consist of a related set of numbers.

A TCP session is initialized and ended through a three-way handshake. TCP uses sliding windows to buffer data for transmission between two hosts. The size of the window indicates the amount of data that can be buffered on a computer.

Lesson 6: UDP

User Datagram Protocol (UDP) provides a connectionless datagram service that offers unreliable, "best effort" delivery. This means that the arrival of datagrams or correct sequencing of delivered packets is not guaranteed.

After this lesson, you will be able to:
- Define UDP and describe the UDP packet structure.

Estimated lesson time: 5 minutes

UDP is used by applications that do not require an acknowledgment of data receipt. These applications typically transmit small amounts of data at one time. Examples of services and applications that use UDP are the NetBIOS name service, NetBIOS datagram service, and SNMP.

UDP Ports

To use UDP, the application must supply the IP address and port number of the destination application. A port provides a location for sending messages and is identified by a unique number. A port functions as a multiplexed message queue, meaning that it can receive multiple messages at a time. It is important to note that the UDP ports listed in the following table are distinct and separate from TCP ports even though some of them use the same port number.

Port	Keyword	Description
15	NETSTAT	Network status
53	DOMAIN	Domain Name Server
69	TFTP	Trivial File Transfer Protocol
137	NETBIOS-NS	NetBIOS name service
138	NETBIOS-DGM	NetBIOS datagram service
161	SNMP	SNMP network monitor

Note UDP is defined in RFC 768. For a copy of this RFC, see the *Course Materials* Web page on the course compact disc.

UDP Packet Structure

The fields in the following table are combined in the 8-byte UDP header.

Field	Function
Source Port	UDP port of sending host. The sending port value is optional. If not used, it is set to zero.
Destination Port	UDP port of destination host. This provides an endpoint for communications.
Message Length	The size of the UDP message. The minimum UDP packet contains only the header information (8 bytes).
Checksum	Verifies that the header is not corrupted.

Summary

UDP is a connectionless datagram service that does not guarantee delivery of packets. It is used by applications that do not require an acknowledgment of data receipt.

Review

The following questions are intended to reinforce key information presented in this chapter. If you are unable to answer a question, review the appropriate lesson and then try the question again.

1. What are the layers in the four-layer model used by TCP/IP?

2. What core protocols are provided in the Microsoft TCP/IP transport driver?

3. Which protocol is used to inform a client that a destination network is unreachable?

4. When an IP datagram is forwarded by a router, how is the datagram changed?

5. When is the User Datagram Protocol used?

6. When an ARP request is sent out, to what address is it sent?

_____

7. What address is requested in the ARP request packet for a local host? For a remote host?

_____

_____

For More Information
- Review all referenced RFCs on the course compact disc.

CHAPTER 4

IP Addressing

Lesson 1   The IP Address . . . 56

Lesson 2   Address Classes . . . 60

Lesson 3   Addressing Guidelines . . . 64

Lesson 4   Subnet Mask and the IP Address . . . 71

Lesson 5   IP Addressing with IP Version 6.0 . . . 75

Review . . . 77

About This Chapter

In this chapter, you review the components in an IP address, the address classes supported by Microsoft Windows NT, and addressing guidelines. The focus of this chapter is on a LAN environment. During the lessons, you identify valid and invalid IP addresses, assign IP addresses to hosts, and identify common IP addressing problems.

Before You Begin

There are no prerequisites in order to complete the lessons in this chapter.

Lesson 1: The IP Address

The IP address identifies a system's location on the network in the same way a street address identifies a house on a city block. Just as a street address must identify a unique residence, an IP address must be unique and have a uniform format.

After this lesson, you will be able to:
- Define the network ID and host ID portions of an IP address.
- Convert IP addresses from binary code to decimal format.

Estimated lesson time: 25 minutes

Each IP address has two parts—a network ID and a host ID. The network ID identifies a physical network. All hosts on the same network require the same network ID, which should be unique to the internetwork.

The host ID identifies a workstation, server, router, or other TCP/IP host within a network. The host ID must be unique to the network ID. Each TCP/IP host is identified by a logical IP address. A unique IP address is required for all hosts and network components that communicate using TCP/IP, as shown in the following illustration.

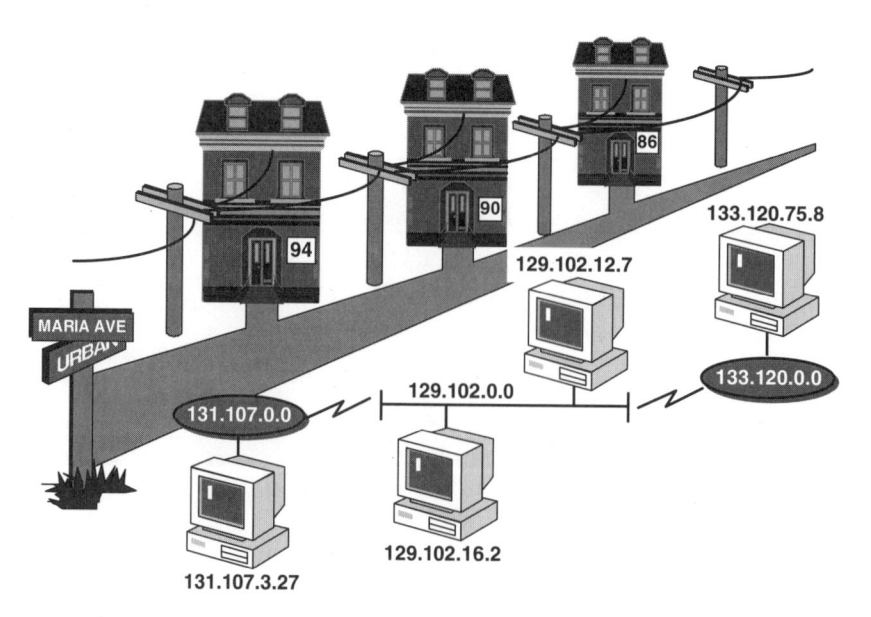

Network ID and Host ID

There are two formats for referencing an IP address—binary and dotted decimal notation. Each IP address is 32 bits long and is composed of four 8-bit fields, called octets. The octets are separated by periods and represent a decimal number in the range 0–255. The 32 bits of the IP address are allocated to the network ID and host ID.

The human-readable format of an IP address is referred to as *dotted decimal notation*. The following table contains an example of an IP address in binary and dotted decimal formats.

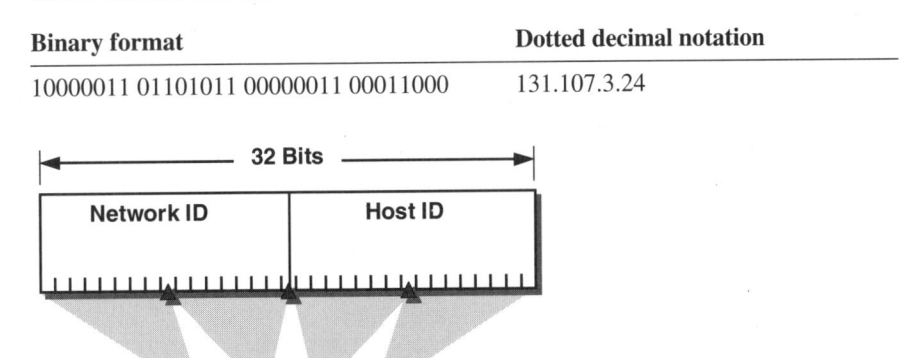

Binary format	Dotted decimal notation
10000011 01101011 00000011 00011000	131.107.3.24

w. x. y. z.

Example: **131.107.3.24**

Converting IP Addresses from Binary to Decimal

You should be able to define the assigned bit values in an octet and convert the bits from binary code to a decimal format. In binary format, each bit in an octet has an assigned decimal value. When each bit is converted to decimal format, the highest value in the octet is 255. Each octet is converted separately.

A bit that is set to 0 always has a zero value. A bit that is set to 1 can be converted to a decimal value. The low-order bit represents a decimal value of one. The high-order bit represents a decimal value of 128. The highest decimal value of an octet is 255—that is, when all bits are set to 1.

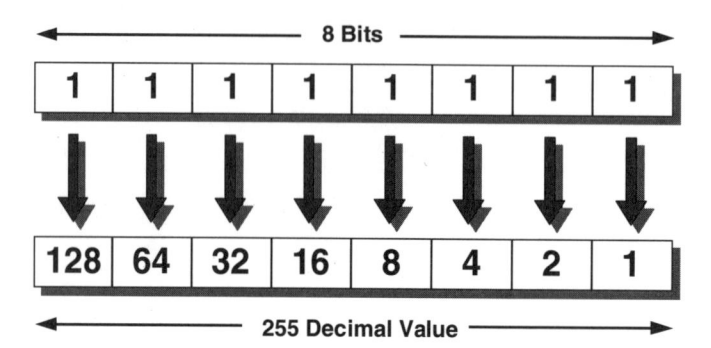

The following table shows how the bits in one octet are converted from binary code to a decimal value.

Binary code	Bit values	Decimal value
00000000	0	0
00000001	1	1
00000011	1+2	3
00000111	1+2+4	7
00001111	1+2+4+8	15
00011111	1+2+4+8+16	31
00111111	1+2+4+8+16+32	63
01111111	1+2+4+8+16+32+64	127
11111111	1+2+4+8+16+32+64+128	255

Practice

In this practice, you convert binary codes to decimal values and vice versa.

1. Convert the following binary numbers to decimal format.

   Tip You can use the calculator (scientific view) in the **Accessories** group to convert decimal format to binary format, and vice versa. However, you may want to first convert some of these numbers manually until you are comfortable with the process.

Binary value	Decimal value
10001011	
10101010	
10111111 11100000 00000111 10000001	
01111111 00000000 00000000 00000001	

2. Convert the following decimal values to binary format.

Decimal value	Binary value
250	
19	
109.128.255.254	
131.107.2.89	

Summary

Each TCP/IP host is identified by a logical IP address, and a unique IP address is required for each host and network component that communicate using TCP/IP. Each IP address defines the network ID and host ID. An IP address is 32 bits long and is composed of four 8-bit fields, called octets.

Lesson 2: Address Classes

There are different classes of IP addresses. Each class defines the part of the IP address which identifies the network ID and the part which identifies the host ID. In this lesson, you learn about the A, B, and C IP address classes.

After this lesson, you will be able to:
- Identify the network ID and host ID in a class A, B, or C IP address.
- Determine the correct address class for various IP addresses.

Estimated lesson time: 15 minutes

The Internet community has defined five IP address classes to accommodate networks of varying sizes. Microsoft TCP/IP supports class A, B, and C addresses assigned to hosts. The class of address defines which bits are used for the network ID and which bits are used for the host ID. The class also defines the possible number of networks and the number of hosts per network.

You can identify the class of address by the number in the first octet. The 32-bit IP addressing scheme supports a total of 3,720,314,628 hosts. The following chart shows the network and host ID fields for class A, B, and C IP addressing.

Class	IP address	Network ID	Host ID
A	w.x.y.z	w	x.y.z
B	w.x.y.z	w.x	y.z
C	w.x.y.z	w.x.y	z

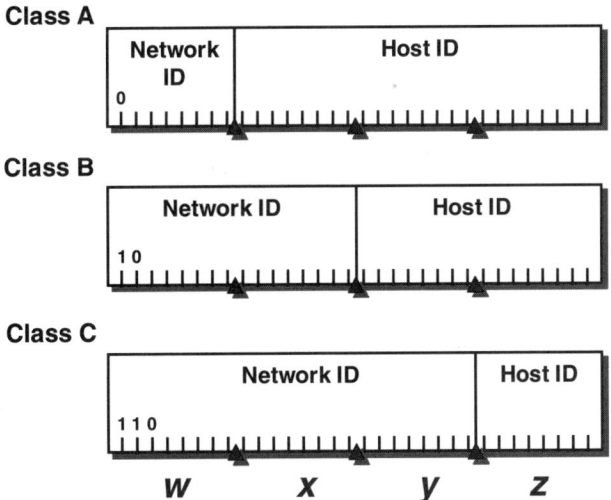

Class A

```
Network ID | Host ID
0
```

Class B

```
Network ID | Host ID
1 0
```

Class C

```
Network ID | Host ID
1 1 0
```

w   x   y   z

Class A

Class A addresses are assigned to networks with a very large number of hosts. The high-order bit in a class A address is always set to zero. The next 7 bits (completing the first octet) complete the network ID. The remaining 24 bits (the last three octets) represent the host ID. This allows for 126 networks and approximately 17 million hosts per network.

Class B

Class B addresses are assigned to medium-sized to large-sized networks. The two high-order bits in a class B address are always set to binary 1 0. The next 14 bits (completing the first two octets) complete the network ID. The remaining 16 bits (last two octets) represent the host ID. This allows for 16,384 networks and approximately 65,000 hosts per network.

Class C

Class C addresses are used for small LANs. The three high-order bits in a class C address are always set to binary 1 1 0. The next 21 bits (completing the first three octets) complete the network ID. The remaining 8 bits (last octet) represent the host ID. This allows for approximately 2 million networks and 254 hosts per network.

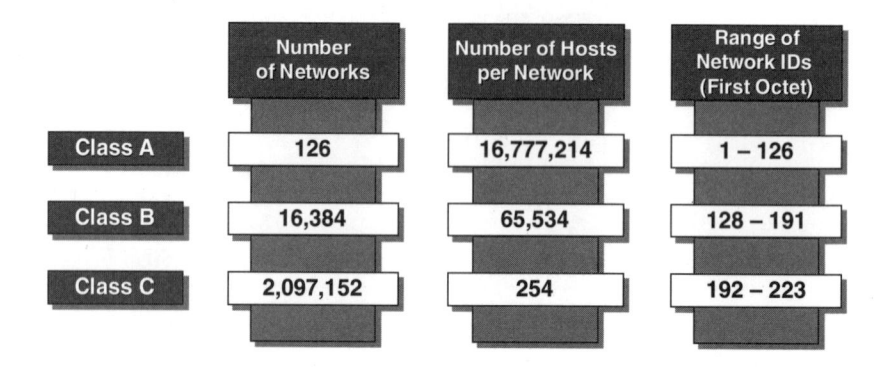

	Number of Networks	Number of Hosts per Network	Range of Network IDs (First Octet)
Class A	126	16,777,214	1 – 126
Class B	16,384	65,534	128 – 191
Class C	2,097,152	254	192 – 223

Note The network ID cannot be 127. This ID is reserved for loopback and diagnostic functions.

Class D

Class D addresses are used for multicast group usage. A multicast group can contain one or more hosts, or none at all. The four high-order bits in a class D address are always set to binary 1 1 1 0. The remaining bits designate the specific group in which the client participates. There are no network or host bits in the multicast operations. Packets are passed to a selected subset of hosts on a network. Only those hosts registered for the multicast address accept the packet. Microsoft supports class D addresses for applications to multicast data to hosts on an internetwork, including WINS and Microsoft NetShow™.

Class E

Class E is an experimental address not available for general use because it is reserved for future use. The high-order bits in a class E address are set to 1111.

Note For more information on multicasting, see the Multicasting white paper in the Additional Readings section of the *Course Materials* Web page on the course compact disc.

Practice

In this practice, you determine the correct address class for a given IP address and scenario.

1. Write the address class next to each IP address.

Address	Class
131.107.2.89	
3.3.57.0	
200.200.5.2	
191.107.2.10	

2. Which address class(es) allow you to have more than 1,000 hosts per network?

3. Which address class(es) allow only 254 hosts per network?

Summary

There are five address classes. Microsoft supports class A, B, and C addresses assigned to hosts. Each address class can accommodate networks of different sizes.

Lesson 3: Addressing Guidelines

Although there are no rules for how to assign IP addresses, you should follow certain guidelines to ensure that you are assigning valid network IDs and host IDs. This lesson explains how to assign IP addresses in a LAN environment.

After this lesson, you will be able to:
- Understand the guidelines for assigning valid IP addresses.
- Identify network components that require a network ID.
- Identify TCP/IP hosts that require a host ID.

Estimated lesson time: 35 minutes

There are several general guidelines you should follow when assigning network IDs and host IDs:

- The network ID cannot be 127. This ID is reserved for loopback and diagnostic functions.
- The network ID and host ID bits cannot all be 1's. If all bits are set to 1, the address is interpreted as a broadcast rather than a host ID.
- The network ID and host ID bits cannot all be 0's. If all bits are set to 0, the address is interpreted to mean "this network only."
- The host ID must be unique to the local network ID.

Assigning Network IDs

A unique network ID is required for each network and wide area connection. If you are connecting to the public Internet, you are required to obtain a network ID from the Internet Network Information Center (InterNIC). If you do not plan to connect to the public Internet, you can use any valid network ID.

The network ID identifies the TCP/IP hosts that are located on the same physical network. All hosts on the same physical network must be assigned the same network ID to communicate with each other.

If your networks are connected by routers, a unique network ID is required for each wide area connection. For example, in the following illustration:

- Networks 1 and 2 represent two routed networks.
- Network 2 represents the WAN connection between the routers.
- Network 2 requires a network ID so that the interfaces between the two routers can be assigned unique host IDs.

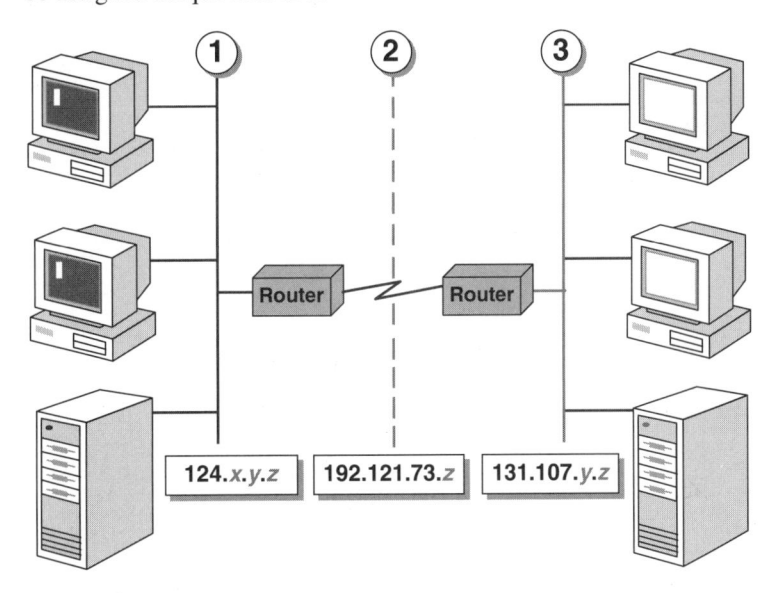

Note If you plan to connect your network to the Internet, you must obtain the network ID portion of the IP address. This will guarantee IP network ID uniqueness. For domain name registration and IP network number assignment, visit InterNIC's online registration services at http://internic.net. If you have any questions, call their registration help line at (703) 742-4777.

IP address allocation for private networks is defined in RFC 1918. For a copy of this RFC, see the *Course Materials* Web page on the course compact disc.

Assigning Host IDs

The host ID identifies a TCP/IP host within a network and must be unique to the network ID. All TCP/IP hosts, including interfaces to routers, require unique host IDs. The host ID of the router is the IP address configured as a workstation's default gateway. For example, for the host on subnet 1 with an IP address of 124.0.0.27, the IP address of the default gateway is 124.0.0.1.

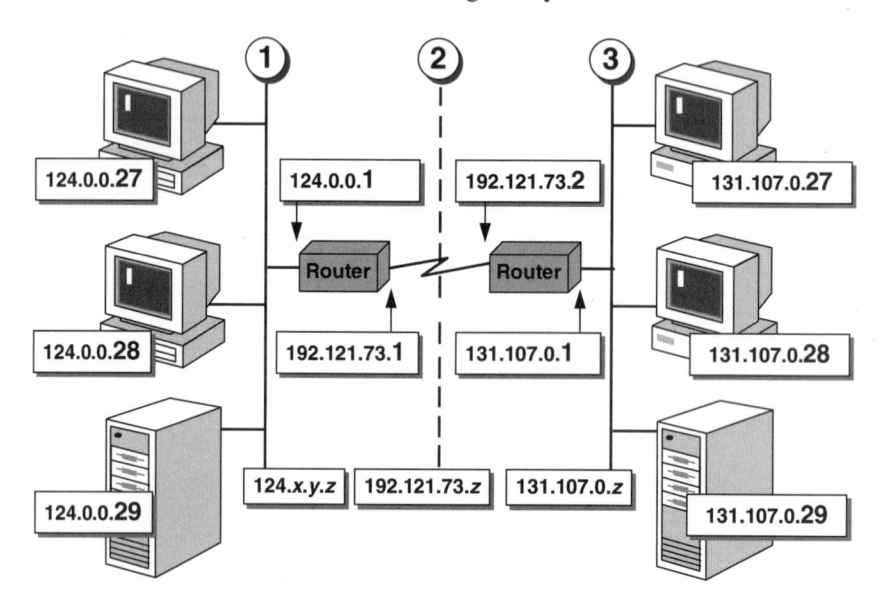

Valid Host IDs

The following table lists the valid ranges of host IDs for a private network.

Address class	Beginning range	Ending range
Class A	w.0.0.1	w.255.255.254
Class B	w.x.0.1	w.x.255.254
Class C	w.x.y.1	w.x.y.254

Suggestions for Assigning Host IDs

There are no rules for how to assign valid IP addresses. You can number all TCP/IP hosts consecutively, or you can number them so they can easily be identified—for example:

- Assign host IDs in groups based on host or server type.
- Designate routers by their IP address.

Organized numbering approaches such as these can help you prevent address conflicts from assigning duplicate IP addresses on a network.

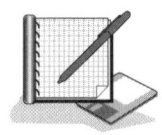

Practice

In this practice, you identify which of the following IP addresses cannot be assigned to a host. Identify the IP addresses that would be invalid if it were assigned to a host, and then explain why it is invalid.

a. 131.107.256.80 _____

b. 222.222.255.222 _____

c. 231.200.1.1 _____

d. 126.1.0.0 _____

e. 0.127.4.100 _____

f. 190.7.2.0 _____

g. 127.1.1.1 _____

h. 198.121.254.255 _____

i. 255.255.255.255 _____

In this next practice, you decide which network components require IP addresses in a TCP/IP network environment. When a protocol is listed, assume it is the only protocol installed on the host. Review the following network components and circle the letter that corresponds to the components that do not require an IP address.

a. Microsoft Windows NT computer running TCP/IP

b. LAN Manager workstation that connects to a Windows NT computer running TCP/IP

c. Computer running Windows 95 that requires access to shared resources on a Windows NT-based computer running TCP/IP

d. UNIX host that you want to connect to using TCP/IP utilities

e. Network interface printer running TCP/IP

f. Router for connecting to a remote IP network

g. Ethernet port on local router

h. Microsoft LAN Manager workstation that is attempting to connect to a LAN Manager server running NetBEUI

i. Computer running Windows for Workgroups that requires access to shared resources on a LAN Manager server running NetBEUI

j. Serial plotter on a Windows NT-based computer running TCP/IP

k. Network printer shared off a LAN Manager server running NetBEUI

l. Communications server providing terminal access to TCP/IP host computers

m. Your default gateway

In this next practice, you decide which class of address will support the following IP network. Next, you assign a valid IP address to each type of host to easily distinguish it from other hosts (for example, UNIX, Windows NT servers, or Windows NT workstations). In this scenario, all computers are on the same subnet.

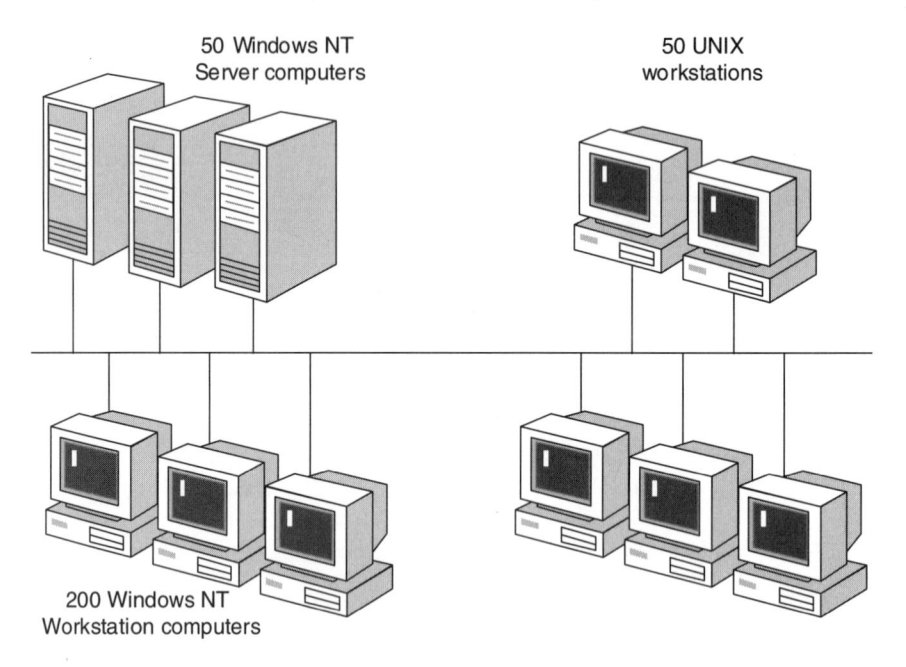

50 Windows NT Server computers

50 UNIX workstations

200 Windows NT Workstation computers

Which address classes will support this network?

___

Which of the following network addresses support this network?

a. 197.200.3.0
b. 11.0.0.0
c. 221.100.2.0
d. 131.107.0.0

Using the network ID that you chose, assign a range of host IDs to each type of host, so that you can easily distinguish the Windows NT Server computers from the Windows NT Workstation computers and the UNIX workstations.

Type of TCP/IP host	IP address range
Windows NT Server computers	
Windows NT Workstation computers	
UNIX workstations	

In this next practice, you decide how many network IDs and host IDs are required to support this network. Use the following illustration for reference.

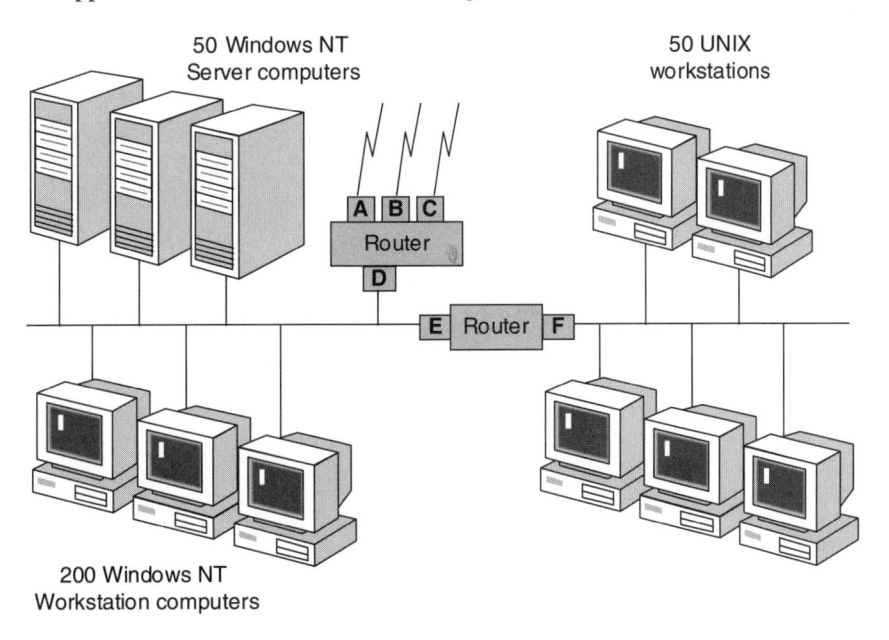

50 Windows NT Server computers

50 UNIX workstations

200 Windows NT Workstation computers

How many network IDs does this network environment require?

How many host IDs does this network environment require?

Which default gateway (router interface) would you assign to the Windows NT Workstation computers that communicate primarily with the UNIX workstations?

Summary

There are several guidelines you should follow to make sure you assign valid IP addresses. All hosts on a given network must have the same network ID to communicate with each other. All TCP/IP hosts, including interfaces to routers, require unique host IDs.

Lesson 4: Subnet Mask and the IP Address

Each host on a TCP/IP network requires a subnet mask. This lesson describes the purpose of a subnet mask and how it is part of the process IP uses to route packets. You learn more about subnet masking in Chapter 5, "Subnetting."

After this lesson, you will be able to:
- Describe the function and purpose of a subnet mask.
- Use the ANDing process to determine an IP address destination.

Estimated lesson time: 15 minutes

A subnet mask is a 32-bit address used to block or "mask" a portion of the IP address to distinguish the network ID from the host ID. This is necessary so that TCP/IP can determine whether an IP address is located on a local or remote network.

Each host on a TCP/IP network requires a subnet mask—either a default subnet mask, which is used when a network is not divided into subnets, or a custom subnet mask, which is used when a network is divided into subnets.

Default Subnet Masks

A default subnet mask is used on TCP/IP networks that are not divided into subnets. All TCP/IP hosts require a subnet mask, even on a single-segment network. The default subnet mask you use depends on the address class.

In the subnet mask, all bits that correspond to the network ID are set to 1. The decimal value in each octet is 255. All bits that correspond to the host ID are set to 0.

Address Class	Bits Used for Subnet Mask	Dotted Decimal Notation
Class A	11111111 00000000 00000000 00000000	255.0.0.0
Class B	11111111 11111111 00000000 00000000	255.255.0.0
Class C	11111111 11111111 11111111 00000000	255.255.255.0

Class B Example

IP Address	131.107.	16.200
Subnet Mask	255.255.	0.0
Network ID	131.107.	y.z
Host ID	w.x.	16.200

Determining the Destination of a Packet

ANDing is the internal process that IP uses to determine whether a packet is destined for a host on a local or remote network. Because ANDing is used internally by IP, you do not normally need to perform this task.

When TCP/IP is initialized, the host's IP address is ANDed with its subnet mask. Before a packet is sent, the destination IP address is ANDed with the same subnet mask. If the results of ANDing the source IP address and destination IP address match, IP knows that the packet belongs to a host on the local network. If the results do not match, the packet is sent to the IP address of an IP router.

To AND the IP address to a subnet mask, TCP/IP compares each bit in the IP address to the corresponding bit in the subnet mask. If both bits are 1's, the resulting bit is 1. If there is any other combination, the resulting bit is 0, as shown in the examples in the following table.

Bit combination	Result
1 AND 1	1
1 AND 0	0
0 AND 0	0
0 AND 1	0

IP Address	10011111	11100000	00000111	10000001
Subnet Mask	11111111	11111111	00000000	00000000

Result	10011111	11100000	00000000	00000000

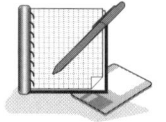

Practice

In this practice, AND the following IP addresses to determine whether the destination IP address belongs to a host on a local network or a remote network.

Source (host) IP address	10011001 10101010 00100101 10100011
Subnet mask	11111111 11111111 00000000 00000000
Result	

Destination IP address	11011001 10101010 10101100 11101001
Subnet mask	11111111 11111111 00000000 00000000
Result	

1. Do the results match?

2. Is the destination IP address located on a local or remote network?

Summary

A default subnet mask is used on TCP/IP networks that are not divided into subnets. A custom subnet mask is used when a network is divided into subnets. ANDing is an internal IP process that determines whether a packet should be sent to a host on a local or remote network.

Lesson 5: IP Addressing with IP Version 6.0

Under the current 32-bit addressing scheme implemented in IP version 4.0 (IPv4), network IDs have become scarce. In this lesson, you learn about the future direction of IP addressing.

After this lesson, you will be able to:
- Explain how IP version 6.0 can help solve current network addressing problems.

Estimated lesson time: 5 minutes

The current IP header (known as version 4) has not been changed or upgraded since the 1970s. This is a tribute to its initial design. However, the initial design did not anticipate the growth of the Internet and the eventual exhaustion of the IP version 4.0 address space.

Therefore, a new version of IP called IPv6 has been developed. This new version, once known as IP—The Next Generation (IPng), incorporates the ideas of many different proposed methods of creating a newer version of the IP protocol.

IPv6 was created to solve the current network addressing problems and provide a long-term solution for address space depletion. IPv6 uses 16 octets. When written, it is divided into 8 octet pairs, separated by colons. The octets are represented in hexadecimal.

IPv6 is an entirely new packet structure which is incompatible with IPv4 systems, but has several benefits such as an extended address space, a simplified header format, support for time-dependent traffic, and the ability add new features.

Extended address space is one primary feature of IPv6. IPv6 has 128-bit source and destination IP addresses (four times larger than IPv4). 128 bits can express over 3×10^{38} possible combinations, thereby allowing an abundance of addresses for the foreseeable future. With IPv6, a valid IP address may appear as:

    4A3F:AE67:F240:56C4:3409:AE52:440F:1403

The IPv6 headers are designed to keep the IP header overhead to a minimum by moving nonessential fields and option fields to extension headers that are placed after the IP header. Anything not included in the base IPv6 header can be added through IP extension headers placed after the base IPv6 header.

A new field in the IPv6 header allows the preallocation of network resources along a path so that time-dependent services such as voice and video are guaranteed a requested bandwidth with a fixed delay.

One final benefit is that IPv6 can easily be extended for unforeseen features through the adding of extension headers after the IPv6 base header. Support for new hardware or application technologies is built in.

Note IPv6 is defined in RFC 1883. For a copy of this RFC, see the *Course Materials* Web page on the course compact disc.

Summary

Under the current implementation of IP, network IDs have become scarce. IPv6 is an entirely new packet structure which has several benefits such as extended address space, a simplified header format, support for time-dependent traffic, and the ability to be extended for new features.

Review

The following questions are intended to reinforce key information presented in this chapter. If you are unable to answer a question, review the appropriate lesson and then try the question again.

1. In class A, class B, and class C addresses, which octets represent the network ID and which represent the host ID?

2. Which numbers are invalid as a network ID and why? Which numbers are invalid as a host ID and why?

3. When is a unique network ID required?

4. In a TCP/IP internetwork, what components require a host ID besides computers?

Review Practice

In this review practice, you examine two examples of IP networks, identify hidden IP addressing problems, and explain the possible effects caused by the problems.

For the following illustration, list all IP addressing problems, and explain how each problem may affect communications. Are the IP addresses and default gateway addresses appropriate for each situation?

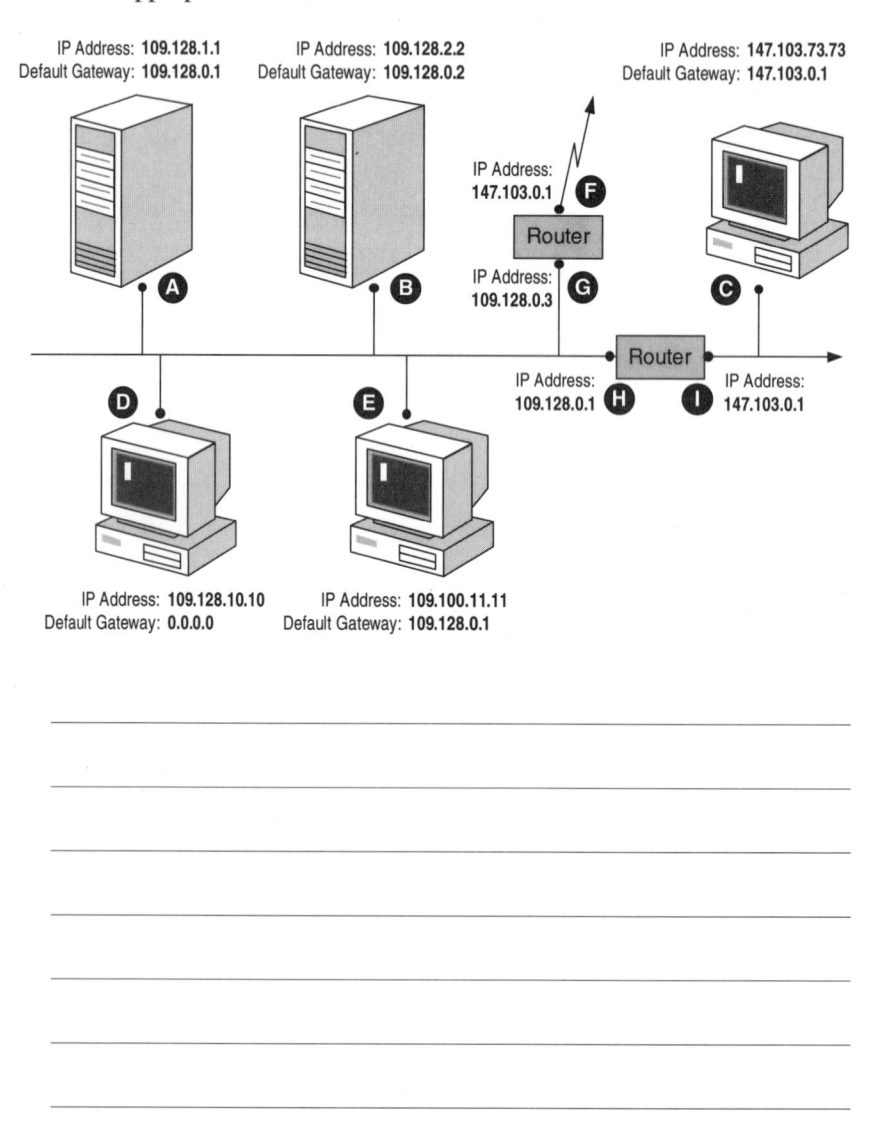

IP Address: **109.128.1.1**
Default Gateway: **109.128.0.1**

IP Address: **109.128.2.2**
Default Gateway: **109.128.0.2**

IP Address: **147.103.73.73**
Default Gateway: **147.103.0.1**

IP Address: **147.103.0.1** **F**

IP Address: **109.128.0.3** **G**

IP Address: **109.128.0.1** **H**

IP Address: **147.103.0.1** **I**

IP Address: **109.128.10.10**
Default Gateway: **0.0.0.0**

IP Address: **109.100.11.11**
Default Gateway: **109.128.0.1**

For the following illustration, list all IP addressing problems, and explain how each problem may affect communications. Are the IP addresses and default gateway addresses appropriate for each situation?

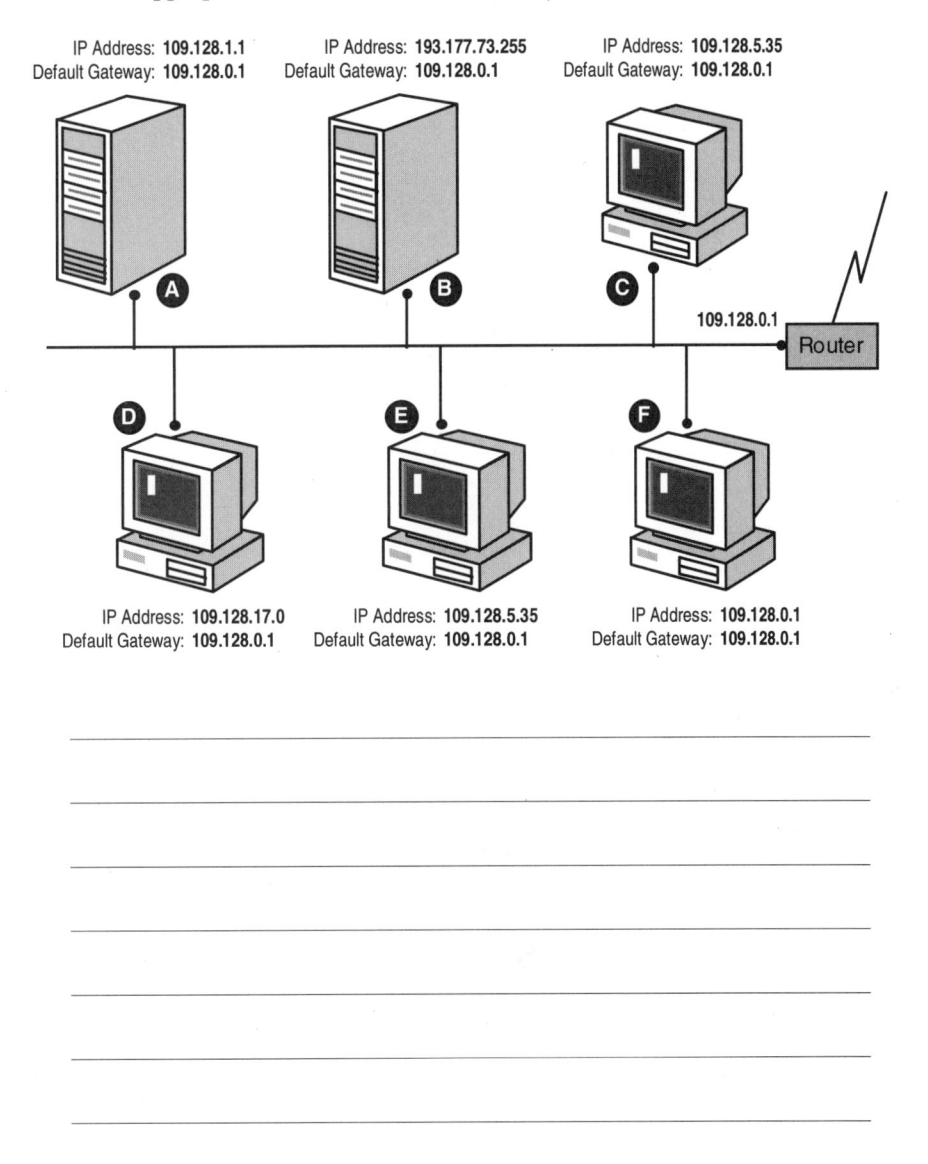

A
IP Address: **109.128.1.1**
Default Gateway: **109.128.0.1**

B
IP Address: **193.177.73.255**
Default Gateway: **109.128.0.1**

C
IP Address: **109.128.5.35**
Default Gateway: **109.128.0.1**

Router: 109.128.0.1

D
IP Address: **109.128.17.0**
Default Gateway: **109.128.0.1**

E
IP Address: **109.128.5.35**
Default Gateway: **109.128.0.1**

F
IP Address: **109.128.0.1**
Default Gateway: **109.128.0.1**

For More Information
- Review all referenced RFCs on the course compact disc.

CHAPTER 5

Subnetting

Lesson 1   Subnet Overview . . . 82

Lesson 2   Defining a Subnet Mask . . . 85

Lesson 3   Defining Subnet IDs . . . 93

Lesson 4   Defining Host IDs for a Subnet . . . 96

Lesson 5   Supernetting . . . 103

Review . . . 106

About This Chapter

In this chapter, you learn how to assign IP addresses to multiple TCP/IP networks with a single network ID. The lessons provide fundamental concepts and procedures for implementing subnetting and supernetting. During the lessons, you learn when subnetting is necessary, how and when to use a default subnet mask, how to define a custom subnet mask, and how to create a range of valid IP addresses for each subnet.

Before You Begin

To complete the lessons in this chapter, you must have:

- An understanding of the ANDing and IP addressing concepts presented in Chapter 4, "IP Addressing."
- Installed Microsoft Windows NT Server 4.0 with TCP/IP.

Lesson 1: Subnet Overview

A subnet is a physical segment in a TCP/IP environment that uses IP addresses derived from a single network ID. Typically, an organization acquires one network ID from the InterNIC. In this lesson, you learn the requirements for subnetting.

After this lesson, you will be able to:
- Explain the purpose and benefits of a subnet.

Estimated lesson time: 10 minutes

Dividing the network into subnets requires that each segment use a different network ID, or subnet ID. As shown in the following example, a unique subnet ID is created for each segment by partitioning the bits in the host ID into two parts. One part is used to identify the segment as a unique network, and the other part is used to identify the hosts. This is referred to as *subnetting* or *subnetworking*. Subnetting is not necessary if your network is private.

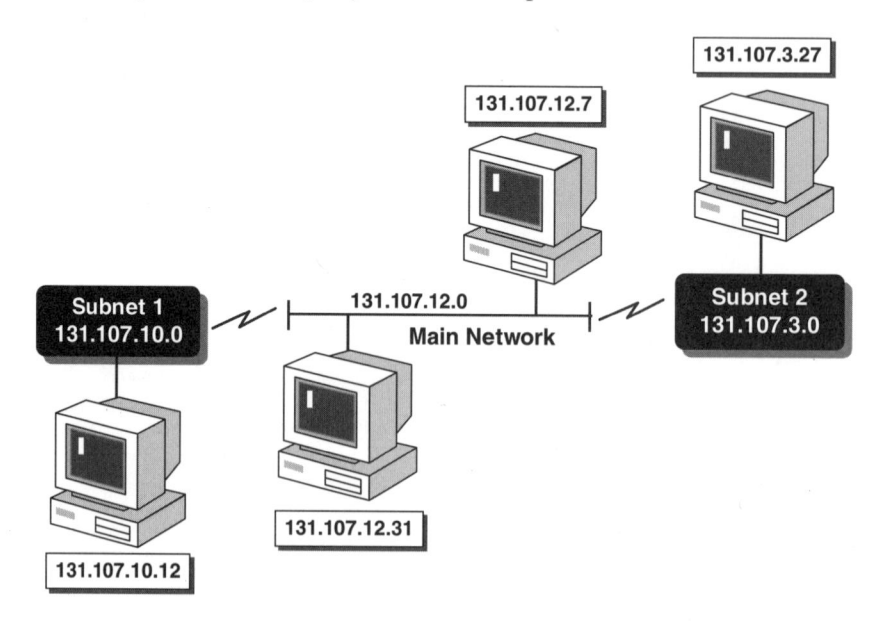

There are several benefits to subnetting. Organizations use subnetting to apply one network across multiple physical segments. With subnetting you can:

- Mix different technologies, such as Ethernet and Token Ring.
- Overcome limitations of current technologies, such as exceeding the maximum number of hosts per segment.
- Reduce network congestion by redirecting traffic and reducing broadcasts.

Note Subnetting is defined in RFC 950. For a copy of this RFC, see the *Course Materials* Web page on the course compact disc.

Implementing Subnetting

Before you implement subnetting, you need to determine your current requirements and plan for future requirements. Follow these guidelines:

1. Determine the number of physical segments on your network.
2. Determine the number of required host addresses for each physical segment. Each TCP/IP host requires at least one IP address.
3. Based on your requirements, define:
    - One subnet mask for your entire network.
    - A unique subnet ID for each physical segment.
    - A range of host IDs for each subnet.

Subnet Mask Bits

Before you define a subnet mask, you should determine the number of segments and hosts per segment you will require in the future.

When more bits are used for the subnet mask, more subnets are available, but fewer hosts are available per subnet. For example, the following class B examples show the correlation between the number of bits and the number of subnets and hosts:

  3 bits=6 subnets=8,000 hosts per subnet

  8 bits=254 subnets=254 hosts per subnet

If you use more bits than needed, it will allow for growth in the number of subnets, but will limit the growth in the number of hosts. If you use fewer bits than needed, it will allow for growth in the number of hosts, but will limit the growth in the number of subnets.

Summary

A subnet is a physical segment in a TCP/IP environment that uses IP addresses from a single network ID. The IP addressing scheme used for subnets is referred to as *subnetting*. The number bits in the subnet mask will determine the number of subnets and hosts per subnets available to you.

Lesson 2: Defining a Subnet Mask

Defining a subnet mask is a three-step process. In this lesson, you learn the three steps and perform several practices to define subnets.

After this lesson, you will be able to:
- Explain the function of a custom subnet mask.
- Define a valid subnet mask for a variety of situations.

Estimated lesson time: 45 minutes

Defining a subnet mask is required if you are dividing your network into subnets. Follow these steps to define a subnet mask:

1. Once you have determined the number of physical segments in your network environment, convert this number to binary format.

2. Count the number of bits required to represent the number of physical segments in binary. For example, if you need six subnets, the binary value is 110. Representing six in binary requires 3 bits.

3. Convert the required number of bits to decimal format in high order (from left to right). For example, if 3 bits are required, configure the first 3 bits of the host ID as the subnet ID. The decimal value for binary 11100000 is 224. The subnet mask then is 255.255.224.0 (for a class B address).

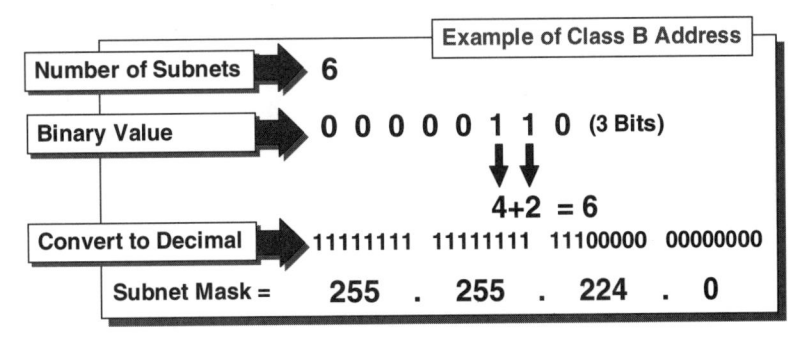

```
                                    Example of Class B Address
Number of Subnets     →  6

Binary Value          →  0 0 0 0 0 1 1 0   (3 Bits)
                                     ↓ ↓
                                    4+2 = 6
Convert to Decimal    →  11111111  11111111  11100000  00000000
Subnet Mask =            255    .  255    .  224    .  0
```

Contiguous Mask Bits

Because subnets are defined by the subnet mask, there is nothing to prevent an administrator from using low-order or unordered bits to determine the subnet ID. When subnetting was initially defined in RFC 950, it was recommended that subnet IDs be derived from high-order bits. Today, however, few router vendors support the use of low-order or non-order bits in subnet IDs. Furthermore, it is now a requirement that the subnet ID make use of contiguous, high-order bits of the local address portion of the subnet mask.

Conversion Tables

The following table lists the subnet masks already converted using one octet for class A networks.

Number of subnets	Required number of bits	Subnet mask	Number of hosts per subnet
0	1	Invalid	Invalid
2	2	255.192.0.0	4,194,302
6	3	255.224.0.0	2,097,150
14	4	255.240.0.0	1,048,574
30	5	255.248.0.0	524,286
62	6	255.252.0.0	262,142
126	7	255.254.0.0	131,070
254	8	255.255.0.0	65,534

The following table lists the subnet masks already converted using one octet for class B networks.

Number of subnets	Required number of bits	Subnet mask	Number of hosts per subnet
0	1	Invalid	Invalid
2	2	255.255.192.0	16,382
6	3	255.255.224.0	8,190
14	4	255.255.240.0	4,094
30	5	255.255.248.0	2,046
62	6	255.255.252.0	1,022
126	7	255.255.254.0	510
254	8	255.255.255.0	254

The following table lists the subnet masks already converted using one octet for class C networks.

Number of subnets	Required Number of bits	Subnet mask	Number of hosts per subnet
Invalid	1	Invalid	Invalid
1–2	2	255.255.255.192	62
3–6	3	255.255.255.224	30
7–14	4	255.255.255.240	14
15–30	5	255.255.255.248	6
31–62	6	255.255.255.252	2
Invalid	7	Invalid	Invalid
Invalid	8	Invalid	Invalid

Subnetting More Than One Octet

During this lesson, you have worked within one octet to define a subnet mask. At times, it may be advantageous to subnet using more than one octet, or more than 8 bits. This will give you greater addressing flexibility.

For example, suppose you are configuring an intranet for a large corporation. The corporation plans to internally connect its sites that are distributed across Europe, North America, and Asia. This totals approximately 30 geographical locations with almost 1,000 subnets and an average of 750 hosts per subnet.

It is possible to use several class B network IDs and further subnet them. To meet your host requirements per subnet with a class B network address, you need to use a subnet mask of 255.255.252.0. Adding our requirement of subnets, you need at least 16 class B addresses.

However, there is an easier way. Because the computers you are using are on an intranet, you can use a private network. If you choose to allocate a class A network ID of 10.0.0.0, you can plan for growth and meet your requirements at the same time. Obviously, subnetting only the second octet will not meet your requirements of one thousand subnets. However, if you subnet both the second octet and a portion of the third octet, you can meet all of your requirements with one network ID.

Network ID	Subnet mask	Subnet mask (binary)
10.0.0.0	255.255.248.0	11111111 11111111 11111000 00000000

Using 13 bits for the subnet ID in a class A address, you have allocated 8,190 subnets, each with up to 2,046 hosts. You have met your requirements with flexibility for growth.

Practice

In this practice, you define a subnet mask for several situations. Remember that not every situation requires subnetting.

1. Class A network address on a local network.

2. Class B network address on a local network with 4,000 hosts.

3. Class C network address on a local network with 254 hosts.

4. Class A address with 6 subnets.

5. Class B address with 126 subnets.

6. Class A network address. Currently, there are 30 subnets that will grow to approximately 65 subnets within the next year. Each subnet will never have more than 50,000 hosts.

7. Using the subnet mask from the preceding scenario, how much growth will this subnet mask provide?

8. Class B network address. Currently, there are 14 subnets that may double in size within the next two years. Each subnet will have fewer than 1,500 hosts.

9. Using the subnet mask from the preceding scenario, how much growth will this subnet mask provide?

Practice

In this practice, you review two invalid subnet masks to see what would happen when you try to communicate with a host on a local network and a remote network.

Using the information below, convert your computer's IP address and the IP address of your second computer to binary format, and then AND them to the subnet mask to determine why the subnet mask is invalid.

Your IP address	131.107.y.z	1 0 0 0 0 0 1 1 0 1 1 0 1 0 1 1
Subnet mask	255.255.255.248	1 1 1 1 1 1 1 1 1 1 1 1 1 1 1 1 1 1 1 1 1 1 1 1 1 1 1 1 1 0 0 0
Result		
Destination IP address	131.107.y.z	1 0 0 0 0 0 1 1 0 1 1 0 1 0 1 1
Subnet mask	255.255.255.248	1 1 1 1 1 1 1 1 1 1 1 1 1 1 1 1 1 1 1 1 1 1 1 1 1 1 1 1 1 0 0 0
Result		

Did the result of ANDing indicate that the destination IP address and subnet mask were for a local or remote network?

_____

Why would you not be able to successfully ping your default gateway?

_____

Using the information below, convert your IP address and the IP address of a remote host to binary format, and then AND them to the subnet mask to determine why the subnet mask would be invalid.

Your IP address	131.107.y.z	1 0 0 0 0 0 1 1 0 1 1 0 1 0 1 1
Subnet mask	255.255.0.0	1 1 1 1 1 1 1 1 1 1 1 1 1 1 1 1 0 0 0 0 0 0 0 0 0 0 0 0 0 0 0 0
Result		
Destination IP address	131.107.y.z	1 0 0 0 0 0 1 1 0 1 1 0 1 0 1 1
Subnet mask	255.255.0.0	1 1 1 1 1 1 1 1 1 1 1 1 1 1 1 1 0 0 0 0 0 0 0 0 0 0 0 0 0 0 0 0
Result		

Did the result of ANDing indicate that the destination IP address and subnet mask were for a local or remote network?

_____

Why would you not be able to successfully ping a remote host?

_____

Compare the two results generated using incorrect subnet masks to see how differently TCP/IP responds when the subnet mask indicates a local network versus a remote network. What did you conclude about how TCP/IP uses a subnet mask?

_____

_____

_____

_____

Practice

In this practice, you review the following two examples, identify the hidden problems, and then explain the possible effects caused by the problems.

Example 1

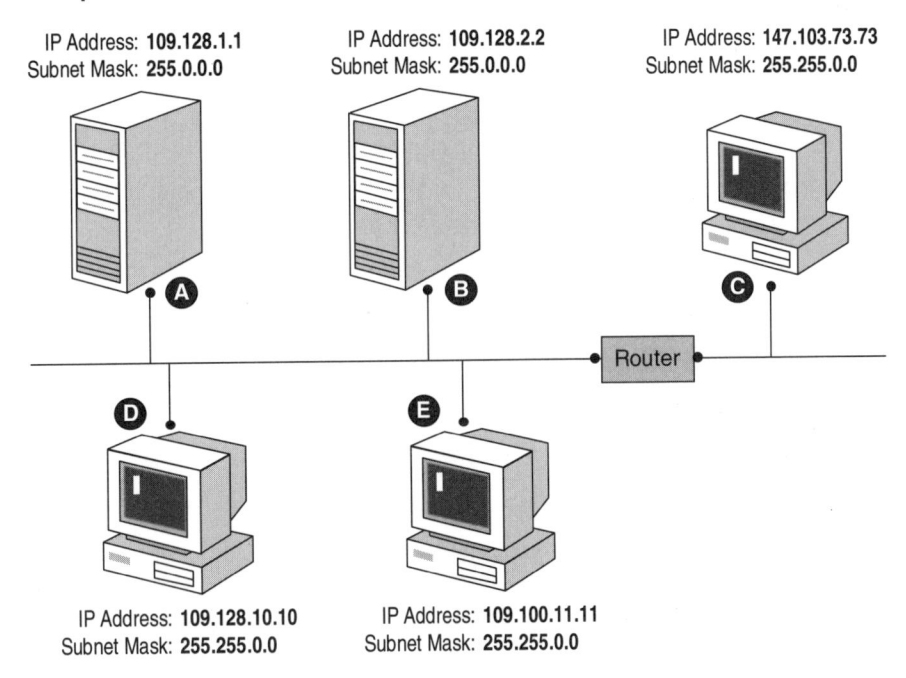

IP Address: **109.128.1.1**
Subnet Mask: **255.0.0.0**

IP Address: **109.128.2.2**
Subnet Mask: **255.0.0.0**

IP Address: **147.103.73.73**
Subnet Mask: **255.255.0.0**

A   B   C

Router

D   E

IP Address: **109.128.10.10**
Subnet Mask: **255.255.0.0**

IP Address: **109.100.11.11**
Subnet Mask: **255.255.0.0**

Which hosts have an incorrect subnet mask?

How will an invalid subnet mask affect these hosts?

What is the correct subnet mask?

Example 2

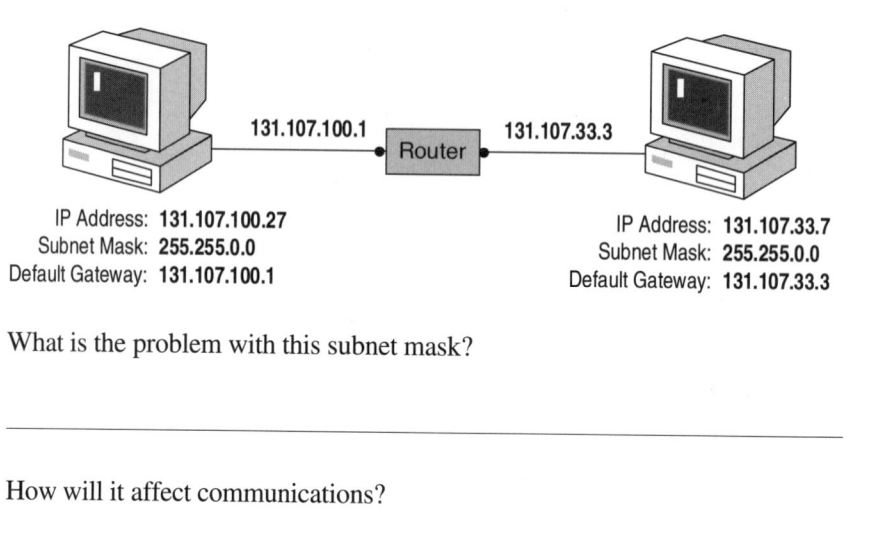

```
131.107.100.1  [Router]  131.107.33.3
```

IP Address: **131.107.100.27**
Subnet Mask: **255.255.0.0**
Default Gateway: **131.107.100.1**

IP Address: **131.107.33.7**
Subnet Mask: **255.255.0.0**
Default Gateway: **131.107.33.3**

What is the problem with this subnet mask?

_____

How will it affect communications?

_____

What is the correct subnet mask?

_____

Summary

If you are dividing your network into subnets, you must define a subnet mask. The steps for defining a subnet mask are converting the number of physical network segments to binary format, counting the number of required bits, and then converting the number of required bits to decimal format. You can subnet more than 8 bits to give you greater addressing flexibility.

Lesson 3: Defining Subnet IDs

Subnet IDs are defined using the same number of host bits as are used for the subnet mask. There are different ways to define a range of subnet IDs for an internetwork. In this lesson, the long and the short methods are discussed.

After this lesson, you will be able to:
- Use different methods to define a range of subnet IDs for an internetwork.
- Define a common subnet mask for a WAN that consists of multiple subnets.

Estimated lesson time: 20 minutes

You can define the subnet ID for a physical segment using the same number of host bits as used for the subnet mask. The possible bit combinations are evaluated and then converted to a decimal format. The following steps and illustration show how to define a range of subnet IDs for an internetwork:

1. Using the same number of bits as are used for the subnet mask, list all possible bit combinations.

2. Cross out values that use all 0's or 1's. All 0's and 1's are invalid IP addresses and network IDs, because all 0's indicate "this network only" and all 1's match the subnet mask.

3. Convert to decimal the subnet ID bits for each subnet. Each decimal value represents a single subnet. This value is used to define the range of host IDs for a subnet.

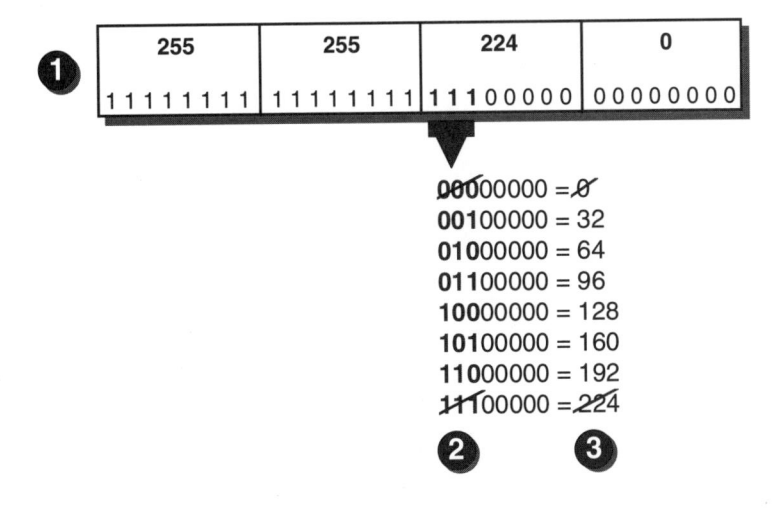

①

255	255	224	0
1 1 1 1 1 1 1 1	1 1 1 1 1 1 1 1	1 1 1 0 0 0 0 0	0 0 0 0 0 0 0 0

~~00~~000000 = ~~0~~
00100000 = 32
01000000 = 64
01100000 = 96
10000000 = 128
10100000 = 160
11000000 = 192
~~111~~00000 = ~~224~~

②   **③**

Special-Case Subnet Addresses

Subnet IDs comprised of all 0's or all 1's are called *special-case subnet addresses*. A subnet ID of all 1's indicates a subnet broadcast, and a subnet ID of all 0's indicates "this subnet." When subnetting, it is recommended not to use these subnet IDs. However, it is possible to use these special-case subnet addresses if they are supported by all routers and hardware on your network. RFC 950 discusses the limitations imposed when using special-case addresses.

Shortcut to Defining Subnet IDs

Using the preceding method to define a subnet ID is impractical when you are using more than 4 bits for your subnet mask because it requires listing and converting many bit combinations. The following steps and illustration demonstrate how to use the shortcut to define a range of subnet IDs:

1. List the number of bits in high order used for the subnet ID. For example, if 2 bits are used for the subnet mask, the binary octet is 11000000.

2. Convert the bit with the lowest value to decimal format. This is the increment value to determine each subnet. For example, if you use 2 bits, the lowest value is 64.

3. Starting with zero, increment the value for each bit combination until the next increment is 256.

Tip If you know the number of bits you need, you can raise 2 to the power of the bit, and then subtract 2 to determine the possible bit combinations.

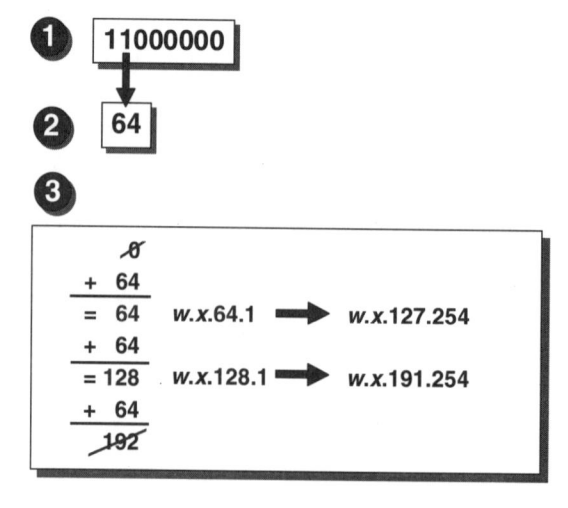

---

① 11000000

② 64

③
```
     0̶
  +  64
  =  64    w.x.64.1  ➡  w.x.127.254
  +  64
  = 128    w.x.128.1 ➡  w.x.191.254
  +  64
    1̶9̶2̶
```

Practice

In this additional practice, you determine the appropriate subnet mask for a given range of IP addresses.

1. Address range of 128.71.1.1 through 128.71.254.254.

   _____

2. Address range of 61.8.0.1 through 61.15.255.254.

   _____

3. Address range of 172.88.32.1 through 172.88.63.254.

   _____

4. Address range of 111.224.0.1 through 111.239.255.254.

   _____

5. Address range of 3.64.0.1 through 3.127.255.254.

   _____

Summary

You can define a range of subnet IDs using a long and short method. Using the long method is impractical when you are using more than 4 bits for your subnet mask.

Lesson 4: Defining Host IDs for a Subnet

You can follow a short procedure to determine the number of hosts per subnet. In fact, if you have defined your subnet IDs, then you have already defined your host IDs for each subnet. This lesson shows you how to define the host IDs for a subnet, and lets you practice the procedure in several practices.

After this lesson, you will be able to:
- Define a range of host IDs for a subnet using the subnet ID.

Estimated lesson time: 30 minutes

The result of each incremented value indicates the beginning of a range of host IDs for a subnet. If you increment the value one extra time, you can determine the end of the range (one less than the subnet mask), as shown in the following illustration.

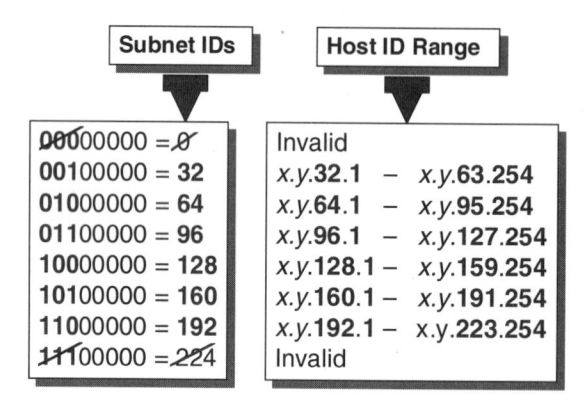

Subnet IDs

```
00000000 = 0
00100000 = 32
01000000 = 64
01100000 = 96
10000000 = 128
10100000 = 160
11000000 = 192
11100000 = 224
```

Host ID Range

```
Invalid
x.y.32.1   - x.y.63.254
x.y.64.1   - x.y.95.254
x.y.96.1   - x.y.127.254
x.y.128.1  - x.y.159.254
x.y.160.1  - x.y.191.254
x.y.192.1  - x.y.223.254
Invalid
```

The following table shows the valid range of host IDs on a class B subnet using 3 bits for the subnet mask.

Bit values	Decimal value	Beginning range value	Ending range value
00000000	0	Invalid	Invalid
00100000	32	x.y.32.1	x.y.63.254
01000000	64	x.y.64.1	x.y.95.254
01100000	96	x.y.96.1	x.y.127.254
10000000	128	x.y.128.1	x.y.159.254
10100000	160	x.y.160.1	x.y.191.254
11000000	192	x.y.192.1	x.y.223.254
11100000	224	Invalid	Invalid

▶ **To determine the number of hosts per subnet**

1. Calculate the number of bits available for the host ID. For example, if you are given a class B address that uses 16 bits for the network ID and 2 bits for the subnet ID, you have 14 bits remaining for the host ID.
2. Convert the binary host ID bits to decimal. For example, 11111111111111 in binary is converted to 16,383 in decimal format.
3. Subtract 1.

Tip If you know the number of host ID bits you need, you can raise 2 to the power of the number of host ID bits, and then subtract 2.

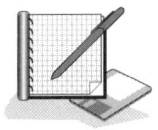

Practice

In the following practices, you define a range of network IDs. Refer to the following illustration to complete the practices.

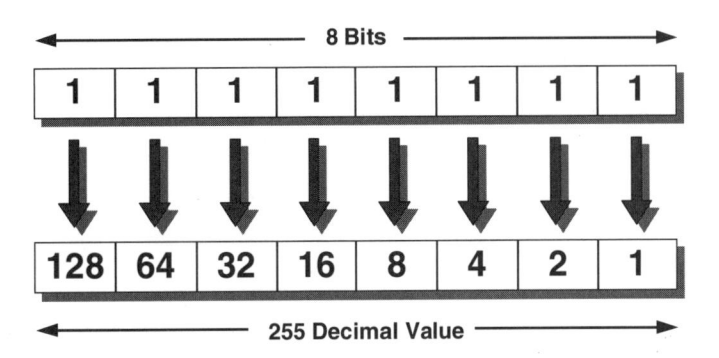

1	1	1	1	1	1	1	1
128	64	32	16	8	4	2	1

← 8 Bits →

← 255 Decimal Value →

Defining a Range of Network IDs for Two Subnets

In this practice, you define a range of network IDs for an internetwork that consists of two subnets, using 2 bits from a class B subnet mask.

1. List all possible bit combinations for the following subnet mask, and then convert them to decimal format to determine the beginning value of each subnet.

255	255	192	0
1 1 1 1 1 1 1 1	1 1 1 1 1 1 1 1	**1 1** 0 0 0 0 0 0	0 0 0 0 0 0 0 0

Invalid	0 0 0 0 0 0 0 0	=	0
Subnet 1	_____	=	____
Subnet 2	_____	=	____
Invalid	1 1 0 0 0 0 0 0	=	192 (subnet mask)

2. List the range of host IDs for each subnet.

Subnet	Beginning value	Ending value
Subnet 1	w.x._____.1	w.x._____.254
Subnet 2	w.x._____.1	w.x._____.254

Defining a Range of Network IDs for 14 Subnets

In this practice, you define a range of network IDs for an internetwork that consists of 14 subnets, using 4 bits from a class B subnet mask.

1. List all possible bit combinations for the following subnet mask, and then convert them to decimal format to determine the beginning value of each subnet.

255	255	240	0
1 1 1 1 1 1 1 1	1 1 1 1 1 1 1 1	1 1 1 1 0 0 0 0	0 0 0 0 0 0 0 0

Invalid	0 0 0 0 0 0 0 0	=	0
Subnet 1	_____	=	____
Subnet 2	_____	=	____
Subnet 3	_____	=	____
Subnet 4	_____	=	____
Subnet 5	_____	=	____
Subnet 6	_____	=	____
Subnet 7	_____	=	____
Subnet 8	_____	=	____
Subnet 9	_____	=	____
Subnet 10	_____	=	____
Subnet 11	_____	=	____
Subnet 12	_____	=	____
Subnet 13	_____	=	____
Subnet 14	_____	=	____
Invalid	1 1 1 1 0 0 0 0	=	240 (subnet mask)

2. List the range of host IDs for each subnet.

Subnet	Beginning value	Ending value
Subnet 1	w.x.____.1	w.x.____.254
Subnet 2	w.x.____.1	w.x.____.254
Subnet 3	w.x.____.1	w.x.____.254
Subnet 4	w.x.____.1	w.x.____.254
Subnet 5	w.x.____.1	w.x.____.254
Subnet 6	w.x.____.1	w.x.____.254
Subnet 7	w.x.____.1	w.x.____.254
Subnet 8	w.x.____.1	w.x.____.254
Subnet 9	w.x.____.1	w.x.____.254
Subnet 10	w.x.____.1	w.x.____.254
Subnet 11	w.x.____.1	w.x.____.254
Subnet 12	w.x.____.1	w.x.____.254
Subnet 13	w.x.____.1	w.x.____.254
Subnet 14	w.x.____.1	w.x.____.254

Defining a Range of Network IDs Using a Shortcut

In this practice, you use a shortcut to define a range of network IDs for 14 subnets. Compare these results to the results in the preceding practice. The two should match. The first step has been done for you.

1. List the number of bits (in high order) that will be used for the subnet mask.

255	255	240	0
1 1 1 1 1 1 1 1	1 1 1 1 1 1 1 1	**1 1 1 1** 0 0 0 0	0 0 0 0 0 0 0 0

2. Convert the bit with the lowest value to decimal format.

3. Convert the number of bits to decimal format (in low order), and then subtract 1 to determine the number of possible subnets.

4. Starting with 0, increment by the value calculated in step 2 the same number of times as the possible bit combinations calculated in step 3.

Practice

In this additional practice, you define a range of host IDs for each of the following subnets.

1. Network ID of 75.0.0.0, subnet mask of 255.255.0.0, and 2 subnets.

2. Network ID of 150.17.0.0, subnet mask of 255.255.255.0, and 4 subnets.

3. Network IDs of 107.16.0.0 and 107.32.0.0, subnet mask of 255.240.0.0, and 2 subnets.

4. Network IDs of 190.1.16.0, 190.1.32.0, 190.1.48.0, and 190.1.64.0, subnet mask of 255.255.248.0, and 4 subnets.

5. Network IDs of 154.233.32.0, 154.233.96.0, and 154.233.160.0, subnet mask of 255.255.224.0, and 3 subnets.

Summary

To determine the number of hosts per subnet you use three steps. First, calculate the number of bits available for the host ID, then convert the binary host ID bits to decimal, and finally, subtract 1.

Lesson 5: Supernetting

To prevent the depletion of network IDs, the Internet authorities devised a scheme called *supernetting*. This lesson gives you an overview of supernetting.

After this lesson, you will be able to:
- Describe the concept of supernetting.

Estimated lesson time: 10 minutes

Supernetting is different than subnetting in that it borrows bits from the network ID and masks them as the host ID for more efficient routing. For example, rather than allocating a class B network ID to an organization that has 2,000 hosts, the InterNIC allocates a range of 8 class C network IDs. Each class C network ID accommodates 254 hosts for a total of 2,032 host IDs.

While this technique helps conserve class B network IDs, it creates a new problem. Using conventional routing techniques, the routers on the Internet now must have an additional seven entries in their routing tables to route IP packets to the organization. To prevent overwhelming the Internet routers, a technique called *Classless Inter-Domain Routing* (CIDR) is used to collapse the eight entries used in the following illustration to a single entry corresponding to all of the class C network IDs used by that organization.

Before Supernetting

Routing Table for Router B
220.78.168.0	255.255.255.0	220.78.168.1
220.78.169.0	255.255.255.0	220.78.168.1
220.78.170.0	255.255.255.0	220.78.168.1
220.78.171.0	255.255.255.0	220.78.168.1
220.78.172.0	255.255.255.0	220.78.168.1
220.78.173.0	255.255.255.0	220.78.168.1
220.78.174.0	255.255.255.0	220.78.168.1
220.78.175.0	255.255.255.0	220.78.168.1

After Supernetting

Routing Table for Router B
220.78.168.0	255.255.248.0	220.78.168.1

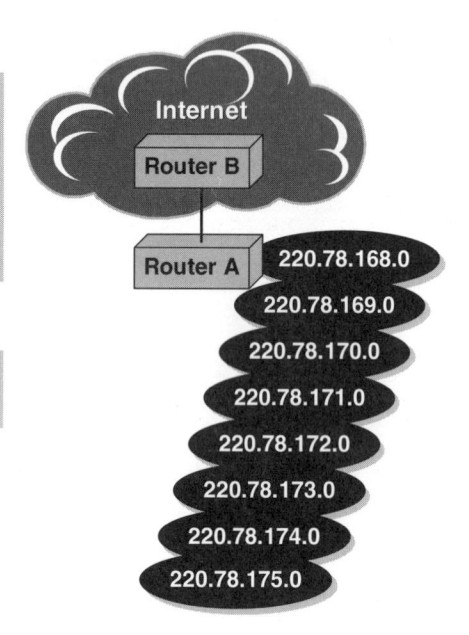

To express the situation in which eight class C network IDs are allocated starting with the network ID 220.78.168.0 and ending with network ID 220.78.175.0, the entry in the routing table becomes:

Network ID	Subnet mask	Subnet mask (binary)
220.78.168.0	255.255.248.0	11111111 11111111 11111000 00000000

In supernetting, the destination of a packet is determined by ANDing the destination IP address and the subnet mask of the routing entry. If a match is found to the network ID, the route is used. This is the same process defined in the preceding lesson.

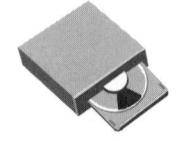

Note *Classless Inter-Domain Routing* (CIDR) is defined in RFCs 1518 and 1519. For copies of these RFCs, see the *Course Materials* Web page on the course compact disc.

Summary

Supernetting borrows bits from the network ID and masks them as the host ID for more efficient routing.

Review

The following questions are intended to reinforce key information presented in this chapter. If you are unable to answer a question, review the appropriate lesson and then try the question again. The scenario-based review practices will help you use key information in real-world situations.

1. What is the purpose of a subnet mask?

2. What requires a subnet mask?

3. When is a default subnet mask used?

4. When is it necessary to define a custom subnet mask?

Review Practice

In the following review practices, you define a subnetting scheme for several scenarios. For each scenario, define the following:

- A subnet mask.
- A range of valid network IDs.
- A default gateway for hosts on each subnet.

After you have defined this information for each scenario, answer the questions that follow.

Scenario 1

You have been assigned one class B address of 131.107.0.0 by the InterNIC. Your intranet currently has 5 subnets. Each subnet has approximately 300 hosts. Within the next year the number of subnets will triple. The number of hosts on three of the subnets could increase to as many as 1,000.

1. How many bits did you use for the subnet mask?

2. How much growth did you allow for additional subnets?

3. How much growth did you allow for additional hosts?

Scenario 2

You have been assigned one class A address of 124.0.0.0 by the InterNIC. Your private internet currently has 5 subnets. Each subnet has approximately 500,000 hosts. In the near future, you would like to divide the 5 subnets into 25 smaller, more manageable subnets. The number of hosts on the 25 new subnets could eventually increase to 300,000.

1. How many bits did you use for the subnet mask?

2. How much growth did you allow for additional subnets?

3. How much growth did you allow for additional hosts?

Scenario 3

You have 5 subnets with approximately 300 hosts on each subnet. Within the next 6 months, the number of subnets could increase to more than 100. The number of hosts on each subnet will probably never be more than 2,000. You do not have any plans to connect to the worldwide public Internet.

1. Which class of address did you use?

2. How many bits did you use for the subnet mask?

3. How much growth did you allow for additional subnets?

4. How much growth did you allow for additional hosts?

Scenario 4

An Internet service provider has just been assigned the block of 2,048 class C network numbers beginning with 192.24.0.0 and ending with 192.31.255.0.

1. What IP address would begin a "supernetted" route to this block of numbers?

2. What net mask would be used to supernet this block of numbers?

_____

Customers of this Internet service provider have the following requirements:

- Customer 1 will not have more than 2,023 hosts.
- Customer 2 will not have more than 4,047 hosts.
- Customer 3 will not have more than 1,011 hosts.
- Customer 4 will not have more than 500 hosts.

Assign the missing IP and subnet mask values for each customer.

1. Customer 1
   Beginning IP address   192.24.0.1
   Ending IP address   192.24.7.8
   Subnet mask   _____

2. Customer 2
   Beginning IP address   _____
   Ending IP address   192.24.31.254
   Subnet mask   255.255.240.0

3. Customer 3
   Beginning IP address   192.24.8.1
   Ending IP address   _____
   Subnet mask   255.255.252.0

4. Customer 4
   Beginning IP address   192.24.14.1
   Ending IP address   192.24.15.254
   Subnet mask   _____

For More Information

- Review all referenced RFCs on the course compact disc.

CHAPTER 6

Implementing IP Routing

Lesson 1   IP Routing Overview . . . 112

Lesson 2   Static IP Routing . . . 115

Lesson 3   Dynamic IP Routing . . . 121

Lesson 4   Implementing a Windows NT Router . . . 126

Review . . . 128

About This Chapter

In this chapter, you review IP routing concepts and describe how to implement IP routing on a computer running Microsoft Windows NT 4.0. The lessons explain how to build a static routing table, configure a Windows NT computer to function as an IP router, detect default gateway failure, and use the Route utility to add static routes to the route table.

Before You Begin

To complete the lessons in this chapter, you must have installed Windows NT Server 4.0 with TCP/IP.

Lesson 1: IP Routing Overview

Routing is the process of choosing a path over which to send packets. Routing occurs at a TCP/IP host when it sends IP packets, and occurs again at an IP router. A *router* is a device that forwards the packets from one physical network to another. Routers are commonly referred to as *gateways*. This lesson explains basic IP routing concepts.

After this lesson, you will be able to:
- Understand basic IP routing concepts.
- Explain the difference between static and dynamic IP routing.

Estimated lesson time: 10 minutes

For both the sending host and router, a decision has to be made as to where the packet is to be forwarded. To make routing decisions, the IP layer consults a routing table that is stored in memory as shown in the following illustration. A routing table contains entries with the IP addresses of router interfaces to other networks that it can communicate with. By default, a router can send packets only to networks to which it has a configured interface.

1. When a host attempts communication with another host, IP first determines whether the destination host is local or on a remote network.
2. If the destination host is remote, IP then checks the routing table for a route to the remote host or remote network.
3. If no explicit route is found, IP uses its default gateway address to deliver the packet to a router.
4. At the router, the routing table is again consulted for a path to the remote host or network. If a path is not found, the packet is sent to the router's default gateway address.

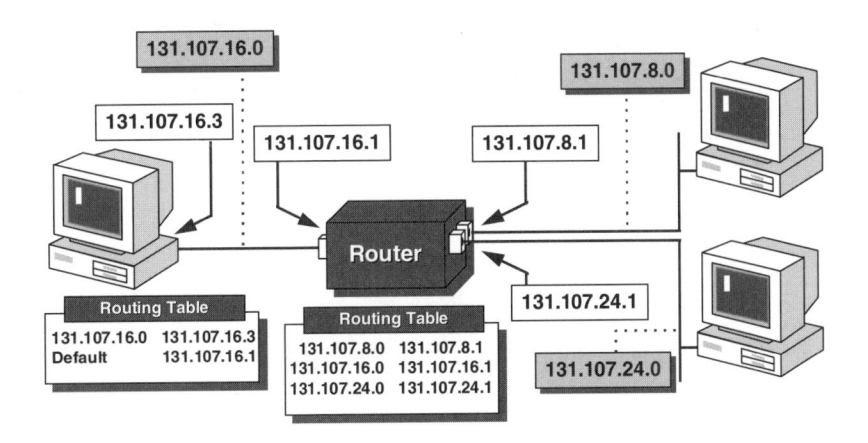

As each route is found, the packet is sent to the next router, called a "hop," and finally delivered to the destination host. If a route is not found, an error message is sent to the source host.

Dead Gateway Detection

TCP can detect the failure of the default gateway and make the necessary adjustments to the IP routing table to use another default gateway. TCP will attempt to send a packet to the default gateway configured on a computer until it receives an acknowledgment. However, if one-half of the *TcpMaxDataRetransmissions* value is exceeded and multiple gateways are configured on the computer, TCP requests that IP switch to the next default gateway in the list.

When you configure a computer running Windows NT with the IP addresses of multiple gateways, by default, dead gateway detection is set to **on**.

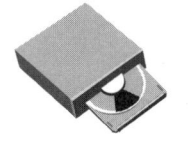

Note The Microsoft implementation of dead gateway detection uses TCP retries and the triggered reselection method described in RFC 816. For a copy of this RFC, see the *Course Materials* Web page on the course compact disc.

Static vs. Dynamic IP Routing

How routers obtain routing information depends on whether the router performs static or dynamic IP routing. Static routing is a function of IP. Static routers require that routing tables are built and updated manually. If a route changes, static routers do not inform each other of the change, nor do static routers exchange routes with dynamic routers.

Dynamic routing is a function of routing protocols, such as the Routing Information Protocol (RIP) and Open Shortest Path First (OSPF). Routing protocols periodically exchange routes to known networks among dynamic routers. If a route changes, other routers are automatically informed of the change.

Windows NT Server version 4.0 can function as an IP router using both static and dynamic routing. A computer running Windows NT can be configured with multiple network adapters and route between them. This type of system, which is ideal for small intranets, is referred to as a *multihomed computer*.

Windows NT Server 4.0 provides the ability to function as an RIP router that supports dynamic management of IP routing tables. RIP eliminates the need to establish static IP routing tables.

Note Microsoft provides support for inter-routing protocols on Windows NT 4.0. RIP is defined in RFC 1723. For copy of this RFC, see the *Course Materials* Web page on the course compact disc.

Summary

Routers forward packets from one physical network to another. The IP layer consults a routing table that is stored in memory. A routing table contains entries with the IP addresses of router interfaces to other networks. Static routers require that routing tables are built and updated manually. With dynamic routing, if a route changes, other routers are automatically informed of the change.

Lesson 2: Static IP Routing

A static router can communicate only with networks to which it has a configured interface. This lesson explains how to configure a static router and modify a routing table.

After this lesson, you will be able to:
- Explain the requirements for communicating with a static IP router.
- Build a static routing table.

Estimated lesson time: 25 minutes

To route IP packets to other networks, each static router must be configured. You should add either an entry in each router's routing table for each network in the internetwork, or a default gateway address of another router's local interface. As shown in the following illustration:

- Computer A has only local connections to networks 1 and 2. As a result, hosts on network 1 can communicate with hosts on network 2, but cannot communicate with hosts on network 3.

- Computer B has only local connections to networks 2 and 3. Hosts on network 3 can communicate with hosts on network 2, but cannot communicate with hosts on network 1.

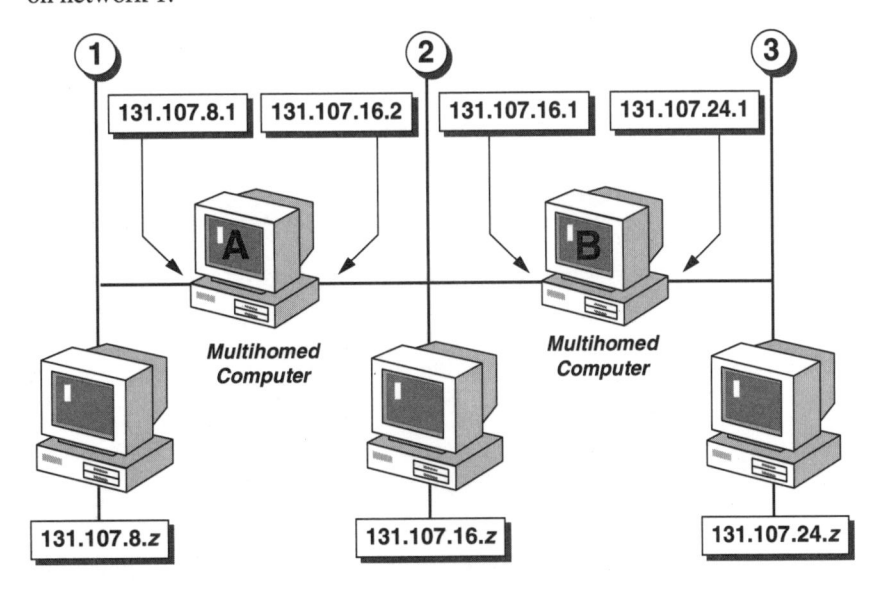

Configuring Static IP Routers

In an internetwork with at least one static router, you will need to configure static routing table entries at each router to all known networks. As shown in the following illustration:

- A static routing table entry is created on computer A. The entry contains the network ID of network 3 and the IP address (131.107.16.1) of the interface computer A can access directly to route packets from network 1 to network 3.

- A static routing table entry is created on computer B. The entry contains the network ID of network 1. The entry also contains the IP address (131.107.16.2) of the interface that computer B can access directly in order to route packets from network 3 to network 1.

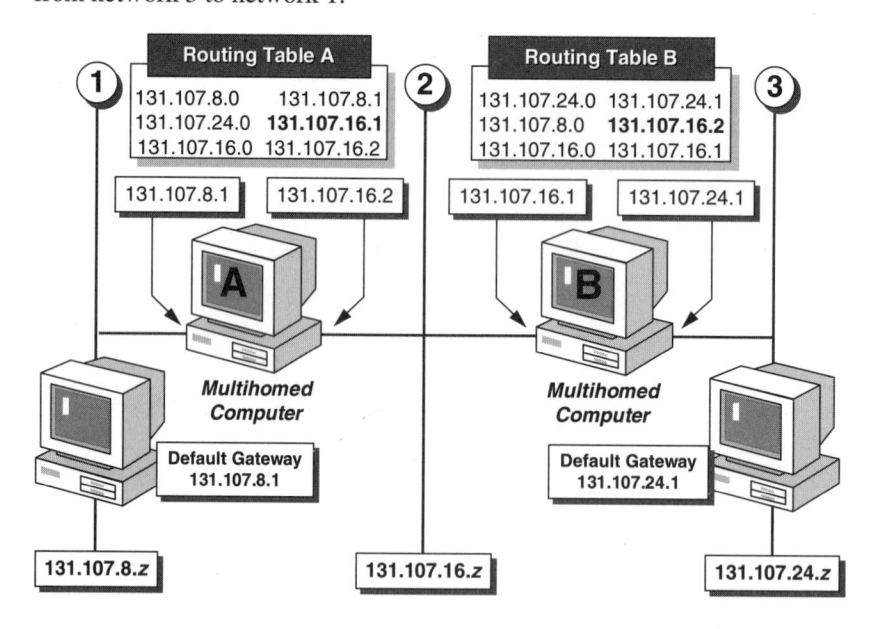

If your internetwork has more than two routers, and at least one of them is a static router, you need to configure a static routing table at each multihomed computer.

For a host to communicate with other hosts on the internetwork, its default gateway address must be configured to match the IP address of the router's local interface.

Using the Default Gateway Address

One method of configuring a static route without manually adding routes to a routing table is to configure each multihomed computer's default gateway address as the local interface to the other multihomed computer on the common network. This method only works effectively with two static routers.

Building a Routing Table

You add information to the routing table using the **route** command. The **route print** command is used to view the default entries in a routing table. A static entry should be added to the static router's routing table for all networks to which it has no configured interface. A static entry includes the following:

- *Network address*. The network ID or network name of the destination network. If a network name is used for the destination, it is looked up in the Networks file.
- *Netmask*. The subnet mask for the network address.
- *Gateway address*. The IP address or host name of the interface to the destination network. If a host name is used for the gateway, it is looked up in the Hosts file.

If you reference a network name or a host name in the routing table, the name must be configured in the appropriate file. Both files are located in the *systemroot*\System32\Drivers\Etc directory.

Default Routing Table Entries

The routing table on Windows NT 4.0 maintains the default entries shown in the following table.

Address	Description
0.0.0.0	The address used as a default route for any network not specified in the route table.
Subnet broadcast	The address used for broadcasting on the local subnet.
Network broadcast	The address used for broadcasting throughout the internetwork.
Local loopback	The address used for testing IP configurations and connections.
Local network	The address used to direct packets to hosts on the local network.
Local host	The address of the local computer. This address references the local loopback address.

Adding Static Entries

You use the **route** command to add static entries to the routing table.

To add or modify a static route	Function
route add [*network*] **mask** [*netmask*] [*gateway*]	Adds a route
route -p add [*network*] **mask** [*netmask*] [*gateway*]	Adds a persistent route
route delete [*network*] [*gateway*]	Deletes a route
route change [*network*] [*gateway*]	Modifies a route
route print	Displays the routing table
route -f	Clears all routes

For example, to add a route to enable communications with network 131.107.24.0 from a host on network 131.107.16.0, you would use the following command:

route add 131.107.24.0 **mask** 255.255.255.0 131.107.16.2

Note Static routes are stored in memory unless the **-p** parameter is used. Persistent routes are stored in the registry. If you restart a computer running Windows NT, you need to recreate all non-persistent routes.

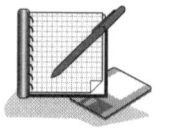

Practice

In this procedure, you use the Route utility to view entries in your local routing table.

▶ **To view the routing table**

- At a command prompt, type **route -p print** and then press ENTER.

What address, other than your IP address and the loopback address, is listed under **Gateway Address**? If you are working with a stand-alone machine, the gateway address will not appear.

In this procedure, you remove the address for the default gateway. This prevents any packets being sent to the default gateway for routing, and requires all routing to be done from existing route entries.

Chapter 6 Implementing IP Routing

▶ **To remove the default gateway address**

1. Double-click the Network icon in Control Panel, and then click the **Protocols** tab.
2. Click **TCP/IP Protocol**, and then click **Properties**.

   The **Microsoft TCP/IP Properties** dialog box appears.
3. Delete the **Default Gateway** address.
4. Click **OK** twice.

▶ **To view the routing table**

- At a command prompt, use the **route print** command.

  Is the default gateway address listed under **Gateway Address**?

  _____

In this procedure, you attempt to communicate with both local and remote hosts.

Note In order to complete this procedure, you must have two networked computers.

▶ **To attempt network communication**

- Ping the IP address of a your second computer or a computer on your local network.

  Was the ping successful?

  _____

  Without a gateway address in the routing table, would you be able to ping the IP address of a remote host?

  _____

In this procedure, you add a static routing table entry for the router.

▶ **To add a route entry**
  1. Type the following command:

     route add 131.107.2.0 mask 255.255.255.0 131.107.2.1
  2. View the entries in the route table, and verify that the route is listed.
  3. If you were to ping a host on another network, would the ping be successful? Why or why not?

In the following procedure, you restore the address for the default gateway. This allows packets to be sent to the default gateway when no route entry exists for the destination network.

▶ **To restore the default gateway address**
  1. Switch to the **Microsoft TCP/IP Properties** dialog box.
  2. In the **Default Gateway** box, type your default gateway address.
  3. Click **OK** twice.

Summary

Static IP routing is a function of IP. This means that routers do not automatically exchange route information. A static route can be configured as either a default gateway address or an entry in a routing table.

Lesson 3: Dynamic IP Routing

With dynamic routing, routers automatically exchange path to known networks with each other. If a path changes, routing protocols automatically update a router's routing table and inform other routers on the internetwork of the change. In large internetworks, dynamic routing plays an important role in network communications.

After this lesson, you will be able to:
- Explain the concept of dynamic IP routing.
- Explain the host configuration requirements for dynamic routing.
- Integrate static and dynamic routing.

Estimated lesson time: 15 minutes

Dynamic routing is typically implemented on large internetworks because minimal configuration is required by a network administrator. Dynamic routing requires a routing protocol such as RIP or OSPF.

The Host Configuration

For a host to communicate with other hosts on the internetwork, its default gateway address must be configured to match the IP address of the local router's interface. No other configuration is required.

As shown in the following illustration, computer A requires a default gateway address configured as 131.107.8.1 (the local interface of the router). Computer B's default gateway address is configured as 131.107.24.1. A host on network 2 can use either 131.107.16.2 or 131.107.16.1 as its default gateway address.

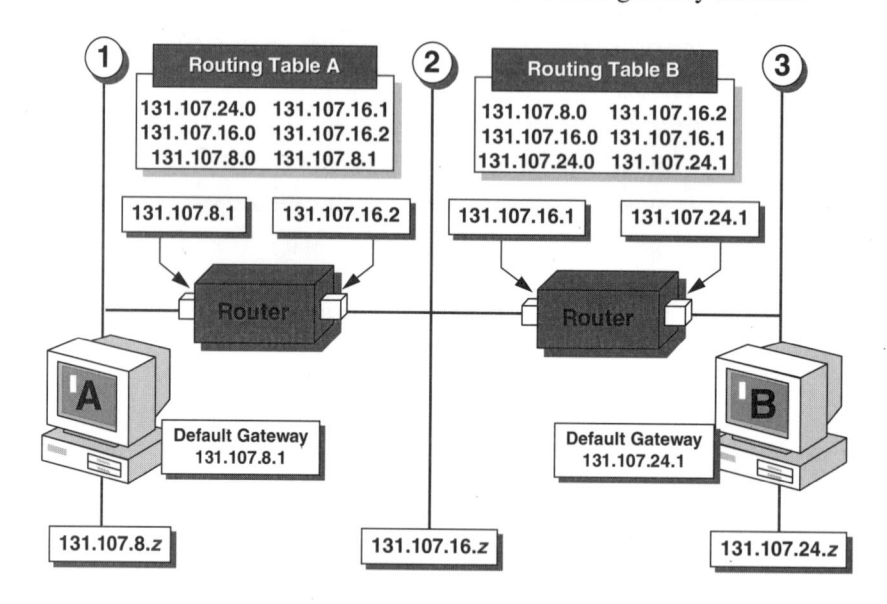

RIP

The Routing Information Protocol (RIP) for IP facilitates the exchange of routing information on an IP internetwork. All RIP messages are sent over UDP port 520.

RIP-enabled routers exchange the network IDs of the networks (that the router can reach), and the distance to these networks. RIP uses a hop-count field, or metric, in its routing table to indicate the distance to a network ID. The hop count is the number of routers that must be crossed to reach the target network ID. The maximum hop count for an RIP entry is 15. Network IDs that require 16 or more hops are considered unreachable. Hop counts can be adjusted to indicate slow or congested links. If multiple entries for a network ID are listed in the routing table, an RIP router will choose the route with the lowest number of hops.

Note An RIP router that receives RIP broadcasts but does not send out any RIP messages is known as a *Silent RIP router*.

The following illustration shows three subnets connected by two computers running Windows NT Server software with RIP routing enabled. Each router is configured with the default update interval; therefore, every 30 seconds each router broadcasts its routing table. Router A sends a limited broadcast to network 2 and all RIP-enabled routers on network 2 informing them about network 1. Router B then adds the new routes to its routing table. If router B has an existing entry in its routing table for a route broadcast by router A, router B will check to see if the new route has a smaller metric. If it is a better route, router B will update its routing table.

Router B also sends a limited broadcast to network 2 and all RIP-enabled routers on network 2 informing them of network 3. Router B then evaluates the new entries and updates its routing table, if necessary.

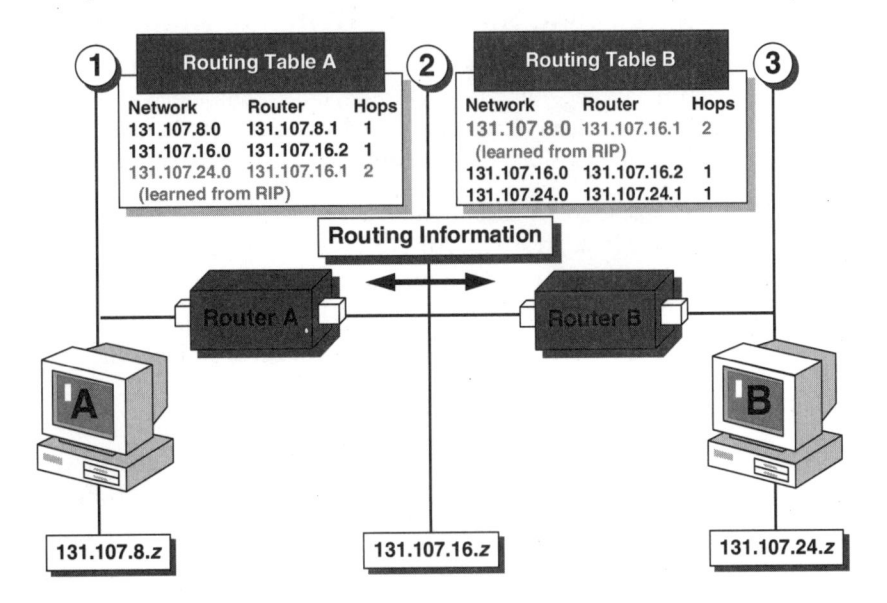

Routing Table A			Routing Table B		
Network	Router	Hops	Network	Router	Hops
131.107.8.0	131.107.8.1	1	131.107.8.0	131.107.16.1	2
131.107.16.0	131.107.16.2	1	(learned from RIP)		
131.107.24.0	131.107.16.1	2	131.107.16.0	131.107.16.2	1
(learned from RIP)			131.107.24.0	131.107.24.1	1

Problems with RIP

While simple and well-supported in the industry, RIP for IP suffers from some problems inherent to its original LAN-based design. These problems make RIP a good solution only in small IP internetworks with a low number of routers.

With RIP, each router's routing table has a complete list of all of the network IDs and all of the possible ways to reach each network ID. This routing table can have hundreds or even thousands of entries in a large IP internetwork with multiple paths. Because the maximum size of a single RIP packet is 512 bytes, large routing tables must be sent as multiple RIP packets.

RIP routers advertise the contents of their routing tables through a Media Access Control-level broadcast on all attached networks every 30 seconds. Large IP internetworks carry the broadcast RIP overhead of large routing tables. This can be especially problematic on WAN links where significant portions of the bandwidth of the WAN link are devoted to the passing of RIP traffic. As a result, RIP-based routing does not scale well to large internetworks or WAN implementations.

Each routing table entry learned through RIP is given a time-out value of 3 minutes past the last time it was last received in an RIP advertisement. When a router goes down, it can take several minutes for the changes to be propagated throughout the internetwork. This is known as the *slow convergence problem*.

Integrating Static and Dynamic Routing

A static router does not trade routing information with dynamic routers. To route from a static router through a dynamic router (such as an RIP-enabled, or OSPF-enabled IP router), you need to add a static route to the routing tables on both the static and dynamic routers. As shown in the following illustration:

- Computer A requires a route added to its routing table. The route must include the IP address (131.107.16.1) of the interface that can access the dedicated IP router to the Internet to route packets from network 1 to the Internet.

- To route packets from networks 2 and 3 to the Internet, a static entry must be added to computer B's routing table that includes the IP address (131.107.24.2) of the interface on the dedicated IP router to the Internet.

- To enable computers on the Internet to communicate with hosts on networks 1 and 2, it is necessary to statically configure the dynamic IP router with the IP address of the interface to computer B. Computer B then acts as a gateway to the other subnets.

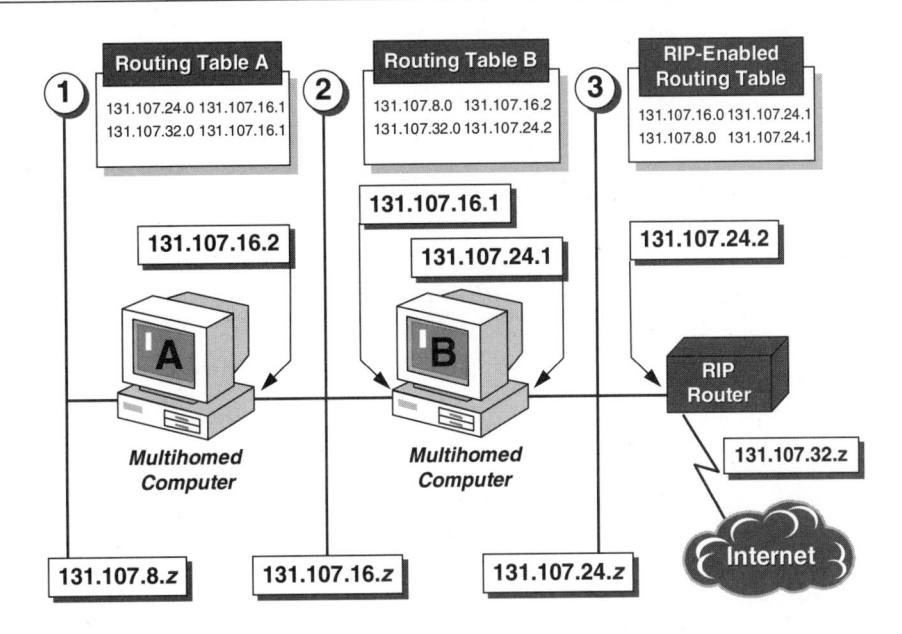

Note Some implementations of RIP do not propagate static routing tables. In this case, it is necessary to statically configure the remote routers in the internetwork. Configuring a static route on an RIP router varies with each router. Refer to the router vendor's documentation for more information.

Summary

Dynamic routing is an important component for large networks. The default gateway address for a host must be configured to match the IP address of the local router's interface. RIP for IP facilitates the exchange of routing information on an IP internetwork; however, RIP is a good solution only in small IP networks.

A static router does not trade routing information with dynamic routers. To route from a static router through a dynamic router, you need to add a static route to the routing tables on both the static and dynamic routers.

Lesson 4: Implementing a Windows NT Router

Static routing can work well for small networks and remote sites, but for large internetworks, the overhead of manually maintaining routing tables is significant. This lesson helps you understand what is required to implement a Windows NT router.

After this lesson, you will be able to:
- Understand how to implement a Windows NT router.
- Understand how the Tracert utility can verify a packet route.

Estimated lesson time: 10 minutes

By enabling the RIP for IP routing protocol, Windows NT Server 4.0 can be a dynamic IP router. Windows NT 4.0 RIP for IP eliminates the manual configuration of routing tables. RIP for IP is suitable for medium-size internetworks, but is not suitable for large IP internetworks because of the significant amount of broadcast traffic it generates.

▶ **To implement a Windows NT router**

1. Install multiple adapter cards and appropriate drivers, or configure multiple IP addresses on a single adapter card.
2. Configure the adapter card(s) with a valid IP address and subnet mask.
3. On the **Routing** tab of the **Microsoft TCP/IP Properties** dialog box, select the **Enable IP Forwarding** check box.
4. Depending on which version of Windows NT you are running:
   - On the **Services** tab of the Control Panel Network program, add the RIP for Internet Protocol service.

   –Or–

   - Add static routes to the static router's routing table for all networks to which the computer has no configured interface.

The TRACERT Utility

The TRACERT utility verifies the route a packet takes to reach its destination. This is useful for determining if a router has failed. If the command is unsuccessful, you can determine where routing failed, possibly indicating router or WAN link problems.

TRACERT is also useful for determining a slow router. The response time is returned in the output, indicating the effectiveness of a router or WAN link. This information can be compared with another route to the same destination.

For example, the following command displays the path taken from the local host to the destination host www.microsoft.com (207.68.137.36):

tracert www.microsoft.com

The output from the preceding command verifies that the router address was used as the route from the local host to the destination host.

```
Tracing route to www.microsoft.com [207.68.137.36]
over a maximum of 30 hops:
1    <10 ms   <10 ms   <10 ms   206.213.84.57
2    30 ms    40 ms    30 ms    fast1.accessone.com [206.213.95.11]
3    30 ms    80 ms    30 ms    198.68.188.1
4    30 ms    40 ms    30 ms    Fddi1-0.GW1.SEA1.ALTER.NET [137.39.63.65]
5    40 ms    40 ms    40 ms    Dist1-Sea.MOSWEST.MSN.NET [137.39.176.22]
6    40 ms    40 ms    40 ms    msft1-f0.moswest.msn.net [207.68.145.46]
7    231 ms   170 ms   170 ms   www.microsoft.com [207.68.137.36]

Trace complete.
```

Summary

Windows NT Server 4.0 can be made a dynamic IP router by enabling the RIP for IP routing protocol. This eliminates the manual configuration of routing tables. The TRACERT utility is useful for determining if a router has failed or if there is a slow router.

Review

The following questions are intended to reinforce key information presented in this chapter. If you are unable to answer a question, review the appropriate lesson and then try the question again.

1. How is IP routing enabled?

2. Is a routing table required on a multihomed computer connecting a two-subnet internet? Why or why not?

3. When is it necessary to build a static routing table?

4. What information is required in a routing table?

5. Why is RIP typically not used in a large internetwork?

For More Information
- Review all referenced RFCs on the course compact disc.

CHAPTER 7

The Dynamic Host Configuration Protocol

Lesson 1　DHCP Overview . . . 130

Lesson 2　Installing and Configuring a DHCP Server . . . 140

Lesson 3　Enabling a DHCP Relay Agent . . . 155

Lesson 4　Managing the DHCP Database . . . 159

Review . . . 162

About This Chapter

In this chapter, you learn how to use the Dynamic Host Configuration Protocol (DHCP) to automatically configure TCP/IP and eliminate some common configuration problems. During the lessons, you install and configure a DHCP server, test the DHCP configuration, install a DHCP relay agent, and then obtain an IP address from a DHCP server.

Before You Begin

To complete the lessons in this chapter, you must have installed Microsoft Windows NT Server 4.0 with TCP/IP.

Lesson 1: DHCP Overview

The Dynamic Host Configuration Protocol (DHCP) automatically assigns IP addresses to computers. DHCP overcomes the limitations of configuring TCP/IP manually. This lesson gives you an overview of DHCP and how it works.

After this lesson, you will be able to:
- Describe the function and benefits of DHCP.
- Explain how a DHCP client obtains IP addresses from a DHCP server.
- Understand how the Ipconfig utility can renew or release a lease.

Estimated lesson time: 35 minutes

DHCP is an extension of the BOOTP protocol. BOOTP enables diskless clients to start up and automatically configure TCP/IP. DHCP centralizes and manages the allocation of TCP/IP configuration information by automatically assigning IP addresses to computers configured to use DHCP. Implementing DHCP eliminates some of the configuration problems associated with manually configuring TCP/IP.

As shown in the illustration below, each time a DHCP client starts, it requests IP addressing information from a DHCP server, including the IP address, the subnet mask, and optional values. The optional values may include a default gateway address, Domain Name Server (DNS) address, and NetBIOS name server address.

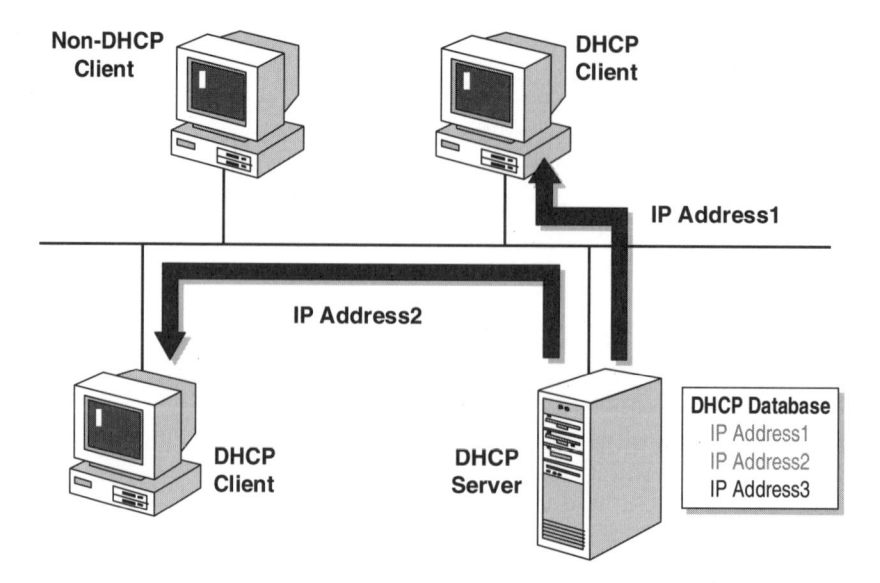

When a DHCP server receives a request, it selects IP addressing information from a pool of addresses defined in its database and offers it to the DHCP client. If the client accepts the offer, the IP addressing information is leased to the client for a specified period of time. If there is no available IP addressing information in the pool to lease to a client, the client cannot initialize TCP/IP.

Note Windows NT 4.0 Service Pack 2 enables support for BOOTP client requests.

The BOOTP protocol is defined in RFC 1532. DHCP is defined in RFCs 1533, 1534, 1541, and 1542. For copies of these RFCs, see the *Course Materials* Web page on the course compact disc.

Manual vs. Automatic Configuration

To understand why DHCP is beneficial in configuring TCP/IP on client computers, it is useful to contrast the manual method of configuring TCP/IP with the automatic method using DHCP.

Configuring TCP/IP Manually

Configuring TCP/IP manually means that users can easily pick a random IP address instead of getting a valid IP address from the network administrator. Using incorrect addresses can lead to network problems that can be very difficult to trace to the source.

In addition, typing the IP address, subnet mask, or default gateway can lead to problems ranging from trouble communicating if the default gateway or subnet mask is wrong, to problems associated with a duplicate IP address.

Another limitation of configuring TCP/IP manually is the administrative overhead on internetworks where computers are frequently moved from one subnet to another. For example, when a workstation is moved to a different subnet, the IP address and default gateway address must be changed for the workstation to communicate from its new location.

Configuring TCP/IP Using DHCP

Using DHCP to automatically configure IP addressing information means that users no longer need to acquire IP addressing information from an administrator to configure TCP/IP. The DHCP server supplies all of the necessary configuration information to all of the DHCP clients. Most of the difficult-to-trace network problems are eliminated by using DHCP.

How DHCP Works

DHCP uses a four-phase process to configure a DHCP client as shown in the following table and illustration. If a computer has multiple network adapters, the DHCP process occurs separately over each adapter. A unique IP address will be assigned to each adapter in the computer. All DHCP communication is done over UDP ports 67 and 68.

Most DHCP messages are sent by broadcast. For DHCP clients to communicate with a DHCP server on a remote network, the IP routers must support forwarding DHCP broadcasts. DHCP configuration phases are shown in the following table.

Phase	Description
IP lease request	The client initializes a limited version of TCP/IP and broadcasts a request for the location of a DHCP server and IP addressing information.
IP lease offer	All DHCP servers that have valid IP addressing information available send an offer to the client.
IP lease selection	The client selects the IP addressing information from the first offer it receives and broadcasts a message requesting to lease the IP addressing information in the offer.
IP lease acknowledgment	The DHCP server that made the offer responds to the message, and all other DHCP servers withdraw their offers. The IP addressing information is assigned to the client and an acknowledgment is sent.
	The client finishes initializing and binding the TCP/IP protocol. Once the automatic configuration process is complete, the client can use all TCP/IP services and utilities for normal network communications and connectivity to other IP hosts.

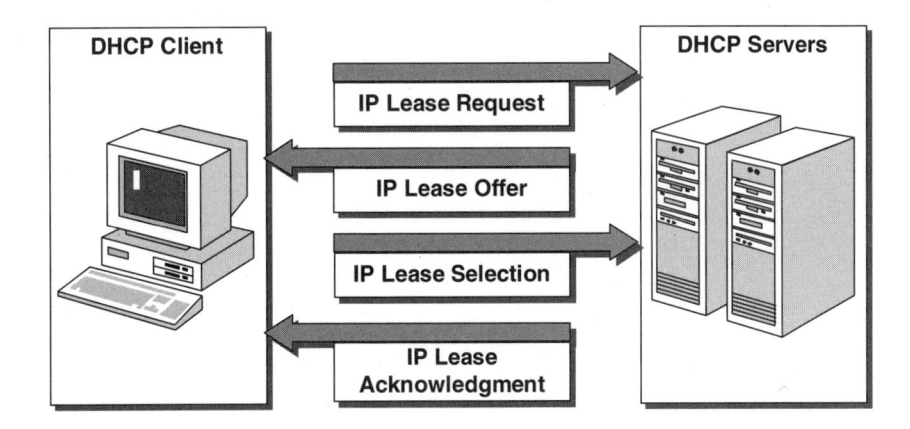

DHCP Client / DHCP Servers

- IP Lease Request
- IP Lease Offer
- IP Lease Selection
- IP Lease Acknowledgment

IP Lease Request and Offer

In the first two phases, the client requests a lease from a DHCP server, and a DHCP server offers an IP address to the client.

IP Lease Request

The first time a client initializes, it requests to lease an IP address by broadcasting a request to all DHCP servers. Because the client does not have an IP address or know the IP address of a DHCP server, it uses 0.0.0.0 as the source address, and 255.255.255.255 as the destination address.

The request for a lease is sent in a DHCPDISCOVER message. This message also contains the client's hardware address and computer name so that DHCP servers know which client sent the request.

The IP lease process is used when one of the following occurs:

- TCP/IP is initialized for the first time as a DHCP client.
- The client requests a specific IP address and is denied, possibly because the DHCP server dropped the lease.
- The client previously leased an IP address, but released the lease and now requires a new lease.

IP Lease Offer

All DHCP servers that receive the request and have a valid configuration for the client broadcast an offer with the following information:

- The client's hardware address
- An offered IP address
- Subnet mask
- Length of the lease
- A server identifier (the IP address of the offering DHCP server)

A broadcast is used because the client does not yet have an IP address. As shown in the following illustration, the offer is sent as a DHCPOFFER message.

The DHCP server reserves the IP address so that it will not be offered to another DHCP client. The DHCP client selects the IP address from the first offer it receives.

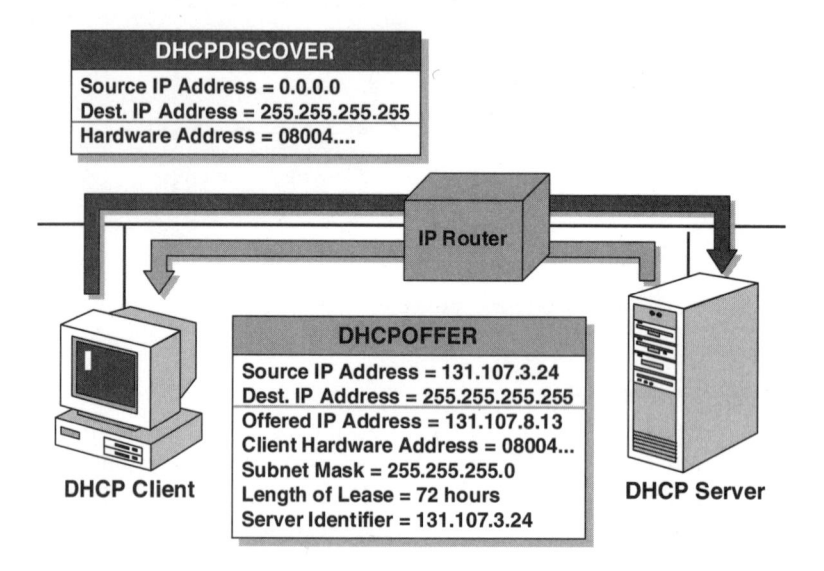

```
DHCPDISCOVER
Source IP Address = 0.0.0.0
Dest. IP Address = 255.255.255.255
Hardware Address = 08004....
```

```
DHCPOFFER
Source IP Address = 131.107.3.24
Dest. IP Address = 255.255.255.255
Offered IP Address = 131.107.8.13
Client Hardware Address = 08004...
Subnet Mask = 255.255.255.0
Length of Lease = 72 hours
Server Identifier = 131.107.3.24
```

When No DHCP Servers Are Online

The DHCP client waits one second for an offer. If an offer is not received, the client will not be able to initialize and it will rebroadcast the request three times (at 9-, 13-, and 16-second intervals, plus a random length of time between 0 and 1,000 milliseconds). If an offer is not received after four requests, the client will retry every five minutes.

IP Lease Selection and Acknowledgment

In the last two phases, the client selects an offer and the DHCP server acknowledges the lease.

IP Lease Selection

After the client receives an offer from at least one DHCP server, it broadcasts to all DHCP servers that it has made a selection by accepting an offer.

The broadcast is sent in a DHCPREQUEST message and includes the server identifier (IP address) of the server whose offer was accepted. All other DHCP servers then retract their offers so that their IP addresses are available for the next IP lease request.

IP Lease Acknowledgment (Successful)

The DHCP server with the accepted offer broadcasts a successful acknowledgment to the client in the form of a DHCPACK message. This message contains a valid lease for an IP address and possibly other configuration information.

When the DHCP client receives the acknowledgment, TCP/IP is completely initialized and is considered a bound DHCP client. Once bound, the client can use TCP/IP to communicate on the internetwork.

The client stores the IP address, subnet mask, and other IP addressing information locally in the registry under the following key:

HKEY_LOCAL_MACHINE\SYSTEM\CurrentControlSet\Services*adapter*\Parameters\Tcpip

IP Lease Acknowledgment (Unsuccessful)

An unsuccessful acknowledgment (DHCPNACK) is broadcast if the client is trying to lease its previous IP address and the IP address is no longer available. It is also broadcast if the IP address is invalid because the client has been physically moved to a different subnet.

As shown in the following illustration, when the client receives an unsuccessful acknowledgment, it returns to the process of requesting an IP lease.

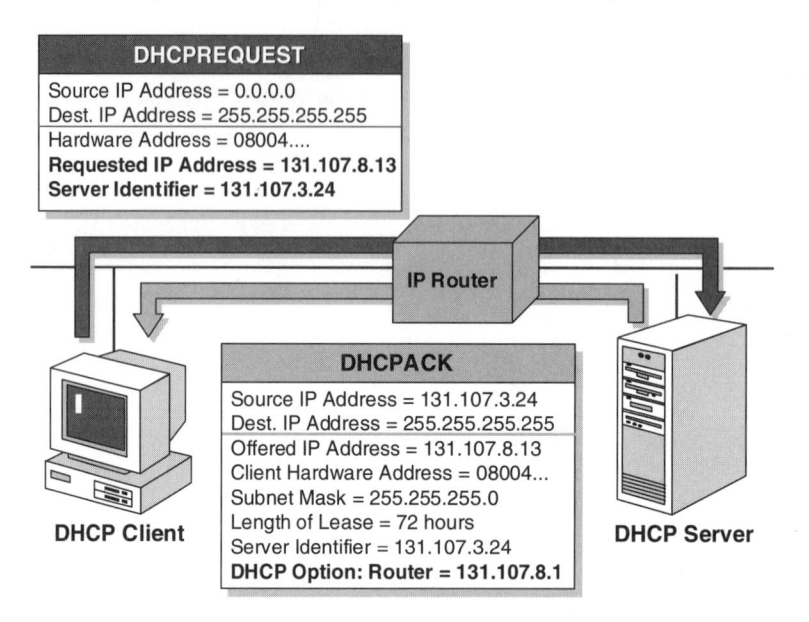

DHCPREQUEST
Source IP Address = 0.0.0.0
Dest. IP Address = 255.255.255.255
Hardware Address = 08004....
Requested IP Address = 131.107.8.13
Server Identifier = 131.107.3.24

IP Router

DHCPACK
Source IP Address = 131.107.3.24
Dest. IP Address = 255.255.255.255
Offered IP Address = 131.107.8.13
Client Hardware Address = 08004...
Subnet Mask = 255.255.255.0
Length of Lease = 72 hours
Server Identifier = 131.107.3.24
DHCP Option: Router = 131.107.8.1

DHCP Client

DHCP Server

IP Lease Renewal

Initial Renewal Attempt

All DHCP clients attempt to renew their lease when 50 percent of the lease time has expired. To renew its lease, a DHCP client sends a DHCPREQUEST message directly to the DHCP server from which it obtained the lease.

If the DHCP server is available, it renews the lease and sends the client a successful acknowledgment (DHCPACK) with the new lease time and any updated configuration parameters.

When the client receives the acknowledgment, it updates its configuration. If a client attempts to renew its lease, but is unable to contact the original DHCP server, the client receives a message indicating that the lease was not renewed. The client can still use the address because 50 percent of the lease life is available.

When a DHCP client restarts, it attempts to lease the same IP address from the original DHCP server. It does this by broadcasting a DHCPREQUEST specifying the last IP address it leased. If it is unsuccessful, and there is still lease time available, the DHCP client continues to use the same IP address for the remainder of the lease.

Subsequent Renewal Attempts

If a lease could not be renewed by the original DHCP server at the 50 percent interval, the client will attempt to contact any available DHCP server when 87.5 percent of the lease time has expired. As shown in the following illustration, the client will broadcast a DHCPREQUEST message. Any DHCP server can respond with a DHCPACK message (renewing the lease) or a DHCPNACK message (forcing the DHCP client to re-initialize and obtain a lease for a different IP address).

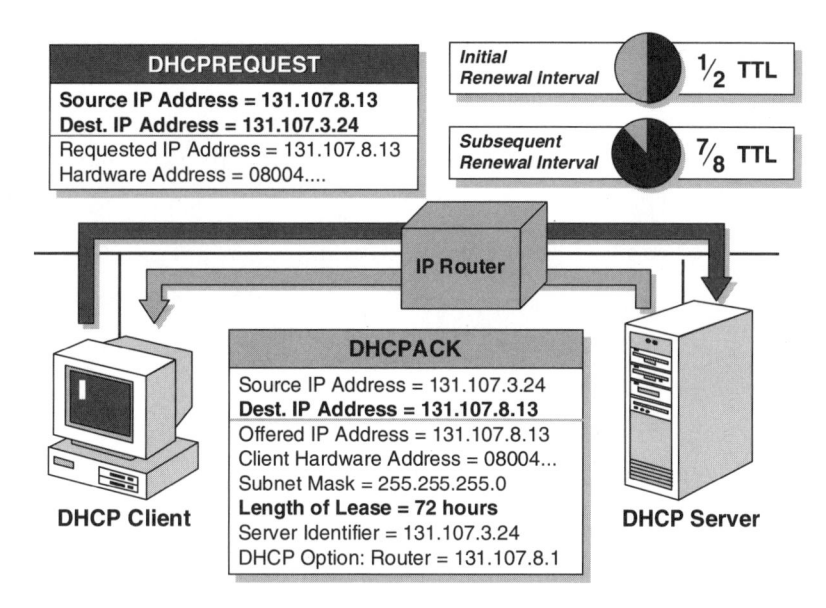

DHCPREQUEST
Source IP Address = 131.107.8.13
Dest. IP Address = 131.107.3.24
Requested IP Address = 131.107.8.13
Hardware Address = 08004....

Initial Renewal Interval — $\frac{1}{2}$ TTL
Subsequent Renewal Interval — $\frac{7}{8}$ TTL

DHCPACK
Source IP Address = 131.107.3.24
Dest. IP Address = 131.107.8.13
Offered IP Address = 131.107.8.13
Client Hardware Address = 08004...
Subnet Mask = 255.255.255.0
Length of Lease = 72 hours
Server Identifier = 131.107.3.24
DHCP Option: Router = 131.107.8.1

DHCP Client — IP Router — DHCP Server

If the lease expires or a DHCPNACK message is received, the DHCP client must immediately discontinue using the IP address. The DHCP client then returns to the process of leasing a new IP address.

If the client's lease expires and it cannot acquire a new lease, communication over TCP/IP stops until a new IP address can be assigned to the client. Network errors occur for any applications that attempt to communicate over the invalid TCP/IP protocol stack interface.

Using the Ipconfig Utility

In addition to its use for verifying a computer's IP configuration, the Ipconfig utility can also be used to renew options and lease time, and to relinquish a lease. At a command prompt, type the following command to verify a computer's IP address, subnet mask, and default gateway:

ipconfig

At a command prompt, type the following command to verify a computer's IP configuration for the operating system and the network adapter:

ipconfig /all

Using the **/all** switch provides the following IP configuration information:

- Host name assigned to the local computer
- IP address of any DNS servers the local computer is configured to use
- NetBIOS node type, such as broadcast, hybrid, peer-peer, and mixed
- NetBIOS scope ID
- Whether or not IP routing is enabled
- Whether or not WINS proxy is enabled
- Whether or not NetBIOS resolution uses DNS

Using the **/all** switch provides the following network adapter IP configuration information:

- Description of the adapter card, such as EtherLink II
- Physical address of the adapter card
- Whether or not DHCP is enabled
- IP address of the local computer
- Subnet mask of the local computer
- Default gateway of the local computer
- IP addresses of the primary and secondary WINS servers

Updating a Lease

The **/renew** switch causes a DHCPREQUEST message to be sent to the DHCP server to get updated options and lease time. If the DHCP server is unavailable, the client will continue using the current DHCP-supplied configuration options. At a command prompt, type:

ipconfig /renew

Releasing a Lease

The **/release** switch causes the DHCP client to send a DHCPRELEASE message to the DHCP server and give up its lease. This is useful when the client is changing to a different network and will not need the previous lease. After this command has been carried out, TCP/IP communications will stop. At a command prompt, type:

ipconfig /release

Microsoft DHCP clients do not initiate DHCPRELEASE messages when shutting down. If a client remains shut down for the length of its lease (and the lease is not renewed), it is possible for the DHCP server to assign that client's IP address to a different client after the lease expires. By not sending a DHCPRELEASE message, the client has a better chance of receiving the same IP address during initialization.

Summary

DHCP was developed to solve configuration problems by centralizing IP configuration information for allocation to clients. DHCP uses a four-phase process to configure a DHCP client. The phases are, in order,: lease request, lease offer, lease selection, and lease acknowledgment.

In addition to verifying a computer's IP configuration, you can use the Ipconfig utility to renew options and lease time, and to relinquish a lease.

Lesson 2: Installing and Configuring a DHCP Server

Before you install DHCP, you should consider several questions about your configuration. This lesson leads you through these questions, helps you understand the server and client requirements for DHCP, and then shows you how to install DHCP.

After this lesson, you will be able to:
- Understand the questions you should ask before implementing DHCP.
- Install DHCP in an internetwork.
- Configure a DHCP scope for multiple subnets.

Estimated lesson time: 75 minutes

Before you install DHCP, answer the following questions:

- Will all of the computers become DHCP clients? If not, consider that non-DHCP clients have static IP addresses, and static IP addresses must be excluded from the DHCP server configuration. If a client requires a specific address, the IP address needs to be reserved.
- Will a DHCP server supply IP addresses to multiple subnets? If so, consider that any routers connecting subnets act as DHCP relay agents. If your routers are not acting as DHCP relay agents, at least one DHCP server is required on each subnet that has DHCP clients.
- How many DHCP servers are required? Consider that a DHCP server does not share information with other DHCP servers. Therefore, it is necessary to create unique IP addresses for each server to assign to clients.
- What IP addressing options will clients obtain from a DHCP server? The IP addressing options might be:
  - Router
  - DNS server
  - NetBIOS over TCP/IP name resolution
  - WINS server
  - NetBIOS scope ID

The IP addressing options determine how to configure the DHCP server, and whether the options should be created for all of the clients in the internetwork, clients on a specific subnet, or individual clients.

Implementing Multiple DHCP Servers

If your internetwork requires multiple DHCP servers, it is necessary to create a unique scope for each subnet. A scope is a range of IP addresses that are available to be leased or assigned to clients.

To ensure that clients can lease IP addresses, it is important to have multiple scopes for each subnet distributed among the DHCP servers in the internetwork. For example:

- Each DHCP server should have a scope containing approximately 75 percent of the available IP addresses for the local subnet.
- Each DHCP server should have a scope for each remote subnet containing approximately 25 percent of the available IP addresses for a subnet.

When a client's DHCP server is unavailable, the client can still receive an address lease from another DHCP server on a different subnet, assuming the router is a DHCP relay agent.

As shown in the following illustration, Server A has a scope for the local subnet with an IP address range of 131.107.4.20 through 131.107.4.150, and Server B has a scope with an IP address range of 131.107.3.20 through 131.107.3.150. Each server can lease IP addresses to clients on its own subnet.

Additionally, each server has a scope containing a small range of IP addresses for the remote subnet. For example, Server A has a scope for Subnet 2 with the IP address range of 131.107.3.151 through 131.107.3.200. Server B has a scope for Subnet 1 with the IP address range of 131.107.4.151 through 131.107.4.200.

When a client on Subnet 1 is unable to lease an address from Server A, it can lease an address for its subnet from Server B, and vice versa.

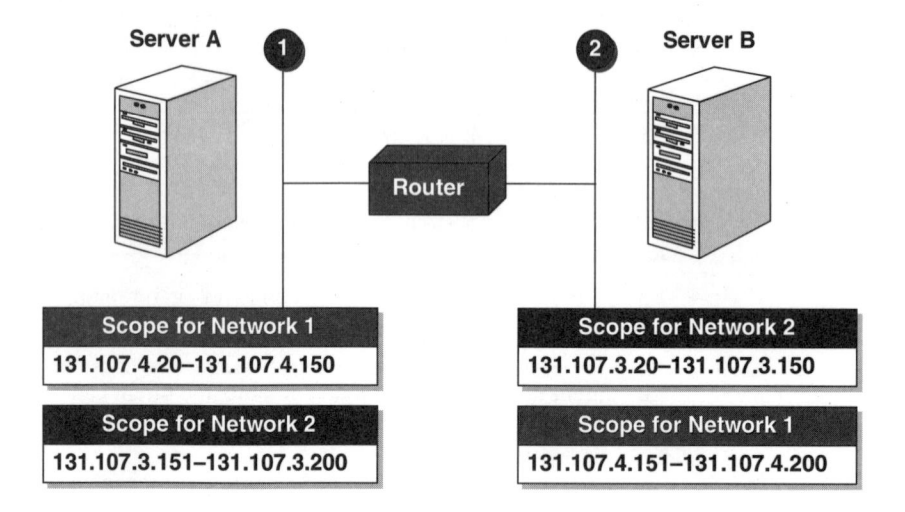

DHCP Requirements

To implement DHCP, both the server and the client require configuration. All routers connecting subnets with DHCP servers and clients must support RFC 1542 and act as BOOTP relay agents.

A DHCP server requires:

- The DHCP Server service configured on at least one computer within the TCP/IP internetwork running Windows NT Server (it does not have to be a domain controller), provided that your IP routers support RFC 1542. Otherwise, you need a DHCP server on each subnet.
- The DHCP server configured with a static IP address, subnet mask, default gateway, and other TCP/IP parameters (it cannot be a DHCP client).
- A DHCP scope created on the DHCP server. A DHCP scope consists of a range, or pool, of IP addresses that the DHCP server can assign, or lease, to DHCP clients—for example, 131.107.3.51 through 131.107.3.200.

A DHCP client requires a computer running any of the following supported operating systems with DHCP enabled:

- Windows NT Server 4.0.
- Windows NT Workstation 4.0.
- Microsoft Windows 95.

- Microsoft Windows for Workgroups 3.11 running Microsoft TCP/IP-32 (provided on the Windows NT Server 3.5 compact disc).
- Microsoft Network Client 3.0 for MS-DOS with the real-mode TCP/IP driver included on the Windows NT Server 3.5 compact disc.
- LAN Manager 2.2c, included on the Windows NT Server 3.5 compact disc. LAN Manager 2.2c for OS/2 is not supported.

Installing and Configuring a DHCP Server

The DHCP Server service must be running to communicate with DHCP clients. Once the DHCP server is installed and started, several options must be configured. The following are the general steps for installing and configuring DHCP:

- Install the Microsoft DHCP Server service.
- A scope, or pool of valid IP addresses, must be configured before a DHCP server can lease IP addresses to DHCP clients.
- Global, scope, and client scope options can be configured for a particular DHCP client.
- The DHCP server can be configured to always assign the same IP address to the same DHCP client.

Note The DHCP server cannot be a DHCP client. It must have a static IP address, subnet mask, and default gateway address.

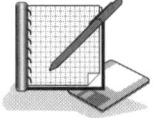

Practice

In this procedure, you install and configure a DHCP server to automatically assign TCP/IP configuration information to DHCP clients.

Note You must have two networked computers to complete this procedure. Complete this procedure from the computer you designate as the DHCP server (Server1). In the next procedure, you work with the second computer (Server2) to configure it as a DHCP client.

Caution It is recommended that you do not perform these procedures if your computer(s) are part of larger network. Installing a DHCP server could conflict with network operations.

In this procedure, you determine the physical hardware address of your network adapter card. This address is used to create a client reservation.

▶ **To determine the network adapter card address**

- At a command prompt, type **ipconfig /all** and then press ENTER.

    Document the physical address here for reference, without the hyphens (–).

    _____

    There are at least two other ways to check the physical address of your network adapter card. What are they?

    _____

    _____

▶ **To install the DHCP Server service**

Note Complete this procedure only from the computer you designate as the DHCP server.

1. Click the **Start** button, point to **Settings**, and then click **Control Panel**.
2. Double-click the **Network** icon.

    The **Network Settings** dialog box appears.

3. Click the **Services** tab.
4. Click **Add**.

    The **Select Network Service** dialog box appears.

5. Select **Microsoft DHCP Server**, and then click **OK**.

    The **Windows NT Setup** box appears, prompting for the full path of the Windows NT distribution files.

6. Type the full path and then click **Continue**.

    The appropriate files are copied to your computer, and then a message box appears, informing you that a static IP address is now required for the network adapter card.

7. Click **OK**.

    The **Network** dialog box appears.

8. Click **Close**.

   The **Network Settings Change** dialog box appears, indicating that the computer needs to be restarted to initialize the new configuration.

9. Click **Yes**.

10. Log on as Administrator.

Configuring a DHCP Scope

Once the DHCP server is installed and started, the next step is to configure a scope of configuration information. As shown in the following illustration, every DHCP server requires at least one scope with a pool of IP addresses available for leasing to clients. You can create multiple scopes for other DHCP servers as a backup method. They are also created for assigning IP addresses specific to a subnet, such as a default gateway address.

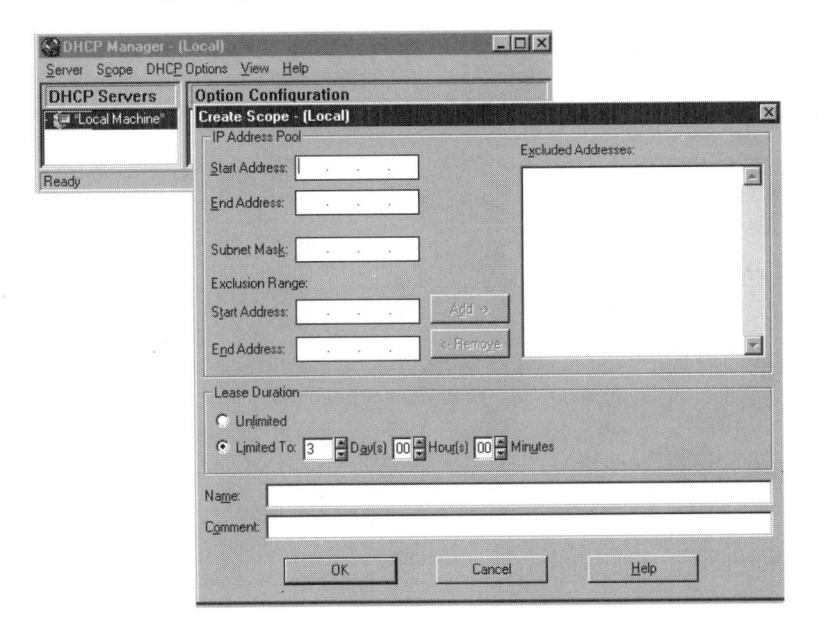

Note Only one scope can be assigned to a specific subnet.

Because DHCP servers do not share scope information, it is important that each scope contain a unique IP address. If more than one scope contains the same IP address, it is possible for both servers to lease the same IP address to different DHCP clients, causing duplicate IP addressing problems.

Practice

In this procedure, you create a DHCP scope that consists of one IP address (your other computer's) with an assigned lease time of one day.

Note Complete this procedure only from the DHCP server.

▶ **To create a DHCP scope**

1. Click the **Start** button, point to **Settings**, and then click **Control Panel**.
2. Double-click the **Services** icon. What are the names of the DHCP services?

   _____

3. Close the **Services** dialog box.
4. Click the **Start** button, point to **Programs**, point to **Administrative Tools**, and then click **DHCP Manager**.

   The DHCP Manager window appears.
5. Under **DHCP** Servers, double-click *Local Machine*.
6. On the **Scope** menu, click **Create**.

   The **Create Scope** dialog box appears. The available options are shown in the following table.

Option	Description
IP Address Pool Start Address	The starting IP address that can be assigned to a DHCP client.
IP Address Pool End Address	The ending IP address that can be assigned to a DHCP client.
Subnet Mask	The subnet mask to be assigned to DHCP clients.
Exclusion Range Start Address	The starting IP address to be excluded from the IP address pool of addresses. The addresses in this exclusion will not be assigned to DHCP clients. This is important if you have static IP addresses configured on non-DCHP clients.
Exclusion Range End Address	The ending IP address to be excluded from the IP address pool of addresses. The addresses in this exclusion will not be assigned to DHCP clients. This is important if you have static IP addresses configured on non-DCHP clients.
Lease Duration Unlimited	The DHCP leases assigned to clients will never expire.

(*continued*)

Option	Description
Lease Duration Limited To	The number of days, hours, and minutes that a DHCP client lease is available before it must be renewed.
Name	A name to be assigned to the DHCP scope. The name displays after the IP address in the DHCP Manager.
Comment	Optional comment for the scope.

7. Configure the scope using the information in the following table.

In this box	Type this
IP Address Pool Start Address	Your second computer's IP address
IP Address Pool End Address	Your second computer's IP address
Subnet Mask	**255.255.255.0**
Lease Duration Limited To (Days)	**1**

8. Click **OK**.

   A **DHCP Manager** message box appears, indicating that the scope was successfully created, and now needs to be activated. The scope must be activated before it is available for lease assignments.

9. To activate the scope, click **Yes**.

   Note Another way to activate the scope is to select the inactive scope in the DHCP Manager window, and then, on the **Scope** menu, click **Activate**.

   The DHCP Manager window appears with the new scope added. Notice the yellow light bulb next to the IP address, indicating an active scope. A message box informs you that no more data is available.

   Important If the internetwork has non-DHCP clients, it is important to exclude their static IP addresses from the scope, or the DHCP server could allocate the same IP address to a DHCP client, causing duplicate addressing problems.

10. Click **OK**.

Configuring DHCP Scope Options

Once you have created the DHCP scope, you can configure options for DHCP clients. You configure these options from the **DHCP Options: Scope** dialog box. There are three levels of scope options—global, scope, and client, as follows:

- *Global*. Global options are available to all DHCP clients. Global options are used when all clients on all subnets require the same configuration information. For example, you might want all clients configured to use the same WINS server. Global options are always used, unless scope or client options are configured.

- *Scope*. Scope options are available only to clients who lease an address from the scope. For example, if you have a different scope for each subnet, you can define a unique default gateway address for each subnet. Scope options override global options.

- *Client*. Client options are created for a specific client using a reserved DHCP address lease. Client options are always used before scope or global options.

Important Even though a Microsoft DHCP server can offer all of the options in the options list, Microsoft DHCP clients will accept only the options in the following table. Non–Microsoft DHCP clients can receive and use any configured option.

Option	Description
003 Router	Specifies the IP address of a router, such as the default gateway address. If the client has a locally defined default gateway, that configuration takes precedence over the DHCP option.
006 DNS Servers	Specifies the IP address of a DNS server.
046 WINS/NBT node type	Specifies the type of NetBIOS over TCP/IP name resolution to be used by the client. Options are: 1 = B-node (broadcast) 2 = P-node (peer) 4 = M-node (mixed) 8 = H-node (hybrid)
044 WINS/NBNS servers	Specifies the IP address of a WINS server available to clients. If a WINS server address is manually configured on a client, that configuration overrides the values configured for this option.
047 NetBIOS Scope ID	Specifies the local NetBIOS scope ID. NetBIOS over TCP/IP will communicate only with other NetBIOS hosts using the same scope ID.

Practice

In this procedure, you create a DHCP scope option that automatically assigns a default gateway address to DHCP clients.

Note Complete this procedure only from the DHCP server.

▶ **To configure DHCP scope options**

1. Click the light bulb icon for the scope you just created.
2. On the **DHCP Options** menu, select **Scope**.

   The **DHCP Options: Scope** dialog box appears.

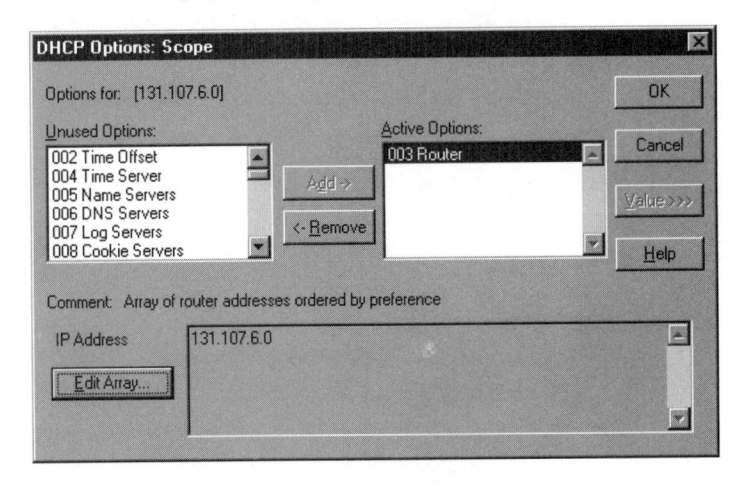

   ![DHCP Options: Scope dialog box]

3. Under **Unused Options**, select **003 Router**, and then click **Add**.

   The **003 Router** option moves to the **Active Options** box.

4. Click **Value**.

   The **DHCP Options: Scope** dialog box expands to add the **Router IP Address** values box.

   The **Router IP Address** box contains six types of values, as shown in the following table.

Type	Description
IP Address	Designates the IP address of a server added to the options. For example: 003 Routers.
Long	Configures a 32-bit numeric value. For example: 035 ARP Cache Time-out.
String	Designates a string of characters. For example: 015 Domain Name.

(*continued*)

Type	Description
Word	Assigns a 16-bit numeric value of specific block sizes. For example: 022 Max DG Reassembly Size.
Byte	Assigns a numeric value consisting of a single byte. For example: 046 WINS/NBT Node Type.
Binary	Specifies a binary value. For example: 043 Vendor-Specific Information.

5. Click **Edit Array**.

    The **IP Address Array Editor** dialog box appears.

6. Under **New IP Address**, type your default gateway address (**131.107.2.1**), and then click **Add**.

    The new IP address appears under **IP Addresses**.

7. Click **OK** to return to the **DHCP Options: Scope** dialog box.

    The new router is listed in the IP address list.

8. Click **OK**.

    A message box informs you that no more data is available.

9. Close DHCP Manager.

Note You must exit and restart DHCP Manager to view the new options in the left pane.

Configuring a Client Reservation

You can configure DHCP so that a DHCP server always assigns the same IP address to a client. This is called a *client reservation*.

For some DHCP clients it is important that the same IP address is reassigned when its lease expires—for example, servers on a network that contain clients that are not WINS-enabled should always lease the same IP address. Clients that are not WINS-enabled must use the LMHOSTS file to resolve NetBIOS computer names of hosts on remote networks. If the IP address of the server changes because it is not reserved, name resolution using LMHOSTS will fail. Reserving an IP address for the server ensures that its IP address will remain the same.

Practice

In this procedure, you create a reservation for your second computer. This ensures that each DHCP server is able to lease an address to a unique DHCP client in an environment of multiple DHCP servers.

Note Complete this procedure only from the DHCP server.

▶ To add a client lease reservation

1. Ping your second computer's IP address, and then type **arp -a** to obtain the physical address of your second computer's network adapter. Document the address here for reference. (Do *not* include hyphens in the physical address.)

   _____

2. Start DHCP Manager.
3. Double-click ***Local Machine***.

   The light bulb icon and the IP address appear.

4. Click the light bulb icon.

   The Option Configuration window displays an active scope option of 003 Router.

5. On the **Scope** menu, click **Add Reservations**.

   The **Add Reserved Clients** dialog box appears.

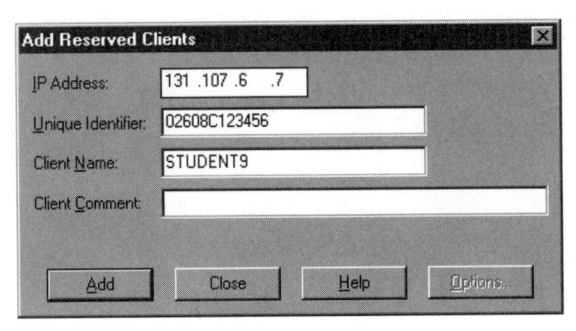

Add Reserved Clients	
IP Address:	131 .107 .6 .7
Unique Identifier:	02608C123456
Client Name:	STUDENT9
Client Comment:	

   Add | Close | Help | Options

6. In the **IP Address** box, type your second computer's IP address.

7. In the **Unique Identifier** box, type the physical address of your second computer's network adapter.

Note Do not include hyphens in the physical address.

Important If the Unique Identifier is incorrectly typed, it will not match the value sent by the DHCP client. As a result, the DHCP server will assign the client any available IP address instead of the IP address reserved for the client.

8. In the **Client Name** box, type **Server2** (where **Server2** is your second computer's name) and then click **Add**.

    This name is used for identification purposes in the DHCP Manager application. The name is associated with the hardware address of the network adapter card.

    The **Add Reserved Clients** dialog box appears.

9. To return to DHCP Manager, click **Close**.

Note If there are multiple DHCP servers in the internetwork, it is important that all DHCP servers have the same client reservations. The client can receive its lease from any DHCP server and will be guaranteed the same IP address.

Practice

In this procedure, you test the DHCP server configuration by starting the DHCP client on your second computer, and determining the TCP/IP configuration information assigned to it by the DHCP server.

Note Perform this procedure from your second computer. This computer will become the DHCP client, and should have the physical address and computer name that was used to create the DHCP client reservation.

▶ **To install the DHCP client**

1. In the **Microsoft TCP/IP Properties** dialog box, click the **IP Address** tab.
2. Click **Obtain an IP address from a DHCP server**.

    You are prompted to enable DHCP.
3. Click **Yes**.
4. Click **OK**.

    This installs and activates the DHCP client on your computer.
5. Click **OK** again.

▶ **To verify the DHCP-assigned TCP/IP information**

Note Complete this procedure only from the DHCP client.

1. At a command prompt, type **ipconfig /all** to view the TCP/IP configuration.
2. What IP address was assigned to the DHCP client computer by the DHCP server?

3. What is the address of the default gateway?

▶ To view DHCP-assigned addresses

In this procedure, you view the DHCP server listing of leased addresses.

Note Complete this procedure from the DHCP server.

1. In the DHCP Manager window, select the local scope (designated by the light bulb icon).
2. On the **Scope** menu, click **Active Leases**.

   The **Active Leases** dialog box appears, displaying the list of IP addresses that have been leased to clients.
3. Click **Properties**.

   The **Client Properties** dialog box appears. The **Lease expires time** is listed as **infinite**.
4. Click **OK** to return to the **Active Leases** dialog box.
5. Click **OK** to return to the DHCP Manager window.

▶ To renew a DHCP lease

In this procedure, you renew the lease assigned to the DHCP client computer.

Note Complete this procedure only from the DHCP client.

1. At a command prompt, type **ipconfig /all**
2. When does the lease expire?

   _____

3. To renew the lease, type **ipconfig /renew** at a command prompt, and then press ENTER.

   The Windows IP Configuration information is displayed.
4. Type **ipconfig /all** to view the lease information.
5. When does the lease expire?

   _____

Summary

A scope is a range of IP addresses that are available to be leased or assigned to clients. Multiple scopes and separate scopes for each subnet can be created to allow DHCP clients to obtain a valid IP address from any DHCP server. To implement DHCP, software is required on both the client and the server. Every DHCP server requires at least one scope.

Lesson 3: Enabling a DHCP Relay Agent

Windows NT Server has the ability to be an RFC 1542–compliant DHCP relay agent. A relay agent, when used in conjunction with either the static or dynamic IP router, relays DHCP messages between DHCP clients and servers on different IP networks.

After this lesson, you will be able to:
- Install and configure a DHCP relay agent.

Estimated lesson time: 25 minutes

If routers separate your DHCP clients and servers, you can configure Windows NT Server to be a DHCP relay agent. A relay agent will intercept DHCP broadcasts and forward the packets to the DHCP server, crossing IP routers. You add Microsoft DHCP Relay Agent through the Control Panel Network program.

When a dynamic client computer on the subnet where the DHCP relay agent resides requests an IP address, the request is forwarded to the subnet's DHCP relay agent as shown in the following illustration. The DHCP relay agent, in turn, is configured to forward the request directly to the correct computer running the Windows NT Server DHCP service. The computer running the Windows NT Server DHCP service returns an IP address directly to the requesting client.

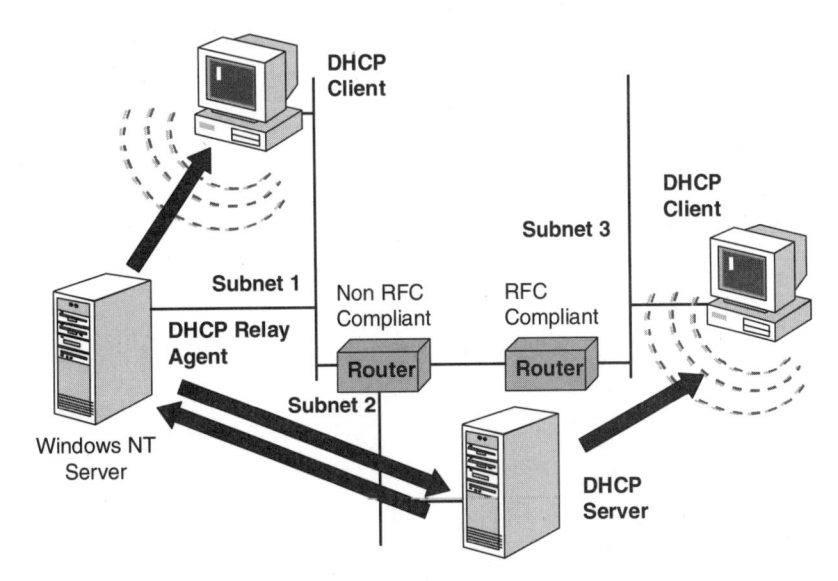

The DHCP relay agent is configured with the IP address of the computer running Windows NT Server DHCP so that the agent will know where to forward requests from clients for available IP addresses.

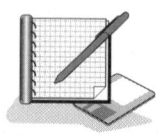

Practice

In this procedure, you use the Control Panel Network program to install the DHCP relay agent, and then configure the relay agent using the DHCP property sheet to specify the IP address of the DHCP server. Keep in mind that in a production environment you will be installing a DHCP relay agent to forward requests from different subnets.

Note Perform this procedure from Server2.

▶ **To install DHCP Relay Agent**

1. Click the **Start** button, point to **Settings**, and then click **Control Panel**.
2. Double-click the **Network** icon.

   The **Network** dialog box appears.
3. Click the **Services** tab.

   The **Services** tab displays the list of Network Services currently running on this computer.
4. Click **Add**.

   The **Select Network Service** dialog box displays the Network Services available.
5. Click **DHCP Relay Agent**.

   The DHCP Relay Agent is highlighted in the list box.
6. Click **OK**.

   The **Windows NT Setup** dialog box appears.
7. Type the path to the Windows NT Server files, and then click **Continue**.

   The **Network** dialog box appears.
8. Click **Close**.

   The **Unattended Setup** dialog box appears.

   You are prompted to add an IP address to the DHCP Servers list.
9. Click **Yes**.

   The **TCP/IP Properties** dialog box appears.
10. Click the **DHCP Relay** tab, and then click **Add**.

    The **DHCP Relay Agent** property sheet appears.

11. Type the IP address of the DHCP Server, and then click **Add**.

    The IP address is added to the **DHCP Servers** list.

12. Click **OK**.

    You are prompted to restart your computer.

13. Click **Yes**.

    Your computer restarts with DHCP Relay Agent enabled.

Practice

In this procedure, you set the computer to its original configuration to prepare for later procedures.

▶ **To disable the DHCP relay agent**

Note Complete this procedure from Server2.

1. Click the **Start** button, point to **Settings**, and then click **Control Panel**.
2. Double-click the **Services** icon.

    The **Services** dialog box appears.
3. Click **DHCP Relay Agent**.
4. Click the **Startup** tab.

    The **Service** dialog box appears.
5. Click **Disabled**.
6. Click **OK**.
7. Click **Close**.
8. Shut down and restart your computer.

▶ **To use a static IP address**

Note Complete this procedure only from the DHCP client computer.

1. Access the **Microsoft TCP/IP Properties** dialog box.
2. Click **Specify an IP address**.
3. Type the configuration information shown in the following table.

In this box	Type
IP Address	131.107.2.211
Subnet Mask	255.255.255.0
Default Gateway	131.107.2.1

4. Click **OK**.

   The **Network** dialog box appears.

5. Click **OK**.

6. Shut down and restart your computer.

Summary

A relay agent relays DHCP messages between DHCP clients and servers on different IP networks.

Lesson 4: Managing the DHCP Database

The DHCP database is automatically backed up every 60 minutes. If the Windows NT Server detects a corrupted database, it automatically restores a backup copy. This lesson explains when to manually back up and compact the database.

After this lesson, you will be able to:
- Back up and restore the DHCP database.
- Use the Jetpack utility to compact the DHCP database.

Estimated lesson time: 10 minutes

Backing Up the DHCP Database

By default, the DHCP database is backed up every 60 minutes. Backup copies are stored in the *systemroot*\System32\Dhcp\Backup\Jet directory.

The default backup interval can be changed by setting the **BackupInterval** value to the appropriate number of minutes and restarting the DHCP Server service. This **BackupInterval** parameter is located in the registry under the following key:

HKEY_LOCAL_MACHINE\SYSTEM\CurrentControlSet\Services
\DHCPServer\Parameters\BackupInterval

A copy of this registry subkey is stored in the *systemroot*\System32\Dhcp\Backup directory as DHCPCFG.

Restoring the DHCP Database

The DHCP database can be restored either automatically or manually. The restore process is done using any of the following methods:

- Restart the DHCP Server service. If the DHCP Server service detects a corrupt database, it automatically restores a backup copy of the database.
- Set the **RestoreFlag** value to **1**, and then restart the DHCP Server service. The **RestoreFlag** parameter is located in the registry under the following key:

  HKEY_LOCAL_MACHINE\SYSTEM\CurrentControlSet\Services
  \DHCPServer\Parameters

  Once the database has been successfully restored, the server automatically changes the value back to the default value of 0.
- Copy the contents of the *systemroot*\System32\Dhcp\Backup\Jet directory to the *systemroot*\System32\Dhcp directory, and then restart the DHCP Server service.

The DHCP Database Files

The files listed in the following table are stored in the *systemroot*\System32\Dhcp directory. You should not tamper with or remove these files.

File	Description
Dhcp.mdb	The DHCP database file.
Dhcp.tmp	A temporary file that DHCP creates for temporary database information while the DHCP Server service is running.
Jet.log and Jet*.log	Logs of all transactions done with the database. These are used by DHCP to recover data if necessary.
System.mdb	Used by DHCP for storing information about the structure of the database.

Compacting the DHCP Database

Windows NT Server 4.0 is designed to automatically compact the DHCP database, so normally you should not need to run this procedure. However, if you are using Windows NT Server version 3.51 or earlier, after DHCP has been running for a while the database might need to be compacted to improve DHCP performance. You should compact the DHCP database whenever its size approaches 30 MB.

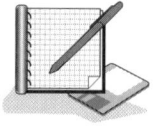

Practice

You can use the Jetpack utility provided with Windows NT Server to compact a DHCP database. Jetpack is a command-line utility that is run in the Windows NT Server command window.

▶ **To compact the DHCP database**

1. Stop the DHCP Server service. This can be done from **Control Panel**, **Services**, **Microsoft DHCP Server**, or at a command prompt. To stop the service at a command prompt, use the following command syntax:

   net stop dhcpserver

2. At a command prompt, go to the *systemroot*\System32\Dhcp directory, and then run the Jetpack utility using the following command syntax (assign any file name to *temporary_name*):

   jetpack dhcp.mdb *temporary_name*.**mdb**

   The contents of Dhcp.mdb are compacted in *temporary_name*, the temporary file is copied to Dhcp.mdb, and then the temporary name is deleted.

3. Restart the DHCP Server service from **Control Panel**, **Services**, **Microsoft DHCP Server**, or at a command prompt. To restart the service at a command prompt, use the following command syntax:

   net start dhcpserver

Note The *Microsoft Windows NT Server Resource Kit* includes a command-line version of DHCP Manager, and a utility that detects unauthorized DHCP servers.

Summary

The DHCP database is automatically backed up every 60 minutes. However, there are some situations when you want to manually back up the database. You can use the Jetpack utility provided with Windows NT Server to compact a DHCP database.

Review

The following questions are intended to reinforce key information presented in this chapter. If you are unable to answer a question, review the appropriate lesson and then try the question again.

1. What are the four steps in the DHCP lease process?

2. At what lease expiration points do DHCP clients attempt to renew their lease?

3. What must be configured on the DHCP server for a DHCP client to receive a lease?

4. In what situations is it necessary to have more than one DHCP server on an internetwork?

5. How are DHCP servers configured to provide backup for each other?

6. In what situations is it necessary to reserve an IP address for a client?

CHAPTER 8

NetBIOS over TCP/IP

Lesson 1   NetBIOS Names . . . 166

Lesson 2   NetBIOS Name Resolution . . . 171

Lesson 3   Using the LMHOSTS File . . . 179

Review . . . 184

About This Chapter

In a preceding chapter, you learned how an IP address is resolved to a hardware address for communicating. In this chapter, you learn NetBIOS name resolution concepts and methods. The lessons clarify how a NetBIOS name is resolved to an IP address using broadcasts, the LMHOSTS file, a NetBIOS name server, a Domain Name Server (DNS), and the HOSTS file. In the lessons in this chapter, you configure and use the LMHOSTS file.

Before You Begin

To complete the lessons in this chapter, you must have installed Microsoft Windows NT Server 4.0 with TCP/IP.

Lesson 1: NetBIOS Names

The NetBIOS name is the name assigned to your computer. This lesson explains how the NetBIOS name is used by Windows NT to communicate with other NetBIOS-based computers.

After this lesson, you will be able to:
- Define NetBIOS and NetBIOS names.
- Describe the types of services provided by NetBIOS over TCP/IP.
- Explain how NetBIOS names are registered, released, and discovered.

Estimated lesson time: 25 minutes

NetBIOS was developed for IBM in 1983 by Sytek Corporation to allow applications to communicate over a network. As shown in the following illustration, NetBIOS defines two entities: a session level *interface* and a session management/data transport *protocol*.

The NetBIOS interface is a standard API for user applications to submit network I/O and control directives to underlying network protocol software. An application program that uses the NetBIOS interface API for network communication can be run on any protocol software that supports the NetBIOS interface.

NetBIOS also defines a protocol that functions at the session/transport level. This is implemented by the underlying protocol software such as NBFP (NetBEUI) or NetBT to perform the network I/O required to accommodate the NetBIOS interface command set. NetBT, or NetBIOS over TCP/IP, is a session-layer network service.

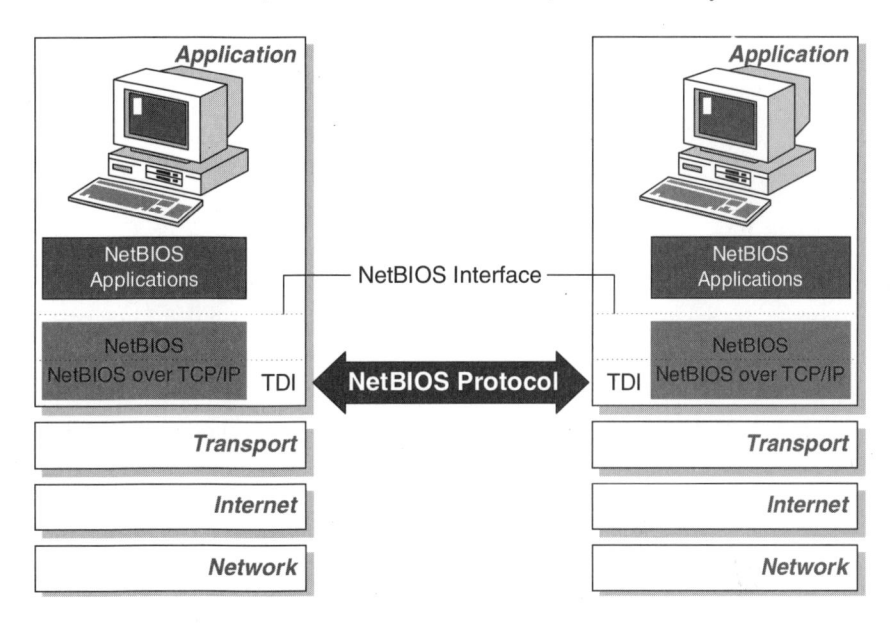

NetBIOS provides commands and support for the following services:

- Network name registration and verification
- Session establishment and termination
- Reliable connection-oriented *session* data transfer
- Unreliable connectionless *datagram* data transfer
- Support protocol (driver) and adapter monitoring and management

NetBIOS Names

A NetBIOS name is a unique 16-byte address used to identify a NetBIOS resource on the network. This name is either a unique (exclusive) or group (non-exclusive) name. Unique names are typically used to send network communication to a specific process on a computer. Group names are used to send information to multiple computers at one time.

You can use the **nbtstat -n** command to view your computer's NetBIOS name.

An example of a process using a NetBIOS name is the server service on a computer running Windows NT. When your computer starts up, the server service registers a unique NetBIOS name based on the computer name. The exact name used by the server is the 15-character computer name plus a 16th character of 20 hexadecimal. Other network services also use the computer name to build their NetBIOS names, so the 16th character is used to uniquely identify each specific service such as the Redirector, Server, or Messenger services.

When you attempt to connect to a computer running Windows NT Server with the **net use** command, the NetBIOS name for the server service is searched for with a *Name Query* request. The matching server process is found and communication is established.

All Windows NT network services register NetBIOS names. All Windows NT network commands (Windows NT Explorer, File Manager, and **net** commands) use NetBIOS names to access these services.

NetBIOS names are also used by other NetBIOS-based computers, such as Windows for Workgroups, LAN Manager, and LAN Manager for UNIX hosts.

Common NetBIOS Names

Viewing the registered names can be helpful in determining which services are running on a computer. The following table describes common NetBIOS names that you see in the Windows Internet Name Service (WINS) database. In Chapter 9, "Implementing Windows Internet Name Service (WINS)," you review WINS.

Registered name	Description
\\computer_name[00h]	The name registered for the Workstation service on the WINS client.
\\computer_name[03h]	The name registered for the Messenger service on the WINS client.
\\computer_name[20h]	The name registered for the Server service on the WINS client.
\\username[03h]	The name of the user currently logged on to the computer. The user name is registered by the Messenger service so that the user can receive **net send** commands sent to their user name. If more than one user is logged on with the same user name (such as Administrator), only the first computer from which a user logged on will register the name.
\\domain_name[1Bh]	The domain name registered by the Windows NT Server primary domain controller (PDC) that is functioning as the Domain Master Browser. This name is used for remote domain browsing. When a WINS server is queried for this name, it returns the IP address of the computer that registered this name.

NetBIOS Name Registration, Discovery, and Release

All nodes of NetBIOS over TCP/IP use name registration, name discovery, and name release for interacting with NetBIOS hosts, such as a Windows NT host.

Name Registration

When a NetBIOS over TCP/IP host initializes, it registers its NetBIOS name using a NetBIOS *name registration request*. This registration can be done using a broadcast or a directed send to a NetBIOS name server.

If another host has registered the same NetBIOS name, either the host or a NetBIOS name server responds with a *negative name registration response*. The initiating host receives an initialization error as a result.

Name Discovery

Name discovery on a local network is handled by local broadcasts or a NetBIOS name server. When Windows NT wants to communicate with another TCP/IP host, a NetBIOS *name query request* containing the destination NetBIOS name is broadcast on the local network or sent to the NetBIOS name server for resolution.

The host that owns the NetBIOS name, or a NetBIOS name server, responds by sending a *positive name query response*.

Name Release

Name release occurs whenever a NetBIOS application or service is stopped. For example, when the Workstation service on a host is stopped, the host discontinues sending a negative name registration response when someone else tries to use the name. The NetBIOS name is said to be *released* and available for use by another host.

Segmenting NetBIOS Names with Scopes

Another useful parameter is the NetBIOS scope ID. The scope ID is used to segment the NetBIOS namespace. Using a scope ID will not increase performance, but it will reduce the number of packets that are accepted and evaluated by a host.

The NetBIOS scope ID is a character string that is appended to the NetBIOS name. It is used to segment the NetBIOS 16-character flat namespace. Without scopes, a NetBIOS name must be unique across all NetBIOS resources on the network. With scopes, a NetBIOS name is unique only within the particular scope, not across the whole namespace.

NetBIOS resources within a scope are isolated from all NetBIOS resources outside the scope. The NetBIOS scope ID on two hosts must match, or the two hosts will not be able to communicate with each other using NetBIOS over TCP/IP. You configure a scope ID from the **WINS Address** tab of the **Microsoft TCP/IP Properties** dialog box.

As shown in the following illustration, two NetBIOS scopes are used—APPS and MIS.

- HOST1.APPS and HOST2.APPS will be able to communicate with SERVER.APPS but not with HOST3.MIS, HOST4.MIS, or SERVER.MIS.
- The NetBIOS scope also allows computers to use the same NetBIOS name (as long as they have a different scope ID). The NetBIOS scope becomes part of the NetBIOS name, making the name unique. In the following illustration, two servers have the same NetBIOS name but different scope IDs.

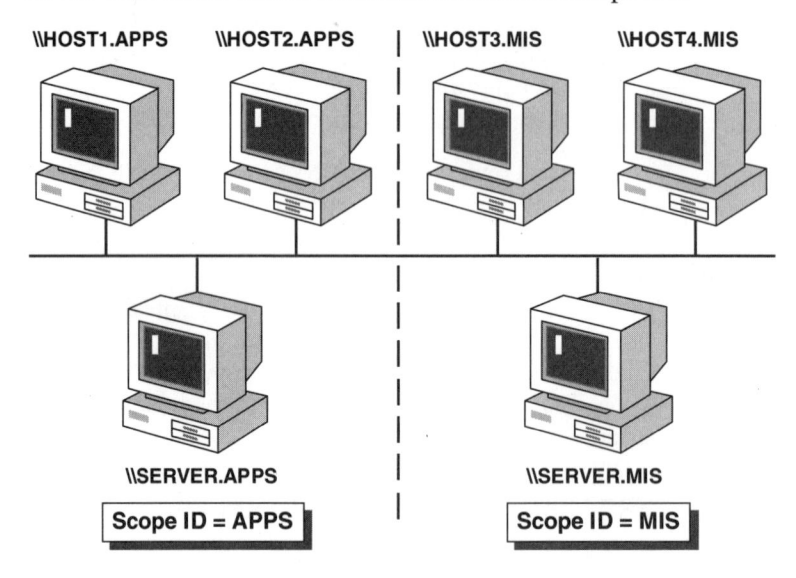

Note The NetBIOS scope ID is defined in RFC 1001. For a copy of this RFC, see the *Course Materials* Web page on the course compact disc.

Summary

NetBIOS defines a session level interface and a session management/data transport protocol. NetBIOS uses name registration, name release, and name discovery for interacting with NetBIOS hosts. The NetBIOS scope ID is used to segment the NetBIOS namespace.

Lesson 2: NetBIOS Name Resolution

Resolving a computer's NetBIOS name to an IP address is called NetBIOS name resolution. This lesson defines NetBIOS name resolution and provides an overview of the different methods used by Windows NT to resolve a NetBIOS name to an IP address. It also provides a brief overview of the NetBIOS name resolution nodes supported by Microsoft TCP/IP.

After this lesson, you will be able to:
- Explain how NetBIOS names of hosts on remote networks are resolved using the LMHOSTS file and a NetBIOS name server.
- Explain how NetBIOS names on a local network are resolved using broadcasts.
- Describe the NetBIOS over TCP/IP node types.

Estimated lesson time: 25 minutes

NetBIOS name resolution is the process of successfully mapping a computer's NetBIOS name to an IP address. Before the IP address can be resolved to a hardware address, a computer's NetBIOS computer name must be resolved to an IP address.

Microsoft TCP/IP can use several methods to resolve NetBIOS names. The type of method depends on whether a host is local or remote.

Standard methods of resolution	Description
NetBIOS name cache	The local cache containing the NetBIOS names that the local computer recently resolved.
NetBIOS Name Server (NBNS)	A server implemented under RFCs 1001 and 1002 to provide name resolution of NetBIOS computer names. The Microsoft implementation of this is WINS.
Local broadcast	A broadcast on the local network for the IP address of the destination NetBIOS name.

Microsoft methods of resolution	Description
LMHOSTS file	A local text file that maps IP addresses to the NetBIOS computer names of Windows networking computers on remote networks.
HOSTS file	A local text file in the same format as the 4.3 Berkeley Software Distribution (BSD) UNIX\Etc\Hosts file. This file maps host names to IP addresses. This file is typically used to resolve host names for TCP/IP utilities.
Domain Name System (DNS)	A server that maintains a database of IP address/computer name (host name) mappings.

Resolving Local NetBIOS Names Using a Broadcast

When the destination host is on the local network, NetBIOS resolves the names of hosts using a broadcast. The following steps and illustration show the process:

1. When a user initiates a Windows NT command, such as **net use**, the NetBIOS name cache is checked for the IP address that corresponds to the NetBIOS name of the destination host. This eliminates extraneous broadcasts on the network. If the name had been resolved recently, a mapping for the destination host would already be in the source host's NetBIOS name cache, and the broadcast would not be sent.

2. If the NetBIOS name is not resolved from the cache, the source host broadcasts a name query request on the local network with the destination NetBIOS name.

3. Each computer on the local network receives the broadcast and checks its local NetBIOS table to see if it owns the requested name.

   The computer that owns the name formulates a name query response. Before the response can be sent, ARP is used (either cache or broadcast) to obtain the source host's hardware address. When the hardware address is obtained, the name query response is sent.

   When the source host receives the name query response, the **net use** session is established.

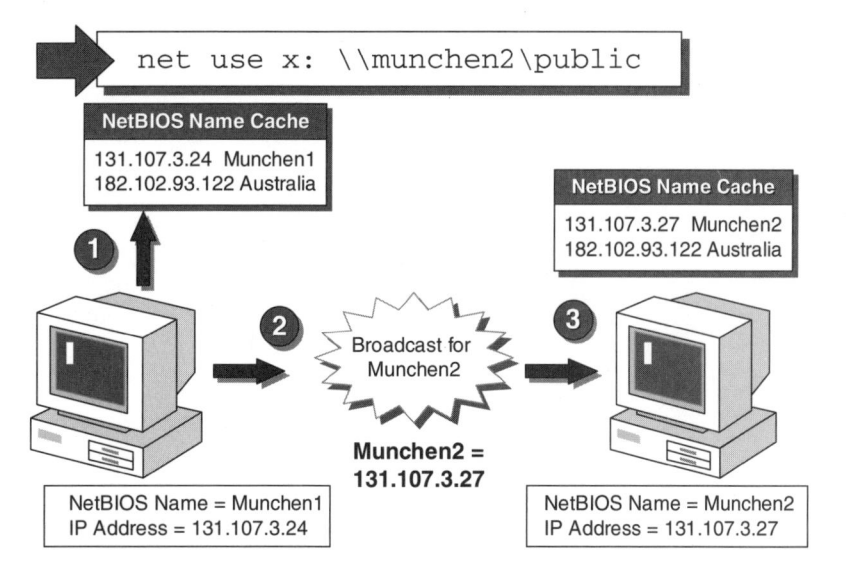

```
net use x: \\munchen2\public
```

NetBIOS Name Cache
131.107.3.24 Munchen1
182.102.93.122 Australia

NetBIOS Name Cache
131.107.3.27 Munchen2
182.102.93.122 Australia

Broadcast for Munchen2

Munchen2 = 131.107.3.27

NetBIOS Name = Munchen1
IP Address = 131.107.3.24

NetBIOS Name = Munchen2
IP Address = 131.107.3.27

Limitations of Broadcasts

Not all routers can forward broadcasts. Those that can typically have this feature disabled because forwarding broadcasts increases internetwork traffic, which can affect network performance. As a result, broadcasts remain on the local network.

Note For a router to forward broadcasts, forwarding of broadcast frames for UDP ports 137 and 138 must be enabled on the router.

Resolving Names with a NetBIOS Name Server

A common method of resolving NetBIOS names to IP addresses is with a NetBIOS name server. The resolution process is as follows:

1. When a user initiates a Windows NT command, such as **net use**, the NetBIOS name resolution process begins. The NetBIOS name cache is checked for the NetBIOS name/IP address mapping of the destination host. If the NetBIOS name is not found in the cache, the Windows NT client will attempt to determine the IP address of the destination host using other methods.

2. If the name cannot be resolved using the NetBIOS name cache, the NetBIOS name of the destination host is sent to the NetBIOS name server that is configured for the source host. When the NetBIOS name is resolved to an IP address, it is returned to the source host.

   By default, the Windows NT client attempts to locate the primary WINS server three times. If there is no response, the Windows NT client attempts to contact the secondary WINS server. If, however, the primary WINS server notifies the client that it does not have a name/IP address mapping for the destination host, the client accepts this as the response and does not attempt to contact the secondary WINS server.

3. After the NetBIOS name is resolved, the source host uses ARP to resolve the IP address to a hardware address for communicating with the source host.

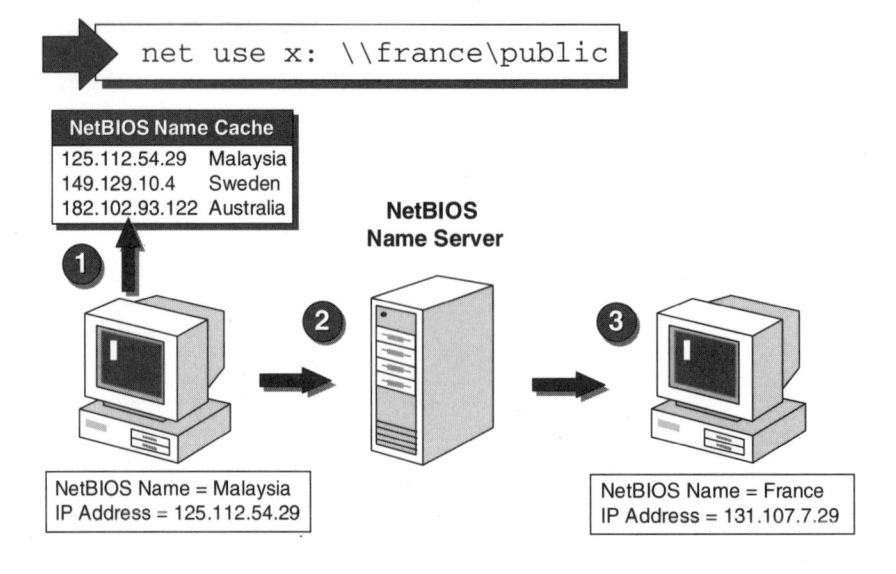

Microsoft Methods of Resolving NetBIOS Names

NetBIOS names can be resolved using a combination of Microsoft-supported methods. Windows NT 4.0 and later can be configured to resolve NetBIOS names using the LMHOSTS file, HOSTS file, and a DNS, in addition to broadcasts and the NetBIOS name server. If one of these methods fails, the other methods provide backup. The following example illustrates how the combined methods might work:

1. When a user types a Windows NT command, such as **net use**, the NetBIOS name cache is checked for the NetBIOS name/IP address mapping of the destination host. If a mapping is found, the name is resolved without generating network activity.

2. If the name is not resolved from the NetBIOS name cache, three attempts are made to contact the NetBIOS name server (if one is configured). If the name is resolved, the IP address is returned to the source host.

3. If the name is not resolved by the NetBIOS name server, the client generates three broadcasts on the local network. If the NetBIOS name is found on the local network, it is resolved to an IP address.

4. If the NetBIOS name is not resolved using broadcasts, the local LMHOSTS file is parsed. If the NetBIOS name is found in the LMHOSTS file, it is resolved to an IP address.

5. If the NetBIOS name is not resolved from the LMHOSTS file, Windows NT begins attempting to resolve the name through host name resolution techniques if the **Enable DNS for Windows Resolution** check box is enabled in the **WINS Address Property** page of the **TCP/IP** protocol dialog box. The first step in host name resolution techniques is to check for a match against the local host name.

    If the host name is found in the HOSTS file, it is resolved to an IP address. The HOSTS file must reside on the local computer.

6. If the name is not resolved from the HOSTS file, the source host sends a request to its configured DNS server. If the host name is found by a DNS server, it is resolved to an IP address.

   If the DNS server does not respond to the request, additional attempts are made at intervals of 5, 10, 20, and 40 seconds.

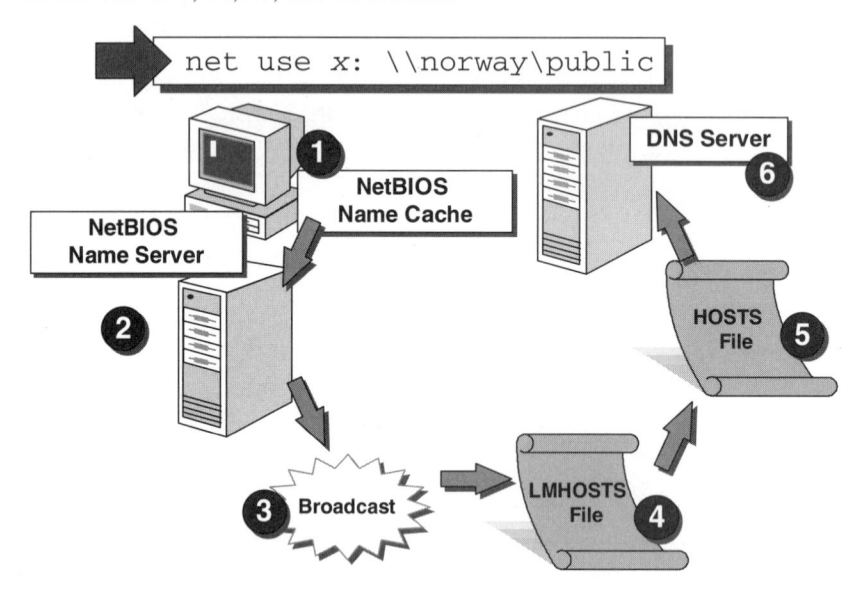

If none of these methods resolve the NetBIOS name, the Windows NT command will return an error to the user, indicating that the computer could not be found.

NetBIOS over TCP/IP Name Resolution Nodes

Windows NT 4.0 provides support for all of the NetBIOS over TCP/IP nodes defined in RFCs 1001 and 1002. Each node resolves NetBIOS names differently.

Node	Description
B-node (broadcast)	B-node uses broadcasts (UDP datagrams) for name registration and resolution. B-node has two major problems: (1) In a large internetwork, broadcasts can increase the network load, and (2) Routers typically do not forward broadcasts, so only computers on the local network can respond.
P-node (peer-peer)	P-node uses a NetBIOS name server (NBNS) such as WINS to resolve NetBIOS names. P-node does not use broadcasts; instead, it queries the name server directly. Because broadcasts are not used, computers can span routers. The most significant problems with P-node are that all computers must be configured with the IP address of the NBNS, and if the NBNS is down, computers will not be able to communicate even on the local network.

(*continued*)

Node	Description
M-node (mixed)	M-node is a combination of B-node and P-node. By default, an M-node functions as a B-node. If it is unable to resolve a name by broadcast, it uses the NBNS of P-node.
H-node (hybrid)	H-node is a combination of P-node and B-node. By default, an H-node functions as a P-node. If it is unable to resolve a name through the NetBIOS name server, it uses a broadcast to resolve the name.
Microsoft enhanced B-node	Microsoft uses an enhanced B-node for resolving NetBIOS computer names of remote hosts. The LMHOSTS file is a static file that maps a remote computer's NetBIOS name to its IP address.
	Entries in the LMHOSTS file designated with "**#PRE**" are cached when TCP/IP initializes. Before a broadcast is sent, the cache is checked for the NetBIOS name/IP address mapping. If the mapping is not found in cache, a broadcast is initiated. If the broadcast is not successful, the LMHOSTS file is parsed in an attempt to resolve the name.

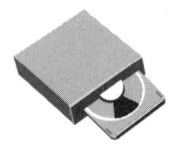

Note NetBIOS over TCP/IP nodes are defined in RFCs 1001 and 1002. For a copy of these RFCs, see the *Course Materials* Web page on the course compact disc.

Configuring Node Types

You can configure which NetBIOS name resolution method NetBT will use to register and resolve names with the following registry parameter:

HKEY_LOCAL_MACHINE\SYSTEM\CurrentControlSet\Services\Netbt\Parameters

Note The system defaults to Microsoft enhanced B-node if there are no WINS servers configured. If there is at least one WINS server configured, the system defaults to H-node.

NBTSTAT Utility

The NBSTAT utility checks the state of current NetBIOS over TCP/IP connections, updates the LMHOSTS cache, and determines your registered name and scope ID. This program is also useful for troubleshooting and pre-loading the NetBIOS name cache.

Command	Description
nbtstat -n	Lists the NetBIOS names registered by the client.
nbtstat -c	Displays the NetBIOS name cache.
nbtstat -R	Manually reloads the NetBIOS name cache using entries in the LMHOSTS file with a **#PRE** parameter.

Summary

NetBIOS name resolution is the process of mapping a computer's NetBIOS name to an IP address. There are several methods available for resolving NetBIOS names, each depending on your network configuration. The methods are NetBIOS name cache, NetBIOS name server (NBNS), local broadcast, LMHOSTS file, HOSTS file, and Domain Name System.

Microsoft supports multiple methods of resolving NetBIOS names. If one method fails, another provides a backup. Windows NT 4.0 supports all of the NetBIOS over TCP/IP nodes.

Lesson 3: Using the LMHOSTS File

Now that you have seen conceptually how the different name resolutions work, you focus on the enhanced B-node implementation using the LMHOSTS file. The LMHOSTS file maps an IP address to its corresponding NetBIOS name of a remote host.

After this lesson, you will be able to:
- Configure an LMHOSTS file for resolving NetBIOS names of hosts on remote networks.

Estimated lesson time: 35 minutes

The LMHOSTS file is a static ASCII file used to resolve NetBIOS names/IP addresses of remote computers running Windows NT and other NetBIOS-based hosts. The LMHOSTS file has the following characteristics:

- It resolves NetBIOS names used in Windows NT commands.
- Entries consist of one NetBIOS name and its corresponding IP address.
- Each computer has its own file. The default directory location is in the form:

    systemroot\System32\Drivers\Etc

    A sample LMHOSTS file (Lmhosts.sam) is included in this directory.
- It is used by Windows NT utilities.

The following is an example of the LMHOSTS file:

```
#This file is used by Microsoft TCP/IP
122.107.9.10     Mexico    # Sales Server
131.107.7.29     France    # Database Server
191.131.54.73    UK   # Training Server
149.129.10.4     Sweden   #PRE     # Main Office Server
182.102.93.122   Australia    #PRE    # MIS Server
```

Predefined Keywords

A Windows NT LMHOSTS file also contains predefined keywords which are prefixed with a #. If you use this LMHOSTS file on an older NetBIOS over TCP/IP system such as LAN Manager, these directives are ignored as comments because they begin with a number sign (#). The following table lists the possible LMHOSTS keywords.

Predefined keyword	Description
#PRE	Defines which entries should be initially preloaded as permanent entries in the name cache. Preloaded entries reduce network broadcasts, because names are resolved from cache rather than from broadcast or by parsing the LMHOSTS file. Entries with a **#PRE** tag are loaded automatically at initialization or manually by typing **nbtstat –R** at a command prompt.
#DOM:[*domain_name*]	Facilitates domain activity, such as logon validation over a router, account synchronization, and browsing.
#NOFNR	Avoids using NetBIOS directed name queries for older LAN Manager UNIX systems.
#BEGIN_ALTERNATE #END_ALTERNATE	Defines a redundant list of alternate locations for LMHOSTS files. The recommended way to **#INCLUDE** remote files is using a UNC path, to ensure access to the file. Of course, the universal naming convention (UNC) names must exist in the LMHOSTS file with a proper IP address to NetBIOS name translation.
#INCLUDE	Loads and searches NetBIOS entries in a separate file from the default LMHOSTS file. Typically, a **#INCLUDE** file is a centrally located shared LMHOST file.
#MH	Adds multiple entries for a multihomed computer.

Note The NetBIOS name cache and file are always read sequentially. Add the most frequently accessed computers to the top of the list. Add the **#PRE** tagged entries near the bottom, because they will not be accessed again once TCP/IP initializes.

Name Resolution Problems Using LMHOSTS

The most common NetBIOS name resolution problems occur when an entry in the LMHOSTS file is incorrect.

Problem	Solution
An entry for a remote host does not exist in the LMHOSTS file.	Verify that the IP address/NetBIOS name mappings of all remote hosts that a computer needs to access are added to the LMHOSTS file.
The NetBIOS name in the LMHOSTS file is misspelled.	Verify the spelling of all names as you add them.
The IP address is invalid for the NetBIOS name.	Verify that the IP address is correct for the corresponding NetBIOS name.
There are multiple entries for the same NetBIOS name.	Verify that each entry in the LMHOSTS file is unique. If there are duplicate names, the first name listed in the file is used. If the first name has an incorrect mapping, the LMHOSTS file will not be re-read for the next entry, and possibly, the correct mapping for the same name.

Tip After you add entries to the LMHOSTS file, use a **net** command with each NetBIOS name to verify that entries were added correctly.

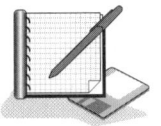

Practice

In this procedure, you configure the LMHOSTS file to resolve NetBIOS names to IP addresses.

Note If you have not already done so, you should remove the NWLink IPX/SPX Compatible Transport Protocol from the **Select Network Protocol** dialog box.

Perform this procedure from your primary computer (Server1).

▶ **To configure LMHOSTS for computer names**

1. Open a command prompt.
2. Using the **edit** command, change the directory and file as follows:

   systemroot\System32\Drivers\Etc\Lmhosts.sam
3. At the beginning of the LMHOSTS file, read the instructions for adding entries.
4. Go to the end of the file, and then add the following entry:

   131.107.2.211   Server2
5. Save the file as LMHOSTS.
6. Start Windows NT Explorer.

7. On the **Tools** menu, click **Map Network Drive**.

   The **Map Network Drive** dialog box appears.

8. In the **Path** box, type **\\Server2** and then click **OK**.

   What was the response?

   _____

If you receive an error message, compare the command syntax to the spelling of the LMHOSTS file entry.

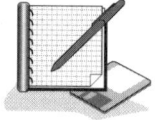

Practice

In this practice, you use the following illustration to determine which entries should be added to an LMHOSTS file for each network, so that hosts on network A can communicate with hosts on network B, and vice versa.

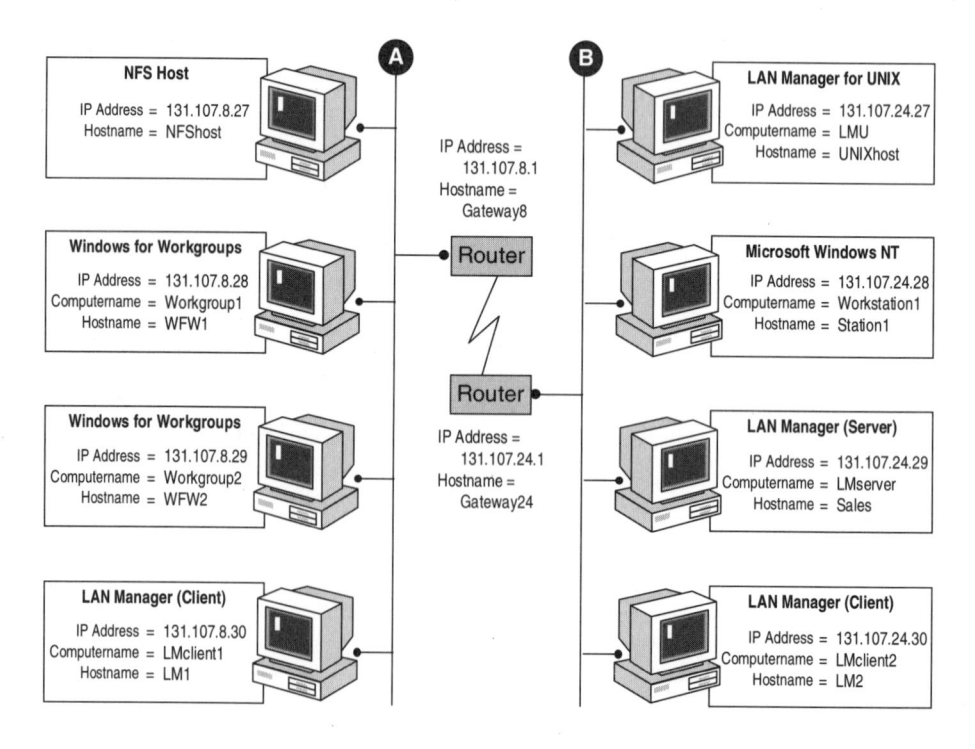

Network A

NFS Host
- IP Address = 131.107.8.27
- Hostname = NFShost

Windows for Workgroups
- IP Address = 131.107.8.28
- Computername = Workgroup1
- Hostname = WFW1

Windows for Workgroups
- IP Address = 131.107.8.29
- Computername = Workgroup2
- Hostname = WFW2

LAN Manager (Client)
- IP Address = 131.107.8.30
- Computername = LMclient1
- Hostname = LM1

Router
- IP Address = 131.107.8.1
- Hostname = Gateway8

Router
- IP Address = 131.107.24.1
- Hostname = Gateway24

Network B

LAN Manager for UNIX
- IP Address = 131.107.24.27
- Computername = LMU
- Hostname = UNIXhost

Microsoft Windows NT
- IP Address = 131.107.24.28
- Computername = Workstation1
- Hostname = Station1

LAN Manager (Server)
- IP Address = 131.107.24.29
- Computername = LMserver
- Hostname = Sales

LAN Manager (Client)
- IP Address = 131.107.24.30
- Computername = LMclient2
- Hostname = LM2

Add the appropriate entries to the following LMHOSTS files so that hosts on both networks can communicate with each other.

LMHOSTS File for Hosts on Network A

IP address	Name

LMHOSTS File for Hosts on Network B

IP address	Name

Summary

The LMHOSTS file maps an IP address to its corresponding NetBIOS name of a remote host. A Windows NT LMHOSTS file contains predefined keywords that facilitate name resolution.

Review

The following questions are intended to reinforce key information presented in this chapter. If you are unable to answer a question, review the appropriate lesson and then try the question again.

1. What methods are used to resolve NetBIOS names?

2. What is the function of the LMHOSTS file?

CHAPTER 9

Windows Internet Name Service (WINS)

Lesson 1 WINS Overview . . . 187

Lesson 2 The WINS Resolution Process . . . 189

Lesson 3 Implementing WINS . . . 196

Lesson 4 Database Replication Between WINS Servers . . . 208

Lesson 5 Maintaining the WINS Server Database . . . 214

Review . . . 222

About This Chapter

The preceding chapters reviewed the different methods of resolving NetBIOS names. In this chapter you will learn how to implement WINS, and understand how WINS reduces broadcast traffic associated with the B-node implementation of NetBIOS over TCP/IP. The lessons in this chapter contain detailed information on installing and configuring a WINS server, WINS client, and WINS proxy agent.

In this chapter, you also learn how to administer a WINS environment. The lessons discuss database replication between WINS servers and maintaining the WINS server database. During the lessons, you configure a push and pull partner, and back up the WINS database.

Before You Begin

To complete the lessons in this chapter, you must have:

- Installed Microsoft Windows NT Server 4.0 with TCP/IP.
- An understanding of the NetBIOS concepts presented in Chapter 8, "NetBIOS over TCP/IP."

Lesson 1: WINS Overview

The Windows Internet Name Service, or WINS, eliminates the need for broadcasts to resolve computer names to IP addresses, and provides a dynamic database that maintains mappings of computer names to IP addresses. In this lesson, you learn the function and purpose of WINS.

After this lesson, you will be able to:
- Explain how a WINS server resolves NetBIOS names.
- Describe the benefits of using WINS.

Estimated lesson time: 5 minutes

WINS is an enhanced NetBIOS Name Server (NBNS) designed by Microsoft to eliminate broadcast traffic associated with the B-node implementation of NetBIOS over TCP/IP. It is used to register NetBIOS computer names and resolve them to IP addresses for both local and remote hosts.

There are several advantages of using WINS. The primary advantage is that client requests for computer name resolution are sent directly to a WINS server. If the WINS server can resolve the name, it sends the IP address directly to the client. As a result, a broadcast is not needed and network traffic is reduced. However, if the WINS server is unavailable, the WINS client can still use a broadcast in an attempt to resolve the name.

Another advantage of using WINS is that the WINS database is updated dynamically, so it is always current. This eliminates the need for an LMHOSTS file. In addition, WINS provides network and interdomain browsing capabilities.

Before two NetBIOS-based hosts can communicate, the destination NetBIOS name must be resolved to an IP address. This is necessary because TCP/IP requires an IP address rather than a NetBIOS computer name to communicate. Resolution uses the following process:

1. In a WINS environment, each time a WINS client starts, it registers its NetBIOS name/IP address mapping with a configured WINS server.
2. When a WINS client initiates a Windows NT command to communicate with another host, the name query request is sent directly to the WINS server instead of broadcasting it on the local network.

3. If the WINS server finds a NetBIOS name/IP address mapping for the destination host in this database, it returns the destination host's IP address to the WINS client. Because the WINS database obtains NetBIOS name/IP address mappings dynamically, it is always current.

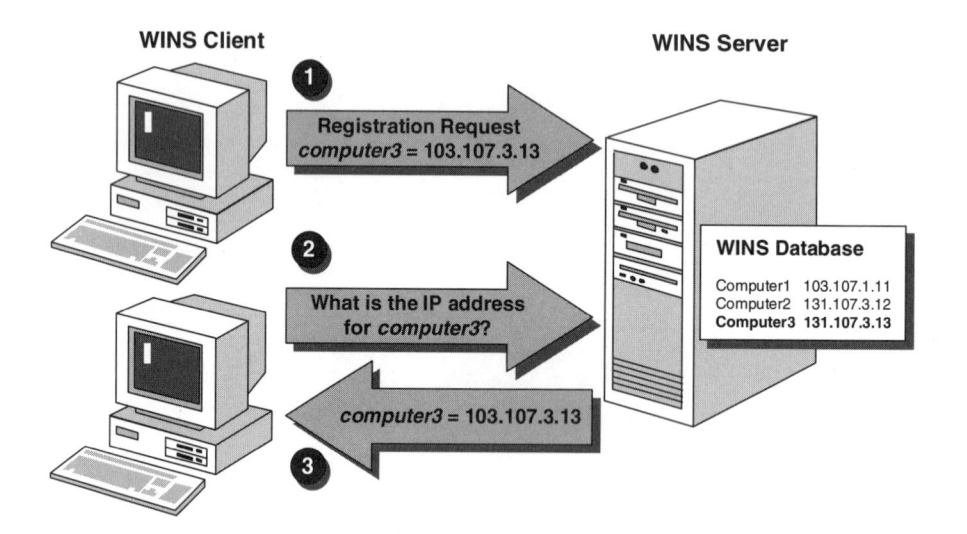

Summary

There are several advantages to using WINS. The primary advantage is that broadcast traffic is reduced because requests for name resolution are sent directly to the WINS server.

Lesson 2: The WINS Resolution Process

WINS uses standard methods of name registration, name renewal, and name release. This lesson introduces the different phases used to resolve a NetBIOS name to an IP address using WINS.

After this lesson, you will be able to:
- Explain how WINS processes name registration, name renewal, and name release.

Estimated lesson time: 25 minutes

The process WINS uses to resolve and maintain NetBIOS names is similar to the B-node implementation. The method used to renew a name is unique to NetBIOS node types that use a NetBIOS name server. WINS is an extension of RFCs 1001 and 1002. The following illustration shows the process of resolving a NetBIOS name.

Note RFCs 1001 and 1002 describe NetBIOS over TCP/IP. For a copy of these RFCs, see the *Course Materials* Web page on the course compact disc.

Name Registration
Each WINS client is configured with the IP address of a primary WINS server and optionally, a secondary WINS server. When a client starts, it registers its NetBIOS name and IP address with the configured WINS server. The WINS server stores the client's NetBIOS name/IP address mapping in its database.

Name Renewal
All NetBIOS names are registered on a temporary basis, which means that the same name can be used later by a different host if the original owner stops using it.

Name Release
Each WINS client is responsible for maintaining the lease on its registered name. When the name will no longer be used, such as when the computer is shut down, the WINS client sends a message to the WINS server to release it.

Name Query and Name Resolution

After a WINS client has registered its NetBIOS name and IP address with a WINS server, it can communicate with other hosts by obtaining the IP address of other NetBIOS-based computers from a WINS server.

All WINS communications are done using directed datagrams over UDP port 137 (NetBIOS Name Service).

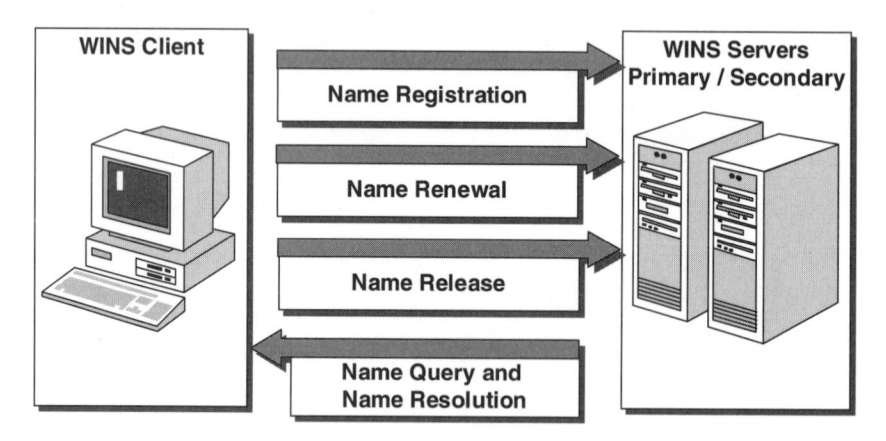

Name Registration

Unlike the B-node implementation of NetBIOS over TCP/IP, which broadcasts its name registration, WINS clients register their NetBIOS names with WINS servers.

When a WINS client initializes, it registers its NetBIOS name by sending a name registration request directly to the configured WINS server. NetBIOS names are registered when services or applications start, such as the Workstation, Server, and Messenger.

If the WINS server is available and the name is not already registered by another WINS client, a successful registration message is returned to the client. This message contains the amount of time the NetBIOS name is registered to the client, specified as the Time to Live (TTL). The following illustration shows the name registration process.

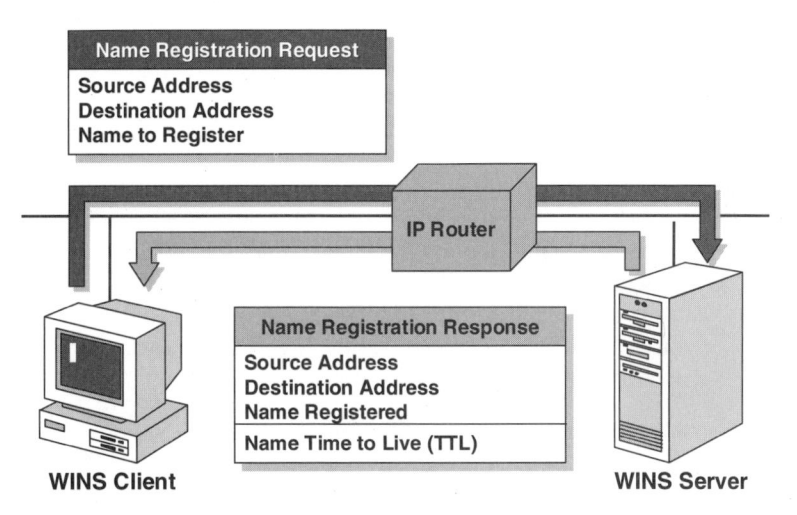

When a Duplicate Name Is Found

If there is a duplicate name registered in the WINS database, the WINS server sends a challenge to the currently registered owner of the name. The challenge is sent as a name query request. The WINS server sends the challenge three times at 500-millisecond intervals.

If the registered computer is a multihomed computer, the WINS server tries each IP address it has for the computer until it receives a response, or until all of the IP addresses have been tried.

If the current registered owner responds successfully to the WINS server, the WINS server sends a negative name registration response to the WINS client that is attempting to register the name. If the current registered owner does not respond to the WINS server, the WINS server sends a successful name registration response to the WINS client that is attempting to register the name.

When the WINS Server Is Unavailable

A WINS client will make three attempts (using ARP) to find the primary WINS server. If it fails after the third attempt, the name registration request is sent to the secondary WINS server, if configured. If neither server is available, the WINS client may initiate a broadcast to register its name.

Name Renewal

To continue using the same NetBIOS name, a client must renew its lease before it expires. If a client does not renew the lease, the WINS server makes it available for another WINS client.

Name Refresh Request

A WINS client first attempts to refresh its name registrations after one-eighth of the TTL has expired. If the WINS client does not receive a name refresh response, it will keep attempting to refresh its registrations every two minutes, until half of the TTL has expired.

At this point, the WINS client will then attempt to refresh its registrations with the secondary WINS server with whose IP address it has been configured. On switching to the secondary WINS server, the WINS client attempts to refresh its registrations as if it were the first refresh attempt—every one-eighth of the TTL until successful, or until half of the TTL has expired, which is four attempts. It then reverts to the primary WINS server.

After a client has successfully refreshed its registration one time, it starts subsequent name registration requests when half of the TTL has expired. The following illustration shows how a WINS client renews its lease to use the same NetBIOS name.

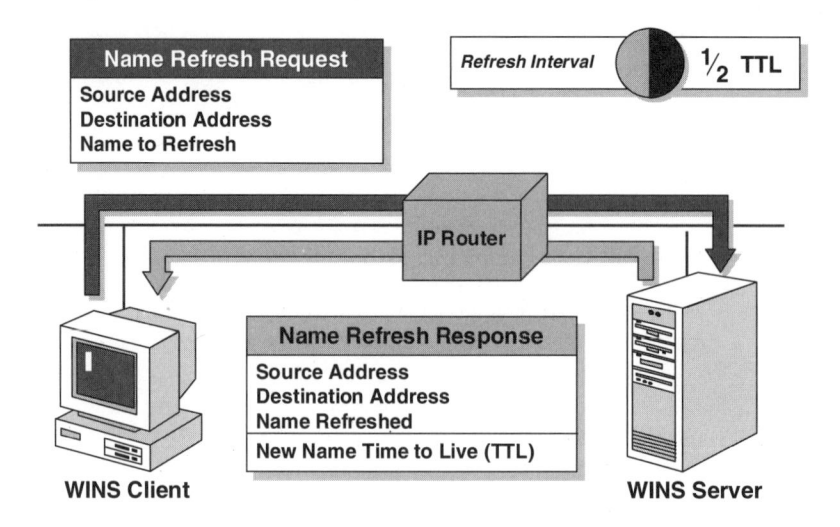

Name Refresh Response

When a WINS server receives the name refresh request, it sends the client a name refresh response with a new TTL.

Name Release

Name Release Request

When a WINS client is properly shut down, it sends a name release request directly to the WINS server for each registered name. The name release request includes the client's IP address and the NetBIOS name to be removed from the WINS database. This allows the name to be available for another client, as shown in the following illustration.

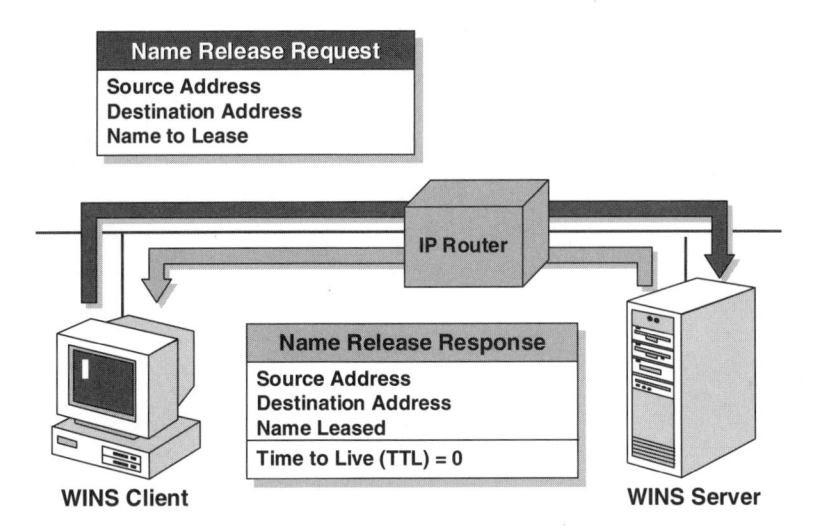

Name Release Request
Source Address
Destination Address
Name to Lease

IP Router

Name Release Response
Source Address
Destination Address
Name Leased
Time to Live (TTL) = 0

WINS Client   WINS Server

Name Release Response

When the WINS server receives the name release request, it checks its database for the specified name. If the WINS server encounters a database error, or if a different IP address maps the registered name, it sends a negative name release to the WINS client.

Otherwise, the WINS server sends a positive name release and then designates the specified name as inactive in its database. The name release response contains the released NetBIOS name and a TTL value of zero.

Name Query and Name Response

A common method of resolving NetBIOS names to IP addresses is with a NetBIOS name server, such as WINS. When a WINS client is configured, by default, the H-node type of NetBIOS over TCP/IP is implemented. The NetBIOS name server is always checked for a NetBIOS name/IP address mapping before initiating a broadcast. The following steps and illustration demonstrate the process:

1. When a user initiates a Windows NT command, such as **net use**, the NetBIOS name cache is checked for the NetBIOS name/IP address mapping of the destination host.

2. If the name is not resolved from cache, a name query request is sent directly to the client's primary WINS server.

    If the primary WINS server is unavailable, the client resends the request two more times before switching to the secondary WINS server.

    When either WINS server resolves the name, a success message with the IP address for the request NetBIOS name is sent to the source host.

3. If no WINS server can resolve the name, a name query response is sent back to the WINS client with the message "Requested name does not exist," and broadcast is implemented.

If the name is not resolved from cache by a WINS server, or broadcast, the name may still be resolved by parsing the LMHOSTS or HOSTS file, or by using a Domain Name System (DNS).

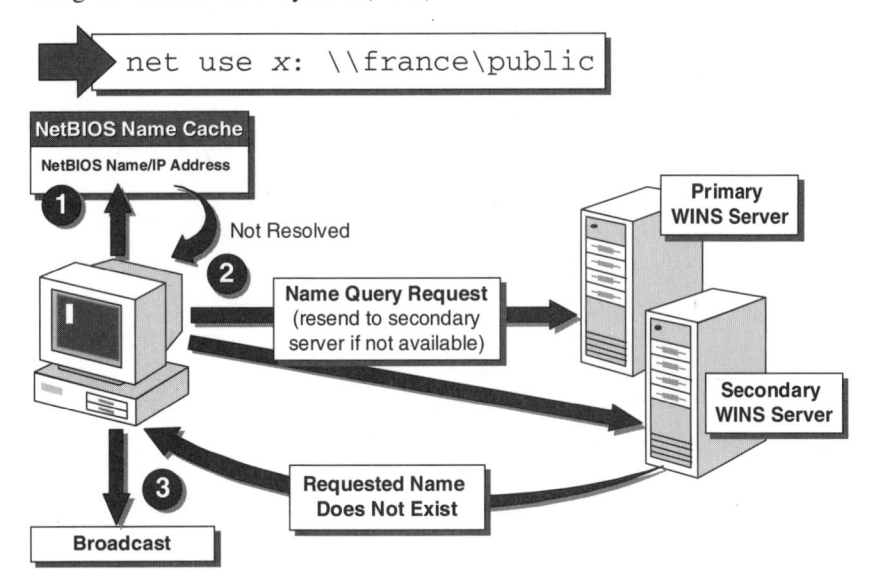

Summary

WINS uses standard name registration, name renewal, and name release methods. To continue using the same NetBIOS name, a client must renew its lease before it expires. When a WINS client is shut down, it notifies the WINS server that it no longer needs its NetBIOS name.

Lesson 3: Implementing WINS

This lesson outlines the considerations for implementing WINS. This lesson shows you how to install the WINS Server service, configure static mappings, and configure a WINS proxy agent.

After this lesson, you will be able to:
- Describe the client and server requirements for implementing WINS.
- Explain how to configure static mappings of non-WINS clients.
- Configure a WINS proxy agent and a DHCP server for WINS.

Estimated lesson time: 60 minutes

Before you implement WINS in an internetwork, consider the number of WINS servers you will need on an internetwork. Only one WINS server is required for an internetwork, because requests for name resolution are directed datagrams that can be routed. Two WINS servers ensure a backup system for fault tolerance. If one server becomes unavailable, the second server can be used to resolve names.

You should also consider the following WINS server recommendations:

- There is no built-in limit to the number of WINS requests that can be handled by a WINS server, but typically it can handle 1,500 name registrations and about 4,500 name queries per minute.
- A conservative recommendation is one WINS server and a backup server for every 10,000 WINS clients.
- Computers with multiple processors have demonstrated performance improvements of approximately 25 percent for each additional processor, as a separate WINS thread is started for each processor.
- If logging of database changes is turned off (through WINS Manager), name registrations are much faster, but if a crash occurs, there is a risk of losing the last few updates.

WINS Requirements

Before you install WINS, you should determine that your server and clients meet the configuration requirements.

WINS Server Requirements

The WINS Server service must be configured on at least one computer within the TCP/IP internetwork running Windows NT Server (it does not have to be a domain controller).

The server must have an IP address, subnet mask, default gateway, and other TCP/IP parameters. These parameters can be assigned by a DHCP server, but statically assigned parameters are recommended.

WINS Client Requirements

WINS is implemented by configuring clients to use WINS and installing and configuring the WINS Server service.

The client can be a computer running any of the following supported operating systems:

- Windows NT Server 4.0 or 3.5*x*
- Windows NT Workstation 4.0 or 3.5*x*
- Windows 95
- Windows for Workgroups 3.11 running Microsoft TCP/IP-32
- Microsoft Network Client 3.0 for MS-DOS
- LAN Manager 2.2c for MS-DOS

The client must have an IP address of a WINS server configured, for a primary WINS server, or for primary and secondary WINS servers.

WINS Server Configuration

- Install WINS.
- Configure a static mapping for all non-WINS clients to enable the WINS clients on remote networks to communicate with the non-WINS clients.
- Configure a WINS proxy agent to extend the name resolution capabilities of the WINS server to non-WINS clients.
- Configure WINS support on a DHCP server.

WINS Client Configuration

The client is configured on the **WINS** tab of the **Microsoft TCP/IP Properties** dialog box. To configure the client, type the IP address of a primary WINS server, and, optionally, the IP address of a secondary WINS server.

Practice

This procedure installs a WINS server to automatically resolve NetBIOS names to IP addresses for WINS clients.

Note Perform this procedure from the computer you designate as the WINS server (Server1).

▶ **To install the WINS Server service**

1. Click the **Start** button, point to **Settings**, and then click **Control Panel**.
2. In Control Panel, double-click the Network icon, click the **Services** tab, and then click **Add**.

   The **Select Network Service** dialog box appears.
3. Select **Windows Internet Name Service**, and then click **OK**.

   The **Windows NT Setup** dialog box appears, prompting for the full path of the Windows NT distribution files.
4. Type the full path to the Windows NT distributions files, and then click **Continue**.

   The appropriate files are copied to your computer, and then the **Network** dialog box appears.
5. Click **Close**.

   A **Network Settings Change** dialog box appears, indicating that the computer needs to be restarted to initialize the new configuration.
6. Click **Yes**.
7. Log on as Administrator.

Configuring Static Entries for Non-WINS Clients

If you have DHCP clients that require a static mapping, you must reserve an IP address for the DHCP client so that its IP address will always be the same.

On an internetwork that has non-WINS clients, it can be beneficial to configure a static IP address/NetBIOS name mapping for each non-WINS client. This ensures that NetBIOS names of non-WINS clients can be resolved by a WINS client without maintaining a local LMHOSTS file. For example, if a WINS client tries to **net use** to a non-WINS client on a remote network, the name cannot be resolved because the non-WINS client is not registered with the WINS server.

▶ **To configure a static mapping**

1. Click the **Start** button, point to **Programs**, point to **Administrative Tools**, and then click **WINS Manager**.

2. On the **Mappings** menu, click **Static Mappings**.

   The **Static Mappings** dialog box appears.

3. Click **Add Mappings**.

   The **Add Static Mappings** dialog box appears.

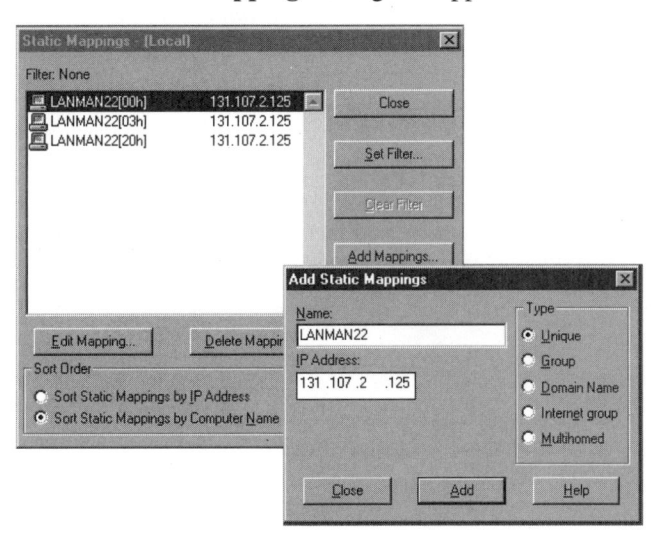

4. In the **Name** box, type the computer name of the non-WINS client.

5. In the **IP Address** box, type the IP address of the non-WINS client.

6. Under **Type**, the options in the following table are available to indicate whether this entry is a unique name or a kind of group with a special name.

Type option	Description
Unique	A unique name maps to a single IP address.
Group	Also referred to as a "Normal" group. When adding an entry to a group by using WINS Manager, you must enter the computer name and IP address. However, the IP addresses of individual members of a group are not stored in the WINS database. Because the member addresses are not stored, there is no limit to the number of members that can be added to a group. Broadcast name packets are used to communicate with group members.
Domain Name	A NetBIOS name-to-address mapping that has 0x1C as the 16th byte. A domain group stores up to a maximum of 25 addresses for members. For registrations after the 25th address, WINS overwrites a replica address or, if none is present, it overwrites the oldest registration.

(*continued*)

Type option	Description
Internet Group	Internet groups are user-defined groups that enable you to group resources, such as printers, for easy reference and browsing. An Internet group can store up to a maximum of 25 addresses for members. A dynamic member, however, does not replace a static member added by using WINS Manager or importing the LMHOSTS file.
Multihomed	A unique name that can have more than one address. This is used for multihomed computers. Each multihomed group name can contain a maximum of 25 addresses. For registrations after the 25th address, WINS overwrites a replica address or, if none is present, it overwrites the oldest registration.

7. Click **Add**.

   The mapping is immediately added to the database for that entry, and then the boxes are cleared so that you can add another entry.

8. Repeat this process for each static mapping, and then click **Close**.

Important Each static mapping is added to the database when you click the **Add** button; you cannot cancel work in this dialog box. If you make a mistake in typing a name or IP address for a mapping, you must return to the **Static Mappings** dialog box and delete the mapping there.

Configuring a WINS Proxy Agent

If you have computers on your internetwork that are not supported as WINS clients, they can resolve NetBIOS names on a WINS server using a WINS proxy agent. A WINS proxy agent extends the name resolution capabilities of the WINS server to non-WINS clients by listening for broadcast name registrations and broadcast resolution requests, and then forwarding them to a WINS server. The following illustration shows how a WINS proxy agent forwards broadcasts to a WINS server.

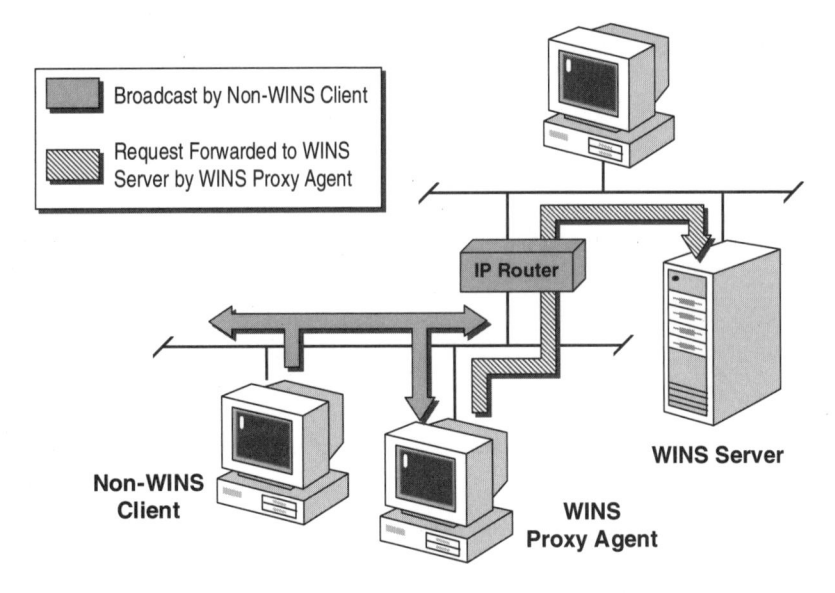

Configuring the WINS proxy agent is accomplished by using the Registry Editor to open HKEY_LOCAL_MACHINE \SYSTEM\CurrentControlSet\Services\ NetBT\Parameters and then setting the **EnableProxy** parameter to **1** (REG_DWORD).

NetBIOS Name Registration

When a non-WINS client broadcasts a name registration request, the WINS proxy agent forwards the request to the WINS server to verify that no other WINS client has registered that name. The NetBIOS name is not registered, only verified.

NetBIOS Name Resolution

When a WINS proxy agent detects a name resolution broadcast, it checks its NetBIOS name cache and attempts to resolve the name. If the name is not in cache, the request is sent to a WINS server. The WINS server sends the WINS proxy agent the IP address for the requested NetBIOS name. The WINS proxy agent returns this information to the non-WINS client.

Implementation Requirements

To use a WINS proxy agent to extend name resolution capabilities of a WINS server requires the following:

- At least one proxy agent on each subnet that has non-WINS clients. This is not required if the routers are configured to forward broadcasts (UDP ports 137 and 138 enabled), but it is recommended to reduce broadcast traffic.
- A maximum of two proxy agents per subnet.
- The proxy agent must be a WINS client but cannot be a WINS server.

▶ To configure a WINS proxy agent

This procedure configures a WINS proxy agent. To be a WINS proxy, the client must first be configured as a WINS client.

1. Click the **Start** button, and then click **Run**.
2. In the **Open** box, type **regedt32.exe** and then click **OK**.

   The Registry Editor window appears.
3. Maximize the HKEY_LOCAL_MACHINE window.
4. Open the following registry key:

   SYSTEM\CurrentControlSet\Services\NetBT\Parameters
5. Double-click the **EnableProxy** value.

   The **DWORD Editor** dialog box appears.
6. In the **Data** box, type **1**
7. Click **OK**.
8. Close the **Registry Editor**.
9. Access the **Microsoft TCP/IP Properties** dialog box.
10. Click the **WINS Address** tab.
11. In the **Primary WINS Server** box, type the IP address of your primary WINS server.
12. Click **OK**.
13. Click **Close**.

    You will be prompted to restart the computer.
14. Click **Yes**.
15. Log on as Administrator.

▶ **To remove the WINS proxy agent**

In preparation for the procedures in next lesson, you remove the WINS proxy agent.

1. Click the **Start** button, and then click **Run**.
2. In the **Open** box, type **regedt32.exe** and then click **OK**.

   The Registry Editor window appears.
3. Maximize the HKEY_LOCAL_MACHINE window.
4. Open the following registry key:

   SYSTEM\CurrentControlSet\Services\NetBT\Parameters
5. Double-click the **EnableProxy** parameter.

   The **DWORD Editor** dialog box appears.
6. In the **Data** box, type **0**
7. Click **OK**.
8. Close the Registry Editor.
9. Access the **Microsoft TCP/IP Properties** dialog box.
10. Click the **WINS Address** tab.
11. In the **Primary WINS Server** box, clear the IP address.
12. Click **OK**.
13. Click **Close**.

    You will be prompted to restart the computer.
14. Click **Yes**.
15. Log on as Administrator.

Configuring a DHCP Server for WINS

If the computer is a DHCP client, WINS support can be configured by using DHCP Manager to add and configure the following two DHCP scope options:

- **044 WINS/NBNS Servers**. Configure the address of primary and secondary servers.
- **046 WINS/NBT Node**. Configure to 0x8 (H-node).

When the DHCP client leases or renews an address lease, it will receive these two DHCP scope options, and the client will be configured for WINS support.

Important The IP addresses that you configure in the primary WINS server and secondary WINS server boxes take precedence over the same parameters configured using DHCP.

Practice

In this procedure, you configure the DHCP server to supply the appropriate WINS server addressing information to DHCP clients.

▶ **To start the DHCP Server service**

Note Complete this procedure only from the DHCP server.

1. Click the **Start** button, point to **Settings**, and then click **Control Panel**.
2. Double-click the **Services** icon.

    The **Services** dialog box appears.
3. Click **Microsoft DHCP Server**, and then click **Start**.
4. Click **Startup**.

    The **Service** dialog box appears.
5. Click **Automatic**, and then click **OK**.
6. Click **Close**.
7. Close Control Panel.

▶ **To configure the DHCP server to assign WINS server addresses**

In this procedure, you configure the DHCP server to automatically assign the WINS server address and NetBIOS node types to DHCP clients.

Note Complete this procedure only from the DHCP server.

1. Click the **Start** button, point to **Programs**, point to **Administrative Tools**, and then click **DHCP Manager**.

    The DHCP Manager window appears.
2. Double-click ***Local Machine***.

    The local scope IP address appears.
3. Click the local scope's IP address.

    The local scope options appear under **Option Configuration**.
4. On the **DHCP Options** menu, click **Scope**.

    The **DHCP Options: Scope** dialog box appears.
5. Under **Unused Options**, select **044 WINS/NBNS Servers**, and then click **Add**.

    A **DHCP Manager** message box appears, indicating that for WINS to function properly, you must add the **046 WINS/NBT Node Type** option.

Chapter 9 Windows Internet Name Service (WINS)

6. Click **OK**.

   The **044 WINS/NBNS Servers** option moves under **Active Options**.

7. Click **Value**.

   The **DHCP Scope: Options** dialog box expands.

8. Click **Edit Array**.

   The **IP Address Array Editor** dialog box appears.

9. Under **New IP Address**, type your server's IP address, and then click **Add**.

   The new IP address appears under **IP Addresses**.

10. To return to the **DHCP Options: Scope** dialog box, click **OK**.

11. Under **Unused Options**, select **046 WINS/NBT Node Type**, and then click **Add**.

    The **046 WINS/NBT Node Type** option moves under **Active Options**, and the **Byte** option box appears.

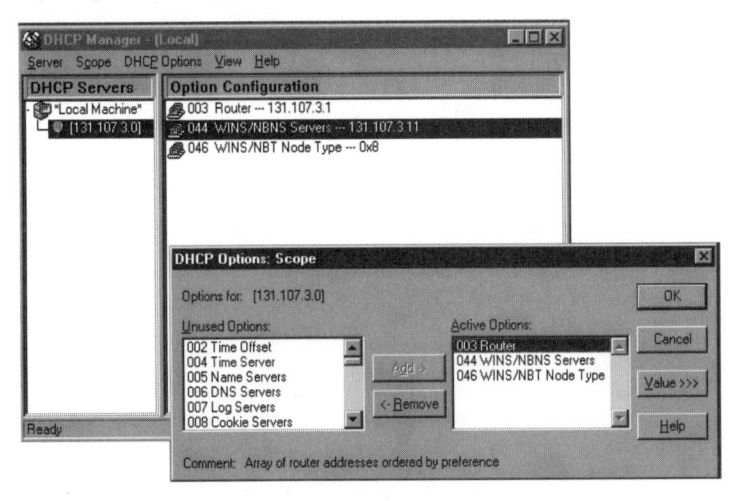

12. In the **Byte** option box, type **0x8** and then click **OK**.

    The DHCP Manager window appears with active scope options of **003 Router**, **044 WINS/NBNS Servers**, and **046 WINS/NBT Node Type** listed under **Option Configuration**.

13. Exit DHCP Manager.

▶ **To update the DHCP client**

In this procedure, you renew your DHCP lease, which automatically assigns the new DHCP scope options of WINS server addresses and node type to the client.

Note Complete this procedure only from the DHCP client.

1. At a command prompt, type **ipconfig /all** and then press ENTER.

   The **Windows IP Configuration** settings appear. The **Node Type** is listed as **broadcast**, and the primary WINS server is not listed.

2. Switch to the **Microsoft TCP/IP Properties** dialog box.
3. Click **Obtain an IP address from a DHCP Server**.

   A message box asks you to confirm the installation of DCHP.

4. Click **Yes**.
5. Click **OK** twice.
6. At a command prompt, type **ipconfig /all** and then press ENTER.

   The **Windows IP Configuration** settings appear. The **Node Type** and **primary WINS server** parameters are updated.

▶ **To use WINS for name resolution**

In this procedure, you use WINS for NetBIOS name resolution. Resolution will be limited to the local subnet, because no remote hosts have registered themselves in the local WINS server database.

1. At a command prompt, verify that the NetBIOS name cache is empty. Type **nbtstat -c** and then press ENTER.
2. If entries appear, clear the NetBIOS name cache. Type **nbtstat -R** and then press ENTER.
3. Start Windows NT Explorer and attempt to browse your other computer.

   Was browsing successful?

   _____

   If you were to browse a remote host computer, would you be successful?

   _____

Summary

To implement WINS, both the server and client require configuration. Configuring a static mapping for non-WINS clients allows WINS clients on remote networks to communicate with them. To resolve a NetBIOS name on a non-WINS client, the WINS proxy agent checks its name cache. If the name is not resolved, the request is sent to the WINS server. At least one, and a maximum of two, proxy agents are required on each subnet with non-WINS clients.

Lesson 4: Database Replication Between WINS Servers

All WINS servers on an internetwork can be configured to fully replicate database entries with other WINS servers. This ensures that a name registered with one WINS server is eventually replicated to all other WINS servers. This lesson explains how WINS database entries are replicated to other WINS servers.

After this lesson, you will be able to:
- Explain when a WINS server should be configured as a push or pull partner.
- Configure a WINS server to replicate database entries.

Estimated lesson time: 40 minutes

Database replication occurs whenever the database changes, including when a name is released. Replicating databases enables a WINS server to resolve NetBIOS names of hosts registered with another WINS server. For example, if a host on Subnet 1 is registered with a WINS server on the same subnet, but wants to communicate with a host on Subnet 2 and that host is registered with a different WINS server, the NetBIOS name cannot be resolved unless the two WINS servers have replicated their databases with each other.

To replicate database entries, each WINS server must be configured as either a pull or a push partner with at least one other WINS server. A *push partner* is a WINS server that sends a message to its pull partners notifying them when its WINS database has changed. When a WINS server's pull partners respond to the message with a replication request, the WINS server sends a copy of its new database entries (replicas) to its pull partners.

A *pull partner* is a WINS server that requests new database entries (replicas) from its push partners. This is done by requesting entries with a higher version number than the last entry it received during the last replication.

Note WINS servers replicate only new entries in their database. The entire WINS database is not replicated each time replication occurs.

Configuring a WINS Server as a Push or Pull Partner

Determining whether to configure a WINS server as a pull partner or push partner depends on your network environment. Keep the following rules in mind when configuring WINS server replication:

- Configure a push partner when servers are connected by fast links, because push replication occurs when the configured number of updated WINS database entries is reached.
- Configure a pull partner between sites, especially across slow links, because pull replication can be configured to occur at specific intervals.
- Configure each server to be both a push and pull partner to replicate database entries between them.

These rules are depicted in the following example and illustration:

- In both Sydney and Seattle, all WINS servers at each site push their new database entries to a single server at their site.
- The servers that receive the push replication are configured for pull replication between each other because the network link between Sydney and Seattle is relatively slow. Replication should occur when the link is the least used, such as late at night.

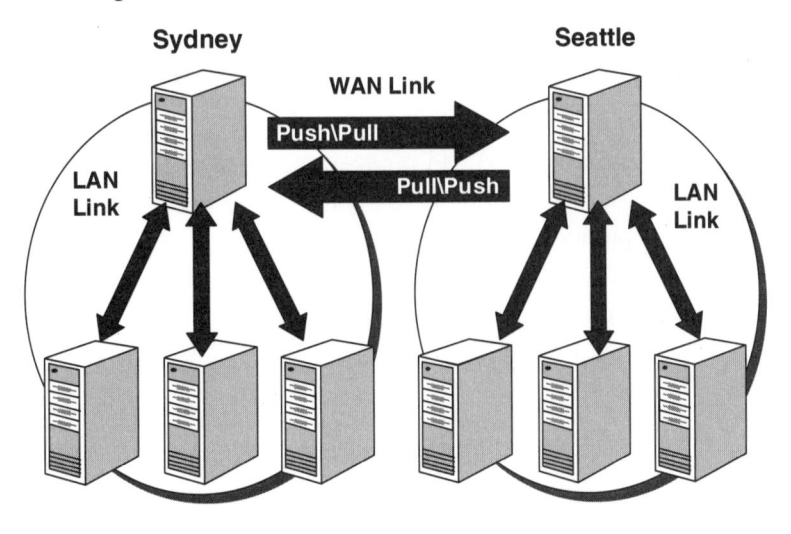

Note You configure a WINS server as a push or pull partner with the WINS Administration tool.

Configuring Database Replication

Database replication requires that you configure at least one push partner and one pull partner. There are four methods of starting the replication of the WINS database:

1. At system start-up. Once a replication partner is configured, by default, WINS automatically pulls database entries each time the WINS Server service is started. The WINS server can also be configured to push on system start-up.
2. At a configured interval, such as every five hours.
3. When a WINS server has reached a configured threshold for the number of registrations and changes to the WINS database. When the threshold (the update count setting) is reached, the WINS server notifies all of its pull partners, who will then request the new entries.
4. By forcing replication through the **WINS Manager Replication Partners** dialog box.

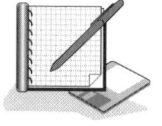

Practice

In these procedures, you configure your WINS server to perform database replication with another WINS server.

Note In order to complete this procedure you first need to configure your second computer (Server2) as a WINS server. Follow the procedure for installing the WINS Server service.

▶ **To configure WINS replication partners**

In this procedure, you configure your second computer (WINS server) as a replication partner.

1. In the WINS Manager window, select the **Server** menu, and then click **Replication Partners**.

    The **Replication Partners** dialog box appears showing the local WINS server.

2. Click **Add**.

    The **Add WINS Server** dialog box appears.

3. In the **WINS Server** box, type **131.107.2.200** and then click **OK**.

   The **Replication Partners** dialog box appears with your IP address added to the list of WINS servers.

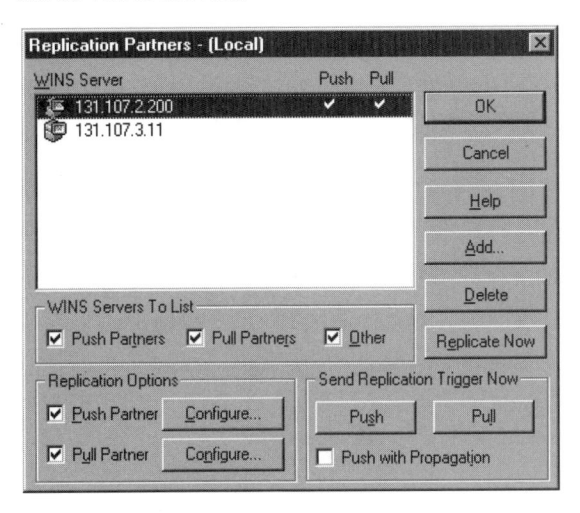

   > **Important** From this computer, you must add your primary WINS server as a replication partner.

4. Under **WINS Server**, click your IP address.
5. Under **Replication Options**, click the **Configure** button next to **Pull Partner**.

   The **Pull Partner Properties** dialog box appears.

   The replication interval is set for 30 minutes.

   > **Note** If this were a push partner, you would type a number in the **Update Count** box for the number of new database entries the WINS server must reach before it will send a push message. An appropriate update count should be based on the number of registrations a server handles. A WINS server that receives hundreds of name registrations when users first log on should not be configured to replicate a small number of registrations.
   >
   > You might also select the **Push with Propagation** check box. This causes the selected WINS servers to obtain any new database entries from the WINS server that sent the message. If the selected WINS servers received any new entries, they propagate the push message to all of their pull partners. If the selected WINS servers did not receive any new entries, they do not propagate the push message.

6. Click **OK**.

▶ **To force replication**

In this procedure, you force WINS to replicate the WINS database with the WINS server.

1. In the **Replication Partners** dialog box, click **Replicate Now**.

   A **WINS Manager** message box appears indicating the replication request has been queued.

2. Click **OK**.

3. Click **OK** to return to the WINS Manager window.

   The WINS Manager window appears with your IP address added as a WINS server.

4. Under **WINS Server**, select the local WINS server.

5. On the **Mappings** menu, click **Show Database**.

   The **Show Database** dialog box appears. Under **Select Owner**, notice the addition of all WINS servers that the replication partner knows about.

   Note If the replicated WINS database shows a version ID of 0, repeat steps 1 through 3 to force replication.

6. Under **Select Owner**, select your IP address.

   Under **Mappings**, the listing of registered names for the WINS server appears.

7. View the information in other WINS server databases, and then click **Close** to return to **WINS Manager**.

WINS Automatic Replication Partners

If your network supports multicasting, the WINS server can be configured to automatically find other WINS servers on the network by multicasting to the IP address 224.0.1.24. This multicasting occurs by default every 40 minutes. Any WINS servers found on the network are automatically configured as push and pull replication partners, with pull replication set to occur every two hours. If network routers do not support multicasting, the WINS server will find only other WINS servers on its subnet.

Automatic WINS server partnerships are turned off by default. To manually disable this feature, use the Registry Editor to set **UseSelfFndPnrs** to **0** and **McastIntvl** to a large value.

Summary

All of the WINS servers on a given network can be configured to communicate with each other so that a name registered with one WINS server will eventually be known by all WINS servers. A pull partner requests WINS new database entries. A push partner sends a message to its pull partners notifying them that its WINS database has changed.

Lesson 5: Maintaining the WINS Server Database

In this lesson, you learn how to view the WINS database and search for specific entries. You also review how to back up and restore the WINS database.

After this lesson, you will be able to:
- Configure WINS to automatically remove obsolete database entries.
- Back up and restore the WINS database.
- Use the Jetpack utility to compact the WINS database.

Estimated lesson time: 40 minutes

WINS Manager provides the ability to view the contents of the WINS database and search for specific entries.

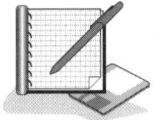

Practice

In this procedure, you view the NetBIOS name-to-address mappings that have been registered in the WINS database.

Note Complete this procedure only from the WINS server.

▶ **To start WINS Manager**

1. At a command prompt, type **nbtstat -R** to purge the NetBIOS name cache (the **-R** is case sensitive).

    This verifies that any names in the cache have been removed prior to using WINS for name resolution.

2. In Control Panel, double-click the **Services** icon.

    The Services dialog box appears.

3. Scroll down the list of services to verify that WINS has started.

4. Close the **Services** dialog box.

5. Click the **Start** button, point to **Programs**, point to **Administrative Tools**, and then click **WINS Manager**.

    The WINS Manager window appears.

▶ To open the WINS database and view IP address mappings

1. On the WINS Manager **Mappings** menu, click **Show Database**.

   The **Show Database** dialog box appears listing all of the NetBIOS names that have been registered in WINS.

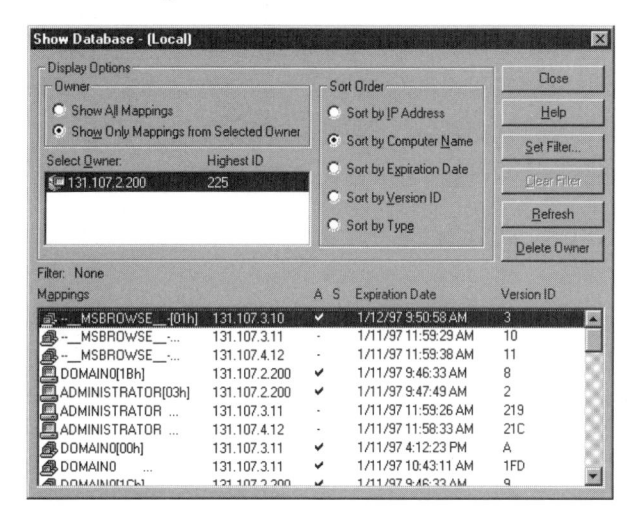

2. To view mappings for a specific WINS server, select **Show Only Mappings from Selected Owner**, and then from the **Select Owner** list, select the WINS server you want to view.

3. Select the **Sort Order** option to sort by IP address, computer name, timestamp for the mapping, version ID, or type. Under **Sort Order**, select how you want mappings sorted.

4. If you want to view only a range of mappings, click **Set Filter**, and then specify the IP addresses or NetBIOS names.

5. View the mappings in the **Mappings** box. Each mapping includes the elements in the following table.

Element	Description
🖳	Indicates that the entry is a unique name.
🖧	Represents a group, internet group, or multihomed computer.
Name	The registered NetBIOS name.
IP Address	The IP address that corresponds to the registered name.
A or S	Indicates whether the mapping is active (dynamic) or static. If there is a cross symbol in the A column, it indicates that the name is no longer active and will soon be removed from the database.

Element	Description
(continued)	
Expiration Date	Shows when the entry will expire. When a replica is stored in the database, its expiration data is set to the current time on the receiving WINS server, plus the renewal interval.
Version ID	A unique hexadecimal number assigned by the WINS server during name registration, which is used by the server's pull partner during replication to find new records.

6. What NetBIOS names have been registered at the WINS server by the client?

   _____

   _____

7. How long will it be before the names expire?

   _____

8. Are there any mappings for remote hosts?

   _____

9. To delete a WINS server and all database entries owned by that server, select a WINS server in the **Select Owner** list, and then click **Delete Owner**.

10. Click **Close**.

Configuring the WINS Server

Each WINS database should be periodically cleared of entries that were released and entries that were registered at another WINS server but were never removed. This process can be done manually by selecting **Initiate Scavenging** on the **Mappings** menu. The WINS administrator can also automatically clean up the database at configured intervals.

Chapter 9 Windows Internet Name Service (WINS)

▶ **To configure the length of time a NetBIOS name is in each phase**

1. On the **WINS Manager Server** menu, click **Configuration**.

    The **WINS Server Configuration** dialog box appears.

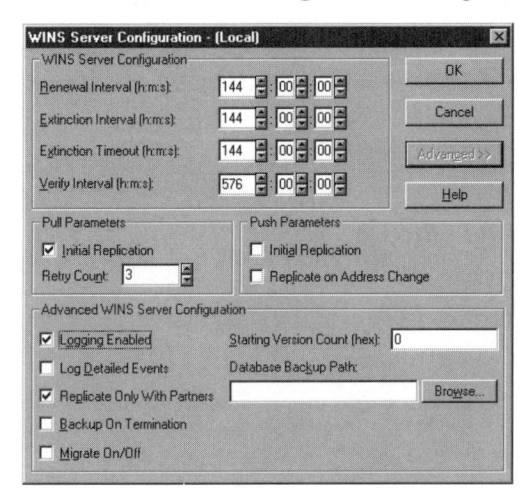

2. To view all of the options in the dialog box, click **Advanced**.

3. Under **WINS Server Configuration**, specify the intervals for each option as described in the following table.

Interval	Description
Renewal Interval	The frequency at which a WINS client will renew its name registration with the WINS server. The default value is 144 hours.
Extinction Interval	The interval between the time an entry in the WINS database is marked as *released* (no longer registered) and the time it is marked as *extinct*. The default value is 144 hours.
Extinction Timeout	The interval between the time an entry is marked *extinct* and the time the entry is scavenged (removed) from the WINS database. The default is the same as the renewal interval, and cannot be less than 24 hours.
Verify Interval	The time after which the WINS server will verify that names it does not own (those replicated from other WINS servers) are still active. The default value is 576 hours (24 days). This is the minimum value that WINS Manager will save.

> **Note** The default values listed in this table are correct; your version of the product documentation or Help may contain incorrect default values for the renewal and extinction intervals.

The WINS server pulls replicas of new WINS database entries from its partners when the computer initializes. By default, **Initial Replication** under **Pull Parameters** is selected.

4. To inform partners of the database status when the computer is initialized, select **Initial Replication** under **Push Parameters**.
5. When finished, click **OK**.

> **Note** The *Microsoft Windows NT Server Resource Kit* includes the Winscl.exe utility, which allows you to delete individual dynamic entries from the WINS database.

Advanced WINS Server Configuration Options

The options in the following table specify how push and pull partners act on start-up as well as perform additional configurations.

Advanced option	Description
Logging Enabled	Specifies whether logging of database changes should be turned on.
Log Detailed Events	Specifies whether logging of events is verbose. If you are tuning for performance, this should be turned off.
Replicate Only With Partners	Specifies that replication will be done only with WINS pull or push partners, and not with a non-listed WINS server partner. This is selected by default.
Backup On Termination	Specifies that the database will be backed up automatically when WINS Manager is closed.
Migrate On/Off	Specifies that static unique and multihomed entries are treated as dynamic when they conflict with a new registration or replica. This means that if they are no longer valid, they will be overwritten by the new registration or replica. Check this option if you are upgrading non–Windows NT computers to Windows NT.
Starting Version Count	Specifies the highest version ID number for the database. Usually, you will not need to change this value unless the database becomes corrupted and needs to be recreated.
Database Backup Path	Specifies the directory where the WINS database backup will be stored. This directory is also used for automatic restoration of the database. Do not specify a network directory.

Backing Up and Restoring the WINS Database

It is important to back up the WINS database in the event of system failure or database corruption. Once you specify a backup directory, the WINS database is automatically backed up every 24 hours.

▶ **To specify the backup directory**

1. On the **WINS Manager Mappings** menu, click **Back Up Database**.

    The **Select Backup Directory** dialog box appears.

2. Specify the location for saving backup files.

3. Click **OK**.

Backing Up the WINS Registry

You should also periodically back up the registry entries for the WINS server.

▶ **To back up the WINS registry entries**

1. Use the Registry Editor to open HKEY_LOCAL_MACHINE\SYSTEM\CurrentControlSet\Services\WINS

2. On the **Registry** menu, click **Save Key**.

3. In the **Save Key** dialog box, specify the path where you store backup versions of the WINS database file.

Restoring a Corrupt WINS Database

In the event that the WINS database becomes corrupt, use one of the following methods to restore the backup database:

- Stop and restart the WINS Server service. If the WINS Server service detects a corrupt database, it automatically restores a backup copy.

- On the **WINS Manager Mappings** menu, click **Restore Database**.

    You then specify the directory where the backup copy is located. The database is restored from the backup copy.

The WINS Database Files

The files in the following table are stored in the *systemroot*\System32\Wins directory.

File	Description
Wins.mdb	The WINS database file.
Winstmp.mdb	A temporary file that WINS creates when you set up a WINS server. This file may remain in the \WINS directory after a software or hardware failure.
J50.log	A log of all transactions processed with the database. This file is used by WINS to recover data, if necessary.
J50.chk	A checkpoint file.

Caution Because these files are necessary for maintaining the WINS database, do not tamper with or remove them, except to manually restore a corrupt WINS database.

Compacting the WINS Database

Because Windows NT Server 4.0 is designed to automatically compact the WINS database, you should not need to run this procedure. If necessary, you can use the Jetpack utility provided with Windows NT Server to compact a WINS database.

▶ **To compact the WINS database**

1. Stop the WINS Server service from **Control Panel**, **Services**, **Windows Internet Name Service**, or at a command prompt. To stop the service from a command prompt, use the following command syntax:

   net stop wins

2. From the *systemroot*\System32\Wins directory, run the Jetpack utility using the following command syntax (assign any file name to *temporary_name*):

   jetpack wins.mdb *temporary_name*.**mdb**

   The contents of Wins.mdb are compacted in *temporary_name*, the temporary file is copied to Wins.mdb, and then the temporary name is deleted.

3. Restart the WINS Server service from **Control Panel**, **Services**, **Windows Internet Name Service**, or at a command prompt. To restart the service from a command prompt, use the following command syntax:

   net start wins

Summary

You can view the contents of the WINS database and search for specific entries through WINS Manager. You can manually remove obsolete database entries, or configure WINS to remove them automatically. Windows NT Server 4.0 is designed to automatically compact the WINS database.

Review

The following questions are intended to reinforce key information presented in this chapter. If you are unable to answer a question, review the appropriate lesson and then try the question again.

1. What are two benefits of WINS?

2. What two methods can be used to enable WINS on a client computer?

3. How many WINS servers are required in an internet of 12 subnets?

4. What methods can non-WINS clients use to resolve NetBIOS names?

5. When should you use a WINS proxy agent?

6. After a default installation of WINS, how often is the WINS database backed up?

7. What types of names are stored in the WINS database?

8. How would WINS replication be configured in an environment with a slow WAN link with limited bandwidth?

9. How would WINS replication be configured in a LAN environment without network traffic problems?

10. When does WINS use multicasting?

CHAPTER 10

IP Internetwork Browsing and Domain Functions

Lesson 1 Browsing Overview . . . 226

Lesson 2 Browsing an IP Internetwork . . . 230

Lesson 3 Domain Functions in an IP Internetwork . . . 235

Review . . . 240

About This Chapter
Previous chapters discussed NetBIOS name resolution using the LMHOSTS file and WINS. In this chapter, you learn about browsing for NetBIOS resources in a TCP/IP internetwork. The lessons in this chapter cover browsing for NetBIOS resources, domain logon, account password changes, and domain synchronization processes. During the lessons, you plan an LMHOSTS implementation to ensure internetwork browsing and domain activity.

Before You Begin
To complete the lessons in this chapter, you must have:

- Installed Microsoft Windows NT Server 4.0 with TCP/IP.
- An understanding of the concepts presented in Chapter 8, "NetBIOS over TCP/IP."

Lesson 1: Browsing Overview

To share resources across a network efficiently, users must be able to find out what resources are available. Windows NT provides the Computer Browser service to display a list of currently available resources. This lesson reviews the operation of the Windows NT Computer Browsing service.

After this lesson, you will be able to:
- Explain the Windows NT Computer Browsing service in terms of collection, distribution, and the servicing of client requests.

Estimated lesson time: 15 minutes

The Computer Browser service is a distributed series of lists of available network resources. These lists are distributed to specially assigned computers that perform browsing services on behalf of browsing clients.

Computers designated as *browsers* eliminate the need for all computers to maintain a list of all of the shared resources on the network. By assigning the browser role to specific computers, the Computer Browser service lowers the amount of network traffic required to build and maintain a list of all shared resources on the network.

The types of browsers differ according to their roles in the overall browsing service.

Computer role	Function
Master browser	The computer that collects and maintains the master list of available servers within its domain or workgroup and a list of other domains or workgroups. It also distributes this list, referred to as the *browse list*, to the backup browsers.
Backup browser	A computer that receives a copy of the browse list from the master browser. It then distributes the list to the browser clients upon request.
Domain master browser	The domain master browser has an additional role besides always being a master browser for its domain. If there are other master browsers for the domain on remote networks, the domain master browser synchronizes the browse list from all of the master browsers within the domain.

Computers running Windows NT Workstation, Windows NT Server, Windows for Workgroups, or Windows 95 can perform the master browser and backup browser roles. Only a computer running Windows NT Server acting as a primary domain controller (PDC) can perform the domain master browser role.

Browsing Collection and Distribution

The browsing services in Windows NT can be understood in terms of three key processes:

- Collection of browsing information
- Distribution of browsing information
- Servicing of browser client requests

The Collection Process

The collection process is performed by the master browser computer. The master browser collects information in its master browse list on an ongoing basis as shown in the following illustration. The information includes a list of servers within its domain, or workgroup, and a list of other domains or workgroups.

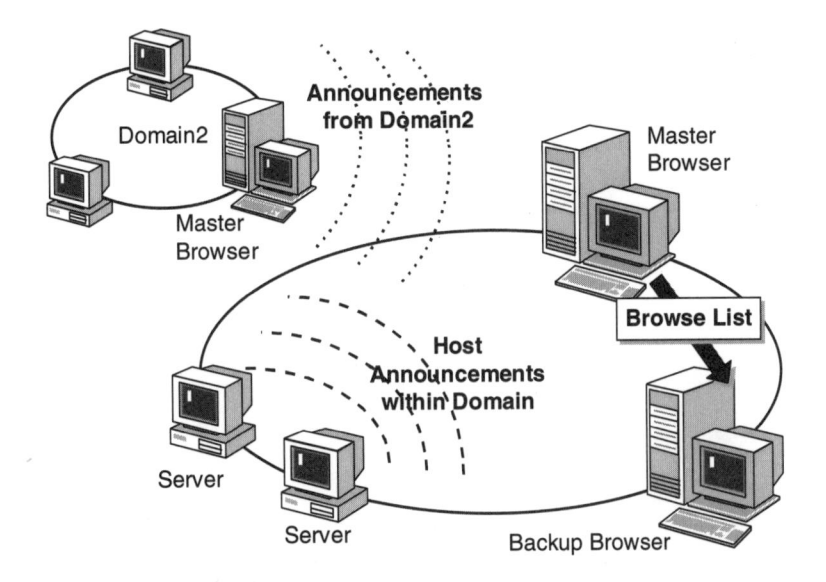

The Distribution Process

The distribution process occurs when the browse lists gathered during the collection process are distributed to the computers that will service the requests from clients. The distribution process occurs through the following:

- Master Browser Announcement

   Periodically, the master browser broadcasts a master browser announcement packet. This packet informs the backup browsers that a master browser still exists. If the master browser does not reply, the election process is initiated to elect a new master browser.

- Browse List Pull Operation from Master Browser to Backup Browser

   Periodically, each backup browser contacts the master browser in its domain and downloads the browse list being kept at the master browser.

Servicing Client Browsing Requests

Once the browse list has been built by the master browser and distributed to the backup browsers, it is ready to begin servicing client requests, as shown in the following process and illustration.

1. When a client attempts to access a domain or workgroup from Windows NT Explorer, it contacts the master browser of the domain or workgroup to which it is attempting to connect.
2. The master browser forwards the client computer a list of three backup browsers.
3. The client then requests the network resource list from a backup browser.

4. The backup browser responds to the requesting client with a list of servers on that domain or workgroup.
5. The client selects a server and receives a list of the server's available resources.

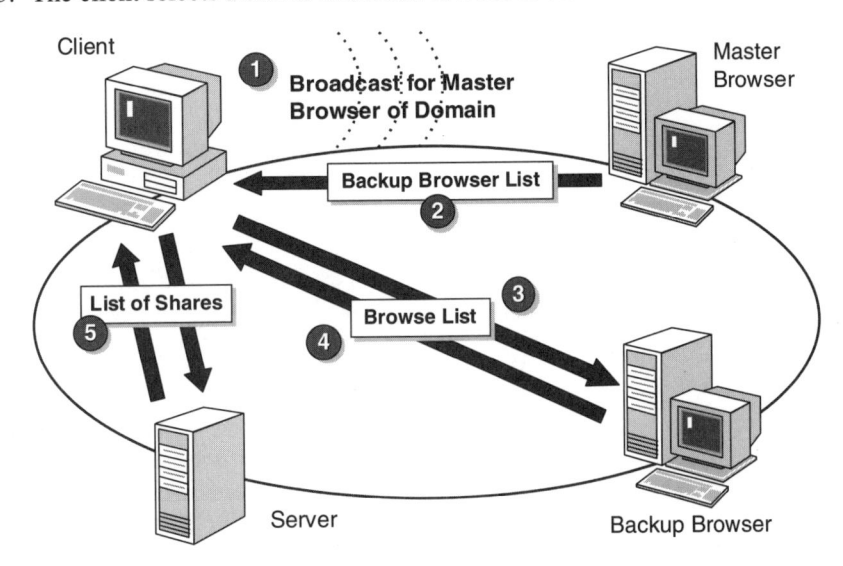

Summary

The Windows NT Computer Browser service provides the ability to view network resources. The types of browsers differ according to their roles in the overall browsing service. The master browser collects a list of servers within its domain and a list of other domains on an ongoing basis. These are compiled in the browse list. Once the browse list has been built by the master browser and distributed to the backup browsers, it is ready to begin servicing client requests.

Lesson 2: Browsing an IP Internetwork

The Computer Browser service uses NetBIOS broadcasts to obtain lists of network resources. This lesson describes the problems associated with browsing an IP internetwork.

After this lesson, you will be able to:
- Describe problems and solutions involved with internetwork browsing.

Estimated lesson time: 15 minutes

Because NetBIOS broadcasts are not routed, it is important that hosts are configured to use WINS or an LMHOSTS file to enable browsing and domain activity across subnets. You can solve browsing problems by using WINS or the LMHOSTS file. However, if your router can forward NetBIOS name broadcasts, it is not necessary to use WINS or the LMHOSTS file.

The Computer Browser service relies on a series of broadcast packets; as a result, browsing across IP routers that do not forward broadcasts can create certain problems. To facilitate client browsing of all network resources in an IP internetwork, there must be mechanisms for the collection, distribution, and servicing of client requests for browse lists.

The IP Router Solution

Some routers can be configured to forward broadcasts from one IP subnet to another. If the IP router is configured to forward these NetBIOS broadcasts, the Browsing service works that same way—as if all of the domains or workgroups were located on the same subnet. All master browsers are aware of all servers in their domains or workgroups—and all other domains or workgroups—and all client browsing requests can be satisfied.

If these settings are enabled on all IP routers in the internetwork, the following information is irrelevant. However, this broadcast forwarding solution is not recommended because it propagates all NetBIOS over TCP/IP broadcast traffic across an internetwork, leading to decreased performance by all nodes on the internetwork. Enabling broadcast forwarding can cause browser election conflicts that report errors in the system log.

Windows NT Solutions

Typically, the IP routers are not configured to forward NetBIOS broadcasts. This means the browsing, collection, distribution, and the servicing of client requests must now take place over *directed* IP traffic rather than *broadcast* IP traffic. There are two ways to facilitate this in Windows NT:

- *WINS.* WINS is used in the collection of browse lists and the servicing of client requests.
- *LMHOSTS Entries.* Special entries in the LMHOSTS file will help facilitate the distribution of browsing information and the servicing of client requests.

Browsing with WINS

WINS solves NetBIOS name broadcast problems by dynamically registering a computer's NetBIOS name and IP address, and storing them in the WINS database. When WINS clients communicate with TCP/IP hosts across subnets, the destination host's IP address is retrieved from the database rather than using a broadcast.

One enhancement WINS adds to this mechanism of collecting domain or workgroup names is that a domain master browser running as a WINS client will periodically query the WINS server to get a list of all of the domains listed in the WINS database.

The advantage of browsing with WINS is that the domain master browser for a given domain now has a list of all domains, including those on remote subnets that are not spanned by its domain as shown in the following illustration.

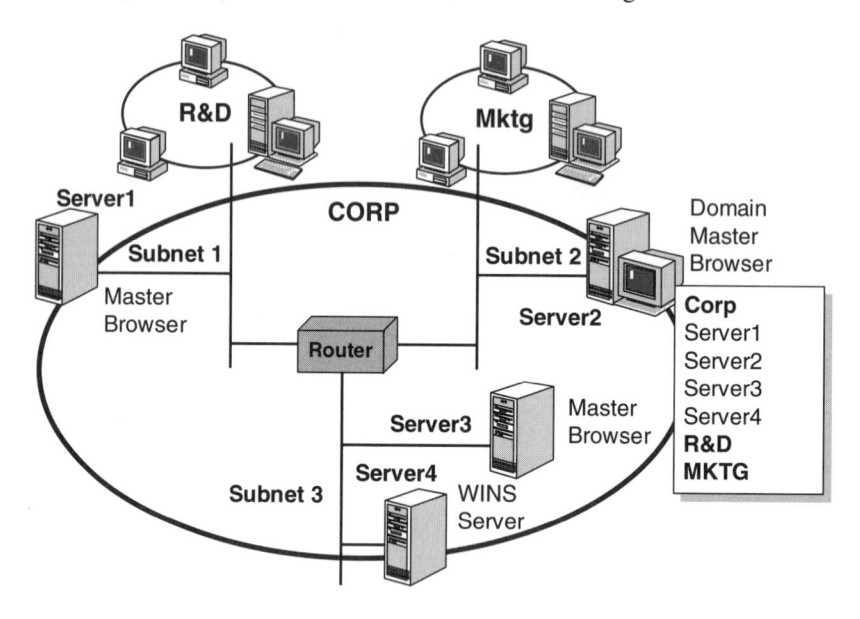

Note The list of domains obtained through the WINS query contains only the domain names and their corresponding IP addresses, but does not include the names of the master browsers that announced those domains.

Browsing Using the LMHOSTS File

To implement direct communication between subnets, non-WINS clients that use broadcasts for NetBIOS name registration and resolution require an LMHOSTS file. The file must be configured with the IP address and NetBIOS name of the domain controllers located on other subnets.

For direct communication between master browsers on remote subnets and the domain master browser, the LMHOSTS file must be configured with the NetBIOS names and IP addresses of the browser computers as shown in the following illustration.

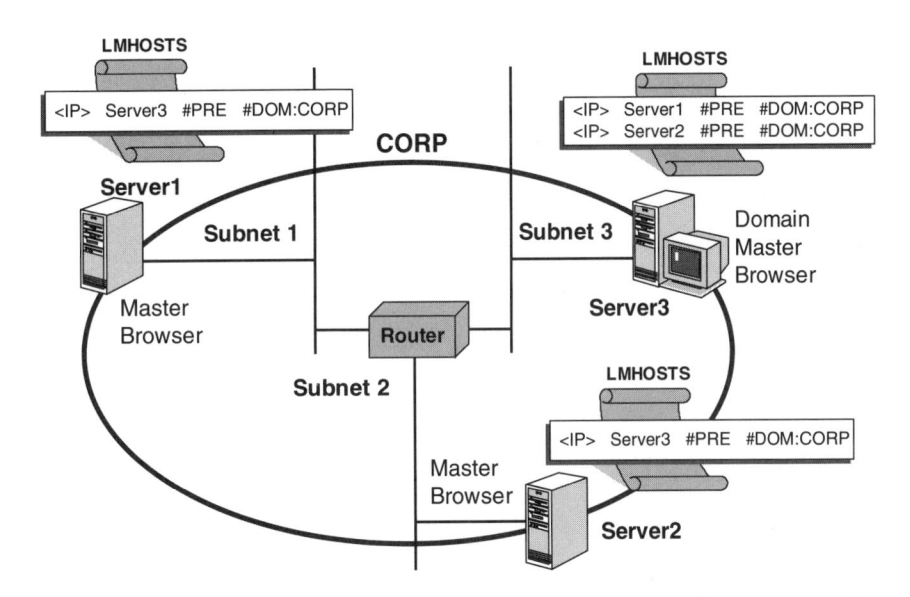

Master Browsers

For computers running Windows NT, the LMHOSTS file on each subnet's master browser should contain the following information:

- IP address and computer name of the domain master browser
- The domain name preceded by the **#PRE #DOM:** tags

For example:

130.20.7.80 *<domain master_browser>* **#PRE #DOM:***<domain_name>*

Domain Master Browsers

At the domain master browser, the LMHOSTS file must be configured with entries for each of the master browsers on remote subnets.

Each master browser computer should have a **#DOM** entry for all of the other master browser in the domain. This way, if one master browser is promoted to the domain master browser, the LMHOSTS files do not need to be changed on the other master browsers.

When multiple LMHOSTS entries exist for the same domain name, the master browser determines which of the entries corresponds to the domain master browser by sending a query to the IP address for each entry. Only the domain master browser will respond. The master browser then contacts the domain master browser to exchange browse lists.

Summary

WINS solves NetBIOS name broadcast problems by dynamically registering a computer's NetBIOS name and IP address, and storing them in the WINS database.

Lesson 3: Domain Functions in an IP Internetwork

This lesson explains how to configure the LMHOSTS file to provide Microsoft domain functions.

After this lesson, you will be able to:
- Describe how domain logon, account password changes, and domain synchronization processes occur in an IP internetwork.
- Plan an LMHOSTS file implementation.

Estimated lesson time: 25 minutes

Besides browsing, some of the other tasks performed by Windows NT network services cause broadcasts to be sent to all computers in a Microsoft domain. These tasks include:

- *Logging on to a domain and password changes.* A broadcast is sent to the domain to locate a domain controller that can authenticate the logon request or to locate the PDC to change the user's password.

- *Domain controllers replicating the domain user account database.* A broadcast is sent from the PDC to the backup domain controllers (BDCs) in the domain instructing them to request replication of the new changes to the domain accounts database.

Because these broadcasts will not cross IP routers, directed traffic must be used to accomplish these tasks. The following illustration shows that when a broadcast is sent to the domain for these tasks, the message is also sent directly to remote domain controllers. The list of computers receiving the direct message is determined by either WINS or LMHOSTS entries.

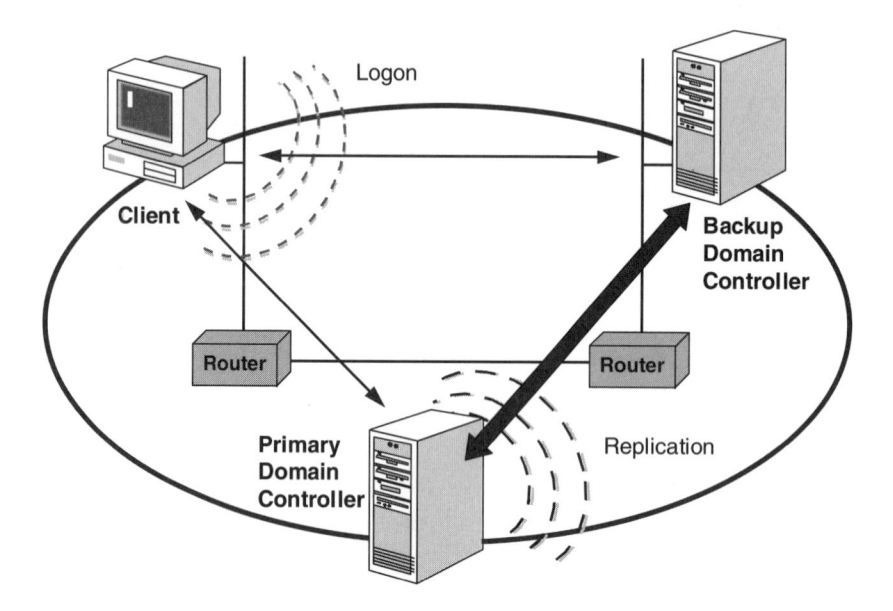

Using the LMHOSTS File

The client broadcasts the message directly to the domain and also looks for any **#DOM** entries in the LMHOSTS file with a matching domain name. If it finds a matching entry, it sends the same message directly to the computer listed.

It is recommended you add remote domain controller **#DOM** entries to each client. This way, if the local domain controllers are offline, the user will still be able to log on. If there are no local domain controllers, a **#DOM** entry is required if the user wants to log on.

A non-WINS PDC must have **#DOM** entries for all BDCs. All of the BDCs must have an entry for the PDC. It is recommended that the domain controllers have **#DOM** entries for each other as well. This way, if a BDC is promoted to a PDC, all of the remaining BDCs will still have a **#DOM** mapping to the new PDC.

Using WINS

Clients contact WINS and ask for the list of domain controllers in the domain. WINS replies with a list of up to 25 domain controllers, called an *Internet group*, registered with that domain. The client then sends the domain message directly to these domain controllers.

Practice

In this practice, you decide which computers require an LMHOSTS file to support browsing, logon validation, domain synchronization, WINS integration, and how each LMHOSTS file must be configured. This practice is based on the following illustration and scenario.

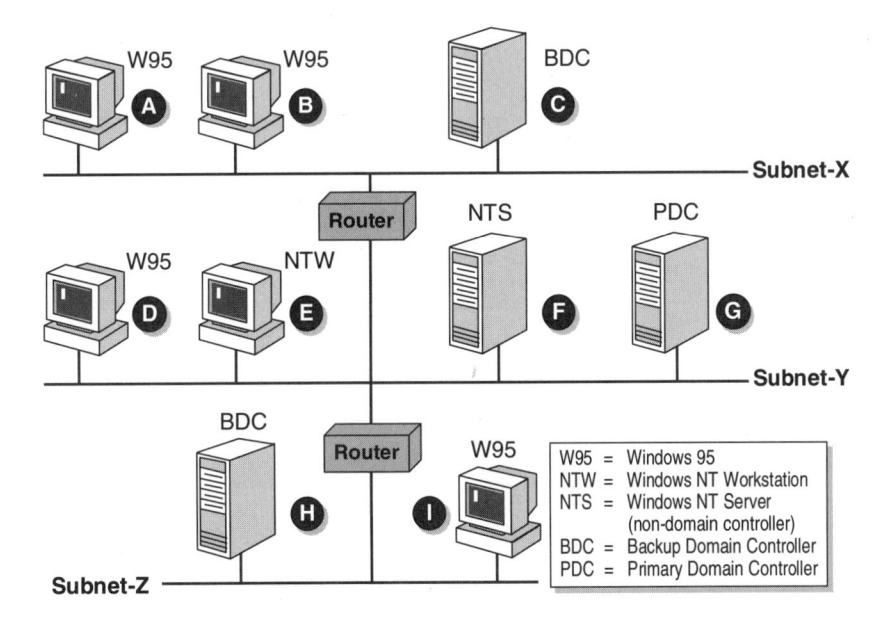

Scenario

As shown in the preceding illustration, the domain spans multiple subnets. Each subnet has a domain controller and various other computers. Hosts on each subnet can only browse and access NetBIOS-based hosts on their own subnets because the routers are not configured to forward broadcasts.

1. Which computers require an LMHOSTS file configured to support internetwork browsing? Which computers should be configured in the LMHOSTS file?

2. Which computers require an LMHOSTS file to support logon validation? Which computers should be configured in the LMHOSTS file?

3. Which computers require an LMHOSTS file configured to support domain account synchronization? Which computers should be configured in the LMHOSTS file?

4. If a WINS server was installed on Subnet-Y, and all computers were configured to use WINS, which computers would require an LMHOSTS file?

Summary

Some of the tasks performed by Windows NT network services cause broadcasts to be sent to all computers in a Microsoft domain. The client broadcasts the message directly to the domain and also looks for any **#DOM** entries in the LMHOSTS file with a matching domain name.

Review

The following questions are intended to reinforce key information presented in this chapter. If you are unable to answer a question, review the appropriate lesson and then try the question again.

1. Why are there problems with browsing in an IP internetwork?

2. How does a master browser on a subnet resolve the IP address of its domain master browser for a domain that spans an internetwork?

3. How does WINS aid in the collection of domains or workgroups?

4. What is required on non-WINS domain controllers to ensure that account synchronization can be accomplished when the domain spans IP internetworks?

CHAPTER 11

Host Name Resolution

Lesson 1 TCP/IP Naming Schemes . . . 242

Lesson 2 Host Names . . . 243

Lesson 3 The HOSTS File . . . 249

Review . . . 252

About This Chapter

This chapter discusses host name resolution concepts and issues. The lessons in this chapter cover how a domain name server, NetBIOS name server, broadcast, and the LMHOSTS file are used to resolve host names. During the lessons, you configure and use the HOSTS file.

Before You Begin

To complete the lessons in this chapter, you must have installed Microsoft Windows NT Server 4.0 with TCP/IP.

Lesson 1: TCP/IP Naming Schemes

Even though TCP/IP hosts require an IP address to communicate, hosts can be referenced by a name rather than an IP address.

After this lesson, you will be able to:
- Explain the different naming schemes used by hosts.

Estimated lesson time: 5 minutes

There are different naming schemes used by Windows NT and UNIX hosts. A Windows NT host can be assigned a host name, but the host name is used only with TCP/IP utilities. UNIX hosts require only an IP address. Using a host or domain name to communicate is optional.

Before communication can take place, an IP address is required on each TCP/IP host. However, the naming scheme affects the way a host is referenced—for example:

- To perform a **net use** command between two computers running Windows NT, a user always specifies the computer's NetBIOS name rather than the IP address, as in the following example:

  net use *x***:** *computer_name*

  The NetBIOS name must be resolved to an IP address before ARP can resolve the IP address to a hardware address.

- To reference a UNIX host running TCP/IP, a user specifies the IP address, host name, or domain name. If a host name or domain name is used, the name is resolved to an IP address. If the IP address is used, name resolution is not necessary and the IP address is resolved to a hardware address.

The main difference in the way you reference the two types of hosts is that you must always communicate using the NetBIOS name with Microsoft network commands and not the IP address. Using TCP/IP utilities to reference a UNIX host allows you to use the IP address.

Note Windows NT 4.0 allows a user to connect to another computer running Windows NT by using an IP address. For example,
\net use *x***:** *131.107.2.200**share_name*.

Summary

Windows NT and UNIX hosts use different naming schemes. Windows NT and other Microsoft network operating systems require a NetBIOS name to communicate with other Windows NT hosts.

Lesson 2: Host Names

A host name simplifies the way a host is referenced because names are easier to remember than IP addresses. Host names are used in virtually all TCP/IP environments. This lesson describes how host name resolution works.

After this lesson, you will be able to:
- Explain how the HOSTS file resolves a host name to an IP address on a local and a remote network.
- Explain how a host name is resolved to an IP address using a DNS server and Microsoft-supported methods.

Estimated lesson time: 20 minutes

A host name is an alias assigned to a computer by an administrator to identify a TCP/IP host. The host name does not have to match the NetBIOS computer name, and can be any 256-character string. Multiple host names can be assigned to the same host.

A host name simplifies the way a user references other TCP/IP hosts. Host names are easier to remember than IP addresses. In fact, a host name can be used in place of an IP address when using PING or other TCP/IP utilities.

A host name always corresponds to an IP address that is stored in a HOSTS file or in a database on a DNS or NetBIOS name server. Windows NT also uses the LMHOSTS file to map host names to IP addresses.

The HOSTNAME utility will display the host name assigned to your system. By default, the host name is the computer name of your computer running Windows NT.

Host Name Resolution

Host name resolution is the process of mapping a host name to an IP address. Before the IP address can be resolved to a hardware address, the host name must be resolved to an IP address.

Windows NT can resolve host names using several methods. These methods are also discussed in Chapter 8, "NetBIOS over TCP/IP."

Microsoft TCP/IP can use any of the methods shown in the following tables to resolve host names. The methods that Windows NT can use to resolve a host name are configurable.

Standard methods of resolution	Description
Local host name	The configured host name for the computer. This name is compared to the destination host name.
HOSTS file	A local text file in the same format as the 4.3 Berkeley Software Distribution (BSD) UNIX\Etc\Hosts file. This file maps host names to IP addresses. This file is typically used to resolve host names for TCP/IP utilities.
Domain Name System (DNS) server	A server that maintains a database of IP address/computer name (host name) mappings.

Microsoft methods of resolution	Description
NetBIOS Name Server (NBNS)	A server implemented under RFCs 1001 and 1002 to provide name resolution of NetBIOS computer names. The Microsoft implementation of this is WINS.
Local broadcast	A broadcast on the local network for the IP address of the destination NetBIOS name.
LMHOSTS file	A local text file that maps IP addresses to the NetBIOS computer names of Windows networking computers on remote networks.

Resolving Names with a HOSTS File

Unlike the LMHOSTS file, which is used for remote hosts only, the HOSTS file maps host names of both local and remote hosts to their IP addresses. As shown in the illustration, the process is as follows:

1. Host name resolution begins when a user types a command using the host name assigned to the destination host.

    Windows NT checks to see if the host name is the same as the local host name. If the two names are different, the HOSTS file is parsed. If the host name is found in the HOSTS file, it is resolved to an IP address.

    If the host name cannot be resolved and no other resolution methods—such as DNS, a NetBIOS name server, or the LMHOSTS file—are configured, the process stops and the user receives an error message.

2. After the host name is resolved to an IP address, an attempt is made to resolve the destination host's IP address to its hardware address.

   If the destination host is on the local network, ARP obtains its hardware address by consulting the ARP cache or by broadcasting the destination host's IP address.

   If the destination host is on a remote network, ARP obtains the hardware address of a router and the request is routed to the destination host.

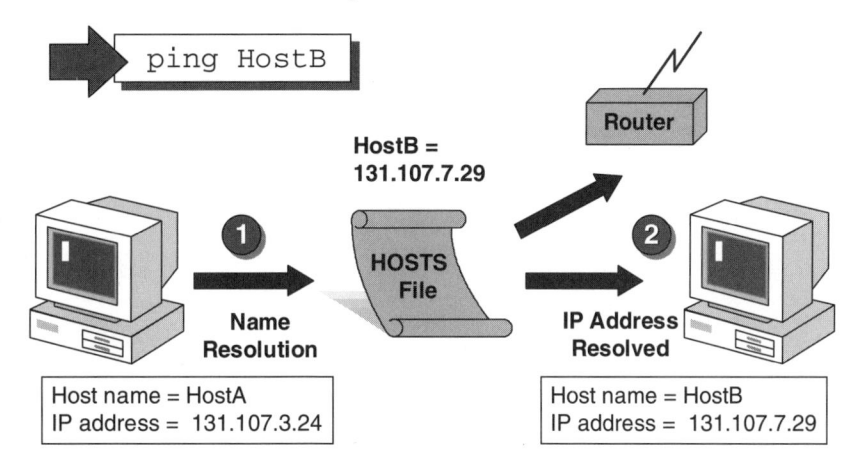

Resolving Names with a DNS Server

A Domain Name System (DNS) server is a centralized online database that is used in UNIX environments to resolve fully qualified domain names (FQDNs) and other host names to IP addresses. Windows NT 4.0 can use a DNS server and provides DNS server services. Resolving a domain name using a DNS server is very similar to using a HOSTS file.

If Windows NT is configured to resolve host names using a DNS server, it uses two steps to resolve a host name as shown in the following process and illustration:

1. When a user types a command using an FQDN or a host name, the DNS server looks up the name in its database and resolves it to an IP address.

   If the DNS server does not respond to the request, additional attempts are made at intervals of 5, 10, 20, 40, 5, 10, and 20 seconds. If the DNS server does not respond to any of the attempts, and there are no other resolution methods configured such as a NetBIOS name server or LMHOSTS, the process stops and an error is reported.

2. After the host name is resolved, ARP obtains the hardware address. If the destination host is on the local network, ARP obtains its hardware address by consulting the ARP cache or by broadcasting the IP address. If the destination host is on a remote network, ARP obtains the hardware address of a router that can deliver the request.

If the DNS server is on a remote network, ARP must obtain the hardware address of a router before the name can be resolved.

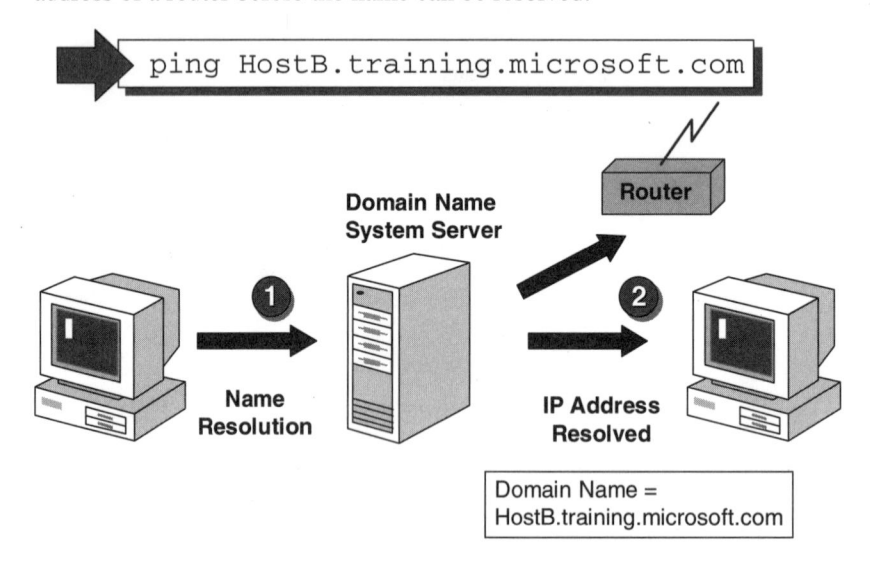

Microsoft Methods of Resolving Host Names

Windows NT can be configured to resolve host names using a NetBIOS name server, broadcast, and LMHOSTS in addition to the HOSTS file and DNS server. If one of these methods fails, the other methods provide a backup, as shown in the following example and illustration.

If NBNS and LMHOSTS are configured, the order of resolution is as follows:

1. When a user types a command referencing a host name, Windows NT checks to see if the host name is the same as the local host name. If they are the same, the name is resolved and the command is carried out, without generating network activity.
2. If the host name and local host name are not the same, the HOSTS file is parsed. If the host name is found in the HOSTS file, it is resolved to an IP address and address resolution occurs. The HOSTS file must reside on the local system.

3. If the host name cannot be resolved using the HOSTS file, the source host sends a request to its configured domain name servers. If the host name is found by a DNS server, it is resolved to an IP address and address resolution occurs.

   If the DNS server does not respond to the request, additional attempts are made at intervals of 5, 10, 20, 40, 5, 10, and 20 seconds.

4. If the DNS server cannot resolve the host name, the source host checks its local NetBIOS name cache before it makes three attempts to contact its configured NetBIOS name servers. If the host name is found in the NetBIOS name cache or found by a NetBIOS name server, it is resolved to an IP address and address resolution occurs.

5. If the host name is not resolved by the NetBIOS name server, the source host generates three broadcast messages on the local network. If the host name is found on the local network, it is resolved to an IP address and address resolution occurs.

6. If the host name is not resolved using broadcasts, the local LMHOSTS file is parsed. If the host name is found in the LMHOSTS file, it is resolved to an IP address and address resolution occurs.

If none of these methods resolve the host name, the only way to communicate with the other host is to specify the IP address.

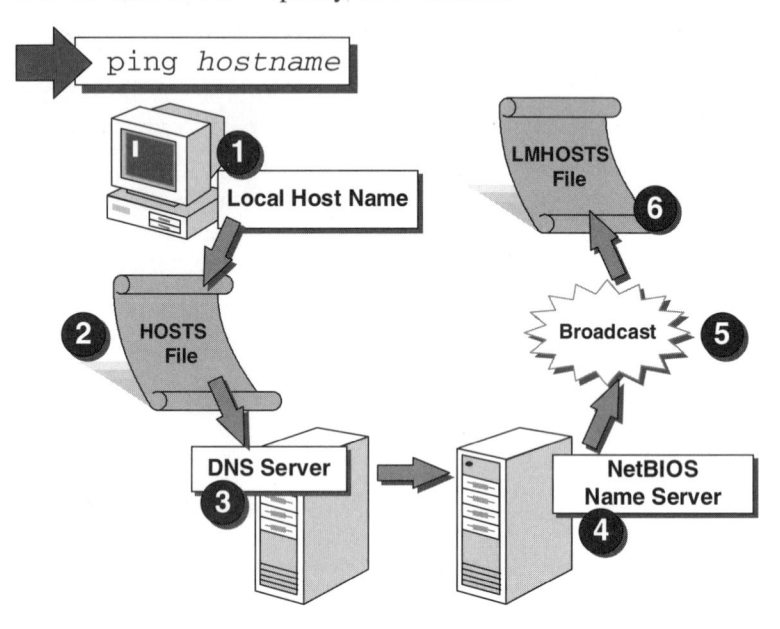

Summary

A host name is used to identify a TCP/IP host or default gateway. Host name resolution is the process of mapping a host name to an IP address. This is necessary before ARP can resolve the IP address to a hardware address.

Lesson 3: The HOSTS File

Now that you have learned the concepts of how host names are solved using different methods, you will look at the HOSTS file. In this lesson, you modify the HOSTS file so that host names are resolved correctly.

After this lesson, you will be able to:
- Configure and use the HOSTS file.

Estimated lesson time: 15 minutes

The HOSTS file is a static file used to map host names to IP addresses. This file provides compatibility with the UNIX HOSTS file. The HOSTS file is used by PING and other TCP/IP utilities to resolve a host name to an IP address on both local and remote networks. The HOSTS file can be used to resolve NetBIOS names (Microsoft TCP/IP-32-specific).

A HOSTS file must reside on each computer. A single entry consists of an IP address corresponding to one or more host names. By default, the host name *localhost* is an entry in the HOSTS file.

The HOSTS file is parsed whenever a host name is referenced. Names are read in a linear fashion. The most commonly used names should be near the beginning of the file.

Note The HOSTS file can be edited with any text editor. It is located in a directory with a name in the following form: *\systemroot*\System32\Drivers\Etc

Each host entry is limited to 255 characters, and entries in the HOSTS file are not case sensitive.

The following is an example of the HOSTS file:

```
#This file is used by Microsoft TCP/IP utilities
#
 127.0.0.1.      localhost loopback

 102.54.94.97    rhino.microsoft.com

 131.107.2.100   unixhost UNIXHOST # LAN Manager UNIX Host

 131.107.3.1     gateway GATEWAY # Default Gateway
```

Practice

In this procedure, you configure and use the HOSTS file, configure Windows NT to use a DNS, and identify problems associated with host name and domain name resolution. In the first part of the procedure, you add host name/IP address mappings to your HOSTS file, and then use the file to resolve host names.

▶ **To determine the local host name**

In this procedure, you determine the local host used for TCP/IP utilities, such as PING.

1. Open a command prompt.
2. Clear the NetBIOS name cache.
3. Type **hostname** and then press ENTER.

   The local host name is displayed.

▶ **To ping local host names**

In this procedure, you ping the name of the local host to verify that Microsoft TCP/IP can resolve local host names without entries in the HOSTS file.

1. Type **ping Server1** (where *Server1* is the name of your computer) and then press ENTER.

   What was the response?

   _____

2. Type **ping Server2** (where *Server2* is your second computer) and then press ENTER.

   What was the response?

   _____

▶ **To attempt to ping a local computer name**

Note Perform this procedure from Server1.

- Type **ping computertwo** and then press ENTER.

  What was the response?

  _____

▶ **To add an entry to the HOSTS file**

Note Perform this procedure from Server1.

1. Change to the following directory by typing:

    cd %*systemroot*%\system32\drivers\etc

2. Use a text editor to modify a file called HOSTS by typing:

    edit HOSTS

3. Add the entry in the following table to the HOSTS file.

Computer IP address	Use this host name
131.107.2.211	computertwo

4. Save the file, and then exit **Edit**.

▶ **To use HOSTS for name resolution**

- Type **ping computertwo** and then press ENTER.

    What was the response?

Summary

The HOSTS file maps host names to IP addresses and provides compatibility with the UNIX HOSTS file.

Review

The following questions are intended to reinforce key information presented in this chapter. If you are unable to answer a question, review the appropriate lesson and then try the question again.

1. What is a host name?

2. What is the purpose of a host name?

3. What does a HOSTS file entry consist of?

4. During resolution, what occurs first, IP address resolution or host name resolution?

CHAPTER 12

Domain Name System (DNS)

Lesson 1   Domain Name System (DNS) . . . 254

Lesson 2   Name Resolution . . . 261

Lesson 3   Configuring the DNS Files . . . 264

Lesson 4   Planning a DNS Implementation . . . 269

Review . . . 278

About This Chapter

This chapter covers the structure and components of the Domain Name System (DNS), including how to resolve TCP/IP addresses, how to configure DNS files, and how to register a DNS server with the parent domain. During the lessons, you design a Domain Name System for various scenarios. This includes making decisions about the number of domains, name servers, zones, and associated DNS files.

Before You Begin

To complete the lessons in this chapter, you must have installed Microsoft Windows NT Server 4.0 with TCP/IP.

Lesson 1: Domain Name System (DNS)

The Domain Name System (DNS) is similar to a telephone book. In DNS, the host computer contacts the name of a computer and a domain name server cross-references the name to an IP address. This lesson describes the architecture and structure of DNS.

After this lesson, you will be able to:
- Describe the structure, architecture, and components of DNS.
- Explain how DNS is used to resolve names and IP addresses.

Estimated lesson time: 30 minutes

Before 1980, the ARPANET had only a few hundred networked computers. The computer name-to-address mapping was contained in a single file called Hosts.txt. This file was stored on the host computer of the Stanford Research Institute's Network Information Center (SRI-NIC) in Menlo Park, California. As the following illustration shows, other host computers on the ARPANET copied the Hosts.txt file from the SRI-NIC to their sites as needed.

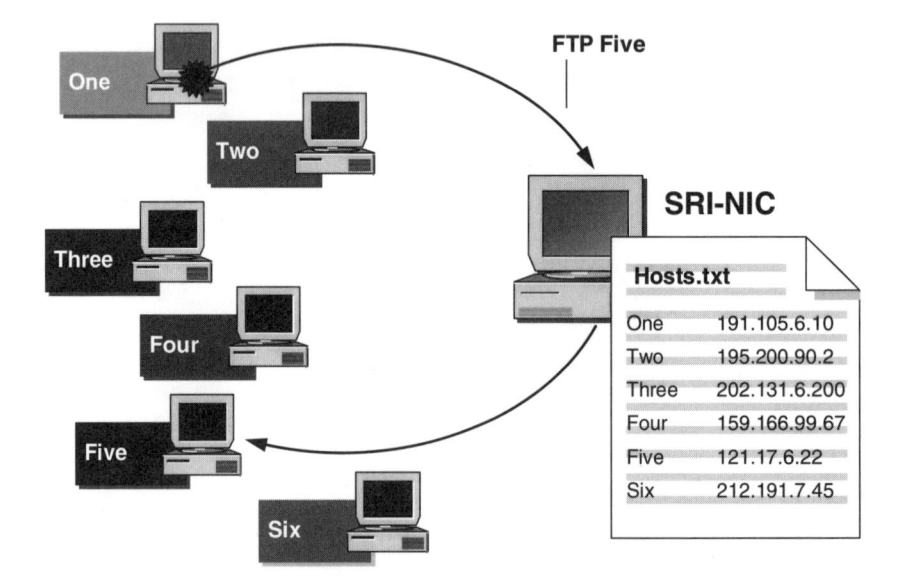

Initially, this scheme worked well because the Hosts.txt list needed to be updated only one or two times a week. However, after a few years, problems arose due to the ever-increasing size of the ARPANET. The problems included the following:

- The Hosts.txt file became too large.
- The file needed to be updated more than once a day.
- Because all network traffic had to be routed through SRI-NIC, maintaining Hosts.txt became a restriction point for the entire network.
- Network traffic on the SRI-NIC host became almost unmanageable.
- Hosts.txt uses a *flat name* structure (name space). This required every computer name to be unique across the whole network.

These and other problems led the governing body of the ARPANET to find a solution to the mechanism surrounding the Hosts.txt file. The decision led to the creation of the Domain Name System (DNS), which is a distributed database using a *hierarchical name* structure (hierarchical name space).

Note The Domain Name System is described in RFCs 1034 and 1035. For copies of these RFCs, see the *Course Materials* Web page on the course compact disc.

How DNS Works

The Domain Name System works using three main components: resolvers, name servers, and the domain name space.

With basic DNS communication, a DNS client, or *resolver*, sends queries to a name server. The server returns the requested information, or a pointer to another name server, or a failure message if the request can not be satisfied.

The Domain Name System is a hierarchical client/server-based distributed database management system. DNS maps to the application layer and uses UDP and TCP as the underlying protocols.

The purpose of the DNS database is to translate computer names into IP addresses as shown in the following illustration. In the DNS, the clients are called *resolvers* and the servers are called *name servers*.

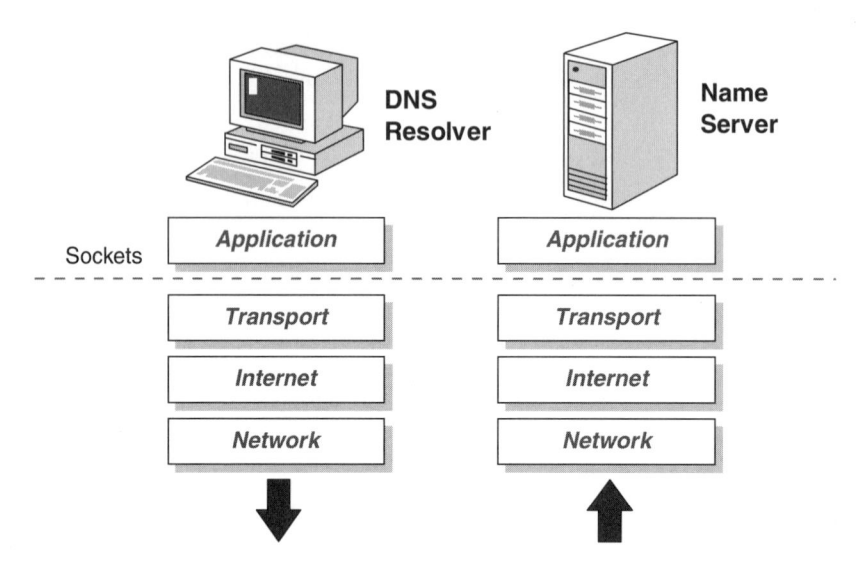

The Domain Name System is analogous to a telephone book. The user looks up the name of the person or organization that he wants to contact and cross-references the name to a telephone number. Similarly, a host computer contacts the name of a computer and a domain name server cross-references the name to an IP address.

Resolvers first send UDP queries to servers for increased performance and resort to TCP only if truncation of the returned data occurs.

Resolvers

The function of the resolvers is to pass name requests between applications and name servers. The name request contains a query. For example, the query might ask for the IP address of a Web site. The resolver is often built into the application or is running on the host computer as a library routine.

Name Servers

Name servers take name requests from resolvers and resolve computer (or domain) names to IP addresses. If the name server is not able to resolve the request, it may forward the request to a name server that can resolve it. The name servers are grouped into different levels that are called *domains*.

Domain Name Space

The domain name space is a hierarchical grouping of names in an inverted-tree-like structure as shown in the following illustration.

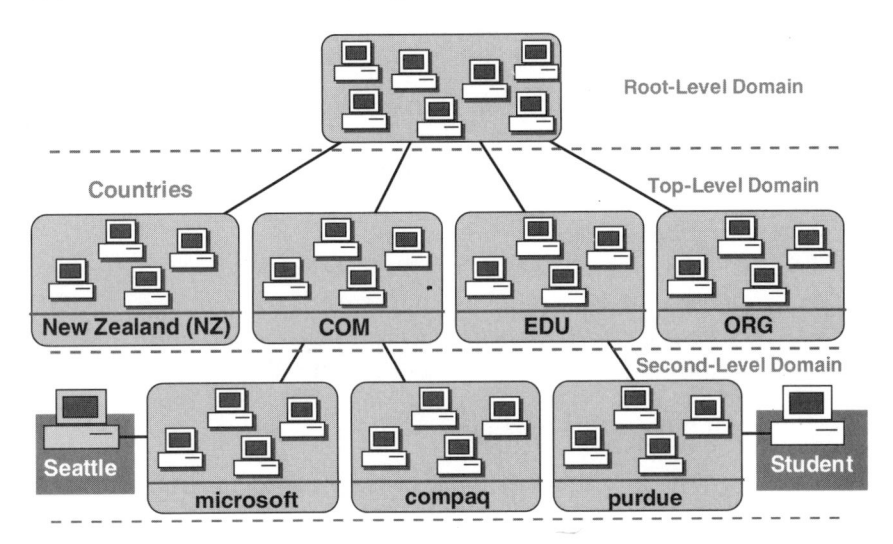

Root-Level Domains

Domains define different levels of authority in a hierarchical structure. The top of the hierarchy is called the *root* domain. The root domain uses a null label, but references to the root domain can be expressed by a period (.).

Top-Level Domains

The following are the present top-level domains:

- com   Commercial organizations
- edu   Educational institutions and universities
- org   Not-for-profit organizations
- net   Networks (the backbone of the Internet)
- gov   Non-military government organizations
- mil   Military government organizations
- num   Phone numbers
- arpa   Reverse DNS
- *xx*   Two-letter country code

Top-level domains can contain second-level domains and hosts.

> **Note** An Internet Society committee is planning several additional top-level domains such as .firm and .web.

Second-Level Domains

Second-level domains can contain both hosts and other domains called *subdomains*. For example, the Microsoft domain, microsoft.com, can contain computers such as ftp.microsoft.com and subdomains such as dev.microsoft.com. The subdomain dev.microsoft.com can contain hosts such as ntserver.dev.microsoft.com.

Host Names

Host names inside domains are added to the beginning of the domain name and are often referred to by their fully qualified domain name (FQDN). For example, a host named fileserver in the microsoft.com domain would have the fully qualified domain name of fileserver.microsoft.com.

Zones of Authority

A *zone of authority* is the portion of the domain name space for which a particular name server is responsible. The name server stores all address mappings for the domain name space within the zone and answers client queries for those names.

The name server's zone of authority encompasses at least one domain This domain is referred to as the zone's *root domain*. The zone of authority may also include subdomains of the zone's root domain. However, a zone does not necessarily contain all of the subdomains under the zone's root domain.

In the following illustration, microsoft.com is a domain, but the entire domain is not controlled by one zone file. Part of the domain is located in a separate zone file for dev.microsoft.com. Breaking up domains across multiple zone files may be needed for distributing management of the domain to different groups, or for data replication efficiency.

A single DNS server can be configured to manage one or multiple zone files. Each zone is anchored at a specific domain node called the zone's root domain.

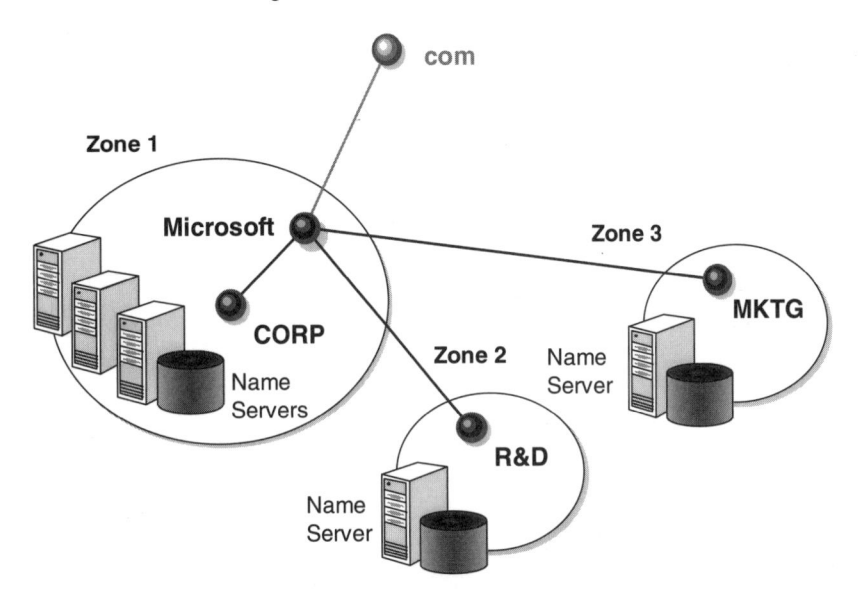

Name Server Roles

DNS name servers can be configured in different roles. DNS servers can store and maintain their database of names in several different ways. Each of the following roles describes a different way a DNS name server can be configured to store its zone data.

Primary Name Servers

The primary name server obtains zone data from local files. Changes to a zone, such as adding domains or hosts, are made at the primary name server level.

Secondary Name Servers

A secondary name server obtains the data for its zones from another network name server that has authority for that zone. Obtaining this zone information across the network is referred to as a *zone transfer*.

There are three reasons to have secondary name servers:

- *Redundancy.* You need at least one primary and one secondary name server for each zone. The computers should be as independent as possible.
- *Faster access for remote locations.* If you have a number of clients in remote locations, having secondary name servers (or other primary name servers for subdomains) prevents these clients from communicating across slow links for name resolution.
- *Reduction of load.* Secondary name servers reduce the load on the primary server.

Because information for each zone is stored in separate files, this primary or secondary designation is defined at a zone level. In other words, a particular name server may be a primary name server for certain zones and a secondary name server for other zones.

Master Name Servers

When you define a zone on a name server as a secondary zone, you must designate another name server from which to obtain the zone information. The source of zone information for a secondary name server in a DNS hierarchy is referred to as a *master name server.* A master name server can be either a primary or secondary name server for the requested zone. When a secondary name server starts up, it contacts its master name server and initiates a zone transfer with that server.

Caching-Only Servers

Although all DNS name servers cache queries that they have resolved, caching-only servers are DNS name servers that only perform queries, cache the answers, and return the results. In other words, they are not authoritative for any domains (no zone data is kept locally) and they only contain information that they have cached while resolving queries.

When trying to determine when to use such a server, keep in mind that when the server is initially started it has no cached information and must build this information up over time as it services requests. Much less traffic is sent across the slow link because the server is not doing a zone transfer. This is important if you are dealing with a slow link between sites.

Summary

Due to the increasing size of the ARPANET, the Domain Name System was created. In DNS, a client, called a resolver, sends queries to a name server. Name servers then take name requests and resolve computer names to IP addresses. The domain name space is a hierarchical grouping of root-level domains, top-level domains, second-level domains, and host names. Specific servers are responsible for a portion of the domain name space called zones of authority.

Lesson 2: Name Resolution

There are three types of queries that a client (resolver) can make to a DNS server: *recursive, iterative,* and *inverse.*

After this lesson, you will be able to:
- Explain how recursive, iterative, and inverse queries work.
- Explain how queries are placed in a cache for future requests.

Estimated lesson time: 10 minutes

Recursive Queries

In a recursive query, the queried name server is petitioned to respond with the requested data, or with an error stating that data of the requested type does not exist or that the domain name specified does not exist. The name server cannot refer the request to a different name server.

Iterative Queries

In an iterative query, the queried name server gives the best answer it currently has back to the requester. This answer may be the resolved name or a referral to another name server that may be able to answer the client's original request.

The following illustration shows an example of both recursive and iterative queries. In this example a client within a corporation is querying its DNS server for the IP address for "www.whitehouse.gov."

1. The resolver sends a recursive DNS query to its local DNS server asking for the IP address of "www.whitehouse.gov." The local name server is responsible for resolving the name and cannot refer the resolver to another name server.

2. The local name server checks its zones and finds no zones corresponding to the requested domain name. It then sends an iterative query for www.whitehouse.gov to a root name server.

3. The root name server has authority for the root domain and will reply with the IP address of a name server for the .gov top-level domain.

4. The local name server sends an iterative query for "www.whitehouse.gov" to the .gov name server.

5. The .gov name server replies with the IP address of the name server servicing the whitehouse.gov domain.

6. The local name server sends an iterative query for "www.whitehouse.gov" to the whitehouse.gov name server.

7. The whitehouse.gov name server replies with the IP address corresponding to www.whitehouse.gov.

8. The local name server sends the IP address of "www.whitehouse.gov" back to the original resolver.

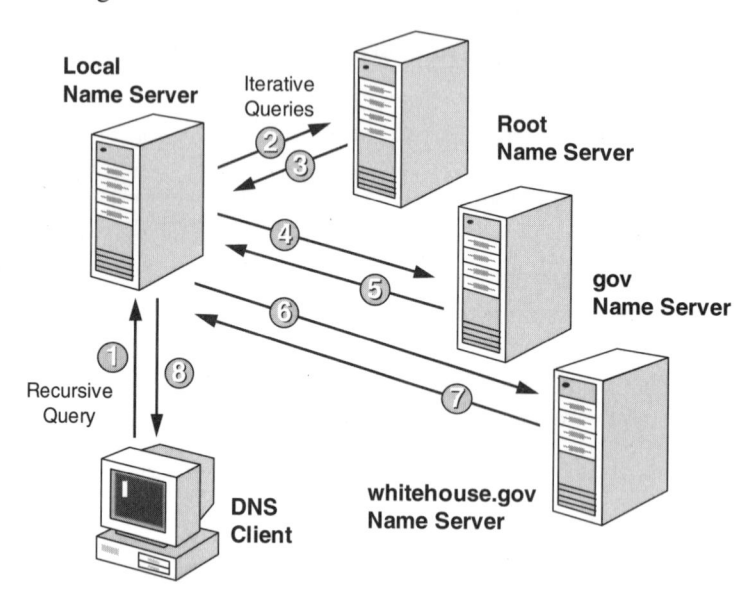

Inverse Queries

In an inverse query, the resolver sends a request to a name server to resolve the host name associated with a known IP address. There is no correlation between host names and IP addresses in the DNS name space. Therefore, only a thorough search of all domains guarantees a correct answer.

To prevent an exhaustive search of all domains for an inverse query, a special domain called "in-addr.arpa" was created. Nodes in the in-addr.arpa domain are named after the numbers in the dotted decimal representation of IP addresses. Because IP addresses get more specific from left to right and domain names get less specific from left to right, the order of IP address octets must be reversed when building the in-addr.arpa domain. With this arrangement, administration of lower limbs of the in-addr.arpa domain can be delegated to organizations as they are assigned their class A, B, or C IP addresses.

Once the in-addr.arpa domain is built, special resource records called *pointer records* (PTR) are added to associate the IP addresses and the corresponding host name. For example, to find a host name for the IP address 157.55.200.51, the resolver queries the DNS server for a pointer record for 51.200.55.157.in-addr.arpa. The pointer record found contains the host name and corresponding IP address 157.55.200.51. This information is sent back to the resolver. Part of the administration of a DNS name server is ensuring that pointer records are created for hosts.

Caching and TTL

When a name server is processing a recursive query, it may be required to send out several queries to find the answer. The name server caches all of the information that it receives during this process for a time that is specified in the returned data. This amount of time is referred to as the *Time to Live* (TTL). The name server administrator of the zone that contains the data decides on the TTL for the data. Smaller TTL values help ensure that data about the domain is more consistent across the network if this data changes often. However, this also increases the load on name servers.

Once data is cached by a DNS server, it must start decreasing the TTL from its original value so that it will know when to flush the data from its cache. If a query comes in that can be satisfied by this cached data, the TTL that is returned with the data is the current amount of time left before the data is flushed from the DNS server cache. Client resolvers also have data caches and honor the TTL value so that they know when to expire the data.

Summary

A client (resolver) can make recursive, iterative and inverse queries to a DNS server. As queries are resolved by the name server, the information is placed in a cache for future requests.

Lesson 3: Configuring the DNS Files

There are four configuration files used by a typical DNS name server. This lesson describes these files in detail.

After this lesson, you will be able to:
- Describe the contents of the DNS database files.

Estimated lesson time: 25 minutes

A typical DNS name server has a database file, reverse lookup file, cache file, and boot file. These configuration files perform a variety of functions on the server.

The Database File

The database file (Zone.dns) stores resource records for a domain. For example, if your zone is "microsoft.com," then this file will be called "microsoft.com.dns." Windows NT 4.0 supplies a sample database file called Place.dns as a template you can work with. This file should be edited and renamed before you use it on a production DNS server. It is generally a good idea to name this file the same as the zone it represents. This is the file that will be replicated between master name servers and secondary name servers.

There are several types of resource records defined in DNS. RFC 1034 defines SOA, A, NS, PTR, CNAME, MX, and HINFO record types. Microsoft has added the WINS and WINS-R Microsoft-specific record types.

Start of Authority Record

The first record in any database file must be the Start of Authority (SOA) record. The SOA defines the general parameters for the DNS zone. The following is an example of an SOA record:

```
@   IN SOA nameserver1.microsoft.com. glennwo.microsoft.com. (
    1        ; serial number
    10800    ; refresh [3 hours]
    3600     ; retry [1 hour]
    604800   ; expire [7 days]
    86400 )  ; time to live [1 day]
```

The following rules apply to all SOA records:

- The at symbol (@) in a database file indicates "this server."
- IN indicates an Internet record.
- Any host name not terminated with a period (.) will be appended with the root domain.
- The @ symbol is replaced by a period (.) in the e-mail address of the administrator.
- Parentheses (()) must enclose line breaks that span more than one line.

Name Server Record

The name server (NS) record lists the additional name servers. A database file may contain more than one name server record. The following is an example of a name server record:

```
@ IN NS nameserver2.microsoft.com
```

Host Record

A Host (A) record statically associates a host name to its IP address. Host records will comprise most of the database file and will list all hosts within the zone. The following are examples of host records:

```
rhino       IN A 157.55.200.143
localhost   IN A 127.0.0.1
```

CNAME Record

A Canonical Name (CNAME) record enables you to associate more than one host name with an IP address. This is sometimes referred to as *aliasing*. The following is an example of a CNAME record:

```
FileServer1 CNAME rhino
www         CNAME rhino
ftp         CNAME rhino
```

Note Database record types are defined in RFCs 1034, 1035, and 1183. For copies of these RFCs, see the *Course Materials* Web page on the course compact disc.

The Reverse Lookup File

The reverse lookup file (*z.y.x.w*.in-addr.arpa) allows a resolver to provide an IP address and request a matching host name. A reverse lookup file is named like a zone file according to the in-addr.arpa zone for which it is providing reverse lookups. For example, to provide reverse lookups for the IP network 157.57.28.0, a reverse lookup file is created with a file name of 57.157.in-addr.arpa. This file contains SOA and name server records similar to other DNS database zone files, as well as pointer records.

This DNS reverse-lookup capability is important because some applications provide the capabilities to implement security based on the connecting host names. For instance, if a client tries to link to a network file system (NFS) volume with this security arrangement, the NFS server would contact the DNS server and do a reverse name lookup on the client's IP address. If the host name returned by the DNS server is not in the access list for the NFS volume or if the host name was not found by DNS, then the NFS request would be denied.

The Pointer Record

Pointer (PTR) records provide an address-to-name mapping within a reverse lookup zone. IP numbers are written in backward order and "in-addr.arpa" is appended to the end to create this pointer record. As an example, looking up the name for "157.55.200.51" requires a pointer query for the name "51.200.55.157.in-addr.arpa." An example might read:

```
51.200.55.157.in-addr.arpa.  IN PTR mailserver1.microsoft.com.
```

The Cache File

The Cache.dns file contains the records of the root domain servers. The cache file is essentially the same on all name servers and must be present. When the name server receives a query outside its zone, it starts resolution with these root domain servers. An example entry might read:

```
.                     3600000  IN    NS    A.ROOT-SERVERS.NET.
A.ROOT-SERVERS.NET.   3600000  A           198.41.0.4
```

The cache file contains host information that is needed to resolve names outside of authoritative domains. It contains names and addresses of root name servers. The default file provided with the Windows NT 4.0 DNS Server has the records for all of the root servers on the Internet. For installations not connected to the Internet, the file should be replaced to contain the name server's authoritative domains for the root of the private network.

Note For a current Internet cache file see ftp://rs.internic.net/domain/named.cache.

The Boot File

The boot file is the start-up configuration file on the Berkeley Internet Name Daemon (BIND)-specific implementation of DNS. This file contains host information needed to resolve names outside of authoritative domains. The file is not defined in an RFC and is not needed in order to be RFC compliant. The Windows NT 4.0 DNS Server can be configured to use a boot file—if administration is to be done through changes to the text files—rather than by using DNS Manager.

The boot file controls the start-up behavior of the DNS server. Commands must start at the beginning of a line and no spaces may precede commands. Recognized commands are: **directory**, **cache**, **primary**, and **secondary**.

The syntax for the boot file is as shown in the following table.

Command	Description
Directory command	Specifies a directory where other files referred to in the boot file can be found.
Cache command	Specifies a file used to help the DNS service contact name servers for the root domain. This command and the file it refers to must be present. A cache file suitable for use on the Internet is provided with Windows NT 4.0.
Primary command	Specifies a domain for which this name server is authoritative and a database file that contains the resource records for that domain (that is, the zone file). Multiple primary command records can exist in the boot file.
Secondary command	Specifies a domain for which this name server is authoritative and a list of master server IP addresses from which to attempt to download the zone information, rather than reading it from a file. It also defines the name of the local file for caching this zone. Multiple secondary command records could exist in the boot file.

The following table shows examples of the commands in a boot file.

Syntax	Example
directory [*directory*]	`directory c:\winnts\system32\dns`
cache.[*file_name*]	`cache.cache`
primary [*domain*] [*file_name*]	`primary microsoft.com microsoft.dns` `primary dev.microsoft.com dev.dns`
secondary [*domain*] [*hostlist*] [*local_file_name*]	`secondary test.microsoft.com` `157.55.200.100 test.dns`

Summary

Four configuration files used by a typical DNS name server. The database file stores resource records for a domain. For the name server to resolve inverse queries, a reverse lookup file is required. The cache file contains the names and addresses for the name servers that maintain the root domain. The boot file is the start-up configuration file on a Berkeley Internet Name Daemon DNS server.

Lesson 4: Planning a DNS Implementation

The configuration of your DNS servers depends on factors such as the size of your organization, organization locations, and fault-tolerance requirements. This lesson gives you an idea of how to configure DNS for your site. It contains scenarios that measure your network planning knowledge prior to installing DNS.

After this lesson, you will be able to:
- Register a DNS server with the parent domain.
- Estimate the number of DNS name servers, domains, and zones needed for a network.

Estimated lesson time: 40 minutes

Rather than maintain a DNS server, an organization with a small network may find it simpler and more efficient to have DNS clients query a DNS name server maintained by an Internet service provider (ISP). Most ISPs will maintain domain information for a fee. Organizations that want to control their domain or cut the costs of using an ISP should maintain their own DNS servers.

If an organization, regardless of size, wants to connect to the Internet as a second-level domain, the InterNIC must be informed of the domain name of the organization and the IP addresses of at least two DNS servers that service the domain. An organization could set up DNS servers within itself independent of the Internet.

For reliability and redundancy, Microsoft recommends that at least two DNS servers be configured per domain—a primary and a secondary name server. The primary name server maintains the database of information, which is replicated to the secondary name server. This replication allows name queries to be serviced even if one of the name servers is unavailable. The replication scheduled can be configured depending on how often names change in the domain. Replication should be frequent enough so that changes are known to both servers. However, excessive replication can tie up the network and name servers unnecessarily.

Registering with the Parent Domain

Once you have your DNS server or servers configured and installed, you need to register with the DNS server that is above you in the hierarchical naming structure of DNS. The following illustration provides an example of registering your DNS server with the domain level above it. The parent system needs the name and addresses of your name servers and may require other information, such as the date that the domain becomes available and the names and mailing addresses of contact people.

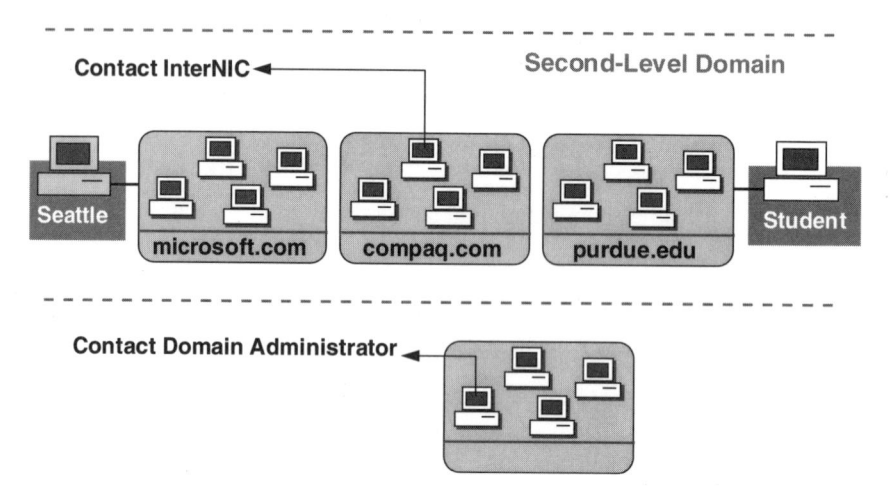

If you are registering with a parent below the second-level domain, check with the administrator of that system to determine the information you need to supply.

Note If you are registering at the subdomain or higher, visit InterNIC's online registration services at http://internic.net. If you have any questions, call their registration help line at (703) 742-477.

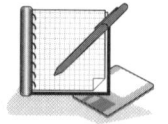

Practice

In this practice, you work through three DNS implementation scenarios. In each scenario, you estimate the number of DNS name servers, domains, and zones needed for a network.

Each scenario describes a company that is migrating to Windows NT Server and wants to implement directory services. You will answer some questions involved in drafting a DNS network design for each company using unique criteria.

The purpose of these practices is to measure your network planning knowledge prior to installing DNS. This will serve as a baseline to measure how much you have learned at the completion of this course and will help you start thinking about DNS network design.

Scenario 1: Designing DNS for a Small Network

The XYZ Company is in the process of replacing their older midrange computer with a computer running Windows NT Server 4.0.

Most employees access the midrange system through terminal devices. Some users have 486 computers and a few have Pentium computers; these computers are not networked. The company has already purchased the hardware for the migration.

The network will be used for basic file and print sharing and will also have one Windows NT server running SQL Server. The majority of users will need access to the computer running Microsoft SQL Server. Desktop applications will be installed on the local computers, but data files will be saved on the servers.

The XYZ Company would like to be connected to the Internet so they can receive e-mail.

Draft a network design using the following criteria

Environmental components	Detail
Users	100
Location(s)	Single office.
Administration	One full-time administrator.
Servers	3 computers, 2 Pentium 120s with 32 MB RAM, 3.2 GB hard disk. 1 Pentium 150 with 128 MB RAM dedicated to Exchange Server.
Clients	All Pentium and 486 computers, running Windows NT 4.0 or Windows 95.
Microsoft BackOffice applications	Exchange Server and DNS.
Server usage	Basic file and print.

The design will take into account:

- Number of users
- Number of administrative units
- Number of sites

1. How many DNS domains will you need to configure?

2. How many subdomains will you need to configure?

3. How many zones will you need to configure?

   _____

4. How many primary name servers will you need to configure?

   _____

5. How many secondary name servers will you need to configure?

   _____

6. How many DNS cache-only servers will you need to configure?

   _____

Scenario 2: Designing DNS for a Medium-Size Network

You are consulting for the WXY Company, which has 8,795 users. There are 8,000 users located in four primary sites, with the remaining employees located in 10 branch offices in major U.S. cities. The company has decided to upgrade their existing LANs to Windows NT servers. The organization has also decided to centralize all user accounts in a single location at the corporate headquarters.

The four primary sites are connected by T1 lines. The branch offices are connected to the nearest primary site by 56 Kbps lines.

Three of the four primary sites are independent business units and operate independently of the others. The fourth is corporate headquarters. Branch offices have between 25 and 250 users needing access to all four of the primary sites but seldom needing access to the other branch offices.

In addition to the 10 branch offices, you have discovered that the company has a temporary research location employing 10 people. The site has one server that connects to Boston using dial-on-demand routers. This site is expected to be shut down within six months. They are a stand-alone operation requiring connectivity for messaging only.

Primary sites will continue to maintain their own equipment and the equipment of the branch offices connected to them. Currently, bandwidth utilization is at 60 percent during peak times. Future network growth is expected to be minimal for the next 12 to 18 months.

Draft a network design using the following criteria

Environmental components	Detail
Users	8,795
Location(s)	Four primary sites, with 10 branch sites in major cities in the U.S. No plans for opening any international locations.
Administration	Full-time administrators at each of the four primary sites. Some of the smaller sites have part-time administrators.
Number of name servers	To be determined.
Number of cache servers	DNS cache servers are needed in each of the remote locations for the same zone.
Clients	386, 486, and Pentium computers running Windows NT and Windows 95.
Server applications	SQL Server, Exchange Server, and DNS.

Primary Site: Portland
Users: 1500
SQL Server
Messaging

Corporate HQ
Primary Site: Boston
Users: 2500
SQL Server, SNA Server
Messaging

Primary Site: Chicago
Users: 2000
SNA Server
Messaging

Primary Site: Atlanta
Users: 2000
Messaging

Branch Office:
San Francisco
Users: 25
Messaging

Branch Office:
Dallas
Users: 250
Messaging

Other branch offices include: Los Angeles, 40 users; Salt Lake City, 25 users; Montreal, 30 users; New Orleans, 25 users; Kansas City, 25 users; Washington, D.C., 100 users; Denver, 200 users; Miami, 75 users.

The design must take into account:

- Number of users
- Number of administrative units
- Number of sites
- Speed and quality of links connecting sites
- Available bandwidth on links
- Expected changes to network
- Line of business applications

1. How many DNS domains will you need to configure?

   _____

2. How many subdomains will you need to configure?

   _____

3. How many zones will you need to configure?

   _____

4. How many primary name servers will you need to configure?

   _____

5. How many secondary name servers will you need to configure?

   _____

6. How many DNS cache-only servers will you need to configure?

   _____

7. Use the following mileage chart to design a zone/branch office configuration based on the geographical proximity between each primary site and branch office. Branch offices should be in the same zone as the nearest primary site.

Portland, OR	Boston	Chicago	Atlanta

Mileage chart	Atlanta	Boston	Chicago	Portland, OR
Dallas	807	1,817	934	2,110
Denver	1,400	1,987	1,014	1,300
Kansas City	809	1,454	497	1,800
Los Angeles	2,195	3,050	2,093	1,143
Miami	665	1,540	1,358	3,300
Montreal	1,232	322	846	2,695
New Orleans	494	1,534	927	2,508
Salt Lake	1,902	2,403	1,429	800
San Francisco	2,525	3162	2,187	700
Washington, D.C.	632	435	685	2,700

Scenario 3: Designing DNS for a Large Network

The ABC Company has 60,000 users located around the world. The corporate headquarters is in Geneva, Switzerland. North and South America headquarters are located in New York City. The Australia and Asia headquarters are located in Singapore. Each of the regional headquarters will maintain total control of users within their areas.

Users require access to resources in the other regional headquarters. The three regional headquarters sites are connected by T1 lines.

Each of the three regional headquarters have lines of business applications that need to be available to all sites within their areas, as well as the other regional headquarters. The Malaysian and Australian subsidiaries have major manufacturing sites to which all regional subsidiaries need access.

These line of business applications are all running on Windows NT servers. These computers will be configured as servers within the domains.

The links between Singapore, Australia, and Malaysia are typically operating at 90 percent utilization. The Asia and Australia region has 10 subsidiaries comprising Australia, China, Indonesia, Japan, Korea, Malaysia, New Zealand, Singapore, Taiwan, and Thailand.

Due to import restrictions with some of the subsidiaries, it has been decided to give control of the equipment to each subsidiary, and to have a resource domain in each subsidiary. Lately most of the computers the subsidiaries have purchased are running Windows NT Workstation. The company has authorized redundant hardware where you can justify it.

In order to keep this scenario reasonable, the questions and answers deal only with the Asia-Australia region.

Draft a network design using the following criteria

Environmental components	Detail
Users in Asia-Australia domain	25,000 evenly distributed across all of the subsidiaries.
Location(s)	Regional headquarters in Singapore, 10 subsidiaries in Australia, China, Indonesia Japan, Korea, Malaysia, New Zealand, Singapore, Taiwan, Thailand.
Administration	Full-time administrators at the regional headquarters and each of the subsidiaries.
Number of domains	To be determined.
Clients	386, 486 and Pentium computers running Windows 95 or Windows NT Workstation.
Server applications	SQL Server, SNA Server, Systems Management Server, Messaging, DNS.
Number of cache servers	To be determined.

The design for the Asia-Australia region must take into account:

- Number of users
- Number of administrative units
- Number of sites
- Speed and quality of links connecting sites
- Available bandwidth on links
- Expected changes to network
- Line of business applications

1. How many DNS domains will you need to configure?

   _____

2. How many subdomains will you need to configure?

   _____

3. How many zones will you need to configure?

_____

4. How many primary name servers will you need to configure?

_____

5. How many secondary name servers will you need to configure?

_____

6. How many DNS cache-only servers will you need to be configure?

_____

Summary

Depending on the size of your organization and configuration, you may want to configure DNS for your site. However, an organization with a small network may want to have DNS clients query a DNS name server maintained by an ISP. If your organization wants to connect to the Internet, you must inform InterNIC.

Review

The following questions are intended to reinforce key information presented in this chapter. If you are unable to answer a question, review the appropriate lesson and then try the question again.

1. Name the three components of the Domain Name System.

2. Describe the difference between primary, secondary, and master name servers.

3. List three reasons to have a secondary name server.

4. Describe the difference between a domain and a zone.

5. Describe the difference between recursive and iterative queries.

6. List the files required for a Windows NT DNS implementation.

7. Describe the purpose of the boot file.

For More Information

- Read *DNS and BIND* by Paul Albitz and Cricket Liu, published by O'Reilly & Associates.
- Read the white paper titled *DNS and Microsoft Windows NT 4.0*.

CHAPTER 13

Implementing DNS

Lesson 1　The Microsoft DNS Server . . . 282

Lesson 2　Administering the DNS Server . . . 286

Lesson 3　Integrating DNS and WINS . . . 296

Review . . . 301

About This Chapter

This chapter addresses installing and configuring DNS, integrating DNS and WINS, and using NSLOOKUP, the DNS diagnostic tool. In the lessons, you install and configure a Domain Name System, configure DNS files, and use DNS servers to resolve host names into IP addresses.

Before You Begin

To complete the lessons in this chapter, you must have:

- Installed Microsoft Windows NT Server 4.0 with TCP/IP.
- An understanding of the concepts presented in Chapter 12, "Domain Name System (DNS)."

Lesson 1: The Microsoft DNS Server

Windows NT 4.0 includes an interoperable, standards-based DNS service. This lesson introduces the Microsoft DNS server implementation.

After this lesson, you will be able to:
- Install the Microsoft DNS Server service.
- Troubleshoot DNS with NSLOOKUP.

Estimated lesson time: 25 minutes

Microsoft DNS is an RFC-compliant DNS server; as a result, it creates and uses standard DNS zone files and supports all standard resource record types. It is interoperable with other DNS servers and includes the DNS diagnostic utility, NSLOOKUP. Microsoft DNS is tightly integrated with WINS and is administered through the graphical administration utility called DNS Manager.

Installing Microsoft DNS Server

Before installing the Microsoft Windows NT DNS Server service, it is important that the Windows NT 4.0 server's TCP/IP protocol be configured correctly. The DNS Server service obtains the default settings for the host name and domain name through the **Microsoft TCP/IP properties** dialog box. The DNS Server service will create default SOA, A, and NS records based on the specified domain name and host name. If the host name and domain name are not specified, only the SOA record is created.

Practice

Note If you have not already installed the Windows NT 4.0 Service Pack 2, you should do so now. To install the service pack, follow the procedure outlined in the Setup Instructions section of About This Book. This procedure shows you how to install the service pack from the course compact disc.

In this procedure, you install the Microsoft DNS Server service. You configure DNS in a later lesson.

Note Complete this procedure from the computer you designate as the DNS server.

▶ **To configure the DNS Server service search order**

1. Log on as Administrator.
2. At a command prompt, type **ipconfig** and then press ENTER.
3. Record the IP address for your computer.

---

4. Switch to the **Microsoft TCP/IP Properties** dialog box, and then click the **DNS** tab.
5. In the **Domain** box, type **Domain1** (or your domain name)
6. Under **DNS Service Search Order**, click **Add**.
7. In the **DNS Server** box, type in the IP address for your computer, and then click **Add**.
8. Click **OK**.

   The **Network** dialog box appears.
9. Click **OK** to close the **Network** dialog box.

▶ **To install the DNS Server service**

1. In Control Panel, double-click the Network icon, and then click **Services**.
2. Click **Add**.

   The **Select Network Service** dialog box appears.
3. In the **Network Service** list, click **Microsoft DNS Server**, and then click **OK**.

   Windows NT Setup displays a dialog box asking for the full path to the Windows NT distribution files.
4. Type the path to the Windows NT distribution files, and then click **Continue**.

   All necessary files, including the sample files, are copied to your hard disk.
5. In the **Network** dialog box, click **Close**.
6. When prompted, click **Yes** to restart your computer.

Troubleshooting DNS with NSLOOKUP

The NSLOOKUP utility, the primary diagnostic tool for DNS, enables users to interact with a DNS server. NSLOOKUP can be used to display resource record on DNS servers, including UNIX DNS implementations. NSLOOKUP is installed with the TCP/IP protocol.

NSLOOKUP Modes

NSLOOKUP has two modes: interactive and non-interactive. If a single piece of data is needed, use non-interactive or command-line mode. If more than one piece of data is needed, interactive mode can be used.

NSLOOKUP Syntax

nslookup [*–option ...*] [*computer-to-find* | – [*server*]]

Syntax	Description
–option ...	Specifies one or more NSLOOKUP commands. For a list of commands, use the **Help** option inside NSLOOKUP.
computer-to-find	If *computer-to-find* is an IP address and the query type is A or PTR, the name of the computer is returned. If *computer-to-find* is a name and does not have a trailing period, the default DNS domain name is appended to the name. To look up a computer outside of the current DNS domain, append a period to the name. If a hyphen (–) is typed instead of *computer-to-find*, the command prompt changes to NSLOOKUP interactive mode.
server	Use this server as the DNS name server. If the server is omitted, the currently configured default DNS server is used.

▶ To use NSLOOKUP in command mode

1. At a command prompt, modify the properties so that it has a screen buffer size of 50.

   Use the **Layout** property page to do this.

2. If the command prompt is not full-screen, press ALT+ENTER.

3. Type the following command:

   nslookup *hostx*

   where *hostx* is a host in your domain.

   NSLOOKUP will return the IP address of the computer *hostx* because the information is stored in the DNS database.

4. Exit the command prompt.

NSLOOKUP Command Help

You can find NSLOOKUP commands using Windows NT Help. To find the commands, start Windows NT Help and search for nslookup. You can then click NSLOOKUP commands to see a list of all commands.

▶ To use NSLOOKUP in interactive mode

1. At a command prompt, type **nslookup** and then press ENTER.

   A > prompt appears.

2. Type **set all** at the > prompt.

   This command lists all of the current values of the NSLOOKUP options.

3. Use Windows NT Help and the **set** commands to change the **time-out** to **1 second** and the **number of retries** to **7**. Use **set all** to verify that the defaults were changed.

    Set ti=1

    Set ret=7

4. Switch to DNS Manager and note the number of hosts in your domain.
5. Switch back to the command prompt.
6. Type the names of the other computers, one at a time, at the **>** prompt. Press ENTER after each name.
7. Switch to DNS Manager, and then press F5.

    All of the computer names that could be resolved are added to the zone database.

8. Exit the command prompt.
9. Close Windows NT Help and DNS Manager.

Summary

Microsoft DNS is interoperable with other DNS servers. Before installing the DNS Server service, you should make sure that the Windows NT 4.0 server's TCP/IP protocol is configured correctly.

The NSLOOKUP utility is the primary diagnostic tool for DNS. It lets you display resource records on DNS servers.

Lesson 2: Administering the DNS Server

There are two ways to administrate the Microsoft DNS server: use the DNS Manager or manually edit the DNS configuration files. This lesson reviews the tools used to administer a DNS server.

After this lesson, you will be able to:
- Administer a DNS server.
- Create a zone file and populate it with resource records.

Estimated lesson time: 60 minutes

Configuring DNS Server Properties

You can use DNS Manager to configure the Microsoft Windows NT DNS server. Because the DNS server has no initial information about a user's network, the DNS server installs as a caching-only name server for the Internet. This means that the DNS server contains only information on the Internet root servers. For most DNS server configurations, additional information must be supplied to obtain the preferred operation, as shown in the following illustration and table.

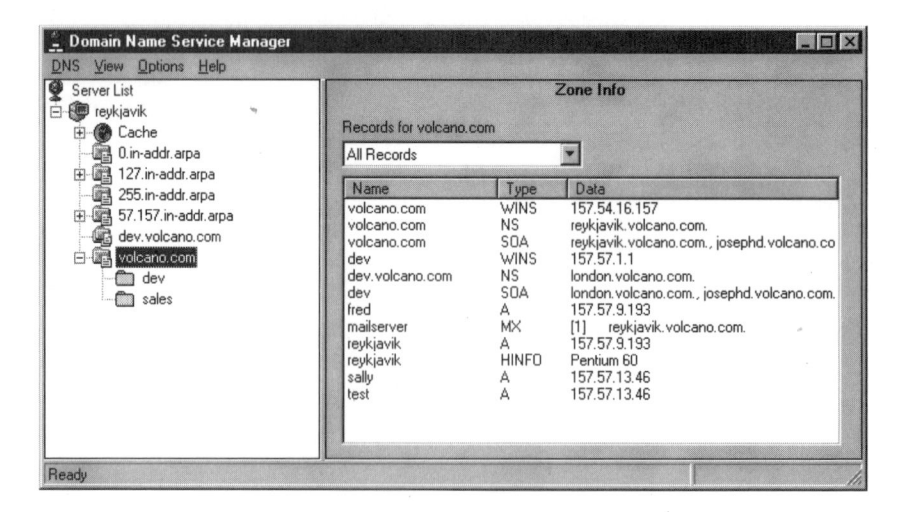

Property	Description
Interfaces	Specifies which interfaces DNS operates over on a multihomed computer. By default, all interfaces are used.
Forwarders	Configures your server to use another name server as a forwarder. The name server can also be configured as a slave to the forwarder.
Boot method	Displays what boot method the name server is using—either from the registry or from the data files.

Practice

In these procedures, you configure DNS, configure DNS files, and use the DNS service to resolve host names into IP addresses.

Note You need two computers for these procedures. One computer functions as a DNS server and the other computer functions as a DNS client.

In this procedure, you view the default installation of the Windows NT DNS Server service.

▶ **To view the default DNS server installation**

Note Complete this procedure from the DNS server computer.

1. Log on as Administrator.
2. Click the **Start** button, point to **Programs**, point to **Administrative Tools**, and then click **DNS Manager**.
3. On the **DNS** menu, click **New Server**.

    The **Add DNS Server** dialog box appears.
4. In the **Add DNS Server** box, type **Server1** and click **OK**.
5. Double-click **Cache**.

    This displays all of the information your DNS server currently has in the cache. All root servers for the Internet are contained in the cache.
6. On the **Options** menu, click **Preferences**.

    The **Preferences** dialog box appears.
7. Click **Show Automatically Created Zones**, and then click **OK**.
8. Click your computer name and then press F5 to refresh the DNS Manager window.

    The three reverse lookup zones appear: **0.in-addr.arpa**, **127.in-addr.arpa**, and **255.in-addr.arpa**.
9. Double-click each of the reverse lookup zones.

    What type of records does each of them contain?

10. Double-click 127.in-addr.arpa.

    A **0** folder appears.

11. Double-click the **0** folder.

    A second **0** folder appears.

12. Double-click the second **0** folder.

    The PTR record for local host appears. This entry is used when the loopback IP address of 127.0.0.1 is looked up.

    At this point, the DNS Server service installed on your computer is configured as a caching-only name server.

Manually Configuring DNS

The DNS server can be configured manually by editing files in the default installation path *system_root*\System32\Dns. Administration is identical to administration of traditional DNS. These files can be modified using a text editor. The DNS service must then be stopped and restarted.

Adding DNS Domains and Zones

The first step in configuring the DNS server is to determine the hierarchy for your DNS domains and zones. Once the domain and zone information has been determined, this information must be entered into the DNS configuration using the DNS Manager.

Adding Primary or Secondary Zones

You add primary and secondary zones through DNS Manager, as shown in the following illustration. After entering your zone information, DNS Manager will construct a default zone file name. If the zone file already exists in the DNS directory, DNS Manager will automatically import these records.

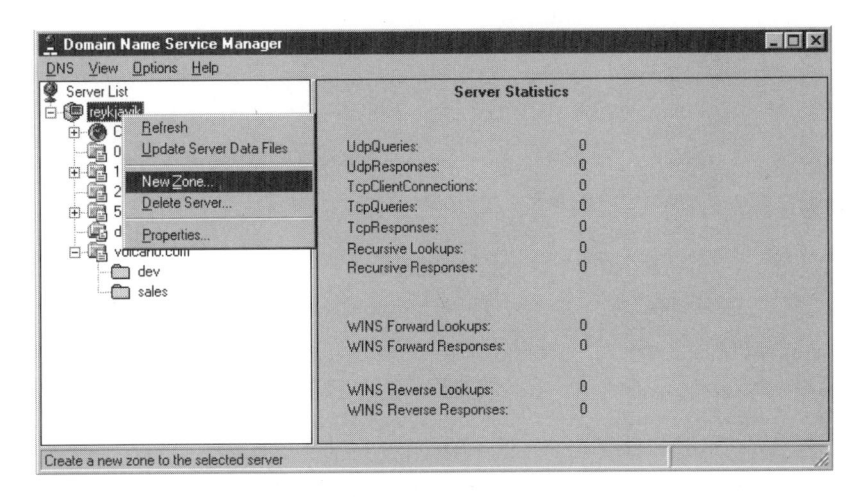

[Screenshot of Domain Name Service Manager window showing Server List with reykjavik server, a context menu with options Refresh, Update Server Data Files, New Zone..., Delete Server..., Properties..., and Server Statistics panel on the right showing counts of UdpQueries, UdpResponses, TcpClientConnections, TcpQueries, TcpResponses, Recursive Lookups, Recursive Responses, WINS Forward Lookups, WINS Forward Responses, WINS Reverse Lookups, WINS Reverse Responses, all showing 0. Status bar reads "Create a new zone to the selected server".]

A primary zone stores name-to-address mappings locally. When you configure a primary zone, you need no information other than the zone name.

Secondary zones obtain name-to-address mappings from a master server by zone transfer. When you configure a secondary zone, you must supply the names for the zone and master name server.

Note The Microsoft Windows NT convention is to create a file called *zonename*.dns, which differs from other DNS servers that create files called Db.zone.

Adding Subdomains

Once all zones have been added to the server, subdomains under the zones can be added. To add a subdomain, on the shortcut menu of the preferred zone, click **New Domain**. Enter the name of the new subdomain, and then click **OK**.

If multiple levels of subdomains are needed, create each successive subdomain through the **New Domain** shortcut menu option for the immediate parent.

There is a key written to the DNS registry entry for each zone for which the DNS will be authoritative. The keys are located under:

HKEY_LOCAL_MACHINE\SYSTEM\ CurrentControlSet\Services\DNS\Zones

Each zone has its own key and the key contains the name of the database file, which indicates whether the DNS server is a primary or secondary name server. For example, for the zone "dev.volcano.com," there is the following registry entry:

HKEY_LOCAL_MACHINE\SYSTEM\\CurrentControlSet\Services\DNS\Zones\dev.volcano.com

Configuring Zone Properties

Property	Description
General	Configures the zone file in which the resource records are stored, and specifies whether this is a primary or secondary name server.
SOA record	Configures zone transfer information and the name server administrator mailbox.
Notify	Specifies the secondary servers to be alerted when the primary server database changes. Also, additional security can be applied to the name server by specifying that only the listed secondary servers can contact this server.
WINS lookup	Enables the name server to query WINS to resolve names. A list of WINS servers can be configured in this dialog. The WINS servers can be set on a per-name-server basis by selecting the **Settings Only Affect Local Server** check box. If this is not selected, secondary servers will also use the configured WINS servers.

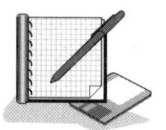

Practice

In this procedure, you configure the DNS server by adding primary zone.

▶ **To add a zone to a server**

Note Complete this procedure from the DNS server computer.

1. Right-click your computer name, and then click **New Zone**.

   The **Creating New Zone for Server1** dialog box appears.

2. Click **Primary**, and then click **Next**.
3. In the **Zone Name** box, type **zone1.com** (where zone1.com is your *zone name*).
4. Press the TAB key.

   zone1.com.dns is automatically entered in the **Zone File** box.

5. Click **Next**, and then click **Finish**.

   The **Server List** now has a zone name, and the **Zone Info** entries have been added.

6. Click each of the resource records.

   What type of records does each of them contain?

   _____

7. Click your zone name.
8. On the **DNS** menu, click **Properties**.

   The **Zone Properties** dialog box appears.

9. Click the **Notify** tab.

   Note If you were configuring a secondary DNS server for your domain, you would indicate it in the **Notify List** box and then click **Add**.

10. Click **OK**.

Adding Resource Records

Once the zones and subdomains are configured, resource records can be added. To add a resource record, select a zone or subdomain and then click **DNS–New Host** or select **New Record** from the menu bar.

New Host

To create a new host, type the host name and IP address, and then select **Create Associated PTR Record** in the associated reverse lookup domain, as shown in the following illustration.

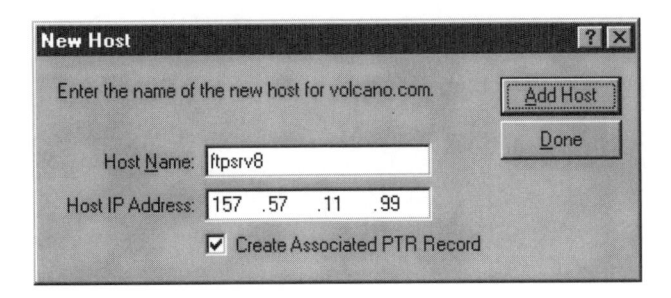

New Record

To create a new record, select which resource record type to create. A dialog box displays various fields specific to record type, as shown in the following illustration. The TTL field displays the default TTL from the SOA record for the zone file. A TTL value will be stored in the record only if it is changed from the default. Enter the information and then click **OK** to add the resource record.

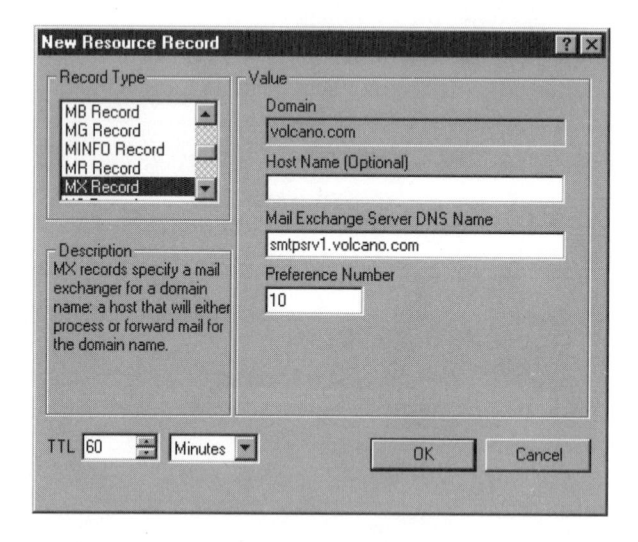

Configuring Reverse Lookup

To find a host name, given the host's IP address, a reverse lookup zone must be created for each network on which hosts in the DNS database reside. Adding a reverse lookup zone is procedurally identical to adding any other type of zone, except for the zone name.

For example, if a host has an address of 198.231.25.89, it would be represented in the in-addr.arpa domain as 89.25.231.198.in-addr.arpa. Furthermore, to enable this host to appear to a client who has its IP address, a zone would need to be added to the DNS for 25.231.198.in-addr.arpa, as shown in the following example.

All pointer records for the network 198.231.25.0 would be added to this reverse lookup zone.

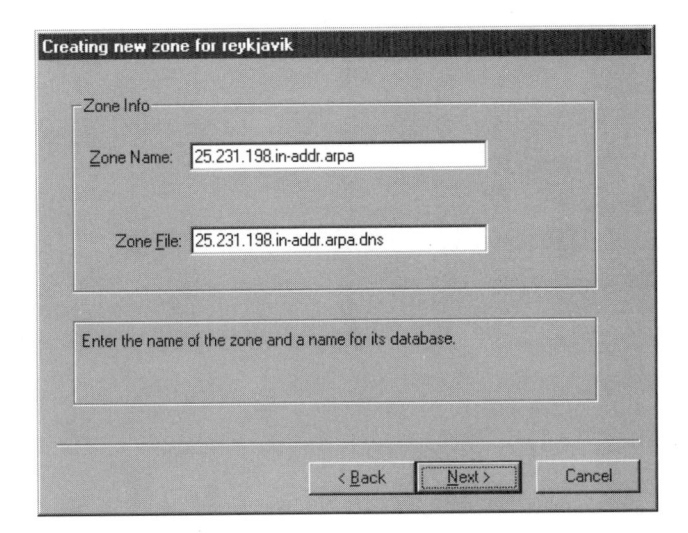

![Creating new zone for reykjavik dialog. Zone Info: Zone Name: 25.231.198.in-addr.arpa; Zone File: 25.231.198.in-addr.arpa.dns. Enter the name of the zone and a name for its database.]

Practice

In this procedure, you create a reverse lookup zone that allows the DNS service to return a name when queried with an IP address from a client.

▶ **To configure a reverse lookup zone for the primary DNS server**

Note Complete this procedure from the DNS server computer.

1. Determine the reverse lookup zone name for your primary DNS server by using one of these three methods:
   - For class A addresses, use your first octet and append to it **.in-addr.arpa** (for example: A class A IP address of 29.122.15.88 would have a reverse lookup zone name of **29.in-addr.arpa**).
   - For class B addresses, use your first two octets in reverse order and append to them **.in-addr.arpa** (for example: A class B IP address of 129.122.15.88 would have a reverse lookup zone name of **122.129.in-addr.arpa**).
   - For class C addresses, use your first three octets in reverse order and append to them **.in-addr.arpa** (for example: A class C IP address of 229.122.15.88 would have a reverse lookup zone name of **15.122.129.in-addr.arpa**).

   What is your reverse lookup zone name?

2. Open the DNS Manager, and then click on your computer name.
3. On the **DNS** menu, click **New Zone**.

   The **Creating New Zone** dialog box appears.
4. Click **Primary**, and then click **Next**.
5. Type your reverse lookup zone name in the **Zone Name** box.
6. Tab to the **Zone File** box.

   The file name is automatically generated.
7. Click **Next**, and then click **Finish**.

> **Note** If you were to configure zone properties for a secondary DNS server, you would enter its IP address using the **Notify** tab in the **Zone Properties** dialog box.

In this procedure, you add a host name to your domain.

▶ **To add your other computer as a host in your domain**

> **Note** Complete this procedure from the DNS server computer.

1. Right-click your zone name.
2. On the menu that appears, click **New Host**.

   The **New Host** dialog box appears.
3. In the **Host Name** box, type your second computer name.
4. In the **Host IP Address** box, type the IP address of your second computer.
5. Click **Create Associated PTR Record**, and then click **Add Host**.
6. Click **Done**.
7. Click the **107.131.in-addr.arpa** zone, and then press F5.

   A plus sign (+) precedes **107.131.in-addr.arpa**.
8. Double-click **107.131.in-addr.arpa**.

   A folder appears beneath **107.131.in-addr.arpa**.
9. Double-click the folder.

   A **PTR** record appears in the **Zone Info** box.
10. Double-click the **PTR** record, examine the contents of the record, and then click **OK**.

    This is the reverse lookup record that is automatically generated when the **Create Associated PTR Record** option is selected.

11. Repeat steps 1 through 10 to add a host record for your computer and refresh the listings.
12. Verify that there are two A records (one record for your first computer, one record for your second computer) in your zone.
13. Verify that there are two PTR records (one record for your first computer, one record for your second computer) in the reverse lookup (107.131.in-addr.arpa) zone.

Summary

The first step in configuring Microsoft Windows NT DNS server is to determine the hierarchy for your DNS domains and zones. Once the zones and subdomains are configured, resource records can be added. To find a host name given the host's IP address, a reverse lookup zone must be created for each network on which hosts in the DNS database reside.

Lesson 3: Integrating DNS and WINS

WINS requires less management than DNS because it dynamically registers name-to-address mappings. This lesson explains why WINS is used and how to use it with DNS.

After this lesson, you will be able to:
- Explain how to integrate DNS with WINS.
- Configure the WINS client.
- Configure WINS host name resolution and reverse lookup resolution.
- Configure an alias for a host name.

Estimated lesson time: 45 minutes

DNS is a static database of name-to-address mappings that must be manually updated. DNS implements a hierarchical model, which allows the administration and replication of the database to be broken into zones.

WINS, on the other hand, allows machines to dynamically register their name-to-address mappings and therefore requires less administration. WINS is a flat name space and requires each WINS server to maintain a complete database of entries through replication.

The WINS Record

A new WINS data record is defined as part of the database file and is unique to the Microsoft DNS server. It is entered into the zone's root domain by placing the record in the database file. If a name-to-address mapping is not found in the database file, DNS queries the WINS database. For example:

1. A client contacts its DNS server and requests an IP address of another host.

    The DNS server searches its database and does not find an address record for the host.

2. Because the database file contains a WINS record, the DNS server converts the host portion of the name to a NetBIOS name and sends a request for this NetBIOS name to the WINS server.

3. If the WINS server is able to resolve the name, it returns the IP address to the DNS server.
4. The DNS server returns the IP address to the requesting client.

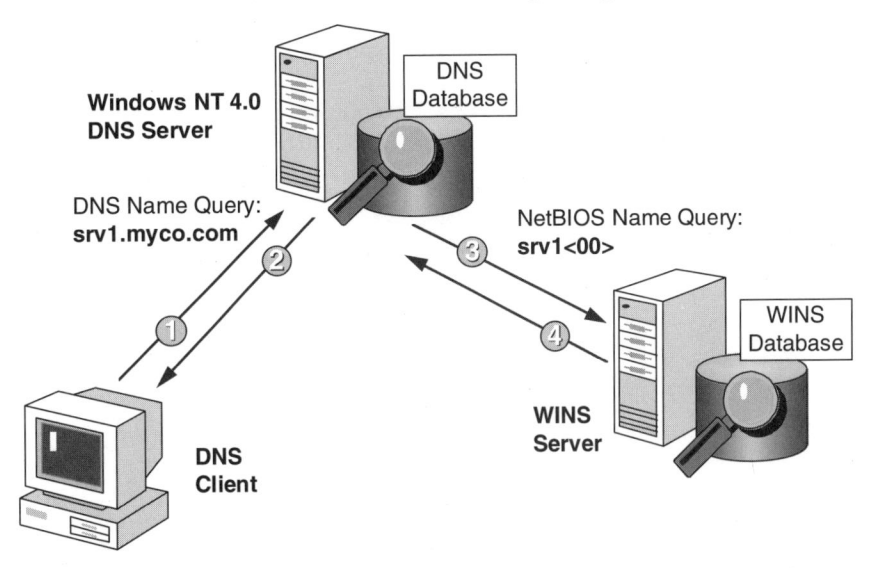

Note If a zone is configured for WINS resolution, all DNS servers that are authoritative for that zone must be configured for WINS resolution.

Enabling WINS Lookup

By enabling WINS Lookup, DNS can be configured to submit queries to a WINS server when a name-to-address mapping cannot be resolved by the DNS server.

You enable WINS Lookup with the DNS Manager by selecting the zone, opening its **Shortcut** menu, and then selecting **Properties**. Click the **WINS Lookup** tab, select the **Use WINS Resolution** check box, and then enter the IP addresses of the preferred WINS servers, as shown in the following illustration.

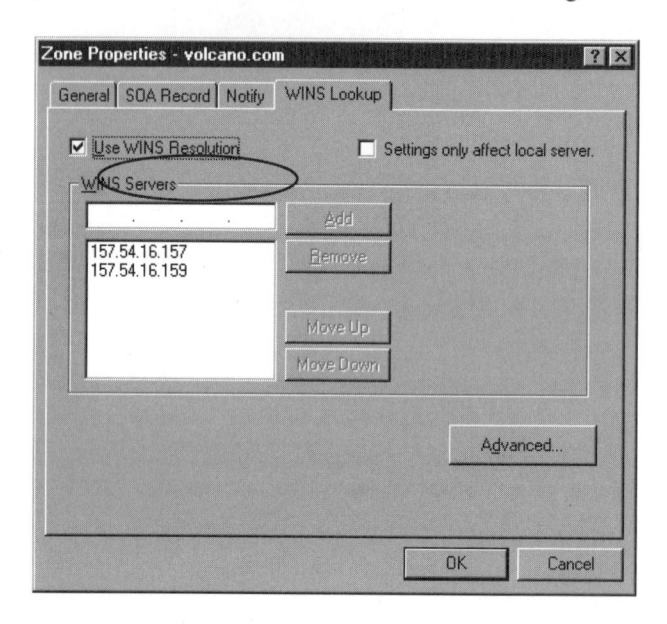

WINS Reverse Lookup

The presence of a WINS-R record at the zone root instructs the DNS server to use a NetBIOS node adapter status lookup. This lookup is for any reverse lookup requests for IP addresses in the zone root which are not statically defined with PTR records.

With DNS Manager, enabling WINS reverse lookup is accomplished by obtaining properties on the appropriate in-addr.arpa zone and selecting the **WINS Reverse Lookup** property page. Enter the **Use WINS Reverse Lookup** check box and enter the **DNS Host Domain** to be appended to the NetBIOS name before returning the response to the resolver.

WINS Time to Live

The WINS TTL can be configured from the **Advanced** dialog box found in the **WINS Lookup** property page of the properties of a zone. When a name-to-address mapping is resolved by the WINS server, the address is cached for the **Cache Timeout Value**. By default, this value is set to 10 minutes. If this address is forwarded to another DNS server, the TTL is also forwarded.

Practice

In these procedures, you configure a Windows NT server to use WINS for host name resolution. In the first procedure, you configure the WINS client so that it uses the primary WINS server.

▶ **To configure the WINS client**

Note Complete this procedure from the DNS client computer.

1. Switch to the **Microsoft TCP/IP Properties** dialog box.
2. Click the **WINS Address** tab.
3. In the **Primary WINS Server** box, type the IP address for your DNS server.
4. Click **OK**, and then click **Close**.

   The **Network Settings Change** message box appears, prompting you to restart the computer.

5. Click **Yes**.

   The computer restarts.

6. Log on as Administrator.

In this procedure, you configure DNS so that it uses WINS to resolve any host names it cannot resolve.

▶ **To configure WINS resolution**

Note Complete this procedure from the DNS server computer.

1. Start DNS Manager.
2. Right-click your zone name, and then click **Properties**.

   The **Zone Properties** dialog box appears.

3. Click the **WINS Lookup** tab.
4. Click **Use WINS Resolution**.
5. In the **WINS Servers** box, type the IP address of your DNS server.
6. Click **Add**, and then click **OK**.

In this procedure, you configure DNS so that it uses WINS to resolve any IP addresses it cannot resolve.

▶ **To configure WINS reverse lookup**

Note Complete this procedure from the DNS server computer.

1. Switch to DNS Manager.
2. Right-click your reverse lookup zone: **107.131.in-addr.arpa**, and then click **Properties**.

   The **Zone Properties** dialog box appears.
3. Click the **WINS Reverse Lookup** tab.
4. Click **Use WINS Reverse Lookup**.
5. Type your zone name in the **DNS Host Domain** box, and then click **OK**.

▶ **To test WINS reverse lookup**

Note Complete this procedure from the DNS server computer.

1. At a command prompt, type:

   nslookup 131.107.2.211

   where *131.107.2.211* is your client IP address.

   The NSLOOKUP utility returns your computer's host name because your host has a record in your reverse lookup database.
2. Type:

   nslookup 131.107.2.200

   where *131.107.2.200* is your server IP address.

   The NSLOOKUP utility returns the host name at 131.107.2.200 because WINS reverse lookup has been configured. DNS automatically adds an address record into the DNS database when it resolves the IP address.

Summary

By enabling WINS lookup, DNS can be configured to submit queries to a WINS server when a name-to-address mapping cannot be resolved. You enable WINS lookup through the **Zone Properties** dialog box in DNS Manager.

Review

The following questions are intended to reinforce key information presented in this chapter. If you are unable to answer a question, review the appropriate lesson and then try the question again.

1. What is the purpose of entering a host name and domain name in the DNS configuration dialog box of the TCP/IP protocol *before* installing the Microsoft DNS Server service?

2. What is the function of the NSLOOKUP utility?

3. Describe the WINS lookup process.

4. Describe a situation where WINS lookup is useful.

For More Information

- Read *DNS and BIND* by Paul Albitz and Cricket Liu, published by O'Reilly and Associates.
- Read the white paper titled *DNS and Microsoft Windows NT 4.0*.

CHAPTER 14

Connectivity in Heterogeneous Environments

Lesson 1 Connectivity in Heterogeneous Environments . . . 304

Lesson 2 Remote Execution Utilities . . . 307

Lesson 3 Data Transfer Utilities . . . 309

Lesson 4 Printing Utilities . . . 316

Review . . . 323

About This Chapter

In this chapter, you review connectivity with NetBIOS-based hosts and foreign hosts. You also review the different connectivity tools provided with Microsoft Windows NT. The lessons in this chapter provide information on installing and configuring Microsoft FTP server software and TCP/IP printing support.

Before You Begin

To complete the lessons in this chapter, you must have:

- Installed Windows NT Server 4.0 with TCP/IP.
- A shared printer to perform the TCP/IP print procedure (optional).

Lesson 1: Connectivity in Heterogeneous Environments

A primary benefit of using TCP/IP is that it provides the ability to connect to and interoperate with different types of hosts, such as a UNIX host. This lesson explains the different requirements for connecting to foreign hosts and connecting to and interoperating with RFC-compliant NetBIOS-based hosts.

After this lesson, you will be able to:
- Explain the connectivity requirements for Microsoft networking.

Estimated lesson time: 10 minutes

Microsoft TCP/IP allows connectivity to many foreign computer systems because it is a common network protocol used by all of them. To communicate with any foreign computer such as OS/2, UNIX, Solaris, or VMS, you need a common network protocol such as TCP/IP. You also need applications (usually client/server) on both ends that communicate using this common network protocol.

Connecting to a Remote Host with Microsoft Networking

In order to use standard Microsoft networking commands and functions (for example, **net use**, Windows NT Explorer, or File Manager) to connect to a remote host, the following requirements must be met:

- *Transport Driver Connectivity.* Both computers must be able to communicate with each other using the same transport driver, such as TCP/IP, NBF, or IPX.
- *SMB Connectivity.* The Workstation service communicates with an *SMB server* process at the remote host. SMB is the file-sharing protocol used on all MS®-Net products.

Note If the NetBIOS scope parameter is configured on the remote host, the scope ID must match the scope ID on your Microsoft clients or they will not be able to communicate with NetBIOS.

Many vendors have implemented NetBIOS over TCP/IP and SMB servers on their operating systems. Examples of these vendors are Digital Equipment Corporation's PATHWORKS on VMS, IBM LAN Server on OS/2, and LAN Manager for UNIX.

Connecting to Windows NT Server from a Remote Host

Windows NT Server provides file services to personal computers through the server message block (SMB) protocol. File service for UNIX clients is available through the network file system (NFS) protocol, the FTP service, or by installing an SMB-based client.

Third-party NFS servers are available for Windows NT. These servers enable Windows NT Server to provide file service for personal computers, UNIX workstations, or other systems acting as NFS clients. They provide support for the Windows NT File System (NTFS), file allocation table (FAT), CD-ROM file system (CDFS), and high-performance file system (HPFS).

Microsoft TCP/IP Utilities

The following Microsoft TCP/IP utilities provide several options for connecting to foreign TCP/IP-based hosts using Windows Sockets.

TCP/IP utility	Function
REXEC	Runs a process on a remote host running REXEC server software. This provides password protection security.
RSH (Remote Shell)	Enables execution of commands on a remote RSH server without logging on. This does not provide password protection.
Telnet	Provides terminal emulation (DEC VT 100, DEC VT 52, and TTY). This provides user and password authentication.
RCP (Remote Copy)	Copies files between a computer running Windows NT and a server running the RCP daemon without logging on, thus providing no user authentication security.
FTP	Provides bidirectional file transfers between a computer running Windows NT and any TCP/IP host running FTP server software. This gives user and password authentication.
TFTP	A subset of FTP that uses the User Datagram Protocol (UDP) instead of TCP; provides bidirectional file transfers between a computer running Windows NT and a TCP/IP host running TFTP server software, and provides no user authentication.
Web Browser	Web browsers access documents stored on a WWW server, and can provide user and password authentication.
LPD	Services LPR requests and submits print jobs to a printer device, and provides user and password authentication.
LPR	Provides the ability to send a print job to a printer connected to a server running the LPD service, and provides user and password authentication.
LPQ	Provides the ability to view the print queue on an LPD server, and provides user and password authentication.

Summary

TCP/IP gives Windows NT the ability to connect to and interoperate with many foreign TCP/IP-based hosts. Microsoft TCP/IP utilities provide several options for connecting to foreign hosts.

Lesson 2: Remote Execution Utilities

Several TCP/IP utilities provide the ability to connect to remote hosts. This lesson explains the requirements for usage of each remote execution utility.

After this lesson, you will be able to:
- Understand how to connect to a remote host with Microsoft networking.

Estimated lesson time: 10 minutes

REXEC

Remote Execution (REXEC) provides remote execution facilities with authentication based on user names and passwords. When the **rexec** command is carried out, it prompts the user for a password on the remote host. After connecting the user to the remote host, it verifies the password. If the password is valid, it then executes the specified command. REXEC normally terminates when the remote command ends. The syntax of REXEC is:

rexec *tcpiphost command*

RSH

Remote Shell (RSH) is used to run commands on a remote server running the RSH daemon (in most cases, a UNIX host). RSH is useful for compiling programs. A user does not have to log on to the UNIX host to run a command. The only security is that the user's name must be configured in the .rhosts file on the UNIX host. RSH does not prompt for passwords. The following is an example of RSH syntax:

rsh *unixhost command*

Telnet

Telnet is a remote terminal emulation protocol that provides Digital Equipment Corporation VT 100, Digital Equipment Corporation VT 52, or TTY emulation. Telnet uses the connection-oriented services of TCP. Any programs or commands you run are processed by the Telnet server and not by the local host.

In order to run Telnet, the host system must be configured with a Telnet server program, also called a daemon. Microsoft does not provide this program. You must also have a user account for the computer running Windows NT.

The client computer must be configured with Telnet client software (provided with Windows NT), and a user account on the Telnet server.

▶ **To make a terminal connection with Telnet**
1. At a command prompt, start Telnet.exe.

    The Telnet window opens.
2. On the **Connect** menu, choose **Remote System**.

    The **Connect** dialog box appears.
3. In the **Host Name** box, type the host name or IP address of the Telnet server, and then click **OK**.
4. When prompted, log on to the Telnet server using the user account and password located on the Telnet server.

    Once you are connected, you can use host commands as if you were at a terminal connected to that host. Any programs or commands you run are processed by the Telnet server and not by the local host.

Note Telnet is defined in RFC 854. For a copy of this RFC, see the *Course Materials* Web page on the course compact disc.

Summary

TCP/IP has several remote execution utilities. Remote Execution starts a process on the remote host and requires a user account. Remote Shell runs commands on a remote host and requires a user name in the .rhosts file on a UNIX host. Telnet runs commands interactively in a terminal emulation application.

Lesson 3: Data Transfer Utilities

TCP/IP provides several data transfer utilities, including the widely-used FTP. This lesson explains the requirements and usage of each data transfer utility.

After this lesson, you will be able to:
- Understand how to use data transfer utilities to connect to and access resources on a TCP/IP-based host.
- Install Microsoft® Internet Information Server (IIS) FTP services.
- Use FTP client software to transfer files.

Estimated lesson time: 25 minutes

RCP

Like RSH, Remote Copy Protocol (RCP) does not require the user to log on to a server running the RCP daemon (in most cases, a UNIX host). However, the user must have a name configured in the .rhosts file on the UNIX host and have remote command execution privileges. RCP is used to copy files between a local and remote UNIX host or two remote hosts. RCP does not prompt for passwords. An example of the syntax for RCP:

rcp *host1.user1:source host2.user2:destination*

FTP

The FTP utility, which uses TCP as its transport, is one of the most commonly used utilities. It provides binary and text file transfers with an FTP server. The FTP server could be a UNIX host or a computer running Windows NT configured with the FTP server daemon. FTP is frequently used to transfer files from the worldwide Internet.

A user account is required on the FTP server, unless the FTP server is configured to all anonymous connections. (A detailed discussion of the Windows NT FTP server follows.) There are many servers on the Internet that allow anonymous connections. The syntax of FTP is:

ftp *[options] host command*

The destination host must be configured with FTP server daemon (provided with Windows NT), and a user account for the Windows NT user.

The client computer must be configured with FTP client software (provided with Windows NT), and a user account on the FTP server.

FTP Commands

An FTP command can be entered on one line or through a command interpreter. If the command is entered on one line, FTP immediately attempts to establish a connection with an FTP server. If it is not entered on one line, FTP enters its command interpreter, from which a user can type an FTP command.

The most common FTP commands are shown in the following table.

Command	Function
binary	Changes the file transfer type to binary
get	Copies a remote file to a local host
put	Copies a local file to a remote host
!	Temporarily returns the user to the command prompt
quit or **bye**	Exits FTP

TFTP

Trivial File Transfer Protocol (TFTP) is used to transfer files to and from a remote or local host. TFTP uses the connectionless services of UDP. The TFTP does not support any user authentication. Files must be world-readable and writable (UNIX permissions) on the remote system.

Microsoft provides only TFTP client software. You must use a third-party TFTP server service (daemon) in order to use TFTP to connect to a computer running Windows NT. An example of the TFTP syntax would be:

tftp -i host get file-one file-two

Note FTP is defined in RFC 959. TFTP is defined in RFC 1350. For copies of these RFCs, see the *Course Materials* Web page on the course compact disc.

Practice

In these procedures, you install the Windows NT FTP server on your workstation and then with a second computer, access the FTP server with FTP. You then use **netstat** to check the status of FTP ports.

Note It is recommended that you have two computers to complete these procedures. However, in many cases you can start an FTP session with your own server by typing **ftp 127.0.0.1**

Use this first procedure to determine if you have installed Microsoft Internet Information Server (IIS) with the FTP service.

▶ **To examine the Windows NT Server environment**

1. Log on as Administrator.
2. Click the **Start** button, point to **Settings**, and then click **Control Panel**.
3. In Control Panel, double-click the Services icon.

    The **Services** dialog box appears.
4. Determine if the **FTP Publishing Service** is listed.

    If the FTP Publishing Service is not listed, you should install Internet Information Server with the FTP service using the following procedure.
5. Close the **Services** dialog box.
6. Close Control Panel.

In this procedure, you install Internet Information Server with the FTP service. Use this procedure if you have not previously installed IIS with the FTP service.

▶ **To install Internet Information Server**

1. Log on as Administrator.
2. On the desktop, double-click the Install Internet Information Server icon.

    The **Internet Information Server Installation** dialog box appears.
3. In the **Installed from** box, type the path to your Windows NT installation files.

    The **Microsoft Internet Information Server 2.0 Setup** dialog box appears.
4. Read the information in the **Microsoft Internet Information Server 2.0 Setup** dialog box, and then click **OK**.

    The following installation options appear:
    - Internet Service Manager
    - World Wide Web Service
    - WWW Service Samples
    - Internet Service Manager (HTML)
    - Gopher Service
    - FTP Service
    - ODBC Drivers and Administration
5. Make sure that at least the **Internet Service Manager** and **FTP Service** options are selected, and then click **OK**.

6. When prompted to create the **C:\Winnt\System32\Inetsrv** directory, click **Yes**.

   The **Publishing Directories** dialog box appears, listing the default directory:

   FTP Publishing Directory   C:\Inetpub\Ftproot

7. Click **OK** to accept the default directory.

8. When prompted to create the default directory, click **Yes**.

   Setup installs the **Internet Information Server FTP Service** software.

9. When Setup is complete, click **OK**.

In this procedure you use FTP client software to copy a file from the FTP server to the FTP client.

▶ **To transfer files using FTP**

1. At a command prompt, type:

   Copy C:\Winnt*.bmp C:\Inetpub\Ftproot

2. Create a temporary directory on your computer named **C:\Ftptemp**.

3. Change to the C:\Ftptemp directory.

4. Start an FTP session with your second computer and ping the computer using the following command:

   ftp server2

5. Log on as Anonymous.

6. When prompted for a password, press ENTER.

   An **ftp>** prompt will appear.

7. Type the following command at the **ftp>** prompt:

   dir

   A listing of all of the files available at the FTP site appears.

8. Use the **get** command to retrieve a single file. Type:

   get lanma256.bmp

9. To view the transferred file on your computer, type the following:

   !dir

   and then press ENTER.

10. Use the **mget** command to retrieve the rest of the files. Type:

    mget *

11. To exit the FTP session, type:

    Bye

    and then press ENTER.

In this procedure you start **netstat** inside an FTP session to check the status of the TCP ports.

▶ **To start an FTP session**

1. At a command prompt, start an FTP session with the second computer by typing the following command:

   ftp server2

2. Log on as Anonymous.

3. When prompted for a password, press ENTER.

   An **ftp>** prompt appears.

4. Type the following command at the **ftp>** prompt:

   !netstat

   This displays the current TCP network connections.

5. Type the following command at the **ftp>** prompt:

   !netstat -n

   This displays the current TCP network connections and the current TCP port connections.

   What TCP port does FTP use on the server side?

   _____

6. To exit the FTP session, type:

   Bye

   and then press ENTER.

Web Browsers

The World Wide Web (WWW) has become one of the most popular ways to transfer data on the Internet. Web browsers access documents stored on a World Wide Web server. The WWW follows a client/server model and uses the Hypertext Transfer Protocol (HTTP) between the client and the server as shown in the following illustration.

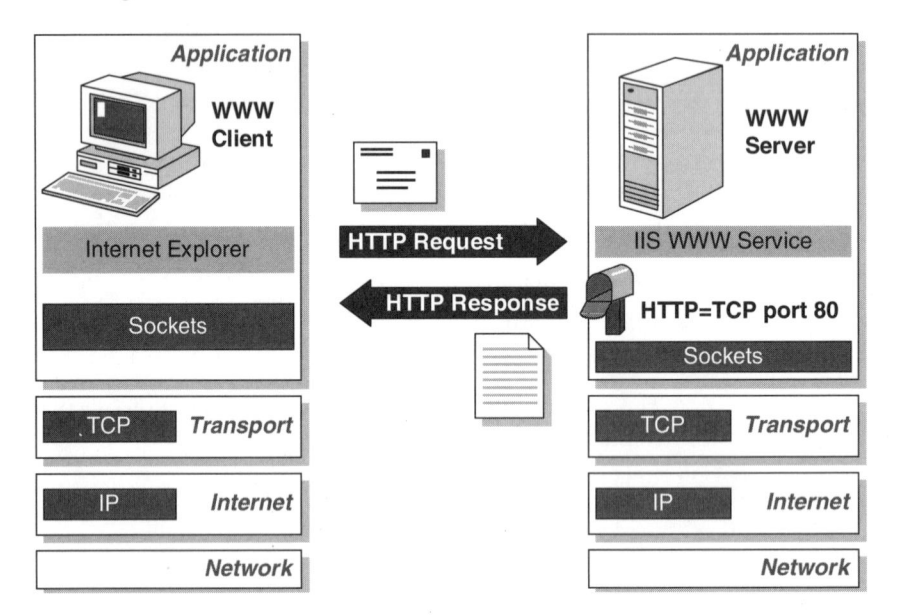

The client must be configured with a Web browser. There are several World Wide Web clients available, some of which can be freely downloaded from the Internet. The server must be configured with the World Wide Web service.

The server responds with the status of the transaction, successful or failed, and the data for the request. After the data is sent, the connection is closed and no state is retained by the server. Each object in an HTTP document requires a separate connection.

Web browsers provide two distinct data transfer benefits. First, Web browsers support many data types. A Web browser can automatically download and display text files and graphics, play video and sound clips, and launch helper applications for known file types.

The second benefit of Web browsers is that they support several data transfer protocols, including FTP, Gopher, HTTP, and Network News Transfer Protocol (NNTP).

Summary

RCP copies files to and from a remote host with no authentication. FTP copies files to and from a remote host reliably over TCP but has user-level authentication. Web browsers such as Microsoft Internet Explorer use HTTP to transfer pages of data from a Web server. TFTP copies files to and from a remote host quickly over UDP. It does not use user-level authentication.

Lesson 4: Printing Utilities

Once you have installed and configured TCP/IP printer support, you can connect to the printer using Print Manager or the LPR command, depending on whether the printer is attached to a computer running Windows NT or a UNIX host. This lesson provides an overview of TCP/IP printing support.

After this lesson, you will be able to:
- Install and configure TCP/IP network printing support.
- Connect and print to a TCP/IP-based printer.
- Use LPQ to view TCP/IP print queues, and use LPR to print a file.

Estimated lesson time: 45 minutes

LPR and LPQ are client applications that communicate with LPD on the server, as shown in the following illustration. These three applications provide the following functions:

- The LPD runs as a service on the computer running Windows NT (LPDSVC) and enables any computer with TCP/IP and LPR to send print jobs to the computer running Windows NT.
- LPR is the client printing application, and enables the Windows NT client to print to any host running LPD.
- LPQ can be used to query the printer once print jobs have been submitted.

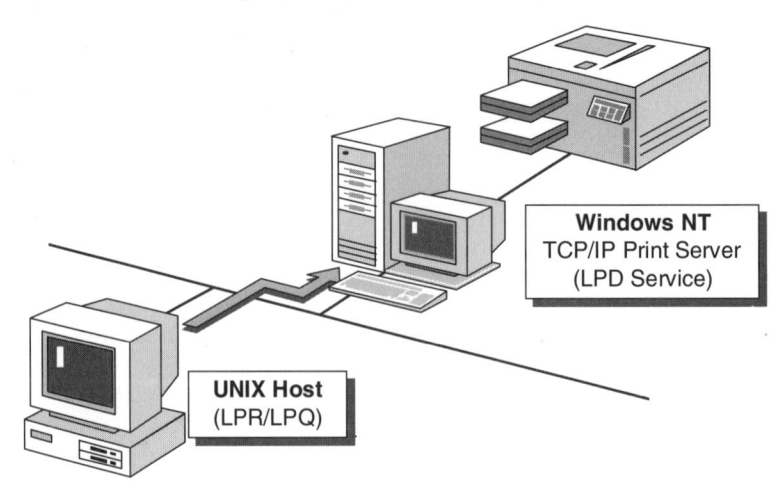

Windows NT
TCP/IP Print Server
(LPD Service)

UNIX Host
(LPR/LPQ)

Note Microsoft TCP/IP printing support is RFC 1179-compliant. For a copy of this RFC, see the *Course Materials* Web page on the course compact disc.

Using the TCP/IP Print Server (LPD)

For Windows NT to accept print jobs from LPR clients, the TCP/IP Printer Server service (LPDSVC) needs to be installed and running. The TCP/IP Printer Server service can be started from the Services program in Control Panel, a command prompt, or Server Manager.

Tip It is recommended that the TCP/IP Print Server service be configured to start automatically, either through the Services program in Control Panel or Server Manager.

TCP/IP Print Server Registry Entries

The configuration parameters for the TCP/IP Print Server are located under the following registry key:

HKEY_LOCAL_MACHINE\SYSTEM\CurrentControlSet\Services\LPDSVC\Parameters

Using LPR and LPQ

Submitting Print Jobs (LPR)

The method you use to print to a TCP/IP-based printer varies according to the environment you are printing from.

- For Windows-based applications, use Print Manager.
- For command-line situations, or when printing from a UNIX host, use the LPR (Lpr.exe) command-line utility.

The LPR utility submits print files to the LPD service running on a Windows NT server or a UNIX host with the following syntax:

lpr –S*ip_address* **–P***printer_name filename*

To send the print job, LPR makes a TCP connection to the LPD service using ports 512 to 1023.

Checking the Print Status (LPQ)

Once a file has been sent to a printer using LPR, you can use the LPQ (Lpq.exe) utility to check the status of the print queue. Use the following syntax:

lpq -**S**ip_address -**P**printer_name -**l**

Note The -**S** and -**P** in both commands are case sensitive, and must be typed in uppercase. The -**l** (the letter l) can be typed in uppercase or lowercase.

Configuring Print Manager with the LPR Print Monitor

To configure Windows NT Print Manager to use an LPD print server, you must add the Microsoft TCP/IP Printing support and configure a printer to use the LPR print monitor. An example of a configuration is shown in the following illustration.

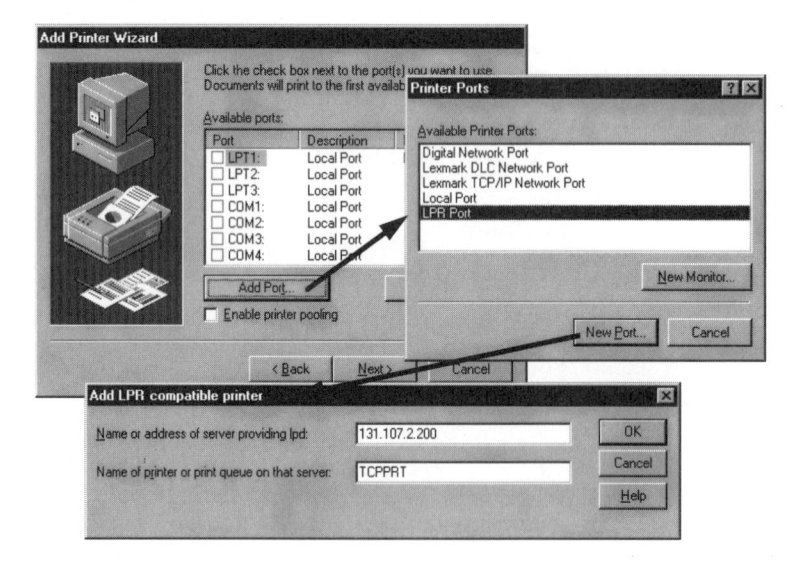

Note Microsoft TCP/IP Printing must be installed before **LPR Port** will appear in the **Printer Port** dialog box of Print Manager.

Using Windows NT as a Print Gateway

A computer running Windows NT with TCP/IP Print services (LPD) installed can perform two gateway functions as shown in the following illustration. First, the computer running Windows NT can receive print jobs from Microsoft clients and then forward them automatically to a TCP/IP-based print server running LPD. The client does not require LPR or TCP/IP.

In addition, the computer running Windows NT can receive print jobs from any LPR client and then forward them to any printer visible to the computer running Windows NT.

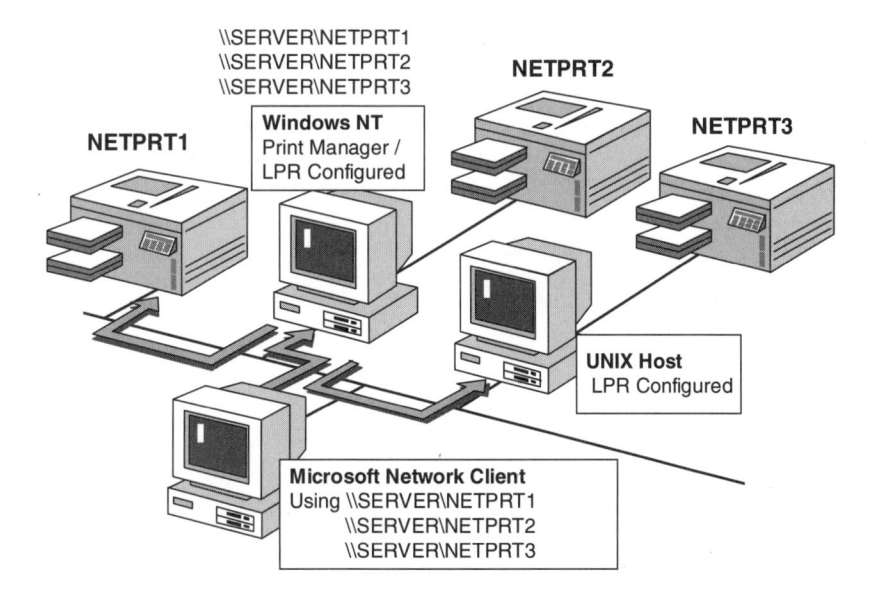

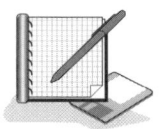

Practice

In these procedures, you install the TCP/IP Print service, create a TCP/IP printer, and then use the LPR utility to print to a printer. You must have a shared printer available to you in order to complete the procedures. You must also know the printer name, printer server IP address, and printer type.

In this procedure, you install the Microsoft TCP/IP Printing service, and then use Print Manager to install a TCP/IP-based printer.

▶ **To install the TCP/IP-based printer**

1. In Control Panel, double-click the Network icon.

    The **Network** dialog box appears.

2. Click the **Services** tab.

    The **Services** property sheet appears.

3. Click **Add**.

    The **Select Network Service** dialog box appears.

4. Click **Microsoft TCP/IP Printing**, and then click **OK**.

    The **Windows NT Setup** box appears, prompting you for the full path of the Windows NT distribution files.

5. Type the path to the Windows NT distribution files, and then click **Continue**.

    The appropriate files are copied to your workstation, and then the **Network** dialog box appears.

6. Click **Close**.

    A **Network Settings Change** message box appears, indicating that the computer needs to be restarted.

7. Click **Yes**.

8. Log on as Administrator.

9. In Control Panel, double-click the Services icon.

    The **Services** dialog box appears.

10. Select **TCP/IP Print Server**, and then click **Start**.

11. Click **Close**.

▶ **To create a TCP/IP-based printer**

1. In Control Panel, double-click the Printers icon.

    The Printers window appears.

2. Double-click **Add Printer**.

    The **Add Printer Wizard** dialog box appears.

3. Click **My Computer**, and then click **Next**.

4. Click **Add Port**.

    The **Printer Ports** dialog box appears.

5. Click **LPR Port**, and then click **New Port**.

    The **Add LPR compatible printer** dialog box appears.

6. In the **Name or address of server providing lpd** box, type your own IP address.

7. In the **Name of printer or print queue on that server** box, type the printer name, and then click **OK**.

8. Click **Close**.

9. Click **Next**.

Chapter 14   Connectivity in Heterogeneous Environments

10. Complete the **Add Printer Wizard** dialog box using the information in the following table.

When prompted for	Use this information
Printer manufacturer and model	*Printer type*
Printer name	*Printer Name*
Shared / Not shared	Shared
Share name	*Printer Name*
Test page	No

    An **Insert Disk** message box prompts you for a floppy disk.

11. Click **OK**.

    A **Windows NT Setup** dialog box appears, prompting you for the location of the Windows NT Server distribution files.

12. Type the path to the Windows NT Server distribution files, and then click **OK**.

    A *printername* icon appears with the TCP/IP printer created.

In this procedure, you connect and print to the TCP/IP-based printer. You use Notepad to send files to be printed. You then use the LPQ command-line utility to view the status of the remote print queue.

▶ **To use Print Manager to connect to a TCP/IP-based printer**

1. In the Printers window, double-click **Add Printer**.

    The **Add Printer Wizard** dialog box appears.

2. Click **Network printer server**, and then click **Next**.

    The **Connect to Printer** dialog box appears.

3. In the **Printer** box, type the path and name of the printer, and then click **OK**.

    The Add Printer wizard prompts you to make this printer the default printer.

4. Click **Yes**, and then click **Next**.

5. Click **Finish**.

    An icon representing the shared computer is created in the Printers window.

6. Double-click the new printer icon.

    The *printername* on *share* window appears.

7. Start Notepad, and then create and print a short document on the shared printer.

8. Switch back to the *printername* on *share* window.

   A **Messenger Service** dialog box appears, notifying you that your print job has finished printing.

9. Click **OK**.

10. Close the *printername* on *share* window.

▶ **To use LPR and LPQ to access a TCP/IP-based printer**

1. At a command prompt, view the remote print queue. Type:

   lpq -S*xxx.xxx.xxx.xxx* **-P***printername* **-l**

   where *xxx.xxx.xxx.xxx* is the printer server IP address, and *printername* is the printer name.

   Important The **-S** and **-P** switches must be in uppercase.

   The **Windows NT LPD Server print queue status** dialog box appears.

2. Send a new job to the print queue. Type:

   lpr -S*xxx.xxx.xxx.xxx* **-P***printername* **c:\config.sys**

   The job is sent to the print queue on *printershare*.

3. View the remote print queue to view new jobs spooled.

   Notice that the new job lists LPR client document as the job name.

4. Exit the command prompt.

Summary

LPD responds to LPR/LPQ requests and sends print job data to the printer device. LPR submits a print job to an LPD print server. LPQ queries the print job list of an LPD print server. Windows NT can gateway traffic among TCP/IP and non-TCP/IP print hosts.

Review

The following questions are intended to reinforce key information presented in this chapter. If you are unable to answer a question, review the appropriate lesson and then try the question again.

1. List the requirements for a computer running Windows NT to connect to a foreign host.

2. List the requirements for a computer running Windows NT to connect to and interoperate with an RFC-compliant NetBIOS-based host, such as LAN Manager for UNIX.

3. List two differences between accessing resources on a TCP/IP-based host using Windows NT commands versus TCP/IP utilities.

4. Which TCP/IP utilities are used to copy files?

5. Which TCP/IP utilities enable you to run commands on a foreign host?

6. What functions does the TCP/IP network printing support provide?

CHAPTER 15

Implementing the Microsoft SNMP Services

Lesson 1　SNMP Defined . . . 326

Lesson 2　The MIB . . . 330

Lesson 3　Installing and Configuring the SNMP Service . . . 333

Review . . . 346

About This Chapter

This chapter reviews the Simple Network Management Protocol (SNMP)—another protocol in the TCP/IP suite. The lessons provide an overview of SNMP, including the functions performed by an SNMP management station and the Microsoft SNMP service (SNMP agent). During the lessons, you install, configure, and test the SNMP service.

Before You Begin

To complete the lessons in this chapter, you must have:

- Installed Microsoft Windows NT Server 4.0 with TCP/IP.
- The Snmputil.exe file from the course compact disc.

Lesson 1: SNMP Defined

Simple Network Management Protocol (SNMP) provides the ability to monitor and communicate status information between a variety of hosts. This lesson defines SNMP and explains management systems and agents.

After this lesson, you will be able to:
- Explain and describe the Microsoft SNMP service.
- Describe the operations performed by an SNMP agent and management system.

Estimated lesson time: 20 minutes

SNMP is part of the TCP/IP protocol suite. It was originally developed in the Internet community to monitor and troubleshoot routers and bridges. SNMP provides the ability to monitor and communicate status information between:

- Computers running Windows NT
- LAN Manager servers
- Routers or gateways
- Minicomputers or mainframe computers
- Terminal servers
- Wiring hubs

SNMP uses a distributed architecture consisting of management systems and agents. With the Microsoft SNMP service, a computer running Windows NT can report its status to an SNMP management system on a TCP/IP network.

The SNMP service sends status information to one or more hosts when the host requests it or when a significant event occurs—for example, when a host is running out of hard disk space.

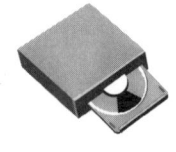

Note SNMP is defined in RFC 1157. For a copy of this RFC, see the *Course Materials* Web page on the course compact disc.

Management Systems and Agents

SNMP monitors various hosts using management systems and agents as shown in the following illustration.

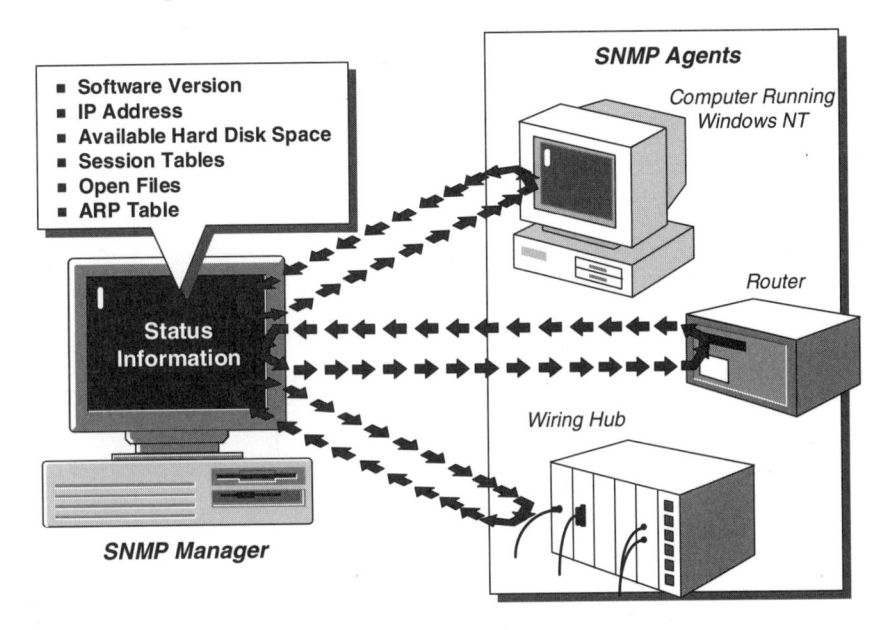

- Software Version
- IP Address
- Available Hard Disk Space
- Session Tables
- Open Files
- ARP Table

SNMP Agents
Computer Running Windows NT
Router
Wiring Hub
Status Information
SNMP Manager

SNMP Management System

The primary function of a management system is to request information from an agent. A management system is any computer running SNMP management software. A management system can initiate the **get**, **get-next**, and **set** operations.

- The **get** operation is a request for a specific value, such as the amount of hard disk space available.
- The **get-next** operation is a request for the "next" value. This operation is used to traverse a conceptual table of objects.
- The **set** operation changes a value. This operation is rarely carried out because most values have read-only access and cannot be set.

SNMP Agent

The primary function of an agent is to perform the **get**, **get-next**, and **set** operations requested by a management system as shown in the following illustration. An agent is any computer running SNMP agent software, typically a server or router. The Microsoft SNMP service is SNMP agent software.

The only operation initiated by an agent is a *trap*. The trap operation alerts management systems to an extraordinary event, such as a password violation.

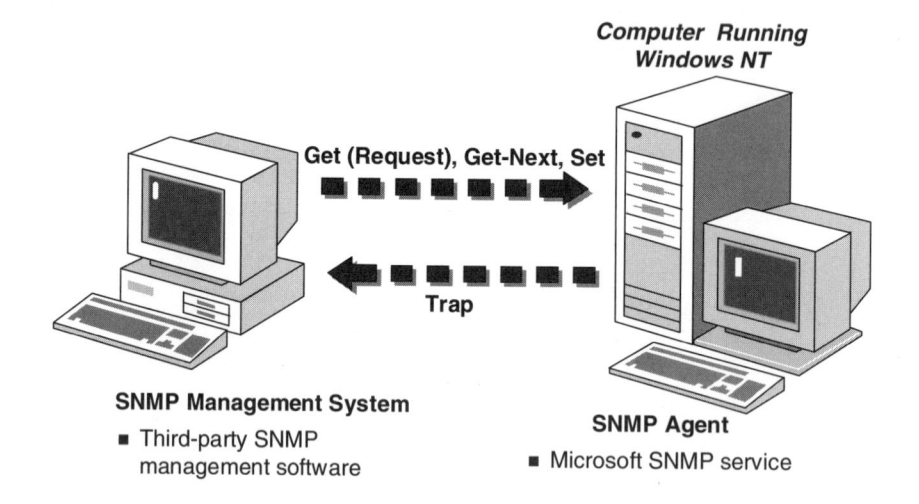

SNMP Management System
- Third-party SNMP management software

SNMP Agent
- Microsoft SNMP service

The Microsoft SNMP Service

The Microsoft SNMP service provides SNMP agent services to any TCP/IP host running SNMP management software. The SNMP service:

- Handles requests for status information from multiple hosts.
- Reports significant events (traps) to multiple hosts as they occur.
- Uses host names and IP addresses to identify the hosts to which it reports information and from which it receives requests.
- Can be installed and used on any computer running Windows NT and TCP/IP.
- Enables counters for monitoring TCP/IP performance using Performance Monitor.

The SNMP Architectural Model

The Microsoft SNMP service is written to the Windows Sockets API. This allows calls from management systems written to Windows Sockets. The SNMP service sends and receives messages using the user datagram protocol (UDP Port 161), and uses IP to support routing of SNMP messages.

SNMP provides extension agent dynamic-link libraries (DLLs) for supporting other Management Information Bases (MIBs). Third parties can develop their own MIBs for use with the Microsoft SNMP service. Microsoft SNMP includes a Microsoft Win32® SNMP manager API to simplify the development of SNMP applications.

Summary

SNMP allows computers running Windows NT to be monitored and to alert management systems of events. The Microsoft SNMP service provides agent services, extension agent DLLs, and a Win32 SNMP manager API to simplify the development of SNMP applications.

Lesson 2: The MIB

The information that a management system can request from an agent is contained in a management information base. This lesson defines the management information base and the Management Information Bases (MIBs) supported by the SNMP service.

After this lesson, you will be able to:
- Describe the management information bases supported by SNMP.

Estimated lesson time: 10 minutes

An MIB is a set of manageable objects representing various types of information about a network device, such as the number of active sessions or the version of network operating system software that is running on a host. SNMP management systems and agents share a common understanding of MIB objects.

The SNMP service supports Internet MIB II, LAN Manager MIB II, DHCP MIB, and WINS MIB.

Internet MIB II

Internet MIB II is a superset of the previous standard, Internet MIB I. Internet MIB II defines 171 objects essential for either fault or configuration analysis.

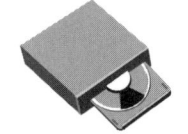

Note Internet MIB II is defined in RFC 1212. For a copy of this RFC, see the *Course Materials* Web page on the course compact disc.

LAN Manager MIB II

LAN Manager MIB II defines approximately 90 objects that include such items as statistical, share, session, user, and logon information. Most LAN Manager MIB II objects have read-only access because of the nonsecure nature of SNMP.

DHCP MIB

Windows NT 4.0 includes a DHCP MIB that defines objects to monitor DHCP server activity. This MIB (Dhcpmib.dll) is automatically installed when the DHCP Server service is installed. It contains approximately 14 objects for monitoring DHCP, such as the number of DHCP discover requests received, the number of declines, and the number of addresses leased out to clients.

WINS MIB

Windows NT 4.0 includes a WINS MIB that defines objects to monitor WINS server activity. This MIB (Winsmib.dll) is automatically installed when the WINS Server service is installed. It contains approximately 70 objects for monitoring WINS, such as the number of resolution requests successfully processed, the number of resolution requests that failed, and the date and time of the last database replication.

The Hierarchical Name Tree

The name space for MIB objects is hierarchical. The following illustration shows how it is structured so that each manageable object can be assigned a globally unique name. Authority for parts of the name space is assigned to individual organizations. This allows organizations to assign names without consulting an Internet authority for each assignment. For example, the name space assigned to LAN Manager is 1.3.6.1.4.1.77. Since the assignment of 1.3.6.1.4.1.77 to LAN Manager, Microsoft as a corporation has been assigned 1.3.6.1.4.1.311, and all new MIBs will be created under that branch. Microsoft has the authority to assign names to objects anywhere below that name space.

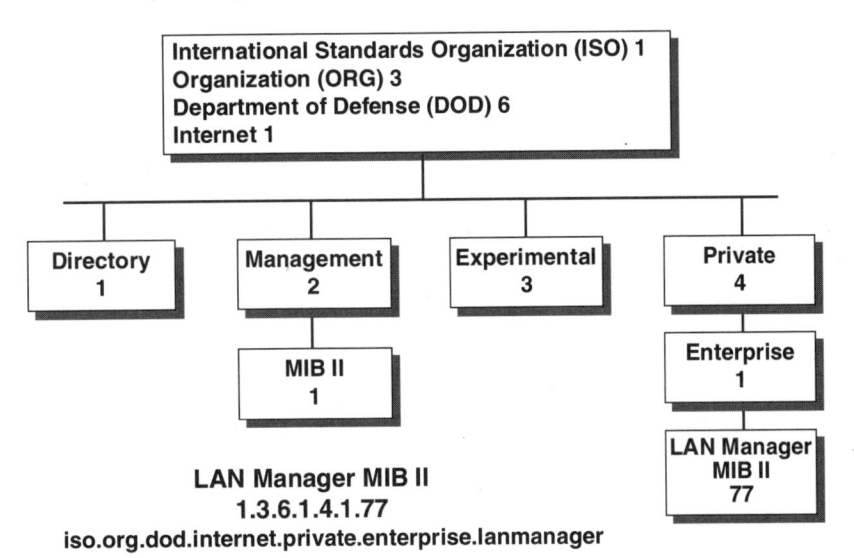

```
International Standards Organization (ISO) 1
Organization (ORG) 3
Department of Defense (DOD) 6
Internet 1
```

- Directory 1
- Management 2
  - MIB II 1
- Experimental 3
- Private 4
  - Enterprise 1
    - LAN Manager MIB II 77

LAN Manager MIB II
1.3.6.1.4.1.77
iso.org.dod.internet.private.enterprise.lanmanager

The object identifier in the hierarchy is written as a sequence of labels beginning at the root and ending at the object. Labels are separated with periods. For example, the object identifier for MIB II is:

Object name	Object number
iso.org.dod.internet.management.mibii	1.3.6.1.2.1

The object identifier for LAN Manager MIB II is:

Object name	Object number
iso.org.dod.internet.private.enterprise.lanmanager	1.3.6.1.4.1.77

Note The name space used to map object identifiers is distinct and separate from the hierarchical name space associated with UNIX domain names.

Summary

An MIB is a set of manageable objects that represent information such as the number of sessions on a host.

Lesson 3: Installing and Configuring the SNMP Service

If you want to monitor TCP/IP with Performance Monitor, you need to install the SNMP service. If you want to use a third-party application to monitor a computer running Windows NT, you also need to configure the SNMP service.

After this lesson, you will be able to:
- Define an SNMP community.
- Install and configure the Microsoft SNMP service.
- Use SNMPUTIL to test communications for the Microsoft SNMP service.

Estimated lesson time: 50 minutes

Defining SNMP Communities

Before you install SNMP, you need to define an SNMP community. A *community* is a group to which hosts running the SNMP service belong. Communities are identified by a *community name*. The use of a community name provides primitive security and context checking for agents that receive requests and initiate traps, and for management systems that initiate requests and receive traps. An agent will not accept a request from a management system outside its configured community.

An SNMP agent can be a member of multiple communities at the same time, allowing for communication with SNMP managers from various communities. For example, in the following illustration there are two defined communities—Public and Public2.

Only the agents and managers that are members of the same community can communicate with each other.

- Agent1 can receive and send messages to Manager2 because they are both members of the Public2 community.
- Agent2 through Agent4 can receive and send messages to Manager1 because they are all members of the default community Public.

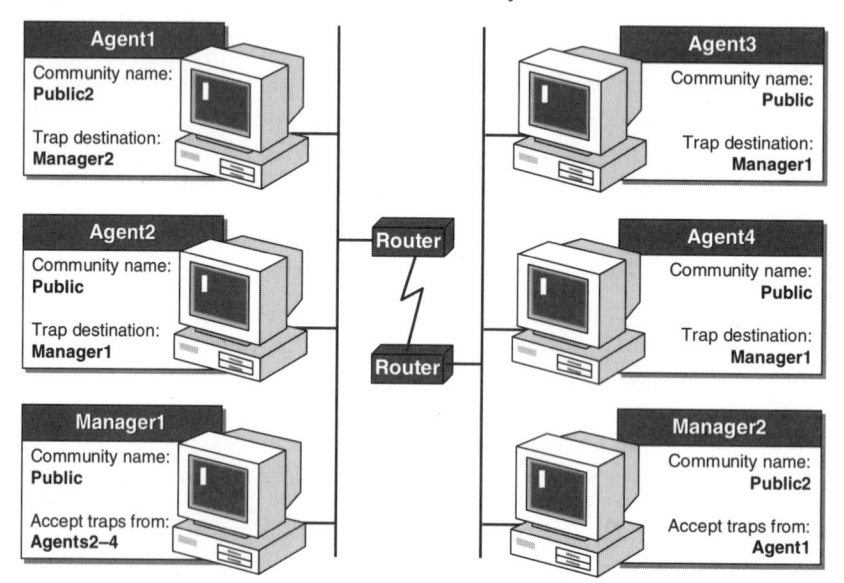

How SNMP Gathers Information

The following steps and illustration outline how the SNMP service responds to management system requests:

1. An SNMP management system sends a request to an agent using the agent's host name (or IP address).

   The request is passed by the application to socket (UDP port) 161.

   The host name is resolved to an IP address using any of the available resolution methods, including HOSTS file, DNS, WINS, broadcast, or LMHOSTS file.

2. An SNMP packet is formed containing the following information:
    a. A **get**, **get-next**, or **set** operation for one or more objects.
    b. A community name and other validating information.

    The packet is routed to socket (UDP port) 161 on the agent.

3. The SNMP agent receives the packet in its buffer.

    The community name is verified. If the community name is invalid or the packet is ill-formed, it is discarded.

    If the community name is valid, the agent verifies the source host name or IP address. (The agent must be authorized to accept packets from the management system, or the packet will be discarded.)

    The request is passed to the appropriate DLL:

If the request is for	This happens
An Internet MIB II object	The TCP DLL retrieves the information.
A LAN Manager MIB II object	The LAN Manager DLL retrieves the information.
A DHCP object	The DHCP MIB DLL retrieves the information.
A WINS object	The WINS MIB DLL retrieves the information.
An extension agent MIB	The DLL for that MIB retrieves the information.

    The object identifier is mapped to the appropriate API function, and the API call is made.

    The DLL returns the information to the agent.

4. The SNMP packet is sent back to the SNMP manager with the requested information.

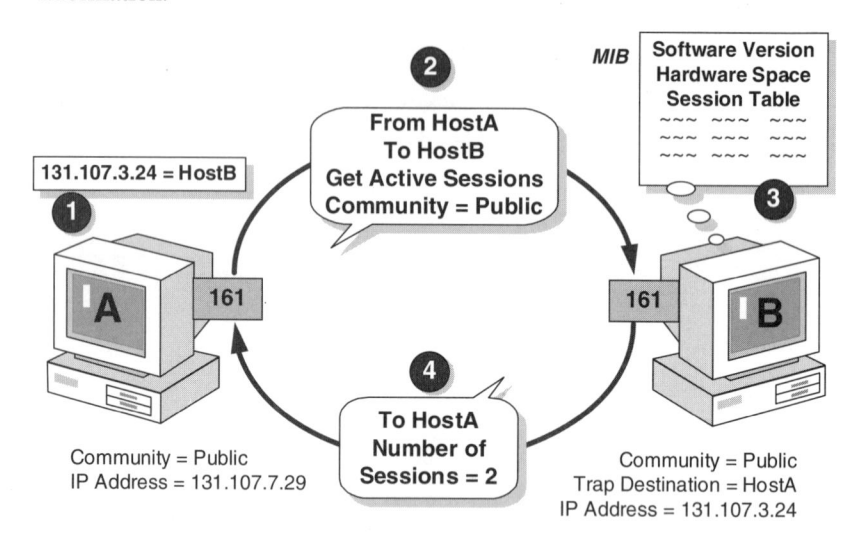

```
131.107.3.24 = HostB

        ②
   From HostA
   To HostB
   Get Active Sessions
   Community = Public

        ④
   To HostA
   Number of
   Sessions = 2

MIB  Software Version
     Hardware Space
     Session Table

A  161                              161  B

Community = Public                  Community = Public
IP Address = 131.107.7.29           Trap Destination = HostA
                                    IP Address = 131.107.3.24
```

Installing SNMP

When you install the SNMP service, you must determine the Send Trap and Trap Destination parameters.

The Send Trap with Community Names parameter defines the community name to which traps are sent. A management system must belong to the designated community to receive traps. The default community name for all hosts is *Public*.

The Trap Destination parameter consists of names or IP addresses of hosts to which you want the SNMP service to send traps. If you use a host name, make sure it can be resolved so that the SNMP service can map it to the IP address.

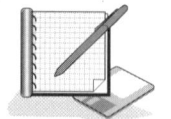

Practice

In this procedure, you install and configure the SNMP service.

▶ **To install the SNMP service**

1. In Control Panel, double-click the Network icon.
2. Click the **Services** tab, and then click **Add**.

   The **Select Network Service** dialog box appears.
3. Click **SNMP Service**, and then click **OK**.
4. When prompted, type the path to the Windows NT distribution files.

5. After the appropriate files are copied to the computer, the **Microsoft SNMP Properties** dialog box appears.

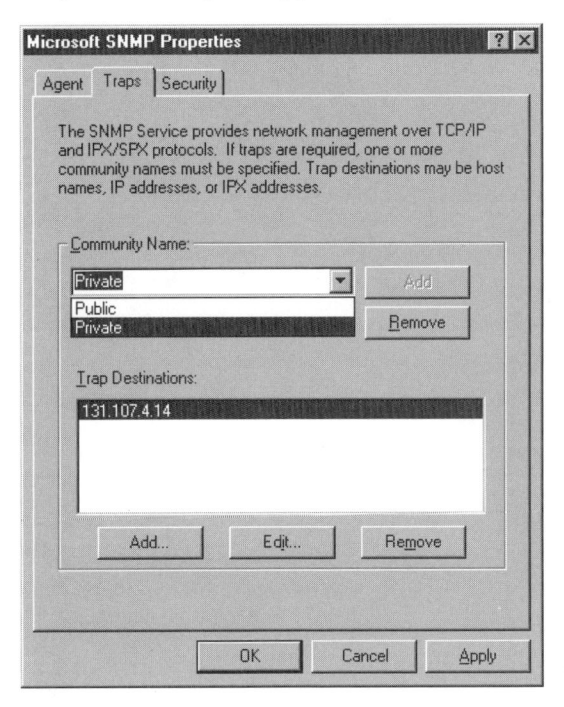

6. Select a Community Name of Public.
7. Click **OK**.

   The **Network** dialog box appears.
8. Click **Close**.

   A **Network Settings Change** message box appears, indicating that you must restart the computer.
9. Click **Yes**.
10. Log on as Administrator.

Configuring SNMP Service Security

The SNMP service provides primitive security and context checking for agents that receive requests and initiate traps, and for management systems that initiate requests and receive traps. An agent will not accept a request from a management system outside the community. Windows NT will send an authentication trap by default.

▶ **To configure SNMP security**

1. In Control Panel, double-click the Network icon.
2. Click the **Services** tab, click the **SNMP Service**, and then click **Properties**.

   The **Microsoft SNMP Properties** dialog box appears.
3. Click the **Security** tab.
4. Configure the parameters shown in the following table.

Parameter	Description
Send Authentication Trap	When the SNMP service receives a request for information that does not contain the correct community name or does not match an accepted host name for the service, the SNMP service can send a trap to the trap destination(s), indicating that the request failed authentication. Select this check box to specify whether this authentication trap is sent.
Accepted Community Names	A host must belong to a community that appears on this list for the SNMP service to accept requests from that host. Typically, all hosts belong to Public, which is the standard name for the common community of all hosts.
Accept SNMP Packets from Any Host	If this option is selected, no SNMP packets are rejected on the basis of the source host ID and the list of hosts in the box below it.
Only Accept SNMP Packets from These Hosts	If this option is selected, SNMP packets are accepted only from the hosts listed.

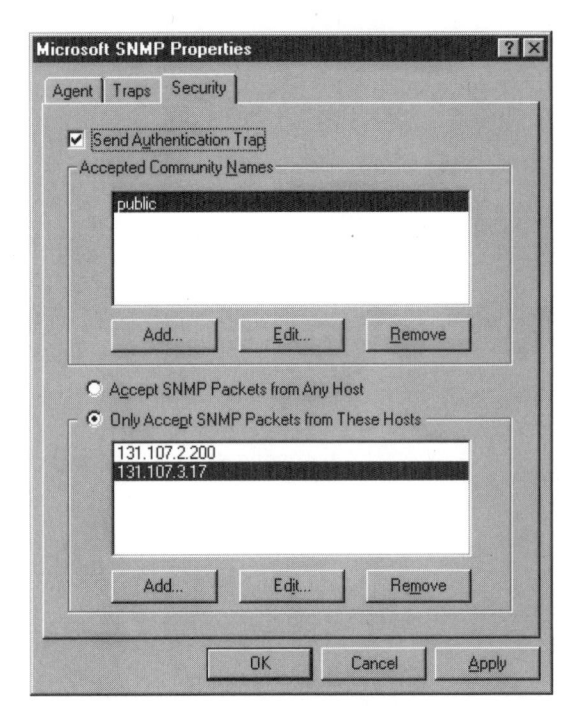

Configuring SNMP Agent Services

SNMP agent services give a computer running Windows NT the ability to provide a management system with information on activity that occurs at different layers of the Internet protocol suite.

▶ **To configure SNMP agent services**

1. In the **Microsoft SNMP Properties** dialog box, click the **Agent** tab.
2. In the **Contact** box, type a contact name.

   This is typically the person who uses the computer.

3. In the **Location** box, type a description for the location of the computer.
4. Under **Service**, select the services to be provided by the agent.

   Each service provides information on activity at the different layers. The default services are Applications, End-to-End, and Internet.

Service	Select this option if
Physical	This computer running Windows NT manages any physical devices, such as repeaters.
Datalink/Subnetwork	This computer running Windows NT manages a bridge.
Internet	This computer running Windows NT acts as an IP gateway (router).
End-to-End	This computer running Windows NT acts as an IP host. This option should always be selected.
Applications	This computer running Windows NT uses any applications that use TCP/IP. This option should always be selected.

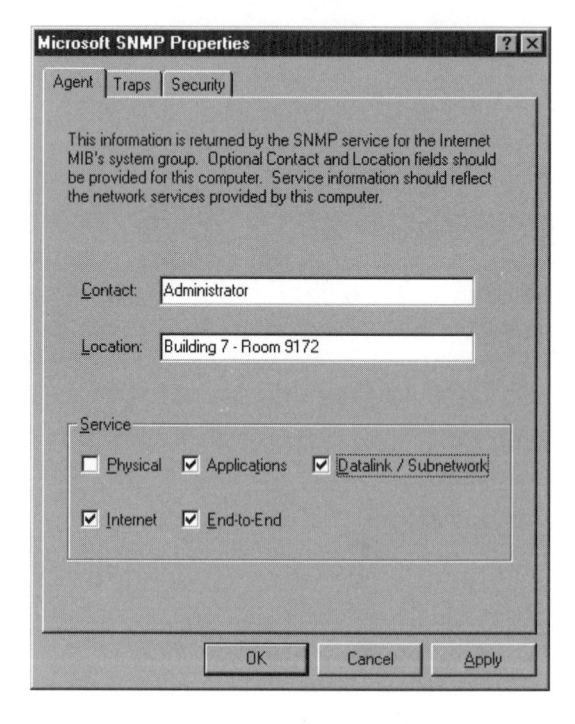

5. Click **OK**.
6. Click **Close**.

Identifying SNMP Service Errors

If the SNMP service fails for any reason, the failure will be documented in the Event Viewer system log as shown in the following illustration. Event Viewer is the first place you should look to identify a problem with the SNMP service.

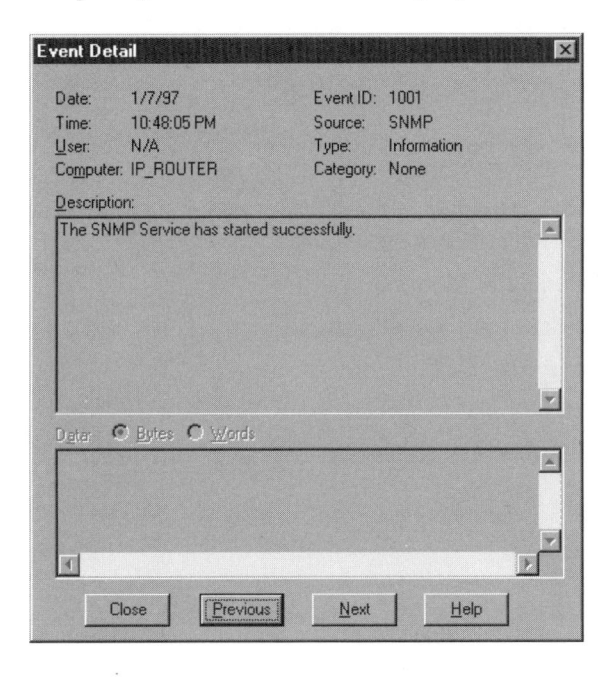

▶ **To see SNMP error messages using Event Viewer**

1. Click the **Start** button, point to **Programs**, point to **Administrative Tools**, and then click **Event Viewer**.
2. Select a message icon to read about an error.

Practice

In these procedures, you use Performance Monitor to view objects added as a result of installing the SNMP service. You then use Performance Monitor to view ICMP and IP counter activity generated by the **ping** command.

Note In order to complete these procedures, you must first install SNMP according to the procedures outlined in this chapter.

▶ **To view the new Performance Monitor objects**

1. Click the **Start** button, point to **Programs**, point to **Administrative Tools**, and then click **Performance Monitor**.

   The Performance Monitor window appears.

2. On the **Edit** menu, click **Add to Chart**.

   The **Add to Chart** dialog box appears.

3. In the **Object** box, click the arrow to display a list of objects.

4. List the TCP/IP-related objects.

   _____

   _____

   _____

▶ **To monitor IP datagrams with Performance Monitor**

1. In the **Object** box, click **ICMP** on the list.

   A list of ICMP counters appears.

2. In the **Counter** box, click **Messages/sec**.

3. In the **Scale** box, set the number to **1.0** and then click **Add**.

4. In the **Object** box, click **IP**.

5. In the **Counter** box, click **Datagrams Sent/sec** from the list.

6. In the **Scale** box, set the number to **1.0** and then click **Add**.

7. Click **Done**.

    Your selections appear in the display area.

8. On the **Options** menu, click **Chart**.
9. Change the **Vertical Maximum** to **10**, and then click **OK**.
10. Move the Performance Monitor window to the top of the screen.
11. At a command prompt, ping your second computer.
12. Return to Performance Monitor, and view the activity that resulted from the ping.

    What activity was recorded as a result of using ping?

    _____

    How many messages per second were recorded for ICMP?

    _____

    How many IP datagrams were sent per second?

    _____

    Why were there twice as many ICMP messages as there were IP datagrams sent?

    _____

13. Close Performance Monitor.

The SNMPUTIL Utility

The *Microsoft Windows NT Resource Kit* includes the SNMPUTIL (Snmputil.exe) utility, which verifies whether the SNMP service has been correctly configured to communicate with SNMP management stations. SNMPUTIL makes the same SNMP calls as an SNMP management station.

The syntax of SNMPUTIL is as follows:

snmputil *command agent community object_identifier_(OID)*

The valid commands are:

get   Get the value of the requested object identifier.
getnext Get the value of the next object following the specified object identifier.
walk   Step through (walk) the MIB branch specified by the object identifier.

For example, to determine the number of DHCP server addresses leased by a DHCP server named DHCPserver in the Public community, you would issue the following command:

snmputil getnext *DHCPserver* Public .1.3.6.1.4.1.311.1.3.2.1.1.1

This command will respond with the object identifier (OID) and counter value for the object ID in question—in this case, the number of IP leases that are issued.

Practice

In this procedure, you view descriptions of MIB objects, and then access SNMP objects to view the data gathered with an SNMP agent and management program. In the first part of the procedure, you use the Snmputil.exe utility to verify that your SNMP agent is configured to communicate with an SNMP manager.

▶ **To view SNMP data**

1. Copy **C:\LabFiles\Chapt15\Snmputil.exe** to **C:\Winnt**.
2. Open a command prompt.
3. Use Snmputil.exe to determine SNMP objects related to DHCP. Type the following command on one line and then press ENTER:

   snmputil getnext 131.107.2.*host_id*
   public .1.3.6.1.4.1.311.1.3.2.1.1.1

   How many IP addresses have been leased?

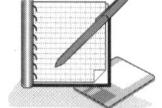

4. Use Snmputil.exe on the WINS object .1.3.6.1.4.1.311.1.2.1.17. Type:

   snmputil getnext 131.107.2.*host_id*
   public .1.3.6.1.4.1.311.1.2.1.17

   How many successful queries have been processed by the WINS server?

5. Use Snmputil.exe on the WINS object **.1.3.6.1.4.1.311.1.2.1.18**. Type:

   snmputil getnext 131.107.2.*host_id*
   public .1.3.6.1.4.1.311.1.2.1.18

   How many unsuccessful queries have been processed by the WINS server?

6. Use Snmputil.exe on the LAN Manager object **.1.3.6.1.4.1.77.1.1.1**. Type:

   snmputil getnext 131.107.2.*host_id* **public .1.3.6.1.4.1.77.1.1.1**

7. Use Snmputil.exe on the LAN Manager Object .1.3.6.1.4.1.77.1.1.2. Type:

   snmputil getnext 131.107.2.*host_id* **public .1.3.6.1.4.1.77.1.1.2**

   What is the version of Windows NT Server running on the computer?

Summary

Before you install SNMP, you must define a community, a group to which SNMP hosts belong. The SNMP service provides basic security and context checking for agents. You can use Event Viewer to monitor SNMP service failures.

Review

The following questions are intended to reinforce key information presented in this chapter. If you are unable to answer a question, review the appropriate lesson and then try the question again.

1. What are the four SNMP operations?

2. Which SNMP operations are initiated by a management system? Which SNMP operations are initiated by an agent?

3. Which MIBs are supported by Windows NT 4.0?

4. Which host name resolution methods does the SNMP employ?

5. What is the purpose of a community name?

CHAPTER 16

Troubleshooting Microsoft TCP/IP

Lesson 1   Windows NT Diagnostic Tools and Guidelines . . . 348

Review . . . 353

About This Chapter

In this chapter, you review guidelines for troubleshooting an IP network. The lesson outlines Microsoft Windows NT and TCP/IP utilities useful in troubleshooting problems. The lesson also covers common TCP/IP-related problems, symptoms, and possible causes.

Before You Begin

There are no prerequisites for completing this chapter.

Lesson 1: Windows NT Diagnostic Tools and Guidelines

There is an orderly process to troubleshooting TCP/IP problems. This lesson explains the process and suggests Windows NT utilities for troubleshooting TCP/IP problems.

After this lesson, you will be able to:
- Identify common TCP/IP-related problems and utilities for troubleshooting.
- Explain the guidelines for troubleshooting TCP/IP.

Estimated lesson time: 20 minutes

Troubleshooting a problem is easiest when you can identify the problem source. TCP/IP-related problems can be grouped into the categories listed in the following table.

Problem source	Common characteristics
Configuration	The host will not initialize or one of the services will not start.
IP addressing	You may not be able to communicate with other hosts. The host could stop responding.
Subnetting	You can ping your workstation, but may not be able to access local or remote hosts.
Address resolution	You can ping your workstation, but not other hosts.
NetBIOS name resolution	You can access a host by its IP address, but not establish a connection with a **net** command.
Host name resolution	You access a host by its IP address, but not by its host name.

Windows NT Utilities

Windows NT includes several utilities that can be helpful for troubleshooting a TCP/IP problem.

Use this tool	To
PING	Verify that TCP/IP is configured correctly and that another host is available.
ARP	View the ARP cache to detect invalid entries.
NETSTAT	Display protocol statistics and the current state of TCP/IP connections.

(*continued*)

Use this tool	To
NBTSTAT	Check the state of current NetBIOS over TCP/IP connections, update the LMHOSTS cache, or determine your registered name and scope ID.
IPCONFIG	Verify TCP/IP configuration, including DHCP and WINS server addresses.
TRACERT	Verify the route to a remote host.
ROUTE	Display or modify the local routing table.
NSLOOKUP	Display information from DNS name servers.
Microsoft SNMP service	Supply statistical information to SNMP management systems.
Event log	Track errors and events.
Performance Monitor	Analyze performance and detect bottlenecks.
Network Monitor	Capture incoming and outgoing packets to analyze a problem.
Registry Editor	Browse and edit the configuration parameters.

Troubleshooting Guidelines

When troubleshooting TCP/IP, it is recommended that you troubleshoot from the bottom layer of the Internet protocol suite to the top layer as shown in the following illustration. The objective is to verify that protocols at each layer can communicate with protocols at the layers above and below them.

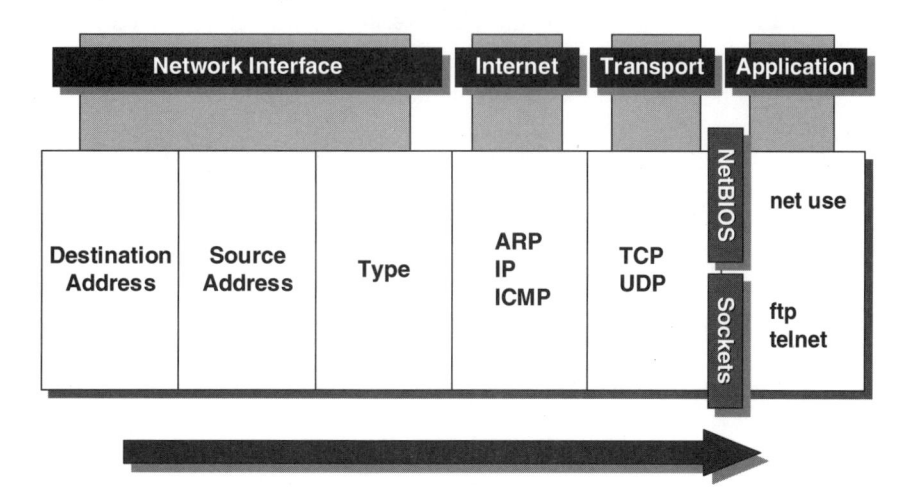

There are two steps in troubleshooting. Make sure you can:

1. Ping successfully.

   If you can ping successfully, you have verified IP communications between the Network Interface layer and the Internet layer. PING uses ARP to resolve the IP address to a hardware address for each echo request and echo reply.

2. Establish a session with a host.

   If you can establish a session, you have verified TCP/IP session communications from the network interface layer through the application layer.

Note If you are unable to resolve a problem, you may need to use an IP analyzer (such as Microsoft Network Monitor) to view network activity at each layer.

Verifying IP Communications

The first goal in troubleshooting is to make sure you can successfully ping an IP address. This verifies communications between the Network Interface layer and the Internet layer. Ping a host using its host name only after you can successfully ping the host using its IP address. The following procedure and illustration show how to troubleshoot connections using Ping.

▶ **To troubleshoot the Network Interface and Internet layers using PING**

1. Ping the loopback address to verify that TCP/IP was installed and loaded correctly. If this step is unsuccessful, verify that the system was restarted after TCP/IP was installed and configured.

2. Ping your IP address to verify that it was configured correctly. If this step is unsuccessful:

   - View the configuration through the Network program in Control Panel to verify that the address was entered correctly.

   - Verify that the IP address is valid and that it follows addressing guidelines.

3. Ping the IP address of the default gateway to verify that the gateway is functioning and configured correctly and that communication is available on the local network. If this step is unsuccessful, verify that you are using the correct IP address and subnet mask.

4. Ping the IP address of a remote host to verify the connection to the WAN. If this step is unsuccessful:
   - Verify that the IP address of the default gateway is correct.
   - Make sure the remote host is functional.
   - Verify that the link between routers is operational.
5. After you can successfully ping the IP address, ping the host name to verify that the name is configured correctly in the HOSTS file.

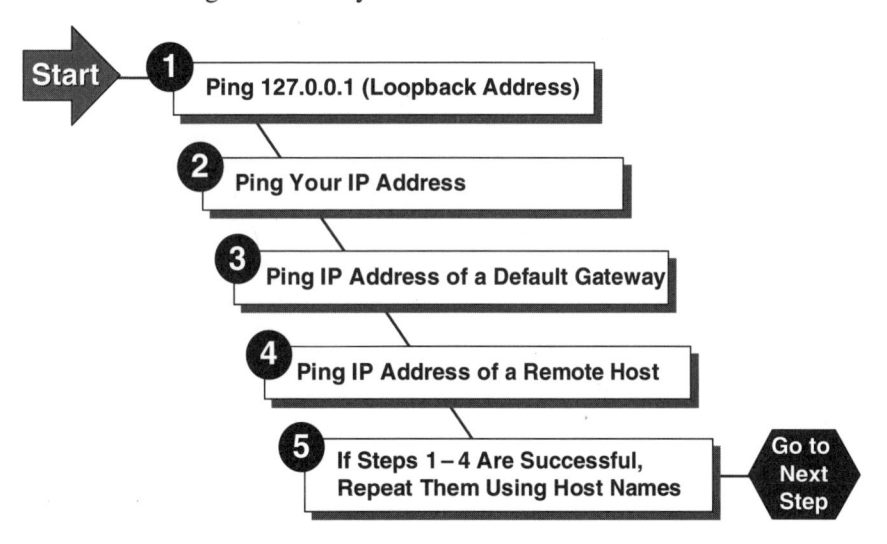

Start → 1. Ping 127.0.0.1 (Loopback Address)
2. Ping Your IP Address
3. Ping IP Address of a Default Gateway
4. Ping IP Address of a Remote Host
5. If Steps 1-4 Are Successful, Repeat Them Using Host Names → Go to Next Step

Verifying TCP/IP Session Communications

The next goal during troubleshooting is to verify communications from the Internet layer through the Application layer by successfully establishing a session. Use one of the following methods to verify communications between the Network Interface layer and the Application layer as shown in the following illustration.

To establish a NetBIOS over TCP/IP session with a computer running Windows NT or other RFC-compliant NetBIOS-based host, make a connection with the **net use** or **net view** command. If this step is unsuccessful:

- Verify that the target host is NetBIOS based.
- Confirm that the scope ID on the target host matches that of the source host.
- Verify that you used the correct NetBIOS name.
- If the target host is on a remote network, verify that a name-to-address mapping is available in either WINS or the LMHOSTS file for the correct entry.

To establish a Windows Sockets session with an IP host, use the Telnet or FTP utility to make a connection. If this step is unsuccessful:

- Verify that the target host is configured with the Telnet daemon or FTP daemon.
- Confirm that you have the correct permissions on the target host.
- Check the HOSTS file or a DNS server for a valid entry if you are connecting using a host name.

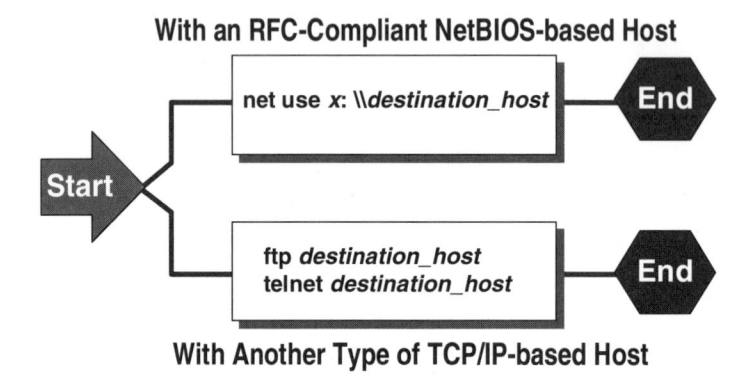

With an RFC-Compliant NetBIOS-based Host

Start → net use *x:* *destination_host* → End

Start → ftp *destination_host*
telnet *destination_host* → End

With Another Type of TCP/IP-based Host

Summary

If you can PING successfully, you have verified communications from the Network Interface layer up through the Internet layer. If you can establish a session, you have verified communications from the Internet layer up through the Application layer.

Review

The following questions are intended to reinforce key information presented in this chapter. If you are unable to answer a question, review the appropriate lesson and then try the question again.

1. What are three Windows NT utilities useful in diagnosing TCP/IP-related problems?

2. Which TCP/IP utility is used to verify communications from the Network Interface layer up to the Internet layer?

3. What are the two procedures for troubleshooting an IP network?

Questions and Answers

Chapter 1: Introduction to TCP/IP

Review Answers

Page 8

1. What is TCP/IP?

   TCP/IP is a suite of protocols that provide routing in WANs, and connectivity to a variety of hosts on the Internet.

2. Are all TCP/IP standards published as RFCs? Do all RFCs specify standards?

   Yes, TCP/IP standards are always published as RFCs. However, not all RFCs specify standards.

Chapter 2: Installing and Configuring TCP/IP

Review Answers

Page 22

1. What TCP/IP utilities are used to verify and test a TCP/IP configuration?

   IPCONFIG and PING.

2. What parameters are required on a Windows NT-based computer running TCP/IP on a WAN?

   IP address, subnet mask, and default gateway.

Chapter 3: Architectural Overview of the TCP/IP Protocol Suite

Practice Answers

▶ **To view the ARP request frame details**

Page 36

5. In the **Detail** window, expand **ETHERNET**.

   The **ETHERNET** frame properties are displayed.

   What is the destination address?

   FFFFFFFFFFFF

   Does the destination address refer to a physical address?

   No, it represents a broadcast address.

   What is the source address?

   The Media Access Control address of the network card in your computer.

   What type of Ethernet frame is this?

   0x0806 – ARP: Address Resolution Protocol

7. In the **Detail** window, expand **ARP_RARP**.

   What is the sender's hardware address?

   Address will vary.

   What is the target's hardware address?

   000000000000 is the address because this is the request packet and the Media Access Control address is unknown at this time.

   What is the target's protocol address?

   131.107.2.211

▶ **To examine an ARP reply frame details**

Page 37

2. In the **Detail** window, expand **ETHERNET: ETYPE**.

   The **ETHERNET: ETYPE** frame properties are displayed.

   What is the destination address?

   Address will vary.

   Does the destination address refer to a physical address?

   Yes.

What is the source address?

The Media Access Control address of the network card in your computer.

What type of Ethernet frame is this?

0x0806 – ARP: Address Resolution Protocol

4. In the **Detail** window, expand **ARP_RARP**.

What is the sender's hardware address?

Address will vary.

▶ To view the ARP cache

2. Document the entry for your default gateway (if configured)—for example: 131.107.2.1 08-00-02-6c-28-93

The entries may vary.

▶ To ping a local host

2. View the new entry in the ARP cache.

What entry was added?

The host that was pinged (your second computer).

What is the entry's type?

Dynamic.

▶ To add an ARP entry

2. View the ARP cache to verify that the entry has been added.

What is the entry's type?

Static.

Why was this entry's type different from preceding entries?

Because the entry was added manually, rather than as a result of a broadcast. Entries that are added manually are static until the computer is restarted.

Review Answers

1. What are the layers in the four-layer model used by TCP/IP?

   Application, Transport, Internet, and Network Interface.

2. What core protocols are provided in the Microsoft TCP/IP transport driver?

   TCP, UDP, ICMP, IGMP, IP, and ARP.

3. Which protocol is used to inform a client that a destination network is unreachable?

   ICMP.

4. When an IP datagram is forwarded by a router, how is the datagram changed?

   Smaller TTL, updated checksum value, and possibly fragmented.

5. When is the User Datagram Protocol used?

   When an application needs to send connectionless traffic—typically sending a messaging to multiple receiving stations.

6. When an ARP request is sent out, to what address is it sent?

   The broadcast address (FFFFFFFF).

7. What address is requested in the ARP request packet for a local host? For a remote host?

   For a local host it is the Media Access Control address of that host. For a remote host it is the Media Access Control address of the gateway to which the IP datagram is being sent (typically your default gateway).

Chapter 4: IP Addressing

Practice Answers

1. Convert the following binary numbers to decimal format.

Binary value	Decimal value
10001011	139
10101010	170
10111111 11100000 00000111 10000001	191.224.7.129
01111111 00000000 00000000 00000001	127.0.0.1

2. Convert the following decimal values to binary format.

Decimal value	Binary value
250	11111010
19	00010011
109.128.255.254	01101101 10000000 11111111 11111110
131.107.2.89	10000011 01101011 00000010 01011001

Practice Answers

Page 63

1. Write the address class next to each IP address.

Address	Class
131.107.2.89	B
3.3.57.0	A
200.200.5.2	C
191.107.2.10	B

2. Which address class(es) allow you to have more than 1,000 hosts per network?

   Class A (16,777,214) and class B (65,534).

3. Which address class(es) allow only 254 hosts per network?

   Class C.

Practice Answers

Page 67

Identify the IP addresses that would be invalid if it were assigned to a host, and then explain why it is invalid.

a. 131.107.256.80

   This is invalid because the highest possible value in an octet is 255.

b. 222.222.255.222

   This is a valid address.

c. 231.200.1.1

   This is invalid because 231 is a class D address, and is not supported as a host address.

d. 126.1.0.0

   This is a valid address.

e. 0.127.4.100

   Zero is an invalid address. It indicated "this network only."

f. 190.7.2.0

   This is a valid address.

g. 127.1.1.1

   This is invalid because 127 addresses are reserved for diagnostics.

h. 198.121.254.255

This is invalid because 255 as a host ID indicates a broadcast.

i. 255.255.255.255

This is invalid because 255 is a broadcast address.

Practice Answers

Page 67

In this practice, you decide which network components require IP addresses in a TCP/IP network environment. When a protocol is listed, assume it is the only protocol installed on the host. Review the following network components and circle the letter that corresponds to the components that do not require an IP address.

a. Microsoft Windows NT computer running TCP/IP

b. LAN Manager workstation that connects to a Windows NT computer running TCP/IP

c. Computer running Windows 95 that requires access to shared resources on a Windows NT-based computer running TCP/IP

d. UNIX host that you want to connect to using TCP/IP utilities

e. Network interface printer running TCP/IP

f. Router for connecting to a remote IP network

g. Ethernet port on local router

h. Microsoft LAN Manager workstation that is attempting to connect to a LAN Manager server running NetBEUI

i. Computer running Windows for Workgroups that requires access to shared resources on a LAN Manager server running NetBEUI

j. Serial plotter on a Windows NT-based computer running TCP/IP

k. Network printer shared off a LAN Manager server running NetBEUI

l. Communications server providing terminal access to TCP/IP host computers

m. Your default gateway

All network components require an IP address except for h, i, j, and k.

Practice Answers

Page 68

In this practice, you decide which class of address will support the following IP network. Next, you assign a valid IP address to each type of host to easily distinguish it from other hosts (for example, UNIX, Windows NT servers, or Windows NT workstations). In this scenario all computers are on the same subnet.

Which address classes will support this network?

Class A or class B.

Which of the following network addresses support this network?

a. 197.200.3.0
b. 11.0.0.0
c. 221.100.2.0
d. 131.107.0.0

B and D will support this network.

Practice Answers

Page 69

Using the network ID that you chose, assign a range of host IDs to each type of host, so that you can easily distinguish the Windows NT Server computers from the Windows NT Workstation computers and the UNIX workstations.

Type of TCP/IP host	IP address range
Windows NT Server computers	**Assign high numbers to all servers, for instance 200–250.**
Windows NT Workstation computers	**Assign low numbers to all UNIX workstations, for instance 150–200.**
UNIX workstations	**Assign numbers to the Windows NT Workstation computers using a different octet than that used by the servers and UNIX workstations.**

Practice Answers

Page 69

In this next practice, you decide how many network IDs and host IDs are required to support this network.

How many network IDs does this network environment require?

2 local networks (E and F) + 3 wide area networks (A, B, and C) = 5 total

How many host IDs does this network environment require?

50 (Windows NT Server computers) + 200 (Windows NT Workstation computers) + 50 (UNIX workstations) + 6 (router interfaces) = 306

Which default gateway (router interface) would you assign to the Windows NT Workstation computers that communicate primarily with the UNIX workstations?

The router interface E.

Practice Answers

Page 73

In this practice, AND the following IP addresses to determine whether the destination IP address belongs to a host on a local network or a remote network.

1. Do the results match?

   No.

2. Is the destination IP address located on a local or remote network?

   Remote.

Review Answers

Page 77

1. In class A, class B, and class C addresses, which octets represent the network ID and which represent the host ID?

   Class A—The network ID uses the first octet. The host ID uses the last three octets.

   Class B—The network ID uses the first two octets. The host ID uses the last two octets.

   Class C—The network ID uses the first three octets. The host ID uses the last octet.

2. Which numbers are invalid as a network ID and why? Which numbers are invalid as a host ID and why?

   As a network ID, 127 is reserved for loopback functions.

   As a network ID and a host ID, all 1's (255) and all 0's are invalid. All 1's are used for broadcasts. All 0's indicate the local network or "this network only."

3. When is a unique network ID required?

   A unique network ID is required for each physical network and for the connection between two routers on a WAN.

4. In a TCP/IP internetwork, what components require a host ID besides computers?

   Each TCP/IP-based host requires a host ID that is unique to the network ID, including routers.

Review Practice

Page 78

For the following diagram, list all IP addressing problems, and explain how each problem may affect communications. Are the IP addresses and default gateway addresses appropriate for each situation?

Host B has an incorrect default gateway address, so communications will be limited to the local network.

Host D has no default gateway assigned, so communications will be limited to the local network.

Hosts F and I have a common IP address. This could cause problems if a host attempts to access the IP address of 147.103.0.1.

Page 79

For the following diagram, list all IP addressing problems, and explain how each problem may affect communications. Are the IP addresses and default gateway addresses appropriate for each situation?

Hosts C and E have duplicate IP addresses (109.128.5.35). Windows NT will detect the duplicate addresses and fail in initializing TCP/IP. If duplicate IP addresses exist on other types of TCP/IP-based hosts (for example, LAN Manager), hosts C and E cannot communicate with each other, hosts could stop responding, and other hosts may not be able to access hosts C and E.

Host B has a different network ID from the other hosts. Host B will not be able to communicate with any other local host. It will not be able to communicate with remote hosts because the network ID for the default gateway is different from its own.

Host F has the same IP address as its default gateway. It may not be able to communicate with local or remote hosts.

Chapter 5: Subnetting

Page 88

Practice Answers

In this practice, you define a subnet mask for several situations. Remember that not every situation requires subnetting.

1. Class A network address on a local network.

   255.0.0.0

2. Class B network address on a local network with 4,000 hosts.

   255.255.0.0

3. Class C network address on a local network with 254 hosts.

   255.255.255.0

4. Class A address with 6 subnets.

   255.224.0.0

5. Class B address with 126 subnets.

   255.255.254.0

6. Class A network address. Currently, there are 30 subnets that will grow to approximately 65 subnets within the next year. Each subnet will never have more than 50,000 hosts.

   Using 7 bits = 255.254.0.0

   Using 8 bits = 255.255.0.0

7. Using the subnet mask from the preceding scenario, how much growth will this subnet mask provide?

   Using 7 bits will provide up to 126 subnets and 131,070 hosts per subnet.

   Using 8 bits will provide up to 254 subnets and 65,534 hosts per subnet.

8. Class B network address. Currently, there are 14 subnets that may double in size within the next two years. Each subnet will have fewer than 1,500 hosts.

   Using 5 bits = 255.255.248.0

9. Using the subnet mask from the preceding scenario, how much growth will this subnet mask provide?

   Using 5 bits will provide up to 30 subnets and 2,046 hosts per subnet.

Questions and Answers

Practice Answers

Page 89

In this practice, you review two invalid subnet masks to see what would happen when you try to communicate with a host on a local and remote network.

Using the information below, convert your computer's IP address and the IP address of your default gateway to binary format, and then AND them to the subnet mask to determine why the subnet mask is invalid.

Your IP address	131.107.y.z	10000011 01101011
Subnet mask	255.255.255.248	11111111 11111111 11111111 11111000
Result		
Destination IP address	131.107.y.z	10000011 01101011
Subnet mask	255.255.255.248	11111111 11111111 11111111 11111000
Result		

Did the result of ANDing indicate that the destination IP address and subnet mask were for a local or remote network?

Remote.

Why would you not be able to successfully ping your default gateway?

IP would determine it was on a remote network, and there would be no gateway available.

Using the information below, convert your IP address and the IP address of the remote host to binary format, and then AND them to the subnet mask to determine why the subnet mask would be invalid.

Your IP address	131.107.y.z	10000011 01101011
Subnet mask	255.255.0.0	11111111 11111111 00000000 00000000
Result		
Destination IP address	131.107.y.z	10000011 01101011
Subnet mask	255.255.0.0	11111111 11111111 00000000 00000000
Result		

Did the result of ANDing indicate that the destination IP address and subnet mask were for a local or remote network?

Local.

Why would you not be able to successfully ping a remote host?

IP tried to route the packet to a host on the local network even though the host was really on a remote network.

Compare the two results generated using incorrect subnet masks to see how differently TCP/IP responds when the subnet mask indicates a local network versus a remote network. What did you conclude about how TCP/IP uses a subnet mask?

The subnet mask is used to determine whether an IP address is located on a local or a remote network. If the destination IP address is on the local network, the datagram is sent directly to that host. If the destination IP address is on a remote network, the datagram is sent to the source host's default gateway.

Example 1

Page 91

Which hosts have an incorrect subnet mask?

D and E are invalid.

How will an invalid subnet mask affect these hosts?

They will not be able to communicate with any host if the second octet is different from their own.

What is the correct subnet mask?

255.0.0.0

Example 2

Page 92

What is the problem with this subnet mask?

The subnet mask indicates that both hosts are on the same network.

How will it affect communications?

Packets sent by either host to the other host will not be routed to the other network, so the two hosts will not be able to communicate with each other.

What is the correct subnet mask?

A correct subnet mask is 255.255.255.0. Other correct subnet masks include:

255.255.254.0
255.255.252.0
255.255.248.0
255.255.240.0
255.255.224.0

Practice Answers

Page 95

In this additional practice, you determine the appropriate subnet mask for a given range of IP addresses.

1. Address range of 128.71.1.1 through 128.71.254.254.

   255.255.0.0

   The only way to get a network ID of 254 is to use the entire octet, in this case the third octet.

2. Address range of 61.8.0.1 through 61.15.255.254.

   255.248.0.0

   A subnet mask of 248 indicates an incremental value of 8.

3. Address range of 172.88.32.1 through 172.88.63.254.

   255.255.224.0

   An incremental value of 32 indicates a subnet mask of 224.

4. Address range of 111.224.0.1 through 111.239.255.254.

   255.240.0.0

   A network range of 224–239 uses an incremental value of 16.

5. Address range of 3.64.0.1 through 3.127.255.254.

   255.192.0.0

   A network range of 64–127 uses an incremental value of 64 using only 2 bits.

Defining a Range of Network IDs for Two Subnets

Page 97

In this practice, you define a range of network IDs for an internetwork that consists of two subnets, using 2 bits from a class B subnet mask.

1. List all possible bit combinations for the following subnet mask, and then convert them to decimal format to determine the beginning value of each subnet.

255	**255**	**192**	**0**
1 1 1 1 1 1 1 1	1 1 1 1 1 1 1 1	**1 1** 0 0 0 0 0 0	0 0 0 0 0 0 0 0
Invalid	0 0 0 0 0 0 0 0	=	0
Subnet 1	**0 1** 0 0 0 0 0 0	=	64
Subnet 2	**1 0** 0 0 0 0 0 0	=	128
Invalid	1 1 0 0 0 0 0 0	=	192 (subnet mask)

2. List the range of host IDs for each subnet.

Subnet	Beginning value	Ending value
Subnet 1	*w.x.*64.1	*w.x.*127.254
Subnet 2	*w.x.*128.1	*w.x.*191.254

Defining a Range of Network IDs for 14 Subnets

In this practice, you define a range of network IDs for an internet that consists of 14 subnets, using 4 bits from a class B subnet mask.

1. List all possible bit combinations for the following subnet mask, and then convert them to decimal format to determine the beginning value of each subnet.

255	255	240	0
1 1 1 1 1 1 1 1	1 1 1 1 1 1 1 1	**1 1 1 1** 0 0 0 0	0 0 0 0 0 0 0 0

Subnet	Bits		Decimal
Invalid	0 0 0 0 0 0 0 0	=	0
Subnet 1	**0 0 0 1** 0 0 0 0	=	16
Subnet 2	**0 0 1 0** 0 0 0 0	=	32
Subnet 3	**0 0 1 1** 0 0 0 0	=	48
Subnet 4	**0 1 0 0** 0 0 0 0	=	64
Subnet 5	**0 1 0 1** 0 0 0 0	=	80
Subnet 6	**0 1 1 0** 0 0 0 0	=	96
Subnet 7	**0 1 1 1** 0 0 0 0	=	112
Subnet 8	**1 0 0 0** 0 0 0 0	=	128
Subnet 9	**1 0 0 1** 0 0 0 0	=	144
Subnet 10	**1 0 1 0** 0 0 0 0	=	160
Subnet 11	**1 0 1 1** 0 0 0 0	=	176
Subnet 12	**1 1 0 0** 0 0 0 0	=	192
Subnet 13	**1 1 0 1** 0 0 0 0	=	208
Subnet 14	**1 1 1 0** 0 0 0 0	=	224
Invalid	1 1 1 1 0 0 0 0	=	240 (subnet mask)

2. List the range of host IDs for each subnet.

Subnet	Beginning value	Ending value
Subnet 1	w.x.16.1	w.x.31.254
Subnet 2	w.x.32.1	w.x.47.254
Subnet 3	w.x.48.1	w.x.63.254
Subnet 4	w.x.64.1	w.x.79.254
Subnet 5	w.x.80.1	w.x.95.254
Subnet 6	w.x.96.1	w.x.111.254
Subnet 7	w.x.112.1	w.x.127.254
Subnet 8	w.x.128.1	w.x.143.254
Subnet 9	w.x.144.1	w.x.159.254
Subnet 10	w.x.160.1	w.x.175.254
Subnet 11	w.x.176.1	w.x.191.254
Subnet 12	w.x.192.1	w.x.207.254
Subnet 13	w.x.208.1	w.x.223.254
Subnet 14	w.x.224.1	w.x.239.254

Defining a Range of Network IDs Using a Shortcut

In this practice, you use a shortcut to define a range of network IDs for 14 subnets. Compare the results to the results in the preceding practice. The two should match. The first step has been done for you.

1. List the number of bits (in high order) that will be used for the subnet mask.

255	255	240	0
1 1 1 1 1 1 1 1	1 1 1 1 1 1 1 1	1 1 1 1 0 0 0 0	0 0 0 0 0 0 0 0

2. Convert the bit with the lowest value to decimal format.

   16.

3. Convert the number of bits to decimal format (in low order), and then subtract 1 to determine the number of possible subnets.

   0 0 0 0 1 1 1 1 = 15 (8+4+2+1)

   15–1=14 (valid subnets)

4. Starting with 0, increment by the value calculated in step 2 the same number of times as the possible bit combinations calculated in step 3.

   The results should match the combinations in the preceding practice.

Practice Answers

Page 101

In this additional practice, you define a range of host IDs for each of the following subnets.

1. Network ID of 75.0.0.0, subnet mask of 255.255.0.0, and 2 subnets.

   Network A: 75.x.0.1 – 75.x.255.254

   Network B: 75.y.0.1 – 75.y.255.254

   (Where x and y are any numbers from 1 through 254, as long as they are unique to each network.)

2. Network ID of 150.17.0.0, subnet mask of 255.255.255.0, and 4 subnets.

   Network A: 150.17.w.1 – 150.17.w.254

   Network B: 150 17.x.1 – 150.17.x.254

   Network C: 150.17.y.1 – 150.17.y.254

   Network D: 150.17.z.1 – 150.17.z.254

   (Where w, x, y, and z are any numbers 1 though 254, as long as they are unique to each of the four networks.)

3. Network IDs of 107.16.0.0 and 107.32.0.0, subnet mask of 255.240.0.0, and 2 subnets.

   Network A: 107.16.0.1 – 107.31.255.254

   Network B: 107.32.0.1 – 107.47.255.254

   A subnet mask of 240 allows for a maximum of 14 subnets; each network ID is incremented by a value of 16.

4. Network IDs of 190.1.16.0, 190.1.32.0, 190.1.48.0, and 190.1.64.0, subnet mask of 255.255.248.0, and 4 subnets.

   Network A: 190.1.16.1 – 190.1.23.254

   Network B: 190.1.32.1 – 190.1.39.254

   Network C: 190.1.48.1 – 190.1.55.254

   Network D: 190.1.64.1 – 190.1.71.254

   A subnet mask of 248 allows for a maximum of 30 subnets; each network ID is incremented by a value of 8.

5. Network IDs of 154.233.32.0, 154.233.96.0, and 154.233.160.0, subnet mask of 255.255.224.0, and 3 subnets.

   Network A: 154.233.32.1 – 154.233.63.254

   Network B: 154.233.96.1 – 154.233.127.254

   Network C: 154.233.160.1 – 154.233.191.254

   A subnet mask of 224 allows for a maximum of 6 subnets; each network ID is incremented by a value of 32.

Review Answers

Page 106

1. What is the purpose of a subnet mask?

   To mask a portion of the IP address so IP can distinguish the network ID from the host ID.

2. What requires a subnet mask?

   Each host on a TCP/IP network requires a subnet mask.

3. When is a default subnet mask used?

   A default subnet mask is used when a TCP/IP host is not part of a subnetwork.

4. When is it necessary to define a custom subnet mask?

   When you divide your network into subnets.

Practices Answers

Scenario 1

Page 107

You have been assigned one class B address of 131.107.0.0 by the InterNIC. Your intranet currently has 5 subnets. Each subnet has approximately 300 hosts. Within the next year the number of subnets will triple. The number of hosts on three of the subnets could increase to as many as 1,000.

1. How many bits did you use for the subnet mask?
2. How much growth did you allow for additional subnets?
3. How much growth did you allow for additional hosts?

Using 5 bits for the subnet mask would allow for 30 subnets and 2,046 hosts per subnet.

Using 6 bits for the subnet mask would allow for 62 subnets and 1,022 hosts per subnet.

Scenario 2

Page 107

You have been assigned one class A address of 124.0.0.0 by the InterNIC. Your private internet currently has 5 subnets. Each subnet has approximately 500,000 hosts. In the near future, you would like to divide the 5 subnets into 25 smaller, more manageable subnets. The number of hosts on the 25 new subnets could eventually increase to 300,000.

1. How many bits did you use for the subnet mask?
2. How much growth did you allow for additional subnets?
3. How much growth did you allow for additional hosts?

Using 5 bits for the subnet mask would allow for 30 subnets and 524,286 hosts per subnet.

Scenario 3

Page 108

You have 5 subnets with approximately 300 hosts on each subnet. Within the next 6 months, the number of subnets could increase to more than 100. The number of hosts on each subnet will probably never be more than 2,000. You do not have any plans to connect to the worldwide public Internet.

1. Which class of address did you use?
2. How many bits did you use for the subnet mask?
3. How much growth did you allow for additional subnets?
4. How much growth did you allow for additional hosts?

In this scenario, subnet addressing is not necessary. You could use a different class A or class B IP address for each network. A class C IP address could not be used because it would only allow 254 hosts per network.

Scenario 4

Page 108

An Internet service provider has just been assigned the block of 2,048 class C network numbers beginning with 192.24.0.0 and ending with 192.31.255.0.

1. What IP address would begin a "supernetted" route to this block of numbers?
   192.24.0.0

2. What net mask would be used to supernet this block of numbers?
   255.248.0.0

Customers of this Internet service provider have the following requirements:

- Customer 1 will not have more than 2,023 hosts.
- Customer 2 will not have more than 4,047 hosts.
- Customer 3 will not have more than 1,011 hosts.
- Customer 4 will not have more than 500 hosts.

Assign the missing IP and subnet mask values for each customer.

1. Customer 1
   Beginning IP address   192.24.0.1
   Ending IP address   192.24.7.8
   Subnet mask   **255.255.248.0**

2. Customer 2
   Beginning IP address   **192.24.16.1**
   Ending IP address   192.24.31.254
   Subnet mask   255.255.240.0

3. Customer 3
   Beginning IP address   192.24.8.1
   Ending IP address   **192.24.11.254**
   Subnet mask   255.255.252.0

4. Customer 4
   Beginning IP address   192.24.14.1
   Ending IP address   192.24.15.254
   Subnet mask   **255.255.254.0**

Chapter 6: Implementing IP Routing

Practice Answers

▶ **To view the routing table**

What address, other than your IP address and the loopback address, is listed under **Gateway Address**? If you are working with a stand-alone machine, the gateway address will not appear.

The address for the default gateway with a network address of 0.0.0.0.

Page 119

▶ **To view the routing table**

Is the default gateway address listed under **Gateway Address**?

No.

Page 119

▶ **To attempt network communication**

- Ping the IP address of a your second computer or a computer on your local network.

Was the ping successful?

Yes.

Without a gateway address in the routing table, would you be able to ping the IP address of a remote host?

No. You would receive an error indicating the destination host is unreachable.

Page 120

▶ **To add a route entry**

3. If you were to ping a host on another network, would the ping be successful? Why or why not?

No, there is no route listed to the other network, and no default gateway configured.

Review Answers

Page 128

1. How is IP routing enabled?

   By adding multiple network adapter cards or configuring multiple IP addresses to a computer, and selecting the Enable IP Forwarding check box.

2. Is a routing table required on a multihomed computer connecting a two-subnet internet? Why or why not?

   No, because the computer already has an interface to both subnets.

3. When is it necessary to build a static routing table?

   When a multihomed computer is not configured with RIP and does not have an interface to a subnet.

Questions and Answers 375

4. What information is required in a routing table?

   Destination network address, subnet mask used with the address, and the address of the router used to reach the destination network. Names can be used in the route table if appropriate entries are in the networks and hosts files.

5. Why is RIP typically not used in a large internetwork?

   Because it creates too much broadcast traffic. It can take a long time for RIP information to propagate among all routers.

Chapter 7: The Dynamic Host Configuration Protocol

Practice Answers

▶ To determine the network adapter card address

Page 144

1. At a command prompt, type **ipconfig /all** and then press ENTER.

   There are at least two other ways to check the physical address of your network adapter card. What are they?

   Go to a command prompt and type net config server

   –Or–

   Click the Start button, point to Programs, point to Administration Tools, and then click Windows NT Diagnostics. Click the Network tab, and then click Transports.

▶ To create a DHCP scope

Page 146

2. Double-click the **Services** icon. What are the names of the DHCP services?

   Microsoft DHCP Server and DHCP Client.

▶ To verify the DHCP-assigned TCP/IP information

Page 153

2. What IP address was assigned to the DHCP client computer by the DHCP server?

   The reserved client address.

3. What is the address of the default gateway?

   131.107.2.1 (as assigned by DHCP).

▶ **To renew a DHCP lease**

Page 154

2. When does the lease expire?

   The answer will vary, but it should be approximately 24 hours from the current time.

5. When does the lease expire?

   The answer will vary, but it should be approximately 24 hours from the current time.

Review Answers

Page 162

1. What are the four steps in the DHCP lease process?

   A DHCP-enabled client broadcasts a request (DHCPDISCOVER) to lease an IP address.

   All DHCP servers respond with an offer (DHCPOFFER).

   The DHCP-enabled client selects an offer (DHCPREQUEST) from the first DHCP server.

   The DHCP server responds with an acknowledgment (DHCPACK) and leases the IP address to the client.

2. At what lease expiration points do DHCP clients attempt to renew their lease?

   Initially, at 50 percent of its lease life with the DHCP server that leased the address, and then at 87.5 percent of its lease life expired with any DHCP server.

3. What must be configured on the DHCP server for a DHCP client to receive a lease?

   A DHCP server must be configured with a scope of available IP addresses and subnet mask.

4. In what situations is it necessary to have more than one DHCP server on an internetwork?

   When all routers do not support RFC 1542 (BOOTP relay agent).

5. How are DHCP servers configured to provide backup for each other?

   Each server is configured with a scope for the local subnet with 75 percent of the available addresses, and a scope for the remote subnet with 25 percent of its available addresses.

6. In what situations is it necessary to reserve an IP address for a client?

   When there are servers on a network that contain clients that are not WINS-enabled. Clients that are not WINS-enabled must use LMHOSTS as a method of resolving NetBIOS computer names of hosts on remote networks. If the IP address of the server changes because it not reserved, name resolution using LMHOSTS will fail.

Chapter 8: NetBIOS Over TCP/IP

Practice Answers

▶ **To configure LMHOSTS for remote computer names**

Page 182

8. In the **Path** box, type **\\Server2** and then click **OK**.

   What was the response?

   A list of shared resources for \\Server2 appears.

Practice Scenario

Page 183

Add the appropriate entries to the following LMHOSTS files so that hosts on both networks can communicate with each other.

LMHOSTS File for Hosts on Network A

IP address	Name
131.107.24.27	LMU
131.107.24.28	Workstation1
131.107.24.29	LMserver

LMHOSTS File for Hosts on Network B

IP address	Name
131.107.8.28	Workgroup1
131.107.8.29	Workgroup2

Review Answers

Page 184

1. What methods are used to resolve NetBIOS names?

   Local broadcast, LMHOSTS file, NetBIOS name server, such as WINS, HOSTS file, and a DNS.

2. What is the function of the LMHOSTS file?

   To resolve NetBIOS names of remote hosts.

Chapter 9: Windows Internet Name Service (WINS)

Practice Answers

▶ **To use WINS for name resolution**

Page 206

3. Start Windows NT Explorer and attempt to browse your other computer. Was browsing successful?

   Yes, browsing should be successful for local hosts.

   If you were to browse a remote host computer would you be successful?

   No, browsing would not be successful for remote hosts.

▶ **To open the WINS database and view IP address mappings**

Page 216

6. What NetBIOS names have been registered at the WINS server by the client?

   Any NetBIOS names registered by your WINS server, the user name, if unique, and WORKGROUP (possibly multiple times).

7. How long will it be before the names expire?

   At least 6 days.

8. Are there any mappings for remote hosts?

   No.

Review Answers

Page 222

1. What are two benefits of WINS?

   Automatic name registration and resolution of NetBIOS names.

   Provides internetwork and interdomain browsing.

   Eliminates the need for local LMHOSTS file.

2. What two methods can be used to enable WINS on a client computer?

   Manually and automatically with DHCP.

3. How many WINS servers are required in an internet of 12 subnets?

   Only one is required. It is recommended to have multiple servers for backup purposes.

4. What methods can non-WINS clients use to resolve NetBIOS names?

   NetBIOS name cache, broadcasts, local LMHOSTS file, central LMHOSTS file(s), local HOSTS file, DNS, and a WINS proxy agent.

5. When should you use a WINS proxy agent?

   When subnets include non-WINS clients. The WINS proxy agent forwards broadcasts for name registration and name resolution to the WINS server.

6. After a default installation of WINS, how often is the WINS database backed up?

   Never, you have to set the backup directory first before it will start backing up automatically every 24 hours.

7. What types of names are stored in the WINS database?

   NetBIOS unique and group names.

8. How would WINS replication be configured in an environment with a slow WAN link with limited bandwidth?

   Configure the replication to occur at off-peak intervals to make best use of the link bandwidth.

9. How would WINS replication be configured in a LAN environment without network traffic problems?

   Configure the replication to occur after a few database changes to keep the servers very synchronized.

10. When does WINS use multicasting?

    To announce itself to other WINS servers and possibly auto configure as a replication partner.

Chapter 10: IP Internetwork Browsing and Domain Functions

Practice Answers

Page 238

1. Which computers require an LMHOSTS file configured to support internetwork browsing? Which computers should be configured in the LMHOSTS file?

   Computer C requires an LMHOSTS file configured with the IP address and NetBIOS name of computers G and H.

   Computer G requires an LMHOSTS file configured with the IP address and NetBIOS name of computers C and H.

   Computer H requires an LMHOSTS file configured with the IP address and NetBIOS name of computers C and G.

2. Which computers require an LMHOSTS file to support logon validation? Which computers should be configured in the LMHOSTS file?

   No computers require an LMHOSTS file because each subnet has a domain controller. If the local domain controller becomes unavailable, the following computers require an LMHOSTS file.

   Computers A and B require an LMHOSTS file configured with the IP address and NetBIOS name of computers G and H.

   Computers D, E, and F require an LMHOSTS file configured with the IP address and NetBIOS name of computers C and H.

   Computer I requires an LMHOSTS file configured with the IP address and NetBIOS name of computers C and G.

3. Which computers require an LMHOSTS file configured to support domain account synchronization? Which computers should be configured in the LMHOSTS file?

   Computer C requires an LMHOSTS file configured with the IP address and NetBIOS name of computers G and H.

   Computer G requires an LMHOSTS file configured with the IP address and NetBIOS name of computers C and H.

   Computer H requires an LMHOSTS file configured with the IP address and NetBIOS name of computers C and G.

4. If a WINS server was installed on Subnet-Y, and all computers were configured to use WINS, which computers would require an LMHOSTS file?

   None.

Questions and Answers 381

Review Answers

Page 240

1. Why are there problems with browsing in an IP internetwork?

   IP routers do not by default propagate domain or workgroup and host announcement packets.

2. How does a master browser on a subnet resolve the IP address of its domain master browser for a domain that spans an internetwork?

   WINS clients query for the NetBIOS name. Non-WINS clients look for entries in the LMHOSTS file with the #DOM tag for their domain.

3. How does WINS aid in the collection of domains or workgroups?

   Domain master browsers query WINS for a list of names to complete its list of domains or workgroups.

4. What is required on non-WINS domain controllers to ensure that account synchronization can be accomplished when the domain spans IP internetworks?

   Each domain controller requires LMHOSTS entries for each of the other domain controllers.

Chapter 11: Host Name Resolution

Practice Answers

▶ **To ping local host names**

Page 250

1. Type **ping Server1** (where *Server1* is the name of your computer) and then press ENTER.

   What was the response?

   Four successful "Reply from IP address" messages.

2. Type **ping Server2** (where *Server2* is your second computer) and then press ENTER.

   What was the response?

   Four successful "Reply from IP address" messages.

▶ **To attempt to ping a local computer name**

Page 250

- Type **ping computertwo** and then press ENTER.

  What was the response?

  Bad IP address computertwo.

▶ **To use HOSTS for name resolution**

- Type **ping computertwo** and then press ENTER.

    What was the response?

    Four successful "Reply from IP address" messages.

Review Answers

1. What is a host name?

    An alias assigned to a TCP/IP host for the purpose of simplifying access to the host.

2. What is the purpose of a host name?

    To simplify how a host is referenced. Host names are used with PING and other TCP/IP utilities.

3. What does a HOSTS file entry consist of?

    The host name or names and the corresponding IP address.

4. During resolution, what occurs first, IP address resolution or host name resolution?

    Host name resolution.

Chapter 12: Domain Name System (DNS)

Practice Answers

Scenario 1

1. How many DNS domains will you need to configure?

    One (or zero if they have an ISP to manage the name server).

2. How many subdomains will you need to configure?

    Zero.

3. How many zones will you need to configure?

    One (or zero if they have an ISP to manage the name server).

4. How many primary name servers will you need to configure?

    One (or zero if they have an ISP to manage the name server).

5. How many secondary name servers will you need to configure?

    One (or zero if they have an ISP to manage the name server).

6. How many DNS cache-only servers will you need to configure?

    Zero.

Scenario 2

Page 274

1. How many DNS domains will you need to configure?

   One.

2. How many subdomains will you need to configure?

   Three.

3. How many zones will you need to configure?

   Four.

4. How many primary name servers will you need to configure?

   Four.

5. How many secondary name servers will you need to configure?

   Four.

6. How many DNS cache-only servers will you need to configure?

   Ten.

7. Use the following mileage chart to design a zone/branch office configuration based on the geographical proximity between each primary site and branch office. Branch offices should be in the same zone as the nearest primary site.

   Zones for each branch office (based on geographical proximity):

Portland, OR	**Boston**	**Chicago**	**Atlanta**
Los Angeles	Montreal	Denver	Dallas
Salt Lake City	Washington, D.C.	Kansas City	Miami
San Francisco			New Orleans

Scenario 3

Page 276

1. How many DNS domains will you need to configure?

   Zero (the domain for this company is in Geneva, Switzerland).

2. How many subdomains will you need to configure?

   11.

3. How many zones will you need to configure?

   11.

4. How many primary name servers will you need to configure?

   11.

5. How many secondary name servers will you need to configure?

   11.

6. How many DNS cache-only servers will you need to be configure?

   Three or more.

Review Answers

Page 278

1. Name the three components of the Domain Name System.

   Domain name space, name servers, and resolvers.

2. Describe the difference between primary, secondary, and master name servers.

   A primary name server has zone information in locally maintained zone files. A secondary name server downloads zone information. A master name server is the source of the downloads for a secondary name server (which could be a primary or secondary name server).

3. List three reasons to have a secondary name server.

   (1) They operate as a redundant name server (you should have at least one redundant name server for each zone). (2) If you have clients in remote locations, you should have a secondary name server to avoid communicating across slow links. (3) A secondary name server reduces the load on the primary name server.

4. Describe the difference between a domain and a zone.

   A domain is a branch of the DNS name space. A zone is a portion of a domain that exists as a separate file on the disk storing resource records.

5. Describe the difference between recursive and iterative queries.

   In a recursive query, the client instructs the DNS server to respond with either the requested information or an error that the information was not found. In an iterative query, the DNS server responds with the best answer it has, typically a referral to another name server that can help resolve the request.

6. List the files required for a Windows NT DNS implementation.

   Database file, cache file, and reverse lookup file.

7. Describe the purpose of the boot file.

   The boot file is used in the BIND implementation to start up and configure the DNS server.

Chapter 13: Implementing DNS

Practice Answers

▶ To view the default DNS server installation

Page 287

9. Double-click each of the reverse lookup zones. What type of records does each of them contain?

   NS records and SOA records.

▶ To add a zone to a server

Page 291

6. Click each of the resource records. What type of records does each of them contain?

   NS records and SOA records.

▶ To configure a reverse lookup zone for the primary DNS server

Page 293

1. Determine the reverse lookup zone name for your primary DNS server by using one of these three methods:

   - For class A addresses, use your first octet and append to it **.in-addr.arpa** (for example: A class A IP address of 29.122.15.88 would have a reverse lookup zone name of **29.in-addr.arpa**).

   - For class B addresses, use your first two octets in reverse order and append to them **.in-addr.arpa** (for example: A class B IP address of 129.122.15.88 would have a reverse lookup zone name of **122.129.in-addr.arpa**).

   - For class C addresses, use your first three octets in reverse order and append to them **.in-addr.arpa** (for example: A class C IP address of 229.122.15.88 would have a reverse lookup zone name of **15.122.129.in-addr.arpa**).

   What is your reverse lookup zone name?

   107.131.in-addr.arpa

Review Answers

Page 301

1. What is the purpose of entering a host name and domain name in the DNS configuration dialog box of the TCP/IP protocol *before* installing the Microsoft DNS Server service?

   The DNS Server uses the host name and domain name to create default SOA, A, and NS records.

2. What is the function of the NSLOOKUP utility?

   NSLOOKUP acts as a command line or interactive resolver that is used to troubleshoot DNS servers.

3. Describe the WINS lookup process.

   A Microsoft DNS Server gets a DNS query that fails DNS resolution. The host name is converted to a NetBIOS name and sent to a configured WINS server for resolution. The results are forwarded back to the original client.

4. Describe a situation where WINS lookup is useful.

   When non-Microsoft TCP/IP clients need resolution to a WINS-registering, DHCP resource such as Internet Information Server.

Chapter 14: Connectivity in Heterogeneous Environments

Practice Answers

▶ **To start an FTP session**

Page 313

What TCP port does FTP use on the server side?

TCP port 21.

Review Answers

Page 323

1. List the requirements for a computer running Windows NT to connect to a foreign host.

   TCP/IP transport and appropriate TCP/IP utilities and services.

2. List the requirements for a computer running Windows NT to connect to and interoperate with an RFC-compliant NetBIOS-based host, such as LAN Manager for UNIX.

   Common transport protocol (TCP/IP or NetBEUI) SMB server.

   Common scope ID.

3. List two differences between accessing resources on a TCP/IP-based host using Windows NT commands versus TCP/IP utilities.

   Windows NT: Use NetBIOS names. Use standard commands.

   TCP/IP utilities: Use commands specific to utilities. IP address or host name can be used.

4. Which TCP/IP utilities are used to copy files?

   FTP, TFTP, and RCP.

5. Which TCP/IP utilities enable you to run commands on a foreign host?
   Telnet, RSH, and REXEC.

6. What functions does the TCP/IP network printing support provide?
   Support for a network interface printer using TCP/IP.

   Access to printers attached to a UNIX host.

Chapter 15: Implementing the Microsoft SNMP Services

Practice Answers

▶ **To view the new Performance Monitor objects**

Page 342

4. List the TCP/IP-related objects.
   ICMP, IP, TCP, UDP, and Network Interface.

▶ **To monitor IP datagrams with Performance Monitor**

Page 343

12. Return to Performance Monitor, and view the activity that resulted from the ping.

    What activity was recorded as a result of using ping?
    ICMP messages and IP datagrams.

    How many messages per second were recorded for ICMP?
    2 (1.997)

    How many IP datagrams were sent per second?
    1 (0.999)

    Why were there twice as many ICMP messages as there were IP datagrams sent?
    Each IP datagram sent results in 2 ICMP messages—one echo request and one echo reply.

▶ **To view SNMP data**

Page 344

3. Use Snmputil.exe to determine SNMP objects related to DHCP. Type the following command on one line and then press ENTER:

   snmputil getnext 131.107.2.*host_id*
   public .1.3.6.1.4.1.311.1.3.2.1.1.1

   How many IP addresses have been leased?
   There should be one address leased.

4. Use Snmputil.exe on the WINS object .1.3.6.1.4.1.311.1.2.1.17. Type:

   snmputil getnext 131.107.2.*host_id*
   public .1.3.6.1.4.1.311.1.2.1.17

   How many successful queries have been processed by the WINS server?

   The answers will vary.

5. Use Snmputil.exe on the WINS object **.1.3.6.1.4.1.311.1.2.1.18**. Type:

   snmputil getnext 131.107.2.*host_id*
   public .1.3.6.1.4.1.311.1.2.1.18

   How many unsuccessful queries have been processed by the WINS server?

   The answers will vary.

7. Use Snmputil.exe on the LAN Manager Object .1.3.6.1.4.1.77.1.1.2. Type:

   snmputil getnext 131.107.2.*host_id* **public .1.3.6.1.4.1.77.1.1.2**

   What is the version of Windows NT Server running on the computer?

   Version 4.0; the first string returned a 4, and the second a 0.

Review Answers

Page 346

1. What are the four SNMP operations?

   get, get-next, set, and trap.

2. Which SNMP operations are initiated by a management system? Which SNMP operations are initiated by an agent?

   Management systems initiate get, get-next, and set operations.

   Agents initiate trap operations.

3. Which MIBs are supported by Windows NT 4.0?

   Internet MIB II, LAN Manager MIB II, Microsoft DHCP MIB, and Microsoft WINS MIB.

4. Which host name resolution methods does the SNMP employ?

   A HOSTS file, DNS, NetBIOS name server, broadcast, or the LMHOSTS file.

5. What is the purpose of a community name?

   To provide primitive security and context checking for agents that send traps and for management systems that receive traps.

Chapter 16: Troubleshooting Microsoft TCP/IP

Review Answers

Page 353

1. What are three Windows NT utilities useful in diagnosing TCP/IP-related problems?

   PING, NBTSTAT, ARP, and NETSTAT.

2. Which TCP/IP utility is used to verify communications from the Network Interface layer up to the Internet layer?

   PING.

3. What are the two procedures for troubleshooting an IP network?

   PING successfully and then establish a session.

Index

A

addresses *See* Address Resolution Protocol (ARP); IP addresses
Address Resolution Protocol (ARP)
    ARP cache 32–33, 38, 39
    capturing packets 34–37
    defined 7, 26, 29
    and frames 35–37
    and IP addresses 30–32
    overview 29
    packet structure 34
    as troubleshooting tool 348
agents *See* relay agents; SNMP agent
ANDing 72–73
Application layer 27, 351
ArcNet 27
ARP *See* Address Resolution Protocol (ARP)
ARPANET 2, 254, 255
ARPCacheLife parameter 33
ATECs xxiii
Authorized Technical Education Centers (ATECs) xxiii

B

backing up databases
    DHCP 159
    WINS 219
backup browser, defined 226
binary notation, converting IP addresses to decimal notation 57–58, 59
B-node 176, 177, 179 *See also* LMHOSTS file
boot file, DNS 267
BOOTP protocol
    vs. DHCP 130
    and Windows NT 131
browse list
    collection process 227
    defined 226
    distribution process 228
    servicing requests 228–29
browsing *See also* Computer Browser; master browser
    internetwork 230–34
    web browsers 305, 314

C

cache
    ARP cache 32–33, 38, 39
    and DNS name servers 260, 263
    NetBIOS name cache 171, 172
Cache.dns file 266
Canonical Name (CNAME) record 265
capturing
    ARP packets 34–37
    network traffic 20–21
certification xxi–xxiii
Class A IP addresses 61
Class B IP addresses 62
Class C IP addresses 62
Class D IP addresses 62
Class E IP addresses 63
classes, IP addresses 60–63
client reservations
    adding 151–52
    defined 150
    when to use 150
CNAME record 265
communities, SNMP 333–34
compacting databases
    DHCP 160–61
    WINS 220
Computer Browser
    collection process 227
    distribution process 228
    and IP internetworks 230–34
    and LMHOSTS file 232–40
    overview 226–29
    servicing client requests 228–29
    types of browsers 226
    and WINS 231–32
copying files 6, 305, 309
course *See* training course

D

DARPA 2
database, DHCP
    backing up and restoring 159
    compacting 160–61
    list of files 160
database, DNS 264–65

database, WINS
    backing up and restoring 219–20
    compacting 220
    configuring server 216–18
    list of files 220
    maintaining 214–21
    replicating between servers 208–13
    viewing contents 215–16
datagrams *See* User Datagram Protocol (UDP)
data transfer utilities
    defined 6
    FTP (File Transfer Protocol) 6, 305, 309–13
    RCP (Remote Copy Protocol) 6, 305, 309
    TFTP (Trivial File Transfer Protocol) 6, 305, 310
    web browsers 305, 314
dead gateways 113
decimal notation, converting IP addresses to 57–58, 59
default gateway
    defined 11
    and dynamic IP routing 121–22
    example 11
    and Microsoft TCP/IP installation 13
    and remote IP addresses 31–32
    removing address 119
    restoring address 120
    and routing 113
    and static IP routers 116
Defense Advanced Research Projects Agency (DARPA) 2
DHCP (Dynamic Host Configuration Protocol)
    configuring for WINS 203–7
    configuring scope 145–50
    enabling relay agents 155–58
    how it works 132–36
    implementing 140–54
    installing servers 143–45, 153
    lease process 132–36
    managing database 159–61
    vs. manual configuration of TCP/IP 12–13, 131
    and MIB 330
    multiple servers 152
    overview 130–39
    system requirements 142–43
Dhcp.mdb file 160
Dhcpmib.dll file 330
Dhcp.tmp file 160
diagnostics utilities *See also* troubleshooting
    Address Resolution Protocol (ARP) 29–39
    defined 7
    FINGER utility 7
    HOSTNAME utility 7, 243
    IPCONFIG utility 7, 15, 16–17, 138–39, 349
    NBTSTAT utility 7, 178, 349
    NETSTAT utility 7, 348
    NSLOOKUP utility 7, 283–85, 349

diagnostics utilities *See also* troubleshooting *(continued)*
    Packet InterNet Groper (PING) utility 7, 15, 16–17, 348, 350
    ROUTE utility 7, 349
    TRACERT utility 7, 126–27, 349
DNS Manager
    adding domains and zones 288–89
    configuring DNS server 286–88
    enabling WINS Lookup 298
DNS servers *See* Domain Name System (DNS); Microsoft DNS Server
domain master browser defined 226
domain name space 257–59
Domain Name System (DNS)
    background 254–55
    configuration files 264–68
    configuring DNS 269–77
    how it works 255–56
    implementing Microsoft DNS Server 282–300
    for large networks 275–77
    for medium-size networks 272–75
    Microsoft DNS Server 282–300
    name resolution 261–63
    and NetBIOS names 172, 176
    registering DNS servers 270
    role of domains 257–58
    role of host names 258
    role of name servers 256, 259–60
    role of resolvers 256
    role of zones of authority 258–59
    for small networks 271–72
    and UNIX 245–46
    and Windows NT 245–46, 247, 264–68
domains
    defined 257
    root-level 257
    second-level 258
    top-level 257, 258
dotted decimal notation 57
downloading *See* data transfer utilities
Dynamic Host Configuration Protocol *See* DHCP (Dynamic Host Configuration Protocol)
dynamic IP routing
    implementing Windows NT router 126–27
    integrating with static IP routing 124–25
    overview 121–22
    and RIP 122–24
    vs. static IP routing 114

E

Ethernet 27
Event log 349

Index   393

F

Fiber Distributed Data Interface (FDDI) 27
fields, header 42, 44–45, 50
File Transfer Protocol *See* FTP (File Transfer Protocol)
FINGER utility 7
four-layer model 26–27
frames
    capturing and viewing data 21, 34–37
    defined 26
    and Network Interface Layer 26, 27
    and Network Monitor 21, 34–37
FTP (File Transfer Protocol)
    defined 6, 305, 309
    installing 311–12
    list of common commands 310
    starting session 313
    syntax 309
    using to transfer files 312–13

G

gateways *See also* routers
    dead 113
    default (*see* default gateway)
    defined 112
    and remote IP addresses 31–32
    and static routing table entries 117

H

handshakes, three-way 48
hardware, course requirements xvi
hardware addresses *See* Address Resolution Protocol (ARP)
header fields 42, 44–45, 50
H-node 176
hops 113, 122
Host (A) record 265
host ID
    assigning IP addresses 66, 67, 69–70
    defined 56
    vs. network ID 56–57
    and subnetting 83, 96–102
host names
    overview 243
    relationship to domains 258
    resolving 243–48
HOSTNAME utility 7, 243
hosts *See also* host ID; host names
    monitoring using SNMP 326–29
    remote 304–8
HOSTS file
    adding entries 251
    defined 10, 244, 251

HOSTS file *(continued)*
    example 249
    and NetBIOS names 172, 175
    resolving host names 244–45, 246, 249–51
HTTP (Hypertext Transfer Protocol) 314

I

IAB (Internet Architecture Board) 3
IANA (Internet Assigned Numbers Authority) 3
ICMP (Internet Control Message Protocol) 26, 40–41
IETF (Internet Engineering Task Force) 3
IGMP (Internet Group Management Protocol) 26, 41
installing
    DHCP servers 143–45, 153
    FTP service 311–12
    Internet Explorer xviii
    Microsoft DNS Server 282–83
    Microsoft Network Monitor 18–19
    Microsoft TCP/IP 12–14
    SNMP service 336–37
    Windows NT Service Pack xviii–xix
    WINS service 198
Internet, TCP/IP history 2
Internet Architecture Board (IAB) 3
Internet Assigned Numbers Authority (IANA) 3
Internet Control Message Protocol (ICMP) 26, 40–41
Internet Engineering Task Force (IETF) 3
Internet Explorer, installing xviii
Internet Group Management Protocol (IGMP) 26, 41
Internet layer 26, 350–51
Internet MIB II 330
Internet Protocol (IP) *See also* IP addresses; IP routing
    defined 26, 42
    list of header fields 42, 44–45
    overview 42–43
    packet structure 44–45
    and routers 43
    versions of 75–76
Internet protocols *See* Address Resolution Protocol (ARP); Internet Control Message Protocol (ICMP); Internet Group Management Protocol (IGMP); Internet Protocol (IP)
Internet Research Task Force (IRTF) 3
Internet service providers (ISPs) 269
Internet Society (ISOC) 3
inverse queries 262–63
IP *See* Internet Protocol (IP); IP addresses
IP addresses
    and Address Resolution Protocol (ARP) 30
    assigning, overview 64
    assigning host IDs 66, 67, 69–70
    assigning network IDs 64–65, 67, 68–69
    binary vs. decimal notation 57–58
    classes 60–63

IP addresses (continued)
    client reservations 150–52
    defined 10, 56
    and DHCP 130–39
    example 10
    IPv6 75–76
    leasing 133–37
    local vs. remote 31–32, 43, 72–73
    and Microsoft TCP/IP installation 13, 14
    network ID vs. host ID 56–57
    overview 56–57
    resolving 30–32
    and subnet masks 71–74
IPCONFIG utility
    and lease activities 139
    testing TCP/IP configuration 15, 16–17, 138
    as troubleshooting tool 7, 349
IP routing See also Routing Information Protocol (RIP)
    implementing Windows NT router 126–27
    overview 112–14
    static vs. dynamic 114, 124–25
IPv4 75
IPv6 75–76
IRTF (Internet Research Task Force) 3
ISOC (Internet Society) 3
ISPs (Internet service providers) 269
iterative queries 261–62

J

Jet.log file 160
Jetpack utility 160

L

LAN Manager MIB II 330
LANs, and TCP/IP 27
layers
    Application layer 27, 351
    Internet layer 26, 350–51
    Network Interface layer 26, 350–51
    Transport layer 27
leases
    acknowledging 135–36
    and client reservations 150, 151–52
    offering 133–34
    releasing 139
    renewing 136–37, 154, 189, 192
    requesting 133
    selecting offers 134
    updating 139
    use of IPCONFIG utility 139
Line Printer Daemon (LPD) 7, 305, 316, 317
Line Printer Queue (LPQ) utility 7, 305, 316, 318, 322

Line Printer Remote (LPR) utility 7, 305, 316, 317–18, 322
LMHOSTS file
    and browsing 232–40
    defined 10, 179, 244
    list of predefined keywords 180
    and NetBIOS names 172, 175, 177, 178, 179–83
    resolving host names 244, 246, 248
    troubleshooting NetBIOS name resolution problems 181
local area networks, and TCP/IP 27
lookup
    enabling WINS lookup 298–300
    NSLOOKUP utility 7, 283–85, 349
    reverse 266, 292–95, 298
LPDSVC See TCP/IP Print Server
LPD utility 7, 305, 316, 317
LPQ utility 7, 305, 316, 318, 322
LPR utility 7, 305, 316, 317–18, 322

M

Management Information Bases (MIBs)
    defined 330
    hierarchical name tree 331–32
    list of MIBs 330–31
masking See subnet masks
master browser
    collection process 227
    defined 226
    distribution process 228
    LMHOSTS file on 233–34
    servicing requests 228–29
MCP (Microsoft Certified Professional) program xxi–xxiii
Metropolitan Area Network (MAN) 27
MIB See Management Information Bases (MIBs)
Microsoft Certified Professional (MCP) program xxi–xxiii
Microsoft DNS Server
    adding domains 289–90
    adding resource records 291–92
    adding zones 288–89, 290–91
    administering 286–95
    configuring manually 288
    configuring reverse lookup 292–95
    configuring server properties 286–88
    configuring zone properties 290
    installing 282–83
    integrating with WINS 296–300
    troubleshooting with NSLOOKUP utility 7, 283–85, 349
    viewing default installation 287–88
Microsoft Network Monitor
    analyzing network traffic 20–21
    capturing and viewing data 21, 34–37
    defined 18, 349
    installing 18–19
Microsoft Online Institute xxiii

Index

Microsoft Roadmap xxii
Microsoft SNMP service *See* SNMP (Simple Network Management Protocol)
Microsoft TCP/IP *See also* TCP/IP protocol suite; Windows NT
   configuration parameters 10–11
   installing 12–14
   lists of utilities 6–7, 305
   overview 2–3
   resolving host names 244
   testing configuration 15–17
M-node 176
multicasting 62, 63, 213
multihomed computers 114, 200
multimedia presentations 25, 49

N

name resolution files, defined 10 *See also* Domain Name System (DNS); HOSTS file; LMHOSTS file
name server (NS) record 265
name servers *See also* Domain Name System (DNS); WINS (Windows Internet Name Service)
   database file record 265
   defined 256
   secondary 259–60
   types of roles 259–60
NBFP 167
NBTSTAT utility 7, 178, 349
NCP (Network Control Protocol) 2
NDIS (Network Device Interface Specification) 27
NetBEUI 27, 167
NetBIOS *See also* NetBIOS names
   defined 27, 166
   and internetwork browsing 230–34
   overview 166–67
   troubleshooting communications 351
NetBIOS names
   discovery 169
   duplicate names 191
   list of common names 168
   and LMHOSTS file 172, 175, 177, 178, 179–83
   overview 167–68
   refreshing registration 189, 192
   registration 169, 189, 190–91
   releasing 169, 189, 193
   renewing lease 189, 192
   resolving 171–78
   segmenting with scopes 169–70
   and WINS 187–207
NetBIOS Name Server (NBNS) 171, 174, 176, 246–47
NetBT 167, 177
NETSTAT utility 7, 348
Network Control Protocol (NCP) 2

network device interface specification (NDIS) 27
network ID
   assigning IP addresses 64–65, 67, 68–69
   vs. host ID 56–57
   and Routing Information Protocol 122–24
   and static routing table entries 117
Network Interface layer 26, 350–51
Network Monitor
   analyzing network traffic 20–21
   capturing and viewing data 21, 34–37
   defined 18, 349
   installing 18–19
network protocols, viewing list 11 *See also* TCP/IP protocol suite
networks *See also* Network Monitor
   capturing network traffic 18–21
   and DNS configuration 269–77
   four-layer TCP/IP model 26–27
   heterogeneous environments 304–6
   IP addresses 56–59
   routing between 112–14
   subnetting 82–84
NETWORKS file, defined 10
nodes *See* B-node; H-node; M-node; P-node
NSLOOKUP utility 7, 283–85, 349

O

objects *See* Management Information Bases (MIBs)
Online Institute xxiii
Open Shortest Path First (OSPF) protocol 114

P

Packet InterNet Groper (PING) utility 7, 15, 16–17, 348, 350
packets
   ARP structure 34
   ICMP structure 40
   IGMP structure 41
   and Internet Protocol 42–43
   IP structure 44–45
   routing 112–14
   TCP structure 50
   UDP structure 52
packet-switched networks 27
Performance Monitor 349
PING (Packet InterNet Groper) utility
   defined 7, 348
   testing TCP/IP configuration 15, 16–17
   as troubleshooting tool 348, 350
P-node 176
Pointer (PTR) record 266
Point-to-Point Protocol (PPP) 28

ports
    port numbers 46, 47
    TCP ports 46, 47
    UDP ports 51
PPP (Point-to-Point Protocol) 28
print gateways 319
printing utilities
    Line Printer Daemon (LPD) 7, 305, 316, 317
    Line Printer Queue (LPQ) utility 7, 305, 316, 318, 322
    Line Printer Remote (LPR) utility 7, 305, 316, 317–18, 322
    overview 7, 316
Print Manager 316, 317, 318, 319, 320–22
PROTOCOL file, defined 10
protocols *See also* data transfer utilities; diagnostics utilities; TCP/IP protocol suite
    Dynamic Host Configuration Protocol (DHCP) 130–39
    Internet Control Message Protocol (ICMP) 26, 40–41
    Internet Group Management Protocol (IGMP) 26, 41
    layers in TCP/IP suite 25–28
    Open Shortest Path First (OSPF) protocol 114
    port numbers 46, 47
    Routing Information Protocol (RIP) 114, 122–24
    viewing list 11
pull partners 208, 209, 210–13
push partners 208, 209, 210–13

Q

queries, name resolution 261–63

R

RAS (Remote Access Server) 27
RCP (Remote Copy Protocol) utility 6, 305, 309
recursive queries 261
Registry Editor 349
relay agents
    configuring 155, 156–57
    defined 155
    disabling 157
Remote Access Server (RAS) 27
Remote Copy Protocol (RCP) utility 6, 305, 309
Remote Execution (REXEC) utility 6, 305, 307
remote hosts 304–8
Remote Shell (RSH) utility 6, 305, 307
Request for Comments (RFC) 4–5
reserving IP addresses 150–52
resolvers, defined 256
restoring
    default gateway address 120
    DHCP database 159
    WINS database 219–20

reverse lookup
    configuring for Microsoft DNS Server 292–95
    file overview 266
    and WINS 298
REXEC utility 6, 305, 307
RFCs 4–5
RIP (Routing Information Protocol)
    and dynamic IP routing 114, 122–24
    troubleshooting 123–24
    when to use 123
Roadmap xxii
routers *See also* Routing Information Protocol (RIP)
    configuring 116
    defined 112
    and Internet Protocol 43
    static 115–20
    static vs. dynamic 114
ROUTE utility 7, 349
routing *See* IP routing
Routing Information Protocol (RIP)
    and dynamic IP routing 114, 122–24
    troubleshooting 123–24
    when to use 123
routing tables
    adding static entries 118, 120
    building 117–20
    default entries 117
    defined 112
    and Routing Information Protocol 123–25
    and static routers 116
    viewing entries 117, 118, 119
RSH (Remote Shell) utility 6, 305, 307

S

scope ID, and NetBIOS names 169–70
scopes, subnet 141–42, 145, 146–47, 148, 149–50
Serial Line Internet Protocol (SLIP) 28
serial lines 27, 28
Service Pack, Windows NT xviii–xix
SERVICES file, defined 10
setup, course xvii–xix
Simple Network Management Protocol (SNMP) *See* SNMP (Simple Network Management Protocol)
sliding windows 49
SLIP (Serial Line Internet Protocol) 28
slow convergence problem, defined 124
SMB servers 304
SNMP agent
    configuring services 339–40
    defined 328
SNMP (Simple Network Management Protocol)
    configuring agent services 339–40
    configuring security 338–39

SNMP (Simple Network Management Protocol) *(continued)*
    defined 326, 349
    defining communities 333–34
    how it works 334–36
    identifying service errors 341–43
    installing service 336–37
    and MIBs 330–32
    overview 326–29
    SNMPUTIL utility 344–45
    viewing data 344–45
SNMPUTIL utility 344–45
sockets, overview 47 *See also* Windows Sockets
software, course requirements xvi
standards 3–5
Start of Authority (SOA) record 264–65
static IP routing
    configuring routers 116
    vs. dynamic IP routing 114
    integrating dynamic IP routing with 124–25
    overview 115
subnet masks *See also* subnets
    and ANDing 72–73
    default 71–72
    defined 11
    defining for subnetting 83, 85–92
    determining requirements 84
    example 11
    and IP addresses 71–74
    and Microsoft TCP/IP installation 13
    overview 71
    and static routing table entries 117
subnets *See also* supernetting
    benefits 83
    creating scope 141–42, 145, 146–47, 148, 149–50
    defining host ID 83, 96–102
    defining subnet ID 83, 93–95
    defining subnet mask 83, 85–92
    vs. supernetting 103–5
subnetting, defined 82
subnetworking *See* subnets
supernetting 103–5
Systek Corporation 166
System.mdb file 160

T

tables *See* routing tables
TCP *See* Transmission Control Protocol (TCP)
TCP/IP Print Server 317, 319–20
TCP/IP protocol suite *See also* Internet Protocol (IP);
   Transmission Control Protocol (TCP)
    configuring manually 131
    configuring using DHCP 131
    and heterogeneous environments 304–6

TCP/IP protocol suite *See also* Internet Protocol (IP);
   Transmission Control Protocol (TCP) *(continued)*
    history 2
    LAN and WAN support 27
    layers of 25–28
    lists of utilities 6–7, 305
    naming schemes 242
    overview 2–5
    resolving host names 243–48
    RFCs 4–5
    SNMP 326–29
    standards process 3–5
    testing configuration 15–17
    troubleshooting 248–52
    Windows NT vs. UNIX naming schemes 242
Telnet 6, 305, 307–8
TFTP (Trivial File Transfer Protocol) 6, 305, 310
Time To Live (TTL) 263, 299
Token Ring 27
TRACERT utility 7, 126–27, 349
training course *See also* Microsoft Certified Professional
   (MCP) program
    hardware requirements xvi
    multimedia presentations 25, 49
    setup xvii–xix
    software requirements xvi
Transmission Control Protocol (TCP)
    and default gateway 113
    defined 27, 46
    and IP routing 113
    list of header fields 50
    overview 46
    packet structure 50
    and ports 46
    sliding windows 49
    three-way handshake 48
Transport layer, defined 27
transport protocols *See* Transmission Control Protocol (TCP);
   User Datagram Protocol (UDP)
troubleshooting *See also* diagnostics utilities
    TCP/IP problems 348–52
    using Network Monitor 18–21, 349
TTL (Time To Live) 263, 299

U

UDP *See* User Datagram Protocol (UDP)
UNIX
    resolving host names 245–46
    TCP/IP naming schemes 242
User Datagram Protocol (UDP)
    defined 27, 51
    overview 51
    packet structure 52

User Datagram Protocol (UDP) *(continued)*
   and ports 51
   and SNMP service 329
utilities, lists of 6–7, 305 *See also* data transfer utilities;
  diagnostics utilities; printing utilities

W

WANs, and TCP/IP 13, 27
web browsers 305, 314
windows, sliding 49
Windows Internet Name Service *See* WINS (Windows
  Internet Name Service)
Windows NT
   Computer Browser service 226–34
   connecting to server from remote host 305
   diagnostic tools (*see* diagnostics utilities)
   and DNS servers 245–46, 247, 264–68
   implementing routers 126–27
   installing Microsoft TCP/IP 10–14
   installing Service Pack xviii–xix
   lists of utilities 6–7, 305
   LMHOSTS file 172, 175, 177, 178, 179–83, 230, 235–
     40, 244
   Microsoft DNS Server 282–300
   Microsoft TCP/IP overview 2–3
   name resolution 10, 243–48
   and NetBIOS names 175–78
   as print gateway 319–22
   and SLIP 28
   and static vs. dynamic routing 114
   TCP/IP naming schemes 242
   troubleshooting TCP/IP problems 348–52
Windows Sockets 3, 27, 47, 329
WINS Manager
   configuring server 216–18
   defined 214
   starting 214
   viewing database contents 215–16
WINS MIB 331
WINS (Windows Internet Name Service)
   configuring client and server 197, 198, 299–300
   configuring DHCP server 203–7
   configuring proxy agents 201–3
   configuring servers as push or pull partners 209
   configuring static IP addresses 198–200
   data record 296–97
   enabling lookup 298–300
   implementing 196–207
   installing server service 198
   integrating Microsoft DNS Server with 296–300
   and internetwork browsing 231–32
   maintaining database 214–21
   name resolution 189–95, 206

WINS (Windows Internet Name Service) *(continued)*
   and non-WINS clients 198–200
   overview 187–88
   relationship to NetBIOS 187–88
   replicating database between servers 208–13
   system requirements 196–200
World Wide Web
   browser as TCP/IP utility 305, 314
   Microsoft Online Institute xxiii

Z

Zone.dns file 264
zones of authority 258–59

The definitive resource for Microsoft Internet Information Server.

This exclusive Microsoft® resource kit was created in cooperation with the Microsoft Internet Information Server (IIS) development and support teams. That makes it comprehensive, authoritative, and indispensable for system administrators and other computer professionals who deman d the best technical information and tools for rolling out and supporting Microsoft IIS within their organizations. Plus, you get more than 40 utilities, ISAPI filters, and components on the enclosed CD-ROMs. For the top performance you want with Microsoft IIS, the essential information you need is inside this kit.

U.S.A. $49.99
U.K.   £46.99 [V.A.T. included]
Canada $71.99
ISBN 1-57231-638-1

Microsoft Press® products are available worldwide wherever quality computer books are sold. For more information, contact your book or computer retailer, software reseller, or local Microsoft Sales Office, or visit our Web site at mspress.microsoft.com. To locate your nearest source for Microsoft Press products, or to order directly, call 1-800-MSPRESS in the U.S. (in Canada, call 1-800-268-2222).

Prices and availability dates are subject to change.

Microsoft Press

This is how Microsoft Windows NT pros become incredibly resourceful.

This three-volume kit provides the valuable technical and performance information and the tools you need for handling rollout and support issues surrounding Microsoft® Windows NT® Server 4.0. You get a full 2500 pages—plus a CD-ROM—loaded with essential information not available anywhere else. For support professionals, MICROSOFT WINDOWS NT SERVER RESOURCE KIT is more than a guide. It's a natural resource.

U.S.A.   **$149.95**
U.K.   £140.99 [V.A.T. included]
Canada $199.95
ISBN 1-57231-344-7

Microsoft Press® products are available worldwide wherever quality computer books are sold. For more information, contact your book or computer retailer, software reseller, or local Microsoft Sales Office, or visit our Web site at mspress.microsoft.com. To locate your nearest source for Microsoft Press products, or to order directly, call 1-800-MSPRESS in the U.S. (in Canada, call 1-800-268-2222).

Prices and availability dates are subject to change.

Microsoft®*Press*

Create **vivid, interactive Web content** with Microsoft **Internet Explorer 4!**

Here's the indispensable volume for site builders, Webmasters, multimedia authors, and anyone else who wants to discover all the technologies that make Microsoft® Internet Explorer 4 a major breakthrough. Inside is a rich exploration of Dynamic HTML, Cascading Style Sheets, the Internet Explorer 4 object model, scripting, multimedia effects and controls, and data binding. You'll discover Dynamic HTML as a multimedia authoring tool for Web, network, or CD-ROM–based productions. And you'll work with plenty of helpful examples on the enclosed CD-ROM. In short, if you want to do great things with Dynamic HTML, you want DYNAMIC HTML IN ACTION.

U.S.A.	$39.99
U.K.	£37.49 [V.A.T. included]
Canada	$57.99
ISBN 1-57231-820-1	

Microsoft Press® products are available worldwide wherever quality computer books are sold. For more information, contact your book or computer retailer, software reseller, or local Microsoft Sales Office, or visit our Web site at mspress.microsoft.com. To locate your nearest source for Microsoft Press products, or to order directly, call 1-800-MSPRESS in the U.S. (in Canada, call 1-800-268-2222).

Prices and availability dates are subject to change.

Microsoft *Press*

Hands-on, self-paced training for supporting Internet Explorer 4!

Here's the ideal way for support professionals to prepare for success on the job *and* on the Microsoft® Certified Professional (MCP) exam. That's because this is Microsoft Official Curriculum—the only self-paced training that's adapted from the corresponding Microsoft-authorized instructor-led course. Here you'll master, at your own pace, the architecture and key features of the Microsoft Internet Explorer 4 suite of products. Through the accompanying labs, you'll gain hands-on experience installing, configuring, using, deploying, and supporting Internet Explorer 4 in a networked environment, with particular emphasis on intranet use. And as you prepare for the real world, you'll also get specific preparation for success on the MCP exam. All of which makes MICROSOFT INTERNET EXPLORER 4 TECHNICAL SUPPORT TRAINING the smart way to advance your career now and well into the future.

U.S.A. $49.99
U.K.   £46.99 [V.A.T. included]
Canada $71.99
ISBN 1-57231-828-7

Microsoft Press® products are available worldwide wherever quality computer books are sold. For more information, contact your book or computer retailer, software reseller, or local Microsoft Sales Office, or visit our Web site at mspress.microsoft.com. To locate your nearest source for Microsoft Press products, or to order directly, call 1-800-MSPRESS in the U.S. (in Canada, call 1-800-268-2222).

Prices and availability dates are subject to change.

Microsoft® Press

Microsoft® Windows NT® Technical Support

Microsoft Press

PUBLISHED BY
Microsoft Press
A Division of Microsoft Corporation
One Microsoft Way
Redmond, Washington 98052-6399

Copyright © 1998 by Microsoft Corporation

All rights reserved. No part of the contents of this book may be reproduced or transmitted in any form or by any means without the written permission of the publisher.

Library of Congress Cataloging-in-Publication Data
Microsoft Windows NT Technical Support Training Kit, Deluxe Multimedia Edition /
   Microsoft Corporation.
       p.   cm.
   Includes index.
   ISBN 1-57231-373-0
   ISBN 1-57231-833-3 (Deluxe Multimedia Edition)
    1. Microsoft Windows NT.   2. Operating systems (Computers)
 I. Microsoft Corporation.
QA76.76.063M52435   1997   97-830
005.74--DC21   CIP

Printed and bound in the United States of America.

1 2 3 4 5 6 7 8 9   WCWC   3 2 1 0 9 8

Distributed to the book trade in Canada by Macmillan of Canada, a division of Canada Publishing Corporation.

A CIP catalogue record for this book is available from the British Library.

Microsoft Press books are available through booksellers and distributors worldwide. For further information about international editions, contact your local Microsoft Corporation office. Or contact Microsoft Press International directly at fax (425) 936-7329. Visit our Web site at mspress.microsoft.com.

ActiveX, BackOffice, DirectDraw, DirectPlay, DirectSound, DirectX, FrontPage, Microsoft, Microsoft Press, MS-DOS, Win32, Windows, the Windows logo, and Windows NT are registered trademarks and MSN is a trademark of Microsoft Corporation. Other product and company names mentioned herein may be the trademarks of their respective owners.

Project Leads: Sandra Alto, Rick Wallace
Instructional Designers: Sandra Alto,
  Suzanne E. Sax, Ph.D. (S&T Onsite)
Subject Matter Experts:
  Beth Nelson, Rick Wallace
Technical Contributors:
  Paul Adare (FYI TechKnowlgy Services),
  Keith Cotton, Andrew Mason,
  Ken Rosen (Ken & Ryan Worldwide)
Software Developer:
  Wendy Wahl (Madrona Software)
Web Page Development: Karen Berge
Web Page Graphics Design:
  Ben Chamberlain (Duck Design), Becky Johnson
Graphic Artist: Julie Stone

Acquisitions Editor: Eric Stroo
Project Editor: Saul Candib

Editor: Shari G. Smith (R & S Consulting)
Editing Contributor: Laurie Pritchard
Indexer: Lori Walker (Star Canyon Consulting)
Production Support:
  Irene Barnett (Barnett Communications)
Manufacturing Support: Bo Galford
Video Producers: Susan Greenberg,
  Beverly Hare (Media Solutions)
Video Development: Digital Post & Graphics
Video Compression & Processing:
  "E.J." John Erickson,
  Brian Snyder (Talent Services)
Product Managers: Dean Murray,
  Robert Stewart, Elaine Stovall

Part No. 097-0002004

Contents

About This Book   **xix**
    Intended Audience xx
    Finding the Best Starting Point for You xxi
    Conventions Used in This Book xxii
        Features of This Book xxii
        Procedural Conventions xxii
        Notational Conventions xxiii
        Keyboard Conventions xxiii
        Icons xxiv
        Notes xxiv
    Chapter and Appendix Overview xxv
        Cross-References to Windows NT Documentation xxix
    Getting Started xxx
        Setup Instructions xxxi
        Network Configuration Used in This Book xxxi
        Description of Course Materials Compact Disc xxxiii
        Removing Self-Paced Training Files xxxv
    The Microsoft Certified Professional Program xxxvii
        MCSE Track xxxviii

Chapter 1   Overview of Windows NT   **1**
    About This Chapter 1
    Before You Begin 1
    Lesson 1: Introduction to Windows NT 2
        What Is Windows NT Server? 2
        What Is Windows NT Workstation? 4
        Windows NT Server vs. Windows NT Workstation 6
    Lesson 2: Overview of Windows NT Directory Services 8
        Video Review 9
    Lesson 3: Workgroups and Domains 10
        What Is a Workgroup? 10
        What Is a Domain? 11
    Summary 13
    Review 14

Answer Key 15
    Video Review 15
    Review Answers.. 15

Chapter 2   Installing Windows NT   17

About This Chapter 17
Before You Begin.. 17
Lesson 1: Preparing for Installation 18
    Hardware Requirements.. 18
    Disk Partitioning During Setup 22
    Selecting a File System During Setup.. 24
    Choosing a Server Role During Setup 26
    Joining a Domain or Workgroup During Installation 31
    Choosing a Licensing Mode During Setup 32
Lesson 2: Installing Windows NT... 34
    Starting a Windows NT Installation 34
    Windows NT Setup Types... 35
    The Windows NT Installation Process 37
    Installing the Course Materials on Server1.. 47
Lesson 3: Adding a Computer Account to a Domain 49
    Installing the Course Materials on Workstation1 54
    Joining a Domain 56
Lesson 4: Logging On to a Computer or Domain...................................... 57
    Logging On to a Computer or Domain 58
Lesson 5: Installing Windows NT Server from a Network Share 64
    Performing a Server-based Installation.. 64
    Installing from a Network Server to a Client Computer Running
    Windows 95 or MS-DOS 67
    Customizing a Server-based Installation 68
    Installing from a Network Server to a Computer Running
    Windows NT 69
    Performing an Unattended Installation 69
    Upgrading from Windows 95 to Windows NT 4.0............................. 76
    Upgrading from Windows NT 3.*x* to Windows NT 4.0...................... 76
    Removing Windows NT 77
Lesson 6: Viewing the Windows NT Documentation 79
Summary.. 81
Review... 83

Answer Key 84
    Procedure Answers 84
    Review Answers 85

Chapter 3   Configuring the Windows NT Environment   87

About This Chapter 87
Before You Begin 87
Lesson 1: The Windows NT Registry 88
    What Is the Registry? 88
    Viewing the Registry 88
    How Windows NT Components Use the Registry 90
    The Registry Structure 92
Lesson 2: Modifying Settings Using Control Panel 97
    System Configuration Overview 98
    Modifying Per-User Settings 99
    Modifying Computer Settings 102
Lesson 3: Modifying System Settings Using Control Panel 111
    Changing Startup and Shutdown Settings 111
    Configuring Hardware Profiles 114
    Configuring Virtual Memory 119
    Setting Environment Variables 122
    Adding and Removing Windows NT Components 125
Lesson 4: Modifying System Settings Using Registry Editor 128
    Guidelines for Using Registry Editor 128
    Useful Registry Editor Commands 129
Summary 134
Review 135
Answer Key 137
    Procedure Answers 137
    Review Answers 139

Chapter 4   Managing System Policies   141

About This Chapter 141
Before You Begin 141
Lesson 1: The Purpose of System Policies 142
    What Is a System Policy? 142
    Computer Policy and User Policy 143
Lesson 2: Implementing a System Policy 146
    Implementing a System Policy in a Domain 147
    Implementing a Local Policy 150

Lesson 3: Using System Policy Editor to Manage a System Policy 151
    System Policy Editor Modes... 152
    Customizing System Policy for Users, Groups, and Computers 157
    Supporting Windows 95 System Policy... 164
    System Policy Templates.. 165
    System Policy Issues 165
Summary.. 167
Review.. 168
Answer Key.. 170
    Procedure Answers... 170
    Review Answers... 170

Chapter 5   Managing File Systems   173

About This Chapter 173
Before You Begin.. 173
Lesson 1: File Systems Supported by Windows NT 174
    FAT File System 175
    NTFS File System 177
    Converting to NTFS 179
    Changing File Systems 181
Lesson 2: Working with File Names... 182
    Autogenerated 8.3 File Names 182
    Long File Names on FAT Partitions.. 184
Lesson 3: Managing NTFS Compression.. 188
    Compressing and Decompressing Files and Folders 188
    Copying and Moving Compressed Files 192
Summary.. 195
Review.. 197
Answer Key.. 199
    Procedure Answers... 199
    Review Answers... 201

Chapter 6   Managing Partitions   203

About This Chapter 203
Before You Begin.. 203
Lesson 1: Partitioning a Disk.. 204
    Primary and Extended Partitions 204
    What Is a Volume Set?.. 208
    Guidelines for Managing Volume Sets 209
    What Is a Stripe Set?... 210

Guidelines for Managing Stripe Sets 211
Comparing a Stripe Set to a Volume Set..211
Other Disk Management Considerations 212
Lesson 2: Managing Partitions Using Disk Administrator.....................213
What Is Disk Administrator?...213
Creating and Formatting Partitions..216
Deleting Partitions..218
Marking Partitions As Active 219
Creating, Formatting, Extending, and Deleting Volume Sets...........220
Creating, Formatting, and Deleting Stripe Sets................................224
Committing Changes 225
Automatic Assignment of Drive Letters by Windows NT 227
Securing the System Partition 229
Lesson 3: General Maintenance and Troubleshooting...........................230
Recovering Disk Configuration Information....................................230
File System Problems and Solutions 231
Summary..233
Review...234
Answer Key 236
Procedure Answers 236
Review Answers...236

Chapter 7 Managing Fault Tolerance   239

About This Chapter 239
Before You Begin...239
Lesson 1: Fault Tolerance 240
RAID Systems..240
Hardware and Software Implementations of RAID 241
RAID 1 vs. RAID 5...245
Implementing RAID 1 and RAID 5 246
Lesson 2: Recovering from Hard Disk Failure......................................248
Regenerating a Stripe Set with Parity 248
Recovering from Mirror Set Failure 249
Creating a Fault Tolerance Boot Disk 251
Understanding ARC Paths...254
Summary..256
Review...257
Answer Key 258
Procedure Answers 258
Review Answers...258

Chapter 8 Supporting Applications   259

- About This Chapter 260
- Before You Begin..260
- Lesson 1: Windows NT Architecture Overview 261
  - User Mode vs. Kernel Mode 261
  - Windows NT Executive 263
  - The Windows NT Memory Model 265
- Lesson 2: Subsystems Overview..268
- Lesson 3: Windows NT Task Manager..270
  - Task Manager Capabilities...271
- Lesson 4: Supporting Win32-based Applications 276
  - Win32-based Applications 276
  - OLE/ActiveX, OpenGL, and DirectX..277
- Lesson 5: Supporting MS-DOS-based and Win16-based Applications..280
  - The NT Virtual DOS Machine (NTVDM).....................................280
  - Configuring the MS-DOS NTVDM 281
  - WOW and Win16-based Applications 283
  - Multiple NTVDMs..288
  - Starting a Win16-based Application in Its Own NTVDM 290
- Lesson 6: Supporting Applications on Different Hardware Platforms ...297
- Lesson 7: Distributed Component Object Model 300
  - DCOM Overview..300
  - Configuring DCOM 303
- Lesson 8: Managing Applications...306
  - Using the Command Prompt...306
  - Configuring the Command Prompt 307
  - Prioritizing Applications 308
  - Changing Foreground Application Responsiveness 310
- Summary...311
- Review...312
- Answer Key 314
  - Procedure Answers..314
  - Review Answers...318

Chapter 9 The Windows NT Networking Environment   319

- About This Chapter 319
- Lesson 1: Windows NT Network Architecture 320
  - Network Component Overview 321
  - NDIS-Compatible Network Adapter Card Drivers 322

Network Device Interface Specification 4.0 323
Protocols 324
Transport Driver Interface 325
File System Drivers 326
Lesson 2: Distributed Processing 328
Distributed Application Overview 328
IPC Mechanisms 329
Lesson 3: Accessing File and Print Resources 330
File and Print Sharing Components 330
File and Print Sharing Process 331
Summary 333
Review 334
Answer Key 335
Review Answers 335

Chapter 10 Configuring Windows NT Protocols   337

About This Chapter 337
Before You Begin 337
Lesson 1: Using the Network Program in Control Panel 338
Installing and Configuring Network Adapter Card Drivers 338
Installing and Configuring Protocols 339
Lesson 2: NWLink 341
NWLink Overview 341
Configuring NWLink 342
Lesson 3: NetBEUI 347
Lesson 4: Microsoft TCP/IP 349
Microsoft TCP/IP Overview 349
Microsoft TCP/IP Protocol Suite 350
Configuring TCP/IP Manually 351
Configuring TCP/IP Automatically 354
Using TCP/IP Utilities 356
Testing TCP/IP with Ipconfig and Ping 357
Lesson 5: Network Bindings 360
Summary 364
Review 365
Answer Key 366
Practice Answers 366
Review Answers 367

Chapter 11 Windows NT Networking Services — 369

About This Chapter 369
Before You Begin... 370
Lesson 1: Installing Network Services... 371
Lesson 2: Dynamic Host Configuration Protocol Overview 373
    What Is DHCP? 373
    Manual vs. Automatic IP Address Configurations............................ 374
    How DHCP Works 375
    DHCP Requirements 376
    Installing and Configuring DHCP 377
Lesson 3: Windows Internet Name Service 390
    Name Resolution 390
    What Is WINS?... 393
    How WINS Works 393
    WINS Requirements 395
    Installing and Configuring WINS 396
Lesson 4: Domain Name System 400
    What Is DNS?... 400
    How DNS Works 401
    Installing and Configuring DNS 404
    Integrating WINS and DNS 409
Lesson 5: Computer Browser Service 412
    The Browser Process 413
    Browser Roles 414
    Browser Elections 415
    Configuring Browsers 416
Summary.. 418
Review... 419
Answer Key 421
    Procedure Answers 421
    Review Answers... 423

Chapter 12 Implementing Remote Access Service — 425

About This Chapter 425
Before You Begin... 426
Lesson 1: RAS and Dial-Up Networking... 427
    WAN Connectivity 428
    Protocols... 433
    Gateways and Routers 437
    RAS Security Features 438

Contents   xi

Lesson 2: Telephony API 440
    TAPI Settings 440
    Configuring a TAPI Location 441
Lesson 3: Installing and Configuring RAS 443
    Installing RAS 443
    Configuring a RAS Server 444
    Configuring a RAS Server to Use NetBEUI 447
    Configuring a RAS Server to Use TCP/IP 448
    Configuring a RAS Server to Use IPX 449
    Granting Remote Access Permissions 453
Lesson 4: Installing and Configuring Dial-Up Networking 454
    Installing Dial-Up Networking 454
    Configuring Phonebook Entries 456
    Logging on Through Dial-Up Networking 460
    AutoDial 462
    Testing the RAS Installation 464
Lesson 5: Troubleshooting RAS 467
    Event Viewer 467
    Problems with PPP Connections 467
    Authentication Problems 467
    Dial-Up Networking Monitor 467
    Multilink and Callback 468
    AutoDial Occurs During Logon 468
Summary 469
Review 470
Answer Key 472
    Procedure Answers 472
    Review Answers 472

Chapter 13   Internetworking and Intranetworking   475

About This Chapter 475
Before You Begin 475
Lesson 1: Internet and Intranet Overview 476
    What Is the Internet? 477
    What Is an Intranet? 477
    Security Considerations When Connecting to the Internet 478
Lesson 2: IIS and PWS Networking Components 479
    Functions of IIS and PWS 479
    Features of IIS and PWS 481
    Installing IIS 482

Installing PWS 484
Configuring IIS and PWS 485
Lesson 3: Microsoft Internet Explorer 489
Lesson 4: Securing Internet and Intranet Sites 490
Summary 498
Review 499
Answer Key 500
Procedure Answers 500
Review Answers 501

Chapter 14 Interoperating with Novell NetWare   503

About This Chapter 503
Before You Begin 503
Lesson 1: Windows NT Connectivity with NetWare 504
NWLink 504
Client Service for NetWare 505
Gateway Services for NetWare 506
File and Print Services for NetWare 508
Remote Administration of Novell Networks 510
Directory Service Manager for NetWare 510
Migration Tool for NetWare 512
Interoperability with Novell NetWare 513
Lesson 2: Installing and Configuring CSNW and GSNW 514
Installing and Configuring CSNW 514
Installing and Configuring GSNW 519
Summary 526
Review 527
Answer Key 528
Review Answers 528

Chapter 15 Implementing Network Clients   529

About This Chapter 529
Before You Begin 530
Lesson 1: Windows NT Server 4.0 Licensing 531
What Is a Client Access License? 531
The Licensing Modes 533
Licensing Administration 537
Lesson 2: Clients Included with Windows NT Server 547
Client Software Provided by Windows NT Server 547
Microsoft Network Client 3.0 for MS-DOS and Windows 548

  LAN Manager 2.2c Clients 549
  Microsoft Windows 95 549
 Lesson 3: Network Client Administrator 551
  What Is Network Client Administrator? 551
  Network Installation Startup Disks 552
  Creating an Installation Disk Set 556
 Lesson 4: Client-based Network Administration Tools 558
  Installing the Administration Tools on Windows NT Workstation ... 558
  Using the Administration Tools on Windows 95 560
 Lesson 5: Services for Macintosh 562
  Services for Macintosh Requirements 562
  Installing Services for Macintosh 563
 Summary 566
 Review 567
 Answer Key 569
  Procedure Answers 569
  Review Answers 570

Chapter 16 Implementing File Synchronization and Directory Replication 573

 About This Chapter 573
 Before You Begin 573
 Lesson 1: The Windows NT Briefcase 574
  Using the Briefcase 576
 Lesson 2: Directory Replication Overview 581
  The Purpose of Directory Replication 581
  Directory Replication Components 584
  The Directory Replication Process 586
 Lesson 3: Preparing for Directory Replication 588
  Preparing an Export Server 588
  Preparing an Import Computer 590
 Lesson 4: Managing Directory Replication 591
  Managing Replication from an Export Server 591
  Managing Replication to an Import Computer 594
 Lesson 5: Troubleshooting Directory Replication 602
  Replication Troubleshooting Overview 602
  Replication Troubleshooting Procedures 603
 Summary 604
 Review 606

Answer Key 607
    Procedure Answers 607
    Review Answers 607

Chapter 17   The Windows NT Boot Process   609

About This Chapter 609
Before You Begin 609
Lesson 1: Overview of the Windows NT Boot Process 610
    Files Required for Windows NT System Boot 610
    The Windows NT Boot Sequence 611
    Windows NT Load Phases 616
Lesson 2: Troubleshooting the Boot Process 621
    Common Boot Process Errors 621
    The Boot.ini File 622
    Troubleshooting Boot.ini Problems 624
    Creating a Windows NT Boot Disk 625
Lesson 3: Last Known Good Configuration 629
    The Function of Last Known Good Configuration 629
    When to Use the Last Known Good Configuration 630
    How to Use the Last Known Good Configuration 632
Lesson 4: Emergency Repair 634
    Creating and Updating an Emergency Repair Disk 634
    The Emergency Repair Process 636
Summary 641
Review 642
Answer Key 644
    Procedure Answers 644
    Review Answers 645

Chapter 18   Windows NT Troubleshooting Tools   647

About This Chapter 647
Before You Begin 647
Lesson 1: Diagnostic Tools 648
    Event Viewer 649
    Windows NT Diagnostics 656
    Performance Monitor 661
    Network Monitor 666
    System Recovery 670

Lesson 2: Resources for Troubleshooting 672
    Microsoft Internet and Online Services 673
Summary 675
Review 676
Answer Key 677
    Procedure Answers 677
    Review Answers 681

Glossary   **683**

Index   **749**

FOREWORD

Microsoft Windows NT Technical Support

For the past eight years a determined Microsoft team has endeavored to raise the Microsoft Windows operating system to a new level of reliability and function. The team's original goal was to deliver an operating system with reliability characteristics of a minicomputer or mainframe combined with the ease of use and responsiveness of a personal computer. Such a system would be suitable for a broad class of uses ranging from the most demanding business desktop scenarios to usage as a system for one's home.

Every release of Microsoft Windows NT® is a single step toward our goal. With Windows NT 4.0, the right mix of performance, networking support, and usability combined with reliability have yielded the most flexible version of Windows NT thus far. Corporate MIS folks have come to love the reliability and security. End users like the Windows 95 style graphical user interface and soon forget the last time they needed to restart their computer because of a software failure. All of this is good news, but we're not done yet. We're hard at work making the end user experience much more simple. on that. "Plug and Play" and Power Management support are in the works too. Expect them in Windows NT 5.0. Integration with the Internet at a fundamental level is in the works too. As we move the system forward with new features and functions we still remain completely focused on reliability and quality. These will never be sacrificed for any reason.

I've been working on system software for the past thirteen years. The software certainly evolves, but many concepts remain the same. An operating system boots up, manages the hardware resources, and provides an environment in which application programs run. Windows NT is no different in that regard, but there are many detailed concepts to learn and explore. To get the most out of an operating system, you need to know everything about it. A system always seems to work best in the hands of an expert. It takes both knowledge and experience to attain expertise. By taking this course, you are taking the first step to attain the knowledge you need. Your next step is to start up Windows NT system and use it every day. Don't worry about being too rough with it. You won't hurt it!

Frank Artale
Director of Windows NT Program Management

January 18, 1997

About This Book

Welcome to *Microsoft® Windows NT® Technical Support*. This book provides the knowledge, concepts, and skills necessary to install, configure, customize, and troubleshoot Windows NT in a single domain Microsoft Windows NT-based network. In addition, you learn how to integrate Windows NT and Novell NetWare networks. This book also provides you with the prerequisite knowledge and skills required for course 689 *Supporting Microsoft Windows NT Server 4.0—Enterprise Technologies*, and helps to prepare you to meet the certification requirements to become a Microsoft Windows NT Certified Professional.

Note For more information on becoming a Microsoft Certified Professional, please see the section "The Microsoft Certified Professional Program" later in this chapter.

The "About This Book" section provides important setup instructions that describe the hardware and software requirements, as well as the networking configuration, for the two computers that are necessary to complete the hands-on procedures. Read through "About This Book" thoroughly before you start the lessons.

Each chapter in this book is divided into lessons. Most lessons integrate the technical information with hands-on procedures that enable you to practice key concepts and skills. A summary is provided at the end of each chapter. In addition, some chapters contain references to additional information or related topics.

Intended Audience

This book is intended for those who support or administer Microsoft Windows NT Server 4.0 and Windows NT Workstation 4.0, plan to take course 689 *Supporting Microsoft Windows NT Server 4.0—Enterprise Technologies,* or who are on the Microsoft Certified Systems Engineer Windows NT 4.0 track.

Prerequisites

- Working knowledge of an operating system, such as Microsoft Windows® version 3.*x*, Windows 95, Windows NT, Windows for Workgroups, Microsoft MS-DOS®, or UNIX.
- Knowledge of basic computer hardware components, including memory, hard disks, CPUs, communication and printer ports, display adapters, and pointing devices. These concepts and skills are covered in course 683, *Networking Essentials—Self-Paced Training Kit.*
- Working knowledge of major networking components, including clients, servers, local area networks (LANs), network adapter cards, drivers, protocols, services, and network operating systems. These concepts and skills are covered in course 683, *Networking Essentials—Self-Paced Training Kit.*
- Proficiency using the Windows 95 or Windows NT version 4.0 interface, including the ability to use Windows NT Explorer to locate, create, and manipulate folders and files.
- Working knowledge of common Windows NT administrative tasks, including creating user and group accounts, assigning permissions, sharing folders, and auditing. These concepts and skills are covered in the instructor-led course 803, *Administering Microsoft Windows NT 4.0* and in course 753, *Microsoft Windows NT 4.0 Network Administration—Self-Paced Training Kit.*
- Working knowledge of network and end-user support.

Finding the Best Starting Point for You

This book has been designed so that you tailor the content and course flow to meet your training needs. If you decide to complete the chapters out of order, keep in mind that Chapters 3 through 18 require that you first complete the procedures in Chapter 2, "Installing Windows NT." The following table provides suggested learning paths for specific training needs.

If you	Follow this learning path
Are preparing to take the Microsoft Certified Professional examinations: Implementing and Supporting Microsoft Windows NT Server 4.0, exam 70–67 or Implementing and Supporting Microsoft Windows NT Workstation 4.0, exam 70–73.	Read "Getting Started" and complete the procedures in "Setup Instructions" (both located later in "About This Book"). Next, complete all of the procedures in the book. Read and review the information contained in Books Online.
Need to install and configure a small network.	Read "Getting Started" and complete the procedures in "Setup Instructions" (both located later in "About This Book"). Read and complete the procedures in Chapters 2, 3, 5, 6, and 9–11.
Need to install and configure multiple departments, groups, or computers.	Read "Getting Started" and complete the procedures in "Setup Instructions" (both located later in "About This Book"). Read and complete the procedures in Chapters 2–11, and 13.
Need to install and configure TCP/IP.	Read "Getting Started" and complete the procedures in "Setup Instructions" (both located later in "About This Book"). Read and complete the procedures in Chapter 2 and Chapters 9–11.
Need to know the definition of a Windows NT term.	Refer to the glossary included in this book, or to Windows NT Help Glossary.
Need information on a specific topic related to Windows NT.	Refer to the table of contents or index in this book, or refer to Windows NT Help.

Conventions Used in This Book

Before you start any of the lessons, it is important that you understand the terms and notational conventions used in this book.

Features of This Book

- Each chapter opens with an "About This Chapter" section, which provides an overview of the chapter content.
- Where appropriate, each chapter opens with a "Before You Begin" section, which describes the other chapters and procedures that must be completed before continuing.
- Whenever possible, lessons contain practices that give you an opportunity to use the skills being presented and explore each component of Windows NT as it is described.
- The "Review" sections at the end of each chapter allow you to test what you have learned in the lessons included in that chapter.
- The "For more information" table at the end of some chapters lists additional resource locations for information on the concepts and skills covered in the chapter.
- The "Answer Key" section at the end of each chapter contains all of the questions and corresponding answers for that chapter. Each question is referenced by page number.
- The glossary presents a set of definitions of most of the technical terms that appear in this book.

Procedural Conventions

- Hands-on procedures are preceded by a *Practice* heading. A triangular bullet (▸) indicates the beginning of a procedure, and the steps of the procedure are given in numbered lists (1, 2, and so on).

  For example:

  ### Practice

  In these procedures, you explore the HKEY_LOCAL_MACHINE subtree to familiarize yourself with the registry hierarchy.

  ▸ **To explore HKEY_LOCAL_MACHINE**

- The word *select* is used for highlighting directories, file names, text boxes, menu bars, and options, and for selecting options in a dialog box.
- The word *click* is used for carrying out a command from a menu or dialog box.

Notational Conventions

- Dialog box names, options, menu names, and menu commands appear in **bold** type.
- Characters or commands that you type appear in **bold lowercase** type.
- Variable information in syntax statements is *italicized*, for example: *cd_rom_drive*:\I386. *Italic* is also used to identify new terms, book titles, and for emphasis in the text.
- Names of files, folders, or directories appear in Title Caps, except when you are to type them directly. Unless otherwise indicated, you can use lowercase letters when you type a folder name or file name in a dialog box or at the command prompt.
- Full capitals are also used for acronyms.
- File name extensions appear in all lowercase.
- Code samples, examples of screen text, or entries that you might type at the command prompt or in initialization files appear in monospace type. For example:

    ```
    I/O Error accessing boot sector file
    multi(0)disk(0)rdisk(0)partition(1):\bootsect.dos
    ```

- Optional items in syntax statements are enclosed in square brackets [ ]. For example, [*filename*] in command syntax indicates that you can choose to type a file name with the command. Type only the information within the brackets, not the brackets themselves.
- Required items in syntax statements are enclosed in braces { }. Type only the information within the braces, not the braces themselves.

Keyboard Conventions

- Names of keys that you press appear in SMALL CAPITALS; for example, TAB and SHIFT.
- A plus sign (+) between two key names means that you must press those keys at the same time. For example, "Press ALT+TAB" means that you hold down ALT while you press TAB.
- A comma (,) between two or more key names means that you must press each of the keys consecutively, not together. For example, "Press ALT, F, X" means that you press and release each key in sequence. "Press ALT+S, R" means that you first press ALT and S together, and then release them and press R.
- You can choose menu commands with the keyboard. Press the ALT key to activate the menu bar, and then sequentially press the keys that correspond to the highlighted or underlined letter of the menu name and the command name. For some commands, you can also press a key combination listed in the menu.

- You can select or clear check boxes or options in dialog boxes with the keyboard. Press the ALT key, and then press the key that corresponds to the underlined letter of the option name. Or you can press TAB until the option is highlighted, and then press SPACEBAR to select or clear the check box or option.
- You can cancel the display of a dialog box by pressing the ESC key.

Icons

The following table describes the icons that are used throughout this book.

Icon	Description
	Identifies content that applies only to computers running Windows NT Server.
	Indicates a hands-on practice.
	Indicates instructions for starting a video clip.
	Identifies content useful when planning.
	Indicates a best practice.
	Identifies content that is useful in identifying and troubleshooting problems.
	Indicates questions that you should answer.

Notes

Notes appear throughout the lessons.

- Notes marked **Tip** contain explanations of possible results or alternative methods.
- Notes marked **Important** are items you should check before completing an action.
- Notes marked **Note** contain supplementary or needed information.
- Notes marked **Caution** contain warnings about possible loss of data.

Chapter and Appendix Overview

This self-paced training kit contains a video, text, hands-on procedures, simulations, and review questions to teach you how to install, configure, and support Windows NT Server and Windows NT Workstation.

The self-paced training book is divided into the following chapters and appendixes:

- Chapter 1, "Overview of Windows NT," provides you with an overview and comparison of the features of Microsoft Windows NT Server 4.0 and Windows NT Workstation 4.0. This chapter also provides you with a review of the components of a Windows NT domain, the administrative differences between a domain and a workgroup, and directory services.

- Chapter 2, "Installing Windows NT," provides you with the hardware requirements and information needed to install Windows NT Server and Windows NT Workstation. The hands-on procedures give you the opportunity to install Windows NT Server from compact disc and configure the computer as a primary domain controller (PDC). You also install Windows NT Workstation from compact disc and then add the computer to the domain. Finally, you create a distribution server for the Windows NT Server source files and use the distribution server to perform an unattended, over-the-network server installation and then configure the computer as a backup domain controller (BDC).

- Chapter 3, "Configuring the Windows NT Environment," provides you with an overview of the registry architecture and introduces you to the tools, Control Panel and Registry Editor, that are used to edit the registry. The hands-on procedures give you an opportunity to use Registry Editor to explore the registry and then use Control Panel to configure the Windows NT environment.

- Chapter 4, "Managing System Policies," introduces you to system policy, a feature of Windows NT Server that enables you to control the user-definable settings in Windows NT user profiles, as well as system configuration settings. The hands-on procedures give you an opportunity to use System Policy Editor to change desktop settings and restrict what users can do from their desktop.

- Chapter 5, "Managing File Systems," provides you with a comparison of the file systems—FAT (file allocation table) and NTFS (Windows NT File System)—and explains issues involved in running them in the Windows NT environment, such as the management of long file names, and file compression. The hands-on procedures give you an opportunity to convert a FAT partition to an NTFS partition, and to create and rename files on a FAT partition and note the effect of these changes on their long file names and aliases. You also use Windows NT Explorer to compress files and folders on an NTFS partition, and then see the effects on compressed files when they are copied or moved into a folder that is not compressed.

- Chapter 6, "Managing Partitions," introduces the types of partitions supported by Windows NT, including primary and extended partitions, volume sets, and stripe sets. The hands-on procedures give you an opportunity to customize Disk Administrator, to create, format, and label the volumes, change the drive letter of a partition, and then extend a partition. Then, you use the Volume Set Simulation to create, format, extend, and delete a volume set.

- Chapter 7, "Managing Fault Tolerance," defines fault tolerance and explains how Windows NT Server provides fault tolerance using two RAID levels: Raid 1–mirror sets, and Raid 5–stripe sets with parity. It also explains the importance of creating a fault tolerance boot disk for use in case of physical disk failure. The hands-on procedures give you the opportunity to use the fault tolerance simulation to implement mirror sets, and stripe sets with parity, and to create a boot disk for the Intel platform that can be used in the event that your computer's boot partition is not accessible.

- Chapter 8, "Supporting Applications," introduces you to the Windows NT operating system architecture. The Windows NT memory model is covered, as well as how Windows NT manages memory and runs applications written for the Windows NT operating system and other operating systems. The hands-on procedures give you the opportunity to manage applications using the Windows NT Task Manager. You determine the effects of a halted Microsoft Win32®-based application on the system, and use Task Manager to end the application that has stopped responding. You observe the effects of a General Protection Fault (GPF) error and the effects of a halted application, and run a Win16-based application in its own memory space.

- Chapter 9, "The Windows NT Networking Environment," describes the components of the Windows NT networking architecture, and how these components communicate with each other and enable a computer running Windows NT to communicate over a network.

- Chapter 10, "Configuring Windows NT Protocols," introduces the Windows network protocols: NWLink IPX/SPX Compatible Transport, NetBEUI, and Transmission Control Protocol/Internet Protocol (TCP/IP). It also describes how network bindings are used to optimize network performance. The hands-on procedures give you an opportunity to install and configure each of these protocols.

- Chapter 11, "Windows NT Networking Services," introduces you to the following services provided by Microsoft Windows NT TCP/IP: Dynamic Host Configuration Protocol (DHCP), Windows Internet Name Service (WINS), and Domain Name Server (DNS). Also covered in this chapter is the Windows NT Computer Browser service which is used by Windows NT to identify and list available network resources. The hands-on procedures give you an opportunity to install and configure DHCP, WINS, and DNS. You create and activate a DHCP scope, use the **ping** and **arp** utilities to help test and troubleshoot DHCP, configure the DHCP server to assign WINS server addresses, and create and configure a DNS Server service primary zone.

- Chapter 12, "Implementing Remote Access Service," introduces you to Microsoft Windows NT Server Remote Access Service (RAS) and the client version of RAS, called Dial-Up Networking. The hands-on procedures give you an opportunity to install RAS and Dial-Up Networking, and include a simulation in which you configure and use Dial-Up Networking.

- Chapter 13, "Internetworking and Intranetworking," introduces you to the Windows NT services used to support publishing and accessing services on the Internet and intranets. These include the Internet Information Server (IIS), Peer Web Services (PWS), and Microsoft Internet Explorer (IE). The hands-on procedures give you an opportunity to install and configure IIS. You examine the Windows NT Server environment before and after installing Microsoft Internet Information Server to determine changes made by IIS. You publish a document on your Web server, and access that document from a client computer running Windows NT Workstation 4.0. Finally, you configure DNS to resolve IP addresses for IIS.

- Chapter 14, "Interoperating with Novell NetWare," explains the Windows NT features and services that enable computers running Windows NT to coexist and interoperate with Novell NetWare servers. Some of these services are included in Windows NT, while others are available as separate products, commonly called add-ons. This chapter describes these NetWare connectivity tools and explains how they can be used to integrate Windows NT and NetWare environments. The hands-on procedures give you the opportunity to install Client Service for NetWare (CSNW). You run a simulation in which you configure CSNW and use it to connect to a NetWare server. You also install and configure Gateway Services for NetWare (GSNW).

- Chapter 15, "Implementing Network Clients," explains the two Windows NT Server client licensing options, Per Server and Per Seat, and introduces you to the tools used to manage client licenses on your network. This chapter describes the client software provided with Windows NT Server 4.0, and the client software that must be installed on a computer so that it can access a computer running Windows NT Server. This chapter also describes Services for Macintosh, which gives you the ability to manage a Windows NT network environment that includes AppleTalk computers. The hands-on procedures give you the opportunity to install the Windows NT Server administrative tools on a client computer, and to install Services for Macintosh.

- Chapter 16, "Implementing File Synchronization and Directory Replication," explains the Microsoft Windows NT Briefcase and the Directory Replicator service used to minimize the administration involved in updating files over a network. The hands-on procedures give you an opportunity to use and configure the Briefcase and the Directory Replicator service.

- Chapter 17, "The Windows NT Boot Process," describes the steps that occur when you start a computer running Windows NT as the operating system and introduces troubleshooting resources that you can use to help you resolve problems when Windows NT will not start. The hands-on procedures give you the opportunity to create a boot disk, and rename system files and reboot to observe error messages. You also disable the keyboard driver and use the Last Known Good configuration to successfully reboot your computer. Finally, you use the **rdisk** utility to update your Emergency Repair Disk and perform an Emergency Repair to inspect your boot sector.

- Chapter 18, "Windows NT Troubleshooting Tools," describes the troubleshooting tools that are available in Windows NT. In addition to learning about these resources, you learn how to use them to diagnose and resolve problems that can occur in administering a Windows NT system or network. The hands-on procedures give you the opportunity to use Event Viewer to view events in the system, security, and application event logs, control the size of the log files, filter events, and search for specific events to locate existing and potential problems. You also use Windows NT Diagnostics (Winmsd) to view configuration information for your local computer and for a remote computer, save a report for the remote computer, and then view the report. You use Performance Monitor to create a chart, and to create and view a log of processor activity. Finally, you install the Network Monitor Tools and Agent, and use them to capture and display network traffic.

- Appendix A, "Comparing Microsoft Windows NT Workstation and Windows 95," provides a comparison of Windows NT Workstation and Windows 95 features and provides criteria to help you choose which operating system will satisfy your organization's requirements.

- Appendix B, "Changes to Kernel Mode, User Mode, and GDI in Microsoft Windows NT 4.0," provides a description of changes to the kernel mode, user mode, and GDI in Windows NT 4.0 and explains how these changes improve the operating system's performance.

- Appendix C, "Implementing DNS Using Microsoft Windows NT 4.0," provides a history of Domain Name Server and explains how to implement DNS in a Windows NT 4.0 network.

- Appendix D, "Using the Point-to-Point Tunneling Protocol," provides detailed information on the function, implementation, and configuration of PPTP in a Windows NT network.

- Appendix E, "The Distributed Component Model," describes how DCOM enhances networking technology over the Internet.

- Appendix F, "Microsoft Services for NetWare," describes each of the Microsoft tools for integrating Windows NT and NetWare networks.
- Appendix G, "Printing from Microsoft Windows NT," examines the Windows NT printing process and describes the components that make it possible.
- Glossary, contains the definitions of most of the technical terms used in this book.

Note The appendixes are located on the *Microsoft Windows NT Technical Support Training Course Materials* compact disc in the Docfiles folder. These files are Microsoft Word for Windows documents and can be viewed and printed with any text editor that can read the RTF file format, such as WordPad.

Cross-References to Windows NT Documentation

You will find references to Windows NT documentation and online Help throughout this book. These references point you to more information about specific tasks.

- Microsoft Windows NT Server *Concepts and Planning* explains how to implement and optimize Windows NT Server. It is designed for new and experienced administrators of small networks and advanced users of operating systems. The online version of Windows NT Server *Concepts and Planning* is included in Books Online on the *Windows NT Server* compact disc.
- The *Microsoft Windows NT Server 4.0 Resource Kit* provides detailed information on the Windows NT Server operating system, and includes utilities and tools that help you to implement and manage Windows NT Server in larger networks.
- The *Microsoft Windows NT Workstation 4.0 Resource Kit* provides detailed information on the Windows NT Workstation operating system, plus topics that are new for version 4.0.
- Help provides references and how-to information for all Windows NT tasks.

Getting Started

This self-paced training contains hands-on procedures to help you learn about Windows NT Server and Windows NT Workstation.

To complete the lessons, you must have two computers. The first computer must be capable of running Microsoft Windows NT Server 4.0. The second computer must be capable of running both Microsoft Windows NT Server 4.0 and Windows NT Workstation 4.0. Both computers must have the following minimum configuration:

- Personal computer with a 486/33 or higher Intel-based processor
- 16 MB of RAM (32 MB recommended)
- A minimum of 450 MB of available hard disk space (on the first computer)
- A minimum of 375 MB of available hard disk space (on the second computer)
- SVGA display adapter and monitor capable of 256 colors
- Microsoft Mouse or compatible pointing device
- Network adapter card and related cables
- One 3.5-inch high-density disk drive
- CD-ROM drive
- Sound card and speakers (optional)
- Null modem cable for testing RAS (optional—for those who do not have the cable, a simulation for RAS is included with the course)
- Serial port for testing RAS practice (optional)

Software Requirements

- *Microsoft Windows NT Server 4.0.* A special 120-day limited use version of Windows NT Server 4.0 is included with this book to enable you to complete the course.
- *Microsoft Windows NT Workstation 4.0.* A special 120-day limited use version of Windows NT Workstation 4.0 is included with this book to enable you to complete the course.

Note Both computers must have an existing Microsoft operating system such as MS-DOS, Windows 3.*x*, Windows 95, or Windows NT 3.*x*. One computer must be able to run multimedia applications so that you can view the video included with the course.

Setup Instructions

1. Set up both computers according to the manufacturer's instructions.
2. The computers need to be networked together, either cabled together using a hub so that the two computers can communicate, or as part of a larger network.
3. Computer1 requires 450 MB of free disk space on drive C.
4. Computer2 requires 200 MB of free disk space on drive C, 125 MB of free disk space on drive D, and 50 MB of unpartitioned disk space in an extended partition.

> **Caution** If your computers are part of a larger network, you *must* verify with your network administrator that the following computer names, domain name, and IP address information do not conflict with network operations. If they do conflict, ask your network administrator to provide alternative values and use those values throughout all of the practices in this book.

Variable	Values used in this course
Computer name for Computer1	Server1
Computer names for Computer2	Server2 and Workstation1
IP address range	131. 107. 2. 200 — 131. 107. 2. 211
Subnet mask	255. 255. 0. 0

Network Configuration Used in This Book

This section provides a description of how your two computers will be configured after completing Chapter 2, "Installing Windows NT," and provides illustrations that show the roles of each computer.

Role of Computer1

Computer1 will act as a server. On Computer1, you install Windows NT Server from the compact disc labeled *Windows NT Server version 4.0 Evaluation Edition 120-day Limit on Use* that is included with this book.

Computer1 will be configured as a primary domain controller (PDC), and will be assigned the computer account name, Server1, and the domain name, Domain1. This computer will act as a domain controller, a file and print server, and an application server in Domain1.

Role of Computer2

Computer2 will act primarily as a workstation for most of the procedures in this course. However, to give you an opportunity to perform an over-the-network installation of Windows NT Server and to perform directory replication, you will also configure Computer2 as a server.

Configuring Computer2 As a Workstation

To configure Computer2 as a workstation, you install Windows NT Workstation from the compact disc labeled *Windows NT Workstation version 4.0 Evaluation Edition 120-day Limit on Use* that is included with this book. This computer is added to Domain1 and is assigned the computer account name Workstation1.

Network Configuration of Server1 and Workstation1

The following illustration shows the roles of Computer1 and Computer2 after installing Windows NT Server on Computer1 and Windows NT Workstation on Computer2.

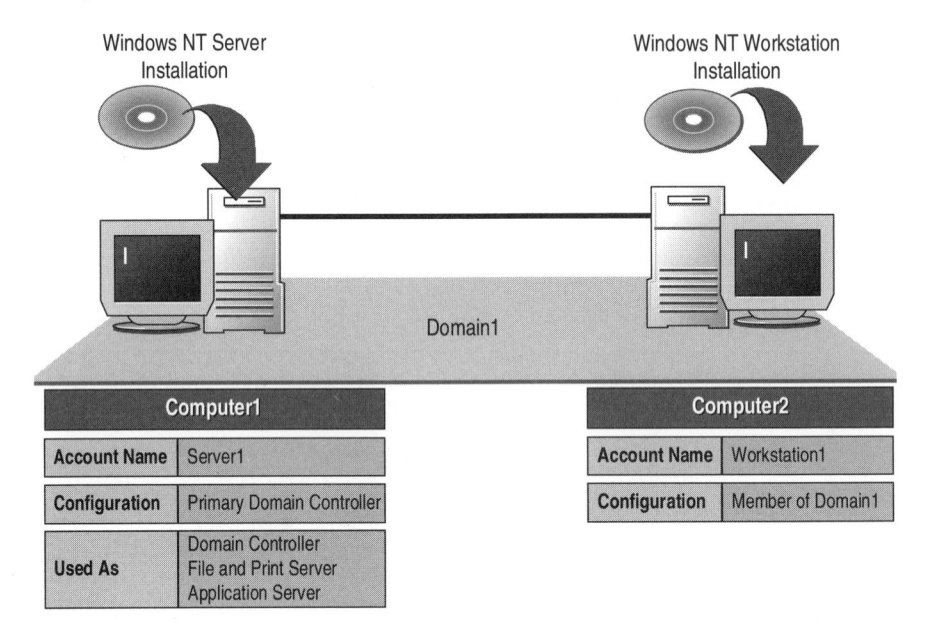

Computer1	
Account Name	Server1
Configuration	Primary Domain Controller
Used As	Domain Controller File and Print Server Application Server

Computer2	
Account Name	Workstation1
Configuration	Member of Domain1

Configuring Computer2 As a Server

To configure Computer2 as a server, you install Windows NT Server. This installation is done during a practice in Chapter 2, "Installing Windows NT." In this practice, Computer2 is configured as a Backup Domain Controller in Domain1 and the computer is assigned the computer account name Server2.

Network Configuration of Server1 and Server2

The following illustration shows the roles of Computer1 and Computer2 after installing Windows NT Server on Computer1 and Computer2.

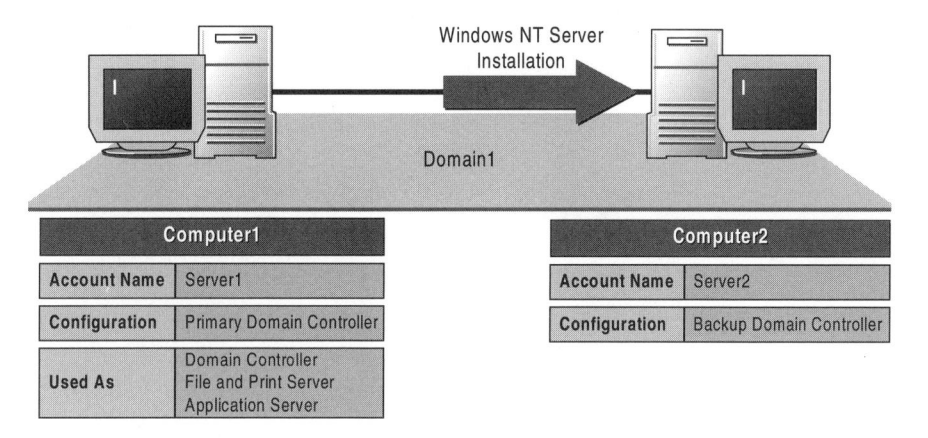

Computer1	
Account Name	Server1
Configuration	Primary Domain Controller
Used As	Domain Controller File and Print Server Application Server

Computer2	
Account Name	Server2
Configuration	Backup Domain Controller

Description of Course Materials Compact Disc

This book includes a compact disc labeled *Microsoft Windows NT Technical Support Training CD-ROM Course Materials*. This compact disc contains the files, simulations, and course Web page that you need in order to complete the procedures in this book. You will install the components on the course materials compact disc onto Server1 and Workstation1 in Chapter 2 "Installing Windows NT."

The following list describes the files that are copied to your computers and the changes that are made to the interface once you have run the course materials Setup program.

1. The lab files used in the procedures are copied to C:\Lab Files.
2. The files required to use the simulations, video, and course Web page are copied to C:\Technical Support Training.

3. The Setup program creates a **Technical Support Training** menu as shown in the following illustration.

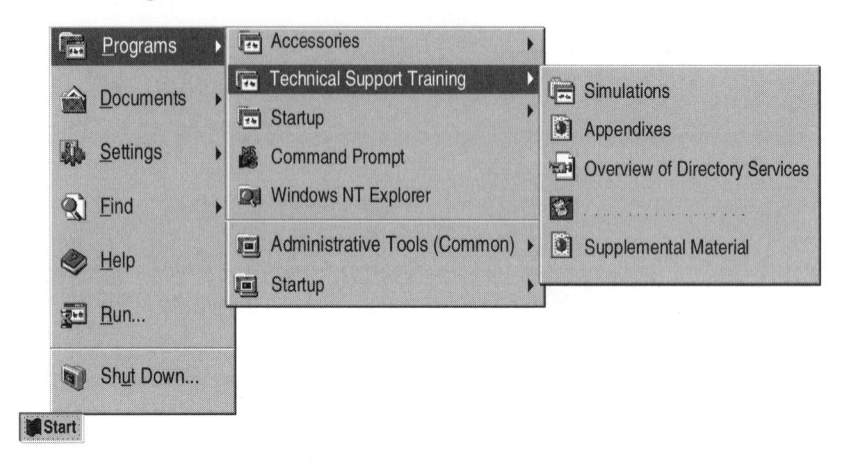

The following list describes the shortcuts on the **Technical Support Training** menu.

- *Simulations.* Pointing to this menu displays the simulations used in this course.
    - *Fault tolerance simulation.* Provides practice using Disk Administrator to create a stripe set with parity, and to create a mirror set.
    - *Novell NetWare simulation.* Provides practice configuring CSNW and then using CSNW to connect to a NetWare server.
    - *RAS simulation.* Provides practice configuring and then using Dial-Up Networking to connect to a RAS server.
    - *Volume set simulation.* Provides practice creating, formatting, extending, and deleting a volume set.
    - *Windows NT Server simulation.* Provides practice installing Windows NT Server as a primary domain controller.
    - *Windows NT Workstation simulation.* Provides practice installing Windows NT Workstation; during this simulation you can choose to install the computer as a member of a workgroup or a domain.
- *Appendixes.* Clicking this option starts the course Web page, and displays a list of the appendixes used in this course. This provides an easy way to view this information online. If you want to print out the appendixes, you can find them on the *Microsoft Windows NT Technical Support Training Course Materials* compact disc in the Docfiles folder. These files are Microsoft Word for Windows documents and can be viewed and printed with any text editor that can read the RTF file format, such as WordPad.

- *Overview of Directory Services.* Clicking this option starts the 7-minute instructional video. The video describes the components in a Windows NT network and the role of user accounts in Windows NT Directory Services. This video can be viewed on either a 32-bit operating system, such as Windows 95 or Windows NT, or on a 16-bit operating system such as Windows 3.1. For more information on running the video, please see the instructions in Chapter 1, "Overview of Windows NT."
- *Self-Assessment Exam.* Clicking this option starts the Microsoft Self-Assessment Program which contains the self-assessment examination for course 803, *Administering Microsoft Windows NT 4.0.* This examination can be used to refresh your knowledge of Windows NT administrative tasks and to identify areas that you may want to study further. If you are interested in learning more about Windows NT administration, you should consider completing the instructor-led course 803, *Administering Microsoft Windows NT 4.0* or course 753, the *Microsoft Windows NT Network Administration* self-paced training kit.
- *Supplemental Material.* Clicking this option starts the course Web page and displays the home page. This Web page provides information on the Microsoft Certified Trainer program, course materials, and links to key Web sites.

Removing Self-Paced Training Files

If you want to remove all files and shortcuts that were created when you installed the self-paced training files, you use the Add/Remove Programs program in Control Panel.

▶ **To remove the self-paced training files**

1. Click the **Start** button, point to **Settings**, and then click **Control Panel**.

    The Control Panel window appears.

2. Double-click the Add/Remove Programs icon.

    The **Add/Remove Programs Properties** dialog box appears.

3. On the **Install/Uninstall** tab, click **Microsoft Windows NT 4.0 Technical Support Training**, and then click **Add/Remove**.

    The **Microsoft Windows NT 4.0 Technical Support Training Setup** dialog box appears.

4. Click **Remove All**.

    A message appears asking if you want to remove Windows NT 4.0 Technical Support Training.

5. Click **Yes**.

   The **Microsoft Windows NT Technical Support Training** menu is removed from **Programs**, and all related files are removed from your hard disk, including the Lab Files folder (which does not appear on the **Technical Support Training** menu).

6. When a message appears stating that the process has successfully completed, click **OK**.

7. Click **OK** to close the **Add/Remove Programs Properties** dialog box.

8. Close Control Panel.

The Microsoft Certified Professional Program

The Microsoft Certified Professional (MCP) program provides the best method to prove your command of current Microsoft products and technologies. Anyone who must prove his or her technical expertise with Microsoft products should consider completing this program, including systems engineers, product developers, support technicians, system and network administrators, consultants, and trainers.

The Four Certifications

The following table describes the four certifications, based on specific areas of technical expertise.

Certification	Description
Microsoft Certified Product Specialist (MCPS)	MCPSs demonstrate in-depth knowledge of at least one Microsoft operating system. Candidates may pass additional Microsoft certification exams to further qualify their skills with Microsoft BackOffice™ products, development tools, or desktop applications.
Microsoft Certified Systems Engineer (MCSE)	MCSEs are qualified to effectively plan, implement, maintain, and support information systems in a wide range of computing environments with Windows NT Server and the Microsoft BackOffice integrated family of server products.
Microsoft Certified Solution Developer (MCSD)	MCSDs are qualified to design and develop custom business solutions with Microsoft development tools, technologies, and platforms, including Microsoft Office and Microsoft BackOffice.
Microsoft Certified Trainer (MCT)	MCTs are instructionally and technically qualified to deliver Microsoft Official Curriculum through Microsoft Authorized Technical Education Centers.

Certification Requirements

The certification requirements differ for each certification and are specific to the products and job functions addressed by the certification. To become a Microsoft Certified Professional, you must pass rigorous certification exams that provide a valid and reliable measure of technical proficiency and expertise.

The following table describes exam requirements.

Certification	Exam requirements
Microsoft Certified Product Specialist (MCPS)	Pass one operating system exam. In addition, individuals seeking to validate their expertise in a program must pass the appropriate elective exam.
Microsoft Certified Systems Engineer (MCSE)	Pass four operating system exams and two elective exams.
Microsoft Certified Solution Developer (MCSD)	Pass two core technology exams and two elective exams.
Microsoft Certified Trainer (MCT)	Required to meet instructional and technical requirements specific to each Microsoft Official Curriculum course they are certified to deliver.[1]

For More Information See the Certification section of the Web page provided on the compact disc or the Microsoft Training and Certification Web site at http://www.microsoft.com/train_cert/

MCSE Track

This course supports the MCSE Windows NT 4.0 track. To complete this track, it is recommended that you do the following.

1. Pass Exam 70-58, *Networking Essentials*

2. Take *Administering Microsoft Windows NT 4.0* Self-Administered Assessment

3. Pass Exam 70-67, *Implementing and Supporting Microsoft Windows NT Server 4.0*
   and
   Pass any Client Exam

4. Pass Exam 70-68, *Implementing and Supporting Microsoft Windows NT Server 4.0 in the Enterprise*

5. Pass Two Elective Exams

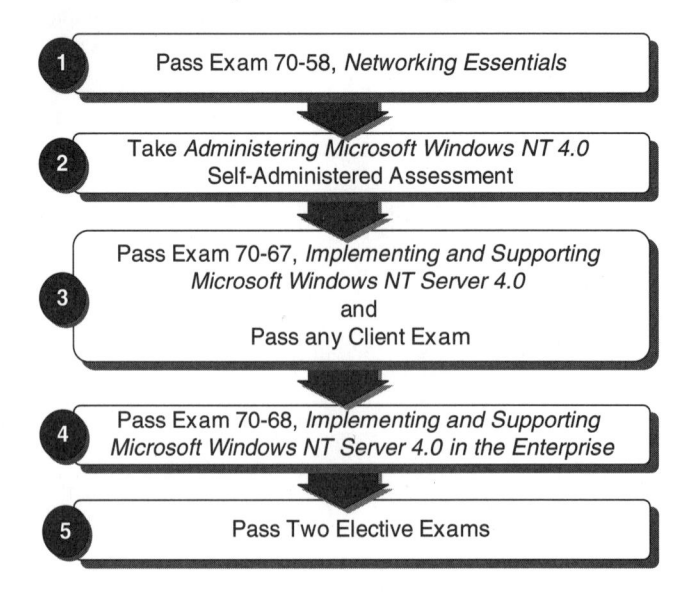

[1] *Inside the United States and Canada call (800) 636-7544 for more information on becoming a Microsoft Certified Trainer. Outside the United States and Canada, contact your local Microsoft subsidiary.*

About This Book   xxxix

The following table outlines the recommended path to certification.

Step	Pass this exam	Preparation
1	70–58, *Networking Essentials*	Course 683, *Networking Essentials—Self-Paced Training Kit*
2	*Administering Microsoft Windows NT 4.0 self-administered assessment*	Course 803, *Administering Microsoft Windows NT 4.0*
		–or–
		Microsoft Windows NT Network Administration Self-Paced Training
3	70–67, *Implementing and Supporting Microsoft Windows NT Server 4.0* and any client exam, such as exam 70–73, *Implementing and Supporting Microsoft Windows NT Workstation 4.0*[2] and exam 70–63, *Implementing and Supporting Microsoft Windows 95*	Course 803, *Administering Microsoft Windows NT 4.0*
		Course 687, *Supporting Windows NT Core Technologies*
		–or–
		Microsoft Windows NT Technical Support Self-Paced Training
		Course 564, *Microsoft Windows 95 Training—Instructor-led training*
4	70–68, *Implementing and Supporting Microsoft Windows NT Server 4.0 in the Enterprise*	Course 689, *Supporting Windows NT Server 4.0 Enterprise Technologies*

Important Microsoft Official Curriculum (MOC) helps you to prepare for Microsoft Certified Professional (MCP) exams. However, no one-to-one correlation exists between MOC courses and MCP exams.

---

[2] For a complete list of client and elective exams, see the Microsoft Training and Certification Web site at http://www.microsoft.com/train_cert/

CHAPTER 1

Overview of Windows NT

Lesson 1   Introduction to Windows NT . . . 2

Lesson 2   Overview of Windows NT Directory Services . . . 8

Lesson 3   Workgroups and Domains . . . 10

Review . . . 14

About This Chapter

This chapter provides an overview and comparison of the features of Microsoft Windows NT Server version 4.0 and Windows NT Workstation version 4.0. You are introduced to several of the key features of Windows NT Server and Workstation, and you will view a video that provides a review of Windows NT Directory Services.

Before You Begin

To complete the lessons in this chapter, you must have a computer running Microsoft Windows 95 or Windows NT version 3.5 or later, with a CD-ROM drive, an audio board, and headphones or speakers. These operating systems enable you to view the "Overview of Windows NT Directory Services" video contained on the *Course Materials* compact disc.

Lesson 1: Introduction to Windows NT

Windows NT is a multipurpose operating system that can act as both a client and a server in a network environment. Windows NT refers to two different products—Windows NT Server and Windows NT Workstation.

This lesson provides an overview of Windows NT Server and Windows NT Workstation, and the key features of both.

After this lesson, you will be able to:
- Explain the key features in Windows NT Server and Windows NT Workstation.
- Describe the features common to Windows NT Server and Windows NT Workstation, and the differences between the two operating systems.

Estimated lesson time: 10 minutes

What Is Windows NT Server?

Microsoft Windows NT Server 4.0 is:

- A powerful, multipurpose server operating system designed for organizations that must implement mission-critical business systems.
- Optimized to be a file, print, and application server that can handle tasks for organizations ranging from small workgroups to enterprise networks.
- Designed to integrate current and future technologies and to provide competitive advantages through better information access.
- The required operating system for the other Microsoft BackOffice server components, including: Microsoft SQL Server™, Microsoft Systems Management Server, Microsoft SNA Server, Microsoft Proxy Server, and Microsoft Exchange Server.

The following illustration shows some of the key features of the Windows NT Server 4.0 operating system.

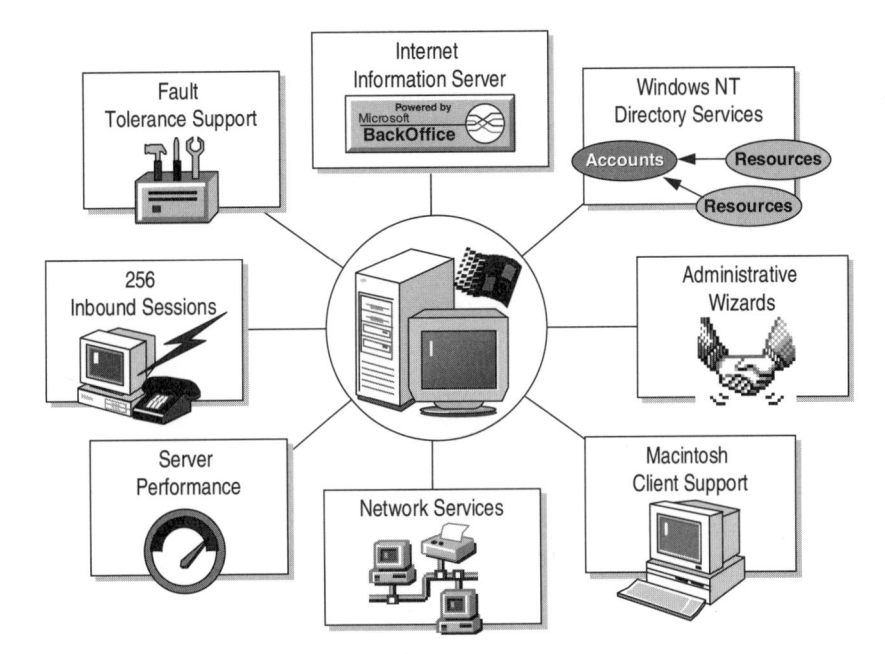

- *The Windows 95 user interface.* Provides a consistent look across desktops and the server, resulting in less training time and a faster rollout of the new network operating system.
- *Internet Information Server (IIS).* The integration of IIS with Windows NT Server 4.0 means that Web server installation and management is simply another part of the operating system. In addition, with IIS 2.0 or later, you can remotely administer your Web site from any computer with a Web browser and provide a fast and secure platform for offering HTTP, FTP, and Gopher services.

  Using Microsoft FrontPage™, a Web authoring and management tool included with Windows NT Server 4.0, you can create Web pages, audit and check the page links, and manage professional-quality Web sites.

- *Windows NT Directory Services.* A directory database that provides a single network logon and a single point of administration.
- *Administrative wizards.* Wizards group the common server management tools, such as User Manager for Domains and Server Manager, in a single place, and walk you through the steps required to add users, create and manage groups of users, manage file and folder access for network clients, and so on.
- *Macintosh client support.* Provides file and print sharing services for Macintosh clients.
- *Network services.* Provides network services, including Microsoft DNS (Domain Name System) Server, Microsoft DHCP (Dynamic Host Configuration Protocol) Server, and Windows Internet Name Service (WINS).
- *Server performance.* Windows NT Server 4.0 is tuned for file, print, and application server performance. The retail version of Windows NT Server supports up to four processors in a symmetric multiprocessing environment. Original equipment manufacturer (OEM) implementations of Windows NT Server support up to 32 processors in a symmetric multiprocessing environment.
- *256 inbound sessions.* Salespeople, home-based employees, traveling workers, and other mobile users connect to Windows NT Server 4.0 using Remote Access Service (RAS), a feature that allows remote users to dial in to their corporate network. Windows NT Server provides support for 256 inbound RAS sessions.
- *Fault tolerance.* Supports software-based *Redundant Array of Inexpensive Disks* (RAID) technology for data protection.

What Is Windows NT Workstation?

Microsoft Windows NT Workstation 4.0 is a powerful desktop operating system for business computing. Optimized for use as a high performance, secure network client and corporate desktop operating system, Windows NT Workstation maximizes the performance of desktop applications running on the local computer. Windows NT Workstation is also designed to improve end-user productivity.

Windows NT Workstation can be used alone as a desktop operating system, networked in a peer-to-peer workgroup environment, or used as a workstation in both a Windows NT Server domain and a Novell NetWare network environment. Windows NT Workstation can be used to access resources on all of the Microsoft BackOffice family of products.

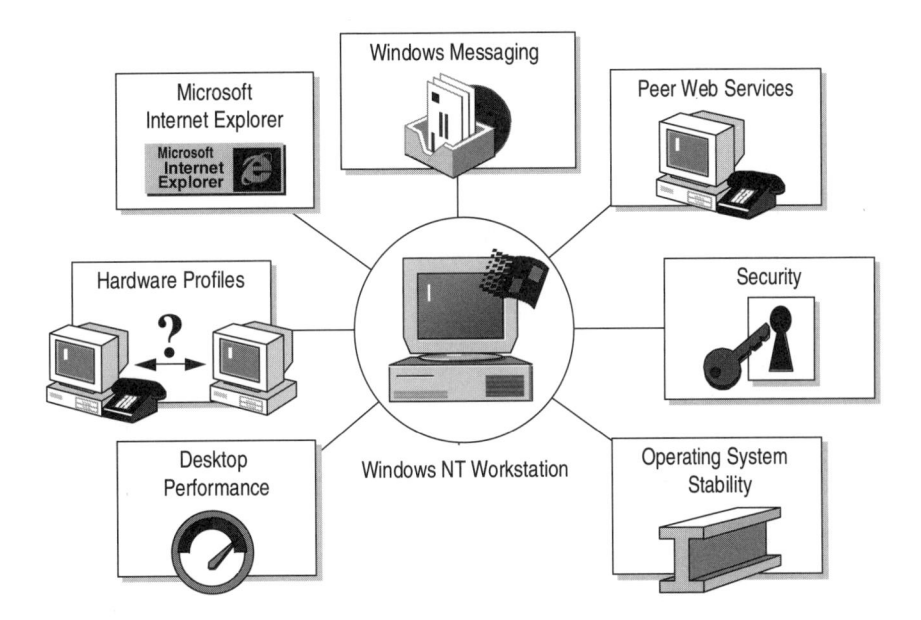

In addition, Windows NT Workstation includes the following features:

- *The Windows 95 user interface.* Provides a consistent look across desktops and the server, resulting in less training time and a faster rollout of the new network operating system.

- *Desktop performance.* Supports preemptive multitasking for all applications. Windows NT Workstation supports multiple processors for true multitasking performance.

- *Hardware profiles.* Creates and maintains a list of hardware configurations to meet specific computer needs.

- *Microsoft Internet Explorer.* Provides a fast and simple-to-use browser for exploring the Internet and the World Wide Web (WWW).

- *Windows messaging.* Receives and stores electronic mail (e-mail), including files and objects created in other applications.

- *Peer Web services.* Provides a personal Web server, optimized to run on Windows NT Workstation 4.0.
- *Security.* Provides local security for files, folders, printers, and other resources. Users must be authenticated by either the local workstation or a domain controller in order to access any resources on the computer or network.
- *Operating system stability.* Supports each application in its own memory address space. Malfunctioning applications will not affect other applications or the operating system.

Windows NT Server vs. Windows NT Workstation

Windows NT Server and Windows NT Workstation have many similar features. For example, both are 32-bit operating systems that provide a fast, multitasking environment. Each operating system also has unique features. This section covers the similarities and differences between Windows NT Server and Windows NT Workstation.

Similarities

The following table describes the common features of both operating systems, and their benefits.

Feature	Benefit
Multiple platforms	Supports Intel or compatible 80486-, Pentium-, and Pentium Pro-based computers, as well as RISC (reduced instruction set computers)-based computers, such as MIPS R4400 and R5000, DEC Alpha AXP, and PowerPC Reference Platform (PReP)-based PowerPC-based systems.
Multitasking and multi-threaded operations	Different applications can run at the same time. Background applications can continue while a user works in the foreground. Multiple threads in an application can operate simultaneously.
Support for MS-DOS-based, Win16-based, Win32-based, OS/2-based, and POSIX-compliant-based applications	Most applications run under Windows NT. Users can work on applications written for other operating systems without having to learn different operating system environments.
Built-in networking	Designed for networking. All utilities are included with the ability to add networking drivers and protocol stacks to meet connectivity requirements. Both systems include a built-in Web browser.

(*continued*)

Feature	Benefit
File systems	Windows NT includes file allocation table (FAT), Windows NT File System (NTFS), and CD-ROM File System (CDFS).
Reliability	Windows NT supports applications in separate memory address spaces. When applications are running in separate memory address spaces, malfunctioning applications will not affect other applications. Furthermore, the Windows NT architecture protects the operating system from applications that attempt to consume too much of the CPU's processing time or to use the operating system's memory address space.

Differences

The primary differences between Windows NT Server and Windows NT Workstation are:

- Windows NT Server contains enhanced features that make it a powerful network server operating system for server-based applications, such as SQL Server, Systems Management Server, SNA Server, and Microsoft Exchange Server. Whereas Windows NT Workstation is designed and tuned as a multitasking desktop operating system.
- The number of concurrent sessions that each operating system can allow. The number of incoming concurrent sessions for Windows NT Server is limited by the number of client licenses, while Windows NT Workstation has a limit of ten incoming concurrent sessions.

Note For a comparison of Windows NT Workstation and Windows 95, see Appendix A, "Comparing Microsoft Windows NT Workstation and Windows 95." You can view this appendix after completing the procedures in Chapter 2, "Installing Windows NT."

Lesson 2: Overview of Windows NT Directory Services

Windows NT Directory Services, one of the services provided by Windows NT Server, allows for centralized administration of the network. Windows NT Directory Services enables each user who has been assigned a unique user name and password to access resources throughout the network. It provides administrators with the ability to view and manage users and network resources from any computer on the network. This lesson provides an instructional video on Windows NT Directory Services, which focuses on a Windows NT environment and the role user accounts play in it.

After this lesson, you will be able to:
- Describe the Microsoft Windows NT Directory Services and the role user accounts play in them.
- Describe the function of the primary domain controller (PDC), backup domain controllers (BDCs), and member servers.
- Explain the function of a trust relationship among domains.

Estimated lesson time: 15 minutes

The video describes the components in a Windows NT network, and defines key terminology used throughout this book. You can view the complete video script on the course Web page, after you have completed the procedures in Chapter 2, "Installing Windows NT."

Practice

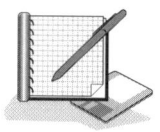

In these procedures, you install the necessary Codec files to run the video, and then you start the video.

Note To view the video, you require a computer running Windows 95 or Windows NT 3.5 or later with a CD-ROM drive.

▶ **To install the Codec files**

1. Insert the *Course Materials* compact disc compact disc in your CD-ROM drive.
2. Using My Computer, Windows NT Explorer, File Manager, or a command prompt, switch to your CD-ROM drive.
3. Change to the Videos\Codec folder.
4. From the Codec folder, run Install.exe.

5. In the **Indeo Video Interactive Install** dialog box, click **Windows 95 or NT**, and then click **OK**.
6. In the **Welcome** dialog box, click **Next**.
7. In the **Software License Agreement** dialog box, click **Yes**.
8. In the **Select Components** dialog box, click the appropriate operating system, and then click **Next**.
9. When prompted to read the Readme file, click **Yes** to read the file or **No** to continue with setup.

   The Codec files are copied to your computer.

▶ **To start the video**

- From the *Course Materials* compact disc, change to the Videos folder, and then double-click **Dirserv.avi**.

Video Review

1. Name three benefits of Windows NT Directory Services.

   _____

   _____

2. Name the three Windows NT Server types.

   _____

   _____

3. How many primary domain controllers can there be in each domain? How many backup domain controllers?

   _____

   _____

4. Name the logical link that combines domains into one administrative unit.

   _____

Lesson 3: Workgroups and Domains

A computer running Windows NT operates in either a workgroup or a domain. This lesson covers the administrative differences between workgroups and domains.

After this lesson, you will be able to:
- List the advantages and disadvantages of the workgroup model.
- List the additional advantages and disadvantages of the domain model.

Estimated lesson time: 10 minutes

What Is a Workgroup?

A workgroup is a logical grouping of typically no more than 10 computers. As part of a workgroup, each computer running Windows NT has its own directory database. One of the main advantages of a workgroup is that it allows its users to share resources. Resources and user accounts are managed at each computer in the workgroup.

The Workgroup Model

In the workgroup model, each computer functions as both a server and a client, and maintains its own accounts, administration, and security policies. The following illustration shows the Windows NT workgroup model.

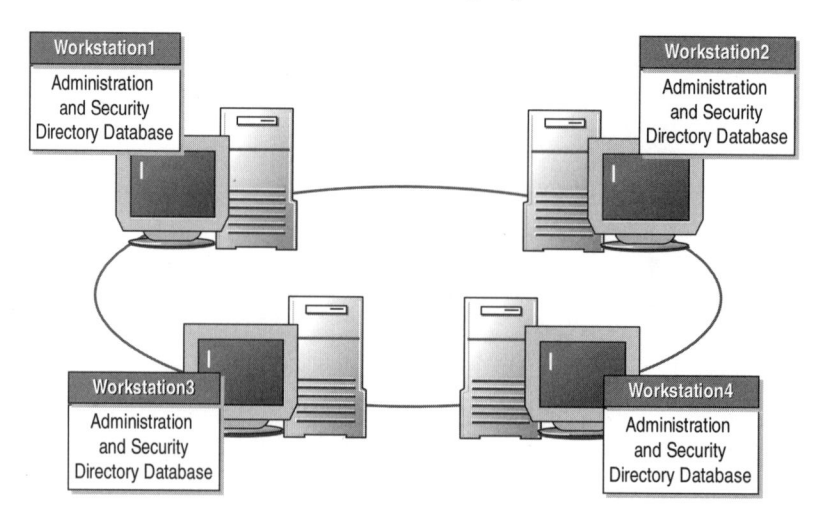

Both Windows NT Workstations and Windows NT Server stand-alone servers can be members of a Windows NT workgroup.

The workgroup model provides the following advantages and disadvantages.

Advantages	Disadvantages
Does not require a Windows NT Server domain controller.	No centralized account management.
Simple design and implementation.	Not recommended for networks that have more than 10 computers.
Convenient for a limited number of computers in close proximity.	

What Is a Domain?

A domain is a collection of computers and users that share a common directory services database. The directory services database allows for central administration of domain account privileges and security and network resources. It is stored on a domain controller.

The Domain Model

While both members of a workgroup and members of a domain can share resources, the domain provides a centralized approach to sharing network resources. The following illustration shows the Windows NT domain model. This example includes one primary domain controller (PDC), two backup domain controllers (BDCs), one computer running Windows NT Server (NTS), and two computers running Windows NT Workstation (NTW).

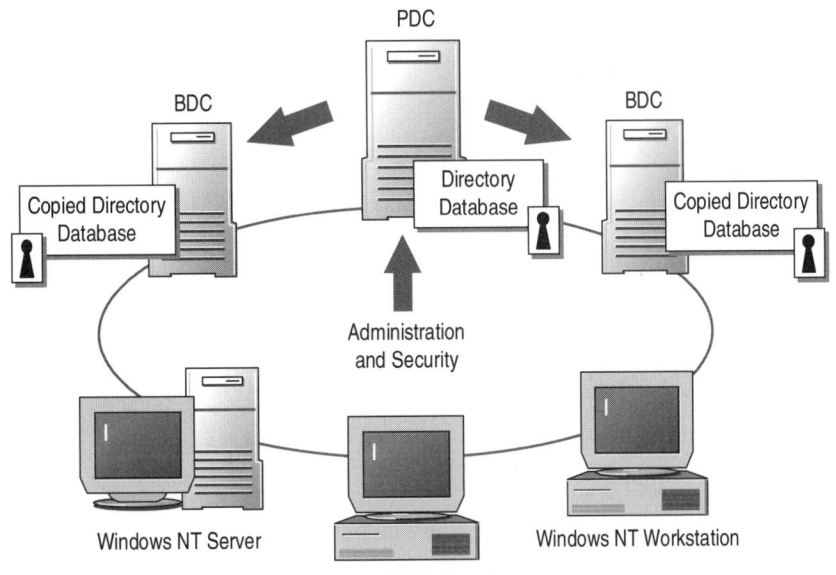

In a domain, computers running Windows NT Workstation and computers running Windows NT Server perform the following tasks:

- Obtain user account validation from the directory database.
- Allow resource access to users defined in the directory database.
- Function as part of a centrally administered group.

Summary

The following information summarizes the key points in this chapter:

- Windows NT refers to two different products—Windows NT Server and Windows NT Workstation.

- Windows NT Server 4.0 is a multipurpose server operating system, optimized to be a file, print, and applications server. Its client/server platform is designed to integrate current and future technologies.

- Windows NT Workstation 4.0 is a desktop operating system that can be used on a stand-alone computer, on a networked computer in a peer-to-peer workgroup environment, or on a networked computer in a Windows NT Server domain or Novell NetWare environment.

- Windows NT Directory Services, one of the services provided by Windows NT Server, allows for centralized administration of the network. The Windows NT Directory Services enables each user who has been assigned a unique user name and password to access resources throughout the network. It provides administrators with the ability to view and manage users and network resources from any computer on the network.

- A workgroup is a logical grouping of typically no more than 10 computers that can share resources. As part of a workgroup, each computer running Windows NT has its own directory database; resources and user accounts are managed at each computer.

- A domain is an administrative unit of Windows NT Directory Services. A domain contains a computer running Windows NT Server configured as a primary domain controller (PDC). The PDC maintains a directory database that stores all of the account and security information for the domain.

Review

1. What is Windows NT Directory Services?

2. Explain the difference between a domain and a workgroup.

3. Which Windows NT operating system provides file and print services for Macintosh clients?

Answer Key

Video Review

Page 9

1. Name three benefits of Windows NT Directory Services.

   Single user logon, universal access to resources, and centralized administration.

2. Name the three Windows NT Server types.

   Primary domain controller, backup domain controller, and member server.

3. How many primary domain controllers can there be in each domain? How many backup domain controllers?

   Each domain must have one and only one primary domain controller. Each domain can have zero or more backup domain controllers; however, at least one is recommended.

4. Name the logical link that combines domains into one administrative unit.

   A trust relationship, or trust.

Review Answers

Page 14

1. What is Windows NT Directory Services?

   Windows NT Directory Services, one of the services provided by Windows NT Server, allows for centralized administration of the network. Windows NT Directory Services enables each user who has been assigned a unique user name and password to access resources throughout the network. It provides administrators with the ability to view and manage users and network resources from any computer on the network.

2. Explain the difference between a domain and a workgroup.

   In a domain, all domain controllers maintain a common directory database, so each user who has been assigned a unique user name and password can log on from any computer that is in the domain. In a workgroup, each computer maintains its own directory database, so a separate user account for each user must exist in each computer's directory database.

3. Which Windows NT operating system provides file and print services for Macintosh clients?

   Windows NT Server.

CHAPTER 2

Installing Windows NT

Lesson 1　Preparing for Installation . . . 18

Lesson 2　Installing Windows NT . . . 34

Lesson 3　Adding a Computer Account to a Domain . . . 49

Lesson 4　Logging On to a Computer or Domain . . . 57

Lesson 5　Installing Windows NT Server from a Network Share . . . 64

Lesson 6　Viewing the Windows NT Documentation . . . 79

Review . . . 82

About This Chapter

This chapter describes the Microsoft Windows NT installation process. You learn what information is required to install Windows NT and how to install it from compact disc or over a network.

Before You Begin

To complete the lessons in this chapter, you must have:

- Two computers that meet the hardware and software requirements as specified in the Getting Started section of "About This Book."
- Nine blank, 1.44 MB high-density disks.

Lesson 1: Preparing for Installation

Before installing Windows NT, you need to determine the computer's configuration, such as the computer's hardware components, the existing partition scheme, existing file systems, and current operating systems. If you are installing Windows NT Server on a computer that will join a domain, you also need to determine the computer's role in that domain. This lesson explains the information that you need to determine before installing Windows NT.

After this lesson, you will be able to:
- Use the NT Hardware Qualifier (NTHQ) program.
- Identify the minimum hardware requirements for installing Windows NT on Intel or RISC-based computers.
- Describe the information required to install Windows NT.

Estimated lesson time: 45 minutes

Hardware Requirements

Before installing Windows NT, you should check to ensure that the computer's hardware is on the Windows NT 4.0 Hardware Compatibility List (HCL). Microsoft supports *only* the devices listed on the HCL. If a device is not on the HCL, contact the device manufacturer to determine if there is a Windows NT driver for the device. The HCL is included on the Windows NT Server and Windows NT Workstation compact disc in a Help file named Hcl.hlp. The most recent version of the HCL is located on the Internet at the following Web site:

http://www.microsoft.com/ntserver/showcase/hwcompatibility.asp

If this Web site is unavailable, please go to the Microsoft home page (http://www.microsoft.com) and search for "compatibility."

Determine the Computer's Hardware

Windows NT provides the NT Hardware Qualifier (NTHQ) to determine the hardware on an Intel *x*86-based computer. NTHQ detects the computer's hardware and can help you avoid installation and start-up problems. You run NTHQ in the following practice. The following illustration shows an example of how NTHQ displays hardware information about a computer.

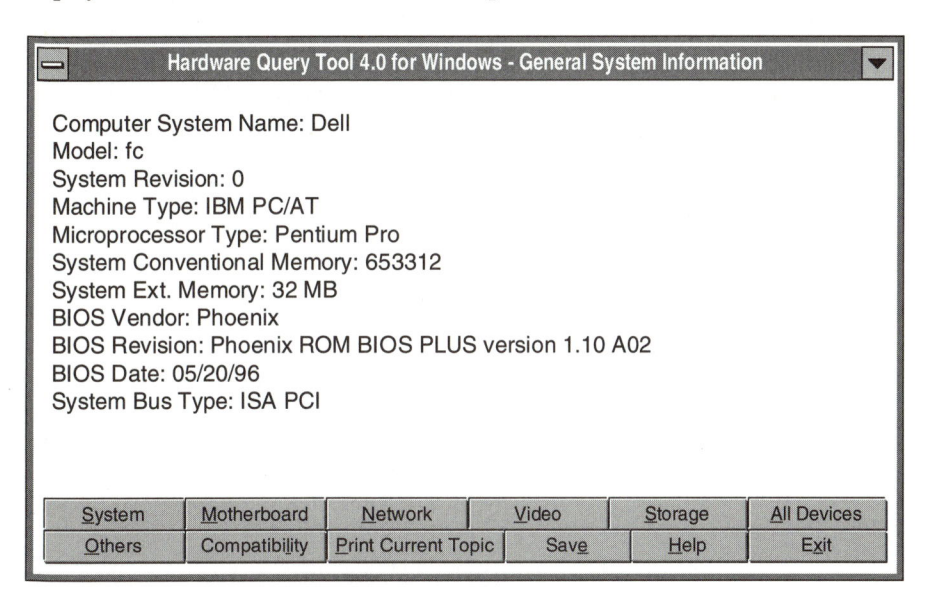

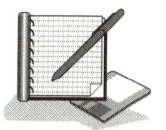

```
Hardware Query Tool 4.0 for Windows - General System Information

Computer System Name: Dell
Model: fc
System Revision: 0
Machine Type: IBM PC/AT
Microprocessor Type: Pentium Pro
System Conventional Memory: 653312
System Ext. Memory: 32 MB
BIOS Vendor: Phoenix
BIOS Revision: Phoenix ROM BIOS PLUS version 1.10 A02
BIOS Date: 05/20/96
System Bus Type: ISA PCI

 [ System ] [ Motherboard ] [ Network ]         [ Video ] [ Storage ] [ All Devices ]
 [ Others ] [ Compatibility ] [ Print Current Topic ] [ Save ]  [ Help ]    [ Exit ]
```

Practice

In these procedures, you create an NTHQ disk and then run NTHQ to determine the hardware components on your system. If any of the hardware components are not on the HCL, your installation of Windows NT Server may not be successful.

Note This procedure requires that you have an operating system installed on a computer that provides the ability to access the CD-ROM drive. This could be the computer that you use to install Windows NT, or a different computer.

▶ **To create an NTHQ disk**

1. Start the computer and insert the *Microsoft Windows NT Server 4.0* compact disc in the CD-ROM drive.
2. Insert a disk in drive A.

   You can use either a formatted or unformatted disk, because a disk image overwrites any information currently on the disk.
3. Start *cd-rom_drive*:\Support\Hqtools\Makedisk.bat

   Makedisk.bat copies the disk image to the floppy disk, creating the NTHQ disk.

▶ **To run NTHQ**

Note Complete this procedure on each of the computers you use to install Windows NT Server or Workstation.

1. Insert the NTHQ disk in drive A, and remove any compact discs from the CD-ROM drive.
2. Shut down and then restart the computer.

   The **Hardware Query Tool 4.0 for Windows** dialog box appears.
3. Read the dialog box, and then click **Yes**.

   The **Detection Method-comprehensive or safe** dialog box appears.
4. Read the dialog box, and then click **Yes**.

   NTHQ runs using comprehensive detection.
5. Explore the NTHQ results for your computer. Use the following table to enter the values for the listed hardware components. You need to click the buttons at the bottom of the display to obtain some of this information.

Hardware component	Value
Computer System Name:	
Model:	
System Revision:	
Microprocessor Type:	
BIOS Vendor:	
BIOS Date:	
System Bus Type:	
Network Device:	
Network Device IRQ:	
Hard Disk Controller Device:	
Video Display Device:	

6. Verify that your entries in the table are on the HCL.

    The HCL can be found by double-clicking the Hcl.hlp file located in the Support folder of your *Microsoft Windows NT Server 4.0* compact disc.

7. Exit the Hardware Query tool, and then remove the NTHQ disk from drive A.

Minimum Hardware Requirements

The following table describes the minimum hardware requirements for installing Windows NT 4.0.

Hardware component	Minimum hardware requirement
CPU	One of the following microprocessors:
	32-bit Intel x86-based (80486/33 or higher) processor or compatible.
	Intel Pentium- or Pentium Pro-based processor.
	MIPS R4400- or R5000-based processor.
	Digital Alpha AXP-based processor.
	PReP-compliant PowerPC-based processor.
Memory	Intel x86-based computers: 16 megabytes (MB) of random access memory (RAM) for Windows NT Server and 12 MB of RAM for Windows NT Workstation.
	RISC-based computers: 16 MB of RAM for Windows NT Server and Windows NT Workstation.
Free hard disk space	Intel x86-based computers: approximately 125 MB for a typical installation of Windows NT Server and 110 MB for Windows NT Workstation.
	RISC-based computers: approximately 160 MB for Windows NT Server and 110 MB for Windows NT Workstation.
	The amount of free disk space required is also dependent upon the sector size in use on the system partition. For example, to install Windows NT Server on a partition using 16 KB clusters the computer would require about 120 MB of free disk space. By comparison, installing Windows NT Server on a partition using 32 KB clusters requires that the computer have about 200 MB of free disk space. A larger cluster size wastes space, because the entire cluster is not used to store data. For this reason, the unused portion of the cluster is wasted.

(continued)

Hardware component	Minimum hardware requirement
Display	Video display adapter with VGA resolution or higher.
Mouse	Microsoft Mouse or other pointing device.
Other drives	Intel *x*86-based computers require a high-density 3.5-inch floppy disk drive and a CD-ROM drive, unless the computer supports the El Torito specification. The El Torito specification does not require the computer to have a floppy disk drive because you can start the computer with a bootable compact disc. For computers without a CD-ROM drive, install Windows NT over a network. RISC-based computers require a CD-ROM drive.
Optional hardware components	Network adapter card and appropriate network cabling.

PowerPC Special Requirements

The version of Windows NT compiled to run on the PowerPC platform is designed to run only on systems that conform to the PReP (PowerPC Reference Platform) specification, created by IBM.

Disk Partitioning During Setup

With Windows NT Setup, you can partition the computer's hard disk during installation. A *partition* is a portion of a physical disk that functions as though it were physically a separate unit. Partitions are assigned their own drive letters, and allow the separation of the operating system and user data into logical units. For example, you could store the operating system on one partition and data on another partition. This would save time when backing up and restoring data.

If only one partition exists, then Windows NT stores all of its files on that partition.

System and Boot Partitions

If there is more than one partition, Windows NT copies the hardware-specific files to the *active* partition (ordinarily drive C), also known as the *system* partition. Setup then prompts you to select a folder in which to install the Windows NT operating system files. This folder can be on the system partition or another partition. The partition that contains the operating system files and its supporting files is called the *boot* partition. If both the hardware-specific files and the operating system and its supporting files are installed on one partition, then that partition would be both the system and boot partition.

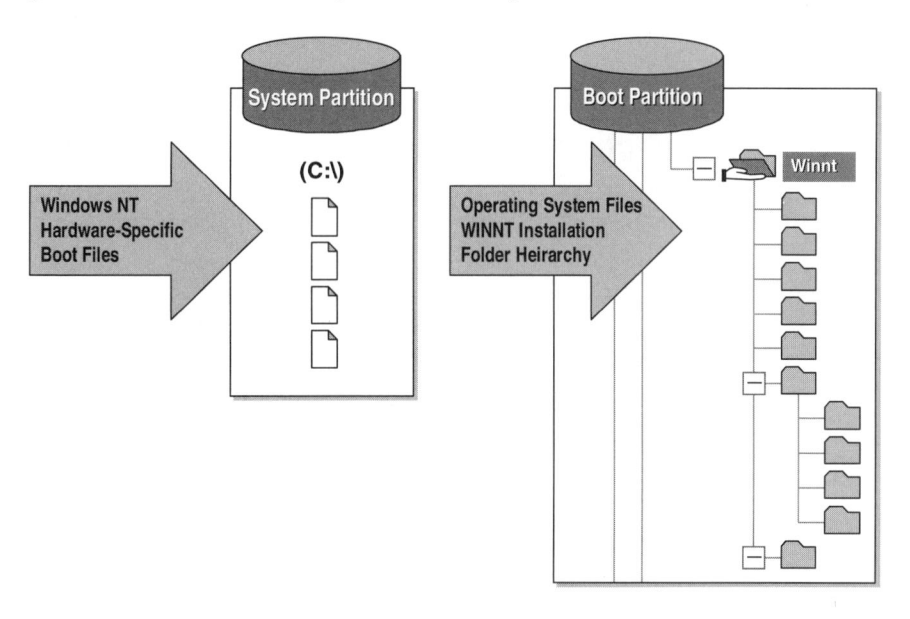

Note If you are familiar with the MS-DOS or Windows 95 operating systems, the Windows NT use of the system and boot partitions may seem confusing. This is because in MS-DOS and Windows 95 the active partition is called the boot drive or partition, whereas in Windows NT, the active partition is called the system partition.

On a RISC-based computer, you use a firmware configuration program to designate the system partition.

Unknown Partition Types

If you are installing Windows NT on a hard disk that already contains *stripe sets, volume sets*, or any areas allocated for *fault tolerance (disk mirroring* and *disk striping with parity)*, they appear on the Setup screen as partitions of an unknown type. If you plan to partition or reformat an unknown partition, but you want to save the data it contains, back up the data before you start Setup, and then restore it after you have completed the Windows NT installation.

Note For more information about stripe sets and volume sets, see Chapter 6, "Managing Partitions." For more information about fault tolerance, see Chapter 7, "Managing Fault Tolerance."

Selecting a File System During Setup

Before installing Windows NT, determine which of the two supported file systems, Windows NT File System (NTFS) or file allocation table (FAT) that you will use for each partition you create.

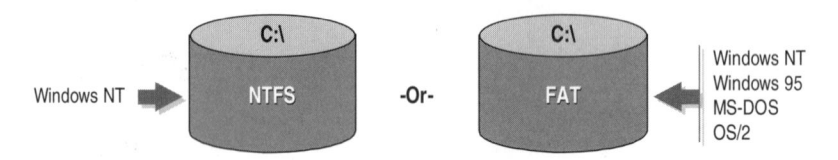

NTFS

NTFS can *only* be accessed by Windows NT and for this reason it provides greater security than the FAT file system. This is because you cannot start the computer with another operating system, such as Windows 95, and access data on an NTFS partition.

Choose NTFS when:

- Windows NT is the only operating system in use.
- Using Services for Macintosh for file sharing.
- File-level security is required.
- Permissions must be preserved while migrating directories and files from a Novell NetWare server.
- Windows NT file compression is required.
- Local security is required.

FAT

The FAT file system can be accessed by Windows NT, Windows 95, MS-DOS, and OS/2 operating systems.

Choose FAT when:

- You require multiple-boot capability between Windows NT and other operating systems, such as Windows 95 or MS-DOS. For this configuration, drive C must be formatted with the FAT file system.
- Installing Windows NT on RISC-based computers. The system partition on a RISC-based computer *must* be formatted with FAT for the firmware to detect the partition as a bootable partition. This partition must be at least 2 MB in size and have enough free hard disk space to store two required Windows NT files: Hal.dll and Osloader.exe.

Common Support Issues

When creating a partition during installation, the partition is always formatted as FAT. Even if you choose to format the partition as NTFS, the initial format is FAT. At the end of the installation, the system restarts and the partition is converted to NTFS.

A problem occurs if you want to create an NTFS partition larger than 4 gigabytes (GB) during installation. Because FAT has a maximum partition size of 4 GB, a partition larger than 4 GB cannot be created during installation.

Solutions

Use one of the following solutions to solve this problem:

- Choose to create a partition of 4 GB or less, then complete the installation. After you finish installing Windows NT, log on as Administrator and start Disk Administrator. You can then use Disk Administrator to extend the NTFS partition. Extending an NTFS partition allows you to add unused disk space to the partition.
- On a different computer that is already running Windows NT, format a partition greater than 4 GB. Remove the drive from that computer and then install it in the computer on which you want to install Windows NT. This computer now has a 4 GB partition where you can install Windows NT.

If you are upgrading from a previous version of Windows NT and want to create an NTFS partition larger than 4 GB, use Disk Administrator to create the partition prior to starting the upgrade.

Note For more information about file systems, see Chapter 5, "Managing File Systems."

Choosing a Server Role During Setup

Prior to installing Windows NT Server, it is important to plan the configuration of your network and the type of servers you need. When you install Windows NT Server you can choose to configure the computer to be one of the following types of servers:

- Primary domain controller (PDC)
- Backup domain controller (BDC)
- Stand-alone (or member server)

PDC
- Only one per domain
- Stores domain directory database
- Validates user accounts

BDC

BDC
- Stores copy of domain directory database
- Validates user accounts
- Can be promoted to a PDC

Member Server   Member Server

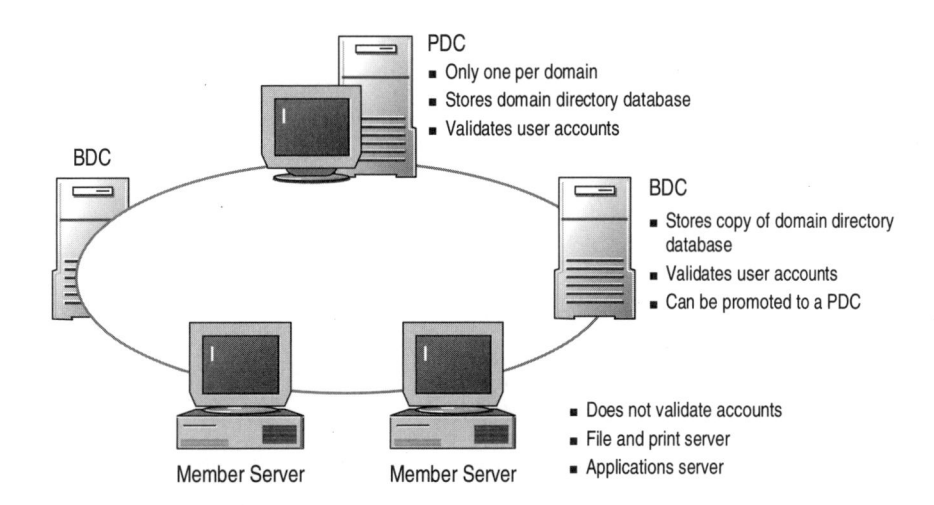

- Does not validate accounts
- File and print server
- Applications server

Primary Domain Controller (PDC)

Each domain requires and can contain *only one* PDC. The PDC contains the directory database for the domain. The PDC also authenticates logon requests.

Once the computer is configured as a PDC it must be online before any other computer can join the domain.

Note Any domain controller can authenticate logon requests from the following clients: MS-DOS clients with *enhanced redirector* installed, Windows NT, Windows 95, Windows for Workgroups, and Microsoft LAN Manager.

Creating a Domain

If you choose to configure the computer as a PDC, the Windows NT Server Setup program prompts you for a unique domain name; entering the domain name automatically creates a new domain. When a domain is created, a domain *security identifier* (SID) is created. A domain SID is a unique numeric value that identifies a domain and is included in all user, group, and computer accounts that are created on the domain.

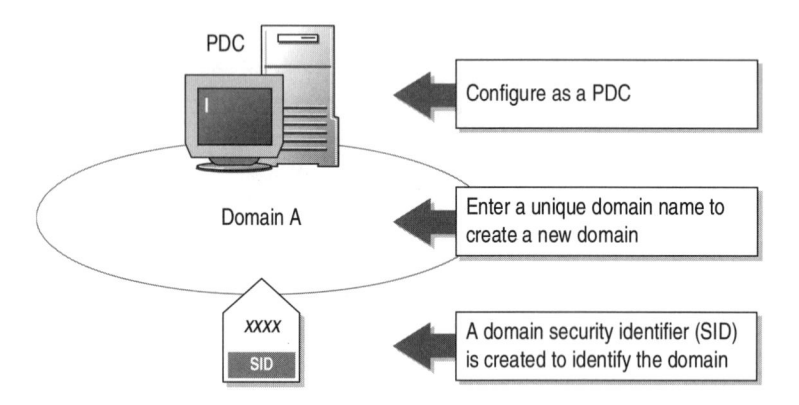

Changing the Domain Name After Installation

You can change the domain name after Windows NT Server is installed, without reinstalling Windows NT Server. This is because the domain SID (rather than the domain name) identifies the domain. The new domain name is associated with the existing SID. However, if you change the domain name you also have to change the domain name for all workstations and servers in the domain. Also, any trust relationships with other domains would have to be re-established.

Computer and domain names are changed using the Network program in Control Panel. Clicking the **Change** button on the **Identification** tab allows you to change the computer name, the domain name, or both.

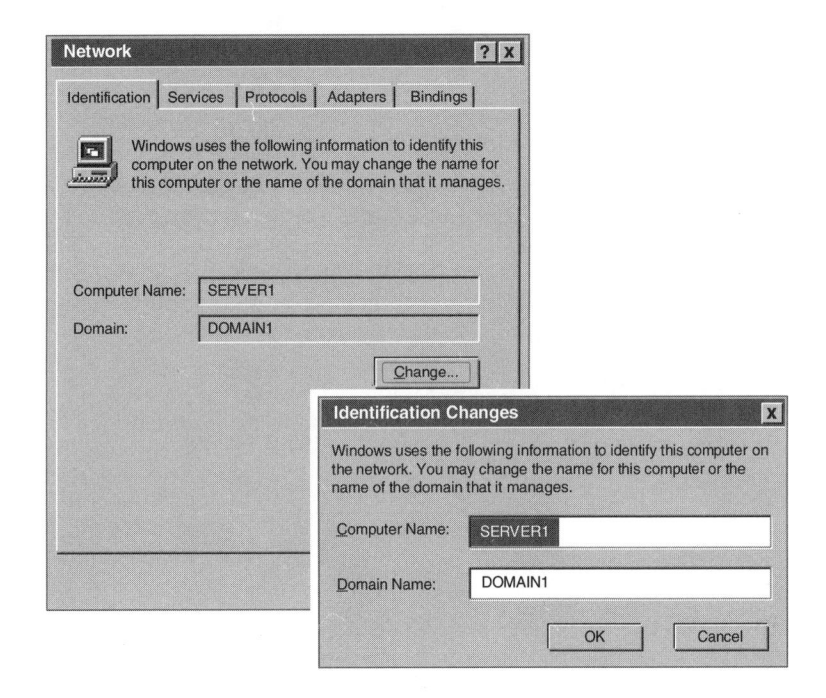

Backup Domain Controller (BDC)

A BDC can also authenticate logon requests; for this reason there are often several BDCs in a domain. If you choose to configure the computer as a BDC, during setup you must supply the name of the domain that the BDC is joining.

Because BDCs can also validate user accounts, the copy of the domain's directory services database, which is stored on the BDC, must be current with the directory services database which is stored on the PDC. To ensure the BDCs remain current, the PDC sends out timed notices that signal the BDCs to request directory changes from the PDC. When the BDC requests changes, it informs the PDC of the last change to the directory database that it received. In this manner, all of the domain controllers remain current.

Furthermore, if the PDC fails, one of the domain BDCs can be promoted to a PDC. The only user account data that would be lost are recent changes that have not yet been replicated to the BDCs.

Moving a Backup Domain Controller to Another Domain

You cannot move a BDC to another domain unless you reinstall Windows NT Server on the BDC. This is because the domain SID cannot be changed without reinstalling Windows NT Server. The best way to avoid reinstallation is to plan your Windows NT network so that PDCs and BDCs remain in the domains in which they were created.

Stand-Alone or Member Server

A stand-alone server may be a member of either a workgroup or a domain. A stand-alone server that is part of a domain is also known as *member* server.

Unlike domain controllers, stand-alone servers do not validate domain user logon requests. For this reason, stand-alone servers provide file, print, and application services more efficiently than domain controllers.

Stand-alone servers and computers running Windows NT Workstation cannot be reconfigured as a BDC or a PDC without reinstalling Windows NT Server.

Moving a Member Server to Another Domain

Unlike a BDC, you can move a member server or a computer running Windows NT Workstation to another domain without reinstalling Windows NT. This is because member servers and computers running Windows NT Workstation maintain their own directory services database. The following illustration shows how the **Identification Changes** dialog box appears when you click the **Change** button on the **Identification** tab. Notice that you can choose to make the computer a member of a workgroup or a domain.

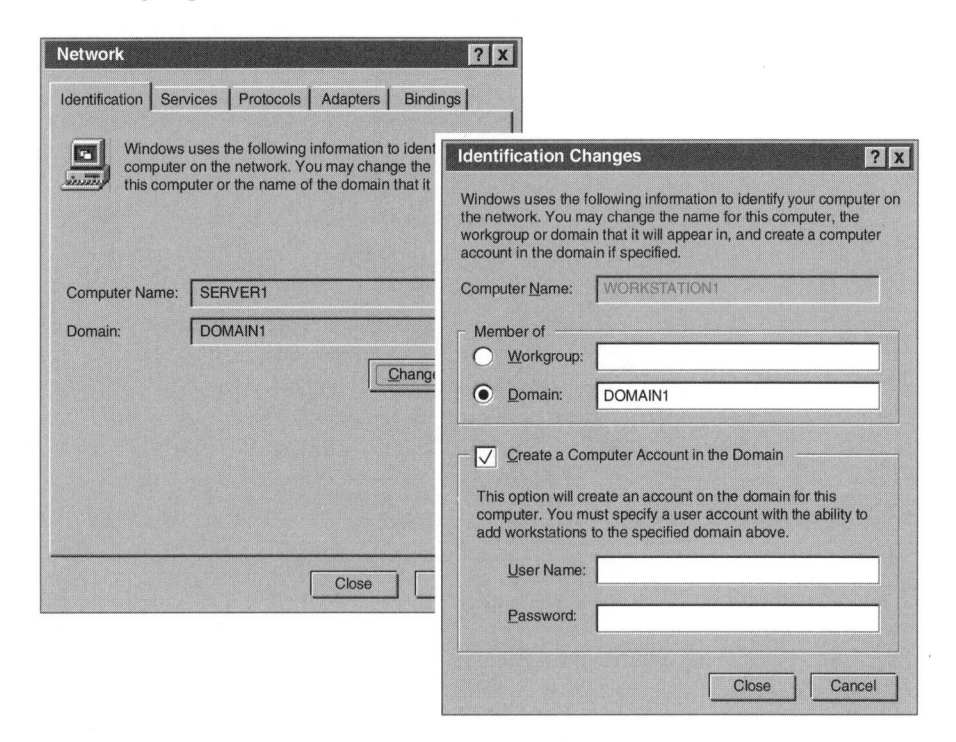

Joining a Domain or Workgroup During Installation

For a BDC, member server, or computer running Windows NT Workstation to participate in a domain, a computer account for that computer must be created and then that computer can join the domain.

For a BDC to join a domain, you must create a computer account on the PDC either prior to or during the installation of the BDC, and supply a computer name and domain name during installation. Stand-alone servers or computers running Windows NT Workstation can join a domain during installation, using the same process as for the BDC. However, stand-alone servers or computers running Windows NT Workstation can also join a domain after installation.

Joining a Workgroup

If the stand-alone server or computer running Windows NT Workstation is joining a workgroup, you supply the name of the workgroup, instead of the name of the domain, during installation. A workgroup does not require a computer account because workgroups do not provide centralized administration of the computer and user accounts in the workgroup.

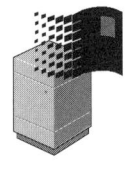

Choosing a Licensing Mode During Setup

During the installation of Windows NT Server you must choose a licensing mode.

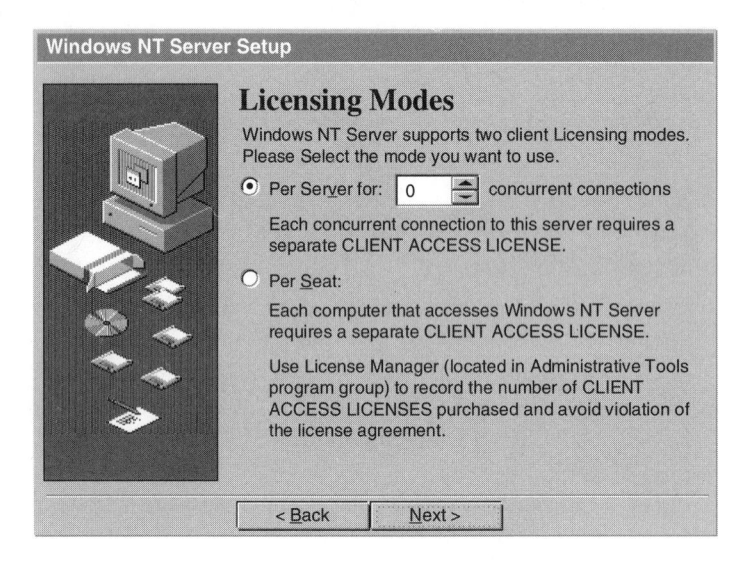

![Windows NT Server Setup - Licensing Modes dialog box. Windows NT Server supports two client Licensing modes. Please Select the mode you want to use. Per Server for: 0 concurrent connections. Each concurrent connection to this server requires a separate CLIENT ACCESS LICENSE. Per Seat: Each computer that accesses Windows NT Server requires a separate CLIENT ACCESS LICENSE. Use License Manager (located in Administrative Tools program group) to record the number of CLIENT ACCESS LICENSES purchased and avoid violation of the license agreement.]

A client access license (CAL) is required in order for a client computer to access resources on a computer running Windows NT Server. A CAL is separate from the desktop operating system software that a client uses to connect to a server. For example, purchasing Microsoft Windows 95, Windows NT Workstation, or any other desktop operating system that connects to a computer running Windows NT Server does not constitute a legal license to connect to a server.

During the installation of Windows NT, you must choose one of the following licensing modes:

- *Per Server licensing mode.* Each CAL is assigned to a specific server and allows one connection to *only* that server for the following basic network services.
    - *File services.* Using and managing files or disk storage.
    - *Printing services.* Using and managing printers.
    - *Macintosh connectivity.* File sharing and printing services.
    - *File and Print Services for NetWare connectivity.* File and printing services for NetWare clients.
    - *Remote access services.* Accessing the server from a remote location through a communication link.

    A connection in Per Server licensing mode is defined as a session between a client and the server. If a client has multiple drive and printer mappings to a single server, the connection would still be considered a single connection for licensing purposes.

- *Per Seat licensing mode.* Requires a separate CAL for each *client* that will access the server for basic network services (file, print, and remote access services). Once a client computer is licensed, it may access any computer running Windows NT Server installed on the network at no additional charge. This means that an unlimited number of computers can have access to a single server, provided each computer is licensed with the appropriate CAL.

    The Per Seat licensing mode is often the most economical one for networks in which clients ordinarily connect to more than one server. For example, in a stock brokerage company users might need persistent connections to an e-mail server, a server running stock quotes, and a server that provides access to the World Wide Web (WWW).

Note If you are not sure which licensing mode to choose, select the Per Server option. After Windows NT Server is installed, you can use the Licensing program in Control Panel for a one-time conversion from the Per Server license to a Per Seat license at no cost. It is not necessary to notify Microsoft to make this change. For more information about client access licenses, see Chapter 15, "Implementing Network Clients."

Lesson 2: Installing Windows NT

This lesson covers the Windows NT installation process and the differences between the installation options when installing Windows NT Workstation or Windows NT Server.

After this lesson, you will be able to:
- Start the setup process on any platform supported by Windows NT.
- Distinguish between the setup types for Windows NT.
- Describe the Windows NT installation process.
- Install Windows NT Server.

Estimated lesson time: 90 minutes

Starting a Windows NT Installation

How you start the Windows NT installation depends on the computer's hardware platform. The Windows NT compact disc includes a version of Windows NT for the Intel x86 and RISC (MIPS, Alpha, and PPC) hardware platforms.

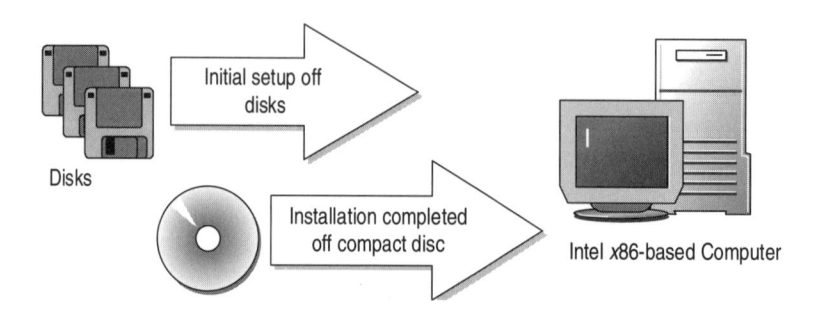

Intel x86-based Computers

To install Windows NT on an Intel x86-based computer, use the three Setup disks and the Windows NT compact disc. The computer must start from the Windows NT Setup Boot Disk (also referred to as Setup Disk #1) and proceed through the other two disks before it can access the Windows NT compact disc. The three Setup disks contain a minimal version of Windows NT, under which the initial Windows NT Setup process runs.

Note If your computer supports the El Torito specification, you do not have to use the disks because you can start the computer with the bootable compact disc.

RISC-based Computers

For RISC-based computers, Windows NT Setup must be invoked directly from the compact disc using the Setupldr program. Depending on the version of the computer's firmware, this may be as simple as clicking **Install Windows NT from CD-ROM** on the firmware's supplementary menu. If the computer does not have this option, click **Run a Program** (or an equivalent command) on the firmware menu and then enter the path to Setupldr. Setupldr loads and initializes Windows NT Setup from the compact disc.

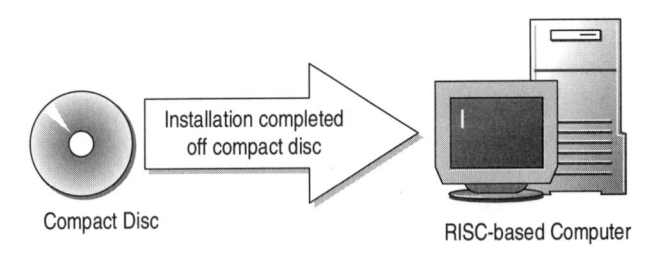

Compact Disc → Installation completed off compact disc → RISC-based Computer

Windows NT Setup Types

Windows NT Workstation provides four setup types: typical, portable, compact, and custom. You can choose one of these types during setup to specify whether or not to include certain components on your computer. Windows NT Server provides only the custom setup type.

The following table describes each setup type.

Setup type	Description
Typical	Designed for most situations, and automatically installs the following components: - Accessibility features. - All Windows NT accessories, except for desktop wallpaper and mouse pointers. - All communications programs. - All multimedia components except Sound Schemes. Windows messaging and games are *not* installed.

(*continued*)

Setup type	Description
Portable	Designed for notebook and other portable computers and *automatically* installs the following components that are useful for mobile computing: • Accessibility features. • All Windows NT accessories except for Desktop Wallpaper and Mouse Pointers. • All communications programs. • All multimedia components supported by the hardware. Dial-Up Networking is also installed by default. Windows messaging and games are not installed.
Compact	Designed to conserve hard disk space, and automatically installs only components required by Windows NT.
Custom	Designed to let you choose which components to install. This setup type is useful when the you require a configuration that is not provided by one of the other setup types.

Components

The following list describes each installation component.

- *Accessibility options.* Includes choices for changing the keyboard, sound, display, and mouse behavior for users with visual, hearing, or mobility impairments.
- *Accessories.* Includes Calculator, Character Map, Dial-Up Networking, Multimedia applications, Notepad, Telnet, WordPad, and others.
- *Communications programs.* Includes accessories to help you connect to other computers and online services.
- *Games.* Includes FreeCell, Minesweeper, Pinball, and Solitaire.
- *Multimedia.* CD Player, Media Player, Sound Recorder, and Volume Control.
- *Windows messaging.* Includes e-mail and messaging utilities.

The Windows NT Installation Process

Installing Windows NT is a step-by-step process that is easy to follow, especially when you are prepared to enter the appropriate information to complete the installation. The following information provides step-by-step information about the different parts of the Windows NT installation process.

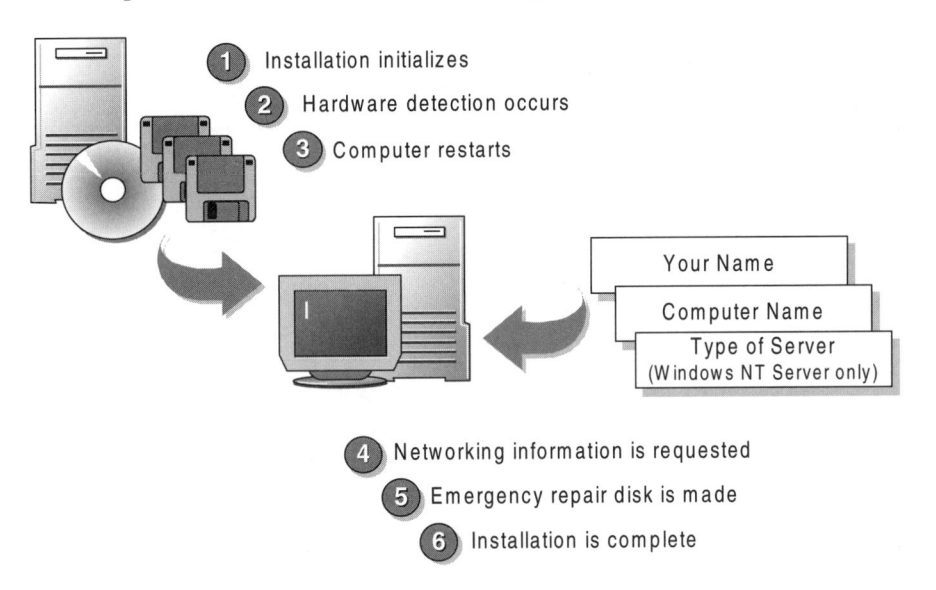

1. Installation initializes
2. Hardware detection occurs
3. Computer restarts

Your Name
Computer Name
Type of Server (Windows NT Server only)

4. Networking information is requested
5. Emergency repair disk is made
6. Installation is complete

Initializing Installation

After you start the installation, if you are doing an over-the-network installation, the setup initialization begins by copying necessary Windows NT files from the source to the hard disk, and then you are prompted to restart the computer.

Whether you are doing an over-the-network installation or a local installation, Windows NT Setup prompts you for the following information:

1. Whether to upgrade a previous version of Windows NT to Windows NT 4.0 (if there is a version of Windows NT already installed on the computer).
2. Confirmation of the detected hardware—it is normal for a computer's video adapter to be detected as VGA at this point. This ensures that the minimum hardware requirement for the video display is available. Near the end of the installation process you can configure a more advanced video adapter.
3. A partition on which to install Windows NT.
4. A file system on which to install Windows NT—by default, the existing file system for the selected partition is retained, but Setup also provides the option to convert FAT partitions to NTFS.
5. A folder to install the Windows NT files—the default folder is \Winnt. After choosing the folder, Setup begins copying the appropriate files to that folder.

Gathering Information

This part of setup begins by displaying the Windows NT Setup wizard. The following table describes the information required by the Setup wizard when installing Windows NT Workstation or Windows NT Server.

Information required by the Windows NT Setup wizard	Windows NT Workstation	Windows NT Server
Setup type (Typical, Portable, Compact, or Custom)	Choose one of the setup types.	This option does not appear on this operating system.
The name and organization of licensee	Enter the name and organization.	Enter the name and organization.
Registration	Enter the 10 digit CD Key found on the yellow sticker on the back of your compact disc case.	Enter the 10 digit CD Key found on the yellow sticker on the back of your compact disc case.
Choose a licensing mode	This option does not appear on this operating system.	Choose either the **Per Server** or **Per Seat** option.
Computer name	Enter a name unique from all other computers, workgroups, and domain names on the network. The name can be 15 characters or less.	Enter a name unique from all other computers, workgroups, and domain names on the network. The name can be 15 characters or less.
Type of server	This option does not appear on this operating system.	Choose the type of server: **PDC**, **BDC**, or **Stand-alone server**.
Password	Enter and confirm a password for the Administrator account.	Enter and confirm a password for the Administrator account.
Floating Point Divide Problem (only on certain computers)	Choose either **Do not enable** *or* **Enable** the floating-point workaround.	Choose either **Do not enable** *or* **Enable** the floating-point workaround.
Emergency Repair Disk	Choose to create an Emergency Repair Disk. This disk can repair missing or corrupt Windows NT files and restore the registry, including the directory database, security information, disk configuration, and other system information.	Choose to create an Emergency Repair Disk. This disk can repair missing or corrupt Windows NT files and restore the registry, including the directory database, security information, disk configuration, and other system information.
Components	Choose the appropriate components to install.	Choose the appropriate components to install.

Installing Windows NT Networking

The Setup wizard continues by prompting you for the appropriate networking information, such as the type of network adapter card in the computer and the protocols used on the network. If the computer is not part of a network, you can skip this part of setup. The following table describes the networking information required to continue installing either Windows NT Workstation or Windows NT Server.

Networking information	Windows NT Workstation	Windows NT Server
How the computer should participate on the network	Choose one of the following: **Do not connect this computer to a network at this time**, *or* **This computer will participate on a network**. If you choose **This computer will participate on a network**, you can then choose the appropriate networking option(s): **Wired to the network**, or **Remote access to the network**.	Choose the appropriate networking option(s): **Wired to the network, Remote access to the network**.
Install Microsoft Internet Information Server (IIS)	This option does not appear on this operating system.	Click **Install Microsoft Internet Information Server** if you want to install this service. You are prompted to configure the appropriate protocols.
Search for installed network adapter cards	Click **Start Search** to have Setup determine the network adapter cards in your computer. If the network adapter card is not automatically detected, click **Select from list** to choose the correct adapter.	Click **Start Search** to have Setup determine the network adapter cards in your computer. If the network adapter card is not automatically detected, click **Select from list** to choose the correct adapter.

(*continued*)

Networking information	Windows NT Workstation	Windows NT Server
Select the appropriate network protocols	Choose the network protocols you want to use on your network: TCP/IP, NWLink IPX/SPX Compatible Transport, NetBEUI Protocol. TCP/IP is the default. If you choose TCP/IP as a protocol, you are prompted as to whether you want to use DHCP. If there is a DHCP server on your network, TCP/IP can be configured to dynamically provide an Internet Protocol (IP) address.	Choose the network protocols you want to use on your network: TCP/IP, NWLink IPX/SPX Compatible Transport, NetBEUI Protocol. TCP/IP and NWLink are the defaults. If you choose TCP/IP as a protocol, you are prompted as to whether you want to use DHCP. If there is a DHCP server on your network, TCP/IP can be configured to dynamically provide an IP address.
Network services	By default, the Computer Browser, NetBIOS Interface, RPC Configuration, Server, and Workstation services are installed. You can click **Select from list** to add other services.	By default, the Computer Browser, NetBIOS Interface, RPC Configuration, Server, and Workstation services are installed. You can click **Select from list** to add other services.
Network Adapter setup	The available options are determined by the network adapter card such as IRQ, I/O Port Address, I/O Channel Ready, and Transceiver type.	The available options are determined by the network adapter card such as IRQ, I/O Port Address, I/O Channel Ready, and Transceiver type.
Configure network bindings	Choose to disable or arrange the order in which the computer finds information on the network.	Choose to disable or arrange the order in which the computer finds information on the network.
Configure the Workgroup or Domain name	Enter a workgroup or domain name. A computer account must exist for the computer to join the domain. If the account does not exist, click **Create computer account in domain** and create the computer account. You must supply a user account, such as the domain Administrator account, and corresponding password, with the ability to add workstations to the specified domain.	Enter a workgroup or domain name. If the computer is a backup domain controller or a member server, a computer account must exist for the computer to join the domain. If the account does not exist, click **Create computer account in domain** and create the computer account. You must supply a user account, such as the domain Administrator account, and corresponding password, with the ability to add workstations to the specified domain.

Finishing Setup

The Setup wizard completes the setup by prompting you for the following information:

1. If you chose to install IIS, you are prompted to specify which IIS options to install.
2. Time zone, date, and time.
3. Video adapter and configuration.

   Your monitor may not support all resolution configurations supported by the video card. If Setup does not recognize the video card, you can install a driver manually after setup using the Display program in Control Panel.

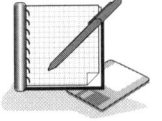

Practice

In these procedures, you install Windows NT Server from the compact disc onto drive C of Computer1. You name the computer Server1, and configure it as a primary domain controller in Domain1. Then you assign Server1 the *IP address* 131.107.2.200 and *subnet mask* 255.255.0.0.

Before you begin the installation, you create the three Setup boot disks needed for the Windows NT Server installation.

To complete these procedures, you need four blank disks. You also need access to a computer that has an operating system and a CD-ROM drive accessible through that operating system.

Important If your computer is part of a larger network, verify with your network administrator that the computer name, domain name, and IP address information do not conflict with network operations. If they do conflict, ask your network administrator to provide alternate values, and use those values for all of the procedures in this book.

▶ **To create Windows NT Server Setup disks**

In this procedure, you create the three Setup disks needed to complete a Windows NT Server compact disc installation.

Note This procedure requires that you have an operating system installed on a computer that provides the ability to access the CD-ROM drive.

1. Insert the *Microsoft Windows NT Server 4.0* compact disc in the CD-ROM drive.
2. Start a command prompt.

   If you are using a computer running Windows 95 or Windows NT, click the **Start** button, point to **Programs**, and then click **Command Prompt**.

3. If you are using a computer running MS-DOS, Windows 3.1, Windows for Workgroups, or Windows 95, at the command prompt, type:

   cd-rom_drive_letter:**\I386\winnt /ox**

   substituting the appropriate letter for your CD-ROM drive.

   If you are using a computer running Windows NT, at the command prompt, type:

   cd-rom_drive_letter:**\I386\winnt32 /ox**

   substituting the appropriate letter for your CD-ROM drive.

   Note For example, if your CD-ROM drive letter is **e**, type **e:\I386\winnt /ox**

4. Press ENTER.

   The **Windows NT 4.00 Upgrade/Installation** dialog box appears, prompting for the location of the Windows NT Server files.

5. In the path or location box, type *cd-rom_drive_letter*:**\I386** and then press ENTER or click **Continue**.

6. When prompted, label a blank disk as Windows NT Server Setup Disk #3, insert the disk in drive A, and then press ENTER or click **OK**.

7. When prompted, label a blank disk as Windows NT Server Setup Disk #2, insert the disk in drive A, and then press ENTER or click **OK**.

8. When prompted, label a blank disk as Windows NT Server Setup Boot Disk, insert the disk in drive A, and then press ENTER or click **OK**.

   When Winnt or Winnt32 has finished creating the disks, the application quits.

9. Remove the disk from drive A and the compact disc from the CD-ROM drive.

▶ **To start the Windows NT Server installation**

In these procedures, you install Windows NT Server.

Note Complete these procedures on Computer1.

1. Insert the Windows NT Server Setup Boot Disk (also referred to as Setup Disk #1) in drive A, and then start your computer.

   You receive the message that Setup is inspecting your computer hardware. Setup then loads files.

2. When prompted, insert the Windows NT Server Setup Disk #2 in drive A, and then press ENTER.

   Setup continues to load files. The **Welcome to Setup** screen appears.

3. Read the **Welcome to Setup** screen, and then press ENTER to continue.
4. Press ENTER to have Windows NT Setup automatically detect mass storage devices.
5. When prompted, insert the Windows NT Server Setup Disk #3 in drive A, and then press ENTER.

   Setup continues to load files, and then displays the recognized mass storage devices.
6. When prompted, press ENTER to confirm the detected devices.
7. When prompted, insert the Windows NT Server CD-ROM in the CD-ROM drive, and then press ENTER.

   The Windows NT Licensing Agreement appears.
8. Use the PAGE DOWN key to scroll through and read the Licensing Agreement.
9. Press F8 to accept the terms of the agreement.

   Setup looks for versions of Windows installed on your computer that can be upgraded.
10. If prompted, press N to cancel the upgrade of any existing version of Windows NT, and instead install a fresh copy of Windows NT.
11. Review the detected hardware and software components, and if you need to make changes, follow the directions on your screen. Press ENTER to confirm the hardware and software components.
12. Select partition C, and then press ENTER to install Windows NT Server on drive C.
13. If there is information on your computer that you need to keep, click **Leave the current file system intact (no changes)**, and then press ENTER.

    If you want to reformat your partition to ensure a clean install, click **Format FAT**, and then press ENTER. You are prompted to press F to begin the format.
14. Press ENTER to confirm the default installation directory of Winnt.
15. Press ENTER to have Setup examine your hard disk.

    Setup copies files to the hard disk. This process may take a few minutes.
16. When prompted, remove the disk from drive A. Also remove the *Windows NT Server CD-ROM* from the CD-ROM drive, and then press ENTER to restart your computer.

▶ **To complete the gathering information part of setup**

1. When prompted, insert the *Windows NT Server CD-ROM* in the CD-ROM drive, and then click **OK**.

   Note If you click **OK** before the CD-ROM drive has had time to read the compact disc, you are prompted to insert the *Windows NT Server CD-ROM*. Click **OK** to continue with setup.

   Setup continues to copy files, and then the Windows NT Server Setup wizard appears.

2. Click **Next**.

   Windows NT Setup creates the folder hierarchy for your installation.

3. Type your name and organization, and then click **Next**.
4. In the **CD-Key** box, type **040** followed by **0048126** and then click **Next**.
5. Click **Per Server**, enter **10** concurrent connections, and then click **Next**.
6. In the **Name** box, type **Server1** and then click **Next**.
7. Click **Primary Domain Controller**, and then click **Next**.
8. In the **Password** and **Confirm Password** boxes, type **password** for the Administrator account password, and then click **Next**.
9. If you see a message indicating that your computer exhibits a floating-point divide problem, click **Do not enable the floating-point workaround**, and then click **Next**.
10. Click **Yes, create an emergency repair disk (recommended)**, and then click **Next**.
11. Click **Next** to accept the default components.

▶ **To install Windows NT Networking**

1. Click **Next** to begin installing Windows NT Networking.
2. Click **Next** to confirm that your computer is wired to the network.
3. Clear the **Install Microsoft Internet Information Server** check box, and then click **Next** to skip installation of Internet Information Server.
4. Click **Start Search** to have Windows NT Server Setup detect your network adapter card.
5. If there is only one network adapter card in your computer, or if you are sure that the network adapter card you want to use has been detected, click **Next** to confirm the detected network adapter card.

   If the wrong network adapter card is detected, you must manually select your network adapter card. For example, if you have two network adapter cards in your computer and your cable is plugged into one card, but the other one is detected, you must click **Select from list**. Then select the appropriate network adapter card and click **OK**.
6. Clear the **NWLink IPX/SPX Compatible Transport** check box, verify that **TCP/IP** is the only protocol selected, and then click **Next**.
7. Click **Next** to confirm the selected network services.
8. Click **Next** to install the selected network components.
9. If prompted, enter the appropriate configuration settings for your network adapter card, and then click **Continue**.
10. Click **No** so that your computer will not use DHCP.

    Windows NT Server Setup installs and configures the networking components. The **Microsoft TCP/IP Properties** dialog box appears on the **IP Address** tab.
11. Click **Specify an IP address**.
12. In the **IP Address** box, type **131.107.2.200**
13. Click **OK** to accept the default **Subnet Mask** of 255.255.0.0 and a blank **Default Gateway**.
14. Click **Next** to accept the default bindings.
15. Click **Next** to start the network.
16. In the **Domain** box, type **Domain1** and then click **Next** to create the domain.

▶ **To complete Windows NT Server setup**
1. In the **Windows NT Server Setup** dialog box, click **Finish**.
2. When prompted, in the **Time Zone** list, click the correct time zone for your location, confirm that the **Date** and **Time** options are correct, and then click **Close**.
3. Click **OK** to confirm the detected video adapter.
4. Click **Test** to test the settings for your video adapter, and then click **OK**.
5. If you did not see the test bitmap, adjust your settings and test them again. If you did see the test bitmap, click **Yes**, and then click **OK**.
6. Click **OK** to confirm the video settings.

    Windows NT Server Setup copies additional files to the hard disk, and saves the configuration to the emergency repair folder.

7. When prompted, label a blank disk as Emergency Repair Disk, insert it in drive A, and then click **OK**.

    Windows NT formats the disk and then copies the emergency repair information.

8. When prompted, remove the disk from drive A and the compact disc from the CD-ROM drive, and then click **Restart Computer**.

    The computer restarts.

9. When the operating system selection list appears, select the default Windows NT Server version 4.0, and then press ENTER.

Installing the Course Materials on Server1

Now that you have installed Windows NT Server, you need to install the course materials to continue with the course. The course materials include lab files, and the course Web page which contains supplemental material, such as appendixes and links to important Microsoft Web sites.

Practice

▶ **To install the course materials on Server1**

1. Insert the *Course Materials* compact disc in the CD-ROM drive of Server1.
2. Log on as Administrator.

Note Throughout this course the password for the administrator is *password*.

3. From the *Course Materials* compact disc, run Setup.exe.

   The **Microsoft Windows NT 4.0 Technical Support** dialog box appears.
4. Click **Continue**.
5. In the **Name** box, type your name.
6. In the **Organization** box, type the name of your organization or leave this box empty, and then click **OK**.
7. Click **OK** to confirm that the Name and Organization information was entered correctly.
8. Click the **Setup** button.

   The required course files are copied to and installed on the hard disk.
9. Click **OK**.

▶ **To install Microsoft Internet Explorer 3.0**

1. In the *Course Materials* compact disc, open the IE_Setup folder, and then run Msie30.exe.

   A **Microsoft Internet Explorer 3.0** dialog box appears prompting if you want to install Microsoft Internet Explorer 3.0.

2. Click **Yes** to install Microsoft Internet Explorer 3.0.

   A **Microsoft Internet Explorer Setup** dialog box appears indicating that files are being copied to a temporary folder on your hard disk.

3. Read the End-User License Agreement for Microsoft Internet Explorer, and then click **I Agree** to accept the terms of the agreement and continue the installation.

   A **Microsoft Internet Explorer Setup** dialog box appears indicating that files are being copied and Microsoft Internet Explorer is being set up on your computer.

4. When prompted to restart your computer, click **Yes**.

Lesson 3: Adding a Computer Account to a Domain

Before a computer running Windows NT can join a domain, a computer account must be created or added to the domain directory database. In this lesson, you configure Computer2 by adding a computer account to Domain1, installing Windows NT Workstation on Computer2, and then configure Workstation1 to join Domain1.

After this lesson, you will be able to:
- Identify who can add computer accounts to a domain.
- Create a computer account.
- Install Windows NT Workstation.
- Join a domain.

Estimated lesson time: 90 minutes

Only users who have the user right *add workstations to a domain* can create a computer account. Members of the Administrators, Domain Admins, or Account Operators groups have this user right, by default. You can use the following methods to create a computer account:

- Create the account during installation.
- Use the **Add to Domain** option in Server Manager—you can add the computer account prior to installation and then delegate the task of actually installing Windows NT by providing the computer account name to the person who completes the installation. This is common in organizations where end-users or help desk technicians install Windows NT but are not granted Administrator privileges.

Once the computer account is added to the domain, the computer must join the domain. This can be done during the Windows NT installation or after installation by using the Network program in Control Panel (on the local computer).

- On the local computer, use the Network program in Control Panel. When you click the **Change** button on the **Identification** tab, the options to change the computer name, join a workgroup or domain, and create a computer account in the domain are displayed. If the computer is configured as a PDC, you can only use this program to rename the computer or domain.

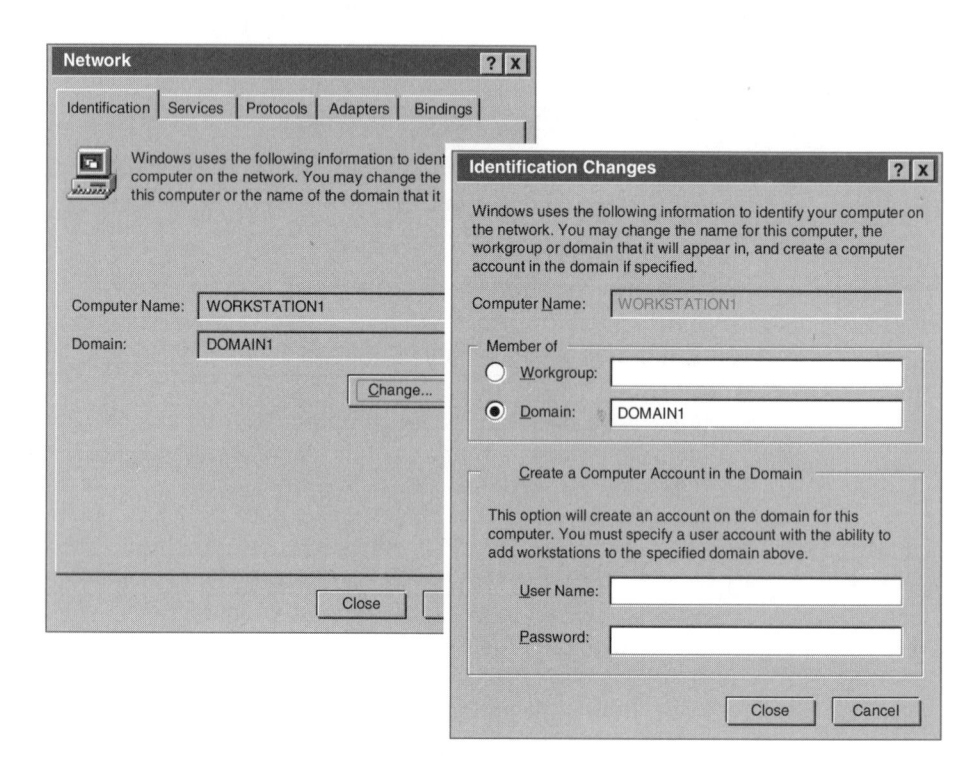

Practice

In this procedure, you use Server Manager to create a computer account named *Workstation1*.

▶ **To add a computer account to a domain**

Note Complete this procedure on Server1.

1. Log on as Administrator.
2. Click the **Start** button, point to **Programs**, point to **Administrative Tools (Common)**, and then click **Server Manager**.
3. On the **Computer** menu, click **Add to Domain**.
4. In the **Add Computer to Domain** dialog box, click **Windows NT Workstation or Server**.
5. In the **Computer Name** box, type **Workstation1** and then click **Add**.

    A computer account for Workstation1 is added to the domain directory database.

6. Click **Close**.

    The computer Workstation1 appears in the Server Manager window.

7. Close Server Manager.

Practice

In these procedures, you install Windows NT Workstation from compact disc on drive C of Computer2. You name the computer Workstation1, and it will join Domain1. You have already created a computer account for Workstation1 in Domain1. Assign the computer the IP address 131.107.2.201 and subnet mask 255.255.0.0. To complete these procedures, you need four blank disks.

Important If your computer is part of a larger network, verify with your network administrator that the computer name, domain name, and IP address information do not conflict with network operations. If they conflict, ask your network administrator to provide alternative values, and use those values throughout all of the procedures in this book.

▶ **To create Windows NT Workstation Setup disks**

In this procedure, you create the three Setup disks needed to complete a Windows NT Workstation compact disc installation.

Note Complete this procedure on Server1.

1. Log on as Administrator.
2. Insert the *Microsoft Windows NT Workstation 4.0* compact disc in the CD-ROM drive, and then close the Microsoft CD-ROM window.
3. Click the **Start** button, and then click **Run**.
4. In the **Open** box, type *cd-rom_drive_letter*:**\I386\winnt32 /ox** substituting the appropriate letter for your CD-ROM drive, and then press ENTER or click **OK**.

   The **Windows NT 4.00 Upgrade/Installation** dialog box appears, indicating the location of the Windows NT Workstation files.
5. Click **Continue**.
6. When prompted, label a blank disk as Windows NT Workstation Setup Disk #3, insert the disk in drive A, and then press ENTER or click **OK**.
7. When prompted, label a blank disk as Windows NT Workstation Setup Disk #2, insert the disk in drive A, and then press ENTER or click **OK**.
8. When prompted, label a blank disk as Windows NT Workstation Setup Boot Disk, insert the disk in drive A, and then press ENTER or click **OK**.

   When Winnt32 has finished creating the disks, the application quits.
9. Remove the disk from drive A and the compact disc from the CD-ROM drive.

▶ **To install Windows NT Workstation**

In this procedure, you install Windows NT Workstation on drive C of Computer2. You name the computer Workstation1, and it will initially be a member of the default workgroup, Workgroup.

Note Complete this procedure on the Computer2.

1. Insert the Windows NT Workstation Setup Boot Disk in drive A, and then start your computer.
2. When prompted, insert the Windows NT Workstation Setup Disk #2 and Disk #3 in drive A, and then press ENTER.
3. When prompted, insert the Windows NT Workstation CD-ROM in the CD-ROM drive, and then press ENTER.

4. Install Windows NT Workstation using the information in the following table.

When this information is requested	Use
MS-DOS-based portion of Setup	
If prompted, upgrade or new fresh copy	**N** to install a fresh copy
Partition to install on	**C**:
File system	Leave the current file system intact (no changes)
Location where files are to be installed	**\WINNT**
Phase 1: Gathering Information	
Setup Options	Typical
Name and Organization	Your name and organization
Computer Name	Workstation1
Administrator Account password	password
Emergency Repair Disk	Yes, create
Windows NT Components	Install the most common components
Phase 2: Installing Windows NT Networking	
How this computer will participate on a network	Wired to the network
Network Adapters	The correct network adapter card for your computer
Network Adapter Properties	The correct network adapter card settings for your computer
Network Protocols	TCP/IP Protocol
Do you wish to use DHCP?	No
IP Address	131.107.2.201
Subnet mask	255.255.0.0
Make this computer a member of workgroup or domain	Workgroup
Workgroup name	Workgroup
Phase 3: Finishing Setup	
Date, time, and time zone	The correct values for your location
Display	The correct display for your computer

5. When the installation has completed, restart your computer.

Installing the Course Materials on Workstation1

Now that you have installed Windows NT Workstation, you also need to install the course materials to continue with the course. The course materials include lab files, and the course Web page which contains supplemental material, such as appendixes and links to important Microsoft Web sites.

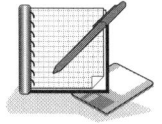

Practice

In these procedures, you install the course materials and Microsoft Internet Explorer 3.0 on Workstation1.

Note Complete this procedure on Workstation1.

▶ **To install the course materials on Workstation1**

1. Insert the *Course Materials* compact disc in the CD-ROM drive of Workstation1.
2. Log on as Administrator.
3. From the *Course Materials* compact disc, run Setup.exe.

   The **Microsoft Windows NT 4.0 Technical Support** dialog box appears.
4. Click **Continue**.
5. In the **Name** box, type your name.
6. In the **Organization** box, type the name of your organization or leave this box empty, and then click **OK**.
7. Click **OK** to confirm that the Name and Organization information was entered correctly.
8. Click the **Setup** button.

   The required course files are copied to and installed on the hard disk.
9. Click **OK**.

▶ **To install Microsoft Internet Explorer 3.0**

1. In the *Course Materials* compact disc, open the IE_Setup folder, and then run Msie30.exe.

   A **Microsoft Internet Explorer 3.0** dialog box appears prompting if you want to install Microsoft Internet Explorer 3.0.
2. Click **Yes** to install Microsoft Internet Explorer 3.0.

   A **Microsoft Internet Explorer Setup** dialog box appears indicating that files are being copied to a temporary folder on your hard disk.

3. Read the End-User License Agreement for Microsoft Internet Explorer, and then click **I Agree** to accept the terms of the agreement and continue the installation.

   A **Microsoft Internet Explorer Setup** dialog box appears indicating that files are being copied and Microsoft Internet Explorer is being set up on your computer.

4. When prompted to restart your computer, click **Yes**.

Joining a Domain

Once the computer account is created or added to the domain, use the Network program in Control Panel to join the computer to the domain.

Note If you want a computer to join to a domain, and the computer currently has a session with the PDC of that domain, the process fails and you receive a message indicating that you already have a connection. Therefore, you must disconnect all sessions that the computer has with the PDC before attempting to have it join the domain.

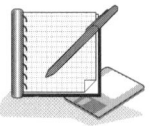

Practice

In this procedure, you have Workstation1 join Domain1.

▶ **To join a domain**

Note Complete this procedure on Workstation1.

1. Log on as Administrator.
2. Double-click the Network icon in Control Panel.
3. Click the **Identification** tab to display the current computer name and the domain or workgroup name to which the computer belongs.
4. Click the **Change** button.

   The **Identification Changes** dialog box appears.

5. In the **Member of** box, click **Domain**, and then type **Domain1** for the name of the domain to join.

Note Because you have already created a computer account in Domain1, you can just click **OK**.

If you had not previously created the computer account, you would have to click **Create Computer Account in the Domain**, supply a user account that has been granted the **Add Workstations to Domain** user right (Administrators and Server Operators have this right by default) and the appropriate password, and then click **OK**.

6. Click **OK**.
7. Click **OK** to acknowledge the **Welcome to the Domain1 domain** dialog box.
8. Click **Close**.
9. Click **Yes** to restart your computer.

Note If the computer has had Windows NT reinstalled on it, or for some other reason needs to rejoin the domain, then the computer name must be deleted and recreated at the domain controller. If this is not done, an error message refers the administrator to check the computer account on the domain.

Lesson 4: Logging On to a Computer or Domain

To access resources on a computer running Windows NT or on a domain, you must log on and be validated by the appropriate directory database. To log on you must provide a user name and password that is unique to the directory database for the computer or the domain. For example, when you log on to a domain, you are validated by the domain directory database and given permission to access resources on the domain. By contrast, when you log on locally to a computer running Windows NT, you are validated by the directory database on that computer and are given access to resources on that computer. The mandatory logon process is a security feature of Windows NT, and cannot be disabled.

After this lesson, you will be able to:
- Describe the resources that are available when you log on to a computer, domain, or workgroup.

Estimated lesson time: 20 minutes

Logging On to a Computer or Domain

The following information describes the logon procedures and the resources available to you when you start Windows NT on a computer that is a domain member.

- *Workstation or member server.* When you log on at a workstation or a member server that is a member of a domain, you can choose to log on to the local computer or to the domain. This is done by clicking either the computer name or the domain name from the **Domain** box in the **Logon Information** dialog box.

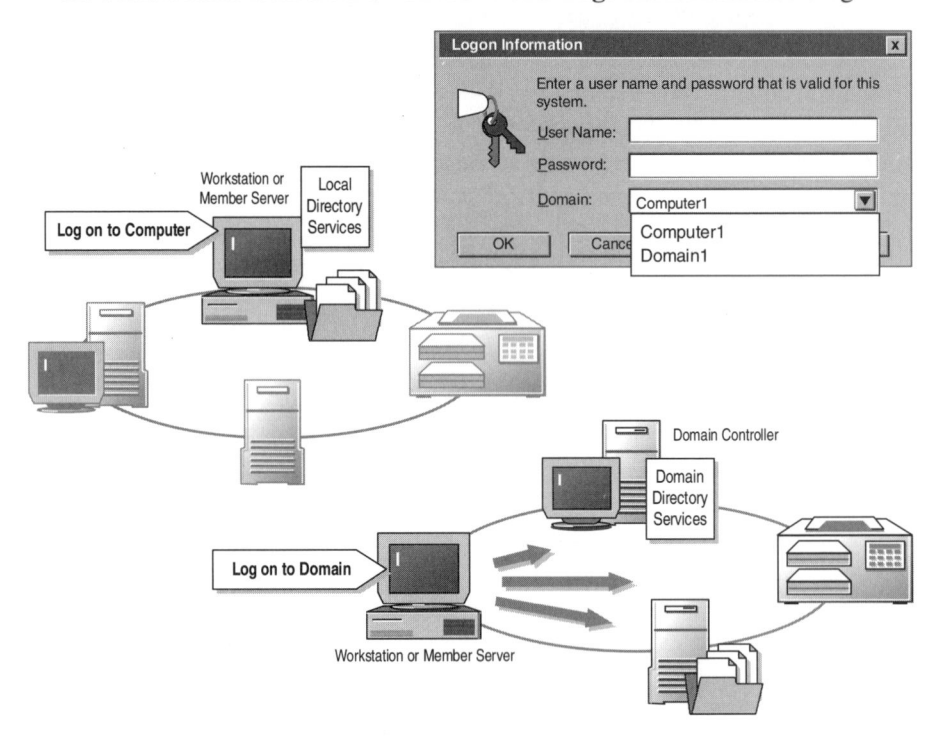

If you specify the computer name in the **Domain** box, then you are specifying the local directory services database stored on that computer. You can still view resources in the domain while logged on to the local computer. For example, you would be able to view the shared folders on another computer in the domain. However, you cannot access the contents of the shared folders unless you connect to a resource on the domain, and specify a valid domain user account and password.

You would use the following steps to map a network drive:

1. Start Windows NT Explorer.
2. On the **Tools** menu, click **Map Network Drive**.
3. In the **Path** box, enter a universal naming convention (UNC) path for the domain resource. For example, *server_name\shared_folder_name*.
4. In the **Connect as** box, enter the domain name and user account name using the following format *domain_name\domain_user_account_name*.
5. You are prompted to enter the appropriate password.

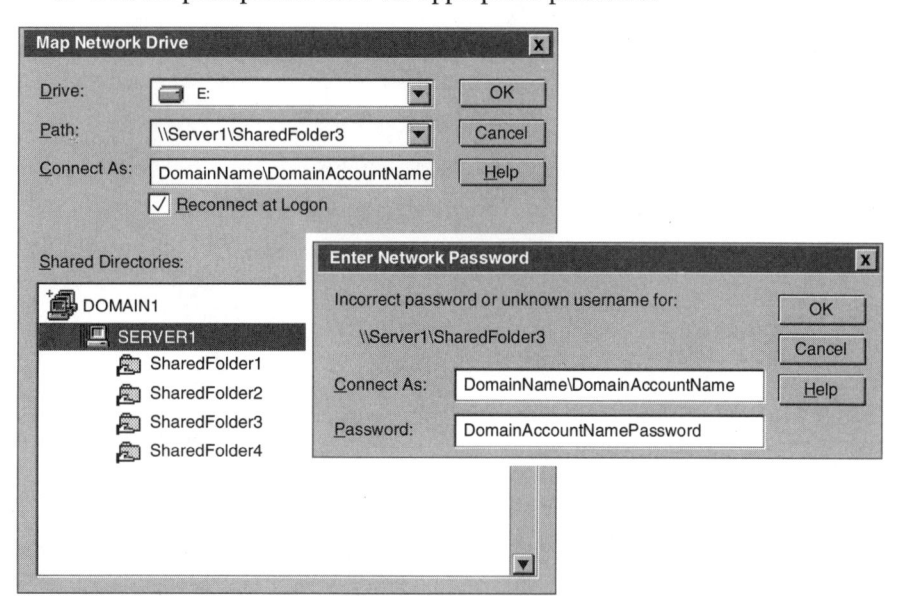

Logging On at a Domain Controller

When you log on at a domain controller, you cannot choose to log on to the local computer, you can only log on to the domain. If the appropriate trust relationships exist with other domains, you can choose to log on to another domain instead. This is because the local directory services database on domain controllers is also the domain directory services database.

When you specify the domain name in the **Domain** box, you are specifying the domain directory services database stored on the domain controllers. This means that you have access to domain resources.

Practice

In this procedure, you log on to Domain1.

▶ **To log on to a domain**

In this procedure, you examine the contents of the **Domain** box in the **Logon Information** dialog box of a domain controller, and then log on to the domain.

Note Complete this procedure on Server1.

1. If you are logged on at Server1, then log off.

   To log off, press CTRL+ALT+DELETE, click **Logoff**, and then click **OK**.

   The **Begin Logon** dialog box appears.

2. Press CTRL+ALT+DELETE to log on.

   The **Logon Information** dialog box appears.

3. In the **Domain** box, click the list box.

   What appears in the list?

4. Log on to the domain as Administrator.
5. Press CTRL+ALT+DELETE.

   The **Windows NT Security** dialog box appears.

   Why does the **Logon Information** dialog box show that you are logged on as DOMAIN1\Administrator?

Practice

In this procedure, you log on to the computer named Workstation1.

▶ **To log on to a computer**

In this procedure, you examine the contents of the **Domain** box in the **Logon Information** dialog box of a computer running Windows NT Workstation that is a member of a domain, and you then log on to the computer.

Note Complete this procedure on Workstation1.

1. If you are logged on at Workstation1, then log off.

    The **Begin Logon** dialog box appears.

2. Press CTRL+ALT+DELETE to log on.

    The **Logon Information** dialog box appears.

3. In the **Domain** box, click the list box.

    What appears in the list?

    _____

    _____

4. In the **Domain** box, click **WORKSTATION1**.
5. Log on to Workstation1 as Administrator.
6. After you have logged on and the Windows NT interface appears, press CTRL+ALT+DELETE.

    The **Windows NT Security** dialog box appears.

    Why does the **Logon Information** dialog box show that you are logged on as WORKSTATION1\Administrator?

    _____

    _____

Logging On to a Computer Running Windows NT in a Workgroup

To log on to a computer running Windows NT in a workgroup, you enter the user name and password in the **Logon Information** dialog box. Unlike logging on to a computer that is a member of a domain, you cannot choose other workgroups to log on to. The user name and password that you enter is validated against the local directory services database on that computer. If you need to access resources on another computer in the workgroup, you would have to have a user account in the directory database on that computer.

If you want to join a different workgroup, you would use the Network program in Control Panel. You would click the **Change** button and, in the **Identification Changes** dialog box, you would type in the name of the workgroup you want to join.

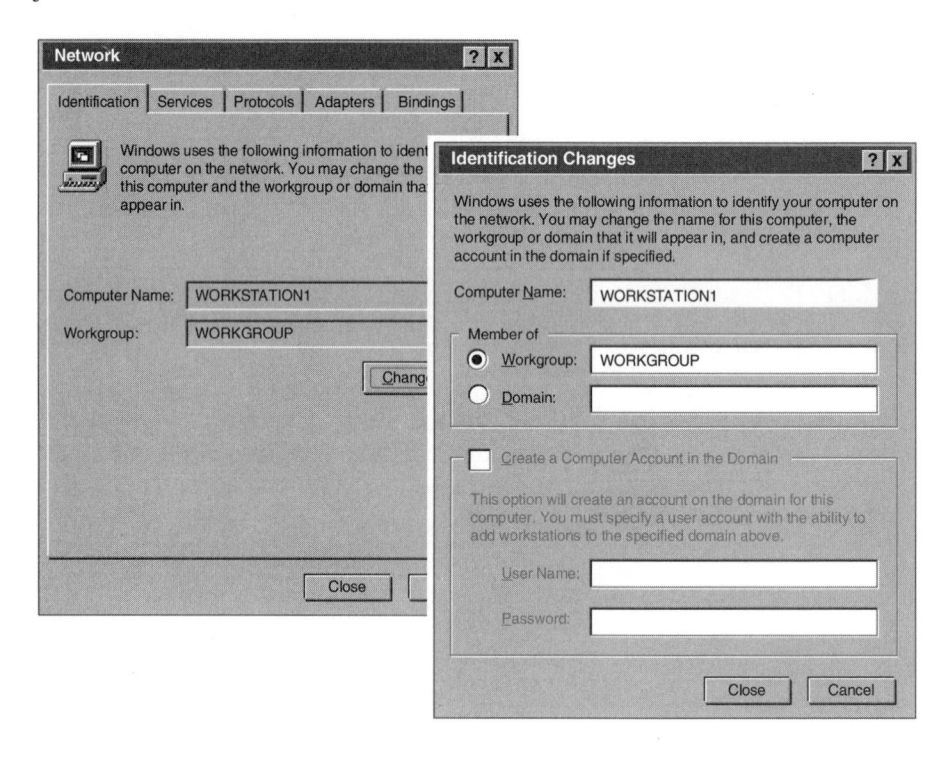

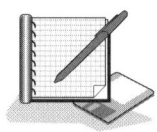

Practice

In this procedure, you log on to the domain named Domain1.

▸ **To log on to a domain from a workstation computer**

In this procedure, you examine the contents of the **Domain** box in the **Logon Information** dialog box of a workstation that is a member of a domain, and you then log on to the domain.

Note Complete this procedure on Workstation1.

1. If you are logged on at Workstation1, then log off.

   The **Begin Logon** dialog box appears.

2. Press CTRL+ALT+DELETE to log on.

   The **Logon Information** dialog box appears.

3. In the **Domain** box, click **DOMAIN1**.

4. Log on as Administrator.

5. After you have logged on and the Windows NT interface appears, press CTRL+ALT+DELETE.

   The **Windows NT Security** dialog box appears.

   Why does the **Logon Information** dialog box show that you are logged on as DOMAIN1\Administrator?

   _____

   _____

Lesson 5: Installing Windows NT Server from a Network Share

If you want to install Windows NT on multiple computers, you can streamline the installation by copying the Windows NT files to a network server. You would then log on to each of the computers, connect to the share containing the Windows NT files, and then run Setup from the server. This installation method, utilizing a network share containing the Windows NT source files, is known as a *server-based installation*. This lesson covers the procedures to perform a server-based installation.

After this lesson, you will be able to:
- Create a *distribution server* that has a network share containing the Windows NT installation files.
- Create an Unattend.txt file to prepare for an unattended installation.
- Install Windows NT on an Intel *x*86-based computer in an unattended installation using a distribution server.
- Explain why Windows NT cannot upgrade a Windows 95 installation.
- Explain how to upgrade from Windows 3.*x* to Windows NT.
- Describe how to remove Windows NT.

Estimated lesson time: 100 minutes

Performing a Server-based Installation

To perform a server-based installation, you need to create a *distribution server*. Create a distribution server by copying the Windows NT source files from the Windows NT compact disc to a shared folder that you created on the distribution server. You determine which source files to copy based on the type of computer on which you install Windows NT. Once you know the required platform(s), copy the appropriate I386, Mips, Ppc, or Alpha folder(s) containing the source files.

Note On RISC-based computers, you can use this server-based installation method only to upgrade or reinstall the operating system when Windows NT is already installed.

To copy the files, use the Windows NT Explorer or the **xcopy** command. If you use the **xcopy** command, include the **/s** switch to make sure that subfolders are copied. Furthermore, if your computer requires any drivers that are located in the Drvlib folder, you need to copy the Drvlib folder to the shared folder on your distribution server.

Note If you are using Windows NT Explorer to copy the files, you must change the Windows NT Explorer default settings in order to allow files with extensions such as .dll, .sys, and .vxd to be displayed. Files that are not displayed are not copied. To change the default settings, click **View**, click **Options**, and then in the **Hidden Files** box, click **Show all files**.

Windows NT provides two Setup programs, named Winnt.exe and Winnt32.exe, that are used for server-based installations.

- *Winnt.exe*. This file is used to install Windows NT on a client computer running Windows 95 or MS-DOS.

- *Winnt32.exe*. This file is used to install or upgrade Windows NT on a computer already running Windows NT. For example, if you are upgrading from Windows NT 3.51 to Windows NT 4.0, then you would install Windows NT 4.0 in the same folder where Windows NT 3.51 was installed, thus preserving your desktop and configuration settings.

  If you want to retain your current version of Windows NT, you should install Windows NT 4.0 in a separate folder. For example, if you are a support engineer that needs to dual boot between Windows NT Workstation and Windows NT Server, or a previous version of Windows NT, you would install Windows NT 4.0 in a separate folder.

Once the files are copied to a network server and the folder is shared, you can connect to the network share from the client computer where you want to install Windows NT, and then run Winnt.exe or Winnt32.exe. The network share method streamlines installation. You can start concurrent installations on several computers by connecting to the server from each client computer and running the Winnt.exe or Winnt32.exe program.

The following illustration shows a distribution server being used to install Windows NT Server on two computers: one to be configured as a PDC and the other as a member server. The distribution server is also being used to install Windows NT Workstation on a third computer. The distribution server would have to have both the Windows NT Server and Windows NT Workstation source files on it.

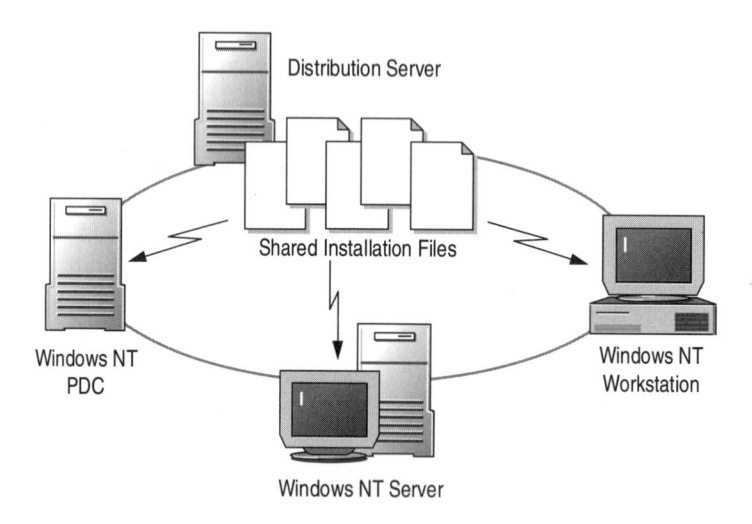

[Figure: Distribution Server sharing installation files with Windows NT PDC, Windows NT Server, and Windows NT Workstation]

Note If you do not have enough hard disk space on a network server to copy all of the appropriate Windows NT installation files, then you could share the I386, Mips, Ppc, or Alpha folder on the Windows NT Server compact disc. To share a folder, connect from the client computers to the shared folder on the compact disc and then run Setup. However, this method is much slower than installing Windows NT from the server's hard disk.

Practice

In this procedure, you create a distribution server for the Windows NT Server source files. You copy the I386 folder on the Windows NT Server compact disc to a folder on Server1, and then share the folder. You use this distribution server later in this chapter to perform an over-the-network installation.

▶ **To create a distribution server for the Windows NT Server files**

Note Complete this procedure on Server1. This procedure typically requires approximately 105 MB of free disk space on a disk partition. If you do not have sufficient free disk space, you can share the compact disc directly.

1. Start Server1 and log on as Administrator.
2. Insert the *Microsoft Windows NT Server 4.0* compact disc in the CD-ROM drive.
3. Create a folder on your hard disk named Nts_source.
4. Use Windows NT Explorer to drag and drop the I386 folder from your *Microsoft Windows NT Server 4.0* compact disc to the Nts_source folder.
5. Use Windows NT Explorer to share the Nts_source folder, assigning the share name of Nts_source, and assigning Read permissions for the group Everyone.
6. Remove the *Microsoft Windows NT Server 4.0* compact disc from the CD-ROM drive.

Installing from a Network Server to a Client Computer Running Windows 95 or MS-DOS

The Windows NT Winnt.exe Setup program is used to install Windows NT from a network server to a client computer running Windows 95 or MS-DOS.

To start the server-based installation, you use the following steps:

1. From the computer where you want to install Window NT, connect to the shared folder containing the Windows NT distribution files.
2. Run Winnt.exe.

Winnt.exe performs the following steps:

1. Winnt.exe creates three Setup boot disks. (These are copies of the disks used for the compact disc installation described earlier in this chapter.) This step requires three blank formatted disks.
2. Winnt.exe creates a Win_nt.~ls temporary folder on the client computer, and then copies Windows NT files from the network shared installation files to this folder.
3. Winnt.exe prompts you to insert the first Setup boot disk in drive A, and then to restart the computer.

Customizing a Server-based Installation

The following table describes switches that can be used with Winnt.exe to control how Setup runs.

Switch	Description
/x	Prevents Setup from creating Setup boot disks. Use this when you have already created Setup boot disks.
/ox	Specifies that Setup only create boot disks for installing from the compact disc. This option can be used to replace the disks that are included with the Windows NT product, if they have been lost or damaged.
/b	Causes the boot files to be loaded on the computer's hard disk rather than on floppy disks, so that floppy disks do not need to be loaded or removed by the user. The /b switch requires an extra 4–5 MB of hard disk space on the computer where Windows NT is being installed. This setup option creates a Ldr file and a Win_nt.~bt temporary folder on the hard disk of the client computer.
/u:answer_file	Specifies the location of an answer file that provides answers for an unattended installation that the user would otherwise be prompted for during the setup process.
/udf:id [,UDF_file]	Specifies the identifier that is to be used by the Setup program to apply sections of the Uniqueness Database File (UDF) file in place of the same section in the answer file. A UDF can be used during an unattended installation to identify settings such as the video adapter or computer name that are unique to a specific computer. If no UDF is specified, the Setup program prompts the user to insert a disk that contains a file named $UNIQUE$.UDF. If a UDF is specified, Setup looks for the identifier in that file.

(continued)

Switch	Description
/s	Specifies the location of the Windows NT source files. This switch can be used in conjunction with the **/u** switch to bypass the normal prompt for the source file location. This switch also allows you to specify multiple source file locations to significantly speed up installation.
/f	Prevents Winnt.exe from verifying files as they are copied. You can use this switch to accelerate installation.
/i:*inffil*	Specifies the file name (no path) of the setup information file. The default is Dosnet.inf. You can modify this file to customize how Setup runs.
/t:*tempdrive*	Forces Setup to place temporary files on the specified drive. If not specified, Setup uses the partition on the computer where Windows NT is being installed that has the most free hard disk space.
/l	Creates a log file named $Winnt.log on the computer where Windows NT is being installed. This file lists any errors encountered when Winnt.exe copies files to the temporary folder.

Installing from a Network Server to a Computer Running Windows NT

The Windows NT distribution files include the Setup program Winnt32.exe for installing Windows NT on computers that are already running Windows NT. It is used to upgrade from earlier version of Windows NT or to install Windows NT in a different folder on the same computer. Winnt32.exe uses all of the switches listed in the preceding table for Winnt.exe, with the exception of the **/f** and **/l** switches.

Performing an Unattended Installation

In an unattended setup, the Setup program runs over a network, using the Winnt.exe or Winnt32.exe programs with the **/u** switch. The **/u** switch is used to specify an *answer file*. The answer file is a script that you create to automate the installation.

Creating Answer Files

You can create different answer files for various computer configurations in an organization. Answer files can be further customized with UDFs. For example, you can create one answer file for each geographic location, or for each corporate division. To customize individual user and computer names you would create a UDF with a section for each computer that specifies the user name and computer name. The user can then run the customized installation by specifying the appropriate answer and UDF file when they run Winnt.exe or Winnt32.exe.

Unattended answer files can be created either by using the Setup Manager utility provided on the Windows NT Server compact disc in the Support\Deptools*platform* folder, or by modifying the sample Unattend.txt file found on the Windows NT Server compact disc in the respective platform folders. An unattended answer file can be given any legal file name.

The unattended answer file is comprised of several sections containing information that is to be used during the installation.

Note For more information on using unattended answer files and installations, see the *Microsoft Windows NT Workstation Resource Kit*.

Practice

In this procedure, you create an Unattend.txt file using Setup Manager, and then modify the file to include additional information. This Unattend.txt file is used later in this lesson to perform an unattended, over-the-network installation.

▶ **To create an Unattend.txt file**

Note Complete this procedure on Server1. This procedure assumes you have created and shared the Nts_source folder on Server1.

1. Run the **Support\Deptools\I386\Setupmgr** program from the *Microsoft Windows NT Server 4.0* compact disc.

    The **Windows NT Setup Manager** dialog box appears.
2. Click **General Setup**.

Chapter 2   Installing Windows NT   71

3. Use the tabs to complete the information in the following table.

On this tab	In this box	Do this action
User Information	User Name	Type your name
	Organization	Type your organization
	Computer Name	Type **Server2**
	Product ID	Type **040-0048126**
Computer Role	Select the role of the computer	Click **Backup domain controller**
	Enter the domain name	Type **Domain1**
Install Directory	Directory	Click **Specify installation directory now**
		Type **Server2**
Display Settings	Automatically use the above settings	Select the check box
Time Zone	Select the time zone for the user's location	Click the time zone for the user location
License Mode	Per Server	Click this option
	users permitted	Type **10**

4. Click **OK**.
5. In the **Windows NT Setup Manager** dialog box, click **Networking Setup**.
6. Use the tabs in the **Networking Options** dialog box to complete the information in the following table.

Note If Setup did *not* correctly detect and install your network adapter card during the Windows NT Workstation installation performed in Lesson 3, then click **Manual Network Installation** and go to step 7.

On this tab	In this box	Do this action
General		Click **Unattended Network Installation**
	Unattended Network Installation	Click **Automatically detect and install first adapter**
Protocols	List of Protocols	Click **Add**; in the drop-down list box, choose **TCP/IP**, and then click **OK**

(*continued*)

On this tab	In this box	Do this action
		Click **Parameters**
	Do not use DHCP	Select the check box
	IP Address	Type **131.107.2.211**
	Subnet	Type **255.255.0.0** and then click **OK**
Internet	Do not install Internet Server	Select the check box

7. Click **OK**.
8. In the **Windows NT Setup Manager** dialog box, click **Advanced Setup**.
9. Use the tabs to complete the information in the following table.

On this tab	In this box	Do this action
General	Reboot	Select the **After Text Mode** and **After GUI Mode** check boxes
	Skip Welcome wizard page	Select the check box
	Skip Administrative Password wizard page	Select the check box
File System	File System	Click **Use current file system**

10. Click **OK**.
11. Click **Save**.

    The **Save as an Answer File** dialog box appears.

12. In the **Save in** box, double-click the **Nts_source** shared folder.
13. In the **File name** box, type **Unattend**
14. In the **Save as type** box, click **Text Files (*.txt)**.
15. Click **Save**, and then click **Exit** to quit Windows NT Setup Manager.
16. In Windows NT Explorer, double-click the **Nts_source\Unattend.txt** file.

    The file is opened in Notepad.

17. Edit the **Nts_source\Unattend.txt** file using the information in the following table.

In this section	Add this line	To bypass this prompt
[unattended]	OEMSkipEula=yes	Licensing agreement
[network]	CreateComputerAccount= Administrator, password	Credentials and password used to create the computer account

18. Save the file and close **Notepad**.

Customizing the Installation with Uniqueness Database Files

When implementing a complete, unattended installation of Windows NT to numerous computers, some of the information that must be supplied through answer files, such as the computer name, must be unique to each computer. With Windows NT, use a single answer file for the information that applies to all users, and use one or more Uniqueness Database Files (UDFs) to supply information that is specific to a single computer or a small group of computers.

UDFs are used to provide replacements for sections of the answer file, or supply additional sections. The replacement sections are specified in a text file similar to the answer file. This file is indexed by means of strings called *uniqueness IDs*.

The UDF is used to specify a set of sections that should be merged into the answer file at the start of Setup. Setup then uses the merged file to perform the customized unattended installation.

The first section of the UDF is the [UniqueIds] section. This section lists all uniqueness IDs that are supported by this database. Following the [UniqueIds] section are the sections referenced in [UniqueIds]. For example:

[UniqueIds]

katedresen = UserData, Unattended

aaronco = UserData, Unattended

elang = UserData, KeyboardDrivers, PointDeviceDrivers

[UserData]

FullName = "Kate Dresen"

...

[Unattended]

NtUpgrade = no

...

Following the [UniqueIds] section are the sections referenced in [UniqueIds].

Specifying a UDF During Installation

To specify a uniqueness ID during setup, the user must run the **Winnt** or **Winnt32** command with the following parameter:

Winnt /U:answer_filename /UDF:ID[,database_filename]

Where *ID* is the uniqueness ID to use while installing Windows NT on this computer, and where *database_filename* is the file name, including the full path, of the UDF.

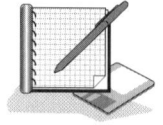

Practice

In this procedure, you install Windows NT Server on drive D of Computer2 by performing an unattended installation. To accomplish this, you connect from Workstation1 to the distribution share \\Server1\Nts_source and run Setup using the Unattend.txt file created earlier in this lesson. This installation configures Computer2 as a BDC in Domain1, and names the computer Server2.

▶ **To perform an unattended setup**

Note Complete this procedure on Workstation1. You must have at least 125 MB of disk space available on drive D.

1. Log on to the domain as Administrator.
2. Use Windows NT Explorer to map network drive S to **\\Server1\Nts_source**. Clear the **Reconnect at Logon** check box.
3. Click the **Start** button, and then click **Run**.
4. In the **Open** box, type **S:\I386\winnt32 /u:S:\unattend.txt /t:D** and then click **OK**.

   The installation starts, and you can watch the progress on the computer's screen.

5. If you configured Unattend.txt for manual network installation, when prompted, configure the network components using the information in the following table.

Note Use the information in the following table *only* if you clicked **Manual Network Installation** in the Unattend.txt file.

When this information is requested	Do this action
How this computer will participate on a network	Check only the **Wired to the network** box
Microsoft Internet Information Server	Clear this check box
Network Adapters	Click **Select from list**, and then select the correct network adapter card for your computer
Network Protocols	Select only the **TCP/IP** protocol
Network Adapter Properties	Select the correct settings for your network adapter card
Do you wish to use DHCP?	Click **No**
IP Address	**131.107.2.211**
Subnet Mask	**255.255.0.0**
Domain	**Domain1**
Administrator Name	**Administrator**
Administrator Password	**password**

When installation is complete, your computer automatically restarts.

6. Start Server2 and log on as Administrator.

Upgrading from Windows 95 to Windows NT 4.0

Because Windows NT and Windows 95 do not use the same *registry* settings or hardware device support, Windows NT cannot upgrade a Windows 95 installation. Instead, you would install Windows NT 4.0 to a separate folder. After Windows NT is installed, you need to start your computer under Windows NT and reinstall all of your applications. Your applications can be installed in the same folders that were used when they were installed under Windows 95. Reinstalling your applications under Windows NT updates the Windows NT registry. After the applications are installed, you can delete the folder where Windows 95 was installed.

Note If you intend to dual boot between Windows 95 and Windows NT, for example, if you are evaluating or supporting both operating systems, then do not delete the Windows 95 folder.

Upgrading from Windows NT 3.x to Windows NT 4.0

If you are installing Windows NT 4.0 on a computer running Windows NT 3.x, Windows NT 4.0 Setup prompts you to upgrade your version of Windows NT. If you decide to upgrade rather than complete a new installation, the following settings are preserved:

- User and group accounts
- Network settings and configuration
- The desktop environment
- Preferences set for administrative tools

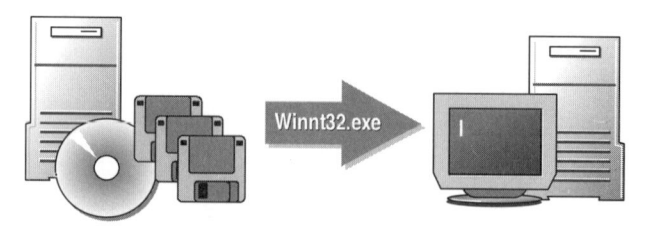

Upgrading preserves the following Windows NT 3.x data:
- User and group accounts
- Network settings and configuration
- Desktop environment
- Administrative tools preferences

To upgrade Windows NT 3.x to Windows NT 4.0, click **Yes** in response to the upgrade question during the setup process, and then follow the upgrade instructions.

Removing Windows NT

You can use one of the following methods to remove Windows NT.

- Remove the partition Windows NT is installed on. This also removes any other information on this partition.
- Remove only Windows NT. This method can only be used on a FAT partition.

Removing a Partition

Use the following procedure to remove a partition.

Caution These steps are provided for your information. If you remove Windows NT, you cannot complete the course without reinstalling Windows NT.

1. Start the computer from the Setup boot disk.
2. When prompted to create or choose a partition, click the partition where the Windows NT files are located, and then press D to delete the partition.
3. When prompted, press F3 to exit Setup.

   The partition is removed from the computer at this time.

The following list contains alternative methods for removing partitions:

- Use the OS/2 1.*x* installation disk A to delete all partitions on the first physical disk.
- Use an MS-DOS 5.0 (or later) boot floppy disk and run **fdisk**.

Note **fdisk** will not remove an NTFS logical drive in an extended MS-DOS partition.

Removing Windows NT from a FAT Partition

If you want to remove Windows NT from a FAT partition on drive C, but you want to leave Windows 95 or MS-DOS on the FAT partition, then use the following procedure.

> **Caution** These steps are provided for your information. If you remove Windows NT, you cannot complete the course without reinstalling Windows NT.

1. Start the computer from a Windows 95 or MS-DOS system disk that contains the Sys.com file.

2. From drive A, type **sys c:**

   This transfers the Windows 95 or MS-DOS system files to the boot track on drive C.

3. After the system files are successfully transferred, restart the system from the hard disk.

4. To free space on the hard disk, delete the following:
   - C:\Pagefile.sys
   - C:\Boot.ini (marked as hidden, system, and read-only)
   - C:\Nt*.* (marked as hidden, system, and read-only)
   - C:\Bootsect.dos (marked as hidden, system, and read-only)
   - *systemroot* folder
   - Program files\Windows NT

Lesson 6: Viewing the Windows NT Documentation

User documentation for Windows NT Workstation and Windows NT Server are included on their corresponding compact discs.

After this lesson, you will be able to:
- Describe the user documentation available on the Windows NT Workstation and Windows NT Server compact discs.
- Install Books Online.

Estimated lesson time: 10 minutes

The Windows NT Workstation compact disc includes support documentation that covers the installation and new features of Windows NT Workstation. The documents are stored in the Support\Books folder. They are Microsoft Word for Windows documents, and can be viewed with applications that can read Word for Windows document files, such as WordPad.

To view the contents of the online documentation, double-click Wfront.doc. The number of each chapter listed in Wfront.doc corresponds to the number in the document name listed in the Support\Books folder. Double-click the document name to view a particular document.

The Windows NT Server compact disc also includes support documentation. The documents are stored in the Support\Books folder. Included in this folder are two books that you might find useful, *Concepts and Planning* (Book_cp.hlp) and *Networking Supplement* (Book_net.hlp). You can view these support files by using the Help viewer, Books Online, which is installed during the Windows NT Server installation.

Note The first time Books Online is run, you are prompted to enter the path to the documentation files. By default, the files are stored on the compact disc. You can copy the files to the local computer or to a network file server and then set the path when you start Books Online. If you move the files to another location after you have set the path, Books Online prompts you to reset the path the next time Books Online is started.

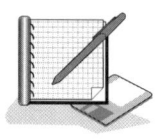

Practice

In this procedure, you start Books Online and review the Windows NT registry topic.

▶ **To use Books Online**

Note Complete this procedure on Server1.

1. Log on as Administrator.
2. Use Windows NT Explorer to create a Support folder in the Nts_source folder on your computer.
3. Use Windows NT Explorer to drag and drop the Support\Books folder from the *Microsoft Windows NT Server 4.0* compact disc to the Nts_source\Support folder on your computer.
4. Remove the *Microsoft Windows NT Server 4.0* compact disc from the CD-ROM drive.
5. Click the **Start** button, point to **Programs**, and then click **Books Online**.
6. In the **Location of Books Online Files** box, type:

   drive_letter:**\nts_source\support\books**

   substituting the correct drive letter for your computer, and then click **OK**.

   The **Help Topics: Windows NT Server 4.0 Books Online** dialog box appears.
7. Open and explore the books available in Books Online.
8. Exit Books Online.

Note Books Online is only available on Windows NT Server.

Summary

The following information summarizes the key points in this chapter:

- Before installing Windows NT on a computer you should determine:
  - That the computer's hardware is listed on the most recent version of the Windows NT Hardware Compatibility List. You can use the Windows NT Hardware Qualifier program to determine the computer's hardware.
  - How the hard disk(s) should be partitioned.
  - Which file system(s), FAT or NTFS, to use.
  - When installing Windows NT Server, whether the computer should be configured as a PDC, BDC, or stand-alone server.
- A domain can contain only one PDC. When you configure a computer as a PDC, you are creating a domain. If the computer is to be configured as a PDC, you must also choose either the Per Server or Per Seat licensing mode.
- Before a computer running Windows NT can join a domain, a computer account must be created or added to the domain directory database. Only users with the right to *add workstations to a domain*, can create computer accounts.
- If a workstation is a member of a domain, a user with the appropriate user rights can choose to log on to either the computer or the domain. If the user logs on to the workstation, the user has access to the resources on that computer. If the user logs on to the domain, the user has access to domain resources.
- When Windows NT must be installed on many computers, copy the Windows NT files to a shared network location. Then connect to the network share from the client computer and run Setup. This installation method is known as a server-based installation.
- By creating answer files and Uniqueness Database Files (UDFs), you can both automate and customize Windows NT installations.
- Windows NT cannot upgrade a Windows 95 installation.
- Windows NT can be removed by removing the partition it was installed on, or Windows NT can be removed from a FAT partition.
- The Windows NT Server compact disc and the Windows NT Workstation compact disc contain supporting documentation.

Review

1. You want to install Windows NT Server on an Alpha-based computer. You want to protect your files and folders with local security, and you will be supporting Macintosh clients. How should you partition your disk or disks?

2. You are installing Windows NT Workstation, and want to include Microsoft Exchange in the installation. What type of installation must you choose?

3. You have been told to automate the setup of Windows NT Workstation 4.0 on multiple machines in your department. You have 40 machines in five different configurations. How can you do this in the easiest possible way?

4. You are trying to install Windows NT Server as a BDC, but Setup reports that a primary domain controller cannot be found. What should you check?

5. Your computer runs only Windows NT Server 3.51. The hard disk is formatted entirely with NTFS. You want to upgrade the operating system to version 4.0 while minimizing the amount of downtime necessary to perform the upgrade. What is the quickest and least disruptive way to upgrade the server?

6. A user sent you an e-mail message asking a question that you cannot answer. How can you get the answer in electronic form, so that you can paste it into your reply?

7. You have been testing Windows NT Workstation on a computer, and now want to return to running Windows 95 only. You delete all of the Windows NT operating system files, including the hidden files in the system partition. But when you start the computer, you receive a messages stating "BOOT: Couldn't find NTLDR. Please insert another disk." The Windows 95 boot process does not proceed. What is causing this behavior?

Answer Key

Procedure Answers

Page 60

▶ **To log on to a domain**

3. In the **Domain** box, pull down the list box.

What appears in the list?

Domain1, which is the domain name of this domain controller.

5. Press CTRL+ALT+DELETE.

The **Windows NT Security** dialog box appears.

Why does the **Logon Information** dialog box show that you are logged on as DOMAIN1\Administrator?

Because the domain's directory services database, stored on the domain controller, validated the logon.

Page 61

▶ **To log on to a computer**

3. In the **Domain** box, pull down the list box.

What appears in the list?

Domain1, which is the domain that this computer has joined, and Workstation1, which is the computer name for this computer.

6. After you have logged on and the **Windows NT** interface appears, press CTRL+ALT+DELETE.

The **Windows NT Security** dialog box appears.

Why does the **Logon Information** dialog box show that you are logged on as WORKSTATION1\Administrator?

Because the workstation's directory services database, stored on the workstation, validated the logon.

Page 63

▶ **To log on to a domain from a workstation computer**

5. After you have logged on and the Windows NT interface appears, press CTRL+ALT+DELETE.

The **Windows NT Security** dialog box appears.

Why does the **Logon Information** dialog box show that you are logged on as DOMAIN1\Administrator?

Because the domain's directory services database, stored on the PDC, validated the logon.

Review Answers

Page 82

1. You want to install Windows NT Server on an Alpha-based computer. You want to protect your files and folders with local security, and you will be supporting Macintosh clients. How should you partition your disk or disks?

   A very small FAT system partition (Alphas require FAT system partitions), with the rest of the disk or disks formatted as NTFS.

2. You are installing Windows NT Workstation, and want to include Microsoft Exchange in the installation. What type of installation must you choose?

   Custom.

3. You have been told to automate the setup of Windows NT Workstation 4.0 on multiple machines in your department. You have 40 machines in five different configurations. How can you do this in the easiest possible way?

   Create an answer file for the generic settings and five UDFs to handle the five configurations for the specific sections. Use the answer file with the appropriate UDF to automate the installations.

4. You are trying to install Windows NT Server as a BDC, but Setup reports that a primary domain controller cannot be found. What should you check?

   Check the spelling of the domain name, make sure the PDC is up and running, make sure the BDC is using the same protocol as the PDC, and make sure that the network adapter card settings for the BDC are correct.

5. Your computer runs only Windows NT Server 3.51. The hard disk is formatted entirely with NTFS. You want to upgrade the operating system to version 4.0 while minimizing the amount of downtime necessary to perform the upgrade. What is the quickest and least disruptive way to upgrade the server?

By using the Winnt32.exe utility, because it copies all of the files from the compact disc or network to the hard disk while the server is still running. Using the Setup disks and compact disc requires the server to be inoperative for a longer period of time.

6. A user sent you an e-mail message asking a question that you cannot answer. How can you get the answer in electronic form, so that you can paste it into your reply?

Look up the topic in Books Online, highlight the text, and then copy and paste it into your reply.

7. You have been testing Windows NT Workstation on a computer, and now want to return to running Windows 95 only. You delete all of the Windows NT operating system files, including the hidden files in the system partition. But when you start the computer, you receive a messages stating "BOOT: Couldn't find NTLDR. Please insert another disk." The Windows 95 boot process does not proceed. What is causing this behavior?

The Windows 95 boot sector must be restored with the Win95 sys command.

CHAPTER 3

Configuring the Windows NT Environment

Lesson 1 The Windows NT Registry . . . 88

Lesson 2 Modifying Settings Using Control Panel . . . 97

Lesson 3 Modifying System Settings Using Control Panel . . . 111

Lesson 4 Modifying System Settings Using Registry Editor . . . 128

Review . . . 135

About This Chapter

One of the most significant challenges for system administrators and technical support engineers is managing and supporting the hardware, operating systems, and applications on personal computers and network servers. Microsoft Windows NT contains a *registry* to help simplify this task by providing a secure, unified database that stores configuration data for the local computer. In this chapter, you learn about the registry architecture and some of the tools provided by Windows NT, such as Control Panel and Registry Editor, which are used to edit the registry on both local and remote computers.

Before You Begin

To complete the lessons in this chapter, you must have:

- Two computers that meet the hardware and software requirements as specified in the Getting Started section of "About This Book."
- Completed all practices in Chapter 2, "Installing Windows NT."

Lesson 1: The Windows NT Registry

This lesson describes the Windows NT registry and how Windows NT uses it to store and access all hardware and software configuration settings.

After this lesson, you will be able to:
- Describe the purpose of the Windows NT registry.
- Describe how Windows NT components use the registry.
- Identify the structural components of the registry hierarchy.

Estimated lesson time: 30 minutes

What Is the Registry?

The *registry* is a unified database where Windows NT stores all hardware and software configuration information for the local computer. The registry controls the Windows NT operating system by providing the appropriate initialization information to start applications and load components such as device drivers and network protocols.

The following list describes the type of information contained in the registry:

- The hardware installed on the computer, including the central processor, bus type, pointing device or mouse, and keyboard.
- Installed device drivers.
- Installed applications.
- Installed network protocols.
- Network adapter card settings. For example, the Interrupt Number, the Memory Base Address, the I/O Port Base Address, I/O Channel Ready, and Transceiver type.
- User account information. For example, the user's group membership, rights, and permissions are stored in the registry.

Viewing the Registry

To view the registry, Windows NT provides Registry Editor. Registry Editor can be used to make direct changes to the registry. However, Windows NT provides applications such as Control Panel, User Manager, and *System Policy Editor* that change the registry based on configuration information you supply. These applications provide an easy-to-use interface to help you to correctly configure your system. As you review this lesson, run Registry Editor so that you can view the contents of the registry on your local computer.

Caution You must be *very* careful when changing values using Registry Editor. Registry Editor does *not* recognize errors in syntax or other semantics, and therefore you are *not* warned if you have made an incorrect entry. If an incorrect entry is made, the operating system may be rendered unusable.

Practice

In these procedures, you create a shortcut for Registry Editor and then start Registry Editor to view the registry on Server1. The following illustration shows how the Registry Editor icon appears on the desktop.

Note Complete this procedure on Server1.

▶ **To create a shortcut for Registry Editor**

1. Right-click the desktop.
2. Click **New**, and then click **Shortcut**.
3. In the **Command line** box, type **regedt32.exe**
4. Click **Next**, and then click **Finish**.

   A shortcut icon for Regedt32.exe appears on your desktop.

▶ **To view the registry**

1. Start Registry Editor by double-clicking the shortcut icon.

   Registry Editor appears.

2. On the **Options** menu, click **Read Only Mode**.

   There should be a check mark by **Read Only Mode** indicating that it is selected. This prevents you from making any unintentional changes to the registry.

   When Registry Editor is opened, it displays five windows. Each window displays a *subtree*; each subtree is used to access different areas of the registry.

3. List the names of the five subtrees displayed by Registry Editor.

   _____

   _____

4. Minimize Registry Editor.

How Windows NT Components Use the Registry

Windows NT stores and checks all configuration information in only one location—the registry. The following illustration shows some of the various Windows NT components that use the registry.

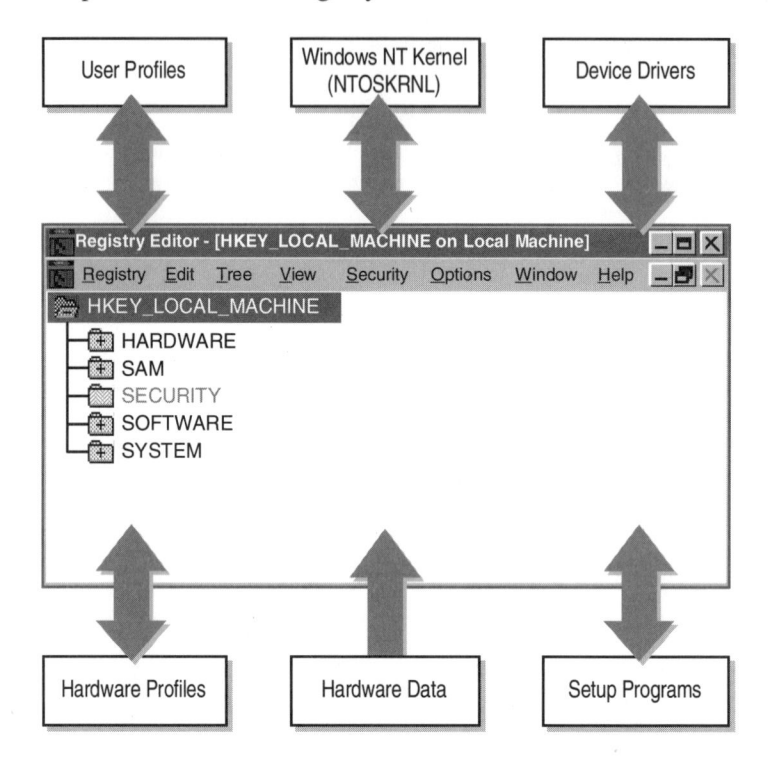

The following table specifies how applications and the Windows NT operating system components use the registry to store and retrieve information.

Component	Description
Hardware profiles	A list of the hardware devices and services to be enabled or disabled when you start Windows NT can be stored in the registry by creating a hardware profile. For example, if you are using a portable computer, you may want to enable particular devices and services, depending on whether your computer is docked or undocked. When you start your computer, you can choose the appropriate hardware profile and when Windows NT starts, it uses that profile.
User profiles	Configuration information is stored on a user-by-user basis in the registry. This information includes all of the per-user settings of the Windows NT environment, such as the desktop arrangement, personal program groups and the program items in those groups, screen saver settings, network connections, printer connections, mouse settings, window size and position, and more.
Windows NT kernel	During startup, the Windows NT kernel (Ntoskrnl.exe) reads information from the registry to determine which device drivers to load and the order that they should be loaded. The kernel also passes back information on itself, such as its version number.
Device drivers	Device drivers pass data to the registry, and also receive load and configuration parameters from the registry. A device driver tells the registry what system resources it is using, such as hardware interrupts or direct memory access (DMA) channels. Device drivers can also report discovered configuration data.
Setup programs	A Setup program can add new configuration data to the registry. It can also query the registry to determine if a component has already been installed, and whether to install a more recent version of the component.
Hardware data	Each time Windows NT is started, hardware and configuration data are collected and the registry is updated. On *x*86-based computers, this hardware detection is done through a program named Ntdetect.com. On RISC-based computers this information is extracted from the computer's firmware and then stored in the registry.

The Registry Structure

The registry is structured as a set of five databases called subtrees that contain per-computer and per-user databases. Access to information in the registry occurs through these subtrees.

The per-computer databases include information about hardware and software installed on the specific computer. The per-user databases include the information in *user profiles*, such as desktop settings, individual preferences for certain software, and personal printer and network settings.

The following table identifies and defines the five registry subtrees.

Subtree	Description
HKEY_LOCAL_MACHINE	Contains all configuration data about the local computer. This data is used by applications, device drivers, and the Windows NT operating system to set computer configuration. Part of the data is used to start Windows NT. Data in this subtree determines which device drivers and services to load during startup. The data in this subtree is constant, regardless of the user.
HKEY_USERS	Contains two subkeys: - DEFAULT—Contains the system default settings (system default profile) used when the CTRL+ALT+DEL logon screen is displayed - The security identifier (SID) of the user currently logged on the computer.
HKEY_CURRENT_USER	Contains data about the user currently logged on interactively. A copy is stored for each user account that has ever been logged on to the computer in the *systemroot*\Profiles*user_name* folder in a file named Ntuser.dat. This subkey points to the same data that can be accessed under HKEY_USERS*SID_of_the_currently_logged_on_user*. This subtree takes precedence over HKEY_LOCAL_MACHINE for duplicated data.
HKEY_CLASSES_ROOT	Contains information about file associations and data associated with COM objects, and points to the CLASSES subkey under HKEY_LOCAL_MACHINE\SOFTWARE.
HKEY_CURRENT_CONFIG	Contains data about the active hardware profile. This data is extracted from the SOFTWARE and SYSTEM keys of HKEY_LOCAL_MACHINE.

The Registry Hierarchy

The registry is organized in a hierarchical structure similar to the hierarchical structure of folders and files on a disk. The following illustration labels each component of the hierarchy.

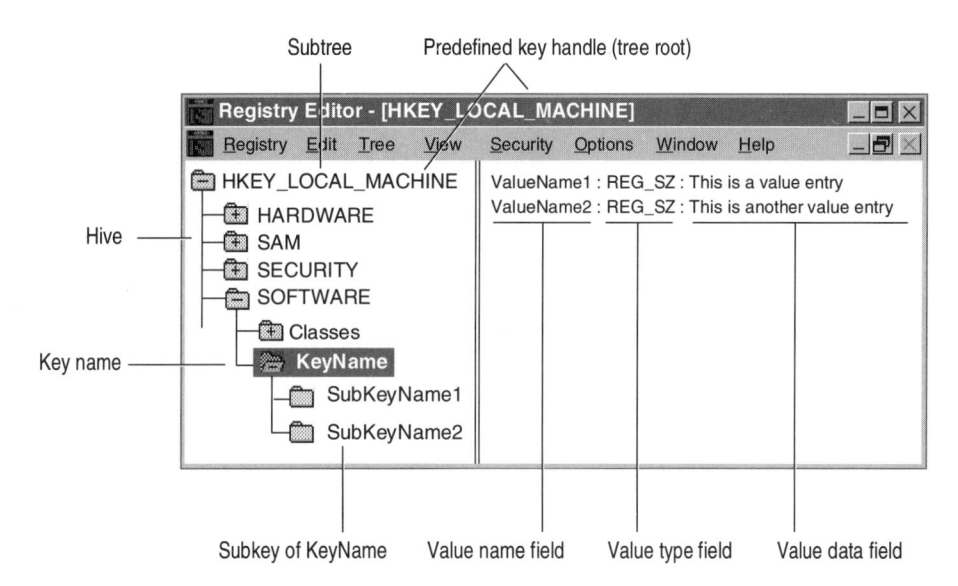

![Registry Editor illustration showing Subtree, Predefined key handle (tree root), Hive, Key name, Subkey of KeyName, Value name field, Value type field, and Value data field labels pointing to parts of the HKEY_LOCAL_MACHINE registry tree with HARDWARE, SAM, SECURITY, SOFTWARE, Classes, KeyName, SubKeyName1, SubKeyName2, and value entries ValueName1 : REG_SZ : This is a value entry and ValueName2 : REG_SZ : This is another value entry]

This section of the lesson describes the hierarchical organization of the registry and defines the overall structure of the *subtrees, hives,* and *value entries.* The following table identifies and describes each of the hierarchical components of the registry.

Hierarchical component	Description
Subtree	A subtree (or subtree key) is analogous to the root folder of a disk. The registry contains the following five predefined subtrees: HKEY_LOCAL_MACHINE HKEY_USERS HKEY_CURRENT_USER HKEY_CLASSES_ROOT HKEY_CURRENT_CONFIG

(*continued*)

Hierarchical component	Description
Hive	A hive is a discrete body of keys, subkeys, and values. Each hive has a corresponding registry file and .log file. By default, most hives, such as Default, SAM, Security, and System, and the corresponding hive files are located in *systemroot*\System32\Config folder. The .log file is used to record changes to the registry and to ensure the integrity of the registry.
Keys and subkeys	Keys and subkeys are analogous to folders and subfolders. Each hive can contain keys and subkeys, just as a folder can have subfolders.
Values	Values are analogous to files because they come at the end of the hierarchy. Keys and subkeys can contain one or more values. A value entry has three parts—the name, data type, and value itself (or configuration parameter).
Value Data Types	**REG_DWORD**. Only one value is allowed, and it must be a string of 1–8 hexadecimal digits. **REG_SZ**. Only one value is allowed, and it is interpreted as the string to be stored. **REG_EXPAND_SZ**. This is similar to **REG_SZ**, except that the text can contain a replaceable variable. For example, in the string %Systemroot%\Ntvdm.exe, %Systemroot% would be replaced with the path to the Windows NT System32 folder. **REG_BINARY**. Only one value is allowed, and it is a string of hexadecimal digits, each pair of which is interpreted as a byte value. **REG_MULTI_SZ**. Multiple values are allowed; each value is a string and is interpreted as a component of the **MULTI_SZ**. Entries are separated by a null character.

Practice

In this procedure, you explore the HKEY_LOCAL_MACHINE subtree to familiarize yourself with the registry hierarchy.

Note Complete this procedure on Server1.

▸ **To explore the HKEY_LOCAL_MACHINE**

1. Maximize Registry Editor.
2. On the **View** menu, verify that **Tree and Data** is selected.
3. Click the HKEY_LOCAL_MACHINE window, and maximize the window.

   Notice that the HKEY_LOCAL_MACHINE subtree has five subkeys—HARDWARE, SAM, SECURITY, SOFTWARE, and SYSTEM.

4. Double-click **HARDWARE** to expand the HARDWARE key.
5. Double-click **DESCRIPTION** to expand the DESCRIPTION key, and then double-click the **System** key.

   Notice the value names, value types, and value listed in the right window.

   For example: **Identifier : REG_SZ : AT/AT COMPATIBLE**

   Identifier is the value name; **REG_SZ** is the value type; and **AT/AT COMPATIBLE** is the value.
6. Explore a few of the other subkeys to see the information they contain.
7. When you are done exploring, close Registry Editor.

Subkeys of HKEY_LOCAL_MACHINE

The HKEY_LOCAL_MACHINE subtree has five subkeys: HARDWARE, SAM, SECURITY, SOFTWARE, and SYSTEM. The SECURITY, SAM, SOFTWARE, and SYSTEM subkeys are all considered *hives* because they have corresponding files located in the *systemroot*\System32\Config folder.

The subkeys in HKEY_LOCAL_MACHINE are described in the following table.

Subkey	Description
HARDWARE	The HARDWARE subkey is volatile. It is constructed from information gathered each time the computer is started. This key contains information that an application can query to determine the type and state of physical devices attached to the local computer. The HARDWARE subkey does not map to a file on the hard disk because the parameter values are volatile, meaning that they are not saved, but built each time the computer is started.
	The information under HKEY_LOCAL_MACHINE\HARDWARE can be used to determine the following information:
	• The appropriate driver to install for a piece of hardware. This is done by starting Windows NT and then seeing what hardware device was detected.
	• Whether a device driver is failing to load because the hardware is no longer being detected. It is possible that there has been a hardware failure or conflict with a new piece of hardware that was installed.

(*continued*)

Subkey	Description
SAM	The SAM (Security Accounts Manager) database hive contains the directory database for the computer. If the computer is a domain controller, the SAM database hive contains the master directory database. The SAM hive maps to the SAM and Sam.log files in the *systemroot*\System32\Config folder. This hive is a pointer to the same data that can be accessed under HKEY_LOCAL_MACHINE\SECURITY\SAM. Data in the SAM or SECURITY keys *cannot* be viewed unless the permissions on the keys are changed. *By default, this data cannot be viewed.* Be careful if you make changes to the permissions on these keys, or you may render your operating system unusable.
SECURITY	The SECURITY database hive contains all of the security information for the local computer. By default, none of the keys contained in SECURITY can be modified by an application. The SECURITY hive maps to the Security and Security.log files in the *systemroot*\System32\Config folder.
SOFTWARE	The SOFTWARE database hive contains information about the software on the local computer that is independent of per-user configuration information. Examples include the manufacturer and version number of software. This hive maps to the Software and Software.log files in the *systemroot*\System32\Config folder and also contains file associations and OLE information.
SYSTEM	The SYSTEM hive contains information about the devices and services on the system. When device drivers or services are installed or configured, they add or modify information under this hive. The SYSTEM hive maps to the System and System.log files in the *systemroot*\System32\Config folder. A backup of the data in the SYSTEM hive is kept in the System.alt file.

Lesson 2: Modifying Settings Using Control Panel

Lesson 1 presented a foundation for understanding where and how Windows NT system changes take place. Many of the settings contained in the registry are configured using the programs in Control Panel.

Users can manage their own environments through programs in Control Panel. For example, each user that can log on to a computer running Windows NT can use the Display program to select a screen saver. These types of settings are called per-user settings, and they are stored in the registry in the Control Panel key under HKEY_CURRENT_USER.

Other Control Panel programs are used to configure computer settings, such as using the Network program to add or configure network adapter cards. These computer settings are stored in the registry in the HKEY_LOCAL_MACHINE subtree, and are in effect regardless of the user that has logged on to the computer. Only administrators can configure these types of system settings.

This lesson identifies the Control Panel programs that are used to modify per-user and computer settings.

After this lesson, you will be able to:
- Identify user and computer programs in Control Panel.
- Configure a user's local profile.
- Configure serial (COM) ports.
- Configure the display.
- Configure SCSI adapters and tape devices.
- Configure an uninterruptible power supply (UPS).
- Configure PC Card devices.

Estimated lesson time: 90 minutes

System Configuration Overview

The following illustration shows the default Windows NT Server Control Panel programs.

[Control Panel window showing icons: Accessibility Options, Add/Remove Programs, Console, Date/Time, Devices, Display, Fonts, Internet, Keyboard, Licensing, Modems, Mouse, Multimedia, Network, PC Card (PCMCA), Ports, Printers, Regional Settings, SCSI Adapters, Server, Services, Sounds, System, Tape Devices, Telephony, UPS]

Note The same default Control Panel programs are installed with Windows NT Workstation, with the exception of the Licensing program; a Client Access License is not required to access Windows NT Workstation.

As you review this lesson, review the Control Panel programs that are covered in this lesson.

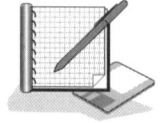

Practice

In this procedure, you start Control Panel.

Note Complete this procedure on Server1.

▶ **To start Control Panel**

1. Log on as Administrator.
2. Click the **Start** button, point to **Settings**, and then click **Control Panel**.

Modifying Per-User Settings

Several Control Panel programs control configuration settings on a per-user basis. The following table describes each Control Panel program that effects user settings.

Program	Description
Accessibility Options	Configures the keyboard, sound, display, and mouse behavior for users with visual, hearing, or mobility impairments.
Console	Configures the display, features, and functionality of the MS-DOS console.
Display	Changes the look of a user's computer desktop, including the wallpaper and screen saver.
Keyboard	Specifies the keyboard repeat rate and delay.
Mouse	Changes mouse settings such as tracking speed, double-click sensitivity, and determining the active mouse button.
Regional Settings	Specifies regional or international settings such as country and language.
Sounds	Assigns sounds to system events.

Changes made through the previous Control Panel programs are saved to the logged-on user's *local profile*. Each user can thus configure the desktop according to individual preferences. Each time a user logs on, the user environment is configured according to the last saved settings in their user profile.

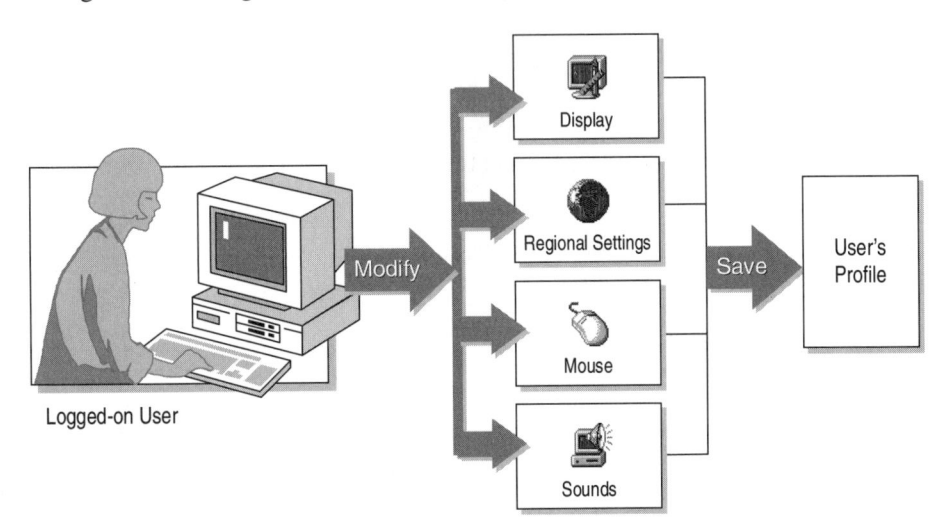

Managing User Profiles

When a user logs on for the first time from a client computer running Windows NT, the system checks to see if a user profile exists for that user. If there is not an existing user profile, the system makes a copy of the default user profile which becomes the user profile for that user. The user profile defines such things as the appearance of a user's desktop environment, and the user's network and printer connections. The user profile ensures that multiple users sharing the same computer can maintain separate desktop environments. When the user logs off, any changes that have been made to the user profile are saved.

Note For more information on configuring user profiles, see Microsoft Windows NT Server *Concepts and Planning*.

Practice

In these procedures, you log on to Server1 and create a new user, User1, in Domain1. You grant the Everyone group the right to log on locally at Server1. You then log on as User1 and change your Display background. When you log back on as User1, you verify that the changes are retained.

Note Complete these procedures on Server1.

▶ **To create a new user**

In this procedure, you create a new user on Domain1. This user is used to test user profiles later in this practice.

1. Click the **Start** button, point to **Programs**, point to **Administrative Tools (Common)**, and then click **User Manager for Domains**.
2. On the **User** menu, click **New User**.
3. Use the following information to complete the fields in the **New User** dialog box.

In this box	Do this action
Username	Type **user1**
Password	Type **password**
Confirm Password	Type **password**
User Must Change Password at Next Logon	Clear this check box

4. Click **Add**.
5. Click **Close**.

Chapter 3 Configuring the Windows NT Environment   101

▶ **To allow the Everyone group to log on locally**

In this procedure, you allow the Everyone group to log on locally.

1. In the **User Manager for Domains** dialog box, on the **Policies** menu, click **User Rights**.
2. In the **Right** drop-down list box, click **Log on Locally**.
3. Click **Add**.
4. In the **Names** box, click **Everyone**, and then click **Add**.

   The group Everyone now appears on the **Add Names** box.
5. Click **OK**.

   The group Everyone now appears on the **Grant To** box.
6. Click **OK**, and then close **User Manager for Domains**.

▶ **To change a user's profile**

In this procedure, you log on as User1, change your desktop configuration, and then log off. You log back on to verify that your changes were retained.

1. Log off, and then log on as User1.
2. Start Registry Editor (Regedt32.exe), and then on the **Options** menu, select **Read Only Mode**.
3. Expand the HKEY_CURRENT_USER\Control Panel\Desktop key.

   What is the value of the **Pattern** field?

   _____

4. Close Registry Editor.
5. Click the **Start** button, point to **Settings**, and then click **Control Panel**.
6. Double-click **Display**.
7. In the **Pattern** box, select a pattern that is not your current pattern, and then click **OK**.

   Notice that the pattern of your display is the one you just selected.
8. Log off, and then log on as User1.

   Notice that the pattern of your display was saved.

9. Start Registry Editor, and then expand the HKEY_CURRENT_USER\Control Panel\Desktop key.

    What is the value of the **Pattern** field?

    _____

10. Close Registry Editor.
11. Log off, and then log on as Administrator.

Modifying Computer Settings

Other Control Panel programs allow you to control per-computer configurations. These configuration settings are used regardless of which user is logged on to the computer running Windows NT.

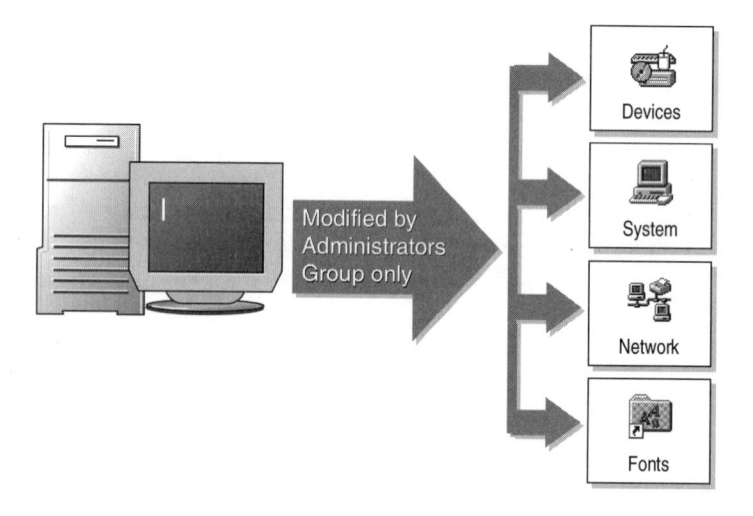

Chapter 3 Configuring the Windows NT Environment

You must be a member of the Administrators group to modify most hardware configuration options. If you are not an administrator, a message appears stating that you do not have administrative permission to change settings or that access is denied. The following table describes the Control Panel programs that are used to configure the hardware on the computer.

Control Panel programs	Description
Date/Time	Changes the date, time, and time zone of your computer's clock. The Time Zone feature allows a correct international time zone to be selected for each computer. Each user thus views time stamps for his or her own time zone. For example, a file saved in New York (US Eastern time) at 6:00 PM shows a 3:00 PM time to a user in Seattle (US Pacific time).
Devices	Starts and stops device drivers, and configures the startup type for each device driver.
Display	Installs and configures the display drivers.
Fonts	Adds and removes fonts, and sets TrueType options.
Internet	Configures settings for Microsoft Internet Explorer.
Multimedia	Installs and removes multimedia device drivers.
Network	Installs and removes network adapter cards, protocols, and software, and configures network bindings.
Ports	Specifies the communications settings for the serial (COM) port(s).
Printers	Installs and removes printers, and sets printer options.
SCSI Adapters	Displays installed SCSI adapters and drivers, adds and removes SCSI adapter drivers.
Server	Displays who is connected to the computer's shared resources. Also controls replication and files that are open.
Services	Configures, starts, pauses, and stops services such as the Computer Browser and Net Logon services. A service can continue to be active even after you log off the computer.
System	Controls the computer's startup settings, such as virtual memory, environment variables, tasking, hardware profiles, and the Boot Loader Operating System Selection menu on Intel x86-based computers. This menu shows the operating systems installed on a computer and lets you choose which operating system to load for a session.
Tape Devices	Displays installed tape backup devices and drivers.
UPS	Installs and configures an uninterruptible power supply (UPS).

Configuring COM Ports

The Ports program in Control Panel is used to specify the communication settings for a selected serial (COM) port. Only administrators can configure the I/O port address and the IRQ options in the **Advanced Settings on COMx** dialog box.

The following table describes the purpose of each option in the **Ports** dialog box.

Option	Description
Settings	Configures port settings, such as baud rate and flow control.
Add	Adds COM ports, up to port 256.
Delete	Deletes the selected port.

The **Ports** dialog box lists only COM ports that are *not in use* by the computer. For example, if a serial mouse is attached to COM1, that port does not appear in the Ports program in Control Panel. The following illustration shows the screens used to configure COM ports. In this specific example, the **Ports** dialog box shows that COM2 is not in use.

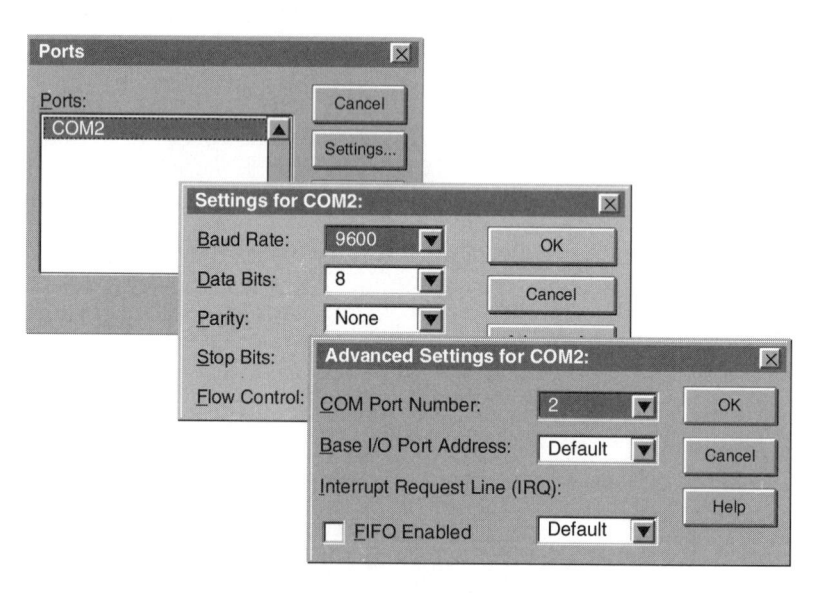

If all COM ports were listed, then none of the COM ports would be in use. Because COM1 is not listed, you know it is in use. If you want to determine which device is using COM1, locate the SerialController key. You can find it by using Registry Editor to view the following key:

HKEY_LOCAL_MACHINE\HARDWARE\Description\System

Below this key, depending on the hardware devices in your computer, you would then look at either the MultifunctionAdapter or EisaAdapter, and then continue to look through their subkeys (0, 1, or 2, depending on your computer) until you find the SerialController key.

Under the SerialController key are subkeys for each port, with 0 for COM1, 1 for COM2, and so on. If you want to determine what is attached to COM1, look at the value 0. For example, if there were a mouse attached to COM1, there would be a PointerPeripheral subkey.

Configuring the Display

The Display program in Control Panel is used to configure user settings such as the background display, screen saver, and the number of colors. It can also be used to configure computer settings, such as video resolution, font sizes, and refresh frequency.

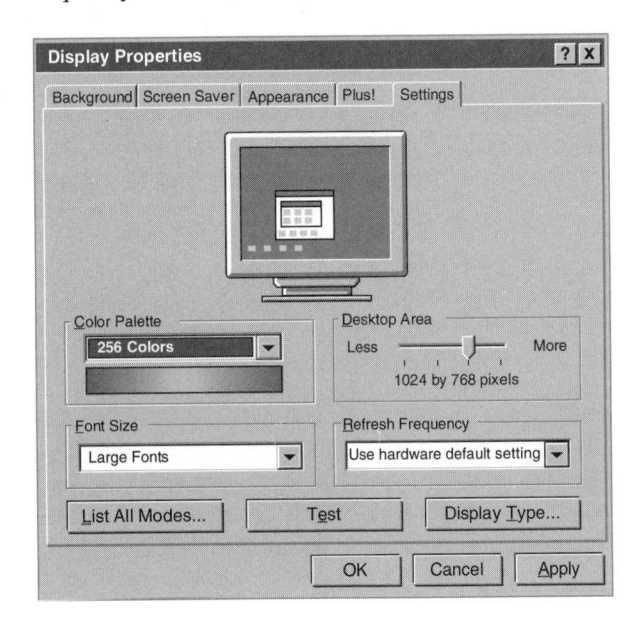

Display Options

The following table describes the options in the **Settings** tab in the **Display Properties** dialog box. Any changes made to these settings affect all users of this computer.

Option	Use to
Color Palette	List color options for the display adapter.
Desktop Area	Configure the screen area used by the display. The larger the desktop area, the smaller the objects will appear on the screen.
Font Size	Change the font size to small or large.
Refresh Frequency	Configure the frequency of the screen refresh rate for high-resolution drivers only. The higher the refresh rate, the less flicker there is on the screen. Do not select a refresh rate that is not supported by the monitor at the selected resolution. If you are unsure what refresh rates your monitor supports, select the lowest refresh rate option.
List All Modes button	Configure color, desktop, and refresh frequency all at once.
Test button	Test screen choices. The Test option works only when old and new drivers do not conflict. For example, if the VGA driver is installed, the SVGA driver cannot be tested because it conflicts with the VGA video driver.
Display Type button	Display information about the display device driver and allows installation of a new driver. Only users with the user right "Load and unload device drivers" can change and test video device drivers. By default, only the Administrators group has this user right.

Configuring SCSI Adapters and Tape Devices

The SCSI Adapters and Tape Devices Control Panel programs are used to install and start the appropriate drivers for each of these devices.

Both utilities have these two tabs:

- Devices
- Drivers

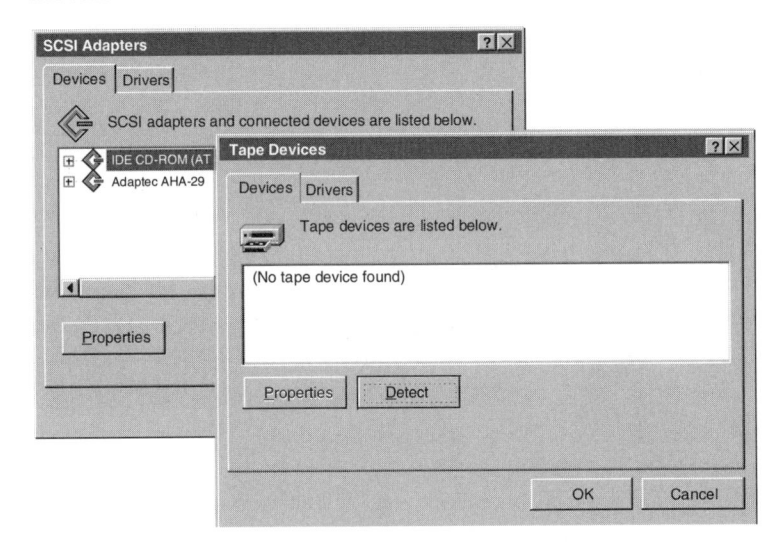

When adding SCSI adapter drivers, the computer must be restarted for the SCSI adapter driver to start.

Windows NT automatically detects tape devices when the **Detect** button on the **Devices** tab in the **Tape Devices** dialog box is clicked. To find tape device information such as SCSI ID number, firmware information, and SCSI host adapter, click the **Properties** button on the **Devices** tab in the **Tape Devices** dialog box. The computer does not need to be restarted for the tape device driver to start.

Configuring a UPS

An *uninterruptible power supply* (UPS) provides uninterrupted power if the main power source fails. The UPS is usually rated to provide power for a specific time period. Power for the UPS comes from batteries that are continuously charged while the main power source is available.

UPS settings are controlled through the UPS program in Control Panel. The following illustration shows the **UPS** dialog box.

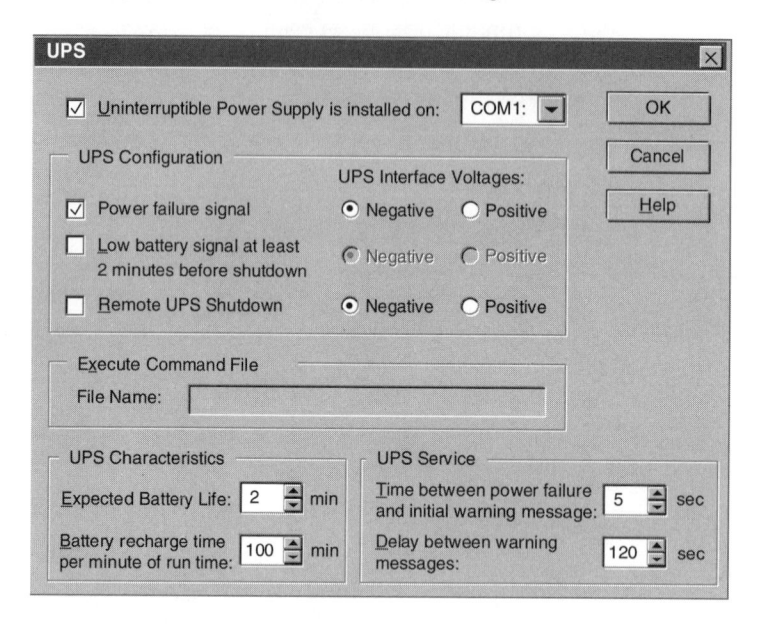

UPS Operation

During a power failure, the UPS service for Windows NT communicates with the UPS to keep the system running until one of the following events occurs:

- Power is restored.
- The system is shut down, either by the administrator or the UPS service.
- The UPS signals that its batteries are low.

The UPS service immediately pauses the Server service during a power failure, so that users do not establish new connections with a failing computer. The UPS service then notifies users of the impending shutdown and advises them to terminate their sessions with the failing server. When signaled to shut down, the UPS service performs a safe system shutdown. If power is restored before the shutdown starts, a message tells users that power is restored and normal operations have resumed.

Note The UPS communicates with the service through a standard RS-232 serial port. However, the cable used between the UPS and the serial port does not use standard pinouts; a special UPS cable is required for the UPS to be able to communicate with the computer. Check the HCL for supported UPSs and their cable part numbers.

Chapter 3 Configuring the Windows NT Environment

Important Be sure to test the UPS service after it has been configured, particularly on Intel *x*86-based computers. During startup, Ntdetect.com sends a detection signal to the serial ports to detect the attached hardware. Some UPS units switch off in response to this signal. If testing the newly configured UPS shows that it shuts off in this way, add the **/NoSerialMice** switch in the Boot.ini file to prevent the detection signal from being sent to the serial port. For more information, see Chapter 3, "Disk Management Basics," in the *Resource Guide* of the *Microsoft Windows NT Server Resource Kit*.

The following table describes the options available in the **UPS** dialog box.

Select this check box	If	Corresponds to
Power failure signal	The UPS device can send a message when the power supply fails.	Clear to send (CTS) cable signal for the UPS serial port connection.
Low battery signal at least 2 minutes before shutdown	The UPS device can send a warning when battery power is low.	Data carrier detect (DCD) cable signal for the UPS serial port connection.
Remote UPS Shutdown	The UPS device can accept a signal from the UPS service to shut down.	Data terminal ready (DTR) cable signal for the UPS serial port connection.

Note For the previous options, the UPS Interface Voltages can be set to either Negative or Positive. The default is Negative. Refer to the UPS manufacturer's instructions for the correct settings.

Select this check box	To	Use these parameters
Execute Command File	Execute a command file immediately before shutdown.	The command file can be any file with a .cmd, .bat, .com, or .exe extension, and has 30 seconds to complete its task.

Use this option	To adjust	Use these parameters
Expected Battery Life	The time, in minutes, that the system can run on battery power.	Range: 2–720 minutes. Default: 2 minutes.

Caution Be sure to enter the number of minutes in the **Expected Battery Life** box when **Power failure signal** is selected but **Low battery signal** is not. Also enter an appropriate number of minutes in the **Battery recharge time per minute of run time** box.

(*continued*)

Use this option	To adjust	Use these parameters
Battery recharge time per minute of run time	The amount of time to recharge the battery, typed as the number of minutes of recharge time per minute of battery run time.	Range: 1–250 minutes. Default: 100 minutes.
Time between power failure and initial warning message	The time between a power failure and the first message sent to notify users of the failure.	Range: 0–120 seconds. Default: 5 seconds.
Delay between warning messages	The interval between power failure messages sent to users notifying them that the system may shut down.	Range: 5–300 seconds. Default: 120 seconds.

Configuring PC Card Devices

The PC Card (PCMCIA) program in Control Panel is used to configure PC card devices. The program shows which PC card devices are installed, in which sockets they are installed, how they are configured, and which resources the PC Card controller is using.

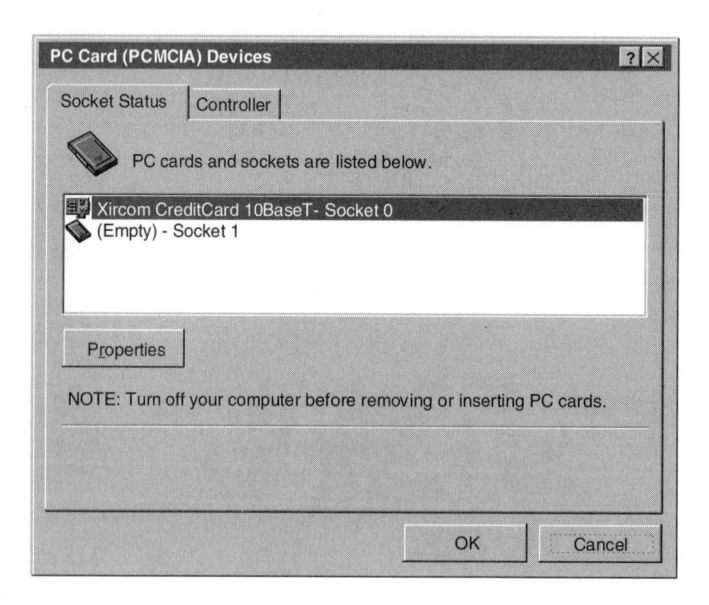

Note Turn the computer off before adding or removing a PC card. When the system restarts, Windows NT recognizes the change in hardware. For many PC card devices, PC Card in Control Panel suggests the correct device driver.

Lesson 3: Modifying System Settings Using Control Panel

This lesson introduces some of the Control Panel programs that are used to configure the operating system and other software on a computer running Windows NT.

After this lesson, you will be able to:
- Use System in Control Panel to change startup and shutdown settings.
- Use System in Control Panel to configure a hardware profile.
- Use System in Control Panel to configure virtual memory.
- Use System in Control Panel to set environment variables.
- Use Add/Remove Programs in Control Panel to customize a Windows NT installation.

Estimated lesson time: 90 minutes

Changing Startup and Shutdown Settings

You can change startup and shutdown settings for a computer running Windows NT by using the System program in Control Panel. These options are configured on the **Startup/Shutdown** tab as shown in the following illustration. There are two groups of information on the tab: **System Startup** and **Recovery**.

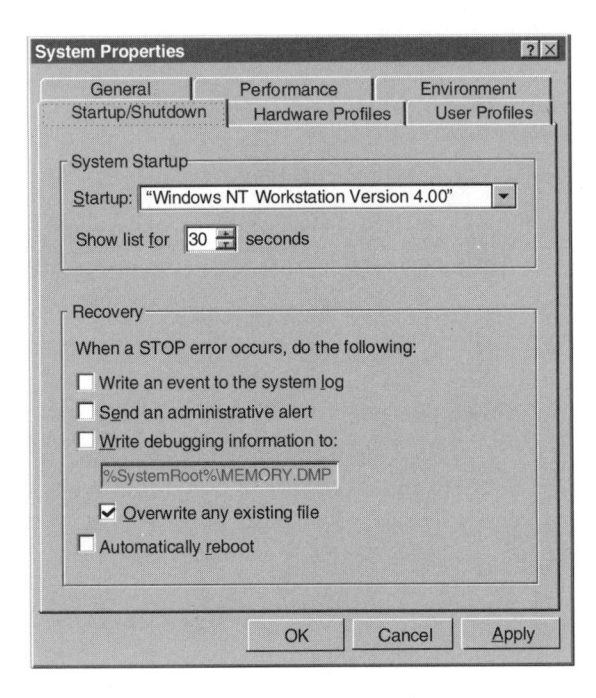

System Startup

If a computer has several operating systems installed, they are displayed when the computer is turned on so that the user can determine which operating system to run. You can configure the order in which the operating systems are displayed, and the number of seconds to pause on this display so that a user can choose which operating system to use. You can specify the default operating system in the **Startup** box and set the number of seconds to wait before the default operating system starts automatically in the **Show list for** box. If the user does not make a selection, then the default operating system initializes when the time set in the **Show list for** box expires.

Note The default setting in the **Startup** box is the last operating system installed. The default setting in the **Show list for** box is 30 seconds. If you do not want users to be able to choose which operating system to run, set the time in the **Show list for** box to 0 seconds.

Recovery

Under **Recovery** there are options to configure Windows NT for specified tasks if a STOP error (Fatal System error) occurs. When a STOP error occurs, Windows NT stops all processes and requires that the computer is restarted. The **Recovery** section includes these options:

- Write an event to the system log.
- Send an administrative alert to the users and computers specified in the **Alerts** dialog box of the Server program in Control Panel.
- Write debugging information to a specified file name. Use of this option requires the following:
  - The paging file must be on the boot partition.
  - The paging file must be at least as big as physical RAM.
  - You must have the necessary disk space for the specified file.

  If you want to overwrite an existing file select the **Overwrite any existing file** check box.
- Automatically reboot. Do this *only* when the **Write debugging information to** check box has been selected.

Note As a best practice, you should *always* select the **Write debugging information to** check box and enter a path and file for this information. The information in this file provides important information that can help Microsoft Technical Support solve reported problems.

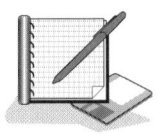

Practice

In this procedure, you set the boot delay by changing the number of seconds of delay before the default operating system is loaded.

Note Complete this procedure on Server1.

▶ **To set the boot delay**

1. Shut down and restart Windows NT Server to observe the number of seconds before Windows NT Server automatically loads.
2. Log on as Administrator.
3. Double-click the System icon in Control Panel.
4. Click the **Startup/Shutdown** tab.
5. In the **Show list for** box, set the number of seconds to **10**, and then click **OK**.
6. Shut down and then restart Windows NT Server to see the results of your boot delay setting.

Practice

In this procedure, you set your default operating system as Windows NT Workstation on the computer that dual-boots as Workstation1 and Server2.

Note Complete this procedure on Server2.

▶ **To change the default operating system**

1. Log on as Administrator.
2. Double-click the System icon in Control Panel.
3. Click the **Startup/Shutdown** tab.
4. In the **Startup** box, click **Windows NT Workstation Version 4.0**, and then click **OK**.
5. Shut down and then restart your computer to see the results.
6. Start your computer as Workstation1.

Configuring Hardware Profiles

A hardware profile stores the configuration for a set of devices and services. Windows NT can store different hardware profiles to meet a user's needs. For example, a portable computer may use different hardware configurations than a desktop computer, depending on whether the portable computer is docked or undocked. A portable computer user could create a hardware profile for each state (docked and undocked), and choose the appropriate profile when starting the operating system. Hardware profiles are created by starting the System program in Control Panel and clicking the **Hardware Profiles** tab as shown in the following illustration.

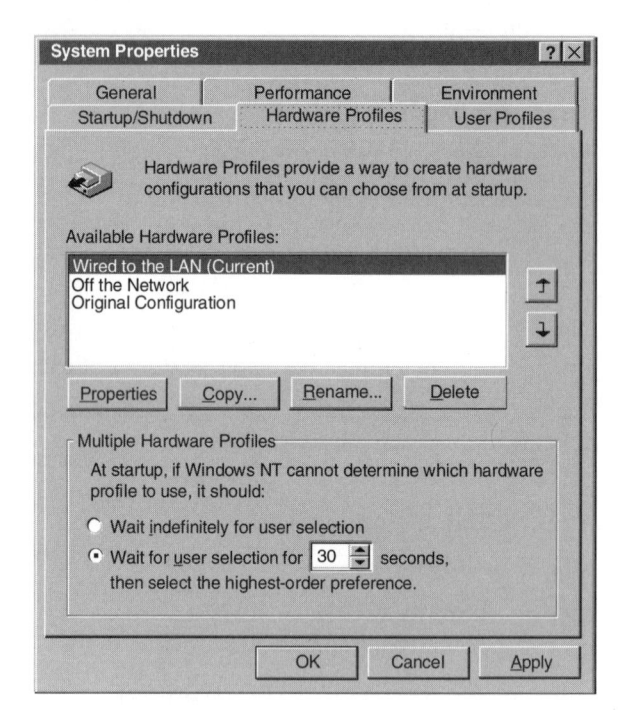

Creating and Modifying Hardware Profiles

You create a hardware profile by copying and then modifying the default hardware profile that is created when Windows NT is installed. The default hardware profile appears as **Original Configuration (Current)** in the **Available Hardware Profiles** list. Once you create a hardware profile, it is added to the **Available Hardware Profiles** list. To configure a specific device or service for a hardware profile, use the Devices and Services programs in Control Panel. Each of these programs contains a **Hardware Profiles** button that allows you to assign the configuration to a specific hardware profile.

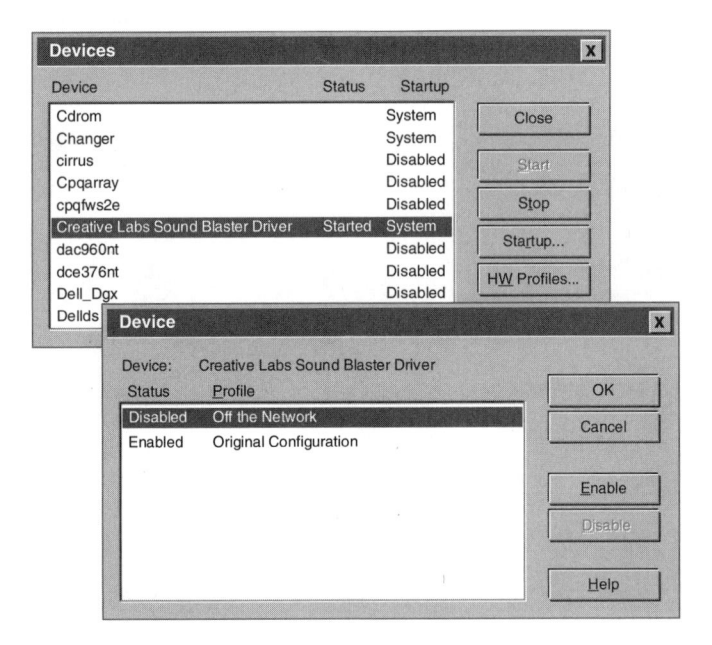

Note As a best practice, make a copy of the default hardware profile and use the copy as your hardware profile. That way, if you make a change or revision to the copy that prevents the system from starting, then you can always start the system with the original default hardware profile. For example, when you modify hardware profiles, be careful not to disable one of the boot devices. If a required boot device is disabled, Windows NT may not start.

Configuring for Multiple Hardware Profiles

When your computer is configured with multiple hardware profiles, you can specify which profile is the default, and how long to wait before automatically starting the default profile.

The first profile in the list is the default profile. To change the order of the profiles, you can use the arrow buttons on the **Hardware Profiles** tab to move the profiles up or down in the list.

To configure the computer to pause for a number of seconds before loading the first hardware profile, click **Wait for user selection for** and enter a number of seconds. The default profile can be configured to start automatically by setting the number of seconds in the **Wait for user selection for** option to 0.

Loading a Hardware Profile

The order in which hardware profiles appear in the **Available Hardware Profiles** list also determines how the profiles appear at startup and which one is loaded. If more than one profile is in the **Available Hardware Profiles** list, Windows NT prompts you to choose a hardware profile during startup. The following illustration shows a computer with two hardware profiles and how those profiles appear when Windows NT is started.

```
Hardware Profile/Configuration Recovery Menu

This menu allows you to select a hardware profile
to be used when Windows NT is started.

If your system is not starting correctly, then you may switch to a previous
system configuration, which may overcome startup problems.
IMPORTANT: System configuration changes made since the last successful
startup will be discarded.
   Original Configuration
   Off the Network

Use the up and down arrow keys to move the highlight
to the selection you want. Then press ENTER.
To switch to the Last Known Good configuration, press 'L'.
To Exit this menu and restart your computer, press F3.

Seconds until highlighted choice will be started automatically: 30
```

To load a hardware profile, you can select the profile when this screen appears. If you do not select a profile, then the first one in the list is loaded.

Configuring a Network-Disabled Profile

For computers that are not always attached to the network, you can configure a hardware profile to disable all networking devices and services. A user could then choose this profile when using a computer when it is not attached to the network. To configure a network-disabled profile, use the System program to copy an existing profile. In the **Properties** dialog box for the copied profile, click the **Network** tab and then click **Network-disabled hardware profile**.

For example, you can create a network-disabled hardware profile for your laptop computer. When not connected to the network, having a network-disabled hardware profile for the laptop can decrease your startup time and prevent startup error messages such as "One or more services failed to start." This error message occurs when starting a computer running Windows NT that is configured to start networking devices and services, but is not attached to a network.

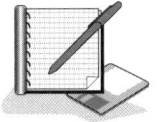

Practice

In these procedures, you create a network-disabled hardware profile for Workstation1. You then test the profile, verifying that the networking functions have been disabled. Finally, you delete the network-disabled hardware profile.

Note Complete this procedure on Workstation1. Server1 must be online.

▶ **To create a network-disabled hardware profile**

In this procedure, you use the System program to create a network-disabled hardware profile for Workstation1.

1. Log on to Domain1 as Administrator.
2. Double-click the System icon in Control Panel.
3. Click the **Hardware Profiles** tab.
4. Click **Rename**.

    The **Rename Profile** dialog box appears.

5. In the **To** box, type **On the Network** and then click **OK**.
6. Click **Copy**.

    The **Copy Profile** dialog box appears.

7. In the **To** box, type **Off the Network** and then click **OK**.
8. In the **Available Hardware Profiles** box, click **Off the Network**, and then click **Properties**.
9. Click the **Network** tab.
10. Select the **Network-disabled hardware profile** check box, and then click **OK**.
11. Under **Multiple Hardware Profiles**, in the **Wait for user selection for** box, change the value to 10 seconds.
12. Click **OK**.

To choose a hardware profile at system startup

In this procedure, you test your Off the Network hardware profile.

1. Shut down and then restart Workstation1.
2. On the **Hardware Profile/Configuration Recovery** menu, select **Off the Network**, and then press ENTER.
3. Log on to Domain1 as Administrator.

What message appears?

_____

_____

_____

_____

Why does this message appear?

_____

_____

_____

_____

4. Click **OK**.
5. Shut down and then restart Workstation1, using the On the Network profile.

To delete a hardware profile

In this procedure, you delete the Off the Network hardware profile that you created.

1. Log on to Domain1 as Administrator.
2. Double-click the System icon in Control Panel.
3. Click the **Hardware Profiles** tab.
4. Under **Available Hardware Profiles**, click **Off the Network**, and then click **Delete**.
5. Click **Yes** to confirm that you want to delete the profile.
6. Click **OK** to close System.

Common Support Issue

When trying to determine why a user cannot connect to the network, remember to first check the hardware profile a user has loaded to make sure that it is *not* configured as a network-disabled profile. The reason you should check the profile is because the Services program in Control Panel and the **net start** command at a command prompt show all network services as started, even when a network-disabled profile is loaded.

Configuring Virtual Memory

Windows NT uses a process called *demand paging* to swap data between RAM and one or more paging files located on one or more hard drives. When Windows NT is installed, Setup creates a virtual-memory paging file, Pagefile.sys, on the partition with the most free disk space.

Paging File Size

The following list specifies the default size of the paging file for Windows NT.

- *Windows NT Server.* The default paging file size is the amount of physical RAM or, if you have less than 22 MB of RAM, the default paging file size is 22 MB or the amount of available disk space, whichever is smaller.

- *Windows NT Workstation.* The paging file size is equal to the total amount of RAM plus 12 MB, or the amount of available disk space, whichever is smaller. The minimum size is 2 MB. A typical paging file is 24 MB or larger.

Often, the size of the paging file can stay at the default value assigned during installation. In some circumstances, such as a large number of applications running simultaneously, a larger paging file or multiple paging files may be advantageous.

Configuring the Paging File

The paging file is configured by clicking the **Change** button on the **Performance** tab of the System program in Control Panel. The **Virtual Memory** dialog box appears, from which virtual memory parameters can be edited. The following illustration shows the **Virtual Memory** dialog box.

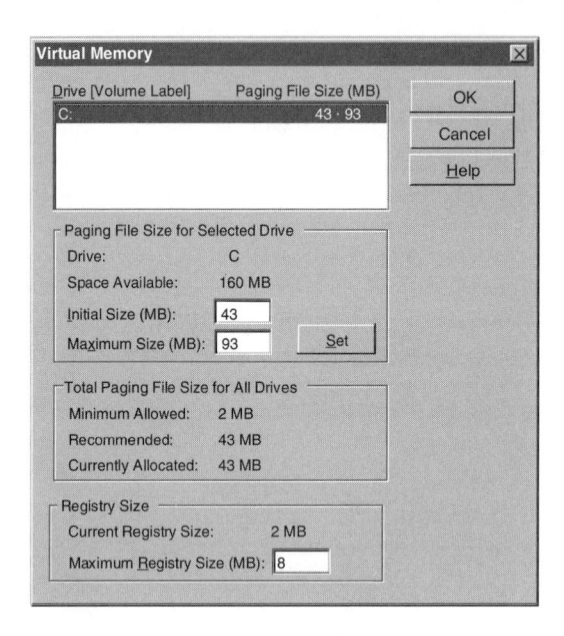

[Virtual Memory dialog box showing:
- Drive [Volume Label] / Paging File Size (MB): C: 43 - 93
- Paging File Size for Selected Drive: Drive: C, Space Available: 160 MB, Initial Size (MB): 43, Maximum Size (MB): 93
- Total Paging File Size for All Drives: Minimum Allowed: 2 MB, Recommended: 43 MB, Currently Allocated: 43 MB
- Registry Size: Current Registry Size: 2 MB, Maximum Registry Size (MB): 8
- Buttons: OK, Cancel, Help, Set]

The **Virtual Memory** dialog box shows the drives on which the paging files reside, and has fields for adjusting the following parameters:

- Paging file size for the selected drive.
- Maximum registry size.

To move the paging file to another partition, or to create a paging file on each hard disk, use the **Virtual Memory** dialog box.

After a paging file is created, it does not shrink below its initial size. Unused space in the paging file is always available to the internal Windows NT Virtual Memory Manager. If the initial paging file is sized significantly below the recommended size, then when you log on, Windows NT displays a Limited Virtual Memory message. You are then prompted to use the System program in Control Panel to create a paging file or increase the initial paging file size. Only an administrator can log on and use the System program to correct this problem.

As needed, a paging file grows from its initial size to the maximum size configured. Once the maximum paging file size is reached, system performance may degrade if additional applications, requiring more virtual memory, are started or continue to run.

When a computer running Windows NT is restarted, all paging files are resized to the initial size specified.

Enhancing Performance

Several options are available to you to increase system performance. For example, if a system has multiple hard disks, consider creating a paging file for each disk. If the hard disk controller can read from and write to multiple hard disks simultaneously, the distribution of information across multiple paging files can significantly improve performance.

You may also be able to improve system performance by moving the paging file off the drive that contains the Windows NT *systemroot* folder. Placing the paging file on a drive that does not contain the boot partition avoids competition between various reading and writing requests. If the paging file is placed on the boot partition to facilitate the recovery feature, you can increase performance by creating multiple paging files that reside on other drives. Because the Virtual Memory Manager alternates write operations between paging files, the paging file on the boot partition is accessed less frequently.

Another way to increase system responsiveness is to set the initial size of the paging file to the optimal size required by the system. This eliminates the time required to enlarge the file.

Note When applying new settings, be sure to click the **Set** button before clicking **OK**.

Remember that changes made to virtual memory are not dynamic. They take effect only after the system restarts.

Practice

In this procedure, you use the System program to change the size of the Windows NT paging file on Server1.

Note Complete this procedure on Server1.

▶ **To change the paging file size**

1. Log on as Administrator.
2. Double-click the System icon in Control Panel.
3. In the **System Properties** dialog box, click the **Performance** tab.

4. Click the **Change** button.

   The **Virtual Memory** dialog box appears.

5. In the **Drive** box, click the drive that currently contains your paging file.

6. In the **Initial Size (MB)** box, increase the value by 10, and then click **Set**.

   If you do not click **Set**, the change does not occur.

7. Click **OK**, and then click **Close**.

   The **System Settings Change** dialog box appears.

8. Click **Yes** to shut down and then restart Windows NT Server.

9. After Windows NT Server restarts, log on as Administrator and confirm the new settings using the System program in Control Panel.

Setting Environment Variables

Environment variables are strings containing information such as a drive, path, or file name. Environment variables provide information that Windows NT requires to control the behavior of various applications. For example, the TEMP environment variable specifies the location where applications place temporary files.

Chapter 3 Configuring the Windows NT Environment

In the **System Properties** dialog box in the System program in Control Panel, the **Environment** tab (as shown in the following illustration) allows administrators to change two types of environment variables:

- System environment variables
- User environment variables for *logged_on_user_name*

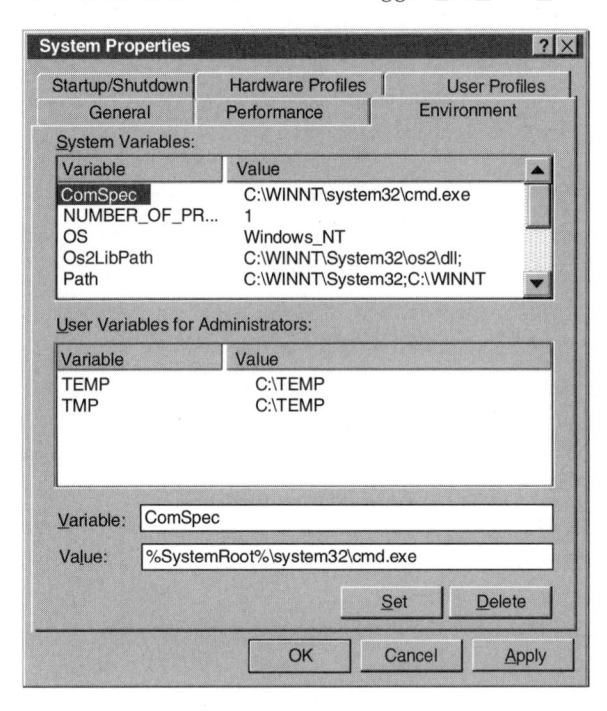

System Environment Variables

Administrators can change or add environment variables that apply to the system, and thus to all users of the system. These are called system environment variables. During installation, Windows NT Setup configures the default system variables, such as the path to the Windows NT files.

User Environment Variables

The user environment variables are different for each user of a particular computer. The variables include any that are set by the user, as well as any variables defined by applications, such as the path to the location of the application files.

How Windows NT Sets Environment Variables

The **Environment** tab in the **System Properties** dialog box displays all of the system and user environment variables currently in effect. Any user can add, modify, or remove a user environment variable, but only an administrator can add, modify, or remove a system environment variable.

By default, Windows NT searches the C:\Autoexec.bat file, if one exists, and sets any environment statements. For example, the PATH statement in the C:\Autoexec.bat file is automatically appended to the default system path every time any user logs on.

Windows NT sets environment variables in this order:

1. Autoexec.bat variables
2. System environment variables
3. User environment variables

For example, if the line "SET TMP=C:\" is placed in Autoexec.bat and a User variable "TMP=X:\TEMP" is set, the User variable setting overrides the prior setting. Therefore, the TMP environment variable is equal to X:\TEMP.

A registry entry can be set to prevent Windows NT from searching the C:\Autoexec.bat file. To enable this feature, an administrator can use Registry Editor to edit the following registry parameter and make the value ParseAutoexec: **REG_SZ = 0**.

\HKEY_CURRENT_USER\Software\Microsoft\
Windows NT\CurrentVersion\Winlogon\ParseAutoexec **REG_SZ = 0**

Optionally, System Policy Editor can be used to edit this registry parameter. Under the Local User hierarchy, choose **Windows NT System** and clear the **Parse Autoexec.bat** check box to prevent parsing of Autoexec.bat.

Note System Policy Editor is covered in Chapter 4, "Managing System Policies."

Adding and Removing Windows NT Components

An administrator can add or remove any of the Windows NT components that are not required by the system through Add/Remove Programs in Control Panel. The **Add/Remove Programs Properties** dialog box contains the following tabs:

- **Windows NT Setup**
- **Install/Uninstall**

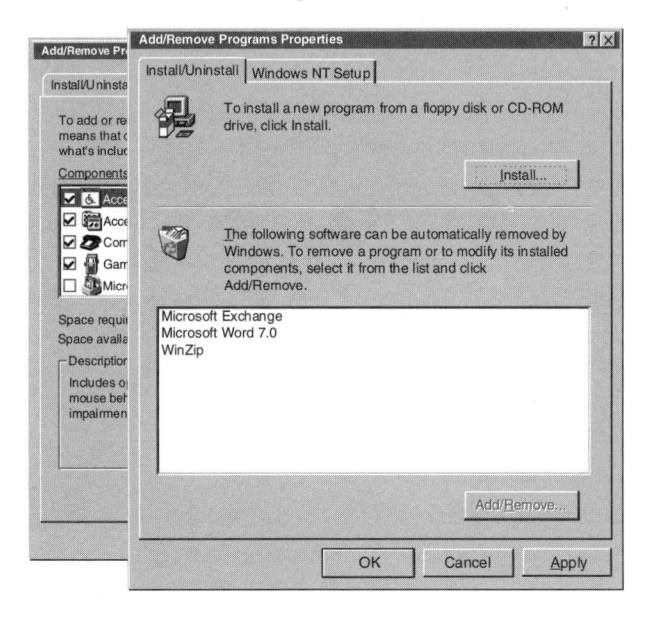

Windows NT Setup

Use the **Windows NT Setup** tab to add or remove Windows NT components. The **Windows NT Setup** tab displays the same list of optional components that is presented during installation. Adding more components or removing existing ones requires the original Windows NT 4.0 compact disc or shared installation files to be available. Restarting the computer may be required following the addition or removal of components, depending on the software that was added or removed.

Install/Uninstall

Use the **Install/Uninstall** tab to install new applications or to uninstall existing applications. Any application that uses Setup.exe or Install.exe to install itself can be both installed and uninstalled.

Clicking the **Install** button on the **Install/Uninstall** tab prompts Windows NT to scan first the floppy disk drives and then the CD-ROM drive for Setup.exe or Install.exe. Windows NT runs the first instance of a program named SETUP or INSTALL that it finds.

Applications that use the Install/Uninstall application programming interface (API) appear on the list of installed programs above the **Add/Remove** button. Clicking the **Add/Remove** button runs the original Setup program for the selected application. Additional components of that application, or the application itself, can then be added or removed, following the application's Setup program.

Practice

In this procedure, you use the Add/Remove Programs program to install the Windows NT games and wallpaper.

Note Complete this procedure on both Server1 and Workstation1.

▶ **To add additional Windows NT components**

1. Log on as Administrator.
2. Double-click the Add/Remove Programs icon in Control Panel.
3. Click the **Windows NT Setup** tab.
4. Select the **Games** check box.
5. Select the **Accessories** check box, and then click **Details**.
6. In the **Components** list, click **Desktop Wallpaper**, and then click **OK**.

7. Click **OK**.

   The **Insert Disk** dialog box appears.

8. Click **OK**.

   The **Files Needed** dialog box appears.

9. In the **Copy files from** box:

   On Server1, type **\\Server1\nts_source\I386** and then click **OK**.

   On Workstation1, insert the *Microsoft Windows NT Workstation 4.0* compact disc, type *cd-rom drive letter***:\I386** and then click **OK**.

   The files are installed.

10. Check the contents of your Accessories folder to confirm that the games have been installed.

11. Using the Display program in Control Panel, click the **Background** tab to confirm that the wallpapers have been installed.

Lesson 4: Modifying System Settings Using Registry Editor

Windows NT Registry Editor is the most powerful tool available for editing the registry. It is the only Windows NT program that can be used to edit all of the local keys in the registry. It also allows an administrator to edit the HKEY_LOCAL_MACHINE and HKEY_USERS keys on a remote computer running Windows NT. This enables administrators to provide either local or remote support of Windows NT.

After this lesson, you will be able to:
- Use Registry Editor to view information in the registry.
- Use various commands of Registry Editor to explore the registry.

Estimated lesson time: 45 minutes

Guidelines for Using Registry Editor

The Windows NT Registry Editor allows administrators to manually edit the registry and it enables troubleshooting by displaying the contents of the registry. Registry Editor (Regedt32.exe) is installed in the *systemroot*\System32 folder during the Windows NT setup but is not added to any of the folders on the **Start** menu.

Appropriate Use of Registry Editor

The primary purpose of Registry Editor is to help with troubleshooting and problem resolution. For example, sections of the registry can be saved to disk and transported to another computer for analysis or system documentation purposes, or the registry can be viewed over the network.

Note For more information on editing the registry, see the *Microsoft Windows NT Server Resource Kit*.

By default, administrators have Full control over the registry. Users have Full control over their HKEY_CURRENT_USER subtree, and have Read access to other parts of the registry. An administrator can change the registry permissions through the **Security** menu in Registry Editor.

Though Registry Editor is a dedicated administrative tool, in most cases it is not the appropriate tool for modifying the system configuration. Most configuration changes can be made through Control Panel or System Policy Editor, as described later in this book. However, some configuration settings can only be set directly through Registry Editor.

Caution Incorrect use of Registry Editor can cause serious problems that may require reinstallation of Windows NT. Microsoft cannot guarantee that problems due to incorrect use of Registry Editor can be solved without reinstallation. When using Registry Editor to view data, click **Read Only Mode** on the **Options** menu to prevent accidental edits to the registry.

Useful Registry Editor Commands

Some of the most useful Registry Editor commands are on the **View** and **Registry** menus of the **Registry Editor** dialog box. The following table describes these commands.

Command	Description
View Menu:	
Find Key	Searches only for keys, not values. Use this command to search the registry for a specific key. Key names appear on the left of the Registry Editor window. The search begins at the currently selected key and parses all descendant keys for the specified key name. The search is local to the subtree in which the search begins; for example, a search for keys under HKEY_LOCAL_MACHINE does not include keys under HKEY_CURRENT_USER.
Registry Menu:	
Save Key	Saves part of the registry in binary format. It saves the currently selected key and all subkeys. This binary file can then be used with the Restore command to reload a set of values after testing a modification.
Restore	Loads the data in the selected file under the currently selected key. If the selected key was saved in the data file, Registry Editor overwrites the key with the values in the file.
Save Subtree As	Saves the selected key and all subkeys in a text file. The text file can then be searched in a text editor for a specific value or key that was added or modified. If an administrator is unsure as to which value may have been modified, this command can be used to determine which keys had values modified and when those modifications were made.

(*continued*)

Command	Description
Select Computer	Accesses the registry of a remote computer. By default, Windows NT Server allows remote access to only the Administrators group; Windows NT Workstation allows remote access by any valid user account. The remote access permissions for either platform can be modified by setting permissions on this registry key: HKEY_LOCAL_MACHINE\SYSTEM\CurrentControlSet\Control\SecuredPipeServers\winreg
	By default, this key exists on Windows NT Server. The key does *not* exist on Windows NT Workstation, but you can add it through Registry Editor.

Windows 95 Registry Editor

Windows NT Setup also installs the Windows 95 Registry Editor (Regedit.exe). Because Regedit.exe does not have a security menu, or a read-only mode, and because it does not support all of the data types that Regedt32.exe supports, it is not the recommended Registry Editor for Windows NT. However, Regedit.exe does contain a more powerful search engine that allows you to find keys, values, and data in the registry. Regedt32.exe allows you to search only for keys.

Practice

In these procedures, you use Registry Editor to locate and view information in the registry.

Note Complete these procedures on Server1.

▶ **To locate information in the registry**

In this procedure, you use Registry Editor to view information in the registry.

1. Verify that you are logged on as Administrator.
2. Start Registry Editor (Regedt32.exe).
3. On the **Options** menu, verify that **Read Only Mode** is selected.
4. On the **View** menu, verify that **Tree and Data** is selected.
5. Minimize all windows except HKEY_LOCAL_MACHINE on Local Machine.

6. Expand the HARDWARE\DESCRIPTION\System subkey. Locate the system subkeys, and value and string for each item in the Hardware configuration column in the second table, using the subkeys under the System key. The first table provides an example of system subkeys, values and strings.

Hardware configuration	System subkeys	Value and string
Processor type (example)	CentralProcessor\0	Identifier:80486
Bus type (example)	MultifunctionAdapter\0	Identifier:ISA
Pointer controller type (example)	MultifunctionAdapter\0\ PointerController\0\ PointerPeripheral\0\	Identifier:MICROSOFT PS2 MOUSE
Pointer controller type (EISA example)	EisaAdapter\0\ PointerController\0\ PointerPeripheral\0\	Identifier:MICROSOFT PS2 MOUSE
Processor type		
Bus type		
Pointer controller type		

7. Expand the SOFTWARE\Microsoft\Windows NT\CurrentVersion subkey and locate the value and string for each item listed under Software configuration in the following table.

Software configuration	Value and string
Current Build Number	
Current Version	
Registered Organization	
Registered Owner	

▶ **To use the Find Key command**

In this procedure, you use Regedt32.exe to find a specified key in the registry.

1. Select the HKEY_LOCAL_MACHINE subkey located at the top of the path. This ensures that the entire subtree is searched.
2. On the **View** menu, click **Find Key**.
3. In the **Find what** box, type **serial** and then click **Find Next**.
   Note the locations in the registry that are found.
4. Click **Find Next** until a **Warning** dialog box appears stating "Registry Editor cannot find the desired key."
5. Click **OK** to close the dialog box.
6. In the **Find** dialog box, click **Cancel** to end the search.

▶ **To view a configuration change in the registry**

In this procedure, you make a change using Control Panel and verify that the configuration information was written to the registry.

1. Double-click the System icon in Control Panel.
2. In the **System Properties** dialog box, click the **Environment** tab.
3. In the **System Variables** box, click any variable.

   The focus is now set on the **System Variables** box.
4. In the **Variable** box, type **TEST**
5. In the Value box, type **yes** and then click Set.
6. Click **OK**.
7. Switch to Registry Editor.

   Does the TEST variable appear in HKEY_LOCAL_MACHINE\SYSTEM\CurrentControlSet\Control\Session Manager\Environment?

8. Close Control Panel.

▶ **To search a subtree for a specific value using Regedt32.exe and Notepad**

In this procedure, you use Regedt32.exe and Notepad to search for a registry value's data.

1. Switch to Registry Editor.
2. Click **HKEY_LOCAL_MACHINE\SOFTWARE**.
3. On the **Registry** menu, click **Save Subtree As**.
4. Save the file with the name Software.txt.
5. Close Registry Editor.
6. Open the Software.txt file that you just created.

   Notepad displays the file.
7. On the **Search** menu, click **Find**.
8. In the **Find what** field, type **CurrentBuildNumber** and then click **Find Next**.
9. Click **Cancel** to close the **Find** dialog box.
10. Scroll down (if necessary) to see the data for **CurrentBuildNumber**. What is the current build?

11. Close Notepad.

▶ **To search the registry for a specific value using Regedit.exe**

The Windows 95 Registry Editor, Regedit.exe, provides an alternate way of viewing data directly in the registry. In this procedure, you use Regedit.exe to search for a registry value's data.

1. Click the **Start** button, and then click **Run**.
2. In the **Open** box, type **regedit.exe** and then click **OK**.
3. On the **Edit** menu, click **Find**.
4. In the **Find what** box, type **CurrentBuildNumber** and then click **Find Next**.

   What is the current build?

   _____

5. Close Regedit.exe.

Summary

The following information summarizes the key points in this chapter:

- The Windows NT registry is a unified database where Windows NT stores all system configuration information for the local computer.
- Windows NT provides tools such as Control Panel, System Policy Editor, and other administrative tools that are used to configure the hardware, software, and operating system settings.
- The Windows NT Registry Editor is a tool that provides access to the entire registry, and should be used to view the registry to identify whether the proper system settings are being loaded. You should be very careful when using Registry Editor to edit the registry. Registry Editor does not check for mistakes made in syntax or semantics, so you are not warned if you have improperly entered a value into the registry.

For more information on	See
The registry	*Microsoft Windows NT Workstation Resource Kit*
	The *Resource Guide* of the *Microsoft Windows NT Server Resource Kit*
	–or–
	"Using Registry Editor" in Microsoft Windows NT Server *Concepts and Planning*

Review

1. Based on what you know of the registry, in which subtrees (HKEY_LOCAL_MACHINE or HKEY_CURRENT_USER) do you think the following configuration parameters reside?

    - TCP/IP:

    - Video:

    - Hardware profiles:

    - Mouse pointer acceleration:

2. You use a portable computer both at home and in a docking station on the network at your office. When you start Windows NT at home, you get the following message: "One or more services failed to start. See Event Viewer for details." This message does not appear when you start Windows NT while your computer is docked at work. What is causing this message, and what can you do to stop it?

3. You configured your computer to dual-boot between Windows NT Workstation and Windows NT Server. You almost always use Windows NT Workstation rather than Windows NT Server. However, because you installed Windows NT Server after Windows NT Workstation, your computer always starts into Windows NT Server by default. How can you configure Windows NT Workstation to start by default?

4. When you attempt to access the registry of a computer running Windows NT Server remotely using Registry Editor, you get an "Access Denied" message. What is the likely cause of the message?

Answer Key

Procedure Answers

Page 89

- **To view the registry**

    3. List the names of the five subtrees displayed by Registry Editor.

       HKEY_LOCAL_MACHINE, HKEY_CLASSES_ROOT, HKEY_CURRENT_USER, HKEY_CURRENT_CONFIG, HKEY_USERS

Page 101

- **To change a user's profile**

    3. Expand the HKEY_CURRENT_USER\Control Panel\Desktop key.

       What is the value of the **Pattern** field?

       (None)

    9. Start Registry Editor, and then expand the HKEY_CURRENT_USER\Control Panel\Desktop key.

       What is the value of the **Pattern** field?

       It is a numeric value for the new pattern.

Page 118

- **To choose a hardware profile at system startup**

    3. Log on to Domain1 as Administrator.

       What message appears?

       **A domain controller for your domain could not be contacted. You have been logged on using cached account information.
       Changes made to your profile since you last logged on may not be available.**

       Why does this message appear?

       This messages appears because network-related services and drivers are not running. This prevents dependent services and drivers from starting, and it also prevents the workstation from communicating with a domain controller during logon.

138   Microsoft Windows NT Technical Support

Page 131

▶ **To locate information in the registry**

6. Expand the HARDWARE\DESCRIPTION\System subkey and locate the information requested in the second table, using the subkeys under the System key.

Hardware configuration	System subkeys	Value and string
Processor type		
Bus type		
Pointer controller type		

Answers will vary.

7. Expand the SOFTWARE\Microsoft\Windows NT\CurrentVersion subkey and locate the information in the following table.

Software configuration	Value and string
Current Build Number	1381
Current Version	4.0
Registered Organization	
Registered Owner	

Answers will vary.

Page 132

▶ **To view a configuration change in the registry**

7. Switch to Registry Editor.

Does the TEST variable appear in HKEY_LOCAL_MACHINE\SYSTEM\CurrentControlSet\Control\Session Manager\Environment?

Yes, if the system environment variable was entered correctly.

Page 132

▶ **To search a subtree for a specific value using Regedt32.exe and Notepad**

10. Scroll down (if necessary) to see the data for **CurrentBuildNumber**. What is the current build?

1381.

Page 133

▶ **To search the registry for a specific value using Regedit.exe**

4. In the **Find what** box, type **CurrentBuildNumber** and then click **Find Next**. What is the current build?

1381.

Chapter 3 Configuring the Windows NT Environment 139

Review Answers

Page 135

1. Based on what you know of the registry, in which subtrees (HKEY_LOCAL_MACHINE or HKEY_CURRENT_USER) do you think the following configuration parameters reside?
   - TCP/IP: **HKEY_LOCAL_MACHINE**
   - Video: **HKEY_LOCAL_MACHINE**
   - Hardware profiles: **HKEY_LOCAL_MACHINE**
   - Mouse pointer acceleration: **HKEY_CURRENT_USER**

2. You use a portable computer both at home and in a docking station on the network at your office. When you start Windows NT at home, you get the following message: "One or more services failed to start. See Event Viewer for details." This message does not appear when you start Windows NT while your computer is docked at work. What is causing this message, and what can you do to stop it?

   The network services are not loading because the network adapter card is in the docking station. Create separate hardware profiles to solve the problem.

3. You configured your computer to dual-boot between Windows NT Workstation and Windows NT Server. You almost always use Windows NT Workstation rather than Windows NT Server. However, because you installed Windows NT Server after Windows NT Workstation, your computer always starts into Windows NT Server by default. How can you configure Windows NT Workstation to start by default?

   Change the startup option on the Startup/Shutdown tab of Control Panel System so that Windows NT Workstation is selected.

4. When you attempt to access the registry of a computer running Windows NT Server remotely using Registry Editor, you get an "Access Denied" message. What is the likely cause of the message?

   You are using an account that is not recognized as an administrator's account on the remote computer. Computers running Windows NT Server restrict registry remote access to members of the Administrators group.

CHAPTER 4

Managing System Policies

Lesson 1 The Purpose of System Policies . . . 142

Lesson 2 Implementing a System Policy . . . 146

Lesson 3 Using System Policy Editor to Manage a System Policy . . . 151

Review . . . 168

About This Chapter
System policies enable you to control the user-definable settings in Windows NT and Windows 95 user profiles, as well as system configuration settings. You can use *System Policy Editor* to change desktop settings and restrict what users can do from their desktops. In this chapter, you learn how to implement a system policy in a domain.

Before You Begin
To complete the lessons in this chapter, you must have:

- Two computers that meet the hardware and software requirements as specified in the Getting Started section of "About This Book."
- Completed all practices in Chapter 2, "Installing Windows NT."
- Completed the practices in Chapter 3, "Configuring the Windows NT Environment," in which you used Add/Remove Programs in Control Panel to install the Windows NT games and wallpaper, and in which you used User Manager for Domains to create User1.

Lesson 1: The Purpose of System Policies

A system policy provides administrators with increased control and manageability of desktop computers running Windows NT or Windows 95 across a domain. This lesson provides an overview of the settings you can control with a policy.

After this lesson, you will be able to:
- Define the function of system policies.
- Identify which Windows NT operating system includes System Policy Editor.
- Identify who can implement system policy.
- Start System Policy Editor.
- Describe what settings are configured in a computer policy.
- Describe what settings are configured in a user policy.

Estimated lesson time: 25 minutes

What Is a System Policy?

A system policy is a set of rules that controls what a user sees on their desktop and what they can do with their computer. When a system policy is used in a domain, it can establish a uniform set of rules, or policy, for all users and computers running Windows NT or Windows 95. System policies can also be configured to provide custom desktop and computer configurations for specific users, groups, and computers.

A system policy gives you the ability to:

- Restrict options in Control Panel, such as hiding the Screen Saver tab in the Display program, which would prevent users from changing or configuring their screen savers.
- Customize parts of the desktop, such as specifying the corporate standard wallpaper on all computers.
- Control network logon and access, such as creating a logon banner to display a message when a user logs on.

Note A system policy is created with an administrative tool, System Policy Editor (Poledit.exe). System Policy Editor is only included with Windows NT Server 4.0 and appears on the **Administrative Tools (Common)** menu. Only administrators can create and change system policies.

As you review this lesson, review the options in System Policy Editor that are covered in this chapter.

Practice

In this procedure, you create a shortcut for System Policy Editor and then start System Policy Editor.

Note Complete this procedure on Server1.

▶ **To create a shortcut for and start System Policy Editor**

1. Log on to as Administrator.
2. Create a shortcut for Poledit.exe.

    The following illustration shows how the shortcut icon appears on your desktop.

    poledit

3. Start System Policy Editor from the shortcut for Poledit.exe.

    System Policy Editor appears. Notice that the System Policy Editor window is empty. This is because a policy file must first be created or opened before it can appear in the System Policy Editor window.

4. On the **File** menu, click **New Policy**.
5. What two icons appear in the System Policy Editor window?

Computer Policy and User Policy

When you create a new policy, System Policy Editor displays two icons, Default Computer and Default User. These icons display the individual policy options that give you the ability to configure a computer policy for all computers in the domain that are running Windows NT or Windows 95 and a user policy for all users that log on to one of these computers.

- *Default Computer.* Computer policy options are used to configure logon and network settings. These options apply to all computers in the domain and effect all users that log on to those computers. When you need to customize a specific computer policy for a specific computer, you can add the computer using the **Edit** menu in System Policy Editor.

- *Default User.* User policy options are used to configure the user's desktop. You can set these options to effect all users that log on to the domain. When you need to customize a specific user policy that is different from the default, you can add users or groups using the **Edit** menu in System Policy Editor.

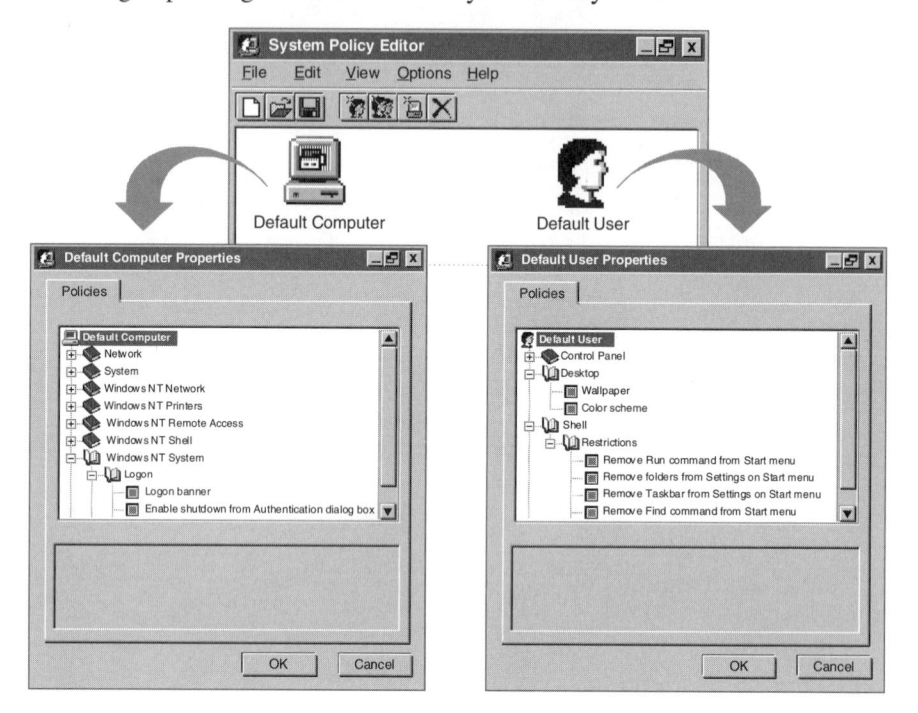

Practice

In this procedure, you explore the policy options in Default User and Default Computer.

Note Complete this procedure on Server1.

▶ **To explore Default User and Default Computer**

1. In System Policy Editor, double-click **Default User**.
2. Expand **Shell** by clicking the plus sign (+) beside **Shell**, and then expand **Restrictions**.
3. Explore the various Default User options.

    The Default User options are explained later in this chapter.
4. Click **Cancel** to close the **Default User Properties** dialog box.
5. Double-click **Default Computer**.

6. Expand **Windows NT System**, and then expand **Logon**.
7. Explore the various Default Computer options.

    These Default Computer options are explained later in this chapter.
8. Click **Cancel** to close the **Default Computer Properties** dialog box.
9. Close System Policy Editor and do *not* save any changes.

Lesson 2: Implementing a System Policy

In this lesson, you learn how a system policy is implemented in a domain. This includes what happens when a user logs on, and the priority order in which policies are implemented. You also learn how to implement a local policy when you want a computer to use a policy other than the domain policy.

After this lesson, you will be able to:
- Describe the process to implement a system policy in a domain.
- Describe how a user policy is implemented when a user logs on to the domain.
- Describe how a computer policy is implemented when a user logs on to a domain.
- Describe how to implement a local policy.

Estimated lesson time: 20 minutes

Implementing a System Policy in a Domain

The following steps provide an overview of how a system policy is implemented in a domain.

1. Use System Policy Editor to create a new policy file. Set the appropriate policy options in Default Computer and Default User.

2. If you need to set specific policy options for a user, group, or specific computer account, use the **Edit** menu to add the account and then set the policy options.

   The following illustration shows a domain system policy that also includes separate policies for a specific computer (Computer1), user (User1), and group (Account Operators).

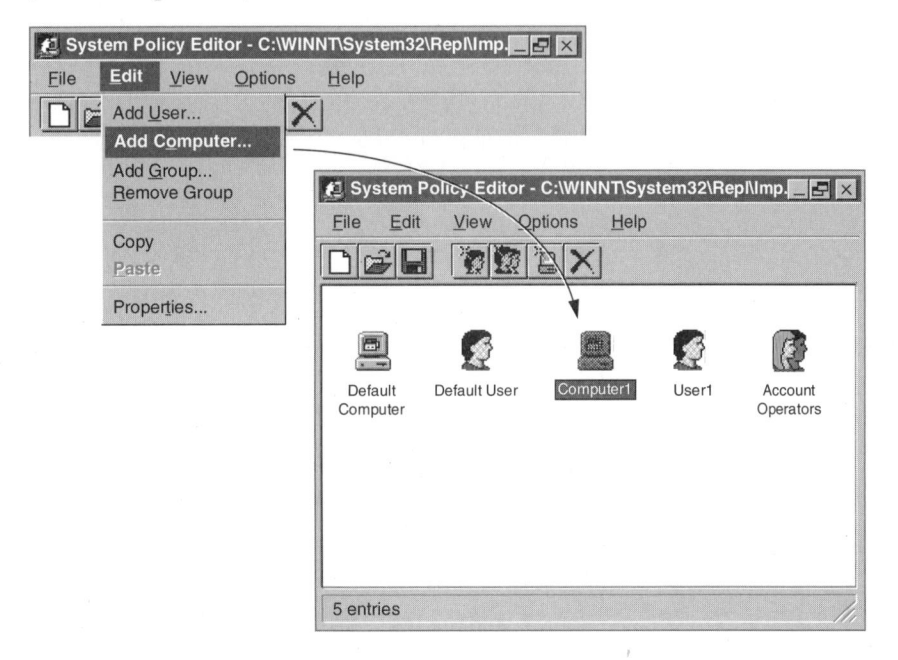

3. By default, Windows NT searches for the Ntconfig.pol policy file stored on the PDC in the Netlogon share. Therefore, name the policy file Ntconfig.pol on the PDC in the following folder:

   systemroot\System32\Repl\Import\Scripts

   On domain controllers, the Windows NT installation automatically shares this folder with the share name Netlogon.

4. Enable *replication* on all domain controllers so that the Ntconfig.pol file is replicated to the same folder on all backup domain controllers.

Note For more information on replication see Chapter 16, "Implementing File Synchronization and Directory Replication."

How a User Policy Is Implemented When a User Logs On

The following list describes the process used by Windows NT to determine which *user* settings to apply to a user logging on to a domain:

- When a users logs on to the domain from a computer running Windows NT, the user's user profile is loaded. Next, Windows NT searches for the Ntconfig.pol file on the domain controller that authenticated the user logon request.

- If a specific user policy exists for that user, those policy settings are merged into the current user portion of the registry (HKEY_CURRENT_USER).

- Even if user policy is not defined for a specific user, the system policy may include a group policy that has been defined for a *group* of which the user is a member. If a user is a member of more than one group, the group with the highest priority defines the policy settings for the user. The group's policy settings are then merged into HKEY_CURRENT_USER.

  A group's priority is configured in System Policy Editor by clicking **Group Priority** on the **Options** menu.

- If system policy is not defined for the user or for the user's group(s), the *Default User policy* settings are merged into HKEY_CURRENT_USER.

Note Policies are applied only at the time a user logs on. If a user is logged on when a system policy change is implemented, the user must log off and log back on for the policy change to take effect.

The following illustration diagrams how user and computer policies are implemented when a user logs on.

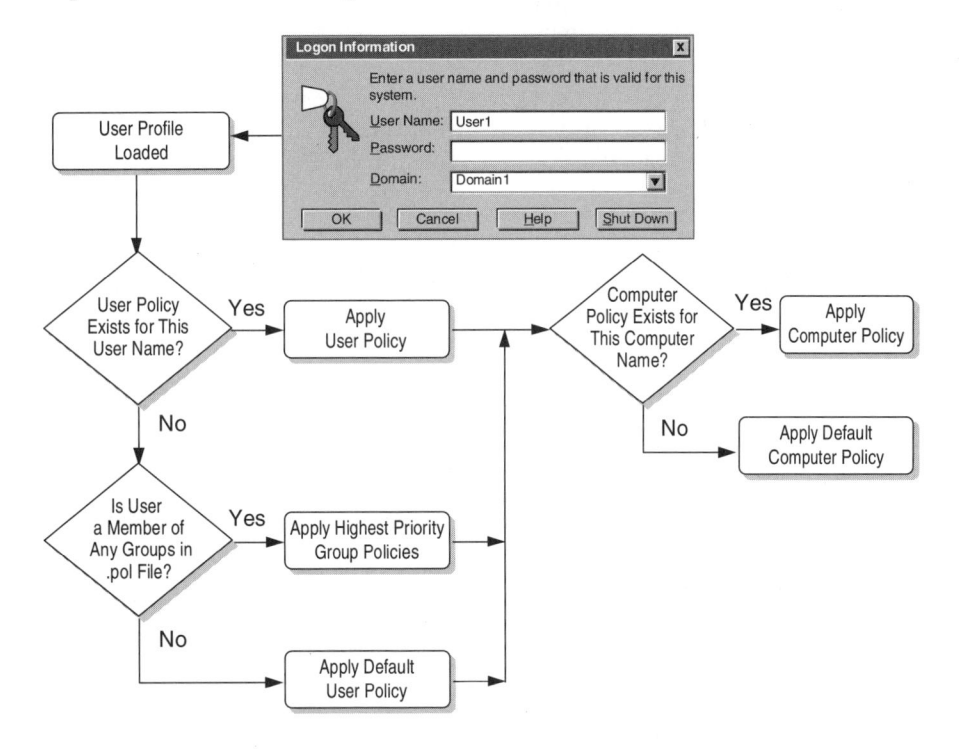

[Flowchart showing logon process: Logon Information dialog → User Profile Loaded → User Policy Exists for This User Name? If Yes → Apply User Policy. If No → Is User a Member of Any Groups in .pol File? If Yes → Apply Highest Priority Group Policies. If No → Apply Default User Policy. Then → Computer Policy Exists for This Computer Name? If Yes → Apply Computer Policy. If No → Apply Default Computer Policy.]

How a Computer Policy Is Implemented When a User Logs On

If a specific computer policy is defined for the computer at which the user is logging on, those policy settings are merged into the local computer portion of the registry (HKEY_LOCAL_MACHINE). Otherwise, the *Default Computer policy* settings are merged into HKEY_LOCAL_MACHINE.

Note To apply system policies in a network that uses both Windows 95 and Windows NT Workstation, System Policy Editor must be run once from each platform. When you use System Policy Editor on a computer running Windows 95, you save the policy settings to a file named Config.pol. This file is similar to the Ntconfig.pol file, but has a different file format and reflects differences in the registries of the two operating systems. Save the Config.pol file to the Netlogon share on the PDC. For more information on using system policy for computers running Windows 95, see the *Microsoft Windows 95 Resource Kit*.

Implementing a Local Policy

You are not restricted to using only one system policy in a domain. However, by default a computer running Windows NT automatically downloads the information in the Ntconfig.pol file from the domain controller that authenticated the user logon request. Therefore, if you want to use a system policy from a computer that is not a domain controller, you would change the **Remote update** setting from *automatic* in the computer policy portion of the system policy to *manual,* and specify the computer and path to the system policy file.

You would use the following steps to set up a manual update path on a computer running Windows NT Workstation. This is done by using System Policy Editor on a computer running Windows NT Server to create a system policy file on the computer running Windows NT Workstation.

Note The following steps are informational and should *not* be performed at this time.

1. Start System Policy Editor on a computer running Windows NT Server.
2. On the **File** menu, click **New Policy**.
3. Double-click **Default Computer**, and then expand **Network**.
4. Expand **System policies update**.
5. Select **Remote update** (there should be a check in the check box).

    Notice at the bottom of the screen that the **Settings for Remote update** dialog box appears.

6. In the **Update mode** box, click the down arrow, and then click **Manual (use specific path)**.
7. In the **Path for manual update** box, enter *path\unique_file_name*.pol. For example, **C:\Ws1.pol**
8. Click **OK**.
9. Click **File** and, then click **Save**.
10. In the **Save in** box, click the down arrow.
11. Click **Network Neighborhood**, and then double-click the name of the computer for which you want to change the remote update setting.

    The name of the computer running Windows NT Workstation now appears in the **Save in** box, so that you can save the policy file on it.

12. In the **File name** box, type the file name that you specified in the system policy file. In our example, it was Ws1.pol.

    By default, Ws1.pol is saved in the root directory of the drive containing *systemroot*. Therefore, you must make sure that the path and file name of the policy file match the one you entered in the **Path for manual update** box.

Lesson 3: Using System Policy Editor to Manage a System Policy

Now that you have learned how a system policy is implemented in a domain, you learn how to create and manage a system policy using System Policy Editor.

After this lesson, you will be able to:
- Describe the two Registry Editor modes: registry mode and policy mode.
- Describe the computer and user policy options.
- Configure a computer policy within a system policy.
- Describe the function of the system policy templates.

Estimated lesson time: 60 minutes

System Policy Editor is available in the Administrative Tools (Common) folder on computers running Windows NT Server 4.0. System Policy Editor is used to:

- Modify default settings for the computer and user policy for the domain.
- Create custom settings that apply to individual users, groups of users, or individual computers.
- Specify the manner and location from which to download policy for some or all users.

Note Educate users about the system policy implemented in the domain or on a computer. If a user is familiar with the default Windows NT interface, they may interpret policy restrictions or customizations as a problem with the operating system. For example, if the policy hides the **Run** command on the **Start** menu, a user may report that the operating system is not working properly, because the user cannot find the **Run** command.

System Policy Editor Modes

System Policy Editor has two modes, registry mode and policy mode. When System Policy Editor starts, it is not in any specific mode.

Registry Mode

In registry mode, you can edit portions of the registry of the local computer or a remote computer. This is a *direct* edit of the local registry and changes are reflected almost immediately. To simplify administration, avoid using this mode and instead make changes to the domain system policy. When the registry is opened (by clicking **Open Registry** or **Connect** on the **File** menu), System Policy Editor is placed in registry mode. The title bar displays **Local Registry**.

Changing Registry Settings on a Local or Remote Computer

When System Policy Editor is used in registry mode, changes are made by selecting or clearing specific registry options in **Local Computer** or **Local User**.

Using registry mode exposes certain keys in HKEY_CURRENT_USER and HKEY_LOCAL_MACHINE. Changes made to the Local Computer or Local User policy are updated in these registry keys when the settings are saved and the registry is closed. The user does not need to log off or restart the computer to see the changes.

To make changes to the Windows NT registry settings on a remote computer, click **Connect** on the System Policy Editor **File** menu. This feature allows remote adjustment to computer registries.

Note To simplify administration, avoid using registry mode to change individual computer registry settings. A uniform system policy for the domain is easier to maintain. If a specific user or computer incompatibility problem occurs, instead of making *direct changes* to registry settings, create a separate policy entry for that user or computer within the domain system policy (Ntconfig.pol).

Policy Mode

Policy mode is the mode you use to create and modify a system policy for a domain. The policy mode is used to create or modify system policy files (.pol). However, changes to the registry on the computers receiving the policy are not implemented for users or computers until the following procedures are completed:

1. The policy file is saved as Ntconfig.pol in the Netlogon share on the PDC.
2. Ntconfig.pol is replicated to the BDCs in the domain.
3. Users log on to the domain.

When you create a policy file by clicking **New Policy** on the **File** menu, System Policy Editor is placed in policy mode. The title bar displays **Untitled**. When you modify an existing system policy by clicking **Open Policy** on the **File** menu and typing in the existing policy file name, System Policy Editor is also placed in policy mode.

Check Box Selection Levels

The check boxes for individual policies can appear dimmed, selected, or cleared as shown in the following illustration.

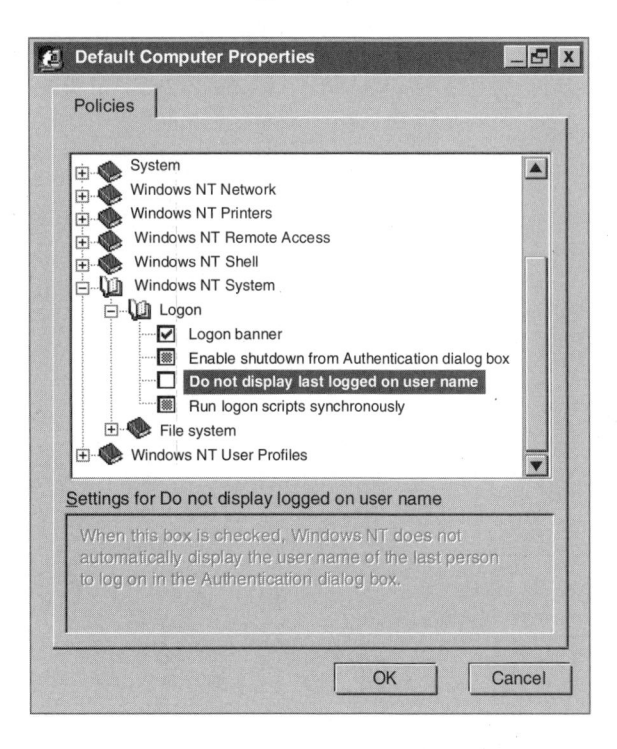

- *Dimmed.* The registry key for the policy is not modified. This is the default setting.
- *Selected.* The policy is implemented.
- *Cleared.* The policy is not implemented.

When the policy file is created, only the selected and cleared policy settings are saved to the policy file (.pol). You would leave a check box dimmed to increase logon speed. This is because dimmed options are not saved to the policy file and are not loaded across the network.

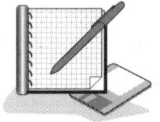

Practice

In these procedures, you use System Policy Editor on Server1 to examine the various options available for creating and modifying system policy.

Note Complete these procedure on Server1.

▶ **To explore the File menu options in System Policy Editor**

1. Start **System Policy Editor**.
2. Click **File**.

    The following table describes the options on the **File** menu.

File option	Allows you to
New Policy	Create a new system policy.
Open Policy	View and modify an existing system policy.
Open Registry	View and modify the information stored in the local registry.
Save	Save any changes you have made to system policy.
Save As	Allows you to create a new system policy based on the one you are currently editing. Any change made since the last save are only saved in the new system policy.
Close	Close the open system policy file.
Connect	To make changes to the Windows NT registry settings on a remote computer.
Exit	Close or exit System Policy Editor.

▶ **To create a new system policy**

- On the **File** menu, click **New Policy**.

    System Policy Editor displays two icons, Default Computer and Default User.

▶ To explore system policy for default computer

1. Double-click **Default Computer**.

   The **Default Computer Properties** dialog box appears.

2. Explore the Default Computer settings.

   The following table describes the system policy settings available for Default Computer.

Computer system policy option	Use the option
Network	To perform system policy updates. Remote Update options include a choice of two modes: an automatic default path (which updates from Ntconfig.pol on a domain controller), or a manually entered path to update system policy from a computer other than a domain controller. There are also options to enable display of error messages if the policy file cannot be found, and to enable *load balancing* for computers running Windows 95.
System	To configure the Simple Network Management Protocol (SNMP) entry and specify the contents of the **Run** entry that is used to specify which applications should run at startup.
Windows NT Network	To enable creation of hidden shares for each drive letter upon system startup.
Windows NT Printers	To disable the print spooler browser, to change the priority of print job assignments, or set the print spooler to beep every 10 seconds if there is an error condition for a print job on a remote print server.
Windows NT Remote Access	To use a remote access server, set a maximum number for unsuccessful authentication retries, and a maximum time limit for authentication. There is also an option for the time interval between call-back attempts and a time limit for automatic disconnection from the server.
Windows NT Shell	To create custom shared folders for all users at the computer.
Windows NT System	To modify **Logon** options: Altering the logon banner, changing the default user name and password, enabling shutdown from the **Authentication** dialog box, and disabling display of the last logged-on user name. To modify **File system** options for enabling or disabling 8.3 file names, for using extended characters for 8.3 file names, and for updating the last access time attribute of a file.

156   Microsoft Windows NT Technical Support

(continued)

Computer system policy option	Use the option
Windows NT User Profiles	To define a slow connection to a logon server and allow the computer to automatically detect a slow connection when a user attempts to log on. Use these settings in conjunction with the options on the **User Profile** tab of the System program in Control Panel to optimize performance when logging on through a slow connection.
FTP System (appears if FTP server service is enabled)	To configure the File Transfer Protocol (FTP) server service.

3. After you have finished exploring the Default Computer options, click **Cancel**. Do not change the default settings at this time.

▶ **To explore system policy for the default user**

1. Double-click **Default User**.

    The **Default User Properties** dialog box appears.

2. Explore the Default User options.

    The following table describes the system policy options in **Default User**.

User system policy option	Use the option
Control Panel	To restrict the user activity in the Display program in Control Panel or to deny any access to the Display program.
Desktop	To specify the background wallpaper and color scheme for the desktop.
Shell	To customize desktop folders and restrict what appears on the desktop, and restrict the use of the **Run**, **Find**, and **Shut Down** commands. You can create custom folders by entering paths to program items, desktop icons, startup items, Network Neighborhood items, and **Start** menu items that you want to come from a location other than user profile folders. You can provide locations for custom desktop icons, applications you want in the Startup folder, or even replace the entire **Start** menu.

(*continued*)

User system policy option

	Use the option
System	To disable Windows NT Registry Editor (Regedt32.exe) and Windows 95 Registry Editor (Regedit.exe) so that users cannot edit the registry files. You can also enter a list of Windows-based applications users can use. Any application *not* in the list is unavailable to the user.
Windows NT Shell	To customize the desktop by specifying a path to a custom Programs folder, desktop icons, Startup folder, Network Neighborhood and **Start** menu, and to hide the **Start** menu subfolders. Also used to remove common program groups from the **Start** menu.
Windows NT System	To merge the environmental variables from the **Parse** Autoexec.bat file with the user's environment variables.

3. After you have finished exploring the Default User options, click **Cancel**.

   Do not change the default settings at this time.

4. Close System Policy Editor.

Customizing System Policy for Users, Groups, and Computers

The default settings established by system policy can affect the entire domain. If you have users, groups, or computers that require settings that are different from the default settings, you can add these accounts to the domain system policy and configure them as needed.

Users, groups, or computers with settings that are different from the default system policy settings receive separate entries in the Ntconfig.pol file. For example, if User1 requires settings different from the default system policy settings, you would need to use System Policy Editor to add a user profile for User1 to the Ntconfig.pol file. The same would be true of a group or computer requiring settings that were different from the default settings.

When a user or group member who has special policy settings in Ntconfig.pol logs on, the system finds Ntconfig.pol and also the special settings that apply specifically to the user or group member. Similarly, if a computer is added and special settings are entered using System Policy Editor, anyone logging on to that computer receives those computer settings.

To add special policies for a user, a group, or a computer, you would use the following steps:

1. Log on as Administrator and start System Policy Editor.
2. On the **Edit** menu, click the appropriate selection:
   - Click **Add User** to create an entry for a specific user.
   - Click **Add Group** to create an entry for a specific group.
   - Click **Add Computer** to create an entry for a specific computer.
3. Enter the appropriate user, group, or computer name.
4. Click **OK**.
5. You would then open the icon for the user, group, or computer and modify the settings for that account.

Example: Configuring a System Policy to Secure Computers

System Policy Editor provides two computer policy options that enable you to configure the **Logon Information** dialog box to secure a computer using the following methods:

- *Prevent the display of the last logged on user.* By default, each time a user presses CTRL+ALT+DELETE, the **Logon Information** dialog box displays the user name of the last person to log on to the system. To prevent the display of the last user that logged on, configure the **Windows NT System\Logon\Do not display last logged on user name** option in the appropriate computer policy.

- *Display a warning to users against unauthorized system use.* This is done by configuring the **Windows NT System\Logon\Logon Banner** option in the appropriate computer policy. You can set this option in the Default Computer policy for all computers in the domain, or in a specific computer name.

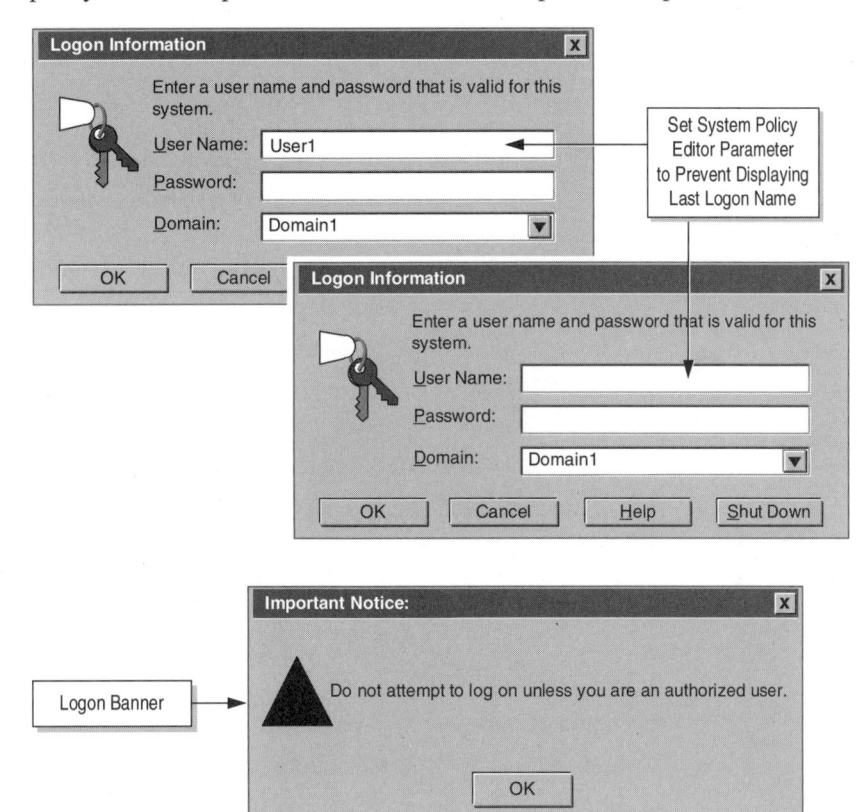

Note You can set these two policy options for all computers in the domain by modifying the Default Computer policy, or for a specific computer by modifying its settings.

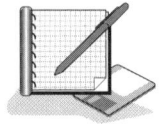

Practice

In these procedures, you use System Policy Editor to create a domain system policy containing a computer policy for Workstation1. You then configure the computer policy to display a logon banner that appears whenever a user logs on to Workstation1, and to prevent the display of the last logged on user name.

Note Complete these procedures on Server1 logged on as Administrator.

▸ **To create a domain system policy for Workstation1 that displays a logon banner**

1. Start System Policy Editor.
2. On the **File** menu, click **New Policy**.
3. On the **Edit** menu, click **Add Computer**.
4. In the **Add Computer** dialog box, type **Workstation1** and then click **OK**.
5. Double-click the Workstation1 icon.

    The **Workstation1 Properties** dialog box appears.

6. Expand **Windows NT System**.
7. Expand **Logon**.
8. Click the **Logon Banner** option.

    Notice at the bottom of the screen that a **Settings for Logon banner** dialog box appears. If this box appears dimmed, you have not yet selected this option (there is not a check mark in the check box).

9. In the **Caption** box, type **Attention:**
10. In the **Text** box, type **Unauthorized use of Workstation1 is prohibited.**
11. Click **OK**.

Note System Policy Editor stores this information in two values (LegalNoticeCaption and LegalNoticeText) in the registry under:

HKEY_LOCAL_MACHINE\SOFTWARE\Microsoft\Windows NT\CurrentVersion\Winlogon

Chapter 4 Managing System Policies   161

▶ **To disable the display of the last logged on user name on Workstation1**
1. Double-click the Workstation1 computer profile icon.
2. Expand **Windows NT System**, and then expand **Logon**.
3. Click the **Do not display last logged on user name** check box.
4. Click **OK**.

▶ **To save the new system policy file in Netlogon**
1. On the **File** menu, click **Save**.
2. Save the file in the C:\Winnt\System32\Repl\Import\Scripts folder, and name it Ntconfig.

    System Policy Editor automatically appends the .pol extension.
3. Close System Policy Editor.

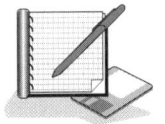

Practice
In this procedure, you test the domain system policy and the computer policy for Workstation1.

▶ **To test the new system policy**

Note Complete this procedure on Workstation1. Server1 must be running.

1. If you are currently logged on at Workstation1, log off.
2. Press CTRL+ALT+DELETE.
3. Are the policy settings in effect? Why or why not?

_____

_____

_____

_____

4. Log on to Domain1 as Administrator, and then log off.

162   Microsoft Windows NT Technical Support

5. Press CTRL+ALT+DELETE to log on.
6. Are the policy settings in effect? Why or why not?

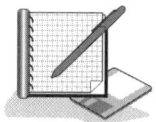

_____

_____

Practice

In these procedures, you use System Policy Editor to add a user policy to the domain system policy, and then you test the user policy for User1.

▶ **To add a user to the Ntconfig.pol system policy**

Note Complete this procedure on Server1 logged on as Administrator.

1. Open System Policy Editor.
2. On the **File** menu, click **Open Policy**.
3. In the **File Name** box, type the following:

    c:\winnt\system32\repl\import\scripts\ntconfig.pol

4. Click **Open**.
5. On the **Edit** menu, click **Add User**.
6. In the **Add User** dialog box, type **User1** and then click **OK**.
7. Double-click the User1 icon.

    The **User1 Properties** dialog box appears.

8. Expand **Desktop**.
9. Select the **Wallpaper** check box.

    The **Settings for Wallpaper** dialog box appears at the bottom of the screen.

10. In the **Wallpaper Name** box, type **C:\Winnt\Blue Monday**

    Note If you did not complete the practice in Chapter 3, "Configuring the Windows NT Environment," in which you used Add/Remove Programs in Control Panel to install the Windows NT games and wallpaper, the Blue Monday wallpaper is not available.

11. Select the **Tile Wallpaper** check box.
12. On the **Policies** tab, select the **Color Scheme** check box.

    The **Settings for Color Scheme** dialog box appears at the bottom of the screen.

13. In the **Scheme name** box, click **Rose 256**, and then click **OK**.
14. Close System Policy Editor, and then save changes to Ntconfig.pol.

▶ **To test the user profile portion of system policy**

Note Complete this procedure on Workstation1.

1. If you are currently logged on at Workstation1, log off.
2. Log on to Domain1 as User1.
3. Are the policy settings in effect? Why or why not?

_____

_____

_____

Restricting the User Environment

System Policy Editor provides policy options that enable you to restrict the user's environment. Use the following steps to enable these options.

Caution The following steps are provided for your information and should *not* be done as part of the course. If you make changes to any of these settings, you may not be able to complete the remainder of the course.

1. Start System Policy Editor.
2. On the **File** menu, click **Open Policy**.
3. Open *systemroot*\System32\Repl\Import\Scripts\Ntconfig.pol.
4. Open **Default User**.
5. Expand **Shell**.
6. Expand **Restrictions**.

    The following table explains some of the Restriction policy options.

Individual policy option	Description
Remove Run command from Start menu	The **Run** command no longer appears as an option on the **Start** menu.
Hide Network Neighborhood	The Network Neighborhood no longer appears on the desktop.
Hide all items on desktop	All items are missing from the desktop.
Disable the Shut Down command	The **Shut Down** command no longer appears as an option on the **Start** menu.

Supporting Windows 95 System Policy

You have learned that system policies allow you to override local registry values for user or computer settings. When a user logs on, system policy settings overwrite the current settings in the user's registry to enable administrators to control individual desktop and registry settings.

For computers running Windows 95, the following rules also apply:

- System policies can only be stored on the domain controllers.
- Group policies, if used, must be enabled on each computer running Windows 95. You can enable group policies when you install Windows 95, using a custom setup script, or use Add/Remove Programs in Control Panel after Windows 95 is installed.
- Windows 95 policy must be saved in a file named Config.pol (*not* Ntconfig.pol), and stored in the Netlogon share of the primary domain controller (PDC).

Note Remember that system policy files created on computers running Windows NT cannot be used on computers running Windows 95, and vice versa. Therefore, when modifying system policy for a computer running Windows 95, you run System Policy Editor on a computer running Windows 95 and you save the policy settings to a file named *Config.pol* in the Netlogon share on the PDC. For more information on using system policy for computers running Windows 95, see the *Microsoft Windows 95 Resource Kit*.

Load Balancing

Ordinarily, computers running Windows 95 get policy settings from the PDC only. Load balancing allows computers running Windows 95 to take policies from multiple domain controllers. Therefore, enabling load balancing can prevent network slowdown when many Windows 95 clients try to access the same policy file.

To enable load balancing, use the Windows 95 System Policy Editor to open Config.pol, then double-click the Default Computer icon, open **Network\Update\Remote Update Policy**, and then check **Load-balanced**.

System Policy Templates

The policies that appear in System Policy Editor are provided by template files. Windows NT requires both the Winnt.adm and the Common.adm system policy templates.

Note Because policy files are basically registry entries, it is possible to add options to System Policy Editor by editing the existing templates or creating and adding in new template files. For more information on the system policy templates, see Microsoft Windows NT Server *Concepts and Planning*, or see "Adding policy templates" in System Policy Editor Help.

System Policy Issues

Verify the following items when troubleshooting problems with system policies:

- The individual policy option is set properly in the policy (.pol) file.
- The policy file is located in the correct network location, and the network location is accessible from the computer running Windows NT or Windows 95.
- The user name, group name, and computer name are correct, and groups contain the appropriate members.

The following table describes common policy issues and their resolutions.

Issue	Resolutions
Downloading system policies is very slow.	Although there is no limit to the number of individual users, groups, or computers that can be added to a policy file, delays may occur if too many users log on at the same time.
	Enable load balancing on the computers running Windows 95 to better balance network resources.
	On computers running Windows NT, in **Remote update**, click **Manual**, and use computers other than the domain controllers to store the system policy files.
User policies are downloaded for a user when logged on to a computer running Windows 95, but are not downloaded when the user logs on to a computer running Windows NT.	Although computers running Windows NT and computers running Windows 95 support system policy files created with System Policy Editor, the policy files are not named the same and are not interoperable. If a user uses a computer running Windows 95 and a computer running Windows NT, you must create a user policy in both system policy files (Config.pol and Ntconfig.pol).

(continued)

Issue	Resolutions
User policies are downloaded for a user when logged on to a computer running Windows NT, but are not downloaded when the user logs on to a computer running Windows 95.	Same as above.
User policies restrict access to Control Panel options, but the icons still appear in Control Panel.	System policies can restrict access to Control Panel options, but they cannot remove the icons. In order to remove the icons from Control Panel, modify the [don't load] section of Control.ini.
The wallpaper assigned in the system policy file does not appear on all client computers.	Some system policy settings require components to be installed locally on the computer where the policy is applied. In this example, the wallpaper bitmap is not present in the path specified by the policy file.
Group policies are not processed by all client computers running Windows 95.	Group Policy must be installed on a computer running Windows 95 not only to create group policies, but to process them. Unlike Windows NT, group policies are not installed by default with System Policy Editor. Add group policy support through the Add/Remove Programs option of Control Panel.

Summary

The following information summarizes the key points in this chapter:

- Prior to implementing a system policy, plan the types of restrictions and customizations that will be implemented by the policy. Identify any specific policies for users, groups, and computers. Notify users and groups before the policy is implemented to avoid possible confusion once the policy is implemented.
- A system policy is made up of computer policy, user policy, group policy, or any combination of these policies.
- By default, to implement a domain system policy on computers running Windows NT, the policy settings must be stored in a file named Ntconfig.pol in the Netlogon share of the PDC.
- By default, to implement a domain system policy on computers running Windows 95, use the Windows 95 System Policy Editor to create system policy on that operating system. These system policy settings must be saved to a file named Config.pol in the Netlogon share of the PDC.
- Both Ntconfig.pol and Config.pol must be stored on the PDC in the following folder: *systemroot*\System32\Repl\Import\Scripts. By default this folder is shared as Netlogon.
- Replication must be enabled for all domain controllers to receive copies of the Ntconfig.pol and Config.pol files. Remember that load balancing must be enabled on computers running Windows 95 in order for them to access Config.pol on BDCs.
- You can specify customized settings for individual users, groups, and computers to meet the needs of your organization.
- System Policy Editor can be used to directly edit portions of the registry.

Review

1. Describe the purpose of system policy.

2. Who can implement system policy?

3. Name two major functions of System Policy Editor.

4. Name two policies that you might create to secure a computer.

5. If a user logs on to a domain that has system policy, but system policy has not been defined for that user, what happens next?

6. Your network has 165 computers running Windows 95, and 200 computers running Windows NT Workstation. The Windows 95 users are complaining that the network is really slow when everyone is trying to log on in the morning. What can cause this problem and how do you resolve it?

Answer Key

Procedure Answers

Page 143

▶ **To create a shortcut for and start System Policy Editor**

5. What two icons appear in the System Policy Editor window?

Default Computer and Default User.

Page 161

▶ **To test the new system policy**

3. Are the policy settings in effect? Why or why not?

No, because system policies are not downloaded until a user logs on. When you complete the logon process, your computer policy is downloaded, and the next time you attempt to log on to the computer the policy settings are in effect.

6. Are the policy settings in effect? Why or why not?

Yes, because the system policy was downloaded when you logged on in step 4.

Page 163

▶ **To test the user profile portion of system policy**

3. Are the policy settings in effect? Why or why not?

Yes, because User1 now has the Blue Monday wallpaper and the color scheme is Rose256. System policy overwrites the local user profile on Workstation1.

Review Answers

Page 168

1. Describe the purpose of system policy.

To establish a uniform set of rules to maintain computer and user environments across a domain.

2. Who can implement system policy?

An administrator.

3. Name two major functions of System Policy Editor.

Modify default settings for the computer and user policy for the domain.

Create custom settings that apply to individual users, groups of users, or individual computers.

Specify the location from which to download system policy.

4. Name two policies that you might create to secure a computer.

   Create a logon banner that is seen by anyone logging on to the computer.

   Disable the display of the last user's logon name.

5. If a user logs on to a domain that has system policy, but system policy has not been defined for that user, what happens next?

   Windows NT checks to see whether system policy exists for a group that the user is in, and if it does exist, the group settings are merged into HKEY_CURRENT_USER. If a group does not exist, then the default user policy settings are merged into HKEY_CURRENT_USER.

6. Your network has 165 computers running Windows 95, and 200 computers running Windows NT Workstation. The Windows 95 users are complaining that the network is really slow when everyone is trying to log on in the morning. What can cause this problem and how do you resolve it?

   A potential slowdown on the network can occur because by default the computers running Windows 95 always search for their policies on the PDC. If load balancing is selected, after the initial logon the Windows 95 client takes its policy from whichever logon server authenticates a user.

CHAPTER 5

Managing File Systems

Lesson 1   File Systems Supported by Windows NT . . . 174

Lesson 2   Working with File Names . . . 182

Lesson 3   Managing NTFS Compression . . . 188

Review . . . 197

About This Chapter

This chapter covers the Microsoft Windows NT file systems—FAT (file allocation table), also used by other operating systems, such as Microsoft MS-DOS; and NTFS (Windows NT File System), used only on computers running Windows NT—and explains the issues involved in running them in the Windows NT environment. In addition, management of long file names (LFNs) is discussed, including how long file names are converted to 8.3 entries and the concerns when using long file names on a FAT partition. Finally, methods of file compression are explained, along with the effects that copying and moving files have on the compression attributes of the files.

Before You Begin

To complete the lessons in this chapter, you must have:

- Two computers that meet the hardware and software requirements as specified in the Getting Started section of "About This Book."
- Completed all practices in Chapter 2, "Installing Windows NT."

Lesson 1: File Systems Supported by Windows NT

Windows NT supports different file systems on the same computer running Windows NT. You can format multiple partitions with different file systems on the same computer running Windows NT. The file system(s) you choose depend on the operating system(s) and the security needs of your organization. This lesson describes the file systems supported by Windows NT and identifies their major distinguishing features.

After this lesson, you will be able to:
- Describe the features of the FAT file system.
- Describe the features of the NTFS file system.
- Identify important considerations in NTFS implementation.
- Compare the advantages and disadvantages of FAT and NTFS.
- Convert FAT partitions to NTFS.

Estimated lesson time: 25 minutes

The following table shows the file systems in Windows NT and the operating systems that support them.

File system	Supporting operating systems
File allocation table (FAT)	Windows NT, Microsoft Windows 95, MS-DOS, and IBM OS/2
Windows NT File System (NTFS)	Windows NT
CD-ROM File System (CDFS)	Windows NT and Windows 95

Note CDFS is used to read from CD-ROM drives. Because CDFS is a read-only, special-purpose file system, it is not described in this course.

FAT File System

The file allocation table (FAT) file system is an enhanced version of the file system that has been used for years with computers running MS-DOS. FAT is required for computers running Windows 95 and MS-DOS. Therefore, if you want to dual-boot a computer running Windows NT with another operating system, such as Windows 95 or MS-DOS, the system partition must be formatted with the FAT file system.

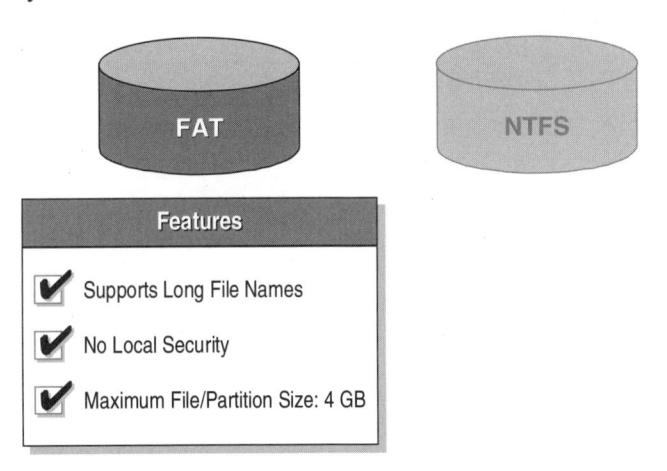

FAT

NTFS

Features

- ✓ Supports Long File Names
- ✓ No Local Security
- ✓ Maximum File/Partition Size: 4 GB

Note Windows NT cannot read FAT32 file systems, which are available on some OEM versions of Windows 95.

Some important considerations when using the FAT file system are naming conventions, security concerns, and file and partition size.

FAT Naming Conventions

Under Windows NT, the FAT file system is enhanced to support long file names (LFNs). The following criteria apply to file names on a Windows NT partition that has been formatted with the FAT file system:

- The file name, including the full path location, can be up to 255 characters.
- The name must start with either a letter or a number, and can contain any characters except the following:

  / \ : | * = ? " ; [ ] , ^

- The name can contain multiple spaces.
- The name can contain multiple periods, with the characters after the last period treated as the extension.
- Names preserve case, but are not case-sensitive.

FAT Security

A FAT partition cannot be protected by *local* file or folder security features of Windows NT. The only security available on FAT partitions is provided through Windows NT directory-level sharing mechanisms.

FAT File and Partition Size

FAT is the preferred file system for partitions less than 200 MB in size. The maximum file and partition size for FAT is 4 GB.

Other FAT File System Considerations

The following considerations are important when implementing a FAT file system for Windows NT:

- You cannot undelete a file because undelete utilities access the hardware directly, which is not allowed under Windows NT. However, if the deleted file is on a FAT partition, and the system is restarted under MS-DOS, it may be possible to undelete the file if it has not been written over.
- FAT has minimal file-system overhead (less than 1 MB per partition).
- Performance declines with large numbers of files because FAT uses a linked list for the folder structure. If the amount of data in a file grows, the file becomes fragmented on the hard disk, and the process of retrieving the file from the disk becomes slower.
- FAT is the required file system for the system partition on ARC-compliant computers, which are RISC-based computers supported by Windows NT.

NTFS File System

The Windows NT File System (NTFS) is the preferred file system under Windows NT for a number of reasons, primarily security. NTFS can only be used on computers running Windows NT.

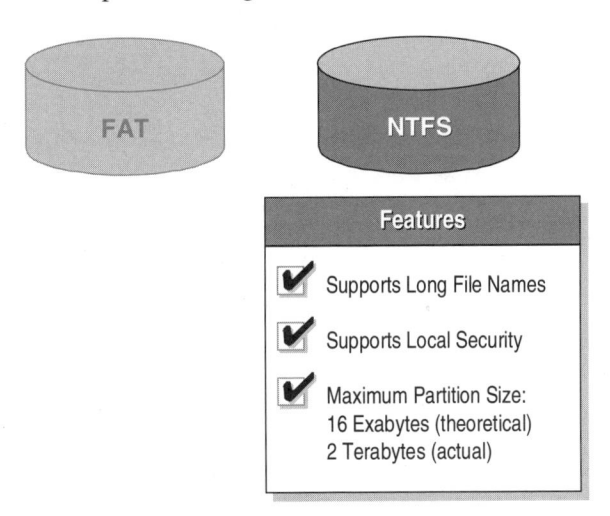

Features

- ✓ Supports Long File Names
- ✓ Supports Local Security
- ✓ Maximum Partition Size:
  16 Exabytes (theoretical)
  2 Terabytes (actual)

NTFS Naming Conventions

The following rules apply to NTFS file names:

- File and folder names can be up to 255 characters, including extensions.

- In general, names are not case-sensitive but are case-preserving. There is an exception: within a POSIX application, NTFS allows the coexistence of two identically named files that differ only in case. POSIX (Portable Operating System Interface) is a standard developed by the Institute of Electrical and Electronics Engineers, Inc. (IEEE).

- Names can contain any characters, including spaces, except the following:
  / \ : | * ? " < >

NTFS Security

NTFS should be used when security is required for servers and personal computers. NTFS supports discretionary access control and ownership privileges important to ensure the integrity of data. While folders shared by a computer running Windows NT can have assigned permissions regardless of the file system used, NTFS files and folders can have assigned permissions whether or not they are shared. NTFS is the only file system on Windows NT that allows permissions to be assigned to individual files and folders.

NTFS File and Partition Size

NTFS supports larger file and partition sizes than the FAT file system, theoretically up to 16 exabytes for both files and partitions.

- The maximum file size is between 4 GB and 64 GB, depending on the computer's hardware. The functional maximum partition size for NTFS on typical hardware is 2 terabytes due to industry-standard limitations on the maximum number and size of disk sectors.

- The recommended minimum partition size for an NTFS partition is 50 MB, because of the overhead involved in using NTFS.

Additional Features

NTFS has the following additional features that make it a powerful and flexible file system:

- *Support for file compression.* File compression reduces text-oriented application or data file size by about 50 percent and reduces executable file size by about 40 percent.

- *Transaction-based recoverability.* NTFS has high reliability. It is a recoverable file system that uses transaction logging to log all folder and file updates automatically. This is used by Windows NT to repeat or undo operations that failed due to system failure or power loss.

- *Support for cluster remapping.* If an error occurs because of a bad sector on the hard disk, NTFS allocates a new cluster to replace the cluster with the bad sector. NTFS then stores the address of the cluster containing the bad sector so that the bad sector is not reused. This is transparent to any applications performing disk I/O.

- *Support for Macintosh files.* You can install Services for Macintosh on computers running Windows NT Server. This allows Macintosh computers to store their files on the computer running Services for Macintosh.

- *Support for POSIX requirements.* NTFS is the Windows NT POSIX.1-compliant supported file system and supports the following POSIX.1 requirements:

  - *Case-sensitive naming.* Under POSIX, file names are case-sensitive, so that README.TXT, Readme.txt, and readme.txt are different files.

  - *Additional time stamp.* This supplies the time the file was last accessed.

  - *Hard links.* A hard link occurs when two different file names, which can be located in different folders, point to the same data.

Note You can run POSIX applications from any Windows NT file system. However, if the application requires access to file system resources, then NTFS is required.

- *Support for file and folder security.*
- *Provides a separate Recycle Bin for each user.*
- *Reduces file fragmentation.* Reduces file fragmentation by attempting to write files contiguously on the partition. A file can become fragmented as it grows in size, depending on the disk's space usage.

For more information on Windows NT file systems, see *Inside the Windows NT File System,* by Helen Custer.

Converting to NTFS

Windows NT includes an executable file, Convert.exe, that converts an existing FAT hard disk partition to NTFS. Note that conversion is a one-way process; there is no way to convert an NTFS partition to FAT.

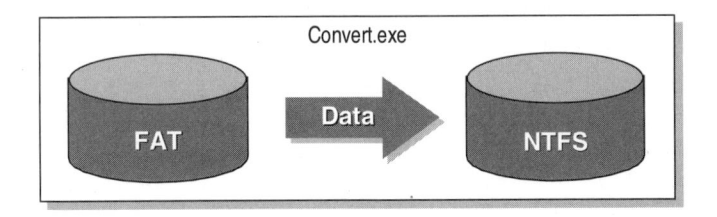

Converting a partition from FAT to NTFS preserves all data on the partition, unlike formatting the partition, which destroys all data.

The **convert** command uses the following command prompt syntax:

convert *drive***: /fs:ntfs**

where *drive* is the letter of the logical drive to be converted to NTFS.

If a process, including Windows NT itself, is currently accessing the drive, an error message appears. The error message provides an option to schedule the drive for conversion when the system restarts.

Practice

In this procedure, you convert your Server2 boot partition (drive D) from FAT to NTFS. You then observe what happens when you attempt to convert a partition on which there are open files.

▶ **To convert a FAT partition to NTFS**

Note Complete this practice on Server2.

1. Start Server2 and log on as Administrator.
2. Click the **Start** button, point to **Programs**, and then click **Command Prompt**.
3. Type **convert d: /fs:ntfs** and then press ENTER.

   A message appears stating the **convert** command cannot gain exclusive access to drive D and cannot convert it now.

   Why does this message occur?

   _____

   _____

4. Type **y** and then press ENTER to schedule the conversion to take place the next time the system restarts.
5. Shut down and then restart the computer as Server2.

   The conversion process occurs.

   Note The system restarts itself a second time. Make sure you start your computer as Server2.

6. After Server2 has restarted, log on as Administrator.
7. Right-click **My Computer**, and then click **Explore**.

   Windows NT Explorer starts.
8. Right-click **drive D**, and then click **Properties**.

   What file system is on drive D?

   _____

   _____

9. Click **Cancel**.
10. Close Windows NT Explorer.

Changing File Systems

File systems can be changed on any partition after running Setup. Windows NT provides Convert.exe to convert a FAT partition to NTFS with no loss of data. You cannot convert an NTFS partition to FAT. If you want to change a partition from NTFS to FAT, you must do the following:

1. Back up all files.
2. Reformat the partition (this action deletes all of the files), specifying the file system, using either the **format** command or Disk Administrator.
3. Restore the files from the backup.

Lesson 2: Working with File Names

Long file name (LFN) support on Windows NT frees users from the limitations of the 8.3 file naming convention used by MS-DOS. This lesson examines how Windows NT handles long file names on FAT and NTFS file systems. This lesson also describes treatment of case-sensitive file names on partitions.

After this lesson, you will be able to:
- Explain the process for converting long file names to 8.3 entries.
- Identify concerns when using long file names on a FAT partition.

Estimated lesson time: 40 minutes

Autogenerated 8.3 File Names

The previous lesson explained that Windows NT supports long file names (LFNs) for both the FAT and NTFS file systems. To allow Windows 3.*x*- and MS-DOS-based applications to recognize and load LFN files, Windows NT automatically generates an 8.3 alias for each long file name.

Generating 8.3 File Names

Converting file names from the LFN to 8.3 format follows this process:

1. All file name characters that are not allowed under MS-DOS are removed, such as spaces.
2. The conversion takes the first six characters of the long file name and uses a *~number* suffix to keep the name unique. For example:
   - My Term Paper A.doc becomes MYTERM~1.DOC.
   - If additional files have the same first six characters, and the same characters after the period, the successive iterations would be: MYTERM~2.DOC, MYTERM~3.DOC, and MYTERM~4.DOC.
3. After the fourth file with the same first 6 characters, and the exact same 3 characters after the last period in the LFN, the naming convention changes. The fifth iteration keeps the first 2 characters of the LFN, but the next 4 characters are generated by a hashing algorithm. The random characters improve seek performance by distinguishing otherwise similar file names. For example:
   - My Term Paper E.doc becomes MY0F58~1.DOC.
   - Only when the hashing of the middle 4 characters (0F58) fails to produce a unique name is the ~1 incremented to ~2, and so on. This method is used on both FAT and NTFS partitions to create aliases for long file names.

The following illustration shows the long file name-to-8.3 alias generation.

LFN Entry	Short (8.3) Entry
1. My Term Paper A.doc	MYTERM~1.DOC
2. My Term Paper B.doc	MYTERM~2.DOC
3. My Term Paper C.doc	MYTERM~3.DOC
4. My Term Paper D.doc	MYTERM~4.DOC
5. My Term Paper E.doc	MY0F58~1.DOC
6. My Term Paper F.doc	MY6968~1.DOC

Long File Name Considerations

There are several important considerations when using long file names:

- When using long file names on files that are read by MS-DOS-based applications, consider creating files with unique combinations of the first six characters.

- Windows NT does not generate an alias for files created by a POSIX-based application. MS-DOS- and 16-bit Windows-based applications are not able to access a file created by a POSIX-based application if its file name exceeds the MS-DOS 8.3 file naming convention.

- When using long file names from the command prompt, if there are any spaces in the path, the path must be in quotes. For example, if Microsoft Word for Windows is installed in the folder D:\Word for Windows, all references to the folder path and files from the command prompt should be in quotation marks. To start Word from a command prompt, you would type the following: "D:\Word for Windows\winword.exe"

  If quotation marks are not placed around the path, an invalid path error message appears. The exception is the **chdir** (or **cd**) command, which does not require quotation marks.

Caution Some 16-bit applications save data to a temporary file, delete the original file, and then rename the temporary file to the original file name. In some cases this deletes the long file name and, when the file is on an NTFS partition, any permissions that were associated with the original file.

Long File Names on FAT Partitions

On a FAT partition, Windows NT automatically creates a short file name, or alias, for each long file name (LFN). The LFNs are retained in secondary folder entries.

Alias Folder Entries

For every LFN on a Windows NT FAT partition, an autogenerated short file name provides an alias for the long file names. Aliases are stored as MS-DOS-compatible FAT folder entries.

There are two ways to view an alias:

- Through Command Prompt
    1. Click the **Start** button, point to **Programs**, and then click **Command Prompt**.
    2. Type **dir /x**

       Both the LFN and the alias are listed for each file.
- Through Windows NT Explorer
    1. Start Windows NT Explorer, and then select the file.
    2. On the **File** menu, click **Properties**.

       The alias appears as the 8.3 character MS-DOS name of the file.

Secondary Folder Entries

On FAT partitions, an LFN creates one folder entry for its alias and a hidden secondary folder entry for every 13 characters of the LFN. For example, the file name, *This is a Long Name.txt*, is 23 characters, and has three folder entries: one folder entry for the alias and two secondary folder entries for the LFN.

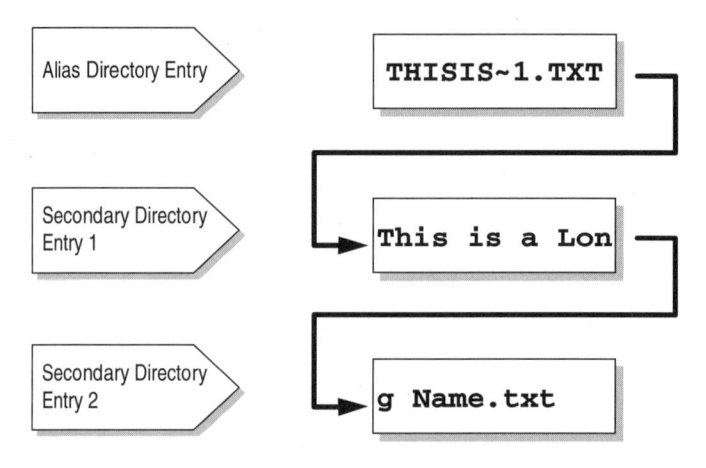

Alias Directory Entry	`THISIS~1.TXT`
Secondary Directory Entry 1	`This is a Lon`
Secondary Directory Entry 2	`g Name.txt`

Caution The FAT root folder has a hard-coded limit of 512 entries. If many LFN files are stored in the root folder, the user could run out of entries in the root folder. As a result, the user would be unable to create any more LFN files, 8.3 files, or folders in the root folder.

Note When a system is started under MS-DOS, some third-party disk utilities that directly manipulate FAT can destroy LFN entries, or even the file itself. Users should be careful when using these utilities. They give errors indicating that there is something wrong with FAT. It is more likely that the LFN entries are causing the error message, rather than FAT.

LFN entries are not harmed by either the MS-DOS version 6.*x* tools, SCANDISK, DEFRAG, and CHKDSK, or the disk utilities designed for Windows 95.

Windows NT can be configured to prevent the use of LFNs on FAT partitions by changing the following registry value to 1:

HKEY_LOCAL_MACHINE\SYSTEM\CurrentControlSet\Control\FileSystem\Win31FileSystem.

Mixed-Case File Names

Windows NT preserves case-sensitive file names. Therefore, on a FAT partition, a mixed-cased file name generates an uppercase alias, even if the original file name meets the other 8.3 naming convention requirements. For example, MyFile.Txt generates an alias of MYFILE.TXT on a FAT partition. However, this same file on an NTFS partition does not generate an alias.

Practice

In this procedure, you create and rename files on a FAT partition (drive C) and note the effect of these changes on their long file names and aliases. When creating the files, type the names exactly as the procedure specifies; remember that Windows NT preserves the uppercase and lowercase formatting of file names.

Note Complete this procedure on Server2.

▶ **To create long file names**

1. Log on as Administrator.
2. Right-click **My Computer**, and then click **Explore**.

   Windows NT Explorer starts.
3. On the **View** menu, click **Options**.

4. On the **View** tab, verify that **Hide file extensions for known file types** is selected, and then click **OK**.
5. Click the icon for drive C.
6. On the **File** menu, point to **New**, and then click **Folder** to create a new folder. Name the folder LFN Lab Exercise.
7. Inside the LFN Lab Exercise folder, create the following text documents using Windows NT Explorer:

   Long filename.lab.exercise

   Long filename.exercise.lab

   Longfilename.exercise.lab

   Exercise.long filename.lab

   Lab.long filename.exercise

   Test.Txt
8. At a command prompt, change to the root folder of drive C (C:\). Use the **dir /x** command to list the root folder.

   How does the LFN Lab Exercise folder that you just created appear in the folder list?

   _____

9. Type **cd LFN Lab Exercise** and then press ENTER to change to the folder you created.
10. Type **dir /x** to list the folder. Record the 8.3 file names below.

8.3 file names	Long file names
_____	Long filename.lab.exercise.txt
_____	Long filename.exercise.lab.txt
_____	Longfilename.exercise.lab.txt
_____	Exercise.long filename.lab.txt
_____	Lab.long filename.exercise.txt
_____	Test.Txt.txt

    Why does Test.Txt have two extensions when listed from the command prompt?

    _____

11. Rename LONGFI~1.TXT to LFN.LAB by typing **ren LONGFI~1.TXT LFN.LAB** and then pressing ENTER.

12. List the folder and note the file name and alias.

    What happened to the file name and alias of the file you renamed?

    _____

13. Type **ren "Long filename.exercise.lab.txt" LONG.TXT** and then press ENTER.

    Be sure to use quotation marks around the long file name because the **ren** command does not recognize blank spaces.

14. List the folder contents.

    What happened to the file name and alias of the file you renamed?

    _____

15. Type **ren LONG.TXT Long.Txt** and then press ENTER.

16. List the folder contents.

    What happened to the file name and alias of the file you renamed?

    _____

    Why does Long.Txt have an alias while LONG.TXT does not?

    _____

17. Minimize the command prompt.

Lesson 3: Managing NTFS Compression

This lesson discusses file compression on NTFS partitions and issues that can result when you compress and decompress files and folders.

After this lesson, you will be able to:
- Compress and decompress files and folders using Windows NT Explorer or the **compact** command.
- Describe the effects that copying and moving files has on the compression attributes of the files.

Estimated lesson time: 30 minutes

Compressing and Decompressing Files and Folders

The NTFS file system supports automatic compression and decompression of files and folders. Compression can be performed on individual files, folders, and even entire drives.

Note By default Windows NT files and folders are decompressed. To compress them you must select the compression attribute.

Although both Windows NT Server and Windows NT Workstation support file compression, performance degradation can occur on systems that experience heavy write traffic, such as some types of dedicated servers.

Note For performance reasons, compression is not supported on NTFS partitions with cluster sizes greater than 4 KB.

Compression Attribute

On an NTFS partition, each file and folder has an attribute for compression. The compression attribute of a file is different from that of a folder in the following ways:

- If the compression attribute is set for a file, it indicates that the file is compressed.
- If the compression attribute is set for a folder, it indicates that any files created in the folder are automatically compressed.

In Windows NT Explorer, files and folders that have a compressed attribute can be configured to display in blue text. To do this, on the **View** menu, click **Options**, click the **View** tab, and then click the **Display compressed files and folders with alternate color** check box.

Note Blue is the only color option that Windows NT Explorer provides to designate compressed files and folders; therefore, using a blue background is not recommended.

Methods for Compressing and Decompressing

Windows NT includes the following two methods to compress and decompress files and folders:

- Windows NT Explorer
- Compact.exe

Note Neither Windows NT Explorer nor Compact.exe will compress an open file.

Windows NT Explorer

When you use Windows NT Explorer to examine the attributes of a folder on an NTFS partition, the **General** tab in the **Properties** dialog box includes a **Compress** check box.

Note The **Properties** dialog box of a *file* on an NTFS partition includes a **Compressed** check box.

The following illustration shows the properties of a folder named Reports.

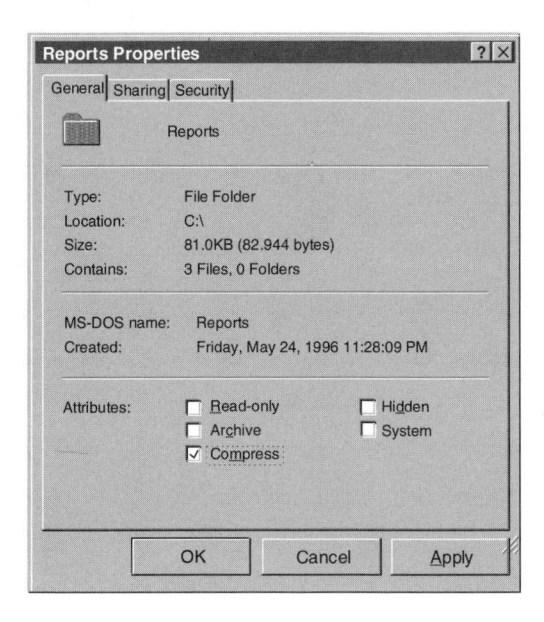

When you compress or decompress a folder, Windows NT Explorer prompts you to indicate whether to compress or decompress existing subfolders in the selected folder. Each existing subfolder in compressed or decompressed folders retains its compression state unless you change it.

Compact.exe

You can also compress files and folders by using Compact.exe from the command prompt. Compact.exe supports the following options.

Option	Action performed
/c	Compresses the specified files. Folders are marked so that files added after the initial compression are compressed.
/u	Decompresses the specified files. Folders are marked so that files added after the decompression are not compressed.
/s	Performs the specified operation on files in the given folder and all subfolders. The default folder is the current folder.
/a	Displays files with the hidden or system attributes. These files are omitted by default.
/i	Continues performing the specified operation even after errors have occurred. By default, Compact.exe stops when an error is encountered.
/f	Forces the compress operation on all specified files, even those that are already compressed. This switch is useful if a large file is being compressed and power is lost. When a file is compressed, it is initially marked as compressed before the compression actually occurs. If the power is lost during compression, the file may not be fully compressed. This switch can be used to complete the compression process on the file.
/q	Reports only the summary information.

If Compact.exe is used without any options, it displays the compression state of the current folder and any files within the current folder.

Note Any user that has Read and Write permissions can use Windows NT Explorer or Compact.exe to compress and decompress files and folders on an NTFS partition.

Compressing the Windows NT Installation

If Windows NT is installed on an NTFS partition, it is possible to compress the entire *systemroot* folder and all subfolders. However, it is not possible to compress the Windows NT Boot Loader (NTLDR) if you are booting from an NTFS partition on an Intel *x*86-based computer.

Paging files cannot be compressed while in use. A closed paging file from another Windows NT installation can be compressed, but when that installation restarts, the paging file is immediately decompressed.

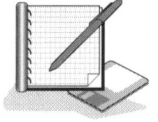

Practice

In these procedures, you use Windows NT Explorer to compress files and folders on an NTFS partition.

Note Complete these procedures on Server2, where drive D is formatted as an NTFS partition.

▶ **To prepare for this practice**

1. Start Windows NT Explorer.
2. Create a new folder in the root of drive D named Student.
3. Copy the C:\Lab Files\Ntfs\Student folder and all of its subfolders and files to D:\Student.

▶ **To compress a folder**

1. Right-click drive D, and then click **Properties**.

    The **Properties** dialog box appears.

    What is the total capacity of drive D?

    _____

    What is the free space for drive D?

    _____

2. Select the **Compress D:** check box, and then click **Apply**.

    An **Explorer** dialog box appears that contains the following messages: "Compress all files in D:\." "This action compresses all files but does not compress subfolders."

3. Select the **Also compress subfolders** check box, and then click **OK**.

    A Windows NT Explorer dialog box appears with a message that Windows NT Explorer cannot change the compress attributes for D:\Pagefile.sys.

4. Click **Ignore All** to continue.

   How much free space is available on drive D after compression?

5. Click **OK**.

▶ **To confirm that files have been compressed**

1. On the **View** menu in Windows NT Explorer, click **Options**.
2. On the **View** tab, select the **Display compressed files and folders with alternate color** check box.
3. Click **OK**.

   The compressed files and folders are displayed in blue.

▶ **To decompress a folder**

1. In Windows NT Explorer, expand the icon for drive D.
2. Expand the Student folder.
3. In the Student folder, right-click the Archives folder.
4. Click **Properties**.
5. Clear the **Compress** check box, and then click **OK**.

   An **Explorer** dialog box appears that contains the following messages: "Uncompress all files in D:\Student\Archives." "This action uncompresses all files but does not uncompress subfolders."

   This dialog box contains a check box option to decompress subfolders.

6. Select the **Also uncompress subfolders** check box, and then click **OK**.

   The Archives folder name should now be displayed in black. If not, press F5 to refresh the display.

Copying and Moving Compressed Files

When files are copied or moved on NTFS partitions, their compression attributes can change.

Copying

When a file is copied from one folder to another, the compression attribute of the file changes to that of the target folder. In the same way that permissions are inherited on a copied file, the file inherits the compression setting of the target folder.

Note When copying a file to a compressed folder, the file is first copied, and then compressed. For this reason, if the partition on which the compressed folder resides does not have enough space for the file in its decompressed state, the copy fails, even though there is enough space for the compressed file.

Moving

When a file is moved from one folder to another on the same NTFS partition, the file retains its compression attribute, regardless of whether or not the target folder is compressed. Again, as was true for permissions, the file retains its compression setting when a file is moved.

When a file is moved between two NTFS partitions, just as with permissions, the file inherits the compression attribute from the target folder. This occurs because a move between partitions is actually a copy-and-delete operation.

Note When a compressed file is moved to a folder that is not compressed, the folder does not appear in blue in Windows NT Explorer. The only time a folder appears in blue is when the folder has the compression attribute set.

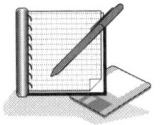

Practice

In these procedures, you see the effects that copying and moving files have on compressed files.

Note Complete these procedures on Server2, where drive D is a compressed NTFS partition containing the Student folder.

▶ **To copy a compressed file to a decompressed folder**

1. Examine the properties for Dna.txt in D:\Student\Reports\Statistics.

   Is Dna.txt compressed or decompressed?

2. Copy Dna.txt to the Archives folder on drive D.

   Make sure you copy (hold down the CTRL key) and do not move the file.

3. Examine the properties for Dna.txt in the Archives folder.

   Is Dna.txt compressed or decompressed?

   _____

   Why?

   _____

4. Close Windows NT Explorer.

▶ **To move a compressed file to a decompressed folder**

1. Examine the properties of Labor.txt in the D:\Student\Reports\Tech folder.

   Is Labor.txt compressed or decompressed?

   _____

2. Move Labor.txt to the Archives folder.
3. Examine the properties of Labor.txt in the Archives folder.

   Is Labor.txt compressed or decompressed?

   _____

   Why?

   _____

Summary

The following information summarizes the key points in this chapter:

- Windows NT 4.0 supports both the file allocation table (FAT) and Windows NT File System (NTFS).
- The following table compares the basic characteristics of FAT and NTFS.

	FAT	NTFS
File name and folder length	255 characters	255 characters
File size	4 GB (2^{32} bytes)	4 GB–64 GB actual, based on current hardware; 16 exabytes (2^{64} bytes) theoretical based on Windows NT software
Partition size	4 GB (2^{32} bytes)	2 terabytes actual, based on current hardware; 16 exabytes (2^{64} bytes) theoretical based on Windows NT software
Attributes	Read Only, Archive, System, Hidden	Further extended and extensible
Accessible through	Windows NT, Windows 95, MS-DOS, and OS/2	Windows NT
Built-in security	No	Yes
Supports file compression	No	Yes

- The following table shows advantages and disadvantages of FAT and NTFS.

	Advantages	Disadvantages
FAT	Low system overhead. Suitable for drives or partitions up to 400 MB.	No file or directory permissions. Using FAT with drives or partitions larger than 400 MB can decrease performance.
NTFS	Suitable for volumes of 400 MB or larger. More robust than FAT. Supports local security.	Not efficient for volumes smaller than 400 MB, because of disk space overhead of an NTFS partition. Disk space overhead ranges from 1–5 MB or more, depending on the size of the partition.

- Windows NT supports long file names (LFNs) for both the FAT and NTFS file systems. Windows NT automatically generates an 8.3 alias for each LFN.
- The NTFS file system supports automatic compression and decompression of files and folders. Compression can be performed on individual files, folders, and even entire drives.

For more information on	See
Windows NT file systems	*Inside the Windows NT File System,* by Helen Custer.

Review

1. If you must support long file names on all partitions, need the ability to dual-boot between MS-DOS and Windows NT Workstation, and want to provide file compression for Windows NT, which file system or systems should you choose?

    a. FAT and NTFS

    b. FAT on all partitions

    c. NTFS on all partitions

2. You get a telephone call from a user, saying that he got a message that something is wrong with the FAT file system. As you ask the user questions, you learn that an error was generated when a third-party disk utility was in use. What do you think caused the problem?

3. You get a telephone call from a user who wants to know why she is unable to create a file in the root folder. She is using LFNs, the root folder is on a FAT partition, and she has 278 entries in the folder. What do you suspect is the problem?

4. You install Windows NT Workstation on a computer that previously ran Windows 95. One of your FAT partitions is not accessible under Windows NT Workstation. Why not? How can you make this partition accessible under Windows NT?

5. You create a folder named Archives on an NTFS partition and compress it. You use this folder to store files that are eventually backed up to tape, but when you move files into this folder, some get compressed and some do not. Why is the compression status not consistent?

Chapter 5 Managing File Systems 199

Answer Key

Procedure Answers

Page 180

▶ **To convert a FAT partition to NTFS**

3. Type **convert d: /fs:ntfs** and then press ENTER.

    A message appears stating the **convert** command cannot gain exclusive access to drive D and cannot convert it now.

    Why does this message occur?

    Drive D is the boot partition and is currently in use by the operating system.

8. Right-click **drive D**, and then click **Properties**.

    What file system is on drive D?

    NTFS.

Page 185

▶ **To create long file names**

8. At a command prompt, change to the root folder of drive C (C:\). Use the **dir /x** command to list the root folder.

    How does the LFN Lab Exercise folder that you just created appear in the folder list?

    The command dir /x shows both the alias and the long file name: LFNLAB~1 and LFN Lab Exercise.

10. Type **dir /x** to list the folder. Record the 8.3 file names below.

8.3 file names	Long file names
LONGFI~1.TXT	Long filename.lab.exercise.txt
LONGFI~2.TXT	Long filename.exercise.lab.txt
LONGFI~3.TXT	Longfilename.exercise.lab.txt
EXERCI~1.TXT	Exercise.long filename.lab.txt
LABLON~1.TXT	Lab.long filename.exercise.txt
TESTTX~1.TXT	Test.Txt.txt

    Why does Test.Txt have two extensions when listed from the command prompt?

    By default, Windows NT Explorer hides extensions. When you created a new text document, a .txt extension was appended to the file name that you provided (Test.Txt). The new file name is Test.Txt.txt.

12. List the folder and note the file name and alias.

    What happened to the file name and alias of the file you renamed?

    The file name was changed to LFN.LAB and the alias was deleted because it was no longer necessary.

14. List the folder contents.

    What happened to the file name and alias of the file you renamed?

    The file was renamed to LONG.TXT and the alias was deleted.

16. List the folder contents.

    What happened to the file name and alias of the file you renamed?

    The file was renamed to Long.Txt with an alias of LONG.TXT.

    Why does Long.Txt have an alias while LONG.TXT does not?

    Aliases are only created when a file name exceeds the FAT 8.3 limitation, or when a mixed-case file name is created.

▶ **To compress a folder**

1. Right-click drive D, and then click **Properties**.

   The **Properties** dialog box appears.

   What is the total disk space for drive D?

   Answers will vary.

   What is the total free disk space for drive D?

   Answers will vary.

4. Click **Ignore All** to continue.

   How much free disk space is available on drive D after compression?

   Answers will vary.

▶ **To copy a compressed file to a decompressed folder**

1. Examine the properties for Dna.txt in D:\Student\Reports\Statistics.

   Is Dna.txt compressed or decompressed?

   Compressed.

3. Examine the properties for Dna.txt in the Archives folder.

   Is Dna.txt compressed or decompressed?

   Decompressed.

   Why?

   A copied file inherits the compression attribute of the target folder.

Page 194

▶ **To move a compressed file to a decompressed folder**

1. Examine the properties of Labor.txt in the D:\Student\Reports\Tech folder.

   Is Labor.txt compressed or decompressed?

   Compressed.

3. Examine the properties of Labor.txt in the Archives folder.

   Is Labor.txt compressed or decompressed?

   Compressed.

   Why?

   When a file is moved to a new folder on the same partition, its compression attribute does not change.

Review Answers

Page 197

1. If you must support long file names on all partitions, need the ability to dual-boot between MS-DOS and Windows NT Workstation, and want to provide file compression for Windows NT, which file system or systems should you choose?

   a. FAT and NTFS

   b. FAT on all partitions

   c. NTFS on all partitions

   Answer a., because FAT is required for MS-DOS, and NTFS is required for file compression.

2. You get a telephone call from a user, saying that he got a message that something is wrong with the FAT file system. As you ask the user questions, you learn that an error was generated when a third-party disk utility was in use. What do you think caused the problem?

   When a system is started under MS-DOS, some third-party disk utilities that directly manipulate FAT and long file name entries are probably causing the error. Check to see whether the user is using LFNs and whether they have been warned that the disk utility could destroy the LFNs and leave only the 8.3 aliases, and possibly destroy the file itself. Determine the reason for running the utility and suggest an alternative such as SCANDISK, DEFRAG, or CHKDSK in Windows 95 or MS-DOS 6.*x*; these utilities do not harm LFN entries.

3. You get a telephone call from a user who wants to know why she is unable to create a file in the root folder. She is using LFNs, the root folder is on a FAT partition, and she has 278 entries in the folder. What do you suspect is the problem?

The FAT root directory has a hard-coded limit of 512 entries. On FAT partitions, an LFN takes one directory entry for each 13 characters, plus another directory entry for its alias. For example, if a file name is 15 characters long, it has two directory entries for the LFN and another for the alias. A 36-character LFN takes three directory entries for the LFN plus another for its alias, for a total of four directory entries. If a large number of the 278 entries in the root directory are LFNs, the user could have run out of entries in the root directory and could be unable to create any more files in the root directory.

4. You install Windows NT Workstation on a computer that previously ran Windows 95. One of your FAT partitions is not accessible under Windows NT Workstation. Why not? How can you make this partition accessible under Windows NT?

The partition is probably FAT32, which is supported by some versions of Windows 95, but not by Windows NT. You must back up any files on the partition that you want to keep. You can then reformat the partition so that Windows NT can access it. Finally, you would need to restore the files you backed up.

5. You create a folder named Archives on an NTFS partition and compress it. You use this folder to store files that are eventually backed up to tape, but when you move files into this folder, some get compressed and some do not. Why is the compression status not consistent?

The files are probably being moved from multiple partitions. Moving files within the same partition does not change the compression attribute, so decompressed files stay decompressed even when they are moved into a compressed folder. Moving a file from one partition to another actually creates a new instance of the file and deletes the original. New files inherit the compression attribute from their parent folder.

CHAPTER 6

Managing Partitions

Lesson 1 Partitioning a Disk . . . 204

Lesson 2 Managing Partitions Using Disk Administrator . . . 213

Lesson 3 General Maintenance and Troubleshooting . . . 230

Review . . . 234

About This Chapter

In this chapter, you learn about the types of partitions supported by Windows NT, including primary and extended partitions, volume sets, and stripe sets. You also learn about and use Disk Administrator—a Windows NT tool used to create, manage, and delete partitions. Finally, you will learn maintenance and troubleshooting solutions for partition management problems.

Before You Begin

To complete the lessons in this chapter, you must have:

- Two computers that meet the hardware and software requirements as specified in the Getting Started section of "About This Book."
- Completed all practices in Chapter 2, "Installing Windows NT."
- At least 50 MB of free space in an extended partition on Workstation1.

Lesson 1: Partitioning a Disk

Before a hard disk can be formatted with a file system, the disk must first be partitioned. Partitioning a disk involves specifying which portion and how much of the hard disk can be formatted with a file system. You can divide a hard disk into a maximum of four partitions. When a partition is created, Windows NT assigns it a drive letter.

Partitioning of disk space serves a number of purposes for computers running Windows NT. You can have the dual-boot capability discussed in Chapter 5, "Managing File Systems," and can manage your disk space to maximize the efficiency and performance of your system.

Windows NT supports several types of partitions. These include primary and extended partitions, volume sets, and stripe sets. This lesson describes the partition options in Windows NT.

After this lesson, you will be able to:
- Explain the differences between primary and extended partitions.
- Explain the benefits and disadvantages of a volume set.
- Explain the benefits and disadvantages of a stripe set.
- Describe hardware-related issues that affect Windows NT when adding additional hard disks.

Estimated lesson time: 30 minutes

Primary and Extended Partitions

Partitions are created in hard disk *free space*. Free space is the unused (or unpartitioned) portion of a hard disk. Free space can be divided into two types of partitions: primary or extended. Multiple primary partitions and one extended partition can coexist on the same disk. There can be up to four partitions on a hard disk.

Primary Partitions

A primary partition is a portion of a disk that can be marked as active and used by the system to start the computer. There can be up to four primary partitions per disk (or up to three, if there is an extended partition). A primary partition cannot be divided into smaller partitions.

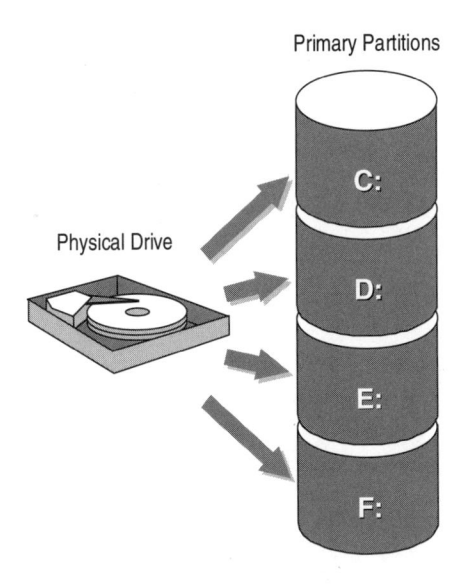

All partitions used by the Microsoft Windows 95 or Microsoft MS-DOS operating system must be formatted with the FAT file system.

On RISC-based computers, the primary partition created by the manufacturer's configuration program must be FAT, and at least 2 MB in size.

Some operating systems, such as MS-DOS version 5.0, can recognize only one primary partition per disk, even if other primary partitions are formatted with a file system that the operating system can use.

Extended Partitions

An extended partition is a method for avoiding the four-partition limit, and for configuring a hard disk into more than four logical volumes. Similar to a primary partition, an extended partition is created from free space on a hard disk.

You can have one extended partition on a hard disk. An extended partition is effectively a logical disk. Unlike a primary partition, you do not format the extended partition, nor is it assigned a drive letter. Instead, you can create one or more logical drives within the extended partition, and each logical drive is assigned a drive letter. You format each logical drive with a particular file system; this allows additional drive letters for organizing applications, data files, e-mail, multiple file systems, and so on. The following illustration shows how disk space can be divided into primary and extended partitions.

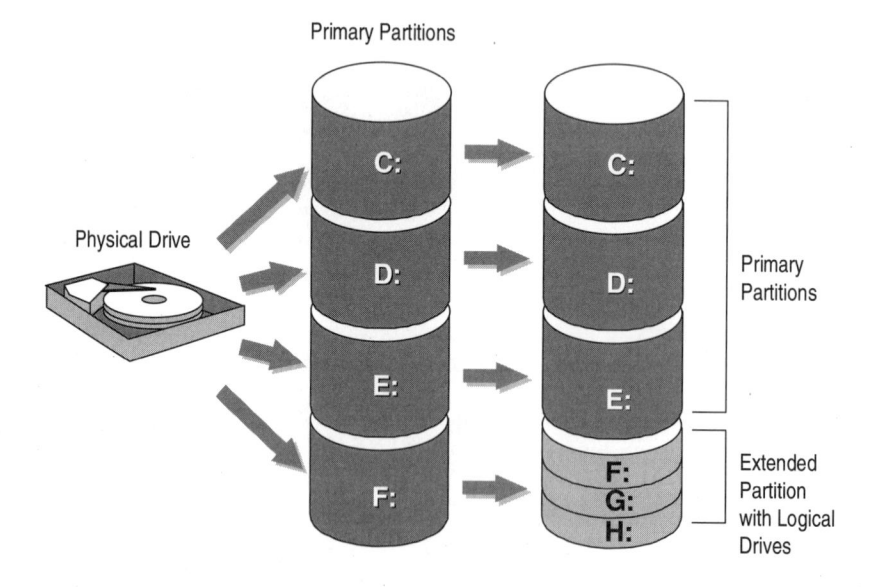

Theoretically, you could allocate disk space according to the preceding illustration, in which one primary partition was replaced by an extended partition divided into logical drives. However, the following illustration represents a more typical distribution of your hard disk space when using both primary and extended partitions. Typically the C partition would contain the system and boot files, and the remaining disk space would be an extended partition with space distributed among one or more logical drives to complement your working environment.

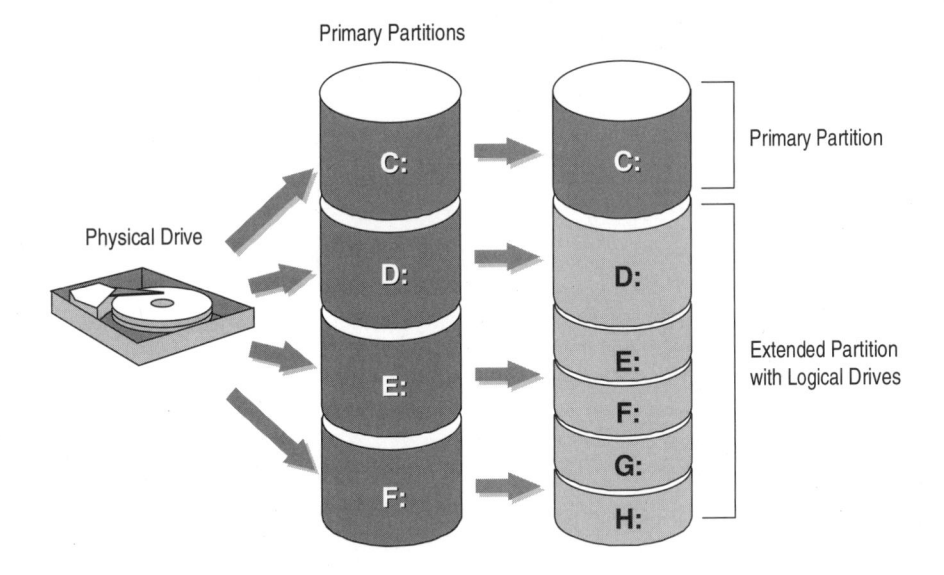

System and Boot Partitions

The Windows NT system partition must be a primary partition. The Windows NT boot partition can be either a primary partition or a logical drive in an extended partition.

What Is a Volume Set?

A volume set is a partition formed by collecting 2 to 32 areas of unformatted free space on one or more hard disks. Each area is referred to as a member of the volume set. The members form one large logical volume set, which is treated as a single partition. Though this does not improve performance, volume sets do increase the disk space available for a single logical drive and free up drive letters for other purposes. For example, in the following illustration, 100 MB of free space from Disk 0 is combined with 50 MB of free space from Disk 1 to create a 150 MB partition called a volume set.

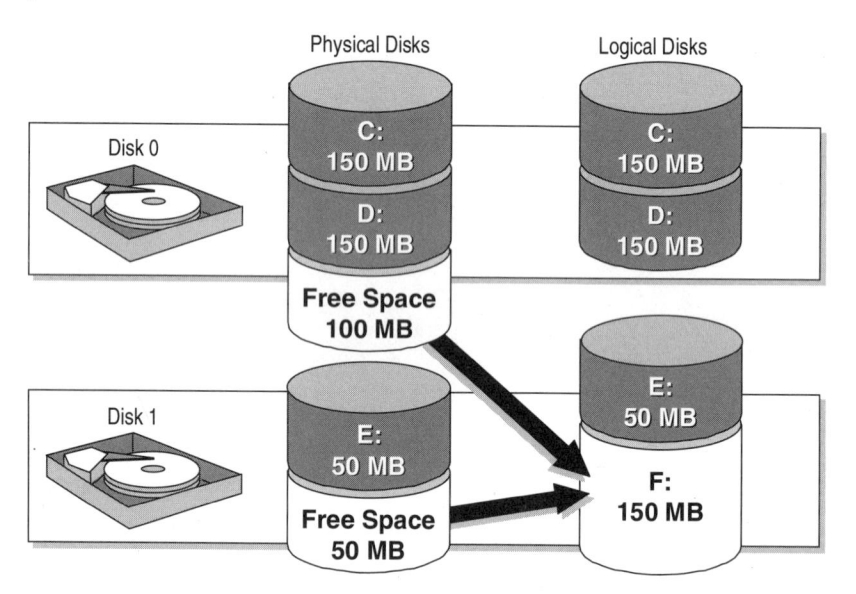

A volume set can combine areas from different types of hard disks, including small computer system interface (SCSI), enhanced small device interface (ESDI), and integrated device electronics (IDE). When creating a volume set, the free space can be an unallocated area within an extended partition, or an unpartitioned area elsewhere on the disk.

Create a volume set when you have disk space from two or more unused areas that can be combined into a single large partition, or when an application requires a larger amount of disk space than you have on any single hard disk.

Guidelines for Managing Volume Sets

Keep the following points in mind when implementing volume sets:

- You cannot reclaim portions of disk space used in a volume set for other purposes without losing the entire volume set and all of the data stored on it.
- The Windows NT boot and system partitions cannot reside in a volume set.
- If a computer running Windows NT is configured to allow booting of another operating system that does not support volume sets, such as Windows 95 or MS-DOS, that operating system cannot access information in a volume set.
- Volume sets do not provide any *fault tolerance* (the ability of a computer or operating system to respond to a catastrophic event, such as a power outage or hardware failure, so that no data is lost and work in progress is not corrupted) because there is no data redundancy. In fact, volume sets spanning multiple hard disks are more susceptible to failure because a failure on any of the hard disks will destroy the full volume set.
- In a volume set, data is written to one member of the set at a time until no space remains on that member. Data is then written to the next member in the volume set, and so on.

Note For more information about fault tolerance, see Chapter 7, "Managing Fault Tolerance."

What Is a Stripe Set?

Stripe sets are similar to volume sets in that they also combine areas of unformatted free space into one large logical drive.

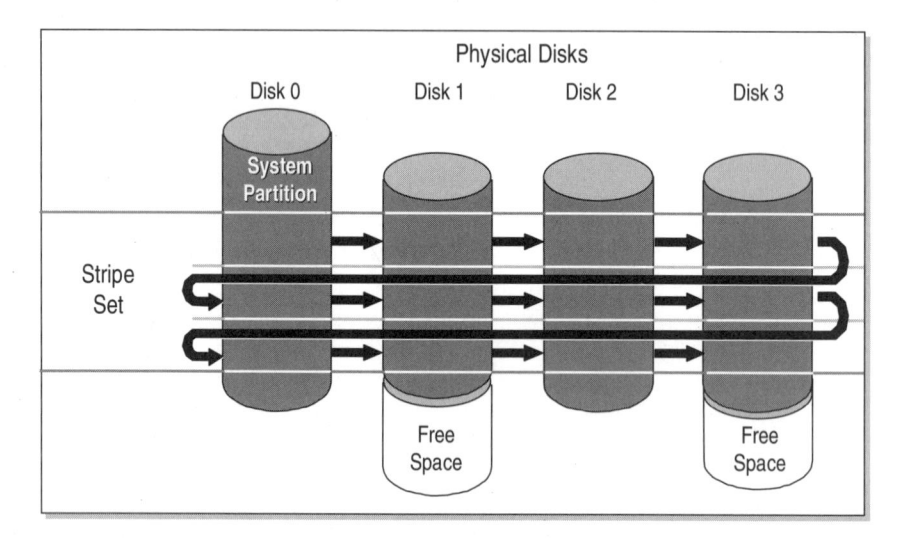

Physical Disks

Disk 0 — System Partition

Disk 1, Disk 2, Disk 3

Stripe Set

Free Space (Disk 2), Free Space (Disk 3)

Unlike a volume set, which can be implemented with a single hard disk, a stripe set requires at least two hard disks. Stripe sets, like volume sets, can include disk space from as many as 32 hard disks and can combine areas on different types of hard disks, such as SCSI, ESDI, and IDE. The amount of space used on each disk will be equal to the smallest unpartitioned space that you selected on the disks.

In a stripe set, data is written evenly across all of the physical disks, one row at a time. The Windows NT implementation of stripe sets writes these in 64 KB units.

All of the hard disks belonging to the stripe set perform the same functions as a single hard disk. This allows concurrent I/O commands to be issued and processed on all hard disks simultaneously. In this way, stripe sets can increase the speed of system I/O.

Guidelines for Managing Stripe Sets

Stripe sets are similar to volume sets in the following ways:

- You cannot reclaim portions of disk space used in a stripe set for other purposes without losing the entire stripe set and all of the data stored on it.
- The Windows NT boot and system partitions cannot reside in a stripe set.
- If a computer running Windows NT is configured to allow booting of another operating system that does not support stripe sets, such as Windows 95 or MS-DOS, that operating system cannot access information in a stripe set.
- Stripe sets inherently do not provide any fault tolerance because there is no data redundancy. In fact, a stripe set is more susceptible to failure because it spans two or more hard disks, and a failure on any of the hard disks will destroy the full stripe set.

Note Windows NT Server includes a mechanism, adding *parity* to stripe sets, that can enable stripe sets to provide fault tolerance. For more information about fault tolerance, see Chapter 7, "Managing Fault Tolerance."

Comparing a Stripe Set to a Volume Set

The following table compares the features of stripe sets and volume sets.

Condition	Stripe set	Volume set
Can it be created on one hard disk?	No	Yes
Can it contain the system or boot partition?	No	No
What is the maximum number of areas that can be combined?	32	32
Must the areas combined be of approximately the same size?	Yes	No
Can it combine areas on different types of hard disks such as SCSI, ESDI, and IDE?	Yes	Yes
Is the area on one hard disk filled before starting to fill the next hard disk?	No	Yes
Can it improve I/O performance?	Yes	No

Note A volume set can appear to slightly improve performance on reads if the controller has the ability to do concurrent reads. The small read performance gains that can occur when using a volume set is actually a function of the hardware, and not the volume set.

Other Disk Management Considerations

In addition to creating, formatting, and deleting partitions, other disk management tasks may have to be performed on a computer running Windows NT. These include adding hard disks and configuring a disk for removable media.

Adding Hard Disks

The number of hard disks that can be added to a computer depends on the following variables:

- The physical configuration of the computer, such as the number of slots or bays available.
- The number of devices that can be connected to a disk controller or SCSI bus controller.
- The number of controllers in the computer.

When a new hard disk is added to the computer, the Disk Administrator program updates the registry when the computer is shut down and restarted. There is no need to indicate to Windows NT that a new hard disk has been added. As long as the drivers are installed for the disk controller, Windows NT automatically detects the hard disk and allows it to be partitioned and used. To partition and format the hard disk, run Disk Administrator.

Removable Media

Removable media can have only one partition, and it must be a primary partition. Removable media cannot be part of a volume set or stripe set, and cannot contain a system or boot partition. Windows NT supports formatting removable media as either FAT or NTFS. However, if the removable disk is formatted as NTFS, the computer must be shut down and restarted to change disks.

Lesson 2: Managing Partitions Using Disk Administrator

You have learned about the different types of file systems and the partitions supported by Windows NT. This lesson describes *Disk Administrator*, the Windows NT tool that is used to manage hard disks. You use Disk Administrator to create, format, and delete partitions, volume sets, and stripe sets.

After this lesson, you will be able to:
- Create, format, and delete partitions.
- Describe the purpose of an active partition.
- Create, format, extend, and delete volume sets.
- Create, format, and delete stripe sets.
- Describe drive letter assignments.
- Commit changes from within Disk Administrator.
- Secure the system partition on a RISC-based computer.

Estimated lesson time: 60 minutes

What Is Disk Administrator?

Disk Administrator is an administrative tool for managing hard disks. Disk Administrator can be thought of as a graphical Windows NT version of the MS-DOS **fdisk** utility.

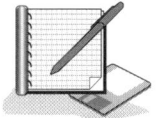

Practice

In this procedure, you start the Disk Administrator program.

- Customize the Disk Administrator legend.
- Set the Disk Administrator window to display disk areas as "equal" regions, rather than as proportional.

▶ **To start Disk Administrator**

Note Complete this procedure on Workstation1.

1. Shut down Server2, and then restart the computer as Workstation1.
2. Log on as Administrator.
3. Click the **Start** button, point to **Programs**, and then point to **Administrative Tools (Common)**.

4. On the **Administrative Tools (Common)** menu, click **Disk Administrator**.

   If this is the first time Disk Administrator has run, you will see one of the following messages:

   ```
   Disk Administrator has determined that this is the first time Disk
   Administrator has been run, or that one or more disks have been added
   to your computer since Disk Administrator was last run....
   ```

   –or–

   ```
   No signature found on Disk 0. Writing a signature is a safe operation
   and will not affect your ability to access this from other operating
   systems, such as DOS....
   ```

5. If you get the first message, click **OK**. If you get the second message, click **Yes**.

   Disk Administrator starts.

Clicking **Yes** creates a 32-bit signature that identifies the disk. The signature is written in the Master Boot Record of the disk. Even if a disk is moved to a different controller, or its identification is changed, Disk Administrator and the Windows NT fault tolerance driver (Ftdisk.sys) recognize it.

Disk Administrator displays the computer's disk resources through a status bar and legend. This legend can be customized by colors and patterns to display disk regions and disk usage.

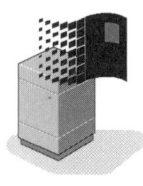

Note The following illustration shows Disk Administrator on Windows NT Server. The **Fault Tolerance** menu is included only on Windows NT Server Disk Administrator. Fault tolerance can only be administered on computers running Windows NT Server.

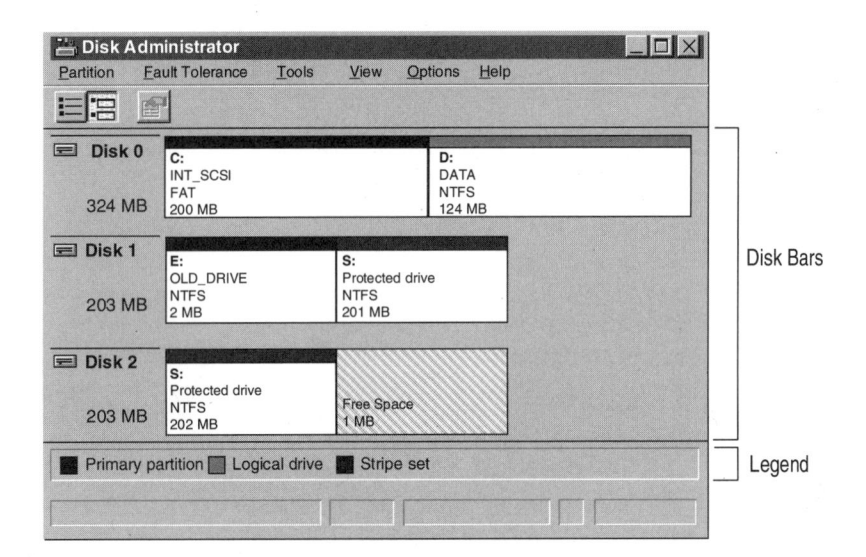

```
Disk Administrator                                    _ □ ×
Partition  Fault Tolerance  Tools  View  Options  Help

Disk 0      C:                      D:
            INT_SCSI                DATA
            FAT                     NTFS
324 MB      200 MB                  124 MB

Disk 1      E:                      S:
            OLD_DRIVE               Protected drive
            NTFS                    NTFS
203 MB      2 MB                    201 MB

Disk 2      S:
            Protected drive
            NTFS              Free Space
203 MB      202 MB            1 MB

■ Primary partition  ▨ Logical drive  ■ Stripe set
```
— Disk Bars
— Legend

Practice

In these procedures, you start Disk Administrator, customize the Disk Administrator legend and set the Disk Administrator window to display disk areas as "equal" regions.

Note Complete these procedures on Workstation1.

▶ **To customize the Disk Administrator legend**

In this procedure, you set the color indicator of the primary partition to white.

1. Verify that Disk Administrator is displayed on your screen.
2. On the **Options** menu, click **Colors and Patterns**.
3. Click the down arrow in the **Color and pattern for:** box.

   List the options for which you can customize the color and pattern.

   _____

   _____

4. In the **Color and pattern for:** box, click **Primary Partition**.
5. In the **Colors** box, click the white box, and then click **OK**.

   The Disk Administrator window appears. Notice that the color indicator of the primary partition C: is now white.

▶ **To use Disk Administrator to set up the display window**

In this procedure, you set the window to display the areas representing the disk space in equal rather than proportional regions.

What file systems are currently used on drives C and D?

_____

According to the information in the Disk Administrator window, how much free disk space does your computer have?

_____

1. On the **Options** menu, click **Region Display**.
2. In the **Which disk** box, click **All disks**.
3. Click **Size all regions equally**, and then click **OK**.

   The Disk Administrator window appears. Notice that the size of block representing all partitions is the same, regardless of the actual size of the partition.

Creating and Formatting Partitions

To create and format partitions, use the Disk Administrator **Partition** and **Options** menus. You specify the location and when prompted, specify the size of the partition. When a partition is created, Windows NT assigns the next available drive letter.

After the hard disk is partitioned, the partitions must be formatted with a file system. A partition can be formatted in one of two ways:

- Use the **format** command in a command prompt with the following syntax:

  format d: /fs:FAT|NTFS

- Use the **Format** option on the **Tools** menu in Disk Administrator.

Both options allow formatting of a partition as either FAT or NTFS and assigning a volume label.

Practice

In these procedures, you use Disk Administrator to do the following:

- Create a new partition.
- Format a partition and label a volume.
- Change the drive letter of the newly-created volume.
- Save the changes.

Note Complete these procedures on Workstation1.

▶ **To create a new partition**

1. Click an area of free space to select it.

   The area should now have a dark outline around it, indicating that it is selected.

2. On the **Partition** menu, click **Create**.
3. In the **Create logical drive of size** box, type **25** and then click **OK**.

   The partition is created using the next available drive letter.

4. On the **Partition** menu, click **Commit Changes Now**.

   A **Confirm** dialog box appears asking if you want to save the changes.

5. Click **Yes**.

   A **Disk Administrator** dialog box appears stating that disks were updated successfully.

6. Click **OK**.

▶ **To format a partition and label a volume**

In this procedure, you format and label the partition that you just created.

1. Click the new unformatted partition, and then on the **Tools** menu, click **Format**.

   The **Format** dialog box appears.

2. In the **File System** box, click **NTFS**.
3. In the **Volume Label** box, type **ntfs-vol**
4. Select the **Quick Format** check box, and then click **Start**.

   A **Format** dialog box appears, warning that formatting will erase all data on this disk.

5. Click **OK**.

    A **Format Complete** dialog box appears.

6. Click **OK**.

7. Click **Close** to close the **Format** dialog box.

    Notice that Disk Administrator now displays the label, the type of file system, and the size of the newly formatted partition.

▶ **To change the drive letter**

In these procedures, you change the drive letter of the 25 MB partition you created.

1. Click the ntfs-vol partition.

2. On the **Tools** menu, click **Assign Drive Letter**.

3. In the **Assign drive letter** box, click **I:**, and then click **OK**.

    A **Confirm** dialog box appears, stating that the new drive letter assignment will happen immediately.

4. Click **Yes**.

5. On the **Partition** menu, click **Exit**.

Deleting Partitions

Use the Disk Administrator **Delete** command, located on the **Partition** menu, to delete partitions. Partitions can be deleted at any time, except under the following conditions:

- The system and boot partitions cannot be deleted from within Windows NT. You can remove the system and boot partitions by either of the following methods:

    • Booting with another operating system such as MS-DOS and then deleting the partitions.

    • Booting from the Windows NT Setup Disk 1, as if doing an installation. You are then prompted to insert Setup Disks 2 and 3, and are asked where to install Windows NT. You can also create and delete partitions from this screen. Select the system partition and then press **d**. Follow the prompts on the screen to finish deleting the partitions.

- A partition containing an open file cannot be deleted. This includes the partition that contains Pagefile.sys, the Windows NT paging file.

Marking Partitions As Active

The active partition contains the system files.

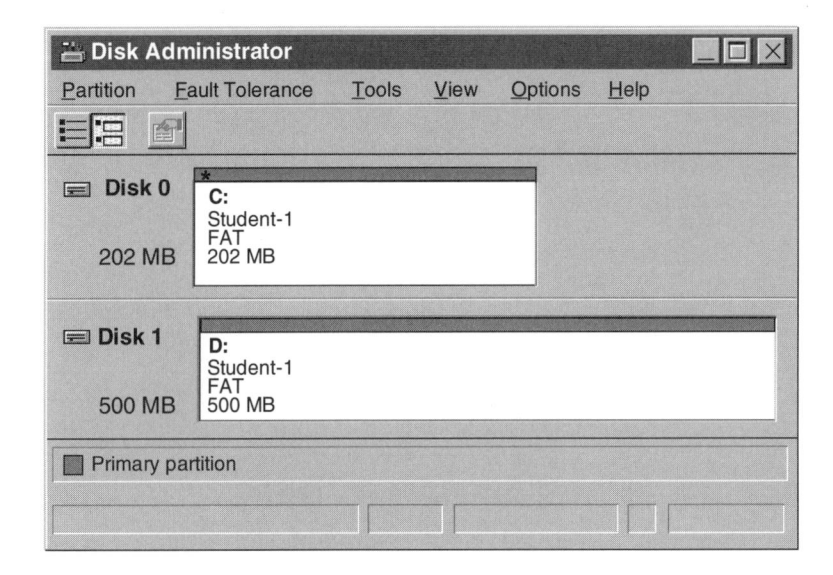

![Disk Administrator screenshot showing Disk 0 (C: Student-1, FAT, 202 MB) marked with asterisk and Disk 1 (D: Student-1, FAT, 500 MB), both primary partitions.]

In order for an operating system to start, the partition containing the startup file must be marked as active. On Intel *x*86-based computers, the active partition is a primary partition containing the system boot files. The active partition is on the disk that the computer accesses when starting up. Use the Disk Administrator **Partition** menu to mark a partition as active. Disk Administrator displays the active partition with an asterisk in its color bar. Only one partition should be marked as active at a time.

Note The default color for primary partitions can make it difficult to see the asterisk. You may want to use the **Colors and Patterns** option on the **Options** menu of Disk Administrator to change the color of the primary partitions, as you did in an earlier procedure.

If you want to use an operating system, for example UNIX or OS/2, that is located on a partition other than the partition currently marked active, you must mark the system partition of the other operating system as active. Then shut down and restart the computer.

When a system partition is marked active, the active designation of any other partition is removed.

Note On RISC-based computers, partitions are not marked active. Instead, they are configured by a hardware configuration program supplied by the manufacturer.

Creating, Formatting, Extending, and Deleting Volume Sets

You have learned that a volume set is a collection of free space combined to create a single logical drive. To create, extend, and delete a volume set you use the **Create Volume Set**, **Extend Volume Set**, and **Delete** commands on the Disk Administrator **Partition** menu.

A volume set is created by selecting free space on the computer's hard disks. After a volume set is created, it must be formatted. Volume sets can be formatted with either FAT or NTFS. This is done by using the Disk Administrator **Format** command, which is located on the **Tools** menu.

Volume sets are also created when an NTFS partition is extended. You can also extend an existing NTFS volume set. In these circumstances, the extended partition is automatically formatted with NTFS when the computer is restarted.

Deleting a volume set deletes all information on all parts of the volume set, and returns free space.

Extending a Volume Set

You add space to an existing volume set by extending it. You can only extend a volume set that is formatted with NTFS.

For example, in the following illustration, a 150 MB NTFS volume set is extended by adding 100 MB of free space to create one 250 MB volume set.

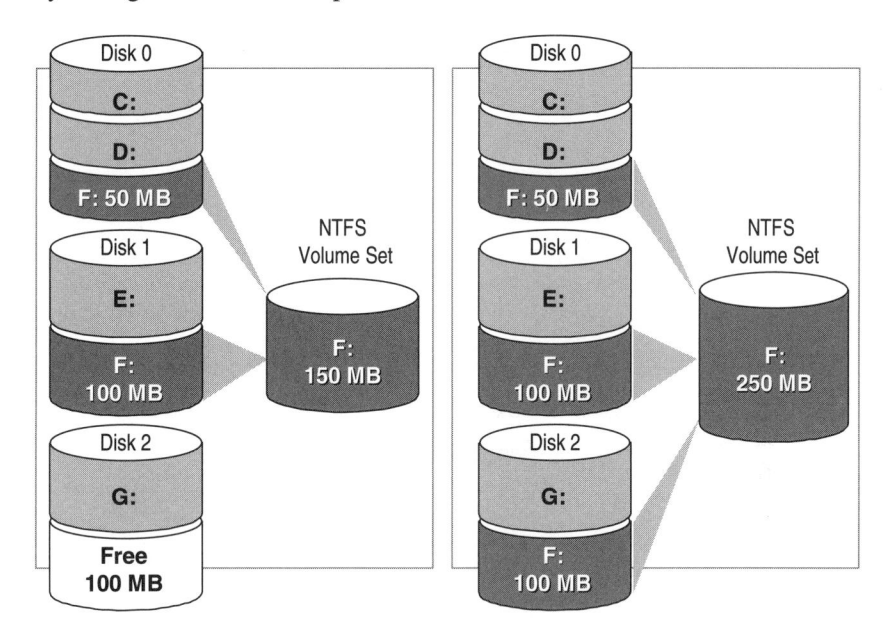

An existing volume set is extended by selecting the volume set and one or more areas of free space, and then clicking **Extend Volume Set** on the **Partition** menu in Disk Administrator.

Note There is no way to extend a FAT volume set. If you have a FAT volume set you want to extend, you must first convert the volume to NTFS. Then you can extend it.

It is necessary to shut down and restart the computer when a volume set is created or extended. Shutting down and restarting the computer after a volume set is extended automatically formats the new area or areas when the computer starts.

Important After a volume set is extended and the configuration is saved, space cannot be reclaimed without deleting the entire volume set.

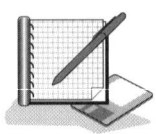

Practice

In these procedures, you use the Volume Set Simulation to create, format, extend and delete a volume set.

Note Complete these procedures on Server1.

▶ **To start the simulation**

1. Log on as Administrator.
2. Click the **Start** button, point to **Programs**, point to **Technical Support Training**, point to **Simulations**, and then click **Volume Set Simulation**.

    The simulations starts, and Disk Administrator appears.

▶ **To create a volume set**

1. Click an area of free space on Disk 0.

    The area should now have a dark outline around it, indicating that it is selected.

2. Hold down the CTRL key, and then click an area of free space on Disk 1.

    Both areas should now appear selected.

3. On the **Partition** menu, click **Create Volume Set**.

    The **Create Volume Set** dialog box appears. Notice in **Create Volume Set of Total Size** that the default is the actual total of the two areas of free space you selected.

4. Click **OK** to create a volume set of the maximum size possible on Disk 0 and Disk 1.

    The new volume set is created. Notice that the next available drive letter, G, has been assigned and the color bar has changed. The new volume set is unformatted.

5. On the **Partition** menu, click **Commit Changes Now**.

    A **Confirm** message box appears, stating that changes have been made to your disk configuration.

6. Click **Yes** to save the changes.

    A **Confirm** message box appears, stating that the changes requested will require you to restart your computer.

7. Click **Yes** to continue with the changes.

    A **Disk Administrator** message box appears, stating that the disks were updated successfully.

8. Click **OK**.

   A **Disk Administrator** message box appears, stating that changes have been made which require you to restart your computer.

9. Click **OK** to initiate system shutdown.

   A **Volume Set Simulation** message box appears, stating that the simulation will proceed as if a shutdown occurs and you have logged on as Administrator.

10. Click **OK**.

    A message box appears prompting you to please wait while the system writes unsaved data to the disk.

    The simulation continues with Disk Administrator open.

▶ **To format a volume set**

1. In Disk Administrator, click the unformatted volume set, drive G, and then on the **Tools** menu, click **Format**.
2. In the **File System** box, select **NTFS**, and then click **Start**.
3. Click **OK** to continue to format the volume set.

   A **Formatting** message box appears indicating the format is complete.

4. Click **OK**.
5. Click **Close**.

   The volume set now appears in Disk Administrator as an NTFS volume set.

▶ **To extend a volume set**

1. In Disk Administrator, click drive G, and then while you hold down the CTRL key, click an area of free space on Disk 2. Both areas should be selected.
2. On the **Partition** menu, click **Extend Volume Set**.

   The **Extend Volume Set** dialog box appears. Notice in **Create Volume Set of Total Size** that the default is the maximum total size of the areas you selected.

3. Click **OK** to extend the volume set.

   You have extended an existing NTFS volume. Notice that drive G appears in all three region displays for this volume set.

4. On the **Partition** menu, click **Exit**, and then click **Yes** to save your changes.

   A **Disk Administrator** dialog box appears, indicating your disks were updated successfully.

5. Click **OK**.

   A **Disk Administrator** dialog box appears indicating that the requested changes require you to restart your computer.

6. Click **OK** to restart your computer.

   A **Volume Set Simulation** dialog box appears, stating that the simulation will proceed as if a shutdown occurs and you have logged on as Administrator.

7. Click **OK**.

   A dialog box appears prompting you to please wait while the system writes unsaved data to the disk.

   The simulation continues with Disk Administrator open.

▸ **To delete a volume set**

1. In Disk Administrator, click drive G. All areas of drive G should now be selected.

2. On the **Partition** menu, click **Delete**.

   A **Confirm** dialog box appears indicating that all data in the volume set will be lost.

3. Click **Yes** to delete the selected volume.

4. On the **Partition** menu, click **Exit**, and then click **Yes** to save your changes.

   A **Disk Administrator** dialog box appears indicating that the disks were updated successfully.

5. Click **OK**.

   Disk Administrator closes, and the Volume Set Simulation ends.

Creating, Formatting, and Deleting Stripe Sets

Procedures for creating and deleting stripe sets are similar to procedures for creating and deleting volume sets.

You have learned the structure and use of stripe sets, and that a stripe set is similar to a volume set. Areas of free space are combined to form a single logical drive. However, while a volume set can consist of space on one or more hard disks (up to a maximum of 32), a stripe set requires space on two or more (up to 32) hard disks. Use the **Disk Administrator** menu commands to create, format, and delete stripe sets. Unlike a volume set, a stripe set cannot be extended.

The partitions combined to create a stripe set must be approximately the same size. If they are not, Disk Administrator makes each partition of the stripe set approximately the same size.

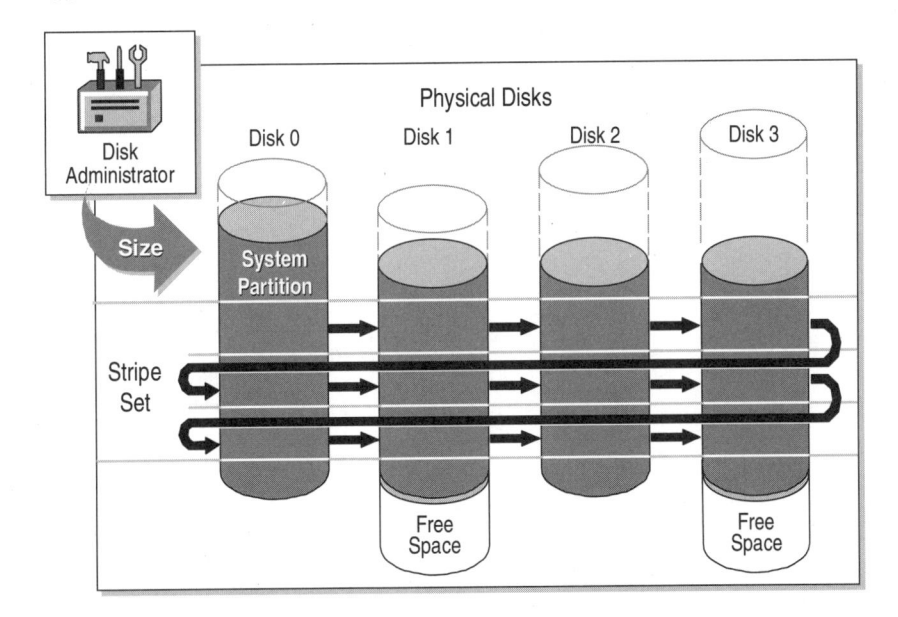

It is necessary to shut down and restart the computer when a stripe set is created.

Caution Deleting a stripe set deletes all of the information stored in the stripe set.

Committing Changes

If you have made changes to partitions using Disk Administrator, on exit, a dialog box appears requiring confirmation before changes are committed, or saved.

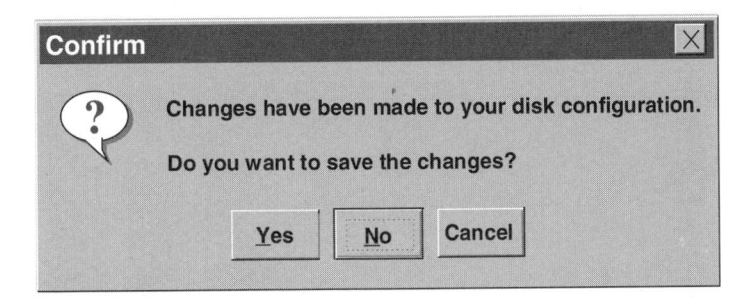

Changes can also be confirmed by using the **Commit Changes Now** command on the **Partition** menu. Changes do not take effect until they have been confirmed.

Primary and extended partitions can be removed, reconfigured, and formatted without restarting the computer. However, it *is* necessary to shut down and restart the computer when a volume set is created or extended, or when a stripe set is created.

Partition Renumbering

Windows NT assigns partition numbers to all primary partitions before assigning partition numbers to any logical drives within an extended partition. The following illustration shows how logical partitions are sequentially numbered after the primary partition.

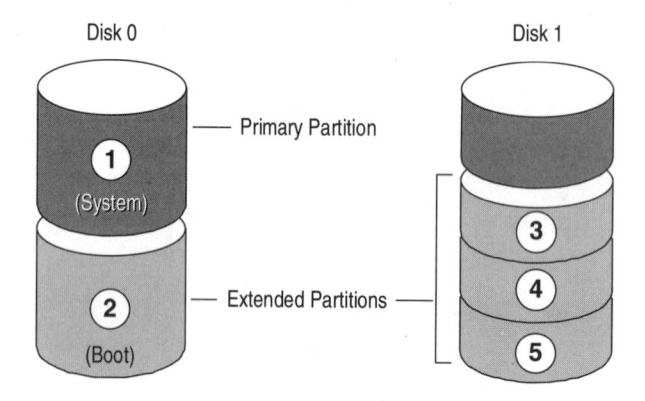

If you create another primary partition, regardless of the hard disk that it is created on, the new primary partition receives a number lower than any logical drive on an extended partition. Then the logical partitions are renumbered. The following illustration shows an example of partition renumbering. A primary partition was created on Disk 1, and was assigned the number 2. The logical partitions were reassigned numbers (3, 4, 5, 6) following the number of the newly-created primary partition (2).

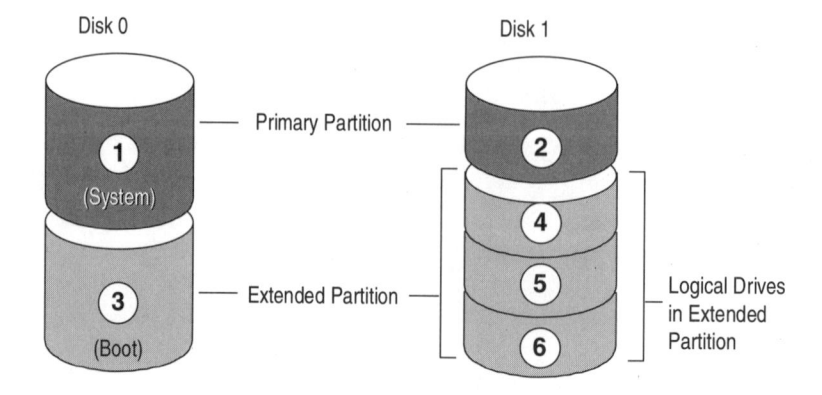

Support Issue

Windows NT uses a file named Boot.ini to find the boot partition. If the boot partition resides on an extended partition that was subsequently renumbered (as shown in the preceding illustration), then the Boot.ini file *must* be manually updated so that it points to the boot partition; otherwise, Windows NT will not start.

If you use Disk Administrator to create additional partitions on computers that are sold with small hidden partitions containing diagnostic utilities, the partition table is rewritten to include the hidden partition as partition 1. In this situation a message appears that prompts you to edit the Boot.ini file. Again, Windows NT will not start unless the Boot.ini file is correctly updated.

Note For more information about editing the Boot.ini file, see Chapter 7, "Managing Fault Tolerance."

Automatic Assignment of Drive Letters by Windows NT

Until Disk Administrator is run for the first time, Windows NT dynamically assigns drive letters using the following procedure:

1. Starting with Disk 0, the first primary partition on each disk is assigned a consecutive drive letter, beginning with the active system partition as drive C. In the following illustration, the primary partition on Disk 0 is assigned C, Disk 1 has no primary partition, Disk 2 is assigned D, and Disk 3 is assigned E.

2. Then, starting with Disk 0, logical drives on each disk are assigned the next consecutive letter(s). In the following illustration, Disk 1 has three logical drives, which are assigned F, G, and H.

3. The remaining primary partitions on each disk with unassigned partitions are each assigned a letter. In the following illustration, Disk 0 has a second primary partition which is assigned the letter I.

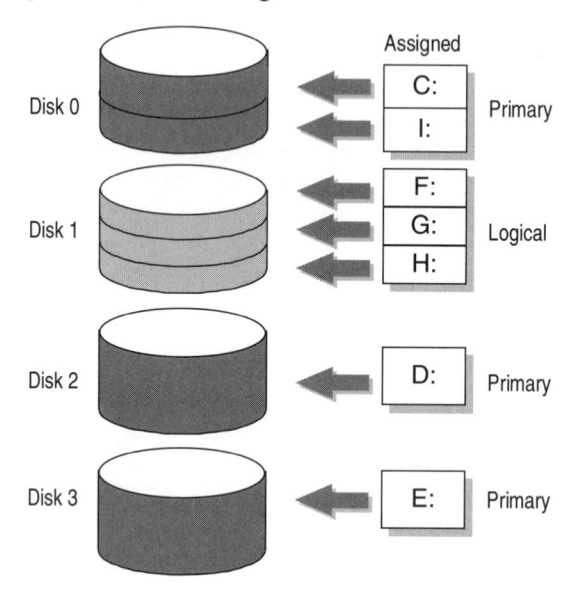

```
Disk 0    ← C:   Primary
          ← I:

Disk 1    ← F:
          ← G:   Logical
          ← H:

Disk 2    ← D:   Primary

Disk 3    ← E:   Primary
```
(Assigned)

After Disk Administrator is run for the first time, it assigns static drive letters to partitions.

Reassigning Drive Letters Through Disk Administrator

Drive letters can be reassigned though the **Drive Letter** command on the Disk Administrator **Tools** menu. A partition can be statically assigned any letter that is not already in use by a local device, such as a CD-ROM drive, or in use by a network connection. Be careful not to change the drive letter of the system partition because many programs make reference to the C drive.

Assigning CD-ROM Drive Letters Through Disk Administrator

A drive letter for a CD-ROM drive can be assigned using the **CD-ROM Drive Letter** command on the **Tools** menu in Disk Administrator.

Note All drive letter modifications made with Disk Administrator can be done without restarting the computer, if the selected partition does not contain Windows NT system files.

Securing the System Partition

You learned about selecting a file system for the system partition in Chapter 2, "Installing Windows NT." Although only NTFS provides local security, FAT may be required for the system partition. For example, RISC-based computers require system partitions to be formatted with FAT, regardless of the operating system. This is because these computers will only start from a FAT file system.

Securing a FAT System Partition on a RISC-based Computer

Because FAT partitions cannot be protected with local security, the system partitions on a RISC-based computer are vulnerable unless the system partition is secured through Disk Administrator or with a third-party utility.

Note The **Secure System Partition** command is only present on RISC-based computers.

On RISC-based computers, when the **Secure System Partition** command is used in Disk Administrator, only members of the Administrators group on that computer are able to access the system partition. All other users receive an access denied message. Security is not applied until the computer is restarted.

Lesson 3: General Maintenance and Troubleshooting

This lesson covers problems that you may encounter with partition management, such as failure to recognize a hard disk or partition, or file corruption, and some potential solutions to these problems. In addition, it introduces a method to restore your current disk configuration.

After this lesson, you will be able to:
- State the solutions for the following maintenance and troubleshooting issues:
  - Recovering disk configuration information
  - Failure to recognize hard disks or partitions
  - Corrupted files or directories
  - Problems with MS-DOS-based disk utilities
  - Problems with 1 GB IDE hard disks

Estimated lesson time: 15 minutes

Recovering Disk Configuration Information

Disk configuration information is initially stored on the Emergency Repair Disk and in the *systemroot*\Repair folder at system installation. After making changes such as assigning drive letters, creating volume sets or stripes sets, and creating new partitions, Disk Administrator provides an option for saving and later restoring this configuration information in the *systemroot* folder. It also prompts you to update your Emergency Repair Disk. You must update the Emergency Repair Disk, or the information will not match the actual hard disk configuration on your computer, if an emergency repair is required.

Restoring saved disk configuration information is useful in the following situations:

- The computer was recently recovered with the Emergency Repair process and the registry was reset to its initial state. At this point, the current disk configuration will be as it was when the system was originally installed.
- A new version of Windows NT is being installed.

The Rdisk.exe utility, in the *systemroot*\System32 folder, can also be used to restore the configuration to its previous state in the last update operation.

Note Use the Rdisk.exe utility to update the Emergency Repair Disk. For more information on Rdisk.exe see Chapter 17, "The Windows NT Boot Process."

File System Problems and Solutions

Further file system problems fall into two categories: failure to recognize the hard disk or partition, and corrupted files. The following table offers solutions to some of these file system problems.

Problem	Solution
Failure to recognize hard disks or partitions.	Check to make sure there are no hardware incompatibility or hard disk problems. If Windows NT does not recognize the disk, then there is probably an incompatibility problem. If Windows NT recognizes the disk but cannot access the partition, then the problem is in either the partition table or the boot sector. Detected hardware appears in the registry under HKEY_LOCAL_MACHINE\HARDWARE.
File system corruption.	In the case of damaged directories, files with scrambled names, and minor corruption, remove the offending folder or file. More serious problems may require use of a file system repair utility. In general, if a logical drive appears corrupted and a backup exists, then reformat the drive and restore the files.
Corrupted or lost files when running MS-DOS-based utilities on dual-boot FAT partitions.	When a computer is booted under MS-DOS, some third-party disk utilities that directly manipulate FAT can destroy long file name (LFN) entries, or even the file itself. Users should be careful when using these utilities; the utilities give errors indicating that there is something wrong with FAT. It is more likely that the LFN entries are causing the error message, rather than FAT.
	LFN entries will not be harmed by either the MS-DOS 6.*x* tools, SCANDISK, DEFRAG, and CHKDSK, or the disk utilities designed for Windows 95.
	Windows NT can be configured to prevent the use of LFNs on FAT partitions by changing the following registry value to 1: HKEY_LOCAL_MACHINE\SYSTEM\CurrentControlSet\Control\FileSystem\Win31FileSystem.

(*continued*)

Problem	Solution
Problems with 1-GB IDE disks. These disks follow the EIDE standard.	Windows NT generally cannot gain access to all of the space on the disk because the disks do not translate in a way that Windows NT recognizes. This is due to a BIOS limit of 1024 cylinders, not an operating system limit.
	To overcome this limit, either the computer's BIOS must be able to circumvent the limit (by sector translation or by using relative cluster addressing, as SCSI hard disks do), or Windows NT must be able to communicate directly with the controller. Windows NT can currently communicate only with WD 1003-compatible controllers.
	Windows NT includes support for the OnTrack Systems Disk Manager partitioning utility in the hard disk device driver, Atdisk.sys.
	Disk Manager provides support for large (greater than 540 MB) IDE hard disks under MS-DOS. Disk Manager works by embedding BIOS extension code into Track 0 (zero) of the hard disk. Disk Manager makes sure that the MBR (Master Boot Record) invokes code that loads the BIOS extensions before anything else, such as NTLDR. The BIOS extensions, combined with the Disk Manager partition type, are used to transparently support large hard disks.

Summary

The following information summarizes the key points in this chapter:

- Windows NT supports primary and extended partitions.
- A physical disk can have as many as four partitions, or as few as one. If there are four partitions, up to four can be primary, but only one can be extended.
- Windows NT also supports volume sets and stripe sets.
- A volume set is a partition formed by collecting areas of free space to form one large logical volume. This both increases the disk space available for a single logical drive and frees up drive letters for other purposes.
- Stripe sets are similar to volume sets in that they also combine areas of unformatted free space into one large logical drive. However, a stripe set requires at least two hard disks.
- Stripe sets, like volume sets, can include disk space from as many as 32 hard disks and can combine areas on different types of hard disks, such as SCSI, ESDI, and IDE.
- In a stripe set, data is written evenly across all of the physical disks, one row at a time. The amount of space used on each disk will be equal to the smallest unpartitioned space that you selected on the disks.
- The hard disks belonging to a stripe set perform the same functions as a single hard disk, allowing concurrent I/O commands to be issued and processed on all hard disks simultaneously, thereby increasing the speed of computer I/O.
- Disk Administrator is the graphical tool provided by Windows NT that is used to create, manage, and delete partitions, volume sets, and stripe sets.
- Problems may arise relating to partitions, such as failure to recognize a hard disk or partition, or file corruption. These problems can usually be resolved by following general maintenance and troubleshooting procedures.
- The Emergency Repair Disk can be used to restore your current disk configuration when emergency repair is required.

Review

1. Name at least two reasons for using volume sets.

2. Name at least two differences between volume sets and stripe sets.

3. If you want to start an operating system that is on your computer, but is not on the active partition, what would you do?

4. If you access Disk Administrator and the **Fault Tolerance** menu is missing, what would you conclude?

5. You have created and formatted a volume set using Disk Administrator, but you are not able to write to the partition. What must you do?

6. If you are installing a new version of Windows NT, and would like to restore your present computer configuration, what should you do?

7. Where would you find information regarding detected hardware?

8. What is the likely cause of a lost file when running an MS-DOS-based utility on dual-boot FAT partitions?

Answer Key

Procedure Answers

Page 215

- **To customize the Disk Administrator legend**

    3. Click the down arrow in the **Color and pattern for:** box.

       List the options for which you can customize the color and pattern.

       Primary partition, Logical drive, Stripe Set, Stripe Set with parity, Mirror set, and Volume set.

Page 216

- **To use Disk Administrator to set up the display window**

    What file systems are currently used on drives C and D?

    Drive C is FAT, and drive D is NTFS.

    According to the information in the Disk Administrator window, how much free disk space does your computer have?

    Answers will vary.

Review Answers

Page 234

1. Name at least two reasons for using volume sets.

   To enable using an application that requires more disk space than you have on any single drive.

   To arrange disk space more efficiently, such as combining several partitions into one.

   To free up drive letters for other functions.

2. Name at least two differences between volume sets and stripe sets.

   Volume sets can reside on a single hard disk; stripe sets require two or more hard disks.

   A volume set can consist of areas of varying sizes; a stripe set requires that the areas included in the partition be of approximately the same size.

   In a volume set, data is written to one member of the set at a time until no space remains; in a stripe set, data is written evenly across all of the physical disks, one row at a time.

   Volume sets can be extended; stripe sets cannot.

3. If you want to start an operating system that is on your computer, but is not on the active partition, what would you do?

   Use Disk Administrator to mark the partition containing the operating system as active.

4. If you access Disk Administrator and the **Fault Tolerance** menu is missing, what would you conclude?

   Your computer is running Windows NT Workstation, rather than Windows NT Server.

5. You have created and formatted a volume set using Disk Administrator, but you are not able to write to the partition. What must you do?

   You must shut down and restart the computer.

6. If you are installing a new version of Windows NT, and would like to restore your present computer configuration, what should you do?

   Use Disk Administrator to save your current computer configuration. Then install the new version of Windows NT and restore the current configuration.

7. Where would you find information regarding detected hardware?

   In the registry under HKEY_LOCAL_MACHINE\HARDWARE

8. What is the likely cause of a lost file when running an MS-DOS-based utility on dual-boot FAT partitions?

   The changes to FAT for long file names may not be supported by the utility.

CHAPTER 7

Managing Fault Tolerance

Lesson 1   Fault Tolerance . . . 240

Lesson 2   Recovering from Hard Disk Failure . . . 248

Review . . . 257

About This Chapter

Fault tolerance is the ability of a computer or operating system to respond to a catastrophic event, such as a power outage or a hardware failure, so that no data is lost, and that work in progress is not corrupted.

Microsoft Windows NT Server provides fault tolerance through a system called Redundant Array of Inexpensive Disks (RAID). Data protected by fault tolerance can be recovered and restored. This chapter covers the two RAID levels that are supported by Windows NT Server: *mirror sets* and *stripe sets with parity*. Furthermore, you will practice configuring these two methods of fault tolerance.

Before You Begin

To complete the lessons in this chapter, you must have:

- Two computers that meet the hardware and software requirements as specified in the Getting Started section of "About This Book."
- Completed all practices in Chapter 2, "Installing Windows NT" and Chapter 6, "Managing Partitions."
- One blank, 1.44 MB high-density disk.

Lesson 1: Fault Tolerance

This lesson discusses the various forms of fault tolerance including hardware and software solutions provided by Redundant Arrays of Inexpensive Disks (RAID).

After this lesson, you will be able to:
- Identify supported RAID levels and features.
- Describe the mirror sets function of RAID 1.
- Describe the disk striping function of RAID 5.
- Compare the features of RAID 1 with the features of RAID 5.
- Implement RAID 1 and RAID 5.

Estimated lesson time: 25 minutes

Fault tolerance is the ability of a system to continue functioning when part of the system fails. Fault tolerance is designed to combat problems with disk failures, power outages, or corrupted operating systems, which can include boot files, the operating system itself, or system files. Fully fault-tolerant systems include redundant disk controllers, power supplies, and uninterruptible power supplies (UPSs), which safeguard against local power failure.

Caution Although the data is available and current in a fault-tolerant system, you still need to make backups to protect the information on your hard disks from erroneous deletions, fire, theft, or other disasters. Always remember that fault-tolerant systems should never be used as a replacement for the regular backup of servers and local hard disks. A carefully planned backup strategy is the best insurance for recovering lost or damaged data.

RAID Systems

Windows NT Server provides a software implementation of a fault tolerance technology known as RAID. RAID technology is standardized and categorized in levels. Each level offers various mixes of performance, reliability, and cost. Windows NT Server supports RAID levels 1 and 5 to provide fault tolerance.

How does RAID operate to protect your system? RAID provides fault tolerance by implementing *data redundancy*. With data redundancy, data is written to more than one disk in a manner that allows recovery of the data in the event of a single hard disk failure. This lesson describes the types of RAID that can be implemented by Windows NT Server, and the implications of using each type.

Hardware and Software Implementations of RAID

RAID fault tolerance can be implemented as either a hardware solution or a software solution. The following are points to consider when deciding whether to implement fault tolerance in hardware or software:

- Fault-tolerant software is available only on Windows NT Server. Windows NT Workstation does not provide fault tolerance.
- Software fault tolerance is less expensive than a hardware fault tolerance solution.
- System performance is usually faster with hardware fault tolerance.
- A hardware fault tolerance solution may lock you into a single hardware vendor.
- In a hardware fault tolerance implementation, some hardware vendors allow replacement of a failed drive without shutting down the system.

Regardless of whether you implement fault tolerance by using hardware or software, implementing fault tolerance does not reduce the need for regular backups.

Furthermore, following a failure, there is no fault tolerance until the fault is repaired. If a second fault occurs before the data lost from the first fault is regenerated, you cannot recover the data without restoring it from a backup.

Hardware Implementations of RAID

In a hardware solution, the disk controller interface handles the creation and regeneration of redundant information. Some hardware vendors implement RAID data protection directly into their hardware, as with disk array controller cards. Because these methods are vendor-specific and bypass the fault tolerance software drivers of the operating system, they usually offer performance improvements over software implementations of RAID.

Note For information about hardware implementation of RAID, consult vendor product documentation.

Software Implementations of RAID

Windows NT Server supports two software implementations of RAID: RAID 1, mirror sets, and RAID 5, stripe sets with parity.

RAID 1: Mirror Sets

Mirror sets (RAID 1) use the Windows NT fault tolerance driver (Ftdisk.sys) to simultaneously write the same data to two physical drives. Through duplication, or mirroring, RAID 1 helps to ensure the survival of data in case of failure.

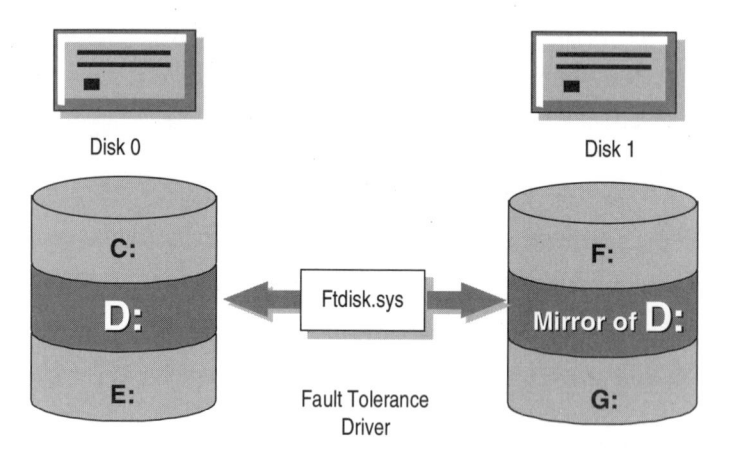

With mirror sets the data on a partition is duplicated on another physical disk. In the preceding illustration, data written to drive D on Disk 0 is duplicated on Disk 1. Any partition, including the boot or system partitions, can be mirrored. This strategy protects a single disk against failure. Windows NT Server configures fault tolerance at the level of the logical drive letter, not the physical disk level. For example, if your computer has one physical disk containing drives C and D, and a second physical disk with sufficient unpartitioned disk space, you can choose to mirror drive C, or drive D, or both.

In terms of cost per megabyte, mirror sets is more expensive than other forms of fault tolerance because disk space use is only 50 percent. However, for peer-to-peer and small server-based LANs, mirror sets usually have a lower initial cost because it requires only two disks.

Mirror sets can provide enhanced read performance because the fault tolerance driver can read from both members of the mirror set at the same time. There can be a slight decrease in write performance when writing to a mirror set because the fault tolerance driver must write to both members simultaneously. When one member of a mirror set fails, read performance returns to normal because the fault tolerance driver works with only the single partition.

Note If either the boot partition or the system partition is part of a mirror set, you should create a fault tolerance boot disk and test it in order to ensure a smooth and rapid data recovery. See the following lesson for the steps to create a fault tolerance boot disk.

Disk Duplexing

A member of a mirror set is one of the physical disk partitions that make up the set. If both physical disks that comprise a mirror set are controlled by the same disk controller, and the disk controller fails, both members of the mirror set are inaccessible. However, a second controller can be installed in the computer so that each disk in the mirror set has its own controller. In this way, the mirror set is protected against both controller failure and disk failure. This arrangement is called *disk duplexing*. Duplexing also reduces bus traffic and potentially improves read performance.

Note Disk duplexing is a hardware enhancement to a Windows NT Server mirror set. No additional software configuration is necessary.

RAID 5: Stripe Sets with Parity

The following illustrations shows stripe sets with parity.

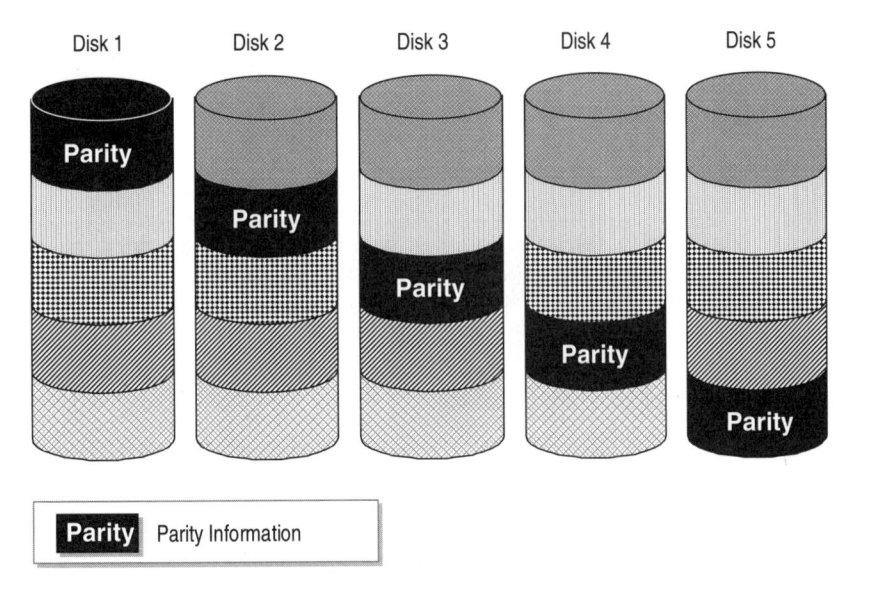

Stripe sets were discussed in Chapter 6, "Managing Partitions." Data written in stripe sets can be protected by the fault tolerance mechanism, stripe sets with parity (RAID 5), which is supported by Windows NT Server.

Parity is a mathematical method of verifying data integrity. Fault tolerance is achieved by adding a parity-information stripe to each disk partition in the volume. In a stripe set with parity, 3 to 32 disks are supported. The parity stripe block is used to reconstruct data for a failed physical disk. If a single disk fails, data is not lost because the Windows NT Server fault tolerance driver has spread the information across the remaining disks. The data can be completely reconstructed. For example, if Disk 3 fails and must be replaced, data for the new disk can be regenerated using the data and parity information in each stripe on the remaining four disks.

All normal write operations on a stripe set with parity are substantially slower than writing to stripe sets without parity due to the parity calculation.

However, stripe sets with parity can offer better read performance than mirror sets, especially with multiple controllers, because data is distributed among multiple drives. However, if a disk fails, the read performance on a stripe set with parity slows because data is being reconstructed using parity information.

Stripe sets with parity can offer a cost advantage over mirror sets because disk utilization is optimized. For example, if there are four disks in a stripe set with parity, the disk space overhead is 25 percent, compared to 50 percent disk space overhead with mirror sets. Stripe sets with parity is currently the most popular approach to fault tolerance.

Note Neither the boot partition nor the system partition can be part of the Windows NT implementation of a stripe set with parity.

RAID 1 vs. RAID 5

The previous section describes RAID 1 (mirror sets) and RAID 5 (stripe sets with parity). The major differences between mirror sets and striping with parity are hardware requirements, performance, and cost. The following illustration shows the major features of the two methods of fault tolerance.

Mirror Sets	Stripe Sets with Parity
■ Supports FAT and NTFS	■ Supports FAT and NTFS
■ Can mirror system or boot partition	■ Cannot stripe system or boot partition
■ Requires two hard disks	■ Requires minimum of three hard disks
■ Has higher cost per megabyte (50 percent utilization)	■ Has lower cost per megabyte
■ Has good read and write performance	■ Has moderate write performance ■ Has excellent read performance
■ Uses less system memory	■ Requires more system memory
	■ Supports up to 32 hard disks

Implementing RAID 1 and RAID 5

Mirror sets and stripe sets with parity can coexist on the same computer. Because a stripe set with parity cannot include the system or boot partition, consider mirroring the system and boot partitions, and protecting the remaining data in stripe sets with parity. For example, as shown in the following illustration, the system and boot partition are located on drive C, which is part of a mirror set. The remaining data on drive D is part of a stripe set with parity.

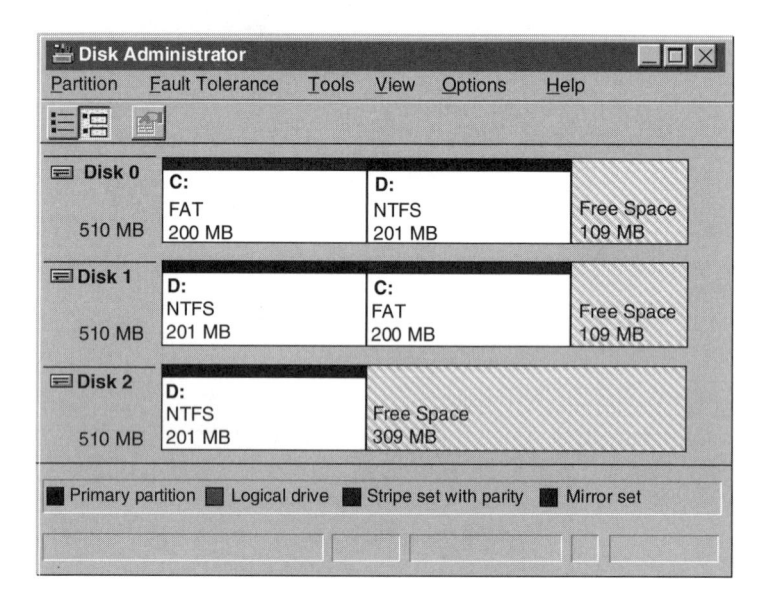

Note that the Windows NT Server Disk Administrator has an additional menu named **Fault Tolerance**, from which both mirror sets and stripe sets with parity are managed.

Considerations When Creating and Deleting a Stripe Set with Parity

The free spaces that are combined to create a stripe set with parity must be the same size. If they are not, Disk Administrator makes each partition of the set approximately the same size and leaves the unused portions of the partitions as usable free space.

Note It is necessary to shut down and then restart the computer after a stripe set with parity is created.

Caution Deleting a mirror set or stripe set with parity deletes all of the information stored in that volume.

Practice

In this procedure, you use the fault tolerance simulation to implement stripe sets with parity, and mirror sets.

Note Complete these procedures on Server1.

▶ **To configure stripe sets with parity**

1. Log on as Administrator.

2. Click the **Start** button, point to **Programs**, point to **Technical Support Training**, point to **Simulations**, and then click **Implementing Fault Tolerance Simulation**.

    The simulation starts, and Disk Administrator appears.

3. Click an area of free space on Disk 0 to be used for creating a stripe set with parity.

4. Hold down the CTRL key and click an area of free space on Disk 1 and an area of free space on Disk 2.

5. On the **Fault Tolerance** menu, click **Create Stripe Set with Parity**.

    The Create Stripe Set with Parity dialog box appears. The default size is three times the size of the smallest area of selected free space.

6. In the **Create stripe set of total size** box, type **300** and then click **OK**.

    The partitions now have the same drive letter (G) and are highlighted in green. This indicates that they are part of a stripe set with parity.

▶ **To configure mirror sets**

1. Click drive D to begin creating a mirror set.

2. Hold down the CTRL key and click an area of free space on Disk 1.

    The area must be equal to or greater than the partition selected in the preceding step.

3. On the **Fault Tolerance** menu, click **Establish Mirror**.

    The partitions should now have the same drive letter (D) and be highlighted in purple. This indicates that they are part of a mirror set.

▶ **To exit and save changes**

- On the **Partition** menu, click **Exit** to end the simulation.

    If this had not been a simulation, Disk Administrator would have prompted you to save your changes.

Lesson 2: Recovering from Hard Disk Failure

Fault tolerance duplicates system and user data in case of disk failure. The previous lesson described the implementation of mirror sets and stripe sets with parity. This lesson describes procedures to recover data that was saved by mirror sets and stripe sets with parity.

When a member of a mirror set or a stripe set with parity fails (as may occur in a power loss or hardware failure), the fault tolerance driver directs all I/O to the remaining members of the fault-tolerant volume. This ensures continuous service. If you have used Server Manager to configure the computer to send administrative alerts, and the Alerter service is running, then an alert message is sent to notify the specified accounts that this failure has occurred.

If the failed disk is part of a mirror set that contains the boot partition, and if the failed disk is the primary physical drive, then a fault tolerance boot disk will be required to restart the system.

After this lesson, you will be able to:
- Describe the procedure for recovering from the failure of a member of a stripe set with parity.
- Describe the procedure for recovering from the failure of a member of a mirror set.
- Create a fault tolerance boot disk.
- Describe how Advanced RISC Computing (ARC) paths identify partitions.

Estimated lesson time: 40 minutes

Regenerating a Stripe Set with Parity

If a member of a stripe set with parity fails, the computer continues to operate and to gain access to all data. However, as data is requested, the Windows NT Server fault tolerance driver uses the parity bits to regenerate the missing data in RAM. When this happens, system performance slows down.

To regenerate the data and return the computer to its previous performance level, use Disk Administrator to select an area of free space to replace the failed member and then click the **Regenerate** command on the **Fault Tolerance** menu. If you do not have sufficient free space, replace the failed drive and then regenerate your data.

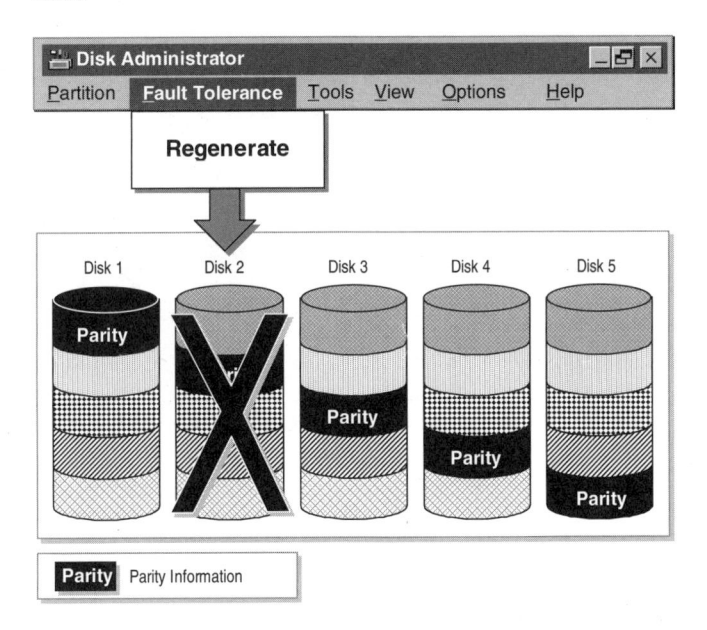

The fault tolerance driver reads the parity information from the stripes on the other member disks. It then recreates the data of the missing member and writes the data to the new member.

Recovering from Mirror Set Failure

Because of the data duplication involved in mirror sets, the system continues to function when a member of the mirror set fails. In order to replace the failed member, an administrator must first "break" the mirror set.

In order to break a mirror set, do the following:

1. From Disk Administrator, use the **Break Mirror** command on the **Fault Tolerance** menu to break the mirror set. Break the mirror set relationship to isolate the remaining *working* partition as a separate volume. Regardless of which disk contains the fault, when the mirror set is broken, Disk Administrator assigns the mirrored volume the next available drive letter.

In the following illustration, drive D on Disk 0 is mirrored on Disk 1. Drive D on Disk 1 is the secondary member of the mirror set. When the mirror set is broken, drive D on Disk 1 is assigned the next available drive letter, H.

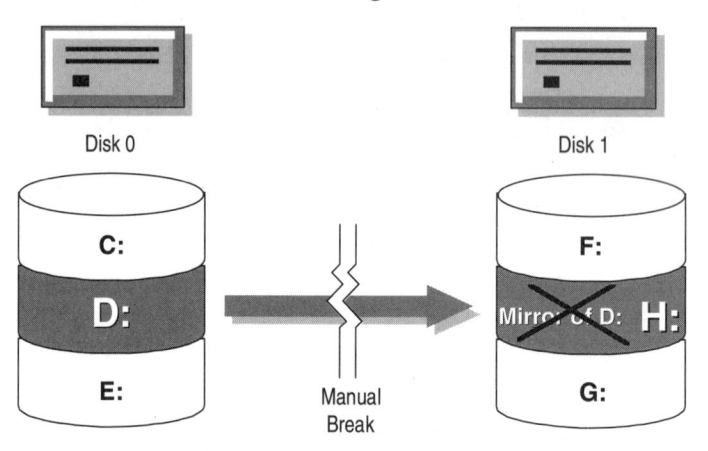

2. If the failed drive is the primary member of the mirror set, it may be necessary to assign the drive letter that was previously assigned to the complete mirror set to the working member of the mirror set. For example, if the disk has any shared resources, or if a shortcut points to a location on a particular drive letter, you would need to reassign the drive letter to maintain your computer's functionality.

   In the preceding illustration, assume that the failure occurred on Disk 0. The working member (now drive H) needs to retain the drive letter D assignment. Using Disk Administrator, first unassign drive D on Disk 0, and then reassign drive letter D to drive H.

3. Delete the *failed* partition.

   Note You can use Event Viewer to look at the System log to determine which partition failed.

4. Using free space on another disk, create a new mirror set relationship.

   For the procedure to establish a mirror set, see "Establishing a Mirror Set" in Windows NT Server Help. When the computer is restarted, the data from the good partition is copied to the new member of the mirror set.

Note Replacing a failed member is not the only reason that you would break a mirror set. You would also break the mirror set if you wanted to reclaim the disk space for other purposes.

Creating a Fault Tolerance Boot Disk

When making a mirror set for the boot partition or system partition of a computer running Windows NT Server, it is important to create a fault tolerance boot disk for use in case of physical disk failure.

Remember that in a software implementation of RAID, the system and boot partitions cannot be members of a stripe set with parity; only mirror sets can provide fault tolerance for the system and boot partitions.

The following illustration outlines the steps involved in creating a fault tolerance boot disk.

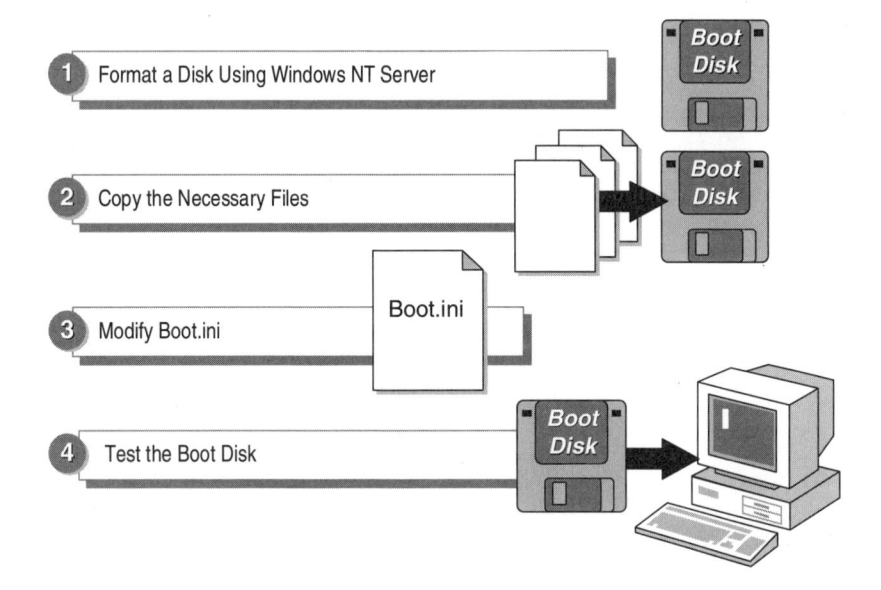

1. Format a Disk Using Windows NT Server
2. Copy the Necessary Files
3. Modify Boot.ini
4. Test the Boot Disk

The following explanation describes the steps used to create a fault tolerance boot disk in detail:

1. Format a floppy disk on a computer running Windows NT Server. This writes information to the boot track of the disk so that it looks for the appropriate loader file when the system is started.

   Note A fault tolerance boot disk must be formatted on a computer running Windows NT Server.

2. Copy the following files from the primary partition of the computer running Windows NT Server to the boot disk. Several of the files are ordinarily hidden in the root folder. Use Windows NT Explorer to display hidden files.

x86-based computers	RISC-based computers
Ntldr	Osloader.exe
Ntdetect.com	Hal.dll
Ntbootdd.sys (for SCSI disks not using SCSI BIOS)*	*.pal (contains PAL code—software subroutines that provide an operating system with direct control of the processor)
Boot.ini	

   *The Ntbootdd.sys file appears only on SCSI systems in which the SCSI BIOS is not used.

3. On Intel x86-based computers, edit Boot.ini to change your operating system entry to point to the mirrored copy of the boot partition.

   On RISC-based computers, modify the firmware variables shown in the following table.

Variable	Value
OSLOADER	multi(0)disk(0)fdisk(0)\Osloader.exe
SYSTEMPARTITION	multi(0)disk(0)fdisk(0)
OSLOADPARTITION	path to the secondary mirrored partition
OSLOADFILENAME	path to the Windows NT Server root directory

4. Test the boot disk to ensure that it works and boots using data from the mirrored copy of the boot partition; do this by shutting down Windows NT Server, inserting the fault tolerance boot disk, and then restarting the computer.

Whenever partition path information has been changed, it is important to update the Boot.ini file on the fault tolerance boot disk.

Note For more information on creating fault tolerance boot disks, see Chapter 7, "Protecting Data," in Microsoft Windows NT Server *Concepts and Planning*.

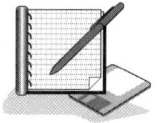

Practice

In these procedures, you create a boot disk for the Intel platform that can be used in the event that your computer's boot partition is not accessible. Then, you test the boot disk by starting the computer using the Windows NT boot disk.

Note Complete these procedures on Server1.

▶ **To create a Windows NT boot disk**

1. Format a floppy disk using the Windows NT Explorer, or go to a command prompt and use the **Format.exe** command.
2. Copy the following files from the root of drive C to the root of drive A.

   Ntldr

   Ntdetect.com

   Boot.ini

   Bootsect.dos (only if it exists)

   Ntbootdd.sys (only if it exists)
3. Do not remove the disk from the drive.

▶ **To test the Windows NT boot disk**

1. Shut down and then restart your computer using the Windows NT boot disk you just created.

   Did Windows NT start successfully?

   _____

   _____

   _____

2. Remove the floppy from the disk drive.

Understanding ARC Paths

Creating a fault tolerance boot disk for recovery of a mirrored boot or system partition requires editing the Advanced RISC Computing (ARC) names in the Boot.ini file. You need to change the ARC path so that it points to the secondary or mirrored partition rather than the primary or boot or system partition. You are familiar with identifying the paths of $x86$-based computers by supplying a drive letter, such as C:\ or D:\. The ARC paths in the Boot.ini file use a different naming convention, which is explained in this section.

When you install Windows NT, a Boot.ini file is generated. The Boot.ini file contains the ARC paths used to point to location(s) of the operating system(s) files. The following represents an ARC path in the boot.ini file:

multi(0)disk(0)rdisk(1)partition(2)

The following table describes the ARC naming conventions used by Windows NT to generate the ARC paths:

Convention	Description
multi/scsi	Identifies the hardware adapter/disk controller as either multi or SCSI.
	SCSI indicates a SCSI controller on which SCSI BIOS is not enabled.
	All other adapters or disk controllers are represented by multi. These include SCSI disk controllers with the BIOS enabled so that the SCSI disk is accessed by the SCSI BIOS. For Windows NT Server, this could be a disk supported by the Atdisk, Abiosdsk, or Cpqarray drivers.
	Remember, use multi in all cases except when Ntbootdd.sys is on your system. The Ntbootdd.sys file appears only on SCSI systems in which the SCSI BIOS is not used.
(x)	Ordinal number of the hardware adapter. For example, if there are two SCSI adapters in the system, the first to load and initialize is assigned the ordinal number 0 and the next adapter is assigned the ordinal number 1.
disk(*y*)	SCSI bus number. For settings of multi, this value is always 0.
rdisk(*z*)	Ordinal number of the disk (ignored for SCSI controllers).
partition(*a*)	Ordinal number of the partition.

RISC-based computers use the SCSI naming convention. In both multi and SCSI conventions, multi/scsi, disk, and rdisk numbers are assigned starting with (0), while partition numbers are assigned starting with (1). All non-extended partitions are assigned numbers first, followed by all logical drives in extended partitions.

Note SCSI and multi ARC naming conventions are similar except that the SCSI notation varies the disk( ) parameter for successive disks on one controller, while the multi format varies the rdisk( ) parameter.

The following illustration shows a computer running Windows NT Server that has three hard disks divided into five partitions. It also shows the ARC path for the boot partition that is located on drive G.

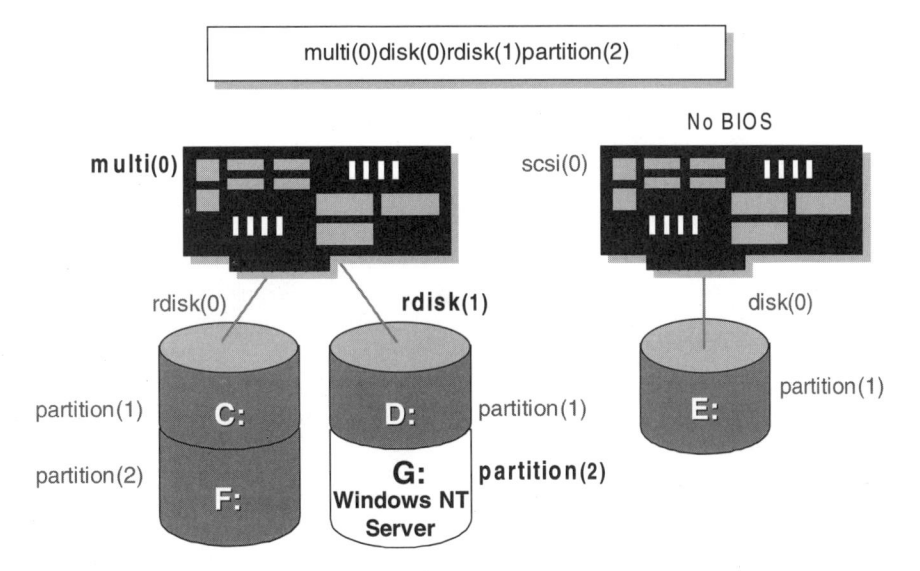

multi(0)disk(0)rdisk(1)partition(2)

multi(0) — rdisk(0) — partition(1) C:, partition(2) F:
rdisk(1) — partition(1) D:, partition(2) G: Windows NT Server

scsi(0) No BIOS — disk(0) — partition(1) E:

What would the ARC path be if the system files were located on drive C?

What would the ARC path be if the system files were located on drive E?

Summary

The following information summarizes the key points in this chapter:

- Fault tolerance is the ability of a system to protect against loss of data when part of the system fails. Both hardware and software fault tolerance solutions are available. While hardware solutions can provide enhanced performance over software solutions, they can also be more costly.

- Windows NT Server supports two software fault tolerance methods, mirror sets and stripe sets with parity. The factors that influence whether to use either one or both methods include cost, performance, and reliability.

- When you implement fault tolerance, keep the following considerations in mind:
  - Fault tolerance is *not* a substitute for regular backups.
  - Following a failure, fault tolerance has not been achieved until the fault is repaired and the data is restored.
  - Create a fault tolerance boot disk to restore the system in the case of a physical disk failure of a mirror set containing the boot or system partition.

For more information on	See
RAID, RAID terminology, and disk arrays	*The RAIDbook, a Source Book for Disk Array Technology*
Stripe sets, mirror sets, and stripe sets with parity on Windows NT Server	Chapter 7, "Protecting Data," in Microsoft Windows NT Server *Concepts and Planning*
Configuring, and recovering from failures of, mirror sets and stripe sets with parity	"Preparing for and Performing Recovery" in the *Resource Guide* of the *Microsoft Windows NT Server Resource Kit*
Creating fault tolerance boot disks	Chapter 7, "Protecting Data," in Microsoft Windows NT Server *Concepts and Planning*

Review

1. Your computer running Windows NT Server has the following disk configuration:
   - Disk 0: drive C (300 MB, system/boot partition), drive D: (700 MB, data), and 500 MB of free space.
   - Disk 1: 750 MB free space.
   - Disk 2: 1 GB free space.

   You want to install additional Microsoft BackOffice components on this computer. How can you protect your computer's data and optimize its performance using Windows NT fault tolerance?

2. The disk containing the system/boot partition for your computer running Windows NT Server failed. The system/boot partition was part of a mirror set, but your computer only tries to boot from the original system/boot partition. How can you successfully boot Windows NT Server from the mirrored system/boot partition?

Answer Key

Procedure Answers

Page 253

▶ **To test the Windows NT boot disk**

1. Shut down and then restart your computer using the Windows NT boot disk you just created.

   Did Windows NT start successfully?

   Yes. The boot disk was created properly.

   No. Verify that you formatted the floppy disk using Windows NT, and then compare the files on your boot disk with those listed in the preceding procedure.

Page 255

Understanding ARC Paths

What would the ARC path be if the system files were located on drive C?

multi(0)disk(0)rdisk(0)partition(1)

What would the ARC path be if the system files were located on drive E?

scsi(0)disk(0)rdisk(0)partition(1)

Review Answers

Page 257

1. Your computer running Windows NT Server has the following disk configuration:

   - Disk 0: drive C (300 MB, system/boot partition), drive D: (700 MB, data), and 500 MB of free space.
   - Disk 1: 750 MB free space.
   - Disk 2: 1 GB free space.

   You want to install additional Microsoft BackOffice components on this computer. How can you protect your computer's data and optimize its performance using Windows NT fault tolerance?

   Mirror drive C on Disk 2, and create a 1.5 GB stripe set with parity spanning all three disks.

2. The disk containing the system/boot partition for your computer running Windows NT Server failed. The system/boot partition was part of a mirror set, but your computer only tries to boot from the original system/boot partition. How can you successfully boot Windows NT Server from the mirrored system/boot partition?

   With a fault-tolerance boot disk. You must edit the Boot.ini file to point to the mirrored boot partition.

CHAPTER 8

Supporting Applications

Lesson 1 Windows NT Architecture Overview . . . 261

Lesson 2 Subsystems Overview . . . 268

Lesson 3 Windows NT Task Manager . . . 270

Lesson 4 Supporting Win32-based Applications . . . 276

Lesson 5 Supporting MS-DOS-based and Win16-based Applications . . . 280

Lesson 6 Supporting Applications on Different Hardware Platforms . . . 297

Lesson 7 Distributed Component Object Model . . . 300

Lesson 8 Managing Applications . . . 306

Review . . . 312

About This Chapter

Microsoft Windows NT is designed to run applications written for existing operating systems such as Microsoft MS-DOS, OS/2, POSIX, and Microsoft Windows 3.*x*. It achieves this through *environment subsystems*, which emulate different operating system environments. This chapter describes each of the Windows NT environment subsystems and their configurations. The chapter also addresses general application management.

Before You Begin

To complete the lessons in this chapter, you must have:

- Two computers that meet the hardware and software requirements as specified in the Getting Started section of "About This Book."
- Completed all practices in Chapter 2, "Installing Windows NT."

Lesson 1: Windows NT Architecture Overview

A working knowledge of Windows NT begins with an understanding of the system architecture. This lesson introduces key aspects of the Windows NT architecture that affect the operating system functionality and performance.

After this lesson, you will be able to:

- Define the two processor modes used by Windows NT: user mode and kernel mode.
- Describe the function of the components that make up the Windows NT architecture.
- Describe the Windows NT memory model.

Estimated lesson time: 20 minutes

User Mode vs. Kernel Mode

Windows NT uses two modes, *user mode* and *kernel mode*, to maintain operating efficiency and integrity. The following illustration shows the components of the Windows NT architecture, separated into user mode components and kernel mode components.

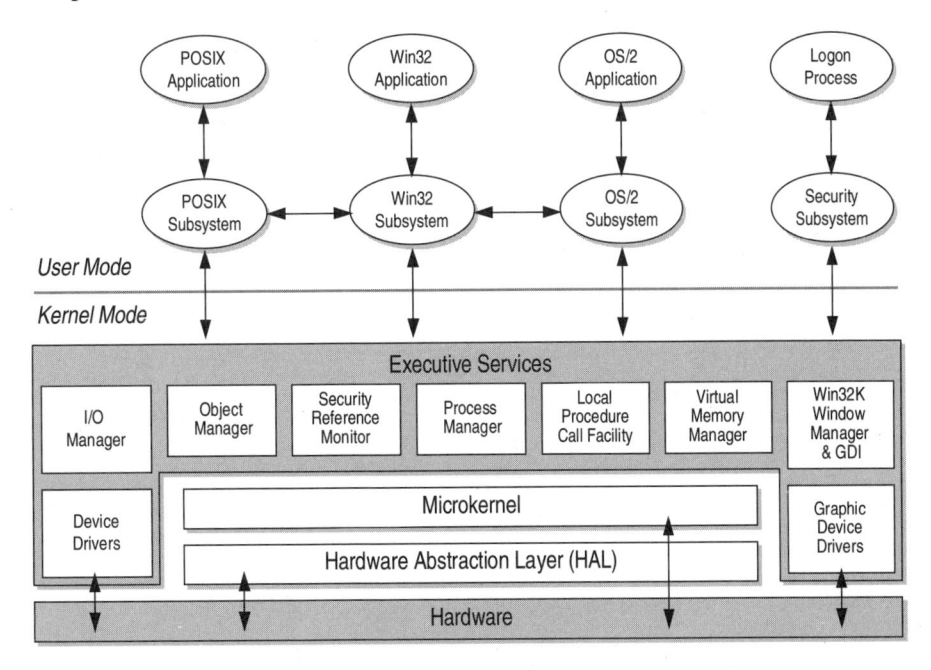

User Mode

User mode is a less privileged processor mode than kernel mode, and has no direct access to hardware. Code running in user mode acts directly only in its own address space. It uses well-defined operating system application program interfaces (APIs) to request system services. Applications, and the subsystems that support them, run in user mode. When an application is started, a Windows NT *process* is created. A process is implemented as an *object*. An object consists of an executable program, a set of virtual memory addresses, and one or more threads.

User mode processes:

- Have no direct access to hardware. To protect against malfunctioning applications or unauthorized user access, user mode processes cannot directly access hardware. Hardware access requests must be granted by a kernel mode component.
- Are limited to an assigned address space. Windows NT helps protect the operating system by limiting the areas of memory that a user mode process can access. This limitation is accomplished by assigning only certain addresses to the user mode process.
- Can be paged out of physical memory into virtual RAM on a hard disk. *Virtual memory,* also known as virtual RAM, allows hard disk space to be used as if it were additional memory. In this manner, the user mode processes have access to more memory than is actually available to them. The details of virtual memory are covered later in this lesson.
- Process at a lower priority than kernel mode components. User mode processes are lower in priority—and therefore typically have less access to the CPU cycles—than processes that run in kernel mode. This ensures that the operating system does not slow down or have to wait while an application finishes processing.

The user mode environment subsystems shown in the preceding illustration are covered in the next lesson.

Kernel Mode

Kernel mode is the privileged mode of operation in which the code has direct access to all hardware and all memory, including the address spaces of all user mode processes. The following list outlines some of the capabilities of the kernel mode components. Kernel mode components:

- Can access hardware directly.
- Can access all of the memory on the computer.
- Are not moved to the virtual memory page file on the hard disk.
- Process at a higher priority than user mode processes.

The kernel mode in Windows NT is comprised of the Windows NT Executive, which includes the Executive Services, the microkernel, and the hardware abstraction layer (HAL).

Windows NT Executive

Windows NT Executive is the generic name for a number of subsystems and components of the operating system that run in kernel mode.

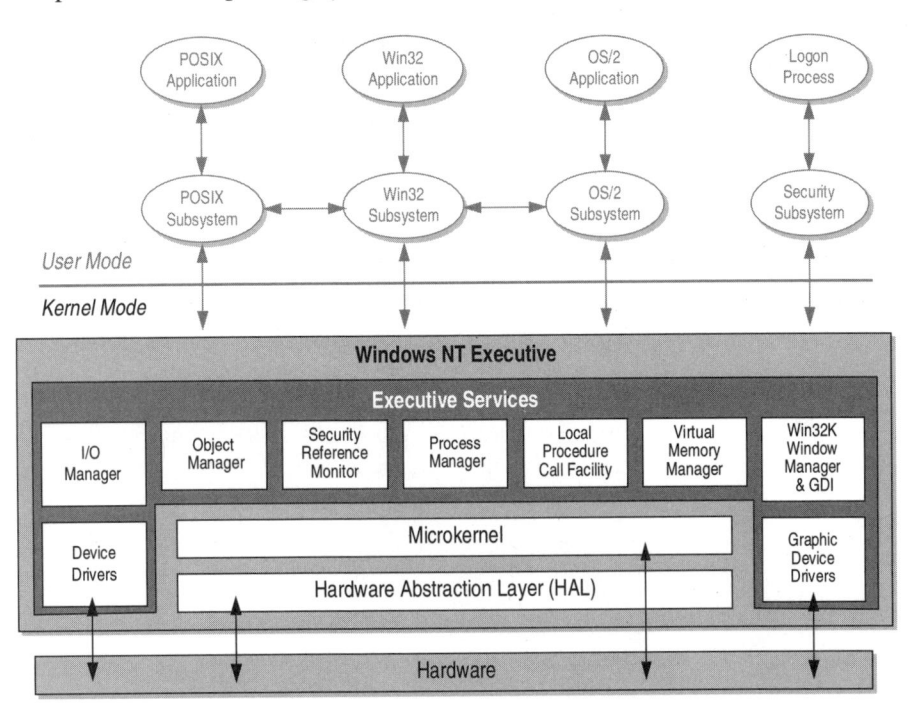

Windows NT Executive provides support for user applications and environment subsystems. Within the Windows NT Executive, basic functions of the operating system are integrated through three layered components; the Executive Services, the microkernel, and the HAL.

Executive Services Components

The Windows NT Executive Services are central to all major operating system functions; therefore, it is important to protect them from user mode applications and subsystems. This is accomplished by having the Executive Services run in kernel mode.

The following table describes the function of each component of Executive Services.

Executive Service	Function
Managers	Various modules that manage I/O, objects, security, processes, interprocess communications (IPC), virtual memory, and window and graphics management.
Device drivers	Software components that control hardware access.

Note If you are familiar with the previous releases of Windows NT, you may notice a change in the components listed as Executive Services. In Windows NT version 3.51 or earlier, the Window Manager and graphics device interface (GDI) were located in the Win32 subsystem. In Windows NT 4.0, this functionality is provided by the Win32K Window Manager and GDI of the Windows NT Executive Services. The Win32K Window Manager and GDI are responsible for handling all graphical user interface (GUI)-related I/O requests, maintaining the display, and providing a common GUI for all applications.

For more information about user mode and kernel mode in Windows NT, see Appendix B "Changes to Kernel Mode, User Mode, and GDI in Windows NT 4.0."

Microkernel

The microkernel provides the most basic operating system services, such as thread scheduling, first-level interrupt handling, and deferred procedure calls. The microkernel resides between the Executive Services and HAL layers.

Hardware Abstraction Layer

The HAL is a kernel-mode library of hardware-manipulating routines provided by Microsoft or by the hardware manufacturer. This software layer hides the characteristics of the platform behind standard entry points so that all platforms and architectures look alike to the operating system. It enables the same operating system to run on different platforms with different processors. For example, it allows Windows NT to run on single or multiprocessor computers and enables higher-level device drivers, such as graphics display drivers, to format data for different kind of monitors.

The Windows NT Memory Model

The memory architecture for Windows NT is a demand-paged, virtual memory system. It is based on a flat, linear 32-bit address space, which allows each process in Windows NT to have access to up to 4 GB of memory.

Virtual Memory Architecture

With *virtual memory*, all applications seem to have a full range of memory addresses available. Windows NT does this by giving each application a private memory range called a *virtual memory space* and by mapping that virtual memory to physical memory.

Windows NT maps physical and virtual memory addresses in 4 KB blocks called *pages*. Each virtual memory space has room for 4 GB of addresses. This address space is made up of 1,048,576 (1 MB) 4 KB pages.

Because few systems contain enough RAM to provide 4 GB for each application, the operating system allocates the available physical RAM pages between the virtual memory spaces. While the application operates as though it is in RAM, in reality, the pages are often in virtual memory. Pages in virtual memory can have one of the following three characteristics:

- Most of the pages are actually empty, because the application is not using them.
- Pages that are being used are redirected by a pointer, invisible to the application, to physical RAM.
- Some pages that have not been used recently contain another pointer, also invisible to the application, to a 4 KB section of the *paging file* on the hard disk.

Note For information on how to configure virtual memory, see Chapter 3, "Configuring the Windows NT Environment."

Virtual Memory Process

The virtual memory process makes use of the paging file(s) on the hard disk (Pagefile.sys). With virtual memory in Windows NT, some of the application code and other information is kept in RAM while other information can be temporarily paged into virtual memory. When the paged information is required again, Windows NT reads it back into RAM, paging other information to virtual memory if necessary.

The process of managing which pages are stored in RAM, and which are stored in the paging file, is called *demand paging*. The Windows NT demand paging procedure is shown in the following illustration.

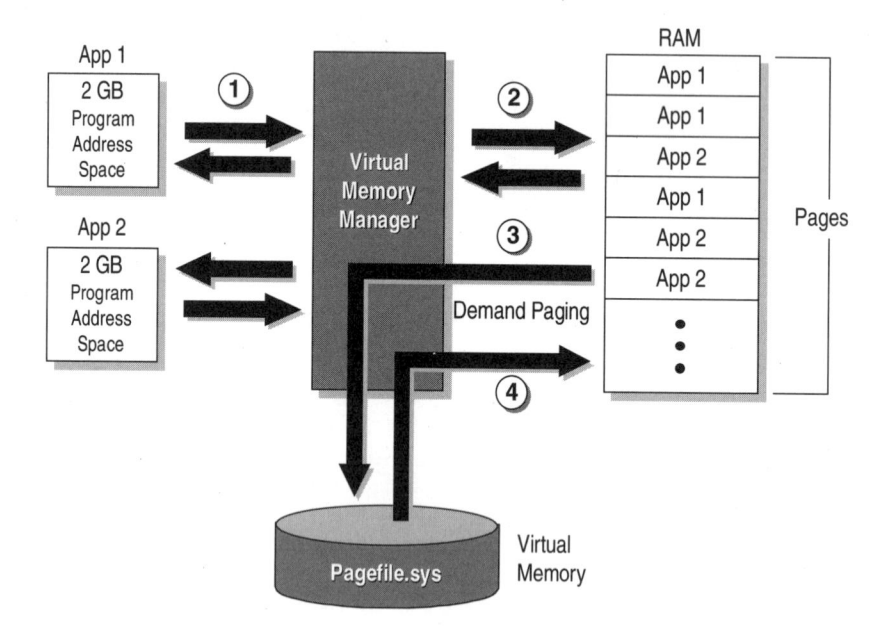

The following steps describe this procedure:

1. An application attempts to store data in memory.
2. The Virtual Memory Manager intercepts the request, determines how many pages are needed to fill the request, and maps unused physical memory to any empty address spaces in the application's virtual memory space, as needed. The Virtual Memory Manager hides the organization of physical memory from the application. When an application calls for a memory location, it maps to a non-conflicting memory address.
3. If there is not enough unused physical memory available, the Virtual Memory Manager uses demand paging to find pages of RAM that have not been used recently. It then copies these pages to the paging file (Pagefile.sys) on the hard disk. The newly freed RAM is remapped to fill the application's request.
4. When data stored in the paging file is needed, the pages are copied back into RAM. The new RAM location is mapped back to the same virtual address required by the application.

Virtual Memory Advantages

The linear addressing scheme used by the Virtual Memory Manager helps make Windows NT portable because it is compatible with the memory addressing of processors such as the MIPS R4000, IBM RS/6000, and DEC Alpha AXP.

Windows NT makes memory use efficient, and consistent. As a result, it allows programmers to write large and concise applications. It also allows users to run more applications at one time than a system's physical memory would otherwise allow.

Note For more information about Windows NT architecture, see Chapter 5, "Windows NT 4.0 Workstation Architecture," in the *Microsoft Windows NT Workstation Resource Kit.*

Lesson 2: Subsystems Overview

Windows NT supports applications by using environment subsystems. An environment subsystem provides API services to applications written for a specific environment or operating system. This lesson describes the subsystem architecture that allows these applications to run, and specifically describes the function of the Win32 subsystem.

After this lesson, you will be able to:
- Explain the purpose and function of the environment subsystems.
- Describe the Windows NT subsystem architecture.

Estimated lesson time: 5 minutes

The following illustration shows the relationships that exist between the environment and Win32 subsystems and Executive Services.

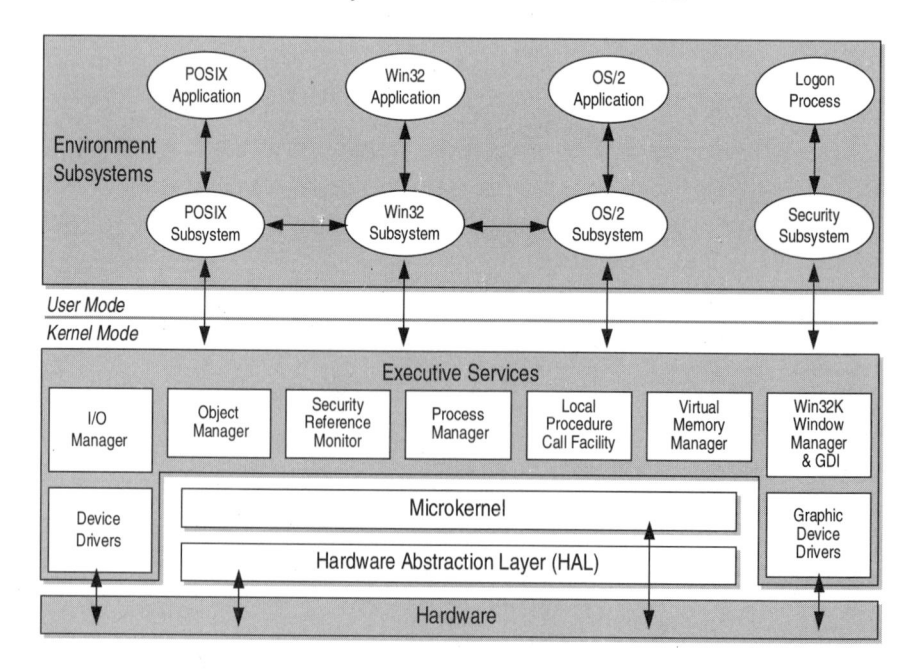

Environment Subsystems

An environment subsystem in Windows NT is an intermediary between an application designed for a specific operating environment, and the Executive Services. The environment subsystem translates environment-specific instructions from an application into instructions that the Executive Services can carry out. There are two Windows NT environment subsystems that support applications designed for other operating environments: the POSIX subsystem and the OS/2 subsystem. These subsystems receive all function requests from the applications that they support. A subsystem either carries out the request itself or passes it to the Windows NT Executive Services.

The Win32 Subsystem

The Win32 subsystem is sometimes referred to as the client/server subsystem, the CSR subsystem, or CSRSS. It supports Win32-, MS-DOS-, and Windows 3.*x*-based applications and the environment subsystems. The Win32 subsystem also supports console applications—applications not written for the Microsoft Windows GUI—application shutdown, and error handling functions.

Note The security subsystem supports the logon process. It does not support other applications.

Subsystems Interactions with Executive Services

The Windows NT Executive Services perform basic operating system functions for all subsystems. The Executive Services reside in kernel mode. This provides stability for the operating system, because no application can directly access the Executive Services. In this way, a malfunctioning user-mode component (such as an application) cannot unintentionally stop a kernel mode component.

All GUI-related I/O requests are channeled to the Win32K Window Manager and GDI component of Executive Services which is responsible for maintaining the display. This provides a common GUI for all applications.

The subsystems build on the Executive Services to produce environments that meet the specific needs of their client applications. In this way, common operating system functions are implemented once in the Executive Services, rather than duplicated in each subsystem. This reduces the effort required to develop new subsystems and makes them easier to maintain.

Lesson 3: Windows NT Task Manager

Task Manager is a Windows NT utility that provides information about the current processes running in Windows NT. In this lesson, you learn the functions of Task Manager and how to use Task Manager to manage applications and processes.

After this lesson, you will be able to:
- Describe the function and capabilities of Task Manager.
- Use Task Manager to view running applications and processes.
- Use Task Manager to prioritize applications.
- Use Task Manager to end a process.
- User Task Manager to view system performance.

Estimated lesson time: 20 minutes

You use Task Manager to monitor and prioritize applications and processes, and to view system performance data.

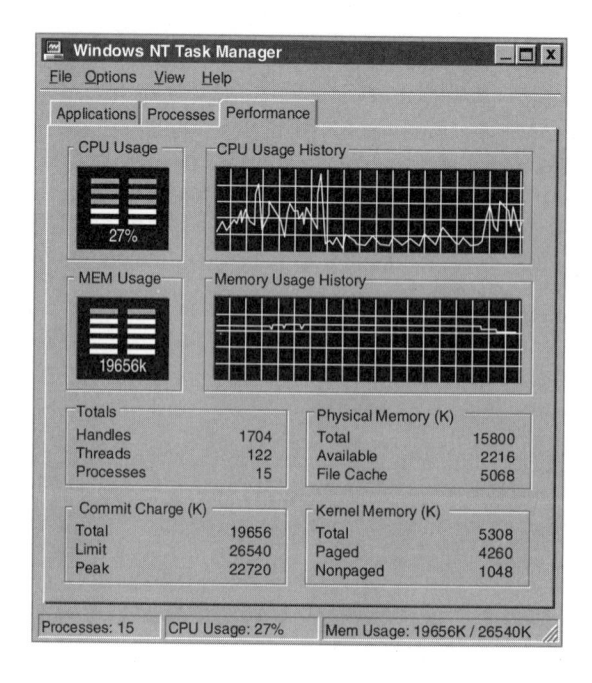

Task Manager Capabilities

Task Manager includes the following capabilities:

- Displays running applications and processes, including 16-bit processes.
- Displays the most commonly used performance measures for processes, including processor time, physical memory usage, virtual memory size, page faults, base priority, and thread count.
- Displays line graphs and instantaneous values of CPU and memory use for the computer.
- Sets processor affinity for an application on a multiprocessor computer, changes the base priority of a process, and activates a debugger if you have one.

Task Manager Tabs

There are three tabs in the **Windows NT Task Manager** dialog box: Applications, Processes, and Performance. The **Applications** tab shows the status of the programs or tasks that are currently running on your computer. From this window you can end, switch to, or start a program. The **Processes** tab shows information about the processes that are currently running on your computer. The **Performance** tab is used to monitor your computer's system performance.

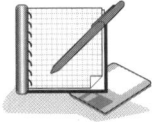

Practice

In these procedures, you use Task Manager to view the applications running on your desktop and the processes executing in the background.

Note Complete these procedures on Workstation1.

▶ **To access Task Manager**
- Start Task Manager using one of these methods:
    - Press CTRL+SHIFT+ESC.
    - Right-click the Windows NT taskbar, and then click **Task Manager**.
    - Press CTRL+ALT+DELETE, and then click **Task Manager**.

▶ **To start applications**

1. Click the **Start** button, point to **Programs**, point to **Accessories**, and then click **Calculator**.
2. Click the **Start** button, point to **Programs**, point to **Accessories**, and then click **Paint**.
3. Click the **Start** button, point to **Programs**, point to **Accessories**, and then click **WordPad**.
4. Minimize Calculator, Paint, and WordPad.

▶ **To view running applications using Task Manager**

1. Switch to Task Manager.
2. Click the **Applications** tab.

   You see a list of the running applications. Notice that there are buttons that allow you to end an application, switch to an application window, or to start a new application.

3. Click **Document - WordPad**, and then click **End Task**.

   WordPad is no longer listed in the task list.

▶ **To view the processes options**

1. In Task Manager, click the **Processes** tab.

   You see a list of running processes and measures of their performance. The Task Manager process table includes every process that runs in its own address space, including all applications and system services.

2. On the **View** menu, click **Select Columns**.

   A **Select Columns** dialog box appears, displaying a list of options that allows you to obtain additional information about a process.

3. Select the **Base Priority** check box, and then click **OK**.
4. On the **Options** menu, select **Show 16-bit tasks**.

   This option allows you to include 16-bit applications in the process table.

5. Use Task Manager to close **Calculator** and **Paint**.

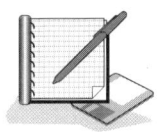

Practice

In these procedures, you use Task Manager to change the base priority of an active process and to end a process.

Note Complete these procedures on Workstation1.

▶ **To view the priority of a running application**

1. From C:\Lab Files\Apps, start **Counter**.
2. Start a second instance of Counter.
3. Arrange Task Manager and the two Counters windows so that you can view them all on the screen.
4. In Task Manager, click the **Processes** tab.
5. If necessary, resize the Task Manager window until you can see the **Base Priority** column.

   What is the priority of each Counter?

▶ **To change the priority of a running application**

1. On the **Processes** tab, right-click either instance of Counter.exe.
2. Point to **Set Priority**, and then click **Low**.

   A **Task Manager Warning** dialog box appears.
3. Click **Yes** to change the priority of Counter.exe.

   The low-priority instance of Counter.exe runs significantly slower than the normal-priority instance.
4. On the **Processes** tab, right-click the instance of Counter.exe that is running at low priority.
5. Point to **Set Priority**, and then click **High**.

   A **Task Manager Warning** dialog box appears.
6. Click **Yes** to change the priority of Counter.exe.

   The high-priority instance of Counter.exe runs significantly faster than the normal-priority instance.

▶ **To end a process using Task Manager**

1. On the **Processes** tab, right-click the instance of Counter.exe that is running at high priority.
2. Click **End Process**.

    A **Task Manager Warning** dialog box appears.

3. Click **Yes** to terminate this instance of Counter.exe.
4. Use Task Manager to end the instance of Counter.exe that is running at normal priority.

Assigning a Process to a Processor

On multiprocessor computers, processor affinity assigns the threads of a process to run on the various processors. The Windows NT microkernel distributes processing over all processors, based on priority. Often, the threads of a single process run on more than one processor. Windows NT uses an algorithm called *soft affinity* to distribute processor load. This means that when possible, Windows NT reassigns threads to the same processor on which they previously ran, but Windows NT does not block the threads to wait for that processor if it is in use.

You can limit the execution of an application to one or more processors. This is known as *hard affinity*. To select processors for a process, right-click the process name on the Task Manager **Processes** tab, click **Set Affinity**, and then click one or more processors from the list. The **Set Affinity** option is visible only on multiprocessor computers. Although it is possible to reserve a processor for a specific thread, this usually results in a decrease in overall performance because all other threads can only use the remaining processors.

Monitoring System Performance

When Task Manager is running, a CPU usage gauge that shows system performance appears on the taskbar in the status area at the end opposite the **Start** button. When the cursor is paused over this icon, the ToolTip displays the percentage of CPU usage.

The status bar at the bottom of the **Performance** tab also displays performance data. It shows the total number of processes, CPU usage, and memory use of the system.

Practice

In this procedure, you use the Task Manager **Performance** tab to monitor your computer's performance.

Note Complete this procedure on Workstation1.

▶ **To view the performance**

1. In Task Manager, click the **Performance** tab.

   Notice the dynamic overview of system performance, including a graph and numeric display of processor and memory usage.

2. Double-click the **CPU Usage History** box.

   The **CPU Usage History** box is expanded.

3. Double-click the **CPU Usage History** box.

   The **Performance** tab appears.

4. Close Task Manager.

Note For additional information on the Task Manager, see the *Microsoft Windows NT Workstation Resource Kit*.

Lesson 4: Supporting Win32-based Applications

The Win32 subsystem maintains the display and manages user input for all applications. This lesson describes the APIs used by Win32-based applications and describes the Microsoft DirectX™ set of APIs supported by Windows NT.

After this lesson, you will be able to:
- Describe how Windows NT supports Win32-based applications.
- Describe Windows NT support for OLE/ActiveX™ and OpenGL (Graphics Language) APIs.
- Describe the DirectX APIs supported by Windows NT.

Estimated lesson time: 10 minutes

Win32-based Applications

Win32-based applications benefit from the inherent reliability of Windows NT and can take full advantage of the following features of Windows NT:

- Multithreading, to enhance system performance
- OLE/ActiveX and OpenGL support
- DirectX set of APIs in Windows NT

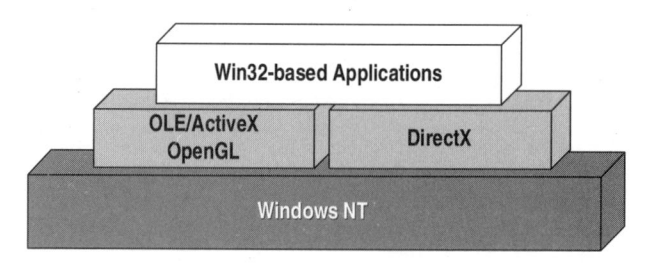

Multithreaded Applications

Win32-based applications can simultaneously execute multiple threads, or execution units of a process. For example, a Win32-based Setup program can be broken into three threads:

- One that decompresses files.
- One that copies files.
- One that modifies the system configuration files.

The threads are completely independent of each other as shown in the following illustration. They run at the same time, thereby increasing system performance.

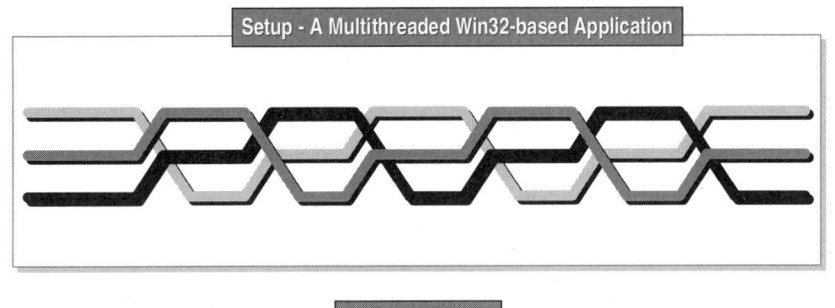

[Setup - A Multithreaded Win32-based Application]

[Multiple Threads]

☐ File Decompression
▨ File Copying
■ System Configuration File Modification

Reliability

Each Win32-based application runs in its own 2 GB address space. For this reason, a Win32-based application cannot corrupt the memory of another Win32-based application. In other words, if one Win32-based application fails, it does not affect other Win32-based applications.

OLE/ActiveX, OpenGL, and DirectX

Windows NT supports OLE/ActiveX and OpenGL APIs and DirectX, a high-performance media interface. This section describes each of these interfaces.

OLE/ActiveX Support

OLE/ActiveX is a method for transferring and sharing information between applications. Windows NT includes both 16-bit and 32-bit versions of OLE, and fully supports interoperability between Win16 and Win32 OLE applications.

While Microsoft ActiveX and OLE are both based on the Component Object Model (COM), they provide substantially different services to developers. COM provides the low-level object-binding mechanism that enables objects to communicate with each other. OLE uses COM to provide high-level application services such as linking and embedding to enable users to create compound documents. ActiveX, on the other hand, provides a substantially pared down infrastructure to enable controls to be embedded in Web sites and respond interactively to events. While OLE is optimized for end-user usability and integration of desktop applications, ActiveX is optimized for size and speed. ActiveX also adds a number of important innovations for the Internet, including a substantial reduction in size (50 to 75 percent) of the controls, and support for incremental rendering and asynchronous connections.

OpenGL

OpenGL (Graphics Language) is an industry-standard software interface for producing two- and three-dimensional graphics. OpenGL allows applications to create high-quality color graphics independent of windowing systems, operating systems, and hardware.

Several 3-D screen savers are included with Windows NT and are examples of OpenGL utilities. Use the Display program in Control Panel to select these 3-D screen savers.

Note The OpenGL screen savers included with Windows NT use more CPU time than a non-OpenGL screen saver. Therefore, it is not recommended to use an OpenGL screen saver on a busy file, print, or application server, as it may affect performance.

DirectX

DirectX is a low-level API designed specifically for high-performance applications such as games. DirectX is designed to provide high-speed, real-time response to the user interface.

The following table describes the three DirectX components included in Windows NT 4.0.

DirectX component	Description
Microsoft DirectDraw™	DirectDraw for Windows NT 4.0 supports a 32-bit API for accelerated drawing. Unlike DirectDraw for Windows 95, DirectDraw for Windows NT does not communicate directly with the display driver or with any hardware. All DirectDraw calls are mediated by the GDI. DirectDraw achieves high performance by providing a thin layer above the video hardware, enabling device-independent access to graphics accelerator hardware.
Microsoft DirectPlay™	DirectPlay simplifies communication between computers, allowing DirectX programs to run over a network or by means of a modem.
Microsoft DirectSound™	DirectSound provides device-independent access to audio accelerator hardware. It provides features such as real-time mixing of audio streams and control over effects such as volume and panning during playback. DirectSound API calls communicate directly with the I/O Manager.

Note For additional information on supporting Win32 applications, or for additional information on DirectX, see the *Microsoft Windows NT Workstation Resource Kit*.

Lesson 5: Supporting MS-DOS-based and Win16-based Applications

Windows NT supports MS-DOS-based applications in an *NT Virtual DOS Machine (NTVDM)*. An NTVDM can also support Win16-based applications in an emulated Win16 on Win32 (WOW) environment. This lesson describes the components and configuration of NTVDMs and the WOW environment.

After this lesson, you will be able to:
- Describe the components of an NT Virtual DOS Machine (NTVDM).
- Configure an NTVDM to run MS-DOS-based applications.
- Describe the components of the Win16 on Win32 (WOW) environment.
- Identify the advantages and disadvantages of running Win16-based applications in multiple NTVDMs.
- Configure a Win16-based application to start in its own memory space in a separate NTVDM.

Estimated lesson time: 60 minutes

MS-DOS-based applications run in a special Win32-based application called an NT Virtual DOS Machine (NTVDM). The NTVDM provides a simulated MS-DOS environment for MS-DOS-based applications.

The NT Virtual DOS Machine (NTVDM)

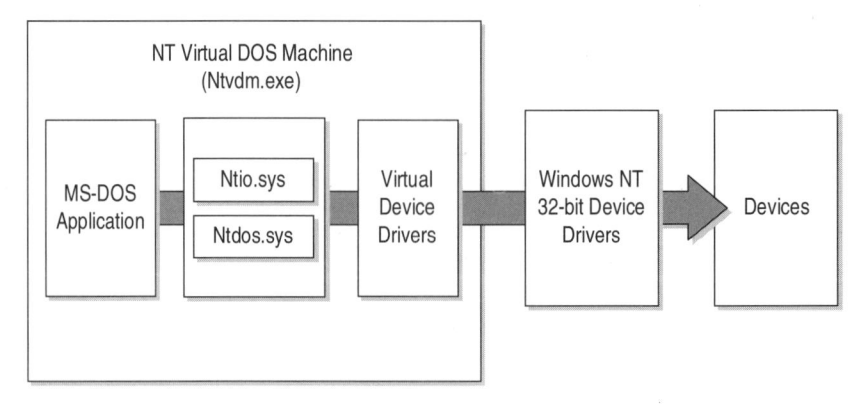

NTVDM Operation and Components

Each MS-DOS-based application has its own NTVDM, and each NTVDM has a single thread. Each NTVDM is independently supported in its own address space, so that if one NTVDM fails, all other NTVDMs remain unaffected. The function of each of the key components of the NTVDM is described in the following table.

Component	Function
Ntvdm.exe	Runs in kernel mode. This program provides the MS-DOS emulation and manages the NTVDM.
Ntio.sys	Equivalent of the MS-DOS Io.sys.
Ntdos.sys	Equivalent of Msdos.sys.

Note On RISC-based computers, the NTVDM also includes an Instruction Execution Unit that emulates an Intel 80486 processor.

MS-DOS Virtual Device Drivers

Many MS-DOS-based applications attempt to access hardware directly. However, you have learned that applications that run in user mode do not have direct access to hardware. The NTVDM uses *virtual device drivers* (VDDs) to allow MS-DOS-based applications to access the system hardware. The VDDs intercept the application's hardware calls and interact with the Windows NT 32-bit device driver. This process of communicating with the hardware is transparent to the application.

Windows NT supplies VDDs for the mouse, keyboard, printer, and COM port. The VDDs are loaded into every NTVDM based on values stored in the registry. Information about the VDDs is found in the following registry path:

HKEY_LOCAL_MACHINE\System\CurrentControlSet\Control\VirtualDeviceDrivers

Configuring the MS-DOS NTVDM

An NT Virtual DOS Machine (NTVDM) can be customized for a specific MS-DOS-based application by changing settings in the application's program information file (PIF). To create, modify, and save PIFs, right-click the application file name in Windows NT Explorer; if you click **OK** after changing any of the settings in the **Properties** dialog box, you create a PIF (a shortcut) for the application.

The settings available in Windows NT PIFs are similar to Windows 3.x PIFs with the addition of two settings: the Autoexec Filename setting and the Config Filename setting. In MS-DOS there was only one Autoexec.bat file and one Config.sys file, while in Windows NT you can have multiple Autoexec files and Config files. These additional settings allow you to specify the Autoexec and Config files to use with a specific application.

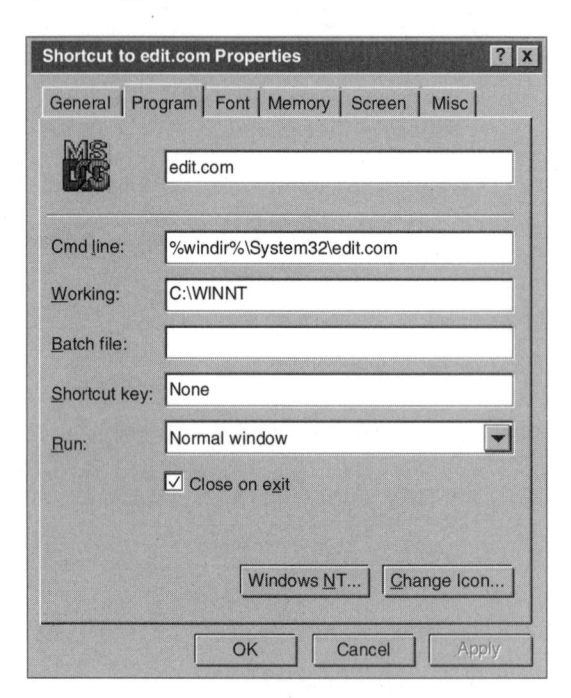

Although most MS-DOS-based commands work under Windows NT, any MS-DOS drivers or executable files that attempt to directly access a device for which there is no VDD will fail. Windows NT protects the system from such access.

Autoexec and Config Windows NT File Names

When an MS-DOS-based application starts, a new NTVDM automatically starts, and its Autoexec and Config files are run. These are the Windows NT equivalents of the MS-DOS files, Autoexec.bat and Config.sys. The default files are Autoexec.nt and Config.nt, and are located in *systemroot*\System32.

To specify different Autoexec and Config files to be used with a specific MS-DOS-based application, click the **Windows NT...** button (as shown in the preceding illustration) on the **Program** tab of the PIF for the application. The dialog box shown in the following illustration appears.

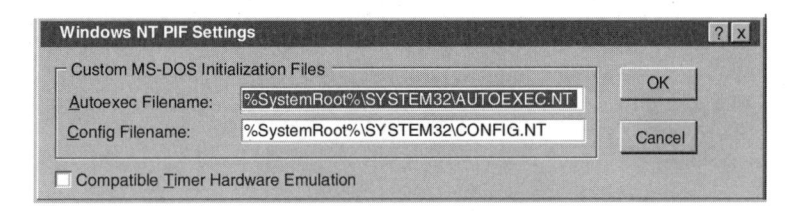

```
┌─ Windows NT PIF Settings ─────────────────────────── ? x ┐
│  ┌─ Custom MS-DOS Initialization Files ──────────┐       │
│    Autoexec Filename:  %SystemRoot%\SYSTEM32\AUTOEXEC.NT    OK    │
│    Config Filename:    %SystemRoot%\SYSTEM32\CONFIG.NT              │
│                                                         Cancel │
│  □ Compatible Timer Hardware Emulation                          │
└──────────────────────────────────────────────────────────┘
```

You must edit the PIF associated with an application to specify different Config and Autoexec files for each application. PIFs can be created for MS-DOS-based applications by modifying the default properties for the applications. A change to a setting in either Autoexec.nt or Config.nt takes effect as soon as the changes are saved and the application restarts.

Windows NT supports the same commands in the Autoexec file that are supported by MS-DOS 5.0. If a command that is not supported by Windows NT is used in the Config file, it is ignored.

Note Remember that there is nothing new added to MS-DOS after version 5.0 that Windows NT does not already have built in. For more information about supported commands, see *What's New and Different from MS-DOS* in Windows NT Help.

WOW and Win16-based Applications

Win16 on Win32 (WOW) is a 32-bit user-mode program in Windows NT that allows Win16-based applications to run in a Win32 environment. Because Windows 3.*x* is itself an MS-DOS-based program, Win16 applications require an NT Virtual DOS Machine (NTVDM). WOW components operate in the context of this NTVDM.

WOW Components

The WOW environment consists of several components, as described in the following table.

Component	Description
Wowexec.exe	Provides the Windows 3.1 emulation for the NTVDM.
Wow32.dll	Provides the DLL portion of the Windows 3.1 emulation layer.
Win16 application	The 16-bit application running in the WOW.
Krnl386.exe	A modified version of the Windows 3.1 386 kernel for Intel x86-based computers, which translates many operations to Win32 services.
User.exe	A modified version of the Windows 3.1 User.exe, which translates API calls to Win32 services.
Gdi.exe	A modified version of the Windows 3.1 Gdi.exe, which translates API calls to Win32 services.

Note 16-bit Windows 3.*x* VDDs are *not* supported under WOW. Win16-based applications that rely on these drivers may not function correctly under Windows NT.

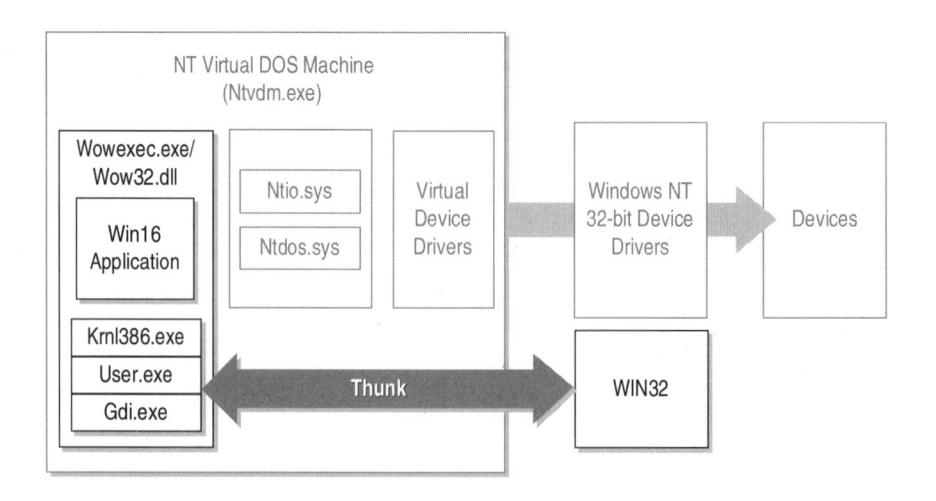

WOW Operation

WOW translates, or *thunks*, 16-bit calls to 32-bit calls. Thunking is the process of translating 16-bit calls into 32-bit calls and vice versa. When an application calls a Windows 3.*x* function, WOW intercepts the call and passes control to the equivalent Win32 function. As a result, Windows 3.*x*-based applications use Win32 functions.

If the Win32 function needs to return anything to the calling application, it must be translated from 32 bits to 16 bits. Although these translations incur some overhead, the loss may be offset by the speed gained by carrying out 32-bit instructions.

WOW provides the nonpreemptive multitasking environment for which Win16-based applications were designed.

By default, a single NTVDM starts when the first Win16-based application is initialized, and all Win16-based applications run in that NTVDM.

WOW Limitations

The WOW environment has these limitations:

- If one Win16-based application fails, it can adversely affect all other Win16-based applications running in the NTVDM. For example, if a Win16-based application does not release the processor, the other Win16-based applications cannot get access to it, because WOW provides nonpreemptive multiprocessing within that environment. Other Windows NT–based applications can still access the processor, but in order for the other Win16-based applications running in that NTVDM to gain access to the processor, the failed Win16-based application must be closed.

- There is no shared memory between the applications running in WOW and other applications running under Windows NT. Win16-based applications cannot call 32-bit DLLs, and Windows NT–based applications cannot call Win16 DLLs.

Practice

In these procedures, you start a few applications, and then use Task Manager to view the active processes and applications on the system. You then determine the effects of a halted Win32 application on the system and end the application that has stopped responding.

Note Complete these procedures on Workstation1.

▶ **To view running applications and system processes**

1. Open the C:\Lab Files\Apps folder.
2. In the Apps folder, start BadApp32, Spind16, and Spind32. Do not close the Apps folder.
3. Click the SpinDIB:32 window, and then click **Open**.
4. Click **Billg.bmp**, and then click **Open**.
5. Click the SpinDIB:16 window, and then click **Open**.

6. Click **Billg.bmp**, and then click **Open**.
7. Arrange your desktop so that you can see the Apps folder, Spind16, Spind32, and BadApp32 (the title bar shows BadApp) at the same time.
8. To verify that the SpinDIB:32 and SpinDIB:16 applications are running, click **Spin!** on each application.
9. Start Task Manager.

   According to the **Applications** tab, what tasks are currently running?

   _____

   _____

   _____

10. Click the **Processes** tab.

    According to Task Manager, what processes are currently running?

    _____

    _____

    _____

    Why does Spind16.exe appear indented under Ntvdm.exe?

    _____

11. On the **Options** menu in Task Manager, select **Always on Top**, so that the check box is *not* selected.

▶ **To view the effects of a Win32 application that has stopped responding**

1. On the BadApp32 **Action** menu, click **Hang**.

   In the BadApp32 window, the fuse burns down, and then the bomb explodes. At this point the application halts.

2. Move the mouse pointer over BadApp32. What is the status of BadApp32?

   _____

3. Are SpinDIB:32 and SpinDIB:16 still active? (Can you spin Bill?)

   _____

▶ **To terminate an application that has stopped responding**

1. Switch to Task Manager, and then click the **Applications** tab.
2. Click **BadApp**, and then click **End Task**.

    The **BadApp** dialog box appears, indicating that the application cannot respond to the End Task request.

3. In the **BadApp** dialog box, click **End Task** to clear the dialog box and end BadApp32.

    SpinDIB:32 and SpinDIB:16 should still be running.

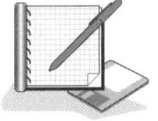

Practice

In these procedures, you observe the effects of a General Protection Fault (GPF) error and the effects of a halted application. You also run a Win16-based application in its own memory space.

Note Complete these procedures on Workstation1.

▶ **To observe the effects of a 16-bit application General Protection Fault**

1. In the Apps folder, open Badapp16.
2. In the Bad App window, click the bomb.

    When the fuse burns down, the bomb explodes. At this point an error message occurs.

3. Do *not* click **Close** or **Ignore**.
4. Click **SpinDIB:32**.

    Is the application active? Why or why not?

5. Click **SpinDIB:16**.

    Is the application active? Why or why not?

6. In the **BADAPP** dialog box containing the error message, click **Close**.

    An **Application Error** dialog box appears.

7. Click **Close**.
8. Click **SpinDIB:16**.

    Is the application active? Why or why not?

▶ **To observe the effects of a Win16 application that halts**

1. With SpinDIB:32 and SpinDIB:16 still active, open Badapp16.
2. On the **Action** menu, click **Hang**.

   When the fuse burns down, the bomb explodes. At this point the application halts.
3. Move the mouse pointer over SpinDIB:16.

   What is the status of SpinDIB:16?

   _____

4. Move the mouse pointer over SpinDIB:32.

   What is the status of SpinDIB:32?

   _____

5. Use Task Manager to end the Bad App application.
6. Switch to SpinDIB:16 to verify that it is still active.
7. Close SpinDIB:16 and SpinDIB:32.

Multiple NTVDMs

Win16-based applications can be configured to run in their own memory spaces, on an application-by-application basis, thereby creating multiple NT Virtual DOS Machines (NTVDMs).

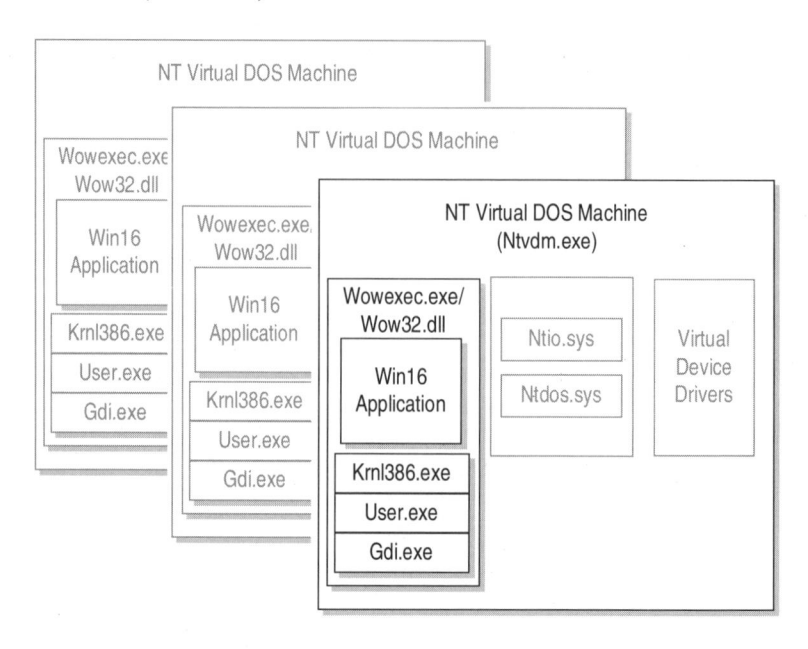

When a Win16-based application is configured to run in its own memory space, a new NTVDM is created when the application starts. Inside the new NTVDM, a new WOW application environment starts. Each Win16-based application configured to run in its own memory space creates another WOW application environment within another NTVDM.

Advantages of Multiple NTVDMs

There are several advantages to running Win16-based applications in separate NTVDMs:

- *Reliability.* A single faulty Win16-based application does not affect any other Win16-based applications.
- *Interoperability.* If Win16-based applications follow the OLE and dynamic data exchange (DDE) specifications, they can interoperate with other applications in separate memory spaces.
- *Preemptive multitasking.* If several Win16-based applications are running in a shared memory space, one busy application prevents the others from being used. Running each Win16-based application in its own memory space, however, keeps all of the applications usable, even when one is busy.
- *Multiprocessing.* Multitasking and true multiprocessing of Win16-based applications is enabled on multiprocessor computers. If all of the Win16-based applications are running in a shared memory space, only one Win16-based application is ever running at one time. Therefore, even on a multiprocessor system, only one Win16-based application can run, and the Win16-based applications do not take advantage of any additional processors on the system. However, if each Win16-based application is configured to run in a separate memory space, it can run simultaneously if the system has enough available processors.

Disadvantages of Multiple NTVDMs

There are potential disadvantages to running Win16-based applications in separate NTVDMs:

- *Additional memory usage.* Starting multiple Win16-based applications in their own memory spaces introduces additional overhead into the system. Each Win16-based application that is started in its own memory space starts another NTVDM and WOW application environment. This overhead can potentially be approximately 2 MB of page file space and approximately 1 MB of RAM per separate memory space used. Depending on the amount of RAM in the computer, this overhead could affect system performance.
- *Lack of interoperability.* If Win16-based applications do not follow the OLE and DDE standards, or if they rely on shared memory to exchange data, these Win16-based applications do *not* function correctly in separate memory spaces. To function properly, such applications must be run in the default (shared) NTVDM and WOW application environment.

Note Once started, the default (shared) NTVDM and WOW application environment remains open, even if all Win16-based applications that were running in it are closed. You can use Task Manager to close the shared NTVDM and WOW application environment.

However, when a Win16-based application is started in a separate memory space, an additional NTVDM and WOW application environment is started. When you close this Win16-based application, its NTVDM and WOW application environment is also closed. The default NTVDM is not affected.

Starting a Win16-based Application in Its Own NTVDM

A Win16-based application can be started in its own NTVDM in the following ways:

- From a command prompt

  Type **start /separate [path] application_executable**

- From the **Start** menu

  Click **Run**, and in the **Open** box, type **[path] application_executable** and then click the **Run in Separate Memory Space** check box.

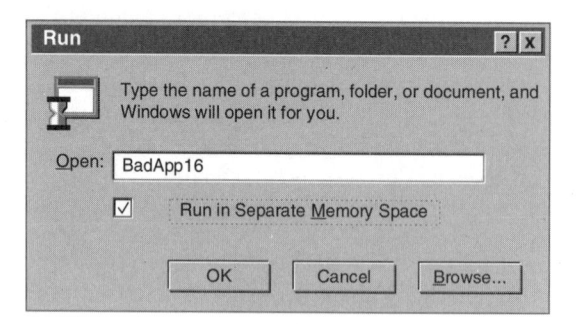

![Run dialog box showing Open field with "BadApp16" entered and "Run in Separate Memory Space" check box selected, with OK, Cancel, and Browse buttons]

Note If the **Run in Separate Memory Space** check box appears dimmed, the application is not a 16-bit Windows application, or the system cannot find the application.

- From a shortcut

  Create a shortcut, and on the **Properties Shortcut** tab, click the **Run in Separate Memory Space** check box.

- By file association

    On the Windows NT Explorer **View** menu, click **Options**, click the **File Types** tab, and then click the Win16-based application to be edited.

    Click **Edit**, and then double-click **Open**.

    Edit the open line to include the **/separate** switch using the following syntax:

    cmd /c start **/separate** <path><application_executable> %1

Note File association can also be done from the command prompt by using the **ftype** and **assoc** commands.

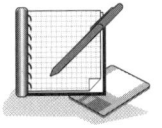

Practice

In these procedures, you run Win16-based applications in separate NTVDMs.

Note Complete these procedures on Workstation1.

▶ **To start a Win16-based application in a separate NTVDM for a single instance from a command prompt**

1. Start a command prompt.
2. Type the following:

    start /separate C:\ "Lab Files"\Apps\Spind16

    and then press ENTER.

▶ **To start a Win16-based application in a separate NTVDM for a single instance from the Start menu**

1. On the **Start** menu, click **Run**.
2. In the **Run** dialog box, type **"C:\Lab Files\Apps\BadApp16"** and then select the **Run in Separate Memory Space** check box.
3. Click **OK**.

    You should now see SpinDIB:16 and BadApp running.
4. Use Task Manager to verify they are running in separate NTVDMs.
5. Close SpinDIB:16 and BadApp.

Note Each Win16-based application runs either in the default shared NTVDM or in its own NTVDM. Only one NTVDM can allow shared Win16-based applications.

If you want to configure a Win16-based application to always start in a separate NTVDM, create a shortcut for the application. Right-click the shortcut and then click **Properties**. In the **Properties** dialog box, click the **Shortcut** tab. On the **Shortcut** tab, click the **Run in Separate Memory Space** check box. Each time you start the application using the shortcut you created, it is automatically started in a separate NTVDM.

Practice

In this procedure, you create and configure a shortcut to start Spind16, a Win16-based application, in a separate NTVDM.

Note Complete this procedure on Workstation1.

▶ **To create and configure a shortcut to start Spind16 in a separate NTVDM**

1. In the Apps folder, right-click **Spind16**, and then click **Create Shortcut**.

    A new Shortcut to Spind16 appears in the Apps folder.

2. Rename the shortcut file name from **Shortcut to Spind16** to **SpinDIB16 (separate WOW)**.

3. Right-click **SpinDIB16 (separate WOW)**.

4. Click **Properties**.

5. Click the **Shortcut** tab.

6. Select the **Run in Separate Memory Space** check box.

7. Click **OK** to close the **SpinDIB16 (separate Wow) Properties** dialog box.

8. Start **SpinDIB16 (separate WOW)**.

    Notice that it takes somewhat longer to start SpinDIB16 this time. This is because a new NTVDM and WOW must be loaded.

You saw earlier in this lesson that when all Win16-based applications are running in a single NTVDM, if one Win16-based application stops responding, it causes the rest of the Win16-based applications to stop responding as well. You now determine what happens when a Win16-based application running in a separate NTVDM stops responding.

Practice

In this procedure, you determine the effect of a non-responding Win16-based application that is running in a separate NTVDM on other Win16-based applications running in the default (shared) NTVDM.

Note Complete this procedure on Workstation1.

▶ **To determine the effect a non-responding Win16-based application, running in a separate NTVDM, has on other Win16-based applications**

1. With the instance of SpinDIB:16 you started from the SpinDIB16 (separate WOW) shortcut still active, start **Badapp16**.
2. Arrange your desktop so that you can see SpinDIB:16 and Bad App at the same time.
3. On the Badapp16 **Action** menu, click **Hang**.
4. When Bad App stops responding, switch to SpinDIB:16.

   Is SpinDIB:16 still active? Why?

5. Use Task Manager to end the Bad App application.
6. Close **SpinDIB:16** and **Task Manager**, and if the **Apps** window is open, close it.

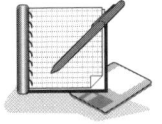

Practice

In these procedures, you rename key subsystem files and observe the resulting effects on running MS-DOS-based, Win16-based, and Win32-based applications.

Note Complete these procedures on Workstation1.

▶ **To observe effects on MS-DOS-based, Win16-based, and Win32-based applications when Ntvdm.exe is missing**

1. In the C:\Winnt\System32 folder, rename Ntvdm.exe to Ntvdm.old.
2. Shut down and then restart Workstation1.
3. Log on as Administrator, and then start a command prompt.
4. From C:\Lab Files\Apps, try to run Edit.com, and record the resulting behavior in the following table.

5. From C:\Lab Files\Apps, try to run Spind16.exe, and record the resulting behavior in the following table.

6. From C:\Lab Files\Apps, try to run Spind32.exe, and record the resulting behavior in the following table.

Application	Record the results here
Edit.com	
Spind16.exe	
Spind32.exe	

7. In the C:\Winnt\System32 folder, rename **Ntvdm.old** to **Ntvdm.exe**.

▶ **To observe effects on MS-DOS-based, Win16-based, and Win32-based applications when Wowexec.exe is missing**

1. In the C:\Winnt\System32 folder, rename Wowexec.exe to Wowexec.old.

2. Shut down and then restart Workstation1.

3. Log on as Administrator, and then start a command prompt.

4. From the C:\Lab Files\Apps folder, try to run Edit.com, and record the resulting behavior in the following table.

5. From C:\Lab Files\Apps folder, try to run Spind16.exe, and record the resulting behavior in the following table.

6. From the C:\Winnt\System32 folder, try to run Spind32.exe, and record the resulting behavior in the following table.

Application	Record the results here
Edit.com	
Spind16.exe	
Spind32.exe	

7. In the C:\Winnt\System32 folder, rename **Wowexec.old** to **Wowexec.exe**.

▶ **To observe effects on MS-DOS-based, Win16-based, and Win32-based applications when Krnl386.exe is missing**

1. In the C:\Winnt\System32 folder, rename Krnl386.exe to Krnl386.old.
2. Shut down and then restart Workstation1.
3. Log on as Administrator, and then start a command prompt.
4. From the C:\Lab Files\Apps folder, try to run Edit.com, and record the resulting behavior in the following table.
5. From C:\Lab Files\Apps folder, try to run Spind16.exe, and record the resulting behavior in the following table.

6. From the C:\Winnt\System32 folder, try to run Spind32.exe, and record the resulting behavior in the following table.

Application	Record the results here
Edit.com	
Spind16.exe	
Spind32.exe	

In which situations did Edit.com fail? Why?

In which situations did Spind16.exe fail? Why?

In which situations did Spind32.exe fail? Why?

7. In the C:\Winnt\System32 folder, rename Krnl386.old to Krnl386.exe.
8. Shut down and then restart Workstation1.

Lesson 6: Supporting Applications on Different Hardware Platforms

Because Windows NT can run on multiple platforms, there are compatibility issues that should be considered. This lesson discusses the compatibility issues you need to understand in deciding which applications to select for a specific platform.

After this lesson, you will be able to:
- List platform capabilities and limitations.
- Choose the appropriate version of an application for a given platform.

Estimated lesson time: 10 minutes

The following illustration summarizes the different hardware platforms that Windows NT runs on, and the compatibility issues that are involved.

Hardware Platform	Win32 Applications	Windows 3.x and MS-DOS Applications	POSIX Applications	OS/2 1.x Applications
Intel x86	Source-compatible	Binary-compatible	Source-compatible	Binary-compatible
RISC - Alpha MIPS PowerPC	Source-compatible	Binary-compatible	Source-compatible	Binary-compatible (Bound Applications Only)

Source Compatibility

A source-compatible application must be recompiled for each hardware platform. For example, the Win32 version of Microsoft Word for Windows runs only on the hardware platform for which it was compiled. Although many Win32-based applications are available for all hardware platforms supported by Windows NT, many other Win32-based applications are specific to the Intel x86-based platform.

Binary Compatibility

A binary-compatible application can run on any hardware platform supported by Windows NT, with no recompilation necessary.

Windows 3.x–based and MS-DOS-based Applications

Many users migrating to Windows NT use applications written for MS-DOS and Windows 3.x. All of these applications contain Intel x86 instructions. One of the goals of Windows NT is to make these existing applications binary-compatible on all computers running Windows NT, including those that do not have built-in support for Intel x86 instructions.

To support this goal, versions of Windows NT developed for non-Intel x86 computers contain code that emulates Intel 80486 instructions. When an MS-DOS- or Windows 3.x–based application runs on RISC-based computers, each instruction the application carries out is emulated by one or more instructions in the processor's native machine language. Emulating these instructions takes time and slows the application's execution. However, the decrease in performance is small, because a RISC-based computer is several times faster than an Intel 80486. Windows 3.x–based and MS-DOS-based applications are binary-compatible across all computers running Windows NT.

OS/2 Applications

The Windows NT OS/2 subsystem supports OS/2 1.x character-based applications on Intel-based computers. OS/2 applications are binary-compatible across all Intel x86-based computers.

Because there is no OS/2 subsystem on RISC-based computers running Windows NT, the only OS/2 applications capable of running on these computers are *bound* applications. Bound applications are applications designed to run under either OS/2 or MS-DOS using a single executable file. OS/2 bound applications can run on RISC-based computers running Windows NT because they run in MS-DOS mode in a NTVDM.

To run the 16-bit OS/2 1.x Presentation Manager application on Windows NT, an add-on subsystem is required. The Windows NT Add-on Subsystem for Presentation Manager is designed to aid in the migration from OS/2 to Windows NT. It is not included with any version of Windows NT, and must be purchased separately. The Windows NT Add-on Subsystem for Presentation Manager is a replacement OS/2 subsystem, and is supported only on Intel x86-based computers.

Win32-based and POSIX-based Applications

POSIX is a standard for versions of UNIX and UNIX-like operating systems. POSIX allows software developers to create applications that meet the U.S. Federal Information Processing Standard 151. POSIX.1 is a library of functions implemented as system calls. Windows NT File System (NTFS) is the only POSIX.1-compliant file system.

Win32 and POSIX are portable APIs. Applications written to these APIs are source-compatible across all Windows NT platforms.

Interoperability

One of the strengths of Windows NT is its support for sharing data between applications. All Windows NT–based applications can share data using the Windows NT Clipboard. Windows 3.*x*-based and Win32-based applications can share data using OLE and DDE. This level of interoperability is possible because all of the subsystems rely on the Win32 subsystem and Win32K Executive Service for user interactions.

Lesson 7: Distributed Component Object Model

Distributed computing users seek a common application infrastructure for building applications made up of multiple components spread across multiple platforms. This lesson explains how the distributed Component Object Model (DCOM) functions and how it can be configured to improve the networking capabilities of a computer running Windows NT.

After this lesson, you will be able to:
- Explain the function and purpose of DCOM.
- Configure DCOM.

Estimated lesson time: 15 minutes

DCOM Overview

DCOM uses remote procedure calls (RPCs) and Windows NT security features, such as permissions, to enable applications to communicate across networks. In addition, DCOM provides a programming model for software developers that can be used to create distributed applications.

One example of an application requiring DCOM would be a stock quote service. Using DCOM on a computer running Windows NT Server, stock quotes are distributed to clients on the network. A second DCOM conversation takes that data and compares it to trading rules from an object on a third computer. For example, you can create a rule specifying when to buy a specific stock. If the price for that stock falls below a predetermined level, a notification to buy would be sent out. The result of the data and rule, "Buy stock," creates a trading advisory that is displayed on a fourth computer. DCOM provides the infrastructure that connects the distributed objects so that clients receive needed information.

DCOM uses the same tools and technologies as COM. Remember that COM is the basis of OLE. COM is the standard by which software components can make use of, or be used by, one another, integrating features among diverse applications. Distributed COM is network OLE—that is, COM with a longer wire. It is a fast transport for distributed applications built with COM.

Note Existing COM (OLE) applications can use DCOM. They require only minor modification to a system's configuration, but none to the application code itself. The programming model is identical to ActiveX technologies, so integration is seamless. However, you should test existing OLE applications before deploying them with DCOM.

DCOM includes the features described in the following table.

Feature	This feature provides Windows NT with the ability to
Distribution	Run applications across a network, including the Internet.
Remote Activation	Start an application by calling a component.
Security	Support launch, access, and context security. Administrators use Windows NT security to set permissions for DCOM applications, and vary them for local and remote execution.
DCOM Configuration Tool	Configure 32-bit applications to communicate over a network and set the applications' properties.

DCOM and Remote Procedure Calls

Remote procedure calls (RPCs) provide the basis of communication and interoperability between the various DCOM services. RPCs allow an application to carry out procedures on a remote computer. In a DCOM application, a program uses the network as a means of carrying out individual components on other hosts at remote locations.

For example, a client application carries out a call to a *stub code* that takes the place of a procedure located on the client computer. The stub code uses both communication and data conversion facilities from an RPC library to carry out the requested routine within a process on a remote server.

Note Stub code is a piece of programming code designed to emulate a local routine that actually resides on a remote computer.

DCOM uses an RPC to enable existing applications to interact across multiple computers in a network. The following illustration shows the flow of a client application call to a server object.

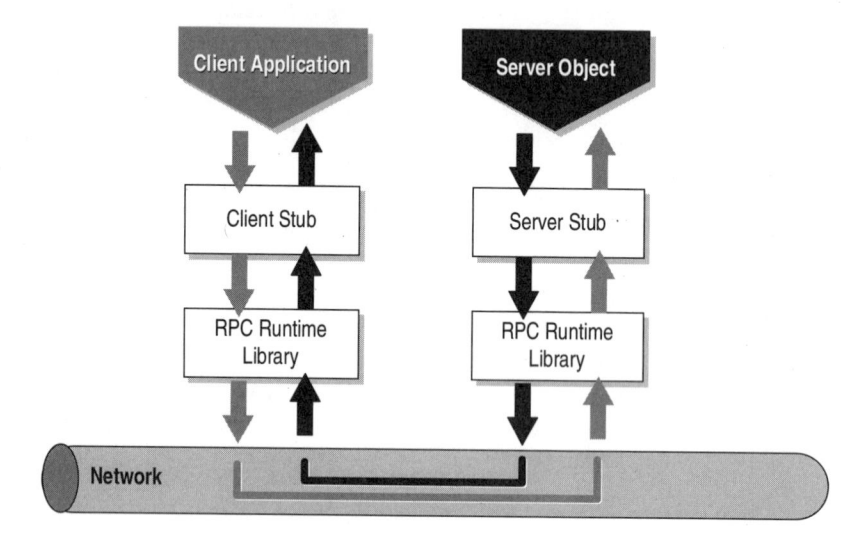

1. A client application initiates an RPC.
2. The RPC client stub packages the call, and the RPC run-time library transmits the package to the server.
3. The server's RPC runtime library receives the package and forwards it to its RPC server stub, which converts the package into the RPC.
4. The RPC is carried out.
5. The RPC server stub packages the procedure results, and the RPC runtime library transmits the package to the client running the application.
6. The client RPC runtime library receives the package and forwards it to the client stub, which unpackages it into the data for the client application.

Configuring DCOM

DCOM is installed during Windows NT setup. Use the **Distributed COM Configuration Properties** dialog box to enable DCOM and to set DCOM properties, such as security and the location for an application. Access this tool through a command prompt by typing **dcomcnfg**. Dcomcnfg.exe is located in the *systemroot*\System32 folder.

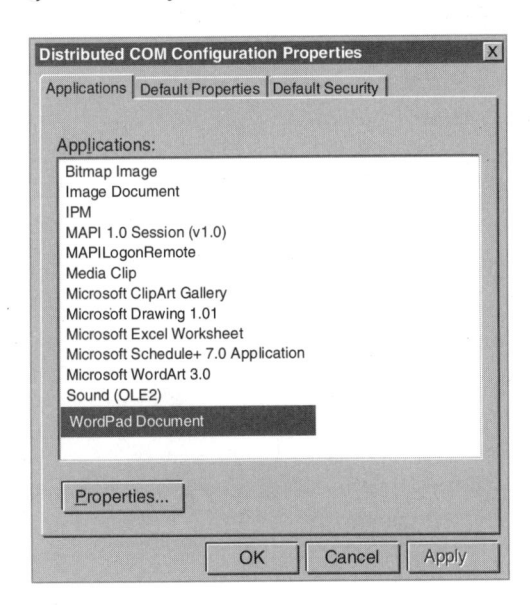

DCOM Configuration Options

The following table lists the DCOM configuration options available through the **Distributed COM Configuration Properties** dialog box.

Tab	Use this tab to
Applications	View current applications and set properties for each application. To view and configure the properties for an application, select the application, and then click the **Properties** button. The following tabs appear: **General** tab. Describes the properties of the DCOM application: the application name, the type of application (including whether the application is on the local computer or on another computer in the network), and the path. **Location** tab. Is used to designate the computer on which the application will run. Using this tab, an administrator can set applications to run on the computer where the data is located, on the local computer, or on another network computer. **Security** tab. Is used to set the following permissions: *access* permissions which allow or deny users or groups access to the application, *launch* permissions which allow or deny users or groups to start the application, and *configuration* permissions which allow users or groups to view or change the application configuration information stored in the registry. **Identity** tab. Contains user account options that allow the administrator to specify whose permissions should be used to run the object. The choices include *interactive user*, *launching user*, or *this user*. The option, *this user*, allows you to specify a specific user or service account.
Default Properties	Enable DCOM on the local computer and set default communication properties, such as Default Authentication and Default Impersonation Level. The Default Authentication properties sets packet-level security on communication between applications. The Default Impersonation Level specifies the level of permissions a client application grants to a server application to perform processing tasks on its behalf.
Default Security	Set default security permissions for Access, Launch, and Configuration.

Note The computers running the client application and the server application must both be configured for DCOM. On the computer running as a client, you must specify the location of the server application that is accessed or started. For the computer running the server application, you must specify the user account that has permission to access or start the application, and the user account that is used to run the application.

For additional information on DCOM, see Appendix E, "The Distributed Component Object Model," included with this book, or Chapter 1, "Windows NT Networking Architecture," in the *Networking Guide* of the *Microsoft Windows NT Server Resource Kit*.

Lesson 8: Managing Applications

In this chapter, you learned about and used Task Manager to manage running applications. This lesson introduces the tools, Command Prompt and the Console and System programs in Control Panel, which are used to start programs and can also be used to manage applications running under Windows NT.

After this lesson, you will be able to:
- Use the Console program in Control Panel to configure the Command Prompt.
- Prioritize applications running under Windows NT.
- Use the System program in Control Panel to change the relative responsiveness of the foreground application.

Estimated lesson time: 20 minutes

Using the Command Prompt

The Windows NT Command Prompt (Cmd.exe) in the Programs folder on the **Start** menu starts a 32-bit character mode interface to Windows NT and all of its subsystems. Starting the Command Prompt does *not* start an NT Virtual DOS Machine (NTVDM). An NTVDM only starts when an MS-DOS-based application is launched.

From the Command Prompt, a user can do the following tasks:

- Start applications, including Windows NT (32-bit), Windows 3.*x* (16-bit), MS-DOS, OS/2 1.*x* character-based, or POSIX applications.
- Start any batch file with the extension .bat or .cmd.
- Issue any Windows NT command.
- Administrate or use network resources.
- Cut and paste information between applications, including applications running in different subsystems.
- Mix commands from the different subsystems (for example, pipe between an MS-DOS and a POSIX application).

Configuring the Command Prompt

Use the **Console** program in **Control Panel** to configure the default settings for any instance of the Command Prompt that the logged-on user runs.

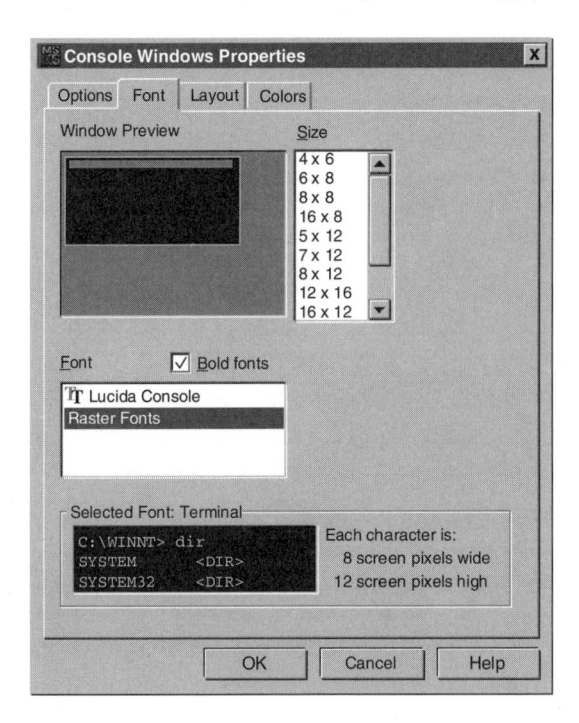

These settings are stored on a user-by-user basis in the registry in the following location:

\HKEY_CURRENT_USER\Console

Each user can configure default settings for the Command Prompt.

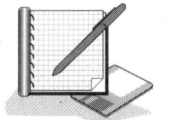

Practice

In this procedure, you configure the default settings for the Command Prompt, and then test your configuration.

Note Complete this procedure on Workstation1.

▶ **To configure the default settings for the Command Prompt**
  1. Log on as Administrator.
  2. Click the **Start** button, point to **Settings**, and then click **Control Panel**.
  3. In Control Panel, start the Console program.

4. Explore the options on each of the tabs.
5. Make one or more changes to default command prompt settings. For example, change the screen background color and screen text color.
6. Click **OK** to apply the change(s); the Console program closes.
7. Start a Command Prompt to test your changes.
8. Close the Command Prompt.

Configuring Individual Command Prompts

In order to configure a Command Prompt that is currently running, click the **MSDOS** icon in the upper-left corner of the Cmd.exe window. Click **Properties** and use the "Command Prompt" **Properties** dialog box to configure a Command Prompt in one of following ways:

- Apply properties to the current window only.

  This applies the settings only to the current Command Prompt window; if another Command Prompt is started, it will have the default settings.

- Modify the shortcut which started this window.

  If you started Command Prompt by means of a shortcut, you can modify the configuration settings for the shortcut. Any Command Prompt started by this shortcut uses these settings. If you start another Command Prompt by clicking the **Start** button, pointing to **Programs**, and clicking **Command Prompt** or by running Cmd.exe, the Command Prompt that starts uses the default configuration set up through the Console program.

Prioritizing Applications

Windows NT prioritizes applications and distributes processing time among them.

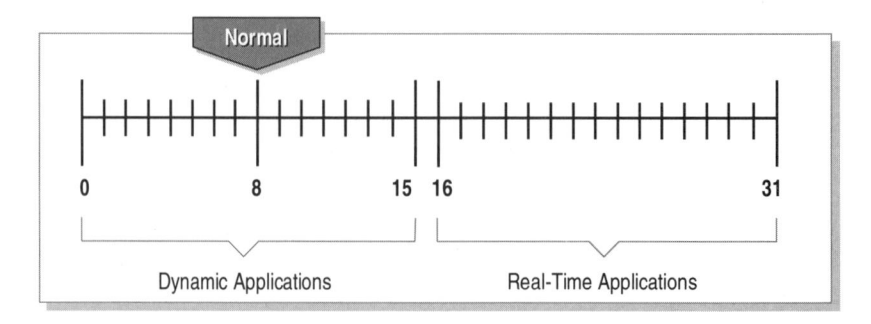

- Normal Priority = 8
- Dynamic Applications Use Priority Levels 0–15
- Real-Time Applications Use Priority Levels 16–31

Priority Levels

Priority levels range from 0 to 31. The base priority is normal (8). Critical system applications use higher priorities; others can use lower levels.

Priority	Used by
0–15	Dynamic applications: User applications and most operating system functions that are not crucial to the performance of the system and can be written to the page file.
16–31	Real-time applications, such as the kernel, that cannot be written to the page file.

Starting Applications at a Specified Priority

In a preemptive, multitasking operating system such as Windows NT, the microkernel schedules threads for the processor in order of their priority and interrupts running threads if a higher priority thread is ready to run. You may want to increase the priority of a process, or decrease the priority of competing processes to improve the response.

If you want to start an application and change its base priority, use the **start** command and one of these options:

/**realtime** (sets base priority to 24)

/**high** (sets base priority to 13)

/**normal** (sets base priority to 8)

/**low** (sets base priority to 4)

For example, to start Notepad.exe at low priority, type the following at the Command Prompt:

start /low notepad

Important Changing the base priority class of a process to Real-Time can destabilize your system. A busy, Real-Time process can prevent other processes and system services from running.

To change the base priority class of a process, click the process name on the Task Manager **Processes** tab, click the highlighted name with the right mouse button, click **Set Priority**, and then click a new priority class from the **Set Priority** menu.

Note Using the **start** command to run an application at high priority may slow performance because other applications get less I/O time. This is why only users with Administrator privileges can use the /**realtime** option.

Changing Foreground Application Responsiveness

Windows NT changes the priorities of applications automatically. To improve system performance, you can manually change the relative priority of foreground and background applications. In **Control Panel**, double-click **System**. On the **Performance** tab in the **System Properties** dialog box, use your mouse or the arrow keys to select one of the three **Application Performance** settings to adjust foreground application responsiveness.

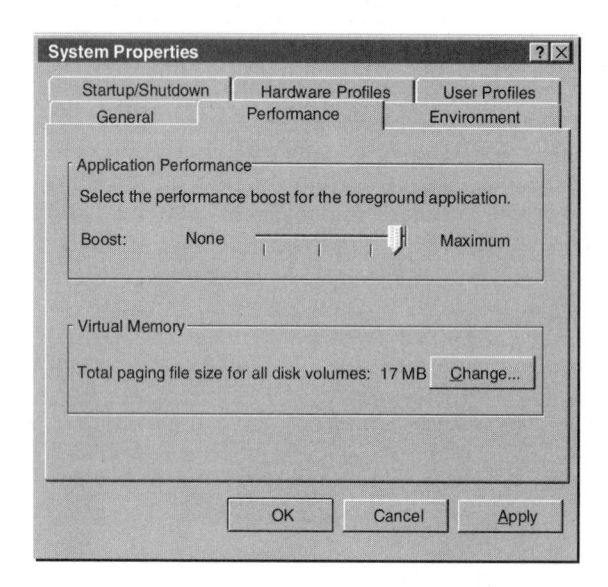

If the **Application Performance** box **Boost** setting is set to **None**, the foreground application priority is not changed. All foreground and background applications retain base priority levels. Use this setting when all applications are equally important to the current task. For example, running an administrative utility on an application server should not slow performance on clients connected to the server.

If the **Application Performance** box **Boost** setting is set to the middle setting, the foreground application's priority increases by one level. Background applications maintain base priority levels. Use this selection for non-critical situations—for example, when a game needs to receive faster response time than a file that is being spell-checked.

If the **Application Performance** box **Boost** setting is set to **Maximum**, the foreground application's priority increases by two levels. Background applications maintain their base priority levels. Use this setting to run an important application that must receive as much CPU time as possible, but still allow background applications to have minimal access to system resources. For example, a mission-critical data file should receive the most CPU time to process mathematical computations, while a file spools on the printer at the same time.

Summary

The following information summarizes the key points in this chapter:

- Windows NT architecture uses a layered approach where applications and the subsystems that support them operate in user mode. The system components, including Executive Services, microkernel, and HAL, operate in kernel mode, which is protected and has a higher priority than user mode. This architecture serves to increase system stability and reliability.

- Windows NT includes enhanced memory management. Virtual RAM allows hard disk space to be used as if it were additional memory. In this manner, the user mode processes have access to more memory than is actually available on the system.

- Through environmental subsystems, Windows NT can support applications written for other operating systems, such as MS-DOS, POSIX, and OS/2. Common operating system functions are implemented once in the Executive Services, rather than duplicated in each subsystem. This consolidation of operating system functions in the Executive Services reduces the effort required to develop new subsystems and makes them easier to maintain.

- In Windows NT 4.0, the Win32K Window Manager and GDI are incorporated into the Windows NT Executive Services. The Win32K Window Manager and GDI are responsible for handling all GUI-related I/O requests, maintaining the display, and providing a common GUI for all applications. Having Window Manager and GDI run in kernel mode enhances system performance.

- There are system compatibility issues involved with supporting applications from a variety of operating systems. For example, some applications attempt to directly access hardware, which is not allowed under the security system of Windows NT.

- Windows NT also includes several system management tools, including Task Manager, Control Panel, and the Command Prompt, which enable you to optimize your system's performance, and prioritize your applications in terms of their access to system resources.

Review

1. You are running several Win32-based applications on a computer running Windows NT Workstation. One of your Win32-based applications encounters an error and stops responding. What impact does this have on the rest of the operating system, and how can you terminate the unresponsive application?

2. You are running two Win16-based applications on a computer running Windows NT Server. Your computer has two processors, but Task Manager shows that only one is being heavily utilized, while the other is relatively idle. How can you improve your system's performance so that both processors are carrying out application code?

3. You download a Win32-based application from the Internet, but it does not run on your PowerPC-based Windows NT Workstation computer. Why?

4. Your company uses a suite of multitier client/server applications. What Microsoft Windows NT service would you configure to let these applications run in a fully distributed, multiple-computer environment? What default parameters must be changed?

5. You have a graphics-intensive program that takes a long time to render when operating in the background. You need to be able to check e-mail and work in other applications, but you do not want to slow the rendering process. How can you optimize your system's performance?

Answer Key

Procedure Answers

Page 273

▶ **To view the priority of a running application**

5. If necessary, resize the Task Manager window until you can see the **Base Priority** column.

   What is the priority of each Counter?

   Normal.

Page 285

▶ **To view running applications and system processes**

9. Start Task Manager.

   According to the **Applications** tab, what tasks are currently running?

   Answers will vary, but should include BadApp, SpinDIB:16, SpinDIB:32, and Exploring–Apps (if you opened Apps through Windows NT Explorer) or Apps (if you did not use Windows NT Explorer).

10. Click the **Processes** tab.

    According to Task Manager, what processes are currently running?

    Answers will vary, but should include Ntvdm.exe, Badapp32.exe, Spind32.exe, Taskmgr.exe, Services.exe, Explorer.exe, Csrss.exe (client/server subsystem services which is the Win32 subsystem), and others.

    Why does Spind16.exe appear indented under Ntvdm.exe?

    Spind16 is a 16-bit application that runs within an NT Virtual DOS Machine (NTVDM), created and maintained by Ntvdm.exe.

Page 286

▶ **To view the effects of a Win32 application that has stopped responding**

2. Move the mouse pointer over BadApp32. What is the status of BadApp32?

   An hourglass appears, meaning that the application has halted.

3. Are SpinDIB:32 and SpinDIB:16 still active? (Can you spin Bill?)

   Yes, both applications should still be active.

Page 287

▶ **To observe the effects of a 16-bit application General Protection Fault**

4. Click **SpinDIB:32**.

   Is the application active? Why or why not?

   Yes. SpinDIB:32 is a 32-bit Windows-based application and has its own memory space.

5. Click **SpinDIB:16**.

   Is the application active? Why or why not?

   No. SpinDIB:16 is a 16-bit Windows-based application and uses the same memory space as Badapp16.

8. Click **SpinDIB:16**.

   Is the application active? Why or why not?

   Yes, Badapp16 is closed.

Page 288

▶ **To observe the effects of a Win16 application that halts**

3. Move the mouse pointer over SpinDIB:16.

   What is the status of SpinDIB:16?

   An hourglass appears, meaning that the application has halted.

4. Move the mouse pointer over SpinDIB:32.

   What is the status of SpinDIB:32?

   SpinDIB:32 is still active.

Page 293

▶ **To determine the effect a non-responding Win16-based application, running in a separate NTVDM, has on other Win16-based applications**

4. When Bad App stops responding, switch to SpinDIB:16.

   Is SpinDIB:16 still active? Why?

   Yes, because it is running in its own memory space.

Page 293

▶ **To observe effects on MS-DOS-based, Win16-based, and Win32-based applications when Ntvdm.exe is missing**

4. From C:\Lab Files\Apps, try to run Edit.com, and record the resulting behavior in the following table.

5. From C:\Lab Files\Apps, try to run Spind16.exe, and record the resulting behavior in the following table.

6. From C:\Lab Files\Apps, try to run Spind32.exe, and record the resulting behavior in the following table.

Application	Record the results here
Edit.com	It fails to run because Windows NT cannot find the file C:\Lab Files\Apps\Edit.com. MS-DOS-based applications require Ntvdm.exe to run.
Spind16.exe	It fails to run because Windows cannot find C:\Lab Files\Apps\Spind16.exe. Win16-based applications require Ntvdm.exe to run.
Spind32.exe	It runs as expected because Win32-based applications are not dependent on Ntvdm.exe to run.

Page 294

▶ **To observe effects on MS-DOS-based, Win16-based, and Win32-based applications when Wowexec.exe is missing**

4. From the C:\Lab Files\Apps folder, try to run Edit.com, and record the resulting behavior in the following table.

5. From C:\Lab Files\Apps folder, try to run Spind16.exe, and record the resulting behavior in the following table.

6. From the C:\Winnt\System32 folder, try to run Spind32.exe, and record the resulting behavior in the following table.

Application	Record the results here
Edit.com	It runs as expected. MS-DOS-based applications are not dependent on Wowexec.exe to run.
Spind16.exe	It fails to run (no error message). Win16-based applications require Wowexec.exe to run.
Spind32.exe	It runs as expected. Win32-based applications are not dependent on Wowexec.exe to run.

Page 295

▶ **To observe effects on MS-DOS-based, Win16-based, and Win32-based applications when Krnl386.exe is missing**

4. From the C:\Lab Files\Apps folder, try to run Edit.com, and record the resulting behavior in the following table.

5. From C:\Lab Files\Apps folder, try to run Spind16.exe, and record the resulting behavior in the following table.

6. From the C:\Winnt\System32 folder, try to run Spind32.exe, and record the resulting behavior in the following table.

Application	Record the results here
Edit.com	It runs as expected. MS-DOS-based applications are not dependent on Krnl386.exe to run.
Spind16.exe	It fails to run (no error message). Win16-based applications are dependent on Krnl386.exe to run.
Spind32.exe	It runs as expected. Win32-based applications are not dependent on Krnl386.exe to run.

In which situations did Edit.com fail? Why?

When Ntvdm.exe was missing. MS-DOS-based applications require Ntvdm.exe to emulate the MS-DOS environment.

In which situations did Spind16.exe fail? Why?

When Ntvdm.exe was missing. Win16-based applications require Ntvdm.exe to emulate the MS-DOS environment, which is required for the WOW component.

When Wowexec.exe was missing. Win16-based applications require Wowexec.exe to emulate the Windows environment.

When Krnl386.exe was missing. Win16-based applications require Krnl386.exe to translate many operations to Win32 services.

In which situations did Spind32.exe fail? Why?

Spind32.exe did not fail because it is a Win32-based application and does not require any of these files to operate.

Review Answers

Page 312

1. You are running several Win32-based applications on a computer running Windows NT Workstation. One of your Win32-based applications encounters an error and stops responding. What impact does this have on the rest of the operating system, and how can you terminate the unresponsive application?

    All other applications, as well as the rest of the operating system, continue to process normally, because each Win32-based application maintains its own threads, separate from all other processes. Use Task Manager to end the unresponsive application.

2. You are running two Win16-based applications on a computer running Windows NT Server. Your computer has two processors, but Task Manager shows that only one is being heavily utilized, while the other is relatively idle. How can you improve your system's performance so that both processors are carrying out application code?

    The Win16-based applications are most likely running in the same NTVDM. Because the Win16-based applications alternate use of a common thread, the microkernel can only schedule this thread on one processor. To optimize performance, start each Win16-based application in its own NTVDM.

3. You download a Win32-based application from the Internet, but it does not run on your PowerPC-based Windows NT Workstation computer. Why?

    The application is probably specific to the Intel platform. Win32-based applications are source-compatible across Windows NT platforms; they must be compiled for a specific platform in order to function on that platform.

4. Your company uses a suite of multitier client/server applications. What Microsoft Windows NT service would you configure to let these applications run in a fully distributed, multiple-computer environment? What default parameters must be changed?

    DCOM. The service must first be enabled, and permissions need to be set so that the appropriate users have permissions to access, change, or delete components as needed.

5. You have a graphics-intensive program that takes a long time to render when operating in the background. You need to be able to check e-mail and work in other applications, but you do not want to slow the rendering process. How can you optimize your system's performance?

    Use the System program in Control Panel to set your dynamic priorities so that the foreground application's threads receive a one-level priority boost rather than a two-level priority boost. The actual setting is the middle setting on the Application Performance slider bar.

CHAPTER 9

The Windows NT Networking Environment

Lesson 1 Windows NT Network Architecture . . . 320

Lesson 2 Distributed Processing . . . 328

Lesson 3 Accessing File and Print Resources . . . 330

Review . . . 334

About This Chapter

Knowledge of the networking components that make up the Microsoft Windows NT networking architecture enhances your ability to support Windows NT. This chapter defines the components of Windows NT networking architecture and describes how these components communicate with each other to enable a computer running Windows NT to communicate over a network.

Lesson 1: Windows NT Network Architecture

The Windows NT operating systems are designed for client/server computing. Client/server computing generally means connecting a single-user, general-purpose workstation (client) to multi-user, general-purpose servers, with the processing load shared between both. The client requests services, and the server responds by providing the services. Windows NT also provides file and print sharing capabilities as well as the ability to use file and print resources on the network. All of these networking capabilities are built into the Windows NT operating system. Because of this integrated network support, a single computer running Windows NT can simultaneously interoperate with the following network environments:

- Microsoft networks, including Windows NT, Microsoft Windows 95, Microsoft Windows for Workgroups, and Microsoft LAN Manager.
- Transmission Control Protocol/Internet Protocol (TCP/IP) networks, including UNIX hosts.
- Remote access systems.
- AppleTalk-based networks (made possible through the Windows NT Server Services for the Macintosh).
- Novell NetWare 3.*x* and 4.*x* networks.

These networking capabilities differentiate Windows NT from other operating systems, such as Microsoft MS-DOS and Microsoft Windows, which install network capabilities separately from the core operating system.

After this lesson, you will be able to:
- Describe the network components that make up the Windows NT network architecture.
- Describe the network transport protocols included with Windows NT.

Estimated lesson time: 30 minutes

Network Component Overview

I/O Manager, a component of Executive Services, contains most of the Windows NT networking components. The components contained within I/O Manager are organized into the following architectural layers:

- *Network adapter card drivers* that are compatible with the network device interface specification (NDIS 4.0). These drivers link computers running Windows NT to the network through corresponding network adapter cards and protocols.
- *Protocols* that enable the reliable flow of data between computers on a network.
- *File system drivers* that enable applications to access local and remote system resources.

The following illustration shows the networking components in I/O Manager.

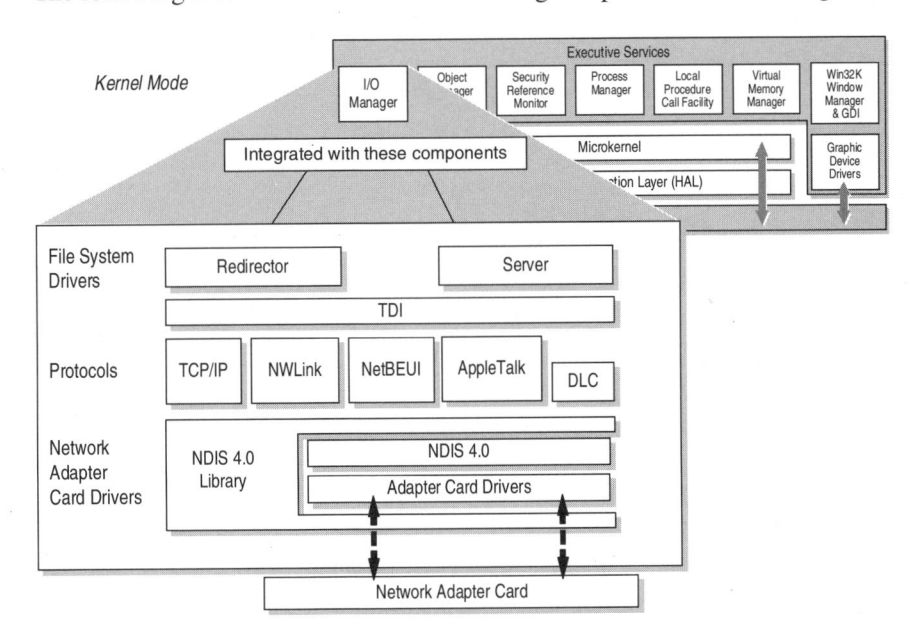

Each component communicates through programming interfaces called *boundaries*. A boundary is the unified interface between the functional layers in the Windows NT network architecture model. Creating boundaries as breakpoints in the network layers helps open the networking components of the operating system to outside development by making it easier for vendors to develop network drivers and services. These boundary layers modularize the Windows NT network architecture and provide a platform for developers to build distributed applications. For example, vendors developing transport protocols need to program only between the boundary layers instead of programming for the entire Open Systems Interconnection (OSI) model.

There are two boundary layers in the Windows NT networking architecture model: transport driver interface (TDI) and network device interface specification (NDIS) 4.0, which are described later in this chapter.

NDIS-Compatible Network Adapter Card Drivers

NDIS-compatible network adapter card drivers coordinate communications between network adapter cards and the computer's hardware, firmware, and software. Network adapter cards are the physical interface between the computer and the network cable.

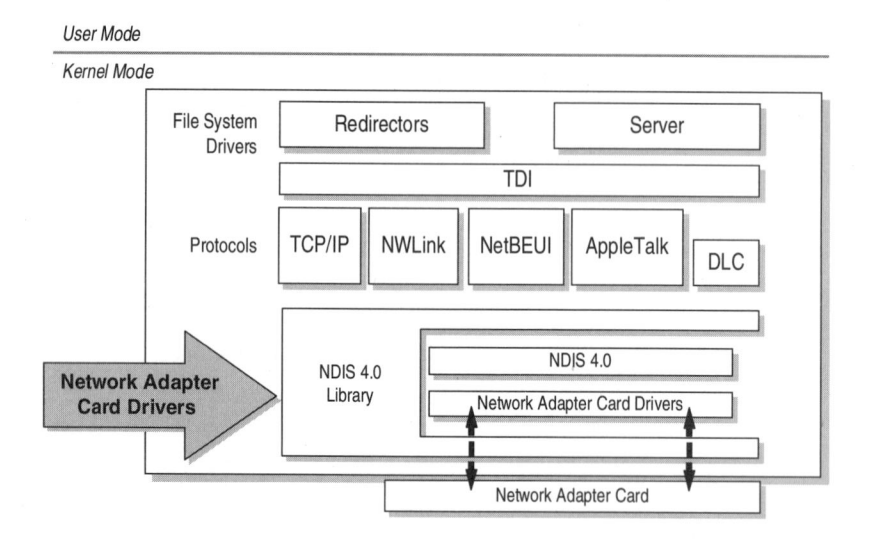

Each network adapter card can have one or more corresponding drivers. These drivers must be compatible with NDIS 4.0 to operate with computers running Windows NT 4.0. With NDIS 4.0, one or more protocols can be bound, independently, to one or more network adapter card drivers.

Because network adapter cards and their corresponding drivers are independent of the protocols, changing protocols does not require a reconfiguration of network adapter cards.

Network Device Interface Specification 4.0

The network device interface specification (NDIS) 4.0 defines the software interface used by protocols to communicate with network adapter card drivers. Any NDIS 4.0–compatible protocol can communicate with any NDIS 4.0–compatible network adapter card driver. Therefore, a protocol does not need to include blocks of code written for specific network adapter card drivers.

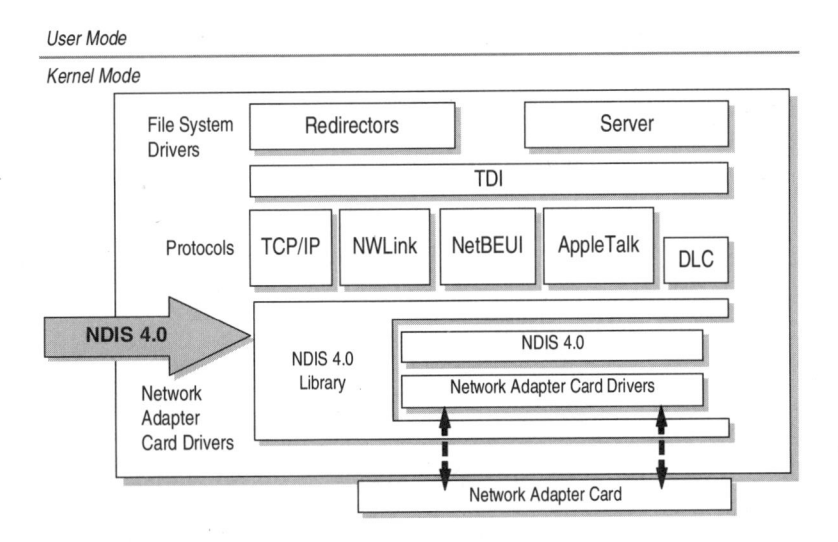

The initial communication channel between the protocol and the network adapter card driver is established through a process called *binding*.

Note For more information on binding, see Chapter 10, "Configuring Windows NT Protocols."

In Windows NT, NDIS 4.0 is implemented in a module called Ndis.sys which is referred to as the NDIS 4.0 library or *wrapper*. The NDIS 4.0 library is code surrounding all of the NDIS device drivers. The library provides a uniform interface between protocol drivers and NDIS device drivers, and contains supporting routines that make it easier to develop an NDIS driver.

In Windows NT, NDIS 4.0 allows:

- Communication links between network adapter cards and associated drivers.
- Protocols and network adapter card drivers to remain independent of each other.
- An unlimited number of network adapter cards.
- An unlimited number of protocols to be bound to a single network adapter card.

Protocols

Protocols govern communication between two or more host computers. Some protocols are commonly referred to as transport protocols. For example, TCP/IP, NWLink, NetBEUI, and AppleTalk are transport protocols. In the Windows NT network architecture, protocols are located above the NDIS 4.0 interface, as shown in the following illustration. Protocols communicate with network adapter cards through NDIS 4.0–compatible network adapter card drivers. Windows NT supports multiple protocols, bound simultaneously to one or more adapters.

In the following illustration, *data link control* (DLC) is also listed as a protocol. However, the DLC protocol is not a transport protocol. DLC is used primarily for accessing printers connected directly to the network and for accessing systems network architecture (SNA) mainframes.

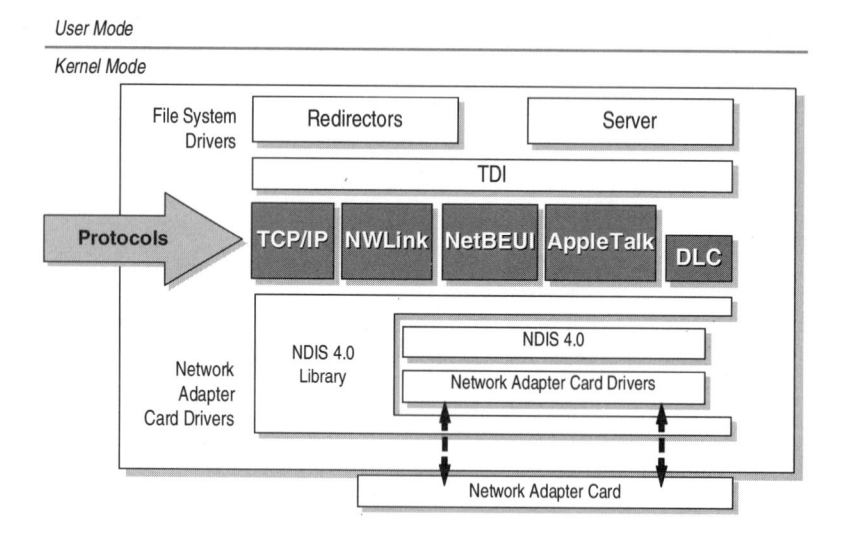

The following protocols are included with Windows NT Server and Windows NT Workstation:

- *Transmission Control Protocol/Internet Protocol (TCP/IP).* A routable networking protocol that supports wide area networks (WANs). TCP/IP is the protocol used on the Internet.
- *NWLink IPX/SPX compatible transport.* An NDIS 4.0–compatible version of the Internetwork Packet Exchange/Sequenced Packet Exchange (IPX/SPX) protocol. NWLink allows users to communicate with MS-DOS, OS/2, Windows, or other computers running Windows NT through remote procedure calls (RPCs), Windows Sockets, or Novell NetBIOS IPX/SPX.

- *NetBEUI.* A very fast and efficient non-routable protocol that relies heavily on broadcasts, and is commonly used in smaller networks. NetBEUI provides compatibility with existing LAN Manager, LAN Server, Windows 95, and Windows for Workgroups installations.
- *AppleTalk.* Used with Services for Macintosh on a computer running Windows NT Server to host connections from Apple Macintosh clients.
- *Data link control (DLC).* Traditionally used as an interface with SNA mainframes and printers that are directly connected to the network. It cannot be used, however, to establish file and print connections to another computer.

Note For more information on protocols, see Chapter 10, "Configuring Windows NT Protocols," or see *Networking Supplement* in Books Online.

Transport Driver Interface

The Transport Driver Interface (TDI) is a boundary layer that provides a common programming interface for file system drivers, such as the Workstation service (Redirector) or Server service (Server), to communicate with the transport protocols. The TDI allows the Redirector and Server to remain independent of the protocols. The Redirector and Service services are covered later in this chapter.

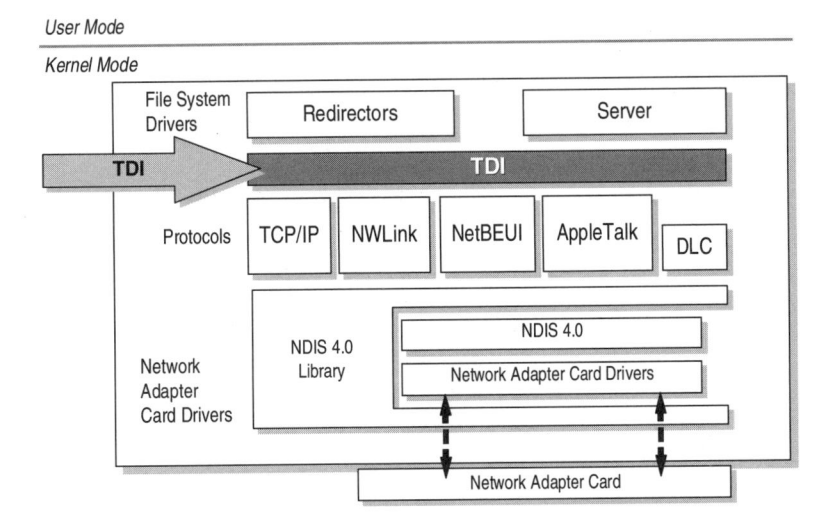

Because the TDI allows networking components to be independent of each other, protocols can be added, removed, or changed without reconfiguring the entire network subsystem.

Note For more information on installing and configuring protocols, see Chapter 10, "Configuring Windows NT Protocols."

File System Drivers

File system drivers are used to access files. Any time you request a file, whether it is a request to perform a read or write operation, a file system driver is involved. For example, if you request a file on an NTFS partition, the Ntfs.sys file system driver is involved in servicing your request. Several major networking components are implemented as file system drivers, such as the Workstation (Redirector) and Server services.

The I/O Manager controls file system drivers. I/O Manager can store files locally on a hard disk, using a file system driver such as Ntfs.sys, or on a remote networked computer using the Redirector file system driver. In the Windows NT network architecture, file system drivers are located above the TDI and allow user-mode applications to access system resources, such as a read call from an I/O operation to an NTFS partition, or a read call to a remote resource that uses the Workstation (Redirector) service.

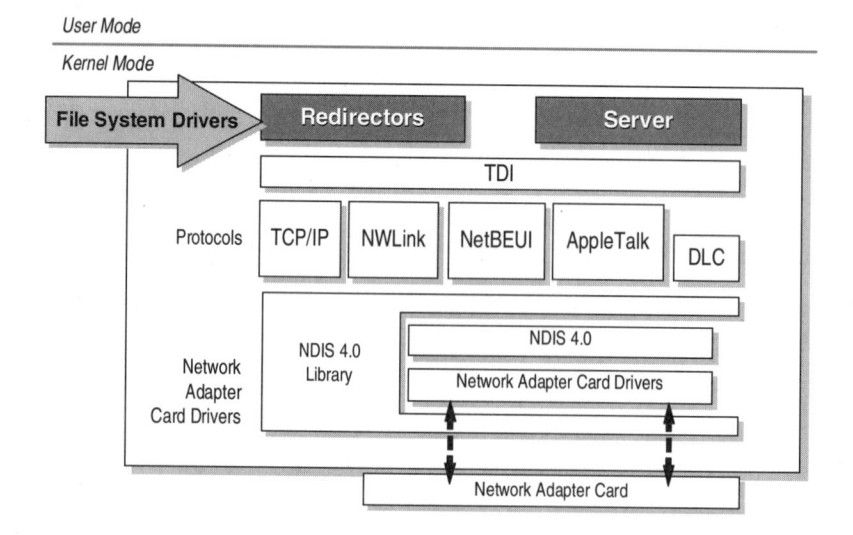

Redirector

The I/O Manager determines if an I/O request is for a local disk or for a network resource. If the I/O request is for a network resource, the Redirector accepts the I/O requests and sends or redirects the request to the appropriate network resource. The Windows NT Redirector (RDR) is a component that resides above the TDI and communicates with the transport protocols by means of the TDI interface. The Redirector allows connection to Windows for Workgroups, LAN Manager, LAN Server, and other Microsoft network-based servers.

The Redirector is implemented as a Windows NT file system driver. Implementing a redirector as a file system driver provides the following benefits:

- Applications can call the Windows NT I/O API to access files on both local and remote computers. From the I/O Manager perspective, there is no difference between accessing files stored locally on a hard disk and using the Redirector to access files stored remotely on a computer on the network.
- The Redirector can run in kernel mode and directly call other drivers and other kernel-mode components, such as Cache Manager, thereby improving the performance of the Redirector.
- The Redirector can be dynamically loaded and unloaded, like any other file system driver.
- The Redirector can easily coexist with other vendor's redirectors that have been installed on your computer.

Server

Windows NT includes a second component, the Server service (Server). Like the Redirector, the Server resides above the TDI, is implemented as a file system driver, and directly interacts with various other file system drivers to satisfy I/O requests, such as reading or writing to a file.

The Server service supplies the connections requested by client-side redirectors and provides them with access to the resources they request.

When the Server service receives a request from a remote computer asking to read a file that resides on the server's local hard drive, the following steps occur:

- The low-level network drivers receive the request and pass it to the Server service.
- The Server service passes a read-file request to the appropriate local file system driver.
- The local file system driver calls lower-level, disk device drivers to access the file.
- The data is passed back to the local file system driver.
- The local file system driver passes the data back to the Server service.
- The Server service passes the data to the lower-level network drivers for transmission back to the client computer.

Lesson 2: Distributed Processing

As more and more enterprises adopt the client/server paradigm for their networks, standards-based distributed processing becomes a key factor in the success of that effort. A computer running Windows NT can divide applications into components: a front-end component that runs on a client, and a back-end component that runs on a server. This distribution allows an application to take better advantage of hardware resources, such as multiple processors or large amounts of RAM, that are distributed on the network. Computers running Window NT use interprocess communication (IPC) mechanisms to create client/server connections that support distributed processing.

After this lesson, you will be able to:
- Explain the function of distributed processing.
- Describe the IPC mechanisms that enable client/server connections.

Estimated lesson time: 10 minutes

Distributed Application Overview

In a typical distributed application, a computing task is divided into processes: front-end processes that require minimal resources and run on a client, and back-end processes that require large amounts of data, number calculations, shared processing rules, or specialized hardware that run on a server. The server shares its processing power, carrying out tasks on behalf of clients.

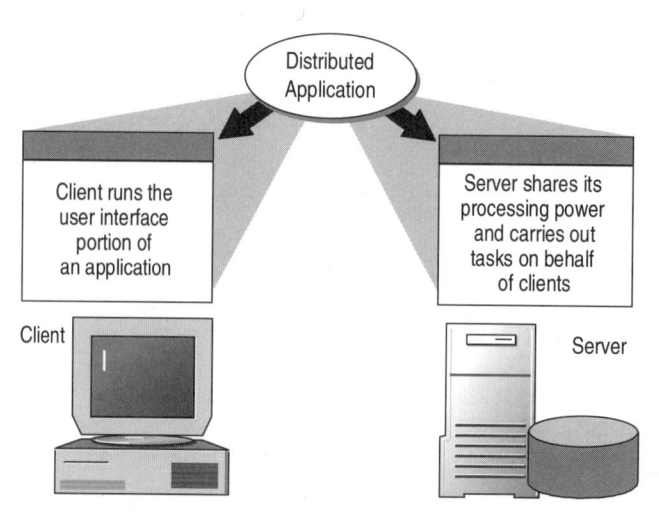

Note Computers running Windows NT can perform the role of either the client or the server for distributed application support. The client and server components can be parts of a common application, such as a Microsoft Exchange Server, or can be parts of different applications, such as Microsoft Access communicating with Microsoft SQL Server.

IPC Mechanisms

In distributed processing, a network connection that allows data to flow in both directions must exist between the client and server portions of a distributed application. The following table describes the Windows NT IPC mechanisms that are used to achieve these connections.

IPC mechanism	This IPC mechanism is used to
Named pipes	Build a bidirectional communication channel between a client and a server. Named pipes provide guaranteed messaging services for distributed applications. Once a pipe is open, both client and server can read data from, and write data to, the pipe. The WinLogon process is an example of an application that uses named pipes.
Mailslots	Build a unidirectional communication channel between a client and server. Mailslots provide second-class, non-guaranteed messaging services for distributed applications. They can be used to identify other computers or services on a network, such as the Browser service.
Windows Sockets (WinSock)	Enable a distributed application to access transport protocols, such as TCP/IP and IPX. WinSock can be used to build a bidirectional, guaranteed communication channel between a client and a server.
Remote procedure calls (RPCs)	Allow a distributed application to call procedures available on various computers in a network.
Network dynamic data exchange (NetDDE)	Share information between applications. NetDDE uses NetBIOS APIs to communicate with the underlying network components. Chat is an example of a NetDDE-based utility.
Distributed Component Object Model (DCOM)	Distribute processes, using RPCs, across multiple computers so that the client and server components of an application can be placed in optimal locations on the network. DCOM is a Microsoft ActiveX technology, and its design enables it to work with both Java™ applets and ActiveX components through use of the Component Object Model (COM).

Lesson 3: Accessing File and Print Resources

Windows NT includes networking components that are necessary to share network resources from a server, and to gain access to network resources from a Windows NT client.

After this lesson, you will be able to:
- Describe the file and print sharing components supported by Windows NT.
- Describe how a computer running Windows NT can access file and print resources on a network.

Estimated lesson time: 10 minutes

File and Print Sharing Components

A computer running Windows NT typically has at least one redirector and a server component that are used for accessing and sharing file and print resources on a network. Along with these components, there are additional components called the multiple universal naming convention provider (MUP) and the Multiple Provider Router (MPR) that are needed to access file and print resources on a network. The following table describes the purpose of each of these components.

Component	Purpose
Workstation service (RDR)	Identify the appropriate service that can provide the resources requested by an application. The redirector does this by accepting I/O requests for remote files, named pipes, or mailslots and redirecting the I/O request to a network service on another computer. The redirector enables a client to gain access to network resources, including the ability to log on to a domain, connect to shared folders and printers, and use distributed applications.
Server service (SRV)	Share and secure resources, such as directories and printers. The Server service accepts incoming I/O requests, such as a request to read or write to a file, and routes the requested resources back to the clients.

(continued)

Component	Purpose
Multiple universal naming convention provider (MUP)	Connect to a remote computer that accepts the universal naming convention (UNC). The UNC is a naming convention for describing network servers. An example of a UNC name is *server_name**share_name**subfolder**file_name*. The MUP frees applications from having to maintain UNC provider listings. This allows a client computer with multiple redirectors installed to browse and access network resources without having to provide a unique syntax to each network redirector.
Multiple Provider Router (MPR)	Support multiple redirectors, including Windows NT, NetWare, and Banyan VINES. For each redirector that is installed, there is also a corresponding *Provider*.dll. The MPR is responsible for routing network requests to the appropriate provider and redirector. For example, if a computer running Windows NT has multiple redirectors installed, Multiple Provider Router is used to direct browser requests to the appropriate redirector for the network that is chosen.

File and Print Sharing Process

When a process on a computer running Windows NT attempts to open a file that resides on a remote computer, the Workstation (Redirector) and Server services complete the following steps to fulfill the I/O request:

1. A client initiates an I/O request through a network command that tells the I/O Manager to open a file.
2. The I/O Manager recognizes the remote file request. With the assistance of the MUP or the MPR, it passes the request to the Redirector.
3. The Redirector (RDR) passes the request to lower-level network drivers, which transmit it to the remote server for processing.
4. The Server service (SRV) receives a request from a remote computer asking it to read a file that resides on the server's local hard disk.
5. The Server service (SRV) passes the request to the I/O Manager.
6. The I/O Manager passes the read request to the local file system driver.
7. The local file system driver calls lower-level disk device drivers to access the file. Once the file is located, it is returned to the client that requested it through the same path.

The following illustration diagrams this process.

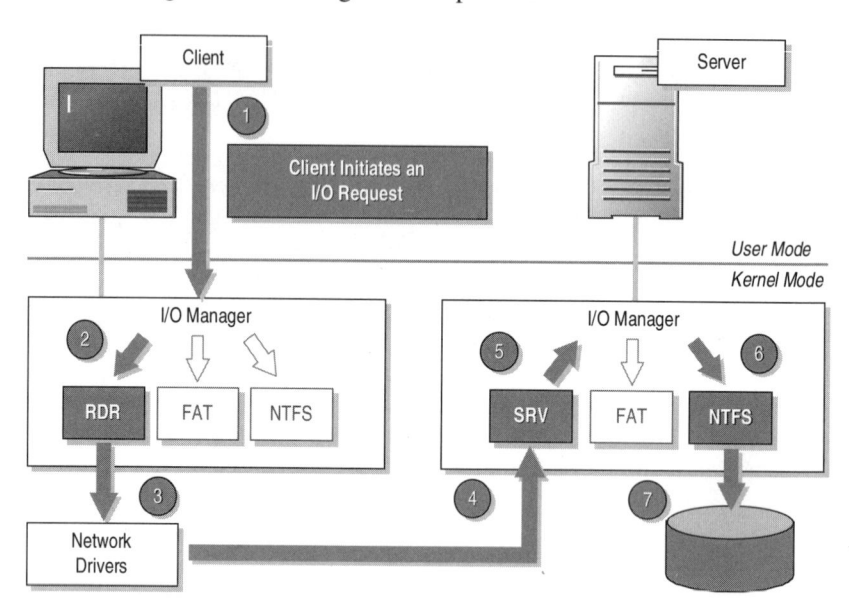

Summary

The following information summarizes the key points in this chapter:

- Networking capabilities are fully integrated into the Windows NT operating system. By providing both client and server capabilities, a computer running Windows NT can be either a client or a server in a distributed application environment. Windows NT also provides file and print sharing capabilities.
- I/O Manager, a component of the Executive Services, contains most of the Windows NT networking components. These components include network adapter cards and their drivers, network protocols, and file system drivers.
- NDIS 4.0 defines the software interface used by protocols to communicate with network adapter card drivers. Any NDIS 4.0–compatible protocol can communicate with any NDIS 4.0–compatible network adapter card driver.
- Computers running Windows NT use IPC mechanisms to create client/server connections that support distributed processing. These include named pipes, mailslots, Windows Sockets, remote procedure calls (RPCs), network dynamic data exchange (NetDDE), and distributed Component Object Model (DCOM).

For more information	See
Windows NT network architecture	Chapter 1 in the *Networking Guide* of the *Microsoft Windows NT Server Resource Kit*

Review

1. Your network includes NetWare-based servers and UNIX-based computers. You must install both the NWLink IPX/SPX compatible transport and TCP/IP protocols on your computer running Windows NT Server so that it can support all of the computers on the network. What is the minimum number of network adapter cards required for the computer running as a Windows NT server to support both protocols?

2. You are able to connect from your computer running Windows NT Workstation to shared folders on any other computer running Windows NT. However, no other computers can connect to the shared folders on your computer. In addition, although you are logged on as an Administrator, your shared folders do not appear with the shared symbol in Windows NT Explorer. What is the likely cause of the problem?

Answer Key

Page 334

Review Answers

1. Your network includes NetWare-based servers and UNIX-based computers. You must install both the NWLink IPX/SPX compatible transport and TCP/IP protocols on your computer running Windows NT Server so that it can support all of the computers on the network. What is the minimum number of network adapter cards required for the computer running as a Windows NT server to support both protocols?

   One. NDIS 4.0 enables multiple transport protocols to be bound to a single network adapter card.

2. You are able to connect from your computer running Windows NT Workstation to shared folders on any other computer running Windows NT. However, no other computers can connect to the shared folders on your computer. In addition, although you are logged on as an Administrator, your shared folders do not appear with the shared symbol in Windows NT Explorer. What is the likely cause of the problem?

   The Server service is probably disabled. Without the Server service, your computer cannot share resources.

CHAPTER 10

Configuring Windows NT Protocols

Lesson 1 Using the Network Program in Control Panel . . . 338

Lesson 2 NWLink . . . 341

Lesson 3 NetBEUI . . . 347

Lesson 4 Microsoft TCP/IP . . . 349

Lesson 5 Network Bindings . . . 360

Review . . . 365

About This Chapter

Microsoft Windows NT includes the following network protocols: NWLink IPX/SPX Compatible Transport, NetBIOS extended user interface (NetBEUI), and TCP/IP. These protocols can be added, removed, or configured using the Network program in Control Panel. In addition, the Network program in Control Panel can be used to optimize network performance by configuring network bindings. This chapter covers the installation and configuration of Windows NT networking protocols.

Before You Begin

To complete the lessons in this chapter, you must have

- Two computers that meet the hardware and software requirements as specified in the Getting Started section of "About This Book."
- Completed all practices in Chapter 2, "Installing Windows NT."

Lesson 1: Using the Network Program in Control Panel

The Network program in Control Panel is used to install and configure Windows NT networking components such as protocols and network adaptercard drivers, and to configure bindings. It is also used to change a computer name, specify a workgroup or domain, and establish a domain account for the computer. This lesson describes how to use the Network program to install and configure network adapter card drivers and protocols.

After this lesson, you will be able to:
- Install and configure network adapter card drivers.
- Install and configure protocols.

Estimated lesson time: 10 minutes

Installing and Configuring Network Adapter Card Drivers

Network adapter card drivers are typically installed during Setup, when hardware is changed, or when drivers need to be updated. Use the **Adapters** tab in the **Network** dialog box in Control Panel to configure network adapter card drivers. The following illustration shows the **Adapters** tab in the **Network** dialog box.

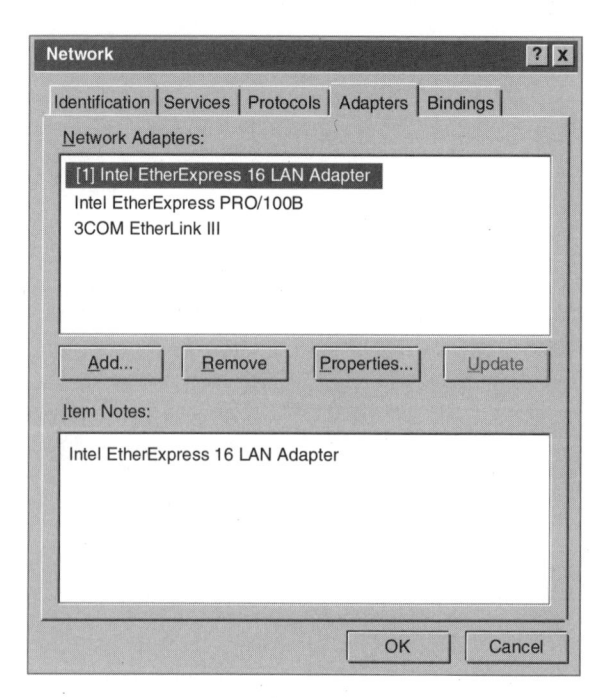

The following table describes the options on the **Adapters** tab.

Option	Use this option to
Add	Add a network adapter card driver to a computer.
Remove	Remove the selected network adapter card driver from the system configuration. Removing the driver does not delete the file from the hard drive. Therefore, you can add the driver again, if necessary.
Properties	View and change the settings for the selected driver. Click the **Properties** button and the **Setup** dialog box appears for the selected network adapter card driver. Use the **Setup** dialog box to configure the appropriate settings, such as the IRQ level, I/O port address, I/O channel, and the transceiver type for a selected network adapter card.
Update	Update the driver information for a selected network adapter card. When you click this button, you are prompted to provide a path to the upgrade driver files.

Installing and Configuring Protocols

Protocols, such as NWLink IPX/SPX Compatible Transport, NetBEUI, and TCP/IP provide a mechanism for computers to connect with each other and exchange information over a network. Protocols communicate with network adapter cards by means of NDIS 4.0–compatible network adapter card drivers. In addition, Windows NT supports multiple protocols, bound to one or more adapters, simultaneously.

Use the **Protocols** tab in the **Network** dialog box in Control Panel to install and configure protocols. The following illustration shows the **Protocols** tab in the **Network** dialog box.

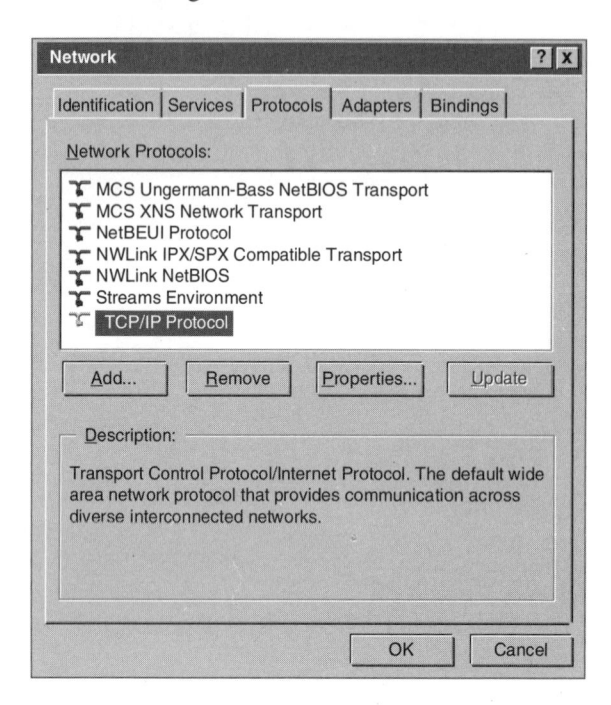

![Network dialog box showing the Protocols tab with Network Protocols list including MCS Ungermann-Bass NetBIOS Transport, MCS XNS Network Transport, NetBEUI Protocol, NWLink IPX/SPX Compatible Transport, NWLink NetBIOS, Streams Environment, and TCP/IP Protocol selected. Buttons for Add, Remove, Properties, and Update are shown, with a Description area describing TCP/IP Protocol.]

The following table defines the functions of each option in the **Protocols** tab.

Option	Function
Add	Add a protocol to the system configuration.
Remove	Remove the selected protocol from the system configuration. Removing the protocol does not delete the protocol files from the hard disk. Although the protocol can be added again by using the files that are currently on the hard disk, the recommended method is to use the original source, such as a network share or the Microsoft Windows NT operating system compact disc.
Properties	View and configure settings for the selected protocol.
Update	Update the selected protocol. When you click the **Update** button, you are prompted for the path to the upgrade files.

Lesson 2: NWLink

NWLink IPX/SPX Compatible Transport protocol is the Microsoft 32-bit NDIS 4.0–compliant version of Novell's Internetwork Packet Exchange/Sequenced Packet Exchange (IPX/SPX) protocol. This lesson describes NWLink's function and configuration in a Windows NT environment.

After this lesson, you will be able to:
- Describe the purpose of the NWLink IPX/SPX Compatible Transport.
- Install and configure NWLink IPX/SPX Compatible Transport.

Estimated lesson time: 20 minutes

NWLink Overview

NWLink is most commonly used in network environments where Microsoft clients need to access client/server applications running on Novell NetWare servers, or NetWare clients need to access client/server applications running on computers running Windows NT. NWLink allows computers running Windows NT to communicate with other network devices that are using IPX/SPX, such as HP JetDirect printers. NWLink can also be used in small network environments that only use Windows NT and Microsoft clients.

NWLink supports the following networking APIs that provide IPC services:

- Windows Sockets (WinSock) support existing NetWare applications written to comply with the NetWare IPX/SPX Sockets interface. WinSock is commonly used for communicating with NetWare Loadable Modules (NLMs). Customers implementing client/server solutions using NLMs can port them to Windows NT Server and still retain compatibility with their clients.

- NetBIOS over IPX, implemented as NWLink NetBIOS, supports communication between a NetWare workstation running NetBIOS and a Windows NT–based computer running NWLink NetBIOS.

Note For more information on configuring computers running Windows NT so that they can access file and print resources on a NetWare server, and on configuring NetWare clients so that they can access file and print resources stored on the computer running Windows NT, see Chapter 14, "Interoperating with Novell NetWare."

Configuring NWLink

The frame type and network number are options that must be configured when installing and configuring NWLink IPX/SPX Compatible Transport.

Frame Types

A frame type defines the way in which the network adapter card formats data to be sent over a network. For computers running Windows NT and NetWare servers to communicate, you need to configure NWLink on the computer running Windows NT with the same frame type as the one used by NetWare servers. Setting an incorrect frame type prevents computers running Windows NT from communicating with NetWare servers.

The following table lists the topologies and frame types supported by NWLink.

Topology	Supported frame type
Ethernet	Ethernet II, 802.3, 802.2, and Sub Network Access Protocol (SNAP), which defaults to 802.2
Token Ring	802.5 and SNAP
FDDI (fiber distributed data interface)	802.2 and SNAP

Note On Ethernet networks, the standard frame type for NetWare 2.2 and NetWare 3.11 is 802.3. Starting with NetWare 3.12, the default frame type was changed to 802.2.

For further information about Ethernet, Token Ring, and FDDI topologies, see *Networking Essentials,* by Microsoft Press®.

Automatically Detected Frame Types

When NWLink is installed on a computer running Windows NT, the frame type is automatically detected. This allows Windows NT to determine the IPX frame type being used on the network and sets the NWLink frame type accordingly. If multiple frame types are detected in addition to the 802.2 frame type, NWLink defaults to the 802.2 frame type.

It is possible for a connection to be established between two computers that are using different frame types on the network, when one of those computers is a NetWare computer acting as a *router*. A router is a device that is used to connect networks of different types, such as those using different architectures and protocols. The NetWare computer could route the network traffic between the two frame types. However, this is not efficient and, depending on the number of computers using the two frame types, this routing could potentially result in a bottleneck. If a connection is successfully established through NWLink but is very slow, verify that the two systems are using the same frame type.

Configuring Frame Types

Frame types are configured through the Network program in Control Panel. Use the **NWLink IPX/SPX Properties** dialog box to designate a frame type for each network adapter card on a computer. Windows NT can be set to automatically detect a frame type for the network. If frame type detection is set to manual, you would need to specify the frame type. A computer running Windows NT can be configured to use multiple frame types simultaneously. The following illustration shows the **General** tab in the **NWLink IPX/SPX Properties** dialog box on a computer running Windows NT Server.

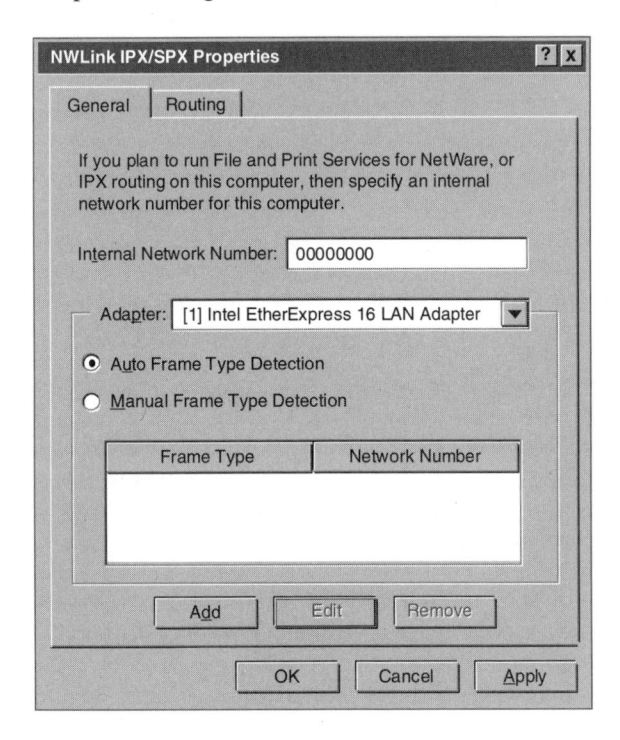

![NWLink IPX/SPX Properties dialog box showing General tab with Internal Network Number field set to 00000000, Adapter set to [1] Intel EtherExpress 16 LAN Adapter, Auto Frame Type Detection selected, and Frame Type/Network Number table.]

Network Number and Internal Network Number

The NWLink IPX/SPX protocol included with Windows NT uses two types of network numbers, the Network Number and the Internal Network Number, each of which serves a distinctly different function. The Network Number identifies the network segment that you need to access; the Internal Network Number identifies your computer on the network.

Network Number

Windows NT uses an IPX network number for routing purposes. This number is sometimes referred to as the *external network number*, and must be unique for each network segment. If you do not know the appropriate network numbers to use, you must obtain them from the NetWare administrator. You then assign a network number to each configured frame type and adapter combination on your computer.

Internal Network Number

Windows NT also uses an internal network number to uniquely identify the computer on the network for internal routing. This internal network number, also known as a *virtual network number*, is represented by an eight-digit hexadecimal number. By default, the internal network number is (00000000).

Windows NT does not automatically detect the internal network number. In each of the following situations, you need to manually assign a unique non-zero internal network number:

- You have File and Print Services for NetWare (FPNW) installed, and you choose multiple frame types on a single adapter.
- You have bound NWLink to multiple adapters in your computer.
- Your computer is acting as a Windows NT server for an application that uses the NetWare Service Advertising Protocol (SAP), such as SQL or SNA.

Routing Information Protocol

Use the **Routing** tab in the **NWLink IPX/SPX Properties** dialog box to enable or disable the Routing Information Protocol (RIP). Using RIP routing over IPX, a Windows NT Server can act as an IPX router.

RIP allows a router to exchange information with neighboring routers. A RIP router is a computer or other piece of hardware that broadcasts routing information, such as network addresses. As a router becomes aware of any change in the internetwork layout—for example, a downed router—it broadcasts the information to neighboring routers.

Practice

In these procedures, you create a shortcut for the Network program. You install the Microsoft NWLink IPX/SPX Compatible Transport protocol on both Server1 and Workstation1, and test the NWLink IPX/SPX Compatible Transport protocol installation.

Note Complete these procedures on both Server1 and Workstation1.

▶ **To create a shortcut to the Network program in Control Panel**

1. Log on to the domain as Administrator.
2. In Control Panel, drag the Network icon to your desktop.

   A dialog box appears, asking if you want to create a shortcut.
3. Click **Yes**.

   A shortcut icon for the Network program appears.

▶ **To install NWLink**

1. Double-click the Shortcut to Network icon.

   The **Network** dialog box appears.
2. Click the **Protocols** tab, and then click **Add**.

   The **Select Network Protocol** dialog box appears.
3. Click **NWLink IPX/SPX Compatible Transport**, and then click **OK**.

   The **Windows NT Setup** dialog box appears.
4. Type the path to your Microsoft Windows NT Setup files in the text box:
   - On Workstation1, insert the *Windows NT Workstation* compact disc, type *cd-rom_drive*:**\I386** and then click **Continue**.
   - On Server1, type **\\Server1\Nts_source\I386** and then click **Continue**.

   All of the files that you need are copied to your computer.

   What are the two new protocols displayed on the **Protocols** tab in the **Network** property sheet?

   _____

   _____

5. Click **TCP/IP Protocol**, and then click **Remove**.

   A **Warning** dialog box appears.

6. Click **Yes**, and then click **Close**.

   Notice that the installation process continues and binds your network adapter card to NWLink IPX/SPX protocol. The **Network Setting Change** dialog box appears when the installation process is completed. It asks if you want to restart your computer now.

7. Click **Yes** to restart your computer.

▶ **To test your installation of the Microsoft NWLink IPX/SPX Compatible Transport protocol**

Note Complete this procedure on Workstation1.

1. Log on to the domain as Administrator.
2. Click the **Start** button, and then click **Run**.
3. Type **\\Server1** and then click **OK**.

   Can you connect to Server1? If a window appears displaying Server1 in the title bar and showing the shares available on Server1, you successfully connected to Server1.

4. Close the Server1 window.

Lesson 3: NetBEUI

NetBIOS extended user interface (NetBEUI) is a protocol developed for small departmental local area networks (LANs) of 20 to 200 computers. NetBEUI is not suitable for wide-area networks because it cannot be routed.

After this lesson, you will be able to:
- Identify the purpose and function of NetBEUI.
- Identify compatible operating systems for NetBEUI.
- Install NetBEUI.

Estimated lesson time: 10 minutes

NetBEUI provides compatibility with existing LANs that use the NetBEUI protocol and provides interoperability with older network systems, such as Microsoft LAN Manager and Microsoft Windows for Workgroups, version 3.11.

NetBEUI provides computers running Windows NT with the following capabilities:

- Connection-oriented and connectionless communication between computers.
- Self-configuration and self-tuning.
- Error protection.
- Small memory overhead.

Windows NT–based computers running NetBEUI must be connected using bridges instead of routers. A bridge is a device that joins two LANs.

NetBEUI is a non-routable, broadcast-based protocol. Because NetBEUI relies on broadcasts for many of its functions, such as name registration and discovery, its use causes more broadcast traffic than other protocols.

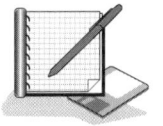

Practice

In these procedures, you install Microsoft NetBEUI and verify that the installation was successful.

▶ **To install Microsoft NetBEUI**

Note Complete this procedure on both Server1 and Workstation1.

1. Log on to the domain as Administrator.
2. Double-click the Shortcut to Network icon.
3. In the **Network** dialog box, click the **Protocols** tab.

4. Click **Add**.
5. Click **NetBEUI Protocol**, and then click **OK**.

   A **Windows NT Setup** dialog box appears and prompts you for the path of the files to be copied.

6. Type the path to your Microsoft Windows NT Setup files in the text box:
   - On Workstation1, insert the *Windows NT Workstation* compact disc, type *cd-rom_drive***:\I386** and then click **Continue**.
   - On Server1, type **\\Server1\Nts_source\I386** and then click **Continue**.

   Once the NetBEUI Protocol is installed, the **Protocols** tab in the **Network** dialog box reappears.

7. Click **NWLink IPX/SPX Compatible Transport**, and then click **Remove**.

   A **Warning** dialog box appears.

8. Click **Yes**, and then click **Close**.

   The binding process starts and finishes and the **Network Settings Change** dialog box appears.

9. When prompted, click **Yes** to restart the computer.

▶ **To verify that your installation was successful**

Note Complete this procedure on Workstation1. Both Workstation1 and Server1 must be restarted after you install NetBEUI on them.

1. Log on to the domain as Administrator.
2. Click the **Start** button, and then click **Run**.
3. Type **\\Server1** and then click **OK**.

   Can you connect to Server1?

4. Close the Server1 window.

Lesson 4: Microsoft TCP/IP

TCP/IP is a networking protocol that provides communication across interconnected networks made up of computers with diverse hardware architectures and various operating systems. Microsoft TCP/IP on Windows NT enables enterprise networking and connectivity on your computer running Windows NT. This lesson provides an overview of the function, installation, and configuration of Microsoft TCP/IP.

After this lesson, you will be able to:
- Explain the purpose and function of Microsoft TCP/IP.
- Identify the components included in the Microsoft TCP/IP protocol suite.
- Configure TCP/IP manually, when given an IP address, the subnet mask, and the default gateway.
- Identify the TCP/IP utilities included with Windows NT.
- Test the TCP/IP configuration and validate connections to other computers.

Estimated lesson time: 45 minutes

TCP/IP is a flexible suite of protocols designed for wide area networks (WANs) and adaptable to a wide range of network hardware. TCP/IP can be used to communicate with Windows NT systems, with devices that use other Microsoft networking products, and with non-Microsoft systems, such as UNIX systems.

Microsoft TCP/IP Overview

Microsoft TCP/IP is a routable, enterprise networking protocol. Adding it to a Windows NT system configuration provides the following capabilities:

- A standard, routable, enterprise networking protocol for Windows NT.
- An architecture that facilitates connectivity in heterogeneous environments.
- Access to the Internet and its resources.

Microsoft TCP/IP Protocol Suite

TCP/IP is a suite of protocols designed for internetworks. The Microsoft TCP/IP core protocols provide a set of standards for how computers running Windows NT communicate in a network environment. The following illustration provides an overview of the Microsoft TCP/IP protocol suite.

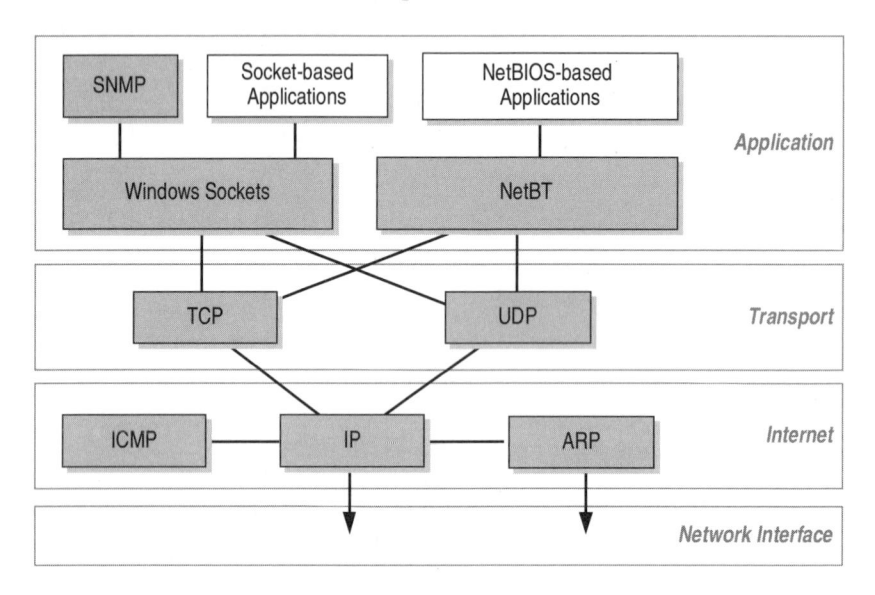

The following table describes the protocols included with Microsoft TCP/IP.

Protocol	This protocol provides
Simple Network Management Protocol (SNMP)	Management Information Base (MIBs) monitoring data contained in SNMP.
Windows Sockets (WinSock)	Standard interface between socket-based applications and TCP/IP protocols.
NetBIOS over TCP/IP (NetBT)	NetBIOS services, including name, datagram, and session services. It also provides a standard interface between NetBIOS-based applications and TCP/IP protocols.
Transmission Control Protocol (TCP)	Connection-oriented, guaranteed packet delivery services.
User Datagram Protocol (UDP)	Connectionless packet delivery services that are not guaranteed.

(*continued*)

Protocol	This protocol provides
Internet Control Message Protocol (ICMP)	Special communication between hosts. Reports messages and errors regarding packet delivery.
Internet Protocol (IP)	Address and routing functions.
Address Resolution Protocol (ARP)	IP address mapping to the media access control sublayer address. An IP address is required for each computer that runs TCP/IP. An IP address is a logical 32-bit address used to identify a TCP/IP host. The media access control sublayer communicates directly with the network adapter card and is responsible for delivering error-free data between two computers on a network.

Configuring TCP/IP Manually

If you are not using Dynamic Host Configuration Protocol (DHCP) to automatically assign the IP addresses, you have to configure TCP/IP manually. To configure TCP/IP manually after it has been installed, you use the **Protocols** tab in the Network program in Control Panel.

The following illustration shows the **Microsoft TCP/IP Properties** dialog box with the **Specify an IP address** option selected.

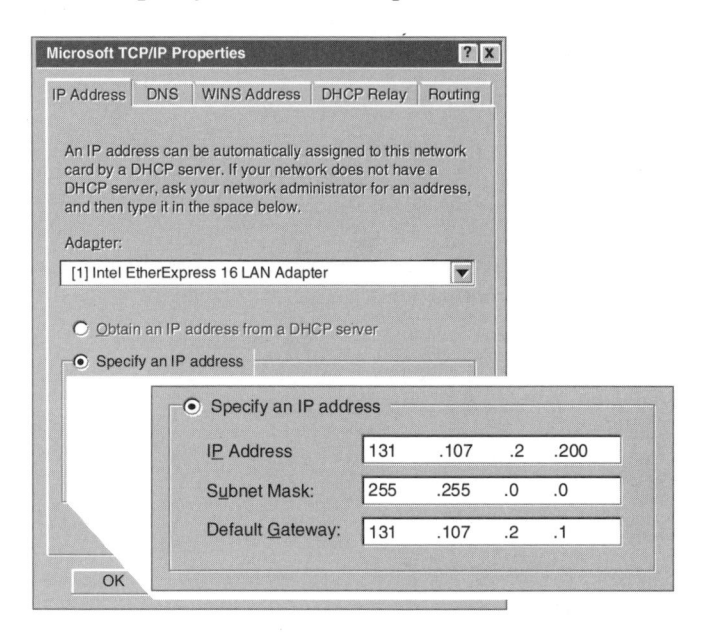

```
Microsoft TCP/IP Properties                          [?][X]
 IP Address | DNS | WINS Address | DHCP Relay | Routing

 An IP address can be automatically assigned to this network
 card by a DHCP server. If your network does not have a
 DHCP server, ask your network administrator for an address,
 and then type it in the space below.

 Adapter:
 [1] Intel EtherExpress 16 LAN Adapter           [▼]

 ○ Obtain an IP address from a DHCP server
 ⦿ Specify an IP address
    ┌─ ⦿ Specify an IP address ──────────────────┐
    │                                             │
    │   IP Address:       131 .107 .2   .200      │
    │                                             │
    │   Subnet Mask:      255 .255 .0   .0        │
    │                                             │
    │   Default Gateway:  131 .107 .2   .1        │
    │                                             │
    [ OK ]
```

When configuring TCP/IP manually, you can:

- Assign an IP address.
- Assign a subnet mask.
- Add a default gateway.

These parameters are required for each network adapter card in the computer that uses TCP/IP. The following table describes these parameters.

Parameter	Description
IP address	An IP address is a logical 32-bit address that is used to identify a TCP/IP host. Each IP address has two parts: the network ID and the host ID. The network ID identifies all hosts that are on the same physical network. The host ID identifies a host on the network. Each computer running TCP/IP requires a unique IP address, such as 131.107.2.200. In this example, 131.107 is the network ID, and 2.200 is the host ID.
Subnet mask	A subnet is a network in a multiple network environment that uses IP addresses derived from a single network ID. Using subnets, an organization can divide a single large network into multiple physical networks and connect them with routers.
	A subnet mask is used to block out a portion of the IP address so that TCP/IP can distinguish the network ID from the host ID. When TCP/IP hosts try to communicate, the subnet mask is used to determine whether the destination host is located on a local or a remote network. A sample subnet mask is 255.255.0.0. In order for computers to communicate on a network, they must have the same subnet mask.
Default gateway	For communication with a host on another network, an IP address should be configured for the default gateway. TCP/IP sends packets that are destined for remote networks to the default gateway, if no other route is configured on the local host to the destination network. If a default gateway is not configured, communication may be limited to the local network (subnet). A sample default gateway is 131.107.2.1.

Important Be careful when assigning IP addresses; IP communications can fail when multiple devices use the same IP address.

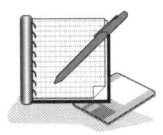

Practice

In these procedures, you remove NetBEUI, install TCP/IP, and then verify your installation.

▶ **To remove NetBEUI, and install and manually configure TCP/IP**

Note Complete this procedure on both Server1 and Workstation1.

1. Log on to the domain as Administrator.
2. Double-click the Shortcut to Network icon.

    The **Network** dialog box appears.
3. Click the **Protocols** tab.
4. Click **NetBEUI Protocol**, and then click **Remove**.

    A **Warning** dialog box appears.
5. Click **Yes**.
6. Click **Add**.

    The **Select Network Protocol** dialog box appears.
7. Click **TCP/IP Protocol**, and then click **OK**.

    The **TCP/IP Setup** dialog box appears. You will not be using DHCP at this time.
8. Click **No**.
9. Type the path to your Microsoft Windows NT Setup files in the text box:
    - On Workstation1, insert the *Windows NT Workstation* compact disc, type *cd-rom_drive***:\I386** and then click **Continue**.
    - On Server1 type **\\Server1\Nts_source\I386** and then click **Continue**.

    All of the files that you need are copied to your computer.
10. Click **Close**.

    The **Microsoft TCP/IP Properties** dialog box appears, with the **IP Address** tab in the foreground.

11. Click **Specify an IP address**, and then complete the configuration settings as indicated in the following table.

In this box	Use
IP Address	131.107.2.200 on Server1
	131.107.2.201 on Workstation1
Subnet Mask	255.255.0.0
Default Gateway	Leave this blank

12. Click **OK**.
13. Click **Yes** to restart your computer.

▶ **To verify that your installation was successful**

Note Complete this procedure on Workstation1. Both Workstation1 and Server1 must have restarted after you installed NetBEUI on them.

1. Log on to the domain as Administrator.
2. Click the **Start** button, and the click **Run**.
3. Type **\\Server1** and then click **OK**.

   Can you connect to Server1?

4. Close the Server1 window.

Configuring TCP/IP Automatically

Windows NT provides a service called the Dynamic Host Configuration Protocol (DHCP) server service. When a DHCP server is configured on a network, clients that support DHCP, such as Windows NT Server and Windows NT Workstation, can request the TCP/IP configuration parameters (IP address, subnet mask, and a default gateway) from the DHCP server.

When a DHCP server is available, TCP/IP can be configured automatically by selecting the **Obtain an IP address from a DHCP server** option on the **IP Address** tab in the **Microsoft TCP/IP Properties** dialog box.

The following illustration shows the **Microsoft TCP/IP Properties** dialog box, with **Obtain an IP address from a DHCP server** selected.

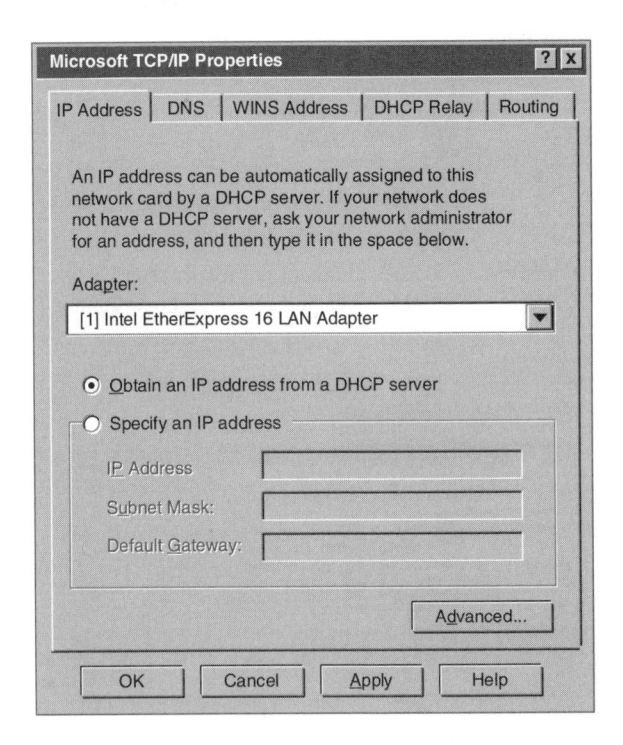

![Microsoft TCP/IP Properties dialog box showing IP Address tab with "Obtain an IP address from a DHCP server" option selected. Adapter shown is [1] Intel EtherExpress 16 LAN Adapter. Tabs: IP Address, DNS, WINS Address, DHCP Relay, Routing.]

When **Obtain an IP address from a DHCP server** is selected, the DHCP client contacts a DHCP server for its configuration information. After receiving this request, the DHCP server assigns an IP address, subnet mask, and default gateway to the DHCP client.

Note The Windows NT Server's DHCP Server service is discussed in more detail in Chapter 11, "Windows NT Networking Services."

Using TCP/IP Utilities

The following table describes the Windows NT utilities that work with TCP/IP protocols to provide networking capabilities.

Utility	Function
Packet Internet Groper (PING)	Verifies configurations and tests connections.
File Transfer Protocol (FTP)	Provides bidirectional file transfers between a computer running Windows NT and any TCP/IP host running FTP.
Trivial File Transfer Protocol (TFTP)	Provides bidirectional file transfers between a computer running Windows NT and a TCP/IP host running TFTP.
Telnet	Provides terminal emulation to a TCP/IP host running Telnet.
Remote Copy Protocol (RCP)	Copies files between a computer running Windows NT and a UNIX host.
Remote Shell (RSH)	Runs commands on a UNIX host.
Remote Execution (REXEC)	Runs a process on a remote computer.
Finger	Retrieves system information from a remote computer that supports TCP/IP and the finger service.
Microsoft Internet Explorer (IE)	Locates resources on the Internet.
ARP	Displays a cache of locally resolved IP addresses to physical addresses.
ipconfig	Displays the current TCP/IP configuration.
nbtstat	Displays protocol statistics and connections using NetBIOS over TCP/IP.
netstat	Displays TCP/IP protocol statistics and connections.
Route	Displays or modifies the local routing table.
Hostname	Returns the local computer's host name for authentication by the RCP, RSH, and REXEC utilities.
Tracert	Checks the route to a remote system.

Testing TCP/IP with Ipconfig and Ping

After TCP/IP is configured and the computer is restarted, it is a good idea to test the configuration and connections to other TCP/IP hosts and networks. This is accomplished through the Command Prompt using the ipconfig and ping utilities.

The Ipconfig Utility

The ipconfig utility is used to verify the TCP/IP configuration parameters on a host. This is useful in determining whether the configuration is initialized or if a duplicate IP address has been configured. The ipconfig command syntax is: **ipconfig /all**.

If a configuration has initialized, the IP address, subnet mask, and, if it is assigned, default gateway appear. If a duplicate IP address has been configured, it appears as configured; however, the subnet mask appears as 0.0.0.0. In addition, if DHCP is being used, and the computer is unable to obtain an IP address, the IP address appears as 0.0.0.0.

The Ping Utility

After the TCP/IP configuration is verified with the ipconfig utility, use the Packet Internet Groper (PING) utility to test connectivity. Ping is a diagnostic tool used to test TCP/IP configurations and diagnose connection failures. Ping determines whether a particular TCP/IP host is available and functional. The ping command syntax is: **ping** *IP_address*.

The following steps outline procedures for verifying a computer's configuration and for testing router connections using ping.

1. Ping the loopback address (127.0.0.1) to verify that TCP/IP is installed and loaded correctly.
2. Ping the IP address of your computer to verify that it was added correctly and to check for possible duplicate IP addresses.
3. Ping the IP address of the default gateway to verify that default gateway is up and running, and that you can communicate with the local network.
4. Ping the IP address of a remote host to verify that you can communicate through a router.

Tip If you start with step 4 and can ping successfully, then steps 1 through 3 are successful by default. If the ping is not successful, ping another remote host.

If ping is successful, it responds, by default, with the following message four times: **Reply from** *IP_address*.

Practice

In these procedures, you use ping to verify IP connectivity, and use ipconfig to display the TCP/IP configuration.

Note Complete these procedures on both Server1 and Workstation1.

▶ **To test that the TCP/IP and configuration is correct**

1. Log on to the domain as Administrator.
2. Start a command prompt.
3. To test that IP is working and bound to your adapter, type **ping 127.0.0.1** and then press ENTER.

   Four "Reply from 127.0.0.1" messages should appear indicating that the internal loop-back test was successful.
4. Type **ping 131.107.2.200** and then press ENTER.

   Four "Reply from 131.107.2.200" messages should appear.

   Note If you are on Workstation1, you are testing the connectivity to Server1 by pinging the Server1 IP address.

   If you are on Server1, you are testing to verify that the IP address was added correctly and to check for possible duplicate IP addresses.

5. Type **ping 131.107.2.201** and then press ENTER.

   Four "Reply from 131.107.2.201" messages should appear.

   Note If you are on Server1, you are testing the connectivity to Workstation1 by pinging the Workstation1 IP address.

   If you are on Workstation1, you are testing to verify that the IP address was added correctly and to check for possible duplicate IP addresses.

6. Type **ping 131.107.2.222** and then press ENTER.

   Four "Request timed out." messages should appear. This is an invalid IP address; if it is a valid address on your network repeat step 6 using an invalid address.

Chapter 10 Configuring Windows NT Protocols

▶ **To use ipconfig to verify the TCP/IP configuration**

1. Type **ipconfig /all** and then press ENTER.
2. Fill in the following tables.

Windows NT IP configuration	Server1	Workstation1
Host name		

Adapter	Server1	Workstation1
Description		
Physical address		
DHCP enabled		
IP address		
Subnet mask		
Default gateway		

Lesson 5: Network Bindings

Network *bindings* are links that enable communication between network adapter card drivers, protocols, and services. This lesson describes the function of bindings in a network and the process of configuring them.

After this lesson, you will be able to:
- Define the function of bindings in a network.
- Configure bindings for a network that uses NetBEUI, NWLink, and TCP/IP.

Estimated lesson time: 15 minutes

As you have learned, the Windows NT network architecture consists of a series of interdependent layers. The bottom layer of the network architecture ends at the network adapter card, which places the information on the cable, allowing information to flow between computers.

Binding is the process of linking network components on different levels to enable communication between those components. You can bind a network component to one or more network components above or below it. The services each component provides can be shared by all other components bound to it. For example, the installed protocols are bound to the Workstation service as well as the Server service.

In the following illustration all three protocols are bound to the Workstation service, but only the routable protocols, NWLink and TCP/IP, are bound to the Server service. You can also select which protocols to bind to the network adapter cards. Network adapter card (0) is bound to all three protocols, while network adapter card (1) is only bound to the routable protocols. Administrators have full control over which components are bound together.

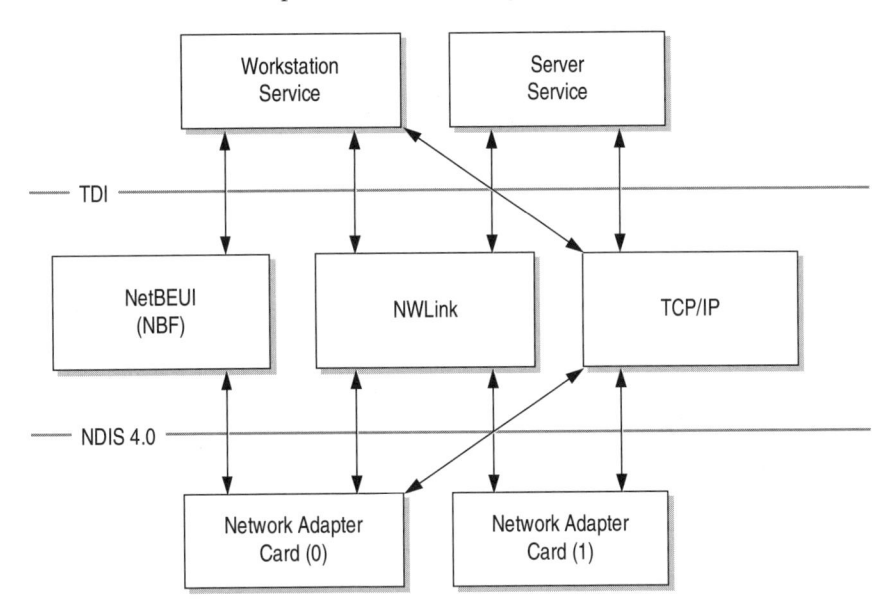

When adding network software, Windows NT automatically binds all dependent network components. NDIS 4.0 provides the capability to bind multiple protocols to multiple network adapter card drivers.

Configuring Network Bindings

To configure network bindings, click the **Bindings** tab in the **Network** dialog box in Control Panel. The **Bindings** tab shows the bindings of the installed network components, from the upper-layer services and protocols to the lowest layer of network adapter card drivers. Bindings can be enabled and disabled, based on your use of the network components installed on your system. The following illustration shows the **Bindings** tab in the **Network** dialog box.

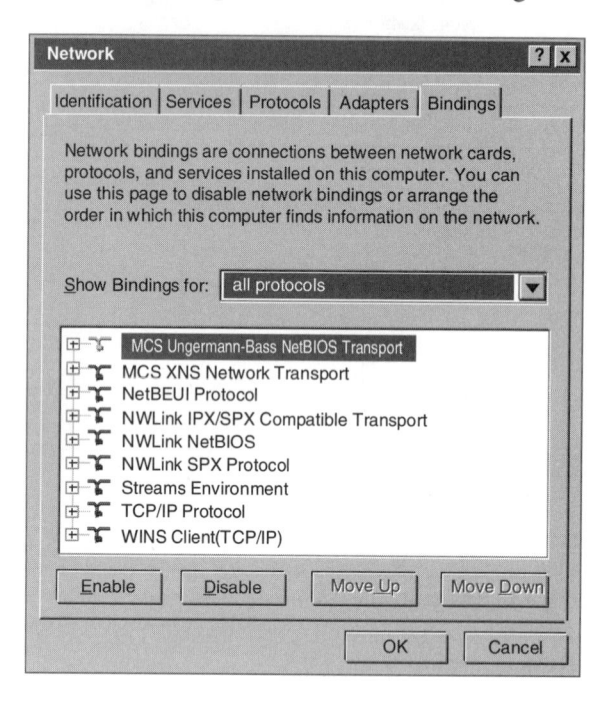

Bindings can also be ordered to optimize the network. For example, if a computer running Windows NT Workstation has NetBEUI, NWLink IPX/SPX, and TCP/IP installed on it, and the majority of servers that it is connected to are running only TCP/IP, the Workstation bindings should be examined. In looking at the Workstation bindings, verify that the Workstation binding to TCP/IP is listed *before* the Workstation binding to NetBEUI, as shown in the following illustration. In this way, when a user attempts to connect to a server, the Workstation service first tries using TCP/IP to establish connection.

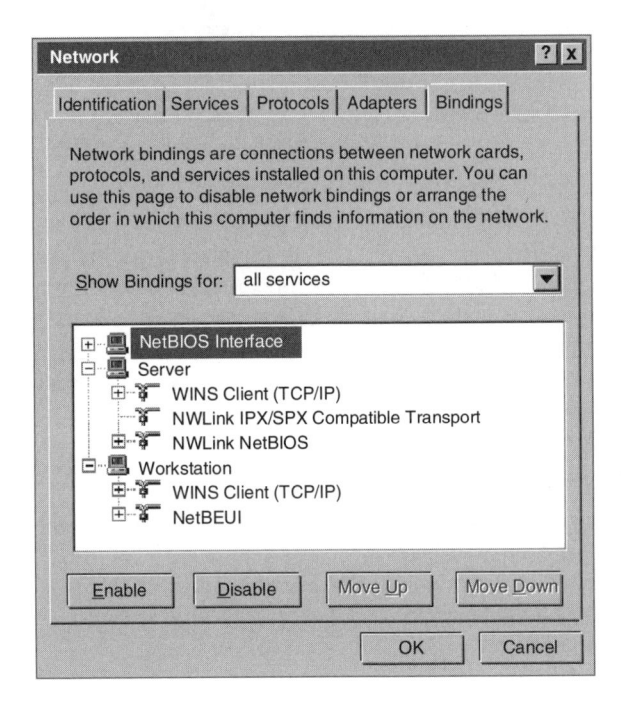

The following table describes the options available on the **Bindings** tab.

Option	Use this option to
Show Bindings for	View bindings for installed services, protocols, and adapters installed on the computer.
Enable	Enable the selected binding path. It also enables all connections in the hierarchy beneath the selected component.
Disable	Disable the selected binding path. It also disables all connections in the hierarchy beneath the selected component.
Move Up or **Move Down**	Move the selected binding up, or down, in the binding list, for computers using more than one network protocol or adapter.

Summary

The following information summarizes the key points in this chapter:

- Windows NT network protocols, network adapter card drivers, and bindings are added, removed, and configured using the Network program in Control Panel.

- NWLink is the Microsoft implementation of the IPX/SPX protocol. NWLink allows NetWare clients to access client/server applications on computers running Windows NT, and allows Microsoft clients to access client/server applications on a NetWare server.

- NetBEUI is a protocol used to support small LANs. It is not suitable for wide area networks because it cannot be routed. NetBEUI is mostly used for older, existing LANs because it is compatible with the NetBEUI protocol driver shipped with older Microsoft networking products.

- Microsoft TCP/IP enables networking and connectivity on computers running Windows NT. To configure TCP/IP manually you must supply an appropriate value for the IP address and the subnet mask. For communication with a remote network, you must also specify a default gateway. The default gateway is where the IP sends packets that are destined for remote networks. If you do not specify a default gateway, communications are limited to the local network. TCP/IP configuration values can also be configured automatically by using a DHCP server. Use the Ping utility to test network connections after TCP/IP is configured.

- Network bindings provide the links between the protocols, network adapter card drivers, and services and enable communication between these components. Windows NT automatically binds all dependent network components. However, bindings can be enabled, disabled, and ordered to optimize network communication.

For more information on	See
DHCP	Chapter 11, "Windows NT Networking Services."
File and Print Services	Chapter 14, "Interoperating with Novell NetWare."

Review

1. Your computer running Windows NT Server can communicate with some, but not all, of the NetWare servers on your network. Some of the NetWare servers are running frame type 802.2 and some are running 802.3. What is the likely cause of the problem?

2. Your computer running Windows NT Workstation was configured manually for TCP/IP. You can connect to any host on your own subnet, but you cannot connect or even **ping** any host on a remote subnet. What is the likely cause of the problem, and how would you fix it?

3. Your computer running Windows NT Server runs TCP/IP as its primary protocol. The server also has NWLink installed, for the sole purpose of hosting connections from NetWare clients. How would you optimize the bindings for this server?

Answer Key

Practice Answers

Page 345

▶ **To install NWLink**

4. Type the path to your Microsoft Windows NT Setup files in the text box:

    On Workstation1, insert the *Windows NT Workstation* compact disc, type *cd-rom_drive***:\I386** and then click **Continue**.

    On Server1, type **\\Server1\Nts_source\I386** and then click **Continue**.

    All of the files that you need are copied to your computer.

    What are the two new protocols displayed on the **Protocols** tab in the **Network** property sheet?

    The two new protocols displayed are NWLink IPX/SPX Compatible Transport and NWLink NetBIOS.

Page 346

▶ **To test your installation of the Microsoft NWLink IPX/SPX Compatible Transport protocol**

3. Type **\\Server1** and then click **OK**.

    Can you connect to Server1? If a window appears displaying Server1 in the title bar and showing the shares available on Server1, you successfully connected to Server1.

    Yes, if your NWLink IPX/SPX Compatible Transport installation is working.

Page 348

▶ **To verify that your installation was successful**

3. Type **\\Server1** and then click **OK**.

    Can you connect to Server1?

    Yes, if both computers are running NetBEUI.

Page 354

▶ **To verify that your installation was successful**

3. Type **\\Server1** and then click **OK**.

    Can you connect to Server1?

    Yes, if TCP/IP is configured correctly on both computers.

Chapter 10   Configuring Windows NT Protocols   367

Page 359

▶ **To use ipconfig to verify the TCP/IP configuration**

2. Fill in the following tables.

Windows NT IP configuration	Server1	Workstation1
Host name	server1	workstation1

Adapter	Server1	Workstation1
Description		
Physical address		
DHCP enabled	No	No
IP address	131.107.2.200	131.107.2.201
Subnet mask	255.255.0.0	255.255.0.0
Default gateway	Blank	Blank

Review Answers

Page 365

1. Your computer running Windows NT Server can communicate with some, but not all, of the NetWare servers on your network. Some of the NetWare servers are running frame type 802.2 and some are running 802.3. What is the likely cause of the problem?

   Although the NWLink implementation in Windows NT can automatically detect a frame type for IPX/SPX compatible protocols, it can only automatically detect one frame type. This network uses two frame types, so both frame types (802.2 and 802.3) will need to be configured manually.

2. Your computer running Windows NT Workstation was configured manually for TCP/IP. You can connect to any host on your own subnet, but you cannot connect or even **ping** any host on a remote subnet. What is the likely cause of the problem, and how would you fix it?

   The default gateway is probably missing or incorrect. It can be added or changed in the Microsoft TCP/IP Properties dialog box accessed through the Network program in Control Panel. Other possibilities: the default gateway is offline, or the subnet mask is incorrect.

3. Your computer running Windows NT Server runs TCP/IP as its primary protocol. The server also has NWLink installed, for the sole purpose of hosting connections from NetWare clients. How would you optimize the bindings for this server?

   For the Server service, order the bindings so that TCP/IP is first, and NWLink is second. Disable the binding between the Workstation service and NWLink, because the server will never need to establish connections or authenticate users over NWLink.

CHAPTER 11

Windows NT Networking Services

Lesson 1 Installing Network Services . . . 371

Lesson 2 Dynamic Host Configuration Protocol Overview . . . 373

Lesson 3 Windows Internet Name Service . . . 390

Lesson 4 Domain Name System . . . 400

Lesson 5 Computer Browser Service . . . 412

Review . . . 419

About This Chapter

In this chapter, you learn how to install and configure the following services provided by Microsoft Windows NT for Transmission Control Protocol/Internet Protocol (TCP/IP): Dynamic Host Configuration Protocol (DHCP), Windows Internet Name Service (WINS), and Domain Name System (DNS).

You also learn about the Computer Browser service, which is used by Windows NT to identify and list the available network resources.

Before You Begin

To complete this chapter, you must have:

- Two computers that meet the hardware and software requirements as specified in the Getting Started section in "About This Book."
- Completed all practices in Chapter 2, "Installing Windows NT."
- Read Chapter 9, "The Windows NT Networking Environment."
- Read and complete all practices in Chapter 10, "Configuring Windows NT Protocols."

Lesson 1: Installing Network Services

Windows NT network services provide a computer running Windows NT with access to the network and its resources. In this lesson, you learn how to install network services.

After this lesson, you will be able to:
- Describe the procedures to add and remove networking services from a computer running Windows NT.
- Identify the options available for installing network services.

Estimated lesson time: 5 minutes

You install network services by using the **Services** tab in the Network program in Control Panel. The following illustration shows the **Services** tab in the **Network** dialog box in Control Panel and the dialog box that appears when you click the **Add** button on the **Services** tab.

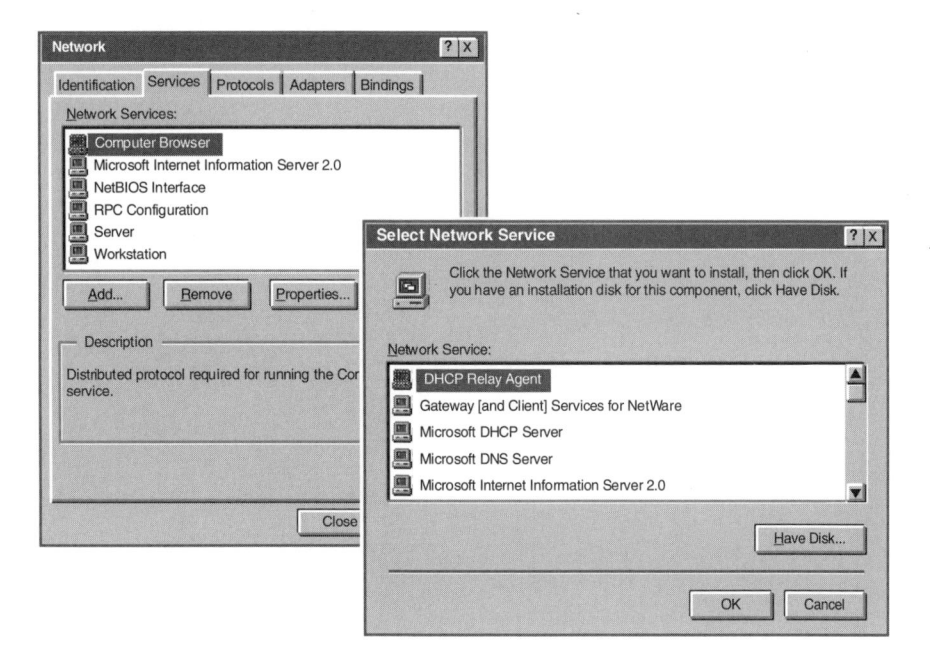

Use the **Services** tab to perform the functions listed in the following table.

Option	Use this option to
Add	Add a service to a computer.
Remove	Remove a selected service.
Properties	View or configure settings for a selected network service.
Update	Update the settings for a service. The system prompts the user for the path of the upgrade files.

Lesson 2: Dynamic Host Configuration Protocol Overview

In order to manually assign and maintain IP address information on a network, you must do the following:

- Maintain a list of the IP addresses assigned to your company.
- Configure or make sure that you correctly configure TCP/IP on each computer on the network and assign a valid IP address to that computer.
- Maintain a list of any unassigned IP addresses.

In this lesson, you learn how the Dynamic Host Configuration Protocol (DHCP) helps reduce administration by *automatically* assigning IP addresses.

After this lesson, you will be able to:
- Explain the function of DHCP.
- List the requirements for using DHCP.
- Explain how DHCP assigns an IP address.
- Install DHCP Server service.
- Create and configure a DHCP scope.
- Configure TCP/IP on a client to obtain an IP address from a DHCP server.

Estimated lesson time: 60 minutes

What Is DHCP?

The Dynamic Host Configuration Protocol (DHCP) is a protocol that centralizes and manages the allocation of TCP/IP configuration information by automatically assigning IP addresses to computers that have been configured to use DHCP. Implementing DHCP eliminates some of the configuration problems and administration associated with manually configuring TCP/IP. In this lesson, you learn how a DHCP server assigns an IP address, and how to install and configure the DHCP Server service.

You use DHCP to define global and subnet TCP/IP parameters for an internetwork. TCP/IP configuration parameters that can be dynamically assigned by a DHCP server include:

- IP addresses for each network adapter card in a computer.
- Subnet masks that identify the portion of an IP address that is the physical segment (subnet) network identifier.
- Default gateway (router) that connects the subnet to other network segments.
- Additional configuration parameters that can be optionally assigned to DHCP clients, such as a domain name.

Each time a DHCP client starts, it requests this TCP/IP configuration information from a DHCP server. When a DHCP server receives a request, it selects an IP address from a pool of addresses defined in its database and offers it to the DHCP client. If the client accepts the offer, the IP address is leased to the client for a specified period of time.

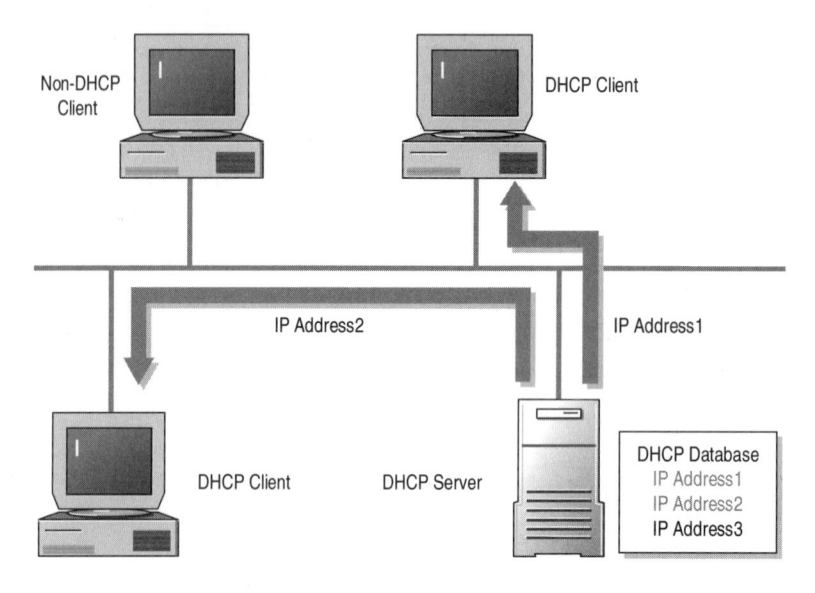

Important If no IP address is available to lease to a client, the client cannot initialize TCP/IP.

Manual vs. Automatic IP Address Configurations

To understand why DHCP is beneficial in configuring IP addresses on client computers, it is useful to contrast the manual method of configuring TCP/IP with the automatic method using DHCP.

Manually Configuring IP Addresses

The impact on administration and the potential problems associated with manually entering and configuring IP addresses include the following:

- The administrator of a client computer can enter a random IP address instead of obtaining a valid, unassigned IP address from the network administrator. Entering an address that is currently in use or that is invalid can lead to network problems that can be difficult to trace to the source of the problem.
- Entering an incorrect subnet mask or default gateway can cause communication problems. For example, if the default gateway is entered incorrectly, you may not be able to communicate beyond your local network.
- There is administrative overhead on internetworks where computers are frequently moved from one subnet to another. For example, the IP address and default gateway address must be changed to enable the computer to communicate from its new location.

Using DHCP to Configure IP Addresses

Using DHCP to automatically configure IP addresses ensures that:

- The client computer always receives a valid IP address.
- The configuration information is correct, thereby eliminating many difficult-to-trace network problems.

How DHCP Works

DHCP uses a four-phase process to configure a DHCP client. The following illustration shows the DHCP process.

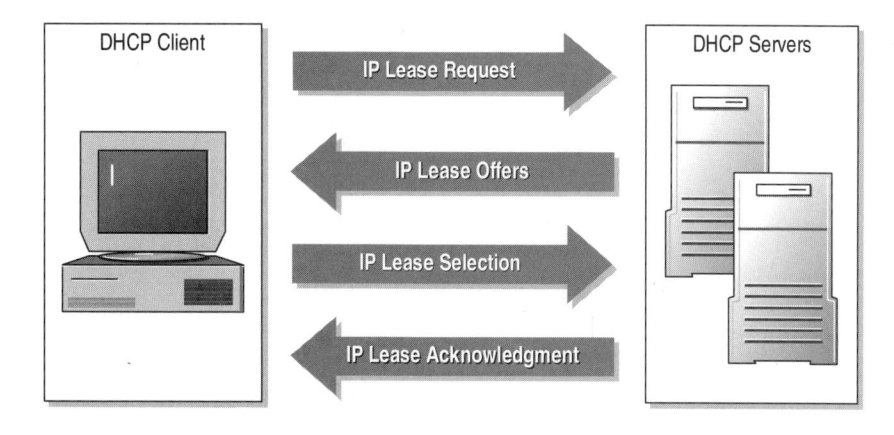

The following table describes the phases of the DHCP process.

Phase	Description
IP lease request	The client initializes a limited version of TCP/IP and broadcasts a request for the location of a DHCP server and IP addresses.
IP lease offers	All DHCP servers that have valid IP addresses available send an offer to the client.
IP lease selection	The client selects the IP address from the first offer it receives and broadcasts a message requesting to lease the IP address in the offer.
IP lease acknowledgment	The DHCP server that made the offer responds to the message, and all other DHCP servers withdraw their offers. The IP addressing information is assigned to the client and an acknowledgment is sent to the client.
	The client finishes initializing and binding the TCP/IP protocol. Once the automatic configuration process is complete, the client can use all TCP/IP services and utilities for normal network communications and connectivity to other IP hosts.

Note If a client has multiple network adapter cards, the DHCP process occurs separately over each network adapter card. A unique IP address is assigned to each adapter in the computer.

DHCP Requirements

To implement DHCP, the following requirements must be met for the DHCP Server service and the DHCP client.

DHCP Server

- The DHCP Server service must be installed and properly configured on a computer running Microsoft Windows NT Server.

   Note The DHCP server does not have to be a domain controller.

- A DHCP server must be configured with a static IP address, subnet mask, and optionally, a default gateway.
- If your IP routers do not support RFC 1542, then a DHCP server is required on each subnet.
- A DHCP scope must be created on the DHCP server. A DHCP scope consists of a range, or pool, of IP addresses that the DHCP server can assign, or lease, to DHCP clients: for example, 131.107.3.51 through 131.107.3.200.

DHCP Client

- A DHCP client must be running one of the following supported operating systems:
  - Windows NT Server 3.5 or later (but not running the DHCP Server service)
  - Microsoft Windows NT Workstation
  - Microsoft Windows 95
  - Microsoft Windows for Workgroups 3.11
  - Microsoft Network Client 3.0 for MS-DOS
  - Microsoft LAN Manager 2.2c
- The TCP/IP protocol must be configured to obtain an IP address from a DHCP server.

Installing and Configuring DHCP

To install the DHCP Server service on your Windows NT Server, use the Network program in Control Panel. On the **Services** tab, click **Add**, and then click **Microsoft DHCP Server**. You need to restart your computer for the service to start.

After installing the DHCP Server service, Windows NT–based DHCP configuration is performed through DHCP Manager. DHCP Manager is located in the Administrative Tools (Common) group on computers running Windows NT Server that have the DHCP Server service installed.

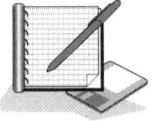

Practice

In this procedure, you install the DHCP Server service.

▶ **To install the DHCP Server service**

Note Complete this procedure on Server1.

1. Log on as Administrator.
2. In Control Panel, double-click the Network icon.

   The **Network** dialog box appears.
3. Click the **Services** tab.
4. Click **Add**.

   The **Select Network Service** dialog box appears.
5. Click **Microsoft DHCP Server**, and then click **OK**.

6. When prompted for the location of the Windows NT distribution files, type **\\Server1\Nts_source\I386** and then click **Continue**.

   The appropriate files are copied to your computer and a dialog box appears stating that if any adapters are using DHCP to obtain an IP address, they are now required to use a static IP address.

7. Click **OK**, and then click **Close**.

8. Click **Yes** to restart the computer.

Configuring a DHCP Scope

Once the DHCP Server service has been installed and started, then you need to create a scope. A scope consists of a range of IP addresses, such as 131.107.3.51 through 131.107.3.200, which the DHCP server can assign or lease to DHCP clients. Every DHCP server requires at least one scope with a pool of IP addresses available for leasing to clients.

To create a DHCP scope, use DHCP Manager. On the **Scope** menu in DHCP Manager, click **Create**. The following illustration shows the **Create Scope** dialog box.

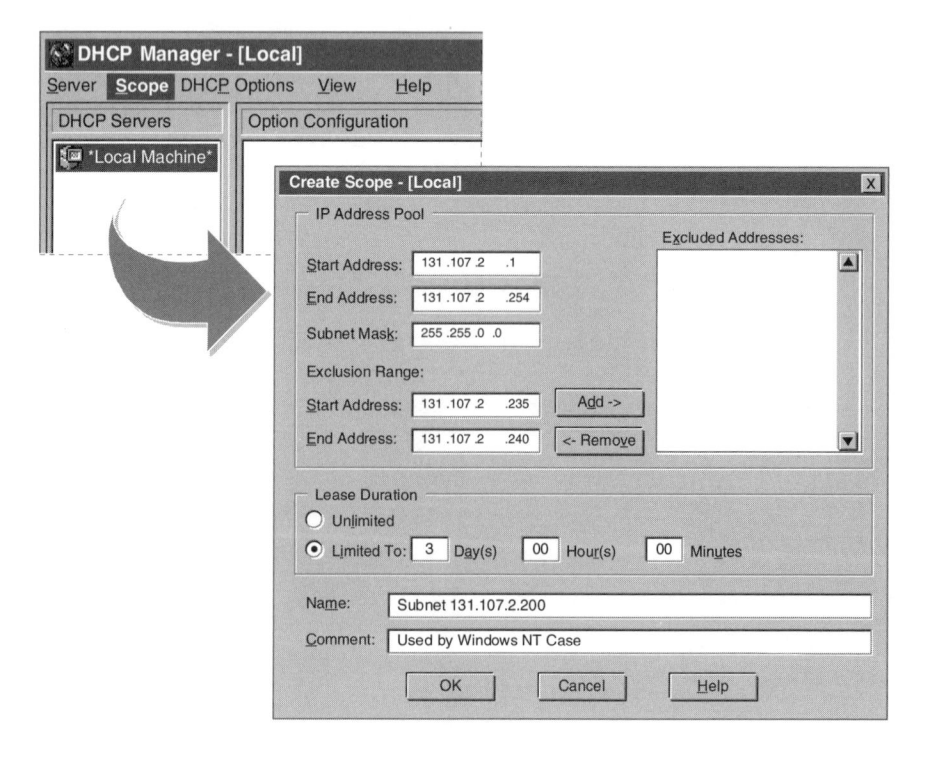

The options listed in the following table can be configured from the **Create Scope** dialog box.

Option	This option configures
IP Address Pool Start Address	First IP address that can be assigned to a DHCP client. This is a required field.
IP Address Pool End Address	Last IP address that can be assigned to a DHCP client. This is a required field.
Subnet Mask	Subnet mask to be assigned to all DHCP clients in this scope. This is a required field.
Exclusion Range Start Address	Starting IP address to be excluded from the IP address pool of addresses. The addresses in this exclusion are not assigned to DHCP clients. This is important if there are static IP addresses configured on non-DCHP clients. This is not a required field.
Exclusion Range End Address	Ending IP address to be excluded from the IP address pool of addresses. The addresses in this exclusion are not assigned to DHCP clients. This is important if there are static IP addresses configured on non-DCHP clients. This is not a required field.
Unlimited	DHCP leases assigned to clients that never expire.
Limited To	Number of days, hours, and minutes that a DHCP client lease is available before it must be renewed.
Name	A name to be assigned to the DHCP scope. The name is displayed after the IP address in the DHCP Manager. This is a required field.
Comment	Optional comments for the scope.

A scope must be activated before the DHCP server can provide a DHCP client with a valid IP address defined by the scope. You can activate the scope when you create it, or at a later time.

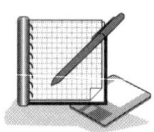

Practice

In this procedure, you create a DHCP scope that consists of a pool of IP addresses and an assigned lease time of 1 day.

▶ **To create a DHCP scope**

Note Complete this procedure on Server1.

1. Log on as Administrator.
2. In Control Panel, double-click the Services icon.

   What are the names of the two DHCP-related services?

   _____

   What are the status and startup values of these two services?

   _____

3. Close **Services**.
4. Click the **Start** button, point to **Programs**, point to **Administrative Tools (Common)**, and then click **DHCP Manager**.

   The DHCP Manager window appears.
5. Click **Scope**.

   Notice that no options on the menu are available because you have not yet specified the computer on which the scope will be created.
6. In the **DHCP Servers** pane, double-click ***Local Machine***

   Now that you have selected this computer, notice that (Local) now appears on the title bar for DHCP Manager.
7. On the **Scope** menu, click **Create**.

   The **Create Scope** dialog box appears.
8. Configure the scope using the following information.

In this box	Type this
IP Address Pool Start Address	131.107.2.201
IP Address Pool End Address	131.107.2.209
Subnet Mask	255.255.0.0
Lease Duration Limited To (Days)	1

9. When you are finished, click **OK**.

   A **DHCP Manager** dialog box appears, indicating that the scope was successfully created, and now needs to be activated.

10. Click **No**. You will activate the scope later in this lesson.

    A dialog box appears stating that no more data is available.

11. Click **OK**.

    The DHCP Manager window appears with the new scope added. Notice the gray light bulb next to the IP address, indicating an inactive scope.

Configuring Client Reservations

You can reserve a specific IP address for a specific client computer. You would do this if the client must use a specific IP address, typically one that was previously assigned using another method of TCP/IP configuration. To create a client reservation, click **Add Reservations** on the **Scope** menu in DHCP Manager. Once you have created a client reservation, you can then configure additional options for the specific client.

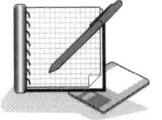

Practice

In this procedure, you use the Ping and Arp utilities to determine the physical address of the network adapter card of the computer running Windows NT Workstation. You then create a reservation for the workstation.

▶ **To add a client reservation**

Note Complete this procedure on Server1.

1. Start a command prompt, type **ping 131.107.2.201** and then press ENTER.
2. Type **arp -a** and then press ENTER to obtain the physical address of Workstation1's network adapter card. Document the address here for reference.

   _____

3. Switch to DHCP Manager and ensure your scope is selected.
4. On the **Scope** menu, click **Add Reservations**.

   The **Add Reserved Clients** dialog box appears.
5. In the **IP Address** box, type **131.107.2.201**
6. In the **Unique Identifier** box, type the physical address (without the hyphens) of Workstation1's network adapter card.
7. In the **Client Name** box, type **Workstation1** and then click **Add**.
8. Click **Close** to return to DHCP Manager.

Other DHCP Options

Many other networking options can be made available to DHCP clients. These options can be configured globally or for a specific scope or client reservation using the DHCP Manager. The following illustration shows the **DHCP Options: Global** dialog box of DHCP Manager.

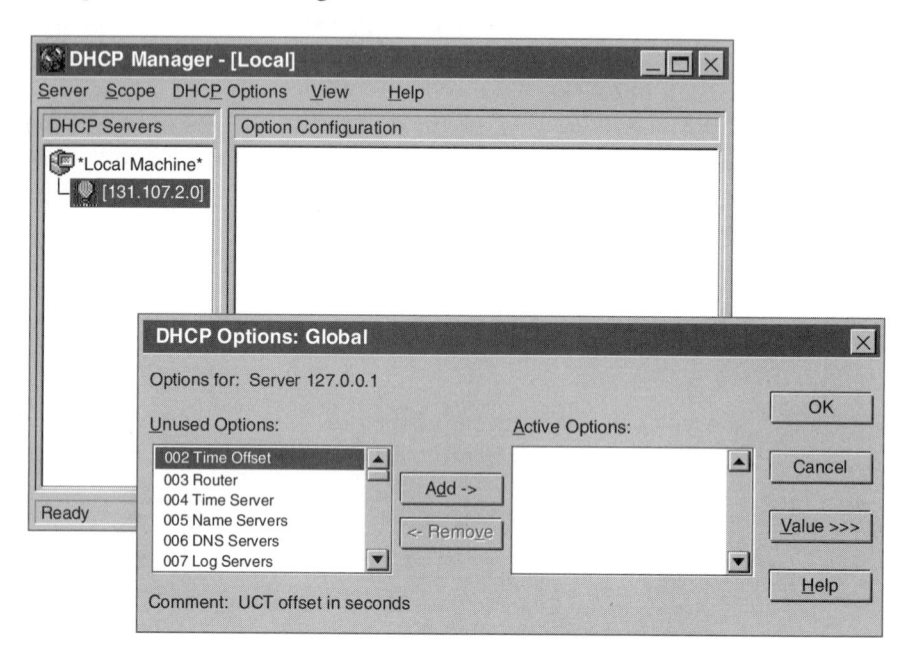

Some common options are listed in the following table.

Option	This option configures a
003 Router	Default gateway.
006 DNS Servers	List of IP addresses for name servers for the client.
044 WINS/NBNS Servers	List of IP addresses for NetBIOS name servers.

Global Options

Global options apply to all DHCP scopes defined on the selected DHCP server and all DHCP clients that lease an address from any of these scopes. Global options are used when all clients on all subnets require the same configuration information. For example, all clients can be configured to use the same WINS server. Global options are always used, unless the Scope or Client options are configured. To configure global options, click **Global** on the **DHCP_Options** menu in DHCP Manager.

Scope Options

Scope options apply to only the specified scope and clients that lease an address from that scope. For example, if there is a different scope for each subnet, you must specify the appropriate default gateway address for each subnet. Scope options override Global options. Therefore, the default gateway specified in the Scope options will be used in place of any specified in the Global options. To configure Scope options, click **Scope** on the **DHCP_Options** menu in DHCP Manager.

Client Options

Client options apply to a specific client that has a reserved DHCP address lease. Client options override Scope or Global options. To configure Client options, first create a client reservation. Then, click **Active Leases** on the **Scope** menu in DHCP Manager. Click the client, click **Properties**, and then click the **Options** button in the **Client Properties** dialog box.

Practice

In these procedures, you activate the DHCP scope option 003 Router. This option automatically assigns a default gateway address for use by the DHCP clients. You then activate the scope.

Note Complete these procedures on Server1.

▶ **To configure a DHCP Scope option**

1. From the **DHCP Options** menu, click **Scope**.

    The **DHCP Options: Scope** dialog box appears.

2. Under **Unused Options**, click **003 Router**, and then click **Add**.

    The **003 Router** option appears in the **Active Options** box.

3. Click **Value**.

    The **DHCP Options: Scope** dialog box expands to add the **IP Address** box.

4. Click **Edit Array**.

    The **IP Address Array Editor** dialog box appears.

5. In the **New IP Address** box, type **131.107.2.200** (your Server1 IP address) and then click **Add**.

    The new IP address appears under **IP Addresses**.

6. Click **OK** to return to the **DHCP Options: Scope** dialog box.

7. In the **DHCP Options: Scope** dialog box, click **OK** to close, and then click **OK** to acknowledge no more data is available.

▶ **To activate the DHCP scope**

1. On the **Scope** menu, click **Activate**.

   Notice the yellow light bulb next to the IP address, indicating an active scope.

2. Close DHCP Manager.

Practice

In these procedures, you configure Workstation1 as a DHCP client, and then test your DHCP server's configuration.

Note Complete these procedures on Workstation1.

▶ **To configure a DHCP client**

1. Log on to the domain as Administrator.
2. In Control Panel, double-click the Network icon.
3. Click the **Protocols** tab.
4. Click **TCP/IP Protocol**, and then click **Properties**.
5. Click **Obtain an IP address from a DHCP server**.

   A **Microsoft TCP/IP Properties** dialog box appears, asking if you want to enable DHCP.

6. Click **Yes**.
7. Click **OK** to close the **Microsoft TCP/IP Properties** dialog box.
8. Click **OK** to close **Network**.

▶ **To test the DHCP configuration**

1. Start a command prompt, type **ipconfig /all** and then press ENTER to view the new TCP/IP configuration.

   What IP address was assigned to the computer running Windows NT Workstation by the DHCP server?

   _____

   What is the DHCP server address?

   _____

What is the address of the default gateway?

___

When does the lease expire?

___

Practice

In these procedures, you explore DHCP and troubleshoot various DHCP configuration errors.

Note These procedures contain procedures for both computers. Make sure that you complete the correct procedure on the correct computer.

▶ **To view DHCP assigned addresses**

In this procedure, you view the DHCP server listing of leased addresses.

Note Complete this procedure on Server1.

1. Start DHCP Manager, and double-click ***Local Machine***
2. Click the local scope.
3. On the **Scope** menu, click **Active Leases**.

    The **Active Leases** dialog box appears, displaying the list of IP addresses that have been leased to clients.

4. Click **Cancel** to return to the **DHCP Manager** window.
5. Close DHCP Manager.

▶ **To renew a DHCP lease**

In this procedure, you release and then renew the lease assigned to Workstation1.

Note Complete this procedure on Workstation1.

1. Start a command prompt, type **ipconfig /all** and then press ENTER to view the lease information.

   When does the lease expire?

   _____

2. Type **ipconfig /release** and then press ENTER.

   What message did you receive?

   _____

3. Type **ipconfig /all** and then press ENTER to view the IP configuration.

   What is your IP address?

   _____

4. Type **ipconfig /renew** and then press ENTER to renew the lease.

   The Windows NT IP configuration information for the assigned address is displayed.

5. Type **ipconfig /all** and then press ENTER to view the lease information again.

   When does the lease expire?

   _____

Practice

In these procedures, you stop the DHCP Server service and then determine what effect this has when a DHCP client attempts to renew a lease.

▶ **To stop the DHCP Server service**

In this procedure, you stop the Microsoft DHCP Server service to prevent IP address lease assignments and renewals.

Note Complete this procedure on Server1.

1. From Control Panel, start Services.
2. Click **Microsoft DHCP Server**, and then click **Stop**.
3. Click **Yes** when prompted.

    The Microsoft DHCP server stops.

▶ **To attempt lease renewal when the DHCP server is unavailable**

In this procedure, you use the **ipconfig** utility to attempt to renew the lease assigned to Workstation1 while the DHCP server is unavailable.

Note Complete this procedure on Workstation1.

1. Start a command prompt, type **ipconfig /renew** and then press ENTER.

    Could you successfully renew the lease?

2. Type **ping 131.107.2.200** and then press ENTER to verify that TCP/IP can still communicate with Server1.

    Ping should respond with four success messages.

    Even though you were unable to renew your IP address lease, it is still a valid lease. The IP address you leased remains active until the lease expires or until you use the **ipconfig /release** command to return the address to the IP address pool. Therefore, TCP/IP communications are still possible using the IP address that you had obtained earlier from the DHCP server.

388　Microsoft Windows NT Technical Support

▶ **To release a DHCP address**

In this procedure, you use the **ipconfig** utility to release the IP address lease assigned to Workstation1.

Note　Complete this procedure on Workstation1.

1. Start a command prompt, type **ipconfig /release** and then press ENTER.

   The Windows IP configuration information appears.

   What message did you receive?

2. Type **ping 131.107.2.200** and then press ENTER to test TCP/IP communications with Server1.

   Ping should respond with four *Destination host unreachable* messages.

3. Shut down and restart Workstation1.
4. Log on to the domain as Administrator.

   A **Logon Message** dialog box appears, stating that a domain controller could not be found.

   Why does this message appear?

5. Start a command prompt, type **ipconfig /all** to view the IP configuration.

   What is the IP address? Why?

▶ **To start the DHCP Server service**

In this procedure, you start the Microsoft DHCP Server service to allow IP address lease assignments and renewals.

Note　Complete this procedure on Server1.

- Use either the **Services** program in Control Panel, or Server Manager to start the Microsoft DHCP Server service.

▶ **To renew a DHCP lease**

In this procedure, you use the **ipconfig** utility to renew the lease assigned to the computer running Windows NT Workstation.

Note Complete this procedure on Workstation1.

1. Start a command prompt, type **ipconfig /renew** and then press ENTER.
2. Type **ipconfig /all** and then press ENTER.

   When does the lease expire?

Lesson 3: Windows Internet Name Service

Computers use IP addresses to identify each other, but computer users usually find it easier to work with computer names. A mechanism must be available on a TCP/IP network to resolve computer names, which are NetBIOS names, to IP addresses. To ensure that both computer name and IP address are unique, the computer running Windows NT using TCP/IP registers its name and IP address on the network during system startup. In this lesson, you learn about NetBIOS name resolution and how Windows NT computers can use the Windows Internet Name Service (WINS) in TCP/IP internetworks to ensure accurate name resolution between Windows NT computer names (NetBIOS names) and IP addresses.

After this lesson, you will be able to:
- Define NetBIOS name.
- Explain the function of WINS.
- Define WINS server and client requirements.
- Install and configure the WINS Server service.
- Configure a WINS client.

Estimated lesson time: 45 minutes

Name Resolution

People typically assign meaningful, easy-to-remember names to their computers. For example, in this book you named the computer running Windows NT Server Server1. Using easy-to-remember names simplifies connecting to resources through the **net use** command or Windows NT Explorer. The Windows NT computer name, assigned during setup, is a NetBIOS name.

TCP/IP devices use IP addresses rather than the computer name to locate a computer on the internetwork. Thus, TCP/IP internetworks require a name resolution method that can match and convert computer names to IP addresses and IP addresses to computer names.

What Is a NetBIOS Name?

A NetBIOS name is used for NetBIOS processes to communicate with each other. In Windows NT, NetBIOS names are created (registered) when services initialize, such as the Server and Workstation services, or when a NetBIOS application starts.

A computer's NetBIOS name:

- Is the computer name, such as Server1, assigned during installation.
- Is stored as an entry in the registry, and can be changed through the Network program in Control Panel.
- Is always specified in Windows NT commands, such as **net use** and **net view**.
- Can be determined by typing **nbtstat -n** at a command prompt.
- Can be 15 characters in length. A 16th character can be added to the name to designate the service or application that registered the name. This extra character is added by the service or application.

What Is NetBIOS Name Resolution?

In order to communicate successfully on a TCP/IP-based network, hosts need to identify each other's media access control address. The media access control address is the physical address assigned to the network adapter card, for example the burned-in address. The physical address is sometimes referred to as the hardware address. The process of converting a computer name to a media access control address is also known as name resolution. Name resolution in a TCP/IP network is really a two-step process. Starting with a computer name, the first step is to resolve the computer name to an IP address. Once the IP address has been determined, the hardware address can be resolved.

Note This lesson only covers name resolution between NetBIOS names and IP addresses.

Microsoft TCP/IP can use any of the methods in the following table to resolve computer names to IP addresses.

Method of resolution	Description
NetBIOS name cache	The local cache containing the locally registered computer names and the computer names that the local computer recently resolved to IP addresses.
NetBIOS Name Server (NBNS), such as the Windows Internet Name Service (WINS)	A server implemented under RFC 1001/1002 to provide name resolution of NetBIOS computer names. The Microsoft implementation of this is WINS.

(*continued*)

Method of resolution	Description
Local broadcast	A broadcast on the local network for the IP address of the destination NetBIOS name.
LMHOSTS file	A local text file that maps IP addresses to the NetBIOS computer names of Windows networking computers on remote networks.
HOSTS file	A local text file in the same format as the 4.3 Berkeley Software Distribution (BSD) UNIX/etc/hosts file. This file maps host names to IP addresses. This file is typically used to resolve host names for TCP/IP utilities.
Domain Name Server (DNS)	A server configured with the DNS daemon that maintains a database of IP address/computer name (host name) mappings. A DNS is common to UNIX environments.

Note This chapter covers the installation and configuration of the WINS and DNS name resolution methods, because they are installed and configured as Windows NT Server services. For more information on name resolution methods, see the *Networking Guide* of the *Microsoft Windows NT Server Resource Kit*.

NetBIOS Over TCP/IP Name Resolution Modes

Windows NT provides support for all of the NetBIOS over TCP/IP name resolution modes defined in the Request for Comments (RFCs) 1001 and 1002. The RFC is a series of documents that contain the standards for TCP/IP. Each mode resolves NetBIOS names differently.

Mode	Description
b-node (broadcast)	Uses broadcasts (UDP datagrams) for name registration and resolution. b-node has two major problems: 1. In a large internetwork, broadcasts can increase the network load, and 2. Routers typically do not forward broadcasts, so only computers on the local network can respond.
p-node (peer-peer)	Uses a NetBIOS Name Server (NBNS), such as WINS to resolve NetBIOS names. p-node does not use broadcasts; instead, it queries the Name Server directly. Because broadcasts are not used, computers can span routers. The most significant problems with p-node are that all computers must be configured with the IP address of the NBNS, and if the NBNS is down, computers will not be able to communicate even on the local network.

(*continued*)

Mode	Description
m-node (mixed)	A combination of b-node and p-node. By default, an m-node functions as a b-node. If it is unable to resolve a name by broadcast, it uses the NBNS of p-node.
h-node (hybrid)	A combination of p-node and b-node. By default, an h-node functions as a p-node. If it is unable to resolve a name through the NetBIOS Name Server, it uses a b-node broadcast to resolve the name.
Microsoft enhanced b-node	An enhanced b-node for resolving NetBIOS computer names of remote hosts. Enhanced b-node utilizes the LMHOSTS file, which is a static file that maps a remote computer's NetBIOS name to its IP address.
	Entries in the LMHOSTS file that marked with #PRE are cached when TCP/IP initializes. Before a b-node broadcast is sent, the cache is checked for the NetBIOS name/IP address mapping. If the mapping is not found in cache, a b-node broadcast is initiated. If the broadcast is not successful, the LMHOSTS file is parsed in an attempt to resolve the name.

What Is WINS?

WINS is a NetBIOS Name Service that is designed to provide a flexible solution to the problem of locating NetBIOS resources in routed TCP/IP-based networks. It is a dynamic database for registering and resolving NetBIOS name-to-IP address mappings in a network.

How WINS Works

Before two NetBIOS-based hosts can communicate, the destination NetBIOS name must be resolved to its IP address. This is necessary because TCP/IP requires an IP address to communicate; TCP/IP cannot establish communication using a NetBIOS computer name.

The procedure for registering and resolving NetBIOS names using WINS is as follows:

1. In a WINS environment, each time a WINS client starts, it registers its NetBIOS name/IP address mapping with a designated WINS server. In the following illustration, Student 3 registers its NetBIOS name and IP address with the WINS server.

2. When a WINS client, Student 1, initiates a NetBIOS command to communicate with another host (Student 3), the name query request is sent directly to the WINS server instead of being broadcast on the local network.

3. If the WINS server finds a NetBIOS name/IP address mapping for the destination host, Student 3, in this database, it returns the destination host's IP address to the WINS client, Student 1. Because the WINS database obtains NetBIOS name/IP address mappings dynamically, it is always current. If the WINS server is unavailable, the client switches to b-node and sends the query as a broadcast message on the local subnet.

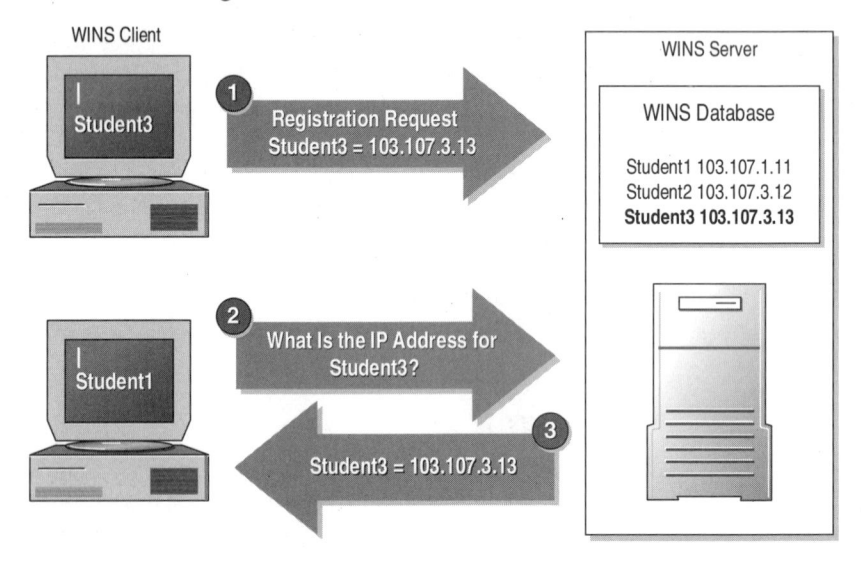

Note For more information on name registration and resolution, see Chapter 3, "Implementation Considerations," in the *Networking Supplement* in Books Online.

WINS Servers

A WINS server handles name registrations and queries. It maintains a database that maps the NetBIOS computer names of WINS clients to their IP addresses. When a WINS client requests an IP address, a WINS server retrieves the IP address from its database and returns it to the client.

WINS Clients

A WINS client registers its computer name and IP address with a WINS server during system startup. It then queries the WINS server for computer name resolution.

Windows-based networking clients, such as WINS-enabled computers running Windows NT, Windows 95, or Windows for Workgroups 3.11, can use WINS directly. Non-WINS computers that use broadcasts can access WINS through proxies. Proxies are WINS-enabled computers that listen to name-query broadcast messages, forward the request to the WINS server, and then respond for names that are not on the local subnet.

WINS Requirements

To implement WINS, both the server and client require configuration.

Server Requirements

A WINS server requires:

- The WINS Server service configured on at least one computer within the TCP/IP internetwork running Windows NT Server. (It does not have to be a domain controller.)
- A static IP address.

Client Requirements

A WINS client requires:

- A computer running any of the following supported operating systems:
  - Windows NT Server 3.5 or later.
  - Windows NT Workstation 3.5 or later.
  - Windows 95.
  - Windows for Workgroups 3.11 running Microsoft TCP/IP-32.
  - Microsoft Network Client 3.0 for MS-DOS with the real-mode TCP/IP driver included on the *Microsoft Windows NT Server* compact disc.
  - LAN Manager 2.2c for MS-DOS (included on the *Microsoft Windows NT Server* compact disc). LAN Manager 2.2c for OS/2 is not supported.
- The IP address of a WINS server.

Installing and Configuring WINS

To install the WINS Server service on a computer running Windows NT Server, use the Network program in Control Panel. On the **Services** tab, click **Add**, and then click **Windows Internet Name Service**. You must shut down and restart your computer for the service to start.

After installing the WINS Server service, all Windows NT-based WINS management and configuration are performed through WINS Manager. WINS Manager is located in the Administrative Tools (Common) group on computers running Windows NT Server that have installed the WINS Server service. WINS Manager (shown in the following illustration) allows you to obtain detailed information about your WINS servers, as well as viewing the mappings database or adding static mappings to the database.

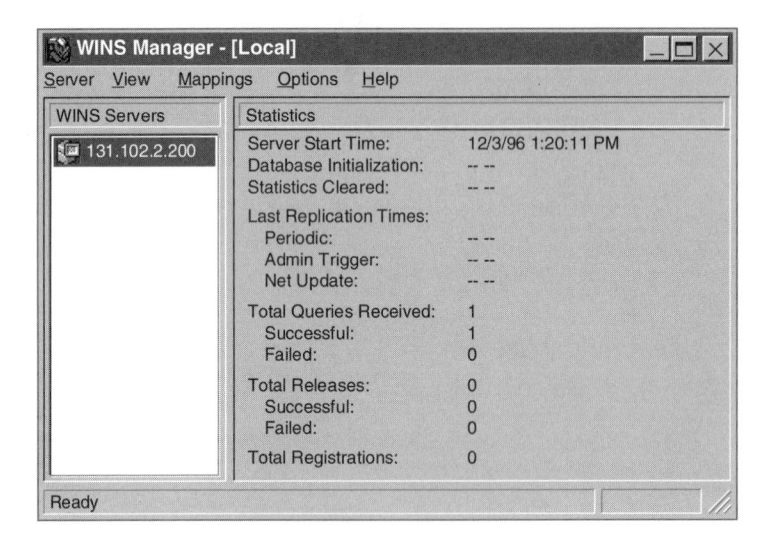

Practice

In this procedure, you install a WINS server on Server1, and you configure Server1 to use itself as its WINS server.

▶ **To install and configure the WINS Server service**

Note Complete this procedure on Server1.

1. Log on as Administrator.
2. In Control Panel, double-click the Network icon.

    The **Network** dialog box appears.
3. Click the **Services** tab, and then click **Add**.

    The **Select Network Service** dialog box appears.

4. Click **Windows Internet Name Service**, and then click **OK**.

   A **Windows NT Setup** dialog box appears asking for the full path to the software.

5. Type **\\Server1\Nts_source\I386** and then click **Continue**.

   The appropriate files are copied to your computer.

6. Click the **Protocols** tab.

   You now configure Server1, which is not a DHCP client, to use its own address for a WINS server.

7. Double-click **TCP/IP Protocol**.

   The **Microsoft TCP/IP Properties** dialog box appears.

8. Click the **WINS Address** tab.

9. In the **Primary WINS Server** box, type **131.107.2.200** (your IP address) and then click **OK**.

   The **Network** dialog box appears.

10. Click **Close**.

    A **Network Settings Change** dialog box appears, indicating that the computer needs to be restarted to initialize the new configuration.

11. Click **Yes** to restart Server1.

Configuring a WINS client

There are two ways to configure a WINS client, either manually or in conjunction with DHCP.

Manually

You can manually configure a WINS client by using the Network program in Control Panel. On the **Protocols** tab, click **TCP/IP**, and then click **Properties**. In the **Microsoft TCP/IP Properties** dialog box, click the **WINS Address** tab. You then provide the address of the primary, and optionally secondary, WINS server.

In Conjunction with DHCP

When you configure your DHCP server to work in conjunction with your WINS server, you save the administrative overhead of individually configuring your DHCP clients to also be WINS clients.

You can use DHCP Manager to add and configure the following DHCP options:

044 WINS/NBNS Servers. Your DHCP server can provide the address of a WINS server to be used for name registration and resolution to the DHCP clients.

046 WINS/NBT Node Type. Must be used to automatically configure the client's node type for use in name resolution.

Note For more information about installing, configuring, and managing WINS servers, see the *Network Guide* of the *Microsoft Windows NT Server Resource Kit*.

Practice

In this procedure, you configure the DHCP server to supply the appropriate WINS server addressing information and node type to DHCP clients.

Note Complete this procedure on Server1.

▶ **To configure the DHCP server to assign WINS server addresses**

1. Log on as Administrator.
2. From the Administrative Tools (Common) group, start DHCP Manager.

   The DHCP Manager window appears.
3. Double-click *Local Machine*

   The local scope IP address appears.
4. Click the local scope's IP address.

   The local scope options appear under **Option Configuration**.
5. On the **DHCP Options** menu, click **Scope**.

   The **DHCP Options: Scope** dialog box appears.
6. Under **Unused Options**, click **044 WINS/NBNS Servers**, and then click **Add**.

   A **DHCP Manager** message box appears, indicating that for WINS to function properly, you must add the **046 WINS/NBT Node Type** option.
7. Click **OK**.

   The **044 WINS/NBNS Servers** option now appears under **Active Options**.
8. Click **Value**.

   The **DHCP Scope: Options** dialog box expands.
9. Click **Edit Array**.

   The **IP Address Array Editor** dialog box appears.
10. Under **New IP Address**, type **131.107.2.200** (your IP address) and then click **Add**.

    The new IP address appears under **IP Addresses**.
11. To return to the **DHCP Options: Scope** dialog box, click **OK**.
12. Under **Unused Options**, click **046 WINS/NBT Node Type**, and then click **Add**.

    The **046 WINS/NBT Node Type** option now appears under **Active Options**.

13. In the **Byte** box, type **0x8** and then click **OK**.

    The DHCP Manager window appears. Under **Option Configuration**, the following active scope options appear: **003 Router**, **044 WINS/NBNS Servers**, and **046 WINS/NBT Node Type**.

14. Exit DHCP Manager.

Practice

In this procedure, you test the configuration of the DHCP server to automatically assign the WINS server address and NetBIOS node types to DHCP clients. At Workstation1, your DHCP client, you renew your IP address, view the information supplied, and ping a computer using the computer name.

Note Complete this procedure on Workstation1.

▶ **To test the configuration of the DHCP server to assign WINS server addresses**

1. Log on to the domain as Administrator.

2. Start a command prompt, type **ipconfig /renew** and then press ENTER to renew your IP address.

3. Type **ipconfig /all** and then press ENTER to view your IP addressing information.

    What is the address of the primary WINS server?

    _____

    What is the node type?

    _____

4. Type **ping server1** and then press ENTER.

    Why were you successful in pinging a NetBIOS computer name?

    _____

5. Close the command prompt.

Lesson 4: Domain Name System

This lesson explains the function of the Domain Name System (DNS) Server service and how it can be configured to locate resources on an internetwork. In addition, it examines how WINS is integrated with DNS, which allows computers running Windows NT to access information on the Internet using Internet naming conventions.

Note DNS is a complex topic, and this book does not attempt to explain it fully. For more information on DNS, see the *Microsoft Windows NT Server Resource Kit,* or *DNS and BIND,* by Paul Albitz and Cricket Liu, published by O'Reilly and Associates.

After this lesson, you will be able to:
- Describe the purpose of DNS.
- Install and configure the DNS Server service.
- Explain the advantages of integrating WINS and DNS.

Estimated lesson time: 45 minutes

What Is DNS?

The Domain Name System (DNS) is a distributed database providing a hierarchical naming system for identifying hosts on the Internet. DNS was developed to solve the problems that arose when the number of hosts on the Internet grew dramatically in the early 1980s. DNS specifications are defined in RFCs 1034 and 1035. DNS computer names consist of two parts: a host name and a domain name, which combine to form the fully qualified domain name (FQDN). For example, research.widgets.com is a FQDN where *research* is the host name and *widgets.com* is the domain name.

Note The term *domain,* when used in the context of DNS, is not related to the term domain used when discussing Windows NT Directory Services.

An Internet domain is a unique name that identifies an Internet site. In order to register a domain name, you must contact the Internet Network Information Center (InterNIC). Visit the InterNIC home page on the Internet at http://internic.net.

What Is the DNS Server Service?

The DNS Server service is a name resolution service that resolves a FQDN to the IP address that is then used by the internetwork. For example, you can use Microsoft Internet Explorer to open research.widgets.com, and a DNS server can resolve this friendly name to the correct IP address on the Internet.

Comparing WINS and DNS

Although DNS might seem similar to WINS, there are two major differences. The following table summarizes the differences.

DNS	WINS
Resolves Internet names to IP addresses.	Resolves NetBIOS names to IP addresses.
Static database of computer name to IP address mappings. It must be manually updated.	Dynamic database of NetBIOS names and IP addresses. It is dynamically updated.

DNS Benefits

Using DNS on your computer running Windows NT allows you to:

- Access UNIX-based systems using friendly names.
- Connect to Internet systems using Internet naming conventions.
- Maintain a consistent hierarchical naming scheme across your organization.

How DNS Works

DNS uses a client/server model, where DNS servers (name servers) contain information about a portion of the DNS database (zone) and make this information available to clients (resolvers).

DNS name servers perform name resolution by interpreting network information to find a specific IP address. The name resolution process is outlined below:

1. A resolver (or client) passes a query to its local name server.
2. If the local name server does not have the data requested in the query, it queries other name servers on behalf of the resolver.
3. When the local name server has the address requested, it returns the information to the resolver.

The Domain Name Space

The DNS database is a tree structure called the *domain name space*. Each domain (node in the tree structure) is named and can contain subdomains. The domain name identifies the domain's position in the database in relation to its parent domain. A period (.) separates each part of the name for each network node in the DNS domain. For example, in the following illustration, the DNS domain name csu.edu, specifies the csu subdomain whose parent is the edu domain; microsoft.com specifies the microsoft subdomain whose parent is the com domain. The following illustration shows the parent-child relationships of DNS domains.

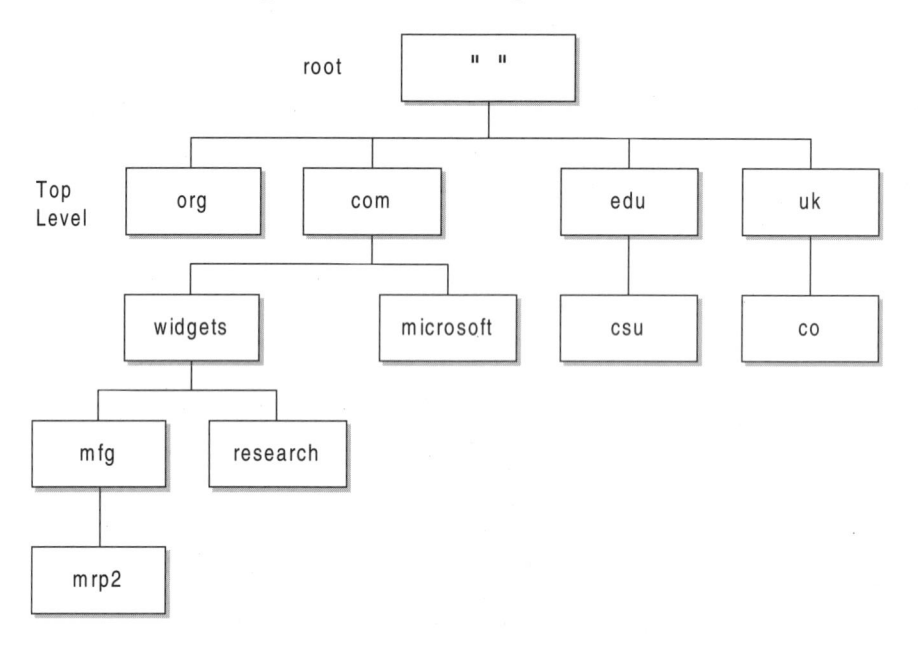

```
                        root  [" "]
                          |
Top      +--------+-------+-------+--------+
Level    |  org   |  com  |  edu  |   uk   |
                     |                |
                  widgets           microsoft    csu       co
                     |
              +------+------+
              | mfg  | research |
                |
              mrp2
```

As shown in the preceding illustration, the root node of the DNS database is unnamed (" " which is used to represent null).

The root node is referenced in DNS names with a trailing period (.). For example, in the name: "research.widgets.com." it is the period after com that denotes the DNS root node.

Top-Level Domains

The root and top-level domains of the DNS database are managed by the InterNIC. In most of the world, top-level domain names consist of geographical 2-character country codes such as .uk for the United Kingdom. In the United States many top-level domains are organizational, 3-character names, for example .com for commercial organizations and .edu for educational organizations.

Delegation

Responsibility for managing the DNS name space below the top level is delegated to other organizations by the InterNIC. These organizations further subdivide the name space and delegate responsibility down the hierarchical tree structure. This decentralized administrative model allows DNS to be autonomously managed at the levels that make the most sense for each organization involved.

Zones

The administrative unit for DNS is the zone. A zone is a subtree of the DNS database that is administered as a single separate entity. It can consist of a single domain or a domain with subdomains. The lower-level subdomains of a zone can also be split into separate zone(s). The following illustration shows the relationship between DNS domains and zones.

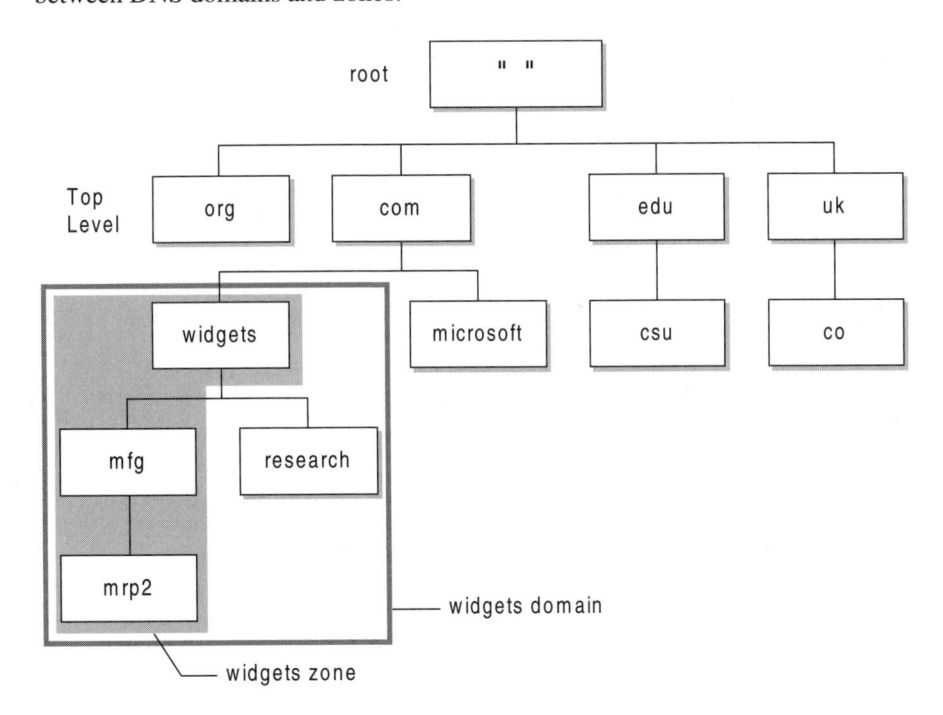

Fully Qualified Domain Names

With the exception of the root, each node in the DNS database has a name (label) of up to 63 characters. Each subdomain must have a unique name within its parent domain. This ensures name uniqueness throughout the DNS name space. DNS domain names are formed by following the path from the bottom of the DNS tree to the root. The node names are concatenated, and a period (.) separates each part. An optional period (.) that signifies the root can appear at the end of the name. Such names are known as fully qualified domain names (FQDN). The following is an example of an FQDN:

mrp2.mfg.widgets.com.

Note For more information about DNS, see Appendix C, "Implementing DNS Using Microsoft Windows NT 4.0."

Installing and Configuring DNS

To install the DNS Server service on a computer running Windows NT Server, use the Network program in Control Panel. On the **Services** tab, click **Add**, and then click **Microsoft DNS Server**. You must restart your computer for the service to start. DNS servers require a static IP address.

All DNS management and configuration is performed through DNS Manager located in the Administrative Tools (Common) group. Its primary function is to configure DNS objects. Each of these objects has a defined set of manageable properties (or attributes). DNS Manager can be used to visually identify any one of these objects, and to view, add, or modify associated properties.

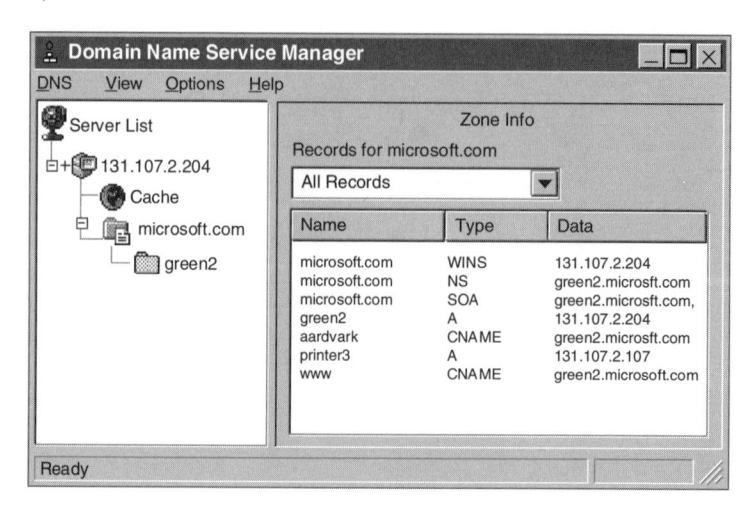

```
┌─────────────────────────────────────────────────────────────────┐
│ 👤 Domain Name Service Manager                      _ □ ×       │
│ DNS   View   Options   Help                                     │
│ ┌──────────────────┬──────────────────────────────────────────┐ │
│ │ 🖥 Server List    │              Zone Info                   │ │
│ │ ⊟─🖳 131.107.2.204│  Records for microsoft.com               │ │
│ │    │              │  ┌────────────────────────────────┐ ▼   │ │
│ │    ├─📁 Cache     │  │ All Records                    │     │ │
│ │    ⊟─📁 microsoft.com │ ┌──────────┬────────┬──────────────┐ │ │
│ │       └─📁 green2 │  │ Name     │ Type   │ Data         │ │ │
│ │                   │  ├──────────┼────────┼──────────────┤ │ │
│ │                   │  │microsoft.com│ WINS │ 131.107.2.204│ │ │
│ │                   │  │microsoft.com│ NS   │ green2.microsft.com│
│ │                   │  │microsoft.com│ SOA  │ green2.microsft.com,│
│ │                   │  │green2    │ A      │ 131.107.2.204│ │ │
│ │                   │  │aardvark  │ CNAME  │ green2.microsft.com│
│ │                   │  │printer3  │ A      │ 131.107.2.107│ │ │
│ │                   │  │www       │ CNAME  │ green2.microsoft.com│
│ │                   │  └──────────┴────────┴──────────────┘ │ │
│ ├──────────────────┴──────────────────────────────────────────┤ │
│ │ Ready                                                       │ │
│ └─────────────────────────────────────────────────────────────┘ │
```

The following table lists the objects that are configured using DNS Manager.

Object	Description
DNS Resource Record (RR)	The RR is the principal object in DNS. It is the component that contains the actual information elements managed by DNS. Three common properties are common to all RR types: owner, class, and TTL (Time to Live).
DNS Domain	A node in the DNS tree. It contains all of the resource records for that domain.
DNS Zone	A subtree of the DNS database that is administered as a single entity. It may contain a single domain, or a domain with subdomains.
DNS Server	Administers at least one DNS zone.
Server List	Contains the DNS servers that can be administered with DNS Manager. New DNS servers can be added as needed.

The Resource Record (RR) property set depends on the RR type. The three properties listed in the following table, however, are common to all RR types.

Property	Function
Owner	Identifies the DNS domain or host to which the RR applies.
Class	Identifies a defined and standardized family of RR types. Almost all RRs in use today are of the 'IN' or Internet class.
TTL (Time to Live)	Indicates how long the information in the RR will remain valid.

Note DNS servers contain a database that Windows NT searches for computer names. Servers are searched in the order they appear in DNS Manager.

Configuring a DNS Client

Windows NT Server, Windows NT Workstation, Windows 95, and Windows for Workgroups 3.11 with Microsoft TCP/IP-32 installed all include DNS-resolver functionality.

There are two ways to configure a Windows NT client to use the DNS server to resolve Internet names, either manually or in conjunction with DHCP.

Manually

You can manually configure a DNS client by using the Network program in Control Panel. On the **Protocols** tab, click **TCP/IP Protocol**, and then click **Properties**. In the **Microsoft TCP/IP Properties** dialog box, click the **DNS** tab. You then provide the domain name for the client, and the IP addresses and search order for all DNS servers that you want to use to resolve host names.

In Conjunction with DHCP

When you configure your DHCP server to work in conjunction with your DNS server, you save the administrative overhead of individually configuring your DHCP clients to also be DNS clients. By using DHCP Manager to add and configure the DHCP option, 006 DNS Servers, your DHCP server can provide the address of a DNS server to be used for Internet name resolution to the DHCP clients.

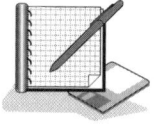

Practice

In these procedures, you install, configure, and test the Microsoft DNS Server service on Server1. Your DNS domain name is corp1.com.

Note Complete these procedures on Server1.

▶ **To install the Domain Name System Server service**

1. Log on as Administrator.
2. In Control Panel, double-click the Network icon.

    The **Network** dialog box appears.
3. Click the **Services** tab, and then click **Add**.

    The **Select Network Service** dialog box appears.
4. In the **Network Service** list, click **Microsoft DNS Server**, and then click **OK**.

    Windows NT Setup displays a dialog box requesting the full path to the Windows NT distribution files.
5. Type **\\Server1\Nts_source\I386** and then click **Continue**.

    All necessary files, including the sample files, are copied to your hard disk.
6. In the **Network** dialog box, click **Protocols**.
7. On the **Protocols** tab, double-click **TCP/IP Protocol**.

    The **Microsoft TCP/IP Properties** dialog box appears.
8. Click the **DNS** tab.
9. In the **Domain** box, type **corp1.com** and then click **OK**.
10. In the **Network** dialog box, click **Close**.
11. When prompted, click **Yes** to restart Server1.

▶ **To configure the DNS Service search order**

In this procedure, you configure the DNS search order by entering the IP address of Server1.

Note Complete this procedure on Server1.

---

1. Log on as Administrator.
2. In Control Panel, double-click the Network icon.

   The **Network** dialog box appears.
3. Click the **Protocols** tab, and then double-click **TCP/IP Protocol**.
4. Click the **DNS** tab.
5. In the **DNS Service Search Order** box, click **Add**.
6. In the **DNS Server** box, type **131.107.2.200** which is the IP address for Server1, and then click **Add**.
7. Click **OK**.

   The **Network** dialog box appears.
8. Click **OK** to close the **Network** dialog box.

▶ **To configure the DNS Server service primary zone**

In this procedure, you create a primary zone within your domain.

Note Complete this procedure on Server1.

---

1. Click the **Start** button, point to **Programs**, point to **Administrative Tools (Common)**, and then click **DNS Manager**.

   The Domain Name Service Manager window appears.
2. On the **DNS** menu, click **New Server**.

   The **Add DNS Server** dialog box appears.
3. In the **DNS Server** box, type **Server1** and then click **OK**.
4. Right-click **Server1**, and then click **New Zone**.

   The **Creating new zone for Server1** dialog box appears.

5. Click **Primary**, and then click **Next**.
6. In the **Zone Name** box, type **corp1.com**
7. Press the TAB key.

   Corp1.com.dns is automatically entered in the **Zone File** box.
8. Click **Next**, and then click **Finish**.

   Notice that the Server List now shows a zone name, corp1.com. In the right pane, notice the Zone Info entries that have been added.

▶ **To add your workstation computer as a New Host in your domain**

In this procedure, you add a host name, Workstation1, for your workstation computer to your domain.

Note Complete these procedure on Server1.

1. In the left pane, right-click your zone name, **corp1.com**.
2. On the menu that appears, click **New Host**.

   The **New Host** dialog box appears.
3. In the **Host Name** box, type **Workstation1**
4. In the **Host IP Address** box, type **131.107.2.201** which is your workstation's IP address, and then click **Add Host**.
5. Click **Done**.

▶ **To add an alias for your workstation computer to your zone**

In this procedure, you add an alias, work1, for Workstation1. The only reason you are creating this alias is to test that DNS is correctly installed and configured.

Note Complete these procedure on Server1.

1. Right-click your zone name, and then click **New Record**.

   The **New Resource Record** dialog box appears.
2. Under **Record Type**, click **CNAME Record**.
3. In the **Alias Name** box, type **work1**
4. In the **For Host DNS name** box, type **workstation1.corp1.com**
5. Click **OK**.

▶ **To add a Name Server record to your domain**

In this procedure, you add a Name Server record for Workstation1 to your domain.

Note Complete these procedure on Server1.

1. Right-click your zone name, and then click **New Record**.

   The **New Record** dialog box appears.

2. Under **Record Type**, click **NS Record**.

   Notice that the domain is already filled in with your domain name.

3. In the **Name Server DNS Name** box, type **workstation1**
4. Click **OK**.
5. Close DNS Manager.

▶ **To resolve an IP address using DNS**

In this procedure, you ensure that DNS is correctly installed and configured by resolving the alias work1. The alias name, work1, only exists in the DNS entries, and not in the WINS database. When the alias is resolved, your installation and configuration of DNS is now verified.

Note Complete these procedure on Server1.

1. Start a command prompt.
2. Type **ping work1** and then press ENTER.

   What IP address did it return?

Integrating WINS and DNS

The structure of a DNS zone changes whenever a new host is added or when an existing host is moved to a different subnet. Because DNS is not dynamic, you must manually change the DNS database files if the zone is to reflect the new configuration. This results in increased administrative overhead, especially on zones that change frequently.

The Windows NT DNS Server service can be configured to use WINS for host name resolution. You can install WINS and DNS on the same computer or on different computers running Windows NT Server 4.0.

This integration creates a form of dynamic DNS Server service that takes advantage of the best features of both DNS and WINS. With it, you can direct DNS to query WINS for name resolution of the lower levels of the DNS tree in your zones. This final WINS resolution is transparent to the client, which perceives the DNS name server as handling the entire process.

The following illustration shows how name resolution works when WINS is integrated with DNS. A user at the resolver computer is trying to connect to the widgets.universal.com host.

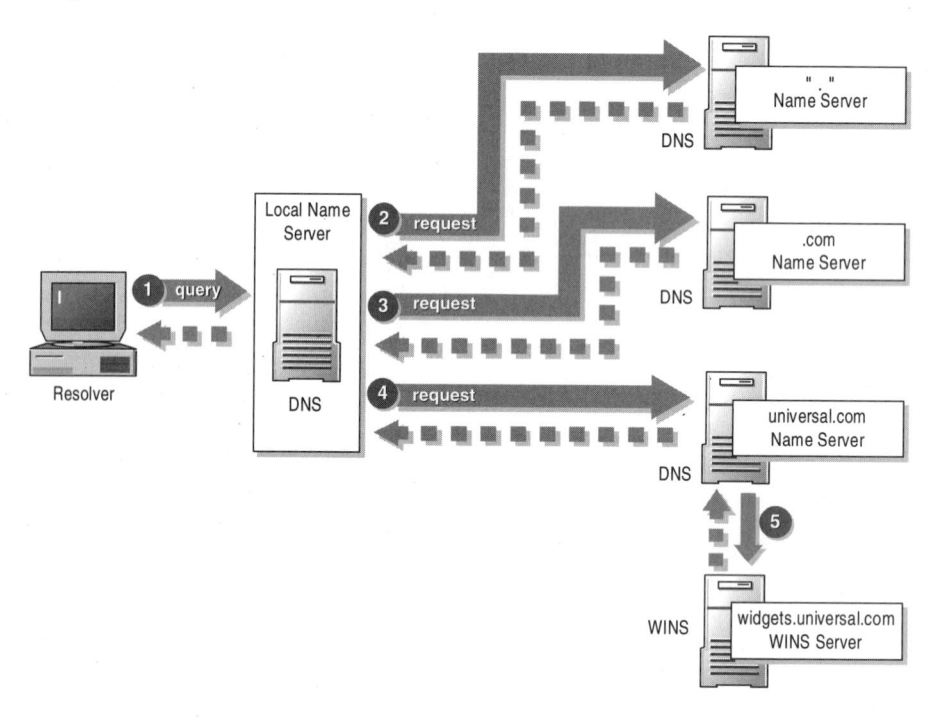

1. A resolver (or client) passes a query to its local name server.
2. The local name server sends an iterative request to one of the DNS root servers requesting resolution of the FQDN. The DNS root server returns a referral to the name servers that are authoritative for the *com* DNS domain.
3. The local name server sends an iterative request to one of the *com* name servers, which responds with a referral to the *universal* name servers.

4. The local name server sends an iterative request to one of the *universal* name servers.

5. The *universal* name servers are running the DNS server on a computer running Windows NT Server. They are configured to use WINS to resolve the leftmost portion (host name) of the FQDN. When the *universal* name server receives the request from the local name server, it passes the *widgets* piece of the DNS name to its local WINS server for resolution. WINS returns the IP address for *widgets* to the *universal* name server, which returns the IP address of the FQDN to the local DNS server, which then sends it back to the client resolver.

To configure DNS to use WINS to resolve the host name of a FQDN, use DNS Manager. Right-click the zone that will consult the WINS database for name resolution, and then click **Properties**. Click the **WINS Lookup** tab, and then select the **Use WINS Resolution** check box and type the WINS server IP address that will be used for resolution.

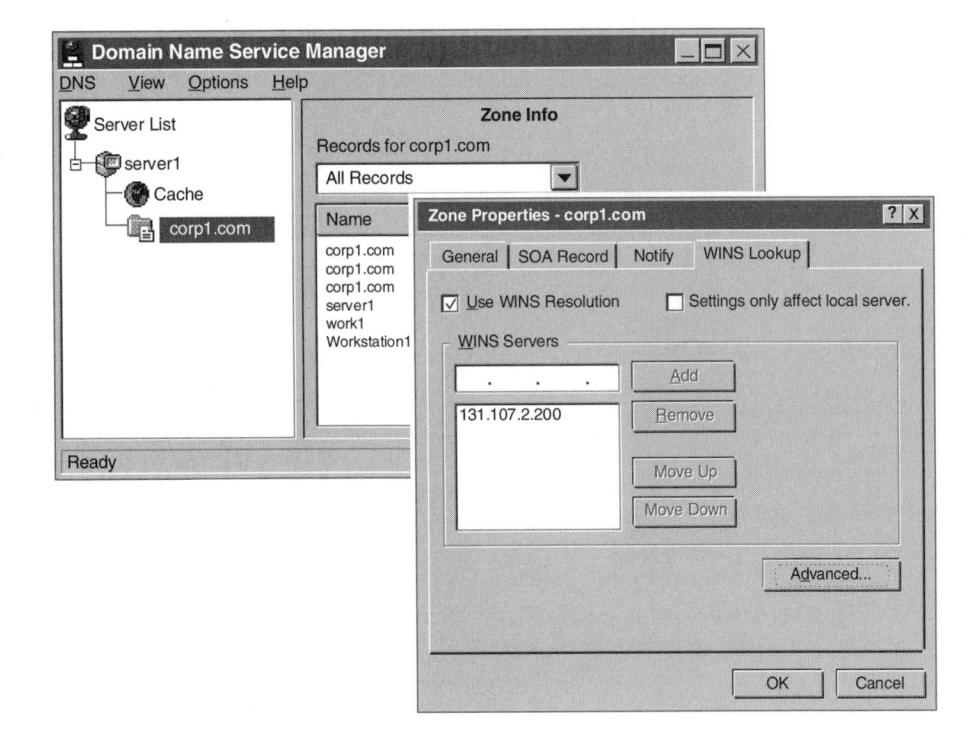

Lesson 5: Computer Browser Service

In this lesson, you learn how browsing for NetBIOS resources occurs in a internetwork.

After this lesson, you will be able to:
- Identify the roles a computer running Windows NT can perform in the browser process.
- Explain how the Windows NT Computer Browser service locates available servers on the network.
- Configure a computer to become a browser.

Estimated lesson time: 15 minutes

To use resources across a network efficiently, users must be able to find out what resources are available. Windows NT uses the Computer Browser service to display a list of currently available network resources.

The Computer Browser service maintains a centralized list of available network resources. This list is distributed to specially assigned computers that perform browsing services, along with their other normal services. Browser computers eliminate the need for all computers to maintain a list of all shared resources on the network. By assigning the browser role to specific computers, the Computer Browser service reduces the amount of network traffic required to build and maintain a list of all shared resources on the network. This also frees the CPU time each computer would have had to use in creating a network resource list.

Note For this lesson, a server is defined as any computer that provides resources to the network. For example, in the context of the Browser service, a computer running Windows NT Workstation is a server if it shares file or print resources with other networked computers.

The Browser Process

The following illustration shows the browser process.

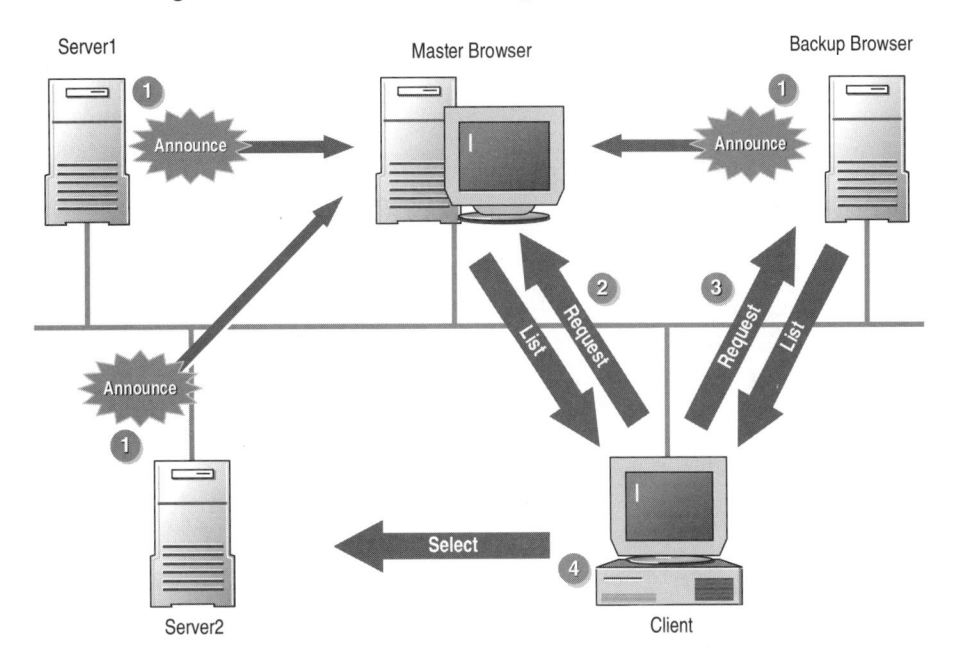

The Windows NT Computer Browser service operates as follows:

1. After startup, all computers that are running a Server service announce their presence to the master browser in their workgroup or domain. This happens regardless of whether or not they have shared resources to advertise.

2. The first time a client computer attempts to locate available network resources, it contacts the master browser of the domain or workgroup for a list of backup browsers.

3. The client then requests the network resource list from a backup browser, which responds to the requesting client with a list of domains and workgroups and the list of servers local to the client's domain or workgroup.

4. The user at the client selects a server, searches for the appropriate resource, and contacts the appropriate server to establish a session to use that resource.

Browser Roles

The responsibility of providing a list of servers to clients is distributed among multiple computers on a network. The browsing roles of these computers are known to the Browser service as potential browser, master browser, backup browser, and browser clients (non-browsers). Computers running Windows NT can perform any of the Browser service roles. These computers collect and maintain a list of available network resources, as defined in the following table.

Browser role	Description
Domain Master Browser	The domain master browser is the computer that collects and maintains the master list of available network servers, as well as the names of other domains and workgroups. It distributes this list to the master browser of each subnet in the Windows NT domain. There is only one domain master browser in a Windows NT domain, and it is the primary domain controller (PDC).
Master Browser	The master browser is the computer that collects and maintains the list of available network servers in its workgroup or subnet. It shares this list with the domain master browser, and receives information on other workgroups, domains, and subnets from the domain master browser, incorporating the information into its list of available resources. It distributes its list, referred to as the browse list, to the backup browsers. There is one master browser for each workgroup or subnet of a domain.
Backup Browsers	A backup browser is a computer that receives a copy of the browse list from the master browser. It then distributes the list to the browser clients upon request.
Potential Browser	A potential browser is not a browser server at all. It is, however, a computer that is capable of becoming a browser (either backup or master) if instructed to do so by a master browser.
Non-Browser	A non-browser is a computer that has been configured so that it will not maintain a browse list. Peer-to-peer networking computers are commonly non-browsers despite their having server services.

Browser Elections

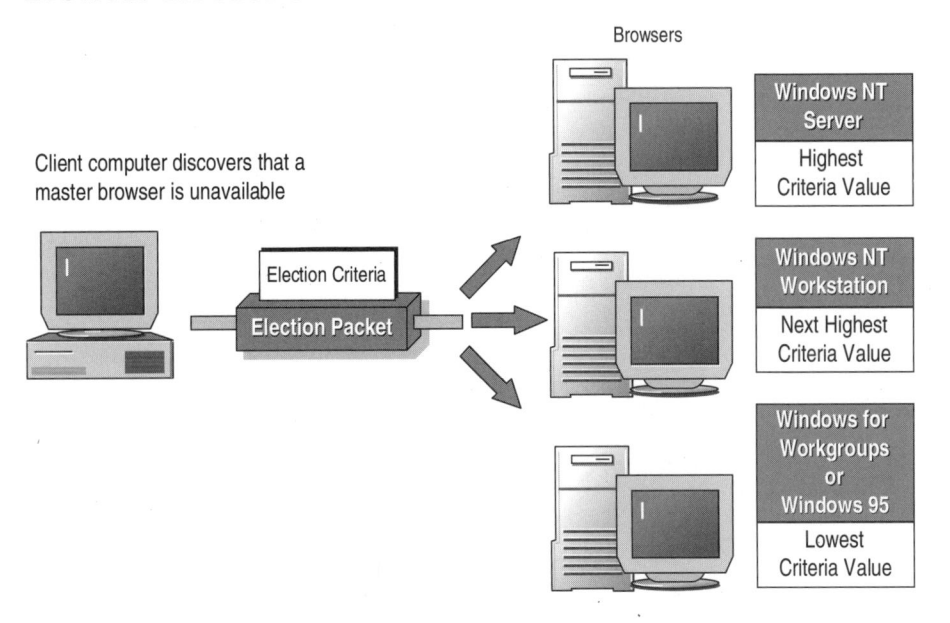

Client computer discovers that a master browser is unavailable

Election Criteria
Election Packet

Browsers

Windows NT Server — Highest Criteria Value

Windows NT Workstation — Next Highest Criteria Value

Windows for Workgroups or Windows 95 — Lowest Criteria Value

When a client computer cannot locate a master browser, or when a backup browser attempts to update its network resource list and cannot locate the master browser, a new master browser must be selected. This selection process is called a browser election. The election process ensures that *only one* master browser exists per workgroup or segment in a domain.

Election Process

Network computers can initiate an election by broadcasting a special message called an election packet. This election packet contains the requesting computer's criteria value. All browsers process the election packet.

When a browser receives an election packet, it examines the packet and compares the requesting computer's criteria value with its own election criteria. If the receiving browser has a higher election criteria than the issuer of the election packet, the browser issues its own election packet and enters what is referred to as an "election-in-progress" state. This process continues until a master browser is elected, based on the highest ranking criteria value.

Browser Criteria

Browser criteria determine the hierarchical order of the different types of computer systems that are in the workgroup or domain. Each browser computer has certain criteria, depending on the type of system it is. Among other things, the criteria include:

- The operating system:
  - Windows NT Server
  - Windows NT Workstation
  - Microsoft Windows 95
  - Microsoft Windows for Workgroups
- The operating system version, for example, Windows NT 4.0, 3.51, 3.5, or 3.1.
- Its configured role in the browsing environment:
  - Browser
  - Potential browser
  - Non-browser

The criteria ranking is used during an election. An election is used to determine which computer should be the master browser if the current master browser is unavailable.

Configuring Browsers

Computers running Windows NT can be configured to be a browser, to never participate as a browser, or to be a potential browser. Use Registry Editor to configure the following parameter:

\HKEY_LOCAL_MACHINE\SYSTEM\CurrentControlSet\Services
\Browser\Parameters**MaintainServerList**

The following table describes the value entries you can set for **MaintainServerList**.

Value entry	This value entry configures the computer to
No	Never participates as a browser server. Use this value entry to prevent computers that are frequently taken offline, such as mobile or test computers, from becoming a browser server.
Yes	Attempt to become a browser server. Yes is the default value entry for Windows NT Server domain controllers.
Auto	Possibly become a browser server, depending on the number of currently active browsers. This computer, referred to as a potential browser, is notified by the master browser as to whether it should become a backup browser. Auto is the default value for computers running Windows NT Server (non-domain controllers) and Windows NT Workstation.

Note To determine whether a computer running Windows NT will become a browser, when the computer initializes, the Computer Browser service looks in the registry for the value entry that has been configured for the computer.

Note For more information about browsing, see Chapter 3, "Windows NT Browser Service," in the *Networking Guide* of the *Microsoft Windows NT Server Resource Kit*.

Summary

The following information summarizes the key points in this chapter:

- Windows NT provides the following related services for TCP/IP that are added and configured using the **Services** tab in the Network program in Control Panel.
    - *DHCP.* Reduces administration by automatically assigning IP addresses to computers configured to use DHCP.
    - *WINS.* Is a name resolution service. It maintains a dynamic database for registering and resolving NetBIOS name-to-IP address mappings in a network.
    - *Windows NT DNS Server service.* Is a name resolution service. It uses a static database that resolves host names to IP addresses as required by the internetwork.
- The Windows NT DNS Server service is not dynamic, but it can be configured to use WINS for host name resolution, thereby creating a form of dynamic DNS Server service that takes advantage of the best features of both DNS and WINS.
- You can configure your DHCP server to work in conjunction with your WINS server and save the administrative overhead of individually configuring your DHCP clients to also be WINS clients.
- You can configure your DHCP server to work in conjunction with your DNS server and save the administrative overhead of individually configuring your DHCP clients to also be DNS clients.
- The Computer Browser service maintains a centralized list of available network resources. This list is distributed to specially assigned computers that perform browsing services, which reduces the amount of network traffic required to build and maintain a list of all shared resources on the network. It also reduces the CPU time each computer would have had to use in creating a network list, and allows users to locate network resources.

Review

1. How do you install Windows NT network services?

2. What role does the DHCP Server service play in the Windows NT networking environment?

3. Explain how the DHCP Server service assigns an IP address.

4. Your new computer running Windows NT Workstation cannot view or access any network resources. You have tried pinging other hosts unsuccessfully. Upon examining your TCP/IP configuration, you discover that your IP address is 0.0.0.0, even though it is a DHCP client. What do you suspect is the cause of the problem?

5. You are experiencing duplicate IP addressing problems. When you troubleshoot the problems, you discover that you accidentally assigned the same IP address to multiple scopes. Why did this create a problem?

6. What roles do WINS and DNS services play in the networking environment, and how do they differ?

7. Explain the advantages of integrating WINS and DNS.

8. You have a Windows NT network with TCP/IP as the only protocol available on your network. You have a computer running Windows NT Workstation that is configured to use DNS and WINS. Although you can connect to the computers running Windows NT Server in your domain, you are unable to **ftp** to any UNIX host on your network using the UNIX host's host name. What do you suspect is the cause of the problem?

Answer Key

Procedure Answers

Page 380

▶ **To create a DHCP scope**

2. In Control Panel, double-click the Services icon.

   What are the names of the two DHCP-related services?

   DHCP Client and Microsoft DHCP Server.

   What are the status and startup values of these two services?

   DHCP Client: blank status, and Disabled startup. Microsoft DHCP Server: Started status and Automatic startup.

Page 384

▶ **To test the DHCP configuration**

1. Start a command prompt, type **ipconfig /all** and then press ENTER to view the new TCP/IP configuration.

   What IP address was assigned to the computer running Windows NT Workstation by the DHCP server?

   The reserved client address, 131.107.2.201

   What is the DHCP server address?

   It is 131.107.2.200, the IP address of the Server1 DHCP server.

   What is the address of the default gateway?

   131.107.2.200 (as assigned by DHCP).

   When does the lease expire?

   Approximately 24 hours from the current time.

Page 386

▶ **To renew a DHCP lease**

1. Start a command prompt, type **ipconfig /all** and then press ENTER to view the lease information.

   When does the lease expire?

   Approximately 24 hours from the time you last renewed your lease.

2. Type **ipconfig /release** and then press ENTER.

   What message did you receive?

   IP address 131.107.2.201 successfully released for adapter "*network_adapter_card*".

3. Type **ipconfig /all** and then press ENTER to view the IP configuration.

   What is your IP address?

   0.0.0.0

5. Type **ipconfig /all** and then press ENTER to view the lease information again.

   When does the lease expire?

   Approximately 24 hours from the current time.

Page 387

▶ **To attempt lease renewal when the DHCP server is unavailable**

1. Start a command prompt, type **ipconfig /renew** and then press ENTER.

   Could you successfully renew the lease?

   No. You receive the following error message: "Error: DHCP Server Unavailable: Renewing adapter '*network_adapter_card*'".

Page 388

▶ **To release a DHCP address**

1. Start a command prompt, type **ipconfig /release** and then press ENTER.

   The Windows IP configuration information appears.

   What message did you receive?

   IP address 131.107.2.201 successfully released for adapter "*network_adapter_card*".

4. Log on to the domain as Administrator.

   A **Logon Message** dialog box appears, stating that a domain controller could not be found.

   Why does this message appear?

   Your computer does not have an IP address and therefore cannot communicate with other computers.

5. Start a command prompt, type **ipconfig /all** to view the IP configuration.

   What is the IP address? Why?

   The IP address is 0.0.0.0 because the DHCP server is disabled, so no IP address was assigned.

Page 389

▶ **To renew a DHCP lease**

2. Type **ipconfig /all** and then press ENTER.

   When does the lease expire?

   Approximately 24 hours from the current time.

Chapter 11   Windows NT Networking Services   423

Page 399

- **To test the configuration of the DHCP server to assign WINS server addresses**

    3. Type **ipconfig /all** and then press ENTER to view your IP addressing information.

       What is the address of the primary WINS server?

       It is the IP address of the \\SERVER1 DHCP server.

       What is the node type?

       It is hybrid, indicating that it is h-node.

    4. Type **ping server1** and then press ENTER.

       Why were you successful in pinging a NetBIOS computer name?

       The WINS server resolved the NetBIOS name to its IP address.

Page 409

- **To resolve an IP address using DNS**

    2. Type **ping work1** and then press ENTER.

       What IP address did it return?

       Your workstation's address.

Review Answers

Page 419

1. How do you install Windows NT network services?

   From the Network program in Control Panel, click the Services tab, and then click Add. Select the required service and then click OK.

2. What role does the DHCP Server service play in the Windows NT networking environment?

   It automatically assigns IP addresses to computers, eliminating common configuration problems that can occur when manually configuring TCP/IP.

3. Explain how the DHCP Server service assigns an IP address.

   The client sends out a request. Each of the DHCP servers that receives the request selects an address from the pool of addresses defined in its database and offers the address to the client. The client then accepts one of the offers, and the IP address is leased for a specific period of time.

4. Your new computer running Windows NT Workstation cannot view or access any network resources. You have tried pinging other hosts unsuccessfully. Upon examining your TCP/IP configuration, you discover that your IP address is 0.0.0.0, even though it is a DHCP client. What do you suspect is the cause of the problem?

   Either a DHCP server is unavailable or all IP addresses in the scope for your subnet are already being leased.

5. You are experiencing duplicate IP addressing problems. When you troubleshoot the problems, you discover that you accidentally assigned the same IP address to multiple scopes. Why did this create a problem?

   Because the same address is being leased by multiple computers.

6. What roles do WINS and DNS services play in the networking environment, and how do they differ?

   Both WINS and DNS are name resolution services.

   WINS is used to register NetBIOS computer names and resolve them to IP addresses. The WINS database is updated automatically.

   The DNS service is used to resolve fully qualified domain names to IP addresses. DNS computer names consist of two parts, a host name and a domain name, which together form the fully qualified domain name. The DNS database is static.

7. Explain the advantages of integrating WINS and DNS.

   It significantly decreases the administrative burden of updating DNS zone changes. The integration creates a dynamic DNS service that takes advantage of the best features of both DNS and WINS.

8. You have a Windows NT network with TCP/IP as the only protocol available on your network. You have a computer running Windows NT Workstation that is configured to use DNS and WINS. Although you can connect to the computers running Windows NT Server in your domain, you are unable to **ftp** to any UNIX host on your network using the UNIX host's host name. What do you suspect is the cause of the problem?

   The DNS server is either unavailable or does not contain a resource record for the UNIX host. Because DNS is not dynamic, you must manually enter resource records for your hosts. Connections to computers running Windows NT are successful because these connections use WINS, not DNS.

CHAPTER 12

Implementing Remote Access Service

Lesson 1 RAS and Dial-Up Networking . . . 427

Lesson 2 Telephony API . . . 440

Lesson 3 Installing and Configuring RAS . . . 443

Lesson 4 Installing and Configuring Dial-Up Networking . . . 454

Lesson 5 Troubleshooting RAS . . . 467

Review . . . 470

About This Chapter

This chapter introduces you to Microsoft Windows NT *Remote Access Service* (RAS). When RAS is installed on Windows NT Server, clients can connect over telephone lines through the Remote Access Service to a remote network. The RAS server acts as a gateway between the remote client and the network. After a user has made a connection, the telephone lines become transparent to the user, and the user can access all network resources as if sitting at a computer in an office that is directly attached to the network. For example, RAS makes a modem act like a network adapter card, projecting your remote computer onto a local area network (LAN).

In Windows NT version 4.0, RAS on the client side is called *Dial-Up Networking* and has a user interface that is consistent with Microsoft Windows 95. Thus, RAS is installed on Windows NT servers and Dial-Up Networking is installed on clients.

You will learn the basic operation of Windows NT RAS and Dial-Up Networking, as well as how to install and configure the key components that are required to support remote networks.

Before You Begin

To complete the lessons in this chapter, you must have:

- Two computers that meet the hardware and software requirements as specified in the Getting Started section of "About This Book."
- Completed all practices in Chapter 2, "Installing Windows NT."

Lesson 1: RAS and Dial-Up Networking

RAS and Dial-Up Networking enable you to extend your network beyond a single location and meet the diverse business needs of remote and mobile employees.

- RAS enables incoming connections from remote clients that are using Dial-Up Networking or other Point-to-Point Protocol (PPP) or Serial Line Internet Protocol (SLIP) dial-up software.

- Dial-Up Networking provides low-speed connections and is used by clients connecting to a RAS server or Internet service provider (ISP).

After this lesson, you will be able to:
- Describe the purpose of RAS and Dial-Up Networking.
- Explain the WAN support included in RAS.
- Identify the remote access protocols that are included in RAS.
- Explain the function of the NetBIOS gateway and routers.
- Describe the Point-to-Point Tunneling Protocol.
- Explain the security features included with RAS.

Estimated lesson time: 40 minutes

Using Windows NT RAS and Dial-Up Networking, a business can extend its networks over Public Switched Telephone Networks (PSTN), Integrated Services Digital Networks (ISDN), X.25, and the Internet. RAS provides an organization with a standards-based, remote networking system that supports computing for remote clients.

Because RAS supports wide area network (WAN) connections, protocols, and Windows NT security features, remote clients can use the network as if they were directly connected to it.

The following illustration lists some of the principal features of RAS and illustrates the resources that are made available to the Dial-Up Networking client.

- WAN Connectivity
- Remote Access Protocols
- Gateways and Routers
- Point-to-Point Tunneling Protocol (PPTP)
- RAS Security Features

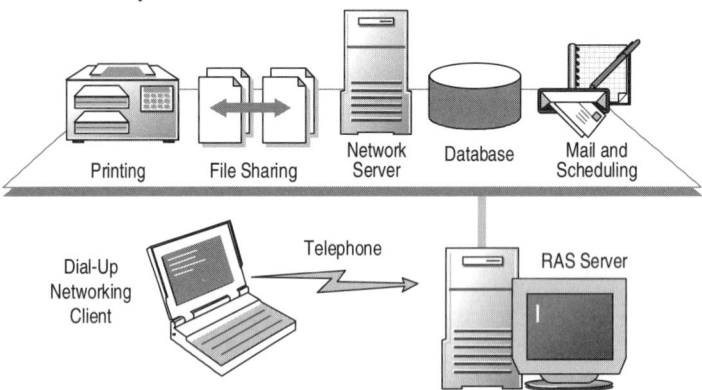

Furthermore, with Dial-Up Networking installed, clients can use the phonebook feature of Dial-Up Networking to record telephone numbers that are needed to connect to remote networks.

WAN Connectivity

Remote clients can connect directly to a RAS server through a Public Switched Telephone Network (PSTN), X.25 network, or Integrated Services Digital Network (ISDN). They may also connect remotely over a TCP/IP (Transmission Control Protocol/Internet Protocol) network, such as the Internet, using the Point-to-Point Tunneling Protocol (PPTP).

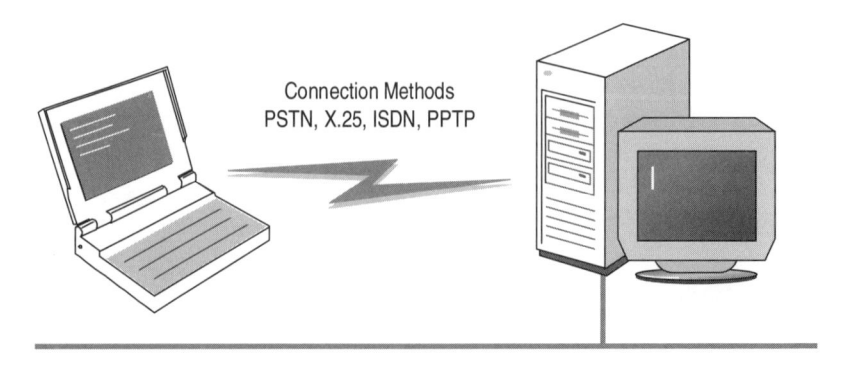

Public Switched Telephone Networks and Modems

Windows NT RAS uses standard modem connections over Public Switched Telephone Networks (PSTNs). A key advantage of PSTN is worldwide availability.

Most modems that comply with industry standards can interoperate with other modems. However, many difficult-to-diagnose problems can result from incompatible modems.

Windows NT can automatically detect modems. This is especially useful for remote clients, when users are not sure which modem is installed (for example, if their computer has an internal modem installed). If there is a problem detecting a modem automatically, it is possible to install a modem manually through the Modems program in Control Panel.

Integrated Services Digital Network

Integrated Services Digital Network (ISDN) is a digital system that offers much faster communication speed than a PSTN, communicating at speeds of 64 kilobits per second (Kbps) or faster. ISDN lines must be installed at both the server and remote site. ISDN requires that an ISDN adapter be installed in both the server and the remote client.

X.25

An X.25 network transmits data with a packet-switching protocol. This protocol relies on data communications equipment (DCEs), an elaborate worldwide network of packet-forwarding nodes that participate in delivering an X.25 packet to its designated address, for example, a modem.

Dial-Up Networking clients can directly access an X.25 network by using an X.25 packet assembler/disassembler (PAD). Dial-Up asynchronous PADs constitute a practical choice for remote access clients because they do not require an X.25 line plugged into the back of the computer. Their only requirement is the telephone number of the PAD service for the carrier.

RAS provides access to the X.25 network in one of two ways, depending on the operating systems involved.

Client/server	Configuration
Client (for Windows 95 or Windows NT operating systems)	Asynchronous packet assemblers/disassemblers (PADs)
Server and client (for Windows NT systems only)	Direct connection to the X.25 network through an X.25 smart card

Note The ISDN adapter and the X.25 adapter are treated as network adapter cards, thereby giving remote computers a direct data feed across a WAN to the LAN.

Packet Assemblers/Disassemblers

The PAD converts serially transmitted data into X.25 packets. When the PAD receives a packet from an X.25 network, it puts the packet out on a serial line making communication possible between the client and the X.25 network.

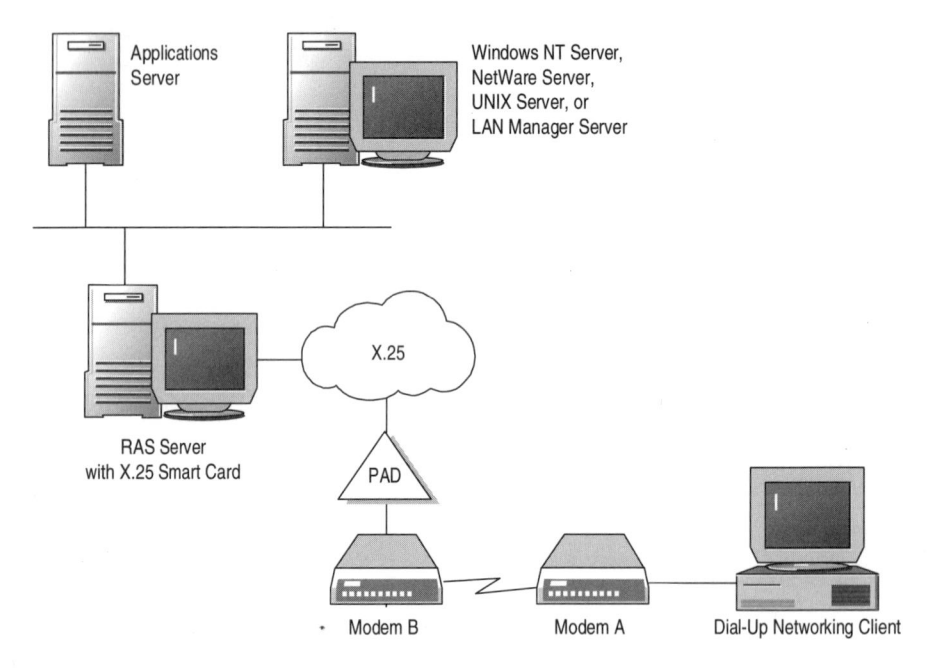

Smart Cards

An X.25 smart card is a hardware card with a PAD embedded in it. The smart card acts like a modem. To the personal computer, a smart card looks like several communication ports attached to PADs.

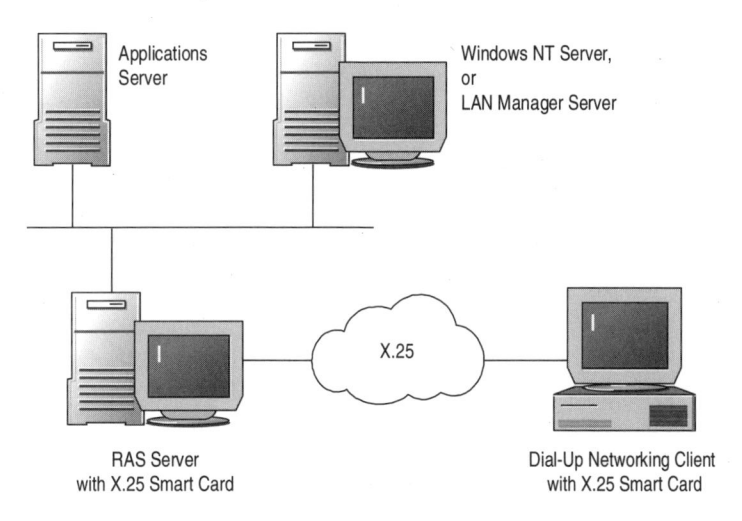

Point-to-Point Tunneling Protocol

Point-to-Point Tunneling Protocol (PPTP) is a technology that supports multiprotocol virtual private networks (VPNs). This support enables you to remotely access your corporate network securely across the Internet. Using PPTP, you establish a connection to the Internet and then establish a connection to the RAS server on the Internet using PPTP.

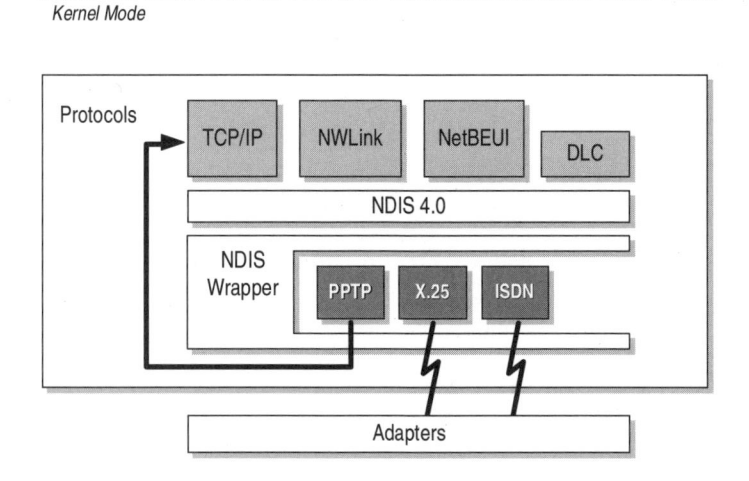

PPTP Advantages

Using PPTP to connect to a remote network offers computers running Windows NT the following advantages:

- *Lower Transmission Costs.* If you have local access through an Internet Service Provider (ISP), access to the remote network will be less expensive than a long-distance telephone call or using an 800 number.
- *Lower Hardware Costs.* If PPTP is used, a RAS server needs only a connection to the Internet. It is not necessary for the RAS server to have multiple modems, ISDN, or X.25 cards.
- *Lower Administrative Overhead.* With PPTP in Windows NT 4.0, you manage and secure your network at the RAS server. You need to manage only the user accounts and RAS dial-in permissions.
- *Security.* PPTP provides security through data encryption. A PPTP connection over the Internet is encrypted and works with the NetBEUI, TCP/IP, and IPX protocols. Data sent by means of a PPTP tunnel consists of encapsulated PPP packets. If Dial-Up Networking is configured to use data encryption, the data sent by means of PPTP is encrypted when sent.

How PPTP Works

PPTP provides a way to route IP, IPX, or NetBEUI PPP packets over a TCP/IP network. Because PPTP allows multiprotocol encapsulation, any of these packets can be sent over the TCP/IP network.

PPTP treats the existing corporate network as a PSTN, ISDN, or X.25 network. This virtual WAN is supported through public carriers, such as the Internet.

Comparing PPTP to Other WAN Protocols

When using PSTN, ISDN, or X.25, a remote access client establishes a PPP connection with a RAS server over a switched network. After the connection is established, PPP packets are sent over the switched connection to the RAS servers to be routed to the destination LAN.

In contrast, when using PPTP instead of a switched connection to send packets over the WAN, a transport protocol such as TCP/IP is used to send the PPP packets to the RAS server over the virtual WAN.

The resulting benefit for the corporation is a savings in transmission costs by using the Internet rather than long distance dial-up connections.

PPTP Access Over the Internet

A Dial-Up Networking client that has a PPTP driver as its WAN driver can connect to a Windows NT 4.0 RAS server using the Internet by either connecting directly to the Internet or calling an ISP.

If a direct connection to the Internet is required, the client must have a PPTP driver, and the RAS server must have a PPTP-enabled adapter.

If an ISP provides the connection, and the ISP's Point of Presence (POP) supports PPTP, then PPTP does not have to be installed on the client. (A POP is a physical site in a geographical area where an ISP has equipment to which users connect to get access to the Internet. This is typically done by dialing in over a modem and telephone line.) The client establishes a connection to the ISP and calls the Windows NT RAS server to establish the PPTP tunnel.

Note For more information about PPTP, see Appendix D, "Using the Point-to-Point Tunneling Protocol."

Protocols

You learned about Windows NT protocols in Chapter 10, "Configuring Windows NT Protocols." This discussion will focus upon the protocols that are specifically relevant to RAS, including which protocols to install, and their implications in implementing RAS.

Protocols supported by RAS can be examined according to their functions: those protocols that transmit data over LANs and those that transmit data over WANs. Windows NT supports LAN protocols such as TCP/IP, IPX/SPX, NWLink, and NetBEUI; and remote access protocols such as PPP, SLIP, and the Microsoft RAS protocol.

The Microsoft RAS protocol is a proprietary remote access protocol supporting the NetBIOS standard. The Microsoft RAS protocol is supported in all previous versions of Microsoft RAS and is used on Windows NT version 3.1, Windows for Workgroups, MS-DOS, and LAN Manager clients. A RAS client dialing in to an older version of Windows (for example, Windows NT version 3.1 or Windows for Workgroups) must use the NetBEUI protocol. The RAS server then acts as a "gateway" for the remote client, providing access to servers that use the NetBEUI, TCP/IP, or IPX protocols.

LAN Protocols

Windows NT RAS supports NetBEUI, TCP/IP, and IPX. Thus, you can integrate Windows NT RAS into existing Microsoft, UNIX, or NetWare networks using the PPP remote access standard. Windows NT RAS clients can also connect to existing SLIP-based remote access servers (primarily UNIX servers).

When you install and configure RAS, any protocols already installed on the computer (such as NetBEUI, TCP/IP, and IPX) are automatically enabled for RAS.

Remote Access Protocols

RAS connections can be established through SLIP or PPP.

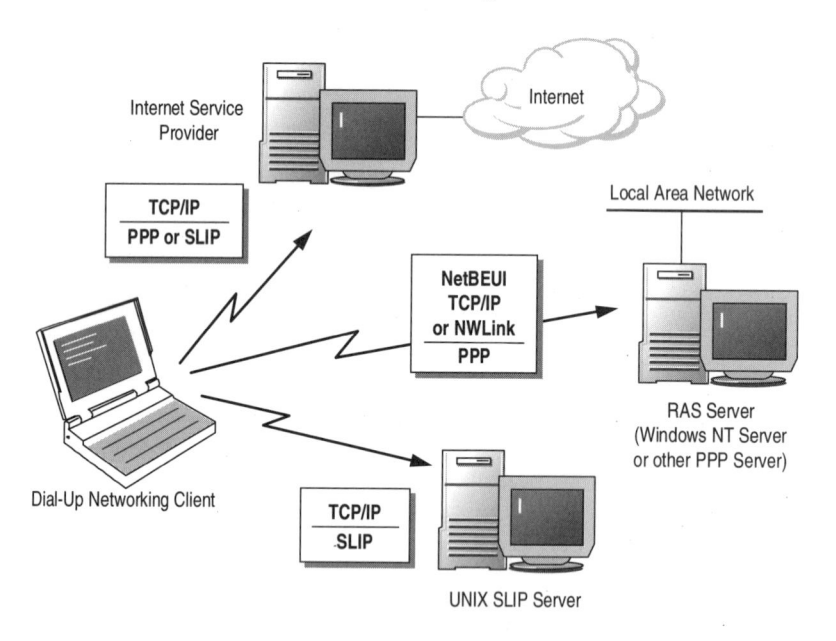

Serial Line Internet Protocol

Serial Line Internet Protocol (SLIP) is an industry standard that addresses TCP/IP connections made over serial lines. SLIP was first developed in 1984 to support TCP/IP networking over low-speed serial interfaces. SLIP is supported by Windows NT Dial-Up Networking and gives Windows NT clients easier access to Internet services.

SLIP has several limitations when compared to the newer Point-to-Point Protocol (PPP). SLIP servers cannot utilize DHCP/WINS. SLIP connections typically rely on text-based logon sessions and usually require a scripting system to automate the logon process. Although SLIP supports TCP/IP, it does not support IPX/SPX or NetBEUI. In addition, unlike PPP, SLIP transmits authentication passwords as clear text, thereby making the system less secure.

Note Windows NT RAS server does not have a SLIP server component, so it cannot be used as a SLIP server.

Point-to-Point Protocol

The Point-to-Point Protocol (PPP) was designed as an enhancement to the original SLIP specification. PPP is a set of industry standard framing and authentication protocols that enable RAS clients and servers to interoperate in a multivendor network. It provides a standard method of sending network data over a point-to-point link. PPP supports several protocols, including AppleTalk, DECnet, Open Systems Interconnection (OSI), NetBEUI, TCP/IP, and IPX. Windows NT supports NetBEUI, TCP/IP, and IPX.

Windows NT Protocol Support Over PPP

PPP support enables computers running Windows NT to dial in to remote networks through any server that complies with the PPP standard. PPP compliance also enables a computer running Windows NT Server to receive calls from, and provide access to, other vendors' remote access software.

The PPP architecture enables clients to load any combination of NetBEUI, TCP/IP, and IPX. Applications written to the Windows Sockets (WinSock), NetBIOS, or IPX interface can be run on a remote computer running Windows NT Workstation.

Supporting TCP/IP makes Windows NT "Internet ready," and allows remote clients to access the Internet through WinSock applications.

RAS clients that have both the IPX interface and Client Service for NetWare (CSNW) installed can access NetWare servers.

RAS clients that do *not* have CSNW installed can still access a NetWare server if Gateway Services for NetWare (GSNW) is installed on a RAS server. The RAS server then functions as a gateway to a NetWare server. In this case, IPX is not required.

RAS Setup automatically binds to NetBEUI, TCP/IP, and IPX if they are already installed on the computer when RAS is installed. After RAS is installed, each protocol can be configured separately for use with RAS.

PPP Multilink Protocol

The PPP Multilink Protocol (MP) provides the means to increase data transmission rates. MP accomplishes this by combining multiple physical links into a logical bundle to increase bandwidth. Based on the Internet Engineering Task Force (IETF) standard RFC 1717, RAS using PPP Multilink Protocol lets you easily combine analog modem paths, ISDN paths, and even mixed analog and digital communications links on both your client and server computers. For example, a client with two 28.8 Kbps modems and two PSTN lines can use MP to establish a single 57.6 Kbps connection to an MP server. This will speed up your access to the Internet or to your intranet, and cut down on the amount of time you have to be remotely connected, thus reducing your costs for remote access.

Both the Dial-Up Networking client and RAS server need to have MP enabled for this protocol to be used.

Remote access protocol standards are defined in RFCs, which are published by the IETF and other working groups. The RFCs supported in this version of Windows NT RAS are listed in the following table.

Request for Comment	Subject
RFC 1662	PPP in HDLC-like Framing
RFC 1552	The PPP Internetwork Packet Exchange Control Protocol (IPXCP)
RFC 1334	PPP Authentication Protocols
RFC 1332	The PPP Internet Protocol Control Protocol (IPCP)
RFC 1661	Link Control Protocol (LCP)
RFC 1717	PPP Multilink Protocol
RFC 1144	Compressing TCP/IP Headers for Low-Speed Serial Links
RFC 1055	A Nonstandard for Transmission of IP Datagrams Over Serial Lines: SLIP

Gateways and Routers

Windows NT RAS can act as a gateway or router in several situations.

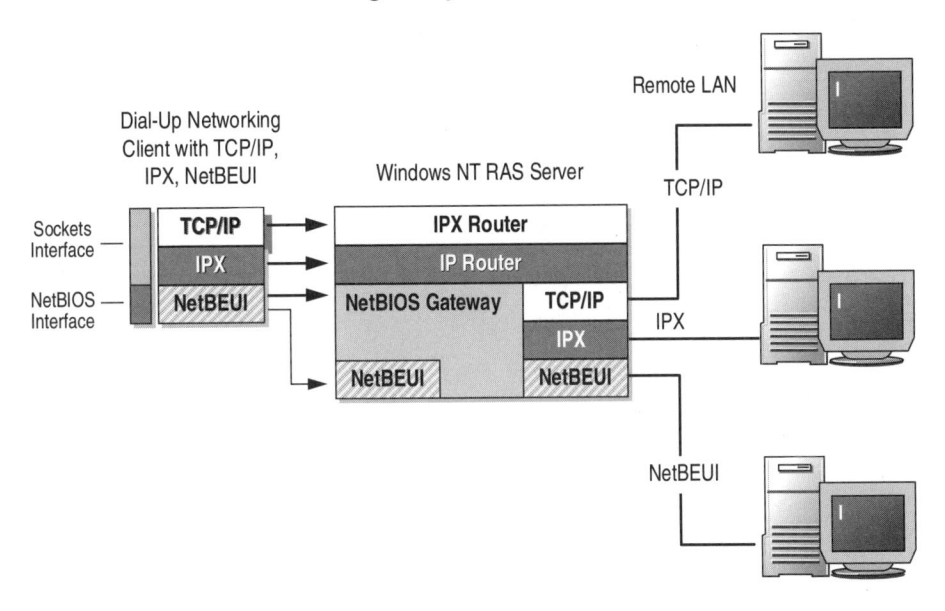

NetBIOS Gateway

Windows NT RAS includes a NetBIOS gateway that enables remote clients to access NetBIOS resources, such as file and print services, on a network. This enables clients running NetBEUI to access remote servers regardless of which protocol is installed on the remote server. The NetBIOS gateway does this by translating the NetBEUI packets into IPX or TCP/IP formats that can be understood by remote servers.

IP and IPX Routers

Windows NT enhances the RAS architecture by adding IP and IPX router capabilities. RAS servers that have IP and IPX routers installed can perform the following functions:

- Act as a router to link LANs and WANs.
- Connect LANs that have different network topologies such as Ethernet and Token Ring.

In addition, a RAS server can be an IPX router and Service Advertising Protocol (SAP) agent for Dial-Up Networking clients. SAP is similar in functionality to the Windows NT Browser service. Once configured, RAS servers enable remote clients to access NetWare file and print services, and to take advantage of Windows Sockets applications.

RAS Security Features

Windows NT RAS implements a number of security measures to validate remote client access to a network.

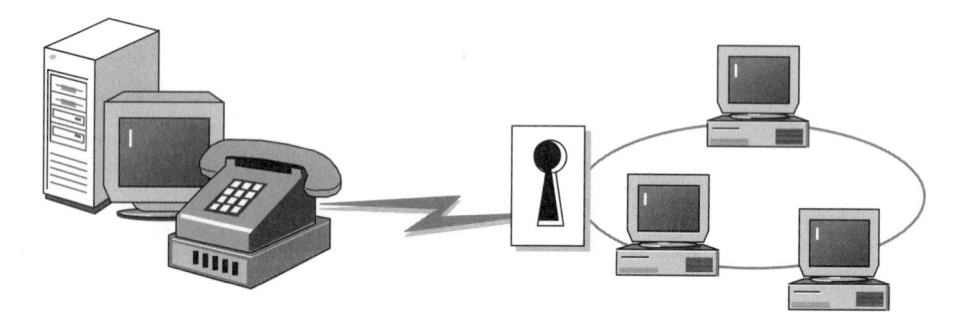

Integrated Domain Security

Windows NT Server provides for enterprise-wide security using a trusted domain, single-network logon model. This eliminates the need for duplicate user accounts across a multiple-server network. The single-network logon model extends to RAS users. The RAS server uses the same user account database as the computer running Windows NT. This allows easier administration, because clients can log on with the same user accounts that they use at the office. This feature ensures that clients have the same privileges and permissions they ordinarily have while in the office.

To connect to a RAS server, clients must have a valid Windows NT user account as well as the RAS dial-in permission. Clients must first be authenticated by RAS before they can log on to Windows NT.

Encrypted Authentication and Logon Process

By default, all authentication and logon information is encrypted when transmitted over RAS. However, it is possible to allow any authentication method, including clear text. In addition, it is possible to configure RAS and Dial-Up Networking so that all data that passes between a client and server is encrypted.

Auditing

With auditing enabled, RAS generates audit information on all remote connections, including processes such as authentication and logging on.

Intermediary Security Hosts

It is possible to add another level of security to a RAS configuration by connecting a third-party intermediary security host between the RAS client or clients and the RAS server or servers. When an intermediary security host is used, clients must type a password or code to get past the security device before a connection is established with the RAS server.

Callback Security

The RAS server can be configured to provide callbacks as a means of increasing security. When callback security is used, the server receives the call from the client computer, disconnects the connection, and then calls the client back either at a preset telephone number or at a number that was provided during the initial call. This allows another level of security by guaranteeing that the connection to the local network was made from a trusted site, such as a branch office.

PPTP Filtering

When using PPTP, the RAS server must have a direct connection to the Internet and a company's corporate network. This could pose a security risk because the corporate network could be accessed through the RAS server. Use PPTP filtering to help ensure security on a corporate network. When PPTP filtering is enabled, all protocols other than PPTP will be disabled on the selected network adapter card.

Note The following steps are presented for informational purposes only and are not intended to be completed as a practice.

To enable PPTP filtering, you would do the following:

1. Click the **Start** button, point to **Settings**, and click **Control Panel**.
2. Double-click the Network icon in Control Panel.
3. Click the **Protocols** tab.
4. Click **TCP/IP Protocols**, and then click the **Properties** button.
5. Click the **IP Address** tab in the **Microsoft TCP/IP Properties** dialog box.
6. Click the **Advanced** button.
7. Select the **Enable PPTP Filtering** check box in the **Advanced IP Addressing** dialog box.

   PPTP filtering would now be enabled.

Lesson 2: Telephony API

The Windows NT Telephony API (TAPI) provides a standard way for communications applications to control telephony functions for data, fax, and voice calls. TAPI virtualizes the telephone system by acting as a device driver for a telephone network. TAPI manages all signaling between a computer and a telephone network, including such basic functions as establishing, answering, and terminating calls. It can also include supplementary functions such as hold, transfer, conference, and call park, found in Private Branch Exchanges (PBXs), ISDN, and other telephone systems.

After this lesson, you will be able to:
- Describe the function of TAPI.
- Describe the TAPI settings.
- Configure a TAPI location.

Estimated lesson time: 10 minutes

TAPI Settings

TAPI allows you to centrally configure your computer for local dialing parameters. The basic TAPI settings for a system are set up when a TAPI-aware program is run for the first time. Dial-Up Networking is a TAPI-aware application. If a TAPI-aware application has not been run, the TAPI configuration will be automatically installed when you install Dial-Up Networking.

Location Setup

A *location* in Windows NT Dial-Up Networking is a set of information that TAPI uses to analyze telephone numbers in international number format, and to determine the correct sequence of numbers to be dialed. A location does not need to correspond to a particular geographic location, although it usually does. A location could include the special numbers needed to dial out from an office or hotel room. Locations can be named anything that is helpful for remembering them later.

Location information includes:

- Area (or city) code.
- Country code.
- Outside line access codes, for both local and long distance calls.
- Preferred calling card.

Calling Card

TAPI uses calling cards to create the sequence of numbers to be dialed for a particular card. The number is stored in scrambled form and will not be displayed once it is entered. This is a security feature that is used to prevent unauthorized access to the number. Multiple calling cards can be defined.

Drivers

TAPI drivers, also known as TAPI Service Providers (TSPs), are software components that control TAPI hardware (for example, a PBX, voice mail card, telephone system, or other equipment). Usually, TAPI drivers are installed with the TAPI hardware. However, the TAPI driver for modems (Unimodem.tsp) is automatically installed with the operating system.

Note All TAPI Service Providers (TSPs) run in the same memory space, so it is possible for a malfunctioning TSP to affect other TSPs.

Configuring a TAPI Location

You can configure a single TAPI location and use it from any TAPI-aware application.

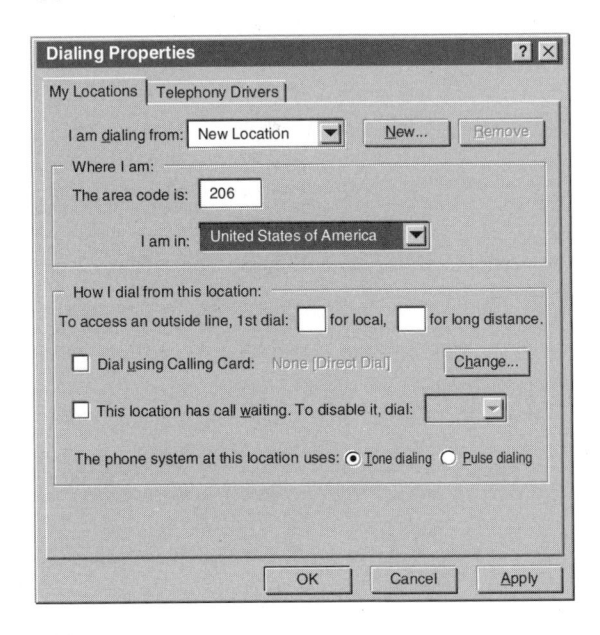

Preparing a computer running Windows NT to use TAPI involves configuring a TAPI location. Configure TAPI locations through the **Dialing Properties** dialog box accessible through the **Telephony** program in Control Panel. This **Dialing Properties** dialog box contains tabs through which various TAPI options can be configured.

The following table lists the configuration options available through the **My Locations** tab in the **Dialing Properties** dialog box.

Option	Use this option to
I am dialing from list and **New** button:	List the locations that are currently set up. To set up an additional location, click **New**.
The area code is	Enter the area code for the TAPI location. If the location is in a country other than the United States, type the city code, without leading 0(s). For example, if the city code is 071, type 71.
I am in	Select the current country name.
To access an outside line	Type the number(s) required to access an outside line for local and long distance calls. In many cases, these two numbers will be the same. If no number is required to access an outside line, leave both spaces blank.
Dial using Calling Card	Specify that the displayed calling card will be used when calling from this location. In the preceding illustration, a calling card has not been specified.
Change button	Change the calling card to be used for this location.
This location has call waiting. To disable it, dial	Specify whether this location uses call waiting. Call waiting should be turned off when dialing from a computer. Contact the local telephone company for information about how to disable call waiting.
The phone system at this location uses	Specify either tone or pulse dialing.

Lesson 3: Installing and Configuring RAS

RAS can be installed either during or after the installation of Windows NT 4.0. If you select "Remote access to the network" during setup, both RAS and Dial-Up Networking will be automatically installed. You can install either one or both services manually after installation. This lesson will cover the installation and configuration of RAS on Server1.

After this lesson, you will be able to:
- Install RAS software.
- Use the automatic modem detection feature of RAS.
- Configure the RAS server to support the various protocols.
- Grant RAS permission to clients.

Estimated lesson time: 50 minutes

Installing RAS

Whether you install RAS during Windows NT installation or later through the Network program in Control Panel, RAS requires the following information for installation:

- The model of modem that will be used.
- The type of communication port to use for the RAS connection.
- Whether this computer will be used to dial in, dial out, or both.
- The protocols to be used.
- Any modem settings such as baud or Kbps rate.
- Security settings including callback.

Note Windows NT 4.0 Server supports 256 simultaneous inbound RAS connections, while Windows NT 4.0 Workstation supports only one.

Configuring a RAS Server

Configuring a RAS server differs from configuring Dial-Up Networking clients. While Dial-Up Networking clients are configured primarily to dial in to remote networks, RAS servers are configured to provide access to network services for these clients. RAS server configuration involves configuring communication ports, network protocols (such as NetBEUI, TCP/IP, and IPX), and encryption settings.

The first step in configuring a RAS server is to specify the hardware that RAS will use, including the type of modem and the port to which the modem will be connected. In the following illustration, the modem is a Hayes Optima 288 V.34 and it is connected to COM1.

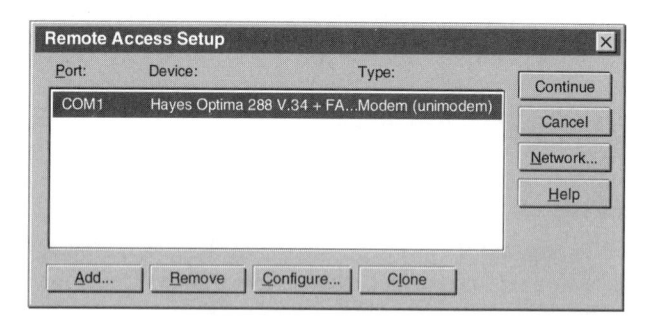

![Remote Access Setup dialog box showing COM1 port with Hayes Optima 288 V.34 + FA...Modem (unimodem), with buttons Continue, Cancel, Network..., Help, Add..., Remove, Configure..., Clone]

The drivers and ports used by RAS servers are configured through the **Remote Access Setup** dialog box. To access this dialog box, start the Network program in Control Panel. Click the **Services** tab and select the Remote Access Service. Then click the **Properties** button. The **Remote Access Setup** dialog box appears. The following table lists the configuration options available through this dialog box.

Option	Use this option to
Add	Make a port available to RAS and install a modem or X.25 PAD.
Remove	Make a port unavailable to RAS.
Configure	Change the RAS settings for the port, such as the attached device or the intended usage (dialing out only, receiving calls only, or both).
Clone	Copy the same modem setup from one port to another.
Network	Configure network protocol, Multilink, and encryption settings.

RAS Server Port Configuration Options

Click the **Configure** button in the **Remote Access Service** dialog box to configure the RAS server ports. The following illustration shows a possible configuration.

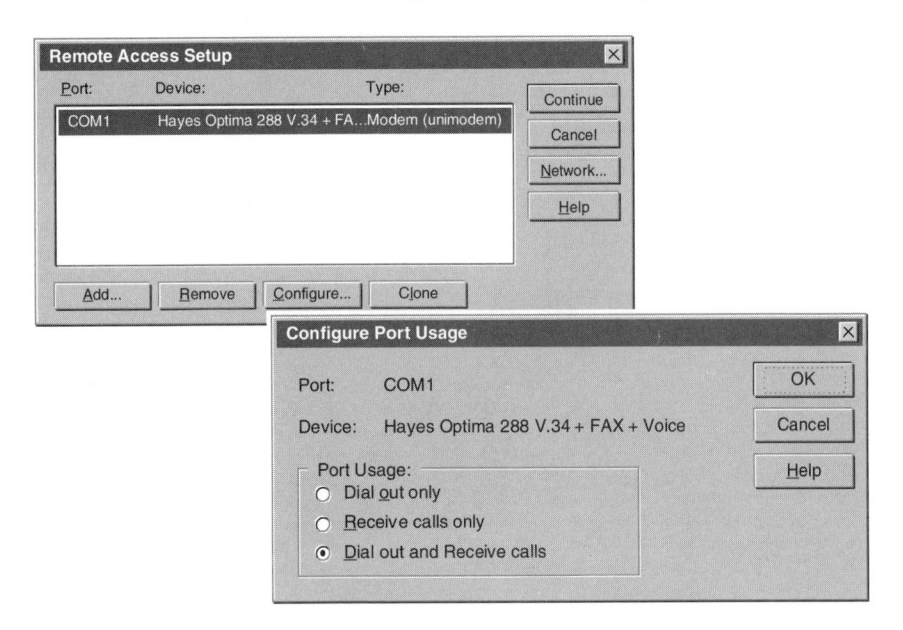

The following table explains the options listed in the **Configure Port Usage** dialog box.

Option	Use this option to enable
Dial out only	Dial-Up Networking clients to use that port to initiate calls.
Receive calls only	RAS servers to receive calls from Dial-Up Networking clients on that port.
Dial out and Receive calls	RAS servers to use that port for either Dial-Up Networking client or server functions.

Port configuration options affect only the specified port. For example, if the server's COM1 port is configured to receive calls and the COM2 port is configured to dial out and receive calls, a remote client could call in on either COM port, but a local user could only use COM2 for outbound RAS calls.

Once you select the appropriate Port Usage option, click **OK** and the **Remote Access Setup** dialog box reappears.

Configuring Protocols on the Server

Click the **Network** button in the **Remote Access Setup** dialog box, and the **Network Configuration** dialog box appears. In the following illustration, one of the dial-out options has been selected and all three protocols are being used.

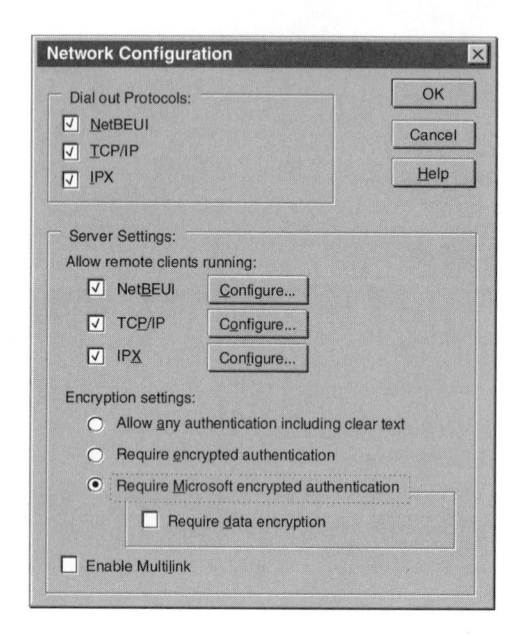

Note In the preceding illustration, the **Enable Multilink** check box is only available on computers running Windows NT Server.

Use the **Network Configuration** dialog box to select and configure the LAN protocols. Network protocol configuration applies to RAS operations on all RAS-enabled ports.

The following table describes the protocol configuration options available through the **Network Configuration** dialog box.

Options	Use this option to
Dial out Protocols	Select the dial-out protocols.
Server Settings	Select and configure the protocols the RAS server can use for servicing remote clients.
Encryption settings	Select an authentication level ranging from clear text for down level clients to Microsoft Encrypted Authentication for Windows NT and Windows 95 clients.
	If **Require Microsoft encrypted authentication** is selected, **Require data encryption** can also be selected.
Enable Multilink	Enable the Dial-Up Networking PPP Multilink Protocol. To use Multilink, both the client and the server must have Multilink enabled.

Note The next lesson provides an explanation of how Dial-Up Networking clients enable the Multilink Protocol.

Configuring a RAS Server to Use NetBEUI

If the NetBEUI protocol has been installed, the RAS Setup enables NetBEUI and the NetBIOS gateway by default. RAS servers use NetBEUI to provide remote clients with access to small workgroups or department-sized LANs.

To configure a RAS server to use NetBEUI, in the **Network Configuration** dialog box, make sure that NetBEUI is selected and then click **Configure** next to **NetBEUI**. The **RAS Server NetBEUI Configuration** dialog box appears.

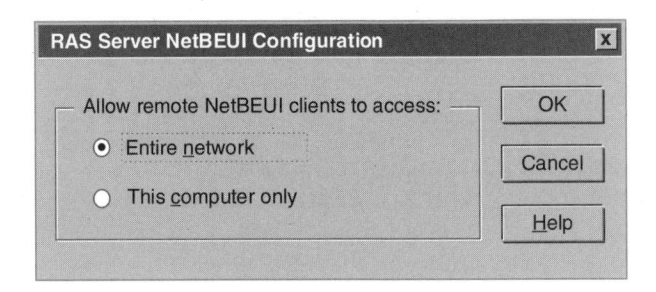

Use the **RAS Server NetBEUI Configuration** dialog box to allow remote NetBEUI clients to access:

- **Entire network**. This option grants remote clients permission to access resources on the network.
- **This computer only**. This option grants remote clients permission to access only the resources on the RAS server.

Configuring a RAS Server to Use TCP/IP

Servers can be configured to support not only Microsoft clients but also PPP clients from other vendors.

Dial-Up Networking clients and servers are assigned to the same WINS and DNS servers. Also, Dial-Up Networking clients in small networks where IP addresses do not change can use a Hosts or Lmhosts file for name resolution.

To configure a RAS server to use TCP/IP, on the **Network Configuration** dialog box, make sure that TCP/IP is selected and then click **Configure** next to **TCP/IP**. The **RAS Server TCP/IP Configuration** dialog box appears.

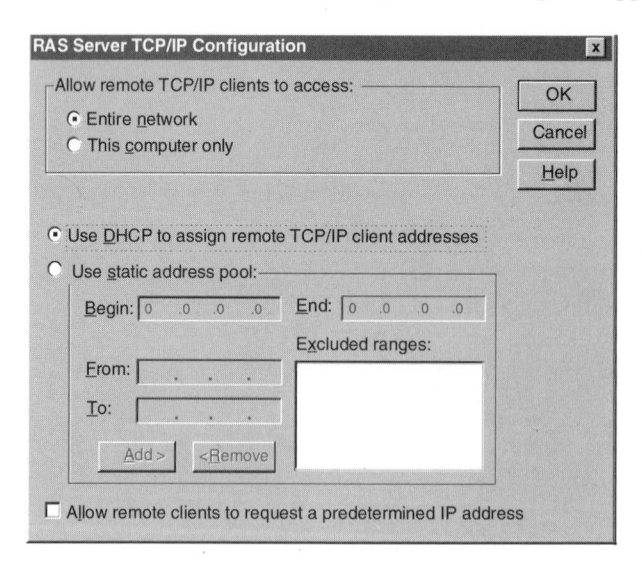

Use the **RAS Server TCP/IP Configuration** dialog box to grant network access permissions and IP addresses to Dial-Up Networking clients. The following table describes the configuration options available through this dialog box.

Option	Use this option to
Allow remote TCP/IP clients to access	Allow Dial-Up Networking clients to access the **Entire network** or the **This computer only** options.
Use DHCP to assign remote TCP/IP client addresses	Use a DHCP server to dynamically assign an IP address to a Dial-Up Networking client. Dial-Up Networking clients require an IP address to communicate on TCP/IP networks.
Use static address pool	Configure the IP address range. Designate beginning and ending values for the IP address range. Use the Add and Remove buttons to exclude any IP addresses that are not to be used.
Allow remote clients to request a pre-determined IP address	Enable Dial-Up Networking clients to request a predetermined IP address.

Configuring a RAS Server to Use IPX

Use the **RAS Server IPX Configuration** dialog box to grant remote IPX clients access to the network and to allocate network numbers.

To configure a RAS server to use IPX, on the **Network Configuration** dialog box, make sure that IPX is selected. Click **Configure** next to **IPX**, and the **RAS Server IPX Configuration** dialog box appears.

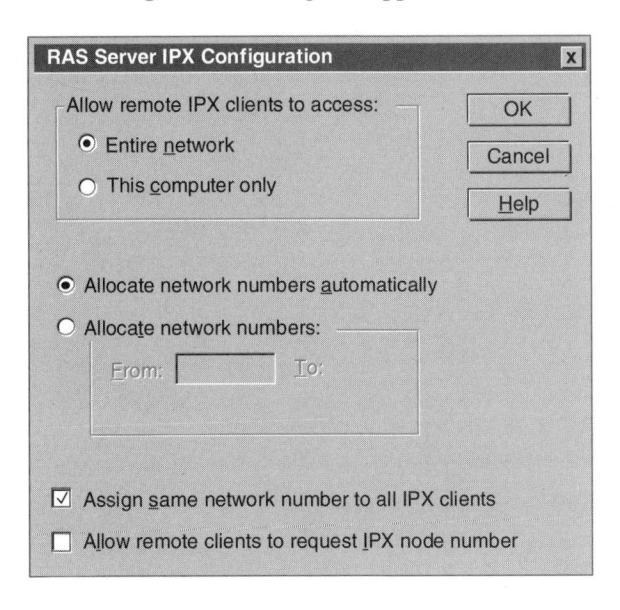

Dial-Up Networking clients can access Novell NetWare server file and print sharing resources through RAS servers that support IPX.

Use the **RAS Server IPX Configuration** dialog box to grant network access permissions and allocate Novell network numbers to Dial-Up Networking clients. The following table outlines the configuration options available through this dialog box.

Option	Use this option to
Allow remote IPX clients to access	Allow Dial-Up Networking clients to access the **Entire network** or **This computer only**.
Allocate network numbers automatically	Assign network numbers automatically to Dial-Up Networking clients. The same network number can be assigned to all IPX clients.
Allocate network numbers	Assign network numbers manually to Dial-Up Networking clients.
Assign same network number to all IPX clients	Assign a single network number to all IPX clients. Only one network number will be added to your routing table for all active Dial-Up Networking clients.
Allow remote clients to request IPX node number	Enable Dial-Up Networking clients to request an IPX node number rather than use the node number assigned by the RAS server.

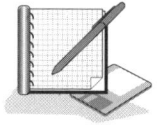

Practice

In these procedures, you install RAS and configure it to use a serial modem cable.

Note Complete these procedures on Server1, logged on as Administrator.

▸ **To prepare to install RAS**

1. Log on as Administrator.
2. In Control Panel, double-click the Network icon.
3. Install NetBEUI Protocol and NWLink IPX/SPX Compatible Transport.
4. Shut down and then restart Server1 for your changes to take effect.

▸ **To install RAS**

1. Log on as Administrator.
2. In Control Panel, double-click the Network icon.
3. Click the **Services** tab, and then click **Add**.
4. In the **Select Network Service** dialog box, click **Remote Access Service**, and then click **OK**.

5. When prompted for the path to the distribution files, type **\\Server1\Nts_source\I386** and then click **Continue**.

   A **Remote Access Setup** dialog box appears, asking if you want RAS Setup to invoke the modem installer.

6. Click **Yes**.

   The Install New Modem wizard appears.

7. Select the **Don't detect my modem, I will select it from a list** check box, and then click **Next**.

   The Install New Modem wizard continues.

8. Under **Manufacturers**, click **(Standard Modem Types)**. Under **Models**, click **Dial-Up Networking Serial Cable between 2 PCs**, and then click **Next**.

   The Install New Modem wizard continues.

9. Click **Selected ports**, click **COM1**, and then click **Next**.

Important If COM1 is already in use on your computer and is therefore not available, you must select an available COM port. All other references to COM1 in these procedures would have to change to the selected COM port.

Note If you have already configured TAPI, you will not be prompted for the options in steps 10–13.

---

10. In the **Location Information** dialog box, select the appropriate country under **What country are you in now?**

11. In the **What area (or city) code are you in now?** box, type your area or city code.

12. If you are in a location where you need to dial a number or numbers to access an outside line, type in the appropriate number(s) in the specified box.

13. Click **Tone dialing** or **Pulse dialing**, depending on your telephone.

14. Click **Next**.

15. Click **Finish**.

    The **Add RAS Device** dialog box appears. You should see **COM1-Dial-Up Networking Serial Cable between 2 PCs** in the **RAS Capable Devices:** box.

16. Click **OK**.

    The **Remote Access Setup** dialog box appears. You have finished installing RAS, and will complete the configuration in the next practice.

▶ **To configure RAS**

Note Complete this procedure on Server1, logged on as Administrator.

1. Click **Configure** in the **Remote Access Setup** dialog box.

    The **Configure Port Usage** dialog box appears.

2. Click **Dial out and Receive calls**, and then click **OK**.

    The **Remote Access Setup** dialog box appears.

3. Click the **Network** button.

    The **Network Configuration** dialog box appears.

4. In the **Dial out Protocols** box, verify that **NetBEUI**, **TCP/IP**, and **IPX** are selected.

5. Under Server Settings, verify that the **Allow remote clients running** check boxes for **NetBEUI**, **TCP/IP**, and **IPX** are selected.

6. Next to **NetBEUI**, click **Configure**.

    The **RAS Server NetBEUI Configuration** dialog box appears.

7. Click **Entire network**, and then click **OK**.

    The **Network Configuration** dialog box appears.

8. Next to **TCP/IP**, click **Configure**.

    The **RAS Server TCP/IP Configuration** dialog box appears.

9. Under **Allow remote TCP/IP clients to access**, click **Entire network**.

10. Click **Use DHCP to assign remote TCP/IP client addresses**.

11. Click **OK**.

    The **Network Configuration** dialog box appears.

12. Next to **IPX**, click **Configure**.

    The **RAS Server IPX Configuration** dialog box appears.

13. Under **Allow remote IPX clients to access**, click **Entire network**.

14. Click **Allocate network numbers automatically**.

15. Select the **Assign same network number to all IPX clients** check box, and then click **OK**.

    The **Network Configuration** dialog box appears.

16. Click **OK**.

    The **Remote Access Setup** dialog box appears.

17. Click **Continue**.

    An **RIP for NWLink IPX Configuration** dialog box appears asking if you want to enable NetBIOS Broadcast Propagation.

18. Click **No**.

    A **Setup Message** dialog box appears indicating that RAS has been successfully installed.

19. Click **OK**.

    The **Network** dialog box appears.

20. Click **Close**.

21. An **NWLink IPX/SPX** dialog box appears offering you the chance to change the internal network numbers now, click **No**.

22. Click **Yes** to restart the computer.

Granting Remote Access Permissions

After installing RAS on a server, you must grant Remote Access permissions to users before they can to connect through Dial-Up Networking. You use the Remote Access **Admin** utility or User Manager for Domains to grant RAS permission.

Practice

▶ **To assign permission to RAS users**

> **Note** Complete this procedure on Server1.

1. Log on as Administrator
2. Click the **Start** button, point to **Programs**, point to **Administrative Tools (Common)**, and then click **Remote Access Admin**.

   This starts the **Remote Access Admin** program on your server.

3. On the **Users** menu, click **Permissions**.

   The **Remote Access Permissions** dialog box appears.

4. Click **Grant All**.

   A **Remote Access Admin** dialog box appears, with the "Grant Remote Access permission to all SERVER1 users?" prompt.

5. Click **Yes**.

   The **Remote Access Permissions** dialog box appears.

6. Click **OK**.
7. Exit the **Remote Access Admin** program.

Lesson 4: Installing and Configuring Dial-Up Networking

Dial-Up Networking enables remote clients to connect to a network from a remote site, such as home or a hotel. It functions by calling the RAS server and establishing a telephone connection with the network. After the connection has been made, a Dial-Up Networking client can work as if connected directly to the network.

There are a number of configuration options that can be set in Dial-Up Networking. You learned about TAPI configuration earlier in this chapter. Other configuration options include configuring phonebook entries, logging on using a dial-in entry, and the AutoDial feature.

After this lesson, you will be able to:
- Install Dial-Up Networking.
- Configure a phonebook entry.
- Log on to a Windows NT domain through Dial-Up Networking.
- Explain the AutoDial feature.

Estimated lesson time: 30 minutes

Installing Dial-Up Networking

You learned earlier that Dial-Up Networking is automatically installed during Windows NT installation if you selected **Remote access to the network** during Setup. It is also automatically installed when you install Remote Access Service if you configure RAS to dial out and receive calls, or dial out only.

You can also manually install Dial-Up Networking by double-clicking the Dial-Up Networking icon in My Computer.

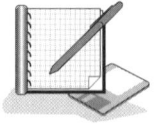

Practice

In these procedures, you install and configure Dial-Up Networking on Workstation1.

Note Complete these procedures on Workstation1, logged on to the domain as Administrator.

▶ **To prepare to install Dial-Up Networking**
1. Double-click the Shortcut to Network icon.
2. Install **NetBEUI Protocol** and **NWLink IPX/SPX Compatible Transport**.
3. Shut down, and then restart Workstation1 for your changes to take effect.

▶ **To install Dial-Up Networking**

1. Log on to the domain as Administrator.

2. On the desktop, double-click My Computer, and then double-click Dial-Up Networking.

3. Click **Install**.

4. If a **Files Needed** dialog box appears, insert the *Microsoft Windows NT Workstation* compact disc, type *cd-rom_drive*:**\I386** and then click **OK**.

5. When the **Remote Access Setup** dialog box appears, asking if you want RAS Setup to invoke the modem installer, click **Yes**.

   The Install New Modem wizard appears.

6. Select the **Don't detect my modem, I will select it from a list** check box, and then click **Next**.

   The Install New Modem wizard continues.

7. Under **Manufacturers**, click **(Standard Modem Types)**. Under **Models**, click **Dial-Up Networking Serial Cable between 2 PCs**, and then click **Next**.

   The Install New Modem wizard continues.

8. Click **Selected ports**; click **COM1** (if COM1 is already in use, select an available COM port on your computer), and then click **Next**.

   A **Location Information** dialog box appears.

   Note Steps 9–12 are not necessary when using a null modem cable to connect two computers, as you are doing in this procedure.

9. In the **What country are you in now?** box, select the appropriate country.

10. In the **What area (or city) code are you in now?** box, type your area or city code.

11. In the **If you dial a number to access an outside line, what is it?** box, type the appropriate number(s).

12. Click **Tone dialing** or **Pulse dialing** depending on your telephone, and then click **Next**.

13. Click **Finish**.

    The **Add RAS Device** dialog box appears. You should see **COM1-Dial-Up Networking Serial Cable between 2 PCs** in the **RAS Capable Devices:** box.

14. Click **OK**.

    The **Remote Access Setup** dialog box appears.

▶ **To configure Dial-Up Networking**

1. Click **Configure**.

    The **Configure Port Usage** dialog box appears.

2. Click **Dial out only**, and then click **OK**.

    The **Remote Access Setup** dialog box reappears.

3. Click the **Network** button.

    The **Network Configuration** dialog box appears.

4. In the **Dial out Protocols** box, verify that **NetBEUI, TCP/IP,** and **IPX** are selected, and then click **OK**.

5. Click **Continue**.

    A **Dial-Up Networking** dialog box appears asking if you would like to restart your computer.

6. Click **Restart**.

Configuring Phonebook Entries

Dial-Up Networking connects a client to remote networks using a modem, ISDN, or other WAN adapter. A *phonebook* entry stores all of the settings needed to connect to a particular remote network.

The Dial-Up Networking client stores all of its configuration data for a single connection in a phonebook file. Phonebooks can be specific to an individual user or shared among all users on the computer. When a phonebook is shared among all users, it is called a system phonebook. To create or edit phonebook entries, you can access Dial-Up Networking through either My Computer or the **Accessories** menu, which is accessed through clicking the **Start** button, and then pointing to **Programs**.

The first time a new phonebook entry is created, you should use the New Phonebook Entry wizard. After you feel comfortable creating phonebook entries, you can turn off the wizard by selecting the **I know all about phonebook entries and would rather edit the properties directly** check box.

Note If you would like to use the New Phonebook Entry wizard again, access **Dial-Up Networking** and click the **More** button. Click **User Preferences**, and then click the **Appearance** tab. On the **Appearance** tab, select **Use wizard to create new phonebook entries**, and then click **OK**. The next time you create a new phonebook entry, the wizard will automatically start.

To create or configure a phonebook entry, double-click the Dial-Up Networking icon in **My Computer**, and then click **New**. If you have disabled the New Phonebook Entry wizard, when you click **New**, the **New Phonebook Entry** dialog box appears.

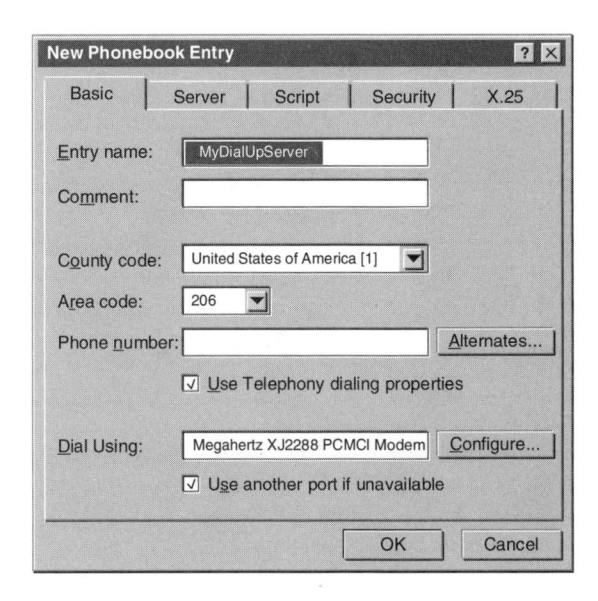

Note In the preceding illustration, if the **Use Telephony dialing properties** option is *not* selected, the **Country code** and **Area code** boxes will not appear.

New Phonebook Entry Configuration

Use the tabs in the **New Phonebook Entry** dialog box to configure the parameters described in the following table.

Tab	Use this tab
Basic	To configure a name for the phonebook entry.
	To enter the telephone number and any alternate telephone numbers, and to use Telephony dialing properties, such as when you are calling long distance or are using a credit card.
	To specify and configure the device used by the phonebook entry. To enable the PPP Multilink Protocol, select **Multiple Lines** in the **Dial Using** box, and then click **Configure**. In order to use the Multilink Protocol, you must have multiple devices installed, such as modems.
Server	To select the Dial-up server, type PPP, SLIP, or an older RAS protocol.
	To select a network protocol, click NetBEUI, TCP/IP, or IPX/SPX Compatible Transport.
Script	To specify a terminal window or script file if manual intervention is required before or after dialing to establish a remote access session.
Security	Select a level of authentication and encryption.
X.25	Select an X.25 network provider and configure connectivity information required by the X.25 network provider.

In addition, the following TCP/IP settings (available on the **Server** tab) may need to be configured, based on the **Dial-up server type** selected. The TCP/IP settings are only available for PPP and SLIP servers.

Option	Description
IP address	Automatically assigned by the dial-up server, or manually configured on clients.
Name server addresses	Assign DNS and WINS server addresses. These can be assigned by a DHCP server or manually configured at the client.
Use IP header compression	Enable header compression for low-speed serial links.
Use default gateway on remote network	Select this check box if the Dial-Up Networking client is using a network adapter card to connect simultaneously to a LAN. When it is checked, packets that cannot be routed on the local network are forwarded to the default gateway on the remote network. In addition, address conflicts between the remote and local networks are resolved in favor of the remote network.

Practice

In this procedure, you create a phonebook entry.

▶ **To create a phonebook entry**

Note Complete this procedure on Workstation1, logged on as Administrator.

1. Log on as Administrator, and then double-click the Dial-Up Networking icon in **My Computer**.

    The **Dial-Up Networking** dialog box appears, stating that the phonebook is empty.

2. Click **OK**.

    The New Phonebook Entry wizard starts.

3. In the **Name the new phonebook entry** box, type **Server1** and then click **Next**.

    A **Server** dialog box appears.

4. Verify that all check boxes are cleared, and then click **Next**.

    A **Phone Number** dialog box appears.

5. Leave the Phone number box blank, and then click **Next**.

    You have just created a phonebook entry for Server1. In this case, the telephone number is blank because this computer is configured for a direct connection to Server1, using the **Dial-Up Networking Serial Cable between 2 PCs** option.

6. Click **Finish** to exit the New Phonebook Entry wizard.

    The **Dial-Up Networking** dialog box appears.

7. Click **New**.

    The **New Phonebook Entry Wizard** dialog box appears.

8. Select the **I know all about phonebook entries and would rather edit the properties directly** check box, and then click **Finish**.

    The **Dial-Up Networking** dialog box appears.

9. Click **New**.

    The **New Phonebook Entry** dialog box appears.

10. Click **Cancel** to close the **New Phonebook Entry** dialog box and to return to the **Dial-Up Networking** dialog box.

Logging on Through Dial-Up Networking

When Dial-Up Networking is installed, Windows NT includes a logon option that enables users to log on to a domain using Dial-Up Networking. When this check box is selected, users have the opportunity to select a Dial-Up Networking phonebook entry that will be used for logging on. Dial-Up Networking will then establish a connection to the RAS server so that a domain controller for the specified domain can validate the client's logon request.

The dial-up settings for establishing a connection for logging on are configured using the **Logon Preferences** dialog box in the Dial-Up Networking client. To access this dialog box, click the **More** button in the **Dial-Up Networking** dialog box, and then select **Logon Preferences** on the **More** menu.

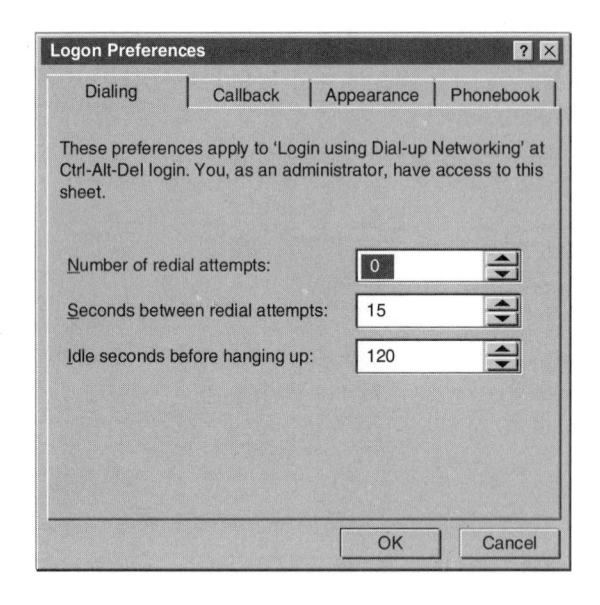

The following table describes the logon options that can be configured using the **Logon Preferences** dialog box.

Tab	Use this tab to
Dialing	Specify the number of and interval between redial attempts. It can also be used to set an idle connection timeout period.
Callback	Configure the server to disconnect and call the client back following authentication to reduce telephone charges and increase security.
Appearance	Configure the Dial-Up Networking interface that appears while logging on, including options to allow you to preview the number before dialing it, to show the location setting before dialing, to allow location edits during the logon process, to show connection progress while dialing, to close on dial, to allow phonebook edits during the logon process, and to use the wizard to create new phonebook entries.
Phonebook	Specify the system phonebook or an alternate phonebook to be used when logging on.

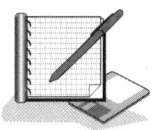

Practice

In this procedure, you configure logon preferences on your Dial-Up Networking client.

▶ **To configure logon preferences**

Note Complete this procedure on Workstation1, logged on as Administrator.

1. If you closed the **Dial-Up Networking** dialog box, double-click the Dial-Up Networking icon in My Computer.

    The **Dial-Up Networking** dialog box appears.

2. Under the **Phonebook entry to dial** box, click **More**.
3. On the **More** menu, click **Logon preferences**.

    The **Logon Preferences** dialog box appears.

4. On the **Dialing** tab, in the **Number of redial attempts** box, set the number to **3**.
5. Click **OK** to close the **Logon Preferences** dialog box.

User Profiles with Dial-Up Networking

The same logon process is used by Windows NT to log on to a LAN directly or through Dial-Up Networking. The reason this process is identical for direct and remote logon is that a copy of a user's profile is cached on the client each time the user logs off.

You may want to use the locally-cached user profile rather than the server-based profile when logging on through Dial-Up Networking. For example, if the server containing your server-based profile is unavailable, any customization of your desktop that is stored in that profile will not occur. However, if you have a locally-cached user profile, these customizations will occur. In order to configure Windows NT to use your locally-cached user profile, access the **User Profiles** tab through System on Control Panel.

AutoDial

Windows NT version 4.0 Dial-Up Networking supports a feature known as *AutoDial*. Windows 95 and Windows NT versions 3.51 and earlier do not support the AutoDial feature.

RAS AutoDial maps and maintains network addresses to phonebook entries, allowing them to be automatically dialed when referenced from an application or from the command line.

The database can include IP addresses (for example, "127.95.1.4"), Internet host names (for example, "www.microsoft.com"), or NetBIOS names (for example, "products1"). Associated with each address in the AutoDial database is a set of one or more entries. Each of these entries specifies a phonebook entry that RAS can dial to connect to the address from a particular TAPI dialing location.

AutoDial automatically creates entries in the AutoDial mapping database in two situations:

- When an attempt to connect to a network address fails.

    If there is no entry for the address in the mapping database, and the computer is not connected to a network (either directly or through RAS), AutoDial prompts the user to specify the information necessary to establish a dial-up connection. If the user provides the information and the dial-up connection operation is successful, AutoDial stores the information in the mapping database.

- When the computer is connected to a network through RAS.

    Whenever the user connects to a network address, AutoDial creates an entry in the database. The entry maps the network address to the phonebook entry that was used to establish the RAS connection.

AutoDial is enabled by default. A user can disable AutoDial in the **User Preferences** dialog box for a phonebook entry. To disable AutoDial, select an entry to dial from the phonebook list. Click **More**, and then click **User Preferences**. On the **Dialing** tab, clear each location listed in the **Enable auto-dial by location** list.

RAS AutoDial works only when the Remote Access AutoDial service is running. To determine if the Remote Access AutoDial service is running, use the Services program in Control Panel. If the Remote Access Autodial Manager is running, then the Remote Access AutoDial service is running. If the Remote Access Autodial Manager is not running, you can start it by selecting it, clicking **Startup**, setting the Startup Type to Automatic or Manual, and then clicking **Start**.

Note AutoDial does not support IPX connections. AutoDial only works with the TCP/IP and NetBEUI protocols. For more information on AutoDial, see Dial-Up Networking (RAS) Help.

The following illustration shows the User Preferences dialog box, with AutoDial enabled for Home and disabled for Hotel.

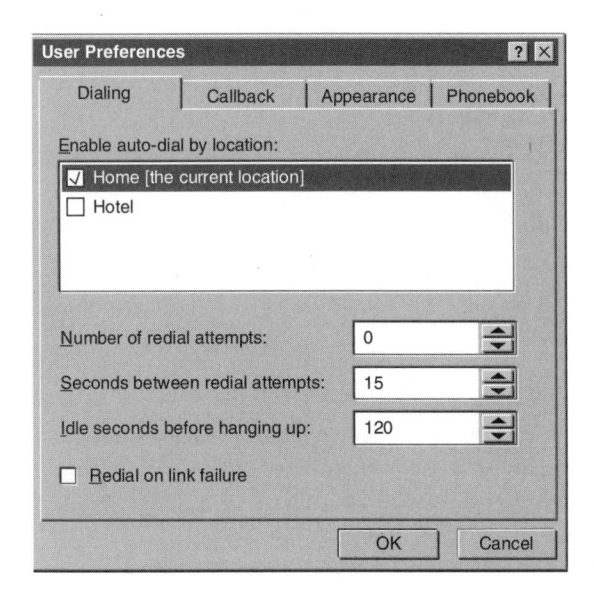

AutoDial also keeps track of all connections made over a Dial-Up Networking connection so that clients can be automatically reconnected.

AutoDial will attempt to make a connection in the following situations:

- When a user is disconnected from the network, AutoDial will attempt to establish a connection whenever an application references a network connection.
- When a user is connected to a network, AutoDial will attempt to create a network connection for addresses that it has previously learned.

Configuring AutoDial Preferences

Practice

In this procedure, you configure AutoDial preferences on your Dial-Up Networking client.

▶ **To configure AutoDial preferences**

Note Complete this procedure on Workstation1, logged on as Administrator.

1. If you closed the **Dial-Up Networking** dialog box, double-click the Dial-Up Networking icon in My Computer.

    The **Dial-Up Networking** dialog box appears.

2. Under the **Phonebook entry to dial** box, click **More**.
3. On the **More** menu, click **User preferences**.

    The **User Preferences** dialog box appears.

4. On the **Dialing** tab, in the **Number of redial attempts** box, set the number to **3**.
5. Click **OK** to close the **User Preferences** dialog box.
6. Click **Close** to close the **Dial-Up Networking** dialog box.

Testing the RAS Installation

To ensure that RAS has been properly installed and configured, you can perform a test procedure. There are two methods of testing your RAS installation: using a modem and telephone lines to dial in to a RAS server from your Dial-Up Networking client, or using a null modem cable to connect a Dial-Up Networking client and a RAS server.

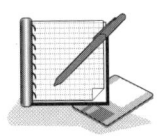

Practice

In this procedure, you use the RAS simulation to practice the procedure you would normally use to test your RAS and Dial-Up Networking installations.

▶ **To run the RAS simulation**

Note Complete this procedure on Workstation1.

1. Click the **Start** button, point to **Programs**, and then point to **Technical Support Training**. Point to **Simulations**, and then click **RAS Simulation**.

    The simulation starts, and the **Logon Information** dialog box appears.

2. Click to select **Log on using Dial-Up Networking**.
3. Verify that the Domain is **Domain1**.
4. Log on as Administrator using *password* as the password, and then click **OK**.

    The **Dial-Up Networking** dialog box appears.

5. Verify the **Phonebook entry to dial** box contains **SERVER1**, and then click **Dial**.

    The **Connect to Server1** dialog box appears.

6. In the **Password** box, type **password** and then click **OK**.

    A **Connecting to Server1** dialog box appears, and the Remote Access Service connects to the RAS server.

    Note You are now looking at Server1. Whether you log on locally or remotely using RAS, your desktop is the same. Your desktop is controlled by your user profile and any System Policy settings that apply to your user account name or the computer to which you log on.

7. Double-click **Network Neighborhood**.
8. Double-click **Server1**.

    What shares are available on Server1?

9. In My Computer, double-click **Dial-Up Networking**.
10. Click **Hang-Up**.

    A **Dial-Up Networking** dialog box confirming that you want to disconnect from Server1 appears.

11. Click **Yes**, and then click **Close**.

    A **Windows NT RAS Simulation** dialog box appears.

12. Click **Continue** to close the simulation.

Note If you have a null modem cable, you can perform the actual test procedure on Server1 and Workstation1. First disconnect Workstation1 from the network by unplugging the network cable. Then connect Workstation1 to Server1 by plugging one end of the null modem cable into Workstation1's appropriate COM port (usually COM1) and the other end into Server1's appropriate COM port. You can then test your RAS installations by following the procedure listed in the practice.

Lesson 5: Troubleshooting RAS

This lesson describes some of the common errors that can occur when using RAS, along with guidelines and tools for solving these problems. Using the Event Viewer, which is accessed from the Administrative Tools (Common) group, and viewing the system log will be helpful as a first line of information in troubleshooting RAS.

After this lesson, you will be able to:
- Describe several of the tools that will enable you to diagnose and solve problems that may arise when using RAS.

Estimated lesson time: 15 minutes

Event Viewer

The Event Viewer is used to view the system log, which contains events for all Windows NT internal services and drivers. Event Viewer is useful in diagnosing RAS problems, because many RAS events are logged in the system log. For example, if the Windows NT Dial-Up Networking client fails to connect, or if the RAS server fails to start, you should check the system log.

Problems with PPP Connections

If the user is having problems being authenticated over PPP, a Ppp.log file can be created to provide debugging information to troubleshoot the problem. The Ppp.log file is stored in the *systemroot*\System32\Ras folder, and it is enabled by changing the following registry parameter to a value of 1:

\HKEY_LOCAL_MACHINE\SYSTEM\CurrentControlSet\Services\Rasman\PPP**Logging**

Authentication Problems

If a Dial-Up Networking client is having problems being authenticated over RAS, try to change the authentication settings for that client. Try the lowest authentication option on each side, and if successful, start increasing the authentication options to determine the highest level of authentication that can be used between the two systems.

Dial-Up Networking Monitor

The Dial-Up Networking Monitor, accessed through the Dial-Up Monitor program in Control Panel, shows the status of a session that is in progress. It shows the duration of the call, amount of data that is being transmitted and received, and the number of errors. In addition, it can show which lines are being used for Multilink sessions.

Multilink and Callback

If a client uses a Multilink-enabled phonebook entry to call a server and that server is configured to call the user back, when the callback is made it will be to one of the Multilink devices. The reason for this is that the RAS **Admin** utility allows only one number to be stored for callback purposes for each user account. Therefore, the RAS server calls only one of the devices and Multilink functionality is lost.

If the link between the Dial-Up Networking client and RAS server is made using ISDN with two channels that have the same telephone number, then Multilink will work with callback.

AutoDial Occurs During Logon

During the logon process, when Windows NT Explorer initializes, any persistent network connections or desktop shortcuts that reference network locations will cause AutoDial to attempt a connection. The only way to avoid this is to disable AutoDial or remove the persistent connections and shortcuts.

Note In order to set up your computer for the rest of the lessons in this book, perform the following procedure to remove RAS from Server1.

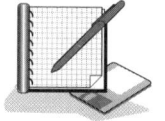

Practice

In this procedure, you remove RAS from Server1 to save resources.

Note Complete this procedure on Server1.

▶ **To remove RAS**

1. Double-click the Shortcut to Network icon.
2. Click the **Services** tab.
3. Click **Remote Access Service**, and then click **Remove**.

   A **Warning** dialog box appears, indicating that this action will permanently remove the component from your system, and asking if you still want to continue.
4. Click **Yes**, and then click **Close**.
5. When prompted to restart your computer, click **Yes**.

Note If you used a null-modem cable to test RAS using Server1 and Workstation1, remove the null-modem cable from the computers and plug the network cable into Workstation1.

Summary

The following information summarizes the key points in this chapter:

- RAS permits users who are not physically connected to the network to have network access through modems and telephone lines. The RAS server acts as a gateway between the remote client and the network. Any Microsoft Dial-Up Networking client can connect to any Microsoft RAS server.
- RAS can establish connections using standard telephone lines, X.25, and ISDN. RAS supports the SLIP and PPP protocols for WAN connections.
- An additional protocol, PPTP, enables you to remotely access your corporate network securely across the Internet. First you establish a connection to the Internet, and then establish a connection to the RAS server using PPTP.
- RAS provides several security features, including integrated domain security, encrypted logon, auditing, intermediary security hosts, and callback security.

Review

1. You would like to enable remote users to connect to your company's LAN through the Internet. However, your manager is concerned about potential unauthorized access from the Internet. How would you implement your plan while relieving your manager's concerns?

2. You are a frequent traveler, and you require dial-up access to your company's network through any of five remote access telephone numbers maintained by a RAS server. Changing all five access number properties to match your area code and dialing conditions is tedious; how can you simplify the process?

3. You use Dial-Up Networking frequently to access your company's network from home. You use a 28.8 Kbps modem to connect, and it takes a very long time to log on. Without buying another modem, how can you speed up the process?

4. Your network supports users who often work from home. These users only require remote access to their home directories, which are maintained on a RAS server. For security reasons, you do not want these users to be able to access the rest of your intranetwork from a remote location. What is the best way to implement this?

5. You receive a help desk call from a remote user who is having trouble connecting to the RAS server using PPP. How would you troubleshoot the problem?

Answer Key

Procedure Answers

Page 465

▶ **To run the RAS simulation**

8. Double-click **Server1**.

   What shares are available on Server1?

   PRINTERS and NETLOGON.

Review Answers

Page 470

1. You would like to enable remote users to connect to your company's LAN through the Internet. However, your manager is concerned about potential unauthorized access from the Internet. How would you implement your plan while relieving your manager's concerns?

   Implement PPTP, which uses the Internet as a connection medium but does not necessarily expose your network on the Internet. Only the RAS server needs to be on the Internet, and PPTP filtering can be enabled to prevent any packets other than PPTP packets from reaching the internal network.

2. You are a frequent traveler, and you require dial-up access to your company's network through any of five remote access telephone numbers maintained by a RAS server. Changing all five access number properties to match your area code and dialing conditions is tedious; how can you simplify the process?

   Configure a TAPI location with your local country and area code and any other necessary dialing properties. This location can be applied to all five of the Dial-Up Networking connections.

3. You use Dial-Up Networking frequently to access your company's network from home. You use a 28.8 Kbps modem to connect, and it takes a very long time to log on. Without buying another modem, how can you speed up the process?

   Configure your computer so that it does not download your server-based profile during logon across RAS.

4. Your network supports users who often work from home. These users only require remote access to their home directories, which are maintained on a RAS server. For security reasons, you do not want these users to be able to access the rest of your intranetwork from a remote location. What is the best way to implement this?

   Configure the RAS server so that it only allows access to itself and not to the entire network. If you apply permissions to other network servers and resources to restrict the remote users, these permissions would also apply when the users work at the office, restricting them unnecessarily.

5. You receive a help desk call from a remote user who is having trouble connecting to the RAS server using PPP. How would you troubleshoot the problem?

   Enable PPP logging for the RAS server and see how far the user is able to get in the connection process.

CHAPTER 13

Internetworking and Intranetworking

Lesson 1 Internet and Intranet Overview . . . 476

Lesson 2 IIS and PWS Networking Components . . . 479

Lesson 3 Microsoft Internet Explorer . . . 489

Lesson 4 Securing Internet and Intranet Sites . . . 490

Review . . . 499

About This Chapter

Supporting Microsoft Windows NT requires a knowledge of how computers running Windows NT can both access resources and distribute them over the Internet or a private intranet. In this chapter, you will learn about the Windows NT tools to support publishing and accessing services on the Internet and intranets. These include Internet Information Server (IIS), Peer Web Services (PWS), and Microsoft Internet Explorer.

Before You Begin

To complete the lessons in this chapter, you must have:

- Two computers that meet the hardware and software requirements as specified in the Getting Started section of "About This Book."
- Completed all practices in Chapter 2, "Installing Windows NT."
- Server1 configured with the DNS service, as directed in Chapter 11, "Windows NT Networking Services."

Lesson 1: Internet and Intranet Overview

This lesson introduces you to the Internet and a private intranet and discusses their functions and characteristics. You will learn about the World Wide Web (WWW), a graphical interface that overlays the Internet to create a virtual network, or Web, of information. Finally, you will learn of the security issues that you should consider when connecting to the Internet as well as when integrating a local intranet with the Internet.

After this lesson, you will be able to:
- Describe the Internet and an intranet.
- Identify security considerations for integrating an intranet site with the Internet.

Estimated lesson time: 10 minutes

The *Internet* is a network of computers located around the world that are able to communicate with one another through telephone lines. An *intranet* exists at a local level, and consists of computers that are connected by means of LANs. The following illustration shows both Internet and intranet connectivity.

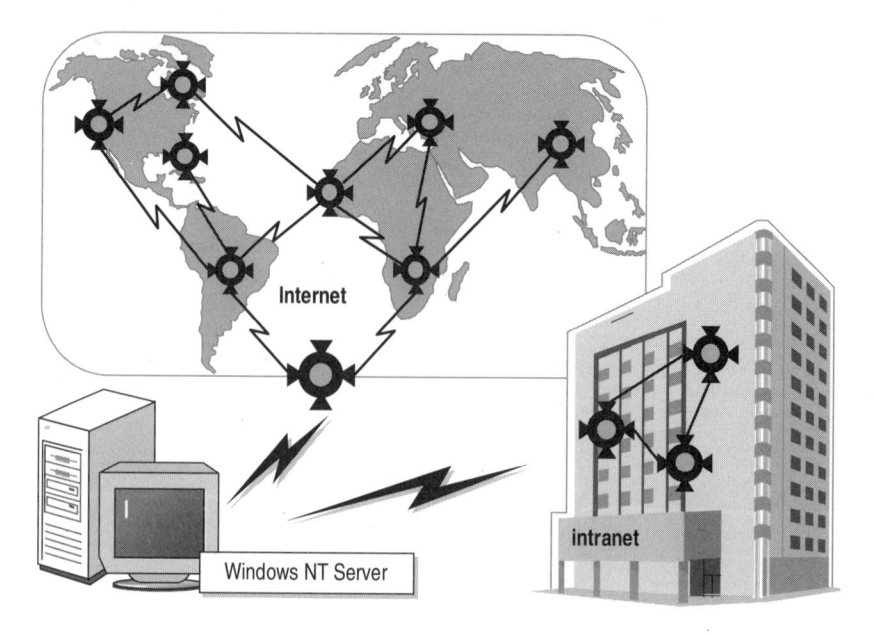

What Is the Internet?

The Internet is a global network of computers that communicate using common languages and protocols.

The Internet has been evolving since the early 1970s. Early servers on the Internet conformed to original Internet protocols, such as the File Transfer Protocol (FTP) or Virtual Terminal Protocol (VTP, now called Telnet). These protocols generally provide a way to copy files or issue commands or start programs through a character-based interface.

Internet technology has grown beyond the simple file transfers on character-based FTP or Telnet servers and incorporates graphical interfaces.

A key graphical network service on the Internet is the World Wide Web (WWW, or the Web). The user creates *Web pages* that are then linked together by means of the *Hypertext Transfer Protocol* (HTTP). Every Web page, including a Web site's *home page*, has a unique address called a *Uniform Resource Locator* (URL). The following shows a sample URL:

http://www.microsoft.com/ntserver/

Web pages are *hypertext* documents—files that have been formatted by using the *Hypertext Markup Language* (HTML)—that contain hyperlinks. *Hyperlinks* have Web addresses embedded in them and are represented as underlined or bordered words and graphics. When you click a hyperlink, you "jump" to the location on the Internet that was specified in the hyperlink.

Web servers automatically provide formatted text, graphics, sounds, and animation to Internet users. In order to connect to Web servers and view the information, you must use a Web *browser* such as *Microsoft Internet Explorer*. Microsoft Internet Explorer also supports the older standards, such as FTP, so you can use Microsoft Internet Explorer to access multiple servers and data types.

What Is an Intranet?

Intranets are networks, internal to a company or organization, that use Internet technology, such as the HTTP servers and Web browser services, to improve an organization's internal communications, information publishing, and application development process. In this chapter, intranet refers to any TCP/IP network using Internet technology that is not connected to the Internet.

Security Considerations When Connecting to the Internet

It is important to remember that the Internet, like other networks, provides two-way communication. When you are connected to the Internet, other computers can see your computer. By default, Windows NT security protects your computer from casual intrusion. However, while it is very unlikely that your computer will be attacked while you are browsing the Internet, it is still a good idea to configure your computer securely. Before you install and configure TCP/IP and Dial-Up Networking, you should review the security configuration of your computer.

Security Considerations for Integrating an Intranet Site with the Internet

It is possible to integrate a corporate intranet with the Internet. Both can be supported by the same network system. If your computer is also connected to an in-house network (an intranet), it is especially important to prevent access to your intranet from the Internet.

The following are security issues to keep in mind if you intend to integrate an intranet with the Internet:

- Usually, intranet sites are casual and informal, while Internet sites generally reflect the organization's public image.

- Separate the information that is downloaded to an intranet site from that distributed over the Internet. For example, proprietary documents are often distributed on intranets but would violate trade secrets if they were released to the Internet.

- It is usually not advisable to grant full intranet access to Internet users.

Lesson 2: IIS and PWS Networking Components

Windows NT is equipped with several components that support interoperability with the Internet and private intranets. You have learned about the Web browser, Microsoft Internet Explorer. Additional Internet and intranet components supported by Windows NT are the Internet Information Server (IIS) and Peer Web Services (PWS).

IIS and PWS provide computers running Windows NT with the ability to publish resources and services on the Internet and on private intranets. Use IIS and PWS for publishing hypertext Web pages and client/server applications, and for interactive Web applications. This lesson discusses IIS and PWS functions and features, and how they provide publishing services and resources to clients. In addition, you will learn how to install and configure both IIS and PWS.

After this lesson, you will be able to:
- Describe Internet Information Server (IIS) and Peer Web Services (PWS).
- Describe the procedures to install and configure IIS and PWS.

Estimated lesson time: 20 minutes

Functions of IIS and PWS

The following illustration shows the roles of IIS and PWS in Internet and intranet communications.

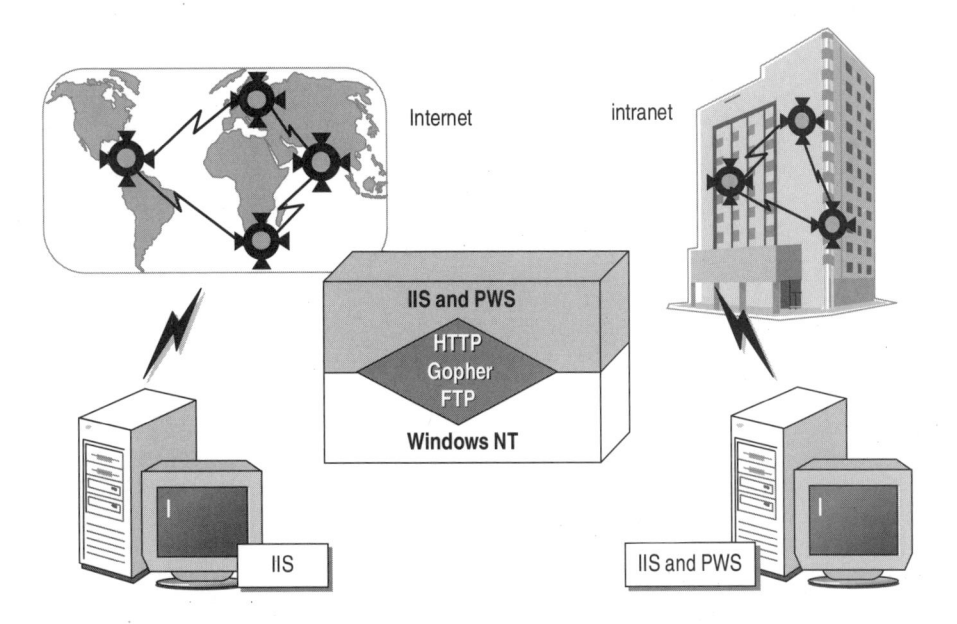

The IIS and PWS are network file and application servers that use HTTP, the Gopher service, and FTP to provide information over the Internet or an intranet.

- HTTP is used to link to and navigate Web hypertext documents and applications.
- The Gopher service is a hierarchical system used to create links to other computers or services, to put these links into custom menus, and to annotate files and directories.
- FTP is used to transfer files between two computers on a TCP/IP network.

Using IIS and PWS, it is possible to publish information or services such as Web pages, interactive applications, and catalogs for customers, and to post and track databases on the Web.

IIS and PWS support the Internet Server application programming interface (ISAPI). ISAPI is used to create interfaces that can be used for client/server applications. For example, ISAPI can be used to create applications that allow clients to access and enter information into a Web page.

IIS and PWS Comparison

Any computer running Windows NT Server can support IIS, and any computer running Windows NT Workstation can support PWS. IIS is designed to support the heavy usage that can occur on the Internet. PWS, on the other hand, is optimized for use as a small scale Web server suitable for exchanging information for a small department or individuals on an intranet.

Features of IIS and PWS

Among the features included with IIS and PWS are file publication, network management, and security. The following table provides an overview of some of the key features that IIS and PWS offer to a computer running Windows NT.

Feature	Use this feature to
File Publication	Publish existing files from Windows NT and other file servers.
Network Management	Monitor and record network activity and provide clients with access to valuable network resources such as HTML pages, shared files and printers, corporate databases, and legacy systems.
Security	Provide clients with secure access to Internet and intranet resources.
Support for common Internet standards	Enable development of Web applications, using such languages as CGI (Common Gateway Interface) and PERL (Practical Extraction and Report Language).
Microsoft Internet Explorer	Enable clients such as Microsoft Windows 3.11, Microsoft Windows for Workgroups, Windows NT, Microsoft Windows 95, and Macintosh to gain easy access to information on the Web.
Scalability	Enable Internet access to multiple platforms running on standard hardware packages, including single and multiprocessor servers using Intel 486, Pentium, Pentium Pro, Digital Alpha AXP, PowerPC, and MIPS processors.
Support for Microsoft BackOffice applications such as Microsoft SQL Server™ and Microsoft SNA Server	Provide businesses with the ability to deliver commercial solutions on the Web to customers.

Installing IIS

IIS can be installed when Windows NT Server is installed, or at a later time using either the Network program of Control Panel or the Install Internet Information Server icon located on the Windows NT Server desktop.

IIS Installation Requirements

Microsoft IIS has the following requirements for IIS installation:

- A computer running Windows NT Server 4.0 with TCP/IP.
- A CD-ROM drive for the *Windows NT Server* compact disc or a LAN connection to a server sharing the installation files.
- Adequate disk space for the published information content. It is recommended to use NTFS file and directory permissions to secure all of the disks used with IIS.

Chapter 13 Internetworking and Intranetworking 483

Changes can be made to a current installation of IIS through the Internet Information Server Setup icon located in the Microsoft Internet Server (Common) folder. Before adding or removing components, or reinstalling IIS, disable any previous versions of FTP, Gopher, or other Web service that may be installed on Windows NT Server.

Note See Windows NT Help for documentation on how to disable these services.

The following illustration shows the components available when installing IIS.

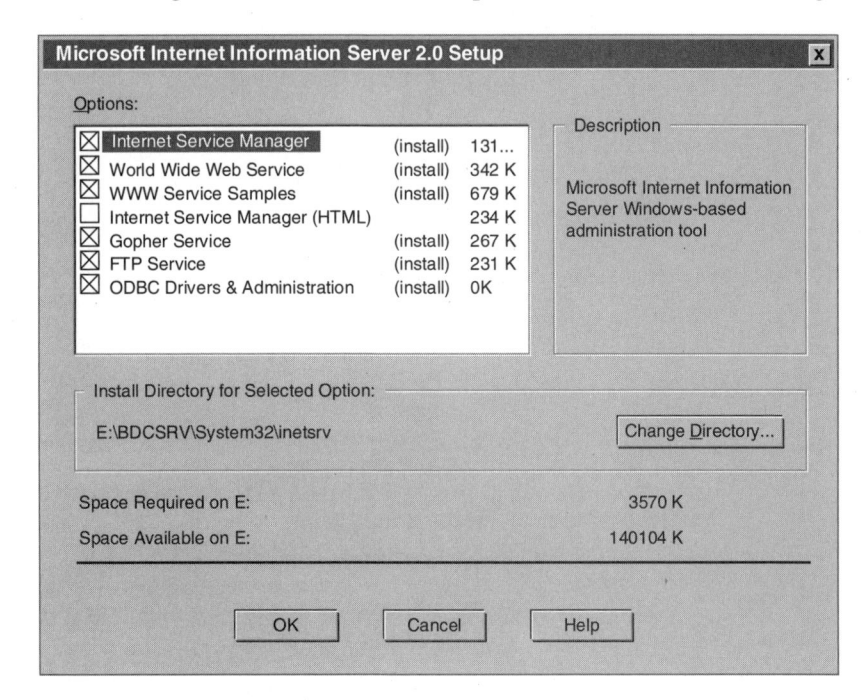

```
Microsoft Internet Information Server 2.0 Setup                                [x]

 Options:
   ☒ Internet Service Manager          (install)   131...    ┌─ Description ──────────┐
   ☒ World Wide Web Service            (install)   342 K     │                        │
   ☒ WWW Service Samples               (install)   679 K     │ Microsoft Internet Information
   ☐ Internet Service Manager (HTML)               234 K     │ Server Windows-based   │
   ☒ Gopher Service                    (install)   267 K     │ administration tool    │
   ☒ FTP Service                       (install)   231 K     │                        │
   ☒ ODBC Drivers & Administration     (install)   0K        └────────────────────────┘

 Install Directory for Selected Option:
   E:\BDCSRV\System32\inetsrv                                         [ Change Directory... ]

 Space Required on E:                            3570 K
 Space Available on E:                           140104 K

              [    OK    ]    [  Cancel  ]    [   Help   ]
```

Installing PWS

Install Peer Web Services through the Network program in Control Panel.

PWS Installation Requirements

PWS requires the following components for installation:

- A computer running Windows NT Workstation 4.0 and TCP/IP.
- A CD-ROM drive for the *Windows NT Workstation* compact disc or a LAN connection to a server sharing the installation files.
- Adequate disk space for the published information content. It is recommended to use NTFS file and directory permissions to secure all drives used with PWS.

The following illustration shows the components that are available when installing PWS.

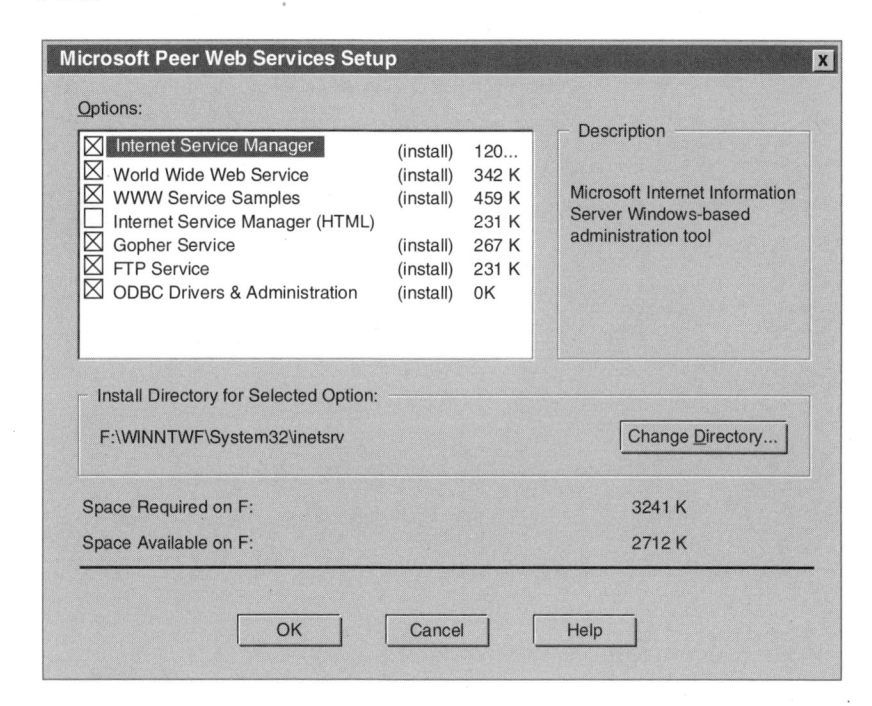

```
┌─ Microsoft Peer Web Services Setup ─────────────────────────────────┐ X
│                                                                     │
│  Options:                                                           │
│   ┌──────────────────────────────────────┐  ┌─ Description ──────┐ │
│   │ ☒ Internet Service Manager  (install) 120... │                  │ │
│   │ ☒ World Wide Web Service    (install) 342 K  │ Microsoft Internet Information │
│   │ ☒ WWW Service Samples       (install) 459 K  │ Server Windows-based │
│   │ ☐ Internet Service Manager (HTML)      231 K │ administration tool │
│   │ ☒ Gopher Service            (install) 267 K  │                  │ │
│   │ ☒ FTP Service               (install) 231 K  │                  │ │
│   │ ☒ ODBC Drivers & Administration (install) 0K │                  │ │
│   └──────────────────────────────────────┘  └────────────────────┘ │
│                                                                     │
│  ┌─ Install Directory for Selected Option: ──────────────────────┐ │
│  │  F:\WINNTWF\System32\inetsrv                  [ Change Directory... ] │
│  └───────────────────────────────────────────────────────────────┘ │
│                                                                     │
│   Space Required on F:                          3241 K             │
│   Space Available on F:                         2712 K             │
│                                                                     │
│           [   OK   ]   [ Cancel ]   [  Help  ]                     │
└─────────────────────────────────────────────────────────────────────┘
```

Changes can be made to a current installation of Peer Web Services through the Peer Web Services Setup icon located in the Microsoft Peer Web Services (Common) folder. Before adding or removing components, or reinstalling PWS, disable any previous versions of Gopher, FTP, or other Web services that may be installed on Windows NT Workstation.

The PWS default setup configurations are suitable for many publishing scenarios without any further modifications.

Configuring IIS and PWS

All of the Internet and intranet services can be configured and managed from one central point using a simple interface.

Use the Microsoft Internet Service Manager (ISM) to enhance IIS and PWS configuration and performance. ISM is located in the Microsoft Internet Server Tools (Common) folder on a computer running Windows NT Server, or in the Microsoft Peer Web Services Tools (Common) folder on a computer running Windows NT Workstation. ISM provides a mechanism to configure and monitor all of the Internet services running on any computer running Windows NT in the network.

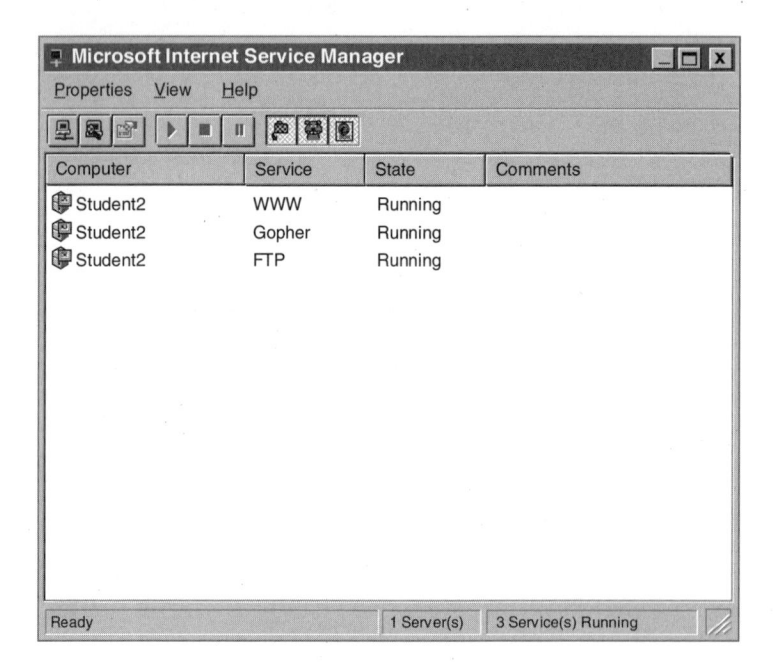

Computer	Service	State	Comments
Student2	WWW	Running	
Student2	Gopher	Running	
Student2	FTP	Running	

Ready — 1 Server(s) — 3 Service(s) Running

Internet Server Manager List Box

Using ISM, it is possible to manage multiple servers from one computer. ISM's default view is the Report view. Report view lists the computers on the network and the services installed on them. Report view also provides users with a mechanism to perform the following tasks:

- Connect to servers and view server properties.
- Start, stop, or pause a service.
- Select which services should be displayed.
- Configure properties of the services, if necessary.

Properties

In ISM, double-click a computer or service name to display its properties. The following illustration shows the WWW service properties displayed on the Service tab.

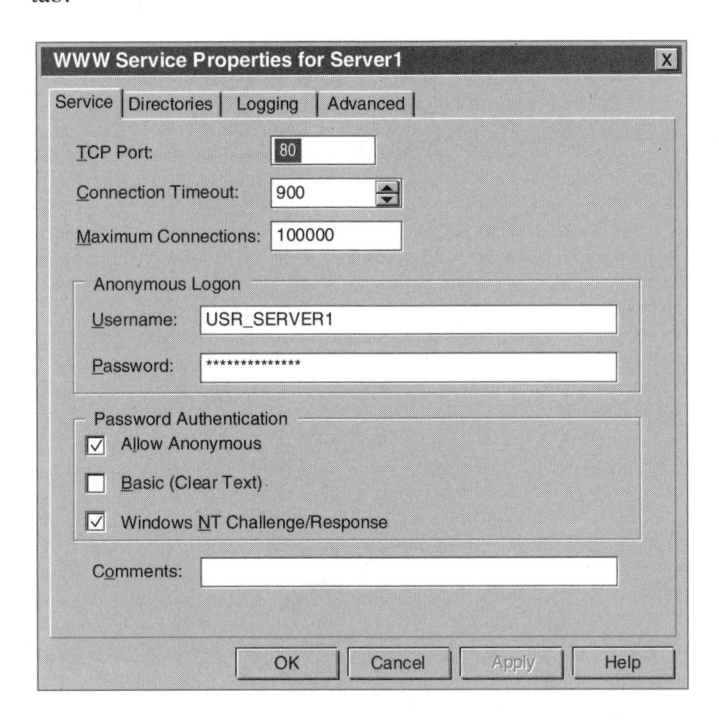

```
┌─ WWW Service Properties for Server1 ─────────────── X ┐
│  Service │ Directories │ Logging │ Advanced │         │
│                                                        │
│    TCP Port:              [ 80 ]                       │
│    Connection Timeout:    [ 900 ] ⬍                    │
│    Maximum Connections:   [ 100000 ]                   │
│                                                        │
│   ┌─ Anonymous Logon ─────────────────────────────┐    │
│   │  Username:   [ USR_SERVER1           ]        │    │
│   │  Password:   [ ************          ]        │    │
│   └───────────────────────────────────────────────┘    │
│                                                        │
│   ┌─ Password Authentication ─────────────────────┐    │
│   │  ☑ Allow Anonymous                            │    │
│   │  ☐ Basic (Clear Text)                         │    │
│   │  ☑ Windows NT Challenge/Response              │    │
│   └───────────────────────────────────────────────┘    │
│                                                        │
│    Comments:  [                              ]         │
│                                                        │
│         [ OK ]   [ Cancel ]   [ Apply ]   [ Help ]     │
└────────────────────────────────────────────────────────┘
```

The different services (WWW, Gopher, FTP) have different properties. The properties that can be configured through the **Properties** dialog box include those listed below:

- **Service** tab. Connections, user logon, and authentication requirements.
- **Directories** tab. Directories used by each service, default document, and directory browsing.
- **Logging** tab. Server activity tracking and log file directory.
- **Advanced** tab. Secured access by IP address and bandwidth. The advanced tab is available only on IIS and not on PWS.

Configuring Services

ISM can also be used to configure the following:

- *WWW Service.* Set a default document so clients who are browsing can always receive the default document if they do not specify a particular file.
- *FTP Service.* Enable FTP clients to view files on NTFS partitions in the same format as a traditional UNIX FTP server.

For more information on	See
IIS	Product documentation available in the Microsoft Internet Server (Common) folder
PWS	Product documentation available in the Microsoft Peer Web Services (Common) folder

Lesson 3: Microsoft Internet Explorer

This lesson introduces you to Microsoft Internet Explorer. It describes the roles and functions of Microsoft Internet Explorer and the processes of accessing, navigating, and browsing the Internet or an intranet.

After this lesson, you will be able to:
- Describe the purpose and use of the Microsoft Internet Explorer.
- Use Microsoft Internet Explorer to access resources on the Internet.

Estimated lesson time: 5 minutes

Microsoft Internet Explorer is a Web browser that is used to navigate and access, or browse, information on the Web. After connecting to the Internet, use Microsoft Internet Explorer to view information on the Internet. Microsoft Internet Explorer can also be used to incorporate Internet information into a document or save the information as a file.

The Microsoft Internet Explorer toolbar provides a range of detailed functions and commands for managing Microsoft Internet Explorer.

The following methods can be used to begin exploring the Internet:

- Click a hyperlink in the Microsoft Internet Explorer main window.
- Enter a URL address directly into the white space on the address bar.
- Enter a URL in the **Run** dialog box available on the **Start** menu.

Windows NT 4.0 includes Microsoft Internet Explorer. In addition, versions of this browser are also available for Windows for Workgroups, Windows 3.1, Macintosh, and Windows 95.

Lesson 4: Securing Internet and Intranet Sites

This lesson describes the issues involved with securing your Internet and intranet sites. It provides guidelines for establishing an account policy to secure your sites from unwanted access and misuse.

After this lesson, you will be able to:
- Understand the major issues of Internet and intranet security.
- Explain how to secure Internet and intranet sites.
- Establish guidelines for creating an account policy.
- Install and configure IIS.

Estimated lesson time: 40 minutes

IIS and PWS are built on the Windows NT security model. Windows NT security helps protect Internet and intranet sites by requiring an assigned user account in order to access the site. When configuring these services, you specify whether to allow anonymous access to your site through the Internet Guest Account or another account designated by you, or to require a Windows NT user name and password. You can enable both anonymous connections and client authentication for the WWW and FTP services.

In addition, it is possible to control access to all computer resources by controlling the permissions assigned for each user or group to NTFS files and folders.

Allow Anonymous Access with the Internet Guest Account

On many Internet servers, access is anonymous; that is, the client request does not contain a user name and password. When you allow anonymous connections to your WWW, Gopher, and FTP services, Windows NT uses the user name and password configured for the service to make the anonymous connections.

The Internet Guest account, IUSR_*computername*, is created during the IIS or PWS installation. By default, this account is used when allowing anonymous connections.

Note The Internet Guest account is added to the Guests group. Changes to the Guests group user rights and resource permissions also apply to the Internet Guest account. Review the user rights and resource permissions for the Guests group to ensure that they are appropriate for the Internet Guest account.

If remote access is available only to the Internet Guest account, remote users do not provide a user name and password, and have only the permissions assigned to the Internet Guest account. This prevents unauthorized users from gaining access to sensitive information with fraudulent or illegally-obtained passwords.

Require a User Name and Password

The WWW and FTP services can be configured to require a valid user name and password to access your site's Internet resources. When this option is configured, the client request must contain a user name and password.

There are two types of authentication available when requiring a user name and password: Basic and Windows NT Challenge/Response.

- Basic authentication does not encrypt transmissions between the client and server, so names and passwords are sent in clear text over the networks. Intruders sniffing your transmissions could discover valid user names and passwords.
- Windows NT Challenge/Response authentication, supported by Microsoft Internet Explorer version 2.0 or later, protects the password, thereby providing for secure logon over the network. In this method, the user account obtained from the client is the one that the user is logged on with at the client computer.

Note The FTP service only supports basic authentication, so your FTP site is more secure if you only allow anonymous connections.

Guidelines for Securing an Internet and Intranet Site

The following are guidelines for creating an account policy for securing an Internet or intranet site:

- Do not allow blank passwords.
- Require a minimum password length.
- Require users to change their passwords frequently.
- Require users to use different passwords each time they are changed.
- Lock out accounts after multiple failed logon attempts.
- Require an administrator to unlock all locked accounts.
- Require users with restricted hours to be automatically disconnected.

Note For more information about securing your network, see Chapter 5, "Securing Your Site Against Intruders," in the *IIS Installation and Administration Guide*, or in the *PWS Installation and Administration Guide*. If you have IIS or PWS installed on your computer, click the **Start** button, point to **Programs**, point to **Microsoft Internet Server (Common)** or **Microsoft Peer Web Services (Common)**, and then click **Product Documentation**.

492 Microsoft Windows NT Technical Support

Practice

In these procedures, you examine the Windows NT Server environment before installing Microsoft Internet Information Server. You then install IIS, and again examine the Windows NT Server environment to determine changes made by IIS. You publish a document on your Web server, and access that document from Workstation1. Finally, you configure DNS to resolve IP addresses for IIS.

▶ **To examine the Windows NT Server environment**

In this procedure, you examine the Windows NT Server environment before installing Microsoft Internet Information Server.

Note Complete this procedure on Server1.

1. Log on as Administrator.
2. Click the **Start** button, point to **Settings**, and then click **Control Panel**.
3. Double-click the Services icon.

   The **Services** dialog box appears.
4. Scroll through the list of services available.

   Are there any publishing services listed? (Hint: Does the word *publishing* appear in the service name?)

5. Close the **Services** dialog box and minimize Control Panel.
6. Click the **Start** button, point to **Programs**, point to **Administrative Tools (Common)**, and then click **User Manager for Domains**.
7. In User Manager for Domains, examine the list of names.

   Is there an Internet Guest account listed?

8. Close User Manager for Domains.
9. In **Administrative Tools (Common)**, click **Performance Monitor**.
10. On the **Edit** menu in Performance Monitor, click **Add to Chart**.

    The **Add to Chart** dialog box appears.

11. In the **Object** box, scroll through the available objects.

    Are there any Internet-related items in the list?

    _____

12. Click **Cancel** to close the **Add to Chart** dialog box.
13. Close Performance Monitor.

▶ **To install Internet Information Server**

In this procedure, you install Internet Information Server.

Note Complete this procedure on Server1.

1. Double-click the Shortcut to Network icon.
2. Click the **Services** tab, and then click **Add**.
3. Click **Microsoft Internet Information Server 2.0**, and then click **OK**.

    The installation program prompts you for the path of the installation files.
4. In the **Installed from** box, type **\\Server1\Nts_source\I386** and then click **OK**.

    The **Microsoft Internet Information Server Setup** dialog box appears.
5. Read the information in the **Microsoft Internet Information 2.0 Server Setup** dialog box, and then click **OK**.

    The following installation options appear.
    - Internet Service Manager
    - World Wide Web Service
    - WWW Service Samples
    - Internet Service Manager (HTML)
    - Gopher Service
    - FTP Service
    - ODBC Drivers and Administration
6. Click **Internet Service Manager (HTML)**. Verify that all options are selected, and then click **OK**.

7. Click **Yes** to create the C:\WINNT\System32\Inetsrv directory.

   The **Publishing Directories** dialog box appears listing the following default directories.

Directory	Path
World Wide Web Publishing Directory	C:\InetPub\wwwroot
FTP Publishing Directory	C:\InetPub\ftproot
Gopher Publishing Directory	C:\InetPub\gophroot

8. Click **OK** to accept the default directories.
9. When prompted to create the default directories, click **Yes**.

   Setup installs the Internet Information Server software.

   Note If a dialog box appears prompting you to create an Internet domain name, click **OK**.

10. When prompted to install the Open Database Connectivity (ODBC) drivers, click **SQL Server**, and then click **OK**.
11. When Setup is complete, click **OK**.
12. Click **Close**.

▶ **To identify changes IIS made to the Windows NT Server environment**

In this procedure, you inspect the Windows NT Server environment after installing Microsoft Internet Information Server. If you do not remember how to determine the answers to the following questions, refer to the corresponding questions in the "To examine the Windows NT Server environment" procedure earlier in this lesson.

Note Complete this procedure on Server1.

1. What publishing services are now installed on your computer?

2. What Internet-related user account is on your computer?

3. What Internet-related objects are on your computer that Performance Monitor can monitor?

Chapter 13 Internetworking and Intranetworking

▶ **To verify that your Microsoft Internet Information Server is working**

In this procedure, you verify that IIS is working.

Note Complete this procedure on Workstation1.

1. Log on as Administrator.
2. Double-click **Internet Explorer**.
3. In Microsoft Internet Explorer, on the **File** menu, click **Open**, type **Server1** and then click **OK**.

   Does your Web server start?

   _____

4. In the **Address** box, type **ftp://Server1** and then press ENTER.

   Can you connect through FTP to your server?

   _____

5. Close Microsoft Internet Explorer.

▶ **To publish from a new directory**

In this procedure, you publish a document using a new directory that you create.

Note Complete this procedure on Server1.

1. Right-click **My Computer**, and then click **Explore**.
2. In the root of drive C, create a new folder called **NewWWW**.
3. Copy C:\Lab Files\IIS\Default.htm to C:\NewWWW.
4. Close Windows NT Explorer.
5. Click the **Start** button, point to **Programs**, point to **Microsoft Internet Server**, and then click **Internet Service Manager**.
6. Click **Server1** on the line where **Service** is **WWW**.
7. On the **Properties** menu, click **Service Properties**.

8. In the **WWW Service Properties** dialog box, click the **Directories** tab.

   What directories and aliases are listed?

Directory	Alias

9. Click the **Add** button.

   The **Directory Properties** dialog box appears.

10. Click the **Browse** button.
11. Double-click **NewWWW** on drive C, and then click **OK**.

    The **Directory** box now contains **C:\NewWWW**.

12. Click **Virtual Directory**, and in the **Alias** box, type **Virtual**

    This will be the published name of the new directory.

13. Click **OK** to close the **Directory Properties** dialog box.

    What directory and alias were added?

14. Click **OK** to close the **WWW Service Properties** dialog box.
15. Exit Internet Service Manager.

▶ **To access the document**

In this procedure, you use Microsoft Internet Explorer to access the document you just published.

Note Complete this procedure on Workstation1.

1. On the desktop, double-click **Internet Explorer**.
2. On the **File** menu, click **Open**.
3. In the **Open** box, type **http://server1/virtual** and then click **OK**.

   Microsoft Internet Explorer displays the default page in the virtual share.
4. Close Microsoft Internet Explorer.

Chapter 13 Internetworking and Intranetworking

▶ **To set up DNS for the Internet Information Server**

In these procedures, you use DNS to resolve IP addresses for Internet Information Server.

Note Complete this procedure on Server1.

1. In **Administrative Tools (Common)**, click **DNS Manager**.
2. Double-click **Server1**.
3. Double-click **corp1.com**.
4. Right-click **corp1.com**.
5. On the menu that appears, click **New Record**.
6. Click **CNAME**, and in the **Alias Name** box, type **WWW1**
7. In the **For Host DNS Name** box, type **Server1.corp1.com** and then click **OK**.
8. Verify that a resource record of type A exists for your computer. If not, create a new host resource record for your computer.
9. Close DNS Manager.

▶ **To test DNS name resolution for the Internet Information Server**

Note Complete this procedure on Server1.

1. At a command prompt, type **ping www1** and then press ENTER.

   What is the name of the host, and what is the IP address?

2. Start Microsoft Internet Explorer.
3. On the **File** menu, click **Open**.
4. In the **Open** box, type **WWW1** and then click **OK**.

   Does your Web server start?

5. Close Microsoft Internet Explorer.

Summary

The following information summarizes the key points in this chapter:

- The *Internet* is a network of computers located around the world that are able to communicate with one another through telephone lines; an *intranet* exists at a local level, and consists of computers that are connected by means of LANs.

- The Internet and intranets communicate using common languages and protocols.

- The World Wide Web (WWW) is a graphical interface that overlays the Internet to create a virtual network, or Web, of information. In order to connect to Web servers and view the information, you must use a Web *browser* such as *Microsoft Internet Explorer*.

- Additional Internet and intranet components supported by Windows NT are the Internet Information Server (IIS) and Peer Web Services (PWS). IIS and PWS provide computers running Windows NT with the ability to publish resources and services on the Internet and on private intranets. Use IIS and PWS for publishing hypertext Web pages and client/server applications, and for interactive Web applications.

- There are security issues that you need to be aware of when you connect an intranet to the Internet. The Internet, like other networks, provides two-way communication. When you are connected to the Internet, other computers can see your computer. By default, Windows NT security protects your computer from casual intrusion. However, while it is very unlikely that your computer will be attacked while you are browsing the Internet, it is still a good idea to configure your computer securely.

Review

1. Your company has an intranet for disseminating project information. Some of the executives have been hearing about potential security issues on the Internet and are concerned that external hackers could break in to the corporate network through this intranet. What difference between intranets and the Internet should ease their worries?

2. Your software company has many customers located throughout the world and must ensure that software updates are available to all customers worldwide. Should you install IIS or PWS? Which publishing service(s) would you use?

3. Your manager is concerned about allowing access to the corporate intranet from the Internet, because some internal Web pages contain confidential information. What would you tell your manager?

Answer Key

Procedure Answers

Page 492

▶ **To examine the Windows NT Server environment**

4. Scroll through the list of services available.

    Are there any publishing services listed? (Hint: Does the word *publishing* appear in the service name?)

    No.

7. In User Manager for Domains, examine the list of names.

    Is there an Internet Guest Account listed?

    No.

11. In the **Object** box, scroll through the available objects.

    Are there any Internet-related items in the list?

    No.

Page 494

▶ **To identify changes IIS made to the Windows NT Server environment**

1. What publishing services are now installed on your computer?

    Gopher Publishing Service, FTP Publishing Service, and World Wide Web Publishing Service.

2. What Internet-related user account is on your computer?

    IUSR_SERVER1

3. What Internet-related objects are on your computer that Performance Monitor can monitor?

    Gopher Service, FTP Server, HTTP Service, and Internet Information Services Global.

Page 495

▶ **To verify that your Microsoft Internet Information Server is working**

3. In Microsoft Internet Explorer, on the **File** menu, click **Open**, type **Server1** and then click **OK**.

    Does your Web server start?

    Yes.

4. In the **Address** box, type **ftp://Server1** and then press ENTER.

    Can you connect through FTP to your server?

    Yes.

Chapter 13   Internetworking and Intranetworking   501

Page 495

▶ **To publish from a new directory**

8. In the **WWW Service Properties** dialog box, click the **Directories** tab.

   What directories and aliases are listed?

Directory	Alias
C:\InetPub\wwwroot	<Home>
C:InetPub\scripts	/Scripts
C:\WINNT\System32\inetsrv\iisadmin	/iisadmin

13. Click **OK** to close the **Directory Properties** dialog box.

    What directory and alias were added?

    C:\NewWWW with an alias of /Virtual

Page 497

▶ **To test DNS name resolution for the Internet Information Server**

1. At a command prompt, type **ping www1** and then press ENTER.

   What is the name of the host, and what is the IP address?

   Server1.corp1.com is the name of the host, and the IP address is 131.107.2.200.

4. In the **Open** box, type **WWW1** and then click **OK**.

   Does your Web server start?

   Yes.

Review Answers

Page 499

1. Your company has an intranet for disseminating project information. Some of the executives have been hearing about potential security issues on the Internet and are concerned that external hackers could break in to the corporate network through this intranet. What difference between intranets and the Internet should ease their worries?

   Intranets, by definition, are internal to an organization. Adding WWW, Gopher, and FTP services does not change the security of the site.

2. Your software company has many customers located throughout the world and must ensure that software updates are available to all customers worldwide. Should you install IIS or PWS? Which publishing service(s) would you use?

   Use IIS, because it is optimized for heavy Internet traffic, and use the WWW and FTP publishing services.

3. Your manager is concerned about allowing access to the corporate intranet from the Internet, because some internal Web pages contain confidential information. What would you tell your manager?

   Windows NT security is fully integrated with IIS and PWS. Both IIS and PWS can be configured to require a valid user account and an encrypted authentication in order to access the site. Specific resources can be protected by granting permissions to appropriate users and groups.

CHAPTER 14

Interoperating with Novell NetWare

Lesson 1 Windows NT Connectivity with NetWare . . . 504

Lesson 2 Installing and Configuring CSNW and GSNW . . . 514

Review . . . 527

About This Chapter

Microsoft Windows NT Server and Microsoft Windows NT Workstation provide several features and services that enable computers running Windows NT to coexist and interoperate with Novell NetWare servers. Some of these services are included in Windows NT, while others are available as separate products, commonly called add-ons.

This chapter describes these NetWare connectivity tools and explains how they can be used to integrate Windows NT and NetWare environments.

Before You Begin

To complete the lessons in this chapter, you must have:

- Two computers that meet the hardware and software requirements as specified in the Getting Started section of "About This Book."
- Completed all practices in Chapter 2, "Installing Windows NT."

Lesson 1: Windows NT Connectivity with NetWare

In order for computers running Windows NT to access and share resources with computers running Novell NetWare, you must install some additional software on your computers running Windows NT. The type of connectivity you require determines the software that you must install. The software included with Windows NT is Client Service for NetWare (CSNW), Gateway Services for NetWare (GSNW), and Migration Tool for NetWare. In addition, there is a set of add-on utilities comprised of *File and Print Services for NetWare* (FPNW) and *Directory Service Manager for NetWare* (DSMN). FPNW enables a computer running Windows NT Server to function as a NetWare 3.12-compatible file and print server. DSMN extends Windows NT Server directory service features to NetWare servers.

This lesson explains how computers running Windows NT share file, print, and application services with NetWare-based computers.

After this lesson, you will be able to:
- List the features and services that allow computers running Windows NT to interoperate with computers running Novell NetWare.
- Explain the purpose of NWLink.
- Explain the function of Client Service for NetWare (CSNW).
- Explain the function Gateway Services for NetWare (GSNW).
- Explain the function of File and Print Services for NetWare (FPNW).
- Explain how Novell NetWare networks can be remotely administered by computers running Windows NT.
- Explain the function of Directory Service Manager for NetWare (DSMN).
- Describe the Migration Tool for NetWare.

Estimated lesson time: 30 minutes

NWLink

NetWare uses Internetwork Packet Exchange/Sequenced Packet Exchange (IPX/SPX) as its primary network protocol. Microsoft developed *NWLink IPX/SPX Compatible Transport* (NWLink) to provide computers running Windows NT with the ability to communicate with NetWare servers and clients. NWLink is a native 32-bit Windows NT implementation of IPX/SPX and supports application servers in a NetWare environment. NWLink is included with both Windows NT Server and Windows NT Workstation.

NWLink allows computers running Windows NT to communicate with other computers running Windows NT as well as with NetWare servers. Two networking application programming interfaces (APIs) are supported to allow these communications:

- *Windows Sockets.* This interface supports existing NetWare applications written to comply with the NetWare IPX/SPX Sockets interface.
- *NetBIOS.* This interface supports sending and receiving Novell NetBIOS packets between a computer running Novell NetWare and Novell NetBIOS, and a computer running Windows NT and NWLink NetBIOS.

By itself, NWLink does not provide access to NetWare file and print resources. To enable a computer running Windows NT to access services on NetWare networks, and to provide NetWare clients with the ability to use services on Windows NT servers, Microsoft has developed several tools for NetWare interoperability.

Client Service for NetWare

Client Service for NetWare (CSNW), included with Windows NT Workstation, enables computers running Windows NT Workstation to make direct connections to file and printer resources at NetWare servers running NetWare 2.*x* or later. CSNW supports NetWare 4.*x* servers running either NetWare Directory Services (NDS) or bindery emulation. Login script support is also included.

The following illustration shows two computers running Windows NT Workstation with CSNW and NWLink installed accessing file and print resources on NetWare Server.

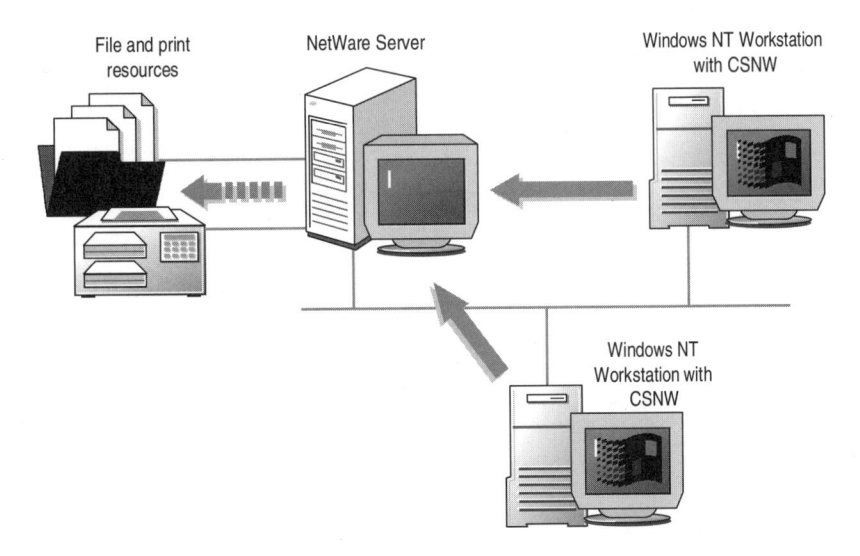

Computers running Windows NT that have CSNW and NWLink installed support the following:

- *NetWare Core Protocol* (NCP), which provides access to file and print services on a NetWare server. NCP provides similar functionality to the Microsoft *server message blocks* (SMBs) protocol, a file sharing protocol designed to allow systems to transparently access files that reside on remote systems.
- *Large Internet Protocol* (LIP), which determines and uses the largest allowable frame size when communicating with a server across a router.
- Long file names (LFNs), which can be used when the NetWare server is running OS/2 Name Space.

CSNW Support for NetWare Directory Services

Client Service for NetWare (CSNW) supports NetWare Directory Services (NDS). NDS organizes shared objects on participating NetWare Servers into a hierarchical tree. Thus, installing CSNW on Windows NT provides Windows NT clients with the ability to browse resources, use authentication, and use printing services on NDS hierarchies.

Note Although Windows NT Server and Windows NT Workstation versions 4.0 support connections to NetWare Directory Services (NDS), they do not support administration of NDS trees.

CSNW Support for Bindery Emulation

CSNW also supports the bindery-based version 3.x of Novell NetWare. User accounts and privileges are stored in the NetWare bindery, which is Novell's equivalent of the Windows NT directory database. Access to the network is validated based on user accounts and passwords in a Windows NT domain through the directory database, or on a Novell NetWare server through the bindery.

Gateway Services for NetWare

Gateway Services for NetWare (GSNW) enables computers running Windows NT Server and using NWLink as a transport protocol to access files and printers at NetWare servers. In addition, you can use GSNW to create gateways to NetWare resources. Creating a gateway enables computers running only Microsoft client software to access NetWare resources through the gateway. Any Microsoft network client, such as Windows NT Workstation, Microsoft Windows 95, or Microsoft Windows for Workgroups, that can access resources on the computer running Windows NT Server can access NetWare services through the Windows NT Server running GSNW.

In the following illustration, Windows clients, using SMBs, communicate with a NetWare Server, using NCPs, through a Windows NT server acting as a gateway.

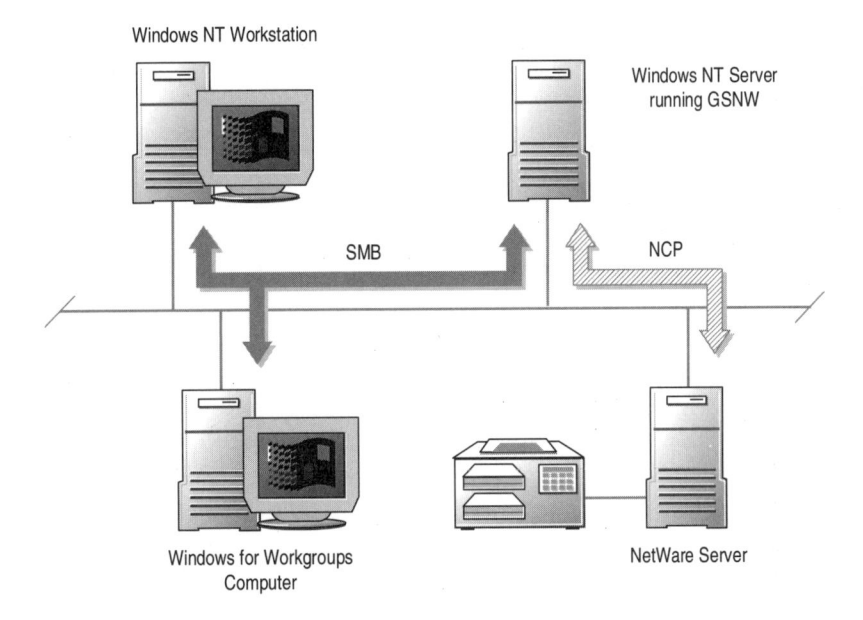

Using GSNW, a computer running Windows NT Server connects to a NetWare file server's directory and then shares it, just as if the directory were on the Windows NT server. Microsoft network clients can then access the directory on the NetWare server by connecting to the share created on the Windows NT server.

Note GSNW is available only on Windows NT Server. When GSNW is installed, CSNW is also installed automatically.

When to Use GSNW

GSNW is designed to provide Windows clients with occasional access to a NetWare network. GSNW is not designed to allow a computer running Windows NT Server to be a user-intensive, high-performance gateway.

GSNW can also serve as a migration path. For example, use GSNW to enable gradual migration from Novell NetWare to Windows NT.

Preparing to Install GSNW

For a computer running Windows NT Server to act as a gateway to resources on a NetWare server, the following steps must be taken on the Novell NetWare network:

1. A user account must be set up on the NetWare server, with the same name and password that the user will use to log on to the computer running Windows NT Server.
2. The user account set up on the NetWare server must have the necessary permissions assigned for the resources that are to be accessed.
3. A group account named NTGATEWAY must be created on the NetWare server.
4. The group NTGATEWAY on the NetWare server must include the user account that was set up in step 1.

Note Use one of the following NetWare utilities—System Console (Syscon), NWAdmin, or NetAdmin—to create the group and user accounts on the NetWare server.

Remote Client Access to NetWare Servers

RAS clients can use GSNW to access NetWare servers. Using GSNW, businesses can use Windows NT Server as a communications server and enable remote users to have reliable and secure remote access to a NetWare local area network (LAN).

Note Like Client Service for NetWare, GSNW supports NetWare Directory Services (NDS) as well as the bindery-based 3.*x* versions.

File and Print Services for NetWare

CSNW and GSNW provide computers running Windows NT with the ability to connect to NetWare servers for file, print, and application resources. To integrate NetWare clients into a Windows NT network and also allow them to access resources on computers running Windows NT Server, Microsoft provides File and Print Services for NetWare (FPNW).

The following illustration shows various connectivity methods between Windows NT networks and NetWare networks. The heavy black line shows the connectivity provided by installing FPNW on a Windows NT server.

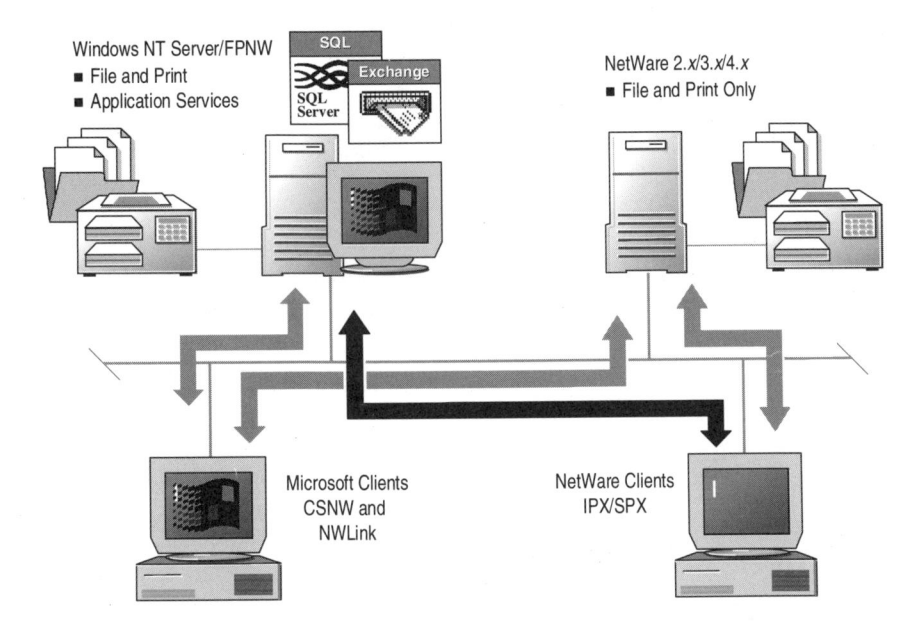

FPNW is not included with Windows NT. It is a Windows NT add-on utility that enables a computer running Windows NT Server to function as a NetWare 3.12-compatible file and print server. The server appears just like any other NetWare server to the NetWare clients, and the clients can access volumes, files, and printers at the server. No changes or additions to the NetWare client software are necessary, making integration with a Windows NT Server environment more cost-effective. You can add FPNW to an existing application server to maximize usage of hardware resources.

In summary, using FPNW, NetWare clients can transparently gain access to file, print, and application services on a Windows NT server. FPNW extends the interoperability of Windows NT Server and makes it easier for NetWare clients to make the transition to Windows NT Server.

Note For more information on FPNW, see the *Microsoft Services for NetWare Reviewer's Guide*.

Remote Administration of Novell Networks

Novell NetWare servers cannot be administered directly; instead, a NetWare client acts as the system console and controls the administration of the NetWare server.

A computer running Windows NT with GSNW or CSNW enabled can also act as a system console to administer the NetWare servers. Access to the NetWare administration utilities, Syscon, RConsole, and PConsole is accomplished on the Windows NT client as if the Windows NT client were a NetWare client.

- System Console (Syscon) is the primary administration tool and is used to set up user accounts, define policies, and grant user access permissions to the NetWare network.
- RConsole provides a remote view of the NetWare system console. The console functions can be performed on the remote console.
- PConsole provides the administrator with the tools necessary to manage print servers.

Multiple sessions of the administration tools can be run on a single Windows NT client. The information about each of the servers to which the client is connected is displayed in a separate window on the client. This ability to run multiple sessions of the administration tools on a single computer running Windows NT allows you to monitor all of the NetWare servers from one system console. This capability is not possible on computers running other operating systems such as Microsoft MS-DOS.

A major benefit of installing and configuring Windows NT Server services is the ability to administer *all* clients and servers on the network from a central point, regardless of the geographic location of the computer or which operating system is running.

Note For a NetWare client to access and administer a Windows NT server, FPNW must be installed on the computer running Windows NT Server. Once FPNW is installed and configured, a NetWare client can sign on to the computer running Windows NT Server and perform administration tasks.

Directory Service Manager for NetWare

Directory Service Manager for NetWare (DSMN) extends Windows NT Server directory service features to NetWare servers. With DSMN, you can centrally manage mixed Windows NT and NetWare 2.*x*, 3.*x*, and 4.*x* (in bindery emulation mode) environments with Windows NT Directory Services.

As can be seen in the following illustration, DSMN copies NetWare user and group account information, such as NWUSER1, NWUSER2, NWGRP1, and NWGRP2, to a primary domain controller (PDC) running Windows NT Server 4.0. DSMN also incrementally propagates any account changes, such as the user account NTUSER1 and group NTGRP1, which are created on the PDC back to NetWare servers.

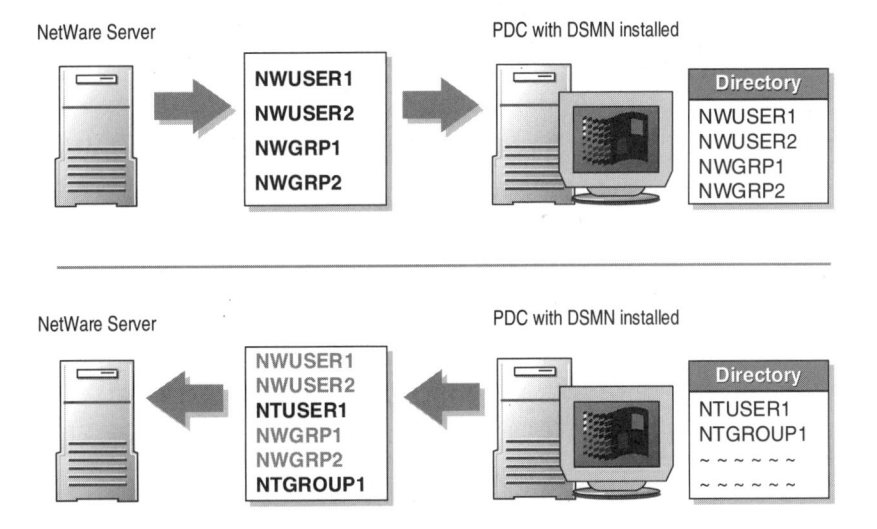

Sharing account information is accomplished without having to install additional software on NetWare servers.

DSMN is not included with Windows NT. It is a Windows NT add-on utility that allows a single network login for NetWare clients by synchronizing accounts across all NetWare servers. Clients need only remember one account name and password to gain access to file, print, and application resources on the network.

Use DSMN to accomplish the following tasks:

- Specify which NetWare user and group accounts to manage centrally from Windows NT Server. The specified accounts are copied to the domain's directory database on the PDC. These NetWare accounts become Windows NT Server accounts and must comply with the account policy of the Windows NT Server domain.

- Merge account names from multiple NetWare servers into one account name. If a client has accounts on two NetWare servers and these accounts have different user names, it is possible to merge the accounts' names when adding them to the domain. For example, DavidS and DavidSm could become DavidS.

- Specify which Windows NT Server domain accounts (user and group) to copy back to NetWare servers. This ensures that changes made to domain accounts are synchronized with the NetWare server.

Note For more information on DSMN, see the *Services for NetWare 4.0 Administrators Guide*.

Migration Tool for NetWare

The Windows NT Server Migration Tool for NetWare, included with Windows NT Server, enables you to easily transfer user and group accounts, volumes, folders, and files from a NetWare server to a computer running Windows NT Server. If the server you are migrating to runs FPNW, you can also migrate users' logon scripts.

The following illustration shows NetWare user and group accounts, folders, and files being transferred to a computer running Windows NT Server.

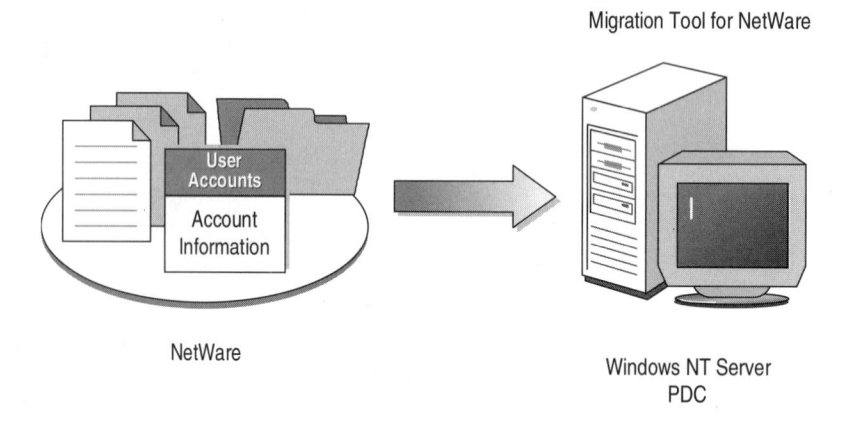

The Migration Tool for NetWare provides a computer running Windows NT with the capability to perform the following functions:

- Preserve appropriate user account information, including NetWare-specific information such as login and station restrictions.
- Preserve login scripts with the user account. Windows NT Server supports NetWare login script commands.
- Control how user and group names are transferred.
- Set passwords for transferred accounts.
- Control how account restrictions and administrative rights are transferred.
- Create a volume for NetWare users.
- Select the directories and files to transfer.
- Select a destination for transferred directories and files.
- Preserve effective rights on directories and files.

Note The executable file for launching the Migration Tool for NetWare is Nwconv.exe. For additional information on the Migration Tool for NetWare, see the *Networking Supplement* portion of Books Online or the Help file included with the source files. You can use the Expand.exe utility to decompress the **expand nwconv.hl_ expand.hlp** Help file.

Interoperability with Novell NetWare

Computers running Windows NT using NWLink can be integrated into Novell NetWare environments. Connections over NWLink can be made through a variety of communication mechanisms, such as Windows Sockets or NWLink NetBIOS.

The following illustration lists the interoperability options.

Platform	Running	Can Connect To
NetWare client	IPX with NetBIOS, Named Pipes, or Windows Sockets support	Windows NT–based computers, with NWLink, running IPX applications such as Microsoft SQL Server
Windows NT–based computer	NWLink	Client/server applications running on a NetWare server
Windows NT–based computer	NWLink and CSNW or NWLink and GSNW	Novell NetWare servers for file and print services
NetWare client	IPX	Windows NT Server, with NWLink and FPNW installed, for file and print services

Novell NetWare Integration

Recall that NWLink provides client/server application support for IPX-based applications, but by itself does not support access to file and print resources. If a Windows NT client requires connections to file and print resources on a NetWare server, CSNW must be installed on the Windows NT client.

If there are computers on the network that are not running NWLink or another IPX/SPX transport, you can create a gateway for these computers on a computer running Windows NT Server by installing and configuring GSNW.

If a Novell NetWare client requires file and print access to a computer running Windows NT, FPNW must be installed on that computer running Windows NT.

Lesson 2: Installing and Configuring CSNW and GSNW

Windows NT tools for NetWare enable file, print, and application sharing between Windows NT–based and NetWare-based computers. This lesson explains how to install and configure two of these tools, CSNW and GSNW.

After this lesson, you will be able to:
- Install and configure CSNW.
- Install and configure GSNW.
- Configure a GSNW gateway.

Estimated lesson time: 45 minutes

Installing and Configuring CSNW

CSNW is installed through the **Services** tab of the Network program in Control Panel.

Note Before installing CSNW, use the **Services** tab of the Network program in the Control Panel to remove any existing NetWare redirectors, such as *NetWare Services for Windows NT* from Novell, and then restart the computer.

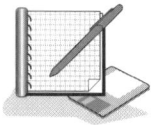

Practice

In this procedure, you install Client Service for NetWare.

Note Complete this procedure on Workstation1.

▶ **To install CSNW**

1. Double-click the Network icon in Control Panel.
2. Click the **Services** tab, and then click **Add**.

   The **Select Network Services** dialog box appears.
3. Click **Gateway (and Client) Services for NetWare**, and then click **OK**.
4. When prompted for the location of the CSNW installation files, type *cd-rom_drive_letter*:**\I386** and then click **Continue**.
5. Click **Close**.

   A series of **Bindings** dialog boxes appears while the binding's configuration, storing, and review occur.

6. Click **Yes** to restart the computer.
7. When Workstation1 restarts, log on to the domain as Administrator.
8. When the **Select NetWare Logon** dialog box appears, click **Cancel**.
9. When the **NetWare Network** dialog box appears indicating that you have not been authenticated by any server and asking if you would like to continue, click **Yes**.

Configuring CSNW

Configuration of CSNW is necessary for computers running Windows NT Workstation to be able to connect to a NetWare server. The CSNW installation creates a new icon, labeled CSNW, and adds it to Control Panel. You use this icon to configure CSNW.

To configure CSNW, double-click the CSNW icon in Control Panel. The **Client Service for NetWare** dialog box appears.

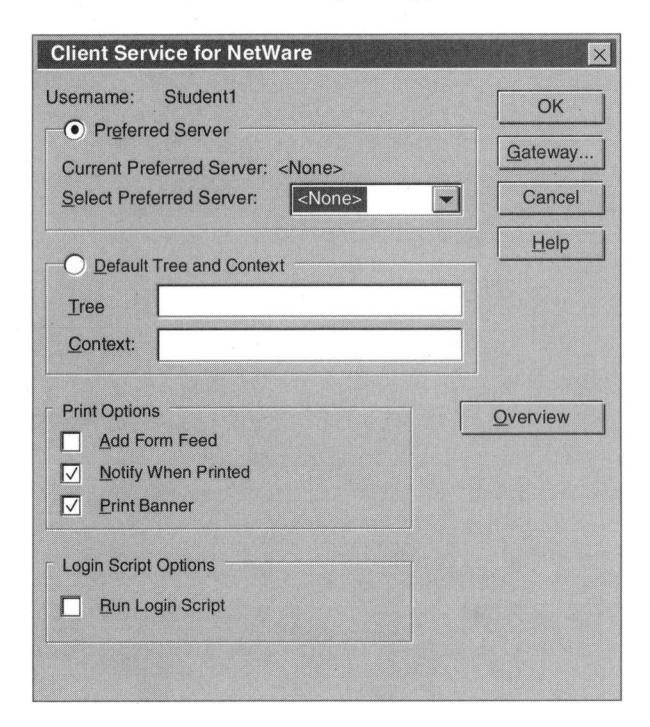

The **Client Service for NetWare** dialog box can be used to configure the options listed in the following table.

Option	Use this option to
Preferred Server	Choose a preferred server that the computer connects to by default during the login process. The preferred server is the one that is queried for information about resources available on the NetWare network. If you have not defined a default tree and context, the name of the NetWare server to which you connect by default when you log in appears in Current Preferred Server. If your network uses NDS, you should have a default tree and context instead of a preferred server.
Default Tree	Enter or change the default tree. In a NetWare Directory Services (NDS) environment, the default tree defines the NDS name of the user name that is used for login. All resources in the default tree can then be accessed without requiring further prompts. NDS is a global, distributed information database that maintains information about every resource on the network—including users, groups, printers, volumes, and other devices—in a hierarchical tree structure.
Default Context	Enter the default context, or position, of the user name used for login. The context can be in either a label or non-labeled format.
Print Options: Add Form Feed	Notify the printer to eject a page at the end of each document that is sent.
Print Options: Notify When Printed	Receive notification when documents have been printed.
Print Options: Print Banner	Notify the printer to print a banner page before each document that is printed.
Run Login Script	Run the user's login script whenever a user logs in to a NetWare server or NDS tree.

Next, you use the Novell NetWare simulation. The purpose of the simulation is to allow you to configure CSNW. The simulation presents two different CSNW configurations:

- *Bindery emulation.* Uses a preferred server. In the first configuration, you access a resource on a Novell NetWare server by specifying a preferred server.
- *NDS.* Uses a default tree and context. In the second configuration, you access a resource on a Novell NetWare server by specifying a default tree and context.

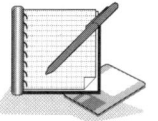

Practice

In these procedures, you use the Novell NetWare simulation to configure CSNW.

Note Complete this procedure on Workstation1.

▶ **To start the Novell NetWare simulation**

- Click the Start button, point to Programs, point to Technical Support Training, point to Simulations, and then click Novell NetWare Simulation.

    The simulation begins, simulating your desktop with Control Panel open.

▶ **To select a preferred server**

1. Double-click the CSNW icon in Control Panel.

    The **Client Service for NetWare** dialog box appears.

2. Click **Preferred Server**.
3. In the **Select Preferred Server** box, select **CANW312DPT01**.
4. Click **OK**.

    A message box appears, indicating your changes will take effect the next time you log in.

5. Click **OK**.

    A **Windows NT NetWare Simulation** dialog box appears stating that the simulation will proceed as if a shutdown occurs and you have logged on as Administrator.

6. Click **OK**.

    A dialog box appears prompting you to wait while the system writes unsaved data to the disk.

    The simulation continues with Control Panel open.

▶ **To use the Syscon resource on a NetWare server running bindery emulation**

1. Right-click My Computer, and then click **Map Network Drive**.
2. Double-click the CANW312DPT01 server.
3. Click the SYS folder, and then click **OK**.

   You are connected to the CANW312DPT01 NetWare server, with the SYS folder mapped to drive E. A window displaying the contents of the SYS folder is open on your desktop.

4. Double-click the Public folder.
5. Double-click **Syscon**.

   You are now running a utility that resides on the NetWare server. For this simulation, the menu options of Syscon have been disabled.

6. To exit Syscon, press ESC, use the arrow keys to select **Yes**, and then press ENTER.
7. Right-click My Computer, and then click **Disconnect Network Drive**.
8. Click **CANW312DPT01\SYS**, and then click **OK**.

▶ **To select a default tree and context**

1. Double-click the CSNW icon in Control Panel.

   The **Client Service for NetWare** dialog box appears.

2. Click **Default Tree and Context**.
3. In the **Tree** box, type **terra_flora**
4. In the **Context** box, type **terra_flora**
5. Click **OK**.

   A message box appears, indicating your changes will take effect the next time you log in.

6. Click **OK**.

   A **Windows NT NetWare Simulation** dialog box appears stating that the simulation will proceed as if a shutdown occurs and you have logged on as Administrator.

7. Click **OK**.

   A dialog box appears prompting you to wait while the system writes unsaved data to the disk.

   The simulation continues with Control Panel open.

▶ **To connect to a NetWare server running NDS**

1. Right-click My Computer, and then click **Map Network Drive**.
2. Double-click the Terra_flora tree.
3. Double-click the Terra_flora organization folder.
4. Click the CANW410DIV01_SYS folder, and then click **OK**.

   A window appears showing the connection to CANW410DIV01_SYS.terra_flora on the Terra_flora tree.

5. Double-click the Public folder.
6. Double-click **Pconsole**.

   You are now running a utility that resides on the NetWare server. In this simulation, the menu options of Pconsole have been disabled.

7. To exit Pconsole, press ESC, use the arrow keys to select **Yes**, and then press ENTER.
8. Right-click My Computer, and then click **Disconnect Network Drive**.
9. Click **TERRA_FLORA\CANW410DIV01_SYS.TERRA_FLORA**, and then click **OK**.

   A **Windows NetWare Simulation** dialog box appears.

10. Click **Exit** to end the Novell NetWare simulation.

Installing and Configuring GSNW

Like CSNW, GSNW is installed through the **Services** tab of the Network program in Control Panel.

Note Before installing GSNW, use the **Services** tab of the Network program in Control Panel to remove any existing NetWare redirectors, such as *NetWare Services for Windows NT* from Novell, and then restart the computer.

Practice

In this procedure, you install Gateway Services for NetWare.

Note Complete this procedure on Server1.

▶ **To install GSNW**

1. Double-click the Network icon in Control Panel.
2. Click the **Services** tab, and then click **Add**.

    The **Select Network Services** dialog box appears.
3. Click **Gateway (and Client) Services for NetWare**, and then click **OK**.
4. When prompted for the location to copy the necessary files, type **\\Server1\nts_source\I386** and then click **Continue**.

    A series of **Windows NT Setup** dialog boxes appear as files are installed on your system. When the installation is complete, the **Network** dialog box appears.
5. Click **Close**.
6. If you have multiple network adapters, you may be prompted to change the default internal network number (if it is 0) to a unique number, and asked if you would like to change that now. Click **No**.

    When the bindings review has completed, a **Network Settings Change** dialog box appears, prompting you to shut down and restart.
7. Click **Yes**.
8. When the computer restarts, log on as Administrator.

    When you log on, a **Select NetWare Logon** dialog box appears, and you are asked to specify a preferred server.
9. Click **Cancel**, and then click **Yes**.

    The GSNW installation creates a new icon, labeled GSNW, and adds it to Control Panel.

Configuring GSNW

Configuration of GSNW is necessary for computers running Windows NT Workstation to be able to connect to a NetWare server.

To configure GSNW, double-click the GSNW program in Control Panel.

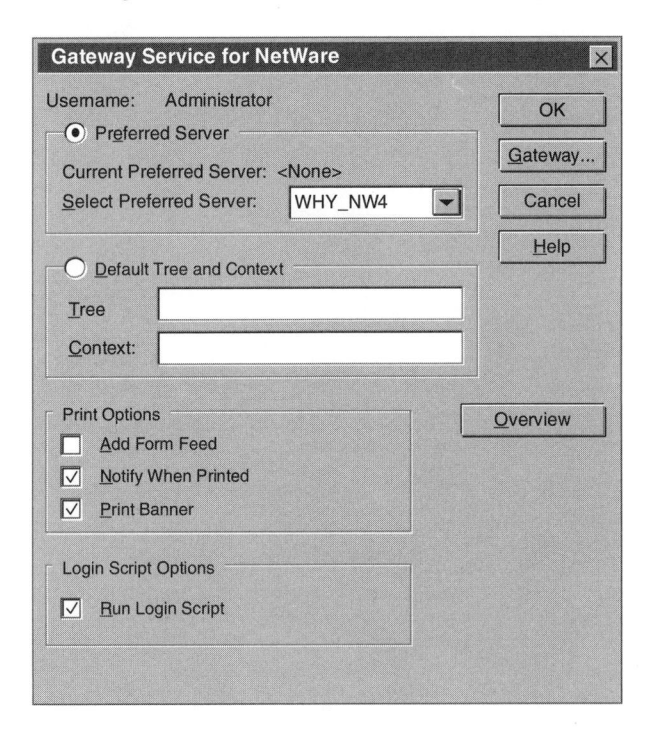

The **Gateway Service for NetWare** dialog box can be used to configure the options listed in the following table.

Option	Use this option to
Preferred Server	Choose a preferred server that the computer connects to by default during the login process. The preferred server is queried for information about resources available on the NetWare network.
Default Tree	Enter or change the default tree. In a NetWare Directory Services (NDS) environment, the default tree defines the NDS name of the user name that is used for login. All resources in the default tree can then be accessed without requiring further prompts.
Default Context	Enter the default context, or position, of the user name used for login. The context can be in either a label or non-labeled format.
Print Options: Add Form Feed	Notify the printer to eject a page at the end of each document that is sent.
Print Options: Notify When Printed	Receive notification when documents have been printed.
Print Options: Print Banner	Notify the printer to print a banner page before each document that is printed.
Run Login Script	Run login scripts.
Gateway	Display the **Configure Gateway** dialog box.
Overview	Display Help topics about Gateway Services for NetWare.

A Windows NT server needs to connect through a gateway to a NetWare server to enable Windows NT clients to transparently gain access to NetWare server file and print resources.

Specifying a Gateway

When you configure GSNW you need to specify a gateway and a gateway account that has supervisory privileges on the NetWare server. To specify a gateway and a gateway account, in the **Gateway Service for NetWare** dialog box, click **Gateway**. The **Configure Gateway** dialog box appears.

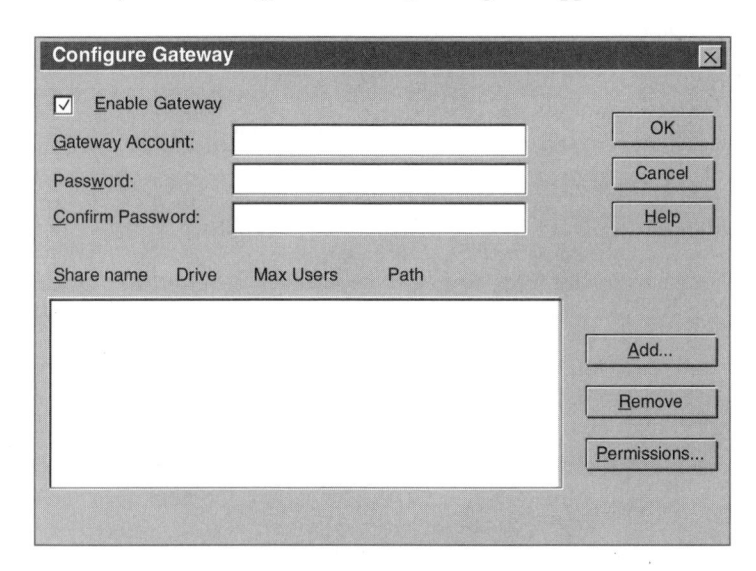

The **Configure Gateway** dialog box is used to enable the gateway to share NetWare file and print resources, to share NetWare volumes and directories, and to set permissions for the gateway. The options listed in the following table can be configured through this dialog box.

Option	Use this option to
Enable Gateway	Enable gateways on this server.
Gateway Account	Enter the user name for a gateway account. This account must exist and be a member of the NTGATEWAY group on all NetWare servers to which this server will have gateways.
Password	Enter the password for the gateway account.
Confirm Password	Retype the password for the gateway account.

(*continued*)

Option	Use this option to
Share name	List the existing gateways to NetWare resources created on this server.
Add	Create gateways to additional NetWare volumes or directories.
Remove	Disconnect clients and stop sharing selected NetWare file resources. You should warn clients before disconnecting them or stopping the sharing of a particular resource.
Permissions	Set permissions to control user access to a gateway.

Note The default permission for a gateway is **Full Control for Everyone**.

Once you have selected Enable Gateway and specified a gateway account and password, click **Add**. The **New Share** dialog box appears.

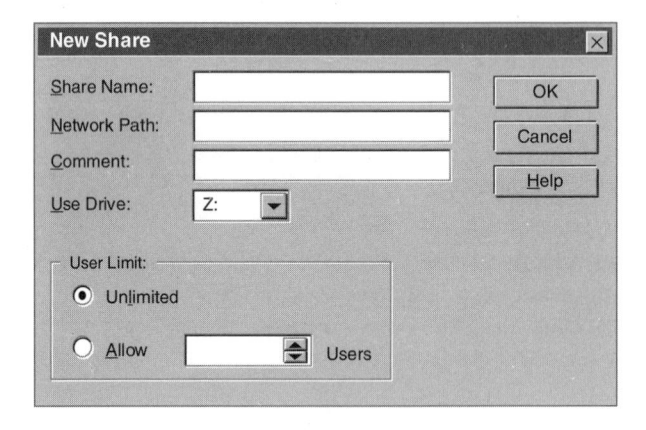

The options listed in the following table can be configured through the **New Share** dialog box.

Option	Use this option to
Share Name	Type the share name that the Microsoft client users will use to connect to the shared directory. In order for MS-DOS-based workstations to connect, the share name cannot exceed eight characters. Otherwise the share name can be as many as 12 characters.
Network Path	Type the path to a NetWare volume, including the name of the NetWare server and volume.

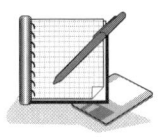

Practice

In this procedure, you view the options you can configure for GSNW. These options include selecting a preferred server, synchronizing your password with the Supervisor password on a Novell NetWare server, and sharing files on a Novell NetWare server.

Note Complete this exercise on Server1.

▶ **To configure GSNW**

1. Double-click the GSNW icon in Control Panel.

   The **Gateway Services for NetWare** dialog box appears.

2. In the **Gateway Services for NetWare** dialog box, click **Gateway**.

   The **Configure Gateway** dialog box appears.

3. Click **Enable Gateway**.
4. In the **Gateway Account** box, type **Administrator**
5. In the **Password** and **Confirm Password** boxes, type **password**
6. Click **Add**.

   The **New Share** dialog box appears.

7. In the **Share Name** text box, type **sysvol**
8. In the **Network Path** text box, type **\\netware1\sys**
9. In the **Use Drive** box, click **Z:**

   Note If you have a NetWare server on your network, you could use it to test this procedure.

10. Click **Cancel** to close the **New Share** dialog box.
11. Click **Cancel** to close the **Configure Gateway** dialog box.
12. Click **Cancel** to close the **Gateway Service for NetWare** dialog box.

    Note If you had entered a new share and clicked **OK** instead of **Cancel**, a dialog box would have appeared, stating that the changes will take effect the next time that you log on.

Summary

The following information summarizes the key points in this chapter:

- Microsoft provides several features and services that enable computers running Windows NT to interoperate with Novell networks and servers so that both computers running Windows NT and Novell-based computers can share resources. Some of these services are included in Windows NT, while others are available as separate products, commonly called add-ons.

- *NWLink protocol.* Microsoft developed NWLink to provide computers running Windows NT with the ability to communicate with NetWare servers and clients. NWLink is included with both Windows NT Server and Windows NT Workstation.

- *Client Service for NetWare* (CSNW). CSNW enables computers running Windows NT Workstation to make direct connections to file and printer resources at NetWare servers. Furthermore, CSNW supports NetWare Directory Services (NDS) which provides Windows NT clients with the ability to browse resources, use authentication, and use printing services on NDS hierarchies.

- *Gateway Services for NetWare* (GSNW). GSNW enables computers running Windows NT Server and NWLink to both directly access files and printers at NetWare servers, and create gateways to NetWare resources for Windows clients.

- *File and Print Services for NetWare* (FPNW). FPNW enables NetWare clients to access file, print, and application resources on computers running Windows NT Server. FPNW extends the interoperability of Windows NT Server and makes it easier for NetWare clients to make the transition to Windows NT Server.

- A computer running Windows NT with GSNW or CSNW enabled can also act as a system console to administer the NetWare servers. Multiple sessions of the NetWare administration tools can be run on a single Windows NT client. This ability to run multiple sessions of the administration tools on a single computer running Windows NT allows you to monitor all of the NetWare servers from one system console.

- *Directory Service Manager for NetWare* (DSMN). DSMN extends Windows NT Server directory service features to NetWare servers. DSMN copies NetWare user and group account information to Windows NT servers and then incrementally propagates any account changes back to NetWare servers.

- *Migration Tool for NetWare.* The Migration Tool for NetWare, included with Windows NT Server, enables the transfer of user and group accounts, volumes, folders, and files from a NetWare server to a computer running Windows NT Server.

Review

1. Your company is deploying Windows NT Workstation on its desktop computers. These computers need to access NetWare servers on the network. What components should be installed on the computers running Windows NT Workstation in order for them to gain access to the NetWare servers?

2. You have established a gateway on a computer running Windows NT Server to a NetWare volume. You have assigned full control permissions to your Domain Users group, and yet your users are complaining that they cannot save files to a directory through the gateway. What is the likely cause of the problem?

3. You want to integrate several NetWare clients into your Windows NT network. These clients need to be able to access printers located on Prntsrv, a computer running Windows NT Server. What software must be installed on the NetWare clients and what software must be installed on Prntsrv?

Answer Key

Page 527

Review Answers

1. Your company is deploying Windows NT Workstation on its desktop computers. These computers need to access NetWare servers on the network. What components should be installed on the computers running Windows NT Workstation in order for them to gain access to the NetWare servers?

   NWLink and CSNW.

2. You have established a gateway on a computer running Windows NT Server to a NetWare volume. You have assigned full control permissions to your Domain Users group, and yet your users are complaining that they cannot save files to a directory through the gateway. What is the likely cause of the problem?

   The NTGATEWAY group on the NetWare server has not been assigned the appropriate level of rights on the NetWare server. The gateway cannot grant greater permissions than the NetWare rights allow.

3. You want to integrate several NetWare clients into your Windows NT network. These clients need to be able to access printers located on Prntsrv, a computer running Windows NT Server. What software must be installed on the NetWare clients and what software must be installed on Prntsrv?

   No additional software needs to be installed on the NetWare clients; Prntsrv must be running NWLink and must have FPNW installed on it.

CHAPTER 15

Implementing Network Clients

Lesson 1   Windows NT Server 4.0 Licensing . . . 531

Lesson 2   Clients Included with Windows NT Server . . . 547

Lesson 3   Network Client Administrator . . . 551

Lesson 4   Client-based Network Administration Tools . . . 558

Lesson 5   Services for Macintosh . . . 562

Review . . . 567

About This Chapter

In order to connect to a computer running Microsoft Windows NT Server, the appropriate client software must be installed and configured on the client computer. In addition, the appropriate licensing for the servers and client computers must be obtained to ensure that network access complies with the Microsoft licensing legal requirements.

In Chapter 2, "Installing Windows NT," you learned that during installation of Windows NT Server you must select either the Per Server or Per Seat licensing mode. However, within a single organization you can choose the Per Server mode on some servers and the Per Seat mode on others. In this chapter, you learn about the Licensing program in Control Panel and License Manager in Administrative Tools (Common) to manage the client access licenses on your network. You learn which client operating systems can access a computer running Windows NT Server. You also learn how to install and configure client software, as well as Services for Macintosh.

Before You Begin

To complete the lessons in this chapter, you must have:

- Two computers that meet the hardware and software requirements as specified in the Getting Started section of "About This Book."
- Completed all practices in Chapter 2, "Installing Windows NT."

Lesson 1: Windows NT Server 4.0 Licensing

With the Microsoft BackOffice licensing model, Windows NT Servers and client computers are licensed separately. You purchase only the licenses required to accommodate your company's networking environment. A server license is required for each server and a Client Access License (CAL) is required for each client computer that accesses a server. Microsoft offers two licensing modes: Per Server licensing and Per Seat licensing. In this lesson, you learn how to determine which is the best licensing solution for a given network environment.

After this lesson, you will be able to:
- Describe a Client Access License.
- Describe Per Server and Per Seat licensing.
- Determine the preferred licensing configuration for a given network environment.
- Explain how to use the Licensing program in Control Panel to specify the licensing mode for a computer running Windows NT Server.
- Explain how to use the Licensing program in Control Panel to configure the license replication load.
- Explain how to use License Manager to manage Client Access Licenses across an organization.

Estimated lesson time: 50 minutes

What Is a Client Access License?

A *Client Access License* (CAL) provides the legal right for a computer to access a computer running Windows NT Server. Client Access Licenses are separate from the desktop operating system software you use to connect to Microsoft server products. Purchasing Microsoft Windows 95, Windows NT Workstation, or any other desktop operating system (such as an Apple Macintosh or any other non-Microsoft operating system) that connects to Microsoft server products does not constitute a legal license to connect to those Microsoft server products.

Example of Client Connections

Licensing is based upon the number of client connections to computers running Windows NT Server.

The following example illustrates how connections are defined for licensing purposes. A company has a computer running Windows NT Server named Products. It contains two shared folders, one named Word and the other named Excel.

- If User1 connects to the Word shared folder and the Excel shared folder from a *single* client computer, this is considered *one* connection to the server for licensing purposes.
- If User1 connects to the Word shared folder on Products from Workstation1 and concurrently logs on to Workstation2, as User1, and connects to the Excel shared folder on Products, that is considered *two* connections.
- Even if a user connects to the Word shared folder on Products from Workstation1 and concurrently logs on to Workstation2, as User1, and connects to the Word shared folder on Products, that is still considered *two* connections.

One Connection

User1 at Workstation1 → Products Server (Word, Excel)

Two Connections

User1 at Workstation1 → Products Server (Word, Excel) ← User1 at Workstation2

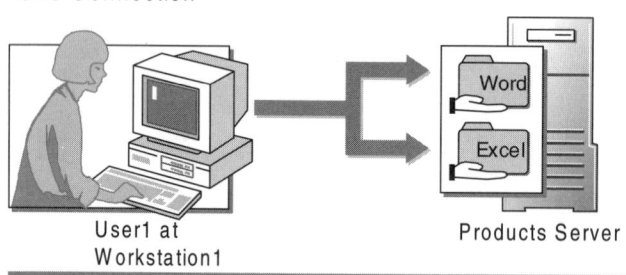

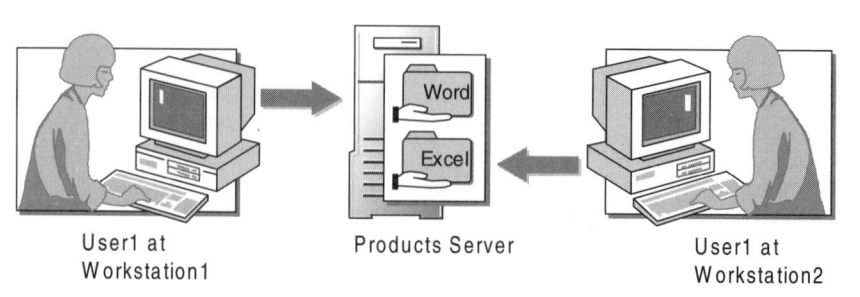

The Licensing Modes

Remember that Windows NT Server provides two licensing modes:

- *Per Server Licensing.* In Per Server licensing, *CALs are assigned to the server.* The number of CALs determines the number of simultaneous connections that can be made to *that* server.

    When you choose the Per Server licensing mode, you must enter the number of CALs purchased for that server. There must be at *least* as many CALs purchased for that server as the maximum number of client computers that connect simultaneously to that server. For example, if the maximum number of clients that will simultaneously connect to the server is 20, then you must have 20 CALs.

    The Per Server licensing mode can be the more economical choice when client computers:

    - Ordinarily connect to only one occasional-use or special-purpose server.
    - Do not all need to connect to the server at the same time.

    Important Under Per Server licensing, if the limit of concurrent connections to the server has been reached, and an additional client tries to connect to the server, Windows NT Server displays an error message on the client computer. This error is logged in the system log. No additional computers can connect to the server until an existing connection is closed or the server is configured for additional Client Access Licenses.

- *Per Seat Licensing.* In Per Seat licensing, *a CAL is purchased for each client computer.* With a Per Seat license, a client can access network resources such as file, print, and communications on *any* computer running Windows NT Server in the network, and can log on to multiple servers simultaneously.

    Thus, a user can legally connect to any server in the network from any client computer for which a CAL has been purchased. If the Per Seat licensing option is chosen, it will not prevent clients from connecting to a server if the number of simultaneous client connections exceeds the number of Per Seat licenses that have been purchased.

Licensing Considerations

The following examples will assist you in deciding whether to select either the Per Server or Per Seat licensing, or a combination of the two for the servers on your network.

If you have 200 clients that need simultaneous access to your server, then you must buy 200 CALs. If you select Per Server licensing, the 200 CALs would be placed on the server. If you purchase a second computer to run Windows NT Server, and continue to use Per Server licensing, you would need to purchase an additional 200 CALs for the second server in order for the clients to access resources on the second server. Thus, you would need a total of 400 CALs.

However, if you switched the first server to Per Seat mode, and you selected Per Seat mode during the Windows NT Server installation on the second server, you could assign the 200 CALs to the 200 clients. The clients would be able to access resources on either of the servers, or both of the servers simultaneously. You would only have to purchase a total of 200 CALs.

If all 200 clients occasionally need access to the two servers, but not all of the clients need access at the same time, you might find it more economical to use Per Server mode licensing. You could buy 100 CALs, with 50 CALs on each server. All 200 clients would have access to both servers, but a maximum of 50 clients at a time could be connected to each of the servers.

Topic Review

Your company is a small, newly created business that has one file and print server and 30 client computers. You configured the server using the Per Server licensing mode and obtained 30 Client Access Licenses, so that all 30 clients could access the server.

1. Your business is growing, so you purchase five new client computers and add them to the network. If 30 clients are currently connected to the server, will another client be able to connect to the server? Why or why not?

2. You decide to add a mail server that *all* clients will connect to. What would be the most economical licensing mode solution for the company?

Choosing Per Server vs. Per Seat Licensing

Use the following guidelines for selecting a licensing mode:

- If your network contains only one server, select the Per Server option and specify the maximum number of simultaneous connections that can be made to the server. The maximum number of simultaneous connections is the number of CALs you have purchased for that server. Any client computer in the network can log on to the server, as long as there are connections available. If you select the Per Seat mode, only those computers for which CALs were purchased would be able to connect to the server.

  If your needs change so that the Per Seat option is more economical, as is often the case when you purchase additional servers for your network, Windows NT Server allows you to perform a *one-time conversion* from a Per Server to a Per Seat configuration. If you chose Per Seat licensing at installation, and you later decide that you prefer the Per Server mode, you would need to reinstall Windows NT Server in order to use Per Server mode.

- If you have multiple servers and the total number of CALs across all servers to support the Per Server mode is equal to or greater than the number of computers or workstations, select or convert to the Per Seat option.

Use the following table to help you determine which licensing mode to use in your networking environment.

Licensing mode and computers	Result
Per Server option:	
Number of simultaneous connections needed to server1	
Number of simultaneous connections needed to server2	
Number of simultaneous connections needed to server*N*	
Total of simultaneous connections needed for all servers: A = server1 + server2 + ... + server*N*	A
Per Seat option:	
Number of seats (computers) that access *any* server is the number of CALs needed for Per Seat licensing	B

The following notes explain how to use the table:

- If A is less than B, then use Per Server licensing.
- If B is less than A, then use Per Seat licensing.

Note When you purchase Windows NT Server, a *server license* is included with the purchase. This server license entitles you to install Windows NT Server on one and only one computer. A server license should not be confused with Per Server licensing for CALs.

Topic Review

1. A company has one computer running Windows NT Server. There are 300 computers running Windows NT Workstation in the company, but only 250 of these will access the server simultaneously.

   What licensing mode would be the best solution for this company?

Licensing mode and computers	Result
Per Server option:	
Number of simultaneous connections needed to server1	
Number of simultaneous connections needed to server2	
Number of simultaneous connections needed to server*N*	
Total of simultaneous connections needed for all servers: A = server1 + server2 + ... + server*N*	A
Per Seat option:	
Number of seats (computers) that access *any* server is the number of CALs needed for Per Seat licensing	B

2. This company now adds an additional computer running Windows NT Server. Up to 200 of the workstations will also access the new server simultaneously.

   What licensing mode would now be the best solution for this company?

Licensing mode and computers	Result
Per Server option:	
Number of simultaneous connections needed to server1	
Number of simultaneous connections needed to server2	
Number of simultaneous connections needed to server*N*	
Total of simultaneous connections needed for all servers: A = server1 + server2 + ... + server*N*	A
Per Seat option:	
Number of seats (computers) that access *any* server is the number of CALs needed for Per Seat licensing	B

Licensing Administration

Tracking licenses manually on local computers within a small domain or across an entire organization with multiple domains can be time-consuming and expensive.

Windows NT Server 4.0 includes two administrative tools that help to reduce these costs and the administrative overhead of license tracking:

- Licensing program in Control Panel
- License Manager program on the Administrative Tools (Common) menu

These tools enable you to automatically replicate licensing data from all of the primary domain controllers (PDCs) in the organization to a centralized database on a specified master server, making it easier for you to comply with legal requirements.

The Licensing Program

The Licensing program is one of the tools that you can use to track licensing data and replicate the licensing data to a centralized database.

Start the Licensing program in Control Panel to access the **Choose Licensing Mode** dialog box shown in the following illustration.

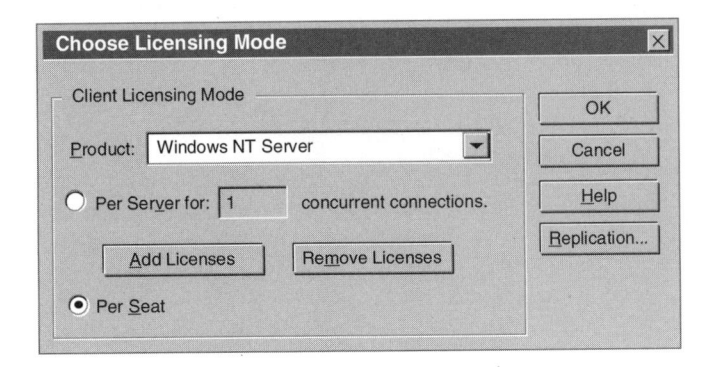

The **Choose Licensing Mode** dialog box allows you to view which licensing mode has been selected for each BackOffice product. The following table describes the tasks that you can perform using the Licensing program in Control Panel.

Option	Use this option to
Product	Specify the server product that requires CALs.
Per Server for x concurrent connections	View the number of concurrent client connections that are configured for a server if Per Server licensing mode has been selected.
Add licenses (Per Server licensing)	Add CALs to increase the number of concurrent client connections.
Remove licenses (Per Server licensing)	Remove CALs to decrease the number of concurrent client connections.
Replication	Display the **Replication Configuration** dialog box, which is used to specify how a computer replicates licensing information to a master server or enterprise server.
Per Seat	View whether the Per Seat licensing mode has been selected.

Note If the server uses the Per Seat licensing mode, use License Manager in the Administrative Tools (Common) group to enter CALs and configure Per Seat licensing options. You would also use License Manager if you want to perform the one-time conversion from a Per Server to a Per Seat configuration. License Manager is covered later in this chapter.

License Replication

You configure license replication on a server so that the server's licensing information is routed to a centralized database on a designated *master server* at specified intervals. The master server may be either the primary domain controller (PDC) for a single domain, or a specified *enterprise server* to which all of the PDCs in the organization replicate their licensing information.

The following illustration shows a PDC acting as a *master server* for license replication in a single domain. There are five stand-alone servers replicating licensing information to the PDC.

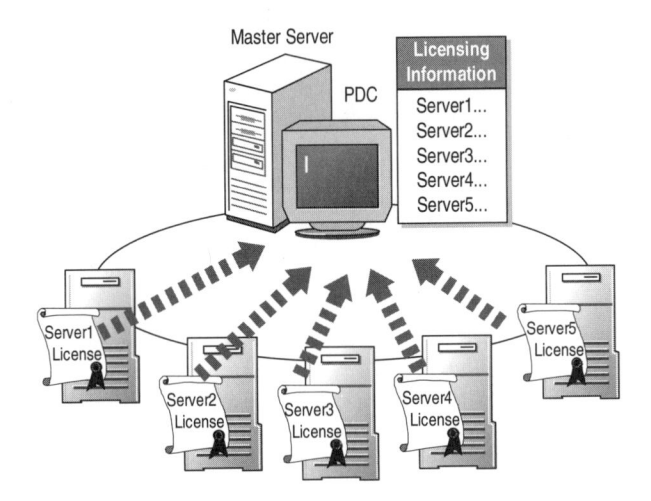

The following illustration shows an enterprise server acting as a *master server* for three domains. Each PDC acts as a master server for its domain. Then each of the three PDCs replicates the licensing information for its domain to the *master server* for the entire enterprise, where the servers' licensing information is stored in a centralized database.

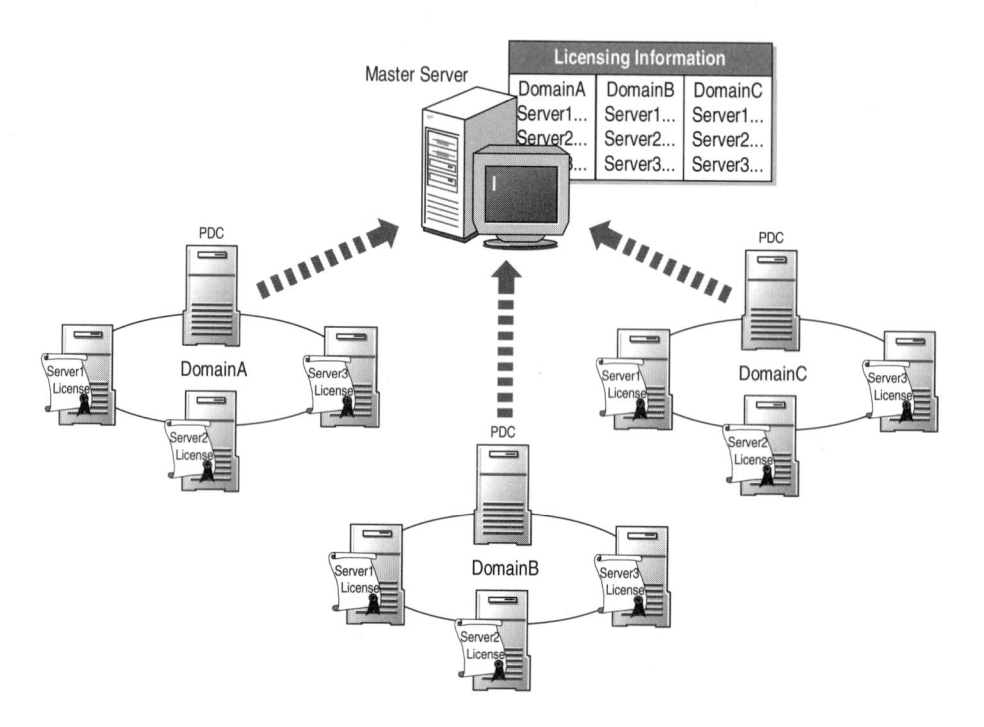

Configuring Licensing Replication

To configure licensing replication, start the Licensing program in Control Panel, and then click **Replication** in the **Choose Licensing Mode** dialog box. The **Replication Configuration** dialog box appears.

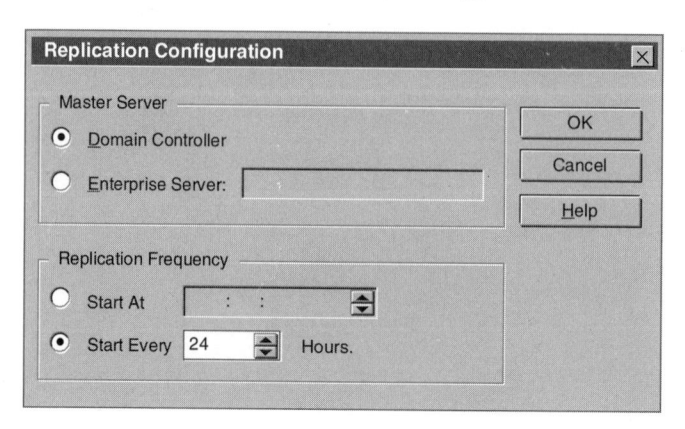

The following table describes the options in the **Replication Configuration** dialog box.

Option	Use this option to	Use this option when
Domain Controller (PDC)	Specify that the master server for this computer is the PDC.	This computer is a stand-alone server in a domain, or is a backup domain controller (BDC).
		This computer is a stand-alone server or a PDC, and you do not want to replicate further.
Enterprise Server	Specify that master server is an enterprise server and enter the name of the enterprise master server.	This computer is a stand-alone server, is part of an enterprise, and you want to replicate its licensing information directly to the enterprise master server.
		The computer is the PDC for its domain, and you want to replicate to an enterprise server.
Start At	Manually designate a time each day when licensing information is replicated to the master server.	You want to manually set a starting time for replication on this computer.
Start Every	Set the frequency for license replication.	The computer running Window NT Server will automatically stagger the replication of licensing data from each server.
		The default is every 24 hours, and the range from 1 to 72 hours.

Note Licensing replication is independent of Directory Replication. Directory Replication is discussed in Chapter 16 "Implementing File Synchronization and Directory Replication."

License Manager

License Manager is another tool that you can use to track licensing data and replicate the licensing data to a centralized database.

License Manager can be used to:

- View your organization's licensing.
- Administer license allocation and usage throughout an organization.
- Perform the one-time, one-way change from Per Server to Per Seat mode for qualifying BackOffice products.

Start **License Manager** from the **Administrative Tools (Common)** menu. The following illustration shows License Manager with the **Server Browser** tab selected.

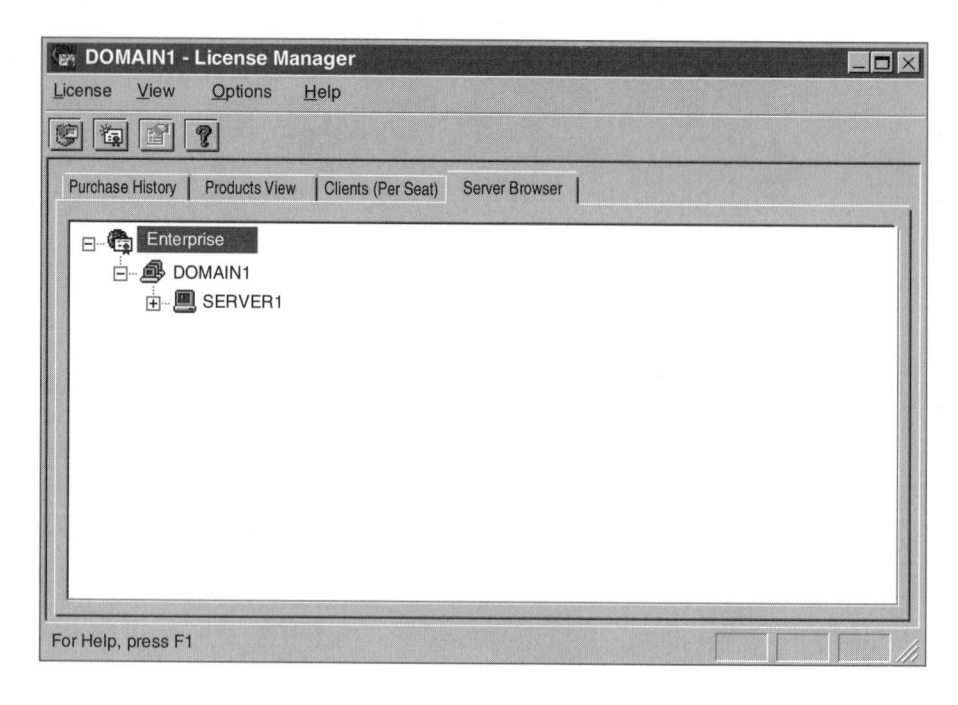

The following table describes the Per Server and Per Seat licensing functions that can be configured through the tabs in License Manager.

Tab	Use this tab to
Purchase History	View the product purchase date, product quantity, and identify the product administrator. This function can be used with either the Per Server or Per Seat licensing mode.
Products View	View the number of Per Server and Per Seat licenses by product in an organization.
Clients (Per Seat)	Survey licensed and unlicensed product usage. Click a user name to view the client's server usage history, to upgrade the user to a BackOffice license, or to revoke permission to access a server.
Server Browser	View servers in a domain or organization. Double-click to expand the domain to display servers in that domain. Double-click a server to display the **Choose Licensing Mode** dialog box.

Adding or Removing CALs for Per Server Licensing

Double-click a domain displayed by the **Server Browser** tab in License Manager to view the servers in that domain. Double-click a server to view the BackOffice products installed on that server. To add or remove CALs through the **Choose Licensing Mode** dialog box, double-click the appropriate BackOffice product.

The following illustration shows the **Choose Licensing Mode** dialog box for Windows NT Server.

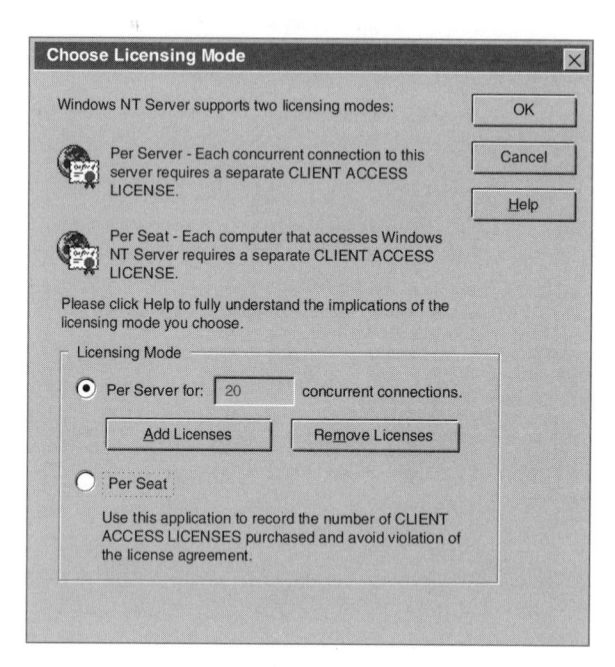

The following table describes the options in the **Choose Licensing Mode** dialog box.

Option	Use this option to
Per Server for *x* **concurrent connections**	View the number of concurrent client connections that are configured for a server, if the Per Server licensing mode has been chosen.
Add licenses (Per Server licensing)	Add CALs to increase the number of concurrent client connections.
Remove licenses (Per Server licensing)	Remove CALs to decrease the number of concurrent client connections.
Per Seat	View whether the Per Seat licensing mode has been selected.

Adding or Removing CALs for Per Seat Licensing

To add CALs for Per Seat licensing, in License Manager, click **New License** on the **License** menu. Select the appropriate product, enter the quantity of Client Access Licenses purchased, and then click **OK**.

To remove CALs for Per Seat licensing, in License Manager, click the **Products View** tab, and then click the appropriate BackOffice product. On the **License** menu, click **Delete**, and the **Select Certificate to Remove Licenses** dialog box appears. Select the appropriate Serial Number. In the **Number of Licenses to remove** box, enter the quantity of CALs to be removed, and then click **Remove**.

Creating License Groups

To obtain correct licensing information when working with Per Seat licenses, it may be necessary to group certain users and make them members of a *license group*.

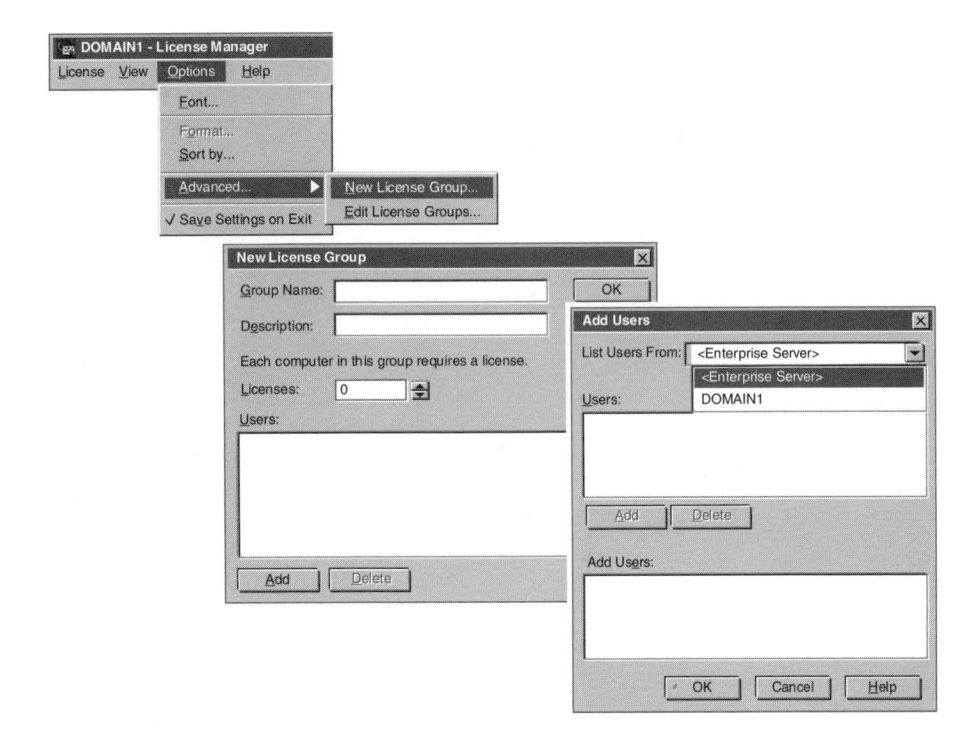

License groups show a relationship (also known as a mapping) between users and computers and should be used only when one of the following configurations is true:

- Multiple users use one computer, such as when people share jobs, or when multiple shifts of workers use the same computers.
- Multiple users use several computers, but there is an unequal number of users and computers, such as may occur in a university computer lab or in a retail store.
- One user uses multiple computers, such as often happens during software development when applications are developed on one computer and tested on several different platforms.

A license group is composed of the following components:

- A descriptive name for the group.
- A specified number of Per Seat licenses assigned to the group. The number of CALs required for a license group corresponds to the number of computers that are being used by the group, rather than the number of users in the group.
- A specific list of users who are members of the group.

Note For more information on licensing, see Chapter 12 of Microsoft Windows NT Server *Concepts and Planning*.

Lesson 2: Clients Included with Windows NT Server

For a computer to access a computer running Windows NT, you must install and configure client software on that computer. On computers running Windows NT Server, Windows NT Workstation, or Microsoft Windows 95, the client software is automatically installed during the installation of the operating system. If you need to set up computers that are running some other operating system, such as Microsoft MS-DOS, that does not include the networking components required to access a computer running Windows NT, Microsoft provides networking client software on the *Windows NT Server 4.0* compact disc. In this lesson, you learn what client software is included on the *Windows NT Server 4.0* compact disc and the protocols and redirectors that are supported by each client.

After this lesson, you will be able to:
- Describe the client software and the corresponding supported protocols for each client that are included with Windows NT Server.

Estimated lesson time: 15 minutes

Client Software Provided by Windows NT Server

The client software provided by Windows NT Server is located in the Clients folder on the *Windows NT Server 4.0* compact disc. The Clients folder contains subfolders that include the following software.

- *Microsoft Network Client 3.0 for MS-DOS and Windows.* Contained in the Msclient folder.
- *Microsoft LAN Manager 2.2c Client.* Contained in the Lanman folder.
- *Microsoft LAN Manager 2.2c Client for OS/2.* Contained in the Lanman.os2 folder.
- *Microsoft Windows 95 operating system.* Contained in the Win95 folder. Includes all operating system files required to install Windows 95.

Note Windows NT Server 4.0 also supports Windows for Workgroups as a client, but does not include the Windows for Workgroups software. Because the version of Transmission Control Protocol/Internet Protocol (TCP/IP) included with Windows for Workgroups does not support Dynamic Host Configuration Protocol (DHCP) and Windows Internet Name Service (WINS), Windows NT Server does include an add-on product, Microsoft TCP/IP-32 for Windows for Workgroups 3.11, which provides support for DHCP and WINS.

Microsoft Network Client 3.0 for MS-DOS and Windows

Microsoft Network Client 3.0 provides network connectivity for MS-DOS-based computers that need to access resources on computers running Windows NT.

The following illustration shows an MS-DOS based computer, with Microsoft Network Client 3.0 installed, accessing resources on a computer running Windows NT Server.

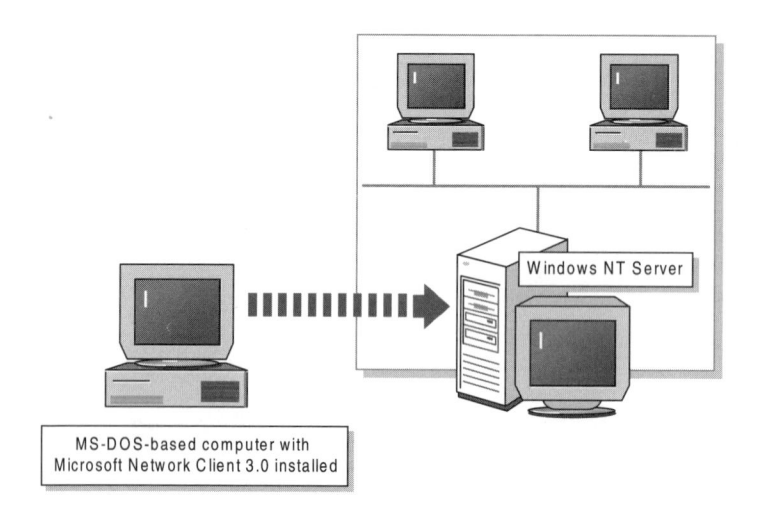

Supported Protocols

Microsoft Network Client 3.0 supports the following protocols:

- NetBEUI
- Internetwork Packet Exchange (IPX) Compatible Transport
- TCP/IP. The TCP/IP protocol included with this client software supports DHCP; it does not support either DNS or WINS name resolution.
- Data link control (DLC)

Full Redirector

By default, Microsoft Network Client 3.0 supports the full redirector, which enables clients to take advantage of the following network services:

- Domain logon capability and logon scripts
- Remote Access Service (RAS) version 1.1
- Messaging
- Interprocess communication mechanisms such as named pipes, remote procedure calls (RPC), and Windows Sockets (WinSock)

Note Neither Microsoft Network Client 3.0 nor MS-DOS have browsing capabilities. Therefore, to browse the network, there must be a Windows for Workgroups–based or a Windows NT–based computer running in the same workgroup.

LAN Manager 2.2c Clients

Windows NT Server includes software for the following two LAN Manager 2.2c clients: LAN Manager 2.2c for MS-DOS and LAN Manager 2.2c for OS/2.

LAN Manager 2.2c for MS-DOS

LAN Manager 2.2c for MS-DOS ships with NetBEUI, Microsoft DLC, and TCP/IP. The TCP/IP protocol stack that is included with LAN Manager 2.2c for MS-DOS supports the DHCP, which is the default setting, but it does not support DNS or WINS name resolution.

In addition, LAN Manager 2.2c for MS-DOS supports the Remoteboot service. MS-DOS and Microsoft Windows 3.x-based computers can be remotely started using the Remoteboot service.

LAN Manager 2.2c for OS/2

LAN Manager 2.2c for OS/2 supports OS/2 1.x and OS/2 2.x. This client ships with NetBEUI and TCP/IP; however, its version of TCP/IP does not support DHCP or WINS.

Microsoft Windows 95

Windows NT Server supports connectivity with Windows 95 clients.

Supported Protocols

Windows 95 supports the following protocols:

- NetBEUI
- Internetwork Packet Exchange/Sequenced Packet Exchange (IPX/SPX) Compatible Transport
- TCP/IP—the TCP/IP protocol supports DHCP, WINS, and DNS name resolution.

Support for 32-bit Networking

Windows 95 clients use a 32-bit protected mode redirector to log on to a network and access resources. The advantage of this redirector is that it supports the 32-bit WinNet32 programming interface and 32-bit protected mode drivers. The combination of the WinNet32 application programming interface (APIs) and 32-bit protected mode drivers provide faster, more robust network access than the corresponding 16-bit APIs and drivers.

Lesson 3: Network Client Administrator

In this lesson, you learn how to use the Network Client Administrator tool to install and configure the network client software and tools contained on the *Windows NT Server 4.0* compact disc.

After this lesson, you will be able to:
- Explain the methods provided by Network Client Administrator that enable you to install and update network client workstations.
- Describe the procedure to create and configure a network installation startup disk.
- Describe the procedure to create an installation disk set.

Estimated lesson time: 20 minutes

What Is Network Client Administrator?

The Network Client Administrator is used to:

- Install network client software by creating a network installation startup disk or an installation disk set.
- Share the installation files contained on the *Windows NT Server 4.0* compact disc.
- Copy the folders and files contained on the *Windows NT Server 4.0* compact disc to a network server and share them. Creating a network share is the recommended method for installing the client software.

The **Network Client Administrator** is located on the **Administrative Tools (Common)** menu on computers running Windows NT Server.

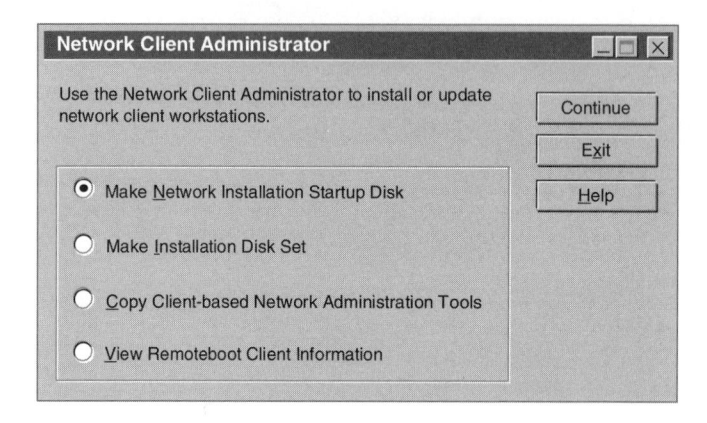

```
Network Client Administrator

Use the Network Client Administrator to install or update
network client workstations.                              [ Continue ]

                                                          [   Exit   ]

  ◉  Make Network Installation Startup Disk               [   Help   ]

  ○  Make Installation Disk Set

  ○  Copy Client-based Network Administration Tools

  ○  View Remoteboot Client Information
```

The following table describes each option in the **Network Client Administrator** dialog box.

Option	Use this option to
Make Network Installation Startup Disk	Create an MS-DOS network installation startup disk that can be used to automatically connect to a server and install Windows 95 or Microsoft Network Client 3.0 for MS-DOS and Windows.
Make Installation Disk Set	Create an installation disk set for Microsoft Network Client 3.0 for MS-DOS and Windows, LAN Manager 2.2c for MS-DOS, LAN Manager 2.2c for OS/2, Remote Access v1.1a for MS-DOS, or TCP/IP 32 for Windows for Workgroups 3.11.
Copy Client-based Network Administration Tools	Install client-based Windows NT administration tools on Windows NT Workstation or Microsoft Windows 95 clients to enable administration from those clients.
View Remoteboot Client Information	View Remoteboot client information. Remoteboot is a Windows NT service that can be used to start MS-DOS, Windows 3.*x*, and Microsoft Windows 95–based computers over the network. The Remoteboot service is installed through the Network program in Control Panel.

Network Installation Startup Disks

If client operating systems are to be installed from a computer running Windows NT Server, by means of either network share or a shared compact disc, then the clients must be able to connect to the Windows NT server. One method of providing access to the server would be to create a network installation startup disk and then start the client computer using that disk.

Creating a Network Installation Startup Disk

To create a network installation startup disk, select **Make Network Installation Startup Disk** in the **Network Client Administrator** dialog box, and then click **Continue**. The **Share Network Client Installation Files** dialog box appears.

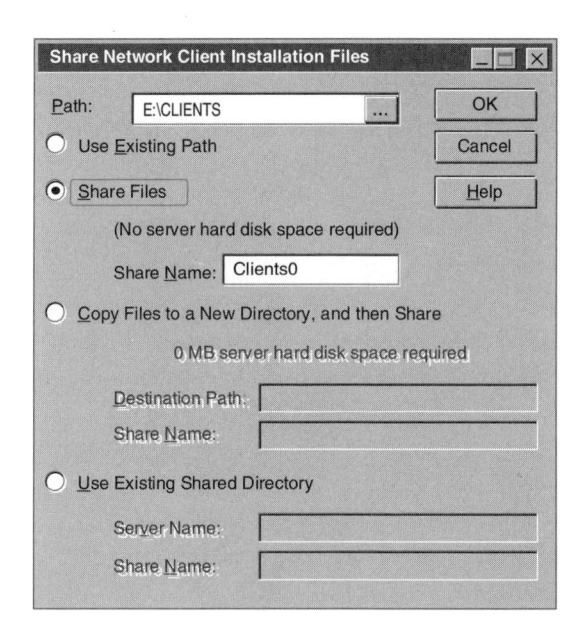

Use the **Share Network Client Installation Files** dialog box to specify how the share should be configured. The following table describes each option in this dialog box.

Option	Use this option to
Path	Indicate the location of the client files.
Use Existing Path	Specify an existing path.
Share Files	Share the client folders and files directly from the compact disc.
Copy Files to a New Directory, and then Share	Specify if files are copied to a new directory and then shared, or shared through an existing server directory.
Use Existing Shared Directory	Use files that have previously been copied and shared.

Note To save hard disk space, delete any folders that are copied from the Clients folder to the network share that are not required. For example, if you do not have any computers that require LAN Manager 2.2 for OS/2, then delete this folder from the network share.

Once the client software files have been shared, you can begin creating network installation startup disks or installation disk sets.

Specifying the Target Workstation Configuration

The next step in creating a network installation startup disk is to specify the configuration on the target workstations.

For example, to share the folders and files on the *Windows NT Server 4.0* compact disc, click **Share Files** in the **Share Network Client Installation Files** dialog box, and then Click **OK**. The **Target Workstation Configuration** dialog box appears.

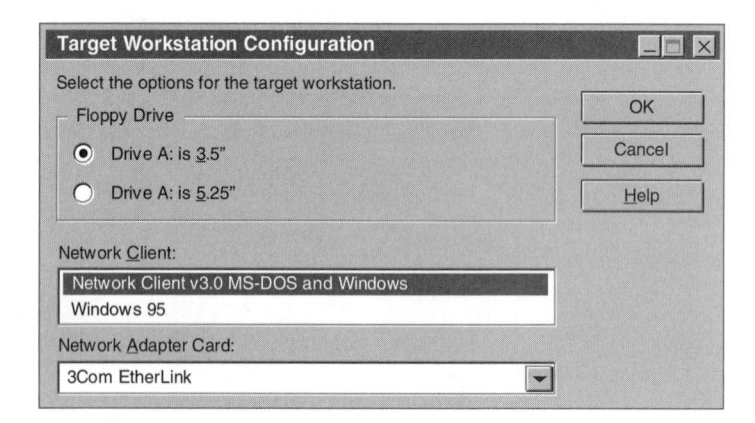

The following table describes the options in the **Target Workstation Configuration** dialog box.

Option	Use this option to
Floppy Drive	Select either 3.5" or 5.25", whichever is compatible with the drive on the target workstation.
Network Client	Identify the network client software that will be installed: Network Client v3.0 for MS-DOS and Windows or Windows 95
Network Adapter Card	Select the correct network adapter card for the client.

Configuring a Network Startup Disk

After you specify the configuration on the target workstation, you must configure the network startup disk.

For example, after specifying the appropriate floppy disk size, network client, and network adapter card, click **OK** in the **Target Workstation Configuration** dialog box. The **Network Startup Disk Configuration** dialog box appears.

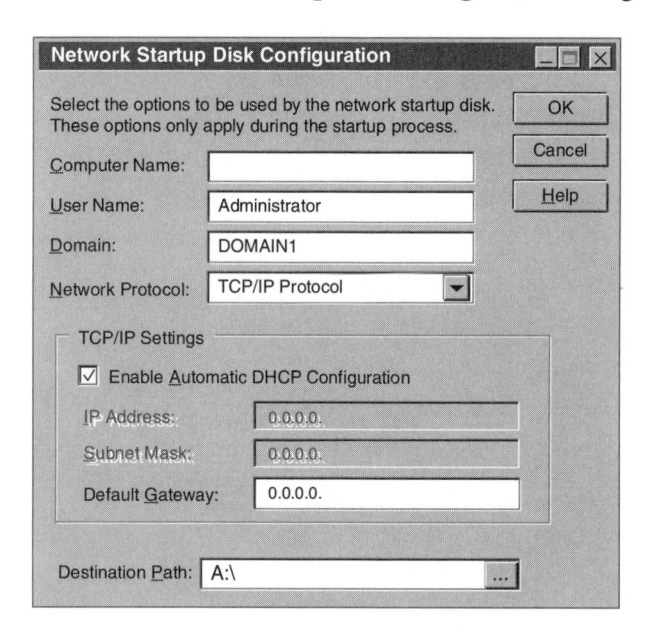

![Network Startup Disk Configuration dialog box showing fields for Computer Name, User Name (Administrator), Domain (DOMAIN1), Network Protocol (TCP/IP Protocol), TCP/IP Settings with Enable Automatic DHCP Configuration checked, IP Address, Subnet Mask, Default Gateway all set to 0.0.0.0, and Destination Path A:\]

The **Network Startup Disk Configuration** dialog box is used to configure the network information described in the following table.

Option	Use this option to
Computer Name	Enter a unique name that identifies the computer on the network.
User Name	Enter a user name that identifies the user to the network.
Domain	Enter a domain name that identifies the domain to the network.
Network Protocol	Select which protocol to use when copying network client administration files.
Enable Automatic DHCP Configuration	Enable automatic DHCP configuration if the network has DHCP servers.
IP Address	Enter the IP address that identifies the computer to other computers on the network.
Subnet Mask	Enter the subnet mask.
Default Gateway	Enter the IP address of the default gateway.
Destination Path	Enter the destination path where files should be copied.

After supplying all information, you are prompted to insert a formatted, high-density system disk in the destination drive. The Network Client Administrator then copies files to the disk according to your specifications. You can then use the floppy disk to start a computer and automatically copy the client software to the computer.

Creating an Installation Disk Set

An installation disk set is used to *manually* install the following client software or service on a computer, as opposed to downloading it from a network server or installing it from the *Windows NT Server 4.0* compact disc:

- Microsoft Network Client 3.0 for MS-DOS and Windows.
- Remote Access v1.1a for MS-DOS.
- TCP/IP-32 for Windows for Workgroups 3.11.
- LAN Manager 2.2c for MS-DOS.
- LAN Manager 2.2c for OS/2.

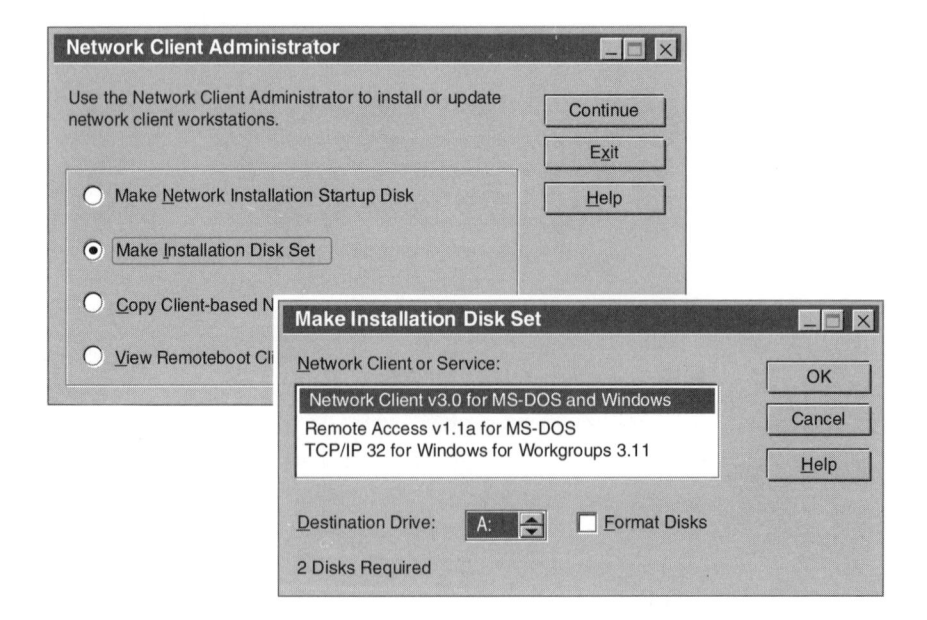

Chapter 15 Implementing Network Clients

To create an installation disk set, start Network Client Administrator, select **Make Installation Disk Set**, and then click **Continue**. The **Make Installation Disk Set** dialog box appears. Select the appropriate options and then click **OK**. The **Share Network Client Installation Files** dialog box appears; configure the **Share Network Client Installation Files** dialog box and then click **OK**. The **Make Installation Disk Set** dialog box appears. The following table explains the options that can be configured in the **Make Installation Disk Set** dialog box.

Option	Use this option to
Network Client or Service	Specify the type of installation disks to create.
Destination Drive	Specify the destination drive for the disk.
Format Disks	Format disks to be used.

After you specify the appropriate information and click **OK**, the client software files are copied to floppy disks. The installation disk set you create can be used only for the specific client or service you selected. If you have multiple computers with different client(s) or service requirements, you must make separate installation disk sets for each network client or service.

Lesson 4: Client-based Network Administration Tools

The *Windows NT Server 4.0* compact disc includes client-based network administration tools that gives you the flexibility to manage computers running Windows NT and domains from either a computer running Windows NT Workstation or Windows 95. Though many of the administrative tools are the same for both operating systems, there are some differences among them. In this lesson, you learn how to install the client-based administration tools on computers running Windows NT Workstation or Windows 95 and learn which tools are installed for each operating system.

After this lesson, you will be able to:
- Explain the system requirements to install the administration tools on Windows NT Workstation and Windows 95 clients.
- Install the administration tools for Windows NT Workstation.
- Explain how to install the administration tools for Microsoft Windows 95.

Estimated lesson time: 25 minutes

Installing the Administration Tools on Windows NT Workstation

In order to use the Windows NT Server administration tools on a computer running Windows NT Workstation, you must first install them. The administration tools are installed in the *systemroot*\System32 folder on the computer's system partition.

System Requirements for Windows NT Workstation Clients

The minimum requirements needed to install the Windows NT Server administration tools for a computer running Windows NT Workstation are:

- A 486DX/33 CPU or higher.
- 12 MB of RAM.
- 2.5 MB of free disk space on the system partition.
- Workstation and Server services installed.

Practice

In this procedure, you install the Windows NT Server client-based administration tools from the *Windows NT Server 4.0* compact disc on Workstation1.

▶ **To install the Windows NT Server client-based administrative tools**

Note Complete this procedure on Workstation1, logged on as Administrator.

1. Insert the *Windows NT Server 4.0* compact disc in the CD-ROM drive on Workstation1.
2. From the *cd_rom_drive***:\Clients\Srvtools\Winnt** folder, run Setup.

   A Command Prompt window is opened, and the administrative tools and their supporting files are copied to the *systemroot*\System32 folder.
3. Read the text in the Command Prompt window, and then press ENTER.
4. Remove the *Windows NT Server 4.0* compact disc from the CD-ROM drive.

The following table describes the administrative tools and their file names that are copied to computer running Windows NT Workstation.

Tool	File name	Use this tool to
DHCP Manager	Dhcpadmn.exe	Manage the DHCP service running on a computer running Windows NT Server. Use DHCP Manager to centrally configure global and scope-specific parameters.
Remote Access Administrator	Rasadmin.exe	Administer the Remote Access Service on a computer running Windows NT.
Remoteboot Manager	Rplmgr.exe	Configure the Remoteboot service on a computer running Windows NT Server.
Server Manager	Srvmgr.exe	Manage Windows NT–based domains and computers.
System Policy Editor	Poledit.exe	Control and change user and system configuration settings.
User Manager for Domains	Usrmgr.exe	Manage users, groups, and security policies for Windows NT–based domains and computers.
WINS Manager	Winsadmn.exe	Administer the Windows Internet Name Service (WINS) on a computer running Windows NT Server.
DNS Manager	N/A	Manage the Microsoft DNS Server service and database.

Note Once the administration tools have been copied to your Windows NT Workstation client computer, create shortcuts for the tools on your desktop.

Using the Administration Tools on Windows 95

System Requirements for Windows 95 Clients

To install the Windows NT Server tools on a computer running Windows 95, the computer must have:

- A 486DX/33 CPU or higher.
- 8 MB of RAM.
- 3 MB of free disk space on the system partition.

Installing the Administration Tools

To install the administration tools on a computer running Windows 95, use the following steps:

1. Insert the *Windows NT Server 4.0* compact disc in the CD-ROM drive on the computer running Windows 95.
2. Click the **Start** button, point to **Settings**, and then click **Control Panel**.
3. Double-click the Add/Remove Programs icon.
4. Click the **Windows Setup** tab, and then click **Have Disk**.
5. In **Copy manufacturer's files from**, type *cd-rom_drive_letter***Clients\Srvtools\Win95** and then click **OK**.
6. Click **Windows NT Server Tools**, and then click **Install**.

   The Windows NT Server client-based network administration tools are installed in a Srvtools folder on the computer's boot drive.

7. Edit the path in the Autoexec.bat file to include the appropriate folder, for example, add C:\Srvtools to the path.

Note You must restart the computer for the new path to take effect.

Chapter 15 Implementing Network Clients

The following table describes the administrative tools and file names that are copied to the computer.

Tool	File name	Use this tool to
Event Viewer	Eventvwr.exe	View, access, manage, and archive event logs. Use Event Viewer to view and manage system, security, and application event logs.
File Security tab added to Windows NT Explorer and My Computer	N/A	Establish file and folder permissions. Use the server tools to view permissions over the network and change them, if required.
Print Security tab added to Windows NT Explorer and My Computer	N/A	Establish print permissions. Set print permissions through the **Properties** dialog box accessed through the **Printers** dialog box.
Server Manager	Srvmgr.exe	Manage shared folders and printers on computers running Windows NT. Use Server Manager to share folders, set permissions on shared folders, view who is using shared resources, and disconnect users from shared resources.
User Manager for Domains	Usrmgr.exe	Create and manage users, groups, and security policies for domains.
User Manager Extensions for Services for NetWare	N/A	Create a NetWare client user account, enable the account, configure account properties, create a NetWare home directory, and set restrictions. Although this tool is included on the *Windows NT Server 4.0* compact disc, it is only installed if File and Print Services for NetWare or Directory Services Manager for NetWare is installed.
File and Print Services for NetWare (FPNW)	N/A	Create and manage FPNW services, user accounts, volumes, printers and queues, and send messages. Although this tool is included on the *Windows NT Server 4.0* compact disc, it is installed only if FPNW is installed.

Note When using the administration tools on a Windows 95 client computer, the system requires the user to log on or enter a password several times for verification.

Lesson 5: Services for Macintosh

Windows NT Server includes Services for Macintosh; these services give you the ability to manage a Windows NT network environment that includes computers using an AppleTalk internetwork. Services for Macintosh also enables computers running Windows NT Server 4.0 to provide file and print services for computers using an AppleTalk internetwork. In addition, once Services for Macintosh are enabled, it is possible to connect networks with Macintosh clients to create an AppleTalk internetwork. In this lesson, you learn how to install and configure Services for Macintosh.

After this lesson, you will be able to:
- Describe the benefits provided by Services for Macintosh.
- Explain the requirements for running Services for Macintosh in a Windows NT Server environment.
- Install Services for Macintosh.

Estimated lesson time: 20 minutes

Services for Macintosh enables Microsoft clients and Apple Macintosh clients to share file, print, administrative, and other network resources. Using Services for Macintosh on a network provides the following benefits.

Function	Description
File sharing	Clients can work on the same documents, even if some clients work with the Macintosh version of an application and others work with the Windows or MS-DOS version.
Printer sharing	Clients can send print jobs to either a printer for personal computers or to a Macintosh-based printer.
Simplified administration	Mixed networks with both Windows-based or MS-DOS-based computers and Macintosh clients can be managed from a computer running Windows NT Server.
AppleTalk routing support	Apple Macintosh networks can be connected to create an AppleTalk internetwork.

Services for Macintosh Requirements

Setting up Services for Macintosh requires a computer running Windows NT Server, with 2 MB of disk space available, and a Windows NT File System (NTFS) partition, which is required for Macintosh-accessible volumes. The procedure for creating Macintosh-accessible volumes is described later in this lesson.

Requirements for Macintosh Clients

To use Services for Macintosh, a client computer must have the Macintosh operating system version 6.0.7 or later, and AppleShare (the Apple networking software for the Macintosh). This includes most Macintosh computers except for the Macintosh XL and Macintosh 128K models.

In addition, Services for Macintosh supports version 6.x or later of the LaserWriter printer driver, and the AppleTalk Filing Protocol versions 2.0 and 2.1.

Note Services for Macintosh supports LocalTalk, Ethernet, Token Ring, and fiber distributed data interface (FDDI). Ethernet and Token Ring are commonly used when integrating a Macintosh computer into a Windows- or MS-DOS-based network.

Installing Services for Macintosh

Services for Macintosh can be installed during the installation of Windows NT Server, or after installation, using the **Services** tab in the Network program located in Control Panel.

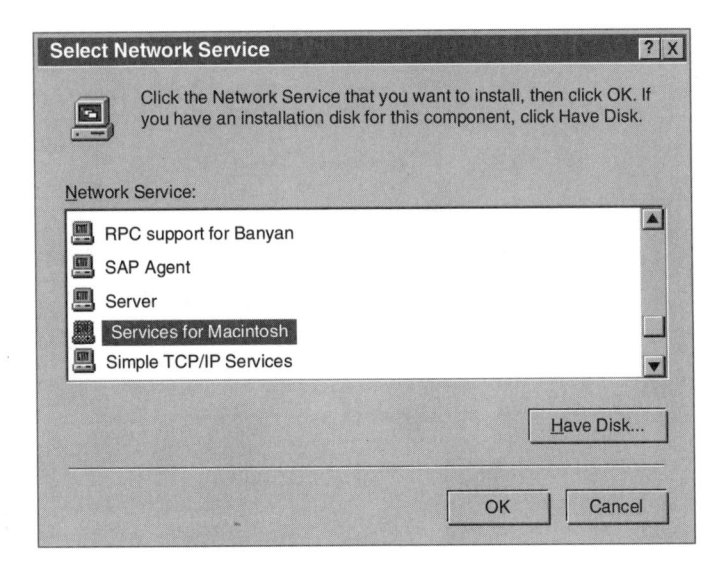

Creating a Macintosh-Accessible Volume

After Services for Macintosh is installed, a **MacFile** menu is added to Server Manager. You use the **MacFile** menu to create Macintosh-accessible volumes.

Note If you want documents that are stored on a Macintosh-accessible volume to also be available to your Windows- and MS-DOS-based network clients, you must share the folder from which the volume was created.

Macintosh computers have a maximum partition size of 2 GB. If Macintosh clients access a computer running Windows NT Server with an NTFS partition of more than 2 GB, the clients may get a message that there are 0 (zero) bytes available.

Practice

In this procedure, you install Services for Macintosh on Server2.

▶ **To install Services for Macintosh**

Note Complete this procedure on Server2, logged on as Administrator.

1. Start Server2, and then log on as Administrator.
2. Double-click the Network program in Control Panel.
3. Click the **Services** tab, and then click **Add**.
4. Click **Services for Macintosh**, and then click **OK**.

   A **Windows NT Setup** dialog box appears.

5. Type **\\Server1\Nts_source\I386** in the path, and then click **Continue**.
6. If you do not have an NTFS partition, a **Setup Message** dialog box appears stating that Services for Macintosh requires an NTFS partition, and that you can create one after you install Services for Macintosh. If this message appears, click **OK**.

   The **Network** dialog box reappears. Notice that Services for Macintosh is now included in the list of Network Services.

7. Click **Close**.

   A **Microsoft AppleTalk Protocol Properties** dialog box appears. This is where you would indicate the Zone.

8. Click **OK**.

   A **Network Settings Change** dialog box appears stating that you must shut down and restart your computer, and prompting you to restart your computer now.

9. Click **Yes**.

Features That Install Automatically with Services for Macintosh

When you install Services for Macintosh, the following features are also automatically installed:

- *The AppleTalk protocol.* Delivers data to its destination on the network. The AppleTalk protocol can be installed and configured through the **Protocols** tab in Control Panel.
- *File Service for Macintosh.* Manages Macintosh volumes, folders, and files.
- *Print Server for Macintosh.* Enables both Windows or MS-DOS clients and Macintosh clients to send print jobs to either AppleTalk (usually PostScript devices) or non-AppleTalk printing devices.

Removing Services for Macintosh

Services for Macintosh can be removed at any time by using the **Remove** button located on the **Services** tab in the Network program in Control Panel.

Summary

The following information summarizes the key points in this chapter:

- With the Microsoft BackOffice licensing model, Windows NT servers and client computers are licensed separately. A server license is required for each server, and a Client Access License (CAL) is required for each client computer that accesses a server.
- When you purchase Windows NT Server, a *server license* is included with the purchase. This server license entitles you to install Windows NT Server on one and only one computer.
- A Client Access License (CAL) provides the legal right for a computer to access a computer running Windows NT Server. CALs are separate from the desktop operating system software you use to connect to Microsoft server products.
- Microsoft offers two licensing modes: Per Server licensing and Per Seat licensing.
  - *Per Server Licensing.* In Per Server licensing, *CALs are assigned to the server.* The number of CALs determines the number of simultaneous connections that can be made to *that* server.
  - *Per Seat Licensing.* In Per Seat licensing, *a CAL is purchased for each client computer.* With a Per Seat license, a client can access network resources such as file, print, and communications on *any* computer running Windows NT Server in the network, and can log on to multiple servers simultaneously.
- Windows NT Server 4.0 includes two administrative tools that you can use to track licensing data and replicate the licensing data to a centralized database: the Licensing program in Control Panel and the License Manager program on the **Administrative Tools (Common)** menu.
- Windows NT Server 4.0 includes the Network Client Administrator, a tool that you can use to install client software.
- The *Windows NT Server 4.0* compact disc includes client-based network administration tools that gives you the flexibility to manage computers running Windows NT and domains from either a computer running Windows NT Workstation or Windows 95.
- Windows NT Server 4.0 includes Services for Macintosh, which enables Microsoft clients and Apple Macintosh clients to share file, print, administrative, and other network resources.

Review

1. You have recently added 50 new desktop computers to your network. Each of these computers requires access to the computers running Windows NT Server on the network. Your servers are licensed in the Per Seat mode. What utility must you use to add the new Client Access Licenses?

2. You are evaluating the clients included on the *Windows NT Server 4.0* compact disc. Your network uses both DHCP and WINS, and you require support for these protocols on your client computers. Which of the clients included with Windows NT Server would you deploy?

3. You must deploy 50 new desktop computers on your network. These computers will all run Windows NT Workstation, and the installation files are located in a shared folder on a computer running Windows NT Server. However, the new computers do not have a network client installed and therefore cannot connect to the server to download Windows NT Workstation. How would you enable the computers to connect to the server so that you can start the installation?

4. You are in charge of network operations for your company. You have many different administrators using various operating systems on their desktop computers. Which operating systems allow the administrators to work at their desktop computers and still be able to apply file and directory permissions to an NTFS partition on a computer running Windows NT Server?

5. Your computer running Windows NT Server provides file and print services to both Windows-based and Macintosh clients. You have installed Services for Macintosh and created a volume in which Macintosh users store their documents. You would like these documents to also be accessible from the Windows-based clients. What must you do?

Answer Key

Procedure Answers

Page 534

Licensing Considerations Review

Your company is a small, newly created business that has one file and print server and 30 client computers. You configured the server using the Per Server licensing mode and obtained 30 Client Access Licenses, so that all 30 clients could access the server.

1. Your business is growing, so you purchase five new client computers and add them to the network. If 30 clients are currently connected to the server, will another client be able to connect to the server? Why or why not?

   No. It will not be able to access the server, because the maximum number of server connections allowed is 30.

2. You decide to add a mail server that *all* clients will connect to. What would be the most economical licensing mode solution for the company?

   The most economical solution is to configure the mail server for the Per Seat licensing mode and then convert the file and print server to the Per Seat licensing mode. In this way, you could purchase 5 more Client Access Licenses and the 35 CALs will be assigned to the clients, allowing them to have access to either server.

Page 535

Choosing Per Server vs. Per Seat Licensing Review

1. A company has one computer running Windows NT Server. There are 300 computers running Windows NT Workstation in the company, but only 250 of these will access the server simultaneously.

   What licensing mode would be the best solution for this company?

Licensing mode and computers	Result
Per Server option:	
Number of simultaneous connections needed to server1	250
Total of simultaneous connections needed for all servers: A = server1 + server2 + ... + serverN	A = 250
Per Seat option:	
Total number of seats (computers) that access *any* server. This the number of CALs needed for Per Seat licensing	B = 300

   A is less than B. Therefore the Per Server Licensing mode is the best licensing solution for this company.

2. This company now adds an additional computer running Windows NT Server. Up to 200 of the workstations will also access the new server simultaneously.

What licensing mode would now be the best solution for this company?

Licensing mode and computers	Result
Per Server option:	
Number of simultaneous connections needed to server1	250
Number of simultaneous connections needed to server2	200
Total of simultaneous connections needed for all servers: A = server1 + server2 + ... + serverN	A = 450
Per Seat option:	
Number of seats (computers) that access *any* server is the number of CALs needed for Per Seat licensing	B = 300

A is now greater than B. Therefore the Per Seat Licensing mode is the best licensing solution for this company when it adds an additional server.

Review Answers

1. You have recently added 50 new desktop computers to your network. Each of these computers requires access to the computers running Windows NT Server on the network. Your servers are licensed in the Per Seat mode. What utility must you use to add the new Client Access Licenses?

   You must use License Manager to enter the information for the new licenses.

2. You are evaluating the clients included on the *Windows NT Server 4.0* compact disc. Your network uses both DHCP and WINS, and you require support for these protocols on your client computers. Which of the clients included with Windows NT Server would you deploy?

   Windows 95 is the only included client that supports both DHCP and WINS. In addition, TCP/IP-32 for Windows for Workgroups (which is included with Windows NT Server) can be added to Windows for Workgroups computers to provide DHCP and WINS support.

   Windows NT Workstation, although not included on the *Windows NT Server 4.0* compact disc, also supports both DHCP and WINS.

3. You must deploy 50 new desktop computers on your network. These computers will all run Windows NT Workstation, and the installation files are located in a shared folder on a computer running Windows NT Server. However, the new computers do not have a network client installed and therefore cannot connect to the server to download Windows NT Workstation. How would you enable the computers to connect to the server so that you can start the installation?

   Use Network Client Administrator to create a network installation startup disk.

4. You are in charge of network operations for your company. You have many different administrators using various operating systems on their desktop computers. Which operating systems allow the administrators to work at their desktop computers and still be able to apply file and directory permissions to an NTFS partition on a computer running Windows NT Server?

   There are Windows NT administrative tools available that run on both Windows 95 and Windows NT.

5. Your computer running Windows NT Server provides file and print services to both Windows-based and Macintosh clients. You have installed Services for Macintosh and created a volume in which Macintosh users store their documents. You would like these documents to also be accessible from the Windows-based clients. What must you do?

   Share the folder from which the volume was created. Both types of clients will be able to access the files contained within the folder.

CHAPTER 16

Implementing File Synchronization and Directory Replication

Lesson 1 The Windows NT Briefcase . . . 574

Lesson 2 Directory Replication Overview . . . 581

Lesson 3 Preparing for Directory Replication . . . 588

Lesson 4 Managing Directory Replication . . . 591

Lesson 5 Troubleshooting Directory Replication . . . 602

Review . . . 606

About This Chapter

In Microsoft Windows NT, the Briefcase and the Directory Replicator service are used to minimize the administration involved in updating files over a network. The Briefcase supports mobile and distributed computing by transparently synchronizing updated files. The Directory Replicator service replicates information such as logon scripts, user profiles, and system policies from a designated export server to one or more import computers.

Before You Begin

To complete the lessons in this chapter, you must have:

- Two computers that meet the hardware and software requirements as specified in the Getting Started section of "About This Book."
- Completed all practices in Chapter 2, "Installing Windows NT."
- One blank, formatted 1.44 MB high-density disk.

Lesson 1: The Windows NT Briefcase

The Windows NT Briefcase, which appears as an icon on the desktop, allows users to copy files to their Briefcase, take their Briefcase with them, either on a disk or portable computer, modify the files in the Briefcase, and then on reconnecting to the network, synchronize the files with the original source.

After this lesson, you will be able to:
- Describe the function of the Windows NT Briefcase.
- Describe the mechanics involved in using the Briefcase.
- Use the Briefcase to synchronize remote file updates with centralized sources.

Estimated lesson time: 30 minutes

The following illustration summarizes the synchronization process that occurs when the Briefcase is used to work on files remotely.

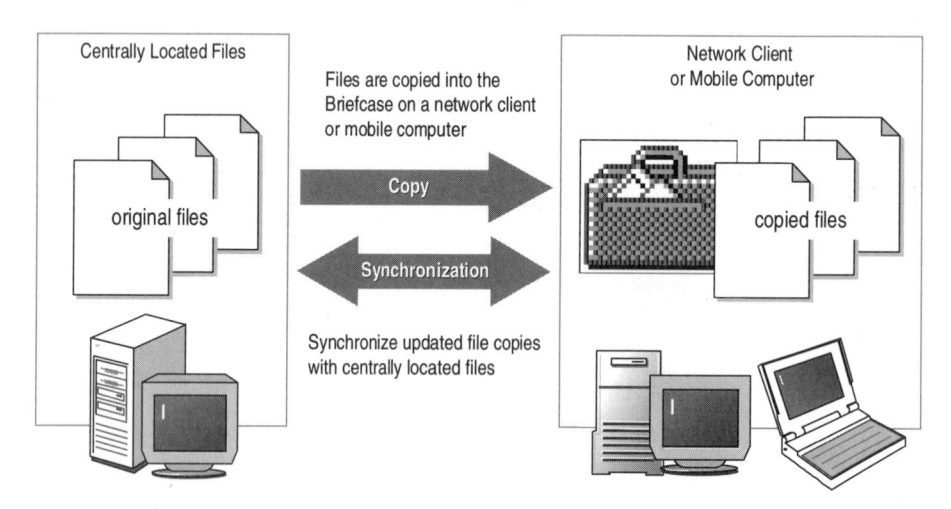

The Windows NT Briefcase can be deployed in any organization where employees spend a significant amount of time working on files off-site. The Briefcase can also be used to synchronize centrally located files with copies on local computers. In addition, it is possible to have a Briefcase synchronized with files on a network server.

For example, network or mobile users can connect to a file source, which could be on any computer that is visible to the user, drag files from it to their Briefcase and then work on these files. When the work on these files is complete, the user synchronizes files without having to move the updated file copies out of the Briefcase or manually replace the original files. The Briefcase notes whether either copy of the file has changed, and then updates the unchanged copy. If both copies of the file have changed, Briefcase notes this, but does not automatically update the copies. You can then choose which, if either, file to replace.

The Briefcase Database

The Briefcase Database stores the information required by Windows NT to synchronize files. If this database is deleted, it is impossible to synchronize updated files.

Note The Briefcase Database files are stored in the Briefcase. When the Briefcase is created, it is, by default, located in the following folder:

systemroot\Profiles*user_name*\Desktop\My Briefcase

These files may be accessed only from the command prompt. They are *not* displayed from Windows NT Explorer.

Using the Briefcase

Synchronizing files through the Briefcase involves copying files to the Briefcase, working on them, and synchronizing the updated files. When you open the Briefcase you see files and folders. These are the files and folders that will be synchronized.

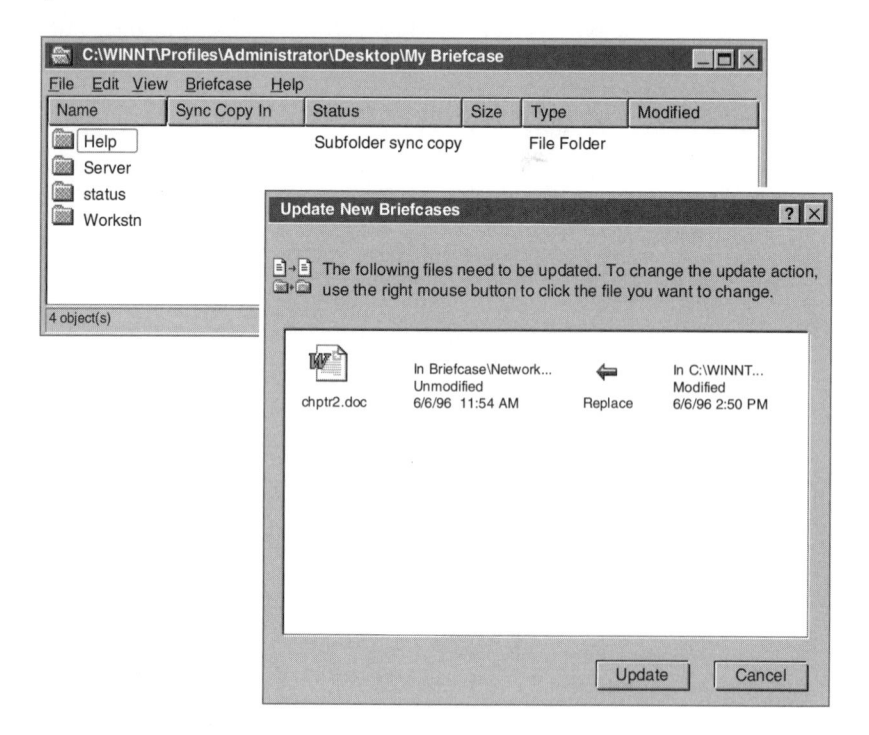

Copying Files to the Briefcase

Files can be copied to the Briefcase through the standard Windows NT methods: by performing a drag-and-drop operation, using the **Copy** and **Paste** commands, using the **Send To** menu command, and so on.

Important Files never get *moved* to the Briefcase; they are always *copied* to the Briefcase.

Working on Files in the Briefcase

To modify files in the Briefcase, open the Briefcase folder on the removable media, and then open the file and do your work. When you save your changes to the file, the changes are written to the file in the Briefcase folder.

Synchronizing Updated Files

If you put your Briefcase on a removable media, such as a floppy disk, drag your Briefcase folder back to your desktop.

You begin the file synchronization process by using the menus in Briefcase. When files are synchronized through the Briefcase **update** command, a dialog box appears requiring one of the following options to be chosen.

Option	This option appears when
Replace	The original file or the Briefcase copy has been updated, but not both.
Skip	Both the original file and the Briefcase copy have been updated.
Delete	The original file or the copy has been deleted.
Merge	Both the original file and the Briefcase copy have been updated, and the application that created the file supports the Briefcase merge feature. Microsoft Access version 7.0 is an example of an application that supports the Briefcase merge feature.

Practice

In these procedures, you use a Briefcase to synchronize files. You populate My Briefcase with four files from your hard disk; you then move My Briefcase to a floppy disk. After you modify some of the existing files in your Briefcase and some of the files on your hard disk, you synchronize the files on the disk with the original files still located on your computer's hard disk.

Note Complete these procedures on Workstation1.

▶ **To enable My Briefcase**

In this procedure, you start Briefcase.

1. Log on to the domain as Administrator.
2. On the desktop, double-click My Briefcase.
3. If this is the first time you have opened My Briefcase, read the directions in the **Welcome to the Windows Briefcase** dialog box, and then click **Finish**.

▶ **To populate My Briefcase with files**

In this procedure, you use My Computer to copy the C:\Lab Files\Briefcas folder to My Briefcase.

1. Open My Computer, locate the C:\Lab Files\Briefcas folder, and then open it to reveal the four files named W, X, Y, and Z (these are .rtf files).
2. For each of the four files, W, X, Y, and Z, right-click the file, and then click **Quick View** to see the data that is currently in the file.
3. Close Quick View when you are done.
4. Drag the entire Briefcas folder to My Briefcase and drop it there. This copies the Briefcas folder and all of the files in the Briefcas folder to My Briefcase.
5. Close My Briefcase.

▶ **To move My Briefcase to another computer**

In this procedure, you move My Briefcase to a floppy disk. This is the first procedure in moving My Briefcase to another computer.

1. Insert a blank disk in your disk drive.
2. Drag the My Briefcase icon to the disk.

    My Briefcase should now be located on the disk.

Chapter 16 Implementing File Synchronization and Directory Replication 579

▶ **To modify the contents of My Briefcase**

The following change relationships are implemented in the following procedures.

	Original	Briefcase
File W	Not Modified	Modified
File X	Modified	Not Modified
File Y	Not Modified	Modified
File Z	Modified	Modified

▶ **To modify the contents of W**

1. In the Briefcas folder located in the Briefcase on your floppy disk, open W.
2. Modify W by inserting the following data at the beginning of the file:

    My name is *your name*. **I have modified this file.**
3. Exit WordPad, saving your changes.

    You have now modified W in your Briefcase. You do *not* modify the original W file.

▶ **To modify the contents of X**

1. In the C:\Lab Files\Briefcas folder, open X.
2. Select all of the text by pressing CTRL+A.
3. Copy the information to the Clipboard by pressing CTRL+C.
4. Position the cursor at the end of the file by pressing CTRL+END.
5. Paste the information from the Clipboard by pressing CTRL+V.
6. Exit WordPad, saving your changes.

    You have now modified your original X file. You do *not* modify the X file in your Briefcase.

▶ **To modify the contents of Y**

1. In the Briefcas folder located in the Briefcase on your floppy disk, open Y.
2. Select all of the text by pressing CTRL+A.
3. Copy the information to the Clipboard by pressing CTRL+C.
4. Position the cursor at the end of the file by pressing CTRL+END.
5. Paste the information from the Clipboard by pressing CTRL+V.
6. Exit WordPad, saving your changes.

    You have now modified the copy of Y in your Briefcase. You will *not* modify the original Y file.

▶ **To modify the contents of Z**

1. In the C:\Lab Files\Briefcas folder, open Z, and type today's date in the file.
2. Exit WordPad, saving your changes.
3. In the Briefcas folder located in the Briefcase on your floppy disk, open Z and type the name of your company in the file.
4. Exit WordPad, saving your changes.

   You have now modified your original Z file, and you have made a different modification to the copy of the Z file in your Briefcase.

5. Close My Briefcase.

▶ **To synchronize your files**

In this procedure, you synchronize the files in your Briefcase with those on your hard disk.

1. Drag My Briefcase from the floppy disk back to the desktop.

   My Briefcase moves to the desktop.

2. Open My Briefcase.
3. On the **Briefcase** menu, click **Update All**.
4. Click **Update**.

   The modified files are synchronized.

5. On the **Briefcase** menu, click **Update All**.

   Z should be the only file listed.

   Why was Z not updated?

   _____

6. Click **Cancel**.
7. Open each of the files (W, X, Y, and Z) to see the changes.
8. Close My Briefcase.
9. Remove the disk from drive A.

Lesson 2: Directory Replication Overview

One of the challenges in supporting multiple dedicated servers in a single-domain or multiple-domain environment is to keep shared resources current. For example, when managing a domain, make certain that all backup domain controllers maintain a copy of the logon scripts and system policy files for that domain. This enables each domain controller to provide a user with a requested logon script or system policy file. If these files are unavailable, then users may experience a problem when logging on to a computer.

Windows NT uses the *Directory Replicator* service to maintain identical folder hierarchies, which could include logon scripts, system policy files, and other commonly used files on multiple servers. This allows users to access multiple servers for their logon files and other information.

After this lesson, you will be able to:
- Describe the purpose of directory replication.
- Identify the directory replication components.
- Describe the directory replication process.

Estimated lesson time: 20 minutes

The Purpose of Directory Replication

Directory replication is a Microsoft Windows NT feature that is used to replicate logon scripts, system policy files, and commonly used information to computers in a domain or to multiple domains. Directory replication is used to set up identical directories on multiple computers running Microsoft Windows NT Server, but can also be set up on computers running Microsoft Windows NT Workstation. The *master directory* is maintained on a designated Windows NT Server. Updates made to the files in the master directory are replicated to the other designated computers.

The following illustration shows the propagation of logon scripts and system policy files to multiple servers by means of directory replication.

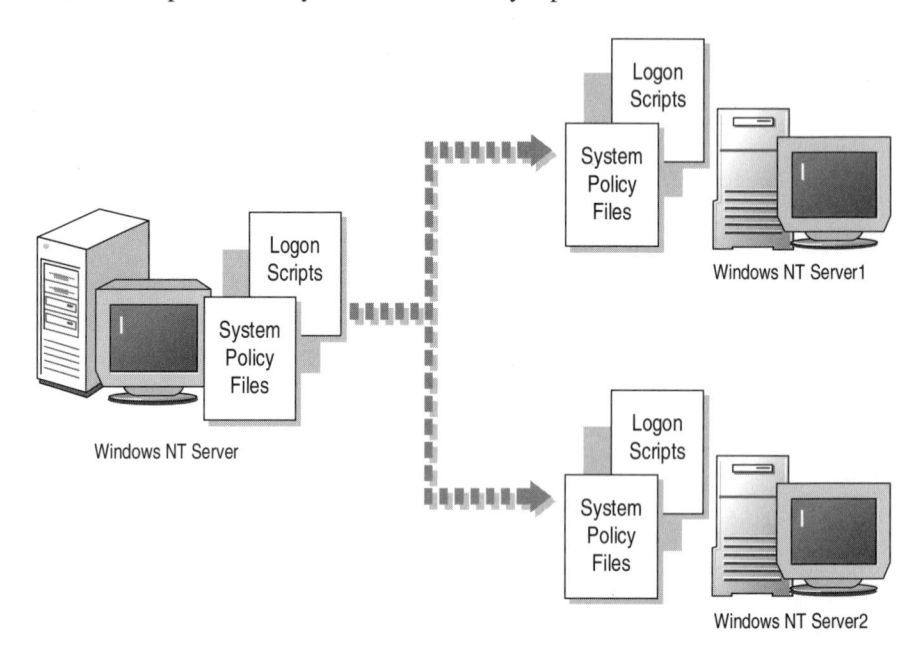

Directory replication makes the same files available at multiple servers. This is useful when a user logs on, because logon scripts must reside on the domain controller that validates the logon. In addition, directory replication helps to balance loads between multiple servers when several users need simultaneous access to a file, typically a read-only file, thereby avoiding overburdening any one server.

Types of Data Maintained by Directory Replication

Directory replication can be used to maintain any type of data. Some common examples of data that is replicated across servers using directory replication are logon scripts and system policy files.

Logon Scripts

Logon scripts are batch files, command files, or executable programs that can be assigned to user accounts. Logon scripts can be used to set up the user's environment without managing all aspects of it.

The logon script must reside on the domain controller that validates the user's logon request. When there is more than one Windows NT Server domain controller in a domain, it is recommended that logon scripts be replicated to all of them. This allows each domain controller to have a copy of all logon scripts. By using replication, only one copy of each script needs to be maintained.

Each time a user logs on, the assigned logon script is run. When a server processes a logon request, the system locates the logon script by combining a file name specified in User Manager for Domains with a path specified in Server Manager.

Note For information about how to manage logon scripts, see "Setting the Logon Script Path" in Server Manager Help.

System Policy Files

System policy files are used to control the user's work environment and implement uniform system configurations for all computers in an organization. Replicating system policy files ensures that proper system policy is downloaded regardless of the server that validates the logon request.

Note For more information on system policy files, see Chapter 4, "Managing System Policies."

Commonly Used Information

If many users need to access a file, such as an online telephone list, replicate the file to several computers. Replicating files to several servers allows you to set up *load balancing*, which can minimize bottlenecks by allowing different groups of users to access the file on different computers. These files are usually marked as read-only, because they typically contain information that is needed by many users, but should not be modified by those users. If any changes are made to the replicated copies of the file, they are overwritten the next time replication occurs.

Directory Replication Components

Replicating directory information in a Windows NT Server network requires an export server that replicates updated information and one or more import computers that receive a copy of these updated files.

The following illustration shows how an export server replicates files to the import servers.

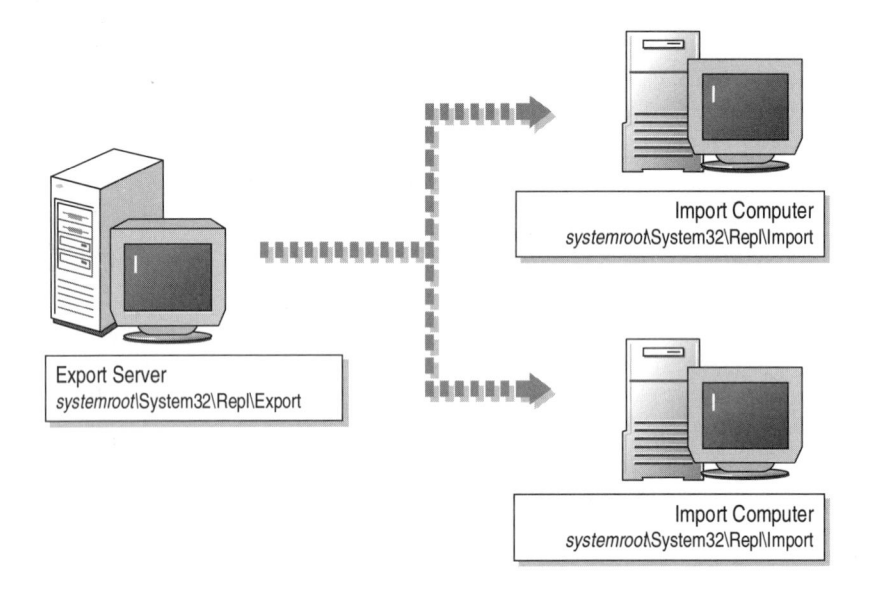

Import Computer
systemroot\System32\Repl\Import

Export Server
systemroot\System32\Repl\Export

Import Computer
systemroot\System32\Repl\Import

The Export Server

Export servers replicate updated files and directories from a designated master directory on an export server to a designated directory on an import computer. Only a computer running Windows NT Server can be an export server.

The Import Computer

Computers that receive updates, which are the replicated files and directories, from the export server are called *import computers*. Updates can be received from specified computers or domains. The following can be designated as import computers:

- Computers running Microsoft Windows NT Server.
- Computers running Microsoft Windows NT Workstation.
- Microsoft LAN Manager OS/2 servers.

Export and Import Directories

The export server keeps the directories to be replicated in a master export directory. By default, this directory is *systemroot*\System32\Repl\Export.

Note The directory *systemroot*\System32\Repl\Export is shared as **Repl$** when the Directory Replicator service is started.

Subdirectories under the *systemroot*\System32\Repl\Export directory must be created by the Administrator for each group of files that need to be replicated. These files are then placed in the appropriate subdirectories.

Caution In order for replication to occur, files must be placed in subdirectories in the *systemroot*\System32\Repl\Export directory. Any files placed directly in the *systemroot*\System32\Repl\Export directory are *not* replicated.

For example, to provide for replication of logon scripts, a computer running Windows NT Server exports logon scripts from the following directory:

systemroot\System32\Repl\Export\Scripts

Each import computer has an import directory that corresponds to the export server's export directory. By default, the import directory is *systemroot*\System32\Repl\Import.

The Directory Replicator service *automatically* creates subdirectories under this directory to match those on the export server.

For example, the logon scripts exported from the master export directory *systemroot*\System32\Repl\Export\Scripts on the export server would be imported to the *systemroot*\System32\Repl\Import\Scripts directory on import computers.

Note You use Server Manager to manage or change the default export or import directory paths.

The Directory Replication Process

After the files and directories have been set up for directory replication, the Directory Replicator service controls the replication process. This service operates on each export server and import computer that participates in replication. The service on each computer logs on using the same user account, for example the repl account, which you create for this purpose.

You configure export servers and import computers to send and receive updated files. An export directory on an export server contains all of the directories and subdirectories of files to be replicated, and when changes are saved to files in these directories, the files automatically replace the existing files on all of the import computers.

Periodically, the export server checks the export directory for changes. If any changes have occurred, the following process occurs, which replicates the updated information from export servers to import computers:

- The export server sends update notices to the import computers or domains.
- When an import computer receives an update notice, it calls the export server and reads the export directory structure.
- The import computer copies any new or changed files to its import directory structure, and deletes any of the import files that are no longer in the export directory structure.

The following illustration summarizes the directory replication process.

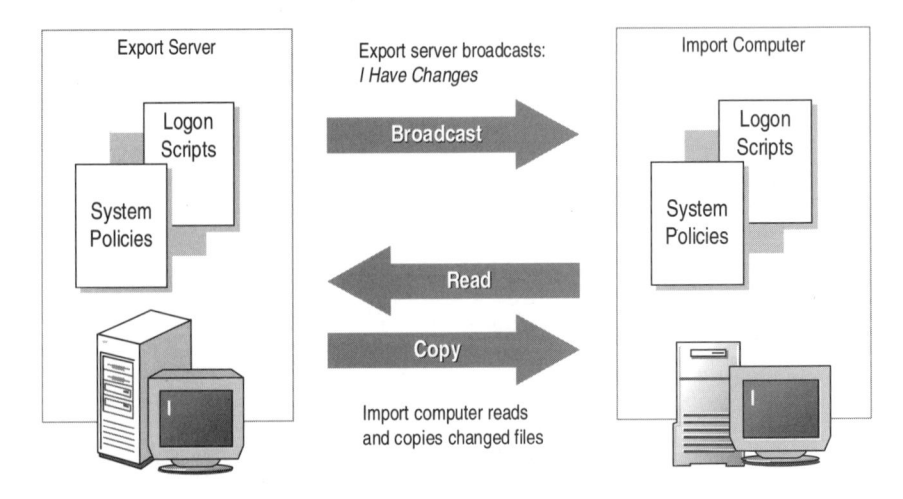

If nothing has changed in the export directories, the export server waits before sending a repeat update notice. The repeat notice allows import computers that missed the original update notice to receive the notice. The timing for checking replicated directories is set by the *Interval* parameter, which is discussed in the "Managing Replication from an Export Server" topic later in this chapter.

The parameters that control the Directory Replicator service are located in the following registry path:

HKEY_LOCAL_MACHINE\SYSTEM\CurrentControlSet\Services\Replicator\Parameters.

Lesson 3: Preparing for Directory Replication

Directory replication begins with the configuration of both the export server and the import computer(s).

After this lesson, you will be able to:
- Prepare an export server to replicate directories to other computers and domains.
- Prepare an import computer to receive directories from an export server.

Estimated lesson time: 10 minutes

Preparing an Export Server

Any computer running Windows NT Server can be set up as an export server.

You would use the following steps to set up replication on an export server:

1. In User Manager for Domains, create a user account, such as repl, for the Directory Replicator service to use, according to the following specifications:
    - All logon hours are allowed.
    - The account is added to the domain's Backup Operators and Replicator groups.
    - The **User Must Change Password at Next Logon** check box is cleared.
    - The **Password Never Expires** option is selected.

Chapter 16 Implementing File Synchronization and Directory Replication

2. From Server Manager, or the Services program in Control Panel configure the Directory Replicator service to start automatically and log on as the directory replicator user account.

   The following illustration shows the **Service** dialog boxes used to configure the Directory Replicator service to start automatically and to use the directory replicator user account.

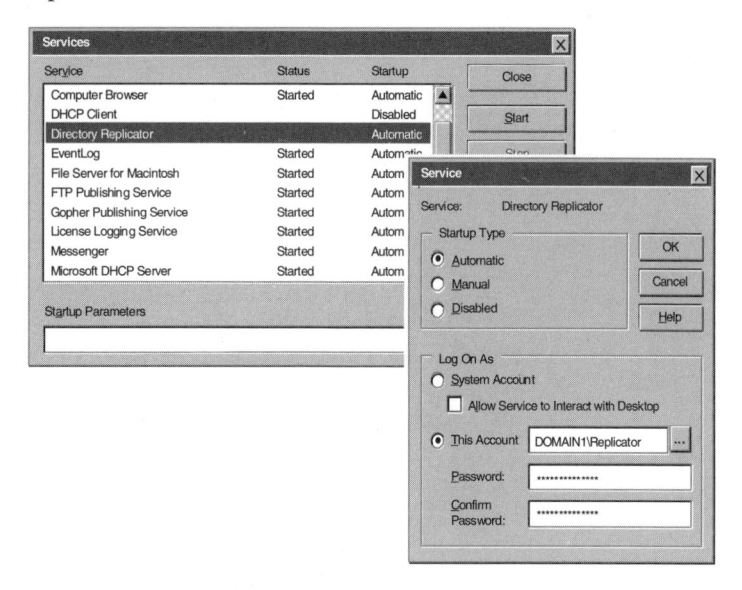

3. Place directories to be replicated in the following folder: *systemroot*\System32\Repl\Export

4. From Server Manager, configure the export server to export files to other computers or domains.

   Note If the export directory is on an (NTFS) partition, the Replicator group on the export server should be granted Full Control to the export directory tree.

Preparing an Import Computer

Computers running Windows NT Server, computers running Windows NT Workstation, and Microsoft LAN Manager OS/2 servers can be set up as import computers. A computer running Windows NT Server that is configured as an export server can also be configured as an import computer.

The following describes the steps that are necessary for setting up replication on an import computer:

1. If the import computer is not part of the export server's domain or a trusting domain, create a replicator user account, using User Manager for Domains.

   - This account must have the same name and password as the account used to configure the export server because the account must have permission to access the export server's Repl$ share.

   - This account must be a member of the local Replicator group and the Backup Operators group.

2. From Server Manager, or the Services program in Control Panel, configure the Directory Replicator service to start automatically and to log on as the directory replicator user account.

3. Using Server Manager, configure the import computer to receive files from other servers or domains.

Lesson 4: Managing Directory Replication

You can manage directory replication between the export server and the import computer.

After this lesson, you will be able to:
- Use Server Manager to manage replication from the export server.
- Use Server Manager to manage replication to the import computer.
- Configure an export server to replicate directories and files.
- Configure an import computer to receive exported files.

Estimated lesson time: 45 minutes

Managing Replication from an Export Server

Server Manager is used to configure a server as an export server, to specify which computers to export to, and to manage the directories to be exported from the export server.

The following illustration shows the dialog boxes displayed in Server Manager that are used to set up an export server.

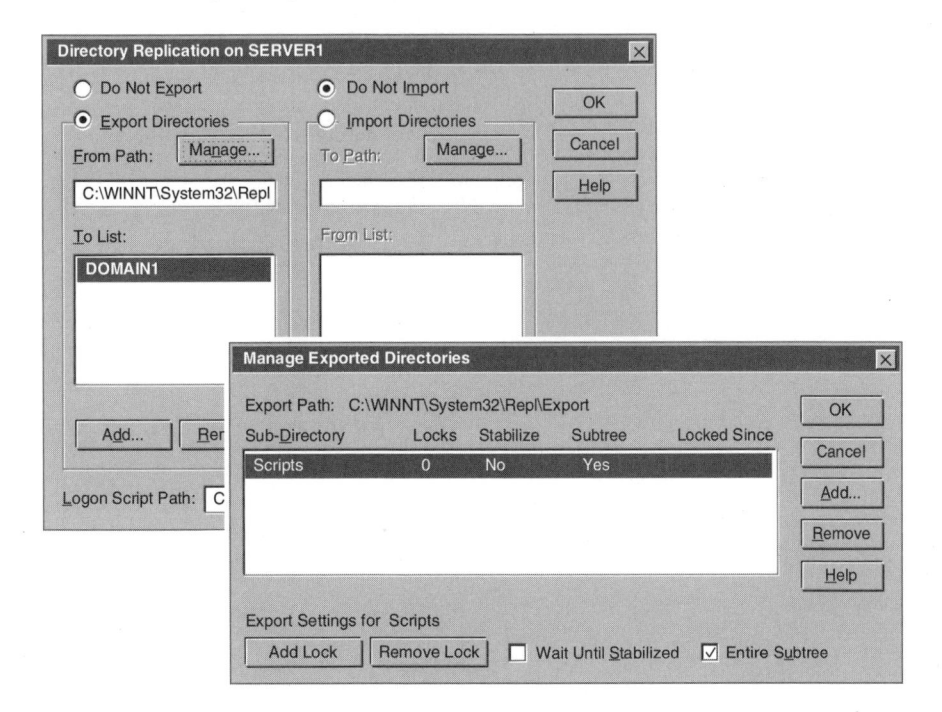

Note Ensure that an appropriate logon account is assigned to the Directory Replicator service before configuring the export options.

When managing directory replication from an export server, consider the following:

- Which computers are to receive the replicated directory. All computers on the network may not need to receive replicated information.
- Which directories are to be exported. Not all directories may need to be exported.
- Whether the entire tree or only top-level directories are to be replicated. In some instances, not all subdirectories need to be replicated.
- How long, if at all, the Directory Replicator service waits for the directory to stabilize before replicating. In many instances, it is not advisable to replicate a changing directory, as file integrity may not be preserved.
- Whether any directories need to be locked while modifications are being made to them. This provides control over when a directory can be replicated.

Use Server Manager to manage the replication options at the export server as shown in the following table.

Option	Description
From Path	Indicates the path from which directories are exported.
To List	Indicates the computers or the domains to which directories can be exported. If blank, replicate to any computer in the same domain configured as an import computer.
Locks	Prevents a directory from being exported. (Directories can be locked by more than one user.)
Stabilize	Indicates whether files in the export directory wait a specified time after changes before being exported.
Subtree	Indicates whether the entire subtree is exported.
Locked Since	Indicates the date and time a lock was placed on a directory.

Chapter 16 Implementing File Synchronization and Directory Replication

The registry contains entries that control various aspects of replication. These are located in HKEY_LOCAL_MACHINE\SYSTEM\CurrentControlSet \Services\Replicator\Parameters.

There are two registry entries that are *not* configurable by Server Manager and that you may want to add to the registry in order to better manage replication are:

- *Interval*: **REG_DWORD** which sets how often an export server checks the replicated directories for changes. The range is from 1 through 60 minutes; the default is 5 minutes.

- *GuardTime*: **REG_DWORD** which sets the number of minutes an export directory must be stable (no changes to any files) before import servers can replicate its files. The range is from 0 through one-half of the Interval minutes; the default is 2 minutes.

Note For more information on registry parameters that control Directory Replication, see the Replicator entry in the Regentry.hlp file on the *Microsoft Windows NT Workstation Resource Kit CD-ROM*.

Managing Replication to an Import Computer

Server Manager allows you to manage replication to the import computer. When managing directory replication to an import computer consider the following:

- Which computers are going to be allowed to replicate to the import computer.
- Which directories are to be imported. Not all directories may be needed.
- Whether any directories need to be locked. This provides control over when a directory can be imported, because a locked directory can not be imported.

The following illustration shows the dialog boxes displayed in Server Manager that are used to set up an import computer.

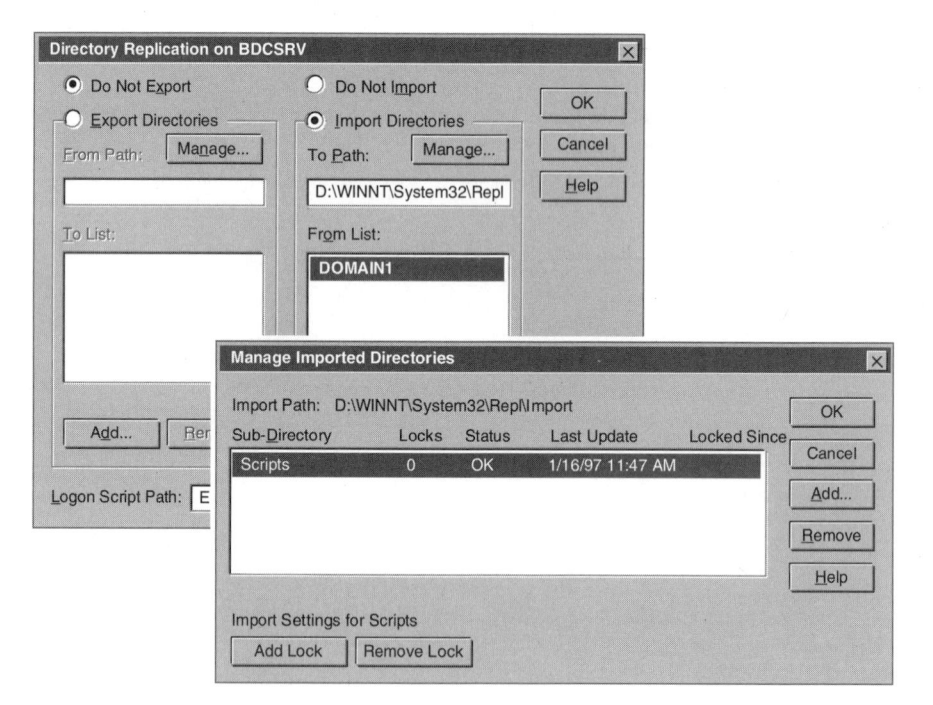

Chapter 16 Implementing File Synchronization and Directory Replication

Use Server Manager to manage aspects of replication at the import computers as listed in the following table.

Option	Description
To Path	Indicates the path in which replicated directories are stored.
From List	Indicates the servers or domains which can export to this computer. If blank, receive replicated data from any export server in the same domain.
Locks	Prevents a directory from being imported.
Status	Indicates the status on receiving updates from the export server. Status options include the following:
	OK. Indicates that the directory is receiving regular updates from the export server and the imported data is identical to that exported.
	No Master. Indicates that the directory is not receiving updates from the export server. The export server may not be running or may have stopped exporting updates.
	No Sync. Indicates that the directory has received updates, but that the data is not up to date. This could be due to a communications failure, open files on the import computer or export server, the import computer not having access permissions to the export server, or an export server malfunction.
	[blank] Indicates that replication has never occurred for the directory. Replication may not be properly configured for this import computer, for the export server, or both.
Last Update	Provides the date and time that the last update was made to a file in the import directory.

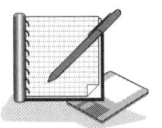

Practice

In these procedures, you configure directory replication. Server1 is your export server, and Server2 is your import computer. In order to complete the procedures in this practice, you need to modify a registry setting on Server1.

▶ **To log on to Server2**

1. Shut down Workstation1, and restart the computer as Server2.
2. Log on at Server2 as Administrator.

▶ **To modify an entry in the registry**

Note Complete this procedure on Server1.

1. Verify that you are logged on to Server1 as Administrator.
2. Open Windows NT Registry Editor (Regedt32.exe).
3. On the **Options** menu, clear **Read Only Mode**.
4. Open the following key:

   HKEY_LOCAL_MACHINE\SYSTEM\CurrentControlSet\Control\SecurePipeServers\winreg\AllowedPaths
5. In the right pane, double-click **Machine: REG_MULTI_SZ**.

   The **Multi-String Editor** dialog box appears with four lines of data.
6. In the **Data** box add a fifth line by pressing the DOWN ARROW key to clear the highlight, and then press ENTER.
7. Type **System\CurrentControlSet\Services\Replicator**

   Caution Verify that you have added a fifth line and typed the information correctly. If you made a mistake, correct it now or click **Cancel** and begin again.

8. Click **OK** to close the **Multi-String Editor** dialog box.
9. Close Registry Editor.
10. Shut down and restart your server.
11. Log on as Administrator.

Chapter 16 Implementing File Synchronization and Directory Replication

▶ **To create an account for the Directory Replicator service**

In this procedure you create an account for the Directory Replicator service to use.

Note Complete this procedure on Server1.

1. Start User Manager for Domains.
2. Create a user account using the information in the following table.

Field	Response
Username	repl
Full Name	Replicator Service Account
Password	password
Confirm Password	password
User Must Change Password at Next Logon	Not selected
Password Never Expires	Selected
Groups	Add as a member of the Replicator group and the Backup Operators group

3. Close User Manager for Domains.

▶ **To configure the Directory Replicator service on an export server**

In this procedure, you configure the Directory Replicator service on your export server, Server1, to start automatically using the repl account.

Note Complete this procedure on Server1.

1. Click the **Start** button, point to **Programs**, point to **Administrative Tools (Common)**, and then click **Server Manager**.
2. Server Manager appears, click to select **Server1**.
3. On the **Computer** menu, click **Services**.
4. Click **Directory Replicator**, and then click **Startup**.

   A **Service** dialog box appears.
5. Under **Startup Type**, click **Automatic**.
6. Under **Log On As**, click **This Account**, and then click the ellipsis (…) button to the right of the **This Account** box.

   The **Add User** dialog box appears.
7. Click **repl**.

8. Click **Add**, and then click **OK**.

   The **Service** dialog box reappears, with **Domain1\repl** in the **This Account** box.

9. In the **Password** and **Confirm Password** fields, type **password**

10. Click **OK**.

    A **Services** dialog box appears, stating that the repl account has been granted the Log On As A Service right.

11. Click **OK**.

12. Click **Close** to close the **Services** dialog box.

▶ **To configure an export server**

In this procedure, you configure Server1 to be an export server for Domain1.

Note Complete this procedure on Server1.

---

1. In Server Manager, double-click **Server1**.
2. Click **Replication**.

   The **Directory Replication on Server1** dialog box appears.

3. Click **Export Directories**.
4. Click the **Add** button located under **Export Directories**.

   The **Select Domain** dialog box appears.

5. In the **Select Domain** list, double-click **Domain1**.

   The list of servers in Domain1 appears.

6. Click **Server2**, and then click **OK**.

   The **Directory Replication on Server1** dialog box reappears, with **Server2** listed in the **To List**.

7. Click **OK**.

   Service Control Manager starts the Directory Replicator service.

8. Click **OK** to close the **Properties for Server1** dialog box.
9. Close **Server Manager**.

Chapter 16 Implementing File Synchronization and Directory Replication

▶ **To create files for replication**

In this procedure, you create files for the Directory Replicator service to replicate.

Note Complete this procedure on Server1, your export server.

1. In the C:\Winnt\System32\Repl\Export directory, create a new folder called Data.
2. Copy two or three files to the Data folder.
3. Close all windows that are open to the export folder or its subfolders.

▶ **To configure the Directory Replicator service on an import computer**

In this procedure, you configure the Directory Replicator service on your import computer, Server2, to start automatically using the repl account.

Note Complete this procedure on Server2.

1. Start Server Manager, and then click **Server2**.
2. On the **Computer** menu, click **Services**.
3. Click **Directory Replicator**, and then click **Startup**.

   A **Service** dialog box appears.
4. Under **Startup Type**, click **Automatic**.
5. Under **Log On As**, click **This Account** and then click the ellipsis (...) button to the right of the **This Account** box.

   The **Add User** dialog box appears.
6. Click **repl**.
7. Click **Add**, and then click **OK**.

   The **Service** dialog box reappears, with **Domain1\repl** in the **This Account** box.
8. In the **Password** and **Confirm Password** fields, type **password**
9. Click **OK**.
10. Click **Close** to close the Services dialog box.

▶ **To configure an import computer**

In this procedure, you configure Server2 to be an import computer for Domain1.

> **Note** Complete this procedure on Server2.

1. In **Server Manager**, double-click **Server2**.
2. Click **Replication**.

   The **Directory Replication on Server2** dialog box appears.
3. Click **Import Directories**.
4. Click the **Add** button located under **Import Directories**.

   The **Select Domain** dialog box appears.
5. In the **Select Domain** list, double-click **Domain1**.

   The list of servers in **Domain1** appears.
6. Click **Server1** and then click **OK**.

   The **Directory Replication on Server2** dialog box reappears with **Server1** listed in the **From List**.
7. Click **OK**.

   Service Control Manager starts the Directory Replicator service.
8. Click **OK**.
9. Minimize **Server Manager**.

Chapter 16 Implementing File Synchronization and Directory Replication

▶ **To verify file replication**

In this procedure, you verify that folders and files have been replicated to your import computer in D:\Server2\System32\Repl\Import directory on Server2.

Note Complete this procedure on Server2, your import computer.

1. Wait approximately six minutes.
2. In **Server Manager**, double-click **Server2**, and then click **Replication**.
3. Under **Import Directories**, click **Manage**.

   What is the status of the Data subdirectory?

   _____

4. If the status is not OK, wait a few more minutes. You may also want to check to see if the files are replicated on the import computer. It may take a while for the status in Server Manager to show that the files have been replicated, even after the files have successfully been copied to the import computer.
5. Close Server Manager.
6. Shut down Server2, and restart the computer as Workstation1.

Lesson 5: Troubleshooting Directory Replication

This lesson describes some of the problems that you may encounter when you use Directory Replication, and it identifies some troubleshooting measures.

After this lesson, you will be able to:
- Describe directory replication problems that can occur.
- Identify solutions to directory replication problems.

Estimated lesson time: 10 minutes

Replication Troubleshooting Overview

When the Directory Replicator service encounters an error, an event is written to the application log. You can use Event Viewer to view the error in the application log. The Event Viewer displays information about the **Status** column in the **Manage Import Directories** dialog box of Server Manager, and information about messages that appear while you are configuring directory replication servers.

The following illustration summarizes some of the common problems that can occur during directory replication, and the possible solutions to these problems.

Error	Possible Solution
Access denied	Use Server Manager to see if the Directory Replicator service is configured to log on using a specific account. Use User Manager for Domains to check logon properties.
Exporting to specific computers	Use Server Manager to make sure that the export servers that will export data, and the Import computers that should receive replicated information, are correctly set up.
Replication over a WAN link	In Server Manager, in the export **To List** and the import **From List**, specify the computer names in addition to the domain name.
Logon scripts are not working	Store logon scripts in a Scripts folder within the Import folder.

Replication Troubleshooting Procedures

Access Denied

If the application log in Event Viewer shows "access denied" errors for the Directory Replicator service, use Server Manager to check the following:

- Make sure that the Directory Replicator service is configured to log on using a specific account.
- Make sure that the account used by the import computer's Directory Replicator service has permission to read the files on the export server.

The default permissions for an export directory grant Full Control to the Replicator local group. If the Full Control permission is removed from the directory, exported files are copied to the import computers but receive the wrong permissions, and an access denied error is written to the event log. If necessary, use Windows NT Explorer and view the properties of the export directory. Then click **Permissions** on the export directory's **Sharing** tab and grant Full Control to the Replicator local group for the export directories.

Exporting to Specific Computers

Be sure to specify the correct export servers and import computers in the **From List** and **To List**, respectively, in the **Directory Replication** dialog box of Server Manager, or the Server program in Control Panel. If you do not specify the export server and import computers, exporting occurs to all import computers in the local domain, and importing occurs from all export servers in the local domain.

Replication to a Domain Name Over a WAN Link

Directory replication to a domain name does not always succeed when some or all replication import computers are located across a wide area network (WAN) bridge from an export server. When adding names to the export **To List** on an export server, and when adding names to the import **From List** on an import computer, specify the computer names (instead of—or in addition to—specifying the domain name) for those computers separated by a WAN bridge.

Logon Scripts Are Not Working

On non-domain controller computers running Windows NT Server or computers running Windows NT Workstation, store the logon scripts in the following local directory: *systemroot*\System32\Repl\Import\Scripts.

Summary

The following information summarizes the key points in this chapter:

- Both the Windows NT Briefcase and Directory Replicator service can provide considerable administrative benefits in managing distributed data.
    - The Briefcase supports mobile and distributed computing by transparently synchronizing updated files.
    - The Directory Replicator service replicates information such as logon scripts, user profiles, and system policies from a designated export server to one or more import computers.
- By copying files to the My Briefcase folder, users are able to work on files on a stand-alone computer, and then synchronize them with the original source upon reconnecting to the network.
- One of the challenges in supporting multiple dedicated servers in a single-domain or multiple-domain environment is to keep shared resources current. Windows NT uses the *Directory Replicator* service to maintain identical folder hierarchies, which could include logon scripts, system policy files, and other commonly used files on multiple servers. This allows users to access multiple servers for their logon files and other information.
- Windows NT Directory Replicator service uses export servers and import computers.
    - Only a computer running Windows NT Server can be an export server. Export servers replicate updated files and directories from a designated master directory on an export server to a designated directory on an import computer.
    - Import computers receive updates, which are the replicated files and directories, from the export server. Updates can be received from specified computers or domains. The following three types of computers can serve as import computers: computers running Microsoft Windows NT Server, computers running Microsoft Windows NT Workstation, and Microsoft LAN Manager OS/2 servers.
- Using the Directory Replicator service, identical directory trees are set up and maintained on the export servers and the corresponding import computers. Only one copy of each file needs to be maintained, yet every computer that participates has an available, identical copy of that file.

- Directory replication also helps alleviate potential bottlenecks through load balancing. If you have many users who need to periodically receive the same file, you can replicate the file to several computers to prevent any one server from becoming a bottleneck.
- When the Directory Replicator service encounters an error, an event is written to the application log. You can use Event Viewer to view the error in the application log. The Event Viewer displays information about the **Status** column in the **Manage Import Directories** dialog box of Server Manager, and information about messages that appear while you are configuring directory replication servers.

Review

1. You copy several files, including the file Qt_rpt01.doc, from a network server to the My Briefcase icon on your desktop computer. Then you copy My Briefcase to a floppy disk so that you can work at home on these files. The next day you copy My Briefcase back on to your desktop computer. When you open My Briefcase and use **Update All** to synchronize the files in My Briefcase with the copies of the files on the network server, all of the file except the Qt_rpt01.doc are updated on the server. What could be the problem?

2. You are one of several administrators on your network. Several of your users call reporting that the end of month reports that the third shift administrator had placed on the export server last night were not replicating correctly. You look in *systemroot*\System32\Repl\Export and find the file, Feb_eom.doc. Why is the file not being replicated?

Answer Key

Procedure Answers

Page 580

▸ **To synchronize your files**

5. On the **Briefcase** menu, click **Update All**.

   Z should be the only file listed.

   Why was Z not updated?

   Because the original and the Briefcase copy were both modified, Briefcase is unable to determine which direction to copy the file.

Page 601

▸ **To verify file replication**

3. Under **Import Directories**, click **Manage**.

   What is the status of the Data subdirectory?

   If the files replicated successfully, the status is OK.

Review Answers

Page 606

1. You copy several files, including the file Qt_rpt01.doc, from a network server to the My Briefcase icon on your desktop computer. Then you copy My Briefcase to a floppy disk so that you can work at home on these files. The next day you copy My Briefcase back on to your desktop computer. When you open My Briefcase and use **Update All** to synchronize the files in My Briefcase with the copies of the files on the network server, all of the file except the Qt_rpt01.doc are updated on the server. What could be the problem?

   The original and the Briefcase copy of Qt_rpt01.doc were both modified, and Briefcase was unable to determine which direction to copy the file.

2. You are one of several administrators on your network. Several of your users call reporting that the end of month reports that the third shift administrator had placed on the export server last night were not replicating correctly. You look in *systemroot*\System32\Repl\Export and find the file, Feb_eom.doc. Why is the file not being replicated?

   You must put the files to be replicated in a subdirectory under the *systemroot*\System32\Repl\Export directory. Files placed in the directory are not replicated.

CHAPTER 17

The Windows NT Boot Process

Lesson 1 Overview of the Windows NT Boot Process . . . 610

Lesson 2 Troubleshooting the Boot Process . . . 621

Lesson 3 Last Known Good Configuration . . . 629

Lesson 4 Emergency Repair . . . 634

Review . . . 642

About This Chapter

Understanding the Microsoft Windows NT boot process facilitates restoring a system if a boot failure occurs. This chapter describes the boot process and introduces troubleshooting resources that help you solve Windows NT boot problems.

Before You Begin

To complete the lessons in this chapter, you must have:

- Two computers that meet the hardware and software requirements as specified in the Getting Started section of "About This Book."
- Completed all practices in Chapter 2, "Installing Windows NT."
- One blank, 1.44 MB high-density disk.

Lesson 1: Overview of the Windows NT Boot Process

The Windows NT boot process occurs in stages: the Power On Self Test (POST) process, the Initial Startup Process, the Boot loader process, the boot sequence, and the load phase. This lesson describes the boot process for the Intel x86 and RISC hardware platforms.

After this lesson, you will be able to:
- Identify the files necessary to boot Windows NT.
- Describe the boot sequence process on an Intel $x86$ platform.
- Describe the boot sequence process on a RISC platform.
- Identify the Windows NT load phases.

Estimated lesson time: 30 minutes

Files Required for Windows NT System Boot

The following illustration summarizes the files that are required for Windows NT system boot on Intel $x86$ platforms and those required by RISC-based systems. Note that some files are platform-specific while others are common to all platforms.

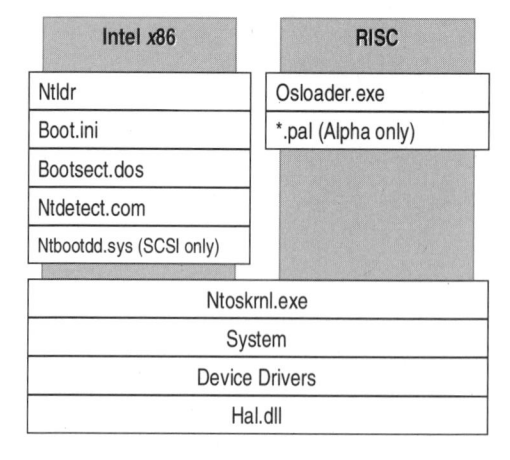

Intel x86	RISC
Ntldr	Osloader.exe
Boot.ini	*.pal (Alpha only)
Bootsect.dos	
Ntdetect.com	
Ntbootdd.sys (SCSI only)	

Ntoskrnl.exe
System
Device Drivers
Hal.dll

Intel x86 Boot Sequence Files

An Intel x86 computer requires all of the following files to be in the root folder of the system partition:

- *Ntldr.* This hidden, read-only system file loads the operating system.
- *Boot.ini.* This is a read-only system file, used to build the **Boot Loader Operating System Selection** menu on Intel x86-based computers.
- *Bootsect.dos.* This is a hidden system file loaded by Ntldr if another operating system, such as Microsoft MS-DOS, Microsoft Windows 95, or O/S 2 version 1.x, is selected instead of Windows NT. This file contains the boot sector that was on the hard disk before installing Windows NT.
- *Ntdetect.com.* This is a hidden, read-only system file used to examine the hardware available and to build a hardware list. This information is passed back to Ntldr to be added to the registry later in the boot process.
- *Ntbootdd.sys.* This hidden, read-only, system file is only on systems that boot from a SCSI hard disk and on which the BIOS on the SCSI adapter is disabled. This driver accesses devices attached to the SCSI adapter during the Windows NT boot sequence.

RISC Boot Sequence Files

RISC-based systems require the following two files:

- *Osloader.exe.* This is the operating system loader (equivalent to Ntldr on Intel x86-based computers).
- **.pal (Alpha only).* These files contain PAL code, software subroutines that provide an operating system with direct control of the processor.

Common Boot Sequence Files

The following files are common to both the Intel x86 and RISC platforms:

- *Ntoskrnl.exe.* This is the Windows NT kernel file, located in the *systemroot*\System32 folder.
- *System.* This file is a collection of system configuration settings. The file is in the *systemroot*\System32\Config folder. It controls which device drivers and services are loaded during the initialization process.
- *Device drivers.* These are files that support various device drivers, such as Ftdisk and Scsidisk.

The Windows NT Boot Sequence

In this section you now learn about the process of booting, and examine the steps that lead up to the Windows NT boot sequence, as well as the boot sequences for Intel x86 computers and those sequences for RISC-based computers.

The Intel *x*86 Boot Sequence

The following illustration presents a global look at the boot sequence for Intel systems.

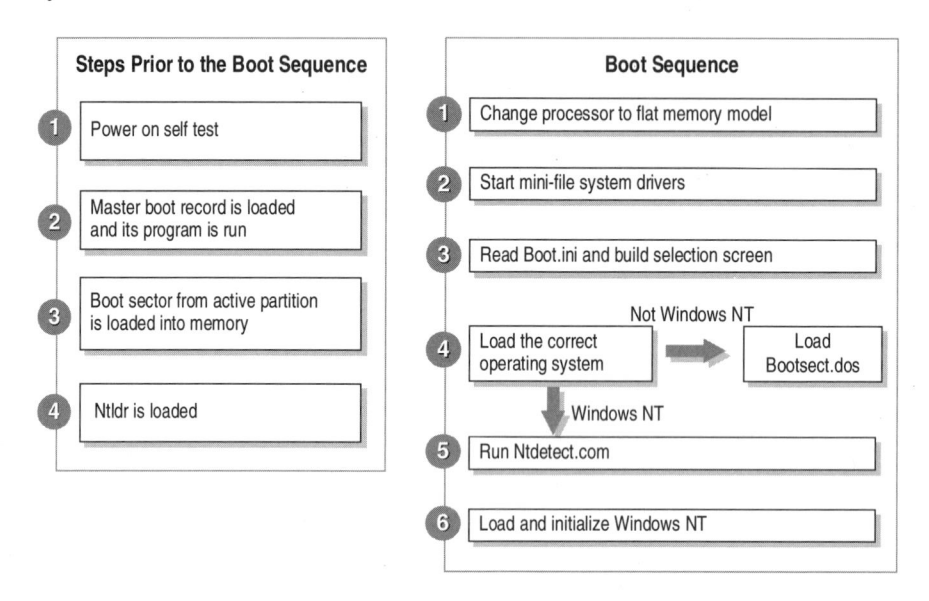

Steps Prior to the Boot Sequence
1. Power on self test
2. Master boot record is loaded and its program is run
3. Boot sector from active partition is loaded into memory
4. Ntldr is loaded

Boot Sequence
1. Change processor to flat memory model
2. Start mini-file system drivers
3. Read Boot.ini and build selection screen
4. Load the correct operating system → (Not Windows NT) Load Bootsect.dos
   ↓ Windows NT
5. Run Ntdetect.com
6. Load and initialize Windows NT

For Intel *x*86-based computers, several steps precede the actual boot sequence.

Steps Prior to the Boot Sequence

When you start a computer that has Windows NT installed on it, the computer initializes and locates the boot portion of the hard disk. The following steps are performed prior to the boot sequence:

1. Power On Self Test (POST) routines are run; for example, the memory check occurs.
2. The boot device is located, and the Master Boot Record (MBR) is loaded into memory. The program contained in the MBR is run.
3. The MBR program scans the Partition Boot Record (PBR) table to locate the active partition. The boot sector from the active partition is loaded into memory.
4. Ntldr is loaded and initialized from the boot sector.

Note When Windows NT is installed, it changes the boot sector so that Ntldr loads on system startup.

Boot Sequence

The boot sequence begins after Ntldr is loaded into memory. The boot sequence gathers information about hardware and drivers in preparation for the Windows NT load phases. The following files are used during the boot sequence: Ntldr, Boot.ini, Bootsect.dos, Ntdetect.com, and Ntoskrnl.exe. The boot sequence follows these steps:

1. Ntldr switches the processor from real mode into 32-bit flat memory mode. Ntldr, as is the case with any 32-bit code, requires this 32-bit flat memory mode before it can carry out any functions.

2. Ntldr starts the appropriate mini-file system drivers. Mini-file system drivers are built into Ntldr to find and load Windows NT from different file system formats (FAT or NTFS).

3. If there is a Boot.ini file, Ntldr reads it and displays the operating system selections contained within the Boot.ini file. This is called the **Boot Loader Operating System Selection** menu.

4. Ntldr loads the operating system. The operating system that is loaded is the one selected by the user or, if no selection is made, the default operating system.

Note If the user selects an operating system other than Windows NT, such as Microsoft Windows 95, Ntldr loads and runs Bootsect.dos and passes control to the selected operating system. The selected operating system then boots. At this point, the Windows NT boot process ends.

5. If Windows NT is selected, Ntldr runs Ntdetect.com. Ntdetect.com scans the hardware and then sends the list of detected hardware back to Ntldr for later inclusion in the registry under HKEY_LOCAL_MACHINE\HARDWARE.

6. Ntldr then loads Ntoskrnl.exe, Hal.dll, and the System hive.

    Ntldr scans the System hive and loads the device drivers configured to start at boot time.

    Finally, Ntldr starts Ntoskrnl.exe, at which point the boot process ends and the load phases begin.

Files Needed for Boot

The following table shows the files and their associated folders that are needed for the Windows NT boot sequence on Intel x86-based computers.

Intel x86-based file	Folder
Ntldr	system partition root
Boot.ini	system partition root
Bootsect.dos	system partition root
Ntdetect.com	system partition root
Ntbootdd.sys	system partition root
Ntoskrnl.exe	*systemroot*\System32
Hal.dll	*systemroot*\System32
System	*systemroot*\System32\Config
Device drivers	*systemroot*\System32\Drivers

The RISC Boot Sequence

The boot sequence for RISC-based computers is slightly different than Intel x86-based computers. The following illustration describes the Windows NT boot process for RISC-based computers.

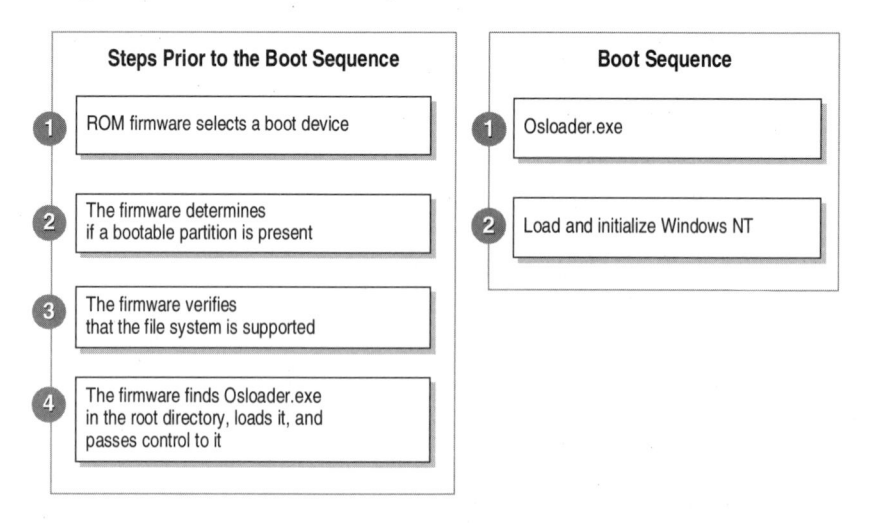

Steps Prior to the Boot Sequence
1. ROM firmware selects a boot device
2. The firmware determines if a bootable partition is present
3. The firmware verifies that the file system is supported
4. The firmware finds Osloader.exe in the root directory, loads it, and passes control to it

Boot Sequence
1. Osloader.exe
2. Load and initialize Windows NT

The Ntldr, Boot.ini, and Bootsect.dos files on Intel x86-based computers are not needed on RISC-based computers. On RISC-based computers, the Ntldr function is built into the firmware. The initial stages of loading the Windows NT operating system, that are controlled by Ntldr on Intel x86-based systems, are performed by Osloader.exe for RISC-based computers.

There is also no need for Ntdetect.com on RISC-based computers. The RISC POST routine collects the hardware information and passes it to Osloader.exe.

Steps Prior to the Boot Sequence

The following steps are performed before the boot sequence:

1. The ROM firmware selects a boot device by reading a boot precedence table from nonvolatile RAM. If the nonvolatile RAM is invalid or blank, the firmware either queries the user for the boot device, or defaults to a floppy or hard disk sequence.
2. For a hard disk boot, the firmware reads the Master Boot Record (MBR), and determines whether a system partition is present.
3. If a system partition exists, the firmware reads the first sector of the partition into memory. It then examines the BIOS Parameter Block (BPB) to determine whether the volume's file system is supported by the firmware.
4. If the file system is supported by the firmware, the firmware searches the root folder of the volume for Osloader.exe, loads the program, and passes control to it, along with a list of the available hardware on the system.

Boot Sequence

1. Osloader.exe loads Ntoskrnl.exe, Hal.dll, the *.pal files, and the System hive.
2. Osloader.exe scans the System hive and loads the device drivers configured to start at boot time.

Osloader.exe passes control to Ntoskrnl.exe, at which point the boot process ends and the load phases begin.

Files Needed for Boot

The following table shows the files and their associated folders that are needed for the boot sequence on RISC-based computers.

RISC file	Folder
Osloader.exe	os\nt40
Ntoskrnl.exe	*systemroot*\System32
Hal.dll	os\nt40
*.pal (Alpha only)	os\nt40
System	*systemroot*\System32\Config
Device drivers	*systemroot*\System32\Drivers

Windows NT Load Phases

The boot sequence for both the RISC and Intel $x86$-based platforms concludes when control is passed to Ntoskrnl.exe. At this point Windows NT begins to load and initializes in the following four phases: the kernel load phase, the kernel initialization phase, the services load phase, and the Win32 subsystem start phase.

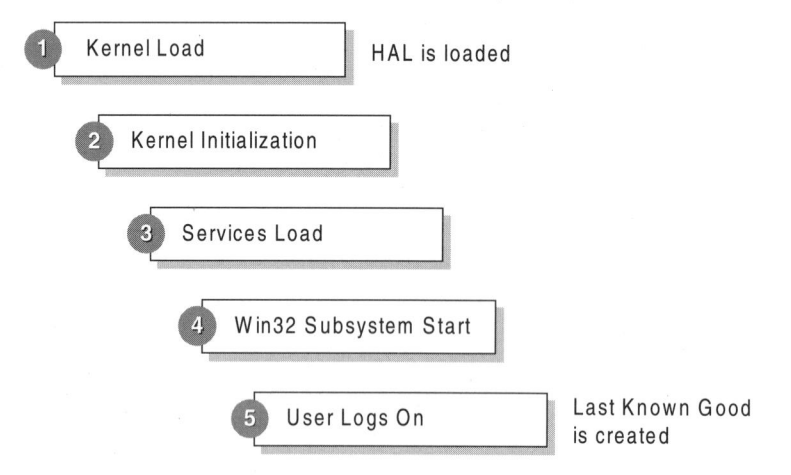

1. Kernel Load — HAL is loaded
2. Kernel Initialization
3. Services Load
4. Win32 Subsystem Start
5. User Logs On — Last Known Good is created

Kernel Load Phase

The kernel load phase begins as soon as Ntoskrnl.exe is loaded. The hardware abstraction layer (HAL), which hides platform-specific hardware issues from Windows NT, is loaded after the kernel.

Next, the System hive is loaded and scanned for drivers and services that should be loaded at this stage. These drivers and services are organized into groups. They are loaded into memory, but not initialized, in the order in which they appear beside "List" in the ServiceGroupOrder subkey. The ServiceGroupOrder subkey is found in the registry under:

HKEY_LOCAL_MACHINE\SYSTEM\CurrentControlSet\Control\ServiceGroupOrder

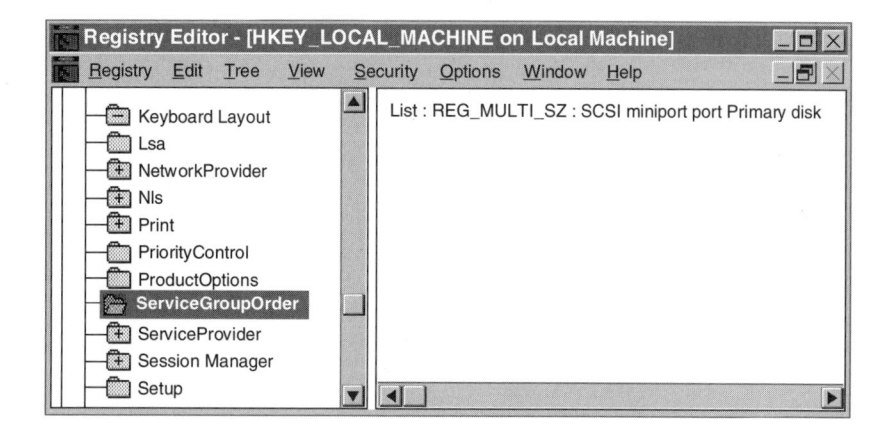

[Screenshot: Registry Editor - HKEY_LOCAL_MACHINE on Local Machine, showing subkeys Keyboard Layout, Lsa, NetworkProvider, Nls, Print, PriorityControl, ProductOptions, ServiceGroupOrder (selected), ServiceProvider, Session Manager, Setup; right pane shows "List : REG_MULTI_SZ : SCSI miniport port Primary disk"]

This portion of the boot sequence occurs when the screen clears after Ntdetect.com has run, and progress dots (...) are displayed across the top of the screen. It is possible to display the names of the drivers being loaded on this screen by adding an **/sos** switch to the appropriate operating system line in Boot.ini.

Kernel Initialization Phase

In this stage of the boot sequence the screen is painted blue. The kernel initialization phase initializes the kernel and the drivers that were loaded during the kernel load phase.

During this phase, the System hive is again scanned to determine which high-level drivers should be loaded. These drivers are initialized and loaded after the kernel has been initialized. The registry's CurrentControlSet is then saved, and the Clone control set is created and initialized, but not saved. The registry hardware list is then created, using the information from Ntdetect.com (for Intel-based computers) or Osloader.exe (for RISC-based computers).

Note A control set contains configuration data used to control the system, such as which device drivers and services to load and start. Control sets are stored in the registry as subkeys of HKEY_LOCAL_MACHINE\SYSTEM\Select.

For more information on the CurrentControlSet subkey, see Chapter 19, "What Happens When You Start Your Computer," in the *Workstation Resource Guide* of Books Online, or Chapter 23, "Overview of the Windows NT Registry," in the *Microsoft Windows NT Workstation Resource Kit*.

ErrorControl Values

If an error is encountered while loading and initializing the drivers for the system, action is taken based on the driver's **ErrorControl** value. There are four different **ErrorControl** levels:

- 0x0 – "Ignore"

    If an error occurs while loading a driver with this **ErrorControl** level, the boot sequence ignores the error and proceeds without displaying an error message.

- 0x1 – "Normal"

    If an error occurs while loading a driver with this **ErrorControl** level, an error message is displayed, but the boot sequence ignores the error and proceeds.

- 0x2 – "Severe"

    If an error occurs while loading a driver with this **ErrorControl** level, the boot sequence fails and then restarts using the LastKnownGood control set. If the boot sequence is currently using the LastKnownGood control set, the error is ignored and the boot sequence continues.

- 0x3 – "Critical"

    If an error occurs while loading a driver with this **ErrorControl** level, the boot sequence fails and then the boot sequence restarts using the LastKnownGood control set. However, if the LastKnownGood control set is being used and is causing the critical error, the boot sequence stops and an error message is displayed.

ErrorControl values are found in the registry under:

HKEY_LOCAL_MACHINE\SYSTEM\CurrentControlSet\Services\ *Name_of_service_or_driver***ErrorControl**

Services Load Phase

The services load phase starts the Session Manager (Smss.exe), which starts the higher-order subsystems and services for Windows NT. Session Manager carries out the instructions under the following four registry entries:

- BootExecute data item
- Memory Management key
- DOS Devices key
- Subsystems key

BootExecute Data Item

Session Manager immediately reads and carries out the list of programs in: HKEY_LOCAL_MACHINE\SYSTEM\CurrentControlSet\Control\Session Manager**BootExecute**

The default entry is: **autocheck autochk ***

Autocheck.exe is the boot-time version of Chkdsk. In this example, the wildcard (*) causes an automatic check of each partition. During system boot, Autocheck displays the check disk information about each partition. This display occurs on the blue screen portion of system boot and is your indication that the services load phase has started.

You can modify the entry for BootExecute. If this entry is changed to read **autocheck autochk /p ***, the **/p** forces the equivalent of a **Chkdsk /f** on each partition on every subsequent restart of the system.

The **BootExecute** value can also contain more than one command. Therefore, you could add a second command, such as the following:

autocheck autochk * autoconv \DosDevices\d: /FS:ntfs

In this example, the second command causes drive d to be converted to NTFS on the next system boot.

Memory Management Key

After all of the checks have been successfully performed on the system's hard disks, Session Manager sets up the paging files defined in:

HKEY_LOCAL_MACHINE\SYSTEM\CurrentControlSet\Control\Session Manager\Memory Management**PagingFiles**

When the partitions are checked and the paging files are set up, the CurrentControlSet and the Clone control set are written to the registry.

DOS Devices Key

Next, the Session Manager creates symbolic links. These links direct certain classes of commands to the correct component in the file system. For example,

PRN : REG_SZ : \DosDevices\LPT1

This link redirects all output sent to PRN to LPT1.

Subsystems Key

The last step performed by Session Manager is to load the required subsystems, as defined in the registry in:

HKEY_LOCAL_MACHINE\SYSTEM\CurrentControlSet\Control\Session Manager\SubSystems**Required**

By default, the only required subsystem is the Win32 subsystem, which appears as Windows in the **Required** data item.

Win32 Subsystem Start Phase

When the Win32 subsystem starts, it automatically starts Winlogon.exe, which starts the Local Security Authority (Lsass.exe) and displays the CTRL+ALT+DEL logon dialog box.

Next, the Service Controller (Screg.exe) is run, which makes a final pass through the registry looking for services that are marked to load automatically, such as the Workstation and Server services. The services that are loaded during this phase are loaded based on their dependencies, that is, their DependOnGroup or DependOnService entries.

User Logs On

The boot is not considered *good* until a user successfully logs on to the system.

Note After a successful logon, the Clone control set is copied to the LastKnownGood control set. The LastKnownGood control set is explained later in this chapter.

Lesson 2: Troubleshooting the Boot Process

Most problems related to booting Windows NT are caused by required files that are either missing or corrupted. Windows NT may also fail to boot if incorrect system configuration changes are made.

After this lesson, you will be able to:
- Identify common Windows NT boot process errors.
- Explain the function of the Boot.ini file.
- Identify troubleshooting strategies related to the Boot.ini file.
- Create a Windows NT boot disk.

Estimated lesson time: 45 minutes

Common Boot Process Errors

The errors presented in this section are the result of files that are missing. Some common boot error messages and symptoms are as follows:

- If the Ntldr file is missing, the following message appears before the **Boot Loader Operating System Selection** menu:

    ```
    BOOT: Couldn't find NTLDR
    Please insert another disk.
    ```

- If Ntdetect.com is missing, the following message appears after the **Boot Loader Operating System Selection** menu (on the same screen):

    ```
    NTDETECT V4.0 Checking Hardware...
    NTDETECT failed
    ```

- If Ntoskrnl.exe is missing, the following message appears after the Last Known Good prompt:

    ```
    Windows NT could not start because the following file is missing
    or corrupt:
    \winnt root\system32\ntoskrnl.exe
    Please re-install a copy of the above file.
    ```

- If Bootsect.dos is missing in a multiple-boot configuration, the following message appears after the **Boot Loader Operating System Selection** menu (on the same screen), when the user attempts to boot an MS-DOS-based system:

    ```
    I/O Error accessing boot sector file
    multi(0)disk(0)rdisk(0)partition(1):\bootss
    ```

In all of these cases, the Emergency Repair process, which is presented later in this chapter, can be used to recover the system and boot files, and to return the computer to a bootable state.

Note Bootsect.dos stores partition information specific to the computer. This file cannot be borrowed from another computer.

The Boot.ini File

If Windows NT does not start, the problem may be that the path for the *systemroot* folder, found in the Boot.ini file, is incorrect. If that is the case, you must edit the Boot.ini file.

However, when Windows NT is installed, it creates Boot.ini in the root of the active partition as a read-only, hidden, system text file. If you want to edit the Boot.ini file by using a text editor, you need to make the file visible, and you need to turn the Read-only option off to be able to make changes to it.

Changing the Attributes of Boot.ini

You can change the attributes of Boot.ini by using My Computer, Windows NT Explorer, or the command prompt.

Using My Computer or Windows NT Explorer to Change the Attributes of Boot.ini

1. Double-click drive C where Boot.ini is located.

   You can not see the Boot.ini file if its *hidden* attribute is set.

2. On the **View** menu, click **Options**.

3. In the **Options** dialog box, click the **View** tab.

4. Click **Show all files,** and then click **OK**.

   The "hidden" files now appear in the folder list.

5. Click **Boot.ini**.

6. On the **File** menu, click **Properties**.

7. In the **Attributes** box of the **General** tab, clear the **Read-only** check box, and then click **OK**.

Using Command Prompt to Change the Attributes of Boot.ini

- At the command prompt, type **attrib -s -h -r boot.ini**

Changing the Path to Windows NT System Files

If you have to change the path to the Windows NT system files, make sure you edit both the default path and the operating system path statements. If you change one but not both, a new choice is added to the **Boot Loader Operating System Selection** menu. The new choice has a DEFAULT designator next to it, indicating that this choice attempts to load the default operating system from the path designated on the default= line of the [boot loader] section of Boot.ini.

Components of the Boot.ini File

Boot.ini is a system file that has two sections: [boot loader] and [operating systems].

The following is an example of a Boot.ini file.

```
[boot loader]
timeout=30
default=multi(0)disk(0)rdisk(0)partition(1)\WINNT
[operating systems]
multi(0)disk(0)rdisk(0)partition(1)\WINNT="Windows NT
Workstation Version 4.0"
multi(0)disk(0)rdisk(0)partition(1)\WINNT="Windows NT
Workstation Version 4.0 [VGA mode]" /basevideo
C:\="Microsoft Windows"
```

[boot loader]

The [boot loader] section specifies the default operating system to start and a timeout value specifying how long to wait before starting automatically. The boot loader section has two parameters, as shown in the following table.

Parameter	Description
timeout	The number of seconds during which the user can select an operating system after the **Boot Loader Operating System Selection** menu appears. If the user does not select an operating system during this time, the default operating system starts.
	If timeout= is set to 0, the **Boot Loader Operating System Selection** menu may appear briefly or not at all, depending on processor speed, and the default operating system boots.
Default	The path to the default operating system that loads when the timeout reaches 0 (zero).

[operating systems]

The [operating systems] section of Boot.ini is a list of operating systems that are displayed in the **Boot Loader Operating System Selection** menu. Each entry includes the path to the operating system, the name displayed in the **Boot Loader Operating System Selection** menu (the text between the quotes), and optional parameters.

For example, if you installed Windows NT 4.0 Workstation, there will be two listings for Windows NT Workstation 4.0. The second listing provides an optional parameter of /BASEVIDEO to allow the user to boot Windows NT Workstation with a standard VGA driver. There will also be an entry of C:\="MS-DOS" on Microsoft MS-DOS-based dual-boot systems.

Troubleshooting Boot.ini Problems

You can use Control Panel to change some of the information in the Boot.ini file, such as the default operating system and the length of time allowed for you to choose which operating system to boot. You can also manually edit the Boot.ini file. However, manual editing errors may prevent Windows NT from booting properly.

The following sections discuss problems that can occur with Boot.ini.

The Boot.ini File Is Missing

If the Boot.ini file is missing, Ntldr automatically tries to boot Windows NT. If Windows NT is installed in the default folder of multi(0)disk(0)rdisk(0)partition(1)\Winnt or scsi(0)disk(0)rdisk(0)partition(1)\Winnt, Windows NT boots successfully. If Windows NT is installed in a folder other than the default, such as Windows, the following message appears after the Last Known Good prompt:

```
Windows NT could not start because the following file is missing
or corrupt:
<winnt root>\system32\ntoskrnl.exe
Please reinstall a copy of the above file.
```

A New Operating System Appears on the Boot Loader Operating System Selection Menu

If the path name for the *default* parameter in the [boot loader] section of Boot.ini does not match any of the path names in the [operating system] section of Boot.ini, the menu selection "NT (default)" appears. This selection is highlighted and loads unless the user selects another operating system.

Invalid Windows NT Path Name

If part of the path name to Windows NT is incorrect in the Boot.ini file, the following message appears:

```
Windows NT could not start because the following file is missing
or corrupt:
<winnt root>\system32\ntoskrnl.exe
Please reinstall a copy of the above file.
```

Invalid Device in Windows NT Path

If there is an invalid device in the path to Windows NT in the Boot.ini file, the following message appears:

```
OS Loader V4.0

Windows NT could not start because of a computer disk hardware
configuration problem.
Could not read from the selected boot disk. Check boot path
and disk hardware.
Please check the Windows NT (TM) documentation about hardware
disk configuration and your hardware reference manuals for
additional information.
```

In all of these cases, Boot.ini can be edited to fix the problem, or an Emergency Repair can restore the Boot.ini file.

Creating a Windows NT Boot Disk

If Windows NT fails to boot because a file is missing or corrupt in the system partition, a boot disk can be used to boot the system and restore the corrupt or missing file or files to the hard disk.

Required Boot Files

The files required on the boot disk depend on the processor in the computer. The following table shows the boot files required for Intel x86-based and RISC-based computers.

Platform	Required Windows NT boot files
Intel x86-based computers	Ntldr, Ntdetect.com, Boot.ini, Ntbootdd.sys (for computers with a BIOS-disabled SCSI adapter)
RISC-based computers	Osloader.exe, Hal.dll, *.pal (Alpha only)

Precautions

Observe the following precautions when creating a Windows NT boot disk:

- A Windows NT boot disk must be formatted on a computer running Windows NT, so that the boot sector on the disk can find and run Ntldr.
- If the computer is Intel x86-based, the Boot.ini file on the boot disk may need to be modified to reflect the ARC path to the system partition on the failed computer. This path includes the disk controller, disk drive, and partition to the Windows NT system files.

Note For additional information on ARC paths, see Chapter 7, "Managing Fault Tolerance."

- After the disk is created, insert it in the disk drive and use it to start Windows NT. It is important to note that only certain files are loaded from a floppy disk. All other files are accessed from the hard disk of the computer running Windows NT. If the Windows NT kernel (Ntoskrnl.exe) or other files are corrupt or missing, the boot disk is of no use. If this is the case, use the Emergency Repair process, as discussed later in this chapter, to restore the missing or corrupt files.

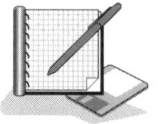

Practice

In these procedures, you create and test a Windows NT boot disk for Workstation1.

Note Complete these procedures on Workstation1.

▶ **To change attributes for Windows NT boot files**

1. Log on to the domain as Administrator.
2. In Windows NT Explorer, click drive C.
3. On the **View** menu, click **Options**.
4. Click **Show all files**.
5. Clear the **Hide file extensions for known file types** check box, and then click **OK**.
6. Select the following files: boot.ini, bootsect.dos, Ntdetect.com, ntldr, and Ntbootdd.sys (only if it exists).
7. On the **File** menu, click **Properties**.
8. Clear the **Hidden** and **Read-only** check boxes, and then click **OK**.

▸ To create a Windows NT boot disk

1. Format a floppy disk using Windows NT Explorer, or go to a command prompt and use the **Format.exe** command.

2. Copy the following files from the root of drive C to the root of drive A.

   Ntldr

   Ntdetect.com

   Boot.ini

   Bootsect.dos (only if it exists)

   Ntbootdd.sys (only if it exists)

3. Do not remove the disk from the drive.

▸ To test the Windows NT boot disk

1. Shut down and then restart your computer using the Windows NT boot disk you just created.

   Did Windows NT start successfully?

   _____

   _____

   _____

2. Remove the floppy from the disk drive, and then restart Workstation1.

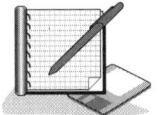

Practice

In these procedures, you rename system files to produce booting problems. You then restart your computer to observe error messages for specific problems.

Note Complete these procedures on Workstation1.

▸ To simulate missing files during system boot

In this procedure, you rename four files that are used to start Windows NT. This enables you to simulate the effects of missing files, as presented in the next procedure.

1. Log on to the domain as Administrator.

2. In Windows NT Explorer, click drive C.

3. Rename each of the following files by adding a .lab extension, for example, Boot.ini.lab. Be sure to write down the new name.

   Boot.ini

   Bootsect.dos

   Ntdetect.com

   Ntldr

▶ **To observe the effect of missing system files**

In this procedure, you observe files in the boot sequence fail. You see an error message that gives appropriate information about the file that failed to load. In the following table, record the error message and the file that you think has failed.

1. Shut down and then restart the computer.

   What error message do you see? Record your answer in the following table.

   What file is missing? Record your answer in the following table.

2. Reboot the computer using the Windows NT Boot Disk that you created earlier, log on as Administrator, and then correct the problem by renaming the file back to its original name.

3. Remove the Windows NT Boot disk from drive A.

   If your solution is successful, the next boot process stops at the next missing file in the boot sequence.

4. Repeat steps 1–3 in this procedure, until you have a successful system boot.

Note The last missing file requires you to select another operating system, such as MS-DOS, from the **OS Loader Operating System Selection** menu.

Error message	Missing file
_____	_____
_____	_____
_____	_____
_____	_____

Lesson 3: Last Known Good Configuration

After a user has successfully logged on to Windows NT, current configuration information from the registry key HKEY_LOCAL_MACHINE is copied to a control set called *Last Known Good*. Last Known Good is a copy of the most recent control set used to successfully boot Windows NT.

If you change the Windows NT configuration and then have problems rebooting, the Last Known Good configuration stored in the registry can be used to boot Windows NT.

After this lesson, you will be able to:
- Describe the Last Known Good configuration and its function.
- Identify the situations in which you would use the Last Known Good configuration.
- Start Windows NT using the Last Known Good configuration.

Estimated lesson time: 25 minutes

The Function of Last Known Good Configuration

Windows NT provides two configurations in which you can start your computer:

- *Default*. The configuration that was saved when you *shut down* the computer.
- *Last Known Good*. The configuration that was saved when you last successfully *logged on* to your computer.

The configurations are stored as control sets in the registry key HKEY_LOCAL_MACHINE\SYSTEM. If you log on and then make changes to your configuration, such as adding drivers, changing services, or changing hardware, the two control sets will contain different information. However, as soon as you shut down, restart Windows NT, and log on again, the information in these control sets will be the same.

Therefore, if you are having problems with startup, and think the problems might be related to the changes that you made to your configuration, *do not log on*. Instead, shut down the computer and restart it. Then, select Last Known Good from the **Hardware Profile/Last Known Good** menu.

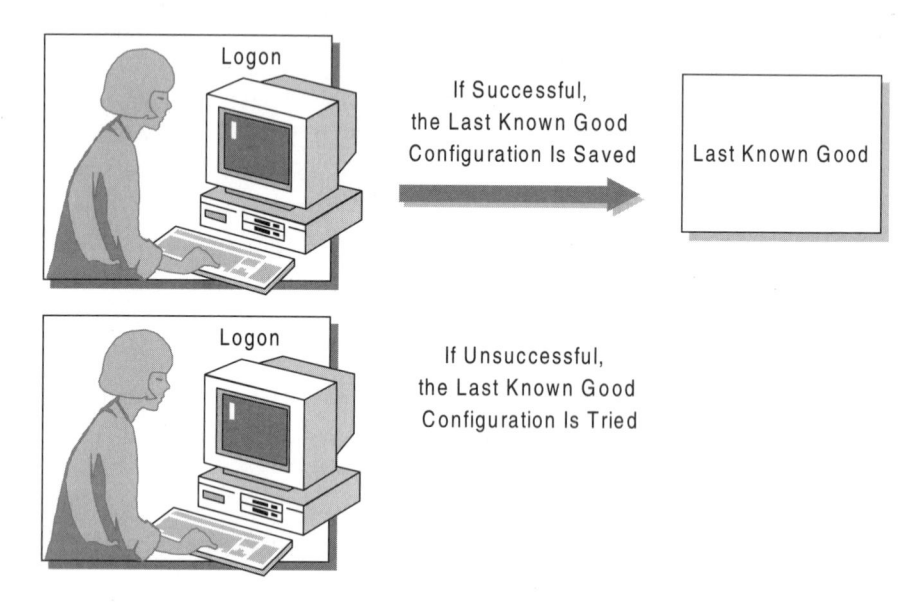

When to Use the Last Known Good Configuration

When Windows NT is selected from the **Boot Loader Operating System Selection** menu, the system loads the default control set. There are only two conditions that cause the system to load the Last Known Good configuration:

- When the system is recovering from a severe or critical device driver loading error.
- When the Last Known Good configuration is selected during the boot process.

Use the Last Known Good control set to recover from the following types of problems:

- You install a new device driver, restart Windows NT, and the system stops responding. The Last Known Good control set enables you to start Windows NT because it does not contain any reference to the new, faulty driver.
- You install a new video driver and are able to restart the system. However, you cannot see anything, because the new video resolution is incompatible with your video adapter. Do not try to log on. If you have the option to shut down the computer without logging on, do so. If that option is not available, you need to restart your computer by turning it off or using the reset button. Wait for all disk activity to stop before you initiate the restart, especially if the computer has FAT volumes.
- You accidentally disable a critical device driver (such as the SCSIport driver). Windows NT is not able to start and automatically reverts to the Last Known Good control set.

Using the Last Known Good control set does *not* help in the following situations:

- Any problem that is unrelated to changes in control set information, such as problems arising from incorrectly configured user profiles or incorrect file permissions.
- After you logged on after making changes. Here, the Last Known Good control set has already been updated to include the changes.
- Switching between different hardware profiles, such as docked and undocked laptops. The Last Known Good control set is only a method to switch between configuration information in the registry.
- Startup failures caused by hardware failures or missing or corrupted files.

In summary, booting from the Last Known Good configuration provides a way to recover from problems such as a newly added driver that may be incorrect for your hardware. It does not solve problems caused by corrupted or missing drivers or files. The Last Known Good option is used only in cases of incorrect configurations.

Important If the Last Known Good configuration is used, all configuration changes you made the last time you were logged on to Windows NT are lost.

How to Use the Last Known Good Configuration

When you have selected the version of Windows NT to start, and the boot loader has collected hardware information, you see the following screen:

OS Loader V4.00

Once you see the OS Loader V4.00 prompt, you have only a few seconds to press the SPACEBAR to invoke the **Hardware Profile/Configuration Recovery** menu.

After you press the SPACEBAR, the **Hardware Profile/Configuration Recovery** menu appears, from which you can do the following:

- Select a hardware profile to be used when Windows NT is started.
- Switch to the Last Known Good configuration.
- Restart the computer.

To switch to the Last Known Good Configuration, press L.

To exit this menu and restart your computer, press F3.

The boot loader uses the registry information that it saved at the completion of the last successful startup to configure this startup. All configuration changes that were made since your system was last successfully started are lost.

Practice

In these procedures, you disable the keyboard driver and use the Last Known Good configuration to successfully reboot your computer.

Note Complete these procedures on Workstation1.

▶ **To disable the keyboard driver**

1. Log on to the domain as Administrator.
2. Start the Devices program in Control Panel.
3. Click **i8042 Keyboard and PS/2 Mouse Port**. If this device is not listed, find your correct keyboard and mouse driver device in the list, and then click it.
4. Click **Startup**.
5. In the **Device** dialog box, click **Disabled**, and then click **OK**.

   A dialog box appears, warning you that changing the startup type for this device may leave the system in an unusable state.
6. Click **Yes**.
7. Click **Close**.
8. Shut down the computer.

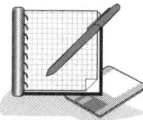

▶ To test the faulty configuration

1. Restart Windows NT Workstation.
2. When the Begin Logon window appears, attempt to log on.

   Were you successful?

   _____

   Why?

   _____

3. Use the power switch to shut off your computer.

▶ To restore the Last Known Good configuration

1. Restart Windows NT Workstation, and when the Press spacebar now to invoke Hardware Profile/Last Known Good prompt appears, press the SPACEBAR.
2. When the **Hardware Profile/Configuration Recovery** menu appears, press L to use the Last Known Good configuration.
3. Press ENTER to select the original configuration.
4. When the Begin Logon window appears, attempt to log on as Administrator.

   Were you successful?

   _____

   Why?

   _____

Lesson 4: Emergency Repair

If Windows NT fails to boot or function correctly, and using the Last Known Good configuration does not solve the problem, you can use the Emergency Repair process in Windows NT Setup to restore Windows NT.

After this lesson, you will be able to:
- Create an Emergency Repair Disk.
- Complete the emergency repair process to restore Windows NT.

Estimated lesson time: 40 minutes

Creating and Updating an Emergency Repair Disk

If you ever have a serious system problem, your best recourse is the Emergency Repair folder or disk.

The Emergency Repair folder and disk are used to return a computer running Windows NT to the state of the last Emergency Repair update. The disk can repair missing or corrupt Windows NT files and restore the registry. Restored registry files include the Security Accounts Manager (SAM) database, security information, disk configuration information, software registry entries, and other system information. The Emergency Repair folder and disk also include a Setup.log file to verify files on the system.

The Repair Disk utility (Rdisk.exe) is used to either update repair information or create a new Emergency Repair Disk. Rdisk.exe is located in the *systemroot*\System32 folder, and has two options:

- Update Repair Info
- Create Repair Disk

Note In order to run Rdisk.exe, the user must be a member of the Administrators or Power Users group or have the appropriate privileges. For non-Administrators or non-Power Users, Rdisk.exe *appears* to work, but as it is saving files, the user gets an error message indicating that the utility could not save all configuration files.

The Update Repair Info Option

The Update Repair Info process overwrites the files in the *systemroot*\Repair folder. During the update process, a $$hive$$.tmp file is created. This file temporarily stores the registry information before it is copied to the appropriate file.

Note Because the Update Repair Info option deletes and creates files under *systemroot*\Repair, if Windows NT is installed on an NTFS partition, the user performing the update must have the appropriate permissions to the folder.

After the contents of the *systemroot*\Repair folder are updated, the repair process prompts the user to create an Emergency Repair Disk. This option formats a floppy disk and creates an Emergency Repair Disk. This has the same result as selecting the Create Repair Disk option.

When the contents of the *systemroot*\Repair folder are updated, copies of Autoexec.nt and Config.nt are also placed in the folder.

Note The Emergency Repair Disk utility (**rdisk**) does not back up the Default, SAM, and Security files, which contain the user accounts and file security, unless you specify the **/s** parameter with the **rdisk** command at the command prompt.

The Create Repair Disk Option

The Create Repair Disk option requests that a disk that can be formatted be inserted in drive A. If the current repair disk is used, the Create Repair Disk option does *not* update the disk; it reformats it and creates a new repair disk.

Setup.log

The Setup.log file is located in the Emergency Repair folder and on the Emergency Repair Disk. Setup.log is used to check the validity of the Windows NT files on the system.

Files Included on the Emergency Repair Disk

The Emergency Repair Disk contains the files listed in the following table.

File	Description
Setup.log	An information file used for verifying the files installed on the system. This file is a read-only, hidden system file. By default, this file does not appear in Windows NT Explorer.
System._	A copy of the System hive from the registry.
Sam._	A copy of the Security Accounts Manager (SAM) from the registry.
Security._	A copy of the Security hive from the registry.
Software._	A copy of the Software hive from the registry.
Default._	A copy of the Default hive from the registry.
Config.nt	The Windows NT version of the Config.sys file used when initializing an NTVDM.
Autoexec.nt	The Windows NT version of the Autoexec.bat file used when initializing an NTVDM.
Ntuser.da_	A compressed version of *systemroot*\Profiles\Default user\Ntuser.dat.

Note The files with an underscore extension (._ or .da_) are compressed versions of the actual files. They can be uncompressed in the same manner as the Windows NT files on the source disks, by using the **expand** utility.

The Emergency Repair Process

This section discusses using the emergency repair process to restore a failed system.

To perform the emergency repair process, you need the following:

- The original installation compact disc, in case any files are detected as missing or corrupt.
- If the Security Account Manager (SAM) database is replaced, the Administrator password stored on the Emergency Repair Disk.

Using the Emergency Repair Process

To repair a Windows NT installation, Windows NT Setup needs either the configuration information that is saved in the *systemroot*\Repair folder or on the Emergency Repair Disk created when you installed Windows NT (or created later using the **rdisk** utility).

If your system becomes corrupt and you cannot repair it using the Emergency Repair Disk or using the information in the Repair folder, you must reinstall Windows NT from the original installation source.

> **Note** For more information about restoring your system, see Chapter 20, "Preparing for and Performing Recovery," in the *Microsoft Windows NT Workstation Resource Kit*.

Restoring Windows NT Server on an Intel *x*86-based Computer

To restore Windows NT on an Intel *x*86-based computer using the repair process in Windows NT Setup, do the following:

1. If you installed Windows NT using the original Setup disks or compact disc, or using Winnt.exe, start Setup just as you did originally. That is, insert the Setup Boot disk in drive A and start the computer.

   If these disks cannot be located, create new disks from the Windows NT compact disc by running either Winnt.exe or Winnt32.exe and use the **/ox** switch. The **/ox** switch creates the Windows NT Setup disks without performing the entire installation.

2. In the text-based Setup screen that asks whether you want to install Windows NT or repair files, type **r** to indicate that you want to repair your Windows NT files.

3. Windows NT Setup prompts you for the Emergency Repair Disk. If you do not have one, Setup presents a list of the Windows NT installations that it found on your computer and lets you select the one you want to repair.

4. Follow the instructions on the screen, inserting the Emergency Repair Disk (if you have one) in drive A and providing any other Windows NT Setup disks as requested.

5. When the final message appears, remove the Emergency Repair Disk from drive A, and then press CTRL+ALT+DEL to restart your computer.

Restoring Windows NT on a RISC-based Computer

To restore Windows NT on a RISC-based computer with an Emergency Repair Disk, do the following:

1. Start the Windows NT Setup program as instructed in your manufacturer-supplied documentation. (How you start Windows NT Setup depends on the type of RISC-based computer you have.)

2. In the text-based Setup screen that asks whether you want to install Windows NT or repair files, type **r** to indicate that you want to repair your Windows NT files.

3. Follow the instructions on the screen, inserting the Emergency Repair Disk (if you have one) in drive A if Setup prompts you for it.

4. When the final message appears, remove the Emergency Repair Disk, and then press ENTER to restart your computer.

Caution Be sure to update the system repair information in the Repair folder on your hard disk and to create and maintain an up-to-date Emergency Repair Disk. This way, your system repair information includes new configuration information such as drive letter assignments, stripe sets, volume sets, mirror sets, and so on. Otherwise, drives can be inaccessible in the event of a system failure.

The repair process in Windows NT Setup enables you to choose what you want to repair. Four options during setup determine which emergency repair tasks are performed:

- *Inspect registry files.* Setup replaces one or more registry files with the files that were created when Windows NT was first installed, or when the Emergency Repair folder or disk was last updated. All changes made to the system since installation or the last update to the repair files are lost.

- *Inspect startup environment.* Select this option if Windows NT is installed but does not appear in the list of bootable systems. For this option, the Emergency Repair Disk is needed.

- *Verify Windows NT system files.* Select this option to verify that each file in the installation is good and matches the file that was installed from the distribution files. The repair process also verifies that files needed to start, such as Ntldr and Ntoskrnl.exe, are present and valid. When the repair process determines that the file on the disk does not match what was installed, it displays a message that identifies the file and asks whether you want to replace it.

- *Inspect boot sector.* Select this option if no system that is installed on the computer boots. Setup copies a new boot sector to the hard disk.

Note For more information about **rdisk** see the Windows NT Server *Start Here* book.

Practice

In these procedures, you use the **rdisk** utility to update your Emergency Repair Disk. Then, you perform an Emergency Repair to inspect your boot sector.

Note These procedures require you to have a CD-ROM drive in your computer, and that you have a *Windows NT Workstation 4.0* compact disc.

Note Complete these procedures on Workstation1.

▶ **To update the Emergency Repair Disk**

1. Log on to the domain as Administrator.
2. On the **Start** menu, click **Run**.
3. Type **rdisk** and then click **OK**.
4. Click **Update Repair Info**.

   A **Repair Disk Utility** dialog box appears, stating that the repair information that was saved when you installed the system or when you last ran this utility will be deleted. This message indicates that the information in the Repair folder will be updated to match the current system configuration.

5. Click **Yes** to continue this operation.

   After the configuration is saved, a **Repair Disk Utility** dialog box appears, stating that you can create an Emergency Repair Disk that contains a copy of the repair information in your system.

6. Click **Yes** to create an Emergency Repair Disk.
7. When prompted, insert the Emergency Repair Disk that was created during installation, and then click **OK**.

   The disk is formatted and the updated repair information is copied.

8. When updating is complete, click **Exit**.
9. Remove the Emergency Repair Disk from drive A.

▶ **To use the Emergency Repair process**

1. Restart your computer using the Windows NT Workstation Setup Boot disk.
2. When prompted, insert the Windows NT Workstation Setup Disk #2.
3. At the Welcome to Setup screen, type **r** to perform the Emergency Repair.

   The following options appear:
   ```
   [X] Inspect registry files
   [X] Inspect startup environment
   [X] Verify Windows NT system files
   [X] Inspect boot sector
       Continue (perform selected tasks)
   ```
4. Select **Inspect boot sector** and clear the other choices.
5. Choose **Continue (perform selected tasks)**, and then press ENTER.
6. Press ENTER to have Setup detect your mass storage devices.
7. When prompted, insert the Windows NT Workstation Setup Disk #3, and then press ENTER.
8. When prompted, press ENTER to confirm the detected mass storage devices.
9. When prompted, press ENTER to confirm that you have an Emergency Repair Disk.
10. When prompted, insert the Emergency Repair Disk, and then press ENTER.

    Setup completes the repair.
11. Remove the Emergency Repair Disk from drive A.
12. Press ENTER to restart your computer and boot Windows NT Workstation.

Summary

The following information summarizes the key points in this chapter:

- The Windows NT boot sequence requires the presence of a number of system files. For example, *Ntldr* is the main component for loading Windows NT on Intel-based computers, and *Osloader* is the main boot component for RISC-based computers.

- Windows NT is loaded and initialized in four phases: the kernel load phase, the kernel initialization phase, the services load phase, and the Win32 subsystem start phase.

- If Windows NT fails to boot, there are several troubleshooting techniques you can try to correct the problem, such as editing the Boot.ini file, using the Last Known Good configuration, and trying an Emergency Repair.

  - The problem may be that the path for the *systemroot* folder, found in the Boot.ini file, is incorrect. If that is the case, you must edit the Boot.ini file.

  - Booting from the Last Known Good configuration provides a way to recover from problems such as a newly added driver that may be incorrect for your system. It does not solve problems caused by corrupted or missing drivers or files. The Last Known Good option is used only in cases of incorrect configurations.

  - The Emergency Repair folder and disk are used to return a computer running Windows NT to the state of the last Emergency Repair update. The Emergency Repair folder and disk also include a Setup.log file to verify files on the system.

Review

1. One of the computers that you support can no longer boot to MS-DOS, even though it appears on the boot menu. You have identified the problem as a corrupted MS-DOS boot sector. Which file, containing the old MS-DOS boot sector, should you suspect has been corrupted?

2. You created a Windows NT boot disk that contains the following files:
   - Ntldr
   - Ntdetect.com
   - Boot.ini
   - Ntbootdd.sys

   When you try to boot Windows NT with the disk, you receive the following error message:

   ```
   Non-System disk or disk error
   Replace and press any key when ready
   ```

   What did you do wrong?

3. You change the settings for your network adapter card. When you reboot, you receive the following message: "One or more services failed to start." When you attempt to log on you receive a message stating that a domain controller could not be found, but you were logged on using cached credentials. After logging on, you discover that you cannot connect to network resources. You shut down your computer and restart using the Last Known Good configuration, but the same behavior results. What went wrong?

4. You need to perform an emergency repair on your computer that is running Windows NT Workstation. You have a CD-ROM drive in your computer, however, you originally installed Windows NT over the network and you do not have the original setup disks. You still have the original Windows NT Workstation compact disc, however, and can access it on other computers. How can you perform the emergency repair?

_____

_____

_____

5. You receive a call from someone who tells you that he forgot the administrator password. He used the Emergency Repair Disk to restore the original administrator password, and now no one else can log on to the system. What happened and how can he correct the problem?

_____

_____

_____

_____

6. You have restarted a computer running Windows NT Workstation, and the following message appears:

```
BOOT: Couldn't find NTLDR
Please insert another disk
```

You suspect that Ntldr is missing or corrupt. How can you replace the file?

_____

Answer Key

Procedure Answers

Page 627

▶ **To test the Windows NT boot disk**

1. Shut down and then restart your computer using the Windows NT boot disk you just created.

   Did Windows NT start successfully?

   Yes. The boot disk was created properly.

   No. Verify that you formatted the floppy disk using Windows NT, and then compare the files on your boot disk with those listed in the preceding procedure.

Page 628

▶ **To observe the effect of missing system files**

1. Shut down and then restart the computer.

   What error message do you see? Record your answer in the following table.

   What file is missing? Record your answer in the following table.

Error message	Missing file
BOOT: Couldn't find NTLDR Please insert another disk	Ntldr
NTDETECT failed	Ntdetect.com
No error message, but the Operating System Select menu failed to appear	Boot.ini
I/O Error accessing boot sector file multi(0)disk(0)rdisk(0)partition(1)\BOOTSS	Bootsect.dos

Page 633

▶ **To test the faulty configuration**

2. When the Begin Logon window appears, attempt to log on.

   Were you successful?

   No.

   Why?

   The keyboard device driver is not running.

▶ **To restore the Last Known Good configuration**

4. When the Begin Logon window appears, attempt to log on as Administrator.

   Were you successful?

   Yes.

   Why?

   Because the Last Known Good configuration contained the correct startup setting for the keyboard device driver.

Review Answers

1. One of the computers that you support can no longer boot to MS-DOS, even though it appears on the boot menu. You have identified the problem as a corrupted MS-DOS boot sector. Which file, containing the old MS-DOS boot sector, should you suspect has been corrupted?

   Bootsect.dos

2. You created a Windows NT boot disk that contains the following files:
   - Ntldr
   - Ntdetect.com
   - Boot.ini
   - Ntbootdd.sys

   When you try to boot Windows NT with the disk, you receive the following error message:

   ```
   Non-System disk or disk error
   Replace and press any key when ready
   ```

   What did you do wrong?

   The disk that you used was not formatted while running Windows NT.

3. You change the settings for your network adapter card. When you reboot, you receive the following message: "One or more services failed to start." When you attempt to log on you receive a message stating that a domain controller could not be found, but you were logged on using cached credentials. After logging on, you discover that you cannot connect to network resources. You shut down your computer and restart using the Last Known Good configuration, but the same behavior results. What went wrong?

   Last Known Good is updated with the current control set following the first successful logon after a reboot. When you notice something wrong following a restart, do not log on.

4. You need to perform an emergency repair on your computer that is running Windows NT Workstation. You have a CD-ROM drive in your computer, however, you originally installed Windows NT over the network and you do not have the original setup disks. You still have the original *Windows NT Workstation* compact disc, however, and can access it on other computers. How can you perform the emergency repair?

   Using another computer, run the Winnt.exe or Winnt32.exe program from the original *Windows NT Workstation* compact disc using the /ox switch. This makes the three setup disks that can be used to start the repair process.

5. You receive a call from someone who tells you that he forgot the administrator password. He used the Emergency Repair Disk to restore the original administrator password, and now no one else can log on to the system. What happened and how can he correct the problem?

   The Emergency Repair process replaces the entire directory database with the original directory database that was created during installation, or with the last updated version from using Rdisk.exe. If he had never updated the directory database stored on the Emergency Repair Disk, the only accounts present after the repair would be the Administrator and the Guest account (and possibly an initial user account) created during installation.

   To correct the situation, he could use the original administrator password to log on, and then restore the directory database from a tape backup.

6. You have restarted a computer running Windows NT Workstation, and the following message appears:

   ```
   BOOT: Couldn't find NTLDR
   Please insert another disk
   ```

   You suspect that Ntldr is missing or corrupt. How can you replace the file?

   Use a Windows NT Boot disk or the Emergency Repair process.

CHAPTER 18

Windows NT Troubleshooting Tools

Lesson 1   Diagnostic Tools . . . 648

Lesson 2   Resources for Troubleshooting . . . 672

Review . . . 676

About This Chapter

This chapter identifies many of the troubleshooting tools that are available in Microsoft Windows NT. In addition to learning about these resources, you will learn how to use them to diagnose and resolve problems that can occur in administering a Windows NT system or network.

Before You Begin

To complete the lessons in this chapter, you must have:

- Two computers that meet the hardware and software requirements as specified in the Getting Started section of "About This Book."
- Completed all practices in Chapter 2, "Installing Windows NT."
- Completed the practice in Chapter 3, "Configuring the Windows NT Environment," in which you used Add/Remove Programs in Control Panel to install the Windows NT games and wallpaper.

Lesson 1: Diagnostic Tools

This lesson describes some of the diagnostic tools included with Windows NT and how to use them to troubleshoot system problems.

After this lesson, you will be able to:
- Identify and use the diagnostic utilities available with Windows NT.
- Describe the contents and options of Event Viewer.
- Analyze system information through the log files.
- View event details to find system information.
- View system information through Windows NT Diagnostics.
- Describe the use of Performance Monitor to troubleshoot performance-related problems.
- Describe the use of Network Monitor to troubleshoot network-related problems.
- Describe the System Recovery utility used to capture information generated by STOP errors.

Estimated lesson time: 60 minutes

To help you troubleshoot system problems, Windows NT provides the following administration tools:

- Event Viewer
- Windows NT Diagnostics
- Performance Monitor
- Network Monitor
- System Recovery

These tools provide information concerning the type of problem and where it occurred.

Event Viewer

Event Viewer provides information about *events* such as errors, warnings, and the success or failure of tasks.

An event is any potentially significant occurrence in the system (or in an application). For example, there are events that can affect system security or network performance. Some critical events, such as a full disk drive or an interrupted power supply, are noted in on-screen messages, as well as in an *event log*. Non-critical events are merely logged. Event logging starts automatically each time you start Windows NT. With an event log and the Event Viewer, you can troubleshoot various hardware and software problems and monitor Windows NT security events.

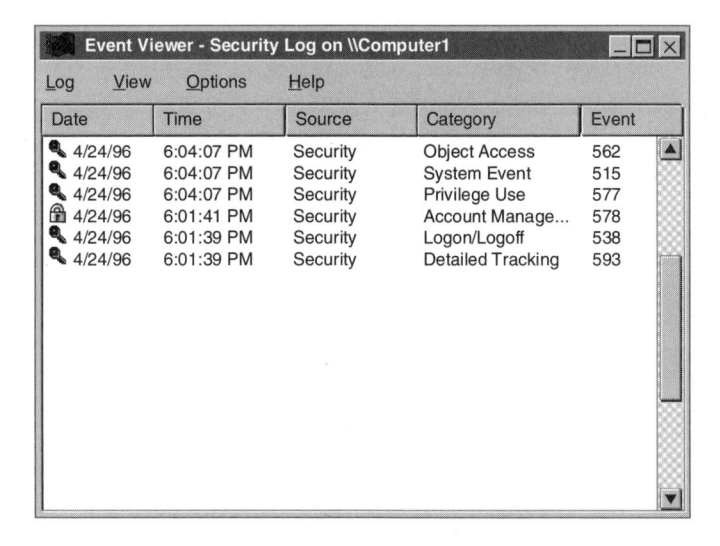

```
Event Viewer - Security Log on \\Computer1              _ □ ×
Log   View   Options   Help

Date       Time         Source      Category             Event
🔑 4/24/96   6:04:07 PM   Security    Object Access        562
🔑 4/24/96   6:04:07 PM   Security    System Event         515
🔑 4/24/96   6:04:07 PM   Security    Privilege Use        577
🔒 4/24/96   6:01:41 PM   Security    Account Manage...    578
🔑 4/24/96   6:01:39 PM   Security    Logon/Logoff         538
🔑 4/24/96   6:01:39 PM   Security    Detailed Tracking    593
```

To start the Event Viewer, click **Start**, point to **Programs**, point to **Administrative Tools (Common)**, and then click **Event Viewer**.

Event Log Files

Windows NT records events in three kinds of logs: the *system log*, the *security log* and the *application log*. The system and application logs are automatically enabled; the security log must be manually enabled.

- The system log (*systemroot*\System32\Config\Sysevent.evt) contains events logged by the Windows NT system components and device drivers. For example, the failure of a driver or other system component to load during startup is recorded in the system log. The event types logged by system components are determined by Windows NT, and those logged by third party drivers are determined by the driver vendor.

- The security log (*systemroot*\System32\Config\Secevent.evt) can contain valid and invalid logon attempts, as well as events related to resource use, such as creating, opening, or deleting files or other objects. For example, if you use User Manager for Domains to enable Logon and Logoff auditing, attempts to log on to and log off of, the system are recorded in the security log.

- The application log (*systemroot*\System32\Config\Appevent.evt) contains events logged by applications. For example, a database program might record a file error in the application log. Application developers decide which events to monitor.

Note System and application logs can be viewed by all users; security logs are accessible only to administrators.

Enabling Security Logging

By default, security logging is turned off. To enable security logging, run User Manager for Domains to enable auditing and to determine what event to audit. You can also set auditing in the registry that causes the system to halt when the security log is full. To do this, use Registry Editor to create the following registry key value:

HKEY_LOCAL_MACHINE\SYSTEM\CurrentControlSet\Control\Lsa
\CrashOnAuditFail

The value type is REG_DWORD and it can have the following data values:

1 - Stop if the audit log is full.

2 - This data value will be set by the operating system just before the system crashes due to a full audit log. While the data value is 2, only the administrator can log on to the computer.

The *CrashOnAuditFail* registry entry directs the operating system to shut down abnormally and display a blue screen when the audit log is full. This assures that no auditable activities, including security violations, occur while the system is unable to log them.

Types of Events

The following table shows Event Viewer icons, event types, and descriptions.

Icon	Event type	Description
	Error	Significant problems, such as loss of data or loss of functionality. For example, an Error event will be logged if a service fails to load during Windows NT startup.
	Warning	Events that are not necessarily significant, but that indicate possible future problems. For example, a Warning event will be logged when disk space is low.
	Information	Infrequent but significant events that describe successful operations of drivers or services. For example, when a network driver loads successfully, it will log an Information event.
	Success Audit	Audited security access attempts that are successful. For example, a user's successful attempt to log on to the system will be logged as a Success Audit event.
	Failure Audit	Audited security access attempts that fail. For example, if a user tries to access a network drive and fails, the attempt will be logged as a Failure Audit event.

Interpreting an Event

Each event stored in the log files can be viewed in greater detail by clicking **Detail** on the **View** menu in Event Viewer. The **Event Detail** dialog box shows the following information:

- Date and time of the event
- Event identification
- Text description of the selected event

In some cases, the **Event Detail** dialog box displays hexadecimal data for the selected event. This information is generated by the component that was the source of the event record. If interpretation of the hexadecimal data is required to resolve a problem, a person who is familiar with the source component should be contacted. Not all events generate such hexadecimal data.

Note For more information about Windows NT Server events, see the Messages Database Help file on the *Windows NT Server Resource Kit 4.0* compact disc.

There are several methods to control the event display and to find specific events in Event Viewer. These methods include filtering, arranging, and searching.

Filtering

When Event Viewer starts, *all* events recorded in the selected log are displayed automatically. To view events with specific characteristics, click **Filter Events** on the **View** menu. Events can be filtered by the following properties:

- View From/View Through: From a specified date and time, or during a time frame
- Type: Error, Warning, Information, Success Audit, Failure Audit
- Source: Alerter, Browser, DLC error, floppy disk, and so on
- User
- Computer
- Event ID

Note Filtering has no effect on the contents of the event log; all events are logged whether the filter is active or not. The filter affects only what will be displayed.

Arranging

Events displayed in Event Viewer are listed in sequence, from the most recent to the oldest. On the **View** menu, the sequence can be changed to display the oldest events first.

Searching

To search for events in large logs, use the **Find** dialog box, which is accessible through the **View** menu. Search for an event by any one or more of the following: Type, Source, Category, Event ID, User, or Computer.

Options in the **Find** dialog box are in effect only during the current session. The settings in the **Find** dialog box can be saved by clicking **Save Settings On Exit** on the Event Viewer **Options** menu.

Archiving Log Files

When you archive an event log, you save it in one of three file formats:

- *Log file format.* This format enables you to view the archived log again in Event Viewer.
- *Text file format.* This format enables you to present the information in a text-oriented application, such as a word processor.
- *Comma-delimited text file format.* This format enables you to manage the information with an application, such as a spreadsheet or database.

Archived event logs can serve a variety of purposes, such as tracking and documenting system performance over time, or providing feedback to system and application developers.

Note For more information on using Event Viewer, see Chapter 9, "Monitoring Events," in Microsoft Windows NT Server *Concepts and Planning*.

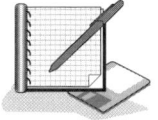

Practice

In these procedures, you use Event Viewer to view events in the system, security, and application event logs, and to control the size of the log files. You then use Event Viewer to filter events and search for specific events to locate existing and potential problems.

Note Complete these procedures on Server1.

▶ **To view events**

1. Log on as Administrator.
2. Click the **Start** button, point to **Programs**, point to **Administrative Tools (Common)**, and then click **Event Viewer**.

    Event Viewer appears.

3. On the **Log** menu, click **System**.

    Different symbols precede different types of events.

4. Double-click one of each of the symbols (Stop sign, exclamation point, and information symbol), one at a time to determine the type of event it represents and to see a description of the event.

    What types of events appear in your system log?

    _____

    _____

5. On the **Log** menu, click **Application**.

    What types of events appear in your application log?

    _____

    _____

▶ To control the size and contents of a log file

1. On the Event Viewer **Log** menu, click **Log Settings**.

   By default, what is the maximum log size for the system, security, and application log files?

   _____

2. In the **Change Settings for** box, select **System**.
3. Click **Overwrite Events As Needed**.

   How will this setting affect the system log?

   _____

4. Click **OK**.

▶ To filter events

1. On the **Log** menu, click **Open**.
2. In the C:\Lab Files\Events folder, open **Sample1.evt**.
3. Under **Open File of Type** window, click **System**, and then click **OK**.
4. On the **View** menu, click **Filter Events**.
5. In the **Source** box, click **Service Control Manager** from the list, and then click **OK**.
6. Double-click the oldest entry.

   What is the description of the problem?

   _____

   _____

   What could be the problem?

   _____

7. Click **Close** to close the event and return to the log.

▶ To search for specific messages

1. On the **Log** menu, click **Open**.
2. In the C:\Lab Files\Events folder, open **Sample2.evt** as a system log.
3. On the **View** menu, click **Filter Events**.
4. In the **Types** box, make sure that only the **Warning** box is checked, and then click **OK**.
5. Double-click the first entry.

   What is the description of the problem?

   _____

   What action is necessary?

   _____

6. Click **Close**.
7. On the **View** menu, click **Filter Events**.
8. In the **Types** box, select the **Error** check box, clear the **Warning** check box, and then click **OK**.
9. Double-click each entry and view its description one at a time until you determine what the problem is.

   What is the problem?

   _____

   What action is necessary?

   _____

10. Close Event Viewer.

Windows NT Diagnostics

Windows NT Diagnostics (Winmsd.exe) is a tool that shows computer hardware and operating system data stored in the Windows NT registry.

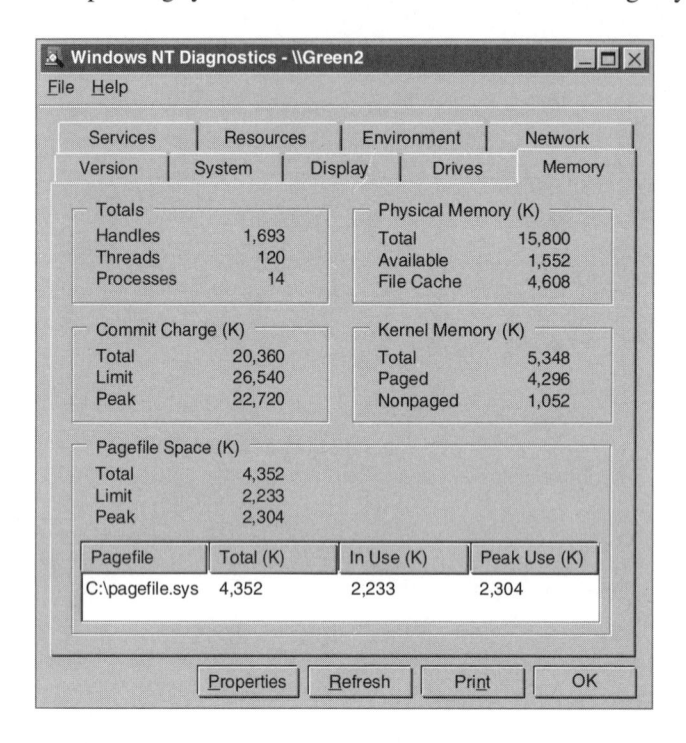

```
Windows NT Diagnostics - \\Green2
File  Help

  Services   |  Resources  |  Environment  |  Network
  Version    |   System    |    Display    |  Drives  | Memory

  ┌ Totals ──────────────────┐  ┌ Physical Memory (K) ──────┐
  │ Handles       1,693      │  │ Total           15,800    │
  │ Threads         120      │  │ Available        1,552    │
  │ Processes        14      │  │ File Cache       4,608    │
  └──────────────────────────┘  └───────────────────────────┘

  ┌ Commit Charge (K) ───────┐  ┌ Kernel Memory (K) ────────┐
  │ Total        20,360      │  │ Total            5,348    │
  │ Limit        26,540      │  │ Paged            4,296    │
  │ Peak         22,720      │  │ Nonpaged         1,052    │
  └──────────────────────────┘  └───────────────────────────┘

  ┌ Pagefile Space (K) ─────────────────────────────────────┐
  │ Total         4,352                                     │
  │ Limit         2,233                                     │
  │ Peak          2,304                                     │
  │                                                         │
  │ Pagefile         | Total (K) | In Use (K) | Peak Use (K)│
  │ C:\pagefile.sys  |   4,352   |   2,233    |    2,304    │
  └─────────────────────────────────────────────────────────┘

              [ Properties ]  [ Refresh ]  [ Print ]  [ OK ]
```

Note Configuration data cannot be modified using Windows NT Diagnostics.

Winmsd.exe is located in the *systemroot*\System32 directory. To start Windows NT Diagnostics, click the **Start** button, point to **Programs**, point to **Administrative Tools (Common)**, and then click **Windows NT Diagnostics**.

The following table describes the types of information displayed by Windows NT Diagnostics.

Tab	Description
Services	Lists services and devices in the CurrentControlSet, along with a state, or status, of running or stopped.
Resources	Displays system resources in use, including IRQs, I/O ports, DMA channels, memory allocation, and device drivers loaded.
Environment	Displays environment variables.
Network	Lists network-related configuration information, including current network statistics.
Version	Contains operating system information with version numbers, such as the build and Service Pack information, and the registered owner.
System	Displays BIOS, HAL, and CPU information.
Display	Contains information about the video adapter, driver, and display settings.
Drives	Lists all available drives and their types, including floppy and other removable drives, local disk drives, CD-ROM drives, and network-connected drives, as well as additional information, such as volume label, serial number, file system, and disk usage, for each drive.
Memory	Contains information about physical and virtual memory, such as the pagefile location, total memory, and available memory are displayed.

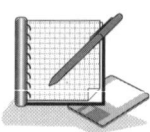

Practice

In these procedures, you use Windows NT Diagnostics (Winmsd) to view configuration information for Server1 and for a remote computer (Workstation1). You then save a report for the remote computer, and view the report.

Note Complete these procedures on Server1.

▶ **To view software configuration information**

In this procedure, you view your computer's configuration information.

1. Click the **Start** button, point to **Programs**, point to **Administrative Tools (Common)**, and then click **Windows NT Diagnostics**.

2. Locate the following information by reviewing the tabs in the Windows NT Diagnostics window. In the following table, record the name of the tab you chose and the value of the requested information.

Requested information	Tab	Value
Registered owner		
Registered organization		
Version number		
Build number		
systemroot (windir)		
Domain name		
CPU type		

3. Locate the following information.

Requested information	Your configuration
Total physical memory	
Available physical memory	
Total pagefile space	
Available pagefile space	
Paging files (location and size)	

4. List the service dependencies for the following services. (Hint: Click the **Services** tab, click the name of the service, and then click **Properties**.)

Service	Dependencies
ClipBook Server	
Network DDE	
Network DDE DSDM	
Server	
Messenger	

▶ **To view configuration information for Workstation1**

1. On the **File** menu, click **Select Computer**.

    The **Select Computer** dialog box appears.

2. In the **Computer** box, type **Workstation1** and then click **OK**.

    What tabs are available for remote computers?

    _____

    _____

3. Locate the following information about Workstation1.

Requested information	Workstation1 configuration
CPU type	
Network adapter IRQ	
Video driver in use	
Domain name	

▶ **To create a Windows NT Diagnostics report for Workstation1**

1. On the **File** menu, click **Save Report**.

    The **Create Report for Workstation1** dialog box appears.

2. Under **Scope**, click **All tabs**.
3. Under **Detail Level**, click **Complete**.
4. Under **Destination**, click **File**.

5. Click **OK**.

   The **Save WinMSD Report** dialog box appears.

6. Save the file as **C:\Msdrpt.txt**.

   The **Generating WinMSD Report** dialog box appears, which contains a status bar indicating the current progress.

7. Click **OK** to exit Windows NT Diagnostics.

▶ **To read a Windows NT Diagnostics report**

1. Start Windows NT Explorer and click drive C.
2. Double-click **Msdrpt.txt** to view your report.

   Notepad starts and displays the file Msdrpt.txt.

3. Use **Find** on the **Search** menu to locate the following information in Msdrpt.txt.

   For example, the results of a Find on PROCESSOR_ARCHITECTURE could be PROCESSOR_ARCHITECTURE=x86.

Requested information	Workstation1 configuration
PROCESSOR_ARCHITECTURE	
PROCESSOR_LEVEL	
PROCESSOR_IDENTIFIER	
PROCESSOR_REVISION	

4. Close Notepad when you have finished viewing your report.

Performance Monitor

Performance Monitor enables you to look at resource use for specific components and application processes through a dynamic display. These dynamic charts can be saved as logs or reports. With Performance Monitor, you can gauge your computer's efficiency, identify and troubleshoot possible problems (such as unbalanced resource use, insufficient hardware, or poor program design), and plan for additional hardware needs. You can also use alerts to notify you when resource use reaches a specified value.

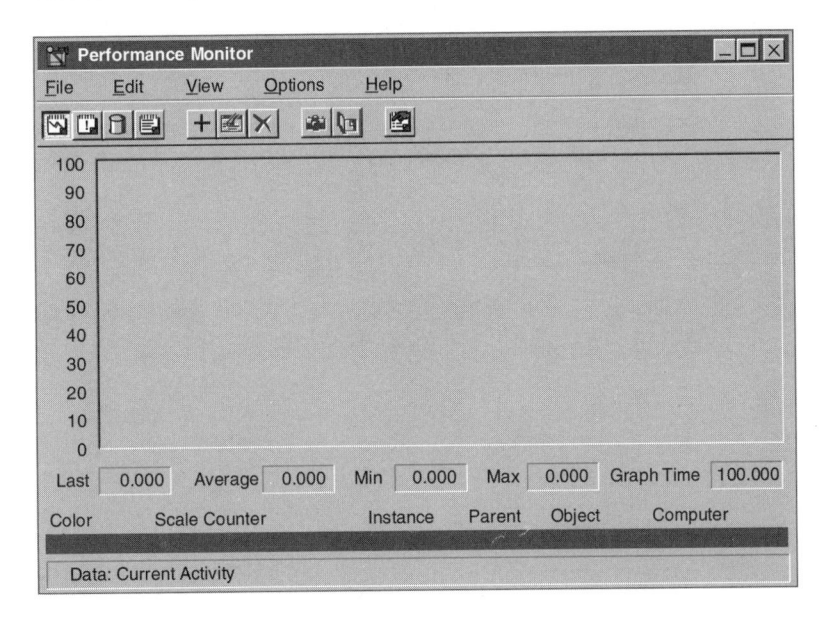

Performance Monitor treats system components as objects in order to track component and application performance. Start Performance Monitor through the Administrative Tools (Common) folder.

Use Performance Monitor by selecting specific features, or *counters*, of these objects for tracking. Counters can be monitored to identify performance problems. Three counters for the Processor and System objects are particularly useful for identifying problems: % Processor Time, Interrupts/Sec, and Processor Queue Length.

Processor: % Processor Time

The % Processor Time counter shows processor activity. During some operations this may reach 100 percent. If the processor returns to a level of use between 0 (zero) and 80 percent, with only occasional increases while loading applications, then the processor is probably not slowing down the performance of your system or network.

Processor: Interrupts/Sec

The Interrupts/Sec counter measures the rate of service requests from I/O devices. A dramatic increase in this value, without a corresponding increase in system activity, shows a hardware problem.

System: Processor Queue Length

The number of threads shown by the processor queue length is an indicator of system performance because each thread requires a certain number of processor cycles. If demand exceeds supply, long processor queues develop and system response slows. Therefore, a consistent processor queue length greater than two may mean that the processor is causing a problem.

Note For more information on Performance Monitor, see Chapter 8, "Monitoring Performance," in Microsoft Windows NT Server *Concepts and Planning*.

Practice

In these procedures, you create a chart in Performance Monitor to display performance data in real time. Real-time charts provide a quick overview of the current performance of your system.

Note Complete these procedures on Server1.

▶ **To configure the chart**

1. Click the **Start** button, point to **Programs**, point to **Administrative Tools (Common)**, and then click **Performance Monitor**.
2. On the **View** menu, click **Chart**.
3. On the **Edit** menu, click **Add To Chart**.

    Notice that Processor is the default object in the **Object** box.

4. In the **Counter** box, click **%DPC Time**, and then click **Explain**.

    Notice that the **Counter Definition** appears at the bottom of the window.

5. Click each of the counters for the **Processor** object, and read the **Counter Definition** for each.
6. In the **Counter** box, select all the counters available for **Processor**, and then click **Add**. (Hint: To select all counters, select the first counter, hold down the SHIFT key, and then select the last counter in the list.)
7. Click **Done**.

    A graph appears displaying the processor's real-time activities.

▸ To generate data and view it on the chart

1. Click the **Start** button, point to **Programs**, point to **Accessories**, point to **Games**, and then click **Pinball**.
2. Play one ball (and *only* one ball) of Pinball.
3. Close Pinball, and switch to Performance Monitor.
4. From the list of counters displayed in the lower part of your screen, click the **% Processor Time**, and notice the changing **Average** value.

> **Tip** While looking at the activity of several counters on the Performance Monitor display, it may be difficult to distinguish a given counter's activity. In order to highlight the activity of a particular counter on the Performance Monitor display, select the counter name, and then press CTRL+H. Once you have turned on highlighting, you can click a different counter name to have its activity highlighted.

5. Minimize Performance Monitor.
6. Start and minimize both Server Manager and Disk Administrator.
7. Restore Performance Monitor.

   Notice the activity, such as spikes, on the chart.

You have created a chart displaying real-time processor utilization. This is useful to determine how your CPU is being used at the current time. In the next procedures, you will collect and save data for future reference, which can then be turned into a graph to compare with real time data to analyze performance.

Practice

In these procedures, you use Performance Monitor to create and view a log of processor activity. Logs gather and record data to a file over a period of time. Logs are useful in predicting long-term trends or in troubleshooting short-term problems. You then view portions of the logged data in the chart to isolate specific information. You also use reports to view data in a non-graphical format.

> **Note** Complete these procedures on Server1.

▸ To create a log

1. On the **View** menu, click **Log**.
2. On the **Edit** menu, click **Add To Log**.

3. In the **Objects** box, click **Processor**, and then click **Add**.

   Note When you select an object for a log, all counters for that object will be recorded in the log automatically.

4. Click **Done**.
5. On the **Options** menu, click **Log**.
6. In the **File Name** box, type **pmlog1.log**
7. In the **Update Time** section, set the **Periodic Update Interval** to 1 second.
8. Click **Start Log**.

   The log window appears with real-time processor activity being collected in the log.

9. Create processor activity by starting applications or moving the mouse.
10. Check the **File Size** box in the Performance Monitor window periodically to determine the size of your data file.
11. Wait until the file has reached 100 KB, and then proceed with the next step.
12. On the **Options** menu, click **Log**, and then click **Stop Log**.

▶ **To view log data in a chart**

1. On the **View** menu, click **Chart**.
2. On the **File** menu, click **New Chart**.
3. On the **Options** menu, click **Data From**.
4. Click **Log File**, and then click the ellipsis (…) button.
5. Click the log file that you just created, and then click **Open**.
6. Click **OK** to return to the Performance Monitor window.

   An empty chart window appears.

7. On the **Edit** menu, click **Add To Chart**.
8. Select all counters available for **Processor**, and then click **Add**.
9. Click **Done**.

   The chart displays the processor counters collected in your log during the log collection period. You will notice data displayed on the chart as well as the status bar. The last, average, minimum, and maximum values are displayed with the total graph time from your log of data.

Chapter 18 Windows NT Troubleshooting Tools 665

▶ **To view isolated segments of log data in a chart**

1. In the list of counters, select **% Processor Time**.
2. Using information from the status bar, record the average of % Processor Time.

---

3. On the **Edit** menu, click **Time Window**.

    The **Input Log File Timeframe** dialog box appears. This dialog box contains a slider that is used to adjust the portion of the chart shown in the Performance Monitor window. By default, the entire chart is shown.

    Note You may need to move the Input Log File Timeframe window to see the entire chart.

4. Click the left section of the slider and drag this section to the middle of the bar.
5. Click **OK**.

    The right half of the original chart is now displayed in the Performance Monitor window.

6. Record the average of % Processor Time again.

---

7. Repeat steps 3–5, this time adjusting the slider so that the last one-quarter of the chart is displayed.
8. Record the average of % Processor Time again.

---

9. Repeat steps 3–5, adjusting the left and right sections of the sliding bar as necessary, until the average % Processor Time for the portion of the chart displayed in the Performance Monitor window is greater than 40 percent.

    How accurate is this representation of the processor's use?

---

10. Edit the time window to view the entire graph.

▶ **To create a report showing the % Processor Time for the entire graph period**

1. On the **View** menu, click **Report**.

    A blank report window appears.

2. On the **Edit** menu, click **Add To Report**.

3. With **Processor** as the default object, select all counters in the **Counter** box, and then click **Add**.

4. Click **Done**.

    A report with the chosen counters is displayed, showing the averages.

    What was the average % Processor Time for the entire graph period?

    _____

5. Close Performance Monitor.

Network Monitor

Network Monitor monitors the network data stream, which consists of all information transferred over a network at any given time. Prior to transmission, this information is divided by the network software into smaller pieces, called frames or packets. Each frame contains the following information:

- The source address of the computer that sent the message.
- The destination address of the computer that received the frame.
- Headers from each protocol used to send the frame.
- The data or a portion of the information being sent.

For security reasons, Windows NT Network Monitor captures only those frames, including broadcast frames and multicast frames, that are sent to or from the local computer.

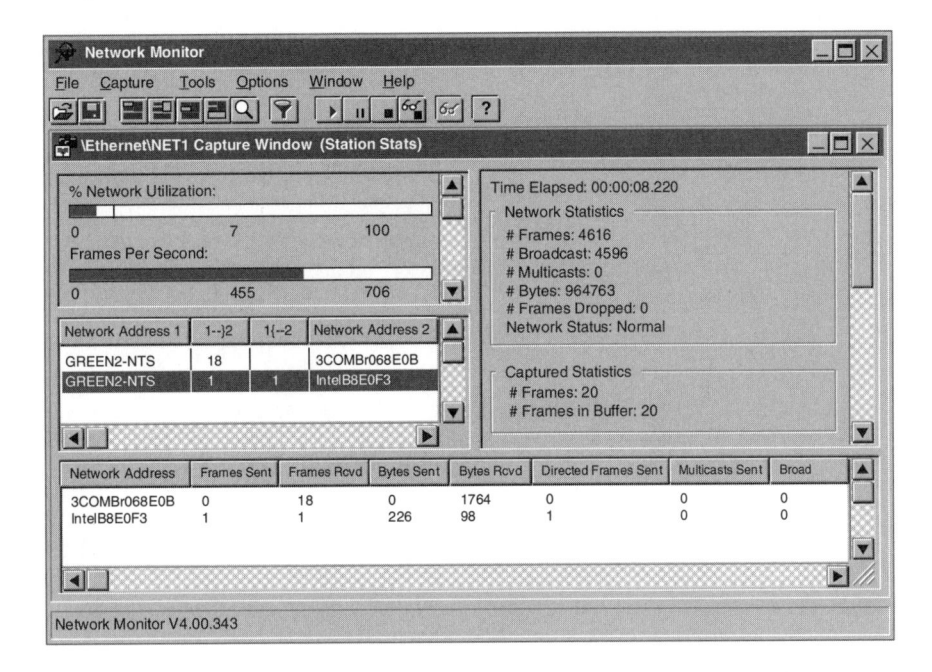

Installing Network Monitor

Network Monitor is installed as a service through the Network program in Control Panel. When Network Monitor is installed, it appears on the **Administrative Tools (Common)** menu.

The Network Monitor Capture Window

The Capture window in Network Monitor displays captured data. Four major *panes*, or sections, of the window display data. The following table describes the four panes.

Pane	Displays
Graph	The current activity as bar charts, showing the following: the percentage of network utilization, frames per second, bytes per second, broadcasts per second, and multicasts per second.
Session Statistics	A summary of the conversations between two hosts, and which host is initiating broadcasts and multicasts.
Total Statistics	Statistics for the traffic detected on the network as a whole, statistics for the frames captured, per second utilization statistics, and network adapter card statistics.
Station Statistics	A summary of the total number of frames initiated by a host, the number of frames and bytes sent and received, and the number of broadcast and multicast frames initiated.

Note For more information on Network Monitor, see Chapter 10, "Monitoring Your Network," in Microsoft Windows NT Server *Concepts and Planning*.

Practice

In these procedures, you install the Network Monitor Tools and Agent. You then use Network Monitor to capture and display network traffic.

Note Complete these procedures on Server1. Workstation1 should be online.

▶ **To install Network Monitor Tools and Agent**

1. Double-click the Shortcut to Network icon.
2. Click the **Services** tab.
3. Click **Add**.
4. In the **Network Service** box, click **Network Monitor Tools and Agent**, and then click **OK**.
5. In the **Windows NT Setup** dialog box, type **\\Server1\Nts_source\I386** and then click **Continue**.

   Windows NT Setup copies the required files.
6. After the files have been copied, click the **Close** button.
7. When prompted, click **Yes** to shut down and then restart your computer.
8. Restart Server1.

▶ To set a trigger

1. Log on as Administrator.
2. Click the **Start** button, point to **Programs**, point to **Administrative Tools (Common)**, and then click **Network Monitor**.

   The Network Monitor **Capture** window appears.
3. On the **Capture** menu, click **Trigger**.

   The **Capture Trigger** dialog box appears.
4. In the **Trigger on** box, click **Buffer Space**.
5. In the **Buffer Space** box, click **50%**.
6. In the **Trigger Action** box, click **Stop Capture**, and then click **OK**.

▶ To capture network data and generate network traffic

1. On the **Capture** menu, click **Start**.
2. On your desktop, click the **Start** button, and then click **Run**.
3. Type **\\Workstation1** and then click **OK**.

   A list of resources on \\Workstation1 appears.
4. Close the Workstation1 window.

▶ To view captured network data

1. On the **Capture** menu, click **Stop**.
2. On the **Capture** menu, click **Display Captured Data**.
3. Scroll through the list of captured frames. You should see your own computer name (**Server1**) and **Workstation1**.
4. Close Network Monitor. Do not save the capture.

System Recovery

When a severe error (called *STOP error*, or fatal system error or blue screen) occurs, Windows NT allows you to configure the way your system responds. This configuration is done through the **Recovery** options found on the **Startup/Shutdown** tab of the System program in Control Panel.

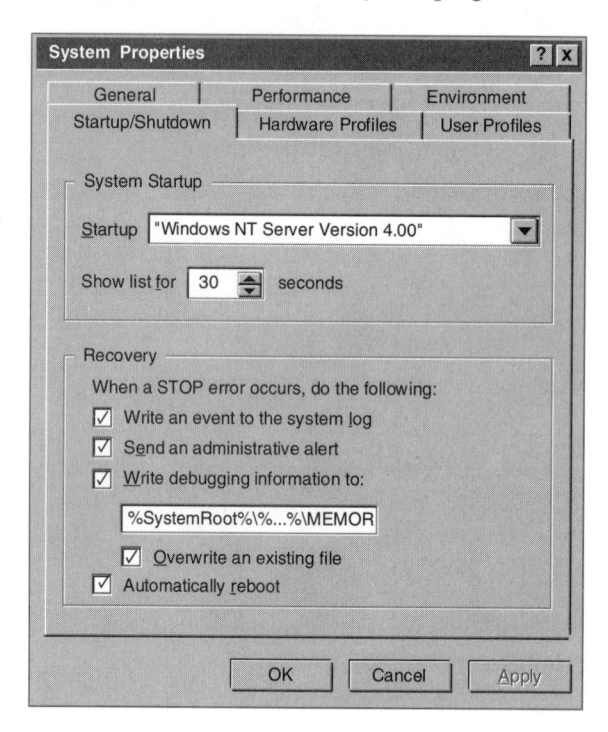

Configuring the Recovery Utility

The **Recovery** box on the **Startup/Shutdown** tab has the following options:

- Write an event to the system log.
- Send an administrative alert to the users and computers specified in the **Alerts** dialog box accessible through the **Server** dialog box in Control Panel.
- Write a debug file to a specified file name. This debug file contains a dump of system memory.
- Restart the system automatically. This allows the server to return to operation after a system crash, instead of requiring a manual reboot.

Recovery Operation

The **Write debugging information to** option is important for troubleshooting. If a STOP error occurs while this option is selected, a program named *Savedump.exe* writes (dumps) the entire contents of memory to the pagefile. For this reason, the pagefile must be at least as large as the amount of physical memory installed in the system. The pagefile must also reside on the partition that contains the *systemroot* folder.

Savedump.exe marks the part of the pagefile that contains the memory dump. When the system restarts, Windows NT automatically copies this part of the pagefile to the specified file name; by default, the file name is *Memory.dmp*. To preserve log files, you should copy them to a new file name after the computer restarts. A support engineer can then use the *Dumpexam.exe* program in the Support folder on the *Microsoft Windows NT Server* compact disc to debug the system.

Lesson 2: Resources for Troubleshooting

Whether you are a technical support engineer or network administrator, you should be aware of the Microsoft resources that are available to help you plan, configure, and troubleshoot Windows NT–based computers and domains. This lesson describes some of the key resources provided by Microsoft to help you maintain your Windows NT network.

After this lesson, you will be able to:
- Describe the purpose of TechNet.
- Name and access Microsoft online technical support resources.

Estimated lesson time: 10 minutes

The *Microsoft TechNet* compact disc is an important technical support tool. It is designed for professionals who perform any of the following tasks:

- Support or train users.
- Administer databases or networks.
- Integrate products and platforms.
- Evaluate and specify new products and solutions.

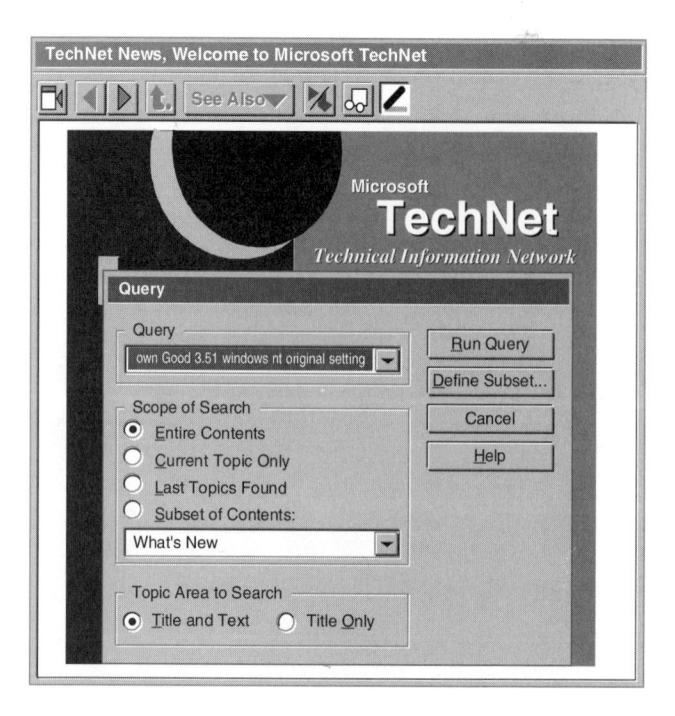

The *Microsoft TechNet* compact disc includes the following components:

- A complete set of online technical references to help install and support *all* Microsoft products. For example, the *Microsoft Windows NT Workstation Resource Kit* documentation describes how to install, configure, and optimize Windows NT Workstation.
- The entire Microsoft Knowledge Base, which is the same library of technical support articles developed and used by Microsoft's own support engineers to support customers.
- *TechNet Supplemental (Drivers & Patches)* compact disc, which contains the Microsoft Software Library. This compact disc includes drivers for the entire line of Microsoft software products, as well as patches and minor software updates for many Microsoft products, including Windows NT. This compact disc also includes code samples, utilities, and templates.

You can subscribe to TechNet by contacting:

Microsoft Corporation
PO Box 10296
Des Moines, IA 50336-0296

(800) 344-2121

Microsoft Internet and Online Services

To get up-to-date information on Microsoft Windows NT, Microsoft maintains online services to provide product and technical support information, such as the Microsoft Web site, the Microsoft Download Service (MSDL), and The Microsoft Network online service, MSN™.

- *Microsoft Web site (www.microsoft.com).* For example, to access articles on Windows NT, use Microsoft Internet Explorer to reach Microsoft support at the following address: http://www.microsoft.com/support
- *The Microsoft Download Service (MSDL).* This Microsoft electronic bulletin board provides support information and products. Access the MSDL by dialing (206) 936-6735. (Note that the modem settings for MSDL are 8 data bits, 1 stop bit, no parity, and no flow control.)

Note The course Web page that you installed from the *Course Materials* compact disc contains links to different Microsoft resources. See the Web Sites page to view this information.

Note The Microsoft Network (MSN) contains answers to the most common technical questions, as well as detailed articles about Microsoft products. In addition, subscribers can join online chat groups to both give and receive advice regarding technical issues from fellow members. Although much of the content of MSN can be accessed using Windows NT and Microsoft Internet Explorer, the full content of MSN can only be accessed from computers running Microsoft Windows 95.

Summary

The following information summarizes the key points in this chapter:

- In order to help you troubleshoot your system and your network, Windows NT provides the following tools: Event Viewer, Windows NT Diagnostics, Performance Monitor, Network Monitor, and System Recovery.

- Event Viewer provides information about events such as errors, warnings, and the success or failure of tasks that are maintained in an event log. An event is any potentially significant occurrence in the system (or in an application). With an event log and the Event Viewer, you can troubleshoot various hardware and software problems and monitor Windows NT security events.

- Windows NT records three kinds of logs: system, security, and application logs. System logs record information about the failure of a driver, or other system component. Security logs record information about valid and invalid logon attempts and events related to resource use such as creating, opening, and deleting files. Application logs record information about applications.

- Windows NT Diagnostics (Winmsd.exe) is a tool that shows computer hardware and operating system data stored in the Windows NT registry.

- Performance Monitor enables you to look at resource use for specific components and application processes through a dynamic display. These dynamic charts can be saved as logs or reports. With Performance Monitor, you can gauge your computer's efficiency, identify and troubleshoot possible problems, and plan for additional hardware needs. You can also use alerts to notify you when resource use reaches a specified value.

- Network Monitor is used to capture and display frames (also called packets) to detect and troubleshoot problems on LANs. For security reasons, Network Monitor captures only those frames, including broadcast frames and multicast frames, that are sent to or from the local computer.

- System Recovery allows you to configure the way your system responds when a STOP error occurs. You can configure the following System Recovery options: write an event to the system log, send an administrative alert, write a debug file that contains a dump of system memory when a STOP error occurs, and restart the system automatically, instead of requiring a manual reboot.

- Microsoft provides various resources, such as TechNet and MSDL, which you can use to get troubleshooting information about Microsoft products. You can also use the Internet to access one of the Microsoft Web sites, such as *www.microsoft.com,* to access the most recent information, as well as to download software, including drivers and Service Packs.

Review

1. A network user calls you and complains that her computer, which is running Windows NT Workstation, is unusually slow. Without going to her computer, what steps can you take to diagnose the problem?

2. Your manager wants you to track all unsuccessful logon attempts. You search the system log, but you cannot find any unsuccessful logon attempts recorded. What is the problem?

3. You are having a problem configuring a device to work with Windows NT. Where can you look for any reported problems?

Answer Key

Procedure Answers

Page 653

▶ **To view events**

4. Double-click one of each of the symbols (Stop sign, exclamation point, and information symbol), one at a time to determine the type of event it represents and to see a description of the event.

   What types of events appear in your system log?

   You may see messages with the following types: Information, Warning, and Errors.

5. On the **Log** menu, click **Application**.

   What types of events appear in your application log?

   You may see messages with the following types: Information, Warning, and Errors.

Page 654

▶ **To control the size and contents of a log file**

1. On the Event Viewer **Log** menu, click **Log Settings**.

   By default, what is the maximum log size for the system, security, and application log files?

   The default maximum log size for each log file is 512 KB.

3. Click **Overwrite Events As Needed**.

   How will this setting affect the system log?

   Older events will now be overwritten by new events.

Page 654

▶ **To filter events**

6. Double-click the oldest entry.

   What is the description of the problem?

   The 3Com EtherLink II Adapter Driver service failed to start due to the following error: A device attached to the system is not functioning.

   What could be the problem?

   The network adapter card is missing, configured incorrectly, or malfunctioning.

678 Microsoft Windows NT Technical Support

Page 655

▶ **To search for specific messages**

5. Double-click the first entry.

   What is the description of the problem?

   The drive D is at or near capacity.

   What action is necessary?

   You need to delete some files. The files can be backed up and then deleted from drive D.

9. Double-click each entry and view its description one at a time until you determine what the problem is.

   What is the problem?

   A duplicate computer name exists on the network.

   What action is necessary?

   Rename the computer and then restart Windows NT Server.

Page 658

▶ **To view software configuration information**

2. Locate the following information by reviewing the tabs in the Windows NT Diagnostics window. In the following table, record the name of the tab you chose and the value of the requested information.

   Answers recorded in the table will vary.

Requested information	Tab	Value
Registered owner	**Version**	**Answers will vary.**
Registered organization	**Version**	**Answers will vary.**
Version number	**Version**	**4.0**
Build number	**Version**	**1381**
systemroot (windir)	**Environment**	**C:\Winnt**
Domain name	**Network**	**Domain1**
CPU type	**System or Environment**	**Answers will vary. Example: *x*86 Family 5 Model 2 Stepping 1**

Chapter 18 Windows NT Troubleshooting Tools 679

3. Locate the following information.

Answers recorded in the table will vary.

Requested information	Your configuration
Total physical memory	**Answers will vary.**
Available physical memory	**Answers will vary.**
Total pagefile space	**Answers will vary.**
Available pagefile space	**(Pagefile Space: Total)** **- (Pagefile Space: Total in Use)**
Paging files (location and size)	**Answers will vary.**

4. List the service dependencies for the following services. (Hint: Click the **Services** tab, click the name of the service, and then click **Properties**.)

Service	Dependencies
ClipBook Server	**NetDDE**
Network DDE	**Network DDEDSDM**
Network DDE DSDM	**None**
Server	**TDI**
Messenger	**LANMAN Workstation, NetBIOS**

Page 659

▶ **To view configuration information for Workstation1**

2. In the **Computer** box, type **Workstation1** and then click **OK**.

What tabs are available for remote computers?

Version, System, Display, Services, Resources, Environment, and Network.

3. Locate the following information about Workstation1:

Answers recorded in the table will vary.

Requested information	Workstation1 configuration
CPU type	**Example: *x*86 Family 5 Model 2 Stepping 1**
Network adapter IRQ	**Example: IRQ 5**
Video driver in use	**Example: Ati.sys**
Domain name	**Domain1**

Page 660

▸ **To read a Windows NT Diagnostics report**

3. Use **Find** on the **Search** menu to locate the following information in Msdrpt.txt.

   For example, the results of a Find on PROCESSOR_ARCHITECTURE could be PROCESSOR_ARCHITECTURE=x86.

Requested information	Workstation1 configuration
PROCESSOR_ARCHITECTURE	Answers will vary.
PROCESSOR_LEVEL	Answers will vary.
PROCESSOR_IDENTIFIER	Answers will vary.
PROCESSOR_REVISION	Answers will vary.

Page 665

▸ **To view isolated segments of log data in a chart**

2. Using information from the status bar, record the average of % Processor Time.

   Answers will vary.

6. Record the average of % Processor Time again.

   Answers will vary.

8. Record the average of % Processor Time again.

   Answers will vary.

9. Repeat steps 3–5, adjusting the left and right sections of the sliding bar as necessary, until the average % Processor Time for the portion of the chart displayed in the Performance Monitor window is greater than 40 percent.

   How accurate is this representation of the processor's use?

   It is accurate for this time slice, but will not reflect overall processor activity.

Chapter 18 Windows NT Troubleshooting Tools   681

Page 666

▶ **To create a report showing the % Processor Time for the entire graph period**

4. Click **Done**.

A report with the chosen counters is displayed, showing the averages.

What was the average % Processor Time for the entire graph period?

Answers will vary.

Review Answers

Page 676

1. A network user calls you and complains that her computer, which is running Windows NT Workstation, is unusually slow. Without going to her computer, what steps can you take to diagnose the problem?

   Use Event Viewer to examine the remote computer's event log to see if any errors have been reported. Then use Performance Monitor to see if any devices report a bottleneck. Finally, you can use Windows NT Diagnostics to document the computer's configuration.

2. Your manager wants you to track all unsuccessful logon attempts. You search the system log, but you cannot find any unsuccessful logon attempts recorded. What is the problem?

   Unsuccessful logon attempts are recorded in the security log, not in the system log. By default, security logging is turned off. To enable security logging, run User Manager for Domains and set the Audit policy.

3. You are having a problem configuring a device to work with Windows NT. Where can you look for any reported problems?

   Look in the Microsoft Knowledge Base available on TechNet, or www.microsoft.com.

Glossary

A

access control entry (ACE) An entry in an access control list (ACL). Each access control entry defines the protection or auditing to be applied to a file or other object for a specific user or group of users. *See also* access control list (ACL).

access control list (ACL) The part of a security descriptor that enumerates both the protections to accessing and the auditing of that accessing that are applied to an object. The owner of an object has discretionary access control of the object and can change the object's ACL to allow or disallow others access to the object. Access control lists are ordered lists of access control entries (ACEs). There are two types of ACLs: discretionary (DACL) and system (SACL). *See also* access control entry (ACE); discretionary access control list (DACL); system access control list (SACL).

access permission A rule associated with an object (usually a directory, file, or printer) to regulate which users can have access to the object and in what manner. *See also* user rights.

access privileges Permissions set by Macintosh users that allow them to view and make changes to folders on a server. By setting access privileges (called *permissions* when set on the computer running Windows NT Server), you control which Macintosh can use folders in a volume. Services for Macintosh (SFM) translates access privileges set by Macintosh users to the equivalent Windows NT permissions.

access token (or security token) An object that uniquely identifies a user who has logged on. An access token is attached to all of the user's processes and contains the user's security ID (SID), the SIDs of any groups to which the user belongs, any permissions that the user owns, the default owner of any objects that the user's processes create, and the default access control list (ACL) to be applied to any objects that the user's processes create. *See also* permissions.

access violation An attempt to carry out a memory operation that is not allowed by Windows NT memory management. This can include an invalid operation (such as writing to a read-only buffer); accessing memory beyond the limit of the current program's address space (a "length violation"); accessing a page to which the system forbids access; or accessing a page that is currently resident but dedicated to the use of an Executive component.

account *See* group account; user account.

account lockout A Windows NT Server security feature that locks a user account if a number of failed logon attempts occur within a specified amount of time, based on account policy lockout settings. (Locked accounts cannot log on.)

account policy Controls the way passwords must be used by all user accounts of a domain or of an individual computer. Specifics include minimum password length, how often a user must change his or her password, and how often users can reuse old passwords. Account policy can be set for all user accounts in a domain when administering a domain, and for all user accounts of a single workstation or member server when administering a computer.

ACK Short for acknowledgment. The Transmission Control Protocol (TCP) requires that the recipient of data packets acknowledge successful receipt of data. Such acknowledgments (ACKs) generate additional network traffic, diminishing the rate at which data passes in favor of reliability. To reduce the impact on performance, most hosts send an acknowledgment for every other segment or when a specified time interval has passed.

acknowledgment *See* ACK.

active Refers to the window or icon that you are currently using or that is currently selected. Windows NT always applies the next keystroke or command you choose to the active window. If a window is active, its title bar changes color to differentiate it from other windows. If an icon is active, its label changes color. Windows or icons on the desktop that are not selected are inactive.

ActiveX An umbrella term for Microsoft technologies that enable developers to create interactive content for the World Wide Web.

adapter card *See* network adapter.

address Within Network Monitor, an address refers to a hexadecimal number that identifies a computer uniquely on the network.

address classes Predefined groupings of Internet addresses, with each class defining networks of a certain size. The range of numbers that can be assigned for the first octet in the IP address is based on the address class. Class A networks (values 1–126) are the largest, with over 16 million hosts per network. Class B networks (128–191) have up to 65,534 hosts per network, and Class C networks (192–223) can have up to 254 hosts per network. *See also* octet.

address pairs Refers to the two specific computers between which you want to monitor traffic by using Network Monitor. Up to four specific address pairs can be monitored simultaneously to capture frames from particular computers on your network. *See also* frame.

Address Resolution Protocol (ARP) A network-maintenance protocol in the TCP/IP suite that provides IP address-to-MAC address resolution for IP packets. Not directly related to data transport. *See also* IP address; media access control (MAC); packet; Transmission Control Protocol/Internet Protocol (TCP/IP).

administrative account An account that is a member of the Administrators local group of a computer or domain.

administrative alerts Administrative alerts relate to server and resource use and warn about problems in areas such as security and access, user sessions, server shutdown due to power loss (when UPS is available), directory replication, and printing. When a computer generates an administrative alert, a message is sent to a predefined list of users and computers. *See also* Alerter service; uninterruptible power supply (UPS).

administrator A person responsible for setting up and managing domain controllers or local computers and their user and group accounts, assigning passwords and permissions, and helping users with networking issues. To use administrative tools such as User Manager or User Manager for Domains, an administrator must be logged on as a member of the Administrators local group of the computer or domain, respectively.

Administrator privilege One of three privilege levels you can assign to a Windows NT user account. Every user account has one of the three privilege levels (Administrator, Guest, and User). *See also* administrator; Guest privilege; User privilege.

Advanced RISC Computing (ARC) ARC names are a generic method of identifying devices within the ARC environment. *See also* reduced instruction set computing (RISC).

agent In SNMP, agent information consists of comments about the user, the physical location of the computer, and the types of service to report based on the computer's configuration. *See also* Simple Network Management Protocol (SNMP).

Alerter service Notifies selected users and computers of administrative alerts that occur on a computer. Used by the Server service and other services. Requires the Messenger service. *See also* administrative alerts; Messenger service.

anonymous-level security token The type of security token used when a server impersonates a client. If, when the client calls the server, the client specifies an anonymous impersonation mode, the server cannot access any of the client's identification information, such as its security identifier (SID) or privileges. The server will have to use an anonymous-level security token when representing the client in successive operations. *See also* access token.

Anonymous user A connection for which the request either did not contain a user name and password or whose user name and password were ignored because authentication is not permitted on the server.

API *See* application programming interface.

AppleShare Client software that is shipped with each Macintosh and with Apple Computer server software. With Services for Macintosh, a Macintosh uses its native AppleShare client software to connect to computers running Windows NT Server that have Services for Macintosh.

AppleTalk Apple Computer network architecture and network protocols. A network that has Macintosh clients and a computer running Windows NT Server with Services for Macintosh functions as an AppleTalk network.

AppleTalk Filing Protocol The presentation layer protocol that manages access of remote files in an AppleTalk network.

AppleTalk Phase 2 The extended AppleTalk Internet model designed by Apple Computer. It supports multiple zones within a network and extended addressing capacity.

AppleTalk Protocol The set of network protocols on which AppleTalk network architecture is based. Setting up Services for Macintosh installs its AppleTalk Protocol stack on a computer running Windows NT Server so that Macintosh clients can connect to it.

AppleTalk Transport The layer of AppleTalk Phase 2 protocols that deliver data to its destination on the network.

application A computer program used for a particular kind of work, such as word processing. This term is often used interchangeably with "program."

application log The application log contains specific events logged by applications. Applications developers decide which events to monitor (for example, a database program might record a file error in the application log). Use Event Viewer to view the application log.

application programming interface (API)
A set of routines that an application program uses to request and carry out lower-level services performed by another component, such as the computer's operating system or a service running on a network computer. These maintenance chores are performed by the computer's operating system, and an API provides the program with a means of communicating with the system, telling it which system-level task to perform and when.

application window The main window for an application, which contains the application's menu bar and work area. An application window may contain multiple document windows.

ARC *See* Advanced RISC Computing.

archive bit Backup programs use the archive bit to mark the files after backing them up, if a normal or incremental backup is performed. *See also* backup types.

ARP *See* Address Resolution Protocol.

ARP reply packet All ARP-enabled systems on the local IP network detect ARP request packets, and the system that owns the IP address in question replies by sending its physical address to the requester in an ARP reply packet. The physical/IP address is then stored in the ARP cache of the requesting system for subsequent use. *See also* Address Resolution Protocol (ARP); ARP request packet; Internet Protocol (IP); MAC address.

ARP request packet If two systems are to communicate across a TCP/IP network, the system sending the packet must map the IP address of the final destination to the physical address of the final destination. This physical address is also referred to as a MAC address, a unique 48-bit number assigned to the network interface card by the manufacturer. IP acquires this physical address by broadcasting a special inquiry packet (an ARP request packet) containing the IP address of the destination system. *See also* Address Resolution Protocol (ARP); Internet Protocol (IP); MAC address; media access control (MAC).

AS/400 A type of IBM minicomputer.

ASCII file Also called a text file, a text-only file, or an ASCII text file, refers to a file in the universally recognized text format called ASCII (American Standard Code for Information Interchange). An ASCII file contains characters, spaces, punctuation, carriage returns, and sometimes tabs and an end-of-file marker, but it contains no formatting information. This generic format is useful for transferring files between programs that could not otherwise understand each other's documents. *See also* text file.

associate To identify a file name extension as "belonging" to a certain application so that when you open any file with that extension, the application starts automatically.

attributes Information that indicates whether a file is a read-only, hidden, system, or compressed file, and whether the file has been changed since a backup copy of it was made.

A-type resource record A line (record) in a computer's Domain Name System database that maps a computer's domain name (host name) to an IP address in a DNS zone.

auditing Tracking activities of users by recording selected types of events in the security log of a server or a workstation.

audit policy For the servers of a domain or for an individual computer, defines the type of security events that will be logged.

authentication Validation of a user's logon information. When a user logs on to an account on a computer running Windows NT Workstation, the authentication is performed by that workstation. When a user logs on to an account on a Windows NT Server domain, authentication may be performed by any server of that domain. *See also* Basic (clear-text) authentication; challenge/response authentication; server; trust relationship.

B

backup domain controller (BDC) In a Windows NT Server domain, a computer running Windows NT Server that receives a copy of the domain's directory database, which contains all account and security policy information for the domain. The copy is synchronized periodically and automatically with the master copy on the primary domain controller (PDC). BDCs also authenticate user logons and can be promoted to function as PDCs as needed. Multiple BDCs can exist on a domain. *See also* member server; primary domain controller (PDC).

backup set A collection of files from one drive that is backed up during a single backup operation.

backup set catalog At the end of each backup set, Windows NT Backup stores a summary of file or directory information in a backup set catalog. Catalog information includes the number of tapes in a set of tapes as well as the date they were created, and the dates of each file in the catalog. Catalogs are created for each backup set and are stored on the last tape in the set. *See also* backup set.

backup set map At the end of each tape used for backup, a backup set map maintains the exact tape location of the backup set's data and catalog.

backup types:

copy backup Copies all selected files, but does not mark each file as having been backed up. Copying is useful if you want to back up files between normal and incremental backups, because copying will not invalidate these other backup operations.

daily backup Copies all selected files that have been modified the day the daily backup is performed.

differential backup Copies those files created or changed since the last normal (or incremental) backup. It does not mark files as having been backed up.

incremental backup Backs up only those files created or changed since the last normal (or incremental) backup. It marks files as having been backed up.

normal backup Copies all selected files and marks each as having been backed up. Normal backups give you the ability to restore files quickly because files on the last tape are the most current.

bandwidth In communications, the difference between the highest and lowest frequencies in a given range. For example, a telephone line accommodates a bandwidth of 3000 Hz, the difference between the lowest (300 Hz) and highest (3300 Hz) frequencies it can carry. In computer networks, greater bandwidth indicates faster data-transfer capability and is expressed in bits per second (bps). Also known as "throughput."

Basic (clear-text) authentication A method of authentication that encodes user name and password data transmissions. Basic authentication is called "clear text" because the base-64 encoding can be decoded by anyone with a freely available decoding utility. Note that encoding is not the same as encryption. *See also* challenge/response authentication; encryption.

batch program An ASCII file (unformatted text file) that contains one or more Windows NT commands. A batch program's file name has a .cmd or .bat extension. When you type the file name at the command prompt, the commands are processed sequentially.

batch queue facility A program that effects a logon without user input, used for delayed logons.

BDC *See* backup domain controller.

binary A base-2 number system, in which values are expressed as combinations of two digits, 0 and 1.

binary-file transfer A method of transferring binary files from Windows NT HyperTerminal to a remote computer. Binary files consist of ASCII characters plus the extended ASCII character set. These files are not converted or translated during the transfer process. *See also* ASCII file.

binding A process that establishes the communication channel between a protocol driver (such as TCP/IP) and a network adapter. *See also* network adapter; Transmission Control Protocol/Internet Protocol (TCP/IP).

bits per second (bps) A measure of the speed at which a device, such as a modem, can transfer data.

blue screen The screen displayed when Windows NT encounters a serious error.

bookmarks A Windows NT feature that enables you to highlight major points of interest at various points in a Performance Monitor log file and then return to them easily when you work with that log file later on during performance monitoring. Bookmarks are also used in other applications, such as Microsoft Word.

boot loader Defines the information needed for system startup, such as the location for the operating system's files. Windows NT automatically creates the correct configuration and checks this information whenever you start your system.

boot partition The volume, formatted for either an NTFS or FAT file system, that contains the Windows NT operating system and its support files. The boot partition can be (but does not have to be) the same as the system partition. *See also* file allocation table (FAT); partition; Windows NT File System (NTFS).

Bootstrap protocol (BOOTP) A TCP/IP network protocol, defined by RFC 951 and RFC 1542, used to configure systems. DHCP is an extension of BOOTP. *See also* Dynamic Host Configuration Protocol (DHCP).

bps *See* bits per second.

branch A segment of the directory tree, representing a directory (or folder) and any subdirectories (or folders within folders) it contains.

bridge Connects multiple networks, subnets, or rings into one large logical network. A bridge maintains a table of node addresses and, based on this, forwards packets to a specific subnet, reducing traffic on other subnets. In a bridged network, there can be only one path to any destination (otherwise packets would circle the network, causing network storms). A bridge is more sophisticated than a repeater, but not as sophisticated as a router. *See also* packet; repeaters; router; subnet.

broadcast datagram An IP datagram sent to all hosts on the subnet. *See also* datagram; Internet Protocol (IP); subnet.

broadcast message A network message sent from a single computer that is distributed to all other devices on the same segment of the network as the sending computer.

broadcast name resolution A mechanism defined in RFC 1001/1002 that uses broadcasts to resolve names to IP addresses through a process of registration, resolution, and name release. *See also* broadcast datagram; IP address.

brouter Combines elements of the bridge and the router. Usually, a brouter acts as a router for one transport protocol (such as TCP/IP), sending packets of that format along detailed routes to their destinations. The brouter also acts as a bridge for all other types of packets (such as IPX), just passing them on, as long as they are not local to the LAN segment from which they originated. *See also* bridge; packet; router.

browse To view available network resources by looking through lists of folders, files, user accounts, groups, domains, or computers. Browsing allows users on a Windows NT network to see what domains and computers are accessible from their local computer. *See also* Windows NT browser system.

browse list A list kept by the master browser of all of the servers and domains on the network. This list is available to any workstation on the network requesting it. *See also* browse.

browse master *See* master browser; Windows NT browser system.

buffer A reserved portion of memory in which data is temporarily held pending an opportunity to complete its transfer to or from a storage device or another location in memory. Some devices, such as printers or the adapters supporting them, commonly have their own buffers. *See also* memory.

built-in groups Default groups, provided with Windows NT Server and Windows NT Workstation, that have been granted useful collections of rights and built-in abilities. In most cases, a built-in group provides all of the capabilities needed by a particular user. For example, if a domain user account belongs to the built-in Administrators group, logging on with that account gives a user administrative capabilities over the domain and the servers of the domain. To provide a needed set of capabilities to a user account, assign it to the appropriate built-in group. *See also* group; User Manager; User Manager for Domains.

bulk data encryption The encryption of all data sent over a network.

C

cache A special memory subsystem that stores the contents of frequently accessed RAM locations and the addresses where these data items are stored. In Windows NT, for example, user profiles have a locally cached copy of part of the registry.

caching In DNS name resolution, caching refers to a local cache where information about the DNS domain name space is kept. Whenever a resolver request arrives, the local name server checks both its static information and the cache for the name to IP address mapping. *See also* Domain Name System (DNS); IP address; mapping.

Callback Control Protocol (CBCP) A protocol that negotiates callback information with a remote client.

capture The process by which Network Monitor copies frames. (A *frame* is information that has been divided into smaller pieces by the network software prior to transmission.) *See also* frame.

capture buffer A reserved, resizable storage area in memory where Network Monitor copies all frames it detects from the network. When the capture buffer overflows, each new frame replaces the oldest frame in the buffer.

capture filter Functions like a database query to single out a subset of frames to be monitored in Network Monitor. You can filter on the basis of source and destination addresses, protocols, protocol properties, or by specifying a pattern offset. *See also* capture; frame.

capture password Required to be able to capture statistics from the network and to display captured data using Network Monitor.

capture trigger Performs a specified action (such as starting an executable file) when Network Monitor detects a particular set of conditions on the network.

catalog *See* backup set catalog.

CBCP *See* Callback Control Protocol.

CCP *See* Compression Control Protocol.

centralized network administration A centralized view of the entire network from any workstation on the network that provides the ability to track and manage information on users, groups, and resources in a distributed network.

CGI *See* Common Gateway Interface.

Challenge Handshake Authentication Protocol (CHAP) A protocol used by Microsoft RAS to negotiate the most secure form of encrypted authentication supported by both server and client. *See also* encryption.

challenge/response authentication A method of authentication in which a server uses challenge/response algorithms and Windows NT security to control access to resources. *See also* Basic (clear-text) authentication; encryption.

change log An inventory of the most recent changes made to the directory database such as new or changed passwords, new or changed user and group accounts, and any changes to associated group memberships and user rights. Change logs provide fault tolerance, so if your system crashes before a write completes, Windows NT can complete the write the next time you boot. This log holds only a certain number of changes, however, so when a new change is added, the oldest change is deleted. *See also* directory database; fault tolerance.

CHAP *See* Challenge Handshake Authentication Protocol.

check box A small box in a dialog box or property page that can be selected or cleared. Check boxes represent an option that you can turn on or off. When a check box is selected, an X or a check mark appears in the box.

checksum The mathematical computation used to verify the accuracy of data in TCP/IP packets. *See also* packet; Transmission Control Protocol/Internet Protocol (TCP/IP).

choose To pick an item that begins an action in Windows NT. You often click a command on a menu to perform a task, and you click an icon to start an application.

circular dependency A dependency in which an action that appears later in a chain is contingent upon an earlier action. For example, three services (A, B, and C) are linked. A is dependent upon B to start. B is dependent upon C to start. A circular dependency results when C is dependent upon A to start. *See also* dependency.

clear To turn off an option by removing the X or check mark from a check box. To clear a check box, you can click it, or you can select it and then press the SPACEBAR.

clear-text authentication *See* Basic (clear-text) authentication.

clear-text passwords Passwords that are not scrambled, thus making them more susceptible to network sniffers. *See also* network sniffer.

click To press and release a mouse button quickly.

client A computer that accesses shared network resources provided by another computer, called a server. *See also* server; workstation.

client application A Windows NT application that can display and store linked or embedded objects. For distributed applications, the application that imitates a request to a server application. *See also* DCOM Configuration tool; Distributed Component Object Module (DCOM); server application.

Client Service for NetWare Included with Windows NT Workstation, enabling workstations to make direct connections to file and printer resources at NetWare servers running NetWare 2.x or later.

Clipboard A temporary storage area in memory, used to transfer information. You can cut or copy information onto the Clipboard and then paste it into another document or application.

close Remove a window or dialog box, or quit an application. To close a window, you can click **Close** on the **Control** menu, or you can click the close button icon in the upper right corner of the dialog box. When you close an application window, you quit the application.

collapse To hide additional directory levels below a selected directory in the directory tree.

color scheme A combination of complementary colors for screen elements.

command A word or phrase, usually found on a menu, that you click to carry out an action. You click a command on a menu or type a command at the Windows NT command prompt. You can also type a command in the **Run** dialog box, which you open by clicking **Run** on the **Start** menu.

command button A button in a dialog box that carries out or cancels the selected action. Two common command buttons are **OK** and **Cancel**. If you click a command button that contains an ellipsis (for example, **Browse...**), another dialog box appears.

Common Gateway Interface (CGI)
A standard interface for HTTP server application development. The standard was developed by the National Center for Supercomputing Applications.

common group Common groups appear in the program list on the **Start** menu for all users who log on to the computer. Only Administrators can create or change common groups.

communications settings Settings that specify how information is transferred from your computer to a device (usually a printer or modem).

community names A group of hosts to which a server belongs that is running the SNMP service. The community name is placed in the SNMP packet when the trap is sent. Typically, all hosts belong to Public, which is the standard name for the common community of all hosts. *See also* packet; Simple Network Management Protocol (SNMP); trap.

compact A command-line utility used to compress files on NTFS volumes. To see command line options, type **compact /?** at the command prompt. To access this utility, you can also right-click any file or directory on an NTFS volume in Windows NT Explorer, then click **Properties** to compress or decompress the files.

compound device A device that plays specific media files. For example, to run a compound device such as a MIDI sequencer, you must specify a MIDI file.

Compression Control Protocol (CCP)
A protocol that negotiates compression with a remote client.

computer account Each computer running Windows NT Workstation and Windows NT Server that participates in a domain has its own account in the directory database. A computer account is created when the computer is first identified to the domain during network setup at installation time.

Computer Browser service Maintains an up-to-date list of computers, and provides the list to applications when requested. Provides the computer lists displayed in the **Network Neighborhood**, **Select Computer**, and **Select Domain** dialog boxes; and (for Windows NT Server only) in the Server Manager window.

computer name A unique name of up to 15 uppercase characters that identifies a computer to the network. The name cannot be the same as any other computer or domain name in the network.

configure To change the initial setup of a client, a Macintosh-accessible volume, a server, or a network.

connect To assign a drive letter, port, or computer name to a shared resource so that you can use it with Windows NT.

connected user A user accessing a computer or a resource across the network.

connection A software link between a client and a shared resource such as a printer or a shared directory on a server. Connections require a network adapter or modem.

connection-oriented protocol A network protocol with four important characteristics: the path for data packets is established in advance; the resources required for a connection are reserved in advance; a connection's resource reservation is enforced throughout the life of that connection; and when a connection's data transfer is completed, the connection is terminated and the allocated resources are freed.

control codes Codes that specify terminal commands or formatting instructions (such as linefeeds or carriage returns) in a text file. Control codes are usually preceded by a caret (^).

controller *See* backup domain controller (BDC); primary domain controller (PDC).

Control menu *See* window menu.

control set All Windows NT startup-related data that is not computed during startup is saved in a registry key. This startup data is organized into control sets, each of which contains a complete set of parameters for starting up devices and services. The registry always contains at least two control sets, each of which contains information about all of the configurable options for the computer: the current control set and the LastKnownGood control set. *See also* current control set; LastKnownGood (LKG) control set.

conventional memory Up to the first 640 KB of memory in your computer. MS-DOS uses this memory to run applications.

CRC *See* cyclic redundancy check.

current control set The control set that was used most recently to start the computer and that contains any changes made to the startup information during the current session. *See also* LastKnownGood (LKG) control set.

current directory The directory that you are currently working in. Also called "current folder."

cyclic redundancy check (CRC) A procedure used on disk drives to ensure that the data written to a sector is read correctly later. This procedure is also used in checking for errors in data transmission.

The procedure is known as a redundancy check because each data transmission includes not only data but extra (redundant) error-checking values. The sending device generates a number based on the data to be transmitted and sends its result along with the data to the receiving device. The receiving device repeats the same calculation after transmission. If both devices obtain the same result, it is assumed that the transmission is error-free.

D

DACL *See* discretionary access control list; *see also* system access control list (SACL).

daemon A networking program that runs in the background.

database query The process of extracting data from a database and presenting it for use.

data carrier In communications, either a specified frequency that can be modulated to convey information or a company that provides telephone and other communications services to consumers.

Data Carrier Detect (DCD) Tracks the presence of a data carrier. *See also* data carrier.

data communications equipment (DCE) An elaborate worldwide network of packet-forwarding nodes that participate in delivering an X.25 packet to its designated address, for example, a modem. *See also* node; packet; X.25.

Data Encryption Standard (DES) A type of encryption (the U.S. government standard) designed to protect against password discovery and playback. Microsoft RAS uses DES encryption when both the client and the server are using RAS.

data fork The part of a Macintosh file that holds most of the file's information. The data fork is the part of the file shared between Macintosh and PC clients.

datagram A packet of data and other delivery information that is routed through a packet-switched network or transmitted on a local area network. *See also* packet.

Data Source Name (DSN) The logical name used by ODBC to refer to the drive and other information required to access data. The name is use by Internet Information Server for a connection to an ODBC data source, such as a SQL Server database. To set this name, use ODBC in the Control Panel.

data stream Windows NT Network Monitor monitors the network data stream, which consists of all information transferred over a network at any given time.

Data Terminal Equipment (DTE) For example, a RAS server or client. *See also* Remote Access Service (RAS).

dbWeb Administrator The graphical user tool for Microsoft dbWeb that allows an administrator to create definition templates referred to as schemas. Schemas control how and what information from a private database is available to visitors who use the Internet to access the public Microsoft dbWeb gateway to the private database. *See also* schemas.

DCD *See* Data Carrier Detect.

DCE *See* data communications equipment.

DCOM *See* Distributed Component Object Model.

DCOM Configuration tool A Windows NT Server utility that can be used to configure 32-bit applications for DCOM communication over the network. *See also* Distributed Component Object Model (DCOM).

DDE *See* dynamic data exchange.

deadlock condition A run-time error condition that occurs when two threads of execution are blocked, each waiting to acquire a resource that the other holds, and both unable to continue running.

decision tree A geographical representation of a filter's logic used by Windows NT Network Monitor. When you include or exclude information from your capture specifications, the decision tree reflects these specifications.

default button In some dialog boxes, the command button that is selected or highlighted when the dialog box is initially displayed. The default button has a bold border, indicating that it will be chosen automatically if you press ENTER. To override a default button, you can click **Cancel** or another command button.

default gateway In TCP/IP, the intermediate network device on the local network that has knowledge of the network IDs of the other networks in the Internet, so it can forward the packets to other gateways until the packet is eventually delivered to a gateway connected to the specified destination. *See also* gateway; network ID; packet.

default network In the Macintosh environment, this refers to the physical network on which a server's processes reside as nodes and on which the server appears to users. A server's default network must be one to which that server is attached. Only servers on AppleTalk Phase 2 internets have default networks.

default owner The person assigned ownership of a folder on the server when the account of the folder or volume's previous owner expires or is deleted. Each server has one default owner; you can specify the owner.

default printer The printer that is used if you choose the **Print** command without first specifying which printer you want to use with an application. You can have only one default printer; it should be the printer you use most often.

default profile *See* system default profile; user default profile.

default user Every user profile begins as a copy of default user, a default user profile stored on each computer running Windows NT Workstation or Windows NT Server.

default zone The zone to which all Macintosh clients on the network are assigned by default.

dependency A situation in which one action must take place before another can happen. For example, if action A does not occur, then action D cannot occur. Some Windows NT drivers have dependencies on other drivers or groups of drivers. For example, driver A will not load unless some driver from the G group loads first. *See also* circular dependency.

dependent service A service that requires support of another service. For example, the Alerter service is dependent on the Messenger service. *See also* Alerter service; Messenger service.

DES *See* Data Encryption Standard.

descendent key All of the subkeys that appear when a key in the registry is expanded. A descendent key is the same thing as a subkey. *See also* key; registry; subkey.

desired zone The zone in which Services for Macintosh appears on the network. *See also* default zone.

desktop The background of your screen, on which windows, icons, and dialog boxes appear.

desktop pattern A design that appears across your desktop. You can create your own pattern or select a pattern provided by Windows NT.

destination directory The directory to which you intend to copy or move one or more files.

destination document The document into which a package or a linked or embedded object is being inserted. For an embedded object, this is sometimes also called the container document. *See also* embedded object; linked object; package.

device Any piece of equipment that can be attached to a network—for example, a computer, a printer, or any other peripheral equipment.

device contention The way Windows NT allocates access to peripheral devices, such as modems or printers, when more than one application is trying to use the same device.

device driver A program that enables a specific piece of hardware (device) to communicate with Windows NT. Although a device may be installed on your system, Windows NT cannot recognize the device until you have installed and configured the appropriate driver. If a device is listed in the Hardware Compatibility List, a driver is usually included with Windows NT. Drivers are installed when you run the Setup program (for a manufacturer's supplied driver) or by using Devices in Control Panel. *See also* Hardware Compatibility List (HCL).

DHCP *See* Dynamic Host Configuration Protocol.

DHCP Relay Agent The component responsible for relaying DHCP and BOOTP broadcast messages between a DHCP server and a client across an IP router. *See also* Bootstrap protocol (BOOTP); Dynamic Host Configuration Protocol (DHCP).

dialog box A window that is displayed to request or supply information. Many dialog boxes have options you must select before Windows NT can carry out a command.

dial-up line A standard dial-up connection such as telephone and ISDN lines.

dial-up networking The client version of Windows NT Remote Access Service (RAS), enabling users to connect to remote networks.

directory Part of a structure for organizing your files on a disk, a directory (also called a folder) is represented by the folder icon in Windows NT, Windows 95, and on Macintosh computers. A directory can contain files and other directories, called subdirectories or folders within folders.

With Services for Macintosh, directories on the computer running Windows NT Server appear to Macintosh users as volumes and folders if they are designated as Macintosh accessible.

See also directory tree; folder.

directory database A database of security information such as user account names and passwords, and the security policy settings. For Windows NT Workstation, the directory database is managed by using User Manager. For a Windows NT Server domain, it is managed by using User Manager for Domains. (Other Windows NT documents may refer to the directory database as the "Security Accounts Manager (SAM) database.") *See also* Windows NT Server Directory Services.

directory replication The copying of a master set of directories from a server (called an export server) to specified servers or workstations (called import computers) in the same or other domains. Replication simplifies the task of maintaining identical sets of directories and files on multiple computers, because only a single master copy of the data must be maintained. Files are replicated when they are added to an exported directory and every time a change is saved to the file. *See also* Directory Replicator service.

Directory Replicator service Replicates directories, and the files in those directories, between computers. *See also* directory replication.

Directory Service Manager for NetWare (DSMN) A component of Windows NT Server. Enables network administrators to add NetWare servers to Windows NT Server domains and to manage a single set of user and group accounts that are valid at multiple servers running either Windows NT Server or NetWare.

directory services *See* Windows NT Server Directory Services.

directory tree A graphical display of a disk's directory hierarchy. The directories and folders on the disk are shown as a branching structure. The top-level directory is the root directory.

disabled user account A user account that does not permit logons. The account appears in the user account list of the User Manager or User Manager for Domains window and can be re-enabled at any time. *See also* user account.

discovery A process by which the Windows NT Net Logon service attempts to locate a domain controller running Windows NT Server in the trusted domain. Once a domain controller has been discovered, it is used for subsequent user account authentication.

discretionary access control Allows the network administrator to allow some users to connect to a resource or perform an action while preventing other users from doing so. *See also* discretionary access control list; system access control list (SACL).

discretionary access control list (DACL) The discretionary ACL is controlled by the owner of an object and specifies the access particular users or groups can have to that object. *See also* system access control list (SACL).

disjoint networks Networks that are not connected to each other.

disk configuration information The Windows NT registry includes the following information on the configuration of your disk(s): assigned drive letters, stripe sets, mirror sets, volume sets, and stripe sets with parity. Disk configuration can be changed by using Disk Administrator. If you choose to create an Emergency Repair Disk, disk configuration information will be stored there, as well as in the registry.

display filter Functions like a database query, allowing you to single out specific types of information. Because a display filter operates on data that has already been captured, it does not affect the contents of the Network Monitor capture buffer. *See also* capture buffer.

display password Required to be able to open previously saved capture (.cap) files in Network Monitor.

Distributed Component Object Model (DCOM) Use the DCOM Configuration tool to integrate client/server applications across multiple computers. DCOM can also be used to integrate robust Web browser applications. *See also* DCOM Configuration tool.

distributed server system In Windows NT, a system in which individual departments or workgroups set up and maintain their own remote access domains.

DLL *See* dynamic-link library.

DNS *See* Domain Name System.

DNS name servers In the DNS client/server model, the servers containing information about a portion of the DNS database, which makes computer names available to client resolvers querying for name resolution across the Internet. *See also* Domain Name System (DNS).

DNS service The service that provides domain name resolution. *See also* DNS name servers.

document A self-contained file created with an application and, if saved on disk, given a unique file name by which it can be retrieved. A document can be a text file, a spreadsheet, or an image file, for example.

document file A file that is associated with an application. When you open a document file, the application starts and loads the file. *See also* associate.

Document file icon Represents a file that is associated with an application. When you double-click a document file icon, the application starts and loads the file. *See also* associate.

document icon Located at the left of a document window title bar, the document icon represents the open document. Clicking the document icon opens the window menu. Also known as the control menu box.

domain In Windows NT, a collection of computers, defined by the administrator of a Windows NT Server network, that share a common directory database. A domain provides access to the centralized user accounts and group accounts maintained by the domain administrator. Each domain has a unique name. *See also* directory database; user account; workgroup.

domain controller In a Windows NT Server domain, refers to the computer running Windows NT Server that manages all aspects of user-domain interactions, and uses information in the directory database to authenticate users logging on to domain accounts. One shared directory database is used to store security and user account information for the entire domain. A domain has one primary domain controller (PDC) and one or more backup domain controllers (BDCs). *See also* backup domain controller (BDC); directory database; member server; primary domain controller (PDC).

domain database *See* directory database.

domain model A grouping of one or more domains with administration and communication links between them that are arranged for the purpose of user and resource management.

domain name Part of the Domain Name System (DNS) naming structure, a domain name is the name by which a domain is known to the network. Domain names consist of a sequence of labels separated by periods. *See also* Domain Name System (DNS); fully qualified domain name (FQDN).

domain name space The database structure used by the Domain Name System (DNS). *See also* Domain Name System (DNS).

Domain Name System (DNS) Sometimes referred to as the BIND service in BSD UNIX, DNS offers a static, hierarchical name service for TCP/IP hosts. The network administrator configures the DNS with a list of host names and IP addresses, allowing users of workstations configured to query the DNS to specify remote systems by host names rather than IP addresses. For example, a workstation configured to use DNS name resolution could use the command **ping remotehost** rather than **ping 172.16.16.235** if the mapping for the system named **remotehost** was contained in the DNS database. DNS domains should not be confused with Windows NT networking domains. *See also* IP address; ping.

domain synchronization *See* synchronize.

dots per inch (DPI) The standard used to measure print device resolution. The greater the DPI, the better the resolution.

double-click To rapidly press and release a mouse button twice without moving the mouse. Double-clicking carries out an action, such as starting an application.

down level A term that refers to earlier operating systems, such as Windows for Workgroups or LAN Manager, that can still interoperate with Windows NT Workstation or Windows NT Server.

downloaded fonts Fonts that you send to your printer either before or during the printing of your documents. When you send a font to your printer, it is stored in printer memory until it is needed for printing. *See also* font; font types.

DPI *See* dots per inch.

drag To move an item on the screen by selecting the item and then pressing and holding down the mouse button while moving the mouse. For example, you can move a window to another location on the screen by dragging its title bar.

drive icon An icon in the All Folders column in Windows NT Explorer or the Names Column in My Computer that represents a disk drive on your system. Different icons depict floppy disk drives, hard disk drives, network drives, RAM drives, and CD-ROM drives.

driver *See* device driver.

drop folder In the Macintosh environment this refers to a folder for which you have the Make Changes permission but not the See Files or See Folders permission. You can copy files into a drop folder, but you cannot see what files and subfolders the drop folder contains.

DSDM Acronym for DDE share database manager. *See also* dynamic data exchange (DDE); Network DDE DSDM service.

DSMN *See* Directory Service Manager for NetWare.

DSN *See* Data Source Name.

DSR Acronym for Data Set Ready signal, used in serial communications. A DSR is sent by a modem to the computer to which it is attached to indicate that it is ready to operate. DSRs are hardware signals sent over line 6 in RS-232-C connections.

DTE *See* Data Terminal Equipment.

dual boot A computer that can boot two different operating systems. *See also* multiple boot.

DWORD A data type composed of hexadecimal data with a maximum allotted space of 4 bytes.

dynamic assignment The automatic assignment of TCP/IP properties in a changing network.

dynamic data exchange (DDE) A form of interprocess communication (IPC) implemented in the Microsoft Windows family of operating systems. Two or more programs that support dynamic data exchange (DDE) can exchange information and commands. *See also* interprocess communication (IPC).

Dynamic Host Configuration Protocol (DHCP) A protocol that offers dynamic configuration of IP addresses and related information. DHCP provides safe, reliable, and simple TCP/IP network configuration, prevents address conflicts, and helps conserve the use of IP addresses through centralized management of address allocation. *See also* IP address.

dynamic-link library (DLL) An operating system feature that allows executable routines (generally serving a specific function or set of functions) to be stored separately as files with .dll extensions and to be loaded only when needed by the program that calls them.

dynamic routing Dynamic routing automatically updates the routing tables, reducing administrative overhead (but increasing traffic in large networks). *See also* routing table.

dynamic Web pages Web pages that are derived or assembled only when the client requests them. Dynamic pages are used to deliver very current information, to deliver responses to forms and queries, and to provide a customized page. They are often associated with databases, such as SQL databases. *See also* static Web pages.

E

EISA *See* Extended Industry Standard Architecture.

embedded object Presents information, created in another application, which has been pasted inside your document. Information in the embedded object does not exist in another file outside your document.

EMS *See* Expanded Memory Specification.

encapsulated PostScript (EPS) file A file that prints at the highest possible resolution for your printer. An EPS file may print faster than other graphical representations. Some Windows NT and non-Windows NT graphical applications can import EPS files. *See also* font types; PostScript printer; print processor.

encryption The process of making information indecipherable to protect it from unauthorized viewing or use, especially during transmission or when it is stored on a transportable magnetic medium.

enterprise server Refers to the server to which multiple primary domain controllers (PDCs) in a large organization will replicate. *See also* primary domain controller (PDC).

environment variable A string consisting of environment information, such as a drive, path, or file name, associated with a symbolic name that can be used by Windows NT. To define environment variables, use System in Control Panel or use the **Set** command from the Windows NT command prompt.

EPS *See* encapsulated PostScript file.

error logging The process by which errors that cannot readily be corrected by the majority of end users are written to a file instead of being displayed on the screen. System administrators, support technicians, and users can use this log file to monitor the condition of the hardware in a computer running Windows NT to tune the configuration of the computer for better performance, and to debug problems as they occur.

event Any significant occurrence in the system or an application that requires users to be notified, or an entry to be added to a log.

Event Log service Records events in the system, security, and application logs. The Event Log service is located in Event Viewer.

exception A synchronous error condition resulting from the execution of a particular computer instruction. Exceptions can be either hardware-detected errors, such as division by zero, or software-detected errors, such as a guard-page violation.

Executive The Executive is the part of the Windows NT operating system that runs in kernel mode. *Kernel mode* is a privileged processor mode in which a thread has access to system memory and to hardware. (In contrast, *user mode* is a nonprivileged processor mode in which a thread can only access system resources by calling system services.) The Windows NT Executive provides process structure, thread scheduling, interprocess communication, memory management, object management, object security, interrupt processing, I/O capabilities, and networking. *See also* Hardware Abstraction Layer (HAL); Kernel.

Executive messages Two types of character-mode messages occur when the Windows NT Kernel detects an inconsistent condition from which it cannot recover: STOP messages and hardware-malfunction messages.

Character-mode STOP messages are always displayed on a full character-mode screen rather than in a Windows-mode message box. They are also uniquely identified by a hexadecimal number and a symbolic string.

Character-mode hardware-malfunction messages are caused by a hardware condition detected by the processor.

(continued)

Executive messages The Executive displays a Windows-mode STATUS message box when it detects conditions within a process (generally, an application) that you should know about.

expand To show hidden directory levels in the directory tree. With My Computer or Windows NT Explorer, directories that can expand have plus-sign icons which you click to expand.

expanded memory A type of memory, up to 8 megabytes, that can be added to an 8086 or 8088 computer, or to an 80286, 80386, 80486, or Pentium computer. The use of expanded memory is defined by the Expanded Memory Specification (EMS). Note: Windows NT requires an 80486 or higher computer.

Expanded Memory Specification (EMS)
Describes a technique for adding memory to IBM PC systems. EMS bypasses the limits on the maximum amount of usable memory in a computer system by supporting memory boards containing a number of 16K banks of RAM that can be enabled or disabled by software. *See also* memory.

Explorer *See* Windows NT Explorer.

export path In directory replication, a path from which subdirectories, and the files in those subdirectories, are automatically exported from an export server. *See also* directory replication.

export server In directory replication, a server from which a master set of directories is exported to specified servers or workstations (called import computers) in the same or other domains. *See also* directory replication.

Extended Industry Standard Architecture (EISA)
A 32-bit bus standard introduced in 1988 by a consortium of nine computer industry companies. EISA maintains compatibility with the earlier Industry Standard Architecture (ISA) but provides for additional features.

extended memory Memory beyond one megabyte in 80286, 80386, 80486, and Pentium computers. Note: Windows NT requires an 80486 or higher computer.

extended partition Created from free space on a hard disk, an extended partition can be subpartitioned into zero or more logical drives. Only one of the four partitions allowed per physical disk can be an extended partition, and no primary partition needs to be present to create an extended partition. *See also* free space; logical drive; primary partition.

extensible counters Performance Monitor counters that are not installed with Windows NT. Extensible counters typically are installed independently. Extensible counters should be monitored to make certain that they are working properly.

extension A file name extension usually indicates the type of file or directory, or the type of application associated with a file. In MS-DOS, this includes a period and up to three characters at the end of a file name. Windows NT supports long file names, up to the file name limit of 255 characters.

extension-type association The association of an MS-DOS file name extension with a Macintosh file type and file creator. Extension-type associations allow users of the PC and Macintosh versions of the same application to share the same data files on the server. Services for Macintosh has many predefined extension-type associations. *See also* name mapping.

external command A command that is stored in its own file and loaded from disk when you use the command.

F

family set A collection of related tapes containing several backup sets. *See also* backup set.

FAT *See* file allocation table.

fault tolerance Ensures data integrity when hardware failures occur. In Windows NT, fault tolerance is provided by the Ftdisk.sys driver. In Disk Administrator, fault tolerance is provided using mirror sets, stripe sets with parity, and volume sets. *See also* mirror set; stripe sets with parity; volume set.

FCB *See* file control block.

Fiber Distributed Data Interface (FDDI) A type of network media designed to be used with fiber-optic cabling. *See also* LocalTalk; Token Ring.

file A collection of information that has been given a name and is stored on a disk. This information can be a document or an application.

file allocation table (FAT) A table or list maintained by some operating systems to keep track of the status of various segments of disk space used for file storage. Also referred to as the FAT file system.

File and Print Services for NetWare (FPNW) A Windows NT Server component that enables a computer running Windows NT Server to provide file and print services directly to NetWare-compatible client computers.

file control block (FCB) A small block of memory temporarily assigned by a computer's operating system to hold information about a file that has been opened for use. An FCB typically contains such information as the file's identification, its location on disk, and a pointer that marks the user's current (or last) position in the file.

file creator A four-character sequence that tells the Macintosh Finder the name of the application that created a file. With Services for Macintosh, you can create extension-type associations that map PC file name extensions with Macintosh file creators and file types. These associations allow both PC and Macintosh users to share the same data files on the server. *See also* extension-type association.

file fork One of two subfiles of a Macintosh file. When Macintosh files are stored on a computer running Windows NT Server, each fork is stored as a separate file. Each fork can be independently opened by a Macintosh user.

file name The name of a file. MS-DOS supports the 8.3 naming convention of up to eight characters followed by a period and a three-character extension. Windows NT supports the FAT and NTFS file systems with file names up to 255 characters. Because MS-DOS cannot recognize long file names, Windows NT Server automatically translates long names of files and folders to 8.3 names for MS-DOS users. *See also* long name; name mapping; short name.

file name extension The characters that follow the period in a file name, following the FAT naming conventions. Filename extensions can have as many as three characters and are often used to identify the type of file and the application used to create the file (for example, spreadsheet files created by Microsoft Excel have the extension .xls). With Services for Macintosh, you can create extension-type associations that map PC file name extensions with Macintosh file creators and types.

File Replication service A Windows NT service that allows specified file(s) to be replicated to remote systems, ensuring that copies on each system are kept in synchronization. The system that maintains the master copy is called the exporter, and the systems that receive updates are known as importers.

File Server for Macintosh service A Services for Macintosh service that enables Macintosh clients and PC clients to share files. Also called MacFile.

file sharing The ability for a computer running Windows NT to share parts (or all) of its local file system(s) with remote computers. An administrator creates share points by using the file sharing command in My Computer or Windows NT Explorer or by using the **net share** command from the command prompt.

file system In an operating system, the overall structure in which files are named, stored, and organized. NTFS and FAT are types of file systems.

File Transfer Protocol (FTP) A service supporting file transfers between local and remote systems that support this protocol. FTP supports several commands that allow bidirectional transfer of binary and ASCII files between systems. The FTP Server service is part of the Internet Information Server. The FTP client is installed with TCP/IP connectivity utilities.

file type In the Macintosh environment, this refers to a four-character sequence that identifies the type of a Macintosh file. The file type and file creator are used by the Macintosh Finder to determine the appropriate desktop icon for that file.

find tab Displays the words you can use to search for related topics. Use this tab to look for topics related to a particular word. It is located in the Help button bar near the top of the Help window.

firewall A system or combination of systems that enforces a boundary between two or more networks and keeps intruders out of private networks. Firewalls serve as virtual barriers to passing packets from one network to another.

flat name space A naming system in which computer names are created from a short sequence of characters without any additional structure superimposed.

floppy disk A disk that can be inserted in and removed from a disk drive. Floppies are most commonly available in a 3.5- or 5.25-inch format.

flow control An exchange of signals, over specific wires, in which each device signals its readiness to send or receive data.

folder A grouping of files or other folders, graphically represented by a folder icon, in both the Windows NT and Macintosh environments. A folder is analogous to a PC's file system directory, and many folders are, in fact, directories. A folder may contain other folders as well as file objects. *See also* directory.

font A graphic design applied to a collection of numbers, symbols, and characters. A font describes a certain typeface along with other qualities such as size, spacing, and pitch. *See also* font set; font types.

font set A collection of font sizes for one font, customized for a particular display and printer. Font sets determine what text looks like on the screen and when printed. *See also* font.

font types:

device fonts Reside in the hardware of your print device. They can be built into the print device itself or can be provided by a font cartridge or font card.

downloadable soft fonts Fonts that are stored on disk and downloaded as needed to the print device.

plotter fonts A font created by a series of dots connected by lines. Plotter fonts can be scaled to any size and are most often printed on plotters. Some dot-matrix printers also support plotter fonts.

PostScript fonts Fonts that are defined in terms of the PostScript page-description language rules from Adobe Systems. When a document displayed in a screen font is sent to a PostScript printer, the printer uses the PostScript version if the font exists. If the font doesn't exist but a version is installed on the computer, that font is downloaded. If there is no PostScript font installed in either the printer or the computer, the bitmapped font is translated into PostScript and the printer prints text using the bitmapped font.

raster fonts Fonts that are stored as bitmaps. If a print device does not support raster fonts, it will not print them. Raster fonts cannot be scaled or rotated.

screen fonts Windows NT fonts that can be translated for output to the print device. Most screen fonts (including TrueType fonts) can be printed as well.

TrueType fonts Device-independent fonts that can be reproduced on all print devices. TrueType fonts are stored as outlines and can be scaled and rotated.

vector fonts Fonts that are useful on devices such as pen plotters that cannot reproduce bitmaps. They can be scaled to any size or aspect ratio. (*See also* plotter fonts, earlier in this entry.)

fork *See* data fork; file fork; resource fork.

FPNW *See* File and Print Services for NetWare.

FQDN *See* fully qualified domain name.

frame In synchronous communication, a package of information transmitted as a single unit from one device to another. *See also* capture.

Frame Relay A synchronous High-level Data Link Control (HDLC) protocol–based network that sends data in HDLC packets. *See also* High-level Data Link Control (HDLC).

framing rules Are established between a remote computer and the server, allowing continued communication (frame transfer) to occur. *See also* frame.

free space Free space is an unused and unformatted portion of a hard disk that can be partitioned or subpartitioned. Free space within an extended partition is available for the creation of logical drives. Free space that is not within an extended partition is available for the creation of a partition, with a maximum of four partitions allowed per disk. *See also* extended partition; logical drive; primary partition.

FTP *See* File Transfer Protocol.

full name A user's complete name, usually consisting of the last name, first name, and middle initial. The full name is information that can be maintained by User Manager and User Manager for Domains as part of the information identifying and defining a user account. *See also* user account.

full-screen application A non–Windows NT application that is displayed in the entire screen, rather than a window, when running in the Windows NT environment.

full synchronization Occurs when a copy of the entire database directory is sent to a backup domain controller (BDC). Full synchronization is performed automatically when changes have been deleted from the change log before replication takes place, and when a new BDC is added to a domain. *See also* backup domain controller (BDC); directory database.

fully qualified domain name (FQDN) Part of the TCP/IP naming convention known as the Domain Name System, DNS computer names consist of two parts: host names with their domain names appended to them. For example, a host with host name **corp001** and DNS domain name **trey-research.com** has an FQDN of **corp001.trey-research.com**. (DNS domains should not be confused with Windows NT networking domains.) *See also* Domain Name System (DNS).

G

gateway Describes a system connected to multiple physical TCP/IP networks, capable of routing or delivering IP packets between them. A gateway translates between different transport protocols or data formats (for example IPX and IP) and is generally added to a network primarily for its translation ability. Also referred to as an IP router. *See also* IP address; IP router.

Gateway Service for NetWare Included with Windows NT Server, enables a computer running Windows NT Server to connect to NetWare servers. Creating a gateway enables computers running only Microsoft client software to access NetWare resources through the gateway. *See also* gateway.

General MIDI A MIDI specification controlled by the MIDI Manufacturers Association (MMA). The specification provides guidelines that authors of MIDI files can use to create files that sound the same across a variety of different synthesizers.

global account For Windows NT Server, a normal user account in a user's domain. Most user accounts are global accounts. If there are multiple domains in the network, it is best if each user in the network has only one user account in only one domain, and each user's access to other domains is accomplished through the establishment of domain trust relationships. *See also* local account; trust relationship.

global group For Windows NT Server, a group that can be used in its own domain, member servers and workstations of the domain, and trusting domains. In all those places it can be granted rights and permissions and can become a member of local groups. However, it can only contain user accounts from its own domain. Global groups provide a way to create handy sets of users from inside the domain, available for use both in and out of the domain.

Global groups cannot be created or maintained on computers running Windows NT Workstation. However, for Windows NT Workstation computers that participate in a domain, domain global groups can be granted rights and permissions at those workstations, and can become members of local groups at those workstations. *See also* domain; group; local group; trust relationship.

globally unique identifier (GUID) *See* universally unique identifier (UUID).

Gopher A hierarchical system for finding and retrieving information from the Internet or an intranet. Similar to FTP, Gopher uses a menu system and enables links to other servers.

group In User Manager or User Manager for Domains, an account containing other accounts that are called members. The permissions and rights granted to a group are also provided to its members, making groups a convenient way to grant common capabilities to collections of user accounts. For Windows NT Workstation, groups are managed with User Manager. For Windows NT Server, groups are managed with User Manager for Domains. *See also* built-in groups; global group; local group; user account.

group account A collection of user accounts. Giving a user account membership in a group gives that user all of the rights and permissions granted to the group. *See also* local account; user account.

group category One of three categories of users to which you can assign Macintosh permissions for a folder. The permissions assigned to the group category are available to the group associated with the folder.

group memberships The groups to which a user account belongs. Permissions and rights granted to a group are also provided to its members. In most cases, the actions a user can perform in Windows NT are determined by the group memberships of the user account the user is logged on to. *See also* group.

group name A unique name identifying a local group or a global group to Windows NT. A group's name cannot be identical to any other group name or user name of its own domain or computer. *See also* global group; local group.

guest Users of Services for Macintosh who do not have a user account or who do not provide a password are logged on as a guest, using a user account with guest privileges. When a Macintosh user assigns permissions to everyone, those permissions are given to the group's guests and users.

guest account On computers running Windows NT Workstation or Windows NT Server, a built-in account used for logons by people who do not have a user account on the computer or domain or in any of the domains trusted by the computer's domain.

Guest privilege One of three privilege levels that you can assign to a Windows NT user account. The guest account used for Macintosh guest logons must have the Guest privilege. *See also* Administrator privilege; user account; User privilege.

GUID Acronym for globally unique identifier. *See* universally unique identifier (UUID).

H

HAL *See* Hardware Abstraction Layer.

handle A handle is a value used to uniquely identify a resource so that a program can access it.

In the registry, each of the first-level key names begins with HKEY_ to indicate to software developers that this is a handle that can be read by a program.

handshaking Refers to flow control in serial communication, which defines a method for the print device to tell Windows NT that its buffer is full. *See also* buffer.

Hardware Abstraction Layer (HAL) A thin layer of software provided by the hardware manufacturer that hides, or abstracts, hardware differences from higher layers of the operating system.

Through the filter provided by the HAL, different types of hardware all look alike to the rest of the operating system. This allows Windows NT to be portable from one hardware platform to another. The HAL also provides routines that allow a single device driver to support the same device on all platforms.

The HAL works closely with the Kernel.

See also Executive; Kernel.

Hardware Compatibility List (HCL) The Windows NT Hardware Compatibility List lists the devices supported by Windows NT. The latest version of the HCL can be downloaded from the Microsoft Web page (microsoft.com) on the Internet.

HCL *See* Hardware Compatibility List.

HDLC *See* High-level Data Link Control.

heterogeneous environment An internetwork with servers and workstations running different operating systems, such as Windows NT, Macintosh, or Novell NetWare, using a mix of different transport protocols.

hexadecimal A base-16 number system that consists of the digits 0 through 9 and the uppercase and lowercase letters A (equivalent to decimal 10) through F (equivalent to decimal 15).

High-level Data Link Control (HDLC) A protocol that governs information transfer. Under the HDLC protocol, messages are transmitted in units called frames, each of which can contain a variable amount of data but which must be organized in a particular way.

high memory area (HMA) The first 64 KB of extended memory (often referred to as HMA). *See also* memory.

High-Performance File System (HPFS) The file system designed for the OS/2 version 1.2 operating system.

hive A section of the registry that appears as a file on your hard disk. The registry subtree is divided into hives (named for their resemblance to the cellular structure of a beehive). A hive is a discrete body of keys, subkeys, and values that is rooted at the top of the registry hierarchy. A hive is backed by a single file and a .log file, which are in the *systemroot*\System32\Config or the *systemroot*\Profiles*user_name* folder. By default, most hive files (Default, SAM, Security, and System) are stored in the *systemroot*\System32\Config folder.

The *systemroot*\Profiles folder contains the user profile for each user of the computer. Because a hive is a file, it can be moved from one system to another but can only be edited by using a Registry Editor.

HMA *See* high memory area.

h-node A NetBIOS implementation that uses the p-node protocol first, then the b-node protocol if the name service is unavailable. For registration, it uses the b-node protocol, then the p-node protocol. *See also* NetBIOS; p-node; registration.

home directory A directory that is accessible to the user and contains files and programs for that user. A home directory can be assigned to an individual user or can be shared by many users.

home page The initial page of information for a collection of pages. The starting point for a Web site or section of a Web site is often referred to as the home page. Individuals also post pages that are called home pages.

hop Refers to the next router. In IP routing, packets are always forwarded one router at a time. Packets often hop from router to router before reaching their destination. *See also* IP address; packet; router.

host Any device that is attached to the network and uses TCP/IP. *See also* Transmission Control Protocol/Internet Protocol (TCP/IP).

host group A set of zero or more hosts identified by a single IP destination address. *See also* host; IP address.

host ID The portion of the IP address that identifies a computer within a particular network ID. *See also* IP address; network ID.

host name The name of a device on a network. For a device on a Windows or Windows NT network, this can be the same as the computer name, but it may not be. The host name must be in the host table or be known by a DNS server for that host to be found by another computer attempting to communicate with it. *See also* Domain Name System (DNS); host table.

HOSTS file A local text file in the same format as the 4.3 Berkeley Software Distribution (BSD) UNIX \etc\hosts file. This file maps host names to IP addresses. In Windows NT, this file is stored in the *systemroot*\System32\Drivers\Etc directory. *See also* IP address.

host table The HOSTS and LMHOSTS files, which contain mappings of known IP addresses mapped to host names.

HPFS *See* High-Performance File System.

HTML *See* Hypertext Markup Language.

HTTP *See* Hypertext Transport Protocol.

HTTP keep-alives An optimizing feature of the HTTP service. HTTP keep-alives maintain a connection even after the initial connection request is completed. This keeps the connection active and available for subsequent requests. HTTP keep-alives were implemented to avoid the substantial cost of establishing and terminating connections. Both the client and the server must support keep-alives. Keep-alives are supported by Internet Information Server version 1.0 and later and by Microsoft Internet Explorer version 2.0 and later. *See also* TCP/IP keep-alives.

hue The position of a color along the color spectrum. For example, green is between yellow and blue. To set this attribute, use Desktop in Control Panel.

hyperlink A way of jumping to another place on the Internet. Hyperlinks usually appear in a different format from regular text. You initiate the jump by clicking the link.

Hypertext Markup Language (HTML)
A simple markup language used to create hypertext documents that are portable from one platform to another. HTML files are simple ASCII text files with codes embedded (indicated by markup tags) to indicate formatting and hypertext links. HTML is used for formatting documents on the World Wide Web.

Hypertext Transport Protocol (HTTP)
The underlying protocol by which WWW clients and servers communicate. HTTP is an application-level protocol for distributed, collaborative, hypermedia information systems. It is a generic, stateless, object-oriented protocol. A feature of HTTP is the typing and negotiation of data representation, allowing systems to be built independently of the data being transferred.

I

ICMP *See* Internet Control Message Protocol.

icon A graphical representation of an element in Windows NT, such as a disk drive, directory, group, application, or document. Click the icon to enlarge an application icon to a window when you want to use the application. Within applications, there are also toolbar icons for commands such as cut, copy, and paste.

IDC *See* Internet Database Connector.

IDE *See* integrated device electronics.

IETF *See* Internet Engineering Task Force.

IGMP *See* Internet Group Management Protocol.

IIS *See* Internet Information Server.

IIS object cache An area of virtual memory that the IIS process uses to store frequently used objects, such as open file handles and directory listings. The IIS object cache is part of the working set of the IIS process, Inetinfo.exe, and it can be paged to disk.

IMC *See* Internet Mail Connector.

impersonation Impersonation occurs when Windows NT Server allows one process to take on the security attributes of another.

import To create a package by inserting an existing file into Object Packager. When you import a file, the icon of the application you used to create the file appears in the Appearance window, and the name of the file appears in the Contents window. *See also* package.

import computers In directory replication, the servers or workstations that receive copies of the master set of directories from an export server. *See also* directory replication; export server.

import path In directory replication, the path to which imported subdirectories, and the files in those subdirectories, will be stored on an import computer. *See also* directory replication; import computers.

Inetinfo A process containing the FTP, Gopher, and HTTP services. This process is about 400 KB in size. In addition to the FTP, Gopher, and HTTP services, this process contains the shared thread pool, cache, logging, and SNMP services of Internet Information Server.

input/output activity (I/O) Read or write actions that your computer performs. Your computer performs a "read" when you type information on your keyboard or you select and choose items by using your mouse. Also, when you open a file, your computer reads the disk on which the file is located to find and open it.

Your computer performs a "write" whenever it stores, sends, prints, or displays information. For example, your computer performs a write when it stores information on a disk, displays information on your screen, or sends information through a modem or to a printer. *See also* I/O addresses.

input/output control (IOCTL) An IOCTL command enables a program to communicate directly with a device driver. This is done, for example, by sending a string of control information recognized by the driver. None of the information passed from the program to the device driver is sent to the device itself (in other words, the control string sent to a printer driver is not displayed on the printer).

insertion point The place where text will be inserted when you type. The insertion point usually appears as a flashing vertical bar in an application's window or in a dialog box.

integrated device electronics (IDE)
A type of disk-drive interface in which the controller electronics reside on the drive itself, eliminating the need for a separate adapter card.

Integrated Services Digital Network (ISDN)
A type of telephone line used to enhance WAN speeds, ISDN lines can transmit at speeds of 64 or 128 kilobits per second, as opposed to standard telephone lines, which typically transmit at only 9600 bits per second (bps). An ISDN line must be installed by the telephone company at both the server site and the remote site. *See also* bits per second (bps).

interactive logon A network logon from a computer keyboard, when the user types information in the **Logon Information** dialog box displayed by the computer's operating system. *See also* remote logon.

intermediary devices Microsoft RAS supports various kinds of intermediary devices (security hosts and switches) between the remote access client and the remote access server. These devices include a modem-pool switch or security host. *See also* Remote Access Service (RAS).

internal command Commands that are stored in the file Cmd.exe and that reside in memory at all times.

internet In Windows NT, a collection of two or more private networks, or private inter-enterprise TCP/IP networks.

In Macintosh terminology, refers to two or more physical networks connected by routers, which maintain a map of the physical networks on the internet and forward data received from one physical network to other physical networks. Network users in an internet can share information and network devices. You can use an internet with Services for Macintosh by connecting two or more AppleTalk networks to a computer running Windows NT Server.

Internet The global network of networks. *See also* World Wide Web (WWW).

Internet Assigned Numbers Authority (IANA)
The central coordinator for the assignment of unique parameter values for Internet protocols. IANA is chartered by the Internet Society (ISOC) and the Federal Network Council (FNC) to act as the clearinghouse to assign and coordinate the use of numerous Internet protocol parameters. Contact IANA at http://www.iana.org/iana/.

Internet Assistant Several Internet Assistant add-on software components are available for Microsoft Office products. Each Internet Assistant adds functionality that is relevant to creating content for the Internet. For example, Internet Assistant for Microsoft Word enables Word to create HTML documents from within Microsoft Word.

Internet Control Message Protocol (ICMP)
A maintenance protocol in the TCP/IP suite, required in every TCP/IP implementation, that allows two nodes on an IP network to share IP status and error information. ICMP is used by the ping utility to determine the readability of a remote system. *See also* ping; Transmission Control Protocol/Internet Protocol (TCP/IP).

Internet Database Connector (IDC)
Provides access to databases for Internet Information Server by using ODBC. The Internet Database Connector is contained in Httpodbc.dll, which is an Internet Server API DLL.

Internet Engineering Task Force (IETF)
A consortium that introduces procedures for new technology on the Internet. IETF specifications are released in documents called Requests for Comments (RFCs). *See also* Requests for Comments (RFCs).

Internet Group Management Protocol (IGMP)
A protocol used by workgroup software products and supported by Microsoft TCP/IP.

Internet group name A name known by a DNS server that includes a list of the specific addresses of systems that have registered the name. *See also* Domain Name System (DNS).

Internet Information Server (IIS) A network file and application server that supports multiple protocols. Primarily, Internet Information Server transmits information in Hypertext Markup Language (HTML) pages by using the Hypertext Transport Protocol (HTTP).

Internet Mail Connector (IMC) The Internet Mail Connector is a component of Microsoft Exchange Server that runs as a Windows NT Server service. You can use the Internet Mail Connector to exchange information with other systems that use the Simple Mail Transfer Protocol (SMTP).

Internet Network Information Center (InterNIC) The coordinator for DNS registration. To register domain names and obtain IP addresses, contact InterNIC at http://internic.net.

Internet Protocol (IP) The messenger protocol of TCP/IP, responsible for addressing and sending TCP packets over the network. IP provides a best-effort, connectionless delivery system that does not guarantee that packets arrive at their destination or that they are received in the sequence in which they were sent. *See also* packet; Transmission Control Protocol (TCP); Transmission Control Protocol/Internet Protocol (TCP/IP).

Internet Protocol Control Protocol (IPCP) Specified by RFC 1332. Responsible for configuring, enabling, and disabling the IP protocol modules on both ends of the point-to-point (PPP) link. *See also* Point-to-Point Protocol (PPP); Requests for Comments (RFCs).

Internet Relay Chat (IRC) A protocol that enables two or more people, each in remote locations, who are connected to an IRC server to hold real-time conversations. IRC is defined in RFC 1459.

Internet router A device that connects networks and directs network information to other networks, usually choosing the most efficient route through other routers. *See also* router.

Internet Server Application Programming Interface (ISAPI) An API for developing extensions to the Microsoft Internet Information Server and other HTTP servers that support ISAPI. *See also* application programming interface (API).

Internet service provider (ISP) A company or educational institution that enables remote users to access the Internet by providing dial-up connections or installing leased lines.

internetworks Networks that connect local area networks (LANs) together.

interprocess communication (IPC) The ability, provided by a multitasking operating system, of one task or process to exchange data with another. Common IPC methods include pipes, semaphores, shared memory, queues, signals, and mailboxes. *See also* named pipe; queue.

interrupt An asynchronous operating system condition that disrupts normal execution and transfers control to an interrupt handler. Interrupts can be issued by both software and hardware devices requiring service from the processor. When software issues an interrupt, it calls an interrupt service routine (ISR). When hardware issues an interrupt, it signals an interrupt request (IRQ) line.

interrupt moderation A Windows NT performance optimizing feature that diverts interrupts from the network adapters when the rate of interrupts is very high. The system accumulates the interrupts in a buffer for later processing. Standard interrupt processing is resumed when the interrupt rate returns to normal.

interrupt request line (IRQ) A hardware line over which devices can send signals to get the attention of the processor when the device is ready to accept or send information. Typically, each device connected to the computer uses a separate IRQ.

intranet A TCP/IP network that uses Internet technology. May be connected to the Internet. *See also* Internet; Transmission Control Protocol/Internet Protocol (TCP/IP).

I/O addresses Locations within the input/output address space of your computer, used by a device such as a printer or modem. *See* also input/output activity (I/O).

IOCTL *See* input/output control.

IP *See* Internet Protocol.

IP address Used to identify a node on a network and to specify routing information. Each node on the network must be assigned a unique IP address, which is made up of the *network ID*, plus a unique *host ID* assigned by the network administrator. This address is typically represented in dotted-decimal notation, with the decimal value of each octet separated by a period (for example, 138.57.7.27).

In Windows NT, the IP address can be configured statically on the client or configured dynamically through DHCP. *See also* Dynamic Host Configuration Protocol (DHCP); node; octet.

IPC *See* interprocess communication.

IPCP *See* Internet Protocol Control Protocol.

IP datagrams The basic Internet Protocol (IP) information unit. *See also* datagram; Internet Protocol (IP).

IP router A system connected to multiple physical TCP/IP networks that can route or deliver IP packets between the networks. *See also* packet; routing; Transmission Control Protocol/Internet Protocol (TCP/IP).

IPX *See* IPX/SPX.

IPX/SPX Acronym for Internetwork Packet Exchange/Sequenced Packet Exchange, which is a set of transport protocols used in Novell NetWare networks. Windows NT implements IPX through NWLink.

IRC *See* Internet Relay Chat.

IRQ *See* interrupt request line.

ISAPI *See* Internet Server Application Programming Interface.

ISDN *See* Integrated Services Digital Network.

ISDN interface card Similar in function to a modem, an ISDN card is hardware that enables a computer to connect to other computers and networks on an Integrated Services Digital Network.

ISO Abbreviation for the International Standards Organization, an international association of member countries, each of which is represented by its leading standard-setting organization—for example ANSI (American National Standards Institute) for the United States. The ISO works to establish global standards for communications and information exchange.

ISP *See* Internet service provider.

iteration One of the three key concepts in DNS name resolution. A local name server keeps the burden of processing on itself and passes only iterative resolution requests to other name servers. An iterative resolution request tells the name server that the requester expects the best answer the name server can provide without help from others. If the name server has the requested data, it returns it, otherwise it returns pointers to name servers that are more likely to have the answer. *See also* Domain Name System (DNS).

In programming, iteration is the art of executing one or more statements or instructions repeatedly.

J

jump Text, graphics, or parts of graphics that provide links to other Help topics or to more information about the current topic. The pointer changes shape whenever it is over a jump. If you click a jump that is linked to another topic, that topic appears in the Help window. If you click a jump that is linked to more information, the information appears in a pop-up window on top of the main Help window.

K

keep-alives *See* HTTP keep-alives; TCP/IP keep-alives.

Kermit Protocol for transferring binary files that is somewhat slower than XModem/CRC. However, Kermit allows you to transmit and receive either seven or eight data bits per character. *See also* XModem/CRC.

Kernel The Windows NT Kernel is the part of the Windows NT Executive that manages the processor. It performs thread scheduling and dispatching, interrupt and exception handling, and multiprocessor synchronization. The Kernel synchronizes activities among Executive-level subcomponents, such as I/O Manager and Process Manager. It also provides primitive objects to the Windows NT Executive, which uses them to create User-mode objects. The Kernel works closely with the Hardware Abstraction Layer (HAL). *See also* Executive; Hardware Abstraction Layer (HAL).

Kernel debugger The Windows NT Kernel debugger (KD) is a 32-bit application that is used to debug the Kernel and device drivers, and to log the events leading up to a Windows NT Executive STOP, STATUS, or hardware-malfunction message.

The Kernel debugger runs on another Windows NT host computer that is connected to your Windows NT target computer. The two computers send debugging (troubleshooting) information back and forth through a communications port that must be running at the same baud rate on each computer.

Kernel driver A driver that accesses hardware. *See also* device driver.

key A folder that appears in the left pane of a Registry Editor window. A key can contain subkeys and value entries. For example: Environment is a key of HKEY_CURRENT_USER. *See also* subkey.

keyboard buffer A temporary storage area in memory that keeps track of keys you typed, even if the computer did not immediately respond to the keys when you typed them.

key map A mapping assignment that translates key values on synthesizers that do not conform to General MIDI standards. Key maps ensure that the appropriate percussion instrument is played or the appropriate octave for a melodic instrument is played when a MIDI file is played. *See also* Musical Instrument Digital Interface (MIDI).

kiosk A computer, connected to the Internet, made available to users in a commonly accessible location.

L

LAN *See* local area network.

LastKnownGood (LKG) control set The most recent control set that correctly started the system and resulted in a successful startup. The control set is saved as the LKG control set when you have a successful logon. *See also* current control set.

lease In Windows NT, the network administrator controls how long IP addresses are assigned by specifying lease durations that specify how long a computer can use an assigned IP address before having to renew the lease with the DHCP server. *See also* Dynamic Host Configuration Protocol (DHCP); IP address.

leased line A high-capacity line (most often a telephone line) dedicated to network connections.

license group License groups show a relationship (also known as a mapping) between users and computers. A license group comprises a single descriptive name for the group, a specified number of Per-Seat licenses assigned to the group, and a specific list of users who are members of the group.

line printer daemon (LPD) A line printer daemon (LPD) service on the print server receives documents from line printer remote (LPR) utilities running on client systems.

linked object A representation or placeholder for an object that is inserted into a destination document. The object still exists in the source file and, when it is changed, the linked object is updated to reflect these changes.

list box In a dialog box, a type of box that lists available choices—for example, a list of all files in a directory. If all of the choices do not fit in the list box, there is a scroll bar.

LMHOSTS file A local text file that maps IP addresses to the computer names of Windows NT networking computers outside the local subnet. In Windows NT, this file is stored in the \systemroot \System32\Drivers\Etc directory. *See also* IP address; subnet.

local account For Windows NT Server, a user account provided in a domain for a user whose global account is not in a trusted domain. Not required where trust relationships exist between domains. *See also* global account; trust relationship; user account.

local area network (LAN) A group of computers and other devices dispersed over a relatively limited area and connected by a communications link that enables any device to interact with any other on the network.

local group For Windows NT Workstation, a group that can be granted permissions and rights only for its own workstation. However, it can contain user accounts from its own computer and (if the workstation participates in a domain) user accounts and global groups both from its own domain and from trusted domains.

For Windows NT Server, a group that can be granted permissions and rights only for the domain controllers of its own domain. However, it can contain user accounts and global groups both from its own domain and from trusted domains.

(continued)

local group Local groups provide a way to create handy sets of users from both inside and outside the domain, to be used only at domain controllers of the domain. *See also* global group; group; trust relationship.

local guest logon Takes effect when a user logs on interactively at a computer running Window NT Workstation or at a member server running Windows NT Server, and specifies Guest as the user name in the **Logon Information** dialog box. *See also* interactive logon.

Local Mail Delivery Agent The component of the SMTP server that processes messages that have been received by the SMTP server and downloads the messages to the user's local computer.

local printer A printer that is directly connected to one of the ports on your computer. *See also* port.

LocalTalk The name given by Apple Computer to the Apple networking hardware built into every Macintosh. LocalTalk includes the cables and connector boxes that connect components and network devices that are part of the AppleTalk network system. LocalTalk was formerly known as the AppleTalk Personal Network.

local user profiles User profiles that are created automatically on the computer at logon the first time a user logs on to a computer running Windows NT Workstation or Windows NT Server.

lock A method used to manage certain features of subdirectory replication by the export server. You can lock a subdirectory to prevent it from being exported to any import computers, or use locks to prevent imports to subdirectories on an import computer. *See also* directory replication; export server; import computers; subtree.

log books Kept by the system administrator to record the backup methods, dates, and contents of each tape in a backup set. *See also* backup set; backup types.

log files Created by Windows NT Backup and contain a record of the date the tapes were created and the names of files and directories successfully backed up and restored. Performance Monitor also creates log files.

logical drive A subpartition of an extended partition on a hard disk. *See also* extended partition.

Logical Unit (LU) A preset unit containing all of the configuration information needed for a user or a program to establish a session with a host or peer computer. *See also* host; peer.

log off To stop using the network and remove your user name from active use until you log on again.

log on To provide a user name and password that identifies you to the network.

logon hours For Windows NT Server, a definition of the days and hours during which a user account can connect to a server. When a user is connected to a server and the logon hours are exceeded, the user will either be disconnected from all server connections or allowed to remain connected but denied any new connections.

logon script A file that can be assigned to user accounts. Typically a batch program, a logon script runs automatically every time the user logs on. It can be used to configure a user's working environment at every logon, and it allows an administrator to affect a user's environment without managing all aspects of it. A logon script can be assigned to one or more user accounts. *See also* batch program.

logon script path When a user logs on, the computer authenticating the logon locates the specified logon script (if one has been assigned to that user account) by following that computer's local logon script path (usually C:\Winnt\System32\Repl\Imports\Scripts). *See also* authentication; logon script.

logon workstations In Windows NT Server, the computers from which a user is allowed to log on.

long name A folder name or file name longer than the 8.3 file name standard (up to eight characters followed by a period and a three-character extension) of the FAT file system. Windows NT Server automatically translates long names of files and folders to 8.3 names for MS-DOS users.

Macintosh users can assign long names to files and folders on the server, and by using Services for Macintosh, you can assign long names to Macintosh-accessible volumes when you create them. *See also* file allocation table (FAT); file name; name mapping; short name.

loopback address The IP address 127.0.0.1, which has been specified by the Internet Engineering Task Force as the IP address to use in conjunction with a loopback driver to route outgoing packets back to the source computer. *See also* loopback driver.

loopback driver A network driver that allows the packets to bypass the network adapter completely and be returned directly to the computer that is performing the test. *See also* loopback address.

LPD *See* line printer daemon.

LPR Acronym for line printer remote. *See also* line printer daemon.

LU *See* Logical Unit.

luminosity The brightness of a color on a scale from black to white on your monitor.

M

MAC *See* media access control.

MAC address A unique 48-bit number assigned to the network adapter by the manufacturer. MAC addresses (which are physical addresses) are used for mapping in TCP/IP network communication. *See also* Address Resolution Protocol (ARP); ARP request packet; media access control (MAC).

MacFile *See* File Server for Macintosh service.

MacFile menu The menu that appears in Windows NT Server when Services for Macintosh is set up. You can create Macintosh-accessible volumes, and set permissions and other options by using commands on this menu.

Macintosh-accessible volume Storage space on the server used for folders and files of Macintosh users. A Macintosh-accessible volume is equivalent to a shared directory for PC users. Each Macintosh-accessible volume on a computer running Windows NT Server will correspond to a directory. Both PC users and Macintosh users can be given access to files located in a directory that is designated as both a shared directory and a Macintosh-accessible volume.

Macintosh-style permissions Directory and volume permissions that are similar to the access privileges used on a Macintosh.

MacPrint *See* Print Server for Macintosh.

Mac volume *See* Macintosh-accessible volume.

Mail Server (MailSrv) The MailSrv utility no longer ships with the *Windows NT Server Resource Kit*.

Make Changes The Macintosh-style permission that gives users the right to make changes to a folder's contents; for example, modifying, renaming, moving, creating, and deleting files. When Services for Macintosh translates access privileges into Windows NT Server permissions, a user who has the Make Changes privilege is given Write and Delete permissions.

Management Information Base (MIB) A set of objects that represent various types of information about a device, used by SNMP to manage devices. Because different network-management services are used for different types of devices or protocols, each service has its own set of objects. The entire set of objects that any service or protocol uses is referred to as its MIB. *See also* Simple Network Management Protocol (SNMP).

mandatory user profile A profile that is downloaded to the user's desktop each time he or she logs on. A mandatory user profile is created by an administrator and assigned to one or more users to create consistent or job-specific user profiles. They cannot be changed by the user and remain the same from one logon session to the next. *See also* roaming user profile; user profile.

mapping In TCP/IP, refers to the relationship between a host or computer name and an IP address, used by DNS and NetBIOS servers on TCP/IP networks.

In Windows NT Explorer, refers to mapping a driver letter to a network drive.

In Windows NT License Manager, refers to the relationship between users and computers in license groups. *See also* Domain Name System (DNS); IP address; license group.

mapping file A file defining exactly which users and groups are to be migrated from NetWare to Windows NT Server, and what new user names and passwords are to be assigned to the migrated users.

Master Boot Record The most important area on a hard disk, the data structure that starts the process of booting the computer.

The Master Boot Record contains the partition table for the disk and a small amount of executable code. On x86-based computers, the executable code examines the partition table and identifies the system (or bootable) partition, finds the system partition's starting location on the disk, and loads an image of its Partition Boot Sector into memory. The Master Boot Record then transfers execution to the Partition Boot Sector. *See also* Partition Table.

master browser A kind of network name server which keeps a browse list of all of the servers and domains on the network. Also referred to as browse master. *See also* browse; Windows NT browser system.

master domain In the master domain model, the domain that is trusted by all other domains on the network and acts as the central administrative unit for user and group accounts.

maximize To enlarge a window to its maximum size by using the **Maximize** button (at the right of the title bar) or the **Maximize** command on the window menu.

Maximize button The small button containing a window icon at the right of the title bar. Mouse users can click the **Maximize** button to enlarge a window to its maximum size. Keyboard users can use the **Maximize** command on the window menu.

maximum password age The period of time a password can be used before the system requires the user to change it. *See also* account policy.

MCI *See* Media Control Interface.

media access control (MAC) A layer in the network architecture that deals with network access and collision detection.

media access control (MAC) driver *See* network card driver.

Media Control Interface (MCI) A standard control interface for multimedia devices and files. Using MCI, a multimedia application can control a variety of multimedia devices and files.

member server A computer that runs Windows NT Server but is not a primary domain controller (PDC) or backup domain controller (BDC) of a Windows NT domain. Member servers do not receive copies of the directory database. Also called a stand-alone server. *See also* backup domain controller (BDC); directory database; primary domain controller (PDC).

memory A temporary storage area for information and applications. *See also* expanded memory; extended memory.

menu A list of available commands in an application window. Menu names appear in the menu bar near the top of the window. The window menu, represented by the program icon at the left end of the title bar, is common to all applications for Windows NT. To open a menu, click the menu name.

menu bar The horizontal bar containing the names of all of the application's menus. It appears below the title bar.

Messenger service Sends and receives messages sent by administrators or by the Alerter service. *See also* Alerter service.

MIB *See* Management Information Base.

Microsoft dbWeb A database publishing gateway provided in the *Windows NT Server Resource Kit*. dbWeb can run under Internet Information Server to provide public access to private enterprise ODBC sources as specified by an administrator of the private enterprise.

MIDI *See* Musical Instrument Digital Interface.

MIDI setup Specifies the type of MIDI device you are using, the channel and patch settings needed to play MIDI files, and the port your device is using. *See also* Musical Instrument Digital Interface (MIDI).

Migration Tool for NetWare Included with Windows NT, it enables you to easily transfer user and group accounts, volumes, folders, and files from a NetWare server to a computer running Windows NT Server.

MIME *See* Multipurpose Internet Mail Extensions.

minimize To reduce a window to a button on the taskbar by using the **Minimize** button (at the right of the title bar) or the **Minimize** command on the **Control** menu. *See also* maximize.

Minimize button The small button containing a short line at the right of the title bar. Mouse users can click the **Minimize** button to reduce a window to a button on the taskbar. Keyboard users can use the **Minimize** command on the **Control** menu.

minimum password age The period of time a password must be used before the user can change it. *See also* account policy.

minimum password length The fewest characters a password can contain. *See also* account policy.

mirror set A fully redundant or shadow copy of data. Mirror sets provide an identical twin for a selected disk; all data written to the primary disk is also written to the shadow or mirror disk. This enables you to have instant access to another disk with a redundant copy of the information on a failed disk. Mirror sets provide fault tolerance. *See also* fault tolerance.

m-node A NetBIOS implementation that uses the b-node protocol first, then the p-node protocol if the broadcast fails to resolve a name to an IP address. *See also* IP address; network basic input/output system (NetBIOS); p-node.

modem Short for modulator/demodulator, a communications device that enables a computer to transmit information over a standard telephone line.

MPR *See* MultiProtocol Routing.

MS-DOS-based application An application that is designed to run with MS-DOS, and therefore may not be able to take full advantage of all Windows NT features.

multicast datagram IP multicasting is the transmission of an IP datagram to a host group (a set of zero or more hosts identified by a single IP destination address). An IP datagram sent to one host is called a unicast datagram. An IP datagram sent to all hosts is called a broadcast datagram. *See also* broadcast datagram; host; IP address.

multihomed computer A system that has multiple network adapters, or that has been configured with multiple IP addresses for a single network adapter. *See also* IP address; network adapter.

multihomed system A system with multiple network adapters attached to separate physical networks.

multilink dialing Multilink combines multiple physical links into a logical "bundle." This aggregate link increases your bandwidth. *See also* bandwidth.

multiple boot A computer that runs two or more operating systems. For example, Windows 95, MS-DOS, and Windows NT operating systems can be installed on the same computer. When the computer is started, any one of the operating systems can be selected. Also known as dual boot.

multiport serial adapter A communications device that enables a computer to simultaneously transmit information over standard telephone lines to multiple computers. Similar to multiple modems contained in one device. *See also* modem.

MultiProtocol Routing (MPR) Enables routing over IP and IPX networks by connecting LANs or by connecting LANs to WANs. *See also* IPX/SPX; local area network (LAN); wide area network (WAN).

Multipurpose Internet Mail Extensions (MIME) A standard mechanism for specifying and describing the format of Internet message bodies. MIME enables the exchanging of objects, different character sets, and multimedia in electronic mail on different computer systems. Defined in RFC 1521.

Musical Instrument Digital Interface (MIDI) An interface that enables several devices, instruments, or computers to send and receive messages for the purpose of creating music, sound, or lighting.

N

named pipe An interprocess communication mechanism that allows one process to communicate with another local or remote process.

name mapping Is provided by Windows NT Server and Windows NT Workstation to ensure access by MS-DOS users to NTFS and FAT volumes (which can have share names of up to 255 characters, as opposed to MS-DOS, which is restricted to eight characters followed by a period and a three-character extension). With name mapping, each file or directory with a name that does not conform to the MS-DOS 8.3 standard is automatically given a second name that does. MS-DOS users connecting the file or directory over the network see the name in the 8.3 format; Windows NT Workstation and Windows NT Server users see the long name. *See also* Domain Name System (DNS); long name; Windows Internet Name Service (WINS).

name resolution service TCP/IP internetworks require a name resolution service to convert computer names to IP addresses and IP addresses to computer names. (People use "friendly" names to connect to computers; programs use IP addresses.) *See also* IP address; Transmission Control Protocol/Internet Protocol (TCP/IP).

NDIS *See* network device interface specification.

NDS *See* NetWare Directory Services.

NetBEUI A network protocol usually used in small, department-size local area networks of 1 through 200 clients. It can use Token Ring source routing as its only method of routing. *See also* router; Token Ring.

NetBIOS *See* network basic input/output system.

NetBT Short for NetBIOS over TCP/IP. The session-layer network service that performs name-to-IP address mapping for name resolution. *See also* IP address; name resolution service; network basic input/output system (NetBIOS); Transmission Control Protocol/Internet Protocol (TCP/IP).

Net Logon service For Windows NT Server, performs authentication of domain logons, and keeps the domain's directory database synchronized between the primary domain controller (PDC) and the other backup domain controllers (BDCs) of the domain. *See also* backup domain controller (BDC); directory database; primary domain controller (PDC).

NetWare Directory Services (NDS) A NetWare service that runs on NetWare servers. The service enables the location of resources on the network.

network adapter An expansion card or other device used to connect a computer to a local area network (LAN). Also called a network card; network adapter card; adapter card; network interface card (NIC).

network adapter card *See* network adapter.

network administrator A person responsible for planning, configuring, and managing the day-to-day operation of the network. This person may also be referred to as a system administrator.

network basic input/output system (NetBIOS) An application programming interface (API) that can be used by applications on a local area network. NetBIOS provides applications with a uniform set of commands for requesting the lower-level services required to conduct sessions between nodes on a network and to transmit information back and forth. *See also* application programming interface (API).

network card *See* network adapter.

network card driver A network device driver that works directly with the network card, acting as an intermediary between the card and the protocol driver. With Services for Macintosh, the AppleTalk Protocol stack on the server is implemented as a protocol driver and is bound to one or more network drivers.

Network DDE DSDM service The Network DDE DSDM (DDE share database manager) service manages shared DDE conversations. It is used by the Network DDE service. *See also* dynamic data exchange (DDE).

Network DDE service The Network DDE (dynamic data exchange) service provides a network transport and security for DDE conversations. *See also* dynamic data exchange (DDE).

network device driver Software that coordinates communication between the network adapter and the computer's hardware and other software, controlling the physical function of the network adapters.

network device interface specification (NDIS) In Windows networking, the Microsoft/3Com specification for the interface of network device drivers. All transport drivers call the NDIS interface to access network cards. With Services for Macintosh, the AppleTalk Protocol stack on the server is implemented as an NDIS-compliant protocol and is bound to an NDIS network driver. All network drivers and protocol drivers shipped with Windows NT Workstation and Windows NT Server conform to NDIS.

network directory *See* shared directory.

network driver *See* network device driver.

network driver interface specification *See* network device interface specification (NDIS).

Network File System (NFS) A service for distributed computing systems that provides a distributed file system, eliminating the need for keeping multiple copies of files on separate computers.

network ID The portion of the IP address that identifies a group of computers and devices located on the same logical network.

Network Information Service (NIS) A service for distributed computing systems that provides a distributed database system for common configuration files.

network interface card (NIC) *See* network adapter.

Network News Transfer Protocol (NNTP) The protocol used to distribute network news messages to NNTP servers and to NNTP clients (news readers) on the Internet. NNTP provides for the distribution, inquiry, retrieval, and posting of news articles by using a reliable stream-based transmission of news on the Internet. NNTP is designed so that news articles are stored on a server in a central database, thus enabling a user to select specific items to read. Indexing, cross-referencing, and expiration of aged messages are also provided. Defined in RFC 977.

network number In the Macintosh environment, the network number (also referred to as the network range) is the address or range of addresses assigned to the network, which is used by AppleTalk routers to route information to the appropriate network. Each physical network can have a range of network numbers.

network protocol Software that enables computers to communicate over a network. TCP/IP is a network protocol, used on the Internet. *See also* Transmission Control Protocol/Internet Protocol (TCP/IP).

network range In the Macintosh environment, a range of network numbers (routing addresses) associated with a physical network in Phase 2. Apple manuals sometimes refer to a network range as a cable range. *See also* network number; routing.

network sniffer A hardware and software diagnostic tool that can also be used to decipher passwords, which may result in unauthorized access to network accounts. Clear-text passwords are susceptible to network sniffers.

NFS *See* Network File System.

NIC Acronym for network interface card. *See* network adapter.

NIS *See* Network Information Service.

NNTP *See* Network News Transfer Protocol.

node In the PC environment, a node is any device that is attached to the internetwork and uses TCP/IP. (A node can also be referred to as a host.) In the Macintosh environment, a node is an addressable entity on a network. Each Macintosh client is a node.

nonpaged memory Memory that cannot be paged to disk. *See also* memory; paging file.

non–Windows NT application Refers to an application that is designed to run with Windows 3.*x*, MS-DOS, OS/2, or POSIX, but not specifically with Windows NT, and that may not be able to take full advantage of all Windows NT features (such as memory management). *See also* POSIX.

NT *See* Windows NT Server; Windows NT Workstation.

NT File System *See* Windows NT File System.

NTFS *See* Windows NT File System.

NWLink IPX\SPX Compatible Transport
A standard network protocol that supports routing, and can support NetWare client/server applications, where NetWare-aware Sockets-based applications communicate with IPX\SPX Sockets-based applications. *See also* IPX/SPX; Sockets.

O

object Any piece of information, created by using a Windows-based application, that can be linked or embedded into another document. *See also* embedded object; linked object.

object-cache scavenger A component of the IIS process that periodically flushes from the cache objects that have changed or that have not been referenced in its last timed interval. The default time interval for the object-cache scavenger is 30 seconds.

octet In programming, an octet refers to eight bits or one byte. IP addresses, for example, are typically represented in dotted-decimal notation, that is, with the decimal value of each octet of the address separated by a period. *See also* IP address.

ODBC *See* Open Database Connectivity.

offset When specifying a filter in Windows NT Network Monitor based on a pattern match (which limits the capture to only those frames containing a specific pattern of ASCII or hexadecimal data), you must specify where the pattern occurs in the frame. This number of bytes (from the beginning or end of the frame) is known as an offset. *See also* frame; hexadecimal.

OLE A way to transfer and share information between applications. *See also* ActiveX; embedded object; linked object.

one-way trust relationship One domain (the trusting domain) "trusts" the domain controllers in the other domain (the trusted domain) to authenticate user accounts from the trusted domain to use resources in the trusting domain. *See also* trust relationship; user account.

opcode Operation code; a code, usually a number, that specifies an operation to be performed. An opcode is often the first component in a contiguous block of data; it indicates how other data in the block should be interpreted.

open To display the contents of a directory, a document, or a data file in a window.

Open Database Connectivity (ODBC)
ODBC is an application programming interface that enables applications to access data from a variety of existing data sources.

Open Systems Interconnection (OSI) model
TCP/IP protocols map to a four-layered conceptual model consisting of Application, Transport, Internet, and Network Interface. Each layer in this TCP/IP model corresponds to one or more layers of the International Standards Organization (ISO) seven-layer OSI model consisting of Application, Presentation, Session, Transport, Network, Data-link, and Physical. *See also* ISO.

orphan A member of a mirror set or a stripe set with parity that has failed in a severe manner, such as in a loss of power or a complete head crash. When this happens, the fault-tolerance driver determines that it can no longer use the orphaned member and directs all new reads and writes to the remaining members of the fault-tolerance volume. *See also* fault tolerance; mirror set; stripe sets with parity.

orphaned member *See* orphan.

OSI *See* Open Systems Interconnection model.

owner In Windows NT, every file and directory on an NTFS volume has an owner, who controls how permissions are set on the file or directory and who can grant permissions to others.

P

package An icon that represents an embedded or linked object. When you choose the package, the application used to create the object either plays the object (for example, a sound file) or opens and displays the object. *See also* embedded object; linked object.

packet A transmission unit of fixed maximum size that consists of binary information representing both data and a header containing an ID number, source and destination addresses, and error-control data.

packet assembler/disassembler (PAD)
A connection used in X.25 networks. X.25 PAD boards can be used in place of modems when provided with a compatible COM driver. *See also* X.25.

packet header The part of a packet that contains an identification number, source and destination addresses, and—sometimes—error-control data. *See also* packet.

PAD *See* packet assembler/disassembler.

page fault In the processor, a page fault occurs when a process refers to a virtual memory page that is not in its working set in main memory.

A *hard page fault* occurs when data that a program needs is not found in its working set (the physical memory visible to the program) or elsewhere in physical memory, and must be retrieved from disk.

A page fault will not cause the page to be fetched from disk if that page is on the standby list, and hence already in main memory, or if it is in use by another process with which the page is shared. In this case, a *soft page fault* occurs.

paging file A special file on a PC hard disk. With virtual memory under Windows NT, some of the program code and other information is kept in RAM while other information is temporarily swapped into virtual memory. When that information is required again, Windows NT pulls it back into RAM and, if necessary, swaps other information to virtual memory. Also called a swap file.

PAP *See* Password Authentication Protocol.

parity Redundant information that is associated with a block of information. In Windows NT Server, stripe sets with parity means that there is one additional parity stripe per row. Therefore, you must use at least three, rather than two, disks to allow for this extra parity information. Parity stripes contain the XOR (the Boolean operation called exclusive OR) of the data in that stripe. Windows NT Server, when regenerating a failed disk, uses the parity information in those stripes in conjunction with the data on the good disks to recreate the data on the failed disk. *See also* fault tolerance; stripe set; stripe sets with parity.

partial synchronization The automatic, timed delivery to all domain BDCs (backup domain controllers) of only those directory database changes that have occurred since the last synchronization. *See also* backup domain controller (BDC); synchronize.

partition A partition is a portion of a physical disk that functions as though it were a physically separate unit. *See also* extended partition; system partition.

Partition Table An area of the Master Boot Record that the computer uses to determine how to access the disk. The Partition Table can contain up to four partitions for each physical disk. *See also* Master Boot Record.

pass-through authentication When the user account must be authenticated, but the computer being used for the logon is not a domain controller in the domain where the user account is defined, nor is it the computer where the user account is defined, the computer passes the logon information through to a domain controller (directly or indirectly) where the user account is defined. *See also* domain controller; user account.

password A security measure used to restrict logons to user accounts and access to computer systems and resources. A password is a unique string of characters that must be provided before a logon or an access is authorized. For Windows NT, a password for a user account can be up to 14 characters, and is case-sensitive. There are four user-defined parameters to be entered in the **Account Policy** dialog box in User Manager or User Manager for Domains: maximum password age, minimum password age, minimum password length, and password uniqueness.

With Services for Macintosh, each Macintosh user must type a user password when accessing the Windows NT Server. You can also assign each Macintosh-accessible volume a volume password if you want, which all users must type to access the volume. *See also* account policy.

Password Authentication Protocol (PAP) A type of authentication that uses clear-text passwords and is the least sophisticated authentication protocol.

password uniqueness The number of new passwords that must be used by a user account before an old password can be reused. *See also* account policy; password.

patch map The part of a channel-map entry that translates instrument sounds, volume settings, and (optionally) key values for a channel.

path A sequence of directory (or folder) names that specifies the location of a directory, file, or folder within the directory tree. Each directory name and file name within the path (except the first) must be preceded by a backslash (\). For example, to specify the path of a file named Readme.wri located in the Windows directory on drive C, you type c:\windows\readme.wri.

PC Any personal computer (such as an IBM PC or compatible) using the MS-DOS, OS/2, Windows, Windows for Workgroups, Windows 95, Windows NT Server, or Windows NT Workstation operating systems.

PCMCIA *See* Personal Computer Memory Card International Association.

peer Any of the devices on a layered communications network that operate on the same protocol level.

Peer Web Services A collection of services that enable the user of a computer running Windows NT Workstation to publish a personal Web site from the desktop. The services include the WWW service, the FTP service, and the Gopher service.

pel Also known as a pixel, which is short for picture element, the smallest graphic unit that can be displayed on the screen.

Perl Practical Extraction and Report Language. A scripting (programming) language that is frequently used for CGI scripts.

permissions Windows NT Server settings you set on a shared resource that determine which users can use the resource and how they can use it. *See also* access permission.

Services for Macintosh automatically translates between permissions and Macintosh access privileges, so that permissions set on a directory (volume) are enforced for Macintosh users, and access privileges set by Macintosh users are enforced for PC users connected to the computer running Windows NT Server.

Personal Computer Memory Card International Association (PCMCIA) A standard for removable peripheral devices (called PC cards) about the size of a credit card, which plug into a special 68-pin connector found most commonly in portable computers. Currently available PCMCIA cards include memory, hard disk, modem, fax, network, and wireless communication devices.

personal group In the **Start** menu on the **Programs** list, a program group you have created that contains program items. Personal groups are stored with your logon information and each time you log on, your personal groups appear. *See also* group.

Physical Unit (PU) A network-addressable unit that provides the services needed to use and manage a particular device, such as a communications link device. A PU is implemented with a combination of hardware, software, and microcode.

PIF *See* program information file.

ping A command used to verify connections to one or more remote hosts. The **ping** utility uses the ICMP echo request and echo reply packets to determine whether a particular IP system on a network is functional. The ping utility is useful for diagnosing IP network or router failures. *See also* Internet Control Message Protocol (ICMP); router.

pipe An interprocess communication mechanism. Writing to and reading from a pipe is much like writing to and reading from a file, except that the two processes are actually using a shared memory segment to communicate data. *See also* named pipe.

pixel *See* pel.

plotter font *See* font types.

p-node A NetBIOS implementation that uses point-to-point communications with a name server to resolve names as IP addresses. *See also* h-node; IP address; network basic input/output system (NetBIOS).

pointer The arrow-shaped cursor on the screen that follows the movement of a mouse (or other pointing device) and indicates which area of the screen will be affected when you press the mouse button. The pointer changes shape during certain tasks.

Point-to-Point Protocol (PPP) A set of industry-standard framing and authentication protocols that is part of Windows NT RAS to ensure interoperability with third-party remote access software. PPP negotiates configuration parameters for multiple layers of the OSI model. *See also* Open Systems Interconnection model (OSI).

Point-to-Point Tunneling Protocol (PPTP)
PPTP is a new networking technology that supports multiprotocol virtual private networks (VPNs), enabling remote users to access corporate networks securely across the Internet by dialing into an Internet service provider (ISP) or by connecting directly to the Internet. *See also* virtual private network (VPN).

POP *See* Post Office Protocol.

pop-up menu *See* window menu.

port A location used to pass data in and out of a computing device. This term can refer to an adapter card connecting a server to a network, a serial 232 port, a TCP/IP port, or a printer port.

port ID The method TCP and UDP use to specify which application running on the system is sending or receiving the data. *See also* Transmission Control Protocol (TCP); User Datagram Protocol (UDP).

POSIX Acronym for Portable Operating System Interface, an IEEE (Institute of Electrical and Electronics Engineers, Inc.) standard that defines a set of operating-system services. Programs that adhere to the POSIX standard can be easily ported from one system to another.

Post Office Protocol (POP) The Post Office Protocol version 3 (POP3) is a protocol that permits a workstation to dynamically access a mail drop on a server in a useful fashion. Usually, this means that a POP3 server is used to allow a workstation to retrieve mail that an SMTP server is holding for it. POP3 is specified in RFC 1725.

PostScript printer A printer that uses the PostScript page description language to create text and graphics on the output medium, such as paper or overhead transparency. Examples of PostScript printers include the Apple LaserWriter, the NEC LC-890, and the QMS PS-810. *See also* font types.

POTS Acronym for plain-old telephone service. Also an acronym for point of termination station, which refers to where a telephone call terminates.

power conditioning A feature of an uninterruptible power supply (UPS) that removes spikes, surges, sags, and noise from the power supply. *See also* uninterruptible power supply (UPS).

PPP *See* Point-to-Point Protocol.

PPTP *See* Point-to-Point Tunneling Protocol.

predefined key The key represented by a registry window, the name of which appears in the window's title bar. *See also* key; registry.

primary domain controller (PDC) In a Windows NT Server domain, the computer running Windows NT Server that authenticates domain logons and maintains the directory database for a domain. The PDC tracks changes made to accounts of all computers on a domain. It is the only computer to receive these changes directly. A domain has only one PDC. *See also* directory database.

primary partition A partition is a portion of a physical disk that can be marked for use by an operating system. There can be up to four primary partitions (or up to three, if there is an extended partition) per physical disk. A primary partition cannot be subpartitioned. *See also* extended partition; partition.

print device Refers to the actual hardware device that produces printed output.

printer Refers to the software interface between the operating system and the print device. The printer defines where the document will go before it reaches the print device (to a local port, to a file, or to a remote print share), when it will go, and various other aspects of the printing process.

printer driver A program that converts graphics commands into a specific printer language, such as PostScript or PCL. *See also* font types.

printer fonts Fonts that are built into your printer. These fonts are usually located in the printer's read-only memory (ROM). *See also* font; font types.

printer permissions Specify the type of access a user or group has to use the printer. The printer permissions are No Access, Print, Manage Documents, and Full Control.

printer window Shows information for one of the printers that you have installed or to which you are connected. For each printer, you can see what documents are waiting to be printed, who owns them, how large they are, and other information.

printing pool Consists of two or more identical print devices associated with one printer.

print processor A PostScript program that understands the format of a document's image file and how to print the file to a specific printer or class of printers. *See also* encapsulated PostScript (EPS) file.

print server Refers to the computer that receives documents from clients.

Print Server for Macintosh A Services for Macintosh service that enables Macintosh clients to send documents to printers attached to a computer running Windows NT; enables PC clients to send documents to printers anywhere on the AppleTalk network; and enables Macintosh users to spool their documents to the computer running Windows NT Server, thus freeing their clients to do other tasks. Also called MacPrint.

print sharing The ability for a computer running Windows NT Workstation or Windows NT Server to share a printer on the network. This is done by using the **Printers** folder or the **net share** command.

print spooler A collection of dynamic-link libraries (DLLs) that receive, process, schedule, and distribute documents.

privilege level One of three settings (User, Administrator, or Guest) assigned to each user account. The privilege level a user account has determines the actions that the user can perform on the network. *See also* Administrator privilege; Guest privilege; user account; User privilege.

process When a program runs, a Windows NT process is created. A process is an object type which consists of an executable program, a set of virtual memory addresses, and one or more threads.

processor affinity mask A Windows NT bit mask that associates processors with network adapters. All deferred procedure calls (DPCs) originating from the network adapter are handled by its associated processor.

program file A file that starts an application or program. A program file has an .exe, .pif, .com, or .bat file name extension.

program group On the **Start** menu, a collection of applications. Grouping your applications makes them easier to find when you want to start them. *See also* common group; personal group.

program icon Located at the left of the window title bar, the program icon represents the program being run. Clicking the program icon opens the window menu.

program information file (PIF) A PIF provides information to Windows NT about how best to run MS-DOS-based applications. When you start an MS-DOS-based application, Windows NT looks for a PIF to use with the application. PIFs contain such items as the name of the file, a start-up directory, and multitasking options.

program item An application, accessory, or document represented as an icon in the **Start** menu or on the desktop.

promiscuous mode A state of a network card in which it passes on to the networking software all of the frames that it detects on the network, regardless of the frames' destination address. *See also* frame; network adapter.

propagate Copy. For example, NetWare user accounts are propagated to the Windows NT primary domain controller when using Directory Service Manager for NetWare (DSMN).

property In Windows NT Network Monitor, a property refers to a field within a protocol header. A protocol's properties, collectively, indicate the purpose of the protocol.

protocol A set of rules and conventions for sending information over a network. These rules govern the content, format, timing, sequencing, and error control of messages exchanged among network devices.

protocol driver A network device driver that implements a protocol, communicating between Windows NT Server and one or more network adapter card drivers. With Services for Macintosh, the AppleTalk Protocol stack is implemented as an NDIS-protocol driver, and is bound to one or more network adapter card drivers.

protocol parser A dynamic-link library (DLL) that identifies the protocols used to send a frame onto the network. *See also* dynamic-link library (DLL); frame.

protocol properties Refers to the elements of information that define a protocol's purpose. Because the purposes of protocols vary, properties differ from one protocol to another.

protocol stack The implementation of a specific protocol family in a computer or other node on the network.

proxy A computer that listens to name query broadcasts and responds for those names not on the local subnet. The proxy communicates with the name server to resolve names and then caches them for a time period. *See also* caching; Domain Name System (DNS); subnet.

PSTN Acronym for public switched telephone network.

PU *See* Physical Unit.

public key cryptography A method of encrypting data transmissions to and from a server.

pull partner A WINS server that pulls in replicas from its push partner by requesting it and then accepting the pushed replicas. *See also* Windows Internet Name Service (WINS).

push partner A WINS server that sends replicas to its pull partner upon receiving a request from it. *See also* Windows Internet Name Service (WINS).

Q

queue In Windows NT terminology, a queue refers to a group of documents waiting to be printed. (In NetWare and OS/2 environments, queues are the primary software interface between the application and print device; users submit documents to a queue. However, with Windows NT, the printer is that interface—the document is sent to a printer, not a queue.)

quick format Deletes the file allocation table (FAT) and root directory of a disk but does not scan the disk for bad areas. This function is available in Disk Administrator or when checking disks for errors. *See also* file allocation table (FAT); root directory.

R

RAID Acronym for Redundant Array of Inexpensive Disks. A method used to standardize and categorize fault-tolerant disk systems. Six levels gauge various mixes of performance, reliability, and cost. Windows NT includes three of the RAID levels: Level 0, Level 1, and Level 5.

RAM An acronym for random-access memory. RAM can be read from or written to by the computer or other devices. Information stored in RAM is lost when you turn off the computer. *See also* memory.

RAS *See* Remote Access Service.

recursion One of the three key concepts in DNS name resolution. A resolver typically passes a recursive resolution request to its local name server, which tells the name server that the resolver expects a complete answer to the query, not just a pointer to another name server. Recursive resolution effectively puts the workload onto the name server and allows the resolver to be small and simple. *See also* Domain Name System (DNS); iteration.

reduce To minimize a window to an icon by using the **Minimize** button or the **Minimize** command. A minimized application continues running, and you can click the icon on the toolbar to make it the active application.

reduced instruction set computing (RISC) A type of microprocessor design that focuses on rapid and efficient processing of a relatively small set of instructions. RISC architecture limits the number of instructions that are built into the microprocessor, but optimizes each so that it can be carried out very rapidly—usually within a single clock cycle.

refresh To update displayed information with current data.

registration In Windows NT NetBT name resolution, registration is the process used to register a unique name for each computer (node) on the network. A computer typically registers itself when it starts.

registry The Windows NT registry is a hierarchical database that provides a repository for information about a computer's configuration on Windows NT Workstation and about hardware and user accounts on Windows NT Server. It is organized in subtrees and their keys, hives, and value entries. *See also* hive; key; subtree; user account.

registry size limit (RSL) The total amount of space that can be consumed by registry data is restricted by the registry size limit, which is a kind of universal maximum for registry space that prevents an application from filling the paged pool with registry data. *See also* hive; paging file.

Remote Access Service (RAS) A service that provides remote networking for telecommuters, mobile workers, and system administrators who monitor and manage servers at multiple branch offices. Users with RAS on a Windows NT–based computer can dial in to remotely access their networks for services such as file and printer sharing, electronic mail, scheduling, and SQL database access.

remote administration Administration of one computer by an administrator located at another computer and connected to the first computer across the network.

remote logon Occurs when a user is already logged on to a user account and makes a network connection to another computer. *See also* user account.

remote procedure call (RPC) A message-passing facility that allows a distributed application to call services available on various machines in a network. Used during remote administration of computers. *See also* remote administration.

Remote Procedure Call service *See* RPC service.

renew Client computers are periodically required to renew their NetBIOS name registrations with the WINS server. When a client computer first registers with a WINS server, the WINS server returns a message that indicates when the client will need to renew its registration. *See also* network basic input/output system (NetBIOS); Windows Internet Name Service (WINS).

repeaters The most basic LAN connection device, repeaters strengthen the physical transmission signal. A repeater simply takes the electrical signals that reach it and then regenerates them to full strength before passing them on. Repeaters generally extend a single network (rather than link two networks).

replication *See* directory replication.

replicators One of the Windows NT built-in local groups for workstations and member servers, used for directory replication functions. *See also* directory replication.

Requests for Comments (RFCs) The official documents of the IETF (Internet Engineering Task Force) that specify the details for protocols included in the TCP/IP family. *See also* Internet Engineering Task Force (IETF); Transmission Control Protocol/Internet Protocol (TCP/IP).

resolution In Windows NetBT name resolution, resolution is the process used to determine the specific address for a computer name.

resolvers DNS clients that query DNS servers for name resolution on networks. *See also* Domain Name System (DNS).

resource Any part of a computer system or a network, such as a disk drive, printer, or memory, that can be allotted to a program or a process while it is running, or shared over a local area network.

resource domain A trusting domain that establishes a one-way trust relationship with the master (account) domain, enabling users with accounts in the master domain to use resources in all of the other domains. *See also* domain; trust relationship.

resource fork One of two forks that make up each Macintosh file. The resource fork holds Macintosh operating system resources, such as code, menu, font, and icon definitions. Resource forks have no relevance to PCs, so the resource forks of files on the server are never accessed by PC clients. *See also* data fork; file fork.

response In Windows NT RAS, responses are strings expected from the device, which can contain macros.

RFC *See* Requests for Comments.

right *See* permissions; user rights.

RIP *See* routing information protocol.

RISC *See* reduced instruction set computing.

roaming user profile User profile that is enabled when an administrator enters a user profile path into the user account. The first time the user logs off, the local user profile is copied to that location. Thereafter, the server copy of the user profile is downloaded each time the user logs on (if it is more current than the local copy) and is updated each time the user logs off. *See also* user profile.

root directory The top-level directory on a computer, a partition, or Macintosh-accessible volume. *See also* directory tree.

router In the Windows NT environment, a router helps LANs and WANs achieve interoperability and connectivity and can link LANs that have different network topologies (such as Ethernet and Token Ring). Routers match packet headers to a LAN segment and choose the best path for the packet, optimizing network performance.

In the Macintosh environment, routers are necessary for computers on different physical networks to communicate with each other. Routers maintain a map of the physical networks on a Macintosh internet (network) and forward data received from one physical network to other physical networks. Computers running Windows NT Server with Services for Macintosh can act as routers, and you can also use third-party routing hardware on a network with Services for Macintosh. *See also* local area network (LAN); packet; wide area network (WAN).

routing The process of forwarding packets to other routers until the packet is eventually delivered to a router connected to the specified destination. *See also* packet; router.

routing information protocol (RIP)
Enables a router to exchange routing information with a neighboring router. *See also* routing.

routing table Controls the routing decisions made by computers running TCP/IP. Routing tables are built automatically by Windows NT based on the IP configuration of your computer. *See also* dynamic routing; routing; static routing; Transmission Control Protocol/Internet Protocol (TCP/IP).

RPC *See* remote procedure call.

RPC Locator service The Remote Procedure Call Locator service allows distributed applications to use the RPC Name service. The RPC Locator service manages the RPC Name service database.

The server side of a distributed application registers its availability with the RPC Locator service. The client side of a distributed application queries the RPC Locator service to find available compatible server applications. *See also* remote procedure call (RPC).

RPC service The Remote Procedure Call service is the RPC subsystem for Microsoft Windows NT. The RPC subsystem includes the endpoint mapper and other miscellaneous RPC services. *See also* remote procedure call (RPC).

RSL *See* registry size limit.

S

SACL *See* system access control list.

SAM Acronym for Security Accounts Manager. *See* directory database; Windows NT Server Directory Services.

SAP In the Windows environment, SAP is an acronym for Service Advertising Protocol, a service that broadcasts shared files, directories, and printers categorized first by domain or workgroup and then by server name.

In the context of routing and IPX, SAP is also an acronym for Service Advertising Protocol, used by servers to advertise their services and addresses on a network. Clients use SAP to determine what network resources are available.

In NetBEUI, SAP is an acronym for Service Access Point, in which each link-layer program identifies itself by registering a unique service access point.

Not to be confused with SAP financial database application software for the mainframe computer.

saturation The purity of a color's hue, moving from gray to the pure color.

scavenging Cleaning up the WINS database. *See also* Windows Internet Name Service (WINS).

Schedule service Supports and is required for use of the **at** command. The **at** command can schedule commands and programs to run on a computer at a specified time and date.

schemas Schemas control how and what information from a private database is available to visitors who use the Internet to access the public Microsoft dbWeb gateway to the private database. *See also* dbWeb Administrator.

Schema Wizard Interactive tool in dbWeb Administrator that leads a user through creation of HTML pages or through implementing an ISAPI application.

screen buffer The size reserved in memory for the command prompt display.

screen dump *See* snapshot.

screen elements The parts that make up a window or dialog box, such as the title bar, the **Minimize** and **Maximize** buttons, the window borders, and the scroll bars.

screen fonts Fonts displayed on your screen. Soft-font manufacturers often provide screen fonts that closely match the soft fonts for your printer. This ensures that your documents look the same on the screen as they do when printed. *See also* font; font types.

screen saver A moving picture or pattern that appears on your screen when you have not used the mouse or the keyboard for a specified period of time. To select a screen saver, either use Display in Control Panel or right-click on the desktop for properties.

scroll To move through text or graphics (up, down, left, or right) in order to see parts of the file that cannot fit on the screen.

scroll arrow An arrow on either end of a scroll bar that you use to scroll through the contents of the window or list box. Click the scroll arrow to scroll one screen at a time, or continue pressing the mouse button while pointing at the scroll arrow to scroll continuously.

scroll bar A bar that appears at the right or bottom edge of a window or list box whose contents are not completely visible. Each scroll bar contains two scroll arrows and a scroll box, which enable you to scroll through the contents of the window or list box.

scroll box In a scroll bar, a small box that shows the position of information currently visible in the window or list box relative to the contents of the entire window.

scroll buffer The area in memory that holds information that does not fit on the screen. You can use the scroll bars to scroll through the information.

SCSI *See* small computer system interface.

Search button *See* find tab.

section header In Windows NT RAS, a section header is a string, comprising up to 32 characters between square brackets, that identifies the specific device to which the section applies.

secure attention sequence A series of keystrokes (CTRL+ALT+DEL) that will always display the Windows NT operating system logon screen.

secure communications channel Created when computers at each end of a connection are satisfied that the computer on the other end has identified itself correctly by using its computer account. *See also* computer account.

Secure Sockets Layer (SSL) A protocol that supplies secure data communication through data encryption and decryption. SSL enables communications privacy over networks by using a combination of public key cryptography and bulk data encryption.

security A means of ensuring that shared files can be accessed only by authorized users.

Security Accounts Manager (SAM) *See* directory database; Windows NT Server Directory Services.

security database *See* directory database.

security host A third-party authentication device that verifies whether a caller from a remote client is authorized to connect to the Remote Access server. This verification supplements security already authorized to connect to the Remote-Access server.

security ID (SID) A unique name that identifies a logged-on user to the security system. Security IDs (SIDs) can identify one user or a group of users.

security identifier *See* security ID (SID).

security log Records security events. This helps track changes to the security system and identify any possible breaches of security. For example, depending on the Audit settings in User Manager or User Manager for Domains, attempts to log on to the local computer might be recorded in the security log. The security log contains both valid and invalid logon attempts as well as events related to resource use (such as creating, opening, or deleting files). *See also* event.

security policies For Windows NT Workstation, the security policies consist of the Account, User Rights, and Audit policies, and are managed by using User Manager.

For a Windows NT Server domain, the security policies consist of the Account, User Rights, Audit, and Trust Relationships policies, and are managed by using User Manager for Domains.

security token *See* access token.

seed router In the Macintosh environment, a seed router initializes and broadcasts routing information about one or more physical networks. This information tells routers where to send each packet of data. A seed router on an AppleTalk network initially defines the network number(s) and zone(s) for a network. Services for Macintosh servers can function as seed routers, and you can also use third-party hardware routers as seed routers. *See also* packet; router.

See Files The Macintosh-style permission that give users the right to open a folder and see the files in the folder. For example, a folder that has See Files and See Folders Macintosh-style permissions is given the Windows NT-style R (Read) permission. *See also* permissions.

See Folders The Macintosh-style permission that gives users the right to open a folder and see the files contained in that folder. *See also* permissions.

select To mark an item so that a subsequent action can be carried out on that item. You usually select an item by clicking it with a mouse or pressing a key. After selecting an item, you choose the action that you want to affect the item.

selection cursor The marking device that shows where you are in a window, menu, or dialog box and what you have selected. The selection cursor can appear as a highlight or as a dotted rectangle around text.

semaphore Generally, semaphores are signaling devices or mechanisms. However, in Windows NT, system semaphores are objects used to synchronize activities on an interprocess level. For example, when two or more processes share a common resource such as a printer, video screen, or memory segment, semaphores are used to control access to those resources so that only one process can alter them at any particular time.

sequence number The identifier with which TCP marks packets before sending them. The sequence numbers allow the receiving system to properly order the packets on the receiving system. *See also* packet; Transmission Control Protocol (TCP).

Serial Line Internet Protocol (SLIP) An older industry standard that is part of Windows NT RAS to ensure interoperability with third-party remote access software.

server In general, refers to a computer that provides shared resources to network users. *See also* member server.

server application A Windows NT application that can create objects for linking or embedding into other documents. For distributed applications, the application that responds to a client application. *See also* client application; DCOM Configuration tool; Distributed Component Object Model (DCOM); embedded object; linked object.

Server Manager In Windows NT Server, an application used to view and administer domains, workgroups, and computers.

server message block (SMB) A file-sharing protocol designed to allow systems to transparently access files that reside on remote systems.

Server service Provides RPC (remote procedure call) support, and file, print, and named pipe sharing. *See also* named pipe; remote procedure call (RPC).

server zone The AppleTalk zone on which a server appears. On a Phase 2 network, a server appears in the default zone of the server's default network. *See also* default network; default zone; desired zone; zone.

service A process that performs a specific system function and often provides an application programming interface (API) for other processes to call. Windows NT services are RPC-enabled, meaning that their API routines can be called from remote computers. *See also* application programming interface (API); remote procedure call (RPC).

Service Access Point (SAP) *See* SAP.

Service Advertising Protocol (SAP) *See* SAP.

Services for Macintosh *See* Windows NT Server Services for Macintosh.

session A link between two network devices, such as a client and a server. A session between a client and server consists of one or more connections from the client to the server.

SFM Acronym for Windows NT Services for Macintosh.

share To make resources, such as directories and printers, available to others.

shared directory A directory that network users can connect to.

shared network directory *See* shared directory.

shared resource Any device, data, or program that is used by more than one other device or program. For Windows NT, shared resources refer to any resource that is made available to network users, such as directories, files, printers, and named pipes. Also refers to a resource on a server that is available to network users. *See also* named pipe.

share name A name that refers to a shared resource on a server. Each shared directory on a server has a share name, used by PC users to refer to the directory. Users of Macintosh use the name of the Macintosh-accessible volume that corresponds to a directory, which may be the same as the share name. *See also* Macintosh-accessible volume.

share permissions Are used to restrict a shared resource's availability over the network to only certain users.

Shiva Password Authentication Protocol (SPAP) A two-way (reversible) encryption mechanism employed by Shiva. Windows NT Workstation, when connecting to a Shiva LAN Rover, uses SPAP, as does a Shiva client connecting to a Windows NT Server. *See also* encryption.

shortcut key A key or key combination, available for some commands, that you can press to carry out a command without first selecting a menu. Shortcut keys are listed to the right of commands on a menu.

short name A valid 8.3 (up to eight characters followed by a period and a three-character extension) MS-DOS or OS/2 file name that the computer running Windows NT Server creates for every Macintosh folder name or file name on the server. PC users refer to files on the server by their short names; Macintosh users refer to them by their long names. *See also* long name; name mapping.

SID *See* security ID.

silent mode During IP routing in silent mode, the computer listens to RIP broadcasts and updates its route table but does not advertise its own routes. *See also* routing; routing information protocol (RIP); routing table.

simple device A device that you use without specifying a related media file. An audio compact-disc player is a simple device.

Simple Mail Transfer Protocol (SMTP)
A member of the TCP/IP suite of protocols that governs the exchange of electronic mail between message transfer agents.

Simple Network Management Protocol (SNMP)
A protocol used by SNMP consoles and agents to communicate. In Windows NT, the SNMP service is used to get and set status information about a host on a TCP/IP network. *See also* Transmission Control Protocol/Internet Protocol (TCP/IP).

single user logon Windows NT network users can connect to multiple servers, domains, and applications with a single network logon.

SLIP *See* Serial Line Internet Protocol.

small computer system interface (SCSI)
A standard high-speed parallel interface defined by the American National Standards Institute (ANSI). A SCSI interface is used for connecting microcomputers to peripheral devices such as hard disks and printers, and to other computers and local area networks.

SMB *See* server message block.

SMS *See* Systems Management Server.

SMTP *See* Simple Mail Transfer Protocol.

SNA *See* System Network Architecture.

snapshot A copy of main memory or video memory at a given instant, sent to a printer or hard disk. A graphical image of the video screen can be saved by taking a snapshot of video memory, more commonly called a screen dump.

sniffer *See* network sniffer.

Sniffer files Files saved from Network General Sniffer, a third-party protocol analyzer. *See also* network sniffer.

SNMP *See* Simple Network Management Protocol.

socket A bidirectional pipe for incoming and outgoing data between networked computers. The Windows Sockets API is a networking API used by programmers creating TCP/IP-based sockets applications. *See also* application programming interface (API); named pipe.

Sockets Windows Sockets is a Windows implementation of the widely used UC Berkeley sockets API. Microsoft TCP/IP, NWLink, and AppleTalk protocols use this interface. Sockets interfaces between programs and the transport protocol and works as a bidirectional pipe for incoming and outgoing data. *See also* application programming interface (API); named pipe; socket.

source directory The directory that contains the file or files you intend to copy or move.

source document The document where a linked or embedded object was originally created. *See also* embedded object; linked object.

SPAP *See* Shiva Password Authentication Protocol.

special access permission On NTFS volumes, a custom set of permissions. You can customize permissions on files and directories by selecting the individual components of the standard sets of permissions. *See also* access permission.

split bar Divides Windows NT Explorer into two parts: The directory tree is displayed on the left, and the contents of the current directory are on the right. *See also* directory tree.

spoofing Refers to a case where an Internet user mimics ("spoofs") the source IP address for an Internet server, proxy server, or firewall of a system to which it is trying to gain access.

spooler Software that accepts documents sent by a user to be printed, and then stores those documents and sends them, one by one, to available printer(s). *See also* spooling.

spooling A process on a server in which print documents are stored on a disk until a printing device is ready to process them. A spooler accepts each document from each client, stores it, then sends it to a printing device when it is ready.

SQL Acronym for structured query language, a database programming language used for accessing, querying, and otherwise managing information in a relational database system.

SSL *See* Secure Sockets Layer.

stabilize During subdirectory replication, when a subdirectory is stabilized, the export server waits two minutes after changes before exporting the subdirectory. The waiting period allows time for subsequent changes to take place so that all intended changes are recorded before being replicated. *See also* directory replication; export server; subtree.

stand-alone server *See* member server.

static mapping A method provided on a WINS server to assign a static (unchanging) IP address to a client.

static object Information that has been pasted into a document. Unlike embedded or linked objects, static objects cannot be changed from within the document. The only way you can change a static object is to delete it from the document, change it in the application used to create it, and paste it into the document again. *See also* embedded object; linked object.

static routing Static routing limits you to fixed routing tables, as opposed to dynamically updating the routing tables. *See also* dynamic routing; routing table.

static Web pages Standard Web pages that are created in advance and stored for later delivery to clients. *See also* dynamic Web pages.

status bar A line of information related to the application in the window. Usually located at the bottom of a window. Not all windows have a status bar.

STATUS message A message displayed by the Executive in a Windows-mode message box when the Executive detects a condition within a process that you should know about.

STATUS messages can be divided into three types:

System-information messages. Just read the information in the message box and click **OK**. The Kernel continues running the process or thread.

Warning messages. Some advise you to take an action that will enable the Kernel to keep running the process or thread. Others warn you that, although the process or thread will continue running, the results might be incorrect.

Application-termination messages. These warn you that the Kernel is about to terminate either a process or a thread.

See also Executive messages; STOP message.

STOP message A character-mode message that occurs when the Kernel detects an inconsistent condition from which it cannot recover. Always displayed on a full character-mode screen, uniquely identified by a hexadecimal number and a symbolic string. The content of the symbolic string can suggest, to a trained technician, the part of the Kernel that detected the condition from which there was no recourse but to stop. However, the cause may actually be in another part of the system. *See also* Executive messages; STATUS message.

string A data structure composed of a sequence of characters, usually representing human-readable text.

stripe set Refers to the saving of data across identical partitions on different drives. A stripe set does not provide fault tolerance; however stripe sets with parity do. *See also* fault tolerance; partition; stripe sets with parity.

stripe sets with parity A method of data protection in which data is striped in large blocks across all of the disks in an array. Data redundancy is provided by the parity information. This method provides fault tolerance. *See also* fault tolerance; stripe set.

subdirectory A directory within a directory. Also called a folder within a folder.

subkey A key within a key. Subkeys are analogous to subdirectories in the registry hierarchy. Keys and subkeys are similar to the section heading in .ini files; however subkeys can carry out functions. *See also* key; registry.

subnet A portion of a network, which may be a physically independent network segment, that shares a network address with other portions of the network and is distinguished by a subnet number. A subnet is to a network what a network is to an internet.

subnet mask A 32-bit value that allows the recipient of IP packets to distinguish the network ID portion of the IP address from the host ID. *See also* IP address; packet.

substitution macros Placeholders that are replaced in command strings.

subtree During directory replication, this refers to the export subdirectory and all of its subdirectories. *See also* directory replication.

swap file *See* paging file.

switched circuit *See* dial-up line.

SYN attack SYN (synchronizing character) messages maliciously generated by an intruder in an attempt to block legitimate access to a server by proliferating half-open TCP port connections. Also called SYN flooding.

synchronize To replicate the domain database from the primary domain controller (PDC) to one backup domain controller (BDC) of the domain, or to all of the BDCs of a domain. This is usually performed automatically by the system, but can also be invoked manually by an administrator. *See also* backup domain controller (BDC); domain; primary domain controller (PDC).

syntax The order in which you must type a command and the elements that follow the command. Windows NT commands have up to four elements: command name, parameters, switches, and values.

system access control list (SACL) The system ACL is controlled by the system administrator, and allows system-level security to be associated with an object. SACL APIs can be used only by a process with System Administrator privileges. *See also* discretionary access control list (DACL).

system default profile In Windows NT Server, the user profile that is loaded when Windows NT is running and no user is logged on. When the **Begin Logon** dialog box is visible, the system default profile is loaded. *See also* user default profile, user profile.

system disk A disk that contains the MS-DOS system files necessary to start MS-DOS.

system log The system log contains events logged by the Windows NT components. For example, the failure of a driver or other system component to load during startup is recorded in the system log. Use Event Viewer to view the system log.

System Network Architecture (SNA) System Network Architecture is a communications framework developed by IBM. Microsoft System Network Architecture (SNA) is an optional solution that provides a gateway connection between personal computer LANs or WANs and IBM mainframe and AS/400 hosts. *See also* AS/400; gateway.

system partition The volume that has the hardware-specific files needed to load Windows NT. *See also* partition.

system policy A policy, created by using the System Policy Editor, to control user work environments and actions, and to enforce system configuration for Windows 95. System policy can be implemented for specific users, groups, computers, or for all users. System policy for users overwrites settings in the current user area of the registry, and system policy for computers overwrites the current local machine area of the registry. *See also* registry.

systemroot The name of the directory that contains Windows NT files. The name of this directory is specified when Windows NT is installed.

Systems Management Server Part of the Windows NT BackOffice suite. Systems Management Server includes desktop management and software distribution that significantly automates the task of upgrading software on client computers.

T

T1 or T3 connection Standard measurement of network bandwidth.

tag file A configuration file that contains information about a corresponding file on a Gopher server or links to other servers. This information is sent to clients in response to a Gopher request.

tape set A tape set (sometimes referred to as a tape family) in Windows NT Backup is a sequence of tapes in which each tape is a continuation of the backup on the previous tape. *See also* backup set; backup types.

TAPI *See* Telephony API.

Task list A window that shows all running applications and their status. View the Task list in the **Applications** tab in Task Manager.

Task Manager Task Manager enables you to start, end, or run applications, end processes (an application, application component, or system process), and view CPU and memory use data. Task Manager gives you a simple, quick view of how each process (application or service) is using CPU and memory resources. (Note: In previous versions of Windows NT, Task List handled some of these functions.)

To run Task Manager, right-click the toolbar and then click Task Manager.

TCP *See* Transmission Control Protocol.

TCP/IP *See* Transmission Control Protocol/Internet Protocol.

TCP/IP keep-alives An optimizing feature of the TCP/IP service. TCP/IP periodically broadcasts messages to determine whether an idle connection is still active. *See also* HTTP keep-alives.

TDI *See* transport driver interface.

Telephony API (TAPI) An API used by programs to make data/fax/voice calls, including HyperTerminal, Dial-up Networking, Phone Dialer, and other Win32 communications applications written for Windows NT.

Telnet (VTP) A terminal emulation protocol for logging on to remote computers. Once referred to as Virtual Terminal Protocol (VTP). Defined in RFC 854, among others.

template accounts Accounts that are not actually used by real users but serve as a basis for the real accounts (for administrative purposes).

terminate-and-stay-resident program (TSR) A program running under MS-DOS that remains loaded in memory even when it is not running so that it can be quickly invoked for a specific task performed while any other application is operating.

text box In a dialog box, a box in which you type information needed to carry out a command. The text box may be blank or may contain text when the dialog box opens.

text file A file containing text characters (letters, numbers, and symbols) but no formatting information. A text file can be a "plain" ASCII file that most computers can read. Text file can also refer to a word-processing file. *See also* ASCII file.

text-file transfer A method for transferring files from HyperTerminal to a remote computer. With this method, files are transferred as ASCII files with minimal formatting characters, such as linefeeds and carriage returns. All font-formatting information is removed. *See also* ASCII file.

text-only An ASCII file that contains no formatting. *See also* ASCII file.

TFTP *See* Trivial File Transfer Protocol.

thread Threads are objects within processes that run program instructions. They allow concurrent operations within a process and enable one process to run different parts of its program on different processors simultaneously.

throughput *See* bandwidth.

time-out If a device is not performing a task, the amount of time the computer should wait before detecting it as an error.

time slice The amount of processor time allocated to an application, usually measured in milliseconds.

title bar The horizontal bar (at the top of a window) that contains the title of the window or dialog box. On many windows, the title bar also contains the program icon and the **Maximize**, **Minimize**, and **Close** buttons.

Token Ring A type of network media that connects clients in a closed ring and uses token passing to enable clients to use the network. *See also* Fiber Distributed Data Interface (FDDI); LocalTalk.

toolbar A series of icons or shortcut buttons providing quick access to commands. Usually located directly below the menu bar. Not all windows have a toolbar.

topic Information in the Help window. A Help topic usually begins with a title and contains information about a particular task, command, or dialog box.

transforms Rules the administrator creates to add, remove, and modify domain names appended to inbound and outbound messages.

Transmission Control Protocol (TCP) A connection-based Internet protocol responsible for breaking data into packets, which the IP protocol sends over the network. This protocol provides a reliable, sequenced communication stream for network communication. *See also* Internet Protocol (IP); packet.

Transmission Control Protocol/Internet Protocol (TCP/IP) A set of networking protocols that provide communications across interconnected networks made up of computers with diverse hardware architectures and various operating systems. TCP/IP includes standards for how computers communicate and conventions for connecting networks and routing traffic.

transport driver interface (TDI) In Windows networking, the common interface for network components that communicate at the Session layer.

trap In SNMP, a discrete block of data that indicates that the request failed authentication. The SNMP service can send a trap when it receives a request for information that does not contain the correct community name and that does not match an accepted host name for the service. Trap destinations are the names or IP addresses of hosts to which the SNMP service is to send traps with community names. *See also* IP address; Simple Network Management Protocol (SNMP).

trigger A set of conditions that, when met, initiate an action. For example, before using Network Monitor to capture data from the network, you can set a trigger to stop the capture or to execute a program or command file.

Trivial File Transfer Protocol (TFTP) A file transfer protocol that transfers files to and from a remote computer running the TFTP service. TFTP was designed with less functions than FTP. Defined in RFC 1350, among others. *See also* File Transfer Protocol (FTP).

Trojan horse A program that masquerades as another common program in an attempt to receive information. An example of a Trojan horse is a program that masquerades as a system logon to retrieve user names and password information, which the writers of the Trojan horse can use later to break into the system.

TrueType fonts Fonts that are scalable and sometimes generated as bitmaps or soft fonts, depending on the capabilities of your printer. TrueType fonts can be sized to any height, and they print exactly as they appear on the screen.

trust *See* trust relationship.

trust relationship A link between domains that enables pass-through authentication, in which a trusting domain honors the logon authentications of a trusted domain. With trust relationships, a user who has only one user account in one domain can potentially access the entire network. User accounts and global groups defined in a trusted domain can be given rights and resource permissions in a trusting domain, even though those accounts do not exist in the trusting domain's directory database. *See also* directory database; global group; pass-through authentication; user account.

trust relationships policy A security policy that determines which domains are trusted and which domains are trusting domains. *See also* trust relationship.

TSR *See* terminate-and-stay-resident program.

two-way trust relationship Each domain trusts user accounts in the other domain to use its resources. Users can log on from computers in either domain to the domain that contains their account. *See also* trust relationship.

type *See* file type.

Type 1 fonts Scalable fonts designed to work with PostScript devices. *See also* font; font types; PostScript printer.

U

UAM *See* user authentication module.

UDP *See* User Datagram Protocol.

unavailable An unavailable button or command is displayed in light gray instead of black, and it cannot be clicked.

UNC name *See* universal naming convention name.

unicast datagram An IP datagram sent to one host. *See also* broadcast datagram; Internet Protocol (IP); multicast datagram.

Unicode A fixed-width, 16-bit character-encoding standard capable of representing the letters and characters of virtually all of the world's languages. Unicode was developed by a consortium of U.S. computer companies.

Uniform Resource Locator (URL) A naming convention that uniquely identifies the location of a computer, directory, or file on the Internet. The URL also specifies the appropriate Internet protocol, such as HTTP, FTP, IRC, or Gopher.

uninterruptible power supply (UPS) A battery-operated power supply connected to a computer to keep the system running during a power failure.

universally unique identifier (UUID) A unique identification string associated with the remote procedure call interface. Also known as a globally unique identifier (GUID).

universal naming convention (UNC) name A full Windows NT name of a resource on a network. It conforms to the *server_name**share_name* syntax, where *server_name* is the server's name and *share_name* is the name of the shared resource. UNC names of directories or files can also include the directory path under the share name, with the following syntax: *server_name**share_name**directory**file_name*.

UPS *See* uninterruptible power supply.

UPS service Manages an uninterruptible power supply connected to a computer. *See also* uninterruptible power supply (UPS).

URL *See* Uniform Resource Locator.

user account Consists of all of the information that defines a user to Windows NT. This includes such things as the user name and password required for the user to log on, the groups in which the user account has membership, and the rights and permissions the user has for using the system and accessing its resources. For Windows NT Workstation, user accounts are managed with User Manager. For Windows NT Server, user accounts are managed with User Manager for Domains. *See also* group.

user account database *See* directory database.

user authentication module Software component that prompts clients for their user names and passwords. *See also* clear-text passwords.

User Datagram Protocol (UDP) A TCP complement that offers a connectionless datagram service that guarantees neither delivery nor correct sequencing of delivered packets (much like IP). *See also* datagram; Internet Protocol (IP); packet.

user default profile In Windows NT Server, the user profile that is loaded by a server when a user's assigned profile cannot be accessed for any reason; when a user without an assigned profile logs on to the computer for the first time; or when a user logs on to the Guest account. *See also* system default profile; user profile.

User Manager A Windows NT Workstation tool used to manage the security for a workstation. User Manager administers user accounts, groups, and security policies.

User Manager for Domains A Windows NT Server tool used to manage security for a domain or an individual computer. User Manager for Domains administers user accounts, groups, and security policies.

user name A unique name identifying a user account to Windows NT. An account's user name cannot be identical to any other group name or user name of its own domain or workgroup. *See also* user account.

user password The password stored in each user's account. Each user generally has a unique user password and must type that password when logging on or accessing a server. *See also* password; volume password.

User privilege One of three privilege levels you can assign to a Windows NT user account. Every user account has one of the three privilege levels (Administrator, Guest, and User). Accounts with User privilege are regular users of the network; most accounts on your network probably have User privilege. *See also* Administrator privilege; Guest privilege; user account.

user profile Configuration information that can be retained on a user-by-user basis, and is saved in user profiles. This information includes all of the per-user settings of the Windows NT environment, such as the desktop arrangement, personal program groups and the program items in those groups, screen colors, screen savers, network connections, printer connections, mouse settings, window size and position. When a user logs on, the user's profile is loaded and the user's Windows NT environment is configured according to that profile. *See also* personal group; program item.

user rights Define a user's access to a computer or domain and the actions that a user can perform on the computer or domain. User rights permit actions such as logging onto a computer or network, adding or deleting users in a workstation or domain, and so forth.

user rights policy Manages the assignment of rights to groups and user accounts. *See also* user account; user rights.

users In the Macintosh environment, a special group that contains all users who have user permissions on the server. When a Macintosh user assigns permissions to everyone, those permissions are given to the groups users and guests. *See also* guest.

UUENCODE (UNIX-to-UNIX Encode) A utility that converts a binary file (such as a word-processing file or a program) to text so that it can be transmitted over a network. UUDECODE (UNIX-to-UNIX Decode) is the utility used to convert the file back to its original state.

UUID *See* universally unique identifier.

V

value entry The string of data that appears in the right pane of a Registry Editor window and that defines the value of the currently selected key. A value entry has three parts: name, data type, and the value itself. *See also* key; subkey.

Van Jacobsen header compression A TCP/IP network layer compression technique, VJ compression reduces the size of IP and TCP headers. *See also* Internet Protocol (IP); Transmission Control Protocol (TCP); Transmission Control Protocol/ Internet Protocol (TCP/IP).

variables In programming, a variable is a named storage location capable of containing a certain type of data that can be modified during program execution. System environment variables are defined by Windows NT Server and are the same no matter who is logged on at the computer. (Administrator group members can add new variables or change the values, however.) User environment variables can be different for each user of a particular computer. They include any environment variables you want to define of variables defined by your applications, such as the path where application files are located.

VDD *See* virtual device driver.

VDM *See* virtual DOS machine.

verify operation Occurs after all files are backed up or restored, if specified. A verify operation compares files on disk to files that have been written to tape. *See also* backup types.

virtual device driver (VDD) A driver that enables MS-DOS-based and 16-bit Windows-based applications to run on Windows NT.

virtual directory An Internet Information Server directory outside the home directory. A virtual directory appears to browsers as a subdirectory of the home directory.

virtual DOS machine (VDM) Simulates an MS-DOS environment so that MS-DOS-based and Windows-based applications can run on Windows NT.

virtual memory The space on your hard disk that Windows NT uses as if it were actually memory. Windows NT does this through the use of paging files. The benefit of using virtual memory is that you can run more applications at one time than your system's physical memory would otherwise allow. The drawbacks are the disk space required for the virtual-memory paging file and the decreased execution speed when paging is required. *See also* paging file.

virtual printer memory In a PostScript printer, a part of memory that stores font information. The memory in PostScript printers is divided into two areas: banded memory and virtual memory. The banded memory contains graphics and page-layout information needed to print your documents. The virtual memory contains any font information that is sent to your printer either when you print a document or when you download fonts. *See also* font types; PostScript printer.

virtual private network (VPN) A remote LAN that can be accessed through the Internet by using the new PPTP. *See also* Point-to-Point Tunneling Protocol (PPTP).

virtual server A computer with several IP addresses assigned to the network adapter card. This configuration makes the computer look like several servers to a browser.

virus A program that attempts to spread from computer to computer and either cause damage (by erasing or corrupting data) or annoy users (by printing messages or altering what is displayed on the screen).

volume A partition or collection of partitions that have been formatted for use by a file system. *See also* Macintosh-accessible volume; partition.

volume password An optional, case-sensitive password you can assign to a Macintosh-accessible volume when you configure the volume. To access the volume, a user must type the volume password. *See also* Macintosh-accessible volume; user password.

volume set A combination of partitions on a physical disk that appear as one logical drive. *See also* logical drive; partition.

VPN *See* virtual private network.

VTP Acronym for Virtual Terminal Protocol. *See* Telnet.

W

WAIS *See* wide area information server.

wallpaper A picture or drawing stored as a bitmap file (a file that has a .bmp extension).

WAN *See* wide area network.

warning beep The sound that your computer makes when you encounter an error or try to perform a task that Windows NT does not recognize.

Web browser A software program, such as Microsoft Internet Explorer, that retrieves a document from a Web server, interprets the HTML codes, and displays the document to the user with as much graphical content as the software can supply.

WebCat Microsoft Web Capacity Analysis Tool. A script-driven utility that tests your client/server configuration by using a variety of predetermined, invariant workloads. WebCat can test how your server responds to different workloads or test the same workload on varying configurations of the server. WebCat is included on the *Windows NT Resource Kit Supplement 1* compact disc.

Web server A computer equipped with the server software to respond to HTTP requests, such as requests from a Web browser. A Web server uses the HTTP protocol to communicate with clients on a TCP/IP network.

Well Known Port Number The standard port numbers used by the Internet community for well known (commonly used) services. Ports are used in TCP to name the ends of logical connections that carry long-term conversations. Well known services are defined by RFC 1060. The relationship between the well known services and the well known ports is described in RFC 1340.

wide area information server (WAIS) A network publishing system designed to help users find information over a computer network. WAIS software has four main components: the client, the server, the database, and the protocol. Discussed in RFC 1625.

wide area network (WAN) A communications network that connects geographically separated areas.

wildcard A character that represents one or more characters. The question mark (?) wildcard can be used to represent any single character, and the asterisk (*) wildcard can be used to represent any character or group of characters that might match that position in other file names.

window A rectangular area on your screen in which you view an application or document. You can open, close, and move windows, and change the size of most windows. You can open several windows at a time, and you can often reduce a window to an icon or enlarge it to fill the entire desktop.

window menu A menu that contains commands you can use to manipulate a window. You click the program icon or document icon at the left of the title bar to open the window menu.

Windows Internet Name Service (WINS) A name resolution service that resolves Windows networking computer names to IP addresses in a routed environment. A WINS server handles name registrations, queries, and releases. *See also* IP address; routing.

Windows NT–based application Used as a shorthand term to refer to an application that is designed to run with Windows NT and does not run without Windows NT. All Windows NT–based applications follow similar conventions for arrangement of menus, style of dialog boxes, and keyboard and mouse use.

Windows NT browser system Consists of a master browser, backup browser, and client systems. The master browser maintains the browse list—of all of the available domains and servers—and periodically sends copies to the backup browsers. *See also* browse; master browser.

Windows NT Explorer A program that enables you to view and manage the files and folders on your computer and make network connections to other shared resources, such as a hard disk on a server. Windows NT Explorer replaces Program Manager and File Manager, which were programs available in earlier versions of Windows NT. Program Manager and File Manager are still available, and can be started in the same way you start other Windows-based programs.

Windows NT File System (NTFS) An advanced file system designed for use specifically within the Windows NT operating system. It supports file system recovery, extremely large storage media, long file names, and various features for the POSIX subsystem. It also supports object-oriented applications by treating all files as objects with user-defined and system-defined attributes. *See also* POSIX.

Windows NT Server A superset of Windows NT Workstation, Windows NT Server provides centralized management and security, fault tolerance, and additional connectivity. *See also* fault tolerance; Windows NT Workstation.

Windows NT Server Directory Services A Windows NT protected subsystem that maintains the directory database and provides an application programming interface (API) for accessing the database. *See also* application programming interface (API); directory database.

Windows NT Server Services for Macintosh A software component of Windows NT Server that allows Macintosh users access to the computer running Windows NT Server. The services provided with this component allow PC and Macintosh users to share files and resources, such as printers on the AppleTalk network or those attached to the Windows NT Server. *See also* File Server for Macintosh service; Print Server for Macintosh.

Windows NT Workstation The portable, secure, 32-bit, preemptive multitasking member of the Microsoft Windows operating system family.

Windows Open Services Architecture (WOSA)
An open set of APIs for integrating Windows-based computers with back-end services on a broad range of vendor's systems. WOSA consists of an extensible set of APIs that enable Windows-based desktop applications to access available information without having to know anything about the type of network in use, the types of computers in the enterprise, or types of back-end services available. As a result, if the network computers or services change, the desktop applications built by using WOSA will not require rewriting. *See also* application programming interface (API).

Windows Sockets *See* Sockets.

WINS *See* Windows Internet Name Service.

workgroup For Windows NT, a workgroup is a collection of computers that are grouped for viewing purposes. Each workgroup is identified by a unique name. *See also* domain.

working set Every program running can use a portion of physical memory, its working set, which is the current number of physical memory bytes used by or allocated by a process.

workstation Any networked Macintosh or PC using server resources. *See also* backup domain controller (BDC); member server; primary domain controller (PDC).

Workstation service Provides network connections and communications.

World Wide Web (WWW) The software, protocols, conventions, and information that enable hypertext and multimedia publishing of resources on different computers around the world. *See also* Hypertext Markup Language (HTML); Internet.

WOSA *See* Windows Open Services Architecture.

WOW Acronym for Win16 on Win32. The translation of Windows 3.1-based application calls to standard mode for RISC-based computers and 386 enhanced mode for x86-based computers.

wrap To continue to the next line rather than stopping when the cursor reaches the end of the current line.

X

X.25 A recommendation published by the Comite Consultatif International de Telegraphique et Telephonique (CCITT) international communications standards organization that defines the connection between a terminal and a packet-switching network. An X.25 network is a type of packet-switching network that routes units of information (packets) as specified by X.25 and is used in public data communications networks. *See also* packet.

X.25 smart card A hardware card with a PAD (packet assembler/disassembler) embedded in it. *See also* packet assembler/disassembler (PAD); X.25.

X.400 system A messaging system that is compliant with the X.400 standards developed under the CCITT and the International Standards Organization (ISO).

XModem/CRC Protocol for transmitting binary files that uses a cyclic redundancy check (CRC) to detect any transmission errors. Both computers must be set to transmit and receive eight data bits per character.

XOR Short for exclusive OR. A Boolean operation in which the Windows NT Server stripe-sets-with-parity form of fault tolerance maintains an XOR of the total data to provide data redundancy. This enables the reconstruction of missing data (on a failed disk or sector) from the remaining disks in the stripe set with parity. *See also* fault tolerance; stripe sets with parity.

Z

zone In the Macintosh environment, a zone is a logical grouping that simplifies browsing the network for resources, such as servers and printers. It is similar to a domain in Windows NT Server networking.

In a DNS (Domain Name System) database, a zone is a subtree of the DNS database that is administered as a single separate entity, a DNS name server. This administrative unit can consist of a single domain or a domain with subdomains. A DNS zone administrator sets up one or more name servers for the zone. *See also* domain; Domain Name System (DNS).

zone data file A Domain Name System database for a zone in the DNS name space.

zone list In the Macintosh environment, a zone list includes all of the zones associated with a particular network. Not to be confused with Windows NT DNS zones.

Index

256 inbound sessions 4
8.3 file naming 182–183

A

Accessibility options, described 36, 99
Accessories, included with setup 36
Active partition 23
Active partitions 219–220
ActiveX 277, 684
Add/Remove Programs Properties dialog box
    Install/Uninstall tab 125–126
    Windows NT Setup tab 125
Address Resolution Protocol (ARP)
    defined 684
    introduced 350
    reply packet 686
    request packet 686
    TCP/IP function 356
Administrative tools
    client-based network administration tools 558
    file names 559
    installing on a Windows 95 computer 561
    installing on a Windows NT Server client-based
      computer 559
    Licensing program 537
    tool function 559
Administrative Tools (Common)
    DHCP Manager 377
    Disk Administrator 213
    DNS Manager
      setting up DNS for IIS 497
    Event Viewer
      logging events 649
      troubleshooting RAS 467
    License Manager 537, 542
    Network Client Administrator 552
    Network Monitor 667
    Performance Monitor 492, 661
    Remote Access Admin utility 453
    Server Manager
      adding a computer account to a domain 51
      configuring the Directory Replicator on
        an export server 597
      creating a computer account 49
      managing replication 591

Administrative Tools (Common) *(continued)*
    System Policy Editor 142, 151
    Upgrading from previous versions of Windows NT 76
    User Manager for Domains
      creating a new user 100
      defined 743
      examining the Windows NT Server environment 492
      setting Everyone group logon privileges 101
    Windows NT Diagnostics 656
    WINS Manager 396
Administrative wizards 4
Affinity
    hard affinity 274
    processor 274
    set affinity option 274
    soft affinity 274
Alerts dialog box 112
    See also Recovery, options
Alias folders
    defined 184
    viewing 184
Anonymous access, Internet 490
Answer files
    creating 70
    defined 69
Appendixes of this course, location xxix
AppleTalk
    description 325, 685
    internetworking 562
    protocol, described 685
    transport, described 685
    See also Services for Macintosh
Application log 650, 685
Applications
    base priority 309
    binary compatibility 297
    bound 298
    compatibility issues for specific platforms 297
    foreground 310
    installing new 126
    managing using the Command Prompt 306
    MS-DOS 280–283, 298
    OS/2 298
    performance 310

Applications *(continued)*
    Presentation Manager 298
    prioritizing 308–310
    priority levels 309
    responsiveness 310
    sharing data 299
    source compatibility 297
    starting at a specified priority 309
    uninstalling existing 126
    Windows 3.x 298
ARC naming conventions 254
ARC-compliant computers
    ARC paths 254–255
    creating a boot disk 254–255
    file system 176
Archiving log files 652
Auditing
    RAS servers 438
Authentication
    Basic 491
    RAS 438
    Windows NT Challenge/Response 491
Autocheck.exe 619
AutoDial 462–464
Autoexec
    Filename setting 282
    Windows NT default name 282
Automated installation 69–74
Available Hardware Profiles list 116

B

Back-end processes, described 328
BackOffice
    components 2
    licensing model 531
    operating system 2
Backup domain controller (BDC)
    defined 687
    described 29
    functions 27
    introduced 11
    moving to another domain 30
    relationship with PDC 29
    stand-alone server 30
Basic (clear-text) authentication 491, 688
BDC *See* Backup domain controller (BDC)
Binary compatibility, application 297
Bindery emulation 506

Binding
    configuring network 362
    defined 360, 688
    introduced 323
    network components 361
Blue screen errors 670
Book_cp.hlp 79
Book_net.hlp 79
Books Online 79–80
Boot delay, setting 113
Boot disk, creating
    ARC-compliant disk 254–255
    fault tolerance disk 251–253
    Windows NT disk 625–626
Boot partition
    defined 688
    described 23
    locating 227
    See also Boot process
Boot process
    boot sequence, Windows NT 616–620
    files required 610–611
    Intel x86 computers
        boot sequence 613
        files required 611, 614
        initializing 612
        overview 610
    RISC-based computers
        boot sequence 615
        files required 611, 615
        initializing 614–615
    successful completion 620
    user logon 620
    Windows NT load phases 616–620, 641
Boot sequence *See* Boot process, boot sequence
Boot.ini
    components
        boot loader 623
        operating systems 624
        overview 623
    editing for ARC computers 254–255
    editing for boot disk 252
    function 611
    locating the boot partition 227
    troubleshooting 622–625
BootExecute data item 619
Bootsect.dos file 611
Bound applications 298
Boundary layers 322

Index   751

Boundary, networking 321
Bridges, defined 347
Briefcase
   copying files to 576
   database 575
   description 574
   dialog box 576
   folder location 575
   introduced 573
   My Briefcase
      location 575
      practices with 578–580
   synchronization process 574–575
   synchronizing updated files 577
   working with files 577
Browser election 415
   See also Computer Browser service
Business computing with Windows NT Workstation 4

C

CAL *See* Client Access License (CAL)
Callback security, RAS 439
Calling cards, TAPI 441
Case-sensitivity 185
CD-ROM
   assigning drive letter to 228
   compact discs included with this course xxxi
   description of course materials included xxxiii
Centralizing network administration 8
Certified Professional program *See* Microsoft Certified Professional program
Certified Systems Engineer *See* Microsoft Certified Systems Engineer (MCSE)
Changing a domain name 28–29
Changing NTFS to FAT file system 181
Changing the drive letter of a partition 218
Client Access License (CAL)
   adding or removing
      Per Seat 545
      Per Server 543–544
   defined 531
   overview 32
   summarized 566
Client connections 532–533
Client Service for NetWare (CSNW)
   configuring 515–517
   defined 691
   described 505–506

Client Server for NetWare (CSNW) *(continued)*
   dialog box 515
   installing 514–515
   options 516
Client/server subsystem 269
Clipboard
   sharing data using 299
Clone control set 617, 620
Cluster remapping 179
Codec files, installing 8
COM *See* Component Object Model (COM)
COM ports
   configuring 104–105
Command Prompt
   characteristics 306
   configuring default settings 307
   configuring individual settings 308
   locating 306
   registry key 307
   start command options 309
   tasks 306
Common.adm 165
Communications programs included with setup 36
Compact setup 36
Compact.exe
   NTFS compression 190
   options 190
Comparing Windows NT Server and Workstation 6–7
Comparing Windows NT Workstation to Windows 95 7
Compatibility
   application and platform 297
   binary-compatible 297
   source-compatible 297
Component Object Model (COM)
   described 278
   OLE and ActiveX uses 278, 300
   See also Distributed Component Object Model (DCOM)
Components
   adding and removing 125–126
   installation 36
Compressing the Window NT installation 191
Compression
   compact.exe 190
   compressing the installation 191
   compression attribute 188
   copying compressed files 193
   file vs. folder 188
   moving compressed files 193

752   Index

Compression *(continued)*
  NTFS methods 189-190
  NTFS support 188
  performance considerations 188
  practice 191-192
  Windows NT Explorer 189-190
Computer accounts
  adding to a domain 49-51
  administrative permissions 49
  creation methods 49-51
  joining a domain 31, 55
  who can create 49
Computer Browser service
  browser criteria 416
  browser election 415-416
  browser roles 414
  configuring browsers 416
  defined 692
  function 412
  master browser 414, 415
  process 413
  providing server list to clients 414
  See also Service Advertising Protocol (SAP)
Computer policy *See* System policy, computer policy
Computer requirements for this course xxx
Computer1 configuration xxxi
Computer2 configuration xxxii
Config.sys
  Filename setting 282
  Windows NT default name 282
Config.pol 149, 164
Configuration information 90-91
Configure Port Usage dialog box 445
Configuring browsers 416
Console
  application support 269
  described 99
Console program 307
Control Panel
  add/remove programs 125-126
  default installed programs 98
  hardware profiles *See* Hardware profiles
  Network program *See* Network program
  operating system startup and shutdown
    changing settings 111-112
  per-computer programs 102-104
  per-user programs 99
  setting environment variables 123-125
  starting 98
Conventions used in this book xxii-xxiv
Convert command syntax 179
Convert.exe 179

Course
  Appendix location xxix
  book organization xix
  chapter and appendix overview xxv-xxix
  computer requirements xxx
  Computer1 configuration xxxi
  Computer2 configuration xxxi-xxxiii
  conventions used in this book xxii-xxiv
  intentions xx
  materials
    installing on Server1 47
    installing on Workstation1 54
    on CD-ROM xxxiii-xxxv
  network configuration xxxi-xxxiii
  overview xix
  prerequisites xx
  removing training files xxxv
  setup xxxi
  software required xxx
  suggested starting points xxi
Creating a fault tolerance boot disk 251-253
Creating a Windows NT boot disk 625-626
CSNW *See* Client Service for NetWare (CSNW)
CSR subsystem 269
CurrentControlSet subkey 617
Custom setup 36
Customizing installation with UDFs 73
Customizing setup switches 68-69

D

Data link control (DLC)
  as a protocol 324
  description 325
Data redundancy 240
Data transmission, increasing rates 436
DCOM *See* Distributed Component Object Model (DCOM)
Decompression *See* Compression
Default computer *See* System policy, default computer
Default gateway 352
Default user *See* System policy, default user
Defragmentation utilities, web site 179
Deleting a partition 218
Demand paging 119, 266
Determining hardware configuration 19
Device drivers
  interaction with the registry 91
DHCP *See* Dynamic Host Configuration Protocol (DHCP)
DHCP Manager
  Create Scope dialog box 378
  DHCP Options
    Global dialog box 382

Index

Dialing Properties dialog box 441–442
Dial-Up Networking
    and RAS 427
    and TAPI 440
    AutoDial 462–464
    configuring 454, 456
    description 426
    encryption 438
    installing 454–456
    location 440
    logging on 460–461
    Logon Preferences dialog box 460
    Monitor 467
    phonebook entries
        configuring 456–458
        creating 459
    resources made available to client 428
Directory replication
    defined 696
    export and import directories 585
    export servers 584
    GuardTime 593
    import computers 584
    interval 593
    managing replication
        from and export server 591–593
        Server Manager 591
        to an import computer 594–595
    master directory 581
    preparation
        export server 588–590
        import computer 590
    See also Directory Replicator
Directory Replicator
    export and import directories 585
    introduced 573
    overview 581
    parameter location 587
    propagating files 581–582
    purpose 581
    replication components 584–585
    replication process 586–587
    summarized 604
Directory Service Manager for
  NetWare (DSMN) 510–511, 526, 696
Directory services database 11, 29

DirectX 278
Disk Administrator
    assigning drive letters 228
    confirming changes 225–226
    creating and formatting partitions 216–218
    customizing 215–216
    defined 231
    deleting a partition 218
    described 213
    dialog box 215
    fault tolerance, implementing 246
    introduced 26
    reassigning drive letters 228
    starting 213–214
    working with stripe sets 224–225
    working with volume sets 220–224
Disk duplexing 243
Disk partitioning *See* Partitions
Display
    configuring 105–107
    described 99, 105
    dialog box 105
    options 106
Distributed application 328
Distributed Component Object Model (DCOM)
    configuration options 304
    configuration properties dialog box 303
    configuring 304
    DCOM Configuration tool 694
    defined 697
    diagrammed 302
    example of an application 300
    features 301
    interoperability 301
    overview 300–301
    remote procedure calls (RPCs) 301–303
Distributed processing 328–329
Distribution server
    creating 67
    defined 64
DNS *See* Domain Name System (DNS)
DNS Manager 405
Documentation, viewing online 79
    See also Books Online

Domain
    adding a computer account 51
    computer tasks 12
    defined 11
    joining a domain 55
    managing computers across 142
    model 11
    propagating policy changes 153
    RAS logon process 438
    replicating commonly used information 581, 583
    system policy
        computer policy, logon process 149
        creating and modifying 153
        implementing 146–150
        running multiple policies 150
        user policy, logon process 148
    vs. Workgroups 10–13
Domain model 11
Domain name space 402
Domain Name System (DNS)
    benefits 401
    client configuration 405–406
    computer names 400
    configuring 404
    defined 400, 698
    DNS Manager 405
    DNS Resource Record (RR) 405
    domain name space 402
    domains
        diagrammed 402
        top-level 402
    fully qualified domain name (FQDN) 404
    hosts 400
    installing 404
    integrating with WINS 409–411
    introduced 4
    name resolution process 401, 410–411
    name uniqueness 404
    Server service
        configuring primary zone 407
        configuring search order 407
        described 401
        host name resolution 409
        installing 406

Domain Name System (DNS) *(continued)*
    vs. WINS 401
    with Internet Information Server 497
    zones 403
Domain naming 28–29
Drive letters
    automated assignment 227
    CD-ROM 228
    reassigning 228
DSMN *See* Directory Service Manager for NetWare (DSMN)
Dynamic Host Configuration Protocol (DHCP)
    advantages 374–375
    client requirements 376
    client reservations 381
    client/server relationship 374
    configuring 378
    configuring DNS clients 406
    configuring TCP/IP 354
    configuring WINS 398
    defined 699
    DHCP Manager
        Create Scope dialog box 378
        DHCP Options
        Global dialog box 382
    DHCP Relay Agent 696
    function 373
    installing DHCP Server service 377
    introduced 4
    options
        client 383
        common 382
        global 382
        scope 383
    parameters administered by DHCP 373
    process 375–376
    reserving specific IP addresses 381
    scope
        activating 384
        configuring 383
        creating 380
        defined 378
        options 379
    server requirements 376

E

El Torito specification 34
Election packet 415
Emergency Repair
    creating with Setup wizard 38
    files included on disk 636
    overview 634
    process 636–639
    recovering disk configuration information 230
    Repair Disk utility (Rdisk.exe)
        Create Repair Disk option 635
        overivew 634
        Update Repair Info 635
    Setup.log 635
    updating repair disk 639
Enhancing operating system performance 121
Enterprise networking 349
Enterprise server 539
Environment subsystems 269
Environment variables
    described 122
    order 124
    restriciting the user variables in a domain 163
    setting 123–125
    system 124
    user 124
ErrorControl Values 618
Ethernet
    frame type 342
    support 563
Event Viewer
    archiving log files 652
    arranging display of events 652
    enabling security logging 650
    event log 649, 650
    event, defined 649
    filtering events 652, 654
    interpreting an event 651
    overview 649
    searching 652, 655
    starting 649
    summarized 675
    troubleshooting RAS 467
Events
    defined 649
    types of 651
    See also Event Viewer
Everyone group
    setting log on privileges 101

Executive Services
    advantages for operating system 269
    components 263
    diagrammed 263
    Executive messages 700
    introduced 264
    subsystem interaction 269
Export servers, replication 584
Extended partitions *See* Partitions, extended
External network number 344

F

Failure Audit 651
FAT file system
    characteristics vs. NTFS 195
    converting 8.3 file names 182–183
    converting to NTFS 179–181
    description 175
    features 175
    file and partition size 176
    implementation considerations 176–175
    installing during setup 25–26
    long file names (LFNs)
        alias folders 184
        on FAT partitions 184
        secondary folders 184–185
    naming conventions 175
    pros and cons vs. NTFS 195
    security 176
    when to use 25
Fatal System errors 112
    See also Recovery, STOP errors
Fault tolerance
    allocating for during Windows NT setup 24
    creating a boot disk 251–253
    data redundancy 240
    defined 239, 240
    implementation considerations 241, 256
    implementing with Disk Administrator 246
    precautions 240
    RAID solutions 241
    recovering from mirror set failure 249–251
    regenerating stripe sets with parity 248–249
    stripe sets 211
    technology supported 4, 239
    volume sets 209
    See also RAID
FDDI support 563

Index

File, sharing on a network 330–331
File and Print Services for NetWare (FPNW) 508, 702
File replication *See* Directory replication
File system
    drivers *See* File system drivers
    selecting 24
    supported by Windows NT 24
File system drivers
    advantages of a redirector 327
    described 326
    diagram 326
    Redirector 326–327
    Server service (Server) 327
Find key, command 131
Finger 356
FPNW *See* File and Print Services for NetWare (FPNW)
FQDN *See* Fully qualified domain name (FQDN)
Frame types
    automatically detected 342
    configuring 343
    defined 342
    supported by NWLink 342
Free space
    defined 204
    partition types 204
Front-end processes, described 328
FrontPage 3
FTP service
    administering with IIS 3
    configuring 488
    See also Protocols, File Transfer Protocol (FTP)
Fully qualified domain name (FQDN) 400, 404, 705

G

Games included with setup 36
Gateway Services for NetWare (GSNW)
    configuring 521
    configuring, step-by-step 525
    defined 705
    dialog box 521
    installation requirements 508
    installing 520
    options 522
    overview 506–507
    specifying a gateway 523–524
    when to use 507
GDI 264, 269
General Protection Fault (GPF)
    observing effects of a 16-bit application 287
Getting started with this course xxx

Gopher service, administering with IIS 3
Group policy *See* System policy, group policy
GSNW *See* Gateway Services for NetWare (GSNW)
GuardTime 593
Guests group 490

H

HAL *See* Hardware Abstraction Layer (HAL)
Hard disk
    considerations 212
    managing 213–229
Hardware Abstraction Layer (HAL) 264, 706
Hardware address 391
Hardware Compatibility List (HCL) site 18
Hardware platforms supported 297
Hardware profiles
    best practice 115
    choosing at system startup 118
    common support issues 119
    configuring 114–119
    configuring a specific device or service 115
    creating and modifying 115
    default profile, configuring 115
    deleting 118
    described 91
    hardware subkey 95
    loading 116
    network-disabled 116–117
    programs in Control Panel 103–104
    registry key 92
Hardware query tool *See* NT Hardware Qualifier (NTHQ)
Hardware requirements
    determining configuration 19
    Hardware Compatibility List (HCL) site 18
    hardware query tool *See* NT Hardware Qualifier (NTHQ)
    minimum configuration 21
Hardware, configuring 103
HCL site 18
Hidden partitions 227
Hive 93, 707
HKEY_CLASSES_ROOT
    description 92
HKEY_CURRENT_CONFIG
    description 92
HKEY_CURRENT_USER
    Console settings 307
    description 92
    subkeys 92
    user policy settings 148

Index

HKEY_LOCAL_MACHINE
    computer policy settings 149
    description 92
    subkeys 95–96
    subsystems key 620
    viewing 94
HKEY_USERS
    description 92
    subkeys 92
Home pages 477, 707
Hostname 356
HTML *See* Hypertext Markup Language (HTML)
HTTP *See* Hypertext Transfer Protocol (HTTP)
Hyperlinks 477
Hypertext Markup Language 477, 708
Hypertext Transfer Protocol (HTTP) 477, 708
    integration with Windows NT Server 3

I

I/O addresses 712
I/O Manager
    components 321–322
    descriptive summary 333
    file system driver control 326
    network process of fulfilling I/O requests 332
I/O requests
    fulfillment process on a network 331
    GUI-related 269
    increasing speed 210
    on partitions 210
    over a network 326
    sharing resources on a network 330
    with fault tolerance 248
Icons used in this book xxiv
Identification Changes dialog box 31
IIS *See* Internet Information Server (IIS)
Import computers, replication 584
Increasing speed of system I/O 210
Information needed for installation 37–41
Initial Startup Process 610
Installation disk sets, creating Server 556–557
Installing from a network share 64
Installing new applications 126
Installing Windows NT
    adding computer accounts to a domain 49–51
    compressing the installation 195–191
    customizing switches for Winnt.exe 68–69

Installing Windows NT *(continued)*
    disk partitioning
        defined 22
        during setup 22
        large partition concerns 25–26
        RISC-based system 23
        system and boot 23
        unknown partition types 24
    file system partitions 24–26
    finishing setup 41
    hardware configuration
        determining 19
        minimum 21
    hardware requirements 18
    initializing installation 34, 37
    installation components 36
    Intel x86-based computers 34
    Internet Explorer
        on Server 47
        on Workstation 54
    joining a domain or workgroup 32
    multiple platform support 64
    networking, required information 39–40
    on a Windows 95 system 76
    on multiple computers 64
    platform dependencies 34
    preparation 17–33
    process 37–47
    required information 38–41
    RISC-based computers 35
    Server *See* Windows NT Server, installing
    setup programs 65
    setup types 35
    setup wizard, required information 38–41
    specifying a UDF during installation 74
    step-by-step
        completing information gathering 44
        completing Server setup 46
        course materials on Server1 47
        course materials on Workstation 54
        creating CD setup completion disks
            for Server 41–42
        initializing Server installation 42
        installing Workstation from setup disks 52–54
        networking 45
        starting Server installation 44
    to a Windows 95 client computer from a server 67
    to a Windows NT computer from a server 69
    to an MS-DOS client computer from a server 67

Installing Windows NT *(continued)*
    unattended customization with UDFs 73
    unattended installation procedure 74
    unattended installations 69–74
    uninstalling *See* Removing Windows NT
    upgrading previous Windows NT versions 76
    Windows NT Boot Loader (NTLDR) 191
    Workstation *See* Windows NT Workstation, installing
Integrating Windows NT with Novell NetWare 513
Intel x86-based computers
    booting the system 611–614
    initiating a Windows NT installation on 34
Internal Network Number 343, 344
Internet
    anonymous access 490
    browsers 477
    configuring services 488
    defined 476, 477
    described 477
    history 477
    Internet Guest Account 490
    Internet Information Server (IIS) *See* Internet Information Server (IIS)
    Internet Service Manager (ISM)
        configuring services 488
        dialog box 486
        introduced 485
        Properties dialog box 487
        Report view 486
    methods of navigating with Microsoft Internet Explorer 489
    Peer Web Services (PWS) *See* Peer Web Services (PWS)
    RAS connections 431
    secure remote access, PPTP 431, 433
    security
        considerations 478
        guidelines 491
        securing a site 490–491
    viewing service or computer properties 487
    Web server management 3
Internet domain, defined 400
Internet Engineering Task Force (IETF) 436, 710
Internet Explorer *See* Microsoft Internet Explorer
Internet Guest Account 490
Internet Information Server (IIS)
    components 483
    enhancing performance 485
    features 481
    installing
        requirements 482–483
        step-by-step 493–494
    integration with Windows NT Server 3
    overview 479

Internet Information Server (IIS) *(continued)*
    security 490
    server functions 480
    usage 480
    vs. Peer Web Services (PWS) 480
Internet Server API (ISAPI) 480, 711
Internet service provider (ISP) 433, 711
InterNIC 400, 402, 711
Interoperability
    DCOM and RPCs 301
    described 299
    NetWare 513
    networking 320
Interpreting errors, warnings, etc. 649
Interval 593
Intranet
    defined 476, 477, 712
    security
        guidelines 491
        issues when connecting to the Internet 478
        securing a site 490–491
    technology 477
IP address
    automated administration with DHCP 373, 375
    defined 352, 712
    manually configuring 375
    name resolution *See* Name resolution
    reserving specific addresses 381
IPC mechanisms
    bidirectional data support 329
    in distributed processing 328
    summarized 333
    supported by Windows NT 329
Ipconfig 356, 357
IPX/SPX protocol 341, 712
    See also NWLink
ISAPI *See* Internet Server API (ISAPI)
ISDN
    defined 710
    use with RAS 429
    WAN connectivity 428
ISM *See* Internet, Internet Service Manager (ISM)
ISP *See* Internet service provider (ISP)
IUSR_computername 490

J

Joining a domain or workgroup during installation 31
Joining a BDC to a PDC 31
Joining a stand-alone server to a workgroup 32

K

Kernel *See* Windows NT Kernel
Kernel initialization phase 617–618
Kernel load phase 616–617
Kernel mode *See* Windows NT, kernel mode
Keyboard, described 99
Keys, registry
  described 93
  hierarchy 93
  subtree keys 92

L

LAN Manager
  2.2c client support 549
  networking compatibility with Windows NT 347
Large Internet Protocol (LIP) 506
Last Known Good configuration
  function 629
  how to use 632
  when to use 630–631
LastKnownGood (LKG) control set 620, 629, 631, 714
  See also Last Known Good configuration
Learning paths for course xxi
LFNs *See* Long file names (LFNs)
License groups 545–546
License Manager
  creating license groups 545–546
  described 542
  Server Browser tab 542–543
Licensing
  administration 537–546
  client connections, defined 532–533
  considerations 534–536
  creating license groups 545–546
  guidelines for selecting a mode 535–536
  License Manager *See* License Manager
  modes 533–534
  options available 32, 531
  program *See* Licensing program
  replication 538
  See also Windows NT Server, licensing
  selecting a mode 32–33
Licensing program
  Choose Licensing Mode dialog box 537–538
  described 537
  Replication Configuration dialog box 540–541
Licensing replication
  configuring 540
  described 539
Limited Virtual Memory message 120
Linking network components 361

Load balancing 164
Load phases 616–620
Local profile 99
Local Security Authority (Lsass.exe) 620
LocalTalk 563, 715
Locating a port device 105
Locating the boot partition 227
Location, RAS 440, 441
Logging of events 649
Logging on to a computer or domain 57–63
Logical drives
  defined 715
  discussed 206–207
  partition renumbering 226
Logon
  at a domain controller 59
  computer policy, logon process in a domain 149
  from workstation or member server 57–59
  last logged on user, disabling display 161
  overview 57
  RAS logon model 438
  through Dial-Up Networking 460
  to a computer 61–62
  to a computer in a workgroup 62–63
  to a domain 60–61
  user policy, logon process in a domain 148
Logon Information dialog box 59
Logon Information dialog box, customizing 158
Logon Preferences dialog box 461
Logon scripts
  defined 715
  function 583
  replicating in a domain 583
  troubleshooting for replication 603
Long file names (LFNs)
  NetWare server support 506
  See also NTFS, long file names (LFNs)
Lsass.exe 620

M

Macintosh client support 4
Macintosh support 179
  licensing option 33
  MacFile menu 564
  Services for Macintosh *See* Services for Macintosh
Managing hard disks 213
Mandatory logon process 57
Manual setup disks, Server 556–557
Map network drive 59
Mapping
  a network drive 59
  computer names to IP addresses 393
  defined 717

Mapping *(continued)*
  name mapping, defined 719
  See also Name resolution
Master browser 415
Master directory 581
Master server 539–540
Media access control address 391
Member server
  defined 30, 718
  functions 27
  See also Stand-alone server
Memory
  addressing scheme 267
  demand paging 266
  management key in system boot 619
  model 265
  pages
    characteristics 265
    size 265
  RAM 265
  virtual
    architecture 265
    memory space 265
Microkernel 264
Microsoft Certified Product Specialist (MCPS)
  description xxxvii
  exam requirements xxxviii
Microsoft Certified Professional program
  cerifications available xxxvii
  certification requirements xxxvii–xxxviii
  for more information xxxviii
  MCSE track xxxviii–xxxix
  overview xxxvii
  preparing for examinations, course paths xxi
Microsoft Certified Solution Developer (MCSD)
  description xxxvii
  exam requirements xxxviii
Microsoft Certified Systems Engineer (MCSE)
  description xxxvii
  exam requirements xxxviii
  MCSE track xxxviii–xxxix
  recommended path to certification xxxix
Microsoft Certified Trainer (MCT)
  description xxxvii
  exam requirements xxxviii
Microsoft Download Service (MSDL) 673
Microsoft Internet Explorer
  as a feature of Workstation 5
  as an Internet browser 477
  installing on Server 47
  installing on Workstation 54
  methods of navigating the Internet with 489

Microsoft Internet Explorer *(continued)*
  overview 489
  use with IIS and PWB 481
  versions 489
Microsoft licensing options 531
Microsoft Network (MSN) 673
Microsoft Network Client 3.0
  described 548
  limitations 548
  protocols 548
  redirector 548
Microsoft Official Curriculum (MOC) xxxix
Microsoft TechNet 672–673
Microsoft Web site 673
Migration Tool for NetWare
  capabilities 512
  description 526, 718
  introduced 504
Minimum hardware configuration for Windows NT 21
Minimum system configuration for course xxx
Mirror sets
  breaking a set 249–251
  configuring 247
  described 242–243
  recovering from failure 249–251
Modems
  RAS connections 429
Monitoring
  applications and processes 270–272
  events 649
  network data stream 666
  resources 661
  system performance 274
Mouse 99
Moving a BDC to another domain 30
MS-DOS
  applications 280–283
  devices key, symbolic links 620
  installing NT from a network share 67
  Microsoft Network Client 3.0 548
  network connectivity 548
  virtual device drivers (VDDs) 281
Msie30.exe 47
Multimedia components 36
Multiple computers
  installing Windows NT on 64
  setting up identical directories on 581
Multiple platform support 6, 297
Multiple Provider Router (MPR) 330
Multiple universal naming convention provider (MUP) 330
Multiple-boot systems 25, 719

Index

Multitasking 6
Multithreading 6, 276–277
My Briefcase *See* Briefcase

N

Name resolution
    DNS process 401
    NetBIOS 391–392
    NetBIOS over TCP/IP modes 392
    overview 390
    process using WINS 393
    TCP/IP 390–392
Name resolution service
    defined 720
    DNS 401
    WINS 418
nbtstat 356
NCPs *See* NetWare Core Protocols (NCPs)
NDIS 4.0 322
NetBEUI
    bridges 347
    capabilities 347
    configuring RAS server 447
    defined 347, 720
    description 324
    function 347
    installing 347
NetBIOS
    defined 720
    extended user interface (NetBEUI) 347
    gateway, RAS 437
    name resolution *See* Name resolution, NetBIOS
    Name Server (NBNS) 391
    over TCP/IP (NetBT) 350
    resource availability *See* Computer Browser service
    support for NetWare, NWLink 341
Netstat utility 356
NetWare
    add-on utilities
        Directory Service Manager for NetWare (DSMN) 504, 510–511
        File and Print Services for NetWare (FPNW) 504, 509
    administering a Windows NT server from 510
    administration 510

NetWare *(continued)*
    application support 341
    bindery emulation 506
    CSNW *See* Client Service for NetWare (CSNW)
    Configure Gateway dialog box 523
    connecting to 504
    connectivity methods, diagrammed 509
    File and Print Services for NetWare (FPNW) 508
    file resources 508
    frame types 342
    GSNW *See* Gateway Services for NetWare (GSNW)
    interoperability options 513
    licensing option 33
    Migration Tool for NetWare 512
    NetWare Loadable Modules (NLMs) 341
    networking protocol 341
    New Share dialog box 524
    NWLink *See* NWLink
    practice simulation 517–519
    printing resources 508
    utilities 510
NetWare Core Protocols (NCPs) 506
NetWare Directory Services (NDS) 506
Network adapter card drivers *See* Networking, adapter card drivers
Network administration
    centralizing resources 8, 11
    directory services database 11
    sharing resources 10–13
Network Client Administrator
    creating network installation startup disks 552–556
    dialog box 552
    overview 551
    uses 551
    See also Windows NT Server, client-based administration tools
Network Configuration dialog box 446
Network device interface specification (NDIS) 4.0 323
Network installation startup disks, creating 552–556
Network Monitor
    Capture window, described 668
    frames 667
    information captured 667

762 Index

Network Monitor *(continued)*
    installing 667
    interface 667
    overview 666
    summarized 675
Network Number 343–344
Network program
    Adapters tab 338–339
    Bindings tab 362–363
    creating a computer account 49–51
    creating a shortcut 345
    Identification Changes tab 49
    Protocols tab 340
    Services tab 371–372
Network services
    DHCP 373
    function 371
    included with Windows NT 369
    installing 371–372
Network services provided by Windows NT Server 4
Network Startup Disk Configuration dialog box 555
Network-disabled hardware profile 116–117
Networking
    adapter card drivers
        described 322
        frame types 342
        installing and configuring 338–339
        software interface 323
    architecture overview 320–327
    binding
        configuring 362
        function 360
        introduced 323
        optimizing 363
    boundary
        defined 321
        layers 322
    bridges 347
    component overview 321–322
    enterprise 349
    environments supported 320
    extending business networks 427
    file and print sharing
        components 330
        process 331
    I/O Manager
        components 321
        file system driver control 326
    improving capabilities through DCOM 300–304
    installing during Windows NT setup 45
    LAN protocol 347
    linking network components 362

Networking *(continued)*
    modem connections with RAS 429
    monitoring data stream over 666
    NDIS 4.0 323
    protocols *See* Protocols
    required information for installation 39–40
    resource availability *See* Computer Browser service
    routers
        defined 342
        IP and IPX 437
    services *See* Network services
    small networks, protocol 347
    updating files over a network 573
    WAN protocol 349
    with Macintosh AppleTalk internetworking *See* Services for Macintosh
New Phonebook Entry dialog box 456
NLMs 341
Notational conventions of this book xxii
Novell NetWare *See* NetWare
NT Hardware Qualifier (NTHQ)
    creating an NTHQ disk 19
    introduced 19
    running NTHQ 18
NT Virtual DOS Machine (NTVDM)
    autoexec file 282–283
    components 281
    config file 282–283
    configuring 281
    diagrammed 280
    for Win16-based applications 289–293
    multiple NTVDMs
        advantages 289
        creating 288
        disadvantages 289
    virtual device drivers (VDDs) 281
Ntbootdd.sys 611
Ntconfig.pol 147, 157, 162
Ntdetect.com 611, 617
NTDS *See* Windows NT Directory Services (NTDS)
NTFS
    advantages 24
    case-sensitive naming 185
    changing to FAT file system 181
    characteristics vs. FAT 195
    compression *See* Compression
    converting FAT partitions 179–181
    features 177, 178–179
    file and partition size 178
    file compression feature 178
    installing during setup 24–26
    large NTFS partitions 25–26

NTFS *(continued)*
  long file name support 177
  long file names (LFNs)
    alias folders 184
    considerations 183
    converting to 8.3 file names 182–183
    on FAT partitions 184
    practice 185
    preventing use on FAT partitions 185
    secondary folders 184–185
    support 182
  naming conventions 177
  permissions 177
  pros and cons vs. FAT 195
  security 177
  when to use 24
Ntldr file 611
Ntoskrnl.exe 616
NTVDM *See* NT Virtual DOS Machine (NTVDM)
NWLink
  APIs supported 341
  configuring 342–344
  description 324
  frame types 342–343
  functions 341
  installing 345–346
  integrating Windows NT with Novell NetWare 513
  limitations 505
  network numbers 343–344
  NWLink IPX/SPX Properties dialog box 343
  overview 504–505
  routing 342, 344
  Routing Information Protocol (RIP) 344
  topologies supported 342

O

Object, defined 262
OLE 277
OpenGL 278
Operating system
  boot delay, changing 113
  enhancing performance 121
  setting default 113
  System Properties dialog box 111
  system shutdown, changing settings 111
  system startup
    changing settings 111
    configuring 112
    with multiple operating systems 113
    with multiple operating systems installed 112
  virtual memory *See* Virtual memory

OS/2 subsystem
  applications 298
  running 16-bit OS/2 1.x Presentation Manager applications 298
  support 269
Other Windows NT documentation resources xxix
Overview of this book xxv

P

Packet assembler/disassemblers (PADs) 429–430, 723
PADs *See* Packet assembler/disassemblers (PADs)
Pagefile.sys 119
Pages, memory 265
Paging file
  changing size 121
  configuring 120–121
  defined 723
  demand paging 266
  moving 120
  Pagefile.sys 119
  role in system boot 619
  role in system recovery 671
  size 119, 120–121
Parity, defined 244
Partitions
  active 23, 219–220
  adding hard disks, considerations 212
  automated drive letter assignment 227–228
  avoiding limitations 206
  boot 207, 227
  changing drive letter 218
  creating new 217
  deleting 218
  Disk Administrator *See* Disk Administrator
  extended
    defined 206
    number allowed 206
  formatting 216, 217
  hidden partitions 227
  increasing speed of system I/O 210
  installing during setup 22
  maximum number 204
  MS-DOS 205
  primary
    defined 204, 727
    file system 205
    system 207
  removable media 212
  renumbering 226
  RISC-based 205
  securing the system partition 229

764   Index

Partitions *(continued)*
   stripe sets
      creating 224
      defined 231
      deleting 224
      described 210–211, 738
      formatting 224
   support issues 25–26
   supported by Windows NT 203, 204
   system 207
   system and boot 23
   troubleshooting 230–231
   typical distribution 207
   volume label 217
   volume sets
      adding space 221
      creating 222
      defined 231
      deleting 224
      described 208–209
      extending 221, 223
      formatting 223
   volume sets vs. stripe sets 211
   Windows 95 205
   See also Installing Windows NT, disk partitioning
PBXs 440
PC Card Devices 110
PCMCIA program 110, 725
PConsole 510
PDC *'See*
Peer Web Services (PWS)
   components 485
   features 481
   installing 484–485
   overview 479
   server functions 480
   usage 480
   vs. Internet Information Server (IIS) 480
   with Windows NT Workstation 5
Per Seat licensing 33
Per Server licensing 33, 533
Per-computer settings
   configuring 97, 102–110
   defined 92
   registry key 97
Performance Monitor
   dialog box 661
   overview 661, 675
   using 661–662
Permissions
   administrative permissions on computer accounts 49
   granting remote access permissions on RAS server 453

Permissions *(continued)*
   Internet Guest account permissions 490
   NTFS 177
Per-user settings
   defined 92
   modifying 97–101
   registry key 97
   See also User profiles
Phonebook entries 456–459
Physical address 391
PIF files
   Autoexec file 282–283
   Config file 282–283
   configuring 281
Ping 356, 357
Planning a network 26–32
Platforms supported 6
Point-to-Point Tunneling Protocol (PPTP)
   advantages 432
   comparison with other WAN protocols 432
   defined 726
   filtering 439
   Internet and RAS connections 431, 433
   process 432
   security 439
   Virtual private networks (VPNs) 431
Poledit.exe 142
Policy mode *See* System Policy Editor, policy mode
POP, description 433, 726
Port configuration, RAS server 445
Portability 267
Portable setup 36
Ports
   configuring 104–105
   dialog box 104
POSIX
   applications 299
   defined 726
   described 299
   LFN naming considerations 183
   naming conventions 177
   requirements 179
   subsystem 269
Power failures *See* Uninterrupted power source (UPS)
Power On Self Test (POST) 610
Power supply *See* Uninterrupted power source (UPS)
PowerPC, special requirements 22
PPP *See* Protocols, Point-to-Point Protocol (PPP)
PPTP *See* Point-to-Point Tunneling Protocol (PPTP)
PReP (PowerPC Reference Platform) 22
Prerequisites for this course xx
Presentation Manager 298

Index

Primary domain controller (PDC)
    as a licensing replication master server 539–540
    changing a domain name 28–29
    creating a domain 28
    defined 27, 727
    domain requirements 27
    functions 27
    introduced 11
    joining a BDC 31
    system policy storage 147
Primary partitions *See* Partitions, primary
Printing
    sharing resources on a network 330–331
Prioritizing applications 273
Priority levels of applications 309
Privilege
    access 128
    Administrator 49, 685
    Everyone group, setting 101
    Guest 706
    levels 727
    User 743
    See also Permissions
Procedural conventions of this book xxii
Processor
    assigning a process to 274
    distributing loads 274
    distributing processing time
        among applications 308–309
    limiting application execution 274
    monitoring activity 661–662
    priority 274
    processes, changing the base priority 309
    selecting for a process 274
Processor modes, defined 262
Product Specialist *See* Microsoft Certified
    Product Specialist (MCPS)
Propagating files 581–582
Propagating policy changes in a domain 153
Protocols
    ARP *See* Address Resolution Protocol (ARP)
    data link control (DLC) 324
    described 324
    File Transfer Protocol (FTP) 356, 477, 703
    function 339
    Hypertext Transfer Protocol (HTTP) 477
    included with Windows NT 324, 337
    installing and configuring 339–340
    Internet Control Message Protocol (ICMP) 350
    Internet Protocol (IP) 350
    NetBIOS over TCP/IP (NetBT) 350
    Network News Transfer Protocol (NNTP) 721
    Point-to-Point Protocol (PPP) 427, 435, 726

Protocols *(continued)*
    PPP Multilink Protocol (MP) 436
    PPTP *See* Point-to-Point Tunneling Protocol (PPTP)
    Remote Copy Protocol (RCP) 356
    routable protocols 361
    Serial Line Internet Protocol (SLIP) 427, 434, 734
    Simple Network Management
        Protocol (SNMP) 350, 736
    Transmission Control Protocol (TCP) 350
    Trivial File Transfer Protocol (TFTP) 356, 741
    User Datagram Protocol (UDP) 350
    Virtual Terminal Protocol (VTP) 477
PSTN *See* Public Switched Telephone Networks (PSTN)
Public Switched Telephone Networks (PSTNs) 429
PWS *See* Peer Web Services (PWS)

R

RAID
    data redundancy 240
    described 240
    for more information 256
    hardware implementations 241
    implementing 246–247
    levels 240
    RAID 1 vs. RAID 5 245–246
    software implementations
        best practice 242
        disk duplexing 243
        mirror sets 242–243
        stripe sets with parity 243–244
    support 4, 239
RAM, swapping data 119
RAS *See* Remote Access Server (RAS)
RConsole 510
Rdisk.exe utility 230, 634
RDR *See* Windows NT Redirector (RDR)
Recovery
    described 112
    introduced 111
    operation 671
    options 112
    STOP errors 112
    system recovery 670
    utility 670
Redirector *See* Windows NT Redirector (RDR)
Regedit.exe 130
Regedt32.exe 128
Regional settings 99
Registry
    component descriptions 91
    components which use 90–91

766   Index

Registry *(continued)*
  creating a shortcut to Registry Editor 89
  databases, described 92
  defined 88
  diagnosing system data 656–658
  editing with System Policy Editor 152
  Find Key command 131
  for more information 134
  hierarchy 93–94
  hives 93, 707
  information contained in 88
  interaction with applications 91
  interfaces 88
  key locating a port device 105
  keys 92, 93
  locating information within 130
  modifying 88
  organization 93
  Registry Editor *See* Registry Editor
  structure 92–96
  subtrees 92–94
  value data types 94
  values
    described 94
    searching for 132–133
  viewing 88–89
  viewing configurations changes 132
  Windows NT Diagnostics tool 656–658
Registry Editor
  access privileges 128
  appropriate uses 128–129
  commands 129
  defined 128
  introduced 88
  troubleshooting with 129
  Windows 95 130
Registry mode *See* System Policy Editor, registry mode
Remote Access Server (RAS)
  and Dial-Up Networking 427
  authentication 438
  AutoDial 462
  configuring server
    configuring protocols 446
    IPX 449–450
    NetBEUI 447
    options 444
    overview 444
    port configuration 445
    step-by-step 452–453
    TCP/IP 448–449
  connection methods 428
  description 425

Remote Access Server (RAS) *(continued)*
  encryption 438
  features 428
  gateways, diagrammed 437
  granting access permissions 453
  installing 443, 450–452
  introduced 4
  logon process 438
  NetWare server access 508
  protocols
    LAN 434
    overview 433
    remote access 434–436
  remote client connections 427
  removing 468
  RFCs supported 436
  routers 437
  security 438–439
  simultaneous inbound connections supported 443
  testing 464
  WAN security 427
Remote Access Service (RAS) *See* RAS
Remote clients
  connection types 427
  enabling WAN connections 427
  Internet Guest account permissions 490
  validating 438
Remote Execution (REXEC) 356
Remote procedure calls (RPCs) 300, 301–303
Remote Shell (RSH) 356
Remote update, system policy 150
Removable media 212
Removing course materials xxxv
Removing self-paced training files xxxv
Removing Windows NT
  alternative methods 77
  basic methods 77
  from a FAT partition 78
  removing a partition 77
Renumbering partitions 226
Repair Disk utility (Rdisk.exe) 634
Replicating files within a domain 581
Resource sharing on a network 330–331
Resources, networking *See* Computer Browser service
Restoring disk configuration 230
RFCs
  1001 and 1002 392
  1034 and 1035 400
  1717 436
  defined 730
  remote access protocol standard RFCs 436

Index

RISC-based computers
    booting the system 611, 614–615
    file system 25, 176
    initiating Windows NT installation 35
    partitions, active 220
    running MS-DOS applications 281
    securing the system partition 229
    server-based installation restrictions 64
    system partitioning 23
Routable protocols 361
Route utility 356
Routers
    defined 342, 731
    IP 437, 712
    IPX 437
    RAS 437
Routing Information Protocol (RIP) 344
RPCs *See* Remote procedure calls (RPCs)

S

SAM *See* Security Accounts Manager (SAM)
SAP 437, 732
Savedump.exe 671
Saving user preferences 99
Screg.exe 620
SCSI Adapters 107
Secondary folders
    defined 184
Securing the system partition 229
Security Accounts Manager (SAM)
    registry subkey, described 95
Security hosts, RAS 439
Security identifier (SID)
    defined 28
    on member servers 31
    registry key 92
    when moving a BDC to another domain 30
Security log 650, 733
Security, registry subkey 95
Selecting a file system 24–26
SerialController key 105
Server *See* Windows NT Server
Server Manager *See* Administrative Tools (Common), Server Manager
Server message blocks (SMBs) 506–507, 734–
Server performance 4
Server service
    description 327
    location within network architecture 327
    network component in resource sharing 330
    network process of fulfilling I/O requests 331
    process 327

Server1, role in course xxxi
Server-based installations 64–74
Service Advertising Protocol (SAP) 437, 732
Service Controller (Screg.exe) 620
ServiceGroupOrder subkey, boot order 616
Services for Macintosh
    benefits 562
    features 565
    installling 563–564
    Macintosh-accessible volume 564
    overview 562
    removing 565
    requirements 562
    sharing networking resources with NT 562
Services load phase 619
Session Manager (Smss.exe) 619
Setup *See* Installing Windows NT
Setup disks
    creating CD setup completion disks
        for Windows NT Server 41
    creating CD setup completion disks
        for Windows NT Workstation 52
Setup for this course xxx
Setup Manager utility 70
Setup programs 65
Setup types 35
Setup.log 635
Shutdown, system 111
SID *See* Security identifier (SID)
SLIP *See* Protocols, Serial Line Internet Protocol (SLIP)
Smart cards 431
SMBs *See* Server message blocks (SMBs)
Software configuration information, viewing 658–659
Software required to complete this course xxx
Software, registry subkey 96
Solution Developer *See* Microsoft Certified Solution Developer (MCSD)
Sounds program, description 99
Source compatibility, applications 297
Stand-alone server
    defined 30
    joining a workgroup 32
    limitations 30
    moving to another domain 31
    vs. domain controllers 30
Startup, system 111
STOP errors 112, 670, 737
Stripe sets
    introduced 24
    partitions 210
Stripe sets with parity
    configuring 247
    described 243–244, 738
    regenerating 248–249

768 Index

Stub code, defined 301
Subnet mask 352
Subsystems
    diagrammed 268
    environment 269
    interaction with Executive Services 269
    overview 268
    Win32 269
    Windows NT Add-on Subsystem
      for Presentation Manager 298
Subsystems key 620
Subtrees *See* Registry, subtrees
Success Audit 651
Supplemental Material for course xxxv
Support documentation, viewing online 79
    See also Books Online
Switches, custom setup 68–69
Synchronizing files 573
System
    application performance 310
    environment variables 122
    See also Operating system
System boot *See* Boot process
System Console (Syscon) 510, 526
System log 650
System partition
    described 23
    securing 229
System policy
    best practice 151
    capabilities 142
    computer policy 143–144
      logon process 149
    customizing for users, groups and computers 157–163
    default computer
      defined 143
      policy options 154–156
      registry key 149
    Default Computer policy 149
    default user
      defined 143
      policy options 156
    defined 142, 739
    group policy
      in Windows 95 164
      priority 148
    implementation diagram 149
    implementing in a domain 146–150
    implementing in a network using both Windows NT
      Workstation and Windows 95 149
    Ntconfig.pol policy file 147–148
    on Netlogon share 147
    planning, summary 167

System policy *(continued)*
    remote update 150
    replicating files in a domain 581, 583
    running multiple policies in a domain 150
    securing computers, example 158
    supporting Windows 95 164
    templates 165
    troubleshooting issues 165
    user policy
      described 143
      logon process 148
    Windows NT storage defaults 147–148
    See also System Policy Editor
System Policy Editor
    creating shortcut 143
    default computer
      dialog box 144
    default computer icon 143–144
    default user
      dialog box 144
    default user icon 143–144
    editing in registry mode 152
    group priority, setting 148
    introduced 142
    location 151
    manual update, setting 150
    modes 152
    policy mode
      check boxes selections 153
      described 153
      file menu options 154
      propagating changes 153
      viewing 153
    registry mode
      best practice 152
      described 152
      editing registry of local or remote computers 152
      keys 152
    remote update 150
    restriciting the user environment 163
    template files 165
    uses 151
    See also System policy
System policy templates 165
System Properties dialog box
    Environments tab 123
    Hardware Profiles tab 114
    Startup/Shutdown tab 111, 670
System Recovery 670, 675
    See also Recovery
System settings
    per-user settings 99
System, registry subkey 96

Index

Systemroot folder
  compressing 191
  repair folder 230

T

Tape devices 107
TAPI
  calling card 441
  configuring 441–442
  defined 739
  Dialing Properties dialog box 441–442
  drivers 441
  location
    configuring 441–442
    defined 440
  overview 440
  Service Providers (TSPs) 441
  settings 440–441
Target Workstation Configuration dialog box 554
Task Manager
  assigning a process to a processor 274
  capabilities 271
  described 270, 739
  interface 270
  monitoring system performance 274–275
  prioritizing 273–274
  selecting a processor for a process 274
  tabs 271
  viewing applications 271
  viewing processes 272
TCP/IP
  architecture 350
  capabilities 349
  configuring
    automatically 354–355
    manually 351–354
  configuring RAS server 448–449
  defined 324, 349
  dialog box 351
  name resolution *See* Name resolution, TCP/IP
  parameters 352
  protocols 350
  routing 349
  testing with Ipconfig and Ping 357–359
  utilities 356
TDI *See* Transport Driver Interface (TDI)
Technical Support Training menu
  Appendixes xxxiv
  Overview of Directory Services xxxv

Technical Support Training menu *(continued)*
  Self-Assessment Exam xxxv
  Simulations xxxiv
  Supplemental Material xxxv
Telephony *See* TAPI
Telnet 356, 477, 740
Template files 165
Thunking 284
Token Ring 563, 740
Tracert 356
Trainer *See* Microsoft Certified Trainer (MCT)
Transport Driver Interface (TDI)
  description 325
  diagram 325
Transport protocols
  diagram 324
  examples 324
  See also Protocols
Trigger, setting 669
Troubleshooting
  1 GB IDE disks 231
  AutoDial 468
  blue screen errors 670
  boot errors 618
  boot process
    boot.ini file 622–625
    common errors 621–622
  diagnostic tools 648–653
  Dial-Up Monitor 467
  directory replication
    access denied 603
    exporting to specific computers 603
    logon scripts don't work 603
    over a WAN 603
  Emergency Repair 634
  ErrorControl values during system boot 618
  failure to recognize hard disks or partitions 231
  file corruption 231
  file system problems 231
  Microsoft resources 672–675
  PPP connections 467
  RAS 465–468
  recovering disk configuration information 230
  recovering from hard disk failure 248–249
  STOP errors 670
  system policy problems 165
  using Registry Editor 129
  Window NT won't start 622, 624, 641
  Windows NT boot problems 609
TSPs 441
Typical setup 35

U

UDF *See* Uniqueness Database File (UDF)
Unattend.txt, creating 70
Unattended installations 69–74
Uniform Resource Locator (URL) 477, 742
Uninstalling applications 126
Uninstalling Windows NT *See* Removing Windows NT
Uninterrupted power source (UPS)
    configuring 107
    defined 742
    described 108–109
    operation 108–109
    options 109–110
Uniqueness Database File (UDF)
    customizing answer files 70
    customizing installation 73
    described 73
    in conjunction with an answer file 73
    setup switch 68
    specifying during installation 74
Uniqueness IDs 73
UNIX 299
Unknown partition types 24
Updating files over a network 573
Upgrading from previous versions
  of Windows NT 65, 69, 76
    large NTFS partition concerns 26
Upgrading from Windows 95 76
UPS *See* Uninterrupted power source (UPS)
URL *See* Uniform Resource Locator (URL)
User Manager for Domains *See* Administrative
  Tools (Common), User Manager for Domains
User mode *See* Windows NT, user mode
User policy *See* System policy, user policy
User preferences, saving 99
User profiles
    changing user settings 99
    creating a new user 100
    defined 743
    described 91, 100
    information stored within 92
    local profile 99
    managing 100–101
    saving user preferences 99
    with Dial-Up Networking 462
User settings *See* User profiles

V

Value data types 94
Value entries 93–94
Virtual device drivers (VDDs)
    defined 281
    registry key 281
Virtual memory
    advantages 267
    architecture 265
    configuring 119–121
    defined 744
    dialog box 120
    process 265–266
    See also Paging file
Virtual Memory Manager
    advantages 267
    compatibilty with other processors 267
    introduced 266
Virtual memory space 265
Virtual network number 344
Virtual private networks (VPNs) 431, 744
Volume label, creating 217
Volume sets
    introduced 24
    partition 208

W

WAN
    connection methods 428
    security over RAS 427
Web *See* World Wide Web (WWW)
Web browsers 489, 745
Web pages 477
Wfront.doc 79
Win16-based applications
    running in their own memory space 288–289
    starting 290–292
    WOW 283–288
Win32 subsystem 269
Win32 subsystem start phase 620
Win32-based applications 276–279, 299
Win32K Window Manager 264, 269
Window NT
    setting up *See* Installing Windows NT

Index 771

Windows 95
   32-bit networking 550
   client-based network administration tools 560–561
   connectivity with NT 549
   dual-boot setup with Windows NT 76
   installing NT from a network share 67
   Registry Editor 130
   supported protocols 549
   system policy 164
   System Policy Editor 195
   upgrading to Windows NT 76
   user interface 5
   user interface comparison 3
Windows for Workgroups 3.11
   networking compatibility with Windows NT 347
Windows Internet Name Service (WINS)
   clients 395
   configuring
      client 397–399
      server 396
   defined 393, 746
   installing 396
   integrating with DNS 409–411
   introduced 4
   process 393
   purpose 390
   requirements
      client 395
      server 395
   servers 394
   vs. DNS 401
   WINS Manager 396
Windows messaging 5, 36
Windows NT
   Add-on Subsystem for Presentation Manager 298
   administration tools for troubleshooting 648
   architecture
      components 261
      networking 320
      overview 311
      virtual memory 265
   binding network components 361
   booting the system *See* Boot process
   Briefcase *See* Briefcase
   common features between Server and Workstation 6
   components
      adding and removing 125–126
      included with installation 36
   compressing the installation 191
   configuration information, storage and retrieval 90–91
   configurations, described 629
   Control Panel *See* Control Panel

Windows NT *(continued)*
   creating a boot disk 253, 625–626
   DCOM features 301
   defined 13
   definition 2
   documentation, other resources xxix
   environment variables 124
   Fatal System errors *See* Recovery, STOP errors
   file systems
      changing 181
      supported 174
   GDI 264
   hardware platforms supported 297
   installing *See* Installing Windows NT
   integrating with Novell Netware 513
   interoperability 299
   kernel mode
      components 262–263
      description 262
   log files 650, 675, 715
   memory model 265–267
   modes of operation 261
   NetWare, connecting to 504
   networking *See* Networking
   object 262
   operating system features 3–4
   overview 1–13
   portability 267
   processor modes, defined 262
   protocols 324–325, 337
   registry *See* Registry
   subsystems *See* Subsystems
   TCP/IP networking utilities 356
   updating files over a network 573
   user mode
      description 262
      processes 262
   virtual device drivers (VDDs) 281
   Workgroups vs. Domains 10–13
Windows NT Boot Loader (NTLDR) 191
Windows NT Challenge/Response authentication 491
Windows NT Diagnostics 656–658
Windows NT Directory Services (NTDS)
   defined 13
   introduced 4
   overview 8
   practice 8
   reference video 8
Windows NT Executive 263, 700
   See also Executive Services

Windows NT Explorer
  described 746
  file compression 189–190
  mapping a network drive 59
Windows NT Kernel
  described 91
Windows NT Kernel
  debugger, defined 713
  defined 713
Windows NT Redirector (RDR)
  advantages as a file system driver 327
  file system driver 326
  I/O requests over a network 326
  location within network architecture 326
  network component in resource sharing 330
  network process of fulfilling I/O requests 331
Windows NT Server
  Books Online 79–80
  Client Access License (CAL) *See* Client Access License (CAL)
  client software included with 547
  client-based administration tools
    Windows 95 558, 560–561
    Windows NT Workstation 558–559
  creating a distribution server 64–67
  creating setup disks 41
  defined 2, 13
  differences to Windows NT Workstation 7
  Directory Service Manager for NetWare (DSMN) 511
  examining the environment 492
  Gateway Services for NetWare (GSNW) *See* Gateway Services for NetWare (GSNW)
  installing *See* Installing Windows NT, Server
    BDC 29–32
    creating an installation disk set 556–557
    from a network share 64–74
    licensing modes 32
    manually 556–557
    moving a member server 31
    PDC 27–29
    planning network 26–32
    server types 26
    stand-alone server 30
  installing client software *See* Network Client Administrator
  Internet Information Server (IIS) support 480
  licensing
    modes 32, 533
    Per Seat 534
    Per Seat (or client) 33
    Per Server 33, 533
  overview 2
  paging file size 119

Windows NT Server *(continued)*
  planning a network 26–32
  RAID fault tolerance 239–245
  server license 566
  server performance 4
  Services for Macintosh *See* Services for Macintosh
  similiarities to Windows NT Workstation 6
  Web server management 3
  See also Windows NT
Windows NT Workstation
  business computing with 4
  Client Service for NetWare (CSNW) *See* Client Service for NetWare (CSNW)
  connecting to NetWare servers 505
  creating CD setup completion disks 52
  customizing within a domain 160
  defined 4, 13
  differences to Windows NT Server 7
  features 5
  installing
    creating CD setup completion disks 52
    joining a domain or workgroup 31
  installing networking administrative tools 558–559
  installing Workstation from setup disks 52–54
  joining a domain or workgroup during setup 31, 55
  optimizing network bindings 363
  overview 5
  paging file size 119
  Peer Web Services (PWS) support 480
  Redirector file system driver 326
  security 5
  similarities Windows NT Server 6
  support documentation 79
  uses 5
  See also Windows NT
Windows Sockets (WinSock)
  as a TCP/IP interface 350
  common use 341
  NetWare support 341, 505
Windows.adm 165
Winmsd.exe 656
Winnt.exe
  concurrent installations 65
  customizing switches 68–69
  description 65
  functions 68
Winnt32.exe 65
WINS *See* Windows Internet Name Service (WINS)
WinSock *See* Windows Sockets (WinSock)
Wizards
  administrative 4
  New Phonebook Entry 456
  Schema 732
  Setup 38–41

Workgroup model 10
Workgroups
    defined 10, 13
    model
        advantages and disadvantages 11
        diagram 10
    vs. Domains 10–13
Workstation *See* Windows NT Workstation
World Wide Web (WWW)
    browsers 489
    configuring service 488
    defined 477, 747
    Microsoft Web site 673
    securing a service site 491
    Web server's function 477
    See also Internet
WOW
    components 284
    described 283
    limitations 285

WOW *(continued)*
    process 284
Wrapper 323
WWW *See* World Wide Web (WWW)

X

X.25
    description 429
    packet assembler/disassemblers (PADs) 429–430
    RAS access methods 429
    smart card 747
    smart cards 431
    WAN connectivity 428
xcopy command 64

Z

Zones, DNS 403

The *ultimate* companion to Microsoft® Windows NT® Workstation version 4.0

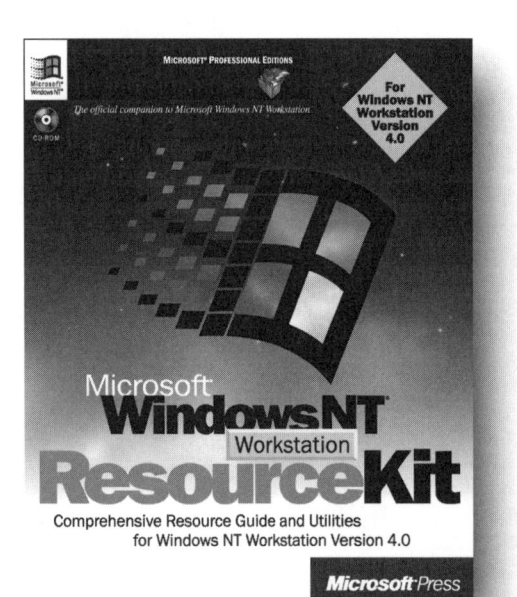

This exclusive Microsoft kit, written in cooperation with the Microsoft Windows NT Workstation development team, provides the complete technical information and tools you need to understand and get the most out of Microsoft Windows NT Workstation version 4.0. The comprehensive technical guide and a CD-ROM containing more than 100 useful tools help you take full advantage of the power of Microsoft Windows NT Workstation version 4.0. Administrators will especially like the section that describes strategies for deployment in large organizations and compatibility with other network and operating systems. Get the MICROSOFT WINDOWS NT WORKSTATION RESOURCE KIT—and get *the* essential reference for installing, configuring, and troubleshooting Microsoft Windows NT Workstation version 4.0.

U.S.A. $69.95
U.K.   £64.99 [V.A.T. included]
Canada $94.95
ISBN 1-57231-343-9

Microsoft Press® products are available worldwide wherever quality computer books are sold. For more information, contact your book retailer, computer reseller, or local Microsoft Sales Office.

To locate your nearest source for Microsoft Press products, reach us at http://mspress.microsoft.com, or call 1-800-MSPRESS in the U.S. (in Canada: 1-800-667-1115 or 416-293-8464).

To order Microsoft Press products, call 1-800-MSPRESS in the U.S. (in Canada: 1-800-667-1115 or 416-293-8464).

Prices and availability dates are subject to change.

Microsoft Press

This is how Microsoft Windows NT pros become incredibly resourceful.

This three-volume kit provides the valuable technical and performance information and tools that you need for handling rollout and support issues surrounding Microsoft Windows NT Server 4.0. You get a full 2500 pages—plus a CD-ROM—loaded with essential information not available anywhere else. For support professionals, MICROSOFT WINDOWS NT SERVER 4.0 RESOURCE KIT is more than a guide. It's a natural resource.

U.S.A.	**$149.95**
U.K.	£140.99 [V.A.T. included]
Canada	$201.95
ISBN	1-57231-344-7

Microsoft Press® products are available worldwide wherever quality computer books are sold. For more information, contact your book retailer, computer reseller, or local Microsoft Sales Office.

To locate your nearest source for Microsoft Press products, reach us at www.microsoft.com/mspress/, or call 1-800-MSPRESS in the U.S. (in Canada: 1-800-667-1115 or 416-293-8464).

To order Microsoft Press products, call 1-800-MSPRESS in the U.S. (in Canada: 1-800-667-1115 or 416-293-8464).

Prices and availability dates are subject to change.

Microsoft®*Press*

Give your Resource Kit the newest resources!

If you own the *Microsoft® Windows NT® Server 4.0 Resource Kit,* here's the quick, economical way to add the most advanced information, tools, and utilities available. Just get this book-and-CD supplement. It provides extensive additional coverage of two important areas—interoperability and the Internet. Plus, the CD is packed with new utilities for your full Resource Kit and more. So get the latest information about the hottest version of Microsoft Windows NT Server. Get MICROSOFT WINDOWS NT SERVER RESOURCE KIT VERSION 4.0, SUPPLEMENT ONE.

U.S.A. $39.99
U.K.   £37.49 [V.A.T. included]
Canada $54.99
ISBN 1-57231-559-8

Microsoft Press® products are available worldwide wherever quality computer books are sold. For more information, contact your book retailer, computer reseller, or local Microsoft Sales Office.

To locate your nearest source for Microsoft Press products, reach us at www.microsoft.com/mspress/, or call 1-800-MSPRESS in the U.S. (in Canada: 1-800-667-1115 or 416-293-8464).

To order Microsoft Press products, call 1-800-MSPRESS in the U.S. (in Canada: 1-800-667-1115 or 416-293-8464).

Prices and availability dates are subject to change.

Microsoft® Press